Historical Origins of International Criminal Law: Volume 3

Morten Bergsmo, CHEAH Wui Ling, SONG Tianying
and YI Ping (editors)

2015
Torkel Opsahl Academic EPublisher
Brussels

Dedicated to my husband CHEN Fang,
for giving me the best years of my life.

YI Ping

EDITORS' PREFACE

The Historical Origins of International Criminal Law ('HOICL') Project has grown beyond all our expectations, and it was difficult to choose from the many high quality contributions that we received. This third volume contains contributions by 28 authors from around the world. Most chapters were first presented as papers at the second conference in the HOICL Project held in New Delhi 29–30 November 2014, co-organized by the Centre for International Law Research and Policy, NALSAR University of Law, O.P. Jindal Global University, Peking University International Law Institute, Waseda University Law School, European University Institute (Department of Law), Indian Society of International Law, Royal Norwegian Embassy in New Delhi, Delegation of the European Union to India, and the Asian-African Legal Consultative Organization.

The preparation of this book for publication has been a comprehensive undertaking for the editorial group and the production experts of the Torkel Opsahl Academic EPublisher. We would like to place on record our sincere gratitude to each member of the diverse and skilled team, in particular, Mr. Gareth Richards (who has made an extraordinary contribution), Assistant Professor ZHANG Binxin, Ms. Pauline Brosch, Mr. CHAN Icarus, Mr. Alf Butenschøn Skre, Ms. Shama Abbasi, Mr. Ryan Nicholas Hong, Mr. Devasheesh Bais, and Dr. WEI Xiaohong. As editors, we are responsible for the final result. But the team stands together in having managed to complete the project in a timely fashion.

We would also like to thank the German Ministry of Foreign Affairs, for support to finalize the editing of this volume, and the Royal Norwegian Ministry of Foreign Affairs, for support in other aspects of the HOICL Project.

Morten Bergsmo
CHEAH Wui Ling
SONG Tianying
YI Ping

FOREWORD BY NARINDER SINGH

It is an honour to write a foreword to this important anthology which happens to be the third volume in the 'Historical Origins of International Criminal Law' series.

This volume brings together papers which were presented at the Historical Origins of International Criminal Law Seminar ('HOICL'), held at New Delhi on 29 and 30 November 2014, which I had the privilege of attending. This was the second of two seminars analysing the main historical origins of international criminal law, the first having taken place in Hong Kong on 1 and 2 March 2014.

The Centre for International Law Research and Policy (acting through her department FICHL), the European University Institute (Department of Law), Peking University International Law Institute, Waseda University Law School, NALSAR University of Law, O.P. Jindal Global University, the Asian-African Legal Consultative Organization, and the Indian Society of International Law co-organized the seminar.

The Seminar brought together more than fifty experts from different parts of the world, covering all continents. Their backgrounds and experiences were equally wide ranging and included: Judges and prosecutors of international and regional courts and tribunals, human rights experts, experts from the International Committee of the Red Cross, professors, and research scholars interested in the subject. The papers presented at the seminar analyse the trials, treaty provisions, national laws, declarations or other acts of States, and publications that constitute significant building blocks of contemporary international criminal law.

The last century especially the period after the establishment of the United Nations has seen a tremendous growth in international law, including in the field of international conventions covering individual criminal responsibility in areas such as trafficking in narcotics, organised crime, money laundering, international humanitarian law, human rights (including prohibition of torture, apartheid and enforced disappearances) and international terrorism.

However, apart from the development of substantive laws identifying various acts as criminal acts under international law – which States Parties to the relevant conventions are required to proscribe as crimes under their national laws, and to co-operate with other States in their prevention, investigation and prosecution – the most important development in this process has been the establishment, after long years of effort, of an International Criminal Court, with the jurisdiction to try persons accused of the most serious crimes of concern to the international community.

Kofi Annan, the United Nations Secretary-General, welcoming the adoption of the Court's Statute, said:

> For nearly half a century – almost as long as the United Nations has been in existence – the General Assembly has recognized the need to establish such a court to prosecute and punish persons responsible for crimes such as genocide. Many thought […] that the horrors of the Second World War – the camps, the cruelty, the exterminations, the Holocaust – could never happen again. And yet they have. In Cambodia, in Bosnia and Herzegovina, in Rwanda. Our time – this decade even – has shown us that man's capacity for evil knows no limits. Genocide […] is now a word of our time, too, a heinous reality that calls for a historic response.

At the start of the Rome Diplomatic Conference, he had stated that "[i]n the prospect of an international criminal court lies the promise of universal justice".

It may be recalled that the draft Statute for the International Criminal Court, together with its commentaries, finalised by the International Law Commission ('ILC') in 1994, had constituted the basis for the work of the Rome Conference, and that the ILC had as early as its second session, in 1950, in response to a request by the General Assembly made in the context of the Genocide Convention, concluded that the establishment of an international judicial organ for the trial of persons charged with genocide or other crimes was both desirable and possible. It took nearly fifty years after this for the International Criminal Court to become a reality.

Another topic of relevance currently being examined by the International Law Commission is "Immunity of State officials from foreign criminal jurisdiction". The question of the immunity of State officials from foreign criminal jurisdiction has attracted greater academic and public discussion as well as State practice, including domestic case law, especially following consideration of the case of former Chilean dictator General A. Pinochet in Great Britain. A number of attempts were made to institute criminal proceedings in domestic courts against senior incumbent and former officials of foreign States. In 2002 the International Court of

Justice rendered a judgment in the case concerning the "Arrest warrant of 11 April 2000" (Democratic Republic of the Congo v. Belgium) which contains a valuable assessment of the state of international law in this field.

Following the above-mentioned judgment of the International Court of Justice, a number of rulings were issued by national courts, which are also of significance for consideration of this issue. The position of various State organs, including those representing the executive branch, on the issue under consideration from the viewpoint of international law was expressed on several occasions recently both during consideration of the above-mentioned court cases and independently of judicial procedures.

The issue of the immunity of senior State officials from foreign criminal jurisdiction was examined by the Institute of International Law at the end of the last century. It adopted a resolution which constitutes an important doctrinal source for the establishment of the content of international law in this field.

Under the United Nations Convention on Jurisdictional Immunities of States and Their Property, the term "State" includes various organs of government, and also representatives of the State acting in that capacity. At the same time, the Convention states that it is without prejudice to privileges and immunities accorded under international law to heads of State *ratione personae*. It is not entirely clear what this means for the immunity *ratione personae* of other officials and, in particular, such senior officials as heads of government and ministers for foreign affairs.

A number of conventions deal with the immunity of State officials from foreign national criminal jurisdiction, including the 1961 Vienna Convention on Diplomatic Relations, the 1963 Vienna Convention on Consular Relations, the 1969 Convention on Special Missions, the 1973 Convention on the Prevention and Punishment of Crimes against Internationally Protected Persons, including Diplomatic Agents, and the 1975 Vienna Convention on the Representation of States in their Relations with International Organizations of a Universal Character.

However, these instruments concern only some specific aspects of the issue under consideration, as each of these conventions apply in respect of certain categories of State officials only. The principal source of international law in relation to the immunity of State officials from foreign criminal jurisdiction is international custom, and was therefore considered a topic suitable for codification and one for which there was a real and immediate need given the attempts by States to exercise universal jurisdiction and other types of domestic criminal jurisdiction, including extraterritorial jurisdiction, in the context of efforts to combat gross human rights violations, terrorism, transnational crime and money laundering.

The debates in the ILC on this topic have reflected divergent positions on the need for immunity, the officials entitled to immunity *ratione personae*, the scope of immunity *ratione materiae*, and the concept of state officials. While some members favour limiting *ratione personae* to only the heads of State and government, the ILC has accepted that it applies to the troika, that is, it also includes the foreign minister, and that the present consideration will not affect the rules in other existing conventions. Members have also referred to the realities of present times where foreign relations are also conducted by other ministers. The next report of the Special Rapporteur will deal with possible exceptions and limitations, and may also include procedural aspects of immunity.

The International Law Commission at its 2015 session started work on a new topic, namely "crimes against humanity". The ILC considers that a global convention on crimes against humanity appears to be a key missing piece in the current framework of international humanitarian law, international criminal law, and international human rights law. The objective of the International Law Commission on this topic, therefore, would be to draft articles for what would become a Convention on the Prevention and Punishment of Crimes against Humanity.

While three core crimes – war crimes, genocide, and crimes against humanity – have been the subject of jurisdiction within the major international criminal tribunals established to date, only two of them have been addressed through global conventions which require States to prevent and punish such conduct and to co-operate among themselves for that purpose: war crimes and genocide, both discussed in considerable detail by chapters in this volume. No comparable convention exists concerning crimes against humanity, even though the perpetration of such crimes continues to occur frequently in numerous conflicts and crises worldwide.

The ILC considered that such a convention would be useful for the following reasons. Firstly, the Rome Statute only regulates relations between its States Parties and the ICC, but does not regulate matters among the Parties themselves (nor among Parties and non-Parties). The Convention would help promote general co-operation among States in the investigation, prosecution, and punishment of persons who commit crimes against humanity.

Secondly, the ICC is based on the principle of complementarity, that is, that national jurisdiction is, in the first instance, the proper place for prosecution. As the ICC does not have the capacity to prosecute all persons who commit crimes against humanity, and as it was envisaged that it would have jurisdiction over the most serious crimes of concern to the international community as a whole, effective prevention and prosecution of such crimes is necessary through the active co-operation among and enforcement by national jurisdictions.

Thirdly, the Convention would require the enactment of national laws that prohibit and punish crimes against humanity, which many States have not done so far. As such, the Convention would help fill a gap in the current legal regime.

Some other topics in the field of international criminal law which have been considered by the International Law Commission include: Formulation of the Nuremberg Principles; draft code of offences against the peace and security of mankind; obligation to extradite or prosecute (*aut dedere aut judicare*); question of defining aggression; and, the prevention and punishment of crimes against diplomatic agents and other internationally protected persons with commentaries.

I commend the organisers of the HOICL project, especially Professor Morten Bergsmo, for the excellent group of experts he has brought together and the theme of the New Delhi Seminar in November 2014, which was spread over twelve sessions and provided rich information from a variety of sources of the manner in which international criminal law has developed and been shaped in the past so that we may learn lessons for the future.

Narinder Singh
Chairman, International Law Commission

FOREWORD BY EIVIND S. HOMME

I am pleased to write this foreword to *Historical Origins of International Criminal Law: Volume 3* which is based on papers presented at a conference in New Delhi on 29 and 30 November 2014. The Norwegian Government has supported the international research project 'Historical Origins of International Criminal Law' from its start, including the first conference in Hong Kong on 1 and 2 March 2014 which formed a solid basis for the subsequent New Delhi conference. Norway also co-sponsored the launch of *Volumes 1 and 2* in the series at the United Nations Headquarters in New York on 12 December 2014.

This book and the wider research project concern a topic that unites rather than divides. Regardless of our views on the International Criminal Court, on universal jurisdiction or the crime of aggression, everyone can gather around the topic of the history of international criminal law. It is a topic that builds bridges between actors from diverse political, legal and economic backgrounds. I hope that this volume will do just that. And I hope that the research project as a whole will contribute towards the development of a sub-discipline of history of international criminal law.

I would like to thank the Centre for International Law Research and Policy for the work it has done on the conference and volume, together with prominent co-organizers in India, China, Japan and the European Union. It has been an ambitious project that is now bearing fruit.

Eivind S. Homme
Former Ambassador of the Kingdom of Norway to India

TABLE OF CONTENTS

PART 1:
Expanding the Historical and Geographical Landscape
of International Criminal Law

By Gregory S. Gordon

PART 2:
Doctrinal Evolution:
Origins of the Core International Crimes

PART 3:
Doctrinal Evolution:
Origins of Modes of Liability

1

Doctrine and the Scope of the Historical Landscape of International Criminal Law

Morten Bergsmo[*], **CHEAH Wui Ling**[**], **SONG Tianying**[§],
YI Ping[‡] **and ZHANG Binxin**[¶]

This volume's enquiry on the historical origins of international criminal law focuses on tracing both the substance of legal rules and the context of their making. In other words, the investigation into the origins of legal doctrines is guided by their constitutive elements and is further nourished by contextual analysis. Authors undertaking such analysis usually take care to inform contemporary theory and practice along these two lines, with different emphases in particular narrative frames. For example, the focus could shift from historical details to technical discussions. This discloses the inner dynamics of the subject matter of the historical origins of international criminal law – the interactions between history and law.

Volume 3 of *Historical Origins of International Criminal Law* ('*HOICL*') carries on the "comprehensive and critical mapping of international criminal law's origins"[1] started in the previous two volumes. Part 1 of this book further expands the landscape of international criminal law in terms of geography, time and the diversity of legal concepts in their early forms. Parts 2 and 3 turn to the origins and evolution of specific doctrines

---

[*] **Morten Bergsmo** is Director of the Centre for International Law Research and Policy, and Visiting Professor at Peking University Law School, China.

[**] **CHEAH Wui Ling** is Assistant Professor at the Faculty of Law, National University of Singapore.

[§] **SONG Tianying** is Legal Adviser at the International Committee of the Red Cross East Asia Delegation in Beijing, China.

[‡] **YI Ping** is Assistant Professor at Peking University Law School, China.

[¶] **ZHANG Binxin** is Assistant Professor at Xiamen University Law School, China, and the inaugural PKU-CILRAP Research Fellow.

[1] CHEAH Wui Ling and CHOONG Xun Ning, "Introduction: Historical Origins of International Criminal Law", in Morten Bergsmo, CHEAH Wui Ling and YI Ping (eds.), *Historical Origins of International Criminal Law*, vol. 1, Torkel Opsahl Academic EPublisher, Brussels, 2014, p. 5 (https://www.legal-tools.org/en/doc/8eb79b/).

of international criminal law, namely, the substantive crimes and principles of individual responsibility. This doctrine-based approach concentrates on the law and – by providing depth of perspective on the evolution of norms and principles – contributes to the vertical consolidation of the discipline and conception of international criminal law. Meanwhile, the historical circumstances as part of the study add flesh and blood to legal doctrines and avoid isolated, overly legalistic interpretations. This doctrinal approach also allows horizontal comparison of crimes and modes of liabilities from a historical perspective.

1.1. Diversity and Inclusiveness of the Historical Landscape

As a sequel to Part 1 of *HOICL*, Volume 1 "Going Beyond Conventional Historical Narratives of International Criminal Law", Part 1 of this volume "Expanding the Historical and Geographical Landscape of International Criminal Law" continues to uncover less well-known trials and practices across history. The chapters touch upon a wide range of contexts in terms of geography, time and social environment: ancient India; ancient Greece; seventeenth- to nineteenth-centuries European powers at sea; seventeenth-century England; post-Civil War United States; post-Khmer Rouge Cambodia; Siam, Ottoman-controlled Crete and China in the late nineteenth century; the post-1860 crisis in Syria; and the Katyn massacre during the Second World War. The diverse contexts add to the mosaic of international criminal law's history, toward whose substance and outcome we remain open-minded.

Rooted in these contexts, Part 1 captures crimes reminiscent of today's core international crimes and other violations treated just as severely and which had an international dimension. For example, Emiliano J. Buis notes in Chapter 3 that torturing prisoners of war was regarded as a violation beyond the concern of a single city-state in ancient Greece. In Chapter 5 Gregory S. Gordon analyses alleged crimes of premeditated murder, the inflicting of severe bodily harm, robbery and arson committed by the Siamese in relation to a French military commander's death in nineteenth-century Siam. On the maritime front, Shavana Musa in Chapter 4 describes "precursors of war crimes" at sea – piracy and violation of neutrality during wartime in the period from the seventeenth to nineteenth centuries.

The historical landscape in Part 1 also offers rich examples of mechanisms designed to address these atrocities. In 405 BCE the Spartan allies set up an *ad hoc* consultation to deal with war crimes perpetrated by the defeated Athenians; two years later, after a regime change, the Athenians implemented a "reconciliation" mechanism that granted a general amnesty to officials of the former regime of the Thirty Tyrants who had carried out the mass killing of citizens.[2] The network of admiralty courts in Europe had tried numerous cases of wartime violations at sea before the development of modern international law.[3] In Cambodia, the People's Revolutionary Tribunal was convened by the new post-conflict regime specifically to try Khmer Rouge leaders in 1979.[4] In 1893 an *ad hoc* French-Siamese Mixed Court sat to hear the circumstances of the death of a French military commander. In the same period, *ad hoc* International Military Commissions of certain European powers were set up in reaction to the intercommunal violence on the island of Crete and the Boxer Rebellion in China.[5] A joint European-Ottoman International Commission of Inquiry oversaw the transitional justice programme following the mass atrocities in the civil war in Syria in 1860.[6]

This kaleidoscope of justice mechanisms reflects rich institutional solutions to crimes of grave concern. Many of these mechanisms bore traits of certain mainstream institutions today. For example, Buis observes that the vocabularies used to justify the Spartan tribunal and the post-Second World War Nuremberg International Military Tribunal ('IMT') are similar. In Gordon's account, the Franco-Siamese Mixed Court and the modern Special Tribunal for Lebanon were both set up in response to the assassination of one individual. Naturally, the distinctive context of the Franco-Siamese trial – the confluence of so-called New Imperialism

---

[2]   See Emiliano J. Buis, "Between *Isonomía* and *Hegemonía*: Political Complexities of Transitional Justice in Ancient Greece", Chapter 3 below.

[3]   See Shavana Musa, "War Crimes Trials and Admiralty Court Precedents", Chapter 4 below.

[4]   See Jens Iverson, "The Trials of Charles I, Henry Wirz and Pol Pot: Why Historic Cases Are Often Forgotten and the Meaning of International Criminal Law", Chapter 5 below.

[5]   See Gregory S. Gordon, "International Criminal Law's 'Oriental Pre-Birth': The 1894-1900 Trials of the Siamese, Ottomans and Chinese", Chapter 6 below.

[6]   See Benjamin E. Brockman-Hawe, "Constructing Humanity's Justice: Accountability for 'Crimes Against Humanity' in the Wake of the Syria Crisis of 1860", Chapter 7 below.

and embryonic pacifism in the late nineteenth century – needs to be considered.

1.2. Doctrinal Evolution Throughout History

Parts 2 and 3 – encompassing most of this volume – continue the narrative transcending post-Second World War trials when it comes to specific crimes and principles of individual responsibility. Part 2 covers the origins and evolution of four categories of core international crimes: war crimes, crimes against humanity, genocide and aggression, while Part 3 turns to modes of liability and principles on sentencing.

The chapters portray the rationales behind the rules, that is, why and how the doctrines were formed. Patryk I. Labuda makes the intriguing argument that the trial of war crimes proliferated as a more humane and productive option to belligerent retaliation during war. The gradual shift in practice was based on lessons learnt that retaliation and counter-retaliation easily provoked an escalation of violence and vicious circles of conflict.[7] Crimes against humanity and genocide originated in a recognition that the persecution of certain groups should not be tolerated. Before then, persecutory acts were regarded more as the domestic affairs of states, not violations of fundamental common values.[8] This rationale is supported by the study of the crime of persecution as a crime against humanity.[9] The persistent tension in the delineation of international and national parameters is discussed further below.

The functional approach features more prominently in other chapters exploring the evolution of the forms and degrees of individual criminal responsibility. For example, forms of liability such as conspiracy, complicity, and the subsequent joint criminal enterprises and co-perpetration correspond to the collective, massive nature of international crimes.[10] Similarly, command responsibility is based on the strict control

---

[7]   See Patryk I. Labuda, "The Lieber Code, Retaliation and the Origins of International Criminal Law", Chapter 9 below.

[8]   See Sheila Paylan and Agnieszka Klonowiecka-Milart, "Examining the Origins of Crimes against Humanity and Genocide", Chapter 13 below.

[9]   See Helen Brady and Ryan Liss, "The Evolution of Persecution as a Crime against Humanity", Chapter 12 below.

[10]   See Marina Aksenova, "Shaping the Definition of Complicity in International Criminal Law: Tensions and Contradictions", Chapter 15 below; Zahra Kesmati, "The Evolution of

structure in military and other organisations that are the primary actors in wars and mass atrocities.[11] On the other hand, sometimes the change of elements may represent inconsistencies in a doctrine, not evolution. This is the case for the criteria of mitigating circumstances in sentencing.[12]

A horizontal comparison of the historical paths taken by the crimes and forms of individual responsibility helps us to discern connections and distinctions between doctrines. Although genocide and crimes against humanity have shared roots, they eventually took on different elements and functions but remain closely related. Crimes against humanity were initially linked to war and, in turn, operated alongside war crimes before achieving autonomy. With regard to forms of liability, conspiracy and complicity were surrounded by controversies when they first emerged. The two forms of liability interacted frequently with each other in the course of development. Eventually, conspiracy did not survive the objections against it and was partly assimilated into variations of complicity.[13]

1.3. Persistent Tensions in International Criminal Law

The chapters in this volume also identify common and timeless tensions in international criminal law. Tension may arise between hegemonic and egalitarian perspectives of justice,[14] between national interests and the independence of international law,[15] between protected values and the demarcation of domains of international and national concerns,[16] from allegations of politicisation,[17] between the drive to punish perpetrators of massacres and the perceived necessity of limiting penalties, between those who would tolerate the inherent political factors in justice and those who

---

Conspiracy as a Mode of Collective Criminal Liability Since Nuremberg", Chapter 16 below.

[11] See Chantal Meloni, "The Evolution of Command Responsibility in International Criminal Law", Chapter 17 below.

[12] See ZHANG Binxin, "Mitigating Circumstances in International Criminal Sentencing", Chapter 20 below.

[13] Kesmati, *supra* note 10.

[14] Buis, *supra* note 2.

[15] Musa, *supra* note 3; Iverson, *supra* note 4; William Schabas, "The Katyn Forest Massacre and the Nuremberg Trial", Chapter 8 below.

[16] Brady and Liss, *supra* note 9.

[17] Iverson, *supra* note 4.

would not, between competing narratives of guilt and victimhood,[18] between the substantive crimes and modes of liability, between the collective wrongdoing and individual criminal responsibility,[19] between the needs of flexibility and predictability.[20]

These tensions may have resulted from interactions of the law with external factors – such as and in particular politics – or intrinsic conflicts within the law itself. Throughout history, the tensions have been symptomatic of the essential struggles in international criminal law, offering parameters for assessment and action. As the cases show, the tensions could be a driving force for change or a stumbling block to progress, depending on the circumstances at the time. For example, the Katyn massacre was charged against the Germans before the Nuremberg IMT as a result of the "efforts by the Soviet Union to use international justice to promote a lie".[21] As the Soviet case was eventually not adequately proven, the final judgment of the IMT was silent on this issue. William Schabas argues that the silence of the judges – including the Soviet judge – on the Katyn charge shows the integrity of the judicial process.[22] In this case, the national interest, in its attempt to instrumentalise international law, failed to be a stumbling block.

1.4. Chapter Contributions

Before tracing the evolution of various doctrines in international criminal law, Part 1 of Volume 3 starts by further expanding the landscape of international criminal law history beyond the common narrative. The contributions in this part take us back some 2,400 years, and cover events that occurred across Eurasia.

In Chapter 2 Manoj Kumar Sinha looks into the ancient Sanskrit text, the *Manusmrti*, or Laws of Manu, in particular its concepts and rules concerning warfare, punishment, the judiciary and administration of justice. Sinha discusses the ancient rules concerning the means and methods of warfare, the king's duty to protect his subjects and the composition of

---

[18] Brockman-Hawe, *supra* note 6.

[19] Aksenova, *supra* note 10; Hitomi Takemura, "The History of the Defense of Superior Orders and its Intersection with International Human Rights Law", Chapter 18 below.

[20] ZHANG, *supra* note 12.

[21] Schabas, *supra* note 15.

[22] *Ibid.*

judicial organs, as enshrined in the *Manusmṛti*, and emphasises the importance of the *Manusmṛti* and other similar texts as examples of key philosophical and legal texts of ancient times.

In Chapter 3 Emiliano J. Buis analyses two case studies from ancient Greece concerning the different approaches – creating *ad hoc* international tribunals and granting general amnesty – that were employed when dealing with violations of "common laws", and especially the individual commission of grave crimes. Buis demonstrates that in ancient Greece there already existed different ways to address mass atrocities, which could help explain the historical and political bases of today's institutions of international criminal justice.

In Chapter 4 Shavana Musa turns to wartime violations at sea. She examines admiralty courts from the seventeenth to nineteenth centuries and their practices, especially their application of the law of nations with respect to wartime misconduct. Musa stresses the importance of the admiralty courts as an early precedent to modern international courts and institutions dealing with crimes committed during wartime. She provides an insight into this overlooked admiralty courts network, which existed across Europe and even expanded to other parts of the world under the colonial rule of the European powers.

In Chapter 5 Jens Iverson discusses three "forgotten" historical trials: those of Charles I, Henry Wirz and Pol Pot. Iverson articulates the reasons why these important trials have been unduly ignored in the narratives of the history of international criminal law. In discussing these reasons, he analyses the inherent tensions of international criminal law. Iverson argues that objective historical studies should also include contested or troubled trials, that a broader approach would be vital both to understanding the past and to shaping the future.

In Chapter 6 Gregory S. Gordon examines three international criminal proceedings by European powers against the Siamese, Ottomans and Chinese at the end of the nineteenth century. He provides detailed accounts of the structure and operation of the tribunals, and the context and proceedings of the trials. Gordon sees these proceedings as forebears of modern international criminal law institutions, and argues that their occurrence could be explained against the overarching historical context of the dawn of the European peace movement juxtaposed ironically with the period of the New Imperialism.

In Chapter 7 Benjamin E. Brockman-Hawe looks to the transitional justice programme established after conflicts between the Druze and Maronite Christian communities of Ottoman Syria in 1860. In this discussion, he highlights how an international body was composed in the aftermath of the atrocities, and how the concept of crimes against humanity was taken one step forward through this process. As a conclusion, Brockman-Hawe calls for more research into these historical events to better understand contemporary social trends and inform today's transitional justice practices.

In Chapter 8 William Schabas traces how the Katyn massacre was dealt with during the Nuremberg Trial. He provides a detailed account of the debates and nuances relating to the massacre charge throughout the IMT trial process. He argues that the Nuremberg judgment's silence on the Katyn massacre should not be perceived as evidence of "victors' justice" but, quite to the contrary, it should be considered a sign of justice being done and the Nuremberg Tribunal's honour remaining intact.

Part 2 looks at the origins of some of the core international crimes. In Chapter 9 Patryk I. Labuda examines criminal trials and belligerent reprisals together as part of a broader turn towards greater individual accountability under international law since the nineteenth century. International criminal justice's qualitative leap is revealed by the evolution of the international legal debate in the period from the American Civil War to the First World War. Labuda in turn argues that the origins of the law of war crimes lie in the second half of the nineteenth century.

Chapter 10 turns to the substantive law of war crimes. GUO Yang looks at the historical developments of the grave breaches regime and its relationship to war crimes under international criminal law. He argues that with the advent of international judicial organs and other categories of war crimes, the grave breaches regime – including its criminal sanctioning system – remains an important domestic tool and is further reinforced by international criminal jurisprudence.

In Chapter 11 Philipp Ambach analyses how the core rules of international humanitarian law were transposed into the legal confines of war crimes before international courts and tribunals. Ambach examines the history of this transposition and the critical steps therein. He concludes that with the rapidly changing reality of armed conflict today, war crimes law will continue to develop and adapt to this reality, and the International

Criminal Court ('ICC') can be instrumental in the enforcement of international humanitarian law in our times.

In Chapter 12 Helen Brady and Ryan Liss provide a detailed history of persecution as a crime against humanity, from the various antecedents of the crime to efforts in the wake of the First and Second World Wars, and finally to contemporary jurisprudence of the United Nations *ad hoc* tribunals and the legal instruments of the ICC. The path persecution took from the domestic domain to international concern offers insights into the evolving parameters of international criminal law as a whole.

In Chapter 13 Sheila Paylan and Agnieszka Klonowiecka-Milart examine the origins of crimes against humanity and genocide. Their inquiry starts with the extermination of Armenians and the failed efforts to punish the perpetrators in its aftermath, and then continues to cover the Jewish Holocaust, the Nuremberg Trial and the Genocide Convention, before turning to contemporary developments of the two crimes. They point to the prevailing geopolitical interests involved in this process, and argue that the prevention and punishment of the crimes should be independent from such interests.

In Chapter 14 Meagan S. Wong focuses on the state act element of the crime of aggression. She compares the definition of the crime of aggression at the Nuremberg Tribunal and the Kampala Amendments to the ICC Statute, and examines the development of this element. Wong concludes that the scope of the crime of aggression is narrower under the ICC Statute than at Nuremberg.

Part 3 analyses the origins and evolution of issues related to modes of liability, defence and sentencing. In Chapter 15 Marina Aksenova explores the evolution of the concept of complicity through the post-Second World War trials and the codification work of the International Law Commission. She analyses the emergence and development of complicity in the light of three tensions inherent in international criminal law: domestic versus international law, collective wrongdoing versus individual criminal responsibility, and substantive crimes versus forms of participation. Aksenova demonstrates how complicity gradually moved to the centre of international criminal law and how this process was deeply influenced by the inherent tensions of international criminal law.

In Chapter 16 Zahra Kesmati examines the development of conspiracy as a mode of liability in international criminal jurisprudence. Her analysis begins with the post-Second World War jurisprudence, and covers later development at the *ad hoc* tribunals, as well as contemporary practices of the ICC. Kesmati argues that the doctrines of joint criminal enterprise and co-perpetration are new forms and manifestations of conspiracy, with the existence of a common plan as the shared denominator of all three doctrines.

In Chapter 17 Chantal Meloni traces the antecedents of command responsibility, from its military origins to its current application before international criminal tribunals. She considers the various issues regarding command responsibility in the light of the fundamental principles of individual and culpable responsibility. Meloni argues that command responsibility could cover a broad spectrum of very different scenarios, and thus should be treated differently depending on different situations.

In Chapter 18 Hitomi Takemura provides a fresh perspective to look into the defence of superior orders. Takemura correlates the defence of superior orders, and especially the duty to disobey manifestly illegal orders, with the human right to selective conscientious objection. Placing the issue against the general background of an increasingly individual-centric international legal order, Takemura argues that an interdisciplinary approach would benefit future research and development of international criminal law.

In Chapter 19 Hae Kyung Kim looks at conspiracy as defined in the Convention against Transnational Organized Crime. Kim compares the acceptance of the Convention and the concept of conspiracy in Japan and South Korea. Through these discussions, she indicates how the embedded historical background of domestic law can influence present-day government policies concerning legal issues and how these could be in conflict with contemporary international policy and developments in international law.

In Chapter 20 ZHANG Binxin examines the evolution of mitigating circumstances in international criminal sentencing. By reviewing the jurisprudence of international courts and tribunals from Nuremberg to the ICC, she observes that the scope of mitigating circumstances has largely been broadened, which reflects an expansion of the underlying goals and ideologies of international criminal justice. ZHANG argues that the inclusion of multiple, and at times internally contradictory goals, and the lack of a clear priority among them, might exacerbate the problems of inconsistency and unpredictability of sentencing in international criminal law.

1.5. Conclusion

While trying to bridge history with contemporary international criminal law, we should be conscious of the intrinsic merits of historical events and norm development. When examined carefully, past events often prove much more complex and nuanced than we may be inclined to assume in an effortless present. Many such events are yet to be comprehensively researched and analysed. The state of knowledge of the history of international criminal law is still tentative. Part 1 of this volume and chapters in Parts 2 and 3 – such as the detailed study of the history of persecution as a crime against humanity by Helen Brady and Ryan Liss – illustrate how thorough research can significantly expand the emerging subdiscipline of history of international criminal law. Much scholarly activity is waiting to be undertaken, hopefully by as diverse a community as the body of contributors to this volume.

As was raised by Chapter 1 of *HOICL* Volume 1, and echoed especially by Patryk Labuda in this Volume 3, we should appreciate relevant historical events within the context of their time and the thinking that prevailed then. We should be cautious of presentist and anachronistic interpretations of history. Such conscious or unconscious efforts to 'illuminate' current study at the cost of a nuanced view of history may be counterproductive. The many topics, histories and analyses undertaken by authors in this volume show that, though there are persistent tensions and challenges, as well as unexpected divergences or gaps, studying the past can nevertheless be illuminating.

2

The *Manusmṛti* and
Laws of Warfare in Ancient India

Manoj Kumar Sinha[*]

2.1. Introduction

Respect for individual dignity and the quest for peace and harmony in society has been an abiding factor within Indian culture.[1] Indian culture has been the product of assimilation of diverse cultures and religions that came into contact over time with the enormous Indian sub-continent.[2] The spirit of unity and universality in this tradition extends to the whole world. It is said in the *Rig Veda*, the sacred collection of Vedic hymns: "There is one race; of human beings". The validity of diverse traditions, religions and indeed of diverse paths to Truth has always been respected. The guiding principles have been *Vasudhaiva Kutumbakam* and *Sarva Dharma Sama Bhava*.[3] The whole universe is one family; it is universal order, and as such its universality is ubiquitous.

An ancient text runs thus: "I seek no kingdom, nor heaven nor rebirth, but I wish that all living beings be spared of the manifold pains and distresses".[4] According to Nagendra Singh, "[t]he individual in ancient

---

[*] **Manoj Kumar Sinha** is Director of the Indian Law Institute in Delhi, on leave from his position as Professor of Law, West Bengal National University of Juridical Sciences, Kolkata, India. He was Visiting Professor at the Raoul Wallenberg Institute of Human Rights and Humanitarian Law, Lund, Sweden (2004–5). He served as Director of the Indian Society of International Law (2006–9). He holds a doctorate in international law from Jawaharlal Nehru University. Among his most recent publications are *Business and Human Rights* (2013), *Implementation of Basic Human Rights* (2013), and *International Criminal Law and Human Rights* (2010).

[1] Mahendra P. Singh, "Human Rights in the Indian Tradition: An Alternative Model", in *NUJS Law Review*, 2009, vol. 2, no. 2, pp. 145–82.

[2] V.S. Mani, *Human Rights in India: An Overview*, Institute for World Congress on Human Rights, Occasional Paper no. 4, January 1997.

[3] L.R. Penna, "Traditional Asian Approaches: An Indian View", in *Australian Yearbook of International Law*, 1985, vol. 9, pp. 168–206.

[4] Mani, 1997, p. 7, see *supra* note 2.

India existed as a citizen of the state and in that capacity he had both rights and obligations".[5] These rights and duties have largely been expressed in terms of duties (*dharma*) – duties to oneself, to one's family, to other fellow humans, to society and the world at large.[6] The Buddhist doctrine of non-violence in deed and thought, according to Nagendra Singh, "is a humanitarian doctrine *par excellence*, dating back to the third century B.C.".[7] Both Buddhism and Jainism emphasised the principles of equality, non-violence and denial of materialistic pleasures.

In ancient times the first and foremost duty of the king was to protect his people. Protection consisted of meeting both internal threats as well as external aggression to man's liberty.[8] Gautama Buddha prescribed that the special responsibility of the king was to protect all beings, to award just punishment and to protect the several *varna* (castes) and *āśrama* (stages of life) according to the *śāstra* (rules), and to bring them round to the path of their proper duties when they swerve from it. Vaśiṣṭha, one of the great patriarchs of Hinduism, also stated that the wise say that protection is a lifelong *sautra* in which the king has to give up fear and softness of heart.[9]

In ancient India there were elaborate provisions for social services such as education, public health, medical attendance, insurance against unemployment, old age, widowhood, becoming orphans and the elimination of poverty. It was believed that it was necessary for the king, representing the state and its resources, to encourage learning, to care for the blind, the decrepit, the old and the widowed and to give employment to those who were unemployed.[10]

An extremely high ideal was placed before the king by Kautilya (also called Chanukah), the Hindu statesman and philosopher, in *Aretha-śāstra* (The Science of Material Gain). He proclaimed the magnificent

---

[5] Nagendra Singh, *India and International Law*, vol. 1, part 1, S. Chand & Co., New Delhi, 1969, p. 46.

[6] Mani, 1997, p. 8, see *supra* note 2.

[7] Nagendra Singh, *Enforcement of Human Rights*, Eastern Law House, Calcutta, 1986, p. 7.

[8] P.V. Kane, *History of Dharmaśāstra*, vol. 2, 2nd ed., Bhandarkar Oriental Research Institute, Poona, 1973, p. 56.

[9] Manoj Kumar Sinha, *Implementation of Basic Human Rights*, Manak Publications, New Delhi, 1999, p. 3.

[10] P.V. Kane, *History of Dharmaśāstra*, vol. 3, 2nd ed., Bhandarkar Oriental Research Institute, Poona, 1973, p. 60.

ideal that "in the happiness of the subjects lies the happiness of the king, in their welfare lies his welfare; the good of the king does not consist in what is pleasing to himself, but what is pleasing to the subjects constitutes his good".[11] The king was also called upon to support helpless and aged people, the blind, the crippled, lunatics, widows, orphans, those suffering from diseases and calamities and pregnant women by giving them medicines, lodging, food and clothing according to their needs.[12] The contribution of ancient India in the development of both domestic and international law is very significant and widely recognised by several Indian scholars.[13]

2.2. The *Manusmṛti*

The *Manusmṛti* (or Laws of Manu), also known as the *Mānava-Dharmaśāstra*, occupies a very significant place among the *Dharmaśāstra* of India, mainly because of its wide coverage and detailed guidelines for various aspects of human living.[14] It probably dates to the period between 200 BCE and 200 CE.[15] Manu was the first Hindu theoretician to treat law in a systematic manner. Hindu philosophy features a bipolar division between *dharma* (right or order) and *adharma* (wrong or unnaturalness). The *Manusmṛti* is one of the 19 *Dharmaśāstra* that belong to the *smṛti* literature.[16] According to Medhātithi, the foremost commentator on the *Manusmṛti*, *dharma* is five-fold: *varnadharma* (duties relating to the four

---

[11] C.H. Alexandrowicz, "Kautilyan Principles and the Law of Nations", in *British Yearbook of International Law*, 1965–66, vol. 41, pp. 301–20.

[12] Kane, 1973, p. 59, see *supra* note 10. King Asoka of the Maurya dynasty had constructed hospitals for men and animals, almshouses, resthouses, watering places, shady trees on the highways and irrigation works, and visited and supported the aged.

[13] C.J. Chacko, "India's Contribution to the Field of International Law Concepts", in *Recueil des cours*, 1958, vol. 93, pp. 117–221; Nagendra Singh, *India and International Law*, S. Chand, New Delhi, 1973.

[14] For a modern annotated translation see Patrick Olivelle, *Manu's Code of Law: A Critical Edition and Translation of the Mānava-Dharmaśāstra*, Oxford University Press, Oxford, 2005. *Dharmaśāstra* refers to the Sanskrit texts of the branch of learning pertaining to religious and legal duties.

[15] See Burjor Avari, India: The Ancient Past: A History of the Indian Sub-Continent from 7000 BC to AD 1200, Routledge, London, 2007, p. 142.

[16] The word *smṛti* which literally means "that which is remembered", in a wider sense is applicable to all ancient, but un-Vedic works such as the *Kalpasūtras*, the *Mahābhārata*, the grammar of Pāṇini, and the works of Manu, Yāgyavalkya and others. However, the word *smṛti* in a narrower sense is concerned with the treatment of *dharma*.

castes, the Brahmin, the Kshatriya, the Vaishya and the Shudra); *āśrama-dharma* (duties relating to the four phases of life, *brahmacarya, gṛhastha, vanaprastha* and *saṁnyāsa*); *varnashramadharma* (duties relating to the caste to which one belongs as well as the stage of life in which one is situated); *naimittikadharma* (unconditionally obligatory duties called for by special occasions (*nimitta*) such as *prāyaścitta* (penance or atonement)); and lastly, *gunadharma* (the duty of a king to protect, no matter whether he is a Kshatriya or not).[17] Gautama, Āpastamba and Vasiṣṭha, among the authors of *Dharmaśāstra,* and Manu and Yāgyavalkya, among the authors of the *Manusmṛti,* all agree in proclaiming that the Vedas are one of the original sources of *dharma.* Manu also regarded the Vedas as a source of *dharma,* while at the same time accepting that *dharma* also owed its origins to the tradition and practice of those who know the Vedas, the usages of virtuous men and righteous individuals.[18]

The *Manusmṛti* is a *Dharmaśāstra* of Hindu *dharma* containing the foundational work of Hindu law and ancient Indian society. The *Manusmṛti* contains the laws (conduct in life) which need to be followed in various orders of life and by persons of various *varna.* The word *smṛti* means "that which have to be remembered".[19] Hindu mythology states that the *Manusmṛti* is the word of Brahma, shadowing authoritative incantations of *dharma.* Manu is presumed to have created this book, which has led the text to be coupled by Hindus with the first human being and the first king in the Indian tradition.[20] The *Manusmṛti* was the first text to adopt the term *vyavahārapadas* or substantive law. The original narrative was divided into 12 chapters and is written in simple verses. The table of contents includes sections on the "Creation of the world", "Sources of *dharma*", "The *dharma* of the four social classes" and "Law of *karma,* rebirth and final liberation".[21]

The *Manusmṛti* is written with a focus on *dharma.* It seems that the book was written in a manner that was aware of the dangers facing the

---

[17] K.L. Bhatia, Concept of Dharma: Corpus Juris of Law and Morality: A Comparative Study of Legal Cosmology, Deep & Deep Publications, New Delhi, 2010.

[18] Olivelle, 2005, p. 169, see *supra* note 14.

[19] M. Rama Jois, *Ancient Indian Law: Eternal Values in Manu Smriti,* Universal Law Publishing, New Delhi, 2012.

[20] George Bühler, *The Sacred Books of the East,* Vol. 25, *The Laws of Manu,* Clarendon Press, Oxford, 1886.

[21] Olivelle, 2005, pp. 8–9, see *supra* note 14.

Brahmin community during a time of social turmoil. The *Manusmṛti* containing the Laws of Manu is both a legal and a religious text that elaborates on the basic Hindu tenets while providing a window into the religion, culture and society of ancient India. It covers topics ranging from the role of women to the definition of sin to an explanation of the caste system and its utility in the maintenance of the universe.

2.3. The *Manusmṛti* and Warfare

Manu followed Kautilya's grand strategic thought by granting importance to coalition warfare.[22] The *Manusmṛti*, following Kautilya's *Arthaśāstra*, an ancient treatise of statecraft, economic policy and military strategy, argues that diplomacy, rather than warfare, should take the pre-eminent role in the formulation of grand strategic policy.[23] Manu's emphasis on *dharmayuddha* was shaped by the epic and *purāṇa* (ancient) literature which came into existence between the fifth and first century BCE.[24] The laws of war, as enunciated in the epic and *purāṇa* literature, distinguish sharply between combatants and non-combatants. Under no circumstances were non-combatants to be harmed.[25] Further, unarmed soldiers were not to be attacked nor a fleeing enemy to be annihilated. Unlike Kautilya's recommendations of *kutayuddha* (unjust war), Manu suggests *dharmayuddha* (just war). *Dharmayuddha* is to be waged by the Kshatriya (warrior caste), because *dharma* is the *kshatra* (duty) of the Kshatriya. If battles become at all necessary, Manu writes that the king should fight with horses and chariots on level ground.[26] Manu, instead of advocating an aggressive war for complete destruction of the enemy by all means, preaches a sort of ceremonial war. Manu was also against the use of deadly weapons, despising horse archery introduced by foreigners. He was

---

[22] M.G. Prasad, "Social Justice in Ancient India: In *Arthaśāstra*", in K.D. Irani and Morris Silver (eds.), *Social Justice in the Ancient World*, Greenwood Press, Westport, CT, 1995, p. 91.

[23] R.P. Kangle, *The Kauṭalya Arthaśāstra*, Part 2, 2nd ed., Motilal Banarsidass, Delhi, 1972.

[24] U.P. Thapliyal, "Military Organization in the Ancient Period", in S.N. Prasad (ed.), *Historical Perspectives of Warfare in India: Some Morale and Materiel Determinants*, New Delhi, Center for Studies in Civilisations, 2002, pp. 45–67.

[25] Nagendra Singh, Enforcement of Human Rights in Peace and War and the Future of Humanity, Martinus Nijhoff, Dordrecht, 1986, p. 105.

[26] Olivelle, 2005, p. 164, see *supra* note 14. See also Nikunja Vihari Banerjee, *Studies in the Dharmaśāstra of Manu*, Manshiram Manoharlal Publisher, New Delhi, 1980.

against the use of deception, treachery and surprise in battle.[27] Manu was also against attacking a retreating army. The *Manusmṛti* warns the king that, while waging war, his soldiers should not kill enemy troops with weapons that are concealed, barbed or smeared with poison or whose tips are ablaze with fire.[28] A righteous warrior should not kill anyone who folds his hands in supplication, asking for mercy or anyone who surrenders. Nor should the righteous king attack enemy soldiers who are without armour or without weapons, or whose weapons are broken. Further, any enemy soldier who is asleep or engaged in combat with someone else should not be attacked.[29]

Manu offers a strong critique of Kautilya's *kutayuddha* on the tactical and strategic planes. The *Manusmṛti* notes that the king should always act without guile. It emphasises constant vigilance on the part of the ruler to guard against fraud by the enemy. The ruler must not let the enemy discover any weakness of his, but rather discover the weakness of the enemy.[30] Unlike Kautilya, who asserts that all alliances and treaties are pieces of paper that are to be torn up if necessary, Manu emphasises the importance of good faith towards one's allies. The *Manusmṛti* advocates fortress warfare. It notes that, when a king launches a military expedition against the realm of an enemy, he should advance towards the enemy's fort. In Manu's paradigm the *giri-durga* (mountain fortress) is the best defensive structure. The best way to defend a fortress is by stationary archers on the walls, and the fortress should be well stocked with weapons money, grain, artisans, fodder and water in order to withstand a long siege.[31]

2.4. The *Manusmṛti* and Punishment

The concept of *dharma* that ruled Indian civilisation from the Vedic period up to Muslim invasion in the twelfth century was that from king to his last servant everyone was bound by *dharma*. The word *dharma* is derived

---

[27] Olivelle, *ibid.*

[28] *Ibid.*, p. 159.

[29] See K.R.R. Sastry, "Hinduism and International Law", in *Recueil des cours*, 1966, vol. 117, pp. 507–614.

[30] Olivelle, 2005, p. 159–60, see *supra* note 14. See also Gregory M. Reichberg, Henrik Sye with Nicole M. Hartwell, *Religion, War, and Ethics: A Sourcebook of Textual Traditions*, Cambridge University Press, New York, 2014, p. 513.

[31] Olivelle, 2005, p. 157–58, see *supra* note 14.

from *dhṛ* which means to uphold, sustain or nourish. The seers often used it in close association with *ṛta* (order, rule) and *satya* (truth). *Dharma* is neither a religion nor religious thought nor is it conservative. It encompasses a progressive movement of societies towards law and morality. It is a movement of righteousness, virtues and virtuous duty. *Dharma* has a broader connotation and ordains law, religion, rectitude and morality regulating life and conduct of human beings so as to fit into the wider context of nature and the cosmos – the world order. The *Manusmṛti* prescribes the *dharmavidhi*, ten essential ethical rules for the observance of *dharma*: patience or steadfastness (*dhriti*), forgiveness (*kshama*), piety or self-control (*dama*), honesty (*asteya*), sanctity or purity (*saucham*), control of senses (*indraiya-nigrah*), wisdom or reason (*dhi*), knowledge or learning (*vidya*), truthfulness (*satya*) and absence of anger (*krodha*). Manu further writes, "Nonviolence, truth, non-coveting, purity of body and mind, control of senses are the essence of *dharma*".[32] Therefore *dharmic* laws govern not only the individual but also everyone in society.

The *Manusmṛti* gives the state the supreme role in human affairs. Manu believed that the maintenance of law and order would not be possible without an effective force behind it. The *daṇḍa* (literally the sceptre) represents the power and coercive dimension of the state, with the king as the judicial administrator.[33] The word *daṇḍa* is very comprehensive in connotation. In a general sense, *daṇḍa* as punishment means coercion. Manu was of the opinion that the king must be knowledgeable about two things, namely *dharma* and *daṇḍa* or chastisement, as the proper maintenance of the rules of *dharma* and imposing punishment on those who violate its rules lay in his hands. Manu followed up his account of the obligations of the king to protect the lives and property of his people by applying the theory of *daṇḍa*. Manu assigns to it the same high divine origin as to the office of kingship. The lord created *daṇḍa* before he appointed a king in order to make the discharge of duties proper and efficient. *Daṇḍa* is considered as the protector of all creatures and of the law. According to Manu, *daṇḍa* rules all people and protects them, as through the fear of *daṇḍa*, criminal tendencies were prevented even when the public was

---

[32] Bhabatosh Bhattacharya, *Studies in Dharmaśāstra: Ancient Period*, Indian Studies Past and Present, Calcutta, 1964.

[33] Haripada Chakraborti, *Criminal Justice in Ancient India*, Vedams, New Delhi, 1996.

asleep.[34] Thus, it was the *daṇḍa* that kept all classes of the society or *varna* and the *āśrama* within the limits of discipline. Moreover, psychologically, the fear of *daṇḍa* was the grand motive for the fulfilment of individual obligations.[35] Manu applied the indiscriminate jurisdiction of the king's *daṇḍa* over his subjects. Thus Manu laid down the principle of the king's unlimited jurisdiction over offenders irrespective of their rank or status or relationship. He felt that the king's mode of application of *daṇḍa* was the key to the prosperity or destruction of the individual and the community. *Dharma* and *daṇḍa* are so integrated that if they are ignored then the law of jungle shall prevail. *Daṇḍa* must be wielded discreetly for the governance of the state as well as a means of its protection, with the sole object of the happiness of all. *Daṇḍa*, with its all-pervading force, keeps thieves and criminals away and hence *daṇḍa* is *dharma*.[36]

It is important to note that Manu sometimes understands law in the sense of duty or obligation and sometimes even in the sense of virtue.[37] Manu emphasised that twice-born men should obey the tenfold law, which includes contentment, forgiveness, self-control, abstention from wrongfully appropriating anything, purification, coercion of the organs, wisdom, knowledge and abstention from anger. Most of these laws are actually virtues signifying duties corresponding to them. Manu mentions the 18 titles of law or grounds for litigation (*vyavahārapada*), namely 1) non-payment of debts, 2) deposits and pledge, 3) sale without ownership, 4) concerns among partners, 5) resumption of gifts, 6) non-payment of wages, 7) non-performance of agreements, 8) rescission of sale and purchase, 9) disputes between owners of cattle and their servants, 10) disputes regarding boundaries, 11) assault, 12) defamation, 13) theft, 14) robbery and violence, 15) adultery and sexual crimes against women, 16) duties of man and wife, 17) partition of inheritance and 18) gambling and betting.[38]

These are the titles of legal issues in connection with which lawsuits may arise, with the demand for a judicial procedure and with a view to their decision. According to Manu, the first step in judicial procedure is

---

[34] Wendy Dongier, *Laws of Manu, with an Introduction and Notes*, Penguin, New Delhi, 1991.
[35] Chakraborti, 1996, see *supra* note 33.
[36] Sastry, 1966, see *supra* note 29.
[37] Olivelle, 2005, p. 154, see *supra* note 14.
[38] *Ibid.*, p. 167; Dongier, see *supra* note 34.

the constitution of the court of justice. At the head of the judicial system stood the king's court.[39] This court was held at the capital, and was sometimes presided over by the king himself, but more often by a learned Brahmin appointed for the purpose; he was known as the *adhyaksha* or *sabhāpati*. The *adhyaksha* perhaps originally selected for each particular occasion in the course of time became a permanent officer of state, and held the position of the chief justice (*prādvivāka*) of the realm. The king, together with the *prādvivāka* and three or four other judges (*dhārmikaḥ*), formed the highest Court of Justice.[40] The aim of the trial of legal cases was the vindication of the cause of justice. Manu insisted that the task of interpreting law should always be undertaken by a Brahmin, no matter whether or not he is qualified to undertake it, but never by a Shudra.[41] Where three Brahmins well versed in the Vedas and a learned judge appointed by the king were present, that place could be called the court. It was found that a jury system existed in Manu's period, and Manu recommended the king to give the power of judicial administration to Brahmins in his absence. It is also surprising to note that the juries in the court of the Brahmin judge were also Brahmins. Manu described such a court where three Brahmins versed in the Vedas and the learned judge appointed by the king sat as the court of four-faced Brahman.[42] The king was to be accompanied by the Brahmins and ministers who were experts in counselling. Since Manu held that the judge should be a person learned in all branches of learning, it was important to notice that scholarship in Vedas alone was not a sufficient qualification for a judge. Manu desired that the king himself had to attend courts.

A very high standard was fixed for rule of law in ancient India. In the *Mahābhārata*, it was laid down that "[a] King who after having sworn that he shall protect his subjects fails to protect them should be executed like a mad dog". And further: "The people should execute a king who does not protect them, but deprives them of their property and assets and who takes no advice or guidance from any one. Such a king is not a king

---

[39] Olivelle, 2005, p. 167, see *supra* note 14; Jois, 2012, p. 77, 82, see *supra* note 19.

[40] M.K. Sharan, *Court Procedure in Ancient India*, Abhinav Publications, New Delhi, 1978, p. 19; Raj Kumar, *Essays on Legal Systems in India*, Discovery Publishing House, New Delhi, 2003, p. 12.

[41] Olivelle, 2005, p. 168, see *supra* note 14.

[42] S.G. Moghe, *History of Dharma-śāstra in Essence*, Bhandarkar Oriental Research Institute, Poona, 2000.

but misfortune".[43] The core concept of rule of law can be traced to the *Upaniṣad*. It provides that the "law is the king of kings".[44] It is more powerful and rigid than the kings. There is nothing higher than the law. By its powers the weak shall prevail over the strong and justice shall triumph. Thus, in a monarchy the concept of law developed to control the exercise of arbitrary powers of the monarchs who claimed divine powers to rule. In a democracy, the concept has assumed a different dimension and means that the holders of public powers must be able to justify publicly that the exercise of power is legally valid and socially just.

2.5. The Judiciary and Administration of Justice

Sacred law (*dharma*), evidence and legal procedure (*vyavahára*), history (*charitra*), and edicts of kings (*rajasasana*) are considered to be the pillars of law; and of these four the last is superior to the others and overrides them. *Dharma* is eternal truth holding sway over the world; *vyavahára* is evidence offered by witnesses; *charitra* is to be found in the tradition (*saṅgraha*) of the people; and the order of kings is what is called *sāsana* (legislation). These principles were administered by the courts in territorial divisions such as the *Sthāna* (which included about 800 villages), *Droṇamukha* (about 400 villages), *Kharvatika* (200 villages) and *Sangrahana* (10 villages), and at places where districts met three members acquainted with sacred law (*dharmastha*) and three ministers of the king (*amātya*) carried on the administration of justice.[45] This arrangement of judiciary suggests that there were sufficient number of courts at different levels of administration, and for district itself (*janapada-sandhishu*) there were circuit courts.[46]

In villages, the local councils (*kulani*), similar to the modern *pancāyat*, consisted of a board of five or more members to dispense justice to villagers. It was concerned with all matters relating to endowments, irrigation, cultivable land, the punishment of crime and so on. Village councils dealt with simple civil and criminal cases. At a higher level, in towns

---

[43] Manoj Kumar Sinha, "Hinduism and International Humanitarian Law", in *International Review of the Red Cross*, 2005, vol. 87, no, 858, pp. 285–94.

[44] M. Rama Jois, Legal and Constitutional History of India: Ancient Legal, Judicial and Constitutional System, Universal Law Publishing Co., New Delhi, 1984, p. 10.

[45] A.S. Altekar, *State and Government in Ancient India*, Motilal Banarsidass, Varanasi, 1949, p. 250.

[46] Kumar, 2003, p. 11, see *supra* note 40.

and districts, the courts were presided over by a government officer under the authority of the king to administer justice. The link between the village assembly in the local and official administration was the headman of the village. In each village, a local headman held hereditary office and was required to maintain order and administer justice. He was also a member of the village council and acted both as the leader of the village and mediator with the government.[47]

In order to deal with disputes among traders or artisans (*sreni*), various corporations trade guilds were authorised to exercise effective jurisdiction over their members. These tribunals, consisting of a president and three or five assistants, were allowed to decide their civil cases regularly just like other courts. It was possible to appeal from the tribunal of the guild to the local court, then to royal judges and finally to the king, though such situations rarely arose.

In the administration of justice, the duties and manners of the king were very clearly laid down in the sacred texts. Manu's code says a king, desirous of investigating law cases, must enter his court of justice, preserving a dignified demeanour, together with Brahmins and with experienced councillors.[48] There, either seated or standing, raising his right arm, without ostentation in his dress and ornaments, he should examine the business of the suitors. Manu cautions the King by saying, in a famous phrase: "Justice, being violated, destroys; justice, being preserved, preserves: therefore justice must not be violated, lest violated justice destroys us". Further he opines: "The only friend of men even after death is justice; for everything else is lost at the same time when the body (perishes)". If the judicial system fails to dispense justice, Manu says that one quarter of the guilt of an unjust decision falls on he who committed the crime, one quarter on the false witness, one quarter on all the judges and one quarter on the king.[49]

Manu felt that judicial administration should not rest in the hands of a feeble-minded king. If judicial administration were given to such a king, he would destroy the whole country. Punishment cannot be inflicted justly by one who has no assistant, by a fool, by a covetous man, by one whose mind is unimproved or by one addicted to sensual pleasures. The legisla-

---

[47] *Ibid.*, p. 12.

[48] R. Lingat, *The Classical Law of India*, University of California Press, Berkeley, 1973.

[49] Bühler, 1886, p. 255, see *supra* note 20.

tive powers of any king were extremely limited. He could not oppress people by means of harsh and unjust laws. This was because he was enjoined to govern the people and to administer justice strictly in accordance with the civil and criminal laws laid down in the *smṛti*.

2.6. Conclusion

The *Manusmṛti* is one of the great achievements of early Indian civilisation. There are in total 2,684 verses divided into 12 chapters and it is considered to be an exemplary treatise on *dharma*, with nine extant commentaries written about it. The *Manusmṛti* was considered such an important source of Hindu law and custom throughout the sub-continent that it was one of the earliest texts earmarked for translation into English to be used in British courts in India. The *Manusmṛti* shows the obvious influence of early *dharmaśāstra* texts and the *Arthaśāstra*.

It is sometimes said that all Hindu law originated from the Vedas (also called the *śruti* or that which is heard). However, this is a fiction. In fact Hindu law really emanated from books called the *smṛti*, such as the *Manusmṛti*, *Yājñavalkya Smṛti* and the *smṛti* of Viṣṇu, Nārada, Parāśara, Apastamba, Vaśiṣṭha, Gautam and so on. These *smṛti* were not laws made by parliament or a legislature. They were books written by Sanskrit scholars in ancient times who specialised in the law. Later, commentaries or digests (called *nibandha* or *tika*) were written on these *smṛti*, such as the commentary of Vijñāneśvara (who wrote a commentary called the *Mitākṣarā* on the *Yājñavalkya Smṛti*), the commentary of Jīmūtavāhana who wrote a law treatise called the *Dāyabhāga* (which is not a commentary on any particular *smṛti* but a digest of several *smṛti*). According to J. Duncan M. Derrett, *dharmaśāstra* literature and specially Manu's code constitutes India's greatest achievement in the field of jurisprudence. Even in the field of comparative law serious researchers, both Eastern and Western, have regarded Manu's work as one of the world's premier compositions in ancient law, more valuable in every sense than Hammurabi and able to hold its own in comparison to the covenant and priestly codes of Moses.[50]

Scholars had also found many contradictions in Manu's statements but instead of dismissing them outright as proofs of inconsistency, they have held that this was inevitable in order to avoid a crude determinism. It

---

[50] J. Duncan M. Derrett, *Religion, Law and State in India*, Faber and Faber, London, 1968.

was necessary to accommodate diverse practices prevalent in different sections of the society. Option was a better policy than elimination. Thus, it could be seen that though it is not very straightforward to accept the views of Manu or Kautilya nowadays, their work could be considered as important examples of key philosophical and legal texts, composed at a time when science and technology were not developed and when ideas of caste and creed superiority (*varnasrama vyavastha*) were at their maximum. They were sincere to their commitments and worked with a view to improving the socio-economic condition of the people of the age. In this sense, their works are unique.

Thus, it is clear from the above discussion that the development of principles of international criminal law had roots in the ancient India and *Manusmṛti* integrated many principles of international criminal law. The contribution of *Manusmṛti* in this field is very significant and widely recognised by scholars.

3

Between *Isonomía* and *Hegemonía*: Political Complexities of Transitional Justice in Ancient Greece

Emiliano J. Buis[*]

> οὔτ᾽ ἂν νομοθέτης ἀκριβής, εἰ μὴ χάριν εἰρήνης τὰ πολέμου νομοθετοῖ μᾶλλον ἢ τῶν πολεμικῶν ἕνεκα τὰ τῆς εἰρήνης.
>
> And he will not make a finished lawgiver unless he designs his warfare legislation for peace rather than his peace legislation for war.
>
> Plato, *Laws*, 628d-e

3.1. Introduction

Sicily, 413 BCE. After a disastrous military campaign the Athenians were severely defeated by the Spartans. It is said that the victors rejected a call for arbitration instead of resorting to war when the enemy had employed weapons (ἐν ταῖς πρότερον ξυνθήκαις ὅπλα μὴ ἐπιφέρειν, ἢν δίκας ἐθέλωσι διδόναι), even if the Athenians had asked for the dispute to be settled peacefully (αὐτοὶ οὐχ ὑπήκουον ἐς δίκας προκαλουμένων τῶν Ἀθηναίων).[1] Similarly, after committing an offence themselves, the Athenians also chose to reject an offer of arbitration shortly afterwards when invited by the Spartans to deal with the controversy (ἐς δίκας

---

[*] **Emiliano J. Buis** received his Ph.D. from the University of Buenos Aires, Argentina, and is Adjunct Professor of Public International Law, International Humanitarian Law, the Origins of International Law in Antiquity and Ancient Greek Language and Literature at the University of Buenos Aires and the Central National University in Azul, Argentina. He is also a Researcher at the National Research Council for Science and Technology. He is a former Fellow at the Department of Classics, Brown University, USA, the Max-Planck-Institut für europäische Rechtsgeschichte, Germany, the Harvard University Center for Hellenic Studies, USA and the Alexander S. Onassis Public Benefit Foundation, Greece. He is currently a Postdoctoral Researcher at the Centre Léon Robin de recherches sur la pensée grecque (CNRS-Paris-Sorbonne).

[1] Thucydides, *The Peloponnesian War*, 7.18.2 ('Thucydides').

προκαλουμένων τῶν Λακεδαιμονίων οὐκ ἤθελον ἐπιτρέπειν).[2] This episode represents, in the first place, an example of how Greeks were capable of appealing to institutionalised methods for solving disputes during armed conflicts at their convenience. Second, it shows that the study of the Peloponnesian War (431–404 BCE) might offer interesting insights into the political realm of international affairs and into the alternative possibilities of putting in place legal mechanisms or deploying physical force to respond to breaches or violations of treaties or customary norms.

Within the broader context of a long-standing neglect of the historical aspects of international law,[3] it should not come as a surprise that very

---

[2] *Ibid.*, 7.18.3.

[3] International legal history was mostly ignored for many centuries. At the beginning of the twentieth century, Lassa Oppenheim, "The Science of International Law", in *American Journal of International Law*, 1908, vol. 2, no. 2, p. 316, complained that "the history of international law is certainly the most neglected province of it". It has only recovered as a discipline in recent decades. In this context, it is possible to refer to seminal works of authors such as Robert Redslob, *Histoire des grands principes du droit des gens depuis l'antiquité jusqu'à la veille de la grande guerre* [History of the Great Principles of the Law of Peoples from Antiquity to the Eve of the Great War], Librairie A. Rousseau, Paris, 1923, or J.H.W. Verzijl, *International Law in Historical Perspective*, vol. 1, A.W. Sijthoff, Leiden, 1968 – whose monumental 11-volume work, written over a period of 24 years, was completed by W.P. Heere and J.P.S. Offerhaus in 1998 – who have constructed the necessary bases to build a true theorisation of international law from a diachronical perspective. Among the contemporary contributions focusing on the history of international law, see the excellent studies of Wilhelm G. Grewe, *Epochen der Völkerrechtsgeschichte*, Nomos, Baden-Baden, 1984 (translated into English as *The Epochs of International Law*, Walter de Gruyter, Berlin, 2000); Martti Koskenniemi, *The Gentle Civilizer of Nations: The Rise and Fall of International Law 1870–1960*, Cambridge University Press, Cambridge, 2002; and the works of Antonio Truyol y Serra, *Historia del Derecho Internacional Público* [History of Public International Law], Tecnos, Madrid, 1998; Slim Laghmani, *Histoire du droit des gens: du* jus gentium *impérial au* jus publicum europaeum [History of the Law of Peoples: From *Jus Gentium* to *Jus Public Europaeum*], Pedone, Paris, 2003; Marie-Hélène Renaut, *Histoire du droit international public* [History of Public International Law], Ellypses, Paris, 2007; Dominique Gaurier, *Histoire du droit international: de l'antiquité à la création de l'ONU* [History of International Law: From Antiquity to the Creation of the UN], Presses Universitaires de Rennes, Rennes, 2014; and Stephen C. Neff, *Justice Among Nations: A History of International Law*, Harvard University Press, Cambridge, MA, 2104, *inter alia*. For an overall vision of the new approaches to the history of international law, see Ingo Hueck, "The Discipline of the History of International Law", in *Journal of the History of International Law*, 2001, vol. 3, no. 2, pp. 194–217. From different points of view, both Martti Koskenniemi, "Why History of International Law Today?", in *Rechtsgeschichte*, 2004, vol. 4, pp. 61–66, and Randall Lesaffer, "International Law and its History: The Story of an Unrequited Love", in Matthew Craven, Malgosia Fitzmaurice and Maria Vogiatzi (eds.), *Time, History and International Law*, Brill, Leiden, 2007, pp. 27–41, agree that the end of the Cold War generated a moment of transi-

few voices have dealt with the legal aspects of interstate relations in pre-modern times. Nevertheless – as the Sicilian example reveals – it seems a well-established fact today that classical Greek antiquity was well aware of the specific functionality and the relative importance of signing treaties and regulating the relations between city-states (*póleis*)[4] according to political interests.[5]

It is not possible to disregard the fact that a heterogeneous set of rules – sometimes explicit, for most times implicit – was agreed and arranged in order to regulate the behaviour of the autonomous and politically organised Hellenic communities between the sixth and first centuries BCE.[6] The existence of written documents, mostly subscribed to under the auspices of religious considerations,[7] and some of which have been pre-

---

tion which facilitated the search for new historical inquiries. On the promising future of these new tendencies, cf. George Rodrigo Bandeira Galindo, "Martti Koskenniemi and the Historiographical Turn in International Law", in *European Journal of International Law*, 2005, vol. 16, no. 3, pp. 539–59.

[4] When transliterated, the original accents of the Greek terms are respected in all cases, with the exception of well-known geographical and personal names (where common English versions are employed).

[5] For a similar intellectual exercise on law in antiquity regarding the norms applicable to Chinese interstate relations, see LIU Daqun, "International Law and International Humanitarian Law in Ancient China", in Morten Bergsmo, CHEAH Wui Ling and YI Ping (eds.), *Historical Origins of International Criminal Law*, vol. 1, Torkel Opsahl Academic EPublisher, Brussels, 2014, pp. 87–113 (https://www.legal-tools.org/doc/8eb79b/).

[6] In this sense, in the face of the traditional denying theory of F. Laurent, *Histoire du droit des gens et des relations internationales: Études sur l'histoire de l'humanité* [History of the Law of Peoples and International Relations: Studies on the History of Humanity], August Durand, Brussels, 1850/1851, who considered that it was impossible to speak of a normative system in force to regulate the relations between the different primitive peoples, I follow the opposing arguments held by Coleman Phillipson, *The International Law and Custom of Ancient Greece and Rome*, 2 vols., Macmillan, London, 1911; Isidoro Ruiz Moreno, *El derecho internacional antes de la era Cristiana* [International Law before the Christian Era], Facultad de Derecho y Ciencias Sociales de la UBA, Buenos Aires, 1946; Elias J. Bickerman, "Remarques sur le droit des gens dans la Grèce classique" [Observations on the Law of Peoples in Classical Greece], in *Revue Internationale des Droits de l'Antiquité*, 1950, vol. 4, pp. 99–127; and, more recently, David J. Bederman, *International Law in Antiquity*, Cambridge University Press, Cambridge, 2001, all of whom recognise certain international law institutions in force in the Graeco-Roman world.

[7] Theodore P. Ion, "The Sanctity of Treaties", in *Yale Law Journal*, 1911, vol. 20, no. 4, p. 268: "In reviewing the practice of the people of ancient times, we see that faith to covenants was in some way their watchword, religious rites being the cardinal feature of their

served in inscriptions or by means of indirect transmission, was useful among Greek cities in order to control the actions of allies or potential enemies when deemed necessary.[8] But the question remains as to whether these agreements were intended to clarify – or rather to hide – the latent inequality of an interstate system systematically characterised by violent invasions and territorial conquest.[9]

By studying the relationship between *póleis* in classical times, especially the tension between the language of equality (as an analogical projection of internal *isonomía*) and hegemonic intention, my purpose here is to analyse how Greek antiquity provides different ways of dealing with violations of common laws (*nómoi*), both externally and internally. In particular, I am interested in exploring how ancient Greeks dealt with the problem of the individual commission of grave crimes such as mass killings. In this sense, I focus my research in the last years of the fifth century BCE, when two examples can show opposing ways in which Spartans and

---

conclusion, although they may, at times, have deviated from the strict observance of their treaty obligations".

[8] Roman practice will draw on this precedent and show a complex development of the practice of signing treaties with a clear political intention: to ensure by all possible means the supremacy of the *urbs* on conquered regions through the implementation of a *ius gentium* created, endorsed and interpreted by Rome herself.

[9] Arthur M. Eckstein, *Mediterranean Anarchy, Interstate War, and the Rise of Rome*, University of California Press, Berkeley, 2006, believes that only a "multi-polar anarchy", which lacked an international law and was characterised by fluid power balances, existed in the Mediterranean interstate system before Roman times. This is the anarchy that was, almost contemporaneously, rejected by Polly Low, *Interstate Relations in Classical Greece. Morality and Power*, Cambridge University Press, Cambridge, 2007, pp. 77–128, when affirming the existence of a Hellenic interstate law with – in my view – substantial irrefutable evidence. Of course, as I will try to show, this legal framework is not incompatible with power politics. On an "international" law among Greek *póleis*, see also Victor Martin, *La vie internationale dans la Grèce des cités (Vie–IVe s. av. J.-C.)* [International Life in Greece in Times of Cities (6th–4th Centuries BCE)], Recueil Sirey, Geneva, 1940; Georges C. Ténékidès, "Droit international et communautés fédérales dans la Grèce des cités (Ve–IIIe s. av. J.C.)" [International Law and Federal Communities in Greece in Times of Cities (5th–3rd Centuries BCE)], *Recueil des cours de l'Academie de droit international de La Haye*, 90 II, Martinus Nijhoff, Leiden, 1956, pp. 475–652; Georges C. Ténékidès, "Esquisse d'une théorie des droits internationaux de l'homme dans la Grèce des cités" [Draft of a Theory of International Human Rights in Greece in Times of Cities], in *Revue des droits de l'homme*, 1970, vol. 213, pp. 195–244; Georges C. Ténékidès, *Les relations internationales dans la Grèce antique* [International Relations in Ancient Greece], Leventis, Athens, 1993; and Frank E. Adcock and Derek J. Mosley, *Diplomacy in Ancient Greece*, Thames and Hudson, London, 1975.

Athenians managed to deal with atrocities originating in the context of international or internal armed conflicts.

As a case study for the international conduct of the *pólis* – and therefore as a sign of the determination to impose local criteria on the adversary – I will address the aftermath of the naval Battle of Aegospotami in 405 BCE. Sources indicate that the Lacedaemonian admiral Lysander decided to transfer the defeated leaders to Lampsacus and established a tribunal – composed of representatives of Spartan allies – in order to try those enemies who had decided to mutilate their prisoners. My second case study relates to the Athenian amnesty law of 403 BCE. Only two years after the condemnation of the generals of the Battle of Aegospotami, the Athenians decided to implement a "reconciliation" mechanism that managed to balance forgiveness and retribution when dealing with the Thirty Tyrants who had planned the extrajudicial killing of almost 10 per cent of all citizens.

On the basis of examining the external and internal dimensions of the classical *pólis*, this chapter intends to shed light on the different manner in which criminal offences in times of armed conflict could be dealt with by a community struggling between democracy and imperialism. As I will try to show, the interplay of criminal tribunals and local remedies translated the complexities of a system in which internal equality among citizens coexisted (and contrasted) – in an international setting – with the aspiration for international supremacy in times of war.

In other words, my purpose here is to show that in Greek antiquity it is already possible to find complementary and simultaneous methods of addressing responsibilities for grave offences against protected people. This ancient milestone, which is complex and similar to more recent experiences, should be fully explained in order to have a better understanding of the historical logics underlying the complexities of *ius post bellum* and the development of international criminal law in modern times.[10] In

---

[10] It is true that the expression *ius post bellum* has been only coined in the last century, as recently suggested by Jens Iverson, "Contrasting the Normative and Historical Foundations of Transitional Justice and *Jus Post Bellum*: Outlining the Matrix of Definitions in Comparative Perspective", in Carsten Stahn, Jennifer S. Easterday and Jens Iverson (eds.), *Jus Post Bellum: Mapping the Normative Foundations*, Oxford University Press, Oxford, 2014, pp. 97–99. This does not preclude the fact that the origins of transitional justice can, in fact, be found in ancient times.

order to be able to consider the different legal reactions to mass atrocities in the case studies (section 3.4.), I shall first explore the conflict between political subjugation and feigned equality in Greek interstate relations (section 3.2.) and then discuss the concept of common laws that settled the ground for a shared juridical system among *póleis* (section 3.3).

3.2. Greek Rules and Armed Conflicts: Negotiation or Imposition?

In Greek antiquity the *pólis* emerged as a city-state – an institutional entity that had control over a certain cultivated territory (*khóra*), possessed a population of citizens composed by adult free men and regulated life under the exercise of power by governmental organs situated in the fortified centre of the city (*ásty*).[11] *Póleis* were clearly independent: concepts such as *autonomía* or *eleuthería* (roughly, "freedom"), frequently mentioned in ancient texts,[12] constitute a preliminary version of what would later be

---

[11] On the notion of the *pólis* as a state, in a broad or in a restrictive sense, the discussions have been very extensive and, *ratione brevitatis*, this cannot be the place to reproduce them. Suffice it to say that in the context of international relations it is clear that these cities behaved as true subjects, capable of acquiring rights and obligations. This international legal personality, however, has not been enough to generate uniformity among scholars regarding the "state" character of the *poleis*. Bearing in mind that today the main characteristics identifying statehood are population, territory and government, I do not believe it appropriate to deny such condition to the Hellenic cities of the classical period, which constituted both a political community and an urban centre. The members of the famous Copenhagen Polis Center have insisted on many occasions on this question; it is held, in fact, that in the Greek world the three elements of the city-state appear in some way in a consolidated hierarchy: first, the community of citizens, then the political institutions, and finally the physical space. See Mogens Herman Hansen, "Introduction. The *Polis* as a Citizen-State", in Mogens Herman Hansen (ed.), *The Ancient Greek City-State*, Munksgaard, Copenhagen, 1993, pp. 7–9. Since the *pólis* will be conceived as the corpus of citizens acting together, the preservation of the city lies in the maintenance of a common spirit of equality, as I will develop in the following pages.

[12] Together with the adjective *autónomos*, it is frequent to find the use of terms to reinforce the independence of the *póleis* such as *autópolis* (applicable to the possibility to individually decide a certain foreign policy), *autotelés* (fiscal autonomy) or *autódikos* (judicial independence). Some emphatic expressions, such as *eleútheroi te kaì autónomoi* ("free and independent") (Thucydides, 3.10.5, see *supra* note 1) or *eleutherotáte* ("very free") (Thucydides, *id.*, 6.89.6, 7.69.2), underscore that independence is presented as one of the essential characteristics of the cities, even protected by customary inter-Hellenic law. Cf. Georges C. Ténékidès, *La notion juridique d'indépendance et la tradition hellénique: Autonomie et fédéralisme aux Ve et IVe s. av. J.C.* [The Legal Concept of Independence and Hellenic Tradition: Autonomy and Federalism in the 5th and 5th Centuries BCE], Presses de l'Institut Français d'Athènes, Athens, 1954, pp. 17–19.

understood as sovereignty.[13] In this sense, each city-state was able to grant itself its own legal rules, considered as *nómoi* (the laws enacted in the context of the political organs of the *pólis*).[14] By the end of the fifth century BCE, Greek men considered themselves, as citizens with full rights, to be living under *isonomía* (political equality before the norms of the *póleis*), distinguishing themselves from the subjects of tyrants and the Persian king.[15]

The acknowledgment of independence in each *pólis* – as well as its self-regulatory nature – explains the creation of a notion of formal equality among them, conceived as a parallel to internal *isonomía*.[16] In this sense, it should not be surprising to find that, almost in a Westphalian environment *avant la lettre*, the international relations among *póleis* were described as the result of a delicate balance between even negotiators.[17] For instance, in Euripides' play *Phoenissae*, represented in Athens in the late fifth century BCE, one of the characters describes the value of justice and the need to honour equality (*isótes*) among friends (*phílous ... phílois*), city-states (*póleis ... pólesi*) and allies (*symmákhous ... symmákhois*)

---

[13]   Adalberto Giovannini, *Les relations entre états dans la Grèce antique, du temps d'Homère à l'intervention romaine (ca. 700–200 av. J.-C.)* [Relations between States in Ancient Greece, From Homer's Time to the Roman Intervention (c. 700–200 BCE)], Franz Steiner, Stuttgart, 2007, p. 98.

[14]   Cf. Jacqueline de Romilly, *La loi dans la pensée grecque* [The Law in Greek Thought], Les Belles Lettres, Paris, 1971, pp. 13–24, defines *nómos* as the law of the classical city.

[15]   Kurt A. Raaflaub, "Zeus Eleutherios, Dionysos the Liberator, and the Athenian Tyrannicides: Anachronistic Uses of Fifth-Century Political Concepts", in Pernille Flensted-Jensen, Thomas Heine Nielsen and Lene Rubinstein (eds.), *Polis & Politics: Studies in Ancient Greek History*, Museum Tusculanum Press, Copenhagen, 2000, pp. 249–75.

[16]   George A. Sheets, "Conceptualizing International Law in Thucydides", in *American Journal of Philology*, 1994, vol. 115, no. 1, p. 53: "Each independent polis had its own territory, its own citizenry and government, and its own defense capacity; each, in theory at least, pursued its own foreign policy, and claimed to enjoy an ostensibly equal standing to other States in the Hellenic community. That community, in turn, was constituted not only by a common culture, but by an intricate web of legal relationships".

[17]   In these remarks, I follow the ideas already presented in Emiliano J. Buis, "Ancient Entanglements: The Influence of Greek Treaties in Roman 'International Law' under the Framework of Narrative Transculturation", in Thomas Duve (ed.), *Entanglements in Legal History: Conceptual Approaches*, Max-Planck Institute for European Legal History, Frankfurt-am-Main, 2014, pp. 151–85.

(verses 535–38). If equality is basically a landmark of personal relations, it can also be useful in describing the balance of international relations.[18]

The first treaty in the Greek world that has been preserved was found in Olympia and dates back to late sixth century BCE. It refers to an agreement of offensive alliance between the Eleians and the Heraians in which the provisions on mutual assistance in case of war or any other circumstance are included in perfect equilibrium:

> ἁ ϝράτρα τοῖρ Ϝαλείοις : καὶ τοῖς Ἐρ-
>
> ϝαοίοις: συνμαχία κ' ἔα ἑκατὸν ϝέτεα :
>
> ἄρχοι δέ κα τοῖ : αἰ δέ τι δέοι : αἴτε ϝέπος αἴτε ϝ-
>
> άργον : συνέαν κ' ἀλ(λ)άλοις : τά τ' ἄλ(λ)<α> καὶ πα-
>
> ρ πολέμο͞ : αἰ δὲ μὰ συνέαν : τάλαντόν κ'
>
> ἀργύρο͞ : ἀποτίνοιαν : τοῖ Δὶ Ὀλυνπίοι : τοὶ κα-
>
> (δ)δαλέμενοι : λατρειόμενον : αἰ δέ τιρ τὰ γ-
>
> ράφεα : ταὶ κα(δ)δαλέοιτο : αἴτε ϝέτας αἴτε τ-
>
> ελεστὰ : αἴτε δᾶμος : ἐν τἐπιάροι κ' ἐνέχ-
>
> οιτο τοἰνταυτ' ἐγραμ(μ)ένοι.[19]

> This is the covenant between the Eleians and the Heraians. There shall be alliance for a hundred years; and this year it shall begin. And if either of us need assistance, whether of word or deed, we shall stand by one another, in all other affairs, and especially in warfare: and if we do not stand by each other, they who have so offended shall pay a silver tal-

---

[18] Indeed, this is the only way to understand the distinction made in the text among persons, cities and "allies" in combat. Some authors even indicate that already in the Greek world an image of natural equality was introduced, based on a sacred law and on a progressive incorporation of equality into the law of peoples as a logical consequence of the fictional analogy created between natural persons and international secondary subjects or legal persons. The frequent appearance of corporal or material metaphors to name organisations created by men finds its source in ancient testimonies and was developed in detail during the Middle Ages, as stated by Edwin Dewitt Dickinson, "Analogy between Natural Persons and International Persons in the Law of Nations", in *Yale Law Journal*, 1917, vol. 26, pp. 564–91.

[19] Hermann Bengston, *Die Staatsverträge des Altertums*, vol. 2: *Die Verträge der griechisch-römischen Welt von 700 bis 338 v. Chr.*, Beck, Munich, 1962 (*StV*), no. 110; Henri van Effenterre and Françoise Ruzé (eds.), *Nomima: Recueil d'inscriptions politiques et juridiques de l'archaïsme grec* [Nomima: Compilation of Political and Legal Inscriptions from Greek Archaic Times], vol. 1, École française de Rome, Rome, 1994, fn. 52. Ténékidès, 1954, p. 19, fn. 3, see *supra* note 12, identifies it as a treaty "*sur pied d'égalité*".

ent to Olympian Zeus, to be confiscated to him. And if any
one shall destroy this inscription, whether private man, or
magistrate, or community, [the offender] shall be liable to
the sacred fine here written.

From this moment onwards, bilateral treaties usually proclaim in
writing that they are agreed and celebrated in balanced terms between the
parties.[20] In the interstate dimension, the prohibition on offending
"equals" (*mè adikeîn toùs homoíous*) was widespread.[21] The Greeks spoke
therefore about symmetry between *póleis*, even if they frequently identified the existence of large and small cities, the former exercising authority, the latter obeying orders.[22] When describing the provisions contained
in the treaty that was signed in 418 BCE between Spartans and Argives,
Thucydides quotes that "all the cities in Peloponnese, both small and
great, shall be independent according to the customs of their country" (τὰς
δὲ πόλιας τὰς ἐν Πελοποννάσῳ, καὶ μικρὰς καὶ μεγάλας, αὐτονόμως ἦμεν

---

[20] It is the meaning of the expression "*epì toîs ísois kaì homoíois*" (Xenophon, *Hellenika*,
7.1.13). According to Peter Hunt, *War, Peace, and Alliance in Demosthenes' Athens*,
Cambridge University Press, Cambridge, 2010, p. 103, "treaties between cities of manifestly different strengths were symmetrical".

[21] Thucydides, 1.42, see *supra* note 1. Gustave Glotz, *Le droit des gens dans l'antiquité
grecque* [The Law of Peoples in Greek Antiquity], Imprimerie nationale, Paris, 1915, p.
98, already mentions the importance of equality among city-states by asserting that "*entre
Grecs, le droit des gens se fondait sur les principes du respect qu'on se doit* entre égaux"
(emphasis added).

[22] This distinction between great and small cities is widespread in the literary sources – see
Ivana Savalli-Lestrade, "Remarques sur les 'grandes' et les 'petites' cités aux époques
classique et hellénistique d'après les sources littéraires et épigraphiques", in *Topoi*, vol. 18,
2013, p. 118 – even if it does not explicitly appear in epigraphical texts, see John Ma,
"Grandes et petites cités au miroir de l'épigraphie classique et hellénistique", in *Topoi*, vol.
18, 2014, p. 67. In this regard, see also the traditional monograph by M. Amit, *Great and
Small Poleis: A Study in the Relations between the Great Powers and the Small Cities in
Ancient Greece*, Latomus, Brussels, 1973. According to Paul MacKechnie, *Outsiders in
the Greek Cities in the Fourth Century BC*, Routledge, London, 1989, p. 1: "City-states
varied in size. The extent of their independence differed: some colonies accepted their
mother city's choice of annual magistrates, for instance, and some small cities, while independent, are not likely to have been able to pursue foreign policies distinct from the foreign policy of a large neighbouring city". It should be said, however, that many *póleis*
were neither great nor small, rather belonging to an intermediate (and maybe less defined)
status; cf. Philippe Gauthier, "Grandes et petites cités: hégémonie et autarcie", in *Opus*,
vols. 6–8, 1987–1989, p. 193.

πάσας καττὰ πάτρια, 5.77.5–7).[23] The treaty also provided that, in case of the territory being invaded from the outside, the parties to the agreement should unite to repel the aggression and all allies of Sparta and Argos would stand on equal terms for both of them.[24]

At least until the mid-fourth century BCE, there is a specific intention of considering independent both the biggest city-states – with a large population – and the smallest ones. It is not unusual, for instance, to find in bilateral conventions a reference to the recognition of sovereignty of all city-states – parties to the agreement and third parties – in terms of legal balance. When Pericles, for instance, had the idea of organising a pan-Hellenic congress in mid-fifth century BCE with the purpose of restoring the temples that had been destroyed by the barbarians, keeping the vows made to the gods and adopting security measures at sea, he summoned all city-states, whether big or small (*kaì mikràn pólin kaì megálen*).[25] The failure of the call, perhaps due to the profound difference of criteria among the communities,[26] does not preclude the fact that, in his speech, *póleis* were referred to as having the same capacity of negotiating in equal conditions.

---

[23] Cf. also Thucydides, 5.79.1, see *supra* note 1. Ida Calabi, *Ricerche sui rapporti fra i poleis* [Research Studies on the Relations Between *Póleis*], La Nuova Italia, Florence, 1953, p. 72, says that, even though it was not a legal distinction, the opposition between large and small cities expressed a relation of superiority linked to the individual "*potenza*" of some *póleis* in terms of interstate relations. In this sense, it is related to the adjective "first" *(prôtos)* which, for example, Thucydides himself uses to identify the "main cities" (*tôn próton póleon*) in 2.8.1, see *supra* note 1.

[24] It should be pointed out, following C.E. Graves, *Commentary on Thucydides Book 5*, Macmillan, London, 1891, that these equitable provisions tended, in essence, to limit the strength of the great powers located outside the area of the Peloponnese, mainly Athens. This means that "equality" of the parties is expressly conceived as a counterweight to the real inequality vis-à-vis third *póleis*.

[25] Plutarch, *Life of Pericles*, 17.1. About this proposal for a congress as a precedent of what would become in the fourth century BCE the Common Peace (*Koinè Eiréne*), cf. Franz Hampl, *Die griechischen Staatsverträge des 4. Jahrhunderts v. Christi geb* [Greek Treaties from the Fifth Century BCE], Hirzel, Leipzig, 1938. Giovannini, 2007, p. 100, fn. 50, see *supra* note 13, says that surely the Periclean proposal was actually a belated intervention, following arguments by Robin Seager, "The Congress Decree: Some Doubts and a Hypothesis", in *Historia*, 1969, vol. 18, pp. 129–41.

[26] According to Malcolm F. McGregor, *The Athenians and their Empire*, University of British Columbia Press, Vancouver, 1987, p. 74, the call failed because Sparta did not want to recognise the Athenian leadership as regards religious piety and common policy.

In the context of the Peace of Antalcidas – signed with Persia in 386 BCE, where some cities in Asia Minor were released to preserve better control over Greece – Xenophon states that King Artaxerxes considered the Asian cities to be their own, together with Clazomenae and Cyprus, whereas the rest of the Greek cities – the big and the small ones (*kaì mikràs kaì megálas*) – would still be independent (*autonómous*).[27] Following a similar reasoning, the orator Isocrates clearly explains how international treaties should be structured in equalitarian provisions and not in unilateral commands:

> ἃ χρῆν ἀναιρεῖν καὶ μηδὲ μίαν ἐᾶν ἡμέραν, νομίζοντας προστάγματα καὶ μὴ συνθήκας εἶναι. τίς γὰρ οὐκ οἶδεν ὅτι συνθῆκαι μέν εἰσιν, αἵ τινες ἂν ἴσως καὶ κοινῶς ἀμφοτέροις ἔχωσι, προστάγματα δὲ τὰ τοὺς ἑτέρους ἐλαττοῦντα παρὰ τὸ δίκαιον.[28]

> We ought to have suppressed asymmetrical provisions and not have allowed them to stand a single day, looking upon them as commands (*prostágmata*) and not as a treaty (*synthékas*); for who does not know that a treaty is something which is fair and impartial to both parties (*ísos kaì koinôs amphotérois ékhosin*), while a command is something which unjustly puts one side at a disadvantage (*tà toùs hetérous elattoûnta parà tò díkaion*)?[29]

Appealing to equality helps to overcome the difficulty of dealing with the unfair – but politically unavoidable – distinction between dominant and subordinate city-states. But even if most sources insist on a balance between city-states which are independent and do not allegedly depend on each other, in practical terms Greek international relations in classical times were determined by a notorious distinction between stronger and weaker *póleis*. In practice, war treaties (concerning alliances or friendship) relied on a feigned co-ordination among equals but tended to hide the unavoidable subordination of subjects to the most powerful.[30]

---

[27] Xenophon, *Hellenika*, 5.1.31; Diodorus Siculus, 14.110.3.

[28] G. Norlin (ed.), *Isocrates*, Harvard University Press, Cambridge, MA, 1980.

[29] Isocrates, *Panegyricus*, 176. Cf. the expression *ex epitagmáton* ("on the basis of impositions") in Andocides, *On the Peace*, 11.

[30] The groundbreaking book by Francisco J. Fernández Nieto, *Los acuerdos bélicos en la antigua Grecia* [War Treaties in Ancient Greece], Universidad de Santiago de Compostela, Santiago de Compostela, 1975, on war treaties is essential for this issue; Víctor Alonso

Some examples show a real hierarchy between the subjects and suggest a much greater negotiating power of the most influential *pólis*, as is the case of some offensive treaties in which a strong city-state – the victor in war, in general – overpowered its weaker counterpart. Thus Sparta was able to enforce its privileged position for most of the fifth century BCE. In 403 – just to mention one specific moment – Spartans imposed severe conditions on the Athenians in an unequal treaty, forcing them to destroy their walls, to surrender almost all of their fleet and to "have the same friends and enemies as the Spartans" (*tòn autòn ekhthròn kaì phílon nomízontas Lakedaimoníois*); they were even obliged to follow the Spartans whenever needed.[31]

The progressive foundation of international organisations during the late fifth and fourth centuries BCE shows autonomous *póleis* participating to a varied degree of interest and commitment.[32] Even if associations among allied city-states respected and guaranteed the formal equality and independence of each member, they also created a practical ground that

---

Troncoso, "Para un corpus de los tratados de alianza de la Grecia Clásica" [For a Corpus of Alliance Treaties in Classical Greece], in *Dike*, 2001, vol. 4, pp. 219–32, already showed, however, that there is still a need for a systematic study of the agreements of alliance.

[31] Xenophon, *Hellenika*, 2.2.20. An analogous obligation to have the same friends and enemies (*tòn autòn [...] ekhthròn kaì phílon Lakedaimoníois nomízein*) and to follow them as allies is included in the treaty imposed by the Spartans on the Olynthians in 379 BCE, taking advantage of the grave famine that affected them (Xenophon, *Hellenika*, 5.3.26). In a similar vein, the Athenians included a parallel clause in the treaties they offered for signature to the Corcyraeans (Thucydides, 3.75.6, see *supra* note 1) or the Thurians (Thucydides, 7.33.6); in both cases Athens called upon them to have the same enemies and friends as they had (*toùs autoùs ekhthroùs kaì phílous toîs Athenaíois nomízein*). Thomas Pistorius, *Hegemoniestreben und Autonomiesicherung in der griechischen Vertragspolitik klassischer und hellenistischer Zeit* [Hegemonic Ambitions and the Protection of Autonomy in Greek Treaty Politics of Classical and Hellenistic Times], Peter Lang, Frankfurt am Main, 1985, pp. 184–85, identifies the two provisions mentioned, which are typical of this type of treaty, as "*Freund-feindklausel*" and "*Heeresfolgeklausel*" respectively. Also P. Bonk, *Defensiv- und offensivklauseln in griechischen Symmakhieverträgen* [Defensive and Offensive Clauses in Greek Symmachy-Treaties], Ph.D. thesis, Rheinischen Friedrich-Wilhelms-Universität, Bonn, 1974, pp. 63–65, examines the content and value of the formulae which establish the need to have the same friends and enemies.

[32] Among these formal organisations there were religious councils (*amphictyonies*) and military associations known as *symmachies*. On the legal nature and functioning of these associations, see Klaus Tausend, *Amphiktyonie und Symmachie: Formen zwischenstaatlicher Beziehungen im archaischen Griechenland* [Amphictionies and Symmachies: Forms of Interstate Relations in Archaic Greece], Franz Steiner, Stuttgart, 1992.

---

ensured the effective supremacy of one of the *pólis* in the group.[33] Leagues and confederations used to be *de facto* under the guidance of a *hegemón* or leader,[34] which was able to decide on the common actions that the organisation would take.[35]

The real unevenness, here again, seems disguised under the legal instruments. When in 431 BCE Sparta requested Athens to give autonomy back to its allies,[36] Athenians replied that Spartans should do the same with their own.[37] In both speeches the concept of autonomy is employed as a rather useful argument for every *hegemón* to resist and fight against its rival's supremacy.[38]

---

[33] A way to obscure and at the same time to highlight the supremacy of a *pólis* in relation to its allies is determined by the inclusion of a "*Dualitätsklausel*" as, for example, the expression "the Athenians and their allies" (*hoi Athenaîoi kaì hoi sýmmakhoi*) in that order; see Pistorius, 1985, p. 183, *supra* note 31. Some authors distinguish between organisations of coordination from those of subordination; cf. Bonk, 1974, pp. 67–68, see *supra* note 31.

[34] Hans van Wees, *Greek Warfare: Myths and Realities*, Duckworth, London, 2004, p. 7, indicates that this informal position of the *hegemón* was also called *arkhé*, which is usually translated in certain contexts as "empire". On hegemony as an complex institution from the point of view of ancient international law, see Víctor Alonso Troncoso, "L'institution de l'hégémonie: entre la coutume et le droit écrit" [The Institution of Hegemony: Between Custom and Written Law], in Gerhard Thür and Francisco J. Fernández Nieto (eds.), *Symposion 1999: Vorträge zur griechischen und hellenistischen Rechtsgeschichte* [Proceedings on Greek and Hellenistic Legal History], Böhlau: Cologne, 2003, pp. 339–54.

[35] In these cases, as noted earlier, there is obviously a voluntary limitation of sovereignty, but it must be recognised that there are different types and grades of connection between city-states. A synthetic charter helps Ténékidès, 1954, p. 179, see *supra* note 12, to identify three methods of association, between which Greek federalism oscillated at the time: he recognises that there were *confederate associations* (composed by autonomous states), *imperial associations* (in which one *pólis* directed the foreign policy of the group) or *fake confederate associations* (in which one of the associates assumed *de facto* directorial powers, although *de iure* the particular sovereignty of each one was respected). We can add to this complex scenario the phenomenon of colonialism. Contrary to what is expected, in the Greek world the relationship between the metropolis and the colony did not imply a clash between a unique central state and a subjugated people, but a nexus of forces similar to that of political associations, in which both parties in the relationship formally behaved as independent cities. As stated by A.J. Graham, *Colony and Mother City in Ancient Greece*, Manchester University Press, Manchester, 1964, p. 5, even though the metropolis had some sort of undefined hegemonic position, "most Greek colonies were founded to be self-sufficient Greek *poleis*".

[36] Thucydides, 1.139.3, see *supra* note 1.

[37] *Ibid.*, 1.144.2.

[38] Giovannini, 2007, p. 102, see *supra* note 13.

A *pólis* acting as *hegemón* within a certain organisation was granted some particular privileges that were very rarely disputed.[39] In the case of the Delian League under the leadership of Athens, the less-important allied city-states pushed their judicial independence (their *autodikía*) into the background, so that their own citizens were tried by Athenian courts on many occasions.[40] An opposition between the hegemonic strategy and the need to respect the sovereignty of subordinated city-states is also visible in the famous Melian Dialogue reproduced by Thucydides. Whereas Athens proposed the celebration of an alliance treaty designed unilaterally, the small island of Melos wanted rather to stabilise mutual relations by means of a peace treaty that should be negotiated jointly between them.[41] The dialogue suggests an interesting clash between the realism of forced imposition – enshrined by the powerful Athenians – and the ideal image of a common sense of justice – promoted by the smaller party.

The consolidation of a maritime empire since the mid-fifth century BCE – as historians usually call the regime of expansionist domination of Athens over the islands – accounts for the separation between entities that were politically unequal. Quite paradoxically, nevertheless, the language used is frequently critical of imperialism[42] and favours instead a democra-

---

[39] The consolidation of federations of states did not emerge in that time from multilateral agreements, but essentially from bilateral agreements, most of the time promoted by the *hegemón* looking to increase its number of allies. See Victor Ehrenberg, *The Greek State*, London, Methuen, 1969, pp. 107, 112.

[40] Cf. Jack M. Balcer, *The Athenian Regulations for Chalkis: Studies in Athenian Imperial Law*, Franz Steiner, Wiesbaden, 1978, pp. 119–44, who advances the existence of an "Athenian Judicial Decree", in force until 412 BCE, which imposed local justice to the *polîtai* of allied cities.

[41] Martin, 1940, pp. 355–56, see *supra* note 9. In this concealment of the imbalance existing under balanced patterns, there is place, however, for mistrust on the part of the less privileged cities: "Interference of some sort in the domestic politics of the allied city was undoubtedly a widely feared consequence of an alliance with a leading state"; Timothy T.B. Ryder, *Koine Eirene: General Peace and Local Independence in Ancient Greece*, Oxford University Press, Oxford, 1965, p. 24). In the opinion of Martin Ostwald, *Autonomia: Its Genesis and Early History*, Scholars Press, New York, 1982 and Peter Karavites, "*Eleuthería* and *Autonomía* in Fifth-Century Interstate Relations", in *Revue Internationale des droits de l'antiquité*, 1982, vol. 29, pp. 145–62, *autonomy* functioned in these cases as a guarantee or efficient mechanism for small cities to protect their independence in the face of the political advance of the hegemonic states.

[42] Pericles himself, promoter of Athenian hegemony, seems to have confessed that the power exercised by Athens over the allies was in violation of the law; cf. Thucydides, 2.60, 2.63, cf. 1.42, see *supra* note 1.

cy that, under expansionist pretensions, is never openly supportive of a superior authority that might destabilise the apparent balance and uncover the real inequalities between the powerful and the weak.[43]

In 351 BCE a speech by Demosthenes mentions that the Greeks signed two treaties with the Persian king: one of them subscribed to by Athens, which was praised by all; the second one by Sparta, which everyone condemned. Demosthenes criticised the disparity of the contracting parties and encourages their formal equalisation. According to this orator, rights happened to be defined differently in both conventional instruments: within each city-state, laws were endorsed by equality, whereas at the international level rights were only defined by the powerful against the will of the feeblest (15.29):

> τῶν μὲν γὰρ ἰδίων τῶν ἐν ταῖς πολιτείαις οἱ νόμοι
> κοινὴν τὴν μετουσίαν ἔδοσαν καὶ ἴσην καὶ τοῖς ἀσθενέσιν
> καὶ τοῖς ἰσχυροῖς· τῶν δ᾽ Ἑλληνικῶν δικαίων οἱ κρατοῦντες
> ὁρισταὶ τοῖς ἥττοσι γίγνονται.[44]

> As far as private rights within a state are concerned, the laws
> of that state grant an equal and impartial share to all, weak
> and strong alike; but the international rights of Greek states
> are defined by the strong against the weak.

It is this opposition between internal *isonomía* and external *hegemonía* that will explain the conceptual construction of *nómos koinós* and, consequently, the varied responses to the individual violation of international rules and customs.

3.3. *Ius Ad Bellum* and *Ius in Bello* in Classical Greece

In spite of the fact that it was not legally forbidden, using force against another Greek city-state seems to have required a valid justification, based

---

[43] At the time there seems to have existed considerable resentment against making evident the supremacy of a city over another one, as rightly indicated by Hunt, 2010, p. 102, see *supra* note 20: "In addition, hegemonic powers bound their subject allies by bilateral treaties or more commonly through a treaty organization such as the Delian League. They tended to emphasize their benefactions to justify their rule over their subject allies. [...] On the other hand, there were various ways that even these obvious superiors tried to obscure their own power. The reason for this obfuscation was the unacceptability of subordinating relationships among status".

[44] S.H. Butcher (ed.), *Demosthenis Orationes* [Speeches], Clarendon Press, Oxford, 1903.

upon religious concerns, legal provisions and political practicalities. However, this explanation or account was frequently stated unilaterally and therefore did not rely on any diplomatic arrangement *inter pares*. Thus, when a *pólis* considered that its own use of violence was in agreement with what the gods or established ancestral customs, there was ample discretion to conduct open aggression based upon unilateral criteria. These arguments show an attempt to overcome the narrative of equality by imposing an international *nómos* upheld by the attacking party against the enemy. According to a late rhetorical treatise attributed to the Aristotelian school, when taking such a decision it was always necessary to convince all others about the convenience of backing an armed attack (*Rhet. ad Alex.* 2, 1425a10–21):

> Προφάσεις μὲν ο ὗν ε ἰσι τοῦ πόλεμον ἐκφέρειν πρός τινας αὗται· δεῖ πρότερον ἀδικηθέντας νῦν καιρῶν παραπεπτωκότων ἀμύνασθαι τοὺς ἀδικήσαντας, ἢ νῦν ἀδικουμένους ὑπὲρ ἑαυτῶν πολεμεῖν ἢ ὑπὲρ συγγενῶν ἢ ὑπὲρ ε ὑεργετῶν, ἢ συμμάχοις ἀδικουμένοις βοηθεῖν, ἢ τοῦ τῇ πόλει συμφέροντος ἕνεκεν ἢ εἰς εὐδοξίαν ἢ εἰς ε ὑπορίαν ἢ εἰς δύναμιν ἢ εἰς ἄλλο τι τ ῶν τοιούτων. Ὅταν μὲν ο ὗν ἐπὶ τῷ πολεμεῖν παρακαλῶμεν, τούτων τε τ ῶν προφάσεων ὅτι πλεῖστα συνακτέον, καὶ μετὰ ταῦτα δεικτέον, ἐξ ὧν ἔστι περιγενέσθαι τ ῷ πολέμῳ, ὅτι τ ὰ πλεῖστα τούτων τοῖς παρακαλουμένοις ὑπάρχοντά ἐστιν. [45]

> The following are the grounds (*propháseis*) for making war on somebody: that we have been wronged (*adikethéntas*) in the past, and now that opportunity offers ought to punish the wrongdoers (*amýnasthai toùs adikésantas*); or, that we are being wronged (*adikouménous*) now, and ought to go to war in our own defence (*hypèr heautôn*) or in defence of our kinsmen and of our benefactors; or, that our allies are being wronged (*adikouménois*) and we ought to go to their help; or, that it is to the advantage of the state in respect of glory or wealth or power or the like. When we are exhorting people to go to war we should bring together as many of these arguments (*propháseon*) as possible, and afterwards show

---

[45] Immanuel Bekker (ed.), *Aristotelis, De Retorica* [On Rhetoric], vol. 3: *De Rhetorica ad Alexandrum* [Rhetoric to Alexander], Oxford, 1837.

that most of the factors on which success in war depends are
on the side of those whom we are addressing.[46]

In 395 BCE the orator Andocides had also explained that arguments
should be presented in order to make a case for Athens and its alleged
"just" war. Resorting to self-defence was therefore suggested as a legitimate means of supporting military action (3.13):

> φασὶ δέ τινες ἀναγκαίως ν ὖν ἡμῖν ἔχειν πολεμεῖν·
> σκεψώμεθα ο ὖν πρῶτον, ὦ ἄνδρες Ἀθηναῖοι, δι ὰ τί καὶ
> πολεμήσωμεν. οἶμαι γὰρ ἂν πάντας ἀνθρώπους ὁμολογῆσαι
> διὰ τάδε δεῖν πολεμεῖν, ἢ ἀδικουμένους ἢ βοηθοῦντας
> ἀδικουμένοις.[47]

> Now it is argued by some that present circumstances oblige
> us to continue fighting. Let us begin, then, gentlemen, by
> considering exactly why we are to fight. Everyone would
> agree (*pántas anthrópous homologêsai*), I think, that war is
> justified only so long as one is either suffering a wrong one-
> self (*adikouménous*) or supporting the cause of another who
> has been wronged (*boethoûntas adikouménois*).[48]

Thucydides – once again – is perhaps the best source to understand
the fair grounds of self-defence in classical Greece.[49] In fact, he seems to
limit all armed response to a previous harm when stating that "we are not
acting improperly in making war against them, nor are we making war
against them without being heavily wronged (*adikoúmenoi*)" (τοῖσδ' ἂν
μόνοις ο ὐκ ὀρθῶς ἀπαρέσκοιμεν, ο ὐδ' ἐπιστρατεύομεν ἐκπρεπῶς μὴ καὶ
διαφερόντως τι ἀδικούμενοι, 1.38.4).[50] Doing wrong is only tolerated

---

[46] According to the text (1425b13–14), however, in order to be respectful of justice, war
should be refrained as soon as one considers that the enemy has just claims (*hótan e tà díkaia axioun toùs enantíous hypolambánosin*).

[47] Michael Edwards (ed.), *Andocides*, Aris & Phillips, Warminster, 1995.

[48] Umberto Albini (ed.), Andocide: De Pace [On Peace], Le Monnier, Florence, 1964, p. 75,
compares the causes to Rhet. Ad Alex. and explains that "la grande novità é dicchiarare
che sono legittime solo le guerre defensive: è un'innovazione etica importantissima". In
contrast, see Anna Missiou, The Subversive Oratory of Andokides: Politics, Ideology and
Decision-making in Democratic Athens, Cambridge University Press, Cambridge, 1992, p.
146: "the distinction between justified and unjustified war-making is only superficial".

[49] The argument, however, is widespread in classical sources; cf. Demosthenes 9.24–25,
10.46, 16.15, *inter alia*.

[50] The possibility of collective self-defence is referred to in the speech of the Corcyraeans
(1.28.4): "First, because you will be helping those who are being wronged (*adikouménois*)

when others have attacked first, as Archidamus's speech seems to discuss in the Plataean dialogue (Thucydides, 2.74):

> θεοὶ ὅσοι γ ῆν τ ὴν Πλαταιίδα ἔχετε καὶ ἥρωες, ξυνίστορές ἐστε ὅτι ο ὔτε τ ὴν ἀρχὴν ἀδίκως, ἐκλιπόντων δ ὲ τῶνδε προτέρων τ ὸ ξυνώμοτον, ἐπὶ γῆν τήνδε ἤλθομεν [...] ο ὔτε νῦν, ἤν τι ποιῶμεν, ἀδικήσομεν· προκαλεσάμενοι γὰρ πολλὰ καὶ εἰκότα ο ὐ τυγχάνομεν. ξυγγνώμονες δ ὲ ἔστε τ ῆς μὲν ἀδικίας κολάζεσθαι τοῖς ὑπάρχουσι προτέροις, τ ῆς δ ὲ τιμωρίας τυγχάνειν τοῖς ἐπιφέρουσι νομίμως.[51]

> All you, Gods and Heros, protectors of Plataeis, be witnesses that we neither invade this territory unjustly (*adíkos*) now in the beginning, because they have first (*protéron*) broken the league they had sworn, [...] nor that we shall further do any wrong (*adikésomen*), because – though we have offered many and reasonable conditions – they have been all refused; assent you also to the punishment of those who first (*protérois*) started the wrong (*adikías*) and to the revenge of those who bear arms lawfully (*nomímos*).

The religious background of this justification is clear,[52] but requires to be complemented by a particular legal dimension.[53] Therefore, when the Plataeans address the Spartans in order to explain their enmity with Thebes, they recall the existence of a generalised acceptance of self-defence which is overtly defined as a *nómos*, that is, as a legal provision (Thucydides, 3.56.2):

> πόλιν γ ὰρ α ὐτοὺς τ ὴν ἡμετέραν καταλαμβάνοντας ἐν σπονδαῖς καὶ προσέτι ἱερομηνίᾳ ὀρθῶς τε ἐτιμωρησάμεθα κατὰ τὸν π ᾶσι νόμον καθεστῶτα, τ ὸν ἐπιόντα πολέμιον

---

and who do not harm others" (πρότερον δ᾽ οὐ καλῶς ἔχειν τοὺς μὲν πολιορκεῖσθαι, αὐτοὺς δὲ δικάζεσθαι).

[51] A commentary on this book is provided by Jeffrey Rusten (ed.), *Thucydides, The Peloponnesian War: Book II*, Cambridge University Press, Cambridge, 1989.

[52] Simon Hornblower, *A Commentary on Thucydides*, vol. 1, Oxford University Press, Oxford, 1991, p. 359. Rusten, 1989, p. 217, see *supra* note 51: "It resembles the Roman *ius fetiale*".

[53] Of course, it should be borne in mind that in ancient times the borders between politics, law and religion were definitely blurred. However, as I have explained, the concept on *nómos* – at least in classical times – indicated in Greece an idea of law that depended on positive regulations created by the relevant legislative bodies in the core of the *pólis*.

ὅσιον εἶναι ἀμύνεσθαι, καὶ νῦν οὐκ ἂν εἰκότως δι᾿ αὐτοὺς βλαπτοίμεθα.[54]

Since they seized our city in time of peace – and, what is more, at a holy time in the month – we punished them as we were fully entitled to do by the universal law (*tòn pâsi nómon*) which says that one may defend oneself against an aggressor without offending the gods; and it cannot now be right for us to suffer on their account.

Described as "universally accepted", the right to self-defence has been compared to natural law,[55] most probably in the light of Sophocles' reference of the unwritten laws about burial of the dead in his play *Antigone* (*ágrapta nómima*, 454).[56] Being qualified as *nómoi*, however, these common laws of the Greeks are not meant to be related to sacred principles, but are rather connected to the legal (human) grounds of actions taken by *póleis* when fighting against each other.[57] In fact, a number of references suggest that *nómos koinós*

---

[54] P.J. Rhodes (ed.), *Thucydides: History III*, Aris & Phillips, Warminster, 1994.

[55] A.W. Gomme, *A Historical Commentary on Thucydides*, vol. 1, Oxford University Press, Oxford, 1959, p. 175.

[56] On the value of *ágrapta nómima*, see Francesco Flumene, *La "legge non scritta" nella storia e nella dottrina etico-giuridica della Grecia classica* [Unwritten Law in the History and Ethical and Legal Doctrine in Classical Greece], L.I.S., Sassari, 1925; M.S. Moore, *The Unwritten Laws of Greece*, University College, Dublin, 1967; and Martin Ostwald, *From Popular Sovereignty to the Sovereignty of Law: Law, Society, and Politics in Fifth-Century Athens*, University of California Press, Berkeley, 1986, pp. 164–69.

[57] Contrary to the opinion of many, these common rules are essentially legal in their scope and nature; their binding force is well attested throughout the classical sources. De Romilly, 1971, pp. 39–40, see *supra* note 14:

En revanche, un système de valeurs cher à un groupe donné, qui se sent différent des autres et supérieur à eux, peut aisément définir un idéal commun. Et, s'il s'agit de corriger la varietés du droit, de cité à cité, s'il s'agit de chercher quelque part, où que ce soit, un ensemble de règles débordant ce cadre, et s'appliquant en particulier aux devoirs simplement humains qui peuvent régir les rapports entre gens de diverses cités, alors on a recours à ce que les auteurs appellent les lois communes des Grecs.

See also Adriaan Lanni, "The Laws of War in Ancient Greece", in *Law and History Review*, 2008, vol. 26, no. 3, pp. 471–72; Alessandro Bonucci, *La legge comune nel pensiero greco* [Common Law in Greek Thought], Bartelli, Perugia, 1903; Demetrius Wogasli, *Die Normen des altgriechischen Völkerrechtes (Nomoi Koinoi tôn Hellénon)* [The Norms of Ancient Greek International Law], diss., Freiburg, 1895.

---

refers to the norms applicable to interstate behavior throughout the late fifth century and afterwards,[58] reflecting the obligatory nature ascribed to customary provisions.[59] If this is so, it should not be forgotten that *nómos koinós* – as broad custom – was in fact liable to be manipulated in speech and action for the selfish interest of a *pólis* attempting to outpace its enemies.

This inter-*póleis* or intra-Hellenic legal system of customs and principles – a useful tool for "legalising" political actions – was not only limited to the regulation of the outbreak of hostilities but also included a number of provisions dealing with the practice of warfare both in situations of hostilities between Greek *póleis* and between Hellenic city-states and barbarian foes.[60]

Some sources show that *nómos koinós* – as a legal order pretending to exceed the domestic law of each *polis* – also included rules related to *ius in bello*.[61] In particular, Polybius differentiates between legal actions – related to the lawful targeting of military objectives – and excessive deeds – which are deemed to be serious offences committed in wartime. Thus, when the Mantineans called for the aid of the Spartans and a garrison was put to death, Polybius explains that spearing those men was part of a "custom by the common laws of men (*katà toùs koinoùs tôn anthrópon nómous*) to grant even to foreign enemies" (τοῦτο γὰρ καὶ τοῖς πολεμίοις ἔθος ἐστὶ συγχωρεῖσθαι κατὰ τοὺς κοινοὺς τῶν ἀνθρώπων νόμους); but

---

[58] Virgilio Ilari, *Guerra e diritto nel mondo antico* [War and Law in the Ancient World], Giuffrè Editore, Milan, 1980, pp. 101–3.

[59] Cf. Sheets, 1994, see *supra* note 16. According to Lanni, 2008, pp. 469–89, see *supra* note 57: "For the Greeks, the notion of applying a customary international law based on state practice was familiar and completely uncontroversial. [...] The laws of war were naturally part of the culture and values of constituent states, and as such could more easily encourage compliance than laws whose legitimacy is based purely on a theory of consent or on the fairness of the procedure by which they were enacted".

[60] In Book V of *Republic*, Plato draws a distinction between international war (*pólemos*), conducted against barbarians, and internal strife within the Greek world (*stásis*), promoting the need to behave in both situations under similar rules of action (469b.5–471b.8). According to the text, even barbarians who were victims of an armed conflict had to be also protected as if they were Greeks, under the application of the same *nómoi*.

[61] This concept was broadly analysed in Emiliano J. Buis, "Las lágrimas de Zeus, la prudencia de Atenea: Normas humanitarias, fuentes históricas y el reconocimiento de un 'derecho internacional' en el mundo griego antiguo" [Zeus's Tears, Athena's Moderation: Humanitarian Norms, Historical Sources and the Acknowledgment of an "International Law" in the Ancient Greek World], in *Revista Jurídica de Buenos Aires*, 2012, pp. 357–83.

instead, the Mantineans are said to have "deliberately, and in violation of the common laws of all men (*tà koinà tôn anthrópon díkaia*), consummated a crime of the most impious description" (τὰ κοινὰ τῶν ἀνθρώπων δίκαια παραβάντες τὸ μέγιστον ἀσέβημα κατὰ προαίρεσιν ἐπετέλεσαν).[62]

According to Thucydides, when the Corinthians were about to wrap up their speech addressed to the Athenians, they contended that their arguments had to be accepted since they expressed "the rightest claims according to the laws of the Greeks" (*katà toùs Hellénon nómous*) (δικαιώματα μὲν οὖν τάδε πρὸς ὑμᾶς ἔχομεν ἱκανὰ κατὰ τοὺς Ἑλλήνων νόμους, 1.41.1). Similarly, the Plataean envoys indicated in 427 BCE that any attack performed in the absence of a previous use of force was contrary to the common laws (3.59.1):

> οὐ πρὸς τῆς ὑμετέρας δόξης, ὦ Λακεδαιμόνιοι, τάδε, οὔτε ἐς τὰ κοινὰ τῶν Ἑλλήνων νό μιμα κα ὶ ἐς το ὺς προγόνους ἁμαρτάνειν ο ὕτε ἡμᾶς το ὺς ε ὑεργέτας ἀλλοτρίας ἕνεκα ἔχθρας μὴ αὐτοὺς ἀδικηθέντας διαφθεῖραι.[63]

> It were not to your glory, Lacedaemonians, either to offend in this way against the common law of the Hellenes (*es tà koinà tôn Hellénon nómima*) and against your own ancestors, or to kill us your benefactors to gratify another's hatred without having been wronged yourselves.

Avoiding the killing of suppliants who surrender[64] or protecting temples and religious facilities during armed conflicts were also considered part of this common set of legal rules.[65] The "common law" was also

---

[62] Theodorus Büttner-Wobst (ed.), *Polybius, Historiae*, Teubner, Leipzig, 1893. Cf. also Diodorus Siculus (13.23–24; 19.63).

[63] Rhodes, 1994, see *supra* note 54.

[64] "To grant us our lives would be, therefore, a righteous judgment; if you consider also that we are prisoners who surrendered of their own accord, stretching out our hands for quarter, whose slaughter the law of the Greeks (*nómos toîs Héllesi*) forbids, and who besides were always your benefactors" (ὥστε καὶ τῶν σωμάτων ἄδειαν ποιοῦντες ὅσια ἂν δικάζοιτε καὶ προνοοῦντες ὅτι ἑκόντας τε ἐλάβετε καὶ χεῖρας προϊσχομένους – ὁ δὲ νόμος τοῖς Ἕλλησι μὴ κτείνειν τούτους – ἔτι δὲ καὶ εὐεργέτας γεγενημένους διὰ παντός, Thucydides, 3.58.3, see *supra* note 1).

[65] The inviolability of these sacred spaces (*asylía*) that safeguarded them from being looted or robbed has been studied by Benedetto Bravo, "Sulân. Représailles et justice privée contre des étrangers dans les cités grecques" [Sulân. Reprisals and Private Justice against Foreigners in the Greek Cities", in *Annuario della Scuola Normale Superiore di Pisa*, 1980, vol. 10, pp. 675–987; cf. Anne Jacquemin, "Droit d'asile et droit d'extradition en

regarded as the applicable legal framework to ensure, whenever neces-sary, the protection of messengers, heralds and ambassadors.[66] The care for these diplomatic officers, based upon clear religious obligations,[67] was legally imposed in public documents. An epigraphical source, dated around 367/6 BCE, has transmitted an Athenian decree on the Aetolian League in which a representative is chosen to file an oral claim for the illegal capture of messengers who had been sent to communicate a cease-fire before the celebration of the Eleusinian Mysteries.[68] The detention by the League was considered to be against the "common laws of the

---

Grèce antique: le fugitif, le dieu, la cité et le tyran" [Laws of Asylum and Extradition in Ancient Greece: The Runaway, the God, the City and the Tyrant], in J.-M. Racault (ed.), *Le territoire, Cahiers CRLH-CIRAOI* 3, Didier érudition, Paris, 1986, pp. 7–12; Anne Jacquemin, *Guerre et religion dans le monde grec (490–322 av. J.-C.)* [War and Religion in the Greek World (490–322 BCE)], Presses Universitaires de Liège, Liège, 2000, pp. 130–32; Raoul Lonis, "Extradition et prise de corps de réfugiés politiques en Grèce" [Extradition and Capture of Political Refugees in Greece], in Raoul Lonis (ed.), *L'étranger dans le monde grec*, Presses Universitaires, Nancy, 1988, pp. 69–88. The best monograph on *asylía* is still Kent J. Rigsby, *Asylia: Territorial Inviolability in the Hellenistic World*, University of California Press, Berkeley, 1996. Honouring the sanctuaries was also a sub-stantial part of the common laws of Greeks (*koinà tôn Hellénon nómima*), according to Diodorus (19.63). Arthur Nussbaum, *A Concise History of the Law of Nations*, Macmillan, New York, 1950, p. 15, considers that "it is difficult to discover recognized lawlike rules of warfare, except perhaps that the protection granted to sanctuaries by amphyctionic trea-ties were particularly intended for war times".

[66] On the treatment of heralds in the Greek world, cf. Raoul Lonis, "L'immunité des agents diplomatiques: hérauts et ambassadeurs" [The Immunity of Diplomatic Agents: Heralds and Ambassadors], in *Les usages de la guerre entre grecs et barbares, des guerres médiques au milieu du IVe siècle avant J.-C.*, Annales littéraires de l'Université de Besançon, Paris, 1969, pp. 63–70; Catherine Goblot-Cahen, "Les hérauts grecs agents et victimes de châtiments" [Greek Heralds as Agents and Victims of Punishment], in *Hypothèses*, 2002, vol. 6, pp. 135–44. The religious protection of heralds has been ana-lysed by Stephen M. Sheppard, "The Laws of War in the Pre-Dawn Light: Institutions and Obligations in Thucydides' Peloponnesian War", in *Columbia Journal of Transnational Law*, 2005, vol. 43, p. 921, and Jonathan M. Hall, "International Relations", in Philip Sa-bin, Hans van Wees and Michael Whitby (eds.), *The Cambridge History of Greek and Roman Warfare*, vol. 1, Cambridge University Press, Cambridge, 2007, p. 94. On the regu-lation of retaliation against foreign envoys, see Yvon Garlan, *La guerre dans l'antiquité* [War in Antiquity], Fernand Nathan, Paris, 1972, pp. 22–23.

[67] Following Pausanias (1.36.3), for instance, the two goddesses punished the Megarians for having killed the herald Antemocritus when he approached them to block a military attack.

[68] A. Geoffrey Woodhead, *Inscriptions: The Decrees* (The Athenian Agora, 16), Princeton University Press, Princeton, NJ, 1997, no. 48. The *editio princeps* corresponds to Eugene Schweigert, "Greek Inscriptions (1–13)", in *Hesperia*, 1939, vol. 8, pp. 5–7, 8.

Greeks", *parà toùs nómous t[oùs koin]oús tôn Hellénon* (παρὰ τοὺς νόμους τ/[ο]ὺς κοι[ν]οὺς τῶν Ἑλλήνων, lines 12–13).

Likewise, according to Herodotus's *Histories*, the Persian king Xerxes refused to retaliate against Athenians and Spartans – who had murdered his envoys – affirming that killing messengers would be illegal according to a universal law (7.136):

> κείνους μὲν γ ὰρ συγχέαι τ ὰ πάντων ἀνθρώπων νόμιμα ἀποκτείναντας κήρυκας, α ὐτὸς δ ὲ τὰ ἐκείνοισι ἐπιπλήσσει ταῦτα ο ὐ ποιήσειν, ο ὐδὲ ἀνταποκτείνας ἐκείνους ἀπολύσειν Λακεδαιμονίους τῆς αἰτίης.[69]

> You made havoc of all human law (*tà pánton anthrópon nómima*) by slaying heralds, but I will not do that for which I censure you, nor by putting you in turn to death will I set the Lacedaemonians free from this guilt.

The fact that the reference to common *nómima* is mentioned here by a barbarian ruler – and not by the Greeks – shows that, if required, there was also the possibility of extending its semantic content to cover not only the Hellenic *póleis* but, more globally, humanity as such.[70]

The treatment of prisoners of war in ancient Greece has been studied by Pierre Ducrey and, despite the fact that in many cases captives and detained are said to have been enslaved, some sources indicate that they were only held in detention until the end of the hostilities.[71] The Peace of Nicias, signed between Athens and Sparta in 421 BCE, included a provision aiming at the exchange of prisoners (Thucydides, 5.18).[72] In Euripides' *Heracleidae* (put on stage around 430 BCE), Eurystheus explains, af-

---

[69] Philippe-Ernest Legrand (ed.), *Hérodote: Histoires* [Herodotus: Histories], vols. 1–9, Les Belles Lettres, Paris, 1963–1968.

[70] Lanni, 2008, p. 472, see *supra* note 57: "the distinction between 'the laws of the Greeks' and 'the laws of mankind' is not consistently applied, and it is not clear whether there was a shared understanding of precisely which laws applied only to Greeks and which were wider in scope".

[71] Pierre Ducrey, *Le traitement des prisonniers de guerre dans la Grèce antique* [The Treatment of Prisoners of War in Ancient Greece], Editions E. de Boccard, Paris, 1968, p. 290.

[72] Cf. Thucydides, 2.103; 5.3, see *supra* note 1. The purpose of truces was sometimes the exchange or release of prisoners of war; Plutarch, *Sol.* 9; Phillipson, 1911, vol. 2, p. 280, see *supra* note 6.

ter his release, that murdering a prisoner of war is an act that goes against the common law in force between *póleis* (1009–11):

> νῦν οὖν ἐπειδή μ᾽ οὐ διώλεσαν τότε / πρόθυμον ὄντα, τοῖσιν Ἑλλήνων νόμοις / οὐχ ἁγνός εἰμι τῷ κτανόντι κατθανών.[73]

> Now, accordingly, since they did not kill me on the battle-field when I was eager to die, by the laws of the Greeks (*toîsin Hellénon nómois*) my death, for the man who kills me, is an unholy act.[74]

In sum, it is possible to claim that in classical times Greek *póleis* have identified *nómos koinós* as an expression that allowed reference to the legal principles and norms applicable to interstate politics. If turning to common customary rules was a frequent mechanism in order to justify the international behaviour of a *pólis*, it is also possible to find cases in which the conduct of an adversary was defined as a violation of the rules in force and thus required a solution designed to put an end to injustice.

3.4. Greek *Ius Post Bellum*: From International Courts to Domestic Amnesties

According to Xenophon's *Hellenica*, in 405 BCE the Spartan admiral Lysander sailed from Rhodes to take action against the cities that had revolted in Aegospotami, on the coasts of Asia Minor. After the Athenians had retired, he launched an attack and captured the Athenian fleet, with the exception of nine ships led by Conon, which escaped the disaster. Once the victory was secured, Lysander brought all prisoners and booty to Lampsacus. Among the prisoners, he had captured the Athenian generals Philocles and Adeimantus. The text shows his next steps concerning the establishment of an *ad hoc* consultation among the Spartan allies in order to decide what destiny the enemies should face (2.1.32–33):

> μετὰ δὲ ταῦτα Λύσανδρος ἀθροίσας τοὺς συμμάχους ἐκέλευσε βουλεύεσθαι περὶ τῶν αἰχμαλώτων. ἐνταῦθα δ ἡ κατηγορίαι ἐγίγνοντο πολλαὶ τῶν Ἀθηναίων, ἅ τε ἤδη παρενενομήκεσαν κα ὶ ἃ ἐψηφισμένοι ἦσαν ποιεῖν, ε ἰ κρατήσειαν τ ῇ ναυμαχίᾳ, τ ὴν δεξιὰν χεῖρα ἀποκόπτειν τῶν

---

[73] James Diggle (ed.), *Euripidis Fabulae* [Euripides' Plays], Oxford University Press, Oxford, 1994.

[74] Lanni, 2008, p. 480–81, see *supra* note 57, considers that these passages reflect a political propaganda aimed at constructing an Athenian "humanitarian" policy concerning prisoners of war.

ζωγρηθέντων πάντων, καὶ ὅτι λαβόντες δύο τριήρεις,
Κορινθίαν καὶ Ἀνδρίαν, τοὺς ἄνδρας ἐξ α ὑτῶν πάντας
κατακρημνίσειαν· Φιλοκλῆς δ᾽ ἦν στρατηγὸς τῶν Ἀθηναίων,
ὃς τούτους διέφθειρεν. ἐλέγετο δ ὲ καὶ ἄλλα πολλά, κα ὶ
ἔδοξεν ἀποκτεῖναι τ ῶν α ἰχμαλώτων ὅσοι ἦσαν Ἀθηναῖοι
πλὴν Ἀδειμάντου, ὅτι μόνος ἐπελάβετο ἐν τ ῇ ἐκκλησίᾳ τοῦ
περὶ τῆς ἀποτομῆς τ ῶν χειρῶν ψηφίσματος· ᾐτιάθη μέντοι
ὑπό τινων προδο ῦναι τ ὰς ναῦς. Λύσανδρος δ ὲ Φιλοκλέα
πρῶτον ἐρωτήσας, ὅς το ὺς Ἀνδρίους καὶ Κορινθίους
κατεκρήμνισε, τί ε ἴη ἄξιος παθεῖν ἀρξάμενος ε ἰς Ἕλληνας
παρανομεῖν, ἀπέσφαξεν.[75]

After this, Lysander gathered the allies (*toùs symmákhous*)
together and told them to decide (*bouleúesthai*) about the
fate of the prisoners of war. In that discussion, many accusations (*kategoríai*) were made against the Athenians, both the
many deeds they had done that were contrary to law
(*parenenomékesan*), and the many resolutions they had
passed in their Assembly concerning how they would their
enemies if they had won the battle – in particular, to cut off
the right hands of those they captured. It was also noted that
the Athenians, when they had captured a Corinthian and an
Andrian trireme, had thrown all the men on those ships
overboard. Philocles was the Athenian general who had sent
these men to their deaths. Many other accusations were made
against the Athenians, and it was finally decided (*édoxen*) to
kill all those prisoners who were Athenians, with the exception of Adeimantus, who alone had attacked the decree in the
Assembly about the cutting off of hands. He was, however,
charged (*eitiáthe*) by some with betraying the ships. Philocles, who had thrown overboard the Corinthians and the An-
drians, was first asked by Lysander what he thought he deserved for having begun uncustomary and illegal actions
against the Greeks (*eis Héllenas paranomeîn*), and then had
his throat cut.

The example – in anticipation of the forthcoming Athenian defeat in
the Peloponnesian War – is relevant since it might show the scope of the
crimes committed in wartime when mistreating the captured enemy

---

[75] Carleton L. Brownson (ed.), *Xenophon*, vol. 1: *Books 1–4*, Harvard University Press,
Cambridge, MA, 1918.

troops. In fact, as scholars such as Georges S. Maridakis have already noted, the vocabulary used to explain the constitution and functioning of this customised trial is similar to the one employed to justify the creation of the Nuremberg International Military Tribunal after the Second World War, and thus represents our earliest known example of an international court dealing with the punishment of war crimes in Western history.[76] The details of the meeting of the allies to discuss the affair is defined as a real council – as the verb *bouleúomai* ("to decide in a council or *boulé*") suggests – and its judicial nature is determined by the existence of indictments (*kategoríai*) proclaimed against the accused. The decision convicting the suspects to the death penalty is presented with the verb *édoxe* ("was resolved"), which was the ordinary formula of contemporary decrees.[77]

As described in the text, the assembly was created *ex post facto* by the victors as a way of condemning the enemy combatants for having breached legal provisions. Twice in the passage the verb *paranomeîn* ("to act against a *nómos*") is mentioned. The international dimension of the alleged offences is clear. The crimes with which the Athenian perpetrators were charged are not presented as representing a breach of the domestic laws of their victims' *póleis*, since no reference is made to the specificities of Corinthian or Andrian law. Quite the opposite, when Lysander asked Philocles about the punishment deserved, he remarked specifically that a violation of the *nómoi* of all Greeks had been committed. In accordance with the sense that was granted to *nómos koinós*, then, it seems quite certain that there is a purpose of presenting the acts performed by the enemy as violations to the whole intra-Hellenic legal system instead of treating them as simple domestic felonies.

---

[76] Cf. Georges S. Maridakis, "Un précédent du procès de Nuremberg tiré de l'histoire de la Grèce ancienne", in *Revue hellénique de droit international*, 1952, vol. 4, pp. 1–16 (translated as Georges S. Maridakis, "An Ancient Precedent to Nuremberg", in *Journal of International Criminal Justice*, 2006, vol. 4, no. 4, pp. 847–52). See also Erich Kraske, "Klassisches Hellas und Nürnberger Prozess" [Classical Greece and the Nuremberg Trials], in *Archiv des Völkerrechts*, 1953, vol. 4, no. 2, pp. 183–89. When exploring the origins of international criminal law, Timothy L.H. McCormack, "From Sun Tzu to the Sixth Committee: The Evolution of an International Criminal Law Regime", in Timothy L.H. McCormack and Gerry J. Simpson (eds.), *The Law of War Crimes: National and International Approaches*, Kluwer Law International, The Hague, 1997, pp. 31–63, also briefly mention this reference.

[77] P.J. Rhodes, *The Athenian Boule*, Clarendon Press, Oxford, 1972, pp. 82–84.

The presentation of this episode shows an international court being settled in order to deal with the war crimes perpetrated by the defeated.[78] As such, the whole trial stands as a demonstration of the political ambition of the Spartans to overtake the power of its rival *póleis*. Far from responding to an equality *inter pares*, the creation of such a judicial body represents a desire to impose justice from a hegemonic wish of superiority.[79] The political motivation is easily perceived if the charges brought are examined. The main alleged reason for condemning the accused was the fact that they had voted a decree according to which in case of victory the Athenians would cut off the right hands of all prisoners.[80] Since this decree was never implemented, the sanction is in fact referring to a mere possibility that had never been put into practice. It should therefore not be surprising to conclude that charges presented against the Athenian generals and officers were politically driven. Moreover, if attention is paid to the Athenian reaction, the absence of consistent grounds for imposing the capital penalty can also be seen in the case of Adeimantus, who objected to the decree in the assembly and was spared by the Spartan allied tribu-

---

[78] Designated a "kangaroo court" by Brian Bosworth, "Massacre in the Peloponnesian War", in Philip G. Dwyer and Lyndall Ryan (eds.), *Theatres of Violence: Massacre, Mass Killing and Atrocity throughout History*, Bergahn Books, New York, 2012, p. 19.

[79] In the history of international relations, realists have always regarded international organisations and courts as "extensions of existing power realities"; David Bosco, *Rough Justice: The International Criminal Court in a World of Power Politics*, Oxford University Press, Oxford, 2014, p. 11. From a Marxist perspective, Danilo Zolo, *La giustizia dei vincitori: da Norimberga a Baghdad* [The Justice of the Winners: From Nuremberg to Baghdad], Laterza, Rome, 2006, argues that international criminal tribunals have always been controlled by powerful states against the will of oppressed nations.

[80] This is also stated in Plutarch, *Lysander*, 9.5: .)5)ds, , Ca, peeches], ondon, niversity), Rwanda], s], ors]y, the God, the City and the Tyrant] of an "International Law" in t"The Athenians were under the command of several generals, among whom was Philocles, the man who had recently persuaded the people to pass a decree that their prisoners of war should have the right thumb cut off that they might not be able to wield a spear, though they might ply an oar" (ἐστρατήγουν δὲ τῶν Ἀθηναίων ἄλλοι τε πλείους καὶ Φιλοκλῆς ὁ πείσας ποτὲ ψηφίσασθαι τὸν δῆμον ἀποκόπτειν τὸν δεξιὸν ἀντίχειρα τῶν ἁλισκομένων κατὰ πόλεμον, ὅπως δόρυ μὲν φέρειν μὴ δύνωνται, κώπην δὲ ἐλαύνωσι); cf. Bernadotte Perrin (ed.), *Plutarch's Lives*, vol. 4, Harvard University Press, Cambridge, MA, 1916. The act of throwing the prisoners over the side of the vessel seems to have been presented as a secondary charge.

nal; for political reasons, again, he was anyway sentenced to death in Athens for betraying the ships to the Spartans.[81]

A similar political explanation can be offered when exploring the consequences of dealing with grave crimes at the domestic level. Greek *póleis* identified the existence of specific military wrongdoings that were dealt with by local tribunals. These major offences against the state included acts of treason (either military or civil), subversion of the constitution and the government – including tyranny – the giving and receiving of bribes and, in democratic times, the deception of the people (*apatê tou dêmou*).[82] All these offences against the administration of the *pólis* could be redressed by a huge number of public actions available to interested citizens.[83] According to Aeschines (3.175), military offences such as cowardice, failure to take the field or desertion of the post could be prosecuted before the courts.[84]

The Athenian judicial body which was in charge of conducting these trials is still subject to an ongoing debate. A passage in Demosthenes suggests that only military superiors were able to receive indictments against soldiers of the lower ranks (39.17):

> ἀπελθόντων δ᾽ ἐξ Ε ὐβοίας τ ῶν στρατιωτῶν λιποταξίου
> προσεκλήθη, κἀγὼ ταξιαρχῶν τῆς φυλῆς ἠναγκαζόμην κατὰ
> τοὐνόματος τοῦ ἐμαυτοῦ πατρόθεν δέχεσθαι τ ὴν λ ῆξιν· καὶ

---

[81] On the accusation against Adeimantus, see Agellos Kapellos, "Adeimantos at Aegospotami: Innocent or Guilty?", in *Historia*, 2009, vol. 58, no. 3, pp. 257–75.

[82] David D. Phillips, *The Law of Ancient Athens*, University of Michigan Press, Ann Arbor, 2013, p. 464.

[83] These actions included the graphè prodosías (in cases of treason), the graphè dóron or dorodokías (corruption) and the graphè klopês (theft). Cf. Mogens Herman Hansen, Eisangelia: The Sovereignty of the People's Court in Athens in the Fourth Century B.C. and the Impeachment of Generals and Politicians, University Press, Odense, 1975; Jennifer T. Roberts, Accountability in Athenian Government, University of Wisconsin Press, Madison, 1982. W. Kendrick Pritchett, *The Greek State at War*, vol. 2, University of California Press, Berkeley, 1974, p. 27, has identified 14 cases of graphaì prodosías and seven cases of graphè dorodokías in the available sources. As far as the accusations for treason during the Peloponnesian War are concerned, see Anne Queyrel Bottineau, Prodosia: La notion et l'acte de trahison dans l'Athènes du Vᵉ siècle [The Concept of Act of Treason in Fifth-Century Athens], Ausonius, Paris, 2010, pp. 180–253.

[84] Cf. A.R.W. Harrison, *The Law of Athens*, vol. 2, Oxford University Press, Oxford, 1971, p. 32; S.C. Todd, *The Shape of Athenian Law*, Oxford University Press, Oxford, 1993, p. 106. Robin Osborne, "Law in Action in Classical Athens", in *Journal of Hellenic Studies*, 1985, vol. 105, p. 56, has identified four situations in which these judicial actions were presented (Lysias, 10 and 14/15; Demosthenes, 21.103 and 59.27).

εἰ μισθὸς ἐπορίσθη τοῖς δικαστηρίοις, εἰσῆγον ἂν δῆλον ὅτι. ταῦτα δ᾽ εἰ μὴ σεσημασμένων ἤδη συνέβη τῶν ἐχίνων, κἂν μάρτυρας ὑμῖν παρεσχόμην.[85]

When the soldiers had come back from Euboea, he was summoned on a charge of desertion (*lipotaxíou*), and I, as taxiarch of our tribe, was forced to receive the summons, since it was against my name, that of my father being added; and if a payment had been available for the juries, I should certainly have had to bring the case into court. If this had not occurred after the boxes had already been sealed, I should have brought you witnesses.

Plato also seems to confirm that all judicial claims had to be presented before the *árkhontes polemikoí* of the army (*Laws*, 12.943a–b).[86]

ἐὰν δέ τις ἐκλείπῃ τινὶ κάκῃ μὴ στρατηγῶν ἀφέντων, γραφὰς ἀστρατείας ε ἶναι πρὸς το ὺς πολεμικοὺς ἄρχοντας, ὅταν ἔλθωσιν ἀπὸ στρατοπέδου, δικάζειν δὲ τοὺς στρατεύσαντας ἑκάστους χωρίς, ὁπλίτας τε καὶ ἱππέας καὶ τἆλλα ἐμπολέμια ἕκαστα ὡσαύτως, καὶ εἰσάγειν ὁπλίτας μὲν εἰς τοὺς ὁπλίτας, ἱππέας δὲ εἰς τοὺς ἱππέας καὶ τοὺς ἄλλους δὲ κατὰ ταὐτὰ εἰς τοὺς αὑτῶν συννόμους·[87]

If anyone, through cowardice, fails to present himself without leave from the commanders, he shall be indicted for desertion (*astrateías*) before the military officers (*toùs polemikoùs árkhontes*) when they return from camp, and each class of those who have served shall sit by themselves as judge – that is, hoplites, cavalry, and each of the other branches – and they shall summon hoplites before the hoplites, cavalrymen before the cavalry, and all others in like manner before soldiers of their own class.

---

[85] W. Rennie (ed.), *Demosthenis Orationes* [Demosthenes' Speeches], Clarendon Press, Oxford, 1931.

[86] Monica Bertazzoli, "Tribunali militari in Atene?" [Military Tribunals in Athens?], in *Aevum*, 2001, vol. 75, no. 1, pp. 57–70, discusses Lysias, 14.5, where a reference to military courts was included. However, by putting forward an alternative explanation for the expression *toùs stratiótas dikázein*, she concludes that no allusion was made to specialised tribunals for generals or soldiers.

[87] R.G. Bury (ed.), *Plato. Laws, Books 7–12*, Harvard University Press, Cambridge, MA, 1926.

The experience of the aftermath of the Battle of Arginusae in 406 BCE – considered to be the greatest naval combat in ancient Greek history[88] – included a trial in which the eight generals who were in charge of the operation were prosecuted for their behaviour in the field. In spite of their victory, the *strategoí* were denounced for not having been able to rescue the shipwrecked and recover the dead. Twenty-five ships and thousands of citizens were lost in this failed attempt,[89] most probably due to a storm that prevented them from accomplishing the mission (βουλομένους ποιεῖν ἄνεμος καὶ χειμὼν διεκώλυσεν αὐτοὺς μέγας γενόμενος, *Hellenica* 1.6.35). Neither the legality of the accusations[90] nor the charges that had been brought were completely clear.[91] However, without being able to make formal speeches in their own defence, the generals seem to have been executed following unjust proceedings and illegal motions.

A later testimony (Lysias, 12.35–36) would suggest that they were tried by the assembly – once the council proposed that it was necessary to vote on whether they were guilty or not – for political reasons: it was stated that they had committed an act of treason since they were intending to subvert democracy. The example of the Arginusae trial shows, once again, that the determination of individual responsibilities for committing crimes related to the circumstances of an armed conflict depended on a political will.[92] Just as the Spartans had done with the Aegospotami proceedings, the Athenians here were ready to take decisions in order to pass a clear message. If in the first example hegemonic ambitions explained the implementation of an *ad hoc* system of justice, in this case Athenians acted for the sake of endorsing their internal democratic policy.

---

[88] Diodorus Siculus, 13.98.5, 102.4; cf. Thucydides, 1.1, 21, 23; 6.31; 7.85.5–6, see *supra* note 1.

[89] Xenophon, *Hell.* 1.6.34; Diodorus, 13.100.1.

[90] Dustin Gish, "Defending *Demokratia*: Athenian Justice and the Trial of the Arginusae Generals in Xenophon's *Hellenica*", in Fiona Hobden and Christopher Tuplin (eds.), *Xenophon: Ethical Principles and Historical Enquiry*, Brill, Leiden, 2012, pp. 191–95, argues that this proceeding was an example of the power of democratic participation through *thórybos*.

[91] On the complexities of the affair and its political implications, cf. Jennifer T. Roberts, "Arginusae Once Again", in *Classical World*, 1977, vol. 71, no. 2, pp. 107–111; Peter Hunt, "The Slaves and the Generals of Arginusae', in *American Journal of Philology*, 2001, vol. 122, no. 3, pp. 359–80; Donald Kagan, *The Peloponnesian War*, Penguin, New York, 2004, pp. 459–66; and Ostwald, 1986, pp. 431–511, see *supra* note 56.

[92] François Rebuffat, *Guerre et société dans le monde grec (490–322 av. J.-C.)* [War and Society in the Greek World (490–322 BCE)], Sedes, Paris, 2000, p. 192.

A final affair that took place a couple of years later can provide additional information on this *modus operandi* of addressing severe crimes. After the Athenian defeat in the Peloponnesian War – which led to a Spartan blockade – in 404 BCE a civil war broke out and an oligarchic group known as the Thirty Tyrants took power after a *coup d'état*. The new violent regime that was imposed lasted for eight months and was characterised by increased mass killing.[93] At the beginning, only political opponents were executed under the orders of the Thirty Tyrants, but soon terror expanded and murders multiplied. Three thousand citizens were chosen by the Thirty Tyrants to participate in the government, and it was decided that the remainder could be put to death without trial. As a result of this widespread extrajudicial and systematic killing operation, more Athenians were put to death than the number of subjects prosecuted during the entire period of its empire (Isocrates, 4.113).[94]

How did Athens deal with the consequences of such a massacre? The only testimony we have referring to the reaction to this behaviour is a passage from Andocides' *On the Mysteries*, written around the autumn of 400 BCE. After being arrested and convicted for having entered a sacred space when it had been forbidden by a decree, the orator argues for the annulment of the legal provision as a consequence of measures taken when democracy was restored in the spring of 403 BCE. When acknowledging the advantages of the new regime, he describes the content of the amnesty (1.81):

> ἐπειδὴ δ' ἐπανήλθετε ἐκ Πειραιῶς, γενόμενον ἐφ' ὑμῖν
> τιμωρεῖσθαι ἔγνωτε ἐᾶν τὰ γεγενημένα, καὶ περὶ πλείονος
> ἐποιήσασθε σῴζειν τὴν πόλιν ἢ τὰς ἰδίας τιμωρίας, καὶ ἔδοξε
> μὴ μνησικακεῖν ἀλλήλοις τῶν γεγενημένων.[95]
>
> When you returned from the Peiraeus, and you were able to seek vengeance (*timoreîsthai*), you decided to let bygones be bygones and placed more value on the salvation of the city than on private retributions. And you resolved not to recall

---

[93] Xenophon, *Hell.* 2.3.12; Aristotle, *Athenaion Politeia*, 35.3.

[94] According to Isocrates (6.67), 1,500 people were executed and around 5,000 were forced to leave the *pólis* and take refuge in the Piraeus. Aristotle, *Athenaion Politeia*, 35.4, agrees that the number of executions involved no less than 1,500 people.

[95] Edwards, 1995, see *supra* note 47.

grievances (*mè mnesikakeîn*) with one another over what had happened.

The prohibition of remembering the bad experiences that had happened (expressed in the text as *mè mnesikakeîn*)[96] is presented as a decision aimed at the protection of the *pólis* and not taken as the result of a private desire for revenge. The speech later addresses the dichotomy between achieving public justice – by means of forgetting – and private retribution – which would lead to an extended suffering. The first objective is qualified as a wise reaction (1.140):

νυνὶ πᾶσι τοῖς Ἕλλησιν ἄνδρες ἄριστοι καὶ εὐβουλότατοι δοκεῖτε γεγενῆσθαι, οὐκ ἐπὶ τιμωρίαν τραπόμενοι τῶν γεγενημένων, ἀλλ᾽ ἐπὶ σωτηρίαν τῆς πόλεως καὶ ὁμόνοιαν τῶν πολιτῶν. συμφοραὶ μὲν γὰρ ἤδη καὶ ἄλλοις πολλοῖς ἐγένοντο οὐκ ἐλάττους ἢ καὶ ἡμῖν· τὸ δὲ τὰς γενομένας διαφορὰς πρὸς ἀλλήλους θέσθαι καλῶς, τοῦτ᾽ εἰκότως ἤδη δοκεῖ ἀνδρῶν ἀγαθῶν καὶ σωφρόνων ἔργον εἶναι.[97]

Now you appear to all the Greeks to be excellent and highly moderate men for not turning to revenge (*timorían*) for what has occurred, but to the preservation of the *pólis* and the unity (*homónoian*) its citizens. Many others have suffered misfortunes no less than ours, but the virtuous reconciliation of

---

[96] On *mè mnesikakeîn* as "recall-wrong", see Edwin Carawan, "The Meaning of *mê mnêsikakein*", in *Classical Quarterly*, 2012, vol. 62, no. 2, pp. 567–81. As expressed by David Cohen, "The Rhetoric of Justice: Strategies of Reconciliation and Revenge in the Restoration of Athenian Democracy in 403 BC", in *European Journal of Sociology*, 2001, vol. 42, no. 2, p. 339: "the relevant phrase which grounds the amnesty is typically translated as 'to forget' or 'not to remember' what the oligarchs had done. In this context, however, the crucial phrase 'not to mnesikakein' actually means not to hold a grudge in the sense in which this is understood in a revenge society: that is, not to seek vengeance". A passage in the *Athenaion Politeia* attributed to Aristotle (39.6) reproduces the same vocabulary when considering that "nobody will be allowed to recall the wrongs (mnesikakeîn) of past events except the Thirty, the Ten, the Eleven, and those that have been governors of Peiraeus, and these will also be obliged if they render account" (τῶν δὲ παρεληλυθότων μηδενὶ πρὸς μηδένα μνησικακεῖν ἐξεῖναι, πλὴν πρὸς τοὺς τριάκοντα καὶ τοὺς δέκα καὶ τοὺς ἕνδεκα καὶ τοὺς τοῦ Πειραιέως ἄρξαντας, μηδὲ πρὸς τούτους, ἐὰν διδῶσιν εὐθύνας). Neverthless, this reference is probably not correct, since in the original agreement there were no exceptions made to the obligation of *mè mnesikakeîn*. According to Edwin Carawan, "Amnesty and Accountings for the Thirty", in *Classical Quarterly*, 2006, no. 56, no. 1 pp. 57–76, the content of the original treaty has been contaminated by exceptions which were added later in time.

[97] Edwards, 1995, see *supra* note 47.

the past differences (*genoménas diaphorás*) may reasonably
be perceived as the work of good and prudent men.

After the civil war, far from establishing *ad hoc* courts, the restored democracy granted amnesty to all officials of the former regime, with the exception of those that had been appointed to the top ranks. At the same time, it is also known to us that ordinary citizens could assist in private arrests and therefore bring "justice" to society by denouncing widespread attacks against civilians under the traditional legal system. As Adriaan Lanni observes: "Athens' unique legal culture permitted the amnesty to be implemented in a way that promoted unity while at the same time avoiding a sense of impunity at the local level".[98] The situation of *stásis* or internal strife was then resolved through the implementation of a delicate balance between retribution and forgiveness. By means of a fictional image of contractual negotiation within the community,[99] a collective narrative was crafted in order to deal with the responsibility for the commission of mass atrocities and at the same time to reconcile democrats and oligarchs.[100] Without resorting to new structures, if individual complaint procedures still permitted accusations against specific oppressors, the formal amnesty was an efficient tool to redirect democratic efforts towards the future and to reintegrate collaborators into the renovated *pólis*.

The enactment of this complex mechanism of transitional justice[101] gave room – in times of political turmoil – to the consolidation of Athenian unity and social pacification without the need to resort to the past for the recovery of truth.[102] In sum, the example of the amnesty law is useful to prove the effectiveness of a particular device created to deal with past cruelties, putting an end to civil war and rescuing the values of democra-

---

[98] Adriaan Lanni, "Transitional Justice in Ancient Athens: A Case Study", in *Journal of International Law*, 2010, vol. 32, no. 2, p. 553.

[99] This is the main thesis of Edwin Carawan, *The Athenian Amnesty and Reconstructing the Law*, Oxford University Press, Oxford, 2013.

[100] There have been different interpretations on the success or effectiveness of this reconciliation; see William Tieman, "'Cause' in History and the Amnesty at Athens: An Introduction", in *Transactions of the American Philological Association*, 2002, vol. 132, nos. 1/2, pp. 63–69.

[101] Jon Elster, *Closing the Books. Transitional Justice in Historical Perspective*, Cambridge University Press, Cambridge, 2004, pp. 7–8.

[102] Lanni, 2010, pp. 593–94, see *supra* note 98.

cy.[103] In this new context, the conciliatory attitude between accountability and pardon that Athenians put in place can be explained through the democratic moderation that the *pólis* intended to enshrine in order to preserve the political harmony and concord. Without eliminating the possibility of addressing local resentment through selected prosecutions, the solution that was imagined when democracy was restored translated a conscious decision to generate a shared fiction in a city-state composed by equals and determined by *isonomía*. Unlike the implementation and enforcement of a tribunal specifically focused to assign responsibility for atrocities committed in the past – as the Spartan court after Aegospotami can show – the Athenian way of dealing with the oligarchic coup rather believed in ensuring a peaceful reconciliation and thus re-establishing the democratic and egalitarian feeling of togetherness.

3.5. Final Remarks: Achieving Justice Between *Isonomía* and *Hegemonía*

Modern history shows that there have been several mechanisms available to face, either nationally or internationally, the effects of past violent experiences. The discussion about the advantages and obstacles of these different mechanisms in order to heal a society that thrives to make its way towards a better future has constituted a landmark of the debate on transitional justice.[104] Greek antiquity can offer here some valuable insights.

In the midst of high tension between democracy at the domestic level and imperialism in the international arena, the last years of the fifth century BCE displayed the coexistence of different social ways in which autonomous *póleis* could react to mass atrocities. As part of a complex response to the phenomenon of *ius post bellum*, inter-*póleis* relations at the end of the Peloponnesian War encouraged under certain circumstances the appeal to "common" laws to enact a hegemonic justice and endorse the victor's resolution by means of the creation of international *ad hoc*

---

[103] Christopher J. Joyce, "The Athenian Amnesty and Scrutiny of 403", in *Classical Quarterly*, 2008, vol. 58, no. 2, pp. 517–18. Other examples of Greek amnesties are mentioned in G. Smith, "The Prytaneum in the Athenian Amnesty Law", in *Classical Philology*, 1921, vol. 16, no. 4, pp. 345–53.

[104] Cf. Ruti G. Teitel, *Transitional Justice*, Oxford University Press, Oxford, 2000, and, more recently, the excellent synopsis by Kora Andrieu, *La justice transitionnelle: de l'Afrique du Sud au Rwanda* [Transitional Justice: From South Africa to Rwanda], Gallimard, Paris, 2012.

tribunals. On the other side, when the internal situation of post-oligarchic Athens is assessed, the solution reached included granting a general amnesty and promoting oblivion but tolerating the exercise of private hearings. Unlike the behaviour of competing *póleis* that fought to impose justice and exert revenge against the enemy, in the specific case of the amnesty law Athenians decided to attain rightness as part of a political will to overturn the social division and rebuild the communitarian web.

To conclude, the examples provided by classical Greek *póleis* clarify the foundations underlying different attitudes towards individual responsibility for the breach of shared *nómoi*, and elucidate the tension of attaining justice by an egalitarian unification of *politai* after a traumatic rupture (equality among citizens) or by a self-centred desire of preeminence over the enemy city-states (inequality among *póleis*). In other words, between democratic self-preservation and hegemonic longing, these experiences demonstrate – to the modern eye – a wide scope of arguments and ideologies that can explain, from the very beginning, the historical and political basis of today's institutions of international criminal justice.

War Crimes Trials and Pre-Nineteenth Century Admiralty Court Precedents

Shavana Musa[*]

4.1. Introduction

War crimes trials are often seen as a product of affairs after the Second World War in which particular heed is paid to the Nuremberg trials. There is, of course, good reason for this. The Charter of the International Military Tribunal ('IMT Charter'), and the subsequent trial, significantly developed the modern interpretation of war crimes.[1] Given the magnitude of events that preceded the Nuremberg trial, it is quite apparent why the nature of war crimes took the turn it did after 1945 and why, since then, international criminal courts, such as the International Criminal Tribunals for the former Yugoslavia and Rwanda and the International Criminal Court, have been created to try war criminals. We are, however, mistaken in thinking that the character of these courts is purely a product of the modern era. In fact, they do have a place in the more distant past than we might think, a past that goes back as far as the Middle Ages, and increases in presence and importance from the seventeenth to nineteenth centuries. This period saw maritime institutions known as admiralty courts occupy a position in the adjudication of wartime violations and crimes. They are therefore important in the discussion of the historical origins of international criminal law. Even the British prosecutor at Nuremberg, David Maxwell Fyfe, recognised that admiralty courts and their prize jurisdic-

---

[*] **Shavana Musa** is a Doctoral Researcher and Lecturer at the Department of Public Law, Jurisprudence and Legal History, Tilburg University, the Netherlands. Her research consists of a comprehensive investigation into reparations for war victims from the mid-seventeenth century to the present, outlining reparative mechanisms at admiralty courts. She also teaches courses on world legal systems, international legal history and international law.

[1] Charter of the International Military Tribunal, 8 August 1945, Art. 6 ('IMT Charter') (https://www.legal-tools.org/doc/64ffdd/).

tion had long been instrumental in punishing those breaching "the laws and usages of war".[2]

Admiralty courts were distinct institutions vested with the authority to deliberate and decide upon issues of prize, namely ships and goods, seized upon the high seas during times of war. They did, however, also deal with other pertinent wartime-related matters, including general violations of the laws of war and the laws of neutrality. Although admiralty courts were not always attributed with explicit criminal law jurisdiction as such, they had the authority to try persons violating the laws of war, hear cases relating to crimes such as piracy and impose punishments depriving culprits of their property, and sometimes life. The pre-twentieth-century world was one where the codification of war crimes had not yet taken place. The term 'war crimes' and its content are therefore used with caution in this chapter. Historically, certain war crimes in the modern sense were committed and viewed as an inevitability of war, and, theologically, as a right that was just in the eyes of God.[3] They were expected and sometimes permitted. Regardless of the religious to legal evolution of war crimes over the centuries, one cannot detract from the role of the admiralty courts in dealing with the *bellum iustum*. Admiralty courts still dealt with many offences that today would be deemed war crimes. Through time, we see cases at admiralty courts involving the attacking of innocent merchantmen, pillaging of non-combatant individuals, violation of the laws of neutrality and other violence on the high seas, especially that connected to matters of prize during wartime. Trials involving pirates could also be conducted within admiralty courts more generally and, on occa-

---

[2] David Maxwell Fyfe, "Foreword", in Robert W. Cooper, *The Nuremberg Trial*, Penguin, London, 1947, pp. 1–6.

[3] For writings on just war theory, see Saint Augustine, *The City of God against the Pagans*, Book IV, Harvard University Press, Cambridge, MA, 1963, p. 151; Thomas Aquinas, *Summa Theologica*, vol. 2, Wiliam Benton, Chicago, 1952; Francisco de Vitoria, "On the American Indians", in Anthony Pagden and Jeremy Lawrence (eds.), *Vitoria: Political Writings*, Cambridge University Press, Cambridge, 1991, pp. xvii, 187, 231–98, 304; Hugo Grotius, "De Jure Belli Ac Pacis" [On the Law of War and Peace], in James Brown Scott (ed.), *The Classics of International Law*, vol. 2, Clarendon Press, Oxford, 1925. For a historical overview of the development of war, see Stephen C. Neff, *War and the Law of Nations: A General History*, Cambridge University Press, Cambridge, 2008.

sion, prohibited wartime actions committed by persons on land would also be tried, within regulations that would allow it.[4]

The workings of the admiralty court, and their application of prize law, were integral to a country's position legally, commercially and politically. Despite each European nation having its own prize jurisdictional body within its admiralty court, each with a different form and structure, it was an innate belief, as was wholeheartedly agreed, that the jurisdiction of each and every prize body in Europe would be determined by the law of nations and not the domestic law of the home country. The law of nations, generally speaking, were the rules governing the practices, behaviours and relations of and between states. In reality, given the geographical domestic situation of each of these admiralty courts, cases would be subject to domestic procedures. However, international rules and regulations deriving from treaties that countries entered into with one another, and sometimes even prominent doctrinal writings, still remained an important source for the legal processes in these courts, which the prize judges frequently referred to.[5] Admiralty courts, with their prize jurisdictions, were institutions that applied international rules and were the epitome of what Henry Wheaton referred to in the nineteenth century as "the most important practical branch of the law of nations".[6]

Both the wartime and peacetime agendas of nations have therefore enveloped prize law for centuries, contributing significantly to the development of international law more generally. It should be highlighted, however, that the internal structure and position of the admiralty court varied depending on the European country in question. Most prize jurisdictions were not isolated prize courts as such, but divisions or separate jurisdictional sections that lay within the broader jurisdiction of an admiralty court. In England, the prize division separated from the Court of Admiralty to stand as a court in its own right around the late seventeenth century. The Dutch, by contrast, had a rather fragmented governmental

---

[4] An Act Concerning Pirates and Robbers of the Sea 1535, 27 Hen 8 c 4 ('Piracy Act'); Offences at Sea Act 1536, 28 Hen 8 c 15 ('Offences at Sea Act'); An Act for the More Effectual Suppression of Piracy 1698, 11 and 12 Will. 3 c 7. This latter Act made amendments to the previous 1536 Act and affirmed piracy as a capital crime. High Court of Admiralty (HCA 1), The National Archives, UK ('TNA').

[5] See examples below involving the English judge Leoline Jenkins.

[6] Henry Wheaton, *A Digest of the Law of Maritime Captures and Prizes*, R. McDermut and D.D. Arden, New York, 1815, p. iii.

structure in the seventeenth century, resulting in prize jurisdiction within five separate admiralty courts in the different Dutch provinces.

Admiralty jurisdiction dealt with broader maritime offences during peacetime. Since prize jurisdictions quite often functioned within an admiralty court to deal with issues of prize during wartime, this chapter uses the term 'admiralty court' to refer not only to the ordinary maritime jurisdiction that the court held during times of peace, but also the prize jurisdiction and consequential prize law that was applied to cases during times of war. One should also bear in mind the civil nature of the admiralty and prize jurisdiction. Although prize law was the body of law dealing specifically with prize during war, legal cases did get complicated when dealing with innately criminal actions such as piracy. The very close connections between privateering and piracy, the amalgamation of the civil aspects of the admiralty courts with additional criminal sentencing from other parts of the same domestic regime, along with the semantically challenged law of nations, means that forming a clear thread on the functioning of these institutions is a challenging task. However, it is for this chapter to bring to light this quite overlooked system of prize as a precedent to war crimes. It will discuss the general function of admiralty courts and outline their role in dealing with wartime misconduct.

This chapter therefore provides an insight into the function of admiralty courts as key overlooked precursors to modern war crimes trials existing as far back as the Middle Ages. It outlines a significant admiralty court network, which functioned throughout Europe. Colonial expansion also resulted in the creation of vice-admiralty courts that extended to the non-European world. Although the international criminal courts today are very different to the admiralty courts here, both substantively and procedurally, it is intended that the discussion will bring attention to a highly regulated, very respected and systemised court network around the world that dealt with offences during wartime before the development of modern international law. Since it is impossible to assess each and every admiralty court dealing with war crimes within a large temporal framework and given the vastness of the global scale, this chapter pays particular attention to a few European admiralty courts and their adjudication of two specific offences, namely piracy and the violation of neutrality, with the latter sometimes even leading to the former. In addition, the final part of the chapter briefly explains the extent to which admiralty courts within the different domestic jurisdictions did in fact adhere to the same rules on issues related to wartime in spite of the exclamations that all prize cases would be dealt with in the same way as their European counterparts under the law of nations.

4.2. Admiralty Courts in Europe

Prize mechanisms have existed in Europe since the Middle Ages, deciding matters of prize during periods of declared war. Prize law was to be applied across admiralty courts in Europe with a degree of consistency under the international sphere of the law of nations. Many domestic admiralty courts adhered to this international law and managed to integrate it into their national agendas. The relationship between the domestic and the international was no doubt a particularly complicated affair with its roots firmly embedded in politics and diplomacy. It is nonetheless interesting to note that just as today states have margins of appreciation, so too did the medieval and early modern states and their admiralty courts.

England, France, the Netherlands and Spain all had prize mechanisms within their admiralty courts, which dealt with issues relating to the capture of ships and property during wartime. Prize was a tool employed by countries to attack the enemy in a bid to damage its commerce and potential for success in a war. Prize law became increasingly expansive and intricate from the fifteenth century onwards. This was as a reflection of the development and necessity of maritime commerce and international relations. It was imperative that crimes such as piracy, unlawful naval attacks and injuries during war were dealt with, and courts administered prize law for the suppression of these types of offences. Doctrinal writers such as Hugo Grotius,[7] Alberico Gentili,[8] and later Cornelius van Bynkershoek,[9] all began writing on issues relating to prize law and its jurisdiction. The intertwining of theoretical conceptions and the practical application of prize law resulted in its further development and significance within admiralty courts.

In England, Acts of Parliament enacted during the time of Henry VIII[10] allowed for the High Court of Admiralty to take its place as the in-

---

[7] Grotius, 1925, see *supra* note 3.

[8] Alberico Gentili, *De Jure Belli Libri Tres*, Clarendon Press, Oxford, 1847 [1589].

[9] Cornelius van Bynkershoek, *A Treatise on the Law of War*, Lawbook Exchange, Clark, NJ, 2008 [1737].

[10] Piracy Act and Offences at Sea Act, see *supra* note 4.

stitution to deal with maritime offences, where "piracy, theft, robbery, murder, and treasons, done on the sea, or within the Admiral's jurisdiction, and Confederacies in the said offences, shall be tried in some County on land, by the King's Commission, directed to the Admiral and others".[11] Prize jurisdiction in England, during the periods of the seventeenth and eighteenth centuries, fell within the realms of the Court of Admiralty and for a time in a stand-alone prize court. It was around the late seventeenth century that a distinct separation between the ordinary side of the Admiralty and the prize court was made. Before this time, the Admiral had more of an amalgamated approach to maritime issues as a whole and did not need additional authority to deal with prize issues during war. Nonetheless, procedural and substantive laws on war offences such as piracy did exist. Instructions dating back to the sixteenth century required the adherence to procedural issues, such as the meticulous inspection of crews, preservation of goods until judgment and penal consequences for any misdeeds.

With the Lord High Admiral towering over its adjudication, the English Court of Admiralty was unique in character, and even before it became a systemised, regulated and commercial prize court in the late seventeenth century it adhered to international laws and considerations. According to the view of the English, every country could sue in the courts of others, as they were all governed by and acquainted with the same law. As far as England was concerned, prize law was instilled in "mutual convenience, eternal principles of justice, wise policy and the consent of nations, which had established a system of procedure, a code of law, and a court for the trial of prize".[12] The general consensus at this time was that the ground of the action prize or no prize gave the Court of Admiralty prize jurisdiction, and excluded the domestic common law.[13]

Within the English Admiralty Court, the process was rather flexible, especially between 1535 and 1759 when there was no regular case

---

[11] Piracy Act and Offences at Sea Act, see *supra* note 4.

[12] Arthur Browne, A Compendious View of the Civil Law, and of the Law of the Admiralty, Being the Substance of a Course of Lectures Read in the University of Dublin, vol. 2, J. Butterworth, London, 1802, p. 224.

[13] For work on prize law at the English Court of Admiralty, see Shavana Musa, "Tides and Tribulations: English Prize Law and the Law of Nations in the Seventeenth Century", in *Journal of the History of International Law*, 2015, vol. 17(1), pp. 47-82.

schedule. The way in which cases were heard was not always the same.[14] This was quite often the case in most European countries with prize jurisdiction, as each war allowed for different circumstances and the procedure would meet the context of that particular war, such as instructions stated explicitly in any relevant treaties. In some cases, claimants and defendants could sue each other simultaneously, or proceed without having libel or allegation, only interrogatories. Upon having heard the case the judge issued decrees. If the decrees were not satisfactory, they could be appealed against, not simply once but even twice. Usually the third decree was the final one, with no further appeals thereafter.

Elizabethan maritime practices during wartime meant that crime at sea was rife during her reign. It is not surprising then that in 1585 a number of instructions were issued regulating prizes. These instructions made explicit actions that were forbidden on the high seas, in turn providing a cause for victims who were injured as a result of these prohibited acts. Letters of reprisal could also be authorised. Instructions were quite often issued at the start of wars. A set of instructions dated 9 July 1585 issued at the start of the Anglo-Spanish War, concerning English subjects injured by Spaniards, provides a good example.[15] A war victim had to prove their loss at the Admiralty Court; all seized property had to be intricately inventoried at the port it arrived at by the vice-admiral, which was thereafter sent to the High Court of Admiralty within six weeks; a security was to be deposited for prizes captured; details of ships, crew members and property; and, the prize value assigned to the owner, officers and crew of the ships. The deliberations and evidentiary rules that judges had to go through at the court itself were not included in the instructions. Later, a proclamation of 1602 was issued for the Admiralty Court in which the judge of the court had the authority to deal with privateers who did not have an authorisation to capture prize.[16] This would be tantamount to pi-

---

[14] R.G. Marsden, "Early Prize Jurisdiction and Prize Law in England", in *English Historical Review*, 1909, vol. 24, p. 675.

[15] SP 12/237, Admiralty warrants: with a list of the Lords High Admiral of England from the reign of Edward II to 1590, with dates of appointment, TNA; R.G. Marsden (ed.), *Documents Relating to Law and Custom of the Sea*, vol. 1: *A.D. 1205–1648*, Navy Records Society, London, 1915, p. 237.

[16] Ordering Execution of Articles against Piracy, 44 Eliz. I, 20 March 1602; Ordering Peace Kept on the Seas, and Pirates Arrested, 6 Eliz. I, 31 July 1564; Penalizing Offences against Allied Shipping, 33 Eliz. I, 3 February 1591, in Paul L. Hughes and James F. Larkin (eds.),

racy and a case involving this crime would be heard at the Admiralty Court.

In France prize jurisdiction was vested in the Admiral from around 1500 and ordinances existed confirming the separation between the ordinary laws of France and the prize jurisdiction. In comparison to England, the French prize system was much more *ad hoc*. The French were, however, very innovative in the way they created consular admiralty tribunals in all of their territories, including those of their allies. The adjudication of captures by French subjects was rendered by the Admiralty officials of the port into which prizes were taken. Any appeals on decisions were made to the Parlement of the province in which the port was situated. During the period from 1627 to 1669, the official of the admiral (or office of the Admiralty) was suspended and replaced by the Grand Master of Navigation. Cardinal Richelieu, Anne of Austria and the Duke of Vendôme were among those who held this title. Since these people were occupied with other matters and not especially qualified to be the Grand Master of Navigation, in 1659, by virtue of letters of patent, the Conseil des Prises (Prize Council) was set up, which commenced the initiation of every war. Appeals from the Conseil des Prises were made to Royal Council.[17]

Unlike in England, there was no unified governmental system in the Dutch Republic. Like most admiralties in Europe, diplomacy was key in the functioning of the establishment, especially given the blurred demarcation between privateers and pirates. Sometimes, the various Dutch admiralties would also hold criminal trials of pirates, as recommended by the Secret Council.[18] Power was derived from the provincial states and municipalities. A 1488 Ordinance placed the Admiral with an authoritative position on maritime issues during war. In the United Provinces during this period, the Admiral could provide a key platform for the practical application of his legal authority, including the appointment of deputies.[19]

Tudor Royal Proclamations, Yale University Press, New Haven, MA, 1964, pp. 71–74, 238–41, 253–55.

[17] R.J. Valin, *Commentaire sur l'ordonnance de la marine* [Commentary on the Ordinance of the Marine], Joubert, Paris, 1841 [1681].

[18] Louis Sicking, Neptune and the Netherlands: State, Economy and War at Sea in the Renaissance, Brill, Leiden, 2004, p. 480.

[19] *Ibid.*, p. 436–37.

The first Dutch admiralty was formed in Veere that year.[20] Much case law can be found on piracy in the Veere Admiralty even later in the sixteenth century.[21] Although initially an Admiral General, the Stadholder was the only consistent figure residing over the admiralties and after the abolition of the Stadholdership in 1650, power was transferred to the States General. Therefore, ships and goods brought into the Dutch admiralty would be seen by the States General after 1650. The adherence to the law of nations can be evidenced in 1658, when we see the States General affirming that

> all the affairs touching prizes and merchandises, which are brought into the ports of this state, and demanded by their owners, acknowledge no other judicature and jurisdiction, than those of the respective admiralties privately, and it is before them, that according to the placards, affairs of this kind, with all circumstances concerning the same, must be discussed and decided, as is usual in all other countries in Europe.[22]

In Spain intendants decided upon the prize and other wartime issues in the ports that the prize was brought into. Alternatively, the intendant of the province could also decide if the port intendant was not available. Appeals for prize cases were dealt with by the Council of War. In 1675 a major disagreement arose between the Council of War and the province of Aragon on the matter of who had exclusive jurisdiction of prizes. Queen Mariana, regent for her son Charles II, after deliberations with the Dutch States General, decided that "the council of war has the exclusive cognizance of all disputes relating to war, as the sending of dispatches and questions relative to salutes and to prizes, which must be determined according to the military laws".[23] Spain also created rules on prize that did not conform to the way other states were behaving according to interna-

---

[20] Nicolaes Wassenaer, *Historisch Verhael Aller Gedenkwaerdiger Geschiedenissen*, vol. 13, Jan Jansz, Amsterdam, 1627–1628, p. 31.

[21] Sicking, 2004, p. 450, see *supra* note 18.

[22] "Resolution of the States General in Answer to Resident Downing's Last Memorial of the Same Date", 2 November 1658, in Thomas Birch (ed.), *A Collection of the State Papers of John Thurloe, Esq; Secretary, First, to the Council of State, and afterwards to the Two Protectors, Oliver and Richard Cromwell*, vol. 7, Fletcher Gyles, London, 1742, p. 458 ('Resolution of the States General').

[23] M.D.A. Azuni, *The Maritime Law of Europe*, vol. 2, George Forman, New York, 1806, p. 264.

tional laws, regardless of the fact that it had entered into treaties declaring that prize would be treated under the law of nations.[24]

As one can see from the description of the admiralty courts and their respective prize jurisdictions, each of the countries structured its courts in a different way, which naturally led to procedural variations. But each admiralty court also dealt with prize issues with international laws in mind "as [was] usual in all other countries in Europe".[25] In dissecting the substantive law of nations, these courts applied a range of legal sources, which ventured beyond the legal and into the political at times. Treaties that states entered into, indicating state practice on any given issue, illustrated this quite well. These included actions that were strictly forbidden during war, culprits of which were penalised thereafter. The courts would also use the more general laws prescribed by doctrine, domestic rules and regulations and ancient maritime sources such as the *Consolato del mare* to deal with wartime issues consistent with their European counterparts.[26] The role of the law of nations in practice within admiralty courts will be discussed below.

4.3. Wartime Offences at the Admiralty Courts

Article 6 of the IMT Charter created in 1945 stated that war crimes were

> violations of the laws or customs of war. Such violations shall include, but not be limited to, murder, ill-treatment or deportation to slave labour or for any other purpose of civilian population of or in occupied territory, murder or ill-treatment of prisoners of war or persons on the seas, killing of hostages, plunder of public or private property, wanton destruction of cities, towns or villages, or devastation not justified by military necessity.[27]

To a degree, much of what was outlined in Article 6 were issues that fell under the jurisdiction of the admiralty court judges. Admiralty judges would deal with murder, plunder of private property and other ac-

---

[24] *Ibid.*

[25] Resolution of the States General, see *supra* note 22.

[26] For ease of reference, *consolato del mare* is the term used here, but in reality there was not one single coherent body of neutrality laws in history, but rather many different *consolati*, not all completely identical in substance.

[27] IMT Charter, Art. 6(b), see *supra* note 1.

tions not "justified by military necessity". Historically, acts constituting later war crimes were not always legally prohibited. At certain points in history they were morally and religiously prohibited. At other times the laws of war allowed many acts of war that would be deemed illegal by international laws today. In the Middle Ages the 'just war' was initiated as a type of law enforcement, and theologians were of the belief that a just side had the right to make war while the unjust side did not. There could never be two just sides and the medieval equivalent of war crimes would be the acts of war perpetrated by the unjust side.[28] As legality started to take root within the war and peace in the sixteenth and seventeenth centuries, acts of war took on a different form, as did the belief that parties to war could now be equal.[29] During this time, admiralty courts begin to take prominent shape, most notably as a reflection of wartime agendas. But a paradigmatic shift in the twentieth century saw aggressive war and related acts of war revert to, in a sense, just war roots. They were to be outlawed. The Kellogg-Briand Pact[30] paved – what at the time was viewed as – the controversial path to the establishment of crimes against peace, war crimes and crimes against humanity, as indicated in Article 6 of the IMT Charter.[31]

A distinction must therefore be made between what today are wartime actions that are criminalised by law and the same historical actions that were not always regarded as crimes in the strictest of sense. Some actions were regarded as violations of the laws of war or neutrality and not necessarily crimes, yet given the same stringent treatment at admiralty courts and therefore justifiably seen as precursors of war crimes. Furthermore, if actions were not authorised by the state as forming part of the war and were committed upon the high seas, then they could be declared as piratical or an offence that again allowed for a severe sanction. Such offences could be brought forward by a victim as a case to be judged at the prize section of the admiralty court or within the wider ordinary admi-

---

[28] See *supra* note 3.

[29] Grotius, 1925, see supra note 3; Emer de Vattel, The Law of Nations, or, Principles of the Law of Nature Applied to the Conduct and Affairs of Nations and Sovereigns, G.G. and J. Robinson, London, 1797.

[30] Treaty between the United States and Other Powers Providing for Renunciation of War as an Instrument of National Policy, 27 August 1928, entered into force 25 July 1929, 94 LNTS 57.

[31] IMT Charter, Art. 6, see *supra* note 1.

ralty jurisdiction depending on the circumstances. Although maritime wartime offences heard at admiralty courts were wide-ranging, there were two particular types of cases that remained markedly dominant: piracy and, most evident in the seventeenth and eighteenth centuries, the violation of neutral rights under the law of neutrality. The following sections will focus primarily on these two offences, on how admiralty courts processed the cases involving them and treated the culprits responsible for their commission.

4.4. Piracy

From time immemorial, piracy has been categorised as one of the most renowned maritime offences, quite often being referred to as *hostis humani generis*. Its definition remains nebulous, not helped by its continuous metamorphosis over time. It has, nevertheless, remained within history a crime, with various European countries employing torturous punishments such as gibbeting, enslavement or, most popularly, capital punishments such as hanging and execution. Historically, pirates could be caught plundering and pillaging non-combatants and committing general violence upon the high seas. Their actions could be regarded as petty treason or even treachery, as was done in England in the seventeenth century by the judge Edward Coke. Admiralty Courts have traditionally been the legal platforms in which these types of culprits have been adjudged. They were of course always laid within the domestic domain, but piracy itself was essentially a 'universal' crime. In this sense, one sees an intertwinement of the domestic and the international when dealing with maritime crimes during war. It is most aptly put by Anne Perotin-Dumon, who states that "crimes of piracy were always handled within a national legal framework. Although they belonged more properly to the domain of international law, they were brought before national admiralty courts or commerce jurisdictions".[32]

Lawful action on the high seas during war was normally characterised by commissions, or *lettres de marque*, issued to privateers authorised to take prizes. If the privateer was caught without a commission then he

---

[32] Anne Perotin-Dumon, "The Pirate and the Emperor: Power and the Law on the Seas, 1450–1850", in James D. Tracy (ed.), *The Political Economy of Merchant Empires: State Power and World Trade, 1350–1750*, Cambridge University Press, Cambridge, 1991, p. 202.

would be regarded as a pirate and treated as such. In the same vein, if goods had been seized and thereafter disposed of without a commission then there would be a probable case for piracy. During the War of the Spanish Succession (1701–14), the admiralty courts in Europe saw an increase in the number of piracy cases and privateers roaming the seas without a fully authorised commission. In some cases, this was even unintentional on the part of the privateer. Regardless, ignorance was never to be a viable justification for a crime. William Dampier was one such person accused of piracy in Amboyna in the Dutch colonies for engaging in piratical acts against the Spanish. He was imprisoned by the Dutch Admiralty as a pirate for want of a commission.[33] Official laws and regulations emphasised the requirement of a commission for legal privateering. In a naval instruction of 1730, any vessel taken "acting as a ship of war or privateer, without having a commission duly authorising her to do so, her crew shall be considered as pirates and treated accordingly".[34]

The process of determining the lawfulness of the action was done in the admiralty court. The Admiralty Court in England did not deal with piracy until at least the fourteenth century, which began first with *ad hoc* arbitrators or councils under maritime law to deal with this crime. Documents from 1357 show Edward III specifically confirming that trials for piracy were done under the jurisdiction of the Admiral: "our admiral has judicially and rightly determined the ownership of the goods claimed by your merchants". In this case, the Portuguese had put forward a complaint of English piratical behaviour.[35] It was only in 1426 that elements of a formal court procedure were actually introduced by a treaty between England and Flanders. Formality within the court was likely due to a high number of piracy complaints made by Philip, Duke of Burgundy and the merchants of Flanders to the Council of England, but also because of complaints by England on underhand Flemish trading with the enemies of the English. A requirement on the admiral's certification of goods was consequently established as part of the prize process.[36]

---

[33] Christopher Lloyd, *William Dampier*, Faber and Faber, London, 1966, p. 21.

[34] Naval Instructions, § 4, 1730, p. 88.

[35] Marsden, 1909, see *supra* note 14, p. 680.

[36] "Rymer's Foedera with Syllabus: 1427", in Thomas Rymer (ed.), *Rymer's Foedera Volume 10*, Apud Joannem Neulme, London, 1739–1745, p. 367–68.

In England, the civil and criminal aspects of the Admiralty were separated with procedural distinctions. Since criminal cases in England would require a jury and the Admiralty functioned according to the civil law, with prize according to the 'law of nations', it was difficult to sentence pirates to death unless an actual confession had been made or a reliable eye witness had confirmed the crime. For this reason, the Piracy Act of 1535 and the Offences at Sea Act of 1536 authorised by Henry VIII allowed for the merger of admiralty cases with a jury-based trial, presided over by the Admiral and declaring piracy a capital crime.[37] It demonstrated a merger of admiralty jurisdiction with the domestic common laws of England to enable the ordering of an appropriate punishment.

Wartime piracy and prize were so closely intertwined that there were instances in which the civil High Court of Admiralty – within the prize jurisdiction for times of war – would try cases of a criminal nature and on some occasions trigger a separate criminal case, if insufficient evidence would prevent a suitably stringent punishment for the culprit. In the case of piracy, death was deemed the most appropriate. The 1536 Act meant that the piracy case would be heard by a jury of 12 'peers' in special sessions at the Court of Admiralty. Since the prize jurisdiction of the English Admiralty Court was limited to ordering the restitution of property, damages or other civil-based remedies, it was very rare that an admiralty judge working on a prize case would in fact sentence a pirate to death. In England this would most likely be transferred as a separate case to the wider admiralty court with its mixed jurisdiction from the common law, as prescribed by the Henrician laws. A century later in 1615 a Dutch ship, which had been first seized by a Swedish privateer, then by a Danish one and finally by English pirates, was taken to the prize body of the English Court of Admiralty and declared as pirate goods. These goods were condemned and confiscated.

Although the prize section of the English Court of Admiralty did not specifically have criminal jurisdiction, it was given powers to make strict orders on property and compensatory matters. Judges on a prize case were authorised to rule on whether the seizure of property during war was lawful or not. Remedies could be ordered *in rem* or *in personam* and those accused of illegally attacking ships during war would have to pay the victim's damages or at least restore the property. Endless English prize cases,

---

[37] Piracy Act and Offences at Sea Act, see *supra* note 4.

especially from the mid-seventeenth century onwards until the court's winding up in the mid-eighteenth century show orders made against persons that had committed depredations against innocent merchants or seamen during war. These attacks were subject to civil adjudication in the prize body of the English Court of Admiralty. Those condemned of the crime might not necessarily be labelled a pirate as such, especially if the attacker's victim received the reparation he was seeking, but at the same time the attacker could be treated as a pirate if the depredation was of the greatest severity and a victim accused the attacker of piracy.

In the Dutch Republic, admiralties would scrutinise the actions of privateers during war to ensure that no illegal activity was taking place. Transgressions would not go unnoticed and Dutch officials at the courts would ensure punishments, which could begin at mild pecuniary penalties and move onto graver ones such as physical torture and death. The Dutch admiralties provided privateers with article letters (*artikel Brieven*), issued proclamations and instructions, which condemned offences such as mutiny, murder and assault. Should privateers be caught committing any of these crimes or violating any of the rules prescribed by the admiralties, they would be tried for the crime of piracy at the courts and, if found guilty, subject to a heavy fine or quite possibly the death penalty.[38]

The practical implementations of admiralty sessions on crimes such as piracy meant that hearing cases during war in far-distant colonies would be a problem. Consequently, vice-admiralty courts were created. In order to apply the universal jurisdiction over piracy practically, vice-admiralty courts began to appear in lands further afield where European countries had established colonial territories. Nations embroiled in expensive wars did not always have the means to send their fleets to patrol the seas with the aim of suppressing piracy, and so the creation of vice-admiralty courts was a very practical method of dealing with cases of piracy there. The surge of piracy in Malta, for example, resulted in the crea-

---

[38] Virginia W. Lunsford, *Piracy and Privateering in the Golden Age Netherlands*, Palgrave Macmillan, New York, 2005, pp. 14–15; Verz. Thysius: Collegien ter Admiralityet, Zeeland Kamer, Instructie ende Articulen, Article 3(2), 21 February 1665. See Treaty of Commerce and Navigation between France and the Netherlands, signed at Nijmegen, 10 August 1678, 14 CTS 399; J.K. Oudendijk, "The Dutch Republic and Algiers, 1662–1664", in Michel Mollat (ed.), *Course et piraterie: Études presentées à la Commission Internationale d'Histoire Maritime à l'occasion de son XVè colloque international pendant le XIVè Congrès International des Sciences Historiques*, Institut de Recherche et d'Histoire des Textes, Centre National de la Recherche Scientifique, Paris, 1975, p. 156.

tion of a Court of Piracy and Vice-Admiralty Court of Malta.[39] A British judge was also sent to hear the cases that were brought to both courts, including ones involving depredations during wartime.

One of the objectives of admiralty courts was to suppress piratical acts during wartime, relating to prize but also issues relating to the general admiralty jurisdiction on piracy in times of peace. The jurisdiction on piracy therefore overlapped between the prize and ordinary jurisdiction of admiralty courts. In certain countries such as England, this was inevitable, given that it was the same person residing over both these different maritime jurisdictions. Since crimes during wartime were embedded within international politics and diplomacy, it was quite normal for kings or other heads of government to complain to the countries where the accused was a national. In 1324 James II of Aragon complained endlessly to Edward II of England about the delay in resolving a piracy case, which prevented the attainment of justice. On this occasion, it was discovered that the reason had been due to an evidentiary obstacle in which the victim had failed to provide the names of the perpetrators. This prevented the conviction of the crime. Interestingly, this case gave rise to a common obstacle to the full and proper adjudication of criminal cases. Prize jurisdiction was recognised as based in the law of nations until the beginning of modern international law. This meant that all states would adhere to the mutual laws extending beyond their domestic frameworks. Evidentiary difficulties resulted in problems when it came to resolving cases at the courts. In this instance, despite agreeing to the same kind of substantive laws in the case, due to England's stricter procedural rules, in which condemnation for a crime had to occur before conviction, the outcome was different to what another country like Spain desired. In medieval Spain, procedural laws simply stated that reprisals could be granted as long as the injury was proven in the Spanish courts. The Spanish were adamant that a miscarriage of justice had occurred.[40]

Another task of the admiralty courts was to deal with crimes committed by non-European and non-Christian states. Admiralty jurisdiction

---

[39] "Conduct of the Vice Admiralty Court at Malta – Arrest of Lord Cochrane", in *Parliamentary Debates*, 18 July 1811, vol. 20, cc. 1017–27, Hansard, London, 1812; Desmond Gregory, *Malta, Britain, and the European Powers, 1793–1815*, Fairleigh Dickinson University Press, Cranbury, NJ, 1996, p. 260–64.

[40] Rymer, 1739–1745, p. 568–90, see *supra* note 36. See also R.G. Marsden, *Select Pleas in the Court of Admiralty*, vol. 1, B. Quaritch, London, 1894, pp. xxiv–xxv.

could be far-reaching, especially when it came to matters of war. In one instance, Leoline Jenkins, an English Admiralty judge, had to decide whether a Muslim crew on an Algerian warship was to be sentenced to death as pirates for having seized an English ship, which was then left wrecked in Ireland. In a letter to Charles II, Jenkins wrote:

> As for the Moors and Turks that are so by birth, and were found on board [...] since the Government of Algiers is owned as well by several Treaties of Peace and Declaration of War, as by the Establishment of Trade, and even of Consuls and Residents among them by so many Princes and States, and particularly by your Majesty; they cannot [...] be proceeded against as Pirates [...] but are to have the Privilege of Enemies in an open War.[41]

Jenkins's letter draws attention to the impact of treaties on the law to be applied within admiralty courts and the stance taken by its respective judges. Foreign relations evidently played a part in the assessment of whether a significant offence had in fact taken place during war and whether the offender should be tried and punished or not. In the absence of treaties, other similar practices between nations would also be taken into account.

Piracy's unique character as a universal crime is evident when established prize law was modified to have a wider jurisdiction. Whereas the general law required cases to be heard at the admiralty court in the country where the crime was committed, in certain instances it had become common practice to deal with piracy under a more universal jurisdiction. Given that piracy was deemed a crime against mankind and the worst kind of depredation possible against the law of nations, many admiralty courts around Europe also broadened their interpretation of when they could try a person accused of piracy. In exemplifying the way in which admiralty courts did this, not even chiefly during wartime, the Scottish High Court of Admiralty sentenced the English captain Thomas Green and two other men for plundering, sinking and disposing of a Scottish vessel and its crew near Calicut, India. The men were hanged, even

---

[41] William Wynne, *The Life of Sir Leoline Jenkins, Judge of the High-Court of Admiralty, and Prerogative Court of Canterbury, &c. Ambassador and Plenipotentiary for the General Peace at Cologn and Nimeguen, and Secretary of State to K. Charles II and a Compleat Series of Letters, from the Beginning to the End of those Two Important Treaties*, vol. 2, Joseph Downing, London, 1724, p. 791.

though the allegations made were somewhat spurious and not based on the most concrete of evidence. Nonetheless, the significance of this case is that neither Green nor the ship in which he sailed was Scottish, with the crime taking place away from Scottish territory. The prosecution for the case gave their reasoning:

> That though the competency of the judge in criminal be ordinarily said, to be found either *in loco delicti* (the place where crime was committed) or *in loco domicilii* (place of habitation of the delinquents) or *in loco originis* (the place of their birth) yet there is a superior consideration, and that is the *locus deprehensionis* (place where they were taken) where the criminal is found and deprehended, which doth so over-rule in this matter, that neither the *locus domicilii* [...] nor the *locus originis* [...] doth found the judges competency, *nisi ibi reus deprehendatur* (except the criminal be apprehended there). And so it is that here the pannels [defendants] were and are deprehended, which happening in the cause of piracy, a crime against the law of nations, and which all mankind have an interest to pursue, wherever the pirates can be found; the Procurator Fiscal's [Prosecutor's] interest to pursue is thereby manifest, and the pannels being here deprehended, cannot decline the admiral's jurisdiction as incompetent.[42]

It is clear that, in this case, the nature of the crime determined the authority of the Admiralty Court to act in a way different to precedent. In general, however, piracy was treated as a crime against the law of nations, which aligned the jurisdiction of the admiralty court away from territorial jurisdiction to a universal one. This also became a common practice of admiralty mechanisms in other countries.[43] It particularly fitted in with the view of the English Admiralty judge Sir Charles Hedges in 1696 on creating a law that would allow pirates to be tried anywhere and not necessarily limited to the English Admiralty Court: "Now piracy is only a sea term for robbery, piracy being robbery committed within the jurisdiction of the

---

[42] "Trial of Captain Green and his Crew", in T.B. Howell, A Complete Collection of State Trials and Proceedings for High Treason and Other Crimes and Misdemeanors from the Earliest Period to the Present, vol. 14, Hansard, London, 1705, p. 1224. See also Alfred P. Rubin, The Law of Piracy, Naval War College Press, Newport, RI, 1988 for a good account on the evolution of the law on piracy.

[43] Rubin, 1888, pp. 93–94, see *supra* note 42.

Admiralty. If any man be assaulted within that jurisdiction, and his ship or goods violently taken away without legal authority, this is robbery and piracy".[44]

4.5. Violation of Neutrality

While belligerent nations and their subjects would inevitably suffer injuries or enter into legal disputes relating to a war, non-belligerent, friendly nations would also often fall victim to wartime injuries. The violations of neutral rights were offences that occurred during war, giving way to legal cases at the admiralty courts for an appropriate remedy. Neutral rights on territorial waters were "the essential basis of sovereignty of any nation".[45] As far as neutrality was concerned, prize law would, especially after the middle of the eighteenth century, give due regard to the law of nations and later modern international law principles. This is because the adherence of neutrality principles during wartime was important to the commercial position of states. Belligerents were aware of the fine line between the way neutrals were and were not permitted to act, but also the duty of the belligerent to the neutral itself. In particular, rules deriving from the ancient *Consolato del mare* prescribed the possibility for belligerents to seize enemy goods from neutral vessels, but not neutral goods from enemy vessels. In time, neutrals, in order to enhance their own commercial success, would surreptitiously carry enemy goods or circumvent laws put in place to restrict certain neutral activity during war. More stringent rules consequentially developed on the prohibition of neutrals carrying enemy goods to enemy ports and also on the way in which cases of neutrality violations would be handled by a prize body within an admiralty court. So strict were some of these rules that if neutrals were commissioned by a belligerent state then they could be deemed and tried as a pirate in the respective admiralty court. In 1559 a French man-of-war captain was convicted as a pirate for the attack of Flemish ships on English waters. It was stated in this case that:

> [I]t is against the lawe and the treatye, as I do remember that in time of warre one ennimye shall annoye thother within the

---

44   Owen Rutter, *The Pirate Wind: Tales of the Sea-Robbers of Malaya*, Oxford University Press, Singapore, 1986, p. 25.

45   Henry J. Bourguignon, *Sir William Scott, Lord Stowell: Judge of the High Court of Admiralty, 1798–1828*, Cambridge University Press, Cambridge, 1987, p. 177.

> territorye or jurisdiction of any prince that is friende to both;
> the Flemyngs beyng within the lymyts of this realme were in
> like case and defense as the subjects of the same.[46]

In the early seventeenth century the same issue arose with regard to many disputes between the Spanish and the Dutch. The disputes again related to violations of neutrality on English waters. It is undoubtedly the case that issues relating to neutrality in admiralty courts were on occasion clothed under politicised decisions and, in this sense, declarations of adherence to the laws of war, necessity and the law of nations were made to justify belligerent actions on neutrality. Nonetheless, it is only important to highlight that violating neutrality rules could lead to cases being heard in the admiralty courts and, in some instances, even being punished for them. Two particular rules instigated by the British in the eighteenth century provide a confined framework from which the admiralty court practices on this crime can be demonstrated.

The rule of 1756 and the doctrine of continuous voyage, both developed during the Seven Years' War, played a part in how neutral property would be subject to capture by a privateer on account of neutral involvement with the enemy. The rules were designed to prevent neutrals from undertaking deceptive practices relating to trading with the enemy during wartime. In addition, all wars involved the prescription of rules on contraband, which were deemed international laws that all countries should respect. In 1790 Britain submitted a strategic rule, previously developed by Emer de Vattel, which stated that neutrals could not carry any food items to enemy states. The legality of the rule was assessed by an international claims commission and subsequently applied. Should food items, or any other contraband, be found on vessels, the case would be heard at the relevant admiralty court and certain punishments such as confiscation would be ordered.[47] Other countries such as France would take punishments further and seize not only the contraband goods but also entire ships, as stated in a French ordinance of 1778.[48] In the case of Yong Vrow Adriana, the judge held that the facts of the cases clearly indicated

---

[46] SP 12/4, Letters and papers sorted and bound in date order, April–June 1559, TNA.

[47] Stephen C. Neff, *The Rights and Duties of Neutrals: A General History*, Manchester University Press, Manchester, 2000, p. 64.

[48] *Règlement concernant la navigation des bâtimens neutres, en temps de guerre* [Regulations Concerning the Navigation of Neutral Vessels in Wartime], 26 July 1778, Art. 1, De l'imprimerie royale, 1778.

that the neutral ship was heading for an enemy port with enemy goods and therefore was liable to condemnation.

In addition, admiralty courts also adjudicated over belligerents that had infringed neutrality principles. Belligerents could not conduct warfare upon neutral territory or waters. Unfortunately, there were endless cases in which belligerents did exactly this, resulting in an enormous number of neutral victims attending admiralty courts to obtain justice and resolution for their injuries. Admiralty courts would hear complaints from neutral states and individuals that had fallen victim to the belligerents during wartime, even when their status meant that they were not officially part of any of the warring states. After 1750 neutral grievances became particularly dominant at admiralty courts in Europe due to the development of neutrality laws in the wartime sphere. In 1760 the English Court of Admiralty deliberated over a case involving a Dutch neutral ship that had been attacked in a Spanish port by an English man-of-war. The neutral ship was eventually restored, but only after the necessary adjudication and case hearing at the court. Violation of neutral territory was a commonplace injury complained of. The Twee Gebroeders case involved British seizures of four Dutch ships from territory that was not precisely neutral.[49] They were seized three miles from Prussian territory that had been neutral at that time. The judge in the case restored the ships and prevented the English culprits from embarking on their own case to claim good prize. Even the Dutch admiralties, where several existed in the entire United Provinces, would be bombarded with neutrality cases. Another case that came before the Admiralty Court in Middelburg, Zeeland in 1602 involved the St. Jago which had been a neutral Italian ship captured by Dutch men-of-war. Although the neutral merchants were not able to reclaim their ship, they did receive compensation from the Dutch Admiralty Court.

Those committing offences in violation of neutrality laws may not have been subject to the death penalty in all cases, but they could be subject to judicial orders depriving them of their property, which was still deemed a serious punishment. In some cases, those violating neutrality laws could indeed also be declared pirates, depending on the admiralty

---

[49] "The Twee Gebroeders, Alberts, master, 29 July 1800, 3 C. Rob.", in Chr. Robinson, *Reports of Cases Argued and Determined in the High Court of Admiralty*, vol. 3, Little, Brown and Company, Boston, 1853, pp. 162–67.

court into which the case was taken. Ultimately, there were rules agreed by nations on neutral and belligerent rights as to the conduct in war and infringements of these would trigger cases at the admiralty courts and thereafter punished if found guilty.

4.6. Admiralty Courts and Sources of Law

The sphere of war has always been governed, at one point or another, by a kind of international legal framework of fluctuating states of evolution. This included the *ius gentium* from antiquarian times or the law of nations and much later modern international law. In terms of practically enforcing the rights under the *iustum bellum* and, in the same vein, punishing violations thereof, admiralty courts, and for specific wartime prize issues the prize jurisdictions, demonstrated the law of nations in action. The term the law of nations is of course quite ambiguous, with Perotin-Dumon stating that a "proper 'law of nations' never existed".[50] Whatever challenges there are in defining the law of nations, it did consist of sources of law that were deemed to be the basis on which admiralty courts in Europe took their jurisdiction on wartime issues of prize and the like. We have already noted an English admiralty judge stating that prize was of mutual convenience and respected among all European nations. Prize mechanisms, although having structural variations depending on which country they were connected to, lay within courts or tribunals that obeyed the law of nations. This was law of an international premise that all countries acknowledged and respected as the rules to follow in prize cases.

In the history of cases at admiralty courts concerning wartime offences, international treaties and declarations played an important part in establishing both procedural and substantive international rules. A treaty between England and Flanders in 1426 affirmed the right of the admiral to deal with the identification of enemy goods found in Flemish ships.[51] This was triggered by the suspicion of England that Flemish ships were carrying French enemy goods. Given that England and France were at war with each other, this was a violation of the *Consolato del mare* that was deemed customary international law at that time and observed by the major European powers such as England, France and Spain. Similar provi-

---

50 Perotin-Dumon, 1991, p. 203, see *supra* note 32.

51 Treaty between England and Flanders 1426, in Rymer, 1739–1745, p. 367, see *supra* note 36.

sions were implemented in the 1498 and 1518 treaties between England and France, in which not only would the Admiral have authority to judge wartime issues but also that bail money would be deposited into the Court of Admiralty for the prevention of any wrongful actions during the war.[52] The bail money would be forfeited if violations of war or neutrality were committed, such as injuries to innocent merchants or their property. This mechanism of depositing security into the court for the prevention of war-time injury and payment of reparations to war victims should injuries take place continued throughout the early modern period at admiralty courts.

The 1518 treaty was particularly important also in light of the fact that it laid out the foundations of procedural law for future wars. Later in the seventeenth century major treaties would outline ways in which belligerent states should deal with neutrals and how the latter could also conduct their commerce in a legal way. The treaty ending the third Anglo-Dutch War is a very good example of how the English and the Dutch provided for an exception to the usual neutral rules laid out by the *Consolato del mare* and was a source utilised by admiralty court judges when dealing with cases relating to the violations of the law of neutrality during war. This is just one example of a plethora of treaties referred to by judges, making treaties a cornerstone of the prize law applied by admiralty courts. One would therefore be right in presupposing the influence of foreign affairs and diplomatic interactions on how a judge would conduct a prize case at an admiralty court. Incidentally, the more at stake for a country in the war, commercially and politically, the more likely it was that the judge would rely upon a favourable treaty from which to draw his judgment, along with the inevitability of interference – and thus influence – from other parts of government on relevant cases. The previously mentioned example on Leoline Jenkins's deliberation over whether a Moor or a Turk was to be regarded as a pirate is illustrative of this.

Besides the treaties that were entered into by countries before, during or after wars, the law of nations also in some respects encompassed the writings of prominent lawyers and scholars. Many admiralty courts around Europe exclaimed that the maritime laws prescribed on issues relating to wartime would adhere to the law of nations. This term was in itself imprecise and did lead to variations between the practices and theories on the subject of crimes such as piracy and other violations of the

---

[52] Marsden, 1894, see *supra* note 40.

laws of war and neutrality. Richard Zouche, the seventeenth-century English judge, referred to the law of nations as "the common element in the law which the peoples of single nations use among themselves; [...] the law which is observed in common between princes or peoples of different nations".[53]

The fact that war crimes such as piracy were offences against all nations did not mean that the admiralty court in England tried piracy in exactly the same way as the admiralty court in Zeeland or in Spain. The law of nations in this case was therefore a law that was respected, prescribed and declared as the underlying law governing war crimes, but variations in state interest, the domestic composition of courts, procedural issues and even national traditions meant that interpretations in the law of nations differed between countries. The marriage between domestic laws and international laws, as applied by admiralty courts throughout history, is crucial in the understanding of how exactly historical 'war crimes' were perceived and handled, and this section shines some light on this complicated relationship.

In order to reconcile the distinctions between international and municipal laws, Samuel von Pufendorf's conception of the law of nations is useful here. He placed the law of nations within the law of nature, so as to allow for the implementation and application of domestic laws on war crimes, by admiralty courts or otherwise, for the prevention of the violation of a universal natural law and not necessarily the law of nations.[54] The domestic courts would essentially be communicators of the universal natural law. Accordingly, admiralty courts would be expressing the natural law on crimes and violations of the law of war. These natural law views, however, quite apparently conflicted with the positivist views on the law of nations.

Cornelius van Bynkershoek's positivist writings in the eighteenth century on piracy included observations on Dutch admiralty law and practices. He referred to the Dutch laws as the authority on determining crimes and punishments. On pirates, he wrote that "we punish as pirates those who sail out to plunder the enemy without a commission from the

---

[53] Richard Zouche, *An Exposition of Fecial Law and Procedure, or of Law between Nations, and Questions concerning the Same*, trans. J.L. Brierly, William Hein, Washington, DC, 1911, part 1, § 1, para. 1 [1650].

[54] Samuel von Pufendorf, *Of the Law of Nature and Nations*, L. Lichfield, Oxford, 1703.

admiral". Despite reference to the authority of the Dutch laws, the idea that piratical actions were determined by the possession of a commission or not was the general consensus of most countries. Bynkershoek's writing on 'war crimes' and the law of nations however are relevant because he claimed that it was state policy that determined international laws on this matter. Of course when one thinks of the nature of war and the sometimes impossible separation between law and power, it is no wonder that wartime offences were adjudicated upon with state interest in mind. It was quite usual for the definition of piracy to be strict or broad, depending on what suited a country best.

Judge William Scott in the English Admiralty Court referred to Grotian and Vattelian principles on numerous occasions when dealing with prize law and wartime injuries.[55] By way of example, he referred to both writers on the lack of a right to capture during innocent passage through neutral waters.[56] Several pieces of correspondence sent from Scott and Judge John Nicholl to John Jay at the end of the American Revolutionary War confirmed the position of the admiralty courts under the law of nations. On the rules of neutrality, according to Scott and Nicholl, enemy goods on a friend's ship were subject to capture, as were contraband goods. They further stated that "by the maritime law of nations, universally and immemorially received, there is an established method of determination whether the capture be, or be not, lawful prize".[57] Here was another eighteenth-century declaration of the international laws and customs to be applied at admiralty courts when dealing with crimes and violations during war, as undertaken by other European countries.

In order to demonstrate continuities and discontinuities in the way different admiralty courts adhered to the international law of that time when hearing cases on wartime violations and offences, the facts of the *Fortune* case can provide insight. Maritime rules dictated that captors would inspect the papers of a ship before full capture was made, in case goods or ships belonged to neutrals. If no papers were found, goods would be instantly condemned. The captor made allegations that the mas-

---

[55] For a more detailed account of the English Admiralty Court's prize law jurisdiction in general in the seventeenth century, see Musa, *supra* note 13.

[56] Bourguignon, 1987, pp. 173–77, see *supra* note 45.

[57] Letter from William Scott and John Nicholl to John Jay, dated 10 September 1794, in Joseph Story, *Notes on the Principles and Practice of Prize Courts*, William Benning, London, 1854, pp. 2–11.

ter of the *Fortune*, which was a Swedish ship, threw his papers overboard deliberately, making the ship and property on board good prize. The General urged condemnation in this instance. However, although the French king had previously stated to the admiral that prize rules must be applied extremely strictly with no leeway to be granted, in this case, the king authorised the release of the ship. It seems here that there was an attempt to maintain neutral goodwill, whilst placing political gains above legal necessity.

A further rule that all nations agreed to was one in which "firm and secure possession" was requisite to a complete capture of ships and property during war. Only then could they be deemed good prize. Without this complete possession, admiralty courts would rule on cases in favour of the victim who had been deprived of its property illegally during war. However, rules of evidence respecting the possession between the various domestic courts in Europe were so variable that this led to opposite conclusions. For some nations it was immediate possession, others such as Portugal and some French admiralties had a 24-hour rule on possession and some an actual sentence of condemnation. England adhered to the rule that the prize was to be legally condemned at an admiralty court. The English felt it necessary to prove that no property had been seized piratically or belonged to the property of a friend. Grotius[58] and other doctrinal writers followed a 24-hour quiet possession rule, but the English Admiralty Court stated that property could only vest in the captor once it had been decided as lawful prize at the court.[59]

There was also discordance between countries on the point of *ius postliminii*; that of restoring a property upon recapture. There were situations according to the law of nations that made this possible, but it was applied in Europe to differing degrees, depending on how some doctrinal writers interpreted the rule. As an example, and not surprisingly, England stated that it would allow the restoration of property under the rule, but only for states that it was friendly with and only under the umbrella of reciprocity. So, if a question of whether restoring a recaptured ship came to the English Admiralty Court, the English judges would not restore it if the questioning nation did not have the same rule to begin with. In this instance, at least on the part of the English, there was evidence of a self-

---

[58] Grotius, 1925, see *supra* note 3.

[59] Browne, 1802, see *supra* note 12.

interested propounding of rules. The Parliament of Paris refused outright to consider any cases of *jure postliminii* at all, but Spain and Venice did allow it. Here there was discordance.

A legal point that all European states and their admiralty courts agreed on was the question of who the captors' property in war belonged to. Grotius on this point argued that states may reserve the property for themselves or give it to the captors and therefore, essentially, captured goods were not always vested in the immediate occupants, but those whose power they were employed under. The right of the sovereign to all captures was acknowledged in France before the Revolution and was always the law of England according to the opinion of the Privy Council. A treaty between France and the United Provinces in 1662 also agreed that prize cases should be judged in the country of the sovereign that authorised the commission. The closeness of legitimate actions and piracy were quite often measured through the checking of whether the man-of-war had the authority of the sovereign. And if not, they would be treated as a pirate.

It is not possible to conclusively give one concrete definition of the law of nations. Admiralty judges did, however, identify it as an important point of reference in their legal deliberations when it came to cases of war crimes, violations of the laws of war, neutrality and other related offences. It embodied the customary international laws of that time, both explicit in treaties and otherwise. In addition, the flourishing writings on the subject by prominent scholars also proved a source of inspiration for the courts. Essentially, though, perceptions of war offences and violations were quite often consistent in most European nations. Consistent practice throughout Europe on war, neutrality and peace was aimed for, but far from being a perfect system, margins of appreciation were also expected by nations, in which there was some digression from the law of nations.

4.7. Conclusion

The intention of this chapter has been to highlight the functional basis of a court network that existed in Europe before the development of modern international law, which adjudicated on issues relating to the crime of piracy and actions deemed in violation of the norms, customs, laws of war, and, especially in the seventeenth and eighteenth centuries, of neutrality. Although each national admiralty court and its usually incorporated prize body varied procedurally, in some ways, in each country, its foundations were firmly within the respected law of nations. The way judgment under the law of nations was reached involved a hybrid process of doctrine, treaties and domestically influenced rules and regulations. Nonetheless, despite the plurality of sources employed by the admiralties, these courts were key establishments in showing how offences during wartime were adjudicated before the rise of modern international criminal institutions.

Among the major offences that comprised the caseload of the admiralty, complaints of piracy and violations of neutrality were certainly prominent. Although violation of neutrality was not a crime as such, it could incur heavy penalties or sometimes be treated as a crime of piracy, in turn resulting in a more severe capital punishment. A trial of the former could be heard within a prize jurisdiction if it was connected to the capture of prize, but also in the wider admiralty jurisdiction as a separate case for want of a more severe punishment, as the prize bodies only allowed civil remedies and not criminal ones. The violation of the laws of neutrality was one type of offence that, especially in the early modern period, admiralty and prize court judges dealt with. Neutral claimants would regularly make a complaint for a case to be heard in the admiralty courts during wartime due to injuries that they had suffered. This was typical of neutral claimants in all prize jurisdictions around the world, as they functioned, or at least ought to have functioned, under a consistent law of nations that provided for the adjudication of these types of cases. Piracy, on the other hand, was universally deemed a war crime and could also be subject to admiralty jurisdiction, in which some admiralties had very severe punishments for the convicted.

It is a given that the notion of war crimes has undergone tremendous metamorphosis over the centuries. But even the variations of what war crimes were or were not, or are or are not, did not preclude them from bring treated with the highest degree of severity in the admiralty courts discussed in this chapter. War criminals such as pirates are a case in point. The uniform practices among a multitude of nations on offences that they deemed reprehensible indicate that trials of perpetrators of wartime offences at an international level were conducted at admiralty courts and remained a platform to which victims of war could resort for the hearing of their grievances and punishment of the offender. If relating to prize, then only a civil remedy (or punishment) could be declared. Indeed, given that war not only had its basis in law, but also politics and international relations, one must not view the admiralty courts as institutions that operated strictly within the confines of morality and justice. It is true that political interference would dictate the outcome of certain ordinary or prize cases. In a sense, the law of nations implicitly inferred that. Different countries would unsurprisingly have differing interests in times of war, and the admiralty courts would occasionally have to interpret the law of nations with political considerations in mind. In this regard, treaties were a crucial source of inspiration for the judges who would refer to agreements made between nations if they had dealt with a specific issue in question, such as neutrality or piracy.

As the sea connects all nations, it makes sense that nations cooperated on matters of mutual interest. It has therefore always been necessary to regulate issues relating to it in an international way. It is unsurprising then that states created a network of admiralty courts that functioned within the national domain, but applied laws that derived from the international. What is surprising, however, is that very little attention has been dedicated to an important precedent to modern international courts and institutions, which dealt with crimes committed during wartime. Of course, we have already established that war crimes in the historical sense of the term should be treated with much caution. Nonetheless one can gain much insight into how states regulated wartime offences more generally and dealt with sanctions and reparations that are too often misperceived as a post-nineteenth-century legal practice.

5

The Trials of Charles I, Henry Wirz and Pol Pot: Why Historic Cases Are Often Forgotten and the Meaning of International Criminal Law

Jens Iverson[*]

5.1. Introduction

Trials involving historic figures such as the King of England, co-conspirators with the President of the Confederacy, and one of the most infamous *génocidaires* of the twentieth century seem like obvious subjects of enduring notoriety and fascination. The subject matter of these trials – crimes against peace, murder in violation of the laws and customs of war, and genocide – are central to international criminal law. The settings of the trials were striking: the High Court of Justice in Westminster Hall, London after the second English Civil War; military proceedings in the Capitol building, Washington, DC after the Civil War in the United States; and the theatre-like Chaktomuk Hall in Phnom Penh, Cambodia after the Khmer Rouge regime was overthrown by Vietnamese intervention. The trials were promoted by the governing authorities as historic events. The trials of Charles I (Charles Stuart), Colonel Henry (Heinrich) Wirz and Pol Pot (Saloth Sar) are nonetheless often absent in studies of international criminal law, and are sometimes even unknown to its scholars and practitioners.

The formation of these lacunae, not in the law itself but in dominant histories of international criminal law, is worthy of additional attention. This chapter first describes the trials themselves, articulating why they should be included in the canon of seminal events in the history of international criminal law. It then explains three reasons why they have not been so included: the contested nature of the circumstances of each trial, the domestic nature of the forum, and the utility of rooting the historiog-

---

[*] **Jens Iverson** is Assistant Professor of Public International Law, Grotius Centre for International Legal Studies, Faculty of Law, University of Leiden, the Netherlands, and an attorney specialising in public international law.

raphy of international criminal law primarily in the post-Second World War order. These proposed reasons for collective scholarly forgetting reveal much about the trials, and illuminate contemporary international criminal law even more. A careful study of the reasons for the absence of these trials in the dominant histories of international criminal law provides its own means of analysing the discipline. International criminal law is a field seized with inherent tensions – tensions that are as present in history as today. These tensions include minimising allegations of politicisation while addressing politically charged subjects, and seeking the imprimatur and apparent independence of international law while maximising the use of domestic judiciaries and authority. This chapter suggests that for the potential of international criminal law to be fully realised, particularly in domestic trials, the history of domestic criminal prosecutions with an international law character must be more carefully considered.

International criminal law is often taught based around the concept of an 'international crime'. For the textbook *An Introduction to International Criminal Law and Procedure*,[1] an international crime is simply "those offences over which international courts or tribunals have been given jurisdiction under general international law".[2] With respect, a better definition of an international crime is a crime created by international law, regardless of whether it is within the jurisdiction of an international court or tribunal.[3] This is the definition emphasised at the International Military Tribunal ('IMT') at Nuremberg, discussing international crimes as "crimes against international law"[4] and emphasising that "individuals have international duties which transcend the national obligations of obe-

---

[1] Robert Cryer, Håkan Friman, Darryl Robinson and Elizabeth Wilmshurst, *An Introduction to International Criminal Law and Procedure*, 3rd ed., Cambridge University Press, Cambridge, 2014.

[2] *Ibid.*, p. 4.

[3] Ibid. See also Bruce Broomhall, International Justice and the International Criminal Court: Between Sovereignty and the Rule of Law, Oxford University Press, Oxford, 2003, pp. 9–10; Robert Cryer, Prosecuting International Crimes: Selectivity and the International Criminal Law Regime, Cambridge University Press, Cambridge, 2005, p. 1; Gerhard Werle, and Florian Jessberger, Principles of International Criminal Law, 2nd ed., Oxford University Press, Oxford, 2009, p. 29.

[4] International Military Tribunal (Nuremberg), Judgment and Sentences, reprinted in *American Journal of International Law*, 1947, vol. 41, pp. 172, 221.

dience imposed by the individual state".[5] This may seem a trivial distinction for students first introduced to the subject, but has profound implications for the history of the field as well as the future of the field, if the main work of international criminal law is not to be relegated to the minute number of trial and appeals chambers belonging to international institutions and instead to be carried forward in and by the uncounted number of domestic judicial fora.

5.2. The Trials

5.2.1. Introduction

There are several problems with drawing conclusions from three historical events, which take place in different centuries, in varied cultures, on separate continents. Each of these events is worth extensive study in its own right. Any encapsulation is necessarily limited. The choice of these three trials is inherently somewhat arbitrary. The specialist who spends their career focused on any of these events might find the brief mention of any of these trials comparatively facile. These are the risks of any comparativist venture, and a risk that must be run should the benefits of comparison be gained. The author is mindful of these difficulties, and hopes that this chapter can serve (for many readers) as an introduction to the subjects addressed, rather than the last word.

More substantially and subtly, the viability of a history of international criminal law that includes such disparate events is not without difficulty. It is tidier to treat the history of international criminal law as a relatively triumphant march of post-Second World War international institutions. One can reasonably read the following with a sceptical mindset, feeling that historical research should ordinarily be limited to discrete periods and locations, and that a more 'global' history is more likely to mislead than clarify. In addition, the use of history in legal scholarship has its own unique difficulties, not the least of which is that few scholars have extensive training in both history and the law.

Nonetheless, the need for the study of legal history remains compelling. Historical jurisprudence emerged as a separate school of legal philosophy in the 1800s in the midst of the debate between positivism and

---

[5]   *Ibid.*

natural law.[6] Friedrich Karl von Savigny is cited as making the first formulation of this school in his response to a German professor of Roman law, A.F.J. Thibaut.[7] Thibaut proposed in 1814 that Germany should adopt a civil code, modelled after the 1804 French Civil Code. Savigny responded that law was "developed first by custom and belief of the people, then by legal science – everywhere, therefore, by internal, silently operating powers, not by the arbitrary will of the legislator".[8] If law, like language, is part of the common consciousness of the nation, then international criminal law, the direct criminalisation of conduct by the 'international community' requires an examination of a more global history. In order to understand the selective forgetting, the primary subject of this chapter, one must first look at the primary history of the events in question – to which we now turn.

5.2.2. The Trial of Charles I

5.2.2.1. The Context

The reign of King Charles I of England lasted from 1625 until the moment of his execution on 30 January 1649.[9] It was a troubled reign, marked by war with Scotland and Ireland. It was also marked by conflict within His Majesty's government. Parliament provided funds for the wars twice – but only reluctantly, partially, and on the condition of a transfer of some authority from the king to Parliament. On the king's third request for war funding, Parliament refused.[10] The royal response was to enter the House of Commons with armed soldiers intending to arrest members of Parliament. He failed, and was forced to flee London and form an army. War was no longer merely between England and neighbouring countries. England was riven by civil war.

Charles lost the civil war. Before it ended, people suffered. At his trial, Charles I was charged with "treasons, murders, rapines, burnings,

---

[6] Harold J. Berman, "The Historical Foundations of Law", in *Emory Law Journal*, 2005, vol. 54, p. 16.

[7] Ibid.

[8] *Ibid.*

[9] Charles Anthony Smith, *The Rise and Fall of War Crimes Trials: From Charles I to Bush II*, Cambridge University Press, Cambridge, 2012, p. 30; C.V. Wedgwood, *The Trial of Charles I*, Collins, London, 1964, p. 13.

[10] Smith, 2012, p. 30, see *supra* note 9.

spoils, desolations, damages and mischiefs to this nation".[11] It was in this raw atmosphere that the House of Commons created a High Court of Justice for one month to try the king.

5.2.2.2. The Accused

Charles I never stopped being king. It was as the King of England that he was charged, put on trial and executed. Unlike Edward II, Henry VI or Mary Stuart, he was not simply killed extrajudicially or deposed. His status as king was recognised by his opponents in war, and by those who charged him, prosecuted him, judged him and signed his death warrant. He was described as the "King of England" in the charges against him, and the warrant for his execution continued to describe him as the "King of England".[12] His last words were an order to the executioner not to behead him until he was ready: "Stay for the sign".[13] The executioner's response indicated his continued royal status: "I will, an' it please Your Majesty".[14]

Aside from his status as king, the nature of the accused is contested. This contestation goes beyond the normal discussions of individual criminal responsibility common in criminal law – the question went to whether he was sacred or damned. For his detractors, he was "Charles Stuart, That Man of Blood"[15] – a phrase that indicated he had shed innocent blood, and thus had blood guilt. Blood guilt indicates spiritual pollution, not ordinary culpability – a man unintentionally guilty of shedding blood could be barred from ordination in the Church.[16]

5.2.2.3. The Prosecution

The most interesting aspect of the collective identity of the prosecution is revealed by their choice not to merely kill or depose the king, but to put the king on trial. Oliver Cromwell, leader of the army, originally favoured

---

[11] Wedgwood, 1964, p. 130, see *supra* note 9.

[12] *Ibid.*, p. 10.

[13] *Ibid.*, p. 193.

[14] *Ibid.*

[15] Patricia Crawford, "Charles Stuart, That Man of Blood", in *Journal of British Studies*, 1977, vol. 16, no. 2, pp. 41–61.

[16] *Ibid.*, p. 42.

a ceremonial kingship, but later backed the destruction of the monarchy.[17] On 20 November 1648 the Puritan army, controlled by Cromwell, demanded that the House of Commons bring the king to trial.[18]

5.2.2.4. The Trial

Charles I declared before the trial began that he would not recognise the authority of the court. As the trial began on 8 January 1649, in the stately Painted Chamber of Westminster Hall, he continued this approach. Not only did the king not recognise the legitimacy of the trial, he refused to plead – which under the procedural requirements at the time meant the trial could not proceed.[19] Normally, this would be remedied by torture. Rather than torture the king, the requirement for the accused to overtly plead was relaxed, with the prosecutor instead arguing he would put in a plea of guilty by implication.[20]

More fundamentally, the tenet of English law that justice proceeded from the sovereign was thrown into doubt by the trial of the sovereign. The House of Commons tried to square this circle with the revolutionary idea of the sovereignty of the people. In this conception, the House of Commons represented the people, and could subject anyone to the law, even the king. The king, in contrast, was described as merely "trusted with a limited power to govern by, and according to the laws of the land, and not otherwise".[21]

The prosecution's theory may remind the scholar of international criminal law of the language used in Nuremberg that starting a war "is the supreme international crime differing only from other war crimes in that it contains within itself the accumulated evil of the whole".[22] The prosecution charged that because the king caused war in furtherance of his "wicked design to erect and uphold in himself an unlimited and tyrannical power to rule according to his Will, and to overthrow the Rights and Liberties

---

[17] Smith, 2012, pp. 31–33, see *supra* note 9.
[18] Wedgwood, 1964, p. 13, see *supra* note 9.
[19] *Ibid.*, pp. 94–95, 103, 109–10.
[20] *Ibid.*, p. 142.
[21] *Ibid.*, pp. 96, 130.
[22] Nuremberg Trial Proceedings, vol. 22, 30 September 1946, available at http://avalon.law.yale.edu/imt/09-30-46.asp, last accessed on 25 November 2014.

of the People",[23] he was responsible for "all the treasons, murders, rapines, burnings, spoils, desolations, damages and mischiefs to this nation, acted and committed in the said Wars, or occasioned thereby".[24]

In contemporary international criminal law, the substantive crimes alleged seem to be less focused on the resort to armed force itself (what might later be described as a violation of *jus ad bellum*, crimes against peace or the crime of aggression), and more on war crimes – with the distinction between what would now be called international and non-international armed conflict made somewhat indistinct between the conflicts with Ireland, Scotland, and within England. The prosecution's theory is also reminiscent of modern crimes against humanity, with a widespread and systematic attack against civilian populations, wickedly designed under governmental plan and policy, criminal under a law supreme to the sovereign even though the crimes were against the sovereign's subjects.

The trial was public, and the galleries were filled, from the lower hall to the galleries above the seats, with some individuals even climbing to the embrasures of the gothic windows. The conduct described before the crowd was damning. One witness gave evidence that those who surrendered to the king were plundered in his presence. Another swore that the king permitted prisoners to be stripped and cut, and that when one of the king's officers tried to stop the cutting of the prisoners the king had said "I do not care if they cut them three times more, for they are mine enemies".[25]

The Act of the House of Commons establishing the High Court of Justice described him as follows:

> Charles Stuart, the now King of England, not content with the many encroachments which his predecessors had made upon the people in their rights and freedom, hath had a wicked design totally to subvert the ancient and fundamental laws and liberties of this nation, and in their place to introduce an arbitrary and tyrannical government, and that besides all other evil ways and means to bring his design to pass, he hath

---

23   Wedgwood, 1964, p. 130, see *supra* note 9.

24   *Ibid.*, p. 130.

25   *Ibid.*, pp. 123, 148–49.

prosecuted it with fire and sword, levied and maintained a
civil war in the land, against the Parliament and Kingdom.[26]

His response was not merely that he was the king but also semi-
sacred, literally anointed at his coronation and reportedly able to heal
through the power of his touch.[27] As the inevitable result of the trial became evident, he declared, "I am the Martyr of the people".[28] His strong-
est arguments at trial, at least to the modern ear, were when he related to
the people of England, and their freedoms and liberties.

> If it were only my own particular case [...] I would have sat-
> isfied myself with the protestation I made the last time I was
> here against the legality of the Court, and that a King cannot
> be tried by any superior jurisdiction on earth. But it is not my
> case alone, it is the freedom and the liberty of the people of
> England; and do you pretend what you will, *I stand more for
> their liberties*. For if power without law may make laws,
> may alter the fundamental laws of the Kingdom, I do not
> know what subject he is in England, that can be sure of his
> life, or anything that he calls his own.[29]

For both sides, then, the approach was not to appeal to revolutionary or counter-revolutionary rhetoric, but to a conservative sensibility. For
the prosecution, this conservative sensibility was grounded in the sovereignty of the people, and the trial was seen as an exercise in reclaiming
and establishing that sovereignty, and re-establishing the universality of
law. The prosecution cited Henry de Bracton and other ancient authorities, and referenced the Barons' War leading to the enshrinement of the
Magna Carta, "[w]hen the nobility of the land did stand out for the liberty
and property of the subject".[30] The prosecution defended their approach
as a defence of sovereignty:

> There is a contract and a bargain made between the King and
> his people, and your oath is taken: and certainly, Sir, the
> bond is reciprocal: for as you are the liege lord, so they liege
> subjects. [...] This we know now, the one tie, the one bond,
> is the bond of protection that is due from the sovereign; the

---

[26] Sean Kelsey, "Politics and Procedure in the Trial of Charles I", in *Law and History Review*, 2004, vol. 22, no. 1, p. 11.

[27] Crawford, 1977, pp. 41–42, see *supra* note 15.

[28] Wedgwood, 1964, p. 192, see *supra* note 9.

[29] *Ibid.*, pp. 137–38 (emphasis added).

[30] *Ibid.*, p.60.

other is the bond of subjection that is due from the subject.
Sir, if this bond be once broken, farewell sovereignty![31]

The idea of 'impunity' for heads of state as a problem begins with
this trial, with the High Court of Justice established so that no one "may
hereafter presume traitorously or maliciously to imagine or contrive the
enslaving or destroying of the English nation, and expect impunity for so
doing".[32] For the accused, this conservative sensibility was grounded
when pressed not only in royal authorities but also in the "freedom and
the liberty of the people of England".[33]

5.2.2.5. The Verdict

To widespread amazement across all of Europe, Charles I was convicted
and executed. While many considered this to be blasphemy against a di-
vinely appointed sovereign,[34] those who chose to subject the king to a trial
defied the theory of divine right, both on religious and (tightly intertwined) legal grounds. On 30 January 1649, less than three months after
the Puritan army made their demand that the king be tried, he was publicly decapitated outside the royal banqueting house of Whitehall.[35]

5.2.2.6. The History

Cromwell's victory did not last long. King Charles II restored the monarchy in 1660, and those deemed responsible for the death of Charles I were
themselves put on trial and killed.[36] The historical approach to the trial of
Charles I has been tied to the author's approach to the royal family ever
since. At a minimum, from a royalist perspective and a plain reading of a
1351 statute, the trial was treason, as treason included the "compassing or
imagining" the death of the king.[37] More than that, it was regicide and the
purest form of revolution. But going further once again, and from the perspective less sympathetic to the monarchy (at least at the time), the trial

---

[31] *Ibid.*, p. 161.
[32] Geoffrey Robertson, The Tyrannicide Brief: The Story of the Man who Sent Charles I to
the Scaffold, 2005, Chatto & Windus, London, p. 12.
[33] Wedgwood, 1964, pp. 137–38, see *supra* note 9.
[34] *Ibid.*, p. 9.
[35] *Ibid.*, pp. 12–13.
[36] *Ibid.*, p. 219.
[37] Robertson, 2005, p. 13, see *supra* note 32.

was a redefinition of sovereignty and the laws of England, and arguably sovereignty and law more generally. The objection to Charles I was rooted in clause 29 of the Magna Carta:

> No free man shall be taken or imprisoned, or be deprived of his freehold, or liberties, or free customs, or be detained, or exiled, or any otherwise destroyed; nor will we pass upon him, or condemn him, but by the lawful judgment of his peers, or by the law of the land. To no man will we sell, to no man will we deny or delay, justice or right.[38]

Because Charles I was seen to have violated this principle, in the Five Knights' case[39] among others, he went from being the source of law and liberty to an individual criminally culpable under the law. He then called upon these ideals of liberty in his defence. While it is anachronistic to imagine this fitting too neatly into the modern framework of human rights, it is not wrong to imagine the connection between rights of the individual and the ideal of sovereignty was felt as keenly then as it is felt today.

The question remains, however, why discussions of international criminal law are highly unlikely to mention the trial of Charles I. One of the most dramatic events in English history is relegated to that history, and not incorporated as part of the discussion of where international criminal law came from, what it is, and what it does. In section 5.3. the question why this trial, as well as other trials, are not remembered as part of international criminal law is dealt with in more detail. In short, the trial of Charles I is often forgotten not because it is intrinsically uninteresting to international criminal law scholars and practitioners, but because of the contemporaneously contested nature of each trial, the domestic nature of the forum and the utility of a post-Second World War narrative. This, in turn, informs the discussion in section 5.4., which further examines the tensions of international criminal law in relation to forgetting, particularly allegations of politicisation and the distrust of domestic authority. But first, additional trials should be examined to provide material for further analysis.

---

[38] Magna Carta, cited in Robertson, 2005, p. 33, see *supra* note 32.
[39] Also known as Darnel's or Darnell's case.

5.2.3. The Trial of Henry Wirz

5.2.3.1. The Context

The trial of Henry (Heinrich) Wirz took place after a public parade of fresh horrors, from the all-encompassing barbarity of the US Civil War, to the widely reported atrocities of the conditions of prisoner of war camps,[40] to the assassination of President Abraham Lincoln. Between February 1864 and May 1865 approximately 13,000 prisoners of war died horribly at Camp Sumter, commonly known as Andersonville prison.[41] Another 2,000 would die after the liberation of the camp before they could return home.[42] These 15,000 were a small fraction of those killed in the Civil War. In terms of American nationals killed, the Civil War remains the deadliest in US history.[43] Despite this, as the war drew to a close, Lincoln's planned post-war policies towards the South were lenient – asking only that citizens pledge not to rebel, that legislatures repudiate Confederate debt and that Southern states ratify the fourteenth amendment.[44] Eight persons were convicted of aiding John Wilkes Booth's assassination of Lincoln.[45] Only three individuals were convicted of war crimes and executed after the Civil War after Lincoln's assassination.[46] Henry Wirz, in charge of the 45,000 prisoners of war in the Andersonville prison camp, was by far the most notorious.[47]

---

[40] Lewis L. Laska and James M. Smith, "'Hell and the Devil': Andersonville and the Trial of Captain Henry Wirz, C.S.A, 1865", in *Military Law Review*, 1975, vol. 68, p. 78, reporting that between 1862 and 1901, over 180 publications discussed the conditions of Southern prisons during the war.

[41] *Ibid.*, p. 78.

[42] *Ibid.*

[43] "U.S. Civil War Took Bigger Toll than Previously Estimated, New Analysis Suggests", in *Science Daily*, 22 September 2011, estimating 750,000 dead, with a margin of 100,000. See also J. David Hacker, "A Census-Based Count of the Civil War Dead", in *Civil War History*, 2011, vol. 57, no. 4, p. 4.

[44] Laska and Smith, 1975, p. 77, see *supra* note 40.

[45] *Ibid.*, p. 84.

[46] The others were Champ Ferguson, see "CHAMP FERGUSON.; Confession of the Culprit", in *New York Times*, 29 October 29, 1865; and Robert Cobb Kennedy, see O. Edward Cunningham, "'In Violation of the Laws of War': The Execution of Robert Cobb Kennedy", in *Louisiana History: The Journal of the Louisiana Historical Association*, 1977, vol. 18, no. 2, pp. 189–201.

[47] Laska and Smith, 1975, p. 84, see *supra* note 40.

5.2.3.2. The Accused

Wirz had a colourful, unsuccessful life before enlisting in the Fourth Louisiana Regiment on 16 June 1861 and eventually becoming responsible for the Civil War's infamous prison camp. He was born in Zurich, Switzerland on 25 November 1823. When he sailed for the United States in 1849 he had already experienced conviction (possibly for embezzlement), divorce and banishment from his native country.[48] As far as can be ascertained, he was an unsuccessful and uncredentialled medical practitioner, reduced to working as a 'doctor' for plantation slaves.[49] Once he joined the Confederate army he was promoted rapidly, and on 27 March 1864 he received the fateful order to Fort Sumter, where he was assigned to command the prison, including supply, physical facilities and prisoner discipline.[50]

5.2.3.3 The Prosecution

The head of the Adjutant General's office and the Bureau of Military Justice was Brigadier General Joseph Holt, Judge Advocate General of the Union army. Holt believed that the deaths at Andersonville were the result of Confederate policy, implemented by Wirz.[51] Witnesses would testify that Wirz had declared, "I'm building a pen here that will kill more damned Yankees than can be destroyed at the front".[52] The alleged nexus to the armed conflict provided the rationale for the trial to be held in a military tribunal. The Judge Advocate General's Office likely relied upon Francis Lieber and the Instructions for the Government of the Armies of the United States in the Field,[53] popularly called the Lieber Code, to frame the charges.[54]

---

[48] *Ibid.*, p. 85.
[49] *Ibid.*
[50] *Ibid.*, p. 86.
[51] *Ibid.*, pp. 88, 90.
[52] *Ibid.*, p. 90. One witness attributed this quote to another individual.
[53] General Order No. 100, 24 April 1863.
[54] Laska and Smith, 1975, p. 99, see *supra* note 40.

5.2.3.4. The Trial

Wirz faced two charges: conspiracy and murder. The allegation that Wirz conspired with Confederate President Jefferson Davis and General Robert E. Lee (along with eight others) was the more explosive charge. The Secretary of War, Edwin Stanton, read the charges in the dramatic setting of the Capitol building, in the spotlight of the national media. Wirz entered a plea of not guilty.[55]

The offences were not against a specific statute or uniform code, but rather committed in "violation of the laws and customs of war".[56] In the history of international criminal law, this is surely worthy of note. The United States was directly incorporating what was held to be effectively customary international law into its criminal jurisdiction. The role of customary international law in the law of the United States is of enduring interest, from the 1789 Alien Tort Statute,[57] to the trial of Wirz, to the (subsequent) decision in the *Paquete Habana*[58], in which the Supreme Court clarified that customary international law was part of the law of the United States to be administered by the courts, "where there is no treaty and no controlling executive or legislative act or judicial decision"[59] to current disputes.

Further, the standard narrative of international humanitarian law holds that it governed international armed conflicts first and foremost with the regulations of non-international armed conflicts coming only with Common Article 3 of the Geneva Conventions of 1949[60] and Addi-

---

[55] *Ibid.*, pp. 97, 100–1.

[56] *Ibid.*, p. 98.

[57] 28 U.S.C. § 1350. Also called the Alien Tort Claims Act. The text simply reads: "The district courts shall have original jurisdiction of any civil action by an alien for a tort only, committed in violation of the law of nations or a treaty of the United States".

[58] 175 U.S. 677, 1900.

[59] *Ibid.*, p. 700.

[60] Geneva Convention for the Amelioration of the Condition of the Wounded and Sick in Armed Forces in the Field (First Geneva Convention), 12 August 1949, 75 UNTS 31; Geneva Convention for the Amelioration of the Condition of Wounded, Sick and Shipwrecked Members of Armed Forces at Sea (Second Geneva Convention), 12 August 1949, 75 UNTS 85; Geneva Convention Relative to the Treatment of Prisoners of War (Third Geneva Convention), 12 August 1949, 75 UNTS 135; Geneva Convention Relative to the Protection of Civilian Persons in Time of War (Fourth Geneva Convention), 12 August 1949, 75 UNTS 287.

tional Protocol II.[61] But the Lieber Code[62] was rooted in customary international law as applied to what would now be called a non-international armed conflict – the US Civil War.

5.2.3.5. The Verdict

Wirz was convicted on both charges.[63] Holt and President Andrew Johnson approved the record of the trial, and Wirz was executed on 10 February 1865.[64] The government issued 250 tickets for spectators, although more viewed the execution from rooftops surrounding the scaffold, within easy sight of the Capitol.[65] Four companies of soldiers chanted "Wirz, remember Andersonville" as Wirz was hung by the neck until dead.[66] Perhaps surprisingly, given the bloodiness of the war and the conviction of Wirz for a conspiracy with Confederate leaders, the leadership of the Confederacy was eventually released without trial.

5.2.3.6. The History

Henry Wirz became a hero to neo-Confederates, as exemplified by the 1908 monument to Wirz by the United Daughters of the Confederacy and continuing memorialisation.[67] The misplaced valorisation of Wirz is often within the context of the denial of Confederate crimes and defence of the Confederate cause. The singular nature of the trial also makes it the subject of reasoned historical treatment, but what was once the most notorious and singular war crimes trial has mostly been forgotten by the general public and ignored outside the community with a specific interest in the Civil War.

The shadow of the Civil War dominates popular and scholarly American history. But like the trial of Charles I, the trial of Wirz is usual-

---

[61] Protocol Additional to the Geneva Conventions of 12 August 1949, and relating to the Protection of Victims of Non-International Armed Conflicts (Protocol II), 8 June 1977, 1125 UNTS 609.

[62] General Order No. 100, 24 April 1863.

[63] Laska and Smith, 1975, p. 126, see *supra* note 40.

[64] *Ibid.*, pp. 127–28.

[65] *Ibid.*, p. 129.

[66] *Ibid.*, p. 129.

[67] Glen W. LaForce, "The Trial of Major Henry Wirz – A National Disgrace", in *The Army Lawyer*, 1988, Department of the Army Pamphlet 27-50-186, p. 3.

ly relegated to an isolated national history, and not incorporated into a broader history of international criminal law. Before turning to the reasons for this lack of incorporation in section 5.3. and an examination of what this forgetting indicates about the tensions within international criminal law in section 5.4., one more example of a forgotten trial will be examined: the trial of Pol Pot.

5.2.4. The Trial of Pol Pot (Saloth Sar)

5.2.4.1. The Context

Between 1975 and early 1979 the Democratic Kampuchea regime – controlled by the Khmer Rouge – murdered millions through forced labour, starvation and execution. Among many others, the jurists of Cambodia were killed. An estimated six to ten legal professionals survived.[68] The Khmer Rouge regime's crimes eradicated the institutions and people who could normally attempt to address those injustices through criminal law. Cities were emptied. Individuals with any type of education were likely targets of persecution, as were ethnic and religious minorities. A nationwide system of imprisonment, torture and murder resulted in over 20,000 mass graves. Economic mismanagement caused widespread starvation and disease. A series of military attacks in southern Vietnam eventually roused Vietnam's ire. Khmer Rouge massacres in Vietnam triggered Vietnam's invasion and occupation of Cambodia, establishing a new regime to administer the devastated country. The new regime held a trial *in absentia* for the top Khmer Rouge leaders, Pol Pot and Ieng Sary.

In August 1979 the People's Revolutionary Tribunal tried Pol Pot and Ieng Sary *in absentia* for genocide.[69] It took place in Phnom Penh, which was virtually a ghost town – emptied by the Khmer Rouge in 1975.[70] It was not a regularly functioning court, but rather a trial specially convened in Chaktomuk Hall to try Khmer Rouge leaders.[71] This theatri-

---

[68] Dolores A. Donovan, Sidney Jones, Dinah PoKempner and Robert J. Muscat, *Rebuilding Cambodia: Human Resources, Human Rights, and Law: Three Essays*, Foreign Policy Institute, Johns Hopkins University, Baltimore, 1993, p. 69.

[69] Howard J. De Nike, John Quigley and Kenneth J. Robinson (eds.), *Genocide in Cambodia: Documents from the trial of Pol Pot and Ieng Sary*, University of Pennsylvania Press, Philadelphia, 2011.

[70] John Quigley, "Introduction", in Nike *et al.*, 2011. p. 1, see *supra* note 69.

[71] *Ibid.*, pp. 1–2.

cal setting would not be equalled until the establishment of the Extraordinary Chambers in the Courts of Cambodia decades later, where Ieng Sary would be retried on similar charges.

A new government was set up by 1981, but the international community largely refused to recognise it. Cambodia remained plagued by guerrilla warfare. Hundreds of thousands of people became refugees. The mass movement represented by the Kampuchean United Front for National Salvation (Renakse) included mass membership organisations of Buddhist monks, nuns, women, youth, workers and other categories. Renakse organised the petitions or 'million documents' which remains the only nationwide opportunity for survivors of the Khmer Rouge regime to describe atrocities they suffered. The million documents were the result of the Renakse research committee that interviewed survivors throughout the country. Various efforts at memorialisation occurred, including famously at Tuol Sleng, Choeung Ek and the annual Day of Remembrance activities on 20 May formerly known as the National Day of Hatred.

5.2.4.2. The Accused

Pol Pot and Ieng Sary were both born in 1925. They studied together in Paris in the early 1950s, met with French communist intellectuals and became dedicated Marxists. Pol Pot became Prime Minister of the Democratic Kampuchea regime as well as the General Secretary of the Central Committee of the Communist Party of Kampuchea, and Ieng Sary became Deputy Prime Minister. They were also brothers-in-law. They were both in hiding at the time of the People's Revolutionary Tribunal. The trial was held *in absentia*.

5.2.4.3. The Prosecution

The trial was not supported by the international community aside from Vietnam, whose army was responsible for the ending of the Khmer Rouge regime. Many participants in the trial focused on China's alleged role in the atrocities of the Khmer Rouge. No one practised law in the country in August 1979, few professional police remained and there were no regular courts.[72] The People's Revolutionary Tribunal relied in part upon foreign lawyers to proceed.

---

[72] *Ibid.*, pp. 7–8.

5.2.4.4. The Trial

The appointed defence attorneys had no contact with the (*in absentia*) accused. The defence did not substantively contest the crime base, instead arguing that China's alleged ultimate responsibility was exculpatory for the accused. There was little cross-examination of prosecution witnesses.[73] Ieng Sary, in an interview in *Le Monde*, acknowledged "excesses" but minimised the role of the Khmer Rouge leadership, denying that atrocities were centrally ordered and instead blaming the Vietnamese.[74] This was the first trial under the Genocide Convention.[75]

5.2.4.5. The Verdict

The Council of Judges of the Revolutionary People's Tribunal ruled that Pol Pot and Ieng Sary were guilty of genocide.[76] It condemned them to death *in absentia*, ruled that all of their properties be confiscated, held that all evidence be handed over to the Ministries of Internal Affairs and National Defence, and allowed the accused to appeal for leniency within seven days of the posting of a public notice.[77] The judgment emphasised the alleged role of China, specifically that "the crime of genocide perpetrated by the Pol Pot-Ieng Sary clique against the Kampuchean people is masterminded by the Peking reactionaries".[78] It based the judgment both on the 1948 Convention on the Prevention and Punishment of the Crime of Genocide and the Decree-Law No. 1 of 15 July 1979 of the Revolutionary People's Council.[79] It found that the consequence of the accused acts was that about 3 million people were killed and the 4 million survivors suffered from physical and "moral" injury.[80] The problem of the specific intent requirement (that an accused must intend to destroy a protected group) was not seriously grappled with in the judgment.

---

[73]   *Ibid.*, pp. 12, 14–15.

[74]   *Le Monde*, 2 June 1979, p. 3.

[75]   Quigley, 2011, p. 17, see *supra* note 70.

[76]   Letter dated 17 September 1979 from the permanent Representative of Viet Nam to the United Nations addressed to the Secretary-General, UN doc. A/34/491, 20 September 1979, Annex, pp. 29–30.

[77]   *Ibid.*

[78]   *Ibid.*, p. 27.

[79]   *Ibid.*

[80]   *Ibid.*, p. 28.

5.2.4.6. The History

The tribunal's judgment was circulated as a UN document,[81] but the trial was largely ignored. The UN General Assembly accepted the Khmer Rouge as the government of Cambodia as of August 1979, despite their loss of territorial control through almost all of the country.[82] Despite the infamy of the crimes and the high-profile subsequent 'hybrid' tribunal on the same subject matter (the Extraordinary Chambers in the Courts of Cambodia), the Revolutionary People's Tribunal has largely been forgotten.

5.2.5. Conclusion

The trials described above deserve a greater place in the history of international criminal law. With the trial of Charles I we see the introduction of several historical themes that continue to resonate: protection for prisoners of war, criminal responsibility for making war, the tension between sovereignty and impunity for the sovereign, and the urge to cast regime change as wholly legitimate and even conservative. The trial of Wirz demonstrated the application of the customary law of armed conflict, as reflected in the Lieber Code, as a criminal code binding upon both parties in a non-international armed conflict. It focused on the protection of prisoners of war and was an interesting application of conspiracy as a substantive crime. It also was an interesting example of the arguably political tactic of prosecuting mid-level commanders while listing the leadership as unindicted co-conspirators. The Revolutionary People's Tribunal may have been the first trial to convict on the basis of the Convention on the Prevention and Punishment of the Crime of Genocide, and was a crucial example of the politically charged nature of international criminal law in a context where the government managing the trial is not widely recognised by other states.

The trials themselves also cannot be properly understood without some concept of international criminal law and the broad issues that inform it. This is perhaps obvious with the genocide trial of Pol Pot and Ieng Sary and the war crimes trial of Wirz. With the trial of Charles I, this connection to international criminal law is perhaps less obvious but argu-

---

81   *Ibid.*
82   Quigley, 2011, p. 9, see *supra* note 70.

ably more important. The subject matter included what were even then seen as violations of the laws and customs of war, notably mistreatment of prisoners of war. More powerfully, the connection between sovereignty, immunity, the use of state power and the protection of individual liberty were all at play in the trial of Charles I. While he was no longer the head of government, Charles remained the king, the sovereign, the head of state. This afforded him no protection at court. The trial was, in the end, not mainly about the accused but about the nature of the authority of the state, the independence of the law and whether individuals' liberties were protected from the state.

5.3. Why Are These Trials Not Remembered as Part of International Criminal Law?

5.3.1. Introduction

This section suggests three reasons why the trials discussed are frequently, but wrongly, neglected in histories of international criminal law. First, the contested nature of each of the trials is analysed. Second, the domestic nature of the forum for each trial is discussed. Third, the utility of a triumphant narrative rooted in the post-Second World War order is explained. While the previous sections were more objective, the following sections are somewhat prescriptive.

5.3.2. The Contemporaneously Contested Nature of Each Trial

While the trial of Charles I proceeded, the country was far from acquiescent. Presbyterian ministers throughout London denounced the not only the trial, but the army, the House of Commons and Cromwell.[83] Eventually the regicides would themselves be tried and executed when Charles II restored the monarchy. Wirz was executed on 10 February 1865, but President Johnson did not proclaim the final suppression of the rebellion in all Southern states except Texas until 2 April 1866, with Texas following in August.[84] The 1908 monument to Wirz by the United Daughters of the Confederacy and continuing memorialisation and valorisation of Wirz[85] demonstrate the continuing contestation of the trial. The People's Revolu-

---

[83] Wedgwood, 1964, p. 111, see *supra* note 9.

[84] Laska and Smith, 1975, p. 96, see *supra* note 40.

[85] LaForce, 1988, p. 3, see *supra* note 67.

tionary Tribunal was not only widely dismissed and ignored, but the government that staged the People's Revolutionary Tribunal was denied a seat at the United Nations, which was instead given to the Khmer Rouge. The civil war in Cambodia would continue until the Paris Peace Accords in 1991. The continued contestation of these trials is part of what has been termed the "meta-conflict"[86] or "the conflict about what the conflict is about". Because the role of the British monarchy, the nature of the US Civil War, and the role of Vietnam and China in Cambodian history and politics continue to be live political issues, the nature of the trials is not settled.

Contrast this with the canonical trials and tribunals celebrated in the normal, triumphal history of international criminal law. Germany and Japan were utterly defeated and (particularly with respect to the Nazi government) discredited before the post-Second World War tribunals. The IMT, tribunals pursuant to Control Council Law No. 10 and the International Military Tribunal for the Far East ('IMTFE') may have been resented by some, but they had nothing like the contemporary and ongoing contested nature of the trials discussed above. The International Criminal Tribunal for the former Yugoslavia ('ICTY') and International Criminal Tribunal for Rwanda ('ICTR') have been canonised with the imprimatur of the UN, together with the defeat of the pre-Kagame regime in Rwanda and the Milošević regime in Serbia, including independence for former Yugoslav Republics and *de facto* Kosovo secession from Serbia. The International Criminal Court ('ICC') is not an *ad hoc* tribunal in the manner that the IMT, IMTFE, ICTY and ICTR were, but nonetheless has enjoyed far less contestation of the legitimacy of its trials when the sovereign power was not subject to its scrutiny.

5.3.3. The Domestic Nature of the Forum

All three trials discussed in this chapter were held in domestic fora. Unlike the IMT, the IMTFE, the ICTY, the ICTR and the ICC, these trials were the projects of single sovereigns. They were of international interest, and with respect to Charles I, Pol Pot and Ieng Sary involved allegations of betrayal or foreign interference. Wirz and Ieng Sary were born outside the territory of the country putting them on trial. With the trial of Ieng

---

[86] Christine Bell, *Peace Agreements and Human Rights*, 2000, Oxford University Press, Oxford, p. 15.

Sary and Pol Pot foreign lawyers played a critical role. They came after civil wars and regime changes. But the forum was nonetheless clearly domestic in each case.

Of course, a domestic forum is not a bar for the application of international criminal law. The Istanbul and Leipzig trials after the First World War were the projects of single sovereigns, as were the trials under US auspices pursuant to Control Council Law No. 10 after the Second World War. It is difficult to determine whether a forum is domestic or not in the case of many 'hybrid' tribunals. Even the IMT has been characterised as a domestic trial, in that it was the sovereign power of the Allies exhibiting a domestic jurisdiction through condominium over Germany. The great hope for an effective system of international criminal law enforcement rests on domestic enforcement, as exemplified in the system of complementarity with the ICC. This of course precedes the ICC Statute, notably in the obligation to prosecute or extradite in the Geneva Conventions of 1949 and the Convention on the Prevention and Punishment of the Crime of Genocide.[87]

With the creation of the ICTY, ICTR and ICC, it was perhaps normal for the focus to be on the particularities of fora created by multiple states. The creation of these institutions was important and their jurisprudence is valuable. But as modern international criminal law loses the glow of novelty, renewed attention to the sources of international criminal law and the long history of proceedings in domestic fora is merited.

5.3.4. The Utility of Rooting the History of International Criminal Law in the Post-Second World War Order

There is an extremely compelling pull towards beginning the narrative of international criminal law with the defeat of Nazi Germany and the prosecution of Nazi officials. Not only are the crimes of Nazi officials of unequalled infamy, but there is a real sense in which the international system was reforged after the Second World War. As argued by William Schabas in his inaugural lecture at the University of Leiden, the Charter of the

---

[87] See also, for example, the Draft Code of Crimes against the Peace and Security of Mankind with Commentaries, 1996, which states in Article 8: "Without prejudice to the jurisdiction of an international criminal court, each State Party shall take such measures as may be necessary to establish its jurisdiction over the crimes set out in articles 17, 18, 19 and 20", that is, genocide, crimes against humanity, crimes against United Nations and associated personnel, and war crimes (https://www.legal-tools.org/doc/5e4532/).

United Nations, Charter of the IMT and the Universal Declaration of Human Rights redefined the association between human rights, justice and peace.[88] The IMT was famously self-promoted by the lead prosecutor, Robert Jackson, as "one of the most significant tributes that Power ever has paid to Reason", which seems like a noble place to start a 'new' area of law.

5.3.5. Conclusion

Despite the appeal of a triumphant, bowdlerised history of international criminal law, the best approach to the history of international criminal law is a broad, humble one. While a compelling history can be crafted by largely focusing on post-Second World War international institutions, and avoiding domestic tribunals that carry historical 'baggage', it is inadvisable. For the objective scholar, a triumphant approach unnecessarily foreshortens the history of the field. For the practitioner, advocate or policymaker, the triumphant approach robs them of perspective. Writing out flawed or contested trials from the history of international criminal law may tend to build unrealistic expectations, leading to inevitable disappointment. If international criminal law is seen as something with a long history, even if that history is somewhat troubled, the disappointments of the day are less likely to be given disproportionate weight. Additionally, the possibility of politicised or otherwise flawed prosecutions may be guarded against with greater vigour.

5.4. The Tensions Within International Criminal Law

5.4.1. Introduction

The author submits that the trials discussed above deserve attention on their own merits. Their absence in standard studies of international criminal law was formed in part because they do not rest easily within a confident, utopian narrative of international criminal law overall. Each trial throws light on two tensions within international criminal law – tensions that may be reduced or managed, but rarely eliminated. First, the allegation of politicisation is never entirely avoidable when dealing with politi-

---

[88] William Schabas, "The Three Charters: Making International Law in the Post-war Crucible", Inaugural Lecture, Leiden University, 25 January 2013 (https://www.legal-tools.org/doc/c3e5cf/).

cally charged subjects. Second, the tension between the independence of
international law and the need for domestic judiciaries and authorities is a
continuing issue. In order for the potential of international criminal law to
be fully realised, particularly in domestic trials, the (sometimes cautionary) history of domestic criminal prosecutions with international law
character must be more carefully considered.

5.4.2. Allegations of Politicisation and Politically Charged Subjects

The trials discussed in this chapter were (and for some are) inherently politically charged. Allegations that the trials were wholly political, mere
predetermined 'show trials' devoid of actual legal substance inherently
diminish their legitimacy. But this is not a problem that will only strike
the occasional international criminal law trial. The subject matter of international criminal law is conduct that has so offended international public
order[89] and the public conscience[90] that it is prohibited not merely domestically but at the international level. Virtually all trials that deal with such
conduct are going to have implications for governmental and public affairs, that is, they have political implications and are inherently politically
charged. That does not mean that the trial must be political, but it likely
means that the suspicion that the prosecution and the bench are politicised
should not simply be ignored. The claims that the prosecution or the
bench are acting for 'the people', for 'civilisation' or even for 'humankind' are unlikely to convince sceptical observers.

Those designing, prosecuting and managing international criminal
law trials will inevitably be tempted to claim that politics have no influence over their purely professional motivations.[91] This chapter does not
seek to follow the common 'critical' approach in which, in the name of
truth telling, the hidden politics of a seemingly apolitical framework is
cleverly revealed. If anything, this chapter suggests an 'anti-critical' approach – rather than seek to expand the realm of politics to cover the entire field, the author suggests it would be helpful for those practising and
analysing international criminal law to attempt to keep politics and law in

---

[89] To use the language of criminal law theory.

[90] To use the language of the Martens Clause.

[91] This section is informed by Jens Iverson, "Springing the Trap: Prosecutorial Discretion
Beyond Politics and Law", available at http://dovjacobs.com/2012/12/20/guest-post-
springing-the-trap-prosecutorial-discretion-beyond-politics-and-law/, last accessed on 25
November 2014.

their respective corners when possible, and instead admit other explanations and criteria for the choices made. Those designing trials and prosecutions are often caught in a rhetorical trap. No one realistically expects that these actors behave as creatures of pure logic, able to rationalise all choices available to them into the single choice they make. When a choice is made, it is easy to portray that decision not as a wholly professional or legal choice but rather a political choice. If the only possible descriptions are legal or political, and the law is not conclusive, the politics will inevitably appear to be (at least to many) the prime mover.

What alternative is there to this dilemma, to this rhetorical trap? How can politics be defined so it does not occupy the field to the detriment of legal processes? The issue of politics as power relations is particularly heated in the context of armed conflict, and indeed has haunted international criminal law in the wake of armed conflict. When Robert Jackson described the IMT as "one of the most significant tributes that Power has ever paid to Reason", he spoke not only to pride in the law but also the concern over victor's justice as a particular politicisation of law that lies at the nexus of international criminal law and international humanitarian law.

If the practice of international criminal law is not to be reduced to mere power relations, it may be helpful to be more overt about the performative, didactic aspects about choices made. It is obvious that some are charged and some are not, some charges are lodged and some are not, not only due to the application of the law to the evidence produced in an unbiased investigation but also due to the economic constraints and policy choices of the state. This need not be wholly an issue of power relations – it also can reflect the prioritisation of contested and colliding values. As stated in Isaiah Berlin's analysis of different choices made by cultures, "[C]ollisions of values are the essence of what they are and what we are".[92] When managing allegations of politicisation, collisions of values should be openly and explicitly addressed, not wished away.

---

[92] Isaiah Berlin, "On the Pursuit of the Ideal", *New York Review of Books*, 17 March 1988, available at http://www.nybooks.com/articles/archives/1988/mar/17/on-the-pursuit-of-the-ideal/, last accessed on 25 November 2014.

5.4.3. International Law and Domestic Authority

Certain specified atrocities are the subject matter of international criminal law. Periods in which these atrocities occur tend to produce social upheaval that can undermine domestic authority. In all of the trials discussed in this chapter, the imprimatur and apparent independence of law beyond the immediate domestic authority was of use to that authority. In the trial of Charles I there was a clear need to appeal to an authority beyond the king himself. For Wirz the Union relied upon the concept that his conduct amounted to a "violation of the laws and customs of war", laws and customs that went beyond domestic statute. For Pol Pot and Ieng Sary the prohibition against genocide was the pivotal basis of an otherwise widely questioned authority.

This willingness of domestic authorities to seek the imprimatur and apparent independence of international law when faced with society-shaking atrocities should be welcome news for those who wish international criminal law to develop. Maximising the use of domestic judiciaries and municipal authority is widely seen as critical for the functioning of international criminal law. But there is a tension inherent in this bargain. International law, translated into domestic judicial systems, may gain local biases and lose the very independence that makes it appealing to local authorities. The more local authorities are used, the greater the potential for international law to be seen as lacking independence, and the weaker its potential imprimatur.

The trials examined in this chapter are important moments in the history of international criminal law. But if the entire history of international criminal law resembled these trials, the imprimatur of international criminal law would be lessened. The ease with which these trials are excluded from the history of international criminal law indicates an uncertainty towards domestic authority among international criminal law scholars, which should be fully reckoned with.

If domestic authorities are increasingly going to take a leading role in the investigation and prosecution of international crimes, some investigations and prosecutions will be less than independent. In addition, as discussed above, different choices will be made in terms of prosecutorial discretion and the emphasis chosen by special tribunal and institutions. The habit of referring almost entirely to the jurisprudence of post-Second World War international institutions is understandable. But a more holistic approach that acknowledges a greater universe of jurisprudence with varying degrees of persuasive authority is more likely to maximise the potential of international criminal law than selective blindness. Even flawed tribunals with poorly reasoned judgments are important in that they show the ways in which international criminal law can be poorly applied. The history of international criminal law should include cautionary tales as well as notes of triumph, just as other areas of legal history allow for noting error and correction.

5.4.4. Conclusion

The trials discussed in this chapter are noteworthy, not only for British, American or Cambodian historians but also for historians of international law. More attention should be paid, both to the particulars of the trials and how they were remembered and interpreted. The trials themselves can only be fully understood within a narrative that includes international law. They are largely ignored as a subject of international criminal law not because they are irrelevant but because they are contested. The further examination of contested trials in domestic fora that do not serve a triumphant narrative should be extremely useful in understanding the field of international law. At worst, the history of international criminal law can devolve to a hagiography of a limited set of post-Second World War institutions. This serves no one well. Broadening the field of analysis is vital both to understand the long-term past developments in international criminal law and to shape them going forward.

6

International Criminal Law's
"Oriental Pre-Birth": The 1894–1900 Trials of the
Siamese, Ottomans and Chinese

Gregory S. Gordon[*]

6.1. Introduction

Conventional wisdom often traces the origins of international criminal law to the 1474 *ad hoc* prosecution for atrocities in Alsace of the Burgundian governor Peter von Hagenbach and then straight to the Nuremberg and Tokyo trials after the Second World War.[1] But this history ignores a remarkable decade at the end of the nineteenth century when three international criminal proceedings with links to the Orient took place: 1) in 1893 a French-Siamese Mixed Court sat in judgment of Phra Yot, a Siamese governor charged with the death of a French military commander;[2] 2) in 1898 International Military Commissions of four European powers prosecuted versions of war crimes and crimes against humanity arising from Muslim–Christian intercommunal violence on the Ottoman-controlled island of Crete;[3] and 3) in 1900 another International Military

---

[*]   **Gregory S. Gordon** is Associate Professor and Director/Assistant Dean (Ph.D.–M.Phil. Programme) at the Faculty of Law, Chinese University of Hong Kong. The author is very grateful to Jan Stone, who once again helped me dig deeply to uncover previously hidden histories and place them into the proper context. He also thanks Icarus CHAN.

[1]   See, for example, Gregory S. Gordon, "The Trial of Peter von Hagenbach: Reconciling History, Historiography and International Criminal Law", in Kevin Jon Heller and Gerry Simpson (eds.), *The Hidden Histories of War Crimes Trials*, Oxford University Press, Oxford, 2013, p. 13, referring to the Hagenbach trial and noting that "the Westphalian order, already on the horizon, would foreclose any such future experiments [in international criminal trials] until Nazi brutality put a chink in the Westphalian armour and inspired an unprecedented transnational justice operation [at Nuremberg] in the wake of a truly global war".

[2]   See generally Benjamin E. Brockman-Hawe, "A Supranational Criminal Tribunal for the Colonial Era: The Franco-Siamese Mixed Court", in Heller and Simpson, 2013, p. 50, see *supra* note 1, describing the trial and situating it historically.

[3]   See generally R. John Pritchard, "International Humanitarian Intervention and Establishment of an International Jurisdiction over Crimes against Humanity: The National and In-

Commission, this one consisting of four powers from Europe, presided over the trial of some participants in the Boxer Rebellion for proto-crimes against humanity.[4] Significantly, and perhaps not coincidentally, these trials took place within the context of the founding of the late nineteenth-century peace movement and the Hague Conferences' transnational endeavour to codify humanitarian law and promote arbitration to resolve disputes. And like those movements, the effort to establish international criminal law, though far-sighted and revolutionary, was ultimately premature. It would take two world wars and unimaginable carnage for the strands of global peace, international humanitarian law and transnational criminal justice to blossom and take root in the fertile human rights soil of the late 1940s.[5]

Moreover, and also not coincidentally, the trials represented the apogee of European imperialism, that period during the late 1800s when industrialisation and gunboat diplomacy fuelled colonisation, especially in Africa and the Orient.[6] Significantly, the efforts at international justice during that century's final decade involved colonial powers sitting in judgment of subjugated or less powerful peoples in the Orient. Thus, in each case, the arguably progressive instinct for global co-operation was adulterated with the ostensibly baser motive of engaging in transnational power politics. That these nascent stabs at international criminal justice arose largely from imperialistic impulses is perhaps best corroborated by the behaviour of the European powers in the period that soon followed. In

---

ternational Military Trials on Crete in 1898", in John Carey, William V. Dunlap and R. John Pritchard (eds.), *International Humanitarian Law*, vol. 1: *Origins*, Transnational Publishers, Ardsley, NY, 2003, pp. 12–13, providing an overview of the Ottoman trials.

[4] See generally Grote Hutcheson, "Report on the Paotingfu Expedition and Murder of American Missionaries at that Place", in *Annual Report of the War Department*, vol. 1, US Government Printing Office, Washington, DC, 1901, p. 460, reporting on the trial as an American military officer attached to the European expeditionary force responsible for prosecuting the perpetrators.

[5] See generally Telford Taylor, *The Anatomy of the Nuremberg Trials: A Personal Memoir*, Knopf, New York, 1992, chronicling the trial of the major Nazi German war criminals before the International Military Tribunal at Nuremberg; Kevin Jon Heller, *The Nuremberg Military Tribunals and the Origins of International Criminal Law*, Oxford University Press, Oxford, 2011, giving an overview and analysis of the Nuremberg Military Tribunals.

[6] See generally Barbara Bush, *Imperialism and Postcolonialism*, Pearson Longman, Harlow, 2006, p. 20, referring to the "New Imperialism" and noting that "a new wave of colonial acquisition opened up with the 'scramble' for Africa and the Far East after 1870".

the wake of the Great War of 1914–1918, although setting out a transnational justice framework in the treaties ending the war, the victorious Allies ultimately refused to put their vanquished fellow Europeans on trial before any international tribunals.[7] Imperialism and international justice were compatible at the turn of the century but Westphalian trepidations foiled far more crucial adjudications less than two decades later.

This chapter explores this little known "Oriental" episode in the formation of international criminal law and proceeds in four sections. Section 6.2. sets the historical context of the trials – the late nineteenth-century apex of European colonialism and relevant political developments in the Near and Far East. Section 6.3. then describes the origins of the three Oriental tribunals, including an overview of the noble and, at turns, cynical rationales that inspired the Great Powers to turn to adjudication efforts and international processes. The structure and operation of the tribunals themselves will also be discussed, including the defendants selected, the rules of procedure applied, the crimes charged, the defences raised and the verdicts issued. Section 6.4. then puts these trials into perspective. It examines the dawn of the European peace movement as curiously juxtaposed with the simultaneous twilight of European imperialism during the closing decade of the nineteenth century.

As will be demonstrated, in significant ways the trials that are the object of this chapter are the odd by-product of this confluence of international pacifism and aggression. To what degree did these tribunals anticipate subsequent developments in substantive and procedural international criminal law? Were the trials themselves the result of cynical machinations on the part of the Great Powers or a genuine attempt to provide for lasting peace or reconciliation through novel processes? How were the verdicts perceived by stakeholders? How should the answers to these questions impact on the development and practice of international law today? The chapter closes by considering these questions.

In the end, the chapter will conclude that colonial power erosion and attempts to preserve it, embryonic indigenous independence drives,

---

[7] See M. Cherif Bassiouni, "International Criminal Justice in Historic Perspective", in M. Cherif Bassiouni (ed.), *International Criminal Law*, vol. 3: *International Enforcement*, Martinus Nijhoff Publishers, Leiden, 2008, pp. 33, 35: "After World War I, the Treaty of Versailles provided for ad hoc tribunals, but none were forthcoming. [...] the post-World War I experience showed the extent to which international justice can be compromised for the sake of political expediency".

and arbitral international dispute resolution advocacy underpin the fascinating formation of these proto-Nuremberg tribunals in such a unique place and time in history. They illuminate an unexplored but vital chapter of international criminal law's past but also provide invaluable insights into its present and future, including the potential spectre of a new imperialism as the International Criminal Court focuses its current work exclusively on Africa.

6.2. Setting the Context: European Imperialism in the Nineteenth Century

6.2.1. Overview

Imperialism has been defined as "the extension of rule or influence by one government, nation, or society over another".[8] There is ample evidence of it in the ancient historical record. The Mesopotamian, Egyptian, Assyrian, Persian and Roman empires all asserted dominion over regional rivals conquered in war or otherwise subjugated through intimidation or aggressive diplomacy.[9] Post-medieval European imperialism, which flowed from maritime exploration and the desire to develop trade,[10] was largely co-extensive with the post-Westphalian rise of the nation state and the after-effects of the Age of Discovery.[11] After a pause in expansion in the wake of the Napoleonic Wars and the subsequent Congress of Vienna,[12] the Industrial Revolution, fuelling demand for cheap labour, raw materials

---

[8] Barbara A. Chernow and George A. Vallasi (ed.), *The Columbia Encyclopedia*, 5th ed., Columbia University Press, New York, 1993, p. 1317.

[9] *Ibid.*

[10] George Edwin Rines (ed.), *The Encyclopedia Americana*, Encyclopedia Americana Corporation, New York, 1920, p. 527.

[11] *Ibid.*: "Imperialism was reborn in the West with the emergence of the modern nation-state and the age of exploration and discovery". See also Piet Strydom, *Discourse and Knowledge: The Making of Enlightenment Sociology*, Liverpool University Press, Liverpool, 2000, p. 100, referring to the "age of exploration and discovery and the subsequent colonialist and imperialist policies and practices of the European states"; William V. Spanos, *American Exceptionalism in the Age of Globalization: The Specter of Vietnam*, State University of New York Press, Albany, NY, 2008, p. xvi, describing "the nation-state system [...] inaugurated by the Treaty of Westphalia in 1648 [...] and the idea of national culture and the imperialism endemic to it".

[12] B.V. Rao, *History of Modern Europe: AD 1789–2002*, New Dawn Press, Elgin, 2005, p. 164: "So around the first half of the nineteenth century the European countries were tired of establishing new colonies".

and new markets, stoked new European colonial ambitions in Africa and Asia.[13]

For some, this era of "New Imperialism" still carried the traditional expansionist justifications of national pride – colonies were considered prestigious – and moral imperative as missionaries sought conversion to Christianity and Europeans zealously assumed the "White Man's Burden" of "civilising" inferior peoples.[14] Control was established through superior arms (especially the rapid-fire machine gun) and transportation (with modern navies on the oceans, steamboats on the inland rivers and railways on the ground). It was maintained through advances in medicine (such as using quinine, with its anti-malarial properties) and communications (primarily the telegraph).[15]

As a result of this New Imperialism, most of Africa and large swathes of Asia were taken over by European powers during the nineteenth century.[16] In Africa, the British asserted dominion over such wide-ranging territories as Nigeria, Gold Coast, Sierra Leone, Egypt, Kenya, Uganda, Swaziland, Zanzibar, Rhodesia and Somaliland. The French took possessions in Algeria, Tunisia, Mauritania, Senegal, Guinea, Mali, Ivory Coast, Benin, Niger, Chad, Central African Republic and Madagascar. German conquests in Africa led to the creation of German East Africa, German South West Africa and German West Africa. The Belgians estab-

---

[13] William J. Duiker and Jackson J. Spielvogel, *World History*, vol. 1: *To 1800*, Wadsworth, Boston, 2006, p. 572.

[14] *Ibid.*

[15] See Keld Nielson, "Western Technology", in Jan Kyrre Berg Olsen Friis, Stig Andur Pedersen and Vincent F. Hendricks (eds.), *A Companion to the Philosophy of Technology*, Wiley-Blackwell, Malden, MA, 2009, p. 27: "[Western] imperialism was much assisted by telegraphs, steam ships, efficient rifles, and railways"; Robert L. O'Connell, *Of Arms and Men: A History of War, Weapons and Aggression*, Oxford University Press, Oxford, 1989, p. 233, explaining that machine guns were so popular with British colonial forces because "from an imperialist standpoint, the machine gun was nearly the perfect laborsaving device, enabling tiny forces of whites to mow down multitudes of brave but thoroughly outgunned native warriors"; Daniel R. Headrick, *The Tools of Empire: Technology and European Imperialism in the Nineteenth Century*, Oxford University Press, Oxford, 1981, p. 71, emphasising the important role played by quinine in combating malaria and thereby enabling nineteenth-century Western imperial expansion.

[16] See generally Richard W. Bulliet, Pamela Kyle Crossley, Daniel R. Headrick, Steven W. Hirsch, Lyman L. Johnson and David Northrup, "The New Imperialism, 1869–1914", in *The Earth and Its Peoples: A Global History*, vol. 2: *Since 1550*, 5th ed., Wadsworth, Boston, 2011, pp. 739–57, tracing the origins and details of the New Imperialism.

---

lished the Belgian Congo. And a formal framework for the division of African possessions among European powers was erected at the 1884 Berlin Conference.[17]

In Asia, among others, the British colonised Afghanistan, Burma, Malaya, Borneo, Hong Kong, Kuwait and Bahrain.[18] Following up on earlier regional conquests, the Dutch subjugated much of modern Indonesia (then called the Netherlands East Indies).[19] And France created French Indochina out of acquisitions in Vietnam, Cambodia and Laos.[20] But the European powers had no equivalent of the Berlin Conference to regulate land-grabs in the Orient. And that would have implications that will be explained below.

6.2.2. French Colonialism and Indochina

France's colonial ambitions during this period are linked in significant ways to its defeat in the Franco-Prussian War of 1870–71. This French military debacle, which brought down Napoleon III, seriously bruised national pride and caused the successor regime, the Third Republic, to look beyond Europe in an effort to find national glory in Africa, Southeast Asia and Oceania (in particular, the colonies of French Polynesia).[21] These flames of imperial ambition were further fanned by the German Chancellor, Otto von Bismarck, who encouraged the French government to expand its overseas possessions in order to divert its attention away from retaking the territory of Alsace-Lorraine it ceded to the new German Empire at the conclusion of the Franco-Prussian War.[22] Related to this,

---

[17] Jeffrey Herbst, *States and Power in Africa: Comparative Lessons in Authority and Control*, Princeton University Press, Princeton, NJ, 2000, pp. 71–72.

[18] Timothy H. Parsons, *The British Imperial Century, 1815–1914: A World History Perspective*, Rowman & Littlefield, Lanham, MD, 1999, p. 5.

[19] Heather Sutherland, "Geography as Destiny? The Role of Water in Southeast Asian History", in Peter Boomgaard (ed.), *A World of Water: Rain, Rivers and Seas in Southeast Asian Histories*, NUS Press, Singapore, 2007, p. 43.

[20] George Fetherling, *Indochina: Now and Then*, Dundurn Press, Toronto, 2012, pp. 10–11.

[21] See Siba N. Grovogui, "Imperialism", in Bertrand Badie, Dirk Berg-Schlosser and Leonardo Morlino (eds.), *International Encyclopedia of Political Science*, vol. 1, Sage, Thousand Oaks, CA, 2011, p. 1155, explaining that "the New Imperialism was a matter of national pride [for] France after defeat in the Franco-Prussian war".

[22] Geoffrey Wawro, *Warfare and Society in Europe, 1792–1914*, Routledge, London, 2000, p. 132: "Bismarck wanted France to forget the humiliating defeats at Sedan and Metz and focus instead on building an overseas empire to rival that of Great Britain".

French officers banished to existing colonial outposts after the 1870–71 military failure often annexed new chunks of territory on their own initiative, without any encouragement from Paris, in order to rehabilitate their reputations and earn promotions. The French government would then accept the new possessions after the fact.[23]

The key French politician sanctioning these developments and often pushing them forward was Jules Ferry, who served variously as Minister of Education, Minister of Foreign Affairs and Prime Minister during the late 1870s and first half of the 1880s.[24] Thanks to Ferry's public education reforms, French literacy increased dramatically and this helped whet the public appetite for stories about colonial conquest and adventure in an expanding French popular press.[25] This, in turn, contributed to French colonial aspirations during the early years of the Third Republic.[26]

In Asia, this imperialist enterprise was realised in the development of what would become French Indochina. Initial French incursions into the region were not by political design. Instead, the first contacts, in the seventeenth century, consisted of French merchants establishing trading posts in southern Vietnam, which was referred to as Cochin-China (the central region was referred to as Annam and the northern as Tonkin).[27] Roman Catholic missionaries followed them in an effort to Christianise the native population.[28] At the end of the eighteenth century, French religious leaders and traders arranged for military aid from Paris memorialised in the 1787 Treaty of Versailles, to assist Prince Nguyễn Ánh, who was attempting to regain power after losing it in a rebellion.[29] In exchange for French assistance, Prince Ánh agreed to let the French use the port of Đà Nẵng and take over Côn Sơn Island, on Vietnam's southeastern coast. With French arms and soldiers, Prince Ánh prevailed and ultimately be-

---

[23] Paul S. Reinsch, World Politics at the End of the Nineteenth Century: As Influenced by the Oriental Situation, Macmillan, New York, 1902, pp. 63–64; Yves Beigbeder, Judging War Crimes and Torture: French Justice and International Criminal Tribunals and Commissions (1940–2005), Martinus Nijhoff, Leiden, 2006, p. 44.

[24] Beigbeder, 2006, pp. 45–46, see supra note 23.

[25] Michael G. Vann, "The Third Republic and Colonialism", in Martin Evans and Emmanuel Godin (eds.), France, 1815–2003, Arnold, London, 2004.

[26] Ibid.

[27] Debbie Levy, The Vietnam War, Lerner, Minneapolis, MN, 2004, p. 7.

[28] Ibid.

[29] Ibid. See also Mark E. Cunningham and Lawrence J. Zwier, The Aftermath of the French Defeat in Vietnam, Twenty-First Century Books, Minneapolis, MN, 2009, pp. 10–11.

came Emperor Gia Long over all of Vietnam in 1802, which helped vali-
date and strengthen France's presence in the region.[30]

Nevertheless, further French expansion was equally desultory. In
addition to the ambition of individual French officers as noted above,
much of the expansion had to do with colonial reactions to animus toward
the occupiers after the death of Gia Long. The French missionaries and
traders were often harassed and subjected to violence.[31] Paris's response
to such attacks would result in imperial expansion. In particular, "a pattern was established [...] when French soldiers, traders, or priests were
attacked, the French [used revenge] as an excuse to extend their power
[and the] Vietnamese were forced to surrender control over their land and
to provide the French with special privileges".[32] In this way, by 1883,
Gallic control was asserted over all of Vietnam and subsequently over the
neighbouring provinces of Cambodia and Laos.[33] The entire region came
to be known as l'Indochine française (or French Indochina).[34]

But French dominion over Laos merits special attention here. That
came about as the result of a brief war in 1893 between France and the
one remaining indigenous sovereign entity in the region, the Kingdom of
Siam. The dispute between the two countries centred on territory along
the eastern bank of the Mekong River referred to as the state of Chieng
Keng (part of modern-day Laos).[35] The Siamese were convinced the territory belonged to them based in part on concessions given to them by the
British. Influenced by politicians belonging to the lobbying group called
the *parti colonial*, who wished for France to annex Laos and check potential British incursions into the area, Paris believed the land was within its
sphere of control as a part of Vietnam.[36] When the demands of the French

---

[30] Cunningham and Zwier, 2009, p. 11, see *supra* note 29.

[31] Levy, 2004, p. 6, see *supra* note 27.

[32] Thomas Ladenburg, "The French in Indochina", *Digital History* (http://www.digitalhist
ory.uh.edu/teachers/lesson_plans/pdfs/unit12_1.pdf).

[33] Levy, 2004, p. 6, see *supra* note 27.

[34] *Ibid.*

[35] Patrick J.N. Tuck, The French Wolf and the Siamese Lamb: The French Threat to Siamese
Independence 1858–1907, White Lotus, Bangkok, 1995, pp. 100, 104.

[36] Sud Chonchirdsin, "Paknam Incident (1893): A Taste of French Imperialism", in Keat Gin
Ooi (ed.), *Southeast Asia: A Historical Encyclopedia from Angkor Wat to East Timor*, vol.
1, ABC-Clio, Santa Barbara, CA, 2004, p. 1015. The *parti colonial* was not a political party in the traditional sense – it was more of a lobbying group of French politicians belonging to different political parties along the political spectrum, but united in their belief that

to surrender the territory, as communicated to Bangkok by the chief French government official in the area, Auguste Pavie, were rebuffed, the French sent a military force into the disputed area.[37]

The Siamese, mistakenly believing the British would come to their aid, offered resistance and fighting took place at various points along the Mekong and on Khong Island (situated in the centre of the capacious river).[38] In the course of the skirmishes, a confrontation between Siamese and French troops at Kham Mouon resulted in the death of a French police inspector by the name of Grosgurin.[39] The French believed the Siamese unjustifiably ambushed Grosgurin and his men and deemed as criminally responsible the Commissioner of the Kham Muon District, Phra Yot Muang Kwang.[40] Once the dispute was resolved via gunboat diplomacy in France's favour (with Laos handed to France as a concession), the French demanded that Phra Yot be put on trial – whence the origin of the first proceeding referred to in this chapter – the Franco-Siamese mixed tribunal.[41]

6.2.3. Incursions into the Ottoman Empire and the Situation in Crete

The Ottoman Empire was established by Turkish tribes in the late theirteenth cenutry in Asia Minor and ultimately expanded to cover vast tracts of land in parts of Europe, Asia and Africa.[42] But nineteenth-century European imperialism often advanced at the expense of Ottoman possessions

---

France should maintain and expand its colonial possessions. See Carl Cavanagh Hodge, *Encyclopedia of the Age of Imperialism, 1800–1914*, Greenwood Press, Westport, CT, 2008, p. 247: "Often lumped together under the general descriptor of *Parti Colonial* – a loose collection of political groups rather than a political organization [...] these groups found a willing audience in the *Groupe Colonial*, a caucus of pro-colonial deputies in the lower house of the National Assembly".

37 Chonchirdsin, 2004, p. 1015, see *supra* note 36.

38 *Ibid.*

39 Charles Gosselin, *Le Laos et le protectorat français*, Perrin, Paris, 1900, pp. 88–89.

40 *Ibid.*

41 Georges Demanche and Édouard Marbeau, "Siam: Procès Phra-Yot", in *Revue française de l'étranger et des colonies et exploration*, 1894, vol. 19, p. 449.

42 Chernow and Vallasi, 1993, pp. 2036–37, see *supra* note 8.

on those continents, including ones in the Balkans, the Near East, the Caucasus, the Maghreb and the Horn of Africa.[43]

In the early 1820s, for example, Britain, France and Russia joined forces with Greek rebels to end Ottoman rule in Greece.[44] After the 1877–78 Russo-Turkish War and the post-conflict Congress of Berlin, which was presided over by various European powers, the Ottomans lost a significant portion of their territorial holdings.[45] Russia succeeded in claiming several provinces in the Caucasus, including Kars and Batumi, as well as the region of Bessarabia on the Black Sea. Austria-Hungary gained possession of Bosnia-Herzegovina and Britain was given Cyprus.[46] The Ottoman Empire was carved up even further in the following decade – this time in Africa. At the beginning of the decade the French invaded Tunisia from Algeria and stripped it from Ottoman control pursuant to the 12 May 1881 Treaty of Bardo.[47] In 1882 Egypt, which had also been a part of the Ottoman Empire, was invaded by combined British and French forces seeking to establish better European control of the Suez Canal.[48] Egypt would remain a British colony for the next four decades.[49]

All this set the stage for a further erosion of Ottoman dominion in 1898, when another group of European powers divested the Turks of the island of Crete, which had been in Turkish possession for over two centuries.[50] But administration of the island during the 1800s had not gone well for the Turks.[51] After a series of uprisings by local Greeks (at least one

---

[43] *Ibid.*

[44] Martin Polley, *A-Z of Modern Europe Since 1789*, Routledge, London, 2000, p. 62.

[45] Mehrdad Kia, *Daily Life in the Ottoman Empire*, ABC-CLIO, Santa Barbara, CA, 2011, pp. 22–23.

[46] *Ibid.*, p. 23.

[47] William E. Watson, *Tricolor and Crescent: France and the Islamic World*, Praeger, Westport, CT, 2003, pp. 27–28.

[48] Glenn E. Perry, *The History of Egypt*, Greenwood, Westport, CT, 2004, pp. 68–69.

[49] James P. Hubbard, *The United States and the End of British Colonial Rule in Africa, 1941–1968*, McFarland, Jefferson, NC, 2010, p. 42: "In 1922, Britain declared Egypt independent". It should be noted, however, that "the British high commissioner in Cairo retained considerable powers and British troops remained". *Ibid.*

[50] Allaire B. Stallsmith, "One Colony, Two Mother Cities: Cretan Agriculture under Venetian and Ottoman Rule", in Siriol Davies and Jack L. Davis (eds.), *Between Venice and Istanbul: Colonial Landscapes in Early Modern Greece*, American School of Classical Studies at Athens Publications, Princeton, NJ, 2007, p. 160.

[51] *Ibid.*

during every decade that century – 1821, 1833, 1841, 1858, 1866, 1878, 1889, 1895 and 1897),[52] the so-called Great Powers of Europe – Russia, France, Italy, Britain, Germany and Austria-Hungary, forming a Council of Admirals – took over administration of the island (leaving the Ottomans as only nominal suzerains).[53]

These developments infuriated the local Turkish population and the situation remained quite volatile. In particular, they resented that a tithe was to be imposed on exports and administered by a Custom House to which a Christian had been appointed.[54] In reaction to this, on 6 September 1898 an unarmed group of Muslims tried to force their way into the associated revenue office in Candia. In repelling them, British troops found it necessary to open fire on the group. The Turks dispersed but returned with weapons and began killing non-Muslims – both British soldiers and Christian civilians.[55] This murderous Muslim mob, which was joined by Ottoman soldiers,[56] also slew the British Vice-Consul Lyssimachus Andrew Calocherino, captain of the British ship *Trafalgar*, who was burnt to death in his house with his family.[57] In all, 800 Christians, including British soldiers, were massacred.[58] The Ottomans were then expelled from Crete, which was eventually united with Greece.[59] But it is important to note here that the 6 September 1898 massacres led to that decade's second effort at international criminal justice that will be the focus of this chapter.

---

[52] Leonidas Kallivretakis, "A Century of Revolutions: The Cretan Question between European and Near Eastern Politics", in Paschalis M. Kitromilides (ed.), *Eleftherios Venizelos: The Trials of Statesmanship*, Edinburgh University Press, 2006, p. 16.

[53] Davide Rodogno, *Against Massacre: Humanitarian Interventions in the Ottoman Empire, 1815–1914*, Princeton University Press, Princeton, NJ, 2012, p. 221.

[54] Harry Thurston Peck, "Crete", in Frank Moore Colby (ed.), *The International Year Book for 1898*, Dodd, Mead and Company, New York, 1899, p. 230.

[55] *Ibid.*

[56] Rodogno, 2013, p. 221, see *supra* note 53.

[57] *Ibid.* See also Pınar Şenışık, *The Transformation of Ottoman Crete: Revolts, Politics and Identity in the Late Nineteenth Century*, I.B. Tauris, London, 2011, p. 169, noting that Vice-Consul Calocherino was captain of the British ship *Trafalgar*; "Situation at Candia", in *Sacramento Daily Union*, 8 September 1898, reporting that "The British Vice Consul, Mr. Calocherino, was burned to death in his house".

[58] Rodogno, 2013, p. 221, see *supra* note 53.

[59] Kallivretakis, 2006, pp. 30–31, see *supra* note 52.

6.2.4. The Plundering of China and the Boxer Rebellion

China, home to one of the world's oldest civilisations, was under dynastic rule for thousands of years.[60] From the fifteenth to eighteenth centuries, as Europeans were sailing around the world in an effort to promote commerce, China severely restricted trade with the West.[61] But by the nineteenth century China's political and social infrastructure was crumbling and its relationship with the West was changing.[62] This decay has been attributed to a number of factors, including corruption, lack of reform, population growth and internal resurrections, but European economic exploitation certainly played an influential role.[63] In particular, it was responsible for the First (1839–1842) and Second (1856–1860) Opium Wars with Britain. The root cause of those wars lay in British efforts to open the Chinese market and redress a trade imbalance (largely owing to the British appetite for tea) by exposing the Chinese to Indian-cultivated opium, addicting them to it, and then selling it to them against the wishes of Chinese authorities.[64] When Chinese officials tried to block British opium merchants from the port in Canton and confiscated their wares, the British launched a naval expedition that, by 1842, had prevailed through superiority of modern arms.[65] The Chinese were forced to sign the Treaty of Nanjing (and the Supplementary Treaty of the Bogue), which forced

---

[60] Michael D. Swaine and Ashley J. Tellis, *Interpreting China's Grand Strategy: Past, Present, and Future*, Rand, Santa Monica, CA, 2000, p. 1, noting that China is "one of the world's oldest civilizations"; Michael Teitelbaum and Robert Asher, *Immigration to the United States: Chinese Immigrants*, Facts On File, New York, 2005, p. 17: "Much of Chinese history is composed of a series of dynasties [...] China was ruled by dynasties for thousands of years".

[61] David Emil Mungello, *The Great Encounter of China and the West, 1500–1800*, 4th ed., Rowman & Littlefield, Plymouth, 2013, pp. 5–7, noting that by 1787 Canton was the sole legal port for trade with the West.

[62] Clive J. Christie, *Southeast Asia in the Twentieth Century: A Reader*, I.B. Tauris, London, 1998, p. 85, commenting on the "crumbling of the Manchu empire" in the "last decade of the nineteenth century".

[63] Duiker and Spielvogel, 2006, p. 571, see *supra* note 13: "[The] Quing dynasty began to suffer from the familiar dynastic ills of official corruption, peasant unrest, and incompetence at court [...] exacerbated by the rapid growth in population"; David S.G. Goodman, *China and the West: Ideas and Activists*, Manchester University Press, Manchester, 1990, p. 1, explaining scholars' perceptions that the "West came saw and conquered" China "in the wake of nineteenth century colonialism and the import of Western ideas".

[64] Duiker and Spielvogel, 2006, p. 571, see *supra* note 13.

[65] *Ibid.*, pp. 571–72.

---

them to open to British trade and allow residence at the ports of Jīnmén, Fuzhou, Ningbo and Shanghai. In addition, China was obligated to cede Hong Kong to Britain.

In turn, following the British example, other Western powers, including France, Germany and Russia, signed similar treaties with the Chinese that also exacted commercial and residential privileges. Nevertheless, in 1856 the Second Opium War broke out in response to an allegedly illegal Chinese search of a British-registered ship. This time, British troops were joined by French in the attack and once again the Chinese were forced to sign a humiliating accord – this time, the Treaty of Tianjin (1858) – to which France, Russia, the United States and Britain were parties. According to the terms of this treaty, China agreed to open 11 more ports, allow foreign legations in Beijing, permit Christian missionary activity and legalise the import of opium.

However, in the end, China tried to prevent the entry of Western diplomats into Beijing and fighting between China and the Western powers recommenced in 1859. This time, an infuriated Britain and France occupied Beijing and burned the imperial summer palace. The Chinese were then forced to sign the Beijing Conventions of 1860, which obligated them to reaffirm the terms of the Treaty of Tianjin as well as make additional concessions.[66] By the close of the century, Chinese resentment over these terms gave rise to the Boxer Rebellion.

The Boxer Rebellion was a violent anti-Christian, xenophobic movement that sought to eradicate European and Japanese influences from Chinese society from 1898 to 1900.[67] Its organisers were called the Yihetuan (or Yihe Quan) movement, which translates as the Righteous and Harmonious Group, and they came to be known in English as the Boxers. Many of them had been farmers who had to leave their homes after crop failures owing to a severe drought during that period. These dispossessed migrants wandered the countryside of northern China looking for food and blaming Westerners for their troubles. Along the way, they began learning the *yihe quan* style of martial arts. The students were taught that the new fighting technique conferred powers on its practition-

---

[66] Chernow and Vallasi, 1993, p. 2015, see *supra* note 8.

[67] Joseph Esherick, *The Origins of the Boxer Uprising*, University of California Press, Oakland, 1987, p. 154.

ers that made them invulnerable to knives and bullets.[68] By 1899 the rising popularity of the fighting style and beliefs, combined with hatred for the foreigners, contributed to violent attacks by Boxers against foreigners and Chinese Christians, primarily in the provinces of Zhílì, Shānxī and Shandong as well as Manchuria and Inner Mongolia.[69] This burgeoning uprising had the support of the Beijing government, primarily through Empress Dowager Cíxǐ, who favoured a last effort to expel the foreigners (as opposed to Emperor Guangxu, who preferred reform but was placed under house arrest by the more powerful Empress Dowager).[70]

The Boxers adopted the slogan "Support the Qing, destroy the foreigner".[71] And by the spring of 1900 they were prepared to carry out this threat on a much larger scale. In May Boxer lynch mobs murdered a large group of Chinese Christians and two British missionaries in Pao Ting Fu (Bǎodìng), the provincial capital of Zhílì (now part of Héběi province), located a little less than 150 kilometres southwest of Beijing.[72] The European powers in the Legation Quarter in Beijing ordered up troops from the coast.[73] Nevertheless, by June a force of nearly 150,000 Boxers, supported by the war party at court, occupied Beijing and surrounded the Legation Quarter, where nearly all foreigners had taken refuge.[74]

During June both the Japanese and German ministers were murdered.[75] Meanwhile, at various points around the countryside in northern China, massacres of Christians and foreign missionaries were still taking place.[76] For instance, at the end of June and beginning of July, 11 adult missionaries and four children were massacred in Pao Ting Fu with the complicity of Chinese civil and military officials.[77] On 30 June members

---

[68] *Ibid.*

[69] Chernow and Vallasi, 1993, p. 348, see *supra* note 8.

[70] *Ibid.* See also Barbara Bennett Peterson (ed.), *Notable Women of China: Shang Dynasty to the Early Twentieth Century*, M.E. Sharpe, New York, 2000, pp. 359–60.

[71] Diana Preston, The Boxer Rebellion: The Dramatic Story of China's War on Foreigners that Shook the World in the Summer of 1900, Berkley Books, New York, 2001, p. 31.

[72] Lynn E. Bodin and Chris Warner, *The Boxer Rebellion*, Osprey, Oxford, 1979, p. 5.

[73] *Ibid.*

[74] Chernow and Vallasi, 1993, p. 348, see *supra* note 8.

[75] William F. Nimmo, Stars and Stripes Across the Pacific: The United States, Japan and Asia/Pacific Region, 1895–1945, Praeger, Westport, CT, 2001, p. 47.

[76] *Ibid.*

[77] Arthur Henderson Smith, *China in Convulsion*, Fleming H. Revell, New York, 1901, pp. 610–11.

of the American Presbyterian Mission, along with three children of one of the missionary couples, were burnt alive in their dwelling.[78] The other missionaries, representing the American Board and the China Inland Mission, were variously shot, stabbed or beheaded the following day.[79] Dozens of their Chinese Christian servants were killed with them.[80]

Finally, the siege of the Legation Quarter in Beijing was lifted in August by an international force of approximately 21,000 British, French, Russian, American, German, Austro-Hungarian, Italian and Japanese troops and the Boxer Rebellion came to an end.[81] Of the besieged defending forces within the Legation Quarter, numbering fewer than 500, 65 had been killed (12 civilians) and 131 wounded (23 of them civilians).[82]

In the aftermath, the Western powers and Japan compelled China to sign the Boxer Protocol, pursuant to which 10 high-ranking Chinese officials were executed, the Chinese had to pay an indemnity of 450,000 taels of silver, modify commercial treaties in favour of the foreigners, and allow foreign troops to be permanently garrisoned in Beijing.[83] In addition, foreign troops were dispatched on "punitive expeditions" to various massacre sites in the northern Chinese countryside.[84] Remarkably, the Pao Ting Fu expedition resulted in the foreigners convening an impromptu international tribunal and holding a trial against Chinese officials deemed responsible for the Boxer massacres.[85] It was the only court proceeding adjudicating criminal liability in the aftermath of the Boxer Rebellion. And it is the subject of the third trial examined in this chapter.

---

[78] *Ibid.*

[79] *Ibid.*

[80] Hutcheson, 1901, pp. 464–5, see *supra* note 4.

[81] Nimmo, 2001, p. 46, see *supra* note 75.

[82] Spencer C. Tucker, *Almanac of American Military History*, vol. 2, ABC-Clio, Santa Barbara, CA, 2013, p. 1196.

[83] Patrick Taveirne, Han-Mongol Encounters and Missionary Endeavors: A History of Scheut in Ordos (Hetao) 1874–1911, Leuven University Press, Leuven, 2004, p. 540.

[84] Peter Harrington, *Peking 1900: The Boxer Rebellion*, Osprey, Oxford, 2001, pp. 87–89.

[85] Raymond Robin, *Des occupations militaires en dehors des occupations de guerre*, Carnegie Endowment for International Peace, Washington, DC, 1942, p. 202: "In Pao-ting-fu, on the other hand, an international tribunal composed of Frenchmen, Germans, and Englishmen was established, under the presidency of the French officer, General Boilloud [sic]".

6.3. The Trials of the Siamese, Ottomans and Chinese

6.3.1. The Franco-Siamese Mixed Court

As will be recalled, the French and Siamese were embroiled in a brief armed conflict regarding the possession of territory in modern-day Laos. The conflict ended when Siam agreed to France's ultimatum to remove Siamese troops from the disputed territory and acknowledge French ownership.[86] To hammer out the details, the parties met at the negotiating table in Bangkok in August 1893.[87] The French were represented by Charles-Marie Le Myre de Vilers, the former Governor of Cochin-China, and the Siamese by Prince Devawongse Varoprakar, the Minister for Foreign Affairs.[88] Foremost among the issues to be worked out concerned territorial possession in the disputed area. The upshot of the negotiations was that Siam renounced its claims to territory east of the Mekong River and to the islands in the river.[89] Siam also consented to a 25-kilometre-wide demilitarised strip along the west bank of the Mekong and promised not to fortify the provinces of Angkor and Battambang.[90] In addition to resolving these larger issues, the French and Siamese also negotiated terms for dealing with Inspector Grosgurin's homicide, which had come to be known as the Affair of Kham Muon.

In the end, a global resolution of all issues between the parties was memorialised in a 2 October 1893 Treaty between France and Siam with an attached Convention ('Franco-Siamese Treaty').[91] Article 3 of the Franco-Siamese Treaty (with an appended *procès-verbal*) provided for adjudication of the Affair of Kham Muon as follows: 1) Phra Yot would be first tried before a specially created Siamese domestic court; and 2) if

---

[86] Adrien Launay, *Siam et les missionnaires français*, Alfred Mame et Fils, Tours, 1896, p. 234.

[87] *Ibid.*

[88] Arthur J. Dommen, The Indochinese Experience of the French and the Americans: Nationalism and Communism in Cambodia, Laos, and Vietnam, Indiana University Press, Bloomington, IN, 2001, p. 18.

[89] Ronald Bruce St John, "The Land Boundaries of Indochina: Cambodia, Laos and Vietnam", in *Boundary of Territory Briefing*, 1998, vol. 2, no. 6, p. 12.

[90] *Ibid.*

[91] Treaty between the Government of France and the Government of His Majesty the King of Siam, 3 October 1893 ('Franco-Siamese Treaty'); Dommen, 2001, p. 18, see *supra* note 88.

the French were not satisfied with the manner or results of those proceedings, they could cause to be convened a "mixed court" presided over by two French judges, two Siamese judges and a French president – in essence, a French majority with three French and only two Siamese judges.[92] Thereafter, feeling the adjudication process outlined in the treaty was unfair, the Siamese urged the French to consider creation of a mixed *international* court, presided over by neutral Dutch, American and British judges.[93] But that proposal fell on deaf ears so the Siamese signed into law a Royal Decree creating a Special and Temporary Court for the domestic trial of Phra Yot ('Royal Decree').[94]

6.3.1.1. The Special and Temporary Court

The Special and Temporary Court ('Special Court') was well designed, combining aspects of both Thai and European law. In particular, the "Court applied existing Siamese legal codes but operated according to procedural rules inspired by the laws of England and France".[95] Moreover, as set forth below, the accused was afforded important guarantees of due process and the French were granted the right to participate in the trial in a meaningful manner. Pursuant to Part I of the Royal Decree, Constitution of the Court, the bench would consist of one chief justice and six judges, all Siamese. In addition, two Siamese prosecutors were designated.[96] According to Part II, Preliminary Process, the accused was to be charged by the prosecutors via an Act of Information, which would inform the accused of the offences imputed to him and the punishments available under Siamese law. A representative of the French government was authorised to confer with the Siamese prosecutors regarding the content of the indictment.[97] For purposes of trial, Part III guaranteed the accused access to the evidence brought against him and translated into Sia-

---

[92] Franco-Siamese Treaty, Art. 3. See also Brockman-Hawe, 2013, pp. 56–57, see *supra* note 2.

[93] Brockman-Hawe, 2013, pp. 57–58, see *supra* note 2.

[94] Royal Decree Instituting a Special and Temporary Court for the Trial of the Affairs of Tong-Xieng-Kham and Keng-Chek (Kham-Muon), in "Full Report, with Documentary Appendices, of the Phra Yot Trial before the Special Court at Bangkok", in *Bangkok Times*, 1894 ('Full Report'); see also Brockman-Hawe, 2013, p. 58, *supra* note 2.

[95] Brockman-Hawe, 2013, p. 58, *supra* note 2.

[96] Full Report, Part I, see *supra* note 94.

[97] *Ibid.*, Part II.

mese, the right to counsel, cross-examination and the right to call witnesses.[98] The French were entitled to a translation of the proceedings into their language and had the right to cross-examine witnesses and give a closing statement independently of the prosecution. However, for the accused was reserved the right to address the Special Court last.[99] Part IV of the Royal Decree stipulated that the final judgment had to be in writing (but not necessarily translated into French) and that any decision as to the guilt or not of the accused had to be by majority. Interestingly, it did not specify burdens or standards of proof.[100]

The trial began on 24 February 1894 and was held in a relatively small room in one of the public buildings within the walled portion of Bangkok. Present in the courtroom, in addition to the accused (represented by two lawyers – one English, the other Ceylonese), the judges, the two Crown prosecutors, court clerks and interpreters, were a French advocate, French consul and French legal expert, who had travelled to Bangkok from Saigon to observe the case.[101] Before a packed courtroom, Phra Yot was arraigned on charges of premeditated murder, infliction of severe bodily harm, robbery and arson. He was informed that conviction could be punished by death, mutilation, scourging with 50 strokes, imprisonment (at the end of which term would be added "cutting grass for the elephants"!), and/or various fines.[102]

In the course of an eight-day trial (in other words, eight public session days – stretching from 24 February to 17 March 1894), with one witness called by the prosecution and seven by the defence (including Phra Yot himself), a clear narrative account of the events at Kham Mouan at last emerged.[103] For eight years prior to the incident in question, Phra Yot had been a Siamese Commissioner in the area of the disputed territory.[104] On 23 May 1893 a French Captain, Luce, arrived there with a contingent of Annamite soldiers, surrounded Phra Yot and ordered him to leave the

---

[98] *Ibid.*, Part III.

[99] *Ibid.*

[100] *Ibid.*, Part IV

[101] John MacGregor, *Through the Buffer State: A Record of Recent Travels through Borneo, Siam, and Cambodia*, F.V. White, London, 1896, p. 100. See also Full Report, "The Trial of Phra Yot, First Day", p. 1, *supra* note 94.

[102] MacGregor, 1896, pp. 99–100, see *supra* note 101.

[103] Brockman-Hawe, 2013, p. 61, see *supra* note 2.

[104] Full Report, "Judgment", p. 56, see *supra* note 94.

territory. He refused. Luce then called in Grosgurin and 20 Annamite soldiers and ordered them to escort Phra Yot away from the disputed territory to Tar Outhene. Luce claimed the escort was necessary to protect Phra
Yot from the local populace, who Luce claimed hated the Siamese Commissioner (whose possessions were also taken by Luce on the grounds
that Luce was safeguarding them pending the parties' arrival at Tar
Outhene). Phra Yot and certain of his underlings left with the escort, but
Phra Yot stated he was doing so pending further instructions from his
government, with which, he claimed, not to have been in communication
to that point.

Midway to their destination, Grosgurin and his escort parted company with Phra Yot, with each party finding lodgings before the final leg
of the trek to Tar Outhene. At that point, Grosgurin was informed by locals that Phra Yot was looking for men and weapons to fight the French.
The locals claimed they learnt this through Phra Yot's interpreter, Luang
Anurak. Two days later, Grosgurin came upon Luang Anurak at Kham
Muon and arrested him. Phra Yot asked for Luang Anurak's release but
this was refused. He then left for Tar Outhene on his own and encountered two Siamese officers accompanied by 50 soldiers, who informed
Phra Yot that the Commissioner of Outhene had orders to fight the French
and expel them from the area. On 3 June 1893 Phra Yot, the officers and
20 of the soldiers then went to Kham Muon and, standing in front of the
house where Grosgurin lay in his sickbed, called for Grosgurin to release
Luang Anurak, return Phra Yot's possessions and then leave the territory.
Grosgurin communicated his refusal.[105]

Luang Anurak then broke free of his captors and fled the house.
Shots were fired from inside the house and a Siamese soldier was struck
(although the French claimed the first shot was fired from the outside –
either way several Siamese soldiers were killed by bullets emanating from
inside the house). The Siamese then conferred and decided to fire shots in
return. In the exchange of gunfire, Grosgurin was shot and killed and the
house caught fire. The Siamese took certain possessions from the house
(including, presumably, those belonging to Phra Yot as well as the soldiers' arms) before it burnt down, during which time some of the Annamite soldiers and an interpreter were wounded by Siamese swords (other

---

[105] *Ibid.*

members of Grosgurin's Annamite escort – a dozen in total – were killed during the firefight).[106]

Having considered all the evidence, the Special Court decided to acquit Phra Yot. With respect to the maiming, arson and robbery charges, the Court found insufficient evidence linking those to any orders by Phra Yot.[107] And, in any event, regarding the supposed stolen goods, a portion of those were arguably Phra Yot's confiscated property that was being retrieved on Phra Yot's behalf.[108] Regarding the homicide charges, the Court held that the accused could bear no liability as the evidence indicated he did not issue orders to the soldiers who fired the shots.[109] Moreover, even if he had, the accused was not in charge of the soldiers who fired the shots, the Siamese military officers were. Therefore, even assuming the homicides entailed criminal liability (which the Court did not assume as it found the Annamites fired first and the Siamese had a duty to defend themselves), the officers would bear sole responsibility for the killings.[110] As a result, Phra Yot was acquitted of all the charges.[111]

6.3.1.2. The Franco-Siamese Mixed Court

Predictably, the French were outraged by the verdict and within three days asserted their right to convene the stipulated Article 3, Mixed Tribunal.[112] The Constitution of the Mixed Court provided that the adjudicative

---

[106] *Ibid.*, p. 58.

[107] *Ibid.*, pp. 59, 61.

[108] *Ibid.*, pp. 59, 61–62.

[109] *Ibid.*, p. 60.

[110] *Ibid.*

[111] *Ibid.*, p. 62. The Special Court did not apply the law of war. It appears this was for political reasons as the French maintained that their assertions of dominion over the Laotian territory, as well as any Siamese resistance thereto, did not place the countries in a state of war. Brockman-Hawe, 2013, p. 63, see *supra* note 2: "[A] ruling by a Siamese court to the contrary would have endangered the fragile *détente* that had prevailed between the two powers since October 1893".

[112] Brockman-Hawe, 2013, p. 64, see *supra* note 2. See also The Case of Kieng Chek Kham Muon before the Franco-Siamese Mixed Court: Constitution of the Mixed Court and Rules of Procedure, "First Part: Constitution of the Mixed Court. – Rules of Procedure" (June 1894), ('Trial of Phra Yot'):

> On the 20th of March 1894, the Minister Resident of the French Republic at Bangkok informed the Siamese Minister of Foreign Affairs that the French Government had decided to submit the Judgment given by the

body would "be composed of a President, assisted by two Siamese Judges and two French Judges".[113] The prescribed Rules of Procedure then laid out a detailed trial framework in three stages.

In Stage One, which I shall call Preliminaries: 1) three days at least before the initial sitting, the Act of Accusation (compared to the more neutral Siamese Act of Information), drawn up by the public prosecutor (French by definition as the position was filled by the *procureur* of the Republic) would be provided to the Accused; 2) pursuant to a date and time chosen by the Court President, the Court would sit in a room in the French legation; 3) interpreters would be provided to assure all parties understood the different languages spoken in court; 4) the accused would then appear before the President, identify himself, be warned to "be attentive to what he is about to hear" and then have the Act of Accusation read to him; 5) the public prosecutor would then lay out the grounds of the accusation and then give a list of both the prosecution and defence witnesses; 6) the witnesses would then be sequestered in a specially designated room and thereafter appear in the courtroom only to give their evidence; 7) the accused, and then each witness one at a time, would be sworn in and examined; 8) after each witness would testify, the accused could respond to the testimony (presumably by addressing the Court directly) and put questions to the witness through the President (not directly through cross-examination); 9) the President would then have the right to question each witness and then each judge and the public prosecutor would have the same right, after asking for and getting leave of the President to question the witness; and 10) during the course of the whole proceeding, the President would have the right to hear all witnesses and obtain all information.[114]

In Stage Two, which I shall call Debates (essentially akin to closing arguments in the British courts): 1) after the hearing of the witnesses, the public prosecutor would address the Court and "develop before the Court the circumstances upon which the accusation is based"; 2) the accused and his counsel would then have the right to answer; 3) the public prosecutor would be allowed to reply but the accused or his counsel would

---

Siamese Court, on the 17th March, 1894, to a Mixed Court, according
to the right given it by the Convention of 3rd October, 1893.

[113] Trial of Phra Yot, 1894, see *supra* note 112. As with the Siamese Special Court, no burden or standard of proof was referenced in the Mixed Tribunal's constituent document.

[114] *Ibid.*, pp. 3–4.

"always have the right to speak last"; and 4) the President would then "declare the debates closed".

In Stage Three, which I shall call Framing the Verdict and Deliberations: 1) the President would put questions "arising from the debates in these words: 'Is the accused guilty of having committed such a deed, with all the circumstances contained in the Act of Accusation?'"; 2) the President would then "put the question of extenuating circumstances"; 3) after the President would frame the questions, the accused and the public prosecutor would be able to "make any observations" on the way the questions were put; 4) the accused or the public prosecutor could then make objections to the way the questions were framed and the Court would then decide on the merits of the objections; 5) the President would then "order the Accused to retire"; and 6) the Court would then "withdraw to the Chamber of deliberations to deliberate upon the solution of the questions and the punishment to be awarded".[115]

The Rules of Procedure then defined the applicable crimes. They began with murder, which was described as "homicide committed voluntarily".[116] They then defined as "assassination" any murder committed with "premeditation or ambush".[117] They went on to define "premeditation" and spelled out details regarding accomplice liability. With respect to the punishment for homicide crimes, the Rules then specified that capital punishment would be imposed on "whoever shall be guilty of assassination, parricide, infanticide, or poisoning" or "murder […] preceded, accompanied or followed [by] another crime".[118] Finally, the Rules stipulated that, in cases of extenuating circumstances, the death penalty could be reduced to hard labour for life or for a time.[119]

It should be noted that the prescribed Rules of Procedure have more of the flavour of a French judge-focused inquisitorial proceeding (with the President controlling most aspects of the proceedings and the accused being called as the first witness) than the Siamese Special Court, which was more adversarial in character (allowing the parties to cross-examine wit-

---

[115] *Ibid.*, p. 4.

[116] *Ibid.*

[117] *Ibid.*

[118] *Ibid.*, p. 5. The Rules also set forth penalties for theft and arson.

[119] *Ibid.*

nesses directly, for example).[120] Also, the crimes, especially with respect to those tied to capital punishment (assassination, for example), were very French in flavour (known as *assassinat* in French).[121]

The trial opened on 4 June 1894. As set forth in the Rules of Procedure, the French prosecutor read the charging instrument, the Act of Accusation.[122] Its text reveals that, from the outset, the deck was stacked against Phra Yot. Contrary to the evidence adduced at the first trial, it avers that the Siamese Commissioner voluntarily submitted to being dispossessed and ejected from his post under armed escort.[123] It then alleges that he had a change of heart once the parties arrived at Kham Muon, where Luang Anurak was legitimately arrested. Phra Yot then gathered Siamese forces near Outhene (as opposed to encountering them by chance), led a "corps" of "over 100 armed men" (as opposed to a mere 20 from the first trial) to Grosgurin's temporary residence, and then, unprovoked and unrelated to Luang Anurak's arrest, gave the order to this "veritable small army" to start firing at Grosgurin and the Annamites.[124] After this premeditated massacre (leaving only two survivors – allegedly taken as prisoners and mistreated en route to Bangkok) and attendant arson, Phra Yot and his troops stole the remaining possessions of the murdered French contingent.[125]

The Act of Accusation acknowledges alternate versions of the facts "produced in the course of the inquiry and during the first trial of this affair" but asserts that "good sense and the concatenation of circumstances indicate" that this is "general and very confused evidence".[126] It then goes on to anticipate and refute Phra Yot's defences averring that "it is in vain […] that he has pretended, for his defence, that his first intentions, on his

---

[120] See Richard S. Frase, "Comparative Criminal Justice as a Guide to American Law Reform: How Do the French Do It, How Can We Find Out, and Why Should We Care?", in *California Law Review*, 1990, vol. 78, no. 3, pp. 539, 628, 673–74, noting that, at trial, defendants testify first in the French system and observing that "another distinctive feature of the French [system] is the active role of the presiding trial judge".

[121] Simon Chesterman, "An Altogether Different Order: Defining the Elements of Crimes against Humanity", in *Duke Journal of Comparative and International Law*, 2000, vol. 10, no. 2, pp. 328–29, discussing the French crime of *assassinat*.

[122] Trial of Phra Yot, 1894, pp. 6–7, see *supra* note 112.

[123] *Ibid.*

[124] *Ibid.*, pp. 8–9.

[125] *Ibid.*, p. 8.

[126] *Ibid.*

arrival at Kieng Chek, were of an absolutely pacific character, that he only came there as an interceder of Luang Anurak".[127] Based on all this, Phra Yot was then charged as an accomplice to murder, theft and arson (referred to as "wilful incendiarism").[128]

The Court then began to hear testimony. The evidence that emerged appeared largely consistent with that from the first trial but the French bullied and harassed witnesses to slant the facts as they wanted them presented. This excerpt from Phra Yot's time on the stand is representative of the tenor of the proceedings:

> Q. – Did Grosgurin explain to you why he arrested Luang Anurak?
>
> A. – He told me because Luang Anurak had spread certain alarming rumours at Kham Muon that the Siamese would return in force.
>
> *The President.* Grosgurin had a perfect right to arrest Luang Anurak after that, in self defence, for he was in an unknown country and only had a handful of men whose fidelity was doubtful. [...]
>
> Q. – It is quite impossible to believe that Grosgurin who was sick and whose party was the weakest would be first to attack. The Siamese witnesses have stated that there were at least 100 men surrounding the house.
>
> A. – I have already stated that there were not more than 50 or 60 men, and the witnesses must have been mistaken.
>
> Q. – Grosgurin was very ill and it is quite incredible that he should have fired upon peaceful men, without any provocation.

On 13 June 1894 the Court found Phra Yot guilty of complicity in the murder of Grosgurin and members of his escort party but acquitted him of the theft and arson charges.[129] Not surprisingly, the three French judges voted in favour of the conviction and the two Siamese judges dissented – in fact, they refused to sign the final verdict form.[130] Nevertheless, the Court did not impose the death sentence in light of extenuating

---

[127] *Ibid.*, p. 9.

[128] *Ibid.*

[129] *Ibid.*, pp. 37–38.

[130] *Ibid.*

circumstances, to wit, that he did not take away "the life of a fellow creature with a view to gratify his cupidity and to satisfy a feeling of hatred or personal vengeance".[131] As a result, Phra Yot was condemned "to the punishment of 20 years hard labour" and ordered to pay the costs of the trial.[132] France wanted the defendant to serve his sentence in a French penal colony but, through a compromise brokered by the British, Phra Yot was confined in a Siamese prison.[133] Five years later, with French permission, Siamese King Chulalongkorn pardoned him and he was released.[134]

6.3.2. The Trial of the Ottomans Before the International Military Commissions

As described earlier, intercommunal violence on the island of Crete, then controlled by the Ottoman Turks, resulted in the murder of nearly one thousand Christians/British soldiers by a vengeful Muslim mob on 6 September 1898. A provisional government of Europeans (or Great Powers), directed by a Council of Admirals representing each of the resident powers – Russia, France, Italy and Britain (Germany and Austria-Hungary had since departed) – had to decide on appropriate justice measures. Prior to this bloodshed, on 31 August 1897, the Great Powers had created a Military Commission of International Police, using as its governing law the Italian Military Code, to handle crimes committed against international citizens (non-Cretans) on the island.[135] This would turn out to be an important cornerstone in the development of a justice solution.

6.3.2.1. Beginning of the Justice Process

The justice process began with officials identifying 172 potential criminal cases.[136] Based on these, 145 people were taken into custody in the imme-

---

[131] *Ibid.*, p. 36.

[132] *Ibid.*, p. 39.

[133] Brockman-Hawe, 2013, p. 69, see *supra* note 2.

[134] Walter E.J. Tips, Gustave Rolin-Jacquemyns and the Making of Modern Siam: The Diaries and Letters of King Chulalongkorn's General Adviser, White Lotus Press, Bangkok, 1996, p. 133.

[135] Robin, 1942, p. 188, see *supra* note 85; Pritchard, 2003, pp. 12–13, see *supra* note 3.

[136] *British Blue Book*, Turkey No. 7 (1898), No. 159, Telegram from Sir Herbert Chermside, British Military Commissioner, Candia, to the Prime Minister and Foreign Secretary, the Marquis of Salisbury, sent 7 October 1898.

diate aftermath of the massacres.[137] In the initial phase, to establish whether authorities had sufficient evidence to prosecute the suspects, Turkish and British Courts of Inquiry were established.[138] To the Great Powers, the Turkish Court of Inquiry appeared ineffectual as Turkish authorities seemed bent on pinning responsibility strictly on lower-level perpetrators and shielding from prosecution the massacre ringleaders.[139]

So the British Court of Inquiry served as the true screening mechanism. Its President was Major Reginald Henry Bertie of the 2nd Royal Welch Fusiliers.[140] Four other British officers also served on the Court: Major J.C. Conway-Gordon of the Highland Light Infantry; Harry Robinson, paymaster of HMS *Isis*; Royal Marine Captain J.H. Lambert of the HMS *Revenge*; and William Ernest Crocker, the assistant paymaster of HMS *Venus*, who acted as secretary to the Court. Reverend Thomas Henderson Chapman, chaplain to the forces, recorded the proceedings via shorthand.[141]

Although conducting proceedings in accordance with the *British Manual of Military Law*, this Court of Inquiry functioned rather akin to a French *juge d'instruction*, an investigating magistrate (somewhat of a cross between a prosecutor and judge), who is charged with conducting an impartial investigation to determine whether a crime worthy of a prosecution has been committed.[142] In serving this function, the British Court of Inquiry heard oral testimony from over 100 witnesses and considered more than 600 deposition transcripts. It disposed of 164 cases and authorised criminal trials for 36 suspects. Beginning on 25 September 1898, it completed its work in two months. In light of this volume, R. John Pritchard, the world's pre-eminent expert on the Cretan trials of the Otto-

---

[137] *Ibid.*

[138] Pritchard, 2003, p. 30, see *supra* note 3. Pritchard refers to an "International Court of Inquiry" being established but it appears that the British Court of Inquiry served as the initial screening mechanism for cases sent to trial before the International Military Commissions. As will be explained below, the International Military Commission at Canea also used a *juge d'instruction* for screening.

[139] *Ibid.*, p. 32.

[140] *Ibid.*

[141] *Ibid.* Interestingly, none of the members had any legal training or degrees.

[142] *Ibid.*, p. 33; Jeremy Shapiro and Bénédicte Suzan, "The French Experience of Counterterrorism", in *Survival*, 2003, vol. 45, no. 1 p. 78. The *juge d'instruction* is not an advocate for the prosecution or the defence and, after making a decision to prosecute, simply hands her case over to the attorneys for adjudication before a *juge de siege* for trial. *Ibid.*

mans, notes that "from a modern perspective, the swiftness of the pro-ceedings in Crete is their most marked characteristic".[143] This feat is all the more remarkable considering that the bulk of suspects were brought before this Court on bogus or extremely flimsy evidence. As Pritchard explains, the screening judges

> were often in considerable doubt as to why the suspects in their custody had been detained by the Turkish authorities, who seem to have been more interested in being seen to co-operate with the Powers in the weeks that followed the ca-lamities of September 6, than they were in completing any paperwork. Put bluntly, the Turks had combed the district for suspicious characters but, in the majority of cases, had failed to charge those whom they apprehended with any offens-es.[144]

6.3.2.2. The British Military Court

The actual trials themselves were conducted before two different judicial bodies. In the first place, prosecutions for the killings of British military personnel as war crimes in violation of the "laws and usages of war" (for example, customary international law) took place before a British Military Court (essentially a military court martial).[145] In the first part of October 1898, Colonel Herbert Chermside, British Military Commissioner and Commandant of the British troops on Crete, appointed Francis Howard, of the 2nd Battalion of the Rifle Brigade, as President of the Court.[146] The Court first tried seven Turks for the 6 September murder of five British soldiers – three men of the Highland Light Infantry killed near the Greek hospital and two outside of what was then called Candia's "new gate".[147] The trial took place on 13–15 October and, at its end, all seven defendants

---

[143] Pritchard, 2003, p. 34, see *supra* note 3.

[144] *Ibid.*, p. 53.

[145] See Instructions given by R.-Adm. Sir Gerard Noel to Col. Sir Herbert Chermside, 10 October 1898, NOE/10, Noel Papers, National Maritime Museum, Greenwich, United Kingdom: order by Britain's chief military commander on Crete to the officer in charge of the Candia sector to "convene a military Court-Martial [...] to try all offenders, charged with having on the 6th [September] carried or used arms against the British forces".

[146] The names and number of other Court members are not known. Pritchard, 2003, pp. 35–36, see *supra* note 3.

[147] *Ibid.*, p. 36.

were convicted and sentenced to death.[148] At the gallows two days later, one British military observer with an imperialist mindset noted, in reference to the condemned Ottoman defendants and their compatriots in attendance: "In England a public execution is unthinkable; as an example to the fantastical hordes to the East it is often imperative for the common safety".[149]

Within days, another British Military Court tried, convicted and sentenced to death five additional Turks in connection with the homicides of British military personnel on the Candia harbour picket and at the British hospital.[150] At the same trial, the Court sentenced four other defendants to 20-year sentences of penal servitude and acquitted one other. Overall, the Court completed all its work in reference to these two separate trials, involving a total of 17 defendants, within the very compressed timeframe of 15 working days.[151] Although the trials were conducted quickly, Pritchard opines that they by no means constituted drumhead justice:

> The accused on trial at Candia were not undifferentiated nor were they jointly tried on any rolled-up conspiracy charges. [...] it is clear that those convicted were connected up with specific crimes committed against particular victims. [...] the investigations, arrests and trials of the accused took place while the events that gave rise to them were extremely fresh in the minds of witnesses.[152]

6.3.2.3. The International Cases

The international cases, involving attacks on Christian civilians (that is, the victims who were not British military personnel) were handled in one of three ways: 1) some were transferred by the British Court of Inquiry to an International Military Commission in Candia; 2) others were initially screened by a separate *juge d'instruction* (not connected to the Court of Inquiry) and those it passed on for trial were heard by a separate International Military Commission based in Canea; and 3) for less serious

---

[148] *Ibid.*, pp. 36–37.
[149] William Price Drury, *In Many Parts: Memoirs of a Marine*, Fisher Unwin, London, 1926, pp. 180–81.
[150] Pritchard, 2003, p. 39, fn. 66, see *supra* note 3.
[151] *Ibid.*, pp. 39–40.
[152] *Ibid.*, pp. 37–38.

crimes, certain suspects were brought to justice in "summary proceedings" – either by Captain Sir H.W. M'Mahon under his powers as British Military Governor of Candia to award sentences of up to 42 days' imprisonment (eight were punished this way) or by the summary powers of the "international military authorities", who could also order short prison sentences (13 suspects were punished this way).[153]

But why were international cases handled separately given that the British Military Court was already up and running? The answer, quite simply, is that the perpetrators funnelled through the international mechanisms had not committed crimes against any foreign or even domestic military forces. In other words, they had not committed war crimes, which, by that time in history, had some basis for prosecution in international law.[154] Logically, the next inquiry would be as to why a domestic court could not have prosecuted these cases. On one level, the answer is rather easy – the Ottoman Empire was being divested of all control of the island and, in any event, by September 1898 its judicial infrastructure had disappeared. That left the *ad hoc* European governing authorities. Digging deeper, however, it is not even clear that existing law, regardless of the forum, adequately dealt with these atrocities that were motivated by religious hatred and shocked the conscience of collective humanity. According to Pritchard:

> The problem arose of how to find a suitable means of prosecuting and punishing the culprits in a manner suitably expressive of the outrage felt by the international community. [The most eminent legal authorities] believed that if international tribunals were set up by the Council of Admirals, these would be "illegal" under international law [...] [So the International Military Commission trials] were thought and in-

---

[153] *Ibid.*, pp. 40–65. Regarding the summary proceedings, see *id.* p. 49. Of all those arrested, 11 prisoners, regarded by the international authorities as notoriously "bad characters" but against whom nothing could be proved at trial, were not prosecuted by the British Military Court or the two International Criminal Tribunals but were summarily banished from the island for life. Some of them served short prison sentences before being exiled. The identities of the "international military authorities" in charge of these summary proceedings is not revealed by surviving documentation.

[154] See Mariya S. Volzhskaya, "*Kononov v. Latvia*: A Partisan and a Criminal – the European Court of Human Rights Takes a Controversial Stance on War Crimes", in *Tulane Journal of International and Comparative Law*, 2011, vol. 19, pp. 651, 653: "The earliest example of the international codification is 'Geneva law,' the collection of Geneva Conventions that provide an evolving set of concepts and definitions of war crimes from 1864".

tended by those responsible for them to mark a new stage in international jurisprudence and statecraft. [These] were exactly the same considerations which were manifest in the declaration of May 28, 1915, by France, Great Britain and Russia in expressing their determination to bring to justice those responsible for perpetrating 'crimes against humanity and civilization for which all members of the Turkish government will be held responsible together with its agents implicated in the massacres' committed against the Armenians.' The 1915 declaration, commonly held to be the first time in which the concept was articulated, proved to be a damp squib. On Crete, however, there was an entirely different outcome in the closing months of 1898.[155]

6.3.2.3.1. The International Military Commission at Candia

Thus, a large portion of those suspected strictly of crimes against civilians were sent for trial by an International Military Commission in Candia convened by the British representative on the four-power Council of Admirals, Rear Admiral Sir Gerard Noel, on 21 October 1898 pursuant to a mandate, specially assigned to him at a 29 September Council meeting, which laid down the ground rules regarding custody of such suspects.[156] The Candia Commission's institutional antecedent, of course, was the Military Commission of International Police, referred to previously. And like this latter Commission, each individual chamber of which consisted of officers of the nationality controlling the sector, the International Military Commission was located in the British sector of Candia. So its members were British.

It is worth noting that the Council of Admirals, through Noel, conferred with the Ottoman Governor of Crete, Djevad Pasha, in advance of the International Military Commission's creation.[157] When informed that the members of the Commission at Candia sitting in judgment of the defendants would consist strictly of British officers (which was presumably true of the International Military Commission at Canea too), Djevad Pasha advocated for a panel of mixed nationalities, including Ottoman – somewhat parallel to the Siamese request of the French in connection with

---

[155] Pritchard, 2003, pp. 40–41, see *supra* note 3.
[156] *Ibid.*, p. 41.
[157] *Ibid.*

the Phra Yot trial. Like that of the Siamese, the Ottoman request was de-nied.[158] Nevertheless, with no options in the face of the power of the Con-cert of Europe, the Ottoman Sultan grudgingly gave his consent to the proposed trials before the International Military Commission at Candia (and by implication, at Canea).[159] It should be noted, however, that, not-withstanding the strictly British composition of the Commission panels at Candia and Canea, final approval of its verdicts and punishments had to be confirmed by the Council of Admirals.[160] In that sense, the Commis-sions still possessed some degree of international character.

The International Military Commission at Candia was created by means of a Convening Order published by Noel on 21 October. The Con-vening Order invested it with powers to

> judge, without appeal, on the basis of the British Military
> Articles of War, all acts arising contrary to the public securi-
> ty, as well as offences of every kind, to the prejudice of the
> land and sea international forces, and the personnel of the in-
> ternational gendarmerie, which may be committed by the na-
> tive subjects of His Imperial Majesty the Sultan, or by for-
> eign subjects in the territory occupied by the Great Pow-
> ers.[161]

Permitting the International Military Commission to adjudicate "all acts arising contrary to the public security" gave it an extremely broad mandate. In practice, this translated into prosecutions for war crimes and a proto-version of crimes against humanity.[162] Its punishments ranged from various terms of imprisonment (with hard labour) to the death penalty.[163]

---

[158] *Ibid.*, p. 42. Two other Ottoman requests – that Ottoman attorneys be sent from Constanti-nople to assist the accused in their defence and that death sentences be commuted to life imprisonment in remote locations – were denied.

[159] *Ibid.*, pp. 43, 55.

[160] *Ibid.*, pp. 47–48. That provision was initially withdrawn at the request of Paris and Saint Petersburg but ultimately put back in. *Id.* p. 48.

[161] Confidential Print No. 234, Sir Evan MacGregor, KCB, Permanent Under-Secretary of State at the Admiralty, to the Foreign Office, sent on 16 November, 1898, received on 18 November 1898, with relevant enclosures ('Confidential Print').

[162] Pritchard, 2003, p. 43, see *supra* note 3, commenting on International Military Commis-sions having war crimes within their subject matter jurisdiction and observing that, in the early stages of the International Military Commissions' creation, the British remained "far less concerned with the punishment of those found guilty of crimes against humanity than with retribution upon those who had attacked the British forces". See also Beth Van Schaack, "The Definition of Crimes against Humanity: Resolving the Incoherence", in *Co-*

The Convening Order also declared that "the procedure of the Commission is to be that of a military court martial with any modifications which are considered by the President [of the Commission] as desirable to suit the special circumstances of the case".[164] In particular, based on the court-martial model, the International Military Commission's rules of procedure were governed by Queen's Regulations, set out in the British *Manual of Military Law*.[165] At the end of the nineteenth century, there were four different types of British courts martial: 1) the regimental courts martial (consisting of a panel of three members); 2) the district courts martial (also had three members but had wider powers than the regimental courts martial; 3) the general courts martial (minimum number of members was five – had the widest powers of punishment and could try an officer or soldier of any rank); and 4) field general courts martial (had the full powers of a general courts martial, although it could sit with a minimum of only three members – convened when accused was on active service or was stationed overseas).[166] Given that, as set forth below, the Commission had a President and four other members (thus five members total), and could issues death sentences, it appears to resemble most a general courts martial.[167]

The procedure in modern British courts martial is identical to that of a civil criminal court – and those of the nineteenth century were not terribly different.[168] This provides insight as to the rough outline of proce-

---

lumbia Journal of Transnational Law, 1999, vol. 37, pp. 787, 796, fn. 28: "These trials exercised jurisdiction over acts, such as the massacre of Christian compatriots by Muslim Cretans, that would later be termed 'crimes against humanity'".

[163] Pritchard, 2003, p. 51, see *supra* note 3, detailing the sentences of men who were sentenced to various terms of imprisonment with hard labour, and *id.*, p. 42, indicating the International Military Commission could sentence to death those found guilty.

[164] Confidential Print, see *supra* note 161.

[165] Pritchard, 2003, p. 45, see *supra* note 3.

[166] Stephen Stratford, "Courts Martial", in British Military and Criminal History in the Period 1900 to 1999 (http://archive.today/LWci6#selection-185.224-185.331).

[167] See Pritchard, 2003, p. 42, *supra* note 3, referring to the availability of the "death sentence" and "capital punishment" for the International Military Commission prosecutions.

[168] Ibid. See also John H. Aulick, Minutes of Proceedings of the Courts of Inquiry and Court Martial in Relation to Captain David Porter, David and Force, Washington, DC, 1825, p. 416:

> The course of proceedings, at British Courts Martial, is said to assimilate more nearly to trials for *high treason* in the Courts of common law: because prisoners, tried for that crime, have greater privileges allowed

dural stages before the International Military Commission. Consistent with what one would see in a typical Crown Court trial, the Commission process probably would have consisted of the following basic steps: 1) the clerk or the President would have read out the charge sheet stating the offences alleged; 2) the prosecution would then have made an opening statement setting out the basic facts; (3) the prosecution would then have put on its case via witnesses testimony (subject to cross-examination) – written affidavits and/or deposition testimony was admitted in certain instances when witnesses were not available (or even if available, perhaps just to save time);[169] 4) the defence case (same process as the prosecution except the defendant may have elected not to give evidence); 5) speeches by the prosecution and the defence urging conviction or acquittal; and 6) deliberation by the judges and passing of sentence.[170]

The surviving documentation from the International Military Commission trials does not reveal the exact identities of the British prosecutors (who would likely have been British military officers) or the defence counsel.[171] But it does tell us who served as members of the Commission at Candia. Admiral Noel appointed Lieutenant Colonel Rowland Broughton Mainwaring of the Royal Welch Fusiliers as the President. He was joined by Commander William Henry Baker-Baker of HMS *Illustrious*, Major S.G. Allen of the Royal Army Medical Corps, Captain Joseph Henry Lachlan White of the First Battalion of the Northumberland Fusiliers, and Lieutenant E. Henslow of HMS *Revenge*. Noel also appointed a Judge Advocate to advise the Commission members on pure matters of law (such as procedure and rules of evidence) – Captain Capel Molyneux Brunker of the 2nd Battalion of the Lancashire Fusiliers.[172] Pritchard explains:

---

them by statute, than what are allowed in criminal prosecutions, for other offences. (emphasis in original)

[169] See Pritchard, 2003, p. 56, *supra* note 3, noting that deposition testimony of certain witnesses was collected.

[170] See UK Criminal Law Blog, "Crown Court Trial", setting out the steps in the procedure (http://ukcriminallawblog.com/crown-court-trial/).

[171] Pritchard, 2003, p. 45, see *supra* note 3. Given that "[local] lawyers would have been entirely unfamiliar with British military law", Pritchard suspects that defence counsel were selected from the ranks of fresh British troops who had arrived after the 6 September massacres. Although they would have had little or no legal training, they likely carried out their duties with great care, diligence and efficacy.

[172] *Ibid.*, pp. 43–44.

> In accordance with the practices of the time, these officers, like those on the preliminary Court of Inquiry, were selected for their fairness, steadiness and intellect. None of them were lawyers by training but all of them would have had a great deal of experience in the application of military law in courts martial, matters generally dealt with by officers selected as men of good sense, few lawyers.[173]

It should be noted that, despite the lingering intercommunal tensions on the island in the wake of the mass violence, no witness protection measures were put in place for the trials.[174] As a result, "there were difficulties in getting witnesses to come forward [and] many remained silent out of a well-justified fear of the consequences they would suffer if they gave evidence".[175] A portion of the International Military Commission testimony was presented by way of deposition and authorities often faced obstacles getting depositions from remote locations such as Athens, Piraeus, Syra and isolated villages in remote parts of Crete's interior.[176] Live witnesses, and all trial participants, were assisted by interpreters given that persons in the courtroom would have spoken English, Greek or Turkish.[177]

From 26 October to 5 November 1898 the International Military Commission at Candia conducted two separate trials. In total, 21 defendants were in the dock on war crimes and/or proto-crimes against humanity charges, which included the murder of the British Vice-Consul Calocherino.[178] In the end, the Commission sentenced five men to death and various others to terms of imprisonment (up to life). Three defendants were acquitted and a number of them were discharged before the conclusion of trial for lack of evidence.[179] The Council of Admirals confirmed the sentences immediately and all five of the death row prisoners were hanged on 7 November 1898.[180]

---

[173] *Ibid.*, p. 44.

[174] *Ibid.*, p. 55.

[175] *Ibid.*, p. 56

[176] *Ibid.*

[177] *Ibid.*, pp. 56–57.

[178] *Ibid.*, pp. 48–51. It would seem the second trial focused more specifically on the murder of the British Vice-Consul and his family. *Id.* p. 51, fn. 89.

[179] *Ibid.*, pp. 51–52.

[180] *Ibid.*, p. 51.

Two of the defendants tried at Candia, also two of the men sentenced to death, are particularly noteworthy. One was Edhem Pasha, the Provincial Governor of Candia, the highest-ranking official to be tried by the International Military Commissions. The other was Churchill Bey, head of the local Ottoman gendarmerie. Both were found to be implicated in the 6 September massacres and were duly executed, notwithstanding their high rank.[181] The principle of liability for government officials for violation of international law is generally thought to have originated at Nuremberg.[182] But the International Military Commission trials on Crete were clearly an important antecedent.

6.3.2.3.2. The International Military Commission at Canea

The European Powers operated a second International Military Commission at Canea. It consisted of the pre-existing Military Commission of International Police converted into an International Military Commission. Available archives do not provide much additional detail regarding this Commission – for example, the identities of its panel members or the prosecutors and defence attorneys who appeared before it are unknown. However, we do know that, given its Military Commission of International Police roots, this Commission's procedures were governed by the Italian Military Code.[183] Thus, unlike International Military Commission at Candia which, as explained above, appears to have used procedures similar to those in British Crown Courts, for example, a more adversarial procedure, the Canea Commission procedure would have been more akin to the inquisitorial Continental European model previously analysed in connection with the Franco-Siamese Mixed Court in the Phra Yot trial. It seems that the Canea Commission was used to try crimes against humanity cases only (as opposed to war crimes cases) – these would appear to implicate murder, arson, rape and theft.[184]

---

[181] *Ibid.*, pp. 59–60.

[182] See John W. Head, "Civilization and Law: A Dark Optimism Based on the Precedent of Unprecedented Crises", in *University of Kansas Law Review*, 2011, vol. 59, p. 1054: "They prosecuted Nazi War leaders at Nuremberg, to make them personally criminally liable for acts they carried out as government officials – the first time such a prosecution had ever even been conceived".

[183] Pritchard, 2003. pp. 12, 60, see *supra* note 3.

[184] *Ibid.*, p. 53: "In the end, 42 prisoners were taken to Canea for trial, all in relation to what today would classify as crimes against humanity".

And, consistent with the inquisitorial template, the Canea Commission's pre-trial screening included examination by a French *juge d'instruction*, Captain L. Berger of the French Marines.[185] In particular, after initial screening by the British Court of Inquiry, 60 of the cases were then sent on to Berger for further review.[186] Of these, 42 were transferred to Canea for trial. Another four defendants were transferred to Canea directly from the British Court of Inquiry.[187]

The Canea trials commenced on 19 November 1898 and were completed within three days. In the end, the International Military Commission sentenced 11 defendants to death (although, in light of efforts to mollify the Sublime Porte,[188] only two were actually executed – Haïder Imanaki and Arap Halil). The Commission also sentenced nine of the accused to life imprisonment.[189] Four were sentenced to terms of 15, 12, 10 and five years' hard labour, respectively. Two others were sentenced to two years' hard labour. Four more were sentenced to relatively short periods of imprisonment (that is, a simple loss of liberty without hard labour). Of those, one was sentenced to only a year in custody. Sixteen were acquitted and a number of those individuals were then banished from the island. The Commission found that, in two other cases, there was insufficient evidence to sustain a prosecution.[190]

6.3.3. The Trial of the Chinese after the Boxer Rebellion

It will be recalled that in the summer of 1900 violence erupted across China as the Boxers slaughtered foreigners in an effort to remove all traces of non-Chinese influence. In the countryside southwest of Beijing, at Pao Ting Fu, in the former Zhílì Province, 11 adult missionaries and four children, along with dozens of their Christian Chinese servants, were killed in horrific fashion. After the expatriate community in Beijing was rescued and order was restored there in August 1900, the Western powers had to decide about security and justice measures to be taken in the surrounding countryside, where Boxer crimes had also been committed.

---

[185] *Ibid.*
[186] *Ibid.*, p. 60.
[187] *Ibid.*
[188] *Ibid.*, p. 63
[189] *Ibid.*, p. 60.
[190] *Ibid.*

6.3.3.1. The Expeditionary Forces Sent to Pao Ting Fu

The Europeans opted to send two separate columns of soldiers from Britain, France, Germany and Italy to Pao Ting Fu as an expeditionary force. One would travel there from Beijing and the other from Tientsin (Tianjin), east of Pao Ting Fu and about the same distance away as Beijing (about 150 kilometres).[191] The decision to send the expeditionary force, as well as measures taken to muster, requisition and dispatch it, required approximately two months of planning. The idea was originally proposed in early September but was postponed for a variety of logistical reasons.[192] At first, it was thought to be a military necessity based on reports of Boxer legions still in force in the countryside and using Pao Ting Fu as a launching point for attacks.[193] But these reports were ultimately found to be unsubstantiated. The Chinese Court, which had fled Beijing and was in Shānxī Province had, by then, issued edicts ordering the people to suppress the Boxers and welcome the foreign troops. In fact, the Boxers were being rounded up by the Chinese authorities and punished.[194]

Nevertheless, there was at least one pressing security issue that required European intervention. A family of missionaries in Pao Ting Fu, the Greens, was allegedly being held hostage by (or, at least, were in the custody of) the *fanti*, the provincial treasurer and chief official in the city. The Green family had sent letters that made it out of Pao Ting Fu and reached Tientsin. The letters stated that the family was being mistreated and were in a wretched condition. They pleaded for help. The British commander in Tientsin had sent a message to the *fanti* warning him that if he did not treat the Greens properly he would be punished by death when the foreign troops arrived. Thus, although perhaps not, on its own, a justification for sending an entire expeditionary force, the Europeans were also interested in assuring the welfare of the Green family.[195] As it turned out, when the expeditionary force arrived, the Greens' condition had dete-

---

[191] Thomas F. Millard, "Punishment and Revenge in China", in *Scribner's Magazine*, 1901, no. 29, p. 190.

[192] *Ibid.*, p. 189.

[193] *Ibid.*, pp. 189–90.

[194] *Ibid.*, p. 190.

[195] *Ibid.*

riorated horribly. Within days after the foreigners reached Pao Ting Fu, the family's little girl had died and her father was on death's door.[196]

Apart from the harrowing situation of the Greens, the security situation had largely stabilised. So the expeditionary mission was then primarily reorientated toward justice objectives as the Europeans looked to investigate the June–July massacres and punish the responsible parties.[197] By the beginning of October, the expedition was ready to embark for Pao Ting Fu but the Germans had been late in arriving in China (having missed the crucial fighting in August) and requested that the parties delay again.[198] In the meantime, Russia, Japan and the United States declined to participate in the operation as they were reducing the number of their troops in China by that point.[199] So the two expeditionary forces – Tientsen and Beijing – consisted of soldiers from Germany, Italy, Britain and France.[200] After some additional delay, the forces, each division of which consisted of about 3,600 men, were finally ready to leave on 12 October 1900.

Much of the Tientsin division was still under the mistaken impression that Boxer forces were massing in the region and spoiling for a fight with any Europeans wishing to enter Pao Ting Fu.[201] As a result, that division's British and German commanders were formulating elaborate strategies for taking Pao Ting Fu.[202] Its French commanders were not as concerned and, while the others were busy planning, sent a battalion on a reconnaissance mission to the targeted city. When the British and Germans

---

[196] *Ibid.*, p. 192.

[197] *Ibid.*

[198] *Ibid.*, p. 190.

[199] "Pao-Ting-Fu Expedition: Australians Included", in *Sydney Morning Herald*, 13 October 1900, p. 9; Millard, 1901, p. 190, see *supra* note 191.

[200] The Italians were unwilling participants. They had no real connection to or interests in China. But owing to their membership in the Treaty of Triple Alliance concluded in 1882 between Italy, Germany and Austria-Hungary, they were bound to German policy. See Ignazio Dandolo, "A Modern Anabasis: The Official Diary of Colonel Garioni, the Commander of the Italian Contingent in China (1900–1901)", in *Bulletin de l'École française d'Extrême Orient*, 1991, vol. 78, pp. 317, 331, describing "how limited […] the Italian adhesion to the idea of an international expedition [was]".

[201] Millard, 1901, p. 190, see *supra* note 191. The division estimated, based on what it perceived as reliable information, that 80,000 Boxers, armed with rifles and artillery, blocked the way to Pao Ting Fu.

[202] *Ibid.*, pp. 190–91.

learned of this, they feared the French would arrive in the city before they could.[203] In exchange for vague French promises to reconnoitre around the city rather than enter it, the British and Germans gave the French General, Maurice Bailloud, command of the entire Tientsin division. The French entered the city anyway![204]

As it turned out, the main contingent of the Tientsin division encountered no resistance en route to Pao Ting Fu.[205] Nevertheless, the division was delayed by dust storms and did not reach Pao Ting Fu until 22 October. It was three days behind the Beijing division, which, in turn had arrived a week after the French battalion had occupied the city. The Beijing division, commanded by the British Lieutenant General, Sir Alfred Gaselee, had an easier time of it. It too left on 12 October but, farsightedly, had not reckoned on continued Boxer resistance. And the division's journey to Pao Ting Fu was not hindered by dust storms. So it arrived at its destination on 19 October and remained billeted outside the city walls for three days.[206]

As the combined expeditionary forces were approaching the Pao Ting Fu gates, the *fanti*, escorted by other Chinese officials, greeted them and assured them that the city would be open to them and they would meet no resistance.[207] He also told them they would be provided with food, shelter and gifts and implored them not to sack, pillage or burn the city.[208] Gaselee, who had assumed command of the combined Tientsin-

---

[203] *Ibid.*, p. 191.

[204] *Ibid.* See also "Marching to Pao Ting Fu: How the Allied Forces Made the Expedition", in *Los Angeles Herald*, 13 December 1900, p. 3, referring to French "bad faith" and noting that Bailloud and his troops had "broken the promise that they would await other commands" ('Marching to Pao Ting Fu'). But see Hutcheson, 1901, p. 462, see *supra* note 4, relating that the French soldiers had "taken possession of the gates but had not entered the city".

[205] Millard, 1901, p. 191, see *supra* note 191. At some point during the trek, however, it was reported that "a regiment of Bombay cavalry hacked to pieces a hundred or so supposed [unarmed] Boxers".

[206] *Ibid.*

[207] Hutcheson, 1901, p. 462, see *supra* note 4.

[208] *Ibid.* But see Marching to Pao Ting Fu, 1900, p. 3, *supra* note 204: "[Upon entering Pao Ting Fu,] Europeans going through the city were received with insolent and insulting remarks, and on several occasions were the objects of spitting, a favorite form of insult".

Beijing expeditionary force,[209] replied that "action would depend upon circumstances" and that he would deal only with the highest officials.[210]

Finally, on 22 October 1900 the newly arrived and combined Tientsin-Beijing expeditionary troops were ready to enter the city and take command.[211] A military chief of police was appointed and Pao Ting Fu was then divided into four sectors with each of the four occupying forces guarding a section of the city gate (and assuming control of security in the sector corresponding to the gate location) – the British in the north, the Italians in the south, the Germans in the east and the French in the west.[212] The Germans, French and Italians quartered their men in their respective districts but the British troops remained in camp outside the city walls and assigned a skeleton force to provide the necessary police protection for its sector inside the city.[213]

6.3.3.2. Establishment and Operation of the International Tribunal

Even before these measures had been taken, while the Europeans were still gathered before the city gates, they put in place arrangements to investigate and prosecute perpetrators of the June–July massacre of the missionaries and their Chinese Christian servants. Given that the missionaries were American, it is curious that the United States refused to join the Europeans on this expedition. Nevertheless, an American officer, Captain Grote Hutcheson of the Sixth Cavalry, had been detailed to the expeditionary forces to observe and provide an American perspective. On 20 October, while the Beijing division was billeted before the gates of Pao Ting Fu and awaiting the arrival of the Tientsin division, Gaselee approached Hutcheson and asked him to opine on potential justice measures. Hutcheson suggested the European powers could establish a joint tribunal "to make an impartial examination into the conduct of the officials and any other accused persons".[214]

---

[209] "The Pao-Ting-Fu Expedition", in *Brisbane Courier*, 18 October 1900, p. 5: "Later information states that General Gaselee will take supreme command of the joint allied expedition after the junction of the two forces".

[210] Hutcheson, 1901, p. 462, see *supra* note 4.

[211] Millard, 1901, p. 192, see *supra* note 191.

[212] *Ibid.* Hutcheson, 1901, p. 463, see *supra* note 4.

[213] Hutcheson, 1901, p. 463, see *supra* note 4.

[214] *Ibid.*

The suggestion was adopted and the following day the European powers created an international Tribunal to adjudicate the guilt or innocence of those implicated in the massacre of the missionaries and their servants.[215] After a preliminary investigation was conducted, five of the top-level leaders were identified as potentially guilty: 1) Ting Yung, the *fanti* (and provincial judge at the time of the massacres); 2) Kuei Heng, the chief Tartar official of the city; 3) Wang Chang-kuei, a Lieutenant Colonel of the Chinese army who was suspected of having stood by with his troops while the massacres were taking place; 4) Shen Chia-pen, the provincial judge at the time of the trial; and 5) T'an Wen-huan, the regional *tao-tai* (an official at the head of the civil and military affairs of a circuit in Imperial China).[216]

Since the trials were held in closed session, and in light of a corresponding paucity of retrospective accounts, details about the specific functioning and character of the Tribunal are not plentiful.[217] That said, certain important information is available. The Tribunal held its sessions in a building within the city and began hearing evidence on or about 22 October.[218] It consisted of five judges, who represented each of the nationalities in the expeditionary force: 1) Bailloud of the French army; 2)

---

[215] *Ibid.* Several sources refer to the adjudicative body as an "international tribunal" or "international military tribunal". See, for example, Arthur Lorriot, *De la nature de l'occupation de guerre*, H. Charles-Lavauzelle, Paris, 1903, p. 341: "*À Pao-ting-Fu, un tribunal international composé de Français, d'Allemands, et d'Anglais fut organisé* (emphasis added); Mechthild Leutner and Klaus Muhlhahn, *Kolonialkrieg in China: Die Niederschlagung der Boxerbewegung 1900–1901*, Ch. Links Verlag, Berlin, 2007, p. 124: "*Ein* internationals Tribunal *erhielt den Auftrag, zu klären, unter welchen Umständen die Missionare gestorben waren*" (emphasis added); Robin, 1942, p. 202, see *supra* note 85: "In Pao-tingfu, on the other hand, an *international tribunal* composed of Frenchmen, Germans and Englishmen was established" (emphasis added). It has also variously been referred to as an "international commission" and "international court of inquiry". See, for example, Hutcheson, 1901, p. 463, see *supra* note 4: "The next day, October 21, an *international commission* was instituted" (emphasis added); Marching to Pao Ting Fu, see *supra* note 204, noting that an "*international court of inquiry* was instituted" (emphasis added). It is referred to as an "international Tribunal" herein.

[216] Report of William W. Rockhill, Late Commissioner to China, with Accompanying Documents, Telegram from Edwin H. Conger, US Ambassador to China, to John Hay, US Secretary of State, 16 November 1900 47 (1901).

[217] Marching to Pao Ting Fu, 1900, see *supra* note 204: "The court sat behind closed doors and no correspondents were allowed to be present or even to be in the vicinity of the building in which the tribunal sat".

[218] *Ibid.*

Colonel D.G. Ramsey of the British (Indian) army; 3) Lieutenant Colonel Salsa of the Italian army; 4) Major von Brixen of the German army; and 5) J.W. Jamison, a civilian, who had been serving as the British consul in Shanghai.[219] Jamison had accompanied the expeditionary force from Beijing. He spoke fluent Chinese and was reputed to be well acquainted with the "customs and character of the Chinese people".[220]

The Tribunal chose Bailloud as its President.[221] Given that the majority of judges on the panel came from Continental European countries, and in light of Bailloud's own Gallic origins as well as his designation as President (akin to the position on the Franco-Siamese Mixed Court), it would be reasonable to assume the Tribunal operated more in line with the inquisitorial model. In other words, Bailloud would have likely exercised strong control with respect to the order and questioning of witnesses. The archives available do not indicate whether a specific prosecutor was appointed or whether the defendants were represented by counsel (even if such counsel was not legally trained). Interpreters were in the courtroom to offer their services.[222]

Based on available sources, we can piece together the trial's essential stages. It began with testimony establishing the specific sequence of events surrounding the June-July slaughter of the missionaries and their Chinese Christian servants. The Presbyterian missionaries, the Simcoxes and their three children, as well as Dr. and Mrs. Hodge, and Dr. George Y. Taylor, lived in a compound located in the village of Changchia-chuang, approximately one mile north of the Pao Ting Fu city gate.[223] On

---

[219] Hutcheson, 1901, p. 463, see *supra* note 4. The available literature is not consistent with respect to the members of the Tribunal. A contemporary Italian chronicler, Mario Valli, identified different judges representing the British and Italians. He listed the British judge as one Captain Poole. As for the Italian judge, he described there being more than one. Italy was initially represented on the bench by a Major Agliardi. He was then replaced by a Captain Ferigo. And then, according to Valli, a Lieutenant Sambuy took the place of Ferigo. Mario Valli, *Gli Avenimenti in Cina nel 1900: e l'azione della R. Marina Italiana*, Urico Hoepli, Milan, 1905, p. 632. With respect to most of these judges, who would not appear to have had any legal training or background, their forenames are lost to history.

[220] Hutcheson, 1901, p. 463, see *supra* note 4.

[221] Lorriot, 1903, p. 341, see *supra* note 215.

[222] See Shirley Ann Smith, *Imperial Designs: Italians in China, 1099–1947*, Fairleigh Dickinson University Press, Plymouth, 2012, p. 40, indicating that interpreters were translating the words of the judges for the defendants and vice versa.

[223] Hutcheson, 1901, p. 463, see *supra* note 4.

---

30 June 1900, between 16:00 and 17:00, a violent mob, led by a local Boxer leader and reputed thug, Chu Tu Tze, surrounded the compound and began attacking it. All of the residents took refuge in one building and tried to defend themselves. All the buildings in the compound were burned but the missionaries put up a valiant defence, wounding 10 Boxers and killing Chu Tu Tze in the process.[224] But the missionaries eventually succumbed. As described by the American observer Hutcheson:

> Dr. Taylor addressed the crowd from one of the upper windows in a vain effort to induce it to disperse, but without avail, and the Boxers being without firearms, could not dislodge and secure possession of their victims. Finally, a successful effort was made to set fire to the building. Soon after the two young sons of Mr. Simcox, Paul and Francis, aged, respectively, about 5 and 7 years, rushed from the building into the open air to escape suffocation from the dense clouds of smoke. They were immediately set upon by the crowd, cut down, and their bodies thrown into the cistern. The other inmates of the house perished in the flames. The Chinese Christians and servants, to the number of perhaps twenty […] also perished.[225]

It was further established that the other American Board missionaries, Revd. Mr. Pitkin, Miss Morrell and Miss Gould, lived in a compound to the south of the city. Residing by them in another compound were the English missionaries, Mr. and Mrs. Bagnall of the China Inland Missionary of England, and their one child, as well as Mr. William Cooper. At approximately 07:00 on 1 July 1900 a group of Boxers, accompanied by a throng of bloodthirsty villagers, attacked the American Board compound. As before, all of the occupants of the compound gathered in one building, which was defended by Pitkin using a revolver. When he ran out of ammunition, the crowd poured into the house, seized the occupants and dragged them out. While a group of about 30 Chinese soldiers looked on, Pitkin was shot, beheaded and thrown in a pit with 10 Chinese Christians and servants who had also been murdered. Miss Morrell and Miss Gould had to endure another few hours of terror. The former fainted and was bound hand and foot and slung on a pole and taken to the city "as pigs are

---

[224] *Ibid.*

[225] *Ibid.*, p. 464.

carried in China".[226] Miss Gould was dragged into the city by her hair. Along the way, angry Chinese ripped and tore at the clothing of the two unfortunate women. They were brought to the Chi-Sheng-An Temple, and were soon joined there by the Bagnall/Cooper party. All of them were then maliciously interrogated by the Boxers to coerce admissions of "guilt".[227] Hutcheson then describes what followed:

> Late in the afternoon, about 6 o'clock, perhaps, the entire party was conducted out of the city. [...] The following method was adopted: The hands were bound and held in front of the body, the wrists about the height of the neck; a rope was then tied about the wrists of the next person behind, thence about the neck, and so on. The child was not bound, but ran along clinging to his mother's dress. The end of the rope in front was seized by two men, and the doomed party, thus led in single file, all bound together like Chinese criminals, viewed by an immense throng of the populace, were led through the streets, passing out by the south gate to the place of execution at the southeast corner of the wall, between the moat and the wall. Here all were executed by being beheaded, except the child, which was speared by a Boxer.[228]

After ascertaining the details regarding the fate of the missionaries, the Tribunal then evaluated the individual guilt of the defendants. The historical record sheds the most light on the case of Ting Yung, the *fanti*. The Tribunal lodged the following specific charges against him:

1. He allowed to be posted in Pao Ting Fu, with his seal affixed to it, an Imperial proclamation encouraging the insurrectionary movement of the Boxers;

2. He castigated and dismissed other local officials who fought the Boxers and protected the Christians;

3. He failed, as requested by the British commander in Tientsin, to protect the Rev. Green and his family;

4. He failed to protect Rev. Bagnall and his family, notwithstanding his being specifically aware of the peril the

---

[226] *Ibid.*
[227] *Ibid.*
[228] *Ibid.*

Bagnall party faced and thus he was indirectly responsible for their murders.[229]

Testimony at trial also determined that the day before the attack on the Simcox compound, Ting Yung had presented to Chu Tu Tze, the city Boxer leader and local ruffian, a gilt button. The button was worn by Chu Tu Tze during the Simcox attack. It was "in the nature of a decoration or badge of distinction, and was presented [as indicating appreciation] of the man's zeal and energy in the Boxer movement [and showing] a certain official sanction to the proceedings of that day and the following".[230]

Ting Yung testified on his own behalf and, at first, did not deny the allegations but did not confess either.[231] He answered questions evasively, claiming ignorance as to some of the allegations against him and asserting the defence of superior orders for others. Unfortunately for Ting Yung, the Tribunal was able to produce a telegram, which he had sent directly to the Court in Beijing. In it Ting Yung complained of "not having enough troops to wipe out the Christians" and recommended killing them because the Europeans would not be coming to their aid.[232] That sealed his fate.

An Italian observer of the trial, Luigi Barzini, provided a vivid description of the courtroom during Ting Yung's ordeal after being confronted with the incriminating telegram:

> The military tribunal interrogates the Fang-tai, a sort of city mayor, who is accused of having sustained the anti-European Boxers. Barzini describes in detail this stout little irascible man loudly declaiming his innocence. In a last-ditch effort to convince the "foreign devils" of his innocence, he grabs the table leg behind which the Western judges are seated in order not to be dragged out of the session when his questioning is over.[233]

The Tribunal also considered the case of Wang Chang-kuei, the Chinese army Lieutenant Colonel. Evidence presented at trial linked him directly to the murders of the Bagnall party. In his defence, he testified

---

[229] Valli, 1905, p. 632, see *supra* note 219.

[230] Hutcheson, 1901, p. 464, see *supra* note 4.

[231] Valli, 1905, p. 632, see *supra* note 219.

[232] *Ibid.*

[233] Smith, 2012, p. 40, see *supra* note 222. Barzini was a journalist so it is not clear whether an exception to the closed-door courtroom policy was made for him or whether he was given this account secondhand by a person or persons who were present.

that, to the contrary, he provided security for these missionaries and transported them to Pao Ting Fu under armed guard.[234] Once in the city, he claimed he transferred them to the care of other Chinese soldiers, who handed the victims over to the Boxers. It was the Boxers who then massacred them near the east gate of the city.[235] Wang Chang-kuei testified that he then witnessed the victims' violent deaths at the hands of the Boxers.[236]

The case against Kuei Heng, the Tartar official (or governor), was much more straightforward. The evidence brought forth before the Tribunal revealed he had clearly approved of the Boxers' agenda, throwing his full support behind them both before and during the attacks on the missionaries and their families.[237]

The evidence regarding T'an Wen-huan, the regional *tao-tai*, centred on his allegedly sending money and arms from Tientsin to the Boxers in Pao Ting Fu.[238] There was apparently no direct evidence implicating him in Pao Ting Fu crimes connected to the missionary massacres. Such evidence was similarly weak in respect of Shen Chia-pen, the provincial judge at the time of the trial but who had been prefect of the city at the time of the murders.[239]

Interestingly, the Tribunal also heard evidence against five alleged Boxers. But it found that these were commonplace criminals who had been taken from local prisons to be offered as sacrificial lambs to help quell European anger regarding the missionary deaths and deflect blame from higher Chinese officials.[240] The Tribunal saw through this ruse and

---

[234] Valli, 1905, p. 633, see *supra* note 219.

[235] G.H.W. O'Sullivan, "Report on the Paotingfu Expedition and Murder of American Missionaries at that Place", in *Annual Reports of the War Department for the Fiscal Year Ended June 30, 1901*, 25 October 1900, p. 466. O'Sullivan was a Lieutenant Colonel and Staff Officer with the US Army who, like Hutcheson, was embedded as an observer with the Pao Ting Fu expeditionary forces.

[236] Valli, 1905, p. 633, see *supra* note 219. But the record does not disclose why he did not intervene to help save them at that point.

[237] *Ibid.*

[238] O'Sullivan, 1900, p. 466, see *supra* note 235.

[239] *Ibid.*

[240] Valli, 1905, p. 633, see *supra* note 219, noting that this was a customary manner of obstructing justice used by local Chinese officials:

> The Chinese authorities always have on hand a few miserable citizens to sacrifice to angry Europeans, when they cannot find, or are trying to

remanded the suspects to local custody for further proceedings, if necessary. It also imposed a 10,000 taels fine on the parties responsible for bringing these individuals as suspects before the Tribunal.[241]

6.3.3.3. The Verdicts and Sentences

In the end, after sitting in session daily until 27 October, the Tribunal convicted Ting Yung, Wang Chang-kuei, Kuei Heng and Shen Chia-pen and sentenced them to death.[242] But, given the comparatively weaker case against Shen Chia-pen, the Tribunal punished him by recommending that he be removed from office, stripped of his rank, and held in military custody until a successor (as provincial judge) could be appointed and assume duties in the city. T'an Wen-huan was ordered to be transferred to Tientsin for trial there regarding his Boxer financing activities.[243]

In addition, as collective punishment for the massacres, the Tribunal recommended that: 1) the gates of the city be destroyed; 2) all pagodas and other buildings on the walls be burnt; and 3) the southeast corner of the city wall be demolished. Similarly, and apart from the Tribunal's order, on 27 October, in accordance with orders from Gaselee, two prominent temples were blown up – Cheng-Huang-Miao (the temple of tutelary divinity and considered the most important in the city and its loss being viewed as a disaster for city residents) and Chi-Sheng-An (where the Bagnall party members were held and interrogated prior to their murder).[244]

The executions were also carried out that day. Replete with gallows humour, Barzini describes the last moments of Kuei Heng, as he was being led to the execution site:

---

shield from culpability, the real culprits. So, after the massacres of Tien-tsin, they executed a dozen criminals who had already been sentenced to death, and with the promise of a gift to their families, and of a beautiful coffin. That would have probably allowed the real perpetrators of massacres enough time to leave the jurisdiction and escape justice. The real killers, or at least many of them [...] escaped the justice of the Europeans.

[241] *Ibid.*

[242] O'Sullivan, 1900, p. 466, see *supra* note 235.

[243] *Ibid.*

[244] *Ibid.*

Another view of local humanity is the depiction of the governor, who has already been condemned to death by beheading. He is an old, completely deaf sixty-year-old man, who can only hear what is being said to him when his servant screams the words into his ear in a high-pitched voice. The scene, even though the executioner is not far away, takes on the slapstick quality of a comedy of errors. The judges ask a question; the interpreters translate it for the servant, who in a shrill voice screams it in the ear of the old governor:

Perchè – gli domandavano – avete concesso delle località nella vostra casa ai boxers per le loro riunioni?

Mi figlio – rispondeva – è a Pechino da sei mesi.

[Why – they asked him – did you allow the Boxers to use some rooms in your house for meetings?

My son – he answered – has been in Beijing for six months].[245]

Barzini then depicts the actual moment of the executions.

The staging of the executions [...] was not at all a gloomy sight. The colorful troops were lined up in their respective formations. The French light infantry with their excessive red pantaloons stood next to the German infantry in their gray overcoats and helmets topped with shiny metal spikes. The Indian cavalry and Italian sailors drew a straight punctuation mark, a sort of hyphen, as they stood in a row in between those old national and political European adversaries. [...] Nothing gloomy about the look of things [...] until the actual beheadings begin. But even these are treated humanely. [...] The executioner is not cruel, cold-blooded, and evil; he is someone who probably has been bribed by the *yang quitze* (European devils) to chop off the heads of his superiors.[246]

---

[245] Smith, 2012, p. 40, see *supra* note 222.

[246] *Ibid.*

6.4. The Trials in Perspective: The Dawn of the European Peace Movement and the Twilight of European Imperialism

This chapter has so far chronicled three international criminal trials in one remarkable decade at the end of the nineteenth century. With the exception of the Hagenbach trial centuries earlier, the world had never seen anything like it. And for another half century it would see nothing like it again. Why did these trials all take place at that time and in that part of the world? Was it merely a coincidence? The historical context suggests it was not. Two overarching historical phenomena in particular played important roles in terms of bringing about these trials in the East: the dawn of the European peace movement and the twilight of imperialism.

6.4.1. The Dawn of the European Peace Movement

Reference in this chapter to the dawn of the European peace movement is rather broad. It is intended to encompass different strands of social activism in the second half of the nineteenth century that sought to curb the incidence of war and lessen its horrors. The genesis of the movement might be said to be the 1864 Geneva Convention.[247] The fruit of the labours of the International Committee of the Red Cross ('ICRC') founder Henri Dunant, a Swiss businessman who had stumbled upon the battlefield suffering of wounded but untended soldiers in the immediate aftermath of the Battle of Solferino in 1859. This event changed Dunant's life and he dedicated it to making war more humane by protecting those *hors de combat*, in other words, fallen soldiers or those otherwise no longer able to engage in the fight.[248] He founded the ICRC in 1863 and, the following year, organised the conference that adopted the first Geneva Convention, which established protections for wounded and sick soldiers.[249]

---

[247] Convention for the Amelioration of the Condition of the Wounded in Armies in the Field, Geneva, 22 August 1864, Art. 6 (https://www.legal-tools.org/doc/59e0f5/; see also Dietrich Schindler and Jiří Toman (eds.), *The Laws of Armed Conflicts*, Martinus Nijhoff, Dordrecht, 1988, pp. 279–83).

[248] Tom Ruys and Christian De Cock, "Protected Persons in International Armed Conflicts", in Christian Henderson and Nigel D. White (eds.), *Research Handbook on International Conflict and Security Law: Jus ad Bellum, Jus in Bello and Jus post Bellum*, Edward Elgar, Cheltenham, 2013, p. 375.

[249] *Ibid.*: "This Convention became the first [international codified] instrument [...] of the law of armed conflict".

Following on this, in November 1868 Tsar Alexander II convened an International Military Commission in Saint Petersburg that drafted a declaration affirming that the only legitimate object of war should be to weaken the military force of the enemy.[250] As a result, the European signatories to the Saint Petersburg Declaration of 1868 agreed to prohibit certain kinds of projectiles and ammunition that caused excessive suffering.[251] Six years later, the Tsar again convened a group of European states to draft the Brussels Declaration of 1874,[252] memorialising and supporting certain fundamental customs and laws of war.[253]

All this set the stage for the Hague Peace Conference of 1899. Once again convened by a Russian Tsar, this time Nicholas II, its object was to seek "the most effective means of ensuring to all peoples the benefits of a real and lasting peace, and, above all, of limiting the progressive development of existing armaments".[254] Twenty-six nations were represented at the Conference, which was held in the seat of the Dutch government from

---

[250] Gary D. Solis, *The Law of Armed Conflict: International Humanitarian Law in War*, Cambridge University Press, Cambridge, 2010, pp. 49–50.

[251] Declaration Renouncing the Use, in Time of War, of Explosive Projectiles Under 400 Grammes Weight, Saint Petersburg, 29 November 1868, reprinted in Schindler and Toman, 1988, pp. 101–3, see *supra* note 247. The preamble declaims:

Considering:

That the progress of civilization should have the effect of alleviating as much as possible the calamities of war;

That the only legitimate object which States should endeavor to accomplish during war is to weaken the military forces of the enemy;

That for this purpose it is sufficient to disable the greatest possible number of men;

That this object would be exceeded by the employment of arms which uselessly aggravate the sufferings of disabled men, or render their death inevitable;

That the employment of such arms would, therefore, be contrary to the laws of humanity [...]

[252] Brussels Conference of 1874, I. Final Protocol, II. Project of an International Declaration concerning the Laws and Customs of War, 27 August 1874, reprinted in in Schindler and Toman, 1988, pp. 25–34, see *supra* note 247.

[253] Megan Eshbaugh, Note, "The Chemical Weapons Convention: With Every Step Forward, We Take Two Steps Back", in *Arizona Journal of International and Comparative Law*, 2001, vol. 18, pp. 209, 216.

[254] "Russian Note Proposing the Program of the First Conference", in James Brown Scott (ed.), *The Hague Conventions and Declarations of 1899 and 1907*, Oxford University press, New York, 1915, p. xvi.

May through June 1899. Although it failed to achieve its main objective, for example, the limitation or reduction of armaments, it adopted three Conventions and an equal number of Declarations, which, overall, generally codified and expanded on the principles set forth in the Saint Petersburg and Brussels Declarations (and adapted them to maritime warfare).[255] One of the treaties had a different focus, however. The Convention for the Pacific Settlement of International Disputes ('Pacific Settlement Convention') created the Permanent Court of Arbitration and marked a normative shift in international relations by aspiring to settle state differences not through war but through adjudication by judges and on the basis of respect for the law.[256] It also stipulated that "in questions of a legal nature [...] arbitration is recognized by the Signatory Powers as the most effective, and at the same time the most equitable, means of settling disputes which diplomacy has failed to settle".[257]

Thanks, in part, to the Pacific Settlement Convention "the idea of resorting to international arbitration as a substitute for war was not new at the turn of the century".[258] And it was part and parcel of the European peace movement of the second half of the nineteenth century. Organised European efforts to *outlaw* war, like efforts to codify regulating it, date

---

[255] Alexander Mikaberidze, "Hague Conference, First", in Alexander Mikaberidze (ed.), *Atrocities, Massacres, and War Crimes: An Encyclopedia*, ABC-Clio, Santa Barbara, CA, 2013, p. 226.

[256] Convention for the Pacific Settlement of International Disputes, The Hague, 29 July 1899, Art. 15 (https://www.legal-tools.org/doc/b1e51f/), in *Statutes at Large*, vol. 32, pp. 1779, 1788–98, and Clive Parry (ed.), *The Consolidated Treaty Series*, vol. 187: *1898–99*, Oceana Publications, Dobbs Ferry, NY, 1980, pp. 410, 416–22 ('Pacific Settlement Convention'): "International arbitration has for its object the settlement of differences between States by judges of their own choice, and on the basis of a respect for law". Another Hague Conference in 1907 updated, revised and expanded the 1899 Conventions but the 1907 Conventions deal with the same subject matter and include a substantially similar Convention on the Pacific Settlement of International Disputes. Howard M. Hensel (ed.), *The Law of Armed Conflict: Constraints on the Contemporary Use of Military Force*, Ashgate, Aldershot, England, 2007, p. 47.

[257] Pacific Settlement Convention, Art. 16, see *supra* note 256.

[258] Christopher R. Rossi, "*Jus Ad Bellum* in the Shadow of the 20th Century", in *New York Law School Journal of International and Comparative Law*, 1994, vol. 15, pp. 49, 58. Of course, in line consistent with the dawn of the European peace movement, arbitrations to settle international disputes had been used with increasing frequency during the second half of the nineteenth century. Notable instances include the Jay Treaty Arbitrations (1794), the Alabama Arbitration (1871–1872), the Behring Sea Fisheries dispute (1893), and the British Guiana Boundary Arbitration (1897). Rossi, *id.*, pp. 58–59.

only from the middle of the nineteenth century.[259] The first "international" peace conference, which consisted of only European and American participants, was held in London in 1843.[260] It concluded with the adoption of two declarations, one favouring use of arbitration to settle international disputes and the other supporting the establishment of a congress of nations.[261]

After similar conferences in succeeding years, the peace movement "expanded significantly in the late nineteenth century".[262] By 1889, in conjunction with the *Exposition Universelle* and the opening of the Eiffel Tower, peace groups from around the globe gathered in Paris for what is considered the first "universal" peace congress. Subsequent congresses were held in each succeeding year leading up to the First World War.[263] At the third one, held in Rome, the participants agreed to set up a permanent headquarters in Bern, which began operations in 1892 as the International Peace Bureau.[264]

The following year, the Austrian peace activist Bertha von Suttner visited with her wealthy Swedish inventor friend, Alfred Nobel, and suggested he could bequeath part of his post-mortem wealth to honour advocates for peace.[265] Nobel apparently thought of von Suttner when he drafted his will, which, as revealed on his death in 1896, set aside money for a prize that would be given "to the person who shall have done the most or the best work for the fraternity between nations, for the abolition or reduction of standing armies, and for the holding of peace congresses".[266] This

---

[259] Chernow and Vallasi, 1993, p. 2091, see *supra* note 8.

[260] David Cortright, *Peace: A History of Movements and Ideas*, Cambridge University Press, Cambridge, 2008, p. 34.

[261] In subsequent conferences over the next couple of decades, final resolutions also included calls for disarmament. *Ibid.*, pp. 34–35.

[262] *Ibid.*, p. 38.

[263] *Ibid.*

[264] *Ibid.* The International Peace Bureau is still in operation today. Its website is located at http://www.ipb.org/web/.

[265] Michelle Benjamin and Maggie Mooney, *Nobel's Women of Peace*, Second Story Press, Toronto, 2008, p. 13: "In 1893, during Arthur and Bertha's final visit with Alfred, the three of them discussed how Alfred could guarantee that his money would continue to do good after his death". Nobel earned much of his fortune from having invented dynamite, blasting caps, smokeless gunpowder and blasting gelatin. Donovan Webster, *Aftermath: The Remnants of War*, Pantheon Books, New York, 1996, pp. 3–6.

[266] Benjamin and Mooney, 2008, p. 14, see *supra* note 265. Von Suttner herself won the award in 1905.

---

was the birth of the Nobel Peace Prize.[267] It was followed three years later by the first Hague Conference, the culmination of a decade's peace movement that stressed "the urging of international arbitration and mediation in disputes between nations".[268] Roger Alford explains the consequences of this:

> The great push for international arbitration had two major consequences. First, it drew together like-minded parliamentarians from different countries to work together to promote peaceful settlement of disputes. This led to the establishment of the Inter-Parliamentary Union, which in turn influenced the convening of the Hague Peace Conferences of 1899 and 1906. Second, the impetus for international arbitration was transformed quickly into a vision of a permanent international judiciary, starting with the Permanent Court of Arbitration and eventually extending to the Permanent Court of International Justice and the International Court of Justice.[269]

This push towards settling disputes via arbitration, and, by extension, through court proceedings, was thus a prominent feature of the decade in which the three sets of trials featured in this chapter took place.

6.4.2. Asia in the Twilight of Imperialism

However, as mentioned previously, imperialism was also a distinguishing characteristic of that decade. In fact, it was implicitly antithetical to the peace movement. Candice Goucher and Linda Walton point out that late nineteenth-century competition related to overseas colonial possessions "fueled tensions that on several occasions nearly led to war between France, Great Britain and Germany".[270] This was especially true in Asia. With respect to Africa, as noted earlier, the European colonial powers met

---

[267] The first awards were conferred in 1901 and given to Henri Dunant and Frédéric Passy. John Stevenson, *The Nobel Prize: Facts You Never Knew About*, John Stevenson, n.p., 2013, pp. 24–25. Roger Alford refers to the early recipients of the Nobel Peace Prize as "parliamentary pacifists" and describes them as most notable for, among other things, "effectively promoting international arbitration". Roger P. Alford, "The Nobel Effect: Nobel Peace Prize Laureates as International Norm Entrepreneurs", in *Virginia Journal of International Law*, 2008, vol. 49, pp. 61, 72.

[268] Chernow and Vallasi, 1993, p. 2091, see *supra* note 8.

[269] Alford, 2008, p. 72, see *supra* note 267.

[270] Candice Goucher and Linda Walton, *World History: Journeys from Past to Present*, Routledge, Abingdon, 2013, p. 295.

at the conference table in Germany and methodically carved out mutually agreeable imperial boundaries pursuant to the 1884–85 Berlin Conference.[271] Colonial Asia was different – it did not have the equivalent of a Berlin Conference. And so imperial rivalries on this far-flung land mass led to even greater tensions than in Africa. As Richard Pomfret observes:

> The concept of Asia […] as a region is relatively modern. In various historical epochs, Chinese cultural influence has been widespread in East Asia and Indian culture has influenced much of Southeast Asia, but none of this was seen as integrating "Asia." Following the Portuguese voyages of discovery from Europe in the 1500s and the establishment of Manila in 1571 as the Asian capital of Spain's New World colonies, European powers […] built up empires in Asia. Although the outside trading nations sometimes collaborated or acquiesced, *these were competing rather than unifying.*[272]

6.4.3. Pacifism, Imperialism and the Oriental Pre-Birth Trials

6.4.3.1. The Franco-Siamese Trial

So what is the relationship between the nascent peace movement and this cresting wave of imperialism in the Orient? The three sets of trials examined in this chapter help explain. Imperialism is the clear subtext of the Franco-Siamese proceeding. The ill-defined border between French Indochina and British Burma led to the 1893 skirmish between the French and Siamese and, ultimately, Grosgurin's homicide.[273] France was outraged by the role Phra Yot played in Grosgurin's demise and, notwithstanding its public stance that its conflict with Siam did not constitute "war", seemingly saw shades of a war crime in the homicide.[274] Tensions between the

---

[271] Gregory H. Maddox, *Sub-Saharan Africa: An Environmental History*, ABC-CLIO, Santa Barbara, CA, 2006, p. 121: "In 1884-1885, the Berlin Conference met to ensure an orderly division of Africa among the European powers".

[272] Richard Pomfret, Regionalism in East Asia: Why Has It Flourished Since 2000 and How Far Will It Go?, World Scientific, Singapore, 2011, p. 8 (emphasis added).

[273] See St. John, 1998, p. 12, see *supra* note 89: "Siam concluded a treaty in October 1893 which was dictated by France *but qualified to some degree by French recognition of the need to take British interests into account*" (emphasis added).

[274] See Brockman-Hawe, 2013, p. 70, *supra* note 2, granting that France and Siam never acknowledged that they were in a state of war but opining that "the conflict between France and Siam falls squarely within the modern conception of war, and crimes of the

two imperial powers flared and, through the British proxy, Siam, "brought Great Britain and France [to] the verge of war".[275]

But in this context, as part of the border settlement, rather than summarily placing Phra Yot before a firing squad, the French channelled the *fin de siècle* judicial settlement *Zeitgeist* and created what Benjamin Brockman-Hawe refers to as "the first modern supranational criminal tribunal".[276] In supporting this conclusion, Brockman-Hawe alludes to "the *ad hoc* nature of the Rules and their appearance in a legal instrument agreed to by two states, the presence of judges from two states on the tribunal, and Siam's agreement (however coerced) to 'mix' its jurisdiction with that of France".[277]

Interestingly, if not symbolically, on the final day of Phra Yot's first trial, when the verdict was announced and the judgment read, present in the courtroom were representatives of various European nations, including France, Britain, Portugal, the Netherlands and Austria-Hungary.[278] Was this Europe's way of assuring that an imperial dispute between two of its states (via a proxy) was resolved amicably? Was this akin to a small segment of a fragmented Berlin Conference for Asia but in a judicial forum? Posing such questions reminds us of what Brockman-Hawe refers to as the "motifs of imperialism" that run through the Phra Yot adjudicative proceedings.[279] At the same time, in light of the contemporaneous peace movement and its attendant push for arbitration to replace war, one appreciates Brockman-Hawe's wondering whether the 1893 trials in Bangkok may have been "inspired by the proliferation of neutral inter-state arbitral tribunals".[280]

6.4.3.2. The Trials of the Ottomans

The trials of the Ottomans on Crete bear similar indicia of this odd mix of imperialist and judicial-irenic leitmotifs. Significantly, determining con-

---

sort Phra Yot was accused of perpetrating are specifically prohibited by contemporary *jus in bello*".

[275] MacGregor, 1896, p. 96, see *supra* note 101.

[276] Brockman-Hawe, 2013, p. 71, see *supra* note 2.

[277] *Ibid.*

[278] Full Report, p. 55, see *supra* note 94.

[279] Brockman-Hawe, 2013, p. 71, see *supra* note 2.

[280] *Ibid.*, p. 69.

trol of Crete was considered an integral part of resolving what was referred to as the Eastern Question. John P. Dunn explains the significance of this historical phenomenon:

> Does the Ottoman Empire have a future? This was the "Eastern Question," an important issue in nineteenth-century diplomatic affairs. As no single answer evolved, great powers sometimes went to war – or became allies – in efforts to present their opinions on the matter. [...] Defeat brought a final answer to the Eastern Question, as the Ottoman Empire was dismembered.[281]

In his analysis of the Eastern Question, Kahraman Sakul perceives the Great Powers attempting to create their own zones of influence in the Turkish realm through the pretext of protecting Christians. He observes:

> [The Great Powers claimed] the status of protector of a particular Christian subject people and [urged] the Sublime Porte to undertake political reforms. The Ottomans, however, viewed all attempts to advance the rights of particular Christian subject peoples through such diplomatic pressures as an encroachment on the rights of their sovereignty. They viewed European intervention in internal Ottoman affairs as a smokescreen that hid the Great Powers' ambitions to dismantle the empire.[282]

Sakul concludes that "simply put, the Eastern Question revolved around the question of how to eliminate the power vacuum in Eastern Europe, the Balkans, and the modern Middle East that emerged with the decline of the Ottoman Empire [...] without harming the delicate balance of power in Europe".[283] And that was essentially the question hovering in the background of the 1898 international criminal trials on Crete. The Ottomans were being removed as part of the next phase of European incursion into the crumbling empire. But Crete was a small island outpost in the Balkans. In the previous decades, various European powers had asserted interests in it. By the time of the massacre of Christians on 6 September 1898, the Europeans decided to put aside existing imperial conflicts else-

---

[281] John P. Dunn, "Eastern Question", in Melvin E. Page (ed.), *Colonialism: An International Social, Cultural, and Political Encyclopedia*, ABC-CLIO, Santa Barbara, CA, 2003, p. 180.

[282] Kahraman Sakul, "Eastern Question", in Gábor Ágoston and Bruce Alan Masters (eds.), *Encyclopedia of the Ottoman Empire*, Facts on File, New York, 2008, p. 191.

[283] *Ibid.*

where and act in harmony with respect to adjudications of the Ottomans. As noted by Pritchard:

> This was, furthermore, a period marked by Great Power rivalries and suspicions, with French forces engaged in enterprises that might conflict with the British adventures in the Sudan, and with problems elsewhere in the Levant that threatened to break out into open conflict among the British, Austro-Hungarians, Germans and Russians. Crete, therefore, provided an opportunity to show that a joint enterprise [...] could harmonize the European Concert.[284]

Once again, the international criminal trials on Crete arguably represented a judicial Berlin Conference-type settling of European differences on the frayed margins of a decaying Ottoman Empire. But it was also seemingly a by-product of the peace movement and constituted another late nineteenth-century expression of the preference for arbitral solutions to international relations problems among European powers. Additionally, the trials on Crete revealed that, in the dying days of the nineteenth century, the Europeans had developed an almost primal affinity for due process over drumhead justice. That instinct for justice was as farsighted as it was instinctive, since within its prescient remit was one of the future cornerstones of international criminal law offences – crimes against humanity. In the words of Beth Van Schaak:

> The 1907 Hague [Conventions] [which also included a revised Pacific Settlement Convention] [have their] roots in many respects in an International Military Commission staged on Crete in 1898 by the six Great Powers (Russia, France, Italy, Great Britain, Germany, and Austria). These trials exercised jurisdiction over acts, such as the massacre of Christian compatriots by Muslim Cretans that would later be termed "crimes against humanity".[285]

---

[284] Pritchard, 2003, p. 6, see *supra* note 3.

[285] Beth Van Schaak, "The Definition of Crimes against Humanity: Resolving the Incoherence", in *Columbia Journal of Transnational Law*, 1999, vol. 37, pp. 787, 796, fn. 28. In fact, only four European powers convened the trials – Britain, France, Italy and Russia. Germany and Austria-Hungary, which had been part of the international governance of the island before the 6 September 1898 massacre, were no longer part of the governing coalition.

6.4.3.3. The Boxer Rebellion Trial

Finally, after the massacres of Christians in the Boxer Rebellion, the two strands of imperialism and pacifism once again exerted an important influence on the creation and operation of the international Tribunal at Pao Ting Fu. In the first place, the colonial undertones in the Pao Ting Fu expedition were unmistakable. As related by Ignazio Dandolo, an Italian colonel, Garioni, who was with the foreign expeditionary force at Pao Ting Fu, described the imperialistic nature of the enterprise:

> Garioni says: "The French and Germans have taken care to furnish their troops with the most recent arms *in order to profit from the colonial enterprise* to experiment their newest offensive weapons, as it is difficult to demonstrate their efficiency on the home firing range. Furthermore, the French and Germans have provided their troops with the best material not only so that they don't look bad in comparison with the others, but also to show the power of the army to which they belong".[286]

Ultimately, however, French and German chauvinism gave way to the spirit of compromise regarding Boxer massacre justice efforts. The expedition to Pao Ting Fu was peripheral to the principal negotiations to resolve Boxer Rebellion issues that took place in Beijing and resulted in the Boxer Protocols. The latter did not provide for trials and stipulated summary execution for certain Imperial Chinese authorities in the capital. And none of the other outlying areas where the Western powers travelled to dispense post-Boxer justice established an international Tribunal.

It is rather amazing, then, that the expeditionary force in the tiny outpost of Pao Ting Fu came up with the idea. Seemingly by osmosis, the European officials there had evidently internalised and acted on the wisdom of their day that meaningful multilateral adjudication was superior to summary execution. That the judges of this international Tribunal took their charge seriously is demonstrated by their acquitting the alleged low-level Boxers brought before them and by their meting out individualised punishments, which ranged from the death penalty to dismissal and stripping of grade. This peripheral band of allies, perhaps influenced by an American staff officer, was subliminally guided by their better angels and they made history.

---

[286] Dandolo, 1991, pp. 317, 331, see *supra* note 200 (emphasis added).

Still, the atavistic imperial instincts were also on display. In collective retaliation for the massacres, the Western allies did demolish precious cultural property at Pao Ting Fu and plundered its wealth. So, by the turn of the century, it appears that pockets of Western actors could boast of learning the most important lessons of the peace movement and applying the rule of law in international relations. But, as the twentieth century's impending world wars would demonstrate, they still had a long way to go.

6.5. Conclusion

Various experts have at times suggested that one or another proceeding before the Nuremberg and Tokyo trials have constituted the true original birth of international criminal justice.[287] But, to date, none has focused on the three sets of trials analysed herein, which took place during the last decade of the nineteenth century and involved transnational hotspots in the Orient. Some scholars have focused on the trials individually (for example, Brockman-Hawe and Pritchard), but none has looked at them as a contemporaneous and thematically linked group. And the post-Boxer Rebellion international Tribunal has been entirely ignored in international criminal law literature. This chapter has explained why these trials should be examined simultaneously and holistically as a defining moment in the development of international criminal law. And it has demonstrated why these subliminally seminal trials took place in the last decade of the nineteenth century, had links to Asia and were international in nature.

In different ways, each of the trials implicated resolution of uncertain power dynamics and territorial claims in the Orient. As we have seen, the trials were the fruit of a unique confluence of late-stage imperialism and embryonic pacifism. The imperialism explains why the European powers were in the various locations where the trials took place and why they sat in judgment of citizens from subjugated countries. And those citizens happened to be from the Orient because, unlike Africa with its Berlin Conference, imperialism in Eastern lands was never formally regulated by

---

[287] See, for example, Gordon, 2013, *supra* note 1, referring to the Hagenbach trial in this regard; Brockman-Hawe, 2013, *supra* note 2, on the Franco-Siamese Mixed Court; Pritchard, 2003, *supra* note 3, on the trials of the Ottomans on Crete; Jenny S. Martinez, *The Slave Trade and the Origins of International Human Rights Law*, Oxford University Press, New York, 2012, p. 148, noting that experts perceive "the International Military Tribunal at Nuremberg as the first international tribunal charged primarily with enforcing humanitarian norms" but suggesting that the antislavery courts preceded the IMT.

and among the European powers. So regulation in the East occurred in dribs and drabs, through *ad hoc* measures, including the trials examined here.

But pacifism played a role, too. Informing and motivating the budding European peace movement, it instilled in the colonial overlords a normative preference for multilateral and judicial dispute resolution. This was the age of international arbitration as the preferred non-bellicose choice for settling interstate disputes. And the trials considered here were arguably inspired by the arbitration ethos of the times.

Nevertheless, examining the modern international criminal law landscape, students of international law can understand how the trials were remarkably ahead of their time. The Franco-Siamese Mixed Court is in many ways procedurally reminiscent of the institution known as the Extraordinary Chambers in the Courts of Cambodia ('ECCC').[288] Apart from the obvious parallel in terms of Southeast Asian courthouse geography, both bodies used mixed rules and judges, were influenced by the French colonial legacy in terms of legal culture, and included much international input and participation.[289] In terms of the Franco-Siamese Mixed Court dealing with the assassination of one individual, it is evocative of the modern Special Tribunal for Lebanon ('STL'), which has focused exclusively on the assassination of Rafik Hariri and also bears the influence of French judicial culture.[290]

---

[288] See Ricarda Popa, "The Contribution of the Extraordinary Chambers in the Courts of Cambodia to the Establishment of a Hybrid Tribunal Model", Research Paper, Faculty of Social Science and Philosophy, Philipps University, Marburg, March 2009, explaining the background and functioning of the ECCC.

[289] See John D. Ciorciari and Jaya Ramji-Nogales, "Lessons from the Cambodian Experience with Truth and Reconciliation", in *Buffalo Human Rights Law Review*, 2012, vol. 19, pp. 193, 206, describing the ECCC as "a mixed tribunal combining international and domestic laws, procedures, and personnel"; David S. Sokol, Note, "Reduced Victim Participation: A Misstep by the Extraordinary Chambers in the Courts of Cambodia", in *Washington University Global Studies Law Review*, 2011, vol. 10, no. 1, pp. 167, 175: "As a former French colony, Cambodian law is premised on the French model of criminal procedure"; Neha Jain, "Between the Scylla and the Charybdis of Prosecution and Reconciliation: The Khmer Rouge Trials and the Promise of International Criminal Justice", in *Duke Journal of Comparative and International Law* , 2010, vol. 20, pp. 247, 255, noting that the ECCC has been the product of "significant international participation".

[290] See Sandra L. Hodgkinson, "Are *Ad Hoc* Tribunals an Effective Tool for Prosecuting International Terrorism Cases?", in *Emory International Law Review*, 2010, vol. 24, pp. 515, 515, referring to the STL as "an *ad hoc* tribunal designed to address the assassination of Lebanese Prime Minister Rafik Hariri on February 14, 2005"; Chris Jenks, "Notice Other-

The International Military Commissions on Crete bear a remarkable resemblance to the Special Panels for Serious Crimes on East Timor.[291] Like the Special Panels, the International Military Commissions were set up to deal with one horrific paroxysm of violence on the eve of the departure from an island of an occupying power (Indonesia in the case of East Timor and the Ottomans in the case of Crete).[292] In both cases, the new "transitional authority" occupiers, the United Nations on East Timor and the Great Powers on Crete, set up panels with international judges (although the Special Panels included East Timorese).[293] And elements of the Panels' legal culture bore the hallmarks of the former Portuguese coloniser in East Timor just as the International Military Commission's incorporated European legal culture.[294] The Boxer Rebellion Tribunal, staffed by four victorious occupying powers in the aftermath of a war, makes one think, though on a much different scale, of the International Military Tribunal at Nuremberg, which was established 46 years later.

So, if we can see these tribunals as impromptu forebears of modern international criminal law institutions, why is it that international criminal justice lay essentially dormant after the great cataclysm of the First World War? If European powers were prepared to join forces and sit in judgment of perpetrators with respect to transnational offences during the last decade of the nineteenth century, why were they incapable of doing it in 1919–1920, after the abysmal atrocities of the Great War?

The precedent was certainly there. But the will was lacking. The trials from 1894 to 1900 involved European powers sitting in judgment of subjugated peoples: the Siamese, the Ottomans and the Chinese. Any true

---

wise Given: Will In Absentia Trials at the Special Tribunal for Lebanon Violate Human Rights?", in *Fordham International Law Journal*, 2009, vol. 33, no. 1, pp. 57, 66, fn. 44, indicating the STL is governed by Lebanese criminal procedure; Helen Chapin Metz (ed.), *Jordan: A Country Study*, Federal Research Division, Library of Congress, Washington, DC., 1991, p. 271, mentioning that the Lebanese legal system is modelled on that of the French.

[291] Suzanne Katzenstein, Note, "Hybrid Tribunals: Searching for Justice in East Timor", in *Harvard Human Rights Journal*, 2003, vol. 16, pp. 245, 253, providing background and information regarding the functioning of the Special Panels.

[292] Nancy Amoury Combs, "Procuring Guilty Pleas for International Crimes: The Limited Influence of Sentence Discounts", in *Vanderbilt Law Review*, 2006, vol. 59, no. 1, pp. 69, 124–25.

[293] *Ibid.*, pp. 125–26.

[294] *Ibid.*

international trials post-1918 would have entailed European powers sitting in judgment of one another. And the Europeans were not ready for that. Only the unimaginable atrocities of the Second World War would finally convince those powers to bring their own to justice. And that was the genesis of the International Military Tribunal at Nuremberg.

7

Constructing Humanity's Justice: Accountability for 'Crimes Against Humanity' in the Wake of the Syria Crisis of 1860

Benjamin E. Brockman-Hawe[*]

> In the interests of justice, of humanity, and of the future government of the Province, it is necessary that a great example should be made of those whose hands are deepest dyed in blood.
>
> *Lord Dufferin, British Commissioner to Syria, to Lord Russell, British Foreign Secretary, 19 December 1860*

7.1. Introduction

In late May 1860 smouldering tensions between the Druze and Maronite Christian communities of Ottoman Syria ignited into full-scale civil war. Reports of the deaths of thousands of Christians under circumstances of unusual barbarity prompted France, Great Britain, Prussia, Russia and Austria, to dispatch troops to the region, as well as an International Commission of Inquiry ('Commission'). Although prosecutions began before the Commissioners arrived in Damascus, they would play a critical role in shaping the (what we would call today) transitional justice process, designing one of the tribunals before which the accused were tried, establishing prosecutorial strategy and ultimately directly deliberating on the guilt of the most high-profile accused, with all of the concomitant agonizing over matters of evidence and law that implies. Over the course of six

---

[*] **Benjamin E. Brockman-Hawe** received his J.D. from Boston University, where he graduated with honours in the concentration of International Law in 2008, and is currently working on his LL.M. at Columbia University. He is the author of "A Supranational Tribunal for the Colonial Era: The Franco-Siamese Mixed Court", in Kevin Jon Heller and Gerry Simpson (eds.), *The Hidden Histories of War Crimes Trials*, Oxford University Press, Oxford, 2013, and his work on international criminal law, amnesties, immunities and state succession has appeared in a various law reviews.

months hundreds of individuals were executed, imprisoned, sentenced to hard labour or banished for their participation in what one Ottoman Porte official described as "crimes against humanity".[1] While these events have recently received some attention from historians, international law scholars have barely given these developments any consideration.[2]

---

[1] Further Papers, Inclosure 5, "Communication made by Abro Effendi to the Members of the Syrian Commission", in No. 40, Dufferin to Russell, sent 10 May 1861, received 23 May 1861, referring to Damascus as "the scene of a great crime, a crime against humanity, which provoked a severe and immediate punishment". This marks, if not the first, then certainly one of the earliest uses of the phrase "crimes against humanity" both in a diplomatic communication and to reference mass atrocities that had come under judicial scrutiny. The Porte – in full the Sublime or Ottoman Porte – is a translation of the Turkish title of the central office of the Ottoman government. All translations from the French in this chapter are by the author.

[2] Leila Tarazi Fawaz, *An Occasion for War: Civil Conflict in Lebanon and Damascus in 1860*, University of California Press, Berkeley, 1994 provides a thorough account of the civil strife and restoration of order in Syria. Ussama Makdisi, *The Culture of Sectarianism: Community, History, and Violence in Nineteenth-Century Ottoman Lebanon*, University of California Press, Berkeley, 2000 expands on this with his expertly written manuscript on the role of sectarianism in the lead up to and aftermath of the events of 1860–61. Ceasar E. Farah, *The Politics of Interventionism in Ottoman Lebanon, 1830–1861*, I.B. Tauris, London, 2000 casts his historian's eye over the "mechanics of disruption" that characterised relations between the Ottoman Porte and Europe over three decades (1830–1861), skilfully placing the 1860 outbreak and the subsequent Ottoman and European response in a proper historic and geopolitical context.

A number of contemporary accounts were published covering the Syria crisis. Four are of particular interest for the perspective they provide on the transitional justice process in post-conflict Syria: Anonymous, *Souvenirs de Syrie (expédition française de 1860) par un témoin oculaire* [Memories of Syria (French Expedition of 1860) by an eyewitness], Plon-Nourrit, Paris, 1903; M. Saint-Marc Girardin, *La Syrie en 1861: condition des Chrétiens en Orient* [Syria in 1861: Condition of Christians of the East], Didier, Paris, 1862; Ernest Louet, *L'Expédition de Syrie, 1860–1861* [The Expedition to Syria, 1860–1861], Amyot, Paris, 1862; Richard Edwards, *La Syrie, 1840–1862: histoire, politique, administration, population, religion et moeurs, événements de 1860 d'après des actes officiels et des documents authentiques* [Syria, 1840–1862: History, Politics, Administration, Population, Religion and Morals, Events of 1860 from Official Acts and Authentic Documents], Amyot, Paris, 1862. The published British Blue Books for this period, which contain more material of interest than I have been able to distil into a single chapter, is another invaluable resource. Houses of Parliament, Parliamentary Papers, *Correspondence Relating to the Affairs of Syria 1860–1861*, Harrison and Sons, London, 1861 ('Papers'); *Part II, Correspondence Relating to the Affairs of Syria (in continuation of Correspondence presented to Parliament in April 1861)*, Harrison and Sons, London, 1861 ('Further Papers').

As best as I can determine, the domestic prosecutions and international involvement in that process that followed have been mentioned only in two other contemporary works related to international law: Gary J. Bass, *Freedom's Battle: The Origins of Humanitarian Intervention*, Alfred A. Knopf, New York, 2008, pp. 192–196, 203–12; Davide Rodongo,

---

The work of the Ottoman courts and the Commission forms part of an underappreciated history of international criminal law. The justice programme in Syria identifies this as an important moment of transition from the era in which states were willing to forswear punishment for atrocities, to one in which massacre would provoke robust military and diplomatic intervention, into matters ostensibly entirely 'local', in humanity's name. Confronted with mass violence, Europeans developed institutions and ways of thinking that are identifiable as progenitors of our modern international criminal law.

The Commission was a physical embodiment of the punitive mandate, but portents of the reasoning that would be critical to subsequent developments in law and policy may also be seen at work in the mind of Europe's educated classes. Sustained interest in the judicial proceedings entangled and entrenched the ideas of appalling bloodshed, crime, punishment and humanity in a manner that moved the concept of 'crimes against humanity' one step closer towards acquiring its contemporary meaning: a repugnant act of violence committed as part of a widespread or systematic attack on a civilian population, in contravention of international law. The questions incumbent to any transitional justice programme were also thought through by European and Ottoman alike: Who to prosecute? How many to punish? What due process rights should be respected? What role, if any, should the international community assume?

Against Massacre: Humanitarian Interventions in the Ottoman Empire 1815–1914, Princeton University Press, Princeton, NJ, 2012, pp. 111–12. Both discuss the punishments of those implicated in the Syria crisis from the point of view of the development of the law of humanitarian intervention. But neither work discusses the trials, the work of the Commission or the intervention in Syria from the standpoint of international criminal law or transitional justice.

The account that follows is based on these sources, as well as a thorough search of material in the US National Archives and Records Administration ('NARA'), the United Kingdom National Archives ('TNA') in Kew, and the Public Record Office of Northern Ireland ('PRONI'). Although it would have been preferable, particularly given that one of the purposes of this volume is to disrupt international criminal law's Western-centric narrative, to consult more of the archives holding relevant materials (particularly the Ottoman archives), lack of knowledge of the relevant languages has prevented me from exploring these sources. I hope that other scholars will pick up where I have left off and continue to investigate this fascinating *caesura* in the development of international criminal law.

Following the lead of Fawaz, I use the terms 'Syria', 'Ottoman Syria' or 'Syria region' throughout this chapter to refer to territory that today comprises Lebanon, Syria, Jordan, Israel and Palestine. 'The Mountain' refers to a region which is today a central part of the state of Lebanon. See Fawaz, 1994, p. xiv; Makdisi, 2000, p. 30.

This chapter proceeds in four sections. In section 7.2. I describe the events, as they were reported to Europe, that triggered international outrage and intervention. In sections 7.3. and 7.4. I attempt to convey the 'flavour' of some of the trials before three Extraordinary Tribunals located in Damascus, Beirut and Moukhtara. In section 7.5. I present the work of the Commission as it related to criminal repression. I then offer some general thoughts on the state of international criminal law in 1860 and identify some areas where the activities of the commissioners still resonate (section 7.6.). The chapter concludes with a brief discussion of the legacy of the Commission and an appeal for additional resources to be put into researching international criminal law's nineteenth-century DNA.

7.2. 1860: "A Year of Fire and Sword, Massacre and Pillage, Desolation and Destruction"

The story of why violence broke out across Greater Syria when it did is complex. The region's occupation by an Egyptian army between 1831 and 1840 had seriously undermined the traditional balance of power, as new laws that disproportionately favoured Maronite Christians pushed the region's traditional power, the Druze, into increasingly dire economic and political straits.[3] By 1850 sectarian conflict had become a regular feature of their relationship between the two communities.[4] The Crimean War (1853–6) had turned Ottoman peripheries into scenes where Great Power rivalries played out, and France and Britain were unabashed in their efforts to influence affairs directly at Constantinople and in Syria through their Maronite and Druze protégés.[5] The war also deprived the Ottoman government of critical cache, blood and treasure, and focused resentment

---

[3] Kais Firro, *A History of the Druzes*, Brill, Leiden, 1992, pp. 61–66, 79–81.

[4] Joseph Abou Nohra, "L'Evolution du système politique libanais dans le context des conflits regionaux et locaux (1840–1864)", in Nadim Shehadi and Dana Haffarmills (eds.), *Lebanon: A History of Conflict and Consensus*, I.B. Tauris, London, 1988, pp. 31–48; Firro, 1992, pp. 88–92, see *supra* note 3.

[5] Makdisi, 2000, pp. 706–7, see *supra* note 2. Leila Fawaz, "The Druze-British Connection in 1840-1860", in *The Druze – Realities & Perceptions*, Druze Heritage Foundation, London, 2005, pp. 105-113. Alfred Schlicht, *The Role of Foreign Powers in the History of Lebanon and Syria from 1799 to 1861*, Journal of Asian History, 14(2) 1980, pp. 97-126.

against foreign powers, a circumstance that disrupted Great Power ambitions not one whit.[6]

The Porte's efforts to reduce foreign influence by eradicating situations that might serve as a pretext for intervention backfired and accelerated the instability. The passage of an edict in 1856 that provided for civil equality and freedom of worship for Christians was regarded with trepidation by Syria's Muslims, who regarded the law as a secular assault on their religious traditions, and feared the loss of their own privileged social status and the injury to their autonomy implied by greater Christian (and by extension French) influence on public affairs.[7] Economic and demographic factors also played a role in undermining the peaceful co-existence of the Druze and Christians. For decades the Druze had resisted the introduction of Western and Ottoman ideas, preferring to hew to their traditional way of life and maintain their status as best they could as feudal landlords of the Mountain.[8] The Maronites benefited from this as the advantages of a modernising and expanding economy, built with French assistance, disproportionately accrued to them.[9] Additionally, the Maronite population had over the span of only a few decades dramatically overtaken that of the Druze. Numerically and commercially, they posed a threat to the traditional Druze elite. These changes, inherently disruptive on their own, also contributed to a perception on the part of Druze and Maronite alike that the other sect was the 'real' minority, and as such had only succeeded by virtue of their own largesse.[10]

Finally, unrest in Montenegro and Serbia in early 1860 had necessitated a reduction in the number of Ottoman troops in Syria.[11] By April the indicia of the sultan's authority had been significantly diminished and, as a practical matter, the risk of punishment as a consequence of violence was significantly reduced.

---

[6] Moshe Mo'az, *Ottoman Reform in Syria and Palestine, 1840–1861: The Impact of the Tanzimat on Politics and Society*, Clarendon Press, Oxford, 1968, pp. 214–15, 218–20; Fawaz, 1994, p. 22, see *supra* note 2; Firro, 1992, pp. 84–85, see *supra* note 3.

[7] Mo'az, 1968, p. 227, see *supra* note 6; Samir Khalaf, *Lebanon's Predicament*, Columbia University Press, New York, 1987, p. 67.

[8] Firro, 1992, p. 115, see *supra* note 3.

[9] *Ibid.*, pp. 115–116; Fawaz, 1995, p. 24, see *supra* note 2. Schlicht, p. 121-2, see *supra* note 5.

[10] Firro, 1992, p. 117, see *supra* note 3.

[11] Farah, 2000, p. 603, see *supra* note 2; Ma'oz, 1968, pp. 51–53, see *supra* note 6.

The match that finally set Syria ablaze was a minor incident in Beit Miri over the question of whether some Druze or Maronite men would yield a path to the other. Around 10 individuals were killed in the resulting brawl.[12] Stories of the incident triggered revenge killings, which spurred sectarian skirmishes, which escalated into interethnic massacres. By late May the situation in the southern, western and eastern Mountain districts was being called a 'civil war' by foreign consuls.[13] Both sides were guilty of warmongering, pillage, murder and other abuses, but the worst excesses (and the actions that ultimately prompted European intervention) were attributed to the Druze. The first of what would become several notorious massacres occurred at Hasbeya, where a band of Druze broke through the gates of the seraglio (with the connivance of the local Ottoman commander, it was reported) and massacred the Christian refugees:

> [The Druze] rushed like hungry tigers upon the unarmed mob in the court-yard. No man was spared. In ten minutes the very stones were inch deep in human blood. No butchery ever known in history equaled this in ferocity and cowardice. In half an hour upwards of a thousand strong men were hacked to death. Some few tried again the escape, but were driven back by the bayonets of Turkish soldiers (regular troops, not Bashi Bazouks [irregular troops]), and the Druses had their revel of blood undisturbed.[14]

Similar scenes played out in the Christian refugee sanctuary of Rasheya and the Christian stronghold of Zahlé.[15] The violence escalated to fever pitch during the Druze attack on the predominantly Christian city of Deir el-Kamar (Deir al-Qamar) on 19 June 1860. Thousands of Christians lost their lives in the attack, vast quantities of goods were plundered, and countless homes and business were destroyed.[16] The descriptions that reached and horrified Europe in the aftermath of the attack

---

[12] Farah, 2000, p. 542, see *supra* note 2; Firro, 1992, p. 119, see *supra* note 3.

[13] The phrase used in F[oreign] O[ffice] 195/655, Moore to Bulwer, 30 May 1860, TNA. For some discussion over the "turning point" that elevated the conflict to a civil war, see Fawaz, 1994, p. 49, see *supra* note 2.

[14] "Syria", *Daily News*, 9 July 1860; Fawaz, 1994, pp. 60–63, see *supra* note 2; Farah, 2000, pp. 566–69, see *supra* note 2.

[15] Farah, 2000, pp. 569, 573–578, see *supra* note 2.

[16] Additional information on and context for these notorious massacres may be found in Fawaz, 1994, pp. 63–74, see *supra* note 2; Farah, 2000, pp. 566–82, see *supra* note 2.

still resonate today. The following from the English *Daily News* represents a typical account:

> Here stood, ninety days ago, a thriving town of 8,000 souls and upwards, and when the troubles in Lebanon broke out nearly two thousand Christians from various parts had sought refuge in the place. Where are now these images of God? Where are the comfortable homes, the thriving trades, the right silk crops, the produce of grapes and of olives, the hundreds of working silk looms that this population possessed? Where are the wives and daughters of these traders and landowners, where the happy children, the hearty welcome which all strangers received, the wealth in dress and jewels with which the matrons were adorned? The men of the place – ay, and some of the women, too, for I counted no less than a dozen in one spot – the men are here, these corrupting masses of putrid skulls are all that remains of them; their houses are all burnt or pulled down; their property all plundered or destroyed; their women beggars in the streets of Beyrout; their male children hacked to pieces by the knives of the Druses. [...]
>
> [In the Turkish Governor's room] in the far interior of the Serai [...] the great slaughter seems to have taken place. Here – two and a half months after these murders – the ground of the room was still discoloured and fat with human blood. Here still lay about fragments of torn dresses and clothing, bearing witness to may fearful deeds of blood. And here, below the large window of the room, lay heap upon heap and pile upon pile of corrupting human bodies, a seething mass of advanced purification.[17]

In mid-July a tenuous Druze-Christian *boyourouldis*[18] (peace accord) arranging for an "oblivion of the past", that is an absolution from any "claim or pretention" for "all that has passed from the beginning of the war to the present date", was signed at the prompting of Khurshid Pa-

---

[17] "Syria", *Daily News*, 21 September 1860; "Syria", *Daily News*, 28 September 1860". The vice-consul of Sidon, Jacob Abela, described the city as "nothing but dead bodies and ruins". Papers, Inclosure 2, in No. 104, Moore to Russell, sent 15 August 1860, received 4 September 1860, see *supra* note 2.

[18] Further Papers, Inclosure 2, in No. 27, Moore to Russell, sent 18 July 1860, received 5 August 1860, see *supra* note 2.

sha, the commander of the Ottoman garrison at Deir el-Kamar.[19] For a moment it looked as though matters had been brought to a decisive, if still unstable, end. But the "year of fire and sword, massacre and pillage, desolation and destruction" was not yet at an end, as became clear when news of fresh outbreaks of violence in Damascus reached the European capitals.[20] The carnage in the Mountain and influx of refugees had aggravated the relationship between the city's Christians and poor Muslims. Over the course of eight days a mob, comprising primarily Muslims, but counting among its members Druze, Kurds and, by many reports, Turkish soldiers, killed between 3,000 and 10,000 Christians, and set ablaze the French, Russian, Greek, Dutch, Austrian and Belgian consulates.[21]

---

[19] Further Papers, Inclosure 4, "Treaty of Peace between the Christians and Druses", in No. 28, Moore to Russell, sent 19 July 1860, received 5 August 1860. The British consul-general, Noel Moore, felt that the terms of the peace had "been forced upon the Christians, who it is impossible should willingly seal their own ruin" [sic]. He also protested that only low-ranking Christian authorities had signed. Further Papers, Inclosure 1, in No. 28, Moore to Russell, sent 19 July 1860, received 5 August 1860, see *supra* note 2.

[20] Papers of the American Board of Commissioners for Foreign Missions ('ABCFM'), ABC 16.8.1, Unit 5, Reel 545, No. 30, "Report of the Beirut Station for the year 1860".

[21] Smylie Robson, Presbyterian Church of Ireland missionary and resident in the Christian quarter in Damascus, described the riots as they unfolded outside his window:

> For the last two hours and a-half the street past my house has presented a terrible scene; first, the rush and running of men armed, and unarmed boys and women shouting imprecations on the infidel; shouts, imprecations on the infidel Christians, and cries of "Kill them! Butcher them! Plunder! Burn! Leave not one! Not a house, not anything! Fear not the solider, fear nothing; the soldiers will not meddle with you". They were right, nobody has interfered. Men, women, boys, and soldiers, for more than two hours have been carrying every sort of thing past my house like fiends from hell. I cannot go to your house. Could I go with my wife and servant into the midst of armed ruffians crying and thirsting for blood? To open my door is as much as my life is worth. I must remain where I am and leave the event with God. Where is your Pasha now? Fifty men could have put the insurrection down. Has any attempt been made to preserve the lives of property of the Sultan's subjects or the subjects of other Powers?

Further Papers, Inclosure 4, in No. 20, Moore to Russell, sent 13 July 1860, received 3 August 1860, see *supra* note 2.

Sir Henry Lytton Bulwer, British Ambassador at Constantinople, described the escalating violence:

> It began by much agitation, the consequence of mutual apprehension; the Christian fearing the Turks, the Turks fearing the Christians and the arrival, forewarned to them, of the French. A slight tumult occurs.

Beginning in early July, the first reports of the violence in the Mountain trickled in to European periodicals.[22] Public support for a humanitarian intervention grew as the massacres unfolded in the press,[23] along with (particularly in the British press), demands for the punishment of the "criminals" responsible.[24] Particular attention was directed at Ottoman officials reported to have been negligent, complicit or participants in the violence. Khurshid Pasha, Governor-General of Sidon, and Ahmad (Achmet) Pasha, Governor-General of Damascus bore the brunt of the

---

> Some boys are arrested and punished: the mob rescue and side; the Pasha and his military do nothing: the mob increases. It murders and pillages. The better classes of the Mussulmans, however, succor the Christians, and save those they can. Others are received in the Citadel. Some houses, however are set on fire, but as yet the disorder was limited. The Arabs and Druses see the flames and pour in to the town.

TNA, 30/22/88, Bulwer to Russell, 27 July 1860. For a more detailed description of the riots, see Fawaz, 1994, pp. 78–100, *supra* note 2; Farah, 2000, pp. 588–92, *supra* note 2. Farah considers it most likely that 3,000 were killed in the Damascus riots. Farah, 2000, p. 592, see *supra* note 2. Fawaz believes that approximately 2,000 local Christians died during the riots but notes that hundreds more may have lost their lives as refugees. Fawaz, 1994, p. 132, fn. 2, see *supra* note 2.

[22] See, for example, *The Times*, 6 July 1860 and *The Times*, 11 July 1860.

[23] See, for example, *The Times*, 25 July 1860: "It is decidedly advisable to treat the Porte as a Government independent and equal with our own, and to occupy the country only under a convention with that Power; but, if such an arrangement cannot be made, then in the name of humanity let us disregard etiquette, and put an end at once to these horrors".

[24] The *Birmingham Daily Post*, 12 July 1860, appears to have been the first to appeal for punitive action against individual offenders, linking the practice with the logic of state-building: "[…] unless the officers in command of the Turkish troops at Zahleh, Hasbeiya, and the other scenes of slaughter, are brought to condign punishment for their infamous treachery in standing idly by while they could have prevented the mischief, or worse still, inducing the Christians to deliver up their arms under promise of protection, and the handing them over to be massacred in cold blood by their remorseless enemies […] a premium is held out for the repetition of similar atrocities at a future day". *The Times*, 25 July 1860, was the next to take up the call: "It will be [the duty of Europe] to insist that the Porte shall punish the chiefs and their accomplices, even though some of the culprits are to be found in the Sultan's own army". The editors of *The Times* would repeatedly insist that the "ringleaders" and "arch-offenders" face Ottoman justice; see "The Massacres in Syria", *The Times*, 17 August 1860 and *The Times*, 16 August 1860. In "The Syrian Questions", the *Saturday Review*, 4 August 1860 was of the opinion that "if the Turkish Government is not wholly corrupt the insurgent [Druze] chiefs and the delinquent Asiatic Pashas will be punished with exemplary rigor". The *Standard*, "The Syrian Massacres", 27 July 1860, forcefully argued that "[t]here must be no oblivion of the past, no 'Syourouldy' [peace agreement with amnesty] until the chief agents, whether they be coward Turks or bloodthirsty Druses, have met the retribution due to their guilt".

reproach and were presented by the press as the arch-villains or architects of the violence.[25] Their peers were the "infamous terrorists of the great French revolution", their hands dyed deeper in blood "than perhaps any men we read of in modern history".[26] Their "extirpation" was accordingly demanded as a "service to Syria and to the cause of humanity".[27]

On 17 July the French Foreign Minister, Edouard-Antoine Thou-venel proposed to the Great Powers the creation of an International Com-mission to "ascertain" the causes of the violence and the degree to which local Ottoman officials were responsible.[28] But the measure was soon overtaken by events on the ground, as news of the Damascus riots quickly convinced Europe's Great Powers that more forceful measures were re-quired. Throughout August the energies of Britain, France, Austria, Prus-sia and Russia – each Power keen to either turn the situation to its ad-vantage or frustrate the ambitions of the other Powers – were directed at obtaining the Porte's consent to a humanitarian mission.[29] Although the

---

[25] There were some marginal efforts to establish a counter-narrative in which the Turkish government was not culpable. See, for example, "The Druses and Maronites", *Liverpool Mercury*, 12 July 1860, asserting that there was no reason to believe Ottoman government was "implicated in the massacre of the Maronite Christians, in any other sense than that in which Sir G. C. Lewis and the London police are implicated in the riots at St. Georges-in-the-East". See also the *Morning Post*, 19 July 1860, whose correspondent blamed "Chris-tian foreign agents" for the uprising.

[26] "Syria", *Daily News*, 3 September 1860.

[27] "The Syrian Intervention", *Saturday Review*, 11 August 1860. See also "Syria", *Daily News*, 20 September 1860, in reference to Khurshid Pasha: "[...] outraged humanity calls for vengeance on the men by whose means and at whose instigation such barbarities have been committed"; "The Fearful Massacre of the Christians", *Morning Post*, 7 September 1860: "No doubt whatever exists as to the complicity of Kurchid Pasha in all those horrors of which the Lebanon has been the scene, and outraged humanity calls for vengeance on the man by whose means and at whose instigation such barbarities have been committed"; "The Syrian Massacres", *Sunday Times*, 19 August 1860: "Now, in the mater of the two miscreants, Kurchid Pasha, late governor of Beyrout, and Achmet Pasha, late governor of Damascus, if there is any meaning whatever in the English language, these men [...] are guilty, directly guilty, of the blood of thousands, and of the misery and beggary of hun-dreds of thousands. If there is law or justice in the empire, these men should pay with their lives the wrong they have done God and man in this land"; "Syria", *Daily News*, 28 Au-gust 1860, reprinted in "Syria", *Irish Times and Daily Advertiser*, 29 August 1860, in ref-erence to Khurshid and Achmet: "If found guilty their sentence must be death – the whole of Christendom will demand no less".

[28] Papers, No. 6, M. Thouvenel to Count Persigny, 17 July 1860, see *supra* note 2.

[29] James Williams, the American minister to the Sublime Porte, wrote of Great Power rela-tions in Constantinople at this time:

Porte had already dispatched its Foreign Minister, Fuad Pasha, and around 15,000 troops to quell the unrest, it begrudgingly assented to the intervention on 3 August 1860.[30] French troops under the command of General Charles de Beaufort d'Hautpoul reached Beirut two weeks later, just as Fuad's efforts to restore order in Damascus were beginning to show results.[31]

7.3. "[T]he Implementation of Imperial Justice": Ottoman Prosecutions in Damascus

The imperial firman (decree) that set out the terms of Fuad's mandate made clear that justice was to be a cornerstone of his post-conflict efforts to restore order:

> You will, by adopting the necessary measures, cause to cease the confusion and civil war which has ensued between the above Maronites and Druses, and procure the return of peace and security to those parts. You will ascertain who have been instrumental in the odious act of shedding human blood, and immediately punish them according to the prescriptions of my Imperial Code. In a word, you are freely entrusted with the adoption of all the military and civil measures, for the extinction of this evil.[32]

> France as usual is prepared for any emergency. She does not absolutely, or at least not ostensibly deal any blows herself, but she smiles upon Turkey, winks at Russia, and stands ready to seize the lion's share when the ripe fruit falls to the ground. England stands apart, frowning and disconsolate, grumbling as usual, at every thing [sic] and every body [sic], unwilling that France and Russia shall seize upon the prey which she does not herself covet, she yet feels that it is a herculean task to uphold the Sultan's government, and she even commences to doubt whether it ought to be upheld. The interests and happiness of the people of Turkey first upon their lips, are last in the hearts of either.

NARA, RG 59 M46 R17, No. 97, James Williams to Lewis Cass, 12 September 1860.

[30] Papers, No. 59, Cowley to Russell, sent 3 August 1860, received 4 August 1860, see *supra* note 2. See also Farah, 2000, pp. 606–8, see *supra* note 2.

[31] Fawaz, 1994, pp. 109–19, see *supra* note 2.

[32] Papers, Inclosure "Firman", in No. 51, Bulwer to Russell, sent 25 July 1860, received 3 August 1860. A slightly different English translation of the firman appears in Inclosure 2, "Imperial Firman", in No. 65, Consul-General Moore to Bulwer, sent July 21, 1860, received 10 August 1860.

Fuad reached Damascus on 29 July, and for several days remained camped outside its gates, rejecting almost all of the efforts on the part of local notables to establish communication.[33] To the outsider Fuad may have looked passive or weak, but in actuality this was a carefully calculated first move in a well-planned raid-and-arrest operation. With an uncommunicative Extraordinary Commissioner from the Sublime Porte outside their walls, the city's elite worked themselves into an anxious froth. Then, after several days:

> A number of the more influential of the inhabitants, about whose conduct unpleasant rumours were current, were invited to wait upon his Imperial Majesty's Commissioner. These men were received with marked politeness, and their opinions as to the measures to be taken were requested. Delighted to find the apprehended storm thus passing over their heads, they manifested a disposition, and even a zeal, to give information against a multitude of their coadjustors.[34]

Doubtless those who co-operated hoped for amnesty. But denunciation did not translate to leniency, and backed by a second imperial firman placing responsibility for the Damascus violence on the shoulders of local officials, the informants were "quietly handed over to the officers of justice".[35] The strategy was employed to great effect among the city's lower-class Muslims as well, and when enough names had been gathered Fuad ordered a telegraphic blackout,[36] the closure and guarding of the city gates,[37] and the deployment of the military into the city.[38] Fuad reported to Consul-General Moore on 4 August 1860 that 330 individuals had been arrested without "striking a blow", and that the number was predicted to swell to 500 by the end of the day.[39] The arrests continued as avenues of

---

[33] "Syria", *Morning Chronicle*, 24 August 1860.

[34] "Turkey", Irish Times and Daily Advertiser, 28 August 1860.

[35] *Ibid.* The second firman may be found in Baron I. de Testa, *Recueil des traités de la Porte ottomane avec les puissances étrangères.* Vol. 6, Muzard, Paris, 1884, pp. 91–92.

[36] "Syria", *Daily News*, 23 August 1860.

[37] "Syria", *Morning Chronicle*, 24 August 1860; "The Massacres in Syria", *The Times*, 23 August 1860.

[38] "Syria", *Morning Post*, 10 September 1860. See also from the Papers: No. 91, Fraser to Russell, sent 8 August 1860, received 22 August 1860; No. 112, "Résumé of Despatches from Fuad Pasha", see *supra* note 2.

[39] Papers, Inclosure 1, in No. 87, Moore to Russell, sent 6 August 1860, received 22 August 1860, see *supra* note 2. The correspondent for the *Morning Chronicle*, however, reported that two individuals who resisted arrest were bayoneted by Turkish soldiers, and one man

escape were carefully surveilled; individuals who fled the city through reopened gates but behaved suspiciously at their destination were identified by Fuad's spies, and those attempting exodus by sea found their passage suspended by Turkish officials.[40] By 10 August 1860 between 700 and 1,000 suspects were in Damascene prisons awaiting trial.[41]

The Extraordinary Tribunal established by Fuad to hear their cases sat in the Silimiye mosque of Damascus. Trials were conducted in secret, so there is scant direct information about its operations and verdicts in the foreign diplomatic or press archives.[42] A private letter to the *Morning Post* reported that the tribunal comprised 13 judges.[43] According to consular communications the judges followed the rules "of a military court", convicted individuals *in absentia*,[44] and heard "any reasonable evidence […] even as far as that of a single Christian against a Moslem".[45] Fuad also reversed the usual burden of proof rules, as, in his own words

> [i]t would be impossible to prove charges for acts of murder which may have taken place in that outbreak by the production of proofs as in other ordinary cases. Therefore a general rule has been adopted towards everybody of allowing the bereaved Christian inhabitants to denounce such murderers of their relatives or plunderers of their property as they might recognise to prosecute their case by the process of confrontation and to prove it upon oath. When the accused party is unable to repel the charge he is pronounced to be guilty and punished according to the degree of his culpability.[46]

---

drowned attempting to hide himself in a well. "Syria", *Morning Chronicle*, 24 August 1860.

[40] "The Massacres in Syria", Freeman's Journal and Daily Commercial Advertiser, 29 August 1860.

[41] Papers, No. 91, reporting "nearly 1000" detained, see *supra* note 38; Papers, No. 92, Moore to Russell, sent 10 August 1860, received 27 August 1860, reporting between 700 and 800 arrests; Papers, No. 106, Fraser to Russell, sent 16 August 1860, received 4 September 1860, reporting that Fuad stated on 11 August that 800 had been arrested.

[42] Papers, No. 91, see *supra* note 38.

[43] "Syria", *Morning Post*, 3 September 1860.

[44] Papers, Inclosure 2, in No. 119, Brant to Russell (sent 25 August 1860, received 13 September 1860); Papers, Inclosure, in No. 138, Brant to Russell (sent 6 September 1860, received 29 September 1860).

[45] Papers, No. 106, Fraser to Russell (sent 16 August 1860, received 4 September 1860).

[46] Papers, Inclosure, in No. 244, Bulwer to Russell (sent 31 December 1860, received 18 January 1861). In the enclosed document, which is a letter from Fuad to the grand vizier,

Hundreds of Damascenes were tried and punished by the Extraordinary Tribunal of Damascus. A note from Fuad dated 23 August 1860 suggests that punishments were doled out on the basis of an accused's culpable acts and, to a lesser extent, professional position:[47]

---

he confirms his understanding that this plan had already been submitted to the Porte and "had met with His Majesty's sanction".

[47] Papers, Inclosure, 2 in No. 119, Brant to Russell, (sent 25 Aug 1860, received 13 September 1860) (list current as of 22 August). According to Fuad perpetual banishment was reserved for those who were proved "to have taken no actual part in the crimes committed"; Papers, No. 112, see *supra* note 38. The Bagnio was a prison in Constantinople for, among others, "Turks as are intended to be secretly executed", captured slaves and prisoners of war. See F.C.H.L. Pouqueville, *Travels in Greece and Turkey, Comprehending a Particular Account of the Morea, Albania, &c*, 2nd ed., Henry Colburn and Co., London, 1820, p. 266. The prison was generally perceived by Europeans as "the *ne plus ultra* of severity and horror" for which "most travelers have exhausted every epithet of the revolting and the terrible". But the traveller Eyre Crowe toured the facility and ultimately determined that prisoners held there were not treated worse than similarly situated prisoners in Italy or Spain. Eyre Evans Crowe, *The Greek and the Turk; Or, Powers and Prospects in the Levant*, Richard Bentley, London, 1853, p. 326. Fifty-six (or 57, depending on the dispatch consulted) individuals were hanged in the public spaces of Damascus on 19 August 1860. Major Fraser reported that among the hanged were "four or five persons above the common class, leader of armed levies, in the pay of the Government". Papers, No. 97. Fraser to Russell, sent 20 August 1860, received 1 September 1860. Attached to the chest of each of those hanged was a paper announcing their crimes, though few citizens could read. Papers, No. 109, Fraser to Russell, sent 23 August 1860, received 6 September 1860. The executions had a profound effect on the Damascus population. The correspondent for *The Times* in "The Massacres in Syria", 5 October 1860, described Damascus as one would a city under siege:

> [W]hen I returned into the bazaars […] we saw how profound was the terror inspired by Fuad Pasha's vigorous measures. One or two were entirely deserted, and all the shops in them closed. The dogs seemed to be badly off, and not to understand the desertion which was rapidly starving them out. In other bazaars some of the shops were opened – one here and there. A few customers might be seen cheapening a yard or two of calico – and they were mostly Christian women – and Bedouins, Kurds, and Metualis, buying staring handkerchiefs, tobacco, and articles they are accustomed to procure in the town. Terror seemed to have acted in different ways upon the Moslems, for in these bazaars the first batch of criminals had been hanged from the rafters which support the roof. Some of the people we passed among were blanched with fear, others were reduced to a state bordering on cretinism, while no inconsiderable proportions seemed to have had their ferocious hatred of Christians intensified, for they muttered to themselves, perhaps curses, and scowled upon us as we passed, looking, I fancied, as if they were brooding over plans for retaliation, and carefully cherishing their vengeance. A few minutes more and we entered the "street called

---

Persons condemned to death, as having openly assassinated Christians, and who have been hung	56
Persons condemned to death for having taken part in the disturbances, armed, and who in their capacity of auxiliary soldiers, zaptiés and bachi-bozouks, have been shot	111
Persons condemned to the bagnio for life, as having taken part in the disturbances, with arms in their hands, and who have been sent to Constantinople	139
Persons condemned to exile, for having taken part in the pillage, without arms	145
Persons condemned to hard labour for a fixed period, and kept at Damascus, to be employed in working on the roads	186
Persons condemned by default [in absentia], and who will be executed as soon as they shall fall into the hands of justice	83
Total	720

Between 23 August and mid-November several dozen more Muslims were sentenced by the Tribunal to death, exile, punishment or hard labour, and thousands more conscripted to fight in the Sultan's armies.[48]

Straight," the via recta of the Romans. With the exception of an apothecary's, nearly all the shops are closed, the doors and windows carefully barred, behind which we fancied we could discern inquisitive eyes peering out upon us, and could hear tremulous voices discussing, scarcely above a whisper, who we were. From a barber's shop an apprentice lolled in the window-sill. His occupation was clearly gone. The garrulous owner was asleep on the bench where customers used to sit waiting to be shaved. The focus of Eastern gossip was silent as the tomb.

For official reports of the public reaction to the capital punishments see Papers No. 91, *supra* note 38; Papers, Inclosure 2, in No. 118: "The people of the town are stricken with terror; they evidently never contemplated what has happened, and are trembling at what may still be impending", see *supra* note 47.

[48] See FO, 195/658, Inclosures, "Extraits du dossier de la procédure des personnes qui ont commis des crimes pendant les événemens de Damas" (listing 181 capital punishments) and "Liste des personnes qui ont été envoyées à Constantinople, et jetées au Bagne à Perpetuite pour leur participation aux événements de Damas" (listing 146 persons, all guilty of looting) in No. 109, Dufferin to Russell, 27 January 1861. Conscription was reserved for those least culpable in the riots. Louet, 1862, p. 71: "They will be worthy com-

The vast majority of those punished were "from the rabble",[49] as it proved difficult to pin crimes on many of the city's elite.[50] This was attributed to fear of retaliation as well as opportunism.[51] There was also a thriving market in "certificates" – attestations of alibi or good character by Christians – as well as testimony that would incline the tribunal toward a guilty verdict.[52] But Fuad, well aware of how impatiently "[t]he world awaits the implementation of imperial justice", refused to let investigative difficulties stand in the way of high-profile arrests and punishments.[53] About a dozen Damascus notables were rounded up, tried and punished by the Extraordinary Tribunal between August and October.[54]

---

panions of the Turkish soldiers who attended impassive, arms in hand, all the cruelties committed in Deir-el-Kamar", see *supra* note 2. See also J. Lewis Farley, *The Massacres in Syria*, 2nd ed., Bradbury and Evans, London, 1861, p. 103, reporting that by 1 September 1860 "upwards of 3,500 mussulman inhabitants of the city have been enrolled as forced conscripts, and sent off to join the army"; Inclsoure 3, in No. 118, reporting that 2,000–3,000 would be conscripted; see *supra* note 47. As of 30 August only 1,000 had been conscripted. Papers, No. 126, Fraser to Russell, sent 30 August 1860, received 19 September, 1860. This is consistent with information sent to the US ambassador to Constantinople. RG 84 Vol. 231, Johnson to Williams, 4 September 1860, NARA. It was reported in the British press that many conscripts bought their way out of their service. "Syria", *Daily News*, 12 January 1861.

49 Papers, No. 91, see *supra* note 38. Fuad Pasha complained to Major Fraser that "it was difficult to get evidence" against even low-level perpetrators. Papers, No. 106, Fraser to Russell, sent 16 August 1860, received 4 September 1860.

50 Papers, No. 109, Fraser to Russell, sent 23 August 1860, received 6 September 1860.

51 Papers, No. 126, Fraser to Russell, sent 30 August 1860, received 19 September 1860; "The Massacres in Syria", *The Times*, 6 October 1860: "The nefarious trade to which I referred in my last, of getting up evidence, is still carried on. [...] The Sheik was arrested, but the Christians are striving to obtain his acquittal, on condition of his restoring to them some portion of their property."

52 As reported in, for example, "Syria", *Chicago Tribune*, 6 November 1860: "Many Christians of Damascus are now selling their souls to the devil by giving Turks and Arabs of that city certificates of good character, knowing full well that they murdered many of their brethren"; "The Massacres in Syria", *The Times*, 5 October 1860: "Unless the Turkish authorities make a signal example of these traffikers in blood and false witness, it is to be feared many innocent men will suffer".

53 Makdisi, 2000, p. 148, *supra* note 2, citing Basbakanlik Devlet Arsivi (Istanbul), Irade-Meclis-I Mahsus [BBA IRADE MM] 851/5, Leff 1, 16 M 1277, 4 August 1860.

54 Papers, No. 109, see *supra* note 50; Papers, Inclosure 3, in No. 118, see *supra* note 47. At least nine of these high-profile arrestees were sentenced to exile or imprisonment despite the complete absence of any evidence against them. Papers, Inclosure 1, in No. 173, Fraser to Russell, sent 20 October 1860, received 8 November 1860; Edwards, 1862, p. 402, see *supra* note 2. The arrest of the 'Sheikh of Damascus', Abdallah el-Halabi, widely regarded as "a descendent of the Prophet" was considered particularly noteworthy. Louis de Baudi-

The trials of Ottoman officials were handled by a separate Council of War.[55] Ahmad Pasha was initially arrested and sent to Constantinople for trial, but at the urging of British consuls he was returned to Damascus[56] where his case proceeded along with those of the commanders and

cour, *La France au Liban*, Dentu, Paris, 1879, p. 167, gives one account of the circumstances of his arrest: "On 22 August, the women who had been shot or hanged surrounded his home, and with cries and lamentations, as only those in Muslim countries know how to make, they shouted at the accused 'It is you who are the cause of everything that happens to us, for the advice you gave to our husbands, following your holy books.' The authority, immediately informed of the fact, arrested the Sheik at home, and after an initial investigation, he was imprisoned with his son". Another source, "The State of Syria", *Freeman's Journal*, 3 September 1860 (republishing correspondence to *Levant Herald* written under the date of 10 August 1860) dates his arrest to earlier in August: "On the forenoon of the 5th, Sheikh Abdullah-el-Halebi, considered to be the prime instigators of the recent slaughters, was arrested, and although he is one of the very leading Mussulmans of the city, and called out lustily to the townspeople to rescue him as he was being dragged by the troops through the bazaars to prison, no movement whatever was made in his behalf, and the soldiers themselves treated him with great indignity". See also Papers, Inclosure 3, in No. 118: Halabi was "considered by the inhabitants in the light of a saint, but in reality a mischievous fanatic and intriguer; although he seeks his pecuniary interest by fraud and chicanery, yet he exercises immense influence over the people. His arrest produced a great sensation"; Papers, Inclosure 10, in No. 175, Dufferin to Russell, sent 26 October 1860, received 8 November 1860: Halabi was "a most influential Moslem". Native Christians and foreign consuls were convinced that "a general massacre never could have been ventured upon, without his consent or connivance"; Papers, No 191, Fraser to Russell, sent 15 November 1860, received 30 November 1860. No evidence could be found to substantiate this claim. Again, this was attributed to self-interest: "a Christian dare not, and a Moslem at the instance of a Christian would not, testify against a man of the Sheikh's position"; *ibid*. Halabi, along with other notables, was condemned to life imprisonment in a fortress despite the admitted absence of evidence against him. Papers, Inclosure 2, in No 173, Fraser to Russell, sent 20 October 1860, received 8 November 1860.

[55] Farah, 2000, p. 612–3, see *supra* note 2. A list of Ottoman functionaries punished by the Council of War in Damascus and their sentences is available in Edwards, 1903, pp. 402–3, see *supra* note 2, and (with slightly more detail) in FO, 195/658, Inclosure, "Extraits des sentences des fonctionnaires ottomans et des notables de Damas" in No. 109, Dufferin to Russell, 27 January 1861, TNA. See also Papers, Inclosure 2, "Memorandum" in No. 131, Dufferin to Russell, sent 8 September 1860, received 20 September 1860.

[56] From a first-hand account published in "The Syrian Massacres", *Sunday Times*, 19 August 1860:

> Before being sent back [...] for trial, he was, according to an order from the Sultan, publicly degraded from his rank in the great square of the Saraskerist. A large body of the troops and civil functionaries were assembled on the ground to witness the ceremony of degradation, which was performed with all the humiliating precision usual on such an occasion. The imperial order having been read aloud, the brass festbutton, epaulets, and sword of the degraded general were roughly tak-

sub-commanders of the Ottoman garrisons at Deir el-Kamar, Racheya (Rashaya), Hasbeya and the Christian quarter in Damascus.[57] A letter from the correspondent for *The Times* suggests that he was convicted es-

---

> en from him, and his deprivation of all rank and honours proclaimed to the spectators. He was then marched back to his prison, and the troops withdrew to their quarters.

[57] Farah, 2000, p. 613, see *supra* note 2. See also Papers, No. 72, Bulwer to Russell, sent 1 August 1860, received 12 August 1860, attributing the decision to send Ahmad back to a local government official who determined that the misconduct could only be inquired into in Damascus; Papers, No. 92, see *supra* note 41. Moore was of the opinion that "nothing short of this measure would have satisfied the exigencies of the case, or even secured the proper trial by affording the necessary evidence direct and circumstantial, which a local inquiry can alone render available". See also Papers, Inclosure 1, in No. 65, Moore to Russell, sent 21 July 1860, received 10 August 1860.

The consuls in Damascus spoke of Ahmad's guilt in terms of negligence, dereliction of duty, pusillanimity and incompetence:

> In my opinion Ahmet Pasha is guilty of gross incapacity in his mode of treating his Medhlis, and in not taking precautionary measures often suggested to him; of obstinacy, in maintaining in his post his Tufenkgee Bashi, who was notoriously incompetent, against the repeated warnings of persons of all classes, for weeks before the outbreak; for not endeavouring to rescue the Christians of Hasbeya and Rasheya, although he repeatedly promised to do so, being warned of their danger: for not making any effort to prevent the attack on Zahleh; for perfect indifference to, at least, if not connivance at, the massacres of the Christians by the Druses, regarding which he is reported to have said that there were two great evils in Syira, the Christians and the Druses, and that the massacres of either party was a gain to the Turkish government for the most extraordinary want to foresight as to the consequences of what was going on, and, when matters became more critical, of being still more obstinate and inactive, until at last he appeared to be paralyzed by fear for never appearing without the Serai at the head of his troops, either to prevent the outbreak at the commencement or to check the massacre afterwards, or even to arrest the conflagration. For such neglect of duty, and incapacity in an employé of his high rank, and for such arrant cowardice in a General Officer, by which the lives of probably 10,000 Christians were sacrificed, besides the intense misery occasioned to twice as many by wounds and sufferings, by loss of parents and relations, and of property; by the disgrace brought on his Sovereign, by the ruin on his country, and the indelible stain on his religious faith, supposing even nothing but incapacity for his high functions and cowardice as an officer by proved, the punishment of a disgraceful death has been merited.

Papers, Inclosure, in No. 138, Brant to Russell, sent Sept. 6 1860, received 29 September 1860.

---

sentially for neglect of duty and gives us some flavour of the proceedings
at the Council of War:

> [Ahmet Agha, né Pasha] was tried by a military tribunal, and
> when the evidence was collected Fuad Pasha summoned, in-
> cluding General Gescer, a Prussian, 40 officers, selected
> from the different corps and of various ranks, to whom he
> confided the duty of pronouncing sentence. His Excellency
> [Fuad] first compelled them to swear the usual Moslem oath
> to give a just and true verdict. He next explained the nature
> of the case and of their duties before giving them the minutes
> of the evidence. The result of the deliberations of this kind of
> supreme Court-martial was a verdict of death. One member
> of the Court voted for hard labour for life, as being a more
> severe and degrading punishment than death for a person in
> the position of the ex-Mushir; but when another member ob-
> served that the Sovereign prerogative of mercy might be ex-
> tended to the culprit, and restore him to the army which he
> had disgraced, the advocate for hard labour gave his vote for
> death. [...]
>
> Ahmed Agha was charged with a military offence – ne-
> glect of duty – convicted of it, and punished for it. He was
> tried by a military tribunal. [...] [I]f I am correctly informed,
> although every facility was afforded for the supply of evi-
> dence, none was offered tending to establish that Ahmed
> Agha had aided or abetted the massacres otherwise than by
> neglecting to do his duty. [...] Consequently, the only crime
> that could be proved against Ahmed Agha was neglect of du-
> ty to his Sovereign, and for that he suffered punishment by
> death.[58]

---

[58] "The Massacres in Syria", *The Times*, 2 October 1860. See also "The Late Massacres in
Syria: Execution of the Turkish Generals", *The Observer*, 23 September 1860. When Fuad
vacillated on following through with the execution of Ahmad Pasha the newly arrived
British Commissioner reminded him that "the greater the rigour he displayed, the less oc-
casion would the Commission have to usurp his authority"; FO 78/1625, No. 4, Dufferin to
Russell, 8 September 1860, TNA.

If the anonymous author of *Souvenirs de Syrie*, 1903, pp. 242–43, see *supra* note 2 is to be
believed, some of these themes ran throughout his trial before the Council of War:

> [I]t would doubtless have been interesting to study [Ahmad's] case, though
> it remained secret. The recitals of the sentence were that he had been
> condemned to death for failing to satisfy his military duty, for failure
> of courage before the riot and for not even having dared to attempt re-
> pression; in a word, he was condemned as a coward. [...]

7.4. The Extraordinary Tribunals of Beyrout and Moukhtara: Punishing Those who "Caused the Most hHarm to Humanity"

In early September 1860 Fuad left Damascus and shifted his attention to the restoration of order in the Mountain. A second extraordinary tribunal was established in Beirut and a number of prosecutions immediately commenced. A small number of Turkish officials, among them the notorious Khurshid Pasha,[59] and 11 Druze chieftains, including the 'supreme head' of the Druze and friend to the British aristocracy, Said Bey Jumblat.[60] At first hearings were confidential like those in Damascus,[61] but the

---

> We asked many questions about this subject of some of the senior officers who were part of the council of war, and with whom we maintained friendly relations. Their answers were always consistent with the version of the extraordinary commissioner: the inquiry showed that Ahmet Pasha had more than once called the attention of the Porte to the troubled situation in the country, and on the impossibility of maintaining order with poorly paid and too few troops at his disposal; the government made no response to its representations and, based on that, he had twice offered his resignation. When the riot broke out, Ahmet Pasha lost his head, thinking he was going to suffer the fate of one of his predecessors, and be torn to pieces in the midst of a popular uprising in Damascus. He consulted his *medjliss* on whether to march against the rioters; the *medjliss* dissuaded him, arguing that if the government did, the whole city would be lost; the sacrifice of a part of the population was therefore deemed preferable to the risk that the entire population would be placed beyond the control of authority and enter into open revolt.

This is consistent with "Extraits des sentences des fonctionnaires ottomans et des notables de Damas", which describes his "type" of accountability as "failing in duties of office", see *supra* note 55. In terms of direct evidence against Ahmad, Brant reported in late August that a "good deal of plunder" was found in the ex-governor-general's house (though this evidence was never mentioned again. Perhaps Brant was reporting the rumour, not the fact). Papers, Inclosure 1, in No. 118, Brant to Russell, sent 25 August 1860, received 13 September 1860.

59 Fuad met with Consul-General Moore and Admiral Martin one week after he arrived in Beirut. Both urged Fuad to remove Khurshid Pasha from his post and punish him for his role in "a most grievous wrong inflicted upon the civilised world"; Papers, No. 82 (and enclosures), Moore to Russell, sent 26 July 1860, received 17 August 1860. This being done, Khurshid was sent to Constantinople. Papers, No. 90, Fraser to Russell, sent 2 August 1860, received 22 August 1860. He was returned to Beirut along with Ahmad Pasha. Papers, No. 92, see *supra* note 41.

60 On Said Bey's connection with the English upper class, see Ann Pottinger Saab, *Reluctant Icon: Gladstone, Bulgaria, and the Working Classes, 1856–1878*, Harvard University Press, Cambridge, MA, 1998, p. 38. The Extraordinary Tribunal determined that he was

trials soon opened to the public (and even became a tourist attraction).[62] The English-language press in Beirut reported extensively on the hearings in Said Bey's case, many of them emphasising aspects of the proceedings that flew in the face of European procedure;[63] even the decidedly anti-Druze correspondent of the *Bombay Times and Standard* decried how the tribunal had deviated from the "forms of a common legal trial":

> The officers of this tribunal, which is to decide on the guilt or innocence of hundreds of men, are as follows:
>
> 1st. The Mufti from Constantinople, name Mustuntik Effendi, a man learned in the Moslem law, speaking the Turkish language, and familiar with the Koran as a classic, but not able to converse in Arabic. He is the President of the Tribunal and conducts the entire examination through an interpreter.
>
> 2nd. Associated with him are Ahmed Pasha, Governor General of the Province (called the Pashalic of Sidon) a man of some energy, ignorant of the Arabic, and of a very coarse, almost brutish countenance; also Mustapha Pasha, Turkish

the "supreme head" of the Druze. Papers, Inclosure 4, "Judgments passed by the Extraordinary Tribunal at Beyrout on the Chief People inculpated in the late Disturbances in the Mountain", in No. 229, Dufferin to Russell, sent 30 December 1860, received 11 January 1860.

[61] "The Massacres in Syria", *The Times*, 6 October 1860; Louet, 1862, p. 86, see *supra* note 2.

[62] *Souvenirs de Syrie*, 1903, pp. 269–70: "From disaster (like the sublime) to the ridiculous there is often a step. The foreheads of European assistants unwrinkle when in the presence of the indiscreet curiosity of tourists, mostly English travelers who, taking advantage of an open court, were sketching the faces of the accused and even those of the Ottoman judges, to the great displeasure thereof", see *supra* note 2.

[63] The correspondents for *The Times* and the *Morning Post* regarded the trials as flawed; "The Massacres in Syria", *The Times*, 6 November 1860; "Syria", *Morning Post*, 3 November 1860. A few correspondents found the trial eminently fair. See for example "Syria", *Morning Chronicle*, 18 December 1860 reprinting a report from the *Levant Herald*, 28 November 1860: "[The proceedings] would bear a most favourable comparison with many state judicial proceedings in Europe – in Italy, and even in France. The public may rely that those who can be proved guilty before this court will not escape, not do I think the innocent will suffer"; "Syria", *Daily News*, 1 January 1861: "nothing can be fairer than the trials seem to be, and certainly nothing more open than the court". A reporter from a local Arab-language paper attended the proceedings and reported on them weekly; "Syria", *Morning Chronicle*, 24 December 1860 reprinting a report from the *Levant Herald*, 3 December 1860.

Admiral, who was trained in the English Navy; Abro Effendi, Private Secretary to Fuad Pasha, and the Mufti of Beirut.

These persons sit at one end of a long room, which is very luxuriously furnished with divans, carpets, &c., and smoke their cigars deliberately, none of them taking notes or even possessed of writing materials. The great Mufti sits in the middle of the upper end of the room quite by himself, with his legs crossed under him in oriental style, and rocks from one side to the other, puffing his tobacco smoke, resembling not a little a steamer rolling at the anchorage in a Syrian harbor. The prisoner Kasim Hassn-ed Dyn, a Druse old man, Private Secretary to Said Jinblat of Mokhtara. He was a confidential agent of his master, and was a most earnest, instrument in bringing about the massacre at Deir-el-Kamr. He sits in a chair in the end of the room opposite the Mufti. By his side sits six or eight Maronite and Greek Christian witnesses, who appear to testify against him. In the middle of the room and nearly half way between the Mufti and the prisoner, sit the clerk and the interpreter, and opposite them, in a row extending along the side of the room from the Mufti and the Pashas down towards the witnesses, are the seats of the agents of the Five Powers and spectators. The Mufti rocking to and fro, looks at the prisoner and asks the interpreter a question in Turkish. The interpreter writes it down carefully, and then repeats it in Arabic to the prisoner. The prisoner replies to the questions to "what he knows about the cause of the war," that he knows absolutely nothing, that he was a private individual, knowing nothing of what was transpiring, and proceeds in a long speech to exculpate himself, and call upon God to witness that he is innocent, and that the resurrection day will reveal all hearts, &c., &c., The interpreter explains the meaning in a few words to the Mufti, who takes another cigarette, and proceeds to mediate. The other Pashas ask questions, and then the witnesses are examined. None of the examiners take notes either of the questions or answers. The prisoner has no counsel. The witnesses and prisoner converse and dispute together, denying each other's statements, and then in a loud voice, and while the Mufti and Pashas are engaged in conversation, the Druse culprit, notoriously guilty, turns to the witnesses and says, "why do you testify this way, oh my children?" They answer, "because it is true and you cannot deny it", and the trial drags along. The prisoner is compelled to defend himself, which he does, keeping up a running fire upon the witnesses and interpreter, abounding in assertions of innocence and pious ejaculations just about in proportion to his own iniquity and complicity in crime.[64]

Most of the Ottoman officials hauled before the tribunal were accused of some form of negligence or omission.[65] Khurshid Pasha was charged with dispatching troops to too few locations to prevent the massacres, failing to confront the Druze or punish their leaders, and neglecting his duty to protect. He objected that sending troops into the Mountain would have left Beirut vulnerable to the violence sweeping through the rest of the region. The tribunal concluded that he had "endeavoured, though imperfectly, to do his duty", and accordingly recommended a sentence of life imprisonment.[66]

---

[64] "News Letters: Syria", *Bombay Times and Standard*, 26 February 1861. Press reports of Druze being subject to unfair trials stirred debate in the British Parliament. Russell assured an agitated Lord Fergusson that the Commission had things well in hand:

> With regard to the sentences, I have already said that the Commissioners in Syria will have all the evidence laid before them, and that if they think that that evidence is insufficient, or has been unfairly taken, it will be in their power to remonstrate with Fuad Pasha against their being carried into effect.

Hansard, House of Commons Debate, 8 February 1861 vol. 161, cc. 197.

[65] The sentencing reports communicated to the Commissioners do not identify which articles of the 1858 Imperial Penal Code the Ottoman defendants were charged with violating, but Article 99 looks like a good candidate:

> Whoever he may be from amongst great or small officials who shall use or cause to be used influence or coercion for the purpose of opposing the carrying out of the orders of the State or of the provisions of the Laws of Regulations or the collection of any kind of public revenues is punished with the punishment of temporary imprisonment; and if the conduct in this way of officials has taken place of necessity or compulsorily by order of their superiors this punishment does not apply to such but is carried out with regard to him from whom the order has first emanated; and if conduct of this kind is the cause of a more grave Jinayet the punishment for that grave Jinayet is awarded and carried out.

John Bucknill and Haig Utidjian, *The Imperial Ottoman Penal Code: A Translation*, Oxford University Press, Oxford, 1913, pp. 77. This provision is found in Part V of the Code: "Those who abuse the influence of their office and position and who do not fulfil the duties of their office".

[66] Papers, Inclosure 4, "Judgments passed by the Extraordinary Tribunal at Beyrout on the Chief People inculpated in the late Disturbances in the Mountain", in No. 229, see *supra* note 60.

Tahir Pasha, military commander at Beirut, was charged with having neglected his duty to question or oppose Christians "with flags flying and other symbols of war" or similarly excited bands of Druze. He was also accused of neglecting to protect the area around his camp, and negligently having believed Druze assurances that they would not attack Deir el-Kamar and subsequently withdrawing protective forces two days before the massacre there took place. His defence, that he did not have orders to protect the towns around his camp, that he was not in Deir el-Kamar at the time of the massacre, and that he had ordered the local military commander to protect that city before the massacres broke out, were treated as mitigating factors by the tribunal, which recommended a sentence of life imprisonment.[67]

Colonel Nuri Bey was accused of having squandered the military assets that had been placed at his disposal to prevent the Druze from marching on Zahlé and having "trusted to the words of the insurgent Druse". Nuri defended by arguing that he had obtained a promise from the Druze chiefs that they would attack the town only if provoked by its Christians, and that he was unable to decamp in Zahlé and protect the city, as he was denied entry by the locals. When word reached him back at his headquarters that fighting had broken out, he felt powerless to intervene "due to the smallness of the force at his disposal, and to the fact that both Christians and Druses were now intermingled". The tribunal treated these as extenuating circumstances, and recommended a sentence of life imprisonment.[68]

The sentencing report on Wasfi Efendi (*kahia* or secretary to Khurshid Pasha) and Ahmad Efendi (comptroller of property at Beirut and agent for the Druzes and Christians to the local government), who were tried together, is the most enigmatic of those found in the National Archives. These two individuals were accused of having "concerted and combined together, and committed various reprehensible acts, and of having contributed by the moral support they afforded to the Druzes, in bringing about the recent outbreak in the Mountain". Though this charge was neither "personal" nor "specific", and there was no "delinquency [...] proved against the individuals which is provided for by the law", the tribunal advised a sentence of temporary confinement in fortress and depri-

[67] *Ibid.*
[68] *Ibid.*

vation of rank, on the grounds that "all the people of the country, and the foreign authorities declare that their mutual accord and agreement was not of an ordinary description, but had reference to the affairs of the country; that they intermeddled in the action and measures of the administration, and occupied themselves reprehensibly in matters which were not within their legitimate cognizance".[69]

Twelve Druze chiefs voluntarily surrendered to the jurisdiction of the tribunal. The most notorious among them was Said Bey Jumblat, a powerful Druze chief with deep connections to the British government. The judges deemed him "the moral organizer and author" of the violence on the basis of circumstantial evidence and, without assessing the exculpatory proofs he had brought in his favour, recommended capital punishment.[70] Only one of the Druze chiefs who surrendered was acquitted;[71] the rest were, like Said, recommended to death.[72]

---

[69] *Ibid.*

[70] *Ibid.* For the minutes of Said Bey's trial see FO 406/11, Inclosure 1, "Interrogatories of the Druse Chiefs tried by the Extraordinary Tribunal at Beyrout", in No. 42, Bulwer to Russell sent 3 April, 1861, received 13 April 1861, TNA.

[71] The only Druze chief acquitted by the tribunal was extrajudicially sentenced to exile by Fuad when a letter allegedly showing his complicity in the massacres was brought to the attention of the Ottoman Commissioner. He was spared this fate at the last minute by the timely intervention of Lord Dufferin, the British commissioner, who argued with Fuad over the fairness of punishing an individual on the basis of documentary evidence that had not been adduced in court, contested the evidentiary value of the proof, and accused Fuad of violating his agreement to let the Commissioners comment on any sentences on a prisoner who had been tried in the presence of European delegates. Additional Papers, Inclosure 3, in No. 6, Dufferin to Russell, sent 24 March 1861, received 4 April 1861.

[72] Thirty-three "leaders of the insurgent bands" who had fled into the Mountain's inaccessible interior were deemed worthy of capital punishment after trials *in absentia*. Papers, Inclosure 4, in No. 229, see *supra* note 60. Said Bey and his cohorts were charged with violations of Articles 55, 56 and 57 of the Penal Code, reproduced below.

Article 55:

> Whoever personally or indirectly incites the subjects of the Imperial Ottoman Government or the inhabitants of the Ottoman dominions in order to make them to revolt in arms against the Ottoman Government is, if the matter of revolt which was his intention comes to effect entirely or the carrying out of the matter of the revolt shall have been commenced, put to death.

Article 56:

> Whoever dares, by making the people of the Ottoman dominions arm themselves against each other, to instigate or incite them to engage in mutual slaughter, or to bring about acts of rapine, pillage, devastation of

On 22 December Ottoman soldiers executed a massive arrest operation, detaining nearly 1,000 Druze men from the rural villages around Beirut and transporting them to Moukhtara for trial before a third extraor-

---

country or homicide in divers places is, if the matter of disorder comes into effect entirely or if a commencement of the matter of the disorder has been made, likewise put to death.

Article 57:

If a gang of ruffians jointly carry out or attempt to carry out any of the riotous acts set forth in the above written Arts. 55 and 56 those from among the persons included in such band of ruffians who are the actual chief ruffians or the agitators of disturbance are put to death wherever they are caught; and such from among the others who are taken and seized at the place of the Jinayet are placed in kyurek perpetually or temporarily according to the degree of their Jinayet or complicity in the matter of the disorder which may become manifest.

Bucknill and Utidjian, 1913, p. 45–49, see *supra* note 65. Inclosure 4, in No. 229, see *supra* note 60. For the minutes of the examinations of the Druze defendants see FO 406/11, Inclosure 1, TNA, see *supra* note 70.

The author of *Souvenirs de Syrie*, 1903, pp. 268–69, see *supra* note 2, attended the trials, including the sentencing hearings:

[...] the meetings of the Special Court presented matters of strong psychological and artistic interest. We were lucky enough to attend, and we retained a deep impression. What a striking example of the vicissitudes of human existence! We found on the dock prominent figures we had admired a few months earlier, in their picturesque attire, at a costume ball of the French consul's. Their theatrical figures had once inspired thoughts of magic enchantments; but the show had turned to drama, as the tragic troupe marched for the second time before our eyes, in the fifth act. These were the same Druze sheikhs, Said Djemblat, Hussein Talhouk and others, along with the same high based Turkish officials, Khourschid Pasha and his cronies.

However, to continue the comparison, the situation and the decorations were much changed; the players were changed no less. You could see on their faces the traces of their emotions. Khourschid Pasha had completely bleached in prison. Said Djemblat had collapsed under the weight of mental suffering and illness that would soon prevail. Of the rest the calm and impassive attitude of many defendants who paraded before the judges cannot be denied for even a moment. They would have told strangers to the outcome of the trial on which their lives depended. They listened to their convictions with complete indifference, some even with a slight smirk. A single individual, a Druze from the low class, lost his composure when reading his death sentence was over, and fell on his knees crying to seek pardon.

dinary tribunal.[73] But when Fuad announced his intention of restricting capital punishment to "a limited number of those who had distinguished themselves by acts of especial atrocity" and asked the Christians to provide evidence against those they considered the "most guilty" the prose-

---

[73] Fuad reported that 949 had been arrested. Papers, Inclosure 2, "Report of the Nineteenth Meeting, held in Beyrout, January 19, 1861", in No. 310, Dufferin to Russell, sent 10 February 1861, received 20 February 1861. The *Morning Post* ("Syria, 12 January 1861) correspondent happened to be in Moukhtara as the prisoners were brought in for trial before the third Extraordinary Tribunal:

> As I stood upon the terrace at different time on Sunday I could see knots of soldiers bringing in Druses from different parts of the valley. […] I have never seen any large bodies of Druses walking together before, and I must confess that their manly carriage, and open, bold countenances, void of any appearance of fear, were calculated to excite one's admiration. Even old men, with fine white beards, walked by the side of the young ones with nearly as elastic a step and as free a gait. A great many of their wives followed in their wake, with very unfavourable impressions as to the result of their arrest. These women were frightened, and could hardly believe that their husbands were going to be put into prison except for some very bloody purpose; crowds of them, white-veiled, were to be seen everywhere in a state of great grief and lamentation. It was duly explained to them, or at least a majority of them, that they need fear nothing, but they were not entirely satisfied by that assurance. It is not, however, unnatural or unreasonable that a women, who has just seen her husband or son shut up in prison and a sentinel mounted before the door, should have her doubts about his fate, and remain weeping near the place; and a great number of these persons have received kindness and consolation […]. The fact of 1,000 men being suddenly thrown into prison certainly sounds rather formidable, but there are some mitigating circumstances to be explained. I was allowed to go through the whole of the prisons the other night, and I found the men comparatively comfortable. They were rather closely packed together in one or two places, but still, on the whole, they were very well treated, and a few evinced the quiet state of their minds by humming and singing songs. Omar Pasha seems willing, also, to be very lenient with them. The men were, in the first instance, allowed to come outside the doors to converse with their wives, a few soldiers only standing round as guard. This favour is now denied them, and the women complain bitterly of the deprivation, though it is partly their own fault that such a measure has been taken. Yesterday intelligence was brought to the pasha that two men had made their escape out of prison by changing dresses with two women, a trick easily performed, and the disguise is not easily betrayed, as they cover up all but one eye with the thick white sheet which the women are accustomed to wear.

cutions ground to a halt.[74] Despite Fuad's best efforts to persuade them, the Christians refused to participate.[75] A bevy of reasons was given for this – fear of retaliation, inability to provide additional evidence, a desire not to invalidate the testimony of those who had already named names, incapacity to call on "the whole" Christian population to furnish evidence – but the most likely scenario is that the Christians were afraid to have their evidence tested, or were gambling that the Ottoman government would capitulate and cave to their demands that those already imprisoned be extra-judicially killed.[76] Cognizant that Europe would never accept 'impunity', Fuad was forced to conduct these trials without the benefit of victim testimony:

> [The prisoners] were divided under three different heads, those supposed to be quite innocent of any participation in the late affairs, those who were supposed to be culpable, and those suspected of being rather deep in the mire. The process of sorting was rather interesting; every morning they were assembled in fifties at a time before Omar Pasha and a commission, in the grand yard of the palace, a guard of Turkish soldiers being assembled round about the place, and each individual was separately asked his name, his village, and

---

74   Inclosure, in No. 258, Dufferin to Russell, sent 13 January 1861, received 24 January 1861.

75   Among other arguments, Fuad attempted to persuade them that Europe would never tolerate a judicially sanctioned massacre, but that "the heads that must fall are those which, by their social position, have had a fatal influence on the ground, or by the number and atrocity of their crimes, have injured humanity". "Fuad Pasha to Abro Efendi", 24 January 1861, to Inclosure 4, "Protocol of the Twentieth Meeting of the Syrian Commission, held in Beyrout, January 24", in No. 310, Dufferin to Russell, sent 10 February 1860, received 20 February 1860.

76   Papers, Inclosure 2, in No. 276, Major Fraser to Lord Dufferin, 14 January 1861. For more on this episode see Farah, 2000, 627–28, see *supra* note 2; Papers, Inclosure 6, in No. 288, Dufferin to Russell, sent 27 January 1861, received 8 February 1861. Most of the Commissioners gave the Maronites the benefit of the doubt. E.P. Novikow, the Russian commissioner, regarded the Christians as genuinely "obliged in conscience" not to participate further. Leon Béclard, the French commissioner, believed that the Tribunal at Moukhtara "inspired in them less confidence than the one at Beiyrout, and they had doubts about the outcome of this procedure, and want to avoid compromising it". P. von (de) Weckbecker, the Austrian commissioner, attributed their abstention to the "special feeling to the people of this country who do not yet understand anything about the formalities of public justice. This is the first time that it works before them, and then proceeds to lead to repression". Only Dufferin perceived deliberate malice in the move; he believed that the Maronites were attempting to force Fuad into imposing a blanket punishment on the Druze. Papers, Inclosure 2, "Protocol of the Seventeenth Meeting, December 31, 1860", in No. 288.

---

where he was at such and such a time, whether he possessed any property belonging to a Christian at all, &c.; and according to the answer he gave he was placed onto the place allotted for his category.[77]

Fuad would subsequently explain to the commissioners that in the absence of evidence, most convictions were based on a "simple presumption of guilt".[78]

It is difficult to determine from the documents available in the British archives how many punishments were actually doled out for crimes in the Mountain. A chart appended to a 7 March 1861 communication from Lord Dufferin contains the names of 58 Druze for whom death was recommended by the Beirut and Moukhtara tribunals.[79] Those cases were commuted in Constantinople to perpetual imprisonment in Belgrade in early July 1861.[80] A list of 248 Druze condemned to deportation or im-

---

[77] "Syria", *Morning Post*, 26 January 1861. Makdisi, 2000, p. 154, quotes a communication from Fuad to the "Ottoman commissioner at the tribunal" from around this time that "the heads which must fall [...] are those of men, who because of their social standing, exercised a grievous influence on the masses, or who, because of the sheer number and atrocity of their crimes, caused the most harm to humanity", citing BBA IRADE MM 935/i, Leff. 3, 24 January1861, see *supra* note 2.

[78] Papers, Inclosure, "Protocol of the Twenty-First meeting of the Syrian Commission, held at Beyrout, January 29, 1861", in No. 372, Dufferin to Russell, sent 4 March 1861, received 26 March 1861. Ali Bey Jumblat, for example, was sentenced by the Moukhtara Tribunal even after "[t]he Court...recorded that it did not find the charge proved [...]". Major Fraser, who observed his trial and would later petition Bulwer to intercede on behalf of the accused, wrote that he was punished "either in unacknowledged deference to his being signalized as a leader in the denunciatory lists presented by the Christians [...], or in consequence of his near relationship to Said Bey Jumblat [...]". FO 195/660, No. 39, Fraser to Bulwer, 10 August 1861, TNA. Ali's sentence was commuted from exile at Tripoli to local imprisonment. FO 195/660, No. 56, Fraser to Bulwer, 2 October 1861. TNA.

[79] FO 195/658, Inclosure, "Tableaux des Druses jugés par les Tribunaux de Beyrout et de Muktara et considérés comme coupables de la 1st catégorie – 1861", in No. 133, Dufferin to Bulwer, 7 March 1861. According to the chart, 39 of those listed were convicted in Moukhtara, 13 were condemned by the Beirut tribunal for actions related to the massacres, and six were condemned by the Beirut Tribunal for contumacy. See Papers, Inclosure 2, "Protocol of the Twenty-Second Meeting of the Syrian Commission, held at Beyrout, February 27, 1861", in No. 375, Dufferin to Russell, sent 10 March 1861, received 26 March 1861, during which Fuad states that 58 individuals have been recommended to death by the Moukhtara tribunal. The chart does not include the names of the Druze chiefs who appeared before or were condemned *in absentia* by the Beirut Tribunal.

[80] FO Inclosure, "List of Druse prisoners condemned to perpetual imprisonment, and sent from Beyrout to Belgrade for detention in that fortress (with the exception of those since dead) on the 10th July 1861", in FO 78/1625, No. 3, Dufferin to Bulwer, 8 September

prisonment also appears as an annex to the notes of the Commission's twenty-sixth meeting of March 1861.[81] These are probably the same persons referenced in a 23 March 1861 letter mentioning 245 Druze exiled to Tripoli.[82] A dispatch from Tripoli a month later reports on the condition of 260 Druze that had arrived.[83]

7.5. Justice at the International Commission of Inquiry: "The Goddess Themis Never Kinks Beneath the Waves. Tho' in the Swell of the Great Popular Ocean She is Now and Then Lost Sight of"

In July 1861 the French Foreign Minister Thouvenel suggested the creation of a body to (1) "ascertain the circumstances which brought about the late conflicts"; (2) "determine the share of responsibility of the Chiefs of the insurrection and of the Agents of the local administration", as well as (3) "the compensation due to the victims"; and (4) "study for the purpose of submitting them to the approbation of their Governments and of the

---

1860, TNA. These cases were sent for review at Dufferin's urging. FO 195/658, No. 133, Dufferin to Bulwer, 7 March 1861, TNA. These are probably the 68 cases referred to in Dufferin's dispatch of 15 March; FO 406/11, Inclosure 1, in No. 525, Dufferin to Russell, sent 15 March 1861, received 28 March 1861, TNA.

[81] FO 406/11, Inclosure 14, "Annex No. 3 to the Protocol of the Twenty-Sixth Meeting of the Syrian Commission", in No 105, Dufferin to Russell, sent 26 April 1860, received 11 May 1860, TNA. Fawaz notes a mistake in the numbering of the chart. The correct number of entries is 248. Fawaz, 1994, p. 272, fn. 57, see *supra* note 2. Some 205 of these prisoners are listed as having been "detained" at Moukhtara, the remainder at Beirut.

[82] FO 406/11, Inclosure 7, in No. 15, Dufferin to Russell, sent 24 March 1861, received 4 April 1861, TNA. Fifty-five of these were sentenced to some term of imprisonment, 155 "simply exiles, merely removed from the country until quieter times should arrive". The rest were too ill to travel. Dufferin felt that most of those sent to Tripoli could not be considered criminals "in the legal acceptation of the term, inasmuch as very little evidence was produced against any of them". But despite his misgivings, he conceded that setting the accused at liberty would be disastrous. "Some satisfaction must be given to the Christians, and if persons who are known to have dipped their hands up to their elbows in human blood are immediately allowed to return to the villages where [...] it would give rise to an amount of panic and clamour against the Government which might become extremely embarrassing". Dufferin was relieved to learn that these individuals would not be treated as prisoners in Tripoli, that they might be permitted to return to the Mountain, in the future, that climate in Tripoli was healthy, and that provision would be made for the prisoners and their families in their place of exile. FO 406/11, Inclosure 1, in No. 525, TNA, see *supra* note 80.

[83] FO 406/11, Inclosure, in No. 110, Dufferin to Russell, sent 3 May 1860, received 16 May 1860, TNA. Only 26 arrived as "criminals". The remainder were "exiles".

Porte the arrangements which should be adopted with the view of averting fresh misfortunes". Only through an International Commission of Inquiry, Thouvenel argued, could Europe "form a correct idea of past occurrences and the necessities of the situation".[84] The proposal was immediately accepted by British Foreign Minister Lord Russell with one slight (and seemingly unpremeditated) alteration. Russell agreed to a Commission "to determine the responsibility of all persons concerned in those proceedings; to consider what compensation or punishment may be due; and finally to submit to the Sultan their opinion upon the measures best calculated to prevent further calamities".[85] Thouvenel's language suggesting that the primary purpose of the commissioners was to produce reports that would enable the governments of Europe to act sensibly was left out, and his four subjects of inquiry now presented as ends to be pursued by the commissioners themselves. The semantic shift stuck, and from this point on the French Foreign Minister would consider it the job of the Commission "to see that the authors and abettors in the massacres were properly punished".[86]

Dufferin, a 34-year-old aristocrat whose experience in the Middle East was limited to hunting on the Nile, organising excavations, and appropriating antiques to his country house in Clandeboye, was the first commissioner appointed by any of the Powers.[87] On 30 July 1860 he was instructed to proceed to Constantinople and await further instructions from the British ambassador to Turkey, Sir Henry Bulwer. The purpose of the Commission, he was informed at that time, "will be to obtain security for the future peace of Syria". This, he was told, would require "a speedy, pure, and impartial administration of justice. Those who suffer wrong and see that wrong committed with impunity take punishment into their own hands or rather substitute revenge for due and legal retribution".[88]

---

[84] Papers, No. 6, "M Thouvenel to Count Persigny – (Communicated to Lord J Russell by Count Persigny, July 17)".

[85] Papers, No. 7, Russell to Bulwer, 17 July 1860.

[86] Papers, No 54, Cowley to Russell, sent 2 August 1860, received 3 August 1860; Papers, No. 56, Cowley to Russell, sent 3 August 1860, received 4 August 1860; No. 61, Cowley to Russell, sent 7 August 1860, received 9 August 1860.

[87] Sir Alfred Comyn Lyall, *The Life of the Marquis of Dufferin and Ava*, vol. 1, John Murray, London, 1905, p. 93.

[88] Papers, No. 42, Russell to Dufferin, 30 July 1860.

Thouvenel, concerned that separate instructions increased the risk of "discordant opinions" among the commissioners, suggested that identic notes be sent directly from their governments.[89] Russell's counter-proposal that the representatives of the intervening Powers in Constantinople should draw up the proposed instructions was rejected by the French Minister, who fretted that "the character of the Commission which is intended to institute an inquiry [...] would be altered, if the instructions to the members of it were not [...] furnished directly by their different Governments".[90] Privately, Russell grew suspicious that the French had proposed the Commission merely as a legitimating cover for military intervention: "If the French had been sincere in wishing to stop the murder of Christians they would have followed up their proposal of the 16th of July by immediate appointment of a Commissioner and instructions accordingly. It looks as if they relied only on the sword".[91] But he openly professed not to care whence the instructions issued[92] and Thouvenel shortly produced draft language by which the delegates would propose a political reorganisation of the Mountain, "examine in concert with [the others], into the origin and the causes of events, to determine the amount of responsibility of the leaders of the insurrection, and of the agents of the Government[,] and [...] call for the punishment of the guilty".[93]

These instructions were issued by the Powers to their representatives without input from the Porte. When the Ottoman government caught

---

[89] FO 406/10, No. 69, Cowley to Russell, sent 2 August 1860, received 3 August 1860, TNA.

[90] FO 406/10, No. 72, Cowley to Russell, sent 3 August 1860, received 4 August 1860, TNA. See also FO 406/10, No. 78, Cowley to Russell, sent 7 August 1860, received 9 August 1860, TNA. Thouvenel was primarily concerned "that if the Commission was to act upon instructions emanating from Constantinople it would not carry with it the same weight as a Commission acting upon identic instructions coming direct from the several Governments furnishing Commissioners". Count Rechberg of Austria found himself in agreement with Thouvenel, as in his opinion, "the conflicting jealousies and intrigues which were always rife in that capital [Constantinople] would render the adoption of an identic draft of instructions by all the Ambassadors a matter of difficult achievement". FO 406/10, No. 109, Fane to Russell, sent 16 August 1860, received 20 August 1860, TNA. The Russians sided with the British, and announced that their commissioner, Novikow, would receive instructions from the Russian envoy at Constantinople. FO 406/10, No. 133, Erskine to Russell, sent 21 August 1860, received 3 September 1860, TNA.

[91] PRO 30.22.104. Russell to Cowley, 9 August 1860, TNA.

[92] FO 406/10, No. 80, Russell to Cowley, 9 August 1860, TNA.

[93] Papers, No. 70, "Proposed Instructions to the French Commissioner in Syria. – Communicated by the Count de Jaucourt, August 11".

wind of the directive, which memorialised a grant of authority over matters of punishment in excess of what they had envisioned when they had consented to the Commission in late July 1860, they pushed for a declaration that the commissioners had "no judicial functions" and were not "authorized to re-investigate cases on which Fuad Pasha has already pronounced judgment".[94] A draft of instructions sent by the Porte to Fuad on 17 September found in the US and UK archives suggests that the Ottoman government achieved this and provides some insight into how the Commission was justified to the Ottoman authorities:

> As for the joint inquiry into the events which have occurred, here too it is evident that everyone [Great Britain, Russia, Prussia, France, Austria] will acknowledge the principle that so long as the two contending parties are subjects of the Ottoman Government alone the inquiry in such a case belongs exclusively and independently to their Government. But as in the above deplorable events certain persons who were subjects and inhabitants of Foreign Governments sustained wrong and injury, and as at Damascus some of the Consulates were laid waste, the necessity of a joint inquiry has arisen therefrom. It is owing to these reasons that the participation of the mixed Commission in the requisite investigations cannot be declined.* But this Commission is only authorized to inquire into and make known the information it may have acquired, it has no power to give judgment as a Tribunal. Therefore it is evident that the trial and punishment according to the established laws of the realm of any offenders whom the Commission may think proper to accuse in the course of its inquiries will be exclusively within your special competency.

---

[94] FO 406/10, No. 66, Bulwer to Rusell, sent 25 July 1860, received 3 August 1860, TNA; FO 406/10, No. 164, Fane to Russell, sent 13 September 1860, received 17 September 1860, TNA. There was also discussion among the ambassadors and Porte officials over whether Fuad was properly considered part of the Commission. Initially the Russian and Prussian ambassadors said no, the French and British Ambassadors yes. "The important point to secure", wrote Bulwer, "is that the Five Powers and the Porte should seem to be acting together". Ultimately the 'yes' voices won the day. D1071/H/C/3/8/3, Bulwer to Dufferin, 11 September 1860, PRONI.

> * Therefore an inquiry into all the crimes which have been committed cannot naturally be removed from their collective action.[95]

There was some variation in the ostensibly identical notes that were sent out. In his dispatch to Dufferin, for example, Russell added to the original language the directive that his work should result in justice "with regard to the Chiefs, as well as the subordinate instruments of crime".[96] Moreover, each commissioner almost certainly received some private directives that ordered them to prioritise aspects of their mandate over others or instructed them to adopt a particular ideology, cause or perspective. Dufferin, for example, reached out to Russell to ask him whether he should make an effort to place the Druze, the longstanding "object of the solicitude of the English Government", in an advantageous position and act as "the apologist of a friend who has put himself in the wrong", or whether he should "postpone all political considerations to the interests of Humanity" and act impartially to end the internecine warfare on the Mountain.[97] Russell instructed Dufferin to adopt an impartial attitude toward the Druze and "let them suffer the penalties due to their crimes", but added that "Koorchid Pasha, Achmet Pacha, and Osman Pacha ought to be shot" as the "Turkish Government and officers are still more to blame

---

[95] R59 M46 R17, "Draft of Instructions to Fuad Pasha. Communicated Sept 17th 1860 by the Sublime Porte", NARA; also available in FO 195/656, TNA. On 8 September 1860 Fuad Pasha met Dufferin for the first time and asked him "whether the Commission was itself to become a tribunal before whom the accused were to be arraigned, and to what extent its functions were to supersede his own as Military and Civil Governor of the Province [...]". Fuad proposed "that he should be allowed to adjudicate on the cases brought before him, becoming himself responsible to the Commission for the manner in which he carried on the investigations, that on the same terms he should be permitted to determine on the mode of conducting the military operations against the Druzes, and that before the Commission entered upon the discussion of any arrangements for the future, it should be competent for him to take the initiative, submitting to their consideration whatever plan of his own he might be prepared to proposed". Dufferin replied that he could not know "in what way the Commission might eventually interpret their instructions" but in his personal opinion the commissioners "would be anxious to adopt whatever course would be most likely to preserve in the eyes of its subjects the dignity of the Porte and the authority of its representative". FO 78/1625, No. 3, TNA, see *supra* note 80. The message was passed along to Russell, but an exhaustive review of the relevant National Archives files has not revealed any reply that addressed this concern.

[96] Compare FO 406/10, No. 70 "Proposed Instructions to the French Commissioner in Syria Communicated by the Count de Jaucouri August 11" to FO 406/10, No. 99, Russell to Dufferin, 14 August 1860, TNA.

[97] PRO 30/22/94, Dufferin to Russell, 28 August 1860, TNA.

than the bloody Druses".[98] Another example may be found in the Archives des affaires étrangères. Upon learning that the French commissioner had clashed with Dufferin during the first few meetings of the Commission, the former was commended by his ambassador for "reminding Dufferin that the official aim of the commission might be to help reestablish the sultan's authority, but its real purpose was to come to the aid of the Christians who had been 'abandoned by the very government which was supposed to protect them'".[99] Messages like these coloured the views of each delegate and set the stage for subsequent showdowns over the scope of the Commission's punishment powers.

The Commission, comprising Fuad Pasha (represented by Abro Efendi when he was otherwise occupied), Lord Dufferin (Britain), P. von (de) Weckbecker (Austria), L. Béclard (France), Guido von (de) Rehfues (Prussia) and E.P. Novikow (Russia), would sit for 29 sessions over seven months, during the course of which it would be transformed into a quasi-court in which European delegates acted as "Assessors with his Excellency [Fuad Pasha] on the cases brought before him and responsible for whatever verdict might be rendered upon each".[100] This process began even before all of the commissioners had arrived. Dufferin, who reached Beirut just in time for the commencement of the trials of the Ottoman officials there,[101] armed with a mandate of (limited) impartiality, expressed an unqualified disdain for the Ottoman justice even before the trials of the Druze had begun:

> When those designated for trial by public opinion are declared guilty, the disagreeable conviction forces itself upon one, that though the verdict may be just, its relation to the crime is almost accidental. The Turkish authorities are aware that Europe requires satisfaction for what has occurred, that a certain amount of punishment must take place and that the reputation of the Porte must be cleansed in the blood of the guilty.

---

[98] PRO 30/22/116, Russell to Dufferin, 8 September 1860, TNA.

[99] Fawaz, 1994, p. 199, see *supra* note 2, citing CP/T/348, La Valette-Thouvenel, No. 1, 1 January 1861, Archives des affaires étrangères.

[100] Papers, Inclosure 2, "Minute on the Judgments proposed to be passed on the Turkish Officials and Druse Chiefs by the Extraordinary Tribunal of Beyrout", in No. 351, Dufferin to Russell, sent 24 February 1861, received 13 March 1861.

[101] Papers, Inclosure 1, in No. 141, Dufferin to Russell, sent 14 September 1860, received 29 September 1860.

The tribunal acts under pressure; the defendant considers himself a victim surrendered to a political exigency; the plaintiff feels that it is rather a politic propitiation that has been made than that the ends of justice have been satisfied.

The better nature of every one revolts against such blundering jurisprudence.

In the case of the Druse Chiefs it is particularly necessary that those who judge them should be persons who have not only the will to decide impartially, but the intelligence to discriminate sagaciously.

The number of lies which will be ratified by the most solemn oaths will probably be enormous, the mass of conflicting testimony considerable, the distinctions to be drawn extremely subtle. I hardly think a native tribunal will have either the patience, the conscientiousness, or the freedom of opinion necessary to deal with the cases brought before them.[102]

He closed out his communiqué with a suggestion that the Commission "interfere" or discover some other remedy to the "crying evil[s]" of dishonesty, incompetence, politicisation that marred the Tribunal. He would soon get his wish. Two weeks later, at the Commission's first meeting (5 October 1860), the commissioners challenged Abro over the decision to allow Husni Bey, who was suspected of complicity in some of the massacres before the Beirut tribunal, to serve as a judge[103] and not to

---

[102] Papers, Inclosure 2, in No. 147, Dufferin to Russell, sent 23 September 1860, received 26 October 1861.

[103] Papers, Inclosure 1, "Protocol of the First Meeting of the Syrian Commission, held at Beyrout, October 5, 1860", in No. 163, Dufferin to Russell, sent 12 October 1860, received 25 October 1860. Fuad announced he would be removed and his role in the massacres investigated during the sixth meeting. The *procès-verbal* of the Commission's meetings are a mere summary of the statements of the commissioners, and a partial (pro-French, the secretary being a Frenchman) summary at that. FO 406/10, Inclosure 5, in No. 240, Dufferin to Russell, sent 4 November 1860, received 19 November 1860, TNA. The records have a clipped and disorganised feel that makes the lines of inquiry pursued by the commissioners difficult to follow. Utterances that may appear spontaneous or disjointed on the record were probably logical in the context of the actual conversations that took place. Likewise, when it appears that a line of argument simply petered out without resolution, an understanding may have been reached and simply gone unrecorded. Dufferin's communiqués to London fill some of the gaps, as they sometimes reveal leitmotifs or analytic processes beyond those recorded in the official summaries.

bring any witnesses in the case against Khurshid Pasha.[104] When Abro prevaricated, they addressed a note to Fuad requesting files "related to the proceedings against the accused or guilty", which would serve as the basis for an opinion on the question of whether new proceedings were "necessary", demanded clarification of the "nature of the investigation" against Khurshid, other Ottoman authorities and the Druze, and asserted their "right to intervene" in the investigation in a communication.[105] The scope of the "right" in question emerged as a theme at the second meeting (9 October). Weckbecker was convinced that the commissioners lacked the authority to "directly summon" witnesses absent the presence of Fuad, a position shared with Abro, who urged the commissioners to await Fuad's reply to their joint communiqué, but objected to by the French, Russian and Prussian commissioners as contrary to the "formal admission of the Porte of the principle of collective inquiry, as clearly expressed in its instructions to [Fuad]".[106]

In a letter to the other commissioners, Fuad consented to provide them with information about the trials but balked at conceding a right to participate in the proceedings. He suggested instead that the Commission was intended to first undertake a "general investigation", that is a "trial between the [Druze and Christian] population to first establish the cause of these events, the general guilt" and then identify "those culpable individuals not yet in the hands of justice".[107] At their third meeting (11 October) the commissioners unanimously rejected Fuad's distinction between the "general investigation" and the "judicial inquiry" as artificial and declared that they would attend the trials.[108] Fuad reserved "the opinion of his government" but accepted that the delegates or their proxies could attend the proceedings in Beirut.[109]

---

[104] Abro countered that it "would have been difficult to admit evidence against the premier authority in the province", by which he probably means that it would have been difficult to find people to testify; *ibid.*

[105] Papers, Annex to Inclosure 1, in No. 163, see *supra* note 103.

[106] Papers, Inclosure 2, "Protocol of the Second Meeting of the Syrian Commission, held at Beyrout, October 9, 1860", in No. 163, see *supra* note 103.

[107] Papers, Annex 1 to Inclosure, "Protocol of the Third Meeting of the Syrian Commission, held at Beyrout, October 11, 1860", in No. 168, Meade to Hammond, sent 22 October 1860, received 1 November 1860.

[108] "Protocol of the Third Meeting", in No. 168, see *supra* note 107.

[109] Papers, Inclosure 12, "Protocol of the Fourth Meeting of the Syrian Commission, held at Beyrout, October 15, 1860", in No. 175, Dufferin to Bulwer, sent 26 October 1860, re-

The sixth meeting (26 October) was the first time that Fuad attended in person. Naturally, the discussion was principally concerned with the extent to which the foreign representatives could meddle in the administration of Turkish justice at Beirut. Dufferin suggested that delegates be allowed to question defendants and witnesses directly. The Austrian commissioner disagreed, and suggested that intervention should be limited to spectator-like observation on the part of delegates, with the Commission communicating any recommendations to Fuad. The British commissioner considered this unnecessarily wasteful, as the attending delegates themselves were in the best position to provide advice immediately helpful to the judges. The Russian and French Ministers agreed with their continental colleague, citing the risk that the delegates would prejudice the Ottoman judges. Fuad reiterated his rejection of direct intervention in the proceedings, referring to his duty to protect the integrity of Ottoman justice.[110]

The foreign representatives were able to reach an agreement that the Commission was "vested with a right of exactly the same procedure as those operating in the Turkey Missions and Consulates in any joint trial

---

ceived 8 November 1860. Dufferin was granted the right to attend or send a representative as a spectator, though he instructed his delegate not to remain passive: "Should you remark any irregularities or partiality in the procedure of the Court, whether in a sense favourable or inimical to the accused, you will subjoin a memorandum on the subject at the foot of your daily report. Should the impropriety which attracts your notice be of a nature to admit of correction on the spot, you will hand to the President of the Court a private communication calling his attention to the circumstance: but in the exercise of this function you will be careful not to transgress the bounds of due discretion". Inclosure 2, in No. 175, *ibid.* I have not been able to determine whether other commissioners issued similar instructions to their delegates. Dufferin's desire to interfere did not stem entirely from a concern with the integrity of the proceedings. He was also anxious that the commissioners use the opportunity presented by the trials to root out those members of the Turkish government most implicated in the massacres. Papers, Inclosure 1, in No. 175, Dufferin to Russell, sent 26 October 1860, received 8 November 1860: "[T]o render our intervention in these judicial proceedings really useful and effectual it would seem necessary that our delegates should have the privilege of suggesting to the Court whatever supplementary questions it may appear to them desirable should be addressed to the prisoner or the witnesses. As the members of the Tribunal will be prepared to quash any evidence at all discreditable to the Turkish Government, and even refuse to the prisoner whatever benefit he might derive from being able to prove he acted under instructions, the exigencies of justice would seem to require some such precaution being taken".

110 Papers, Inclosure 8, "Protocol of the Sixth Meeting of the Syrian Commission, held at Beyrout, October 26, 1860", in No. 182, Dufferin to Russell, sent 4 November 1860, received 19 November 1860.

judged by the courts of the country", and unanimously requested that "no final judgment be pronounced before [the commissioners] had an opportunity to formulate its opinion on the whole of the investigation, and to suggest, if any, to Fuad Pasha elements of a re-examination it finds necessary to inform his conscience". In the face of an otherwise unanimous ultimatum Fuad had to concede something. His dispensation was narrow as could be: he would "not decline to communicate the reports to the Commissioners, which would tell him what She thought". This pronouncement met with the approval of all foreign commissioners.[111]

The sixth meeting also saw some discussion of whether Said Bey Jumblat should be granted access to counsel. Fuad rejected the suggestion as impractical given that the Ottoman Empire had never developed the "institution of defence advocates", and the likelihood that counsel would resort to use of "the less-than-worthy" to procure favourable testimony.[112] An effort on the part of Dufferin to demand additional procedural safeguards in Said Bey's case was denied by Fuad, and prompted Weckbecker to exclaim that the Commission was not here to advocate for the innocent.[113] "She is here", he remarked "only to cause the punishment of the guilty". Dufferin and Rehfues disagreed: "the Commission is interested above all in discovery of truth".[114]

Dufferin also pressed Fuad to improve the procedural quality of the Beirut tribunal behind the scenes through private letters. The Ottoman commissioner was willing to provide Said Bey with summaries of each day's proceedings and an opportunity to voice his objections to the trial,[115] but balked at providing the accused with counsel despite Dufferin's protests that the privilege was "accorded even to prisoners in trial by

---

[111] *Ibid*. Fuad explained that the Extraordinary Tribunal itself did not make final judgments, but rather issued recommendations which become final only when confirmed by him.

[112] Fuad also expressed concern that Said Bey could use his wealth to suborn witnesses. FO 406/10, Inclosure 5, in No. 240, TNA, see *supra* note 103.

[113] *Ibid*.

[114] "Protocol of the Sixth Meeting of the Syrian Commission", see *supra* note 110. From Dufferin's communiqué home: "although the Commission collectively may be considered to discharge the duty of prosecutors on behalf of Europe and Christianty [...] from the moment our Delegates entered Court, the discovery of truth and the attainment of the ends of justice was the sole object that they ought to propose to themselves, and that the acquittal of the innocent was as essentially the logical consequence of this principle as the condemnation of the guilty". FO 406/10, Inclosure 5, in No. 240, TNA, see *supra* note 103.

[115] Papers, Inclosure 3, in No. 175, Dufferin to Bulwer, 26 October 1860.

courts-martial whose procedures are the most summary known to European law".[116] The British commissioner later admitted that there had been some visible improvement in the conduct of the proceedings against Said Bey, but nevertheless vowed to continue pushing his colleagues towards obtaining permission to handle witnesses directly. His concerns were partly borne of altruism and a genuine desire to see justice done, and partly from his conviction that the Beirut tribunal was actively hiding evidence which would impugn the Turkish government, and that only direct control over the proceedings would reveal the "absolute truth".[117]

By mid-November attention had shifted to the punishment of the lower-level Druze participants in the bloodshed. After the drubbing Fuad had been subjected to over the deficiencies of the Beirut tribunal, he must have relished the prospect of forcing his colleagues to confront the same difficult choices he had. At the tenth meeting (14 November) Fuad presented the commissioners with the option of applying "summary and expeditious" or "regular methodical" proceedings, noting that the former "does not give time to weigh the evidence, or always accurately result in proportion between the sentence and the degree of guilt", while the latter were only rarely subject to post-trial suspension or revision. The commissioners were unanimous in their support for the summary proceedings. The Austrian commissioner concluded that extraordinary proceedings were justified by the nature of the crimes themselves: "the beginnings of extermination of one race of the Empire by another" amounting to "a fact of civil war, an act of rebellion, a crime of lèse-majesté" as opposed to a "civil" or "individual to individual" offence. The Prussian and French commissioners agreed that only "swift and exemplary" punishment would be effective in restoring peace; Novikow approved on the grounds that Fuad had inoculated himself from reproach, but suggested that "subordinate" culprits should be dealt with in a way that avoided the "excesses of

---

[116] Inclosure 6, Dufferin to Fuad Pasha, 25 October 1860, in No. 175. Dufferin did not want to be perceived as having "at all wished to insist that the formalities and complications known to European law should be practiced on the present occasion". In his own words: "I am well aware that in such a crisis it is more humane to administer a rough and speedy justice than to allow those manifestly deserving of punishment to escape on any quibble or mere legal pretext. But of any excess in this direction I see no danger". Inclosure 5, in No. 240, see *supra* note 103.

[117] FO 406/10, Inclosure 5, in No. 240, in No. 240, TNA, see *supra* note 103: "[...] one is naturally anxious to take care that Justice while she grasps the sword with one hand should not let her scales slip from the other".

justice that might be branded as exaggeration"; Dufferin conceded that the method chosen by his colleagues was "painful but inevitable, as the method of due process would not be feasible", but quickly backtracked and noted that even the summary process should be somewhat compatible with due process lest punishment begin to follow "a barbaric principle of decimation". Moreover, he added, those who were not caught up in or survived the summary process should receive the benefit of amnesty, and those found guilty should not have their suffering prolonged, but should be put to death quickly.[118]

The commissioners also agreed that the trials should take place at the scene of the crime (in the Mountain, as opposed to Beirut), the tribunal's proceedings should be limited in number and brought against "only those whose hands are deeply dyed in blood", non-eyewitness accounts could serve as the basis for indictments, accusers must swear to the truth of their claims before "the Bishop of the rite to which the witness might belong", and Fuad should pay community leaders most likely to solicit helpful testimony to keep quiet about the ongoing investigations in order to reduce the number of accused taking flight.[119] Three classes of criminal would be pursued – "instigators who did or did not personally take part in the massacres; gang leaders who led the assassins and arson; individuals denounced by the public voice who committed the largest number of killings or acted in circumstances that aggravate their guilt" – and all three were subject to the death penalty.[120]

---

[118] Fuad was sensitive to allegations by his fellow commissioners that he had been "striking blindly" through his "summary procedure in Damascus", but was concerned that if his proposals went too far in respsecting "the formalities of due process" he would be accused of "going too far the other direction". Papers, Inclosure 2, "Protocol of the Tenth Meeting of the Syrian Commission held at Beyrout, November 14, 1860", in No. 195, Dufferin to Russell, sent 23 November 1860, received 6 December 1860. Béclard bristled at use of the word "amnesty", but relaxed when it was explained to him that what Dufferin proposed was an amnesty from future prosecution, and not, as he had supposed, a reprieve from the anticipatedcurtailment of the political advantages that they had hitherto enjoyed.

[119] "Protocol of the Tenth Meeting", see *supra* note 118; Inclosure 8, Dufferin to Fraser, 28 November 1860, in No. 199, Dufferin to Russell, sent 28 November 1860, received 15 December 1860.

[120] "Protocol of the Tenth Meeting", see *supra* note 118. The Moukhtara tribunal's (initial) jurisdiction only over crimes worthy of capital punishment was envisioned by Dufferin as a humane measure intended to ensure that the judges would reject all but "the most direct and trustworthy evidence", that "imperfect" summary procedure would not be applied to "complicated or doubtful case", would exclude Druze who "took up arms only in their own defence", even as it ensured the punishment of the most "blood-stained of the assas-

Two months later a letter from Fuad containing a list of 287 Druze investigated by the Moukhtara Tribunal reached the Commission. In light of the difficulties he had faced in procuring evidence the execution of the capital-punishment-only policy ran the risk of degenerating into judicial massacre, and Fuad solicited the opinion of the foreign commissioners *"pour s'éclairer par ses lumières"*.[121] By his estimation 20 prisoners were eligible for the death penalty. The remaining cases were broken down based on strength of evidence; 57 "of whose greater or lesser complicity in late events, though there was no proof, there was a fair presumption"; 230 "rendered liable to suspicion" by a "few meagre indications". It was also up to the commissioners to decide what was to be done with the remaining 400 prisoners, against whom there was "not a tittle of evidence".[122]

On 24 January 1861 the Commission met to discuss Fuad's proposal. The European commissioners agreed that there should be fewer executions than at Damascus, but differed over the final number and the rationale that should be applied to calculate it. Weckbecker expressed that a mere 30 to 40 prisoners should be executed in light of the poor quality of evidence at trial. Béclard and Rehfues chastised Fuad for attempting to implicate the Commission in a decision which should have remained his

---

sins". Inclosure 9, in No. 288, see *supra* note 76. Dufferin proposed four additional rules applicable to the work of the Moukhtara tribunal:

> That no Druse shall be capitally tried by court martial except on the charge of having murdered in cold blood an unarmed man, woman, or a child.

> That the evidence of two eyewitnesses be considered necessary to secure a capital conviction.

> That in determining the proportion of those who are to suffer capitally due regard be had to the numbers of the Druse nation who have been murdered with impunity by the Christians since the arrival of the Commission in Syria.

> That a less severe measure of capital punishment shall be dealt out to the Druse nation than that which has been considered adequate at Damascus.

These rules were "generally accepted" by the other commissioners at the sixteenth meeting. Papers, Inclosures 2 and 9, "Communication addressed by Lord Dufferin to his Colleagues in the Syrian Commission", in No. 229, see *supra* note 60.

121 Meaning "to light by its lights". Papers, Annex, "Fuad Pasha to Abro Efendi", in No. 310, see *supra* note 75.

122 Papers, Inclosure 4, in No. 306, Dufferin to Russell, sent 1 February 1860, received 16 February 1860.

---

alone. The former recommended that all those who confessed to crimes be executed, and the later proposing that only those who murdered women, children and priests be put to death. Novikow suggested that, in light of the evidentiary difficulties, the Commission renege on its earlier determination that the Moukhtara tribunal could only impose the death penalty and agree that minor punishments could be doled out by the tribunal as necessary.[123] The other commissioners rallied to this idea, including Dufferin, but only with the caveat that even minor punishments inflicted on the innocent, of which he observed there were many on the list of 287, "would be ridiculous, odious, and provoke the indignation of the civilized world". He reminded the commissioners that he had not consented to the creation of a tribunal that was "divested of rules observed even by court-martials of Europe". A joint response to Fuad was prepared including, at Dufferin's urging, language to the effect that only the guilty should be punished:

> As a political matter, the twenty death sentences proposed by the Tribunal of Mokthara are not enough.
>
> It would be appropriate to apply a lower sentence, such as that deportation, those among the 290 individuals included on the Mokhtara list who were not sentenced to capital punishment, and whose guilt would be recognized by the court.[124]

The discussion of the absolute number of Druze to be punished continued through the twenty-first meeting (29 January 1861). Dufferin reiterated his appeals to his peers' better nature to put justice before politics and focus only on the chastisement of the genuinely guilty, as determined by a fair process, even as his foil, Béclard, pushed for acceptance of the principle that the normal niceties of justice had to be set aside in order to achieve "social justice": "[i]t may be that eyewitness accounts are often lacking, which is only natural, since the Druze mercilessly massacred anything that did not flee. But in such a situation, and when 6,000 corpses appear [...] the duty of the courts is to bow to circumstances and convict

---

[123] "Protocol of the Twentieth Meeting", see *supra* note 75.

[124] *Ibid.* The 400 against whom there was no evidence were allowed to go free. Dufferin reported that the commissioners agreed that under no circumstances should the number of those of capital sentences exceed 50. Papers, Inclosure 4, in No. 306, see *supra* note 22.

on evidence other than that needed in ordinary times".[125] The French commissioner changed his tune, however, when he received a communiqué from his home government that his arguments "savoured too much of unnecessary vengeance".[126]

The transmission of the Beirut tribunal's sentencing recommendations to the foreign commissioners provoked a second round of intense debates. The kaleidoscope of opinions that emerged over the course of several conferences is summarised in Table 7.1., taken from the official papers:

Prisoners	Béclard (France)	Dufferin (Britain)	Weckbecker (Austria)	Rehfues (Prussia)	Novikow (Russia)
Khurshid Pasha	Death	Death	Perpetual imprisonment	Death	Death
Tahir Pasha	Death	Death	Perpetual imprisonment	Death	Death
Nuri Bey	Death	'Revised' to mercy	Perpetual imprisonment	Death	Death
Wasfi Effendi	Death	Confirmation of sentence	Acquitted	Death	Imprisonment for life
Ahmad Efendi	Death	Confirmation of sentence	Acquitted	Imprisonment for life	Imprisonment for life
Said Bey Jumblat	Death	Acquitted	Acquitted	Death	Death
Husayn Talhuq	Mercy on account of age	Acquitted	Acquitted	Recommends mercy	Recommends mercy
Assad Tehuk	Death	Acquitted	Acquitted	Death	Declined to give opinion

---

[125] "Protocol of the Twenty-First Meeting", see *supra* note 78. Weckbecker agreed with Béclard and expressed the opinion that in the absence of direct evidence "the public voice can serve as an indication to justice". Bulwer was a constant source of encouragement to Dufferin. When the commissioner complained of the challenges of undertaking his duties in the prevailing anti-Druze environment to Her Majesty's ambassador, he was reminded that "[t]he Goddess Themis never sinks beneath the waves. Tho' in the swell of the great popular ocean she is now and then lost sight of. As the wind abates she is seen riding as sublime and majestically as ever and those who have clung to her robes are with her". D1071/H/C/3/8/38, Bulwer to Dufferin, 9 January 1861, PRONI.

[126] Papers, No. 291, Cowley to Russell, sent 7 February 1860, received 8 February 1860. He called for clemency for those convicted at Moukhtara at the twenty-second meeting. Papers, Inclosure 2, "Protocol of the Twenty-Second Meeting of the Syrian Commission, held at Beyrout, February 27, 1861", in No. 375, see *supra* note 79. Russell concurred with Thouvenel's opinion that the execution of a few of the "most criminal" would be sufficient to satisfy justice and "inspire a wholesome fear". FO 406/10, No. 397, Russell to Cowley, 8 February 1861, TNA.

Hassim Nakad	Death	Acquitted	Acquitted	Death	Death
Asad Imad	Death	Acquitted	Acquitted	Death	Declined to give opinion
Emir Mu-hammad Qasim Raslan	Death	Acquitted	Acquitted	Death	Declined to give opinion
Salim Janbalat	Death	Recommends mercy	Acquitted	Death	Death
Jamal al-Din Hamdan	Death	Recommends mercy	Declined to give opinion	Death	Declined to give opinion
Muhy al-Din Shibli	Death	Death	Death	Death	Death
Ali Said	Recommends mercy	Recommends mercy	Revision of trial	Recommends mercy	Declined to give opinion
Bashir Miri	Death	Death	Death	Death	Death

Table 1: Commissioners' opinions at the Beirut tribunal.[127]

The fault lines that isolated each commissioner from the others were whether: (1) the Ottoman defendants deserved the benefit of the mitigating factors that had been taken into account in their case; (2) the evidence had shown that the Ottoman officials and Druze chiefs were guilty; (3) the trial proceedings had been fair and the judges impartial; (4) the commissioners were behaving capriciously by insisting on capital punishments of the Druze chiefs but considering commuting the death sentences handed down by the Moukhtara tribunal; (5) the Druze chiefs had merely acted consistently with "the ordinary hostile encounters which in this country are dignified by the name of war", that is, in self-defence from a Christian attack, or they had "organized the massacres and dipped their hands in the blood"; and whether (6) "murderers who have stuck indiscriminately" or "those who, rather than stop evil, favoured it, either by a decisive impulse or a loose inaction" deserved, as a matter of principle, a more serious punishment.[128]

---

[127] Papers, Inclosure 5, "Table of Prisoners, with their Sentences", in No. 375, see *supra* note 79; also available in FO 195/698, Inclosure in No. 132, Dufferin to Bulwer, 7 March 1861, TNA. See also Papers, Inclosure 1, in No. 351, see *supra* note 100.

[128] Papers, Annexes, as well as "Protocol of the Twenty-Second Meeting", see *supra* note 79. See also Papers, Inclosure 1 in, as well as, No. 375, see *supra* note 79: "But if a distinction is to be drawn between mountain warfare and savage massacre; if each prisoner's case is to be decided on its own individual merits; and if the verdict is to depend on the evidence adduced before the Court by whom the case is examined, of the eleven Druse prisoners tried by the Extraordinary Tribunal of Beyrout, six, including Said Bey must be acquitted. The sentences of three more ought to be commuted and two may be allowed to suffer the just

As consensus eluded the foreign commissioners, Fuad announced at the twenty-third meeting that although their opinions were all "equally respectable" his conscience prevented him from aggravating the suggested sentences on the Ottoman officials.[129] Moreover, as his task was to "give legal force to the awards made by the Tribunal in accordance with law", were he to revise the sentences in the direction desired by the majority of the commissioners he "would assume such responsibility with respect to his government that under no circumstances could he take this resolution". The French Minister testily replied that if Fuad did not use his "full powers to revise the sentence of the Tribunal in the direction of aggravation, then he and his colleagues compelled him to accept a Démarche and the resulting delays".[130]

The conversation then deadlocked over the appropriate sentences for the Druze chiefs. Weckbecker suggested that the gulf between the commissioners was a consequence of their independent readings of the verdict and proposed a "collective reading and exchange of ideas" to reconcile their views. Fuad added that he would make two members of the tribunal available to the Commission to answer any questions they might have. The foreign commissioners unanimously agreed to this over Béclard's remonstrance that the Commission was "about to lose its true nature, that of a diplomatic body responsible not for judging the guilty but only for causing their punishment, and turn into a court".[131]

---

penalty of their crimes". See also Inclosure 2, "Minute on the Judgments proposed to be passed on the Turkish Officials and Druse Chiefs by the Extraordinary Tribunal of Beyrout", in No. 351, see *supra* note 100. Fuad defended the difference in the sentences between the Druse and the Ottoman officials by referencing the Criminal Code, which called for the death for those who incited rebellion against one of the Empire's peoples, but imprisonment for officials who did not perform their duties. Papers, Annex 3, in "Protocol of the Twenty-Second Meeting", see *supra* note 79.

[129] Papers, Annexe 3 to Inclosure 2, "Protocol of the Twenty-Second Meeting of the Syrian Commission", see *supra* note 79.

[130] Papers, Inclosure 3, "Protocol of the Twenty-Third Meeting of the Syrian Commission, held at Beyrout, February 28, 1861", in No. 375, see *supra* note 79.

[131] *Ibid*. The Prussian government had instructed its representative to act in concert with Dufferin. When discrepancies in the views of the two commissioners were brought to the attention of Baron Alexander von Schleinitz, the Foreign Minister of Prussia demurred that this was an area where the Prussian Government necessarily maintained independence from that arrangement:

[...] the question of the sentences to be passed on the prisoners at Beyrout was one of conscience, and...the course taken by the Prussian Com-

The twenty-fourth meeting (2 March 1861), attended by two judges from the Beirut tribunal, was devoted exclusively to a consideration of Said Bey Jumblat's case. Over the course of seven and a half hours the commissioners considered whether Said Bey was guilty, and if so whether it was by virtue of his position of authority in the Druze community, in which case he contributed to the violence through his deliberate indifference, or whether he had directly instigated or encouraged the massacres. The possibility that his efforts to quell the fighting and save Christian lives, as well as his voluntary appearance at the tribunal, were part of a master plan to avoid prosecution was debated, the statements of witnesses who had testified at his trial were read and their credibility questioned or championed. There was also at least one disagreement over what evidence the commissioners could take into account. Novikow's reliance on "public knowledge" prompted Dufferin to object that only evidence "collected judicially [and] authenticated" could be used during their "collective revision of the trial".[132] Ultimately, none of the commissioners changed their minds, a fact which prompted a sententious I-told-you-so moment from the French commissioner:

> The Commissioner of France recalls that it had accepted M. Weckbecker's proposal with reservations [...]. In reality, the commission could not be in court. Justice in the Ottoman Empire should be made and has been made in this case by an Ottoman court. The Commissioners role is only to provoke the work of local justice. The awards were rendered, and

---

missioner was dictated solely by a conscientious feeling of duty. He [Weckbecker] had to act the part of a juror, and his decision was guided solely by the evidence brought before him; it was impossible to judge these matters at a distance, and each Government must therefore rely on the judgment of their Agents.

FO 406/11, No. 84, Loftus to Russell, sent 27 April 1861, received 29 April 1861. In response to a letter from Dufferin, Bulwer noted that "when two out of three Judges are against Capital Punishment it cannot be inflicted. Nor do I think it ought even to be so inflicted except on the perfect unanimity of the Judges. A difference implies that there is doubt in the mind of a competent party as to the justice of Capital punishment, and the infliction of that punishment unjustly is murder". D/1071/H/C/3/8/31, Bulwer to Dufferin, 23 March 1861, PRONI.

[132] Papers, Inclosure 4, "Protocol of the Twenty-fourth Meeting of the Syrian Commission, held at Beyrout, March 2, 1861", in No. 375, see *supra* note 79.

opinions expressed on these awards. It is for the Ottoman Plenipotentiary to enforce them or not.[133]

In the absence of a unanimous opinion, Fuad announced that he would maintain the verdicts *ad interim* and refer a decision on all of the Beirut tribunal's verdicts to the sultan in Constantinople.[134]

Fuad's decision shifted the locus of European action from Beirut to Paris and London, where the Druze sentences quickly became a political bone of contention between the two governments. On learning of the decision to leave the fate of the Druze and Ottoman authorities in the hands of the sultan, Russell explained to Dufferin that

> [w]hen a tribunal, pretty fairly chosen, has condemned the Turkish officials to a sentence short of death, it would be repugnant to our feelings to demand their execution in pursuance of the requisition of foreign agents who have not heard the evidence, and do not pretend to have examined the proofs of guilt, in a judicial spirit. [...] With regard to the Druses if two of the most criminal and who have been fully and satisfactorily proved to have been guilty of active participation in the massacres are executed in pursuance of their sentence it ought to be sufficient for the purposes of justice and of example. Her Majesty's Government could not give their consent to the execution of the six whom their Commissioner believes to be innocent of the massacres.[135]

---

[133] *Ibid.*

[134] Papers, Inclosure 1, in No. 375, see *supra* note 79. Dufferin invited Russell to charge Bulwer with taking advantage of the opportunity to push for the "correction" of the "absurd and iniquitous" verdicts, based as they were on "false interpretation of the law and on insufficient evidence".

[135] Papers, No. 366, Russell to Dufferin, 18 March 1861. Russell also explained in a 28 March communiqué to Bulwer, that he was in agreement with the French ambassador to London:

> That the ends of justice would be satisfied by the execution of four or five Druses.

> That as we did not object to the Tribunal constituted in Syria we cannot pretend to aggravate the sentence which the Tribunal has pronounced, or to set aside its decisions.

Additional Papers, No. 2, Russell to Bulwer, 28 March 1861. The second point was consistent with the views of Austria. FO 406/11, No. 8, Bloomfield to Russell, sent 28 March 1861, received 1 April 1861, TNA: "[Count Rechberg] said that he must consider that where the Porte was striving to administer justice in a fair spirit, those Powers were rendering a bad service to Turkey who called on her to inflict greater measure of punishment on the prisoners than had been awarded by those charged with their trial, whilst this proceeding fur-

Precisely how interfering with one class of verdicts but not the other was less "repugnant" was not explained, but Russell seems to have been acting on an impulse that to intervene in favour of aggravation of a sentence was reprehensible in a way that interference for the purpose of mitigation was not. Untroubled by this suspicious logic, he immediately took steps to ensure that Said Bey would not be among those executed, instructing Bulwer to threaten to break off relations with the Porte if Said Bey were put to death.[136] This put the Porte in an awkward position, as the French ambassador, Charles de la Valette, was demanding precisely the opposite.[137]

Thouvenel defended the position of the French government as a matter of principle and politics. The normal course of Turkish justice having been followed and the sentences confirmed by three of the five commissioners, the judgments should be sanctioned by the Porte.[138] His primary concern, however, was that effective British intervention on Said Bey's behalf would result in a loss of face for France, and he expressed a willingness to accept a commutation as long as Britain's influence was exercised from the shadows.[139] Russell was unwilling to concede. He wished it to be known that Her Majesty's government inclined to mercy, particularly given the flimsy nature of the evidence that had formed the basis of Said Bey's sentence.[140]

When Thouvenel learned that Bulwer had been instructed to threaten to break off relations with the Porte unless Said Bey were freed, he renewed his protest that the Powers ought not to interfere with Ottoman justice:

---

nished another proof of their desire to bring disrepute on the acts of the Porte, and to seek to undermine its authority".

[136] FO 406/11, No. 12, Russell to Bulwer, 3 April 1861, TNA. Russell was informed on 30 March that Thouvenel did not, in fact, agree with the position of the French ambassador in London. The Foreign Minister's opinion was that the capital sentences imposed on the Druze condemned by the Beirut tribunal should be maintained. FO 406/11, No. 6, Cowley to Russell, sent 29 March 1861, received 30 March 1861, TNA.

[137] FO 406/11, No. 21, Russell to Cowley, 5 April 1861, TNA.

[138] FO 406/11, No. 27, Cowley to Russell, sent 8 April 1861, received 9 April 1861, TNA.

[139] FO 406/11, No. 33, Cowley to Russell, sent 9 April 1861, received 10 April 1861, TNA.

[140] FO 406/11, No. 34, Russell to Cowley, 10 April 1861, TNA. His assessment of the case against Said Bey was based on Dufferin's comments and media reports. The Interrogatories of the Druze chiefs only reached Russell on 13 April. FO 406/11, No. 42, TNA, see *supra* note 70.

The Commission had neither the quality of a Tribunal or a jury. The Commissioner of the Porte communicated to his colleagues a judgment pronounced by an Ottoman Court of Justice against Ottoman subjects. All that Fuad Pascha could do was ask the delegates if the repairs and changes were sufficient. Four out of five [commissioners] have found the conviction by the Turkish authorities of the Druse chiefs too strong. I am convinced of their sincerity and conscientiousness, but I do not know how they engage the judicial responsibility of those who have formulated [the sentences], and doubt their divergence alters anything, as in my opinion the Porte has the exclusive right to decide freely and without foreign pressure on the cases that Fuad Pasha brought before it [...]. Any constraints in this regard would seem to infringe the dignity and moral independence of the Sultan.

This character [Said] [is] surely not worthy of a particular interest. Two things: if he is guilty of the crimes alleged against him, he merits death. If he is innocent, a commutation of the sentence would not redress the legal error, and this error should be invoked in favour of the others sentenced.[141]

An apoplectic Russell fired off a reply that same day. After a reminder that one of the objects of the Commission had been to "obtain the punishment of those guilty of directing or participating in the massacre", he acidly observed out that the Commission had been intimately involved with the two Mountain tribunals almost from the start, and that Thouvenel had himself interposed on the side of mercy in the proposed executions of those condemned at Moukhtara:

If the Sultan was competent to appoint a Tribunal, and to be the sole judge of the decisions of that Tribunal, why was the Commission appointed? Why did it constantly interfere in the trials? Why did M. Thouvenel give his opinion in favour of saving from condign punishment the assassins condemned at Mokhtara? Her Majesty's Government consider that if Turkish officials who were in command of troops, and who

---

[141] FO 406/11, No. 60, M. Thouvenal to Count de Flahault – (Communicated to Lord J. Russell by Count de Flahault, April 23, 12 April 1861, TNA. Thouvenel also suggested a retrial for all of the accused before a new court of justice. Russell had previously rejected the idea of a retrial for Said Bey as "unjust". FO 406/11, No. 45, Russell to Cowley, 14 April 1860, TNA.

allowed and connived at the massacres, are not to be punished with death, the execution of Druses who were far less
culpable is likely to shake the authority of the Sultan, and
disturb the peace of Syria for many years to come. These
considerations, and the particular circumstances of the case
of Said Bey Joublat, have induced Her Majesty's Government to interfere, and will induce them to continue to interfere at Constantinople, with a view to save the life of that
Druse Chief.[142]

But as Thouvenel had, however, promised not to steer the Porte in
the direction of capital punishment, Russell informed Bulwer that he
could withdraw his threat to sever relations.[143]

Said Bey died in prison before the Porte could make a final decision
in his case.[144] The capital sentences were eventually commuted to exile.[145]
An amnesty, applicable to all but the Druze found guilty *in absentia* by
the Extraordinary Tribunal at Beirut and still at large, was declared in
June 1861.[146] The Sultan sentenced Khorshid and Tahir Pashas (and likely

---

[142] FO 406/11, No. 61, Russell to Cowley, 23 April 1861, TNA.

[143] FO 406/11, No. 62, Russell to Cowley, 23 April 1861, TNA. Dufferin ordered Bulwer to
inform the Porte that executing Said Bey would injure British-Ottoman relations. *Ibid.*
Thouvenel later explained that, in his view, the interference with the verdicts passed by the
tribunal at Moukhtara was distinguishable from Said's case, inasmuch as Russell was pro-
posing to interfere in the case of a "particular individual". FO 406/11, No. 81, Cowley to
Russell, sent 24 April 1861, received 26 April 1861, TNA. In the opinion of Russia "the
Sultan should be left, without influence or bias, to decide upon the fate of the accused".
FO 406/11, No. 99, Napier to Russell, sent 28 April 1861, received 6 May 1861, TNA.

[144] FO 406/11, Inclosure 1, in No. 105, Dufferin to Russell, sent 26 April 1861, received 11
May 1861, TNA.

[145] FO 195/660, No. 61, Fraser to Bulwer, 17 October 1861, TNA; FO 195/660, No. 75, Fraser to Bulwer, 29 November 1861, TNA; ABCFM, ABC 16.8.1, Unit 5, Reel 546, No.
141. Hunter to Aiken, 13 July 1861: "On the 10th inst. All the Druse Sheikhs in prison
(excepting Sheikh Yusef Abd el Melek and the Emir Muhammed Raselan, who are pardoned) were sent into exile to Belgrade, it is said, and about 60 Druses and Muhammedans
were exiled at the same time".

[146] Papers, No 65, Rogers to Russell, sent 1 June 1861, received 20 June 1861: "This notification was received without any excitement being produced"; Additional Papers, Inclosure 7,
in No. 46, Dufferin to Russell, sent 11 May 1861, received 24 May 1861. The condemned
but uncaptured Druze leaders in the Hawran received amnesty in 1865 in exchange for
payment of outstanding taxes and accepting an Ottoman administrator in the stronghold.
Leila Hudson, *Transforming Damascus: Space and Modernity in an Islamic City*, I.B. Tauris, London, 2008, p. 21.

the other accused Ottoman officials as well) to life imprisonment in the Empire's far-flung fortresses.[147]

7.6. "Vindicating at Once the Claims of Humanity": Events in Syria and the Idea of International Criminal Law

There is a certain appeal to casting the International Commission as an "international crimes court" in response to those who would denigrate international criminal law as an unpedigreed, and by extension illegitimate, brach of the law. But efforts to apply *any* of these appellations will be thwarted by the ambiguous, shifting and inconsistent pronouncements and practices of the commissioners and their home governments, the lack of a complete factual record, and the spectre of sliding into anachronism. Consider just one of these terms: court.[148] Do the perceptions of the foreign commissioners, to the extent they considered themselves judicial actors in a legal drama, transform them into judges, as would be found at a tribunal? Is an entity with no formalised rules of procedure, articulated jurisdictional limits, or instructions to apply a particular body of law, a court? Would the relevant stakeholders have considered it a court in 1860? Had a consensus been reached on all of the Beirut verdicts, would Fuad have been bound by the determination of the Commission? Or was their decision merely precatory? Does it matter that the assumption of a judicial role by foreign commissioners was only endorsed by some of their home governments? Does the September understanding reached between the Great Powers and the Sublime Porte, enshrined in the instructions to Fuad and which reserved to him all judicial authority, mean that

---

[147] FO, 195/660, No. 3, Fraser to Bulwer, 9 July 1861, TNA; No. 141, Hunter to Aiken, see supra *note* 145: "Khurshed Pasha, Tahir Pasha, and other officials have been sent, it is said, to Cyprus or Crete".

[148] The Commission's nebulous mandate bedevilled the analytical efforts of its contemporaries as well. According to Girardin, 1862, p. 92, see *supra* note 2:

> The right of supervision and review of the actions of the special tribunal of Beirut that is claimed by the commission is constantly challenged and more difficult to exercise. Fuad Pasha said, it is true, through his delegate Abro Effendi, that members of the Commission may attend the court sessions; but he adds that foreigners without this distinction may also attend, so there is room to doubt whether the members of the International Commission attend meetings of the court as a matter of right or only by courtesy and as foreigners of distinction.

the commissioners were acting *ultra vires* when they considered the evidence against Said Bey? If the 'court' capacity of the Commission was illegal, was it in fact not a court at all? Did the sultan's ultimate discretion over the enforcement of the commissioners' recommendations negate the independent control over verdicts that is the hallmark of a court? Did any of the commissioners have the freedom of action that is the *sine qua non* of a court? How real was the Sultan's discretion over sentences given the willingness of the Great Powers to 'guide' his decisions? How strong was the commitment of the Great Powers to enforcing their commissioners' recommendations?

To pursue this line of inquiry is to willingly throw oneself off a cliff with no bottom. Heaven help the poor scholar who attempts to tackle "international" and "crimes" as well.

Setting aside insoluble matters of taxonomy, the response to the events in Syria suggests a number of interesting things about the state of 'international criminal law' in the mid-nineteenth century. First, it seems that by 1860 at least a few Great Powers had accepted two principles: (1) that a body comprising representatives of various states can assume jurisdiction over matters beyond those affecting their nationals or consulates, and (2) that this body can be endowed with the power to trigger local prosecutions, review national proceedings, correct errors made before national courts, review evidence and allocate punishment. Interestingly, this understanding does not appear to have been limited to Europe's politicians and diplomats. In late July 1860 Sir John Gardner Wilkinson, a well-known British traveller-adventurer and pioneer Egyptologist, suggested in a letter to *The Times* the establishment of a true *ad hoc* international criminal court:

> I am sorry to say it, but the truth is there is little difference between the Maronites and the Druses in their vindictive spirit; the former, though the aggressors and confiding in their number, have been worsted, and most cruelly have they been visited for their indiscretion, but it is not by inflicting similar miseries on the Druses that an effectual remedy is to be applied; this can only be done by making the Turks responsible for the future peace of Syria, and, to show that we are in earnest, we should demand that "the Turkish officials" of Damascus and those who treacherously induced the Christians at Dar-el-Kamar to give up their arms, as well as all who commanded Turkish troops in the attack on Zahleh and

other places, be brought down to Beyrout and there tried by a court composed equally of English, French, and Turks, when, if proved guilty, every one according to the magnitude of his offence, should be summarily punished on the spot; in addition to which, the Porte should be immediately forced to make good the whole of the losses sustained by the Christians; the money being delivered to the English and French for distribution among the families of the sufferers. It is useless to say this is an interference in the internal affairs of an independent country. Armed intervention is so, too, but it must be made. The case is peculiar, and we are bound to prevent the recurrence of similar outrages, on a greater scale; which, though others may be the immediate actors, will only be the result of Turkish ill-will against the Christians.[149]

Although I can find no evidence that Wilkinson's (remarkably prescient) proposal was picked up by policymakers, or impelled any of the events that followed, his letter to *The Times* confirms that 'international criminal justice' was in the air and that the prospect had some appeal to the chattering classes.[150]

In some cases, the violence also precipitated an expanded understanding of the sorts of behaviours that could fall under the auspices of 'crimes against humanity'. The concept of the crime against humanity was not new when the crisis in Syria broke out; by 1842 trafficking in slaves had been identified as "justly stigmatized by every civilised and Christian people as a crime against humanity",[151] and slavers, analogised to pirates, were regarded by many states (and some international law scholars) as *hostis humani generis*.[152] But the notion was underdeveloped

---

[149] "The Massacres in Syria: To the Editor of the Times", *The Times*, 26 July 1860, reprinted, as it was "too interesting to be passed over", as "The Syrian Massacres", *Morning Chronicle*, 14 August 1860.

[150] Further evidence that international justice was accepted by the public may be found in the pages of the *Glasgow Herald*, 14 February 1861. The editors interpreted (and approved of) Russell's 8 February 1861 comments in the House of Lords (see *supra* note 64) as indicating that the commissioners were a "Court of Appeal from the Turkish Court-Martial, who stand as a safeguard against any flagrant injustice being perpetrated by that tribunal".

[151] Jenny S. Martinez, *The Slave Trade and the Origins of International Human Rights Law*, Oxford University Press, Oxford, 2012, p. 115, citing Henry Wheaton, Enquiry into the Validity of the British Claim to a Right of Visitation & Search of American Vessels, Suspected to Be Engaged in the African Slave-Trade, Lea and Blanchard, London, 1842, pp. 4, 16.

[152] *Ibid.*, p. 131.

---

and inexorably linked with maritime outlawry; terrestrial crimes of mass violence had never fallen within its ambit. The brutality of the 1860 conflict, however, began the process of unshackling the expression from its thalassic roots. Reasoning by analogy was key to the process of inbuing this phrase with new shades of meaning; just as the slaver was like the pirate, so was the cruel terrene warrior, like the slaver. Richard Robert Madden, a member of the Anglo-Spanish Court of Mixed Commission in Havana, which heard cases involving intercepted slave ships, upon learning of the violence in Syria mused that:

> In modern times, the cruelties committed by slave dealers on the coast of Africa, caused even the introduction into our official vocabulary of such epithets as "miscreants," "monsters," "enemies of the human race," &c., &c; for with such epithets we find the parliamentary slave trade papers teem. The atrocities, however, committed in Syria on the Maronites who were more immediately entitled to British sympathy, because in point of religious relationship they were bound to us in closer bonds of Christian fellowship, deserved, in my humble opinion, to be placed in the same category of crimes, as those in which are recorded the atrocities of the Spaniards and Portuguese, and to be ranked among the worst outrages on humanity that have ever been committed.[153]

Even as the response to the 1860 massacres enlarged the concept of crimes against humanity, it reinforced among European and Ottoman diplomats, as well as the British public, the bedrock precepts on which this nascent legal category was built; first, that some acts were offensive to the conscience of humanity; second, that mass violence could be framed as criminal, that is, labelled 'crime' or countered with prosecutions; third, that individuals could be punished for their discrete contributions to the

---

[153] Richard Madden, *The Turkish Empire: In its Relations with Christianity and Civilization*, vol. 2, T. Cautley Newby, London, 1862, p. 354. See also Gera Burton, "Liberty's Call: Richard Robert Madden's Voice in the Anti-Slavery Movement (1833–1842)", in *Irish Migration Studies in Latin America*, 2007, vol. 5, no. 3, pp. 199–206. With respect to the development of new categories of crime, an offhand remark of Béclard's to the effect that the massacres at Damascus and Deir el-Kamar were not part of a "civil war" but were rather "veritable butcheries" is interesting. Papers, Inclosure 7, "Protocol of the Ninth Meeting of the Syrian Commission, held at Beyrout, November 10, 1860", in No. 190, Dufferin to Russell, sent 17 November 1860, received 30 November 1860.

carnage; fourth, that punishment could be in the name of humanity.[154] Of equal significance, the British press cultivated the idea that allocating responsibility among and punishing accordingly (proto-)international criminals was not only possibly, but properly, a matter of global concern. Early demands that individuals be held accountable fixed Europe's eyes on and built a shared sense of investment in the transitional justice programme in Syria. Discussions of, for example, the appropriate role for Europe in seeing punishments doled out,[155] the number of those who should be

[154] See *infra* notes 24, 25, 26 and 27. Invocations of "humanity", on the part of British diplomats at least, were not merely rhetorical ploys to palliate public opinion. Rather, humanity was treated a body whose integrity could be wounded, as a rightsholder and as a stakeholder, even in private diplomatic correspondence. Papers, No. 139, Moore to Russell, sent 14 September 1860, received 29 September 1860; in reference to Fuad's imposition of punishment of Ahmad Pasha: "His Excellency merits the highest applause for the firmness which pronounced, and the course which carried out a sentence vindicating at once the claims of humanity and the honour of his Government"; Papers, No. 233, Dufferin to Russell, sent 19 December 1860, received 5 January 1860 (quoted below); No 254, Russell to Cowley, 24 January 1861: "The object of the five Powers was to prevent a renewal of those massacres, and to show the fanatical tribes of Syria that such outrages upon humanity could not be committed without punishment and reparation"; Papers, No. 172, Russell to Cowley, 7 November 1860: European troops "went to support the Sultan's authorities in their task of restoring order, and punishing the principal criminals. By the activity of Fuad Pasha, and the energy of General Beaufort, this work of humanity and justice has been in great part accomplished". For Ottoman pronouncements reflecting a similar understanding see *supra* notes 2, 75 and 76.

[155] The *Liverpool Mercury*, in "The Druses and Maronites", 12 July 1860, only begrudgingly lent its support to the French intervention, and felt that the role of the foreign troops, and indeed Europe as a whole, should be negligible: "we have no right to assume that the Porte will fail to comply with any reasonable demand from a European Government for the suppression and punishment of these atrocious outrages, and it is greatly to be desired that the Sultan's authority in the outlying provinces of his empire should be strengthened by exercise rather that it should be superseded by foreign interference". *The Times*, 10 August 1860, suggested that the French were best utilised as a support to the Porte, as "the Turks are strong enough to execute the Sultan's order [the demand that ringleaders be given up] without help"; "The Massacres in Syria", *The Times*, 17 August 1860: Europe should neither "control nor instigate" punishment, as the exercise of this power spoke directly to the preservation of the Ottoman state. In "The Syrian Question", *Saturday Review*, 4 August 1860 on the news that the British and Turkish governments had acquiesced to the dispatch of a French force, the paper thought it unviable to use Zouaves (French troops) to "punish their [the Ottoman leaders'] remissness" to suppress disorder, as this would amount to "making war on the Power from which they derive their commission", also stating that "[t]he plan of superseding them [Ottoman authorities] in the discharge of their duties can only perpetuate anarchy". The *Morning Post*, September 1860 was sceptical that the Porte was serious about accountability, and suggested that unless the Ottoman government's Foreign Minister Fuad Pasha was "closely watched by European commissioners" he would "naturally allow the large fish to escape and only punish the small fry". "The Syrian Mas-

killed,[156] the sufficiency of the sentence against Khurshid Pasha,[157] and the necessity and timing of an amnesty, all unfolded in the papers.[158] The public experienced such a sense of ownership over the proceedings that when news of the poor quality of Said Bey's trial reached Britain and faith in Ottoman justice was at a nadir, *The Times* apportioned Europe a share of the responsibility and symbolically revoked the Powers' imprimatur of Ottoman justice: "It is quite clear that the public opinion of Europe – and it is in some degree under the public opinion of Europe that these proceedings gained their original sanction – will no longer support the jurisdiction of such tribunals".[159]

---

sacres", the *Standard*, 27 July 1860, suggested to let the Sublime Porte first deal with the punishment, but in the event their efforts failed Europe should administer "swift, impartial, and overwhelming" justice. Both the *Birmingham Daily Post*, 20 July 1860, and the *Daily News*, 17 August 1860, expressed confidence in the Ottoman commissioner, but anticipated that his good faith efforts would come to little without a foreign military presence.

[156] "Syria", *Morning Post*, 2 March 1861: "No sooner was it told to the assembled International Commissioners that only 44 Druses were condemned to death, than many protested loudly that that number was insufficient! As though it was a question of killing so many sheep or pigs instead of human beings. [...] Although I myself do not feel particularly blood thirsty, I think there must be something in the air here which exercises a powerful effect on human beings, as the distinguished gentlemen who represent the European Powers would, when in their own country, be shocked at the bare notion of sending back to their judges the sentences of a couple of hundred poor, ignorant men, for the express purpose of selecting 50 of them for capital punishment"; "Syria", Daily News, 9 February 1861: asserting (inaccurately) that 130 had been condemned to death, and (unbelievably) that "the Druses themselves say that if they can kill off-hand some 10,000 of their enemies – not calculating what they shot in open war, but merely those murdered in cold blood – at a loss of only 130 of their own tribe, they have gained a great victory. This is looking at the subject from a truly Oriental perspective".

[157] "Turkey", *Morning Chronicle*, 9 February 1861; "Syria", *Daily News*, 12 January 1861; *Morning Post*, 25 January 1861.

[158] *Morning Post*, 9 April 1861: "After the wholesale, and in many cases apparently indiscriminate, arrests which have been made in the Lebanon and the Hauran, it is hopeless to expect any of those who may be conscious that a shadow of suspicion hangs upon their past conduct towards the Maronites to renew the natural occupations of their daily life so long as number equal to the population of small towns are liable to be swept off to prison together, and there tried with deplorably little reference to the real merits of the accusations against them. [...] We trust that the Turkish Government will evince the courage to proclaim it, and we are confident that its policy in doing so would receive the sanction, at any rate, of such a proportion of the great Powers as would enable it to persevere in such a course"; *Morning Post*, 26 September 1860.

[159] *Morning Post*, 16 April 1861. In a broad sense, the preoccupation with punishment in Syria, evident in press reports and in Parliamently debates, offers an early example of local justice being conscripted by the foreign community to counter atrocity crimes. See, for ex-

Throughout the transitional justice process, one personality is distinguished by his clarity of vision, ability, attentiveness to due process concerns, and sensitivity to the need for a coherent transitional justice strategy: Frederick Hamilton-Temple-Blackwood, 1st Marquess of Dufferin and Ava. His hands, of course, were not entirely clean. No one could accuse Dufferin of not towing Her Majesty's line with respect to seeing Khurshid executed, though ultimately it is difficult to assess how much of this was driven by his own convictions and how much from his eagerness to prove himself capable during what was his first diplomatic posting.[160] What is more, he was willing to compromise his ideals when he was convinced that the benefit to the region outweighed the harm to individuals, as when he (begrudgingly) tolerated the exile of 155 Druze prisoners "whose guilt was not fully proved" to Tripoli.[161] But of all the players involved in Syria's post-conflict reconstruction Dufferin was the least willing to sacrifice procedural integrity for political purposes. He acted with an awareness of what was at stake and a genuine conviction that law, not force, was the means by which Syria would be restored to order.[162] He perceived himself as a judge, took this responsibility seriously,[163] and ex-

---

ample, Hansard's House of Lords Debate, 14 August 1860, vol. 160, cc. 1241, with Wodehouse remarking that "the conduct of Kurschid Pasha was more than suspicious, and requires strict investigation; and, if it should turn out that he is guilty of those acts of which he is accused, severe punishment".

[160] See text associated with *supra* note 98. FO 406/10, No. 101, Russell to Dufferin, 14 August 1860, TNA: "Pashas like Khoorshid of Beyrout, and Achmet of Damascus, would pervert the best regulations that can be framed".

[161] See FO 406/11, Inclosure 1, in No. 525, TNA, *supra* note 80. He also reluctantly instructed Fraser, his representative authorised to assist Fuad with the Moukhtara proceedings, to content himself with "taking such precautions as the circumstances of the case admit", as "we have to deal with an occasion and with a state of society in which a nice adherence to the refinements of European legal practice would be out of place". Papers, Inclosure 9, Dufferin to Fraser, 23 January 1861, in No. 288, see *supra* note 76.

[162] FO 406/10, Inclosure 3, in No. 188, Dufferin to Russell, sent 23 September 1860, received 6 October 1860, TNA: "I entirely agreed with His Excellency [Fuad] in thinking it advisable that, if possible, his progress through the Druse country should have the character of a Judge holding an assize, rather than of a conqueror claiming vengeance"; and Inclosure 7, From a letter to General Beaufort: "But I cannot but think that to effect this object it will be better to delegate so terrible and responsible a duty to the sword of justice rather than to the bayonets of the soldiery, to invest our vengeance with an awful character of a discriminating retribution rather than that of a passionate reprisal, which if carried too far may acquire some resemblance to the crimes we seek to chastise".

[163] Lyall, 1905, p. 121, see *supra* note 87, quoting a letter from Dufferin to the Duchess of Argyll:

---

pressed frustration when the abilities of his colleagues did not meet his standards: "[I am astonished] at finding how little the elemental rules of the administrations of justice are understood by my colleagues. As far as I have observed, they seem to me quite unused to the investigations connected with legal proceedings, and to possess but a very inadequate knowledge of the mode in which the sifting of evidence, at the cross-examination of witnesses, and the other practices of a tribunal are conducted".[164] His memoranda and dispatches are written in the tone of one who wishes to *convince*, not *defeat*, and call to mind nothing so much as a magistrate working through a problem or making a case to peers. And when confronted with data that did not conform to his preconceived notions, he revised his opinions.[165]

This was the man who would traverse areas of the international criminal law map that would only be charted with any detail in the twentieth century. His pursuit of a justice programme that would restore order and affirm the values of restraint, empathy and humanity forced him to confront many of the same questions encountered by today's community of international criminal law scholars, and it is fascinating to see how closely his answers to the field's most difficult questions hew to our own. His attempt to balance between local and international ownership of the transitional justice programme is particularly on point, for its germinal articulation of the now familiar 'unwilling or unable' test. When he ar-

---

It is a terrible thing to feel the life of many a man will have to depend on one's judgment, pluck and skill. Moreover, my task is the most difficult one of any. The other Commissioner are merely prosecutors. Provided those whom their governments are determined to think guilty do not get off, they need have no other care. *But I am judge, jury, prosecutor, and counsel for the plaintiff all at once.* These unfortunate Druses are in a most pitiable position. They have committed the most horrible crimes, they are being pursued with the extremity of rancor by the Maronites out of revenge, and by the French out of ambition; they are being sacrificed by the Turks out of fear, and in the hope of saving their own people; and yet their only friend is obliged to a certain extent to place himself in the ranks of their accusers. (emphasis added)

[164] FO 406/10, Inclosure 4, in No. 414, Dufferin to Russell, sent 1 February 1861, received 16 February 1861, TNA.

[165] Papers, Inclosure 1, in No. 351, *supra* note 100, in which Dufferin describes how he was initially of the opinion that the Druze were solely responsible for the massacres, but as he investigated matters he learned that there were "two sides to the story".

rived in Beirut, the scales tilted in favour of minimal international intervention:

> I have been informed [...] that Achmet Pacha, late Governor of the city, has been tried, condemned, and sentenced, but that his sentence, whatever it may be, has not been yet made public. [...] In delaying to pronounce sentence upon this egregious offender, His Excellency [Fuad] may be influenced, wither by a desire to await the arrival of the Commission in order to compel them to share the odium he is likely to merit by exercising a due severity [...], or by a habit of hesitation not, I believe, altogether foreign to this His Excellency's character. [In the first event] I shall venture to submit [...] whether it might not be undesirable that so grave a function as the punishment of crime should appear to be exercised at Foreign Dictation rather than proceed from the spontaneous exertion of those plenary powers which have been entrusted to him by his Government.[166]

But familiarity with Ottoman justice (and the placing of Druze in the dock) bred contempt, and by early October he was convinced that the government was unable or unwilling to prosecute cases in a manner that would be perceived as fair or would result in "the discovery of the causes of the late events".[167] Now the scales skewed in favour of direct and international participation:

> The contemplation of the circumstances under which those accused of complicity in the late disturbances – whether at Damascus or in the Lebanon – are tried, gives rise to many painful reflections. It seems impossible to constitute a tribunal, composed of subjects of the Porte, capable of inspiring with confidence either the accuser or the accused.[168]
>
> [T]he only effective way of conducting a *bona fide* investigation into the circumstances out of which the late disturbances arose would be by acquiring for the Delegates of the Commission, appointed to watch the trial of those concerned in them, the privilege of directing the inquiry into whatever channel seemed more likely to lead to the discovery of the

---

[166] FO 78/1625, No. 2, Dufferin to Russell, 4 September 1860, TNA.

[167] FO 406/10, Inclosure 5, in No. 240, TNA, see *supra* note 103.

[168] Papers, Inclosure 2, in No. 147, Dufferin to Russell, sent 23 September 1860, received 6 October 1860.

truth [...]. *Now, even if they had the wish, no Turkish tribunal possess either the experience or the skill necessary to conduct so complicated an investigation. But we have every reason to believe that the real object which the Beyrout Tribunal has at heart is the concealment of the truth, and the destruction, with as much dispatch as possible, of those whose mutual recrimination would bring to the knowledge of Europe facts with which it is their interest to keep her unacquainted.* It becomes, therefore, a matter of great importance that we should have the power of preventing those in the purity of whose intentions we can have so little confidence from stifling inquiry and cooking evidence.[169]

Dufferin's distaste for collective punishment foreshadows the turn toward individual culpability that the field would take. He railed against the exceptionally high "penalty tax" Fuad imposed on the Druze, and contrasted it with the more targeted ongoing prosecutions:

> In the interests of justice, of humanity, and of the future government of the Province, it is necessary that a great example should be made of those whose hands are deepest dyed in blood. It is only by the severity of punishment that these barbarians can be made to comprehend the enormity of their crimes; but an awful and impartial administration of capital punishment, on a certain number of notorious offenders, is a far different thing from that stupid and unscrupulous system of persecution by which the whole [Druze] nation is being driven to despair.[170]

Dufferin encouraged an even-handed process that targeted individuals on the basis of their actions, as opposed to their affiliation with a particular social or religious group:

> It seems to me most essential, that whilst the culpable Turkish authorities and the Druse Chiefs are adequately punished, any leaders amongst the Maronites who excited or commenced the recent civil war should not pass unnoticed or unchastised; [...] Murderers and robbers should, I think, be punished as murderers and robbers, not as Mussulmans or Jews, or as belonging to any religious sect. [...] I would be averse to make religion the difference between the ruffian

---

169 FO 406/10, Inclosure 5, in No. 240, TNA, see *supra* note 103 (emphasis added).
170 Papers, No. 233, Dufferin to Russell, sent 19 December 1860, received 5 January 1861.

and his victim, since such a conviction could only make each feel that there was a gulf of blood between them.[171]

He was also the first among the Commissioners to suggest that both prosecutions and amnesties had a role in rebuilding society.[172]

In other areas his communications merely suggest a future direction for the field without reaching a satisfying conclusion. This is the case with respect to his efforts to square the need to ensure justice for victims with local social norms (anticipating what we would call today the "sociopsychological" or "cultural" defence) and with European practice to the contrary:

> [C]onsiderations of some importance must still be permitted to arrest the descending scale of [Justice's] balance. It is to be remembered that this is a country of vendettas; that in the war carried on between the barbarian tribes which inhabit it, usages prevail as horrible as those which disgraced the middle ages of Europe. It is a principle received and acted upon by all alike that when the "deen" or blood feud exists it is allowable to slay your unarmed enemy, and every male belonging to his house wherever you may find them. In fact beneath the full blaze of modern civilization, we find in Syria habits of thought and practices prevailing for which the only historical parallel can be found in the books of Moses. [...]
>
> In some of the most civilized countries of Europe customs alike hateful to philosophy and religion remain unpunishable by law and uncensured by society: while so great is the allowance it is sometimes found necessary to make for the perversity of human nature that the soldiery of civilized States are occasionally suffered to inflict with impunity on the unoffending women of a city taken by assault horrors equaling in brutality those committed by the Druses during the intoxication of triumph and revenge.
>
> Be that as it may, strict equity would seem to require that in estimating the moral guilt of these unhappy persons the

---

[171] Papers, Inclosure in No. 211, Bulwer to Russell, sent 12 December 1860, received 22 December 1860; Papers, Inclosure 1 and Inclosure 3, in No. 306, Dufferin to Russell, sent 1 February 1861, received 16 February 1861.

[172] Papers, Inclosure 8, in No. 199, Dufferin to Russell, sent 28 November 1860, received 15 December 1860.

standard of European civilization is not altogether applicable. Some allowance must be made for the force of circumstances and of inveterate tradition.[173]

> Notwithstanding that much may be said to excuse the conduct of the Druses, it still remains a fact that they slaughtered in cold blood upwards of 5,000 unarmed men and children. Let the moral guilt attaching to their excesses be extenuated as it may, no penalty which fails to make such an impression as will prevent the repetition of similar atrocities would be adequate to the occasion.[174]

Remarkably, despite the passage of nearly a century and a half, and all of the changes in law, practice and terminology that time has wrought, we can discern in this aspect of the history of the Syrian justice programme echoes of our own international criminal law endeavours. Many of Dufferin's improvised but reflective epistles, like the 'unwilling or unable' test, have evolved into legal norms, or like the sequencing of prosecutions and amnesties or the even-handed dispensation of justice, into best practices or animating principles. This suggests that these formulations have an intuitive appeal that transcends the epochs of international criminal law. Dufferin's letters also raise the spectre of hypocrisy on the part of Great Powers, affirming and anticipating the centrality of this issue to the field. Although powerful states even today remain capable of shielding their nationals from the mechanisms of international justice, it is mildly cheering that even from the earliest days of international criminal law (and from within the 'inner circle' of the Syria mission no less) the double standards generated a certain amount of cognitive dissonance. Pharisaical pushes for justice, it would seem, will always be met with voices of dissent from within.

---

[173] Papers, Inclosure 2, "Substance of an Interpellation addressed by Lord Dufferin to Fuad Pasha, at the Eighth Sitting of the Syrian Commission, November 10, 1860", in No. 190, see *supra* note 153. For more on how these defenses are used today, see Ziv Bohrer, "Is the Prosecution of War Crimes Just and Effective? Rethinking the Lessons from Sociology and Psychology", *Michigan Journal of International Law*, 2012, vol. 33, no. 4. pp. 750–81; Alison Dundes Renteln, "Cultural Defenses in International Criminal Tribunals: A Preliminary Consideration of the Issues", *Southwestern Journal of International Law*, 2012, vol. 18, no. 1, pp. 267–85.

[174] FO 406/10, Inclosure 4, in No. 414, Dufferin to Russell, sent 1 February 1861, received 16 February 1860, TNA.

And, it would seem, from outside as well. I will close this section with a consideration of an editorial from *The Times*, interesting for its implication that the idea that no one guilty of mass crimes is above the law was ultimately exported from the Ottoman Empire back to England. The writer began a paragraph by rejoicing at the punishment of the "malefactors", particularly Ahmad Pasha and his subordinates, but rejecting the view that Fuad, with "his firmness, his enlarged views, and the summary justice he has executed" represented the "triumph of European civilization". Fuad's repressive measures were rather the "justice administered by Eastern despots from the earliest ages", an extension of the "justice of Darius, or Haroun Alraschid, or Suleiman the Magnificent". The author then ruminated on the Ottoman psyche: "The troops supported the Pasha with alacrity; and such is Oriental nature that every execution has been received by Moslems composed of Turkish functionaries, have sent the prisoners to death or banishment by droves, because they knew it was the will of the Pasha. The instinct of obedience and the readiness for unsparing slaughter still mark the race as in former days". Then, an abrupt and odd change of perspective, as the results of Fuad's efforts are contrasted with those of a 'civilised' power in a similar situation: "It would be difficult to induce a European Government to carry out such a sentence on a man so highly placed". Finally, a shift in focus to the cyclic nature of Ottoman justice: "As in the old times no rank or office, no amount of Imperial favour, insured the servants of the Sultan from the bowstring, so we find even now that an official of the highest class may fall in an hour, and that a court-martial, composed, perhaps, of his own subordinates and sycophants, will send him to his doom when it is known that a greater man than he has given the word for severity".[175]

One might perceive the leaps in narrative as manifestations of the author's inner struggle to reconcile his distaste for the bloody vengeance being enacted in Syria with his appreciation for its results. There are a number of questions effervescing just beneath the surface here. Is the imperfect justice of Darius preferable to the unaccountability of European officials? What does 'civilisation' mean in a world where the Porte achieved a more thorough justice than European Powers could? There is a longing in this paragraph for the best of all worlds, fairness and punishment, within and outside Europe. Justice in Syria, at least in one case it

---

[175] *The Times*, 2 October 1860.

seems, prompted some of the early, muddled, stirrings of a sentiment that would eventually evolve into demands for recognition of a truly universal right to justice.

7.7. Conclusion

International criminal law was not moribund during the long nineteenth century. Many states were sensitive to atrocity, and prioritized answering the massacre and pillage in Syria with punishment. The Druse-Maronite conflict inspired among Europe's diplomatic and political constituencies an unprecedented willingness to reject a local amnesty and internationlise punishment, and generated sincere and equally unprecedented rhetoric concerning the values and rights of humanity. In Syria and back home, Europeans drew connections between international judicial processes and atrocity, and refined their legal and social lexicon to encapsulate the horrific nature of the violence and justify the recourse to extraordinary international punitive measures. In these endeavours we may discern some of the first stirrings of what would become, in the twentieth century, a revolution in international law.

Surprisingly, international law's luminaries missed opportunities to encourage these roots to take hold. When Gustave Moynier published (a mere 12 years after the Syria crisis) his proposal for an international criminal court to hear cases involving violations of the Geneva Convention, he passed over the Commission, modelled the proposed institution on interstate arbitral tribunals, and analogised between his suggestion and international copyright treaties with a penal component.[176] Francis Lieber's code of conduct, prepared for use by Union troops in 1863, did not cite the tri-

---

[176] Gustave Moynier, "Note sur la création d'une institution judiciaire internationale propre à prévenir et à réprimer les infractions à la Convention de Genève", *Bulletin international des sociétés de secours aux militaires blessés*, Comité international, 1872, no. 11, pp. 122–31. For more on Moynier's proposal see Christopher Keith Hall, "The First Proposal for A Permanent International Criminal Court", *International Review of the Red Cross*, 1998, vol. 322, pp. 57–74. Moynier was confident as late as 1870 that 'extralegal' sanctions – "retaliation, new hostilities and dishonour" (specifically arraignment "before the tribunal of public conscience" and attendant excommunication from the community of "civilised nations") – would be sufficient to ensure compliance with the Geneva Conventions. Gustave Moynier, *Étude sur la convention de Genève pour l'amélioration du sort des militaires blesées dans les armées en campagne*, Cherbuliez, Paris, 1870, pp. 300–2. The failure of both sides in the Franco-Prussian War to honour the Geneva Convention would disabuse him of this notion, but by then, it seems, the Commission and Syrian trials were lost to the Europe's community of international law scholars.

als in Syria as a precedent for the punishment of war criminals.[177] Indeed, I have been unable to find any reference to the punishments or work of the Commission in any English or French legal text from the nineteenth century. As far as development of doctrine was concerned, the slide into obscurity of the post-conflict experience in Syria was steep and complete.

European and US international lawyers declined to construe transitional justice in Syria as a transformative moment in international law or invoke the Commission as a symbol of the existence of a law of nations rightfully concerned with the conduct of individuals (or, less ambitiously, of an international sentiment to the effect that atrocious conduct demanded condign punishment). But the precedent was not forgotten by Europe's diplomats. The "Bulgarian horrors" of 1876 stimulated, with British encouragement, a series of trials in that Ottoman province.[178] When the

---

[177] Lieber relied primarily on his previous work "reinforced with the notes and files that he had painstakingly built up during his teaching career". Richard Baxter, *Humanizing the Laws of War: Selected Writings of Richard Baxter*, ed. by Detlev F. Vagts, Theodor Meron, Stephen M. Schwebel and Charles Keever, Oxford University Press, Oxford, 2013, p. 136. See generally, Francis Freidel, *Lieber: Nineteenth-Century Liberal*, Louisiana State University Press, Baton Rouge, 1947. Neither Lieber's 1862 essay *Guerrilla Parties* nor the records of his lectures delivered at Columbia University between 1861 and 1862, archived at the Eisenhower Library, Johns Hopkins University, make any mention of the events in Syria. Still, it is obvious that Dufferin and Lieber drew from the same philosophical well. Just as the former recognised the need for rational and fair punishments in Syria, the latter, in considering the applicability of rules designed for interstate conflicts to civil wars, considered it "certain, that no army, no society engaged in war, any more than a society at peace, can allow unpunished assassination, robbery, and devastation without the deepest injury to itself and disastrous consequences which might change the very issue of the war". Francis Lieber, *Guerrilla Parties Considered with Reference to the Laws and Usages of War*, D. van Nostrand, New York, 1862, p. 186.

[178] Midhat Pasha, the grand vizier, refused to accept a Great Power-backed International Commission that would have been empowered to "help the Ottoman authorities discover the perpetrators of the massacres, ensure the punishment of the guilty, and take part of the revision of the sentences of persons condemned by [an Ottoman] Extraordinary Commission", but counter-proposed that the Great Powers could send "agents" to attend the hearings of a Porte-established Commission. Great Britain. Foreign Office, Turkey No. 2, *Further Correspondence Respecting the Affairs of Turkey, presented to both Houses of Parliament by Command of Her Majesty*, Harrison and Sons, London; Great Britain. Foreign Office, Turkey No. 15, *Further Correspondence Respecting the Affairs of Turkey, presented to both Houses of Parliament by Command of Her Majesty*, Harrison and Sons, London ('Turkey No. 15'), Inclosure in No. 207, Elliot to Derby, sent 8 January 1877, received 20 January 1877. Walter Baring attended the trials as agent of the British government. My preliminary review of the relevant Blue Books suggests that he did not directly participate in the proceedings, but when a verdict was reached that he did not agree with he announced his withdrawal from the Ottoman Commission. The fact that this was perceived

Turkish ambassador complained of difficulties in executing capital sentences on individuals "convicted of massacres and atrocities" and expressed hope that Britain would be satisfied with a minor sentence, the British Secretary of State for Foreign Affairs reminded him "what had been done" in response to the Lebanon massacres and insisted that only death would be considered an adequate penalty.[179] I am confident that additional research will reveal connections between the statesmen involved in the Commission and subsequent European responses to outbreaks of mass violence.

The Syrian experience with justice embodies many of the same tensions that play out today: between Great Power and non-Great Power expectations and perceptions of justice; between competing conceptions of the limits of foreign jurisdiction over local affairs; between the drive to punish massacre versus the perceived necessity of limiting penalties; between those who would embrace the inherently political nature of mass justice and those who would seek to remove politics from the equation; between competing narratives of guilt and victimhood; and between the divergent political objectives and consciousness of metropole and periphery, to name but a few.

The research presented here is but a first step to understanding how these tensions played out in response to the crisis in Syria, and how these events relate to modern debates and doctrine. Much empirical study remains to be done on the trials at Beirut, Damascus, and Moukhtara. The question of the process of selecting defendants, the profiles of those involved, the evolution of trial procedures, the crimes charged, the rules of evidence, the "due process" protections applied, the verdicts issued and how they were received by local stakeholders, the defences raised, and their findings on matters of law, will be of intrinsic interest to the growing number of history-minded international lawyers. And perhaps when that work is over, international criminal law will be invigorated by the incorporation of new experiences generated by a state not traditionally associated with the development of international criminal law, and the judgments will prove to be a fresh source of jurisprudence from which contemporary adjudicators draw inspiration.

---

as a sanction suggests that the trials before the Turkish Commission were considered 'international' in some sense. Turkey No. 15, *infra*, Inclosure 5, in No. 156, Jocelyn to Earl of Derby, sent 12 February 1877, received 20 February 1877.

[179] Turkey No. 15, No. 163, Earl of Derby to Mr. Jocelyn, 20 February 1877.

I am confident that further research will result in the discovery of additional linkages between episodes where the toolkit of international criminal law was either considered or put into practice, as well as between those experiences and various contemporary social and jurisprudential trends (for example, liberalism, humanitarianism, internationalism, social Darwinism, colonialism, racism, military professionalisation and so on). Pursuing this line of inquiry will not only improve our understanding of the character, morality, process, promise and limits of transitional justice in the present, but will also allow us to draw the sorts of conclusions, for example regarding the factors affecting the durability of the positive out-comes of transitional justice, that only a truly long-term historical perspective permits.

8

The Katyn Forest Massacre and the Nuremberg Trial

William Schabas[*]

Count III (war crimes) of the indictment of the major war criminals by the International Military Tribunal charged the defendants with "murder and ill-treatment of prisoners of war and of other members of the armed forces of the countries with whom Germany was at war, and of persons on the high seas". It provided nearly two pages of particulars concerning 14 cases, some set out in considerable detail, "by way of example and without prejudice to the production of evidence of other cases". Among them was the following: "In September 1941, 11,000 Polish officers who were prisoners of war were killed in the Katyn Forest near Smolensk".[1] These 19 words, in an indictment of some 65 pages, received disproportionate attention during the trial. Testimony of witnesses, for both the prosecution and the defence, consumed two entire trial days.

The mass grave in the Katyn forest had come to the attention of German troops in early 1943, at a time when their armies were in retreat although they still occupied much of the western part of the Soviet Union. The German news agency Transocean announced the discovery on 12 April 1943. German sources claimed the victims, estimated at 10,000, had been shot in the back of the head in 1940 at a time when the territory was under Soviet control. A few days later the Soviet media charged that the murders had been committed in 1941, by German forces.[2] The Germans

---

[*] **William Schabas** is Professor of International Law, Middlesex University, London; Professor of International Criminal Law and Human Rights, Leiden University; and Emeritus Professor of Human Rights Law, National University of Ireland Galway. He served as adviser to the Polish Government before the Grand Chamber of the European Court of Human Rights in *Janowiec and Others v. Russia*. He is the author of more than twenty books dealing in whole or in part with international human rights law.

[1] Indictment, 1 International Military Tribunal 27, 1947, p. 54 ('IMT'). See also, First Day, Tuesday, 20 November 1945, Afternoon Session, 2 IMT 57, 1947 p. 65.

[2] P.M.H. Bell, "Censorship, Propaganda and Public Opinion: The Case of the Katyn Graves, 1943", in *Transactions of the Royal Historical* Society, 1989, vol. 39, pp. 63–64.

assembled an expert commission of inquiry that visited the site and produced a report that attributed responsibility to the Soviets. A year later, when the German forces had been pushed back, the Soviet regime organised its own commission of inquiry, known as the Burdenko Commission. Its report concluded that the massacre took place subsequent to the German invasion and that therefore Germany, not the Soviet Union, was responsible.

In its final judgment, issued on 30 September and 1 October 1948, the International Military Tribunal dealt at some length with the count in the indictment concerning the murder of prisoners of war. It concluded that the Germans were responsible for the murder of American, British and Soviet prisoners of war although it did not systematically review every factual allegation in the indictment.[3] There was no reference to the murder of Polish officers at Katyn in the final judgment of the International Military Tribunal or in the dissenting opinion of Judge I.T. Nikitchenko. In his memoirs, published in 1962, the American judge, Francis Biddle, described the evidence as "inconclusive".[4] Testifying before a congressional committee in 1952, the American chief prosecutor, Robert Jackson, explained that "guilt for the Katyn Forest Massacre has not been adjudged by the Nuremberg Tribunal".[5] In his history of the Second World War, Winston Churchill wrote that "the Soviet government did not take the opportunity of clearing themselves of the horrible and widely believed accusation against them and of fastening the guilt conclusively upon the German government".[6] Some scholars have gone even further, interpreting the judgment as a tacit acknowledgement of Soviet responsibility.[7] Katyn was one of those relatively rare situations in criminal justice

---

[3] Two Hundred and Seventeenth Day, Monday, 30 September 1946, Morning Session, 1 IMT 411, 1947, pp. 471–75

[4] Francis Biddle, *In Brief Authority*, Doubleday, New York, 1962, p. 417.

[5] Hearings before the Select Committee to Conduct an Investigation of the Facts, Evidence and Circumstances of the Katyn Forest Massacre, Eighty-second Congress, Second Session, on Investigation of the Murder of Thousands of Polish Officers in the Katyn Forest near Smolensk, Russia, Part 7, June 3, 4 and November 11, 12, 13, 14, 1952, p. 1945 ('Select Committee Hearings, Part 7').

[6] Winston S. Churchill, *The Second World War*, vol. 4, *The Hinge of Fate*, Cassel, London, 1951, p. 181.

[7] Annette Wieviorka, *Le procès de Nuremberg*, Editions Ouest-France, Rennes, 1995, p. 92; Alexandra Viatteau, "Comment a été traitéé la question de Katyn à Nuremberg", in Annette Wieviorka (ed.), *Les procès de Nuremberg et de Tokyo*, Editions Complexe,

where, because of the nature and scale of the act, there can only be two plausible suspects. But even if the judges had been inclined to attribute responsibility to the Soviets, there was no legal basis for them to make such a finding. The Tribunal could only exercise jurisdiction over "the major war criminals of the European Axis".[8] The Nuremberg trial left the issue of responsibility for Katyn unresolved.

As the Cold War was coming to a close, Russian historians obtained access to previously secret documents that indicated Soviet responsibility for the Katyn massacre. Ironically, one of the researchers was Iurii N. Zoria, the son of the Soviet assistant prosecutor Nikolai Zoria at the International Military Tribunal. Nikolai Zoria was responsible for presenting the case with respect to German aggression against the Soviet Union and the subject of forced labour and deportation into German slavery.[9] Zoria died in his Nuremberg hotel room midway through the trial under suspicious circumstances.[10]

On 13 April 1990 President Mikhail Gorbachev gave the Polish President, Wojciech Jaruzelski, documents containing the lists of prisoners to be executed that had been prepared by the Soviet secret police commonly known by the acronym NKVD (People's Commissariat for Internal Affairs or Народный комиссариат внутренних дел).[11] At the same time, the official news agency TASS confirmed Soviet responsibility for the Katyn massacre, assigning blame primarily to the NKVD, its chief, Lavrenty P. Beria, and his deputy, Vsevolod N. Merkulov. The Russian admission does not seem to have discouraged some denialists, however, including the grandson of Joseph Stalin, Yevgeniy Yakovlevich Dzhugashvili.[12]

In its October 2013 judgment dismissing an application directed against Russia by relatives of the victims at Katyn, the Grand Chamber of

---

Brussels, 1996, pp. 152–53; Léon Poliakov, *Le procès de Nuremberg*, Gallimard, Paris, 1971, p. 205.

[8] Charter of the International Military Tribunal, 82 *UNTS* 280, 1951, annex, Arts. 1, 6.

[9] Fifty-fourth Day, Friday, Afternoon Session, 8 February 1946, IMT 177, 1948, pp. 196–97.

[10] Anna M. Cienciala, Natalia S. Lebedeva and Wojciech Materski (eds.), *Katyn: A Crime Without Punishment*, Yale University Press, New Haven, NJ, 2007, p. 234.

[11] Eugenia Maresch, Katyn 1940: The Documentary Evidence of the West's Betrayal, Spellmount, Stroud, 2010, p. 261.

[12] *Dzhugashvili v. Russia* (dec.), no. 41123/10, 9 December 2014.

the European Court of Human Rights provided the following useful summary of the relevant events:

> 15. On 1 September 1939 Germany invaded Poland, starting the Second World War. On 17 September 1939 the Soviet Red Army marched into Polish territory, allegedly acting to protect the Ukrainians and Belorussians living in the eastern part of Poland because the Polish State had collapsed under the German attack and could no longer guarantee the security of its own citizens. The Polish Army did not offer military resistance. The USSR annexed the territory newly under its control and in November 1939 declared that the 13.5 million Polish citizens who lived there were henceforth Soviet citizens.
>
> 16. In the wake of the Red Army's advance around 250,000 Polish soldiers, border guards, police officers, prison guards, State officials and other functionaries were detained. After they had been disarmed, some of them were set free; the others were sent to special prison camps established by the NKVD (People's Commissariat for Internal Affairs, a predecessor of the KGB) in Kozelsk, Ostashkov and Starobelsk. On 9 October 1939 it was decided that the Polish officer corps should be billeted at the camps in Kozelsk and Starobelsk and the remaining functionaries, including the police officers and prison guards, in Ostashkov.
>
> 17. In early March 1940 L. Beria, head of the NKVD, submitted to J. Stalin, Secretary General of the USSR Communist Party, a proposal to approve the shooting of Polish prisoners of war on the ground that they were all "enemies of the Soviet authorities filled with hatred for the Soviet system of government" who were "attempting to continue their c[ounter]-r[evolutionary] work" and "conducting anti-Soviet agitation". The proposal specified that the prisoner-of-war camps accommodated 14,736 former military and police officers, of whom more than 97 per cent were Polish by nationality, and that a further 10,685 Poles were being held in the prisons of the western districts of Ukraine and Belorussia.
>
> 18. On 5 March 1940 the Politburo of the Central Committee of the USSR Communist Party considered the proposal and decided as follows:
>
> > "I. Instructs the NKVD USSR as follows:

(1) the cases of the 14,700 persons remaining in the prisoner-of-war camps (former Polish Army officers, government officials, landowners, policemen, intelligence agents, military policemen, settlers and prison guards),

(2) and the cases of the persons arrested and remaining in prisons in the western districts of Ukraine and Belorussia, numbering 11,000 (members of various counter-revolutionary espionage and sabotage organisations, former landowners, factory owners, former Polish Army officers, government officials and fugitives), are to be considered in a special procedure, with the sentence of capital punishment – [execution by] shooting – being imposed.

II. The cases are to be considered without the detainees being summoned or the charges being disclosed, and without any statements concerning the conclusion of the investigation or the bills of indictment being issued to them, in the following manner:

(a) the persons remaining in the prisoner-of-war camps: on the basis of information provided by the Directorate of Prisoner-of-War Affairs, NKVD USSR,

(b) the persons arrested: on the basis of information provided by the NKVD of the Ukrainian SSR and the NKVD of the Belorussian SSR.è

The decision was signed by J. Stalin, K. Voroshilov, A. Mikoyan, V. Molotov, M. Kalinin and L. Kaganovich.

19. The killings took place in April and May 1940. Prisoners from the Kozelsk camp were killed at a site near Smolensk known as the Katyn Forest; those from the Starobelsk camp were shot in the Kharkov NKVD prison and their bodies were buried near the village of Pyatikhatki; the police officers from Ostashkov were killed in the Kalinin (now Tver) NKVD prison and buried in Mednoye. The circumstances of the execution of the prisoners from the prisons in western Ukraine and Belorussia have remained unknown to date.[13]

The treatment of the Katyn issue at Nuremberg has not infrequently been invoked by those who attack the legacy of the International Military

---

[13]   *Janowiec and Others v. Russia* [GC], nos. 55508/07 and 29520/09, 21 October 2013.

Tribunal. For example, French *négationniste* Robert Faurisson, in his unsuccessful application before the United Nations Human Rights Committee, challenged the reference to the Nuremberg judgment in French legislation dealing with Holocaust denial. He had been prosecuted under the Gayssot Act of 1990 by which it is an offence to "deny the existence of one or more crimes against humanity as defined in Article 6 of the Statute of the International Military Tribunal annexed to the London agreement of 8 August 1945 which have been committed either by the members of an organisation declared criminal pursuant to Article 9 of the Statute or by a person found guilty of such crimes by a French or international court".[14] Faurisson argued that "the 'Gayssot Act' promotes the Nuremberg trial and judgment to the status of dogma, by imposing criminal sanctions on those who dare to challenge its findings and premises". This is explained in the decision of the Committee:

> In substantiation of the claim that the Nuremberg records cannot be taken as infallible, he cites, by way of example, the indictment which charged the Germans with the Katyn massacre, and refers to the introduction by the Soviet prosecutor of documents purporting to show that the Germans had killed the Polish prisoners of war at Katyn (Nuremberg document USSR-054). The Soviet authorship of this crime, he points out, is now established beyond doubt. The author further notes that, among the members of the Soviet Katyn (Lyssenko) Commission, which had adduced proof of the purported German responsibility for the Katyn massacre, were Professors Burdenko and Nicolas, who also testified that the Germans had used gas chambers at Auschwitz for the extermination of four million persons (Document USSR-006). Subsequently, he asserts, the estimated number of victims at Auschwitz has been revised downward to approximately one million.[15]

It bears repeating that the International Military Tribunal did not find the Nazi leaders responsible for the Katyn massacre. Consequently, the Gayssot Act is utterly inapplicable. Indeed, the fact that the charge relating to Katyn was not upheld in the judgment ought to enhance, and not detract from, the credibility of the Tribunal.

---

[14] English translation provided in *Lehideux and Isorni v. France*, 23 September 1998, § 27, *Reports of Judgments and Decisions* 1998-VII.

[15] *Faurisson v. France*, UN doc. CCPR/C/58/D/550/1993, para. 2.4.

8.1. Preparation of the Indictment

The Charter of the International Military Tribunal, adopted on 8 August 1945, required each of the parties – France, the Soviet Union, the United Kingdom and the United States – to appoint a chief prosecutor. The four chief prosecutors were to act as the "Committee for the Investigation and Prosecution of Major War Criminals" in the organisation and conduct of the trial. The Committee's tasks included preparation and approval of the indictment.[16] Work on the indictment actually began in late June, more than a month before the London Agreement was finalised. A subcommittee charged with drafting the indictment first met on 23 June 1945, but with only American and British representatives in attendance.[17]

Robert Jackson, at the time a sitting justice of the United States Supreme Court, was designated as his country's chief prosecutor. In November 1952 Jackson testified before a Select Committee of the United States Congress that was investigating the Katyn massacre about the decision to include the charge in the indictment. Explaining the rationale for holding the inquiry, the Committee's chairman, Congressman Ray J. Madden, said that there had been questions about "the operation of the Nuremberg trials".[18] Jackson told the Committee that the four Allied chief prosecutors had decided to divide among themselves primary responsibility for specific issues by subject matter. He said that the preparation of evidence of crimes in Eastern Europe, which was then under Soviet occupation and "to much of which the others of us had no access", was assigned to the Soviets. This included Katyn as well as Poland, although "at that time it was not known that the Katyn massacre would be involved".[19]

As the discussions on the indictment were concluding, the Soviets proposed that the following be added: "In September 1941, 925 Polish officers who were prisoners of war were killed in the Katyn Forest near Smolensk".[20] Jackson said that both the British and the American representatives "protested, but they finally concluded that, despite their personal disapproval, if the Soviet thought they could prove the charge they

---

[16] Charter of the International Military Tribunal, 82 *UNTS* 280, 1951, annex, arts. 14–15.

[17] Sidney S. Alderman, "Negotiating on War Crimes Prosecutions, 1945", in Raymond Dennett and Joseph E. Johnson (eds.), *Negotiating with the Russians*, World Peace Foundation, Boston, 1951, pp. 82–84.

[18] Select Committee Hearings, Part 7, p. 1944, see *supra* note 5.

[19] *Ibid.*, p. 1945.

[20] *Ibid.*, p. 1946.

were entitled to do so under the division of the case".[21] According to Jackson, "[i]n view of what we knew of the over-all Nazi plan to exterminate inhabitants of Poland, it did not seem unlikely that this was part of their programme, and the Soviet claimed to have adequate evidence of Nazi guilt".[22] Jackson told the congressional committee that "[w]hile we did not feel justified in preventing the issue, we warned the Soviet delegation that we did not have evidence to support the charge nor time nor opportunity to investigate it and that, if it met with denial or countercharges, we would keep hands off and leave the entire contest to the Soviet and German lawyers".[23]

Explaining the opposition of the British and American prosecutors to the inclusion of the Katyn charge, Jackson cited a policy decision to rely upon documentary evidence of crimes and only to proceed with charges where guilt could be "fully proved or substantially corroborated by documentary evidence captured from the Germans themselves". In that respect, Jackson said responsibility for the Katyn massacre "did not appear to be capable of documentary proof or substantial corroboration".[24] He said that "[b]ecause this was the first international criminal trial in history and was held in the wake of war when passions were high, we did not want any judgment that would rest solely on oral testimony of witnesses whose interest, bias, memory, and truthfulness would always be open to question". For this reason, the prosecutors passed over "many tempting matters because evidence measuring up to this standard was not then obtainable".[25] Jackson's explanation was confirmed by the British prosecutor, David Maxwell Fyfe, who said in his memoirs that the British and Americans had expressed opposition to including the Katyn charge "based on the sound premise that the charge would depart from the basic plan to develop the case from authentic German documents, and no witnesses were available who, in Jackson's own words, 'would meet the high standards of credibility required in a criminal trial'".[26]

---

21 *Ibid.*

22 *Ibid.*, p. 1946.

23 *Ibid.* See also Sidney S. Alderman, "Negotiating on War Crimes Prosecutions, 1945", in Dennett and Johnson, 1951, pp. 96–97, see *supra* note 17.

24 Select Committee Hearings, Part 7, p. 1946, see *supra* note 5.

25 *Ibid.*

26 David Maxwell Fyfe, *Political Adventure: The Memoirs of the Earl of Kilmuir*, Weidenfeld and Nicolson, London, 1964, p. 96.

Jackson also referred to the possibility of obtaining evidence from Polish sources. He said that "[a]ttitudes of Polish authorities at the time were conflicting", confirming his view that "we should not participate in the trial of the Nazi-Soviet dispute". He said that the Polish government then in power had a delegation at Nuremberg that co-operated with the Soviets, "including, as I understood it, accusing the Nazis of the Katyn murders".[27] Jackson also referred to the United Nations War Crimes Commission, the London-based body established in late 1943 charged with investigating wartime atrocities. Jackson noted that Poland was a member of the Commission but that it never even raised the issue of the Katyn massacre.[28] Recently, researchers have obtained access to many of the records of the United Nations War Crimes Commission, which are archived with the United Nations. There is nothing to suggest that Jackson's observation was incorrect. But Jackson added that in February 1946 a group of Polish parliamentarians submitted a letter and statement that indicated Soviet responsibility for the massacre. It concluded that "it would be ill-advised to include the Katyn case in the tasks of the Nuremberg tribunal. The case is of a special character, and needs in order to be fully elucidated, to be examined and treated independently by an international judicial body".[29]

There has been speculation as to whether at the time the indictment was adopted the Americans and the British "knew" that the Soviets were guilty of the massacre.[30] David Irving's book on the Nuremberg Trial contends that "[t]he British government was well aware of the truth about this atrocity".[31] Of course, at a very basic level everyone had been informed of the truth through Nazi propaganda and the German *White Book* on Katyn. But the government officials and prosecutors could not simply ignore the Soviet denials and their accusations of Nazi responsibility. Jackson told the congressional committee that he had no opinion one way or the other about who was responsible for the massacre. He considered that both Nazi Germany and the Soviet Union were capable of the offence and "perhaps both had opportunity to commit it, and that it was perfectly consistent with the policy of each toward Poland".[32] In 1991 the American prosecu-

---

[27] Select Committee Hearings, p. 1947, see *supra* note 5.

[28] *Ibid.*

[29] *Ibid.*

[30] For example, Viatteau, 1996, p. 146, see *supra* note 7.

[31] David Irving, *Nuremberg: The Last Battle*, Focal Point, London, 1996, p. 36.

[32] Select Committee Hearings, Part 7, p. 1946, see *supra* note 5.

tor Telford Taylor told Allen Paul: "There was a feeling then that the Russians, not the Germans, were guilty".[33] However, Taylor did not say this in his memoirs, published the following year,[34] and his recollection is not confirmed by contemporary materials. For example, Thomas J. Dodd, another one of the American prosecutors, wrote to his wife that the responsibility for Katyn was a "toss up". Like Jackson, Dodd believed that both the Nazis and the Soviets were capable of the crime and had a motive to commit it. "I insist that the dispute between them is of little interest to the world – even less will it interest history", he wrote.[35]

The British archives indicate considerable discussion within the Foreign Office about responsibility for Katyn. In May 1943 Sir Owen O'Malley, who was British ambassador to the Polish government-in-exile during the war, in "a bold, able and emotive despatch",[36] had set out the case for Soviet responsibility. O'Malley relied upon circumstantial evidence drawn from Polish sources in London, in particular the fact that the bodies bore winter clothing. In light of O'Malley's reports, Foreign Minister Anthony Eden wrote to Prime Minister Churchill that there were "serious doubts on Russian disclaimers of responsibility" but that "the evidence is conflicting and whatever we may suspect, we shall probably never know". Churchill answered: "This is not one of those matters where absolute certainty is either urgent or indispensable".[37] On 17 February 1944 Professor B.H. Sumner, "a notable and impartial Russian scholar", prepared a memorandum for the Research Department of the Foreign Office that concluded the report of the Soviet Commission had set out "a good, though not a conclusive, case for the perpetration of the massacres by the Germans".[38] Following the issuance of the indictment, Denis Allen

---

[33] Allen Paul, *Katyn: Stalin's Massacre and the Triumph of Truth*, Northern Illinois University Press, De Kalb, IL, 2010, p. 336.

[34] Telford Taylor, *The Anatomy of the Nuremberg Trials: A Personal Memoir*, Alfred A. Knopf, New York, 1992, p. 117.

[35] Christopher J. Dodd with Lary Bloom, *Letters from Nuremberg: My Father's Narrative of a Quest for Justice*, Crown, New York, 2007, p. 333.

[36] The Katyn Massacre and Reactions in the Foreign Office, Memorandum by the Historical Adviser, 10 April 1973, DS(L) 230, para. 7 ('The Katyn Massacre').

[37] *Ibid.*, para. 9. See also Alastair Noble, "British Reactions to the Katyn Massacre", in Delphine Debons, Antoine Fleury and Jean-François Pitteloud (eds.), *Katyn and Switzerland: Forensic Investigators and Investigations in Humanitarian Crises, 1920–2007*, Georg Editeur, Geneva, 2007, pp. 221–36.

[38] The Katyn Massacre, para. 15, see *supra* note 36.

of the Foreign Office prepared a summary of previous developments concerning the Katyn massacre accompanied by a draft brief for a parliamentary debate that did not in fact take place. It included the following:

> [His Majesty's Government] have no direct evidence on the subject in their own possession. [...] They have of course studied the reports published by the German and Soviet Commission which investigated the scene of the massacres in 1943. In their opinion the Soviet report, which was drawn up after a lengthy period of investigation by very distinguished and highly qualified Russian experts, provides sufficient *prima facie* evidence of German guilt to justify the inclusion of this charge in the indictment against the major German war criminals.[39]

Sir Thomas Brimelow minuted agreement with Allen's paper, but with a reservation:

> The Soviet investigations, if accepted as genuine, show that *some* Poles were killed at Katyn after March 1940. They do not prove that they were *all* killed after that date. In other words, the Soviet investigations inculpate the Germans without entirely exculpating the Soviet authorities. On the other hand, the evidence now available about German mass murders makes it impossible to attach credence to German evidence which might be designed to mask German crimes. We must therefore suspend judgment.[40]

In effect, the Foreign Office took the "considered view" that "the evidence at present available would seem to require a suspension of judgment in regard to the whole affair".[41]

The original figure of 925 victims at Katyn contained in the indictment signed by the chief prosecutors on 6 October was apparently based on the number of corpses examined by the Burdenko Commission. It seems that the Russian text of the indictment, dated 9 October 1945, spoke of 11,000 victims.[42] Perhaps at the time the Soviets did not realise the inconsistency with the English text. Nearly two weeks were spent dealing with discrepancies between the German and English texts of the indictment. But the planned filing of the indictment at the Tribunal's first

---

[39] *Ibid.*, para. 34.

[40] *Ibid.*, para. 35.

[41] *Ibid.*, para. 17, citing C 2957/8/55.

[42] Cienciala *et al.*, 2007, p. 230, see *supra* note 10.

public session in Berlin (in accordance with Article 22 of the Charter), on 15 October, was unexpectedly delayed when the Soviet chief prosecutor, Roman Rudenko, asked for a postponement so that the figure of 925 could be amended to 11,000. According to Robert Conot, the Soviet judge, Iona Nikitchenko, "asked which would be the greater evil: a postponement of a few days, or the harm that would come to Russia if the indictment were filed as it existed?".[43] The American judge, Francis Biddle, told his French and British colleagues that he feared the Soviet judges "might bolt if we didn't agree" to the postponement.[44]

As they prepared for the trial to begin, the four prosecution teams considered the possibility that the German defendants would invoke acts allegedly perpetrated by the Allied governments. In addition to various violations of the laws and customs of war, they were also concerned about the aggression charge with respect to planned or actual military action directed at the sovereignty of Iceland, Norway, Poland, Finland and the Baltic States. All but the French were directly concerned by this issue. At a meeting in early November 1945 the prosecutors agreed that they would collectively defend themselves against defence charges of Allied war crimes. It was agreed that each national team would prepare a memorandum outlining its concerns in order to facilitate preparations. Robert Jackson, writing to the French and the Soviet prosecutors, said "the United States, being late in the war and remote from the scene, was little exposed to attack itself and was perhaps in the best position to lead the effort to restrict the proof closely to the charges and try to stop political discussions".[45] The United Kingdom immediately complied with the commitment, but France and the Soviet Union did not, "perhaps uncertain about what the Americans and the British would do with the information".[46] Only in March 1946 did the Soviets provide a list of topics that they wanted to avoid, including the Molotov-Ribbentrop Pact of August 1939 and "Soviet-Polish relations".[47]

In his testimony before the congressional committee, Jackson noted that after the indictment was filed, the Polish government-in-exile neither

---

[43] Robert E. Conot, *Justice at Nuremberg*, Harper & Row, New York, 1983, pp. 67–68.
[44] Taylor, 1992, p. 125, see *supra* note 34; also Biddle, 1962, pp. 387–88, see *supra* note 4.
[45] Francine Hirsch, "The Soviets at Nuremberg: International Law, Propaganda, and the Making of the Postwar Order", in *American Historical Review*, 2008, vol. 113, p. 718.
[46] *Ibid.*
[47] *Ibid.*, p. 719.

objected to the Katyn charge nor did it provide evidence.[48] However, there are indications of attempts from other quarters, subsequent to issuance of the indictment, to influence the conduct of the prosecution with respect to Katyn. A Northern Irish Member of Parliament, Sir Douglas Savory, provided Foreign Minister Ernest Bevin with a report he had helped prepare on the Katyn massacre that pointed the finger at the Soviet Union. In response to a query from Bevin, the Attorney General, Sir Hartley Shawcross, replied:

> We did our best to persuade the Russians not to include a charge about Katyn in the indictment, but they insisted on doing so, although I believe they are now a little doubtful of the wisdom of their decision. In the circumstances there is nothing that we can do except to try and steer the Russians as carefully as we can over this exceedingly delicate and difficult ground. This we are doing as best we can, but I must confess I am not at all happy about the situation which may eventually arise if evidence is called in regard to Katyn.[49]

Shawcross also wrote to Savory, explaining that the Soviets had decided to attempt to prove German responsibility for the Katyn massascre, "and it will therefore be for the Tribunal after hearing the Russian evidence, and such evidence as the Germans may call in regard to the matter, to decide where the truth lies".[50]

The Foreign Office archives also contain a draft letter from a Polish parliamentarian ("We don't know how this paper reached us", says the minute) expressing concern about the Katyn charge: "The question arises as to whether German propaganda will not in the future be able to allude to the incident when one of the parties publicly accused was the judge in its own case?" The letter warned of anything that could diminish the credibility of the Nuremberg Tribunal. It urged that Katyn be investigated by an independent judicial body.[51] In his testimony before the congressional committee, Robert Jackson referred to a letter he received in February 1946 from a group of Polish parliamentarians that indicated Soviet responsibility for the massacre. This seems to be the final version of the draft letter in the British archives. It concluded that "it would be ill-

---

[48]   Select Committee Hearings, Part 7, p. 1947, see *supra* note 5.
[49]   Sir Hartley Shawcross to Ernest Bevin, 28 December 1945, FO 371/56474.
[50]   Sir Hartley Shawcross to Prof. D.L. Savory, MP, 28 December 1945, FO 371/56474.
[51]   Jozef Godlewski to Jan Kwapinski, Parliamentary Group 74, 7 December 1945 (translation), FO 371/56474.

advised to include the Katyn case in the tasks of the Nuremberg tribunal. The case is of a special character, and needs in order to be fully elucidated, to be examined and treated independently by an international judicial body".[52]

8.2. Preliminaries and Production of the Soviet Report

The first reference in the actual proceedings to the Katyn massacre occurred very early in the trial. On 14 December 1945 Major William F. Walsh of the United States prosecution team was reviewing documentary evidence that had already been produced in the record. The title of his presentation was "The Persecution of the Jews". He drew the attention of the Tribunal to a letter that had been sent by the Reich Minister for the Occupied Eastern Territories to Alfred Rosenberg, one of the defendants, protesting against the treatment of Jews. Walsh explained that "a certain amount of discord existed between the officials of the German Government as to the proper means and methods used in connection with the programme of extermination". The author of the letter wrote:

> The fact that Jews receive special treatment requires no further discussion. However, it appears hardly believable that this was done in the way described in the report of the General Commissioner of 1 June 1943. What is Katyn against that? Imagine only that these occurrences might become known to the other side and be exploited by them! Most likely such propaganda would have no effect, only because people who hear and read about it simply would not be ready to believe it.[53]

The Soviets began presenting their part of the case in February 1946. On 14 February 1946 Colonel Y.V. Pokrovsky, deputy prosecutor for the Soviet Union, introduced the evidence in support of the Katyn charge.

> I should now like to turn to the brutalities committed by the Hitlerites towards members of the Czechoslovakian, Polish, and Yugoslavian Armies. We find, in the Indictment, that one of the most important criminal acts for which the major war criminals are responsible was the mass execution of Polish prisoners of war, shot in the Katyn Forest near Smo-

---

[52]   Select Committee Hearings, Part 7, p. 1947, see *supra* note 5.

[53]   Twentieth Day, Friday, 14 December 1945, 3 IMT 542, 1947, p. 562.

lensk by the German fascist invaders. I submit to the Tribunal, as a proof of this crime, official document of the special commission for the establishment and the investigation of the circumstances which attended the executions. The commission acted in accordance with a directive of the Extraordinary State Commission of the Soviet Union. In addition to members of the Extraordinary State Commission – namely Academicians Burdenko, Alexis Tolstoy, and the Metropolitan Nicolas – this commission was composed of the President of the Pan-Slavonia Committee, Lieutenant General Gundorov; the chairman of the Executive Committee of the Union of the Red Cross and Red Crescent, Kolesnikov; of the People's Commissar for Education in the R.S.S.F.R., Academician Potemkin; the Supreme Chief of the Medical Department of the Red Army, General Smirnov; and the Chairman of the District Executive Committee of Smolensk, Melnikov. The commission also included several of the best known medico-legal experts.[54]

Pokrovsky briefly read excerpts from the Burdenko report into the record.[55] The full report was produced as an exhibit.[56]

On 8 March Otto Stahmer, who was counsel for Hermann Göring, applied to the Tribunal for authorisation to call evidence with respect to the Katyn case.

Another supplementary request is concerned with the following: In the session of 14 February 1946 the Soviet Prosecution submitted that a German military formation, Staff 537, Pioneer Battalion, carried out mass shootings of Polish prisoners of war in the forests near Katyn. As the responsible leaders of this formation, Colonel Ahrens, First Lieutenant Rex, and Second Lieutenant Hodt were mentioned. As proof the Prosecution referred to Document USSR-64. It is an official report of the Extraordinary State Commission of the Soviet Union which was ordered to investigate the facts of the well-known Katyn case. The document I have not yet received. As a result of the publication of this speech by the Prosecution in the press, members of the staff of the Army

---

[54] Fifty-ninth Day, Thursday, Morning session, 14 February 1946, 7 IMT 403, 1947, pp. 425–26.

[55] *Ibid.*, pp. 426–28.

[56] "USSR-54, Report by a Special Soviet Commission, 24 January 1944, Concerning the Shooting of Polish Officer Prisoners of War in the Forest of Katyn", 39 IMT 290, 1949.

Group Center, to which Staff 537 was directly subordinate and which was stationed 4 to 5 kilometers from Staff 537, came forward. These people stated that the evidence upon which the Prosecution have based the statement submitted was not correct.

The following witnesses are mentioned in this connection: Colonel Ahrens, at that time commander of, later chief of army armament and commander of the auxiliary army; First Lieutenant Rex, probably taken as a prisoner of war at Stalingrad; Lieutenant Hodt, probably taken prisoner by the Russians in or near Konigsberg; Major General of intelligence troops, Eugen Oberhauser, probably taken prisoner of war by the Americans; First Lieutenant Graf Berg – later ordnance officer with Field Marshal Von Kluge – a prisoner of war in British hands in Canada. Other members of the units which are accused are still to be mentioned. I name these witnesses to prove that the conclusion as to the complicity of Goring drawn by the Prosecution in the above-mentioned statement is not justified according to the Indictment.

This morning I received another communication bearing on the same question, which calls for the following request: Professor Naville, professor of forensic medicine at the University of Geneva, carried out, with an international commission at Smolensk, investigations of the bodies at that time. He established from the state of preservation of these corpses, from the notes found in the pockets of their clothes, and other means of evidence, that the deed must have been committed in the year 1940.[57]

The President of the Tribunal told Stahmer to submit the request in writing.[58]

The Tribunal granted Stahmer's application on 12 March. Judge Nikitchenko abstained in the vote after throwing "all his weight behind

---

[57] Seventy-seventh Day, Friday, Morning session, 8 March 1946, 9 IMT 1, 1947, pp. 3–4.

[58] *Ibid.*, p. 4. There is a brief description of Stahmer's motion by Robert Kempner, an American prosecutor who was in the courtroom: Hearings before the Select Committee to Conduct an Investigation of the Facts, Evidence and Circumstances of the Katyn Forest Massacre, Eighty-second Congress, Second Session, on Investigation of the Murder of Thousands of Polish Officers in the Katyn Forest near Smolensk, Russia, Part 5, 21, 22, 23, 24, 25, and 26 April 1952, pp. 1540–41 ('Select Committee Hearings, Part 5').

the Soviet prosecutor".[59] Nikitchenko insisted that his reasons be recorded in the minutes: "I cannot participate in this vote as the discussion and putting to vote by the Tribunal of a question as to whether an official Government act may be contested is a flagrant contradiction of Article 21 of the Charter".[60] Article 21 governed the taking of judicial notice of "the acts and documents of the committees set up in the various allied countries for the investigation of war crimes". Nikitchenko contended that the Tribunal was bound to admit such documents as proof of the facts at issue and that contrary evidence was then inadmissible. The consequence would be to deny the defendants the possibility of attacking the conclusions of the Burdenko report, already in evidence.

The Soviet interpretation of Article 21 was "ridiculous", wrote the American prosecutor Telford Taylor in his memoir of the trial.[61] When he testified before the congressional committee in 1952, Robert Jackson was somewhat more charitable to the Soviet position. "Under Soviet law it probably could not, but would be entitled to faith and credit – as a judgment, statute, or public act would be here", explained Jackson, speaking of the Burdenko report. However, "we thought that its nature was such that it was clearly open to contradiction".[62] Writing many years later, Judge Biddle admitted that the phrasing of Article 21 was "unfortunate" in that it seemed to blend "facts of common knowledge" with "government documents", and he said "in the Russian translation the two phrases might have interlocked".[63] The subtleties about judicial notice can be seen in a recent ruling of the Appeals Chamber of the Special Court for Sierra Leone.[64]

After the judges ruled that Article 21 did not apply to the Burdenko report in the manner that the Soviets had contended, Prosecutor Rudenko responded with an application for this question to be reheard. His efforts may have been prompted by criticism from the Soviet journalists covering

---

[59] Biddle, 1962, p. 413, see *supra* note 4.

[60] Taylor, 1992, p. 468, see *supra* note 34. See also Cienciala *et al.*, 2007, p. 231, see *supra* note 10.

[61] Taylor, 1992, p. 469, see *supra* note 34.

[62] Select Committee Hearings, Part 7, pp. 1950–51, see *supra* note 5.

[63] Biddle, 1962, p. 413, see *supra* note 4.

[64] *Prosecutor v. Norman et al.*, Fofana – Decision on Appeal Against Decision on Prosecution's Motion for Judicial Notice and Admission of Evidence, SCSL-04-14-AR73, 16 May 2005, para. 32; *Prosecutor v. Norman et al.*, Separate Opinion of Justice Robertson, SCSL-04-14-AR73, 16 May 2005, para. 9.

the trial. In a report sent to the country's leaders, dated 4 April 1946, the journalists faulted the Soviet legal team for failing to challenge "the defense's request to summon fascist witnesses". They said that "our prosecution lost the opportunity to prevent them from being called".[65] When the judges considered Rudenko's motion, on 6 April, Biddle produced an opinion on the matter from Herbert Wechsler, a distinguished legal scholar and adviser to the American judge, that "in dignified but forceful language, made mincemeat of Rudenko's petition".[66] Biddle considered the language of the petition, accusing the Tribunal of violating its duty and committing "gross error", to be "intemperate". He said that in the United States "the author of such an outrage would be cited for contempt". To make his point, Biddle suggested that first Wechsler's opinion should be read in open court and then Rudenko be arrested and sent to prison. The judges agreed to deny Rudenko's motion for reconsideration without giving reasons.[67]

Several weeks later, Göring's counsel, Stahmer, made a supplementary application to call more witnesses about Katyn. The Soviet prosecutor Pokrovsky informed the Tribunal that the Soviet prosecution "from the very beginning, considered the Katyn Forest incident as common knowledge".[68] This was similar to the argument based on Article 21 of the Charter that the judges had already rejected. However, it seems that the earlier objection relied upon the second rather than the first sentence of Article 21. Pokrosky went on to explain that "by the limited space allotted to this crime in the Indictment and by the fact that we found it possible to limit ourselves to reading into the record only a few short excerpts from the report of the Commission, that we consider this episode to be only an episode".[69]

Pokrovsky, also alluded to remarks made by Maxwell Fyfe, the British prosecutor, a few minutes earlier. Maxwell Fyfe had been referring to the production of evidence in order to impeach the credibility of witnesses, noting the restrictive approach taken by English law in this area. Pokrovsky said that if the defendants were authorised to call witnesses

---

[65] Hirsch, 2008, p. 725, see *supra* note 45.

[66] Taylor, 1992, p. 469, see *supra* note 34.

[67] *Ibid.*

[68] One Hundred and Twenty-seventh Day, Morning Session, Saturday, 11 May 1946, 13 IMT 410, 1947, p. 430.

[69] *Ibid.*, pp. 430–31.

to attack the credibility of the Soviet evidence, then the Soviets would be required to call rebuttal evidence. "Thus, if the Tribunal considers it necessary to admit two new witnesses relative to the Katyn Forest shootings, the Soviet Prosecution will find itself obliged to call about ten more new witnesses who are experts and specialists, and to present to the Tribunal new evidence put at our disposal and which we have recently received – new documents", Pokrovsky argued. He said that, in addition, the Soviet prosecutors would feel compelled to read extensive portions of the Burdenko report into the record, causing great delay to the proceedings that would "not be a matter of hours but of days".[70] A few days later, without giving reasons or explanation, the Tribunal granted Göring's application to call two additional witnesses.[71]

The Tribunal considered yet another defence motion to call three additional witnesses on 3 June. Opposing the motion, the Soviet prosecutorial team returned to the Article 21 argument:

> Our position is that this episode of criminal activity on the part of the Hitlerites has been fully established by the evidence presented by the Soviet Prosecution, which was a communication of the special Extraordinary State Commission investigating the circumstances of the mass shooting of Polish officer prisoners of war by the German Fascist aggressors in Katyn Forest. This document was presented by the Soviet Prosecution under the Document Number USSR-54 on 14 February 1946, and was admitted by the Tribunal; and, as provided by Article 21 of the Charter, it is not subject to argument.[72]

Rudenko went on to discuss the proposed testimony of the three witnesses that Stahmer was requesting. The first, a psychiatrist, had participated in the German fact-finding commission but not, Rudenko insisted, "on the basis of his competence in the field of forensic medicine, but as a representative of the German Fascist military command". The second, said Rudenko, had been a member of the Engineer Corps that carried out the executions. "As he is an interested party, he cannot give any useful testimony for clarifying the circumstances of this matter", Rudenko

---

[70] *Ibid.*, p. 431.
[71] One Hundred and Twenty-ninth Day, Morning Session, Saturday, 14 May 1946, 13 IMT 496, 1947, p. 513.
[72] One Hundred and Forty-fifth Day, Afternoon Session, Monday, 14 May 1946, 15 IMT 288, 1948, pp. 289–90.

argued. The third knew nothing about the detention of the Polish victims and in any event "cannot be considered an unprejudiced witness". Rudenko noted that these objections to calling the three witnesses "express the opinion of all the prosecutors".[73]

Although the Soviets took the view that evidence to contradict the Burdenko report was simply inadmissible pursuant to Article 21 of the Charter, the other three prosecutors agreed that the proposed witnesses should not be heard because their testimony would not be relevant. This distinction was noted by the president of the Tribunal, Sir Geoffrey Lawrence, who invited Stahmer to address the issue. Stahmer said that "[o]ne cannot eliminate a witness by saying that he was involved in the act". When Lawrence asked about the psychiatrist, Stahmer said he thought that the proposed witness was present at the inquiry but was not actually a member of the German fact-finding commission.[74] On 8 June the Tribunal granted Göring's application with respect to the first two witnesses but "on the condition that three witnesses only may be called upon the subject concerned".[75]

By this point in the trial, according to Telford Taylor, with an evidentiary hearing looming on Katyn at which German witnesses would be heard, the Soviets appeared increasingly nervous. He wrote that on 18 June the Soviet judge, Nikitchenko, proposed to his colleagues "that the evidence on the Katyn Forest incident be presented in written form rather than by witnesses". Taylor said that nothing came of this idea.[76] But it appears that the judges held out the hope that the Katyn evidence might be produced in the form of affidavits rather than oral testimony. This would require agreement of the parties. Stahmer told the American congressional committee that he was invited by officials of the Tribunal to meet the Soviet prosecution team for a discussion of the matter. At the meeting, a Soviet lawyer, Colonel Prochownik, told Stahmer and another defence counsel, Franz Exner, that Lawrence had requested that the proceedings be made shorter, the idea being to submit evidence by affidavit instead of live witness testimony. Both Stahmer and Exner refused, "for the result of

---

[73] *Ibid.*, p. 290.

[74] *Ibid.*, pp. 292–93.

[75] One Hundred and Fiftieth Day, Morning Session, Monday, 8 June 1946, 15 IMT 574, 1948, p. 574.

[76] Taylor, 1992, p. 470, see *supra* note 34.

such an action would have been that the documents would have been submitted without the public getting to know anything about their contents".[77] Stahmer explained: "I gave my response for refusing by pointing out that that the Russian prosecution had accused the German Wehrmacht publicly of having murdered eleven thousand prisoners of war, and for the sake of the honour of the German Wehrmacht I thought it imperative that the public should be informed in the same way, that this accusation was without foundation".[78]

On 29 June, Lawrence issued rulings on a number of procedural motions concerning evidence. He referred to three motions by Göring but said a decision on them was postponed "subject to the possibility of agreement being reached upon the question of whether affidavits are to be presented or witnesses called".[79] Later in the session, he asked the Soviet chief deputy prosecutor, Pokrovsky, whether agreement with Göring's counsel had been reached. Pokrovsky replied:

> My Lord, we have had three conferences with the Defense Counsel. After the second meeting I told the Tribunal that, in order to shorten the proceedings, the Soviet Prosecution was willing to read into the record only a part of the evidence submitted. About 15 minutes ago I had a meeting with Dr. Exner and Dr. Stahmer, and they told me that their understanding of the Tribunal's ruling was that the old decision for the summoning of two witnesses was still in force and that only additional documents were now under discussion. In view of this interpretation of the Tribunal's ruling, I do not think that we shall be able to come to an agreement with the Defense. As I see it, the decision in this matter must now rest in the hands of the Tribunal.[80]

Lawrence immediately ruled that unless agreement was reached on submission of evidence by affidavit "the evidence shall not be given entirely by affidavits and that the three witnesses on either side shall be called first thing on Monday morning at 10 o'clock".[81] Erich Räder's counsel, Walter Siemers, intervened to explain that several defence coun-

---

[77] Select Committee Hearings, Part 5, p. 1551, see *supra* note 58.

[78] *Ibid.*, p. 1552.

[79] One Hundred and Sixty-seventh Day, Morning Session, Saturday, 29 June 1946, 17 IMT 244, 1948, p. 244.

[80] *Ibid.*, p. 270.

[81] *Ibid.*

sel interested in the Katyn issue, including Stahmer and Jodl's counsel, Franz Exner, had met earlier that day. He said they had agreed to ask the Tribunal to hear two witnesses, Colonel Friedrich Ahrens and First Lieutenant Reinhard von Eichborn. He said they could dispense with oral testimony of a third witness, whose evidence could be submitted by affidavit, together with affidavits of two other witnesses.

Lawrence was inflexible, however. He said the Tribunal would only allow three witnesses, adding that it was immaterial whether their evidence was submitted orally or by affidavit. Stahmer quarrelled with Lawrence, referring to an "original decision" allowing the defence to produce five witnesses on the Katyn issue. Lawrence challenged him to produce written proof of the Tribunal's decision. He said that "the matter is only a subsidiary allegation of fact; and the Tribunal thinks that at this stage of the proceedings such an allegation of fact ought not to be investigated by a great number of witnesses, and three witnesses are quite sufficient on either side".[82] According to Jackson, the Soviet lawyers had proposed that if the subject was to be opened they wanted to call 10 witnesses.[83]

8.3. The Evidentiary Hearing

With the exception of the Katyn evidence, the case for the defence was completed on 30 June 1946. All that then remained were the submissions. Two trial days, on 1 and 2 July 1946, were devoted to evidence of the Katyn massacre. The British were on alert. One note in the Foreign Office files indicates that the "British prosecution will take no part and British judges are aware of difficulties",[84] and another says "[t]here is nothing more that we can do, and the British judges are aware of the snags. With luck we shall avoid trouble".[85] Signalling the importance of the issue, the Attorney General, Shawcross, travelled from London to Nuremberg and attended the hearings.[86]

As previously ordered by the Tribunal, there were three witnesses for the defence and three for the prosecution. Stahmer had been unable to obtain the co-operation of two of the witnesses he had hoped would ap-

---

[82] *Ibid.*, pp. 272–73.

[83] Select Committee Hearings, Part 7, p. 1951, see *supra* note 5.

[84] P.H. Dean to Frank Roberts, 29 June 1946, FO 371/56476.

[85] P.H. Dean to Sir Orme Sargent, 29 June 1946, FO 371/56476.

[86] "Katyn Forest Crime, Nuremberg Defence Refuted", in *The Times*, 2 July 1946, p. 3.

pear. One of them was François Naville, the Swiss forensic pathologist who had participated in the German commission of inquiry.[87] Naville's role in the German commission was of special importance because he was the only expert who did not come from a country where the Nazis were in power. Maxwell Fyfe told the Tribunal that Naville apparently indicated that "he sees no use in his coming here as a witness for Göring".[88] In his congressional testimony, Jackson said that "at the request of the Germans, we located Dr. Naville. [...] We found him in Switzerland, but he informed the tribunal that he saw no use in coming as a witness for Goering. In other words, some of these witnesses that may be available today were not going to help Goering and his crowd".[89]

The other witness, Władysław Anders, was also unwilling to co-operate with Göring. Anders had been the head of the Polish Military Mission to the Soviet Union at the time of the massacre. On 9 July 1946 Anders' assistant wrote to Colonel John L. Tappin of the United States Army Liaison Section offering to provide documents on Katyn if the Tribunal made an express request. Anders later wrote that he did not receive a reply.[90] Jackson said he did not know of Anders' offer to testify until well after the trial had been completed.[91] Jackson said that Anders "did not know, nor do I, whether the tribunal was ever so advised".[92] He referred to Anders' failure to respond to the defence request as "[f]urther evidence of the complexity of the Polish position". Anders, "while believing in Soviet guilt", manifested "a quite understandable attitude in view of what Poland had suffered at the hands of those who would benefit from his testimony".[93] In his book on the Nuremberg trial, Irving wrote that "Anders' allied superiors forbade him to comply" with the request from

---

[87] Document Göring 61: Extract from Official Material Concerning the Mass Murder at Katyn, published in 1943 by the German Foreign Office. Minutes of the International Medical Commission, 30 April 1943, containing the forensic results of the inspections and investigations, 40 IMT 272, 1949, p. 273.

[88] One Hundred and First Day, Morning Session, Saturday, 6 April 1946, 10 IMT 648, 1947. See also Delphine Debons, "Conditions d'engagements et enjeux personnels de la participation de François Naville à l'enquête de Katyn", in Delphine Debons *et al.*, 2007, p. 73, see *supra* note 37.

[89] Select Committee Hearings, Part 7, p. 1957, see *supra* note 5.

[90] Władysław Anders, *An Army in Exile: Story of the Second Polish Corps*, Macmillan, London, 1949, pp. 297–98.

[91] Select Committee Hearings, Part 7, p. 1955, see *supra* note 5.

[92] *Ibid.*, p. 1947.

[93] *Ibid.*

Göring's lawyer but he did not provide any authority.[94] Irving's disgraceful record as an historian would indicate caution in giving credence to his allegation.[95]

Ahrens was the first witness called by Göring's counsel, Stahmer.[96] A German officer, Ahrens had been in command of Signal Regiment 537 when it was stationed in Katyn from late 1941 until 1943. The Burdenko report had named "Lieutenant Colonel Arnes" of the Engineer Battalion 537 as one of two persons responsible for the massacre. In answer to several of Stahmer's questions, Ahrens denied any knowledge of mass killings conducted by Germans in that location or of orders that any such killings were to be carried out.[97] He then explained the discovery of the mass grave. He said he had heard reports of a mound found in the forest with a birch cross planted above it. During 1942 he had been told by soldiers that killings had taken place in the wood but Ahrens said he did not pay any attention to this.[98] Then, in "January or February" 1943,

> quite accidentally I saw a wolf in this wood and at first I did not believe that it was a wolf; when I followed the tracks with an expert, we saw that there were traces of scratchings on the mound with the cross. I had investigations made as to what kind of bones these were. The doctors told me "human bones". Thereupon I informed the officer responsible for war graves in the area of this fact, because I believed that it was a soldier's grave, as there were a number of such graves in our immediate vicinity.[99]

Ahrens testified that Professor Dr. Butz, a German forensic pathologist who had been made responsible for the investigation, then in-

---

[94] Irving, 1996, p. 174, see *supra* note 31.

[95] Richard J. Evans, *Telling Lies About Hitler: The Holocaust, History and the David Irving Trial*, Verso, London, 2002.

[96] A film of a short excerpt of Ahrens's testimony is available at: https://www.youtube.com/watch?v=8VOPqD_Blqo, last accessed at 14 October 2015.

[97] One Hundred and Sixty-eighth Day, Morning Session, Monday, 1 July 1946, 17 IMT 274, 1948, pp. 276–82.

[98] The Wehrmacht War Crimes Bureau had received reports of the killings and of the mass graves as early as mid-1941, following the invasion of the Soviet Union. See Alfred de Zayas, *The Wehrmacht War Crimes Bureau, 1939–1945*, University of Nebraska Press, Lincoln, 1989, pp. 228–29.

[99] One Hundred and Sixty-eighth Day, Morning Session, Monday, 1 July 1946, 17 IMT 274, 1948, p. 282.

formed him that exhumations were to take place. He said that Butz occasionally gave him details.

> I remember that he told me that he had conclusive evidence regarding the date of the shootings. Among other things, he showed me letters, of which I cannot remember much now; but I do remember some sort of a diary which he passed over to me in which there were dates followed by some notes which I could not read because they were written in Polish. In this connection he explained to me that these notes had been made by a Polish officer regarding events of the past months, and that at the end – the diary ended with the spring of 1940 – the fear was expressed in these notes that something horrible was going to happen.[100]

Ahrens insisted that he was not personally involved in any of the exhumations "on account of the dreadful and revolting stench around our house". He estimated that 40 to 50 Russian prisoners were used to carry out the exhumations.[101] In reply to a question from counsel for Karl Dönitz about whether he had discussed the subject with anyone, Ahrens replied:

> Yes. At the beginning of 1943 a Russian married couple were living near my regimental headquarters; they lived 800 meters away and they were beekeepers. I, too, kept bees, and I came into close contact with this married couple. When the exhumations had been completed, approximately in May 1943, I told them that, after all, they ought to know when these shootings had taken place, since they were living in close proximity to the graves. Thereupon, these people told me it had occurred in the spring of 1940, and that at the Gnesdovo station more than 200 Poles in uniform had arrived in railway trucks of 50 tons each and were then taken to the woods in lorries. They had heard lots of shots and screams, too.[102]

Ahrens was cross-examined by the Soviet assistant prosecutor Smirnov. Ahrens confirmed that he had been at his post in Katyn starting in the second half of November 1941. He had no knowledge of events in the area in September and October of that year.[103] Smirnov then listed

---

[100] *Ibid.*, p. 283.
[101] *Ibid*, p. 283.
[102] *Ibid*, p. 284.
[103] *Ibid.*, pp. 286–87.

several names of German soldiers. Ahrens agreed that they had been at Katyn prior to his own arrival, but said he did not know what they were doing in September and October 1941.[104] Smirnov questioned him at some length about the nature of the forest or wood and the precise location of the mass grave.[105] Then he turned to the discovery of the gravesite. Ahrens specified that when he saw the wolf, he did not then identify human bones, something that happened "months later" after a thaw had taken place.[106] He repeated that he had not been particularly interested in the exhumation, that he could not bear the stench, and that while it was underway he was often travelling because of his military responsibilities. He said that "in the course of 1942 the stories [of graves] became more substantial. I frequently heard about them and spoke about it to Colonel Von Gersdorff, Chief of Intelligence, Army Group Center, who intimated to me that he knew all about this matter and with that my obligation ended".[107]

On redirect, Stahmer asked Ahrens about the evidence of Butz. Ahrens said: "Professor Butz told me that no documents or notes were found which might have given indications of a later date, and he expressed his conviction that these shootings must have taken place in the spring of 1940".[108] Ahrens was also questioned by the Soviet judge, Iona Nikitchenko, about the information he had been given by Butz,[109] as well as by Lawrence. In answer to Lawrence, he explained that when he had first heard reports of graves in the forest, he had not been suspicious. "[F]ighting had taken place there; and at first I did not attach any importance to the stories told to me and did not give this matter any credence. I believed that it was a question of soldiers who had been killed there – of war graves, like several in the vicinity", he said.[110]

The second defence witness was Lieutenant Reinhard von Eichborn. He had been an officer with Signals Regiment 537, posted at Katyn from about 20 September 1941. Von Eichborn confirmed that the sur-

---

[104] *Ibid.*, pp. 287–88.
[105] *Ibid.*, pp. 288–91.
[106] *Ibid.*, p. 292.
[107] *Ibid.*, p. 293.
[108] *Ibid.*, p. 295.
[109] *Ibid.*, p. 296.
[110] *Ibid.*

rounding region had fallen to the Germans in mid-July 1941. The evidence in chief of von Eichborn consisted of a denial that Germany forces had been involved in the Katyn massacre. He told the Tribunal that had there been Polish prisoners in the vicinity, or had there been an order to kill such prisoners, he would have been aware of this and he was not.[111] On cross-examination, he admitted that although he was responsible for Wehrmacht signals traffic, he would not have been privy to communications from the Einsatzgruppen B, which was active in the region.[112]

The third witness for the defence was Lieutenant General Eugen Oberhauser. Oberhauser had been a signals officer in the Smolensk area at the relevant times. He was the superior of Ahrens and with his predecessor, Colonel Albert Bedenck. He and his staff had reached Katyn "[s]ometime during September 1941".[113] When asked about mass executions attributable to Ahrens or Bedenck, he said: "I am not informed, but I consider it absolutely impossible".[114] He said he had been in Katyn "three or four times" but that until the exhumations began in 1943 he had heard nothing about mass killings.[115] Stahmer asked if Regiment 537 had "the necessary technical means, pistols, ammunition, and so on, [...] which would have made it possible to carry out shootings on such a scale".[116] Oberhauser replied:

> The regiment, being a signal regiment in the rear area, was not equipped with weapons and ammunition as well as the actual fighting troops. Such a task, however, would have been something unusual for the regiment; first, because a signal regiment has completely different tasks, and secondly it would not have been in a position technically to carry out such mass executions.[117]

The following exchange took place:

> STAHMER: In view of your knowledge of the place, would you consider it possible that 11,000 Poles could have been

---

[111] *Ibid.*, pp. 297–397.

[112] One Hundred and Sixty-eighth Day, Afternoon Session, Monday, 1 July 1946, 17 IMT 308, 1948, p. 310.

[113] *Ibid.*, p. 312

[114] *Ibid.*

[115] *Ibid.*, p. 313.

[116] *Ibid.*

[117] *Ibid.*

> buried at that spot, people who may have been shot between June and September 1941?
>
> OBERHAUSER: I consider that it is out of the question, for the mere reason that if the commander had known it at the time he would certainly never have chosen this spot for his headquarters, next to 11,000 dead.[118]

The Soviet prosecutor Smirnov cross-examined Oberhauser about the firearms in possession of the signal regiment. Oberhauser conceded that its non-commissioned officers would have been equipped with pistols. He also questioned Oberhauser about the presence of other forces in the region. At one point Lawrence interrupted, asking Smirnov why he needed to go into such detail.[119] On redirect, Stahmer asked Oberhauser about the advance party that was in Katyn prior to arrival of the signal regiment in September 1941. Oberhauser testified that there would then only have been a few non-commissioned officers based in Katyn.[120]

When Stahmer had finished, Lawrence intervened.

> THE PRESIDENT: Were there any Einsatzkommandos in the Katyn area during the time that you were there?
>
> OBERHAUSER: Nothing has ever come to my knowledge about that.
>
> THE PRESIDENT: Did you ever hear of an order to shoot Soviet commissars?
>
> OBERHAUSER: I only knew of that by hearsay.
>
> THE PRESIDENT: When?
>
> OBERHAUSER: Probably at the beginning of the Russian campaign, I think.
>
> THE PRESIDENT: Before the campaign started or after?
>
> OBERHAUSER: I cannot remember having heard anything like that before the beginning of the campaign.
>
> THE PRESIDENT: Who was to carry out that order?
>
> OBERHAUSER: Strictly speaking, signal troops are not really fighting troops. Therefore, they really had nothing to do with that at all, and therefore we were in no way affected by the order.

---

[118] *Ibid.*, p. 314.

[119] *Ibid.*, p. 318.

[120] *Ibid.*, pp. 319–20.

THE PRESIDENT: I did not ask you that. I asked you who had to carry out the order.

OBERHAUSER: Those who came into contact with these people, presumably.

THE PRESIDENT: Anybody who came in contact with Russian commissars had to kill them; is that it?

OBERHAUSER: No, I assume that it was the troops, the fighting troops, the actual fighting troops at the front who first met the enemy. That could only have applied to the army group. The signal regiment never came into a position to meet commissars. That is probably why they were not mentioned in the order or affected by it in any way.[121]

Lawrence's questions were obviously prompted by a change in the Soviet theory of the case. Stahmer's defence was premised on demonstrating that Ahrens and his unit could not have been responsible for the killings. It effectively challenged the explanation in the Burdenko report, at least to the extent that the witnesses who testified were deemed to be credible. The Soviets were improvising by offering a new explanation, by which the killings might be attributable to other German military units, in particular one of the SS units known as the Einsatzgruppen. Earlier in the day, Stahmer had applied to call a fourth witness who was expected to testify that no killings took place between July and September 1941.[122] No decision had yet been taken on whether this would be allowed. With the conclusion of the third German witness, the defence phase of the evidentiary hearing on Katyn had come to an end.

The prosecution phase began with the testimony of Boris Bazilevsky.[123] Bazilevsky had been deputy mayor of the city of Smolensk, which is located about 20 kilometres from Katyn, during the German occupation. A professor of astronomy before the war, he said he had attempted to escape the advancing German armies but was unable to. He was subsequently asked by the German occupiers to participate in the local administration.[124] After the occupation, Bazilevsky returned to his ac-

---

[121] *Ibid.*, pp. 321–22.

[122] *Ibid.*, p. 309.

[123] A film of a short excerpt of Bazilevsky's testimony is available at: https://www.youtube.com/watch?v=Q_UoLtvczqE.

[124] One Hundred and Sixty-eighth Day, Afternoon Session, Monday, 1 July 1946, 17 IMT 308, 1948, p. 323. See also Laurie R. Cohen, *Smolensk Under the Nazis: Everyday Life in Occupied Russia*, University of Rochester Press, Rochester, NY, 2013, pp. 63–64.

ademic work; he said he was not punished by the Soviet authorities for his role during the occupation.[125]

Asked to explain the Katyn forest or Katyn wood, Bazilevsky said: "Actually, it was a grove. It was the favorite resort of the inhabitants of Smolensk who spent their holidays and vacations there".[126] He testified "as an eyewitness" that in 1940 and 1941 the area was not fenced in and was accessible to the public.[127] Bazilevsky testified about the presence of Polish prisoners of war in the area, something the three German witnesses had earlier denied. He said that at the beginning of September 1941 he had intervened with the major, Menschagin, on behalf of a Russian prisoner, only to be told by his superior that "Russians would at least be allowed to die in the camps while there were proposals to exterminate the Poles".[128] He continued:

> BAZILEVSKY: Two weeks later – that is to say, at the end of September – I could not help asking him, "What was the fate of the Polish prisoners of war?" At first Menschagin hesitated, and then he told me haltingly, "They have already died. It is over with them".
>
> MR. COUNSELLOR SMIRNOV: Did he tell you where they were killed?
>
> BAZILEVSKY: He told me that they had been shot in the vicinity of Smolensk, as Von Schwetz [of the German Kommandantur of Smolensk] told him.
>
> MR. COUNSELLOR SMIRNOV: Did he mention the exact place?
>
> BAZILEVSKY: No, he did not mention the exact place.
>
> MR. COUNSELLOR SMIRNOV: Tell me this. Did you, in turn, tell anybody about the extermination, by Hitlerites, of the Polish prisoners of war near Smolensk?
>
> BAZILEVSKY: I talked about this to Professor Efimov, who was living in the same house with me. Besides him, a few days later I had a conversation about it with Dr. Nikolski, who was the medical officer of the city. However, I found

---

[125] One Hundred and Sixty-eighth Day, Afternoon Session, Monday, 1 July 1946, 17 IMT 308, 1948, p. 332.

[126] *Ibid.*, p. 322.

[127] *Ibid.*, pp. 322–23.

[128] *Ibid.*, p. 325.

out that Nikolski knew about this crime already from some other source.

MR. COUNSELLOR SMIRNOV: Did Menschagin tell you why these shootings took place?

BAZILEVSKY: Yes. When he told me that the prisoners of war had been killed, he emphasized once more the necessity of keeping it strictly secret in order to avoid disagreeable consequences. He started to explain to me the reasons for the German behavior with respect to the Polish prisoners of war. He pointed out that this was only one measure of the general system of treating Polish prisoners of war.

MR. COUNSELLOR SMIRNOV: Did you hear anything about the extermination of the Poles from the employees of the German Kommandantur?

BAZILEVSKY: Yes, 2 or 3 days later.

…

BAZILEVSKY: Two or three days later, when I visited the office of Menschagin, I met there an interpreter, the Sonder-führer of the 7th Division of the German Kommandantur who was in charge of the Russian administration and who had a conversation with Menschagin concerning the Poles. He came from the Baltic region.

MR. COUNSELLOR SMIRNOV: Perhaps you can tell us briefly what he said.

BAZILEVSKY: When I entered the room he was saying, "The Poles are a useless people, and exterminated they may serve as fertilizer and for the enlargement of living space for the German nation".

…

MR. COUNSELLOR SMIRNOV: Did you learn from Menschagin anything definite about the shooting of Polish prisoners of war?

BAZILEVSKY: When I entered the room I heard the conversation with Hirschfeld. I missed the beginning, but from the context of the conversation it was clear that they spoke about this event.

MR. COUNSELLOR SMIRNOV: Did Menschagin, when telling you about the shooting of Polish prisoners of war, refer to Von Schwetz?

> BAZILEVSKY: Yes; I had the impression that he referred to Von Schwetz. But evidently – and this is my firm belief – he also spoke about it with private persons in the Komman-dantur.
>
> MR. COUNSELLOR SMIRNOV: When did Menschagin tell you that Polish prisoners of war were killed near Smo-lensk?
>
> BAZILEVSKY: It was at the end of September.[129]

Stahmer cross-examined Bazilevsky, asking about his knowledge of the Katyn site and of the presence of Polish prisoners in the region. Bearing in mind the difficulty in appreciating the dynamics of this interaction from the transcript alone, Stahmer does not appear to have unsettled the testimony of Bazilevsky. Bazilevsky took care to distinguish facts of which he had personal knowledge from things he had been told by others. Stahmer asked if Bazilevsky had himself seen "Polish officers". He answered that he had not, but that his students had told him they had seen them in 1941.[130] Stahmer attempted to impugn Bazilevsky by suggesting that he had not only prepared a written version of his testimony, that he read to the Tribunal, but that he had provided the interpreters with the text before the hearing.[131] Although Bazilevsky denied this, later in the cross-examination Stahmer said "when you read your testimony off [...]". Lawrence rebuked him: "Dr. Stahmer, you are not entitled to say to the witness, 'when you read your testimony off', just now, because he denied that he read his testimony off and there is no evidence that he has read it off".[132] After a recess, Thomas Dodd, one of the American prosecutors, told the Tribunal that he had been told by the lieutenant in charge of the interpretations that "no one there had any answers or questions, and I think it should be made clear on the record". "Yes, I think so too", said Lawrence. Then Stahmer explained he had been told this outside of the courtroom. "If it is not a fact, I wish to withdraw my statement", he said. "I was informed outside the courtroom from a trustworthy source". Stahmer said he could not recall the name of the person who had told him.

---

129 *Ibid.*, pp. 326–27.
130 *Ibid.*, p. 331.
131 *Ibid.*, p. 328.
132 *Ibid.*, p. 329.

Lawrence concluded the discussion: "Such statements ought not be made by counsel until they have verified them".[133]

When Stahmer had concluded his cross-examination, Lawrence asked: "Witness, do you know whether the man, whose name I understand to be Menschagin, was told about these matters or whether he himself had any direct knowledge of them?". Bazilevsky replied: "From Menschagin's own words, I understood quite definitely that he had heard those things himself at the Kommandantur, particularly from Von Schwetz, who was the commander from the beginning of the occupation".[134]

Marko Antonov Markov was the second witness Soviet witness. A Bulgarian, Markov was a professor at the University of Sofia. He had been a member of the German commission of inquiry that visited Katyn in April 1943. Markov explained that while working at the Medico-Legal Institute, he was telephoned, on 24 April 1943, by an official in the office of the Bulgarian Prime Minister informing him that he was to represent the government in an examination of the corpses of Polish officers discovered at Katyn. He said he asked if he could refuse but was told he had no choice in the matter. His role would be to sign, on behalf of the Bulgarian government, a report that had already been drafted. On 26 April he flew to Berlin and then onward, two days later, with the other members of the commission to Smolensk. Two days were spent in Smolensk, on 29 and 30 April. During that time there were two visits to Katyn, each of about three or four hours. On 1 May Markov and the other members of the commission returned to Berlin.

While at Katyn, Markov said the commission was shown bodies that had already been exhumed but it did not witness or participate in any exhumation. Markov said that eight corpses were subjected to autopsies by members of the commission. The commissioners were shown documents that they were told had been removed from the exhumed corpses and placed in glass cases. Markov said: "In my opinion these working conditions can in no way be qualified as adequate for a complete and objective scientific examination. The only thing which bore the character of the scientific nature was the autopsy which I carried out".[135] Markov said that he dictated a report on the condition of the corpse that he had himself autopsied, and that the report was reproduced in the materials published

---

[133] *Ibid.*, p. 333.
[134] *Ibid.*, p. 331.
[135] *Ibid.*, p. 337.

by the Germans. He said that the condition of the corpse suggested that it had been buried for not more than a year and a half.[136]

Markov went on to explain that his autopsy report had not reached any conclusion about the time the body had been buried. He said that "from the papers which were given to us there I understood that they wanted us to say that the corpses had been in the ground for 3 years. This could be deduced from the papers which were shown to us in the little peasant hut about which I have already spoken".[137] He continued: "Inasmuch as the objective deduction regarding the autopsy I performed was in contradiction with this version, I did not make any deductions".[138] Smirnov questioned Markov about the opinions of the other members of the commission who had performed autopsies on the corpses. He testified that most members "made their deductions without answering the essential question regarding the time the corpses had been buried".[139] According to Markov, the Italian expert, Vincenzo Mario Palmieri, had said the body had been in the ground "over a year" and the Croatian, Miloslavich, had estimated three years.[140]

Smirnov asked Markov to explain on what basis he had concluded that the bodies had been in the ground for three years. He was interrupted by the judges, who said that Markov had not said he had reached any such conclusion. Smirnov rephrased the question, asking Markov to give the rationale of the commission in its conclusion about three years. Markov answered that this conclusion was based upon the documents and on witness statements rather than the forensic pathology.[141] Markov testified at some length about the signing of the report, implying that a degree of coercion had been involved.[142]

In cross-examination, Stahmer asked Markov about his initial resistance to participating in the inquiry. "Did you consider the task you had to carry out there a political one or a scientific one?" he said. Markov re-

---

[136] *Ibid.*, p. 338.
[137] One Hundred and Sixty-ninth Day, Morning Session, Tuesday, 2 July 1946, 17 IMT 339, 1948, p. 339.
[138] *Ibid.*, p. 340.
[139] *Ibid.*
[140] *Ibid.*
[141] *Ibid.*, p. 344.
[142] *Ibid.*, pp. 345–47.

plied: "I understood this task from the very first moment as a political one and therefore I tried to evade it".[143] Stahmer then asked the Tribunal to admit the German report into evidence.[144] Lawrence said it would be admitted on the basis of Article 19 of the Charter but not Article 21, in that the Tribunal would not take judicial notice of its contents.[145] Stahmer proceeded to interrogate Markov, reading aloud portions of the German report and asking him for his views.[146] He concluded his cross-examination by challenging Markov's claim to have been hesitant and equivocal about the conclusions of the commission, noting that he had signed the protocol with the other members without making any objection. "Witness, you gave two versions, one in the protocol which we have just discussed, and another here before the Court. Which version is the correct one?", he asked provocatively.[147]

Lawrence concluded the examination of Markov with several questions aimed at establishing whether there was evidence that might suggest the corpses that had been examined did not come from the mass grave in Katyn. He also asked Markov about his personal report on the autopsy he had conducted.[148]

The third witness called by the Soviet prosecution team was Victor Il'ich Prosorovski. A professor of medical jurisprudence, Prosorovski had been the chairman of the medico-judicial commission of experts associated with the Soviet commission of inquiry headed by Burdenko. He described a visit to Katyn that took place in January 1944. He said that exhumations of 925 corpses had taken place in September and October 1943. With the exception of three, which had previously been dissected, the bodies examined by the Soviet commission had not previously been touched, he said. Prosorovski explained that various documents had been found on the bodies, some of them associated with or bearing dates in late 1941 and 1942. "I myself discovered a letter with the date 20 June 1941,

---

[143] *Ibid.*, p. 348.
[144] *Ibid.*, p. 349.
[145] *Ibid.*
[146] *Ibid.*, pp. 350–56.
[147] *Ibid.*, p. 358.
[148] *Ibid.*, pp. 35–60.

with the name of Irene Tutchinski, as well as other documents of the same sort", he said.[149]

Smirnov then questioned Prosorovski about whether bullets had been found in the corpses and, if so, whether their origin could be determined. But before receiving an answer, he read into evidence a document he said had been "offered us by our American colleagues". It was described as a telegramme from an official in the Generalgouvernement (the Nazi occupation regime in Poland):

> Urgent, to be delivered at once, secret.
>
> Part of the Polish Red Cross returned yesterday from Katyn. The employees of the Polish Red Cross have brought with them the cartridge cases which were used in shooting the victims of Katyn. It appears that these are German munitions. The caliber is 7.65. They are from the firm Geco. Letter follows. signed– Heinrich.[150]

Prosovoski said that "the bullets discovered in the bullet wounds were 7.65 caliber. The cases discovered during the exhumation did indeed bear the trademark of the firm Geco".[151] Prosorovski declared that the evidence pointed to a date of late 1941 for the burial of the corpses.[152] He said that a date in 1940 was "completed excluded".[153] He described his experience with other mass graves attributable to the Germans within the Soviet Union, noting the methods of camouflaging the burial sites as well as the method of execution. Prosorovski indicated that Katyn followed a similar pattern.[154]

Stahmer only briefly cross-examined Prosorovski. He asked questions about the identity of the bodies and what was done with the documents that were found on them.[155] Lawrence did not question Prosorovski.

Smirnov then informed the Tribunal that the Soviets could produce affidavits from several more witnesses on the Katyn issue. Stahmer said

---

[149] One Hundred and Sixty-ninth Day, Afternoon Session, Tuesday, 2 July 1946, 17 IMT 362, 1948, p. 365.

[150] *Ibid.*, p. 365.

[151] *Ibid.*

[152] *Ibid.*, p. 366.

[153] *Ibid.*, p. 367.

[154] *Ibid.*, pp. 367–68.

[155] *Ibid.*, pp. 368–70.

he had no objection as long as he would be able to do the same. "The Tribunal has already made its order; it does not propose to hear further evidence", said Lawrence.[156]

Somewhat later in the day, counsel for Dönitz, Otto Kranzbühler, produced a report by the Italian expert on the German commission, Palmieri, dealing with the presence of insect larvae on the corpses exhumed at Katyn. Lawrence allowed its production after confirming that it had been referred to in the German *White Book*.[157] But Lawrence did not permit the production of a book published in English in London in 1946 entitled *Report on the Massacre of Polish Officers in the Katyn Wood*. Noting that it was produced for private circulation, did not bear the name of a printer and was "entirely anonymous", Lawrence said "it would be improper to look at a document of this nature".[158]

Much of the secondary literature, published many years after the Nuremberg trial, presents the two-day hearing of the witnesses as a clear victory for the Germans. For example, George Sanford wrote that "[t]he German witnesses demolished the Soviet case against them".[159] Allen Paul described the German testimony as "a devastating response".[160] Another study says "Stahmer's examination of the German witnesses cleared them of responsibility for the Katyn massacre".[161] Robert Conot reported that the testimony "was anything but conclusive", but that "the German witnesses, however, proved far more credible".[162] "In the end, the Germans had the better of it", wrote Joseph Persico.[163]

These assessments, however, are not consistent with opinions expressed at the time by those who were present at the hearings. Instructed by Philip Deane to report by telephone on the proceedings to the Foreign Office in London, Colonel Harry Phillimore of the British War Crimes Executive concluded "that the Russians were winning". Dean minuted: "So far so good".[164] A more detailed report was to follow: "Soviet case

---

[156] *Ibid.*, p. 371.

[157] *Ibid.*, pp. 382–83.

[158] *Ibid.*, p. 383.

[159] George Sanford, Katyn and the Soviet Massacre of 1940: Truth, Justice and Memory, Routledge, London, 2011, p. 141.

[160] Paul, 2010, p. 335, see *supra* 33.

[161] Cienciala *et al.*, 2007, p. 232, see *supra* note 10.

[162] Conot, 1983, p. 453, see *supra* note 43.

[163] Joseph E. Persico, *Nuremberg: Infamy on Trial*, Penguin, New York, 1994, p. 359.

[164] Report of telephone call from Colonel Phillimore, 1 July 1946, FO 371/56476.

has undoubtedly emerged very much enhanced and they are very pleased with the way it has gone. Altogether although not of course conclusive the evidence emerged strongly in favour of the Soviet case and the German report was largely discredited and their evidence unimpressive". Dean's minute to the file reads: "The British team, who are not very credulous, told me that the Russians had much the best of the argument and in their view rightly so".[165]

Correspondents of the major newspapers reached similar conclusions. Following the first day of hearings, *The Times* reported that "after three of the witnesses which the Tribunal allowed [Göring's] counsel to call had been heard, his attempt to establish that the crime was not committed by the Germans can hardly be said to have prospered".[166] The following day, the special correspondent of *The Times* said that the medical evidence "has enlightened the court but little in the attempt by the defence to unsaddle themselves of responsibility for the crime".[167] The *New York Times* explained that the German defendants had "revived" the argument that the Soviets were to blame, but added: "However, Russian prosecutors at once offered rebuttal testimony which put the controversy back on its previous level".[168] Journalistic accounts of the second day were similar in tone. According to *The Times*, "[w]hile the mystery was left in almost as much confusion as when the defence entered rebuttals, on the weight of the evidence the tribunal heard yesterday and today from six witnesses – three for the defence and three for the prosecution – it cannot be said that the German assertion that the murders were committed before the Smolensk area was occupied in July, 1941, was well maintained".[169] Reporting on the second day, the *New York Times* headline read: "Germans Forced Katyn Testimony: Report on Polish Massacre Faked and Signed Under Duress, Court Hears".[170]

---

[165] Report from British War Crimes Executive, in Nuremberg, to FO, 6 July 1946, FO 371/56476.

[166] "Katyn Forest Crime, Nuremberg Defence Refuted", in *The Times*, 2 July 1946, p. 3.

[167] "Murder of Polish Officers, Medical Conclusions at Nuremberg", in *The Times*, 3 July 1946, p. 3.

[168] "Katyn Forest Issue Revived by Germans", in *New York Times*, 2 July 1946, p. 15.

[169] "Murder of Polish Officers, Medical Conclusions at Nuremberg", in *The Times*, Wednesday, 3 July 1946, p. 3.

[170] "Germans Forced Katyn Testimony: Report on Polish Massacre Faked and Signed Under Duress, Court Hears", in *New York Times*, 3 July 1946, p. 4.

Today we read the transcript with the benefit of hindsight, fully knowledgeable of the eventual admissions of guilt by the Soviets. Probably it colours modern attempts to evaluate the evidence that was before the Tribunal. As a matter of law, although the Burdenko report was of course not irrefutable proof of its contents, despite the Soviet claims to the contrary, it had certainly established a case to be answered. That is why the defence presented its evidence first. An experienced trial lawyer reading the testimony of the three defence witnesses would be unlikely to consider that the findings of the Burdenko commission had been "demolished", or that the evidence was "devastating". In effect, the testimony amounted to little more than an absolute denial, the three witnesses contending – no doubt truthfully, as history has shown – that they knew nothing of the matter. But in trial courts, absolute denials rarely tip the scales unless those doing the testifying are of unimpeachable credibility and integrity, something that would hardly be the case with German military officials in 1946.

Robert Jackson said that after the witnesses had been heard, "neither side was satisfied with its own showing and both asked to call additional witnesses".[171] According to Jackson, "[t]he Tribunal, wisely, I think, refused to hear more of the subject".[172] Indeed, all that remained for this first effort at an international criminal trial were the representations by counsel and then the judgment.

8.4. Submissions and Judgment

Immediately following the two days of testimony about Katyn, on 3 July the German defence lawyers began making their final submissions in the trial. At the outset of his plea, Stahmer told the Tribunal that "I have still to complete the Case Katyn".[173] He meant that his comments had not been included in the written submissions, given that the evidentiary hearing had only taken place during the previous days. Stahmer made his oral submissions about Katyn on 5 July.[174] Stahmer pointed to the flaws in the Soviet account, the implausible nature of some of the allegations and the absence

---

[171] Select Committee Hearings, Part 7, p. 1951, see *supra* note 5.

[172] *Ibid.*

[173] One Hundred and Seventieth Day, Afternoon Session, Wednesday, 3 July 1946, 17 IMT 396, 1948, p. 397.

[174] One Hundred and Seventy-second Day, Morning Session, Friday, 5 July 1946, 17 IMT 516, 1948, pp. 536–45.

of evidence capable of proving the charge to an adequate standard. Noting that the Soviets themselves fixed the crime as having taken place in September 1941, he said that their attribution of responsibility to Ahrens was clearly mistaken given that he had not arrived at Katyn by that time. Stahmer went on to argue that the detention of a large number of Polish prisoners would have necessarily been reported to the army, but he said that there was no evidence of this taking place. He said the transfer of such a large number of prisoners could not have been concealed from the public.[175]

Stahmer provided a brief explanation of the failure of the defence to call any forensic experts. He said only that "it would not have been possible to clarify completely all the medical questions which were decisive for the experts in the facts you have established. Therefore, the Defense has also refrained from calling a medical expert to exonerate the defendant".[176] He argued that the report of the German commission of inquiry should be preferred over that of the Soviet commission given that the former "was given by 12 members of a commission of leading representatives of legal medicine from European universities, while the expert opinion referred to by the Prosecution was deposed by a group of Russian experts only". The German experts "were completely non-political", he said.[177]

Stahmer was interrupted by Lawrence: "Dr. Stahmer, you realize, of course, that you have not offered in evidence the report of this German commission. You expressly refrained, as I understand it, from offering the report of the German commission".[178] Stahmer said this was a mistake. A lengthy exchange ensued about whether the Tribunal had agreed to admit the entire German *White Book* on Katyn, or the protocol adopted by the commission of inquiry, or only the excerpts that Stahmer had read in his cross-examination of Markov. Lawrence left the matter unresolved, saying that the Tribunal would look at the record to see what had been decided.[179] The uncertainty about Stahmer's position on the production of the documents, something seized upon by Lawrence, seems associated with a

---

[175] *Ibid.*, pp. 539–42.

[176] *Ibid.*, p. 542.

[177] *Ibid.*

[178] *Ibid.*

[179] *Ibid.*, p. 544.

strategy of avoiding an explicit allegation that the Soviets were responsible for the crime, which was of course the conclusion of the *White Book*. But rather than base the defence on submitting an alternative theory for the crime, which is certainly a very common and effective way of raising a reasonable doubt in the minds of judges, Stahmer stuck closely to the claim that the prosecutors had simply failed to prove German guilt. Stahmer concluded: "[I]t can be said that the task of this proceeding is solely to determine whether the 11,000 Polish officers were shot after the capture of Smolensk by the Germans, in other words, that this deed could have been committed by Germans. The Prosecution have not succeeded in proving this fact".[180] Several years later, Stahmer told the American congressional committee: "The Russians were not accused, and therefore I had neither the task nor the duty to clear up the matter".[181]

There were a few references to Katyn in the oral submissions of other defendants. In his summation, Robert Servatius, counsel for Fritz Sauckel, presciently observed: "The Katyn case shows how difficult it is to determine the truth of such events when they are made use of as effective weapons of propaganda".[182] Counsel for Dönitz, Otto Kranzbühler, noted that he had been denied the opportunity to participate in the cross-examination of the Katyn witnesses. This led him to conclude that "no one was accusing Admiral Donitz in connection with this case".[183] Walter Siemers made a similar statement with respect to Erich Räder.[184] Alfred Seidl, counsel for Rudolf Hess, began his oral submissions by referring to two exhibits, both of them excerpts from the German *White Book* on Katyn.[185] This was quite strange because in his rambling plea about the origins of the Second World War Seidl never returned to the Katyn issue. In any case, there could be no question of Hess being involved in Katyn given his flight to the United Kingdom several weeks prior to the start of Operation Barbarossa.

---

[180] *Ibid.*

[181] Select Committee Hearings, Part 5, p. 1551, see *supra* note 58.

[182] One Hundred and Eighty-first Day, Afternoon session, Thursday, 18 July 1946, 18 IMT 468, 1948, p. 493.

[183] One Hundred and Seventy-ninth Day, Tuesday, Morning Session, 16 July 1946, 18 IMT 325, 1948, p. 362.

[184] One Hundred and Eightieth Day, Wednesday, Morning Session, 17 July 1946, 18 IMT 403, 1948, p. 424.

[185] One Hundred and Eighty-sixth Day, Thursday, Afternoon Session, 25 July 1946, 19 IMT 353, 1948, pp. 353–54.

The Soviet prosecutor, Roman Rudenko, made only the most per-functory references to Katyn in his final submissions to the Tribunal. When he discussed the evidence against Hans Frank, who had been in charge of occupied Poland, Rudenko said:

> It is not merely incidental that the German fascist assassins who annihilated 11,000 Polish prisoner-of-war officers in Katyn forest should refer to the regime which Frank institut-ed in Poland as an example for their own activities – as the Tribunal has been able to ascertain not so very long ago in this courtroom from the evidence presented by the former deputy mayor of Smolensk – Professor Bazilevsky.[186]

But Rudenko was not addressing the facts of the Katyn massacre. Rather, he was speaking of Frank's responsibility for concentration camps in the Generalgouvernement. He cited Frank himself stating that "unfor-tunately, Polish public opinion, and not the intellectuals alone, compares Katyn to the mass death rate in the German concentration camps, as well as to the shooting of men, women, and even of children and old people, during the infliction of collective punishment in the districts".[187] In other words, the Katyn atrocity paled in comparison with others perpetrated by the Nazis. It was almost as if Rudenko was accepting Soviet responsibility for Katyn. At no point in his oral submissions did Rudenko address the evidence concerning Katyn or attempt to refute the analysis proposed by Stahmer. Testifying before the congressional committee in 1952, Robert Jackson said that "[t]he Soviet prosecutor appears to have abandoned the charge".[188]

Nothing further on Katyn is to be found in the record of the pro-ceedings. None of the other prosecution counsel mentioned the matter. Lawrence never returned to the issue of the production of the German *White Book*. According to the published record, the entire *White Book* was in fact never admitted into evidence. There are several exhibits for the defence: two sketch maps of the grave site,[189] the "autopsy reports" of the

---

[186] One Hundred and Eighty-ninth Day, Monday, Afternoon Session, 29 July 1946, 19 IMT 570, 1948, p. 606.

[187] *Ibid.*, p. 607.

[188] Select Committee Hearings, Part 7, p. 1951, see *supra* note 5.

[189] Gör-50, Sketch in connection with the Katyn investigation made on the instructions of General Oberhäuser, 40 IMT 260, 1949; Gör-58, Drawing by Colonel Ahrens in connec-tion with the Katyn investigation, 40 IMT 264, 1948.

German commission[190] and the "Minutes of the International Medical Commission, 30 April 1943, containing the forensic results of the inspections and investigations", sometimes referred to as the "protocol" of the commission.[191]

8.5. Concluding Observations

The silence of the judgment has been interpreted in various ways. The only comment attributable to one of the judges appeared many years later, in the memoirs of Francis Biddle, the American judge: "The evidence before us was inconclusive and, as I have said, was unrelated to any defendant. Any mention of Katyn Woods was omitted when the judgment was under consideration".[192] The British judge, who also presided at the trial, Geoffrey Lawrence, seemed at times to have manifested impatience with the issue, strictly hewing to the rule whereby only three witnesses from each side could be heard. At the same time, his attentive questioning during the evidentiary phase suggests that he did not view the hearing as merely perfunctory. Statements by diplomats in the archives of the Foreign Office to the effect that the British judges were "aware of the snags" in the case are troublesome, if only because they indicate some sort of inappropriate conduct with the judiciary. As with most of the Nuremberg proceedings, the French judge was a minor player. With respect to Katyn, he was invisible.

The Soviet judge, Iona Nikitchenko, is the real enigma. He issued a dissenting judgment but did not use the occasion to mention Katyn. Thus, along with the others he participated in the silent acquittal of the Nazi defendants for the massacre. Alone among the judges, Nikitchenko had participated in the London Conference where the Charter of the Tribunal was drafted but also where there was preliminary work on the indictment. But because the Soviet prosecution team only introduced the Katyn charge at a later date, it would not be right to suggest he had been part of the decision to prosecute the matter. Nikitchenko participated in the evidentiary

---

[190] Gör-60, Extract from "Official Material Concerning the Mass Murders at Katyn", published in 1943 by the German Foreign Office. Autopsy report by (Italian) Professor Palmieri; Autopsy report by (Bulgarian) Professor Markov, 40 IMT 266, 1949.

[191] Gör-61, Extract from "Official Material Concerning the Mass Murder at Katyn", published in 1943 by the German Foreign Office. Minutes of the International Medical Commission, 30 April 1943, containing the forensic results of the inspections and investigations, 40 IMT 272, 1949.

[192] Biddle, 1962, p. 417, see *supra* note 4.

debate about the scope of Article 21 of the Charter. There, he fought for the position adopted by the Soviet prosecutor with regard to the evidentiary value of the Burdenko report. After registering his dissent, he seems subsequently to have accepted the majority view. If he had not, then logically he would have convicted the defendants for the Katyn massacre because for all intents and purposes he would have been bound by the Burdenko report. Nikitchenko also questioned some of the witnesses during the evidentiary hearing but it is difficult to divine any particular orientation from his interventions.

Was Nikitchenko faithfully following instructions from Moscow to drop the issue of Katyn? This is not implausible but nor is there any evidence to support the hypothesis. Was a compromise reached whereby the majority refrained from commenting about the ambiguities of the Soviet case on Katyn in return for Nikitchenko's silence on the matter? There has been speculation about what went on in the deliberations of the judges, but little in the way of hard and credible evidence. For example, Bradley Smith suggested that the decision to restrict the evidentiary hearing was at the initiative of the Soviet judge, Nikitchenko, who "had to labour diligently and call upon every ounce of his colleagues' goodwill in order to work out formulas that would limit the courtroom presentations on Katyn". He wrote that the Katyn issue "seems to have accentuated the distance between the Soviet and Western judges"[193] and that "the judges split over Katyn".[194] But the authorities do not confirm this in any way. Again, such assessments are purely speculative. If Nikitchenko is given the benefit of the doubt, his failure to mention Katyn in the judgment reflects the conclusions of a jurist of honesty and integrity.

Questions have often been raised about the attitude taken by the American and British prosecutors to the Soviet case on Katyn. The suggestion has been that it was too benign and perhaps even helpful. A leitmotif of the 1952 congressional committee, meeting at the height of the McCarthyite witch-hunts, was the possibility that pro-Soviet elements within the prosecution team or the Department of State might have tilted Washington's attitude. The only real evidence of this is the reference by a Soviet prosecutor to a document he said had been "offered us by our

---

[193] Bradley F. Smith, *Reaching Judgment at Nuremberg*, Basic Books, New York, 1977, p. 104.

[194] *Ibid.*, p. 106.

American colleagues".[195] This was a report from the Polish Red Cross indicating that the ammunition used in the killings was of German manufacture. The congressional inquiry heard testimony from the company that had manufactured the bullets explaining that they had been sold widely and that their German origin did not imply German responsibility for the killings. Jackson concurred, saying that the prosecution did not consider the origin of the weapons to have been significant. "You cannot tell by the gun that is used who shot it", he said.[196] In its final report, the Select Committee of the United States Congress referred to "many allegations [...] that Americans on Mr Jackson's staff at Nuremberg assisted the Soviets in the preparation of this case on Katyn against the Nazis". The final report says that the Select Committee had "desired to clarify this point", and that Jackson had denied the suggestion.[197] Jackson explained: "In fact, there was not a great deal of even conferring between their staff and ours because the Soviets are not very sociable, I might say. [...] They hesitate somewhat to be too much with us".[198] Jackson acknowledged that members of the American prosecution team may have been present at meetings of German and Soviet counsel, "as observers, or something of that sort, because we were very much concerned about not having a situation that would prolong this trial. But we took no part in any arrangements between the Soviets and the Germans about it. We thought that was their fight".[199]

Early in the trial, the British briefly considered whether they should actually assist the Soviets in proving the Katyn charge. Colonel Harry Phillimore, of the British War Crimes Executive in Nuremberg itself, wrote to David Scott-Fox of the Foreign Office on 3 January 1946 with some ideas on how to assist the Soviet prosecution team:

> If we are to give the Soviet Prosecutor any support in this matter it is very desirable that we should have your advice and be furnished with any information available to the Foreign Office. I suppose that the answer to the case prepared by Professor Savory might be on these lines:
>
> 1. It is very strange, if those murdered at Katyn were in Russian hands, that although 4,000 of them have been identi-

---

[195] One Hundred and Sixty-ninth Day, Afternoon Session, Tuesday, 2 July 1946, 17 IMT 362, 1948, p. 365.

[196] Select Committee Hearings, Part 7, p. 1957, see *supra* note 5.

[197] *Ibid.*, pp. 1952–53.

[198] *Ibid.*, p. 1952.

[199] *Ibid.*, p. 1953.

fied by letters, etc., found in the graves, in no case is it stated that any of those so identified were known to have been prisoners in Russian hands.

2. It is also strange that there is no statement that bodies so identified are known not to have been made prisoner of the Germans and that in no single case out of 4,000 is any information apparently available as to their place or date of capture.

3. The fixing of the date of death with such certainty after so long an interval is also obviously open to question. Is it certain that none of the written material found in the graves was dated after Soviet troops had retired from Smolensk.

But Foreign Office officials in London wrote minutes in the file indicating their opposition to any involvement in the Katyn case.[200]

Immediately following the initial Soviet submission and filing of the Burdenko report, in February 1946, the British ambassador to Iran, Sir Reader Bullard, wrote to the Foreign Office to express his own concerns about the Katyn charge in the indictment. "If (as I personally believe) Katyn murders were committed by the Russians (possibly without authority as in the case of the execution of the Czar and his family by Sverdlov) it would be unfortunate if the Russians managed to fob it off on the Germans before a court in which the British share is so important", he said.[201] John E. Galsworthy of the Northern Department wrote a note in the file: "It is difficult to see what action the Ambassador hopes might be taken on this telegram. His doubts may be well-founded – and shared by many others – but there could be no question of our 'blowing' the Russian case either in public or in private, and, in many ways, it might be as well that Katyn should be disposed of once and for all – onto the Germans".[202] Indifferent as to the real truth of the matter, Galsworthy seemed to be welcoming the possibility that "justice" would provide a politically convenient albeit completely false answer to the issue of responsibility. Another official also contributed a minute to the file:

This telegram adds nothing to our knowledge of the affair. The Polish case (against the Russians) has been exhaustively examined by Sir O. O'Malley. There are, as Sir R. Bullard

---

[200] Col. Harry Phillimore to David Scott-Fox, Foreign Office, 3 January 1946, FO 371/56474.
[201] Sir R. Bullard to Foreign Office, telegram, 15 February 1946, FO 371/56474.
[202] *Ibid.*

points out, certain things that are difficult to explain away. But no conclusive case has ever been made and we shall probably never know the whole truth.[203]

The British decided that they would do nothing to undermine or otherwise cast aspersions on the Soviet claims. There were concerns about harm this might do to the increasingly strained bilateral relationship with the Soviet Union. When Bullard wrote to the Foreign Office in February 1946, Frank Roberts, who was posted in the British embassy in Moscow, replied:

> I feel that I should emphasise that the effect on Anglo-Soviet relations of any apparent tendency on our part to accept the German case about Katyn would be calamitous. You will re-call that it was the Katyn affair which finally ruined any hope of collaboration between the Soviet Union and General Sikorski's Government. It would surely be best for the future of Polish-Soviet, and indeed of Anglo-Soviet relations if the matter could be definitely decided once and for all at the Nuremberg trial. I hope, therefore, that the Soviet Government will be able to present a full and convincing case. Even if they do not succeed in doing so, it would I think, be wise for us to refrain so far as possible from showing any scepticism, and to guide public opinion accordingly.[204]

Sir Richard Beaumont concurred:

> [W]e do not wish to stand so obviously aloof that our behaviour could be taken to imply criticism and disapproval of what the Russians are doing. [...] Remembering how thin-skinned the Russians are in matters of this sort, however, you will not doubt agree as to the political desirability of our appearing, in our dealings with the Russians themselves, to accept the Soviet case, and I hope that all concerned at Nuremberg will interpret our general instructions to "hold aloof" in this sense.[205]

These materials provide a rare glimpse of the political manipulation of the proceedings, in this case by the British. It is a feature of international criminal justice about which much is suspected but little is known. Doubtless it has become less significant at the modern international tribunals because of the genuine independence of the prosecutors, something

---

[203] *Ibid.*

[204] Frank Roberts (Moscow) to Foreign Office, telegram, 18 February 1946, FO 371/56474.

[205] R.A. Beaumont to P.H. Dean, 25 February 1946, FO 371/56474.

assured by provisions within the relevant legal instruments as well as by the security of their own tenure of office. For example, a provision in the Statute of the International Criminal Tribunal for the former Yugoslavia states: "The Prosecutor shall act independently as a separate organ of the International Tribunal. He or she shall not seek or receive instructions from any Government or from any other source".[206] But in 1945 and 1946 there was no suggestion that the prosecutors were independent of the governments that appointed them.

The Soviet prosecution was "micromanaged" by the Commission for Directing the Nuremberg Trials, a body that met in Moscow under the chairmanship of Andrei Vyshinskii.[207] The Commission met on 21 March 1946, agreeing to prepare a large number of witnesses, including medical experts, as well as documents that had been found on the bodies. A documentary film was also to be prepared, although the record of the meeting does not indicate whether it was intended to be shown to the Tribunal. The film was produced and shown in Polish cinemas in 1946.[208] It goes without saying that the Soviet leaders, who closely supervised the conduct of the Nuremberg proceedings through Vyshinskii, were in on the dirty secret.[209] Yet even within the Soviet leadership, the truth about Katyn appears to have been closely guarded. It is difficult to know at what level those who were involved in oversight actually knew what had happened. Nevertheless, nothing indicates this cynicism at the diplomatic or governmental level is in any way reflected in the conduct of the prosecutors themselves, or for that matter of the judges.

Robert Jackson told the congressional inquiry into Katyn that "I received very little instruction from anybody. The thing was a lawyer's job, and I had no instructions. If I may be so blunt as to say so, I thought that having once gotten me into it, there was a pronounced disposition to leave everything to me. I will not say exactly that that it was to 'pass the buck', but I was in charge of it".[210] Some scholarly work has been done on the links between the American prosecution staff and the United States intelligence service. Jackson's deputy prosecutor, William Donovan, was the

---

[206] Statute of the International Criminal Tribunal for the former Yugoslavia, UN doc. S/RES/827 (1993), annex, Art. 16(2).

[207] Hirsch, 2008, pp. 712–13, 715, 718, see *supra* note 45.

[208] Viatteau, 1996, pp. 149–50, see *supra* note 7.

[209] Cienciala *et al.*, 2007, p. 229–30, see *supra* note 10.

[210] Select Committee Hearings, Part 7, p. 1954, see *supra* note 5.

wartime head of the Office of Strategic Services and the 'father' of the Central Intelligence Agency. In his testimony before the Select Committee, Jackson noted that his staff included employees of the Office of Strategic Services.[211]

Ultimately, the efforts by the Soviet Union to use international justice to promote a lie did not succeed. The attitude of the American and British prosecution officials might be characterised as indifference, but that is probably an unfair assessment. The explanations, especially those of Jackson in his congressional testimony, make sense. Given the stubborn insistence of the Soviets upon proceeding with the Katyn charge, the other prosecutors had little choice. A refusal to agree upon this in the indictment might well have aborted the entire trial. They provided no real assistance to the Soviet prosecutors who were, in the end, unable to prove their case to the satisfaction of the judges.

In a presentation to the United Nations General Assembly in the early years of the International Criminal Tribunal for the former Yugoslavia, its first president, Antonio Cassese, said the institution was creating "an historical record of what occurred during the conflict thereby preventing historical 'revisionism'".[212] But in *Eichmann in Jerusalem*, Hannah Arendt warned against using criminal justice to establish or clarify historical truth.[213] The International Military Tribunal was unable to peer through the fog of war and thereby clarify the facts of the Katyn massacre. But nor did it distort the historical truth by leaving a distorted or even dishonest record. The silence of the judges ensured that no irreparable damage was done to the historical truth. International justice, still at its very beginnings, and as flawed and imperfect as it then was, survived with its honour intact. Nuremberg's critics, some of them with the most dubious motives, are wrong to invoke the Katyn charge as evidence of 'victors' justice'. Indeed, it shows quite the opposite. Faced with contradictory evidence and an incomplete picture, the judges refused to convict. The system worked. Justice was done.

---

[211] See Michael Salter, Nazi War Crimes, US Intelligence and Selective Prosecution at Nuremberg: Controversies Regarding the Role of the Office of Strategic Services, Routledge-Cavendish, London, 2007.

[212] UN doc. A/52/PV.44, p. 2.

[213] Hannah Arendt, Eichmann in Jerusalem: A Report on the Banality of Evil, Viking, New York, 1964, p. 253.

9

The Lieber Code, Retaliation and the Origins of International Criminal Law

Patryk I. Labuda[*]

9.1. Introduction

The enforcement of norms has always been international law's weakest link. Yet the rise of international criminal justice in the last 20 years has begun to alter the sensibilities of international lawyers. Today's media are flooded with news of high-profile trials and path-breaking convictions arising from wars in the former Yugoslavia, Cambodia and the Democratic Republic of Congo. As conventional wisdoms – encapsulated in slogans such as "no peace without justice", "the most serious crimes [...] must not go unpunished" and "states bear the primary responsibility for preventing impunity" – become part of the accepted vocabulary of the discipline, principles that were only recently contested acquire the status of unassailable truths.[1] The origins of concepts, and the contingency of their meaning, get lost in the fog of history.

Reflecting this 'presentist' tilt in international criminal law, scholarship on war crimes espouses various half-truths and anachronisms about

[*] **Patryk I. Labuda** is a Ph.D. Candidate at the Graduate Institute of International and Development Studies in Geneva. He holds a LL.M. in constitutional and international law from Columbia Law School, New York. The author wishes to thank Charles McCurdy for his guidance, and the students in the University of Virginia Law School's Legal History Seminar for their feedback on the term paper that later became this chapter. Thanks are also due to the participants in the Seminar on the Historical Origins of International Criminal Law (New Delhi, 28–29 November 2014) for their valuable comments and suggestions.
[1] The first quotation is a popular slogan among proponents of international criminal trials, see Howard Ball, *War Crimes and Justice: A Reference Handbook*, ABC-CLIO, Santa Barbara, CA, 2002, pp. 31–32. The second quotation is from the Rome Statute of the International Criminal Court, Preamble. The third quotation is from International Committee of the Red Cross Statement to the United Nations, The Scope and Application of the Principle of Universal Jurisdiction, United Nations, General Assembly, 69th Session, Sixth Committee, 15 October 2014.

its recent and more distant past. A prominent example is the supposedly ancient and, implicitly, immutable lineage of individual criminal responsibility for war crimes.[2] Even though international criminal trials first materialised in the aftermath of the First World War, it is suggested that domestic trials for war crimes have a much longer history. We are told that ancient civilisations accepted "personal responsibility for exceeding" limitations on the conduct of war and established "legal processes for imposing penal sanctions for those convicted of such excesses".[3] In the same vein, it is argued that "the enforcement of international humanitarian law dates back to the Middle Ages",[4] and that "[t]he trials of real and alleged war criminals by victorious opponents can be traced back to the dawn of modern international law".[5] This is usually followed by a customary mention of the trials of Conradin von Hohenstaufen, William Wallace or Peter von Hagenbach.[6]

---

[2] Another example is the belief that all war crimes (the term itself is an anachronism) entail individual criminal responsibility under international law and a duty to prosecute. See, for example, Christine Van den Wijngaert, "War Crimes, Crimes against Humanity and Statutory Limitations", in Cherif Bassiouni (ed.), *International Criminal Law*, vol. 3: *Enforcement*, Transnational Publishers, New York, 1987, p. 89: "The obligation either to extradite or to prosecute exists as of the Fifties for war crimes". For the current law, see generally Antonio Cassese, *International Criminal Law*, 2nd ed., Oxford University Press, Oxford, 2008, pp. 81–97, 27–30.

[3] Timothy L.H. McCormack, "Selective Reaction to Atrocity: War Crimes and the Development of International Criminal Law", in *Albany Law Review*, 1997, vol. 60, pp. 686–89.

[4] Jackson Maogoto, "Early Efforts to Establish an International Criminal Court", in José Doria, Hans-Peter Gasser and M. Cherif Bassiouni (eds.), *The Legal Regime of the International Criminal Court: Essays in Honour of Professor Igor Blishchenko*, Martinus Nijhoff, Leiden, 2009, p. 4.

[5] Georg Schwarzenberger, "The Judgment of Nuremberg", in Guénaël Mettraux (ed.), *Perspectives on the Nuremberg Trial*, Oxford University Press, Oxford, 2008, p. 167. United Nations War Crimes Commission, *History of the United Nations War Crimes Commission and the Development of the Laws of War*, His Majesty's Stationery Office, London, 1948, p. 30, cited in Shane Darcy, *Collective Responsibility and Accountability under International Law*, Transnational Publishers, Ardsley, NY, 2007, p. 190.

[6] Lyal S. Sunga, Individual Responsibility in International Law for Serious Human Rights Violations, Martinus Nijhoff, Dordrecht, 1992, pp. 15–19; Elies van Sliedregt, Individual Criminal Responsibility in International Law, Oxford University Press, Oxford, 2012, pp. 3–5; McCormack, 1997, p. 682–95, especially p. 693, see supra note 3; Benjamin B. Ferencz, Enforcing International Law: A Way to World Peace: A Documentary History and Analysis, vol. 1, Oceana Publications, London, 1980; Timothy L.H. McCormack, "From Sun Tzu to the Sixth Committee: The Evolution of an International Criminal Law Regime", in Timothy McCormack and Gerry Simpson (eds.), The Law of War Crimes: International and National Approaches, Kluwer Law International, The Hague, 1997, pp. 31–

How do isolated trials over the course of thousands of years demonstrate the universality of a legal principle? Why did a debate about an international arbitral body for violations of the laws of war begin only in the 1870s? What explains the legal dispute over whether to prosecute Germany's excesses committed in the First World War? Many conventional renditions of war crimes history read like narratives of linear progress culminating in the modern international criminal justice project.[7] Emphasising continuity over rupture and evolution over contingency, these narratives arguably obscure the convoluted historical processes by which key concepts in modern international criminal law emerged.[8]

In exploring the law, doctrine and practice relating to law of war violations, this chapter seeks to nuance the idea that war crimes trials have an ancient pedigree. It argues that institutionalised criminal justice for such violations emerged as a counterpoint to a much older and established enforcement method: belligerent reprisals.[9] Known primarily as retaliation in the nineteenth century, the intentional infliction of a law of war violation constituted the primary vehicle for sanctioning a prior violation of the same body of law. Imposed not for the sake of revenge but rather to compel compliance with the law, retaliation was a widely used and lawful method of enforcing the laws of war. Yet, as domestic military trials of

---

63; Cenap Cakmak, "Evolution of the Idea of a Permanent International Criminal Court Prior to World War I", in Ulusrarasi Hukuk ve Politica, 2008, vol. 4, no. 13, p. 138; Maogoto, 2009, pp. 3–22, see supra note 4.

[7] To be fair, some works probably performed a dual scholarly-advocacy role when they were published. When international criminal trials still seemed a distant prospect, emphasising the universality of principles aimed to strengthen the argument for reform, irrespective of historical accuracy.

[8] On historical narratives in legal scholarship, see Daniel Marc Segesser, Recht staat Rache oder Rache durch Recht? Die Ahndung von Kriegsverbrechen in der international wissenschaftlichen Debatte 1872–1945, Ferdinand Schöningh, Paderborn, 2010, especially pp. 23–33, 76–79. See generally Martti Koskeniemmi, The Gentle Civilizer of Nations: The Rise and Fall of International Law 1870–1960, Cambridge University Press, Cambridge, 2002, pp. 6–11.

[9] It is important to distinguish between belligerent and peacetime reprisals. Since it is limited to the law of war (ius in bello), this chapter deals only with the former. Henceforth, the terms 'reprisals' and 'retaliation' will be used interchangeably to mean belligerent reprisals. For more on terminology, see below fn. 112 and accompanying text. See generally Shane Darcy, "Retaliation and Reprisal", in Marc Weller (ed.), The Oxford Handbook of the Use of Force in International Law, Oxford University Press, Oxford, 2015, pp. 879–96; Shane Darcy, "The Prohibition of Collective Punishment", in Andrew Clapham, Paola Gaeta and Marco Sassoli (eds.), The 1949 Geneva Conventions: A Commentary, Oxford University Press, Oxford, 2015 (forthcoming).

such violations became more common during the second half of the nineteenth century, the lawfulness of resorting to retaliation – the Gallic name 'reprisals' would come to supersede the atavistic English term – gradually declined before the First World War.

This chapter begins with an analysis of the Lieber Code, the first attempt to codify the custom of war, before turning to the international debate on the law and practice of retaliation and criminal trials from 1865 to 1914. The story of how individual accountability through criminal trials gradually displaced retaliatory measures, a form of collective punishment, is part of a complex historical process. By tracing these debates from the American Civil War to the First World War, this chapter argues that the two phenomena should be viewed together as part of the humanisation and individualisation of international law at the turn of the twentieth century.[10] The chapter concludes with some observations about Lieber's role in catalysing reform and how individual criminal responsibility became the norm in the twentieth century.

9.2. Enforcement of the Laws and Customs of War during the American Civil War

9.2.1. The Lieber Code and International Humanitarian Law

In the United States in 1861 few anticipated the destruction and brutality of the next four years. Partisans of Southern independence and advocates of the Union had convinced themselves that the impending military conflict would be resolved quickly and without much bloodshed.[11] Inaugurated by the firing on Fort Sumter, hostilities were greeted with patriotic fervour on both sides: Confederates believed that "one Southerner could whip five Yankees", while Northerners mistakenly assumed secession was doomed to fail.[12]

---

[10] See Theodor Meron, "The Humanization of Humanitarian Law", in *American Journal of International Law*, 2000, vol. 94, no. 2, pp. 239–78; Anne-Marie Slaughter, "Rogue Regimes and the Individualization of International Law", in *New England Law Review*, 2002, vol. 36, no. 4, pp. 815–24.

[11] This section is based on Patryk I. Labuda, "Lieber Code", in Rüdiger Wolfrum (ed.), *Max Planck Encyclopedia of Public International Law*, Oxford University Press, Oxford, 2015.

[12] James McPherson, *Battle Cry of Freedom: The Civil War Era*, Oxford University Press, Oxford, 1988, pp. 308–68. See also Everard H. Smith, "Chambersburg: Anatomy of a Confederate Reprisal", in *American Historical Review*, 1991, vol. 96, no. 2, p. 432. Hence-

Drafted in just a few months, the Lieber Code ('the Code') was issued at the height of the American Civil War in 1863.[13] Although it is often described as "the first modern codification of the laws of war",[14] the term 'code' was actually dropped from the final version of the document.[15] A restatement of then existing custom, it constituted a non-binding set of best practices for the Union's army, even though the Confederate government subsequently voluntarily applied some of its rules.[16]

Named after its main drafter, Francis Lieber, the Code is notable for its lack of systematicity and brevity (just over 150 provisions). It regulated a number of familiar international humanitarian law topics, including rules applicable to prisoners of war (Articles 56–59, 73–76, 105–110) and proscribed methods of war (Articles 16, 63, 65, 101 and 117). The Code foreshadowed certain core norms of modern international humanitarian law, in particular regarding military necessity, the principles of humanity and distinction, but the scope and nature of these principles differed from their modern equivalents.[17] It also recognised norms that would be illegal

---

forth the terms 'South' and Confederacy' and 'North' and 'Union' will be used interchangeably.

[13] Its full name reads General Orders No. 100: Instructions for the Government of Armies of the United States in the Field, promulgated on 24 April 1863 ('Lieber Code').

[14] Richard Baxter described it in these terms in his influential 1963 article on the centenary of the Lieber Code's promulgation. This phrase has been repeated by a number of authors since then. See R. R. Baxter, "The First Modern Codification of the Law of War: Francis Lieber and General Orders No. 100", in *International Review of the Red Cross*, 1963, vol. 3, no. 25, pp. 171–89, 217–36. See also Lawrence P. Rockwood, *Walking Away from Nuremberg: Just War and the Doctrine of Command Responsibility*, University of Massachusetts Press, Amherst, 2007, pp. 11–44.

[15] Seeking to avoid a debate in Congress, President Abraham Lincoln issued the code as a military order instead of a statutory codification that would have required legislative approval. See also Stephen C. Neff, *Justice in Blue and Gray: A Legal History of the Civil War*, Harvard University Press, Cambridge, MA, 2010, p. 56–58.

[16] Frank Freidel, *Francis Lieber: Nineteenth-Century Liberal*, Louisiana State University Press, Baton Rouge, 1947, pp. 334–35. Lynn Hogue, "Lieber's Military Code and Its Legacy", in Charles R. Mack and Henry H. Lesesne (eds.), *Francis Lieber and the Culture of the Mind*, University of South Carolina Press, Columbia, 2005, pp. 55–57.

[17] A few authors have recently drawn attention to the different understanding of international humanitarian law principles in Lieber's writings. See Rotem Giladi, "A Different Sense of Humanity: Occupation in Francis Lieber's Code", in *International Review of the Red Cross*, 2012, vol. 94, no. 885, pp. 81–116, especially p. 89. See also Betsy Baker Röben, *Johann Caspar Bluntschli, Francis Lieber und das modern Völkerrecht 1861–1881*, Nomos, Baden Baden, 2003; Burrus M. Carnahan, "Lincoln, Lieber and the Laws of War: The Origins and Limits of the Principle of Necessity", in *American Journal of International Law*, 1998, vol. 92, no. 2, p. 213–31.

by modern international humanitarian law standards, for instance the practice of giving no quarter to the enemy (Articles 61–63, 66) or the starvation of non-combatants (Article 17). Most significantly, for the purpose of this chapter, the Code allowed the use of belligerent reprisals or – as it was known to Lieber and his contemporaries – retaliation (Articles 27 and 28).

9.2.2. The Concept and Practice of Retaliation

Although it was widely used during the Civil War by both the Confederacy and the Union, disputes over retaliation emerged as soon as the conflict began.[18] In the first months of the war, Jefferson Davis, President of the Confederacy, started issuing letters of marque to captains who were willing to support the Southern war effort. Without a navy, the newly formed Confederacy depended on privateers for its war-making power on the high seas. In line with nineteenth century international law, these letters shielded private parties from prosecution for piracy.[19]

But recognising the legitimacy of privateers undermined a key plank of the Union's theory of the conflict, which President Abraham Lincoln insisted was "a domestic insurrection, a rebellion by certain lawless citizens, not a war between nations".[20] Lincoln refused to recognise the Confederacy's claims to independence, imposed an embargo on Southern ports, and in June 1862 he initiated prosecutions of the crew of a captured Confederate privateer.[21] Outraged by what he viewed as a violation of the laws of war, Davis wrote to Lincoln:

> [I]f driven to the terrible necessity of retaliation by your execution of any of the officers or crew of the Savannah, that retaliation will be extended so far as shall be requisite to se-

---

[18] There is currently no scholarly work on the Lieber Code's rules regarding retaliation. See generally Gregory A. Raymond, "Lieber and the International Laws of War", in Mack and Lesesne, 2005, p. 72, see *supra* note 16.

[19] The 1856 Declaration of Paris had made privateering illegal, but the United States was not a party. See Mark A. Weitz, *The Confederacy on Trial: The Piracy and Sequestration Cases of 1861*, University Press of Kansas, Lawrence, 2005, pp. 17–21. See also Neff, 2010, pp. 24–25, *supra* note 15.

[20] Quoted in Hogue, 2005, p. 52, see *supra* note 16; see also Baxter, 1963, p. 177, *supra* note 14 and Neff, 2010, pp. 20–23, *supra* note 15.

[21] See Weitz, 2005, *supra* note 19. Though it carried a letter of marque from Davis, the *Savannah* was captured off the coast of South Carolina on 6 June 1861 by the federal authorities, which then brought piracy charges against the crew in New York.

cure the abandonment of a practice unknown to the warfare of civilized man, and so barbarous as to disgrace the nation which shall be guilty of inaugurating it.[22]

In this instance, the threat of tit-for-tat retaliation forced Lincoln to recognise Confederate privateers as legitimate belligerents, which entitled them to the protections of prisoner of war status under the laws and customs of war.[23] However, as the conflict dragged on and recriminations of unlawful warfare multiplied, Lincoln realised that clearer rules governing the conduct of armies would be necessary.

Lieber drafted his Code, with Lincoln's tacit support, on the basis of existing international legal norms.[24] Relying on antebellum commentators who referred to it variously as talion, law of retaliation, rule of reciprocity, vindictive retaliation, *retorsio facti* and reprisal, retaliation was mentioned in five different regulations and became one of the Code's key features.[25] An inherently controversial response to international law's lack of enforcement-mechanisms,[26] Lieber devoted two general provisions to the term:

> Art. 27. The law of war can no more wholly dispense with retaliation than can the law of nations, of which it is a branch. Yet civilized nations acknowledge retaliation as the sternest feature of war. A reckless enemy often leaves to his

---

22. Jefferson Davis to Abraham Lincoln, Richmond, 6 July 1861, in United States, War Department, *The War of the Rebellion: A Compilation of the Official Records of the Union and Confederate Armies*, series 2, vol. 3, part 6, Government Printing Office, Washington, DC, 1898, p. 5 (*'War of the Rebellion'*).

23. See Burrus M. Carnahan, *Act of Justice: Lincoln's Emancipation Proclamation and the Law of War*, University Press of Kentucky, Lexington, 2007, pp. 65–67.

24. On Lincoln's (limited) role in the drafting of the Code, see Paul Finkelman, "Francis Lieber and the Modern Law of War. Review of John F. Witt, *Lincoln's Code*", in *University of Chicago Law Review*, 2013, vol. 80, no. 4, p. 2077.

25. Henry W. Halleck, International Law, or Rules Regulating the Intercourse of States in Peace and War, Bancroft, San Francisco, 1861, ch. 18, paras. 25, 26; Henry Wheaton, *Elements of International Law, with a Sketch of the History of the Science*, vol. 2, B. Fellowes, London, 1836, part 4, ch. 2, para. 6; Theodore D. Woolsey, *Introduction to the Study of International Law*, James Munroe, Boston and Cambridge, 1860, part 2, ch. 1, § 2, para. 126; Emerich de Vattel, *The Law of Nations; or Principles of the Law of Nature applied to the Conduct and Affairs of Nations and Sovereigns*, ed. Joseph Chitty, T. and J.W. Johnson and Co., Philadelphia, 1856, book 3, ch. 8, para. 143.

26. See generally Shane Darcy, "The Evolution of the Law of Belligerent Reprisals", in *Military Law Review*, 2003, vol. 175, pp. 184–185; Frits Kalshoven, *Belligerent Reprisals*, Martinus Nijhoff, Leiden, 1971, pp. 22–26.

---

opponent no other means of securing himself against the repetition of barbarous outrage.

Art. 28. Retaliation will, therefore, never be resorted to as a measure of mere revenge, but only as a means of protective retribution, and moreover, cautiously and unavoidably; that is to say, retaliation shall only be resorted to after careful inquiry into the real occurrence, and the character of the misdeeds that may demand retribution.

Unjust or inconsiderate retaliation removes the belligerents farther and farther from the mitigating rules of regular war, and by rapid steps leads them nearer to the internecine wars of savages.

"The sternest feature of war", in Lieber's own words, the Union recognised that retaliation was a lawful method of enforcing the laws and customs of war, and both the Confederate and Union armies would make abundant use of this 'weapon' throughout the war.[27]

In addition to Articles 27 and 28, four provisions regulated specific instances of retaliation. It was forbidden in just one situation: if a deserter joined an enemy army but was then captured by his former comrades, the death penalty was fully warranted and retaliation for such executions was not permitted.[28] By contrast, and unlike in modern international humanitarian law, retaliation against prisoners of war was expressly permitted (Article 59).[29] Though the Code prohibited mere vengeful acts,[30] there are credible reports of summary executions masking as retaliation, both on the battlefield and after battle, against captured belligerents.[31]

Retaliation was also common in prisoner of war camps. The treatment of prisoners became increasingly contentious as the war wore on, due to the Confederacy's worsening military situation and poor detention conditions in Southern prisons camps.[32] Writing to the Secretary of War,

---

[27]   See Lonnie R. Speer, *War of Vengeance: Acts of Retaliation against Civil War POWs*, Stackpole Books, Mechanicsburg, PA, 2002 and Charles W. Sanders, *While in the Hands of the Enemy: Military Prisons of the Civil War*, Louisiana State University Press, Baton Rouge, 2005. Both authors argue that retaliation against prisoners of war was a hallmark of the Civil War.

[28]   Lieber Code, Art. 48, see *supra* note 13.

[29]   *Ibid.*, Art. 48.

[30]   *Ibid.*, Art. 56.

[31]   Speer, 2002, p. xii, see *supra* note 27.

[32]   *Ibid.*, pp. 121–24; Sanders, 2005, pp. 240–44, *supra* note 27.

Edward M. Stanton, General Henry W. Halleck argued that "the treatment of our prisoners of war by the rebel authorities has been even more barbarous than that which Christian captives formerly suffered from the pirates of Tripoli, Tunis, and Algiers".[33] With Radical Republicans pressing Lincoln to authorise retaliatory measures against Southern prisoners in Northern camps and reports of diminishing rations for Northern prisoners in Southern camps, in 1864 Stanton passed an across-the-board 20 per cent decrease in food rations for all Confederate prisoners of war.[34] It was not the war's last retaliatory measure of this nature, but it did prove to be the most drastic.[35]

The Code also authorised retaliation for outlawry.[36] Still used in the nineteenth century, outlawry meant that a belligerent was stripped of all his rights – civil and military – for violating the laws of war. "[A] sort of juridical excommunication, with the person in question being placed entirely outside the framework of the law", such individuals could be killed with impunity.[37] The Confederacy issued two major proclamations of outlawry against Union generals during the Civil War. Although there were no further proclamations after May 1863, it is not clear whether the Code's ban influenced Confederate policy. By contrast, the Lincoln administration never resorted to outlawry, nor did it resort to retaliation to curb it.[38]

Lastly, the Code authorised retaliation for slavery.[39] The controversy over the legal status of slavery was at its peak when Lieber drafted the Code. By mid-1862 Lincoln's initial opposition to abolishing slavery had

---

[33] General Henry W. Halleck to Edward M. Stanton, September 14, 1863 in *War of the Rebellion,* series 2, vol. 6, p. 524, see *supra* note 22.

[34] Sanders, 2005, pp. 240–46, *supra* note 27; Michael Horigan, *Elmira: Death Camp of the North*, Stackpole Books, Mechanicsburg, PA, 2002, pp. 84–87. See also Chester G. Hearn, *Lincoln, the Cabinet, and the Generals*, Louisiana State University Press, Baton Rouge, 2010, p. 181; James Ford Rhodes, *History of the United States from the Compromise of 1850 to the Final Restoration of Home Rule at the South in 1877*, vol. 5, Macmillan, New York, 1912, pp. 504–5.

[35] Rations were decreased again in August 1864. Though there is only indirect evidence of the Lieber Code being invoked to justify such measures, the harsh treatment of prisoners in Southern camps led to one of the few post-war trials for violations of the laws of war. For more on post-war trials, see below fn. 87.

[36] Lieber Code, Art. 148, see *supra* note 13.

[37] Neff, 2010, p. 67, see *supra* note 15.

[38] *Ibid.*, pp. 67–68.

[39] Lieber Code, Art. 58, see *supra* note 13.

slowly given way to a more pragmatic policy, culminating eventually in the Emancipation Proclamation of 1 January 1863.[40] Union commanders, many of whom opposed freeing slaves, had failed to develop a coherent strategy for dealing with runaway slaves prior to the Code's promulgation. Some returned slaves to their Confederate masters, while others – following General Benjamin Butler's lead – impressed them into Union service by declaring captured slaves 'contraband of war'. But even the Emancipation Proclamation, which only freed slaves behind enemy lines (not in Union states over which Lincoln had actual authority), did not provide guidance on how Union soldiers should treat slaves in the border states.[41]

A fierce opponent of the Confederacy's 'peculiar institution', Lieber's rules on retaliation allowed him to intervene in the debate about the legal status of runaway slaves:

> The law of nations knows of no distinction of color, and if an enemy of the United States should enslave and sell any captured persons of their army, it would be a case for the severest retaliation, if not redressed upon complaint.
>
> The United States cannot retaliate by enslavement; therefore death must be the retaliation for this crime against the law of nations.[42]

Retaliation, Lieber hoped, would help to delegalise and deter the re-enslavement of blacks by the Confederacy. The Code had a direct impact on the conduct of war in at least one instance. The South had consistently argued that interfering with domestic property (slaves were treated as property under US constitutional law) was a violation of the laws of war, and an incitement to "servile insurrection".[43] Responding to the recruitment of black Union regiments and the establishment of the Bureau of Colored Troops, the Confederate Congress declared:

---

[40] Weitz, 2005, pp. 71–94, see *supra* note 19.

[41] See Matthew J. Mancini, "Francis Lieber, Slavery, and the 'Genesis' of the Laws of War", in *Journal of Southern History*, 2011, vol. 77, no. 2, pp. 325–48. See also Freidel, 1947, pp. 317–41, see *supra* note 16.

[42] Hogue, 2005, p. 56, see *supra* note 16.

[43] See Gregory J.W. Urwin, "Colored Troops", in David S. Heidler, Jeanne T. Heidler and David J. Coles (eds.), *Encyclopedia of the American Civil War: A Political, Social and Military History*, ABC-CLIO, Santa Barbara, CA, 2000, pp. 2002–3. See also Labuda, 2015, *supra* note 11.

[T]he proclamations of the President of the United States [...] and the other measures [...] designed or tending to emancipate slavers in the Confederate States, or to abduct such slavers, or to incite them to insurrection, or to employ negroes in war against the Confederate States [...] would, if successful, produce atrocious consequences, and they are inconsistent with the spirit of those usages which in modern warfare prevail among civilized nations. They may, therefore, be properly and lawfully repressed by retaliation.

That in every case wherein, during the present war, any violation of the laws or usages of war among civilized nations shall be or has been done and perpetrated by those acting under the authority of the Government of the United States [...] the President of the Confederate States is hereby authorized to cause full and ample retaliation to be made for every such violation in such manner and to such extent as he may think proper.

That every white person, being a commissioned officer, or acting as such, who during the present war shall command negroes or mulattoes in arms against the Confederate States [...] shall, if captured, be put to death or be otherwise punished, at the discretion of the court.[44]

This resolution authorised practically unlimited retaliation for interference with slavery. White officers of black regiments could be summarily executed, making them *de facto* outlaws. Realising the wide implications of this retaliatory measure, Lincoln reacted swiftly, issuing General Order No. 252:

The law of nations, and the usages and customs of war, as carried on by civilized powers, permit no distinction as to color in the treatment of prisoners of war as public enemies. To sell or enslave any captured person on account of his color, and for no offense against the laws of war, is a relapse into barbarism, and a crime against the civilization of the age.

The Government of the United States will give the same protection to all its soldiers, and if the enemy shall sell or enslave any one because of his color, the offense shall be punished by retaliation upon the enemy's prisoners in our possession. It is therefore ordered, that for every soldier of the

---

[44] Reprinted in James W. Loewen and Edward Sebesta (eds.), *The Confederate and Neo-Confederate Reader: The "Great Truth" about the "Lost Cause"*, University Press of Mississippi, Jackson, 2010, pp. 201–2.

United States killed in violation of the law, a Rebel soldier shall be executed, and for every one enslaved by the enemy or sold into slavery, a Rebel soldier shall be placed at hard labor on the public works, and continued at such labor until the other shall be released and receive the treatment due to a prisoner of war.[45]

Although it did not expressly invoke the Code's rules on retaliation and slavery, Lincoln's Order of Retaliation was nonetheless an endorsement of Lieber's interpretation of the laws of war (the first paragraph is, in all likelihood, a combination of Articles 27 and 58 of the Code). Lincoln's order did not eliminate executions of black soldiers, but it probably deterred some violations of belligerent rights.[46]

An assessment of the Code's rules yields the following insights. Rooted in the law of nations,[47] Lieber stitched together a patchwork of norms drawn from pre-Civil War treatises, and proposed a fragmentary, by modern standards, framework for dealing with retaliation. First, retaliation was a law enforcement measure ("never be resorted to as a measure of mere revenge, but only as a means of protective retribution"). As such, the Code authorised violations of the laws of war if the aim was to prevent the commission of further violations.[48] Second, retaliation could be resorted to only "after careful inquiry into the real occurrence, and the character of the misdeeds that may demand retribution". This distinguished it from mere revenge. Third, the Code implied that the principle of necessity – "unavoidably" (Article 28) and "no other means" (Article 27) – applied to retaliation.

Nonetheless, the Code also left a host of issues unresolved.[49] Even if the underlying violation was inquired into, Lieber did not specify whether the original violator should be requested to desist from committing further violations before retaliation was authorised. Likewise, the

---

[45] General Order No. 252, reprinted in Henry Louis Gates (ed.), *Lincoln on Race and Slavery*, Princeton University Press, Princeton, NJ, 2009, pp. 276–78.

[46] Carnahan, 2007, pp. 127–31, see *supra* note 23. See also Gregory J. Urwin (ed.), *Black Flag Over Dixie: Racial Atrocities and Reprisals in the Civil War*, Southern Illinois University Press, Carbondale, 2004.

[47] Lieber Code, Art. 27, see *supra* note 13.

[48] *Ibid.*, Art. 68: "Unnecessary or revengeful destruction of life is not lawful".

[49] For an overview of the law applicable to reprisals in modern international humanitarian law, see Sandesh Sivakumaran, *The Law of Non-International Armed Conflict*, Oxford University Press, Oxford, 2012, pp. 453–57.

Code failed to clarify who was authorised to order retaliation (commanders, higher-ranking officers or any soldier?). Most significantly, the Code left unresolved whether retaliatory measures should be proportional in kind and degree. In a private letter to Halleck, Lieber argued that "in retaliation it is necessary strictly to adhere to sections twenty-seven and twenty-eight of General Order 100, to the elementary principle which prevails all the world over – tit for tat, or eye for eye – and not to adopt ten eyes for one eye".[50]

But retaliation in the Civil War rarely conformed to Lieber's private hopes. Retaliatory measures did not follow the tit-for-tat model, and the causal connection between retaliation and the original violation of the law of war was not always apparent.[51] In practice, army commanders ordered retaliatory measures against groups of individuals or against specific areas only loosely associated with illegitimate warfare.[52] Destruction of civilian (in addition to military) property by way of retaliation was also common. For instance, in July 1864 the entire town of Chambersburg, Pennsylvania was razed to the ground by Confederate troops after a Union general (unlawfully, as it was then argued) burned three homes of Confederate sympathisers in West Virginia.[53] Another common form of retaliation was to make civilians pay compensation for violations of the laws of war, in the hope that this would dissuade them from supporting the enemy.[54] Forced deportation of civilians, the most extreme form of retaliation, occurred

---

[50] Quoted in G.B. Davis, "Doctor Francis Lieber's Instructions", in *American Journal of International Law*, 1907, vol. 1, no. 1, p. 21.

[51] Belligerents usually resorted to acts that differed from the underlying transgression. See James Molony Spaight, *War Rights on Land*, Macmillan, London, 1911, p. 464.

[52] After his deployment to northern Virginia, General John Pope ordered that "[i]f a soldier or legitimate follower of the army be fired upon from any house the house shall be razed to the ground, and the inhabitants sent prisoners to the headquarters of this army. If such an outrage occurs at any place distant from settlements, the people within 5 miles around shall be held accountable and made to pay an indemnity sufficient for the case". General Order No. 7, Headquarters Army of Virginia, Washington, July 10, 1862, in *War of the Rebellion*, series 1, vol. 12, part 2, p. 51, see *supra* note 22. See also Burrus M. Carnahan, *Lincoln on Trial: Southern Civilians and the Law of War*, University Press of Kentucky, Lexington, 2010, p. 58.

[53] Anna Sarah Rubin, "Chambersburg, Burning Of", in Heidler *et al.*, 2000, pp. 390–91, see *supra* note 43. See also Everard H. Smith, "Chambersburg: Anatomy of a Confederate Reprisal", in *American Historical Review*, 1991, vol. 96, no. 2, pp. 432–35.

[54] General Orders No. 159, Headquarters Department of the Missouri, in *War of the Rebellion*, series 1, vol. 41, part 3, p. 8, see *supra* note 22. See also Carnahan, 2010, p. 68, *supra* note 52.

primarily in border states such as Missouri. For instance, in 1863 almost 20,000 civilians were forcibly displaced and many of their homes burned, and though the order prompted outrage in the North (and South) it was never formally rescinded.[55]

Even if contemporaries viewed some retaliatory measures as stretching the limits of acceptable warfare, it must be remembered that they were not unlawful *per se*. Contrary to modern international humanitarian law, collective punishment was a lawful method of war. In Article 15 the Code legitimised "all destruction of property, and obstruction of the ways and channels of traffic travel, or communication, and of all withholding of sustenance or means of life from the enemy".[56] The extremely broad scope, by subsequent standards, of retaliation during the Civil War is best reflected in a letter discovered in Halleck's papers after his death:

> 1. That retaliation is a well-settled principle of the modern law of war, and is resorted to by the most civilized and Christian people.
>
> 2. It must not be applied in a spirit of revenge nor, unnecessarily as a punishment; the object of its use being to prevent a repetition of the offence or crime which is retaliated on the enemy.
>
> 3. Retaliation may be, as the word indicates, literally in kind, that is, "an eye for an eye and a tooth for a tooth," or in a more general sense, other countervailing measures being adopted by way of retaliation.
>
> 4. The law of retaliation in war has its limits, as well as criminal law in time of peace, the object of both being, not revenge, but prevention; not primarily the punishment of the individual offender, but to deter others from a like crime.
>
> 5. As in time of peace we generally punish only the guilty party, so in time of war we generally retaliate only on the individual offender. But there are exceptions in both cases. Thus, all the members of a town or corporation are held responsible in damages for the neglect or carelessness of their

---

[55] See Edward E. Leslie, *The Devil Knows How To Ride: The True Story of William Clarke Quantrill and His Confederate Raiders*, Random House, New York, 1996, pp. 193–244. See also Carnahan, 2010, pp. 63–66, *supra* note 52; Neff, 2010, p. 93, see *supra* note 15.

[56] Lieber Code, Art. 15, see *supra* note 13.

agents; so, in war, a city, an army, or an entire community, is sometimes punished for the illegal acts of its rulers or individual members.

6. Retaliation is limited in extent by the same rule which limits punishment in all civilized governments and among all Christian people – *it must never degenerate into savage or barbarous cruelty.*[57]

Halleck's letter, the most comprehensive legal analysis of retaliation from this period, is noteworthy for three reasons. First, according to Halleck, retaliation in war was the mirror image of criminal justice in peace. Second, he acknowledged that, while individual punishment should be the norm, collective responsibility for violations of the laws of war was fully justified. Third, Halleck, like Lieber before him, recognised that there were limits to the lawfulness of retaliation.[58] Post-Civil War scholars and diplomats would pick up on these three fundamental insights to develop the idea of punishment for violations of law of war norms.

9.2.3. Institutional Justice: Military Commissions

Halleck's juxtaposition of retaliation as a wartime measure and criminal law as a peacetime measure could be read to imply that no judicial sanction was available for violations of the laws of war. That, however, would be misleading. Prosecutions of offences committed in war were recognised as a legitimate enforcement method in the United States and elsewhere in the mid-nineteenth century. There is a history of domestic military tribunals holding individuals accountable for wartime conduct, although contrary to the 'continuity thesis' supported by some scholars,[59] this chapter argues that the Civil War marked a significant qualitative and quantitative departure from earlier practice in this area.

According to Stephen C. Neff: "Of all wars in recorded history, none equals – or even comes close to equalling – the Civil War in the role played by law [...] [it] was unique in that a remarkably large proportion of the legal issues and disputes that arose were actually litigated and decided in the courts".[60] This is partly true for violations of the laws of war

---

[57] Henry W. Halleck, "Retaliation in War", in *American Journal of International Law*, 1912, vol. 6, no. 1, p. 110.

[58] Lieber Code, Art. 28, see *supra* note 13.

[59] On the 'continuity' thesis, see *supra* fn. 5 and 6.

[60] Neff, 2010, p. 1, see *supra* note 15.

committed during the Civil War. Though retaliation remained the primary method of enforcement, American military tribunals meted out punishment on a significant scale, with estimates ranging from 3,000 to over 4,000 trials by military commission, some grounded directly in the international laws and customs of war.[61] Further military trials were administered by courts martial for violations of domestic military law (yet more trials probably took place in Southern territory).[62]

The Lieber Code made two important and lasting contributions to the administration of military justice in the United States. First, it appears to have introduced the idea that combatants incurred criminal responsibility for violations originating directly in the (international) laws and customs of war. Second, the Code institutionalised the criminal repression of such violations through military commissions. The legal framework applicable to military trials can be found in Article 13:

> Military jurisdiction is of two kinds: First, that which is conferred and defined by statute; second, that which is derived from the common law of war. Military offenses under the statute law must be tried in the manner therein directed; *but military offenses which do not come within the statute must be tried and punished under the common law of war*. The character of the courts which exercise these jurisdictions depends upon the local laws of each particular country.
>
> In the armies of the United States the first is exercised by courts-martial, while cases which do not come within the "Rules and Articles of War," or the jurisdiction conferred by statute on courts-martial, are *tried by military commissions*.[63]

---

[61] See Mark E. Neely, *The Fate of Liberty: Abraham Lincoln and Civil Liberties*, Oxford University Press, New York, 1991, pp. 160–79; see also David W. Glazier, "Precedents Lost: The Neglected History of the Military Commission", in *Virginia Journal of International Law*, 2005, vol. 46, no. 1, pp. 7–8, 40. But see also John Fabian Witt, *Lincoln's Code: The Laws of War in American History*, Free Press, New York, 2012, p. 267, where Witt suggests there were only around 1,000 trials of violations of the laws of war during the Civil War.

[62] There is still very little research into how the Confederate justice system operated. See generally William R. Robinson, *Justice in Grey: A History of the Judicial System of the Confederate States of America*, Harvard University Press, Cambridge, MA, 1941. See also Segesser, 2010, p. 76, *supra* note 8, regarding lack of data on pre-Civil War conflicts.

[63] Lieber Code, Art. 13, *supra* note 13, emphasis added. In this chapter, the term 'common law of war' is treated as synonymous with 'international law of war'.

The United States inherited a bifurcated system of military justice from Britain, where two types of institutions had tried offences committed in armed conflict. Courts martial, responsible for adjudicating military offences as defined by statutory law, were themselves creatures of statute (during the Civil War court-martial jurisdiction was governed by the 1806 Articles of War). By contrast, military commissions owed their existence and their jurisdiction to the more amorphous customary international law of war (supplemented, where applicable, by statutory law or the Constitution).[64] Writing after the Civil War, William Winthrop explained the difference in these terms:

> MILITARY LAW PROPER or, that law, almost wholly enacted or written, by which the Army is governed at all times, in peace as well as in war. [...] By the term LAW OF WAR is intended that branch of International Law which prescribes the rights and obligations of belligerents, or more broadly those principles and usages which, in time of war, define the status and relations not only of enemies [...] but also of persons under military government or martial law [...] and which authorizes their trial and punishment when offenders. Unlike Military Law Proper, *the Law of War in this country is not a formal written code, but consists mainly of general rules derived from International Law, supplemented by acts and orders of the military power and a few legislative provisions. In general it is quite independent of the ordinary law.*[65]

As a result, military commissions had residual jurisdiction over those offenses that fell outside the scope of court-martial jurisdiction. This is significant because the law and practice of Union military commissions shed light on the nature and scope of the international law of war in the nineteenth century, in particular what norms governed violations of the laws of war and criminal enforcement. Translated into modern legal terms, the Code reflected contemporaneous ideas about what constituted a war crime giving rise to individual criminal responsibility under international law.[66]

---

[64] Glazier, 2005, pp. 6–10, see *supra* note 61.

[65] William Winthrop, *Military Law and Precedents*, 2nd ed., Government Printing Office, Washington, DC, 1896, p. 1203, emphasis added.

[66] It should be noted that, though there is considerable disagreement as to the scope and nature of the 'common law of war' in US doctrine and case law, these disputes reflect *subsequent* developments in US military law and practice. From a historical perspective, there is

Since 1806 courts martial had jurisdiction over ordinary military offences, such as knowingly harbouring the enemy or espionage.[67] By contrast, the jurisdiction of military commissions remained nebulous at the outset of the Civil War. Rejecting pre-Civil War precedent from the Mexican-American War (1846–1848), Lieber endowed the military commission with personal and subject matter jurisdiction over "violations of the laws of war".[68] In doing so, the Code endorsed the military practice of several border states, where military commissions had assumed wide powers to try Confederate sympathisers in the first years of the conflict. In 1861 Halleck issued a military order in Missouri that empowered military commissions to try "persons charged with aiding and assisting the enemy, the destruction of bridges, roads and buildings, and the taking of public or private property for hostile purposes".[69] In September 1862 Lincoln ordered that "during the existing insurrection and as a necessary measure for supressing the same, all Rebels and Insurgents, their aiders and abettors [...] shall be subject to martial law and liable to trial and punishment by Courts Martial or Military Commission".[70]

Notwithstanding the troubled legacy of military commissions,[71] the Code's more momentous innovation appeared to be that "military offenses which do not come within the statute must be tried and punished under

---

little doubt Lieber and Winthrop equated the term with international law (the law of war among nations). For current controversies before military commissions in Guantánamo, see generally Jonathan Hafetz, "What's in a Name? – Military Commissions and Criminal Liability under a U.S. Common Law of War", in *Opinio Juris*, 12 September 2013 and Jens David Ohlin, "What is the Common Law of War?", in *Opinio Juris*, 28 July 2014. See also Stephen I. Vladeck,

ourts and Article III", in *Georgetown Law Journal*, 2015, vol. 103, pp. 933–1001.

[67] Articles of War 1806, arts. 56 and 57, reprinted in Winthrop, 1896, pp. 1509–22, see *supra* note 65.

[68] Established for the first time during the Mexican-American War of 1846–1848, military commissions tried American soldiers and enemy civilians for ordinary crimes over which courts martial and local courts lacked jurisdiction. By contrast, it was the Councils of War that were responsible for the residual category of violations of the laws of war in the Mexican-American War. However, Councils of War were subsequently abandoned as an institutional form of military criminal justice. See Glazier, 2005, pp. 31–40, *supra* note 61.

[69] General Order No. 13, Department of Missouri, 4 December 1861.

[70] *War of the Rebellion*, vol. 3, part 2, p. 587, see *supra* note 22.

[71] See Gideon Hart, "Military Commissions and the Lieber Code: Toward a New Understanding of the Jurisdictional Foundations of Military Commissions", in *Military Law Review*, 2010, vol. 203, pp. 1–2.

the common law of war".[72] If taken at face value, this rule implied that the source of certain offences could be traced directly to international law.[73] It suggested that the common law of war – in contradistinction to domestic statutes (that is, courts-martial jurisdiction) – established the criminal responsibility of individuals who violated its norms. Thus, at first sight, the Code's regulation of military commission jurisdiction seems to be a precursor to the modern idea of individual criminal responsibility, under international law, for war crimes.

Tempting though it is, such a conclusion would be anachronistic. Upon closer scrutiny, Lieber's regulation of criminal sanctions is fragmentary and contradictory: What was the nature and scope of these offences grounded in the common law of war? What distinguished them from statutory offences? Was there a norm of individual criminal responsibility grounded directly in international law? The Code provides no answers to these questions, which are critical for determining the nature and scope of war crimes law.

In reality, while the Code criminalised a wide range of offences, various provisions mixed and conflated "ordinary" military crimes with "offenses under the common law of war".[74] Under Article 58, re-enslavement was a "crime under the law of nations", for which death was mandatory. Article 38 referred to a "serious breach of the law of war", while Article 114 classified the abuse of a flag of truce as an "especially heinous offense".[75] Article 47 appeared to establish *in fine* a distinction between "crimes punishable by all penal codes" and other crimes (grounded, presumably, in international law). Elsewhere, the Code proscribed acts that did not amount to crimes, leaving unanswered the question of what constituted the "common law of war".[76] Most importantly, while the Code established a few absolute prohibitions against violations of the laws of war, such as the use of torture, perfidy, poison or outlawry,

---

[72] Lieber Code, Art. 13, see *supra* note 13.

[73] A common misperception is that the Code codified the law of war applicable to non-international armed conflict, on the assumption that the American Civil War was an internal conflict. In fact, the Code's rules almost all applied to international armed conflict (except Arts. 149–57, which were added against Lieber's wishes). Likewise, in line with Art. 13, the rules regarding law of war violations, the 'common law of war', were grounded in international (not domestic) law. See Labuda, 2015, *supra* note 11.

[74] Lieber Code, arts. 44, 47, see *supra* note 13.

[75] *Ibid.*, Art. 38.

[76] *Ibid.*, Art. 77.

such acts did not entail any specific criminal sanction.[77] On the contrary, the Code explicitly endorsed retaliation for some of these more serious offences, suggesting retaliation – not trial – was the preferred method of deterrence and punishment.[78]

Focusing on the pure text of the Code, some scholars overinterpret the significance of its criminal provisions. For instance, Silja Vöneky argues that the Code should be read as establishing the principle of individual criminal responsibility under international law, with a concomitant duty of states to prosecute offenders for violations of the laws of war.[79] The International Committee of the Red Cross includes the Code among its examples of state practice regarding individual criminal responsibility (although it cites different provisions than Vöneky).[80]

But none of these claims stands up to closer scrutiny of the historical record. Reflecting the hurried manner in which the Code was prepared, the legal framework applicable to military trials, and criminal sanctions specifically, remains incomplete and inconclusive. More importantly, military practice does not substantiate the more ambitious interpretations of Lieber's ideas. On the contrary, the exercise of jurisdiction by military commissions during the Civil War demonstrates the narrow role of criminal trials in the mid-nineteenth century.

Military commissions were used first and foremost to try violations of the laws of war committed by civilians. According to Mark Neely, the military commission "amounted to little more than courts-martial for civilians".[81] With courts-martial jurisdiction reserved for Union troops, mil-

---

[77] The Code included several general rules on punishment. See *ibid.*, Arts. 11, 44, 47. For instance, according to Art. 11(3) offences "shall be severely punished, and especially so if committed by officers". But see also Art. 16, 66, 71 and 148. Silja Vöneky, "Der Lieber's Code und die Wurzeln des modernen Kriegsvölkerrechts", in *Zeitschrift für ausländisches öffentliches Recht und Völkerrecht*, 2002, vol. 62, pp. 445–49.

[78] In *ibid.*, Art. 44, the Code also clarified that a trial was not always required. If caught disobeying a superior's order "a soldier, officer or private [...] may be lawfully killed on the spot by such superior". But see Art. 12, which suggests that trials should be conducted "whenever feasible".

[79] See Vöneky, 2002, pp. 445–54, *supra* note 77, where the author analyses international agreements 1880 and 1907 and applies their rules retroactively to the American Civil War.

[80] International Committee of the Red Cross, Rules of Customary International Humanitarian Law, Practice relating to Rule 151: Individual Responsibility, available at: https://www.icrc.org/customary-ihl/eng/docs/v2_cha_chapter43_rule151.

[81] Neely, 1991, p. 162, see *supra* note 61.

itary commissions operated in areas under martial law, where they tried Confederate sympathisers. Crucially, they appear not to have tried Confederate soldiers.[82] Thus, the military commission's *raison d'être* was to sanction disloyal conduct committed by opponents of the Union. In the vast majority of cases, their only offence was being a 'guerrilla', rather than any specific act against the laws of war. In other words, the commissions tried out-of-uniform Confederates for supporting the Southern war effort. This understanding of what amounted to a violation of the laws and customs of war is quite different from modern international humanitarian law and international criminal law, which explicitly reject status-based criminalisation of participation in hostilities as a war crime (or other violation of the law of war).[83]

This point is illustrated by the case law of military commissions. As reported by Mark Neely, one Samuel Brytan was accused of

> violating the law of war by belonging to a guerrilla band in Newton Country, that he had aided the band to rob a man [...] and that he had shot at a loyal citizen. When the commission asked for a statement from the defendant after the testimony, he said only "I am a soldier in the Southern army".[84]

As in many other trials, the military commission rejected Brytan's defence and sentenced him to hard labour. The transcript shows that the commission's inquiry stopped at whether the defendant could lawfully wage war, rather than the distinct question of whether his conduct violated any specific norms. As explained by Gideon Hart, "the commissions provided Union authorities a means of targeting guerrillas and other insurgents, who could not be easily countered with traditional armies. In these trials, the charge 'Violations of the Laws of War' was liberally used to capture a wide variety of violent offenses".[85]

---

[82] I have found only one mention of a military commission that tried a Confederate soldier, and even then he was convicted of being a "military insurgent" recruiting inside Union lines. See Hart, 2010, p. 49, *supra* note 71.

[83] Nils Melzer, *Interpretive Guidance on the Notion of Direct Participation in Hostilities under International Humanitarian Law*, International Committee of the Red Cross, Geneva, 2009, pp. 83–84. See also David J.R. Frakt, "Direct Participation in Hostilities as a War Crime: America's Failed Efforts to Change the Law of War", in *Valparaiso University Law Review*, 2012, vol. 46, no. 3, pp. 729–64.

[84] Neely, 1991, p. 169, see *supra* note 61.

[85] Hart, 2010, p. 16, see *supra* note 71.

A flexible term rather than a fixed legal category, Lieber and his contemporaries did not use "violations of the laws of war" to define a regime of criminal responsibility. Unlike the Geneva Conventions' grave breaches regime, or the International Criminal Court ('ICC') Statute's war crimes provisions, trials did not perform the same deterrent and retributive function they do in modern international law. This explains why there are no reported cases of Lincoln threatening Confederates with trial for violating the laws of war (likewise, Davis never used this threat against Northerners).[86] Unlike the threat of retaliation, which, as we have seen, was publicly brandished to influence the enemy's conduct, trials for violations of the laws of war were not part of the legal vocabulary in the 1860s.[87] A far better and time-tested method of deterring and sanctioning violations already existed. Though frequently overlooked by legal scholars, for whom war crimes trials seem self-evident, retaliation is critical to understanding the nature of wartime justice in the nineteenth century.[88]

That being said, even if the Lieber Code did not give criminal trials a leading role in sanctioning law of war violations, it foreshadowed key developments in international humanitarian law and international criminal law. Contrary to suggestions that the Code was a legal document with no impact on the conduct of hostilities, there is little doubt that Lieber's ideas influenced the administration of military justice.[89] Numerous military commission records cite the Code, and there is evidence that military commanders consulted Lieber on some aspects of military law and juris-

---

[86] Trials of law of war violations must be distinguished from treason trials. The Union government regularly threatened to try Southerners for treason. However, treason is a domestic offence, that is, it is a crime under the domestic law of a state, rather than an international legal norm entailing criminal sanction.

[87] This is illustrated by what happened after the Civil War. Allegations of a Confederate conspiracy in Lincoln's assassination prompted calls for trials of Southern violations of the laws of war. Though a few trials were eventually held, most notably against Lincoln's assassins and Henry Wirz (the commander of an infamous prisoner of war camp in the South) the project never gained much traction. Amnesty remained the time-tested solution to questions of post-conflict accountability. According to legal historian John Witt: "in 1865 and 1866, prosecuting high Confederate officials for crimes against black Union soldiers was so politically implausible that it did not even generate substantial internal debate"; see Witt, 2012, pp. 320 and 285–87, *supra* note 61.

[88] In the same sense, see *ibid.*, pp. 128–29; and Mark Lewis, *The Birth of the New Justice: The Internationalization of Crime and Punishment, 1919–1950*, Oxford University Press, Oxford, 2014, pp. 14–18.

[89] On the impact of the Lieber Code, see Labuda, 2015, paras. 23–25, *supra* note 11.

diction.[90] Most importantly, the mere fact that criminal trials occurred was already a fundamental development in international humanitarian law and a precursor to the development of modern international criminal law. In giving military commissions the power to adjudicate violations of the laws of war, Lieber broke with an earlier tradition in international law that left little space for criminal trials.[91] It would take 50 more years of discussion at the international level to generate further interest in criminal enforcement regarding law of war of violations.

9.3. From Collective Punishment to Individual Criminal Responsibility

9.3.1. The International Debate from the Civil War to the First World War

This section traces the evolution of legal thought and international norms on how to sanction violations of the laws and customs of war in the second half of the nineteenth century. Focusing on international agreements, domestic military codes and the writings of prominent international lawyers, it argues that between the American Civil War and the First World War a clear shift occurred in the international community's understanding of retaliation and criminal sanctions. While retaliation gradually lost legitimacy, military trials of law of war violations steadily gained importance, with a rich debate ensuing as to how accountability can best be achieved.

Although a more detailed study of domestic practice in various conflicts is beyond the scope of this chapter, the key military engagements should be briefly noted at the outset. The 1870–1871 Franco-Prussian War catalysed the first sustained debate on the European continent regarding accountability and reprisals (as retaliation was known in the Francophone world) at the 1874 Brussels Conference. The war between Russia and Turkey in 1877–1878 provided further material for discussion at the Institut de droit international's 1880 meeting. After a brief lull, the debate resumed in the mid-1890s, with the the two Hague Conferences (1899 and

---

[90] Hart, 2010, p. 41–49, see *supra* note 71; Neely, 1991, pp. 160, 171, see *supra* note 61.

[91] Many pre-Civil War treatises on international law had little or nothing to say about criminal trials for violations of the laws and customs of war. This meant that *de facto* the issue of enforcement was understood as limited to retaliation. See, for example, Wheaton, 1836, pp. 249–251, 368–69, *supra* note 25; Georg Frederic de Martens, *Précis du droit des gens moderne de l'Europe fondé sur les traités et l'usage*, 3rd ed., Dieterich, Göttingen, 1821, paras. 253–59.

1907) taking place amid the Philippine-American War of 1899–1902, the Second Boer War of 1899–1902 and the Russo-Japanese War of 1904–1905.[92] On the eve of the First World War (1914), the vexed question of how to sanction violations of the laws and customs of war differed markedly from the status quo Lieber left behind at the end of the American Civil War (1865).

9.3.2. From Retaliation and Reprisals to Criminal Enforcement

"[A] harbinger of modern war in its mass destructive scale", there is little doubt that the American Civil War had a transformative impact on the law applicable to armed conflict.[93] Three significant developments characterise the international debate in the post-Civil War period: first, a reluctance to codify and thereby legitimise the use of retaliation; second, the imposition of additional conditions on the lawful exercise of retaliation; third, and most significantly, the gradual recognition that retaliation should not be a primary but rather a subsidiary means of enforcing the law of war.

Convened by the Russian Czar and attended by 15 countries, the 1874 Brussels Conference aimed to produce an international agreement on the laws and customs of war.[94] Under the title "general principles", a draft text of the convention submitted by the Russian delegation recognised reprisals as the primary method of enforcement. Article 5 authorised reprisals "in case the enemy fails to observe the laws and customs of war, as defined in this Convention".[95] In comparison to the Lieber Code, the use of reprisals was subject to several stringent conditions: they should be resorted to only in extreme cases (necessity), authorised by military commanders and be proportional to the original law of war violation.

An early draft allowed a policy of no quarter by way of reprisal, but the delegations attending the conference quickly rejected this proposal.[96]

---

[92] See generally Segesser, 2010, pp. 76–142, *supra* note 8. See also Lewis, 2014, pp. 14–26, *supra* note 88.
[93] Witt, 2012, p. 3, see *supra* note 61. See also Carnahan, 1998, *supra* note 17.
[94] The participants were all European (the United States did not attend). See Thomas Erskine Holland, *The Laws of War on Land (Written and Unwritten)*, Clarendon Press, Oxford, 1908, appendix.
[95] Original Draft, para. 5, in Brussels Conference, *Collection of Documents from 1874 Conference*, Les Frères van Cleef, The Hague, 1890, p. 2. See also para. 3, which touches on the issue of punishment ('Brussels Conference'). All translations by the author.
[96] *Ibid.*, para. 11 (C) (struck out subsequently).

Arguing that "in general, the law of humanity requires that an innocent person should not suffer for the guilty", this seemed to be an early acknowledgement of the principle of individual responsibility for violations of the laws and customs of war.[97] During a confused debate on the Russian draft, the Belgian delegation objected that any recognition of reprisals in the Convention would legitimate "the odious practice".[98] Despite concerns that eliminating the provision would relegate reprisals to an ill-defined grey area of the law, the delegations ended up rejecting it. Significantly, the discussion of reprisals also broached the topic of criminal sanctions for law of war violations for the first time.[99]

Criminal enforcement of the law of war would resurface later in the conference. Lamenting the discrepancies between the military codes of various countries, especially the differences in applicable punishments, General Eugène Arnaudeau of France suggested a "penal code for crimes, violations and contraventions of the laws and customs of war". As an alternative, he proposed to harmonise domestic military laws. However, most delegations proved reluctant to even discuss the topic. For instance, the Dutch delegation, arguing it had no instructions from its government, declined to support an international codification (or transnational harmonisation) and insisted that only the French be associated with the initiative in the conference minutes.[100] A "*simple voeu*", as Arnaudeau described it afterward, trials of law of war violations soon became an unavoidable element of the international legal debate.[101]

Anticipating its importance, Gustave Moynier had launched a discussion among international lawyers on criminal enforcement two years earlier (see also below).[102] In 1875 the Institut de droit international, a

---

[97] *Ibid.*, § 4. Des represailles [Reprisals], para. 69, text proposed 7 August 1874, p. 221.

[98] *Ibid.*, p. 152.

[99] *Ibid.*, Session, 20 August 1874, pp. 152–53. See generally Kalshoven, 1971, pp. 46–51, *supra* note 26.

[100] *Ibid.*, Session, 26 August 1874, pp. 198–99.

[101] *Ibid.*, p. 199.

[102] Moynier presented his project in "Note sur la création d'une institution judiciaire internationale propre à prévenir et à réprimer les infractions à la Convention de Genève", in *Bulletin international des Sociétés de la Croix-Rouge*, 1872, vol. 3, no. 11, pp. 122–31, which spawned a discussion among leading figures of the Red Cross movement, including Gustave Rolin-Jaequemyns, John Westlake, Conrad von Holtzendorff as well as Francis Lieber. See generally Christopher Keith Hall, "The First Proposal for a Permanent International Criminal Court", in *International Review of the Red Cross*, 1998, vol. 322, pp. 57–74.

non-governmental research institute, of which Moynier was a founding member, created a special committee to examine the Declaration of Brussels. Among its stated aims was the adoption of a legal framework for reprisals and a "criminal law of war".[103]

Endorsed by the Institut de droit international at its Oxford meeting in 1880, the "Manuel des lois de la guerre sur terre" was more a handbook for soldiers than a legalistic convention.[104] Also known as the Oxford Manual, the text expressly affirmed the primacy of criminal enforcement and the subsidiarity of reprisals, clarifying that "offenders against the laws are liable to the punishments specified in the penal law".[105] The drafters conceded that, although "reprisals are an exception to the general rule of equity", in some situations "the criminal law is powerless" and then "no other recourse than a resort to reprisals remains".[106] The Manual sought to limit the use of reprisals through a strict legal framework. Reprisals "must in all cases take account of the laws of humanity and morality" and be "absolutely necessary", and they are "formally prohibited in case the injury complained of has been repaired".[107] Likewise, "their nature and scope shall never exceed the measure of the infraction of the laws of war committed by the enemy", and "[t]hey can only be resorted with the authorisation of the commander-in-chief".[108]

Though vague on how criminal enforcement should take place, the Oxford Manual marked an important step forward in the development of international criminal law. By affirming the centrality of (military) trials for law of war violations, it reversed the presumption that reprisals best served this purpose. Moreover, this change occurred in the space of just a

---

[103] Institut de Droit International, Resolution on Brussels Declaration, Art. 11(1): "Nous sommes très décidément d'avis que plus le droit des représailles est terrible, plus il convient de le réglementer". See Annuaire de l'Institut de Droit International, Pedone, Paris, 1875, pp. 509–10 ('IDI Resolution').

[104] See Kalshoven, 1971, p. 51–55, *supra* note 26.

[105] Institut de Droit International, "Manuel des lois de la guerre sur terre" [Manual on the Laws of War on Land], 9 September 1880, Art. 84, in *Annuaire de l'Institut de Droit International*, 1881–1882, vol. 5, pp. 149–74 ('Laws of War on Land'). The text is translated in Spaight, 1911, p. 464, see *supra* note 51.

[106] Laws of War on Land, Art. 84, see *supra* note 105.

[107] *Ibid.*, Arts. 85 and 86.

[108] *Ibid.*

few years, given that the draft text of the Brussels Conference still listed reprisals as the primary method.[109]

This shift can also be traced in the doctrine. William Winthrop, a leading authority on American military law after the Civil War, illustrated the gradual evolution of legal ideas in this area. While the first edition of his monumental study *Military Law* still maintained that retaliation was "the usual remedy" for violations of the laws of war,[110] the second edition cited the Oxford Manual for the proposition that retaliation should be a subsidiary means of enforcement:

> In the event of violations of any of the laws of war above set forth, the offenders, as a matter both of justice and policy, should be brought to punishment if they can be reached. As it is expressed in the Manual of the Institute. [...] Offenders of this class have, with us, been brought to trial by MILI-TARY COMMISSION and punished with death or imprisonment. Where the offender cannot be reached [...] the only remedy of the belligerent against which, or against a citizen or citizens of which, the infraction of law has been injuriously committed, is by retaliation or reprisal.[111]

Reflecting the Francophone overtones of the international debate, Winthrop's second edition incorporated the Oxford Manual's concept of reprisals, but mistakenly assumed that they differed from retaliation.[112] Aside from the terminological confusion, which also appears in other Anglophone studies, the influence of the Institut de droit international's ideas is clear. Some authors endorsed the subsidiarity of reprisals, others gave them co-equal status with criminal enforcement, but the question *per se* – how should violations of the laws of war be sanctioned – could no longer be omitted from any discussion of the law of war.

Meanwhile, the lawfulness of reprisals as such continued to be debated in the late nineteenth century. The two Hague Conventions of 1899

---

[109] Also mentioned by Kalshoven, 1971, p. 53, see *supra* note 26.

[110] William Winthrop, *Military Law*, 1st ed., W.H. Morrison, Washington, DC, 1886, p. 10.

[111] Winthrop, 1896, p. 1241, see *supra* note 65.

[112] It is beyond the scope of this chapter to explore the conceptual differences between retaliation and reprisals in nineteenth-century doctrine. Generally speaking, the Gallic term 're-prisal' was synonymous with retaliation. See Geoffrey Best, *Humanity in Warfare: The Modern History of the International Law of Armed Conflicts*, Weidenfeld and Nicolson, London, 1980, p. 167. However, confusion in the literature persists to this day. See Neff, 2010, p. 286, fn. 36, *supra* note 15.

and 1907 left the issue shrouded in silence,[113] with only one provision addressing reprisals indirectly (the term reprisals as such was not used).[114] But treatises uniformly condemned reprisals. Ever longer lists of conditions were attached to their lawful use in order to limit their relevance. Key rules included: a) an emphasis on their law enforcement character,[115] b) allowed only for serious violations or offences,[116] c) requiring an investigation of the underlying violation,[117] d) a deliberation or precaution requirement, that is, that reprisals should not be used with undue haste,[118] e) a proportionality requirement, that is, reprisals should be similar in nature and extent to the underlying violation,[119] f) a necessity requirement,[120] g) authorised by a commanding or more senior officer,[121] and h) a prohibition of reprisals that would amount to barbarity or violate principles of humanity.[122]

Authors also explored whether specific instances of reprisal could be lawful. There was unanimity that barbarous practices could not be condoned, with some treatises listing serious examples such as enslave-

---

[113] See Kalshoven, 1971, p. 56–66, *supra* note 26. After meticulously analysing the *travaux preparatoires* from both Hague conferences, Kalshoven concluded there was no substantive discussion of reprisals.

[114] Convention IV, respecting the Laws and Customs of War on Land and its annex, The Hague, 18 October 1907, Art. 50. See Kalshoven, 1971, pp. 57–58, *supra* note 26.

[115] Johann Caspar Bluntschli, *Das moderne Kriegsrecht der civilisierten Staaten* [The Modern Law of War of Civilised Nations], C.H. Beck, Nordlingen, 1866, Art. 56 (*Repressalien* [Reprisals]). David Dudley Field, *Draft Outlines of an International Code*, Baker, Voorhis and Company, New York, 1872, para. 758. See also Laws of War on Land, Art. 85, *supra* note 105.

[116] Laws of War on Land, Art. 86, see *supra* note 105.

[117] Field, 1872, Art. 758, *supra* note 115; Brussels Conference, 1874, draft Art. 69, see *supra* note 95.

[118] Field, 1872, Art. 758, see *supra* note 115.

[119] Winthrop, 1896, p. 1244, see *supra* note 65; Brussels Conference, draft Art. 70, see *supra* note 95; IDI Resolution, Art. 9, see *supra* note 103; Laws of War on Land, Art. 86, see *supra* note 105; Percy Bordwell, *The Law of War between Belligerents: A History and Commentary*, Callaghan & Co., Chicago, 1908, p. 306.

[120] Field, 1872, Art. 758, see *supra* note 115; Winthrop, 1896, p. 1244, see *supra* note 65.

[121] Winthrop, 1896, p. 1244, see *supra* note 65; Brussels Conference, 1874, draft Art. 71, see *supra* note 95; IDI Resolution, Art. 9, see *supra* note 103; Laws of War on Land, Art 86, see *supra* note 105.

[122] Bluntschli, 1866, Art. 56, see *supra* note 115; Winthrop 1896, pp. 1243–44, see *supra* note 65.

ment, mutilation and unlawful weapons,[123] while others included more minor offences.[124] Disagreement persisted as to the lawfulness of retaliatory measures against non-combatants and prisoners of war,[125] with the majority of writers arguing against the former but allowing the latter.[126] Another recurrent theme was whether it ought to be permissible, and under what circumstances, to refuse quarter to surrendering troops; retaliation was usually viewed as an exceptional justification, but the issue remained undecided before the First World War.[127]

In developing the rules and prohibitions on reprisals, many authors referred to the Lieber Code as one of their sources of inspiration. Though Lieber's ideas were sometimes rejected, his influence on the doctrinal debate is not in doubt. By contrast, the Code's impact on codification attempts at the international level is less obvious. Although the first chairman of the 1874 Brussels Conference claimed that "the idea of a draft convention was inspired by what happened in the United States during the Civil War", no explicit references to the Code survive in the conference records.[128] It also appears the Code played a marginal, if any, role in the drafting of the Oxford Manual.[129]

---

[123] Field, 1872, para. 759, see *supra* note 115.

[124] *Ibid.*

[125] The 1929 Geneva Convention finally banned reprisals against prisoners of war. See Darcy, 2003, p. 157, *supra* note 26. The issue was also discussed in The Hague, see Kalshoven, 1971, p. 61, *supra* note 26.

[126] William Edward Hall, *A Treatise on International Law*, Clarendon Press, Oxford, 1880, part 3, ch. 2, para. 135; Field, 1872, Art. 815, see *supra* note 115; Winthrop 1886, p. 16 (*in fine*), see *supra* note 110; Winthrop 1896, pp. 1234, 1241–42, see *supra* note 65; Antoine Pillet, *Le droit de la guerre: conférences faites aux officiers de la garnison de Grenoble pendant l'année, 1891–1892*, Librairie Arthur Rousseau, Paris, 1892, pp. 275–99; Henry Bonfils, *Manuel de droit international public*, Librairie Arthur Rousseau, Paris, 1894, pp. 575–79; Franz von Holtzendorff, *Handbuch des Völkerrechts: auf Grundlage Europäischer Staatspraxis unter Mitwirkung*, Carl Habel, Berlin, 1889, pp. 80–83. See also Spaight, 1911, pp. 460–70, see *supra* note 51 and James Wilford Garner, *The German War Code: Contrasted with the War Manuals of the United States, Great Britain, and France*, Committee on Public Information, Washington, DC, 1918.

[127] See Field, 1872, Arts. 758–59, *supra* note 115. See also War Office, *Manual of Military Law*, War Office, London, 1894, Art. 31.

[128] Brussels Conference, pp. 23, 55, see *supra* note 95.

[129] Most of the Oxford Manual's provisions resembled the Russian draft proposal from the 1874 Brussels Conference. Only the last paragraph, emphasising humanity and morality in warfare, followed the humanitarian language embedded in the Lieber Code. See Kalshoven, 1971, pp. 52–54, *supra* note 26. This is hard to square with George B. Davis' claim at the time of the Second Hague Conference that "the Brussels code bears in every article a

Lieber's impact is most visible elsewhere. The Code served as a model for domestic military manuals in the Netherlands (1871), France (1877), Serbia (1879), Spain (1882), Portugal (1890) and Italy (1896).[130] Most manuals contained norms on reprisals that appear to reflect the evolving doctrinal debates taking place in the post-Civil War period.[131] For instance, according to the 1879/1881 British manual (known then as Army Law and Rules of Procedure):

> Retaliation is military vengeance. It takes place where an outrage committed on one side is avenged by the commission of a similar act on the other side. [...] Retaliation is the extreme right of war, and should only be resorted to in the last necessity.[132]

By contrast, the French manual for officers from 1877 (so just a few years later) included a more comprehensive chapter, stipulating that reprisals 1) need not be identical with the original violation, 2) were a subsidiary measure, 3) must be proportional, or "battle can quickly become barbaric", and 4) should respect the laws of humanity.[133]

In sum, post-Civil War trends regarding reprisals imply that the international community did not have a common view of the laws of war. On the one hand, the principle of humanity appears to play an increasingly important role. Starting in the 1870s, international lawyers denounced reprisals as a means of collective responsibility and collective punishment.[134] The Oxford Manual's recognition that reprisals were "an exception to the general rule of equity, that an innocent person ought not to suffer for the guilty"[135] was echoed in the writings of scholars such as Lassa

---

distinct impression that of the [Lieber Code]", and that it in turn influenced the 1907 Hague Convention as well; George B. Davis, *The Elements of International Law, with an Account of Its Origin, Sources and Historical Development*, 3rd ed., Harper, New York, 1907, pp. 22–23. Repeated by Cakmak, 2008, pp. 138–39, see *supra* note 6. Other authors make the same claim, but provide no evidence. See James Brown Scott, *The Hague Peace Conferences of 1899 and 1907*, vol. 1, Johns Hopkins University Press, Baltimore, 1909, pp. 525–26.

[130] Holland, 1908, p. 72, see *supra* note 94. See also Hogue, 2005, p. 58, see *supra* note 16.

[131] Spaight, 1911, p. 463, see *supra* note 51.

[132] War Office, 1894, Art. 31, see *supra* note 127.

[133] *Manuel de droit international à l'usage des officiers de l'armée de terre*, Librairie militaire de J. Dumaine, Paris, 1877, pp. 25–27.

[134] IDI Resolution, Art. 9, see *supra* note 103.

[135] Laws of War on Land, Art. 84, accompanying text, see *supra* note 105.

Oppenheim, who defined reprisals as "terrible means [...] directed against innocent enemy individuals, who must suffer for real or alleged offences for which they are not responsible".[136] On the other hand, this humanising sentiment was far from uniform. Diplomats and politicians failed to limit the use of reprisals at Brussels (1874) and The Hague (1899 and 1907). Reflecting the international community's failure to regulate reprisals, the 1902 Prussian military manual affirmed that the laws and customs of war should be viewed not as positive law but rather as a voluntary transnational pact restricting national egocentrism, in which "fear of reprisals" (*Furcht von Repressalien*) remained the ultimate authority.[137] The struggle to reconcile the dictates of humanity and the necessities of war would continue, with several generations of international lawyers labouring to complete the task of codification after the First World War.[138]

9.3.3. Criminal Enforcement, or the Primary Method of Sanction

Although no conflict in the second half of the nineteenth century produced as many prosecutions as the American Civil War, the debate at the international level continued against the backdrop of a growing number of domestic trials. As explained above, some authors and institutions went so far as to accept the primacy of criminal trials and the subsidiarity of reprisals. Nonetheless, several theoretical and practical questions as to the nature and scope of trials remained unresolved.

Five major legal questions emerged in the second half of the nineteenth century: first, what specific violations of the laws and customs of war could be sanctioned by a criminal tribunal; second, whether prosecuting violations was a right or a duty; third, whether and how criminal sanctions could be used to punish enemy violations; fourth, the nature and type of punishment for such violations; and fifth, whether it was possible to try soldiers who committed violations in furtherance of superior orders. In the background of all these contentious topics was the nascent question of whether some sort of international body could or should exercise jurisdiction over such violations.

---

[136] Lassa Oppenheim, *International Law: A Treatise*, vol. 2, Longmans, Green & Co., London, 1906, para. 247, p. 259. See also Bordwell, 1908, p. 305, *supra* note 119.

[137] Prussia, Grossen Generalstabe, *Kriegsbrauch im Landkriege*, Mitter und Sohn, Berlin, 1902, pp. 2–3, 16.

[138] See also Shane Darcy, *Collective Responsibility and Accountability under International Law*, Transnational Publishers, Ardsley, NY, 2007, pp. 131–37.

With domestic criminal prosecutions proliferating in the Franco-Prussian War, the Philippine-American War and the Boer War, many commentators began to seriously reflect on the scope of military tribunal jurisdiction. Domestic practice varied greatly from state to state, with some countries enacting domestic military codes and others resorting to ill-defined custom to try offenders. One problem appeared to stand out: What violations of the laws of war actually merited criminal sanction? Legal instruments, including international agreements and domestic military manuals, employed the vague notion of "violations of the laws and customs of war", but often left the term undefined.[139] Some commentators defined the term generally, and then provided long or short enumerations of violations.[140] Even then, examples of violations were usually given without explicit reference to criminal enforcement, so their instructive value for understanding the scope of criminal jurisdiction remains limited. Given that criminal enforcement was an emerging norm, it would be an anachronism to assume that all violations *ipso facto* established the criminal responsibility of individuals or the subject matter jurisdiction of tribunals.[141]

This question emerged forcefully after the Franco-Prussian War.[142] Though he proposed an "international judicial institution" to punish violators of the 1864 Geneva Convention, Moynier expressly declined to specify which violations should give rise to criminal responsibility before this body. Recognising the contentious nature of the question, he suggested a separate "international penal law" (*loi pénale internationale*) that would have to be negotiated and accepted by states.[143] Arnaudeau, who drew

---

[139] For instance, the Oxford Manual suggests that "offenders against the laws of war are liable to the punishments specified in the penal law". Laws of War on Land, Art. 86, see *supra* note 105.

[140] Field, 1872, Arts. 754 and 756, see *supra* note 115, though not in relation to criminal enforcement (Art. 719).

[141] It would be incorrect to assume that any violation of the laws and customs of war empowered a tribunal to exercise jurisdiction. This does not reflect nineteenth-century practice. Likewise, in modern international humanitarian law not all violations give rise to (international) criminal responsibility entailing a tribunal's jurisdiction. See Cassese, 2008, pp. 84–86, *supra* note 2.

[142] Lewis, 2014, pp. 16–19, see *supra* note 88.

[143] Moynier, 1872, Art. 5, see *supra* note 102. Many commentators declined to specify which violations gave rise to criminal enforcement. See, for example, Field, 1872, para. 719, *supra* note 115.

attention to the need to establish a common criminal code at the 1874 Brussels conference,[144] named several core violations he considered especially problematic: pillage (individual and collective), theft, inflicting injury on the wounded, parole violations by prisoners of war, espionage, fighting in neutral and allied territory, extension of hostilities beyond deadline and hold-ups (*attaque à main armée*).[145] In his treatise on international law, William E. Hall highlighted discrepancies in state practice regarding the types of violations sanctioned and penalties enforced by belligerents. Citing controversies from the Franco-Prussian War, he argued that trials could raise "no objection [...] so long as the belligerent confines himself to punishing breaches of universally acknowledged laws", such as poisoning wells, assassination, marauding, abuse of flags of truce and the use of weapons which cause unnecessary suffering.[146] However, for other acts "not universally thought to be illegitimate", argued Hall, belligerents should not impose their own views. The death penalty and other disgraceful punishments were expressly prohibited for such "non-universal" offences.[147]

While nineteenth-century authors mainly used the terms 'violations' or 'offences' against the laws and customs, various notions of 'crimes' also emerged.[148] George B. Davis used the term "crimes and offences against the laws of war" to describe espionage, guerrilla warfare, pillage and "other crimes of violence".[149] Winthrop's first edition created a distinction between "violations of the laws of war" and "crimes against the modern law of war". The first category encompassed illegitimate weapons or means, including poison,[150] stratagem and deception, the abuse of flags of truce or improper treatment of prisoners of war,[151] as well as

---

[144] Brussels Conference, see *supra* note 95.

[145] *Ibid.*, Session, 26 August 1874.

[146] Hall, 1880, para. 135, pp. 351–52, see *supra* note 126. See also William E. Hall, *A Treatise on International Law*, 4th ed., Clarendon Press, Oxford, 1895, para. 135, p. 431.

[147] *Ibid.*

[148] Lieber Code, see *supra* note 13.

[149] George B. Davis, *The Elements of International law, with an account of Its Origin, Sources and Historical Development*, 2nd ed., Harper and Brothers, New York, 1900, pp. 319–24. However, Davis conflated ordinary military crimes such as rape, burglary and murder with offences against the laws of war in the proper sense.

[150] Winthrop, 1886, vol. 2, p. 12, see *supra* note 110.

[151] *Ibid.*, pp. 14–16.

> selling to, buying from, or contacting with enemies, furnishing them with supplies, corresponding, mail carrying, passing the lines without authority […] [which] are violations of the laws of war, more or less grave in proportion as they render material aid and information to the enemy or attempt to do so, and […] are among the most frequent of the offences triable and punishable by military commission.[152]

By contrast, crimes against the modern law of war, were "forbidden by the usages of civilized nations" and included

> tak[ing] the lives of, or commit[ing] violence against, non-combatants and private individuals not in arms, including women and children and the sick, as also persons taken prisoners or surrendering. Soldiers committing such offences forfeit their right to be treated as belligerents and become liable to capital punishment as violators of the laws of war.[153]

In the narrow legal sense, the term 'war crime' appeared only in 1906.[154] Highlighting that "[w]riters on the Law of Nations have hitherto not systematically treated of the questions of War Crimes and their punishment",[155] Oppenheim argued that war crimes encompassed acts which were "crimes in the moral sense of the term" but also "others which, such as taking part in a levy *en masse* […] may be highly praiseworthy patriotic acts" and thus crimes "only in a technical legal sense".[156] His treatise established four categories of war crimes: 1) violations of recognised rules regarding warfare committed by members of the armed forces, 2) hostilities in arms committed by non-combatants, 3) espionage and 4) marauding.[157] War crimes, Oppenheim argued, could be punished by belligerents regardless of "the motive, the purpose, and the moral character of the respective act".[158] Oppenheim's catalogue of war crimes, with 20 acts falling into just the first category, marked the culmination of the nineteenth-century legal debate about which violations should give rise to military trials.

---

[152] *Ibid.*, p. 5.

[153] *Ibid.*, pp. 6, 10. But see also Winthrop, 1896, pp. 1222–24, *supra* note 65, where he provides an updated list of crimes, with references to international treaties.

[154] See Segesser, 2010, pp. 49–58, *supra* note 8.

[155] Oppenheim, 1906, para. 251, p. 263, fn. 2, see *supra* note 136.

[156] *Ibid.*, p. 252.

[157] *Ibid.*

[158] *Ibid.*

Notwithstanding his advanced legal framework, Oppenheim wavered on the separate question of how and when belligerents could exercise jurisdiction over war crimes. In a key passage he suggested that "[b]ecause every belligerent can and actually must in the interest of his own safety punish these acts, they are termed war crimes".[159] Though it could be interpreted as imposing a duty to prosecute, Oppenheim did not explore this issue further.[160] His hesitant stance reflected a split in the doctrine between proponents of a duty to try war criminals and the (more limited) view that states merely had a right to punish offenders.

The idea that belligerents *must* try violations of the laws of war emerged shortly after the American Civil War. Rejecting pre-Civil War doctrine, Johann Caspar Bluntschli argued in 1868 that "the military power is obliged [...] to punish offenders".[161] This was endorsed by David Dudley Field, who argued in 1872 that "the nation is bound, through its military or other tribunals, to punish those guilty of violating [the laws of war for the protection of enemies and neutrals]".[162] However, the majority of international opinion appeared to reject this expansive interpretation of what the law of war required. Winthrop and George B. Davis agreed that violators "may be punished" by belligerents, but devoted little space to the issue.[163] While the discussions at the 1874 Brussels Conference remained too general for this topic to surface, the 1880 Oxford Manual made it clear that there was no obligation to punish violators.[164] The Institut de droit international proceedings in 1894–1895 proposed a far-reaching harmonisation of domestic criminal norms, but failed to address this question.[165]

---

[159] *Ibid.*, para. 251, p. 264.

[160] The verb 'must' appears to refer to a state's 'own safety'. It is unlikely Oppenheim believed prosecution was an existing duty under international law.

[161] Bluntschli, 1866, para. 575, p. 321, see *supra* note 115.

[162] Field, 1872, para. 721, see *supra* note 115. It should be remembered that Field's ambitious project to codify the entirety of law was a restatement of existing law and a series of proposals for reform. See Preamble.

[163] George B. Davis, *Outlines of an International Law, with an Account of its Origins and Sources of Historical Development*, Harper and Brothers, New York, 1887, p. 319. Winthrop, 1886, p. 10 ("may punish"), see *supra* note 110.

[164] "[O]ffending parties should be punished, after a judicial hearing" stated the text, but even the hortatory 'should' (instead of 'shall') was tempered by the recognition that the criminal law was powerless in some instances. Laws of War on Land, see *supra* note 105.

[165] *Ibid.*

Writers also broached the (closely related) issue of who could lawfully initiate investigations. There appeared to be consensus at the international level that violations, if they were to be punished, could be tried only by a belligerent who had custody of the violator. Commentators agreed that trials were possible only if the state could secure control of the violator,[166] with some highlighting that retaliation remained the only available alternative.[167] The Oxford Manual stated that "the belligerent in whose hands they are" could exercise jurisdiction over violators, adding later that criminal law was "powerless" in the absence of the accused.[168] A separate resolution of the Institut de droit international, adopted in Oxford in 1880, affirmed that "[e]xtradition ought not to be applied to the desertion of military persons [...] nor to purely military offenses".[169] Even Field, who endorsed a duty to punish violations, restricted it to those enemy combatants who "fall into the power of [military] tribunals".[170]

This confirms that, while violations of the laws of war in the second half of the nineteenth century gave rise to some form of individual criminal responsibility, the nature and scope of this concept were very different from the modern iteration of the term.[171] Even the minority view, which posited a duty to prosecute, accepted that criminal responsibility did not create a separate right or duty to demand extradition of the suspect. Individual criminal responsibility remained an embryonic idea, whose enforcement was left to the discretion of belligerents who had custody of the violator. In the absence of prosecution, retaliation remained a legitimate sanction. Moreover, individual criminal responsibility in the nineteenth century did not create a separate right to a fair trial. Summary execution was expressly allowed for some violations.[172]

---

[166] Winthrop, 1886, p. 10 ("if captured"), see *supra* note 110; Hall, 1895, para. 135, see *supra* note 146; Winthrop 1896, p. 1241, see *supra* note 65; Oppenheim, 1906, para. 251, p. 264, see *supra* note 136.

[167] Winthrop 1896, p. 1241, see *supra* note 65.

[168] Laws of War on Land, part 3, Penal Sanction, and introductory text, and Art. 84 with comment. The Manual also added that reprisals were allowed if apprehending the violator proved impossible. See *supra* note 105.

[169] IDI Resolution, Art. 16, *supra* note 103.

[170] Field, 1872, Arts. 719, 810, see *supra* note 115,

[171] This issue is explored in greater depth in the conclusion.

[172] See Winthrop 1886, pp. 10–11, see *supra* note 110. However, the problematic nature of summary execution was recognised. See Brussels Conference, p. 47, *supra* note 95.

These qualitative differences in the scope of criminal responsibility are illustrated and amplified by the debate about the nature of criminal punishment. Violations of the laws of war were seen not as a *malum in se*, an evil meriting punishment in its own right, but rather as a temporary problem. Writing in 1880, Hall expressed the conventional view of his times: criminal prosecution, like retaliation, served a deterrent purpose in war. Violations generated the right to try violators, but that right extinguished at the end of hostilities, after which amnesty was compulsory. According to Hall, offenders should be "protected by the conclusion of peace from all civil or criminal processes to which they might be otherwise exposed in consequence of their conduct in the war [...] the immunity thus conceded is called an amnesty".[173] Likewise, Davis argued that "[a]s these offenses derive their criminal character from the existence of war, and only retain it during its continuance, it follows that they lose that quality at the close of war, when they cease to be punishable".[174]

Even if this remained the conventional view some writers proposed intriguing adjustments to this rule. Acknowledging that his proposal went beyond the law "in the books", Field argued that responsibility for illegal warfare, including "a criminal violation of the laws of war", must be decided in a "special compact, or decree".[175] Thus, while he rejected an automatic amnesty, belligerents could lawfully choose that option in a peace agreement. Oppenheim's views on the subject were complex. In a key passage, he argued that "[a]ll so-called war crimes which have not been punished before the conclusion of peace can now no longer be punished. Individuals who have committed such war crimes and are arrested for them must be liberated".[176] Yet he disagreed that a peace agreement extinguished *de jure* the possibility of enforcing convictions for violations that were already judicially ascertained. If states knew violators had to be freed after the war, he suggested, the prospect of a post-war amnesty would encourage use of the death penalty, which would then be promptly (and irreversibly) carried out.[177] So, even though Oppenheim believed a prior conviction could be enforced "beyond the duration of the war", this

---

[173] Hall, 1880, para. 201, p. 487, see *supra* note 126.

[174] Davis, 1900, p. 350, see *supra* note 149.

[175] Field, 1872, Art. 945, see *supra* note 115.

[176] Oppenheim, 1906, para 274, p. 287, see *supra* note 136. Oppenheim clarified in a footnote that amnesty should not apply to offenders serving a sentence (for a prior conviction) at the end of the war.

[177] *Ibid.*, para. 257, p. 270.

was guided by pragmatism rather than a belief in the inherent evil of, and the concomitant need to punish, war crimes.[178] It was simply meant to deter use of the death penalty.[179]

It should be remembered that these debates unfolded against the backdrop of conflicts, in which belligerents resorted to both reprisals and trials to sanction violations of the laws of war. As explained above, though some international opinion appeared to advocate greater restrictions on reprisals, efforts to reconcile the two methods produced surprising results. Recognising the subsidiarity of retaliation, Winthrop argued that trials could be used to sanction all violations of the laws of war, whereas retaliation was limited to crimes against the modern law of war.[180] Oppenheim, writing 20 years later, appeared to endorse the opposite solution. Violations of the laws of war gave rise to "reprisals between belligerents [which] are at once admissible for every and any act of illegitimate warfare",[181] whereas military tribunals could prosecute only war crimes (that is, the more serious category of violations in Oppenheim's catalogue).

The distinction had an important practical implication regarding the limits of individual criminal responsibility. According to Oppenheim, war crimes trials were not permitted "when members of the armed forces commit violations *by order* of their Government, [as] they are not war criminals and cannot be punished by the enemy". The enemy "can, however, resort to reprisals", he concluded.[182] Though surprising to the modern reader, the prominence of reprisals as an enforcement method echoed the views of most scholars in the late nineteenth century, who continued to view them as a legitimate enforcement mechanism, albeit subject to more stringent conditions.

---

[178] *Ibid.*

[179] Though it exceeds the scope of this chapter, it should be noted briefly that concerns about punishment, especially the death penalty, were another prominent and recurrent theme in the debate. Rolin-Jaequemyns suggested there was a need for greater uniformity in how states sanctioned violations arising from the 1864 Geneva Convention, but decried international penalisation as suggested by Moynier. See Moynier, 1872, *supra* note 102. Discrepancies between penalties enforced by various states also lay at the heart of Arnaudeau's intervention at the Brussels conference in 1874, see *supra* note 99.

[180] Winthrop, 1886, pp. 5–16, see *supra* note 110; Winthrop, 1896, p. 1211–44, see *supra* note 65. However, for major crimes, Winthrop suggested either retaliation or trial was allowed.

[181] Oppenheim, 1906, para. 248, p. 260, *supra* note 136.

[182] *Ibid.*, para. 253, p. 264.

Oppenheim's interpretations also reflected the majority view of the defence of 'superior orders' in this period. Hall explicitly endorsed the defence, and though Winthrop did not deal with it directly, his treatise was peppered with references to historical cases that recognised superior orders as a defence.[183] Even Field, whose draft international code proposed various progressive interpretations of the law, believed that "the orders of a superior are a justification to an inferior officer or to a soldier in disobeying [the laws of war]". Significantly, Field added that "[t]he superior is, however, responsible".[184] Other commentators acknowledged that superiors issuing unlawful orders could be held accountable, even if their subordinates carried out the illegal act.[185] Thus, although the idea of superior responsibility began to take shape well before 1914, it would take the tragic experience of the First World War to prompt a reconsideration of superior orders as a legal defence under the law of war.[186]

On the eve of the First World War, the law of war crimes – as it became known in the twentieth century – was in a state of flux. Reprisals retained their vitality, despite mounting critique and failed efforts to circumscribe their use in binding legal documents. A turn to individual criminal responsibility was readily discernable in the writings of international lawyers and international projects to regulate the laws of war. However, considerable disagreement still persisted as to the nature, scope and doctrines applicable to criminal trials of violations of the laws of war.

9.4. Conclusion

By analysing the evolution of the international legal debate from the American Civil War to the First World War, this chapter sheds light on an unexplored aspect of the legal history of war crimes and nuances some of the discipline's conventional narratives about its past. Its primary argument is that criminal trials and belligerent reprisals should be examined together as part of a broader turn toward individual accountability under international law. Described elsewhere as the process of "individualisa-

---

[183] Winthrop, 1886, pp. 18, 68, 125, 147, see *supra* note 110.

[184] Field, 1872, para. 723, see *supra* note 115. However, Field also suggested that orders that were "not necessarily and manifestly illegal" could be justified.

[185] *Ibid.*; Oppenheim, para. 253, p. 265, see *supra* note 136.

[186] But see War Department, *Rules of Land Warfare*, Government Printing Office, Washington, DC, 1914, § 366: "Commanders ordering the commission of such acts, or under whose authority they are committed by their troops, may be punished by the belligerent into whose hands they fall" (quoting Oppenheim).

tion of international law" and the "humanisation of international humanitarian law", the chapter argues that the origins of the law of war crimes lie not in antiquity or the Middle Ages but rather in the second half of the nineteenth century.[187] Moreover, contemporaneous attempts to define law of war violations and institutionalise military jurisdiction over individuals committing them can only be understood in the context of parallel efforts to curtail the ancient practice of retaliation. "The sternest feature of war", in Lieber's words, remained the primary enforcement method until international lawyers began chipping away at its foundations and proposing alternative solutions in the aftermath of the American Civil War.

The interplay between retaliation and criminal sanctions places the development of international law within a historical perspective. Only now do we fully appreciate the words of Ronnie Speer, a historian of the American Civil War, who argues:

> Ultimately, there were times that [the Civil War] was often reduced to a "war of retaliation" with "official" threats of retaliation met with 'official' threats of counter-retaliation. Unfortunately, it was seldom conducted against the guilty. Most often it was conducted against the innocent.[188]

Yet, if the unprecedented brutality of the Union and Confederacy's war effort signalled the heyday of retaliation, the turn to criminal trials began well before the Versailles Treaty, which is the conventional point of reference for international criminal lawyers. Often portrayed as the symbolic birth of international criminal law, the post-First World War efforts to prosecute the German emperor actually mark the culmination of a much longer legal process of delegitimising retaliation and encouraging criminal enforcement. These parallel developments are captured poignantly by Elisabeth Hull, a historian of military culture, who argues: "The First World War directly produced these developments in international law: instead of reprisals, trials for war criminals, including heads of state".[189]

Building on these key insights, the chapter draws attention to a few other aspects of the development of war crimes law. First, it re-evaluates

---

[187] See Meron, 1998, especially pp. 247–51, *supra* note 10.

[188] Speer, 2002, pp. xii–xiii, see *supra* note 27.

[189] Isabel V. Hull, *A Scrap of Paper: Breaking and Making International Law during the Great War*, Cornell University Press, Ithaca, NY, 2014, p. 329.

the significance of the American Civil War, and in particular the Lieber Code, for modern international humanitarian law and international criminal law. On the one hand, most histories of international criminal law do not even mention the Civil War or the late nineteenth century;[190] on the other, the Code's purportedly inspirational role in crafting the Hague Conventions and the Geneva Conventions leads some scholars to uncritically accept that it "is the foundation of the modern laws of war".[191] His myth-like status firmly entrenched,[192] few attempt to explore Lieber's ideas in their proper historical context or how his famous Code evolved after the Civil War.[193] The first part of this chapter explains that the Code's rules on retaliation should be viewed as part of the *status quo* of the law of war in the mid-nineteenth century, but its innovations – piecemeal and improvised though they were – regarding the criminal jurisdiction of military commissions launched a debate that international lawyers pursued in the second half of the nineteenth century.

Second, the chapter historicises some international criminal law notions, especially the scope and nature of war crimes law in the late nineteenth century. While the term 'war crime' was first used in the technical legal sense in Oppenheim's 1906 treatise, more significant is the fact that

---

[190] See Gary Jonathan Bass, *Stay the Hand of Vengeance: The Politics of War Crimes Tribunals*, Princeton University Press, Princeton, NJ, 2000; Remigiusz Bierzanek, "War Crimes: History and Definition", in Cherif Bassiouni, 1987, pp. 29–31, see *supra* note 2; Bierzanek, "War Crimes: History and Definition", in Cherif Bassiouni (ed.), *International Criminal Law*, vol. 3: *Enforcement*, 2nd ed., Transnational Publishers, Ardsley, 1999, pp. 87–89; Cherif Bassiouni, "International Criminal Justice in Historical Perspective", in Cherif Bassiouni (ed.), *International Criminal Law*, vol. 3: *Enforcement*, 3rd ed., Martinus Nijhoff, Leiden, 2009, p. 31; Michael Wahid Hanna, "An Historical Overview of National Prosecutions for International Crimes", in Bassiouni, 2009, pp. 297–28.

[191] See Christopher Greenwood, "Historical Development and Legal Basis", in Dieter Fleck (ed.), *The Handbook of Humanitarian Law in Armed Conflicts*, Oxford University Press, Oxford, 1995, p. 18; Richard Shelly Hartigan, "Introduction: Francis Lieber and the Law of War", in Richard Shelly Hartigan (ed.), *Lieber's Code and the Law of War*, Precedent, Chicago, 1983, p. 1; Baxter, 1963, see *supra* note 14; Hogue, 2005, pp. 51, 58, see *supra* note 16; Neff, 2010, pp. 57–58, see *supra* note 15. For a more neutral stance, see Hilaire McCoubrey, *International Humanitarian Law: Modern Developments in the Limitation of Warfare*, 2nd ed., Ashgate, Aldershot, 1998, p. 18.

[192] On mythology in the history of international (humanitarian) law, see Rotem Giladi, "The Enactment of Irony: Reflections on the Origins of the Martens Clause", in *European Journal of International Law*, 2014, vol. 25, no. 3, pp. 847–69, especially p. 869.

[193] But see Giladi, 2012, *supra* note 17; Röben, 2003, *supra* note 17; Carnahan, 1998, *supra* note 17. See also Richard Sallet, "On Francis Lieber and His Contribution to the Law of Nations Today", in Hans Werner Bracht (ed.), *Recht im Dienste der Menschenwürde: Festschrift für Herbert Kraus*, Holzner Verlag, Würzburg, 1964, pp. 279–305.

---

a rich debate about criminal sanctions for law of war violations developed well before the First World War. Understanding the origins of the shift from collective to individual responsibility explains why and how criminal trials became part of the international legal debate in the second half of the nineteenth century. The decline of retaliation and the rise of individual criminal responsibility are two sides of the same coin, although intense contestation persisted as to the merits of both enforcement methods well into the twentieth century.[194] Likewise, the normative scope of individual criminal responsibility remained disputed, with views ranging from international criminalisation to purely domestic repression (that is, trials as a purely state prerogative) that attached during war and extinguished with peace.

Lastly, this chapter is relevant for readers interested in the modern contours of international criminal justice. The establishment of the ICC has produced, in the words of one commentator, "the absorption of grave breaches into war crimes law".[195] Meanwhile, the evolving nature of the ICC's jurisdictional regime based on complementarity has created an expectation that national courts have a duty *tout court* to prosecute all international crimes.[196] It is impossible to appreciate the revolutionary nature of these phenomena without understanding the complex historical process by which such norms emerged. In 1968 Georg Schwarzenberger still argued:

> It corresponds probably most closely to the evolution of the laws of war to view jurisdiction over war criminals under international customary law as an individualised form of reprisals. [...] If it is understood that reprisal is the legal foundation of war crimes jurisdiction, three of the characteristic features of this jurisdiction become readily explicable: (1) Under international customary law, the exercise of jurisdiction over war criminals is optional. War crimes are not crimes under international law in the sense that international

---

[194] From being the norm for sanctioning violations, collective punishment in the guise of reprisals became a violation in its own right and the object of sanction. See generally Darcy, 2007, *supra* note 138.

[195] Marko Divac Öberg, "The Absorption of Grave Breaches into War Crimes Law", in *International Review of the Red Cross*, 2009, vol. 91, no. 873, pp. 163–83.

[196] See Sarah M.H. Nouwen, *Complementarity in the Line of Fire: The Catalysing Effect of the International Criminal Court in Uganda and Sudan*, Cambridge University Press, Cambridge, 2013, pp. 34–110.

> law postulates their punishment. It merely provides for an extraordinary type of jurisdiction which belligerents may exercise at their discretion.[197]

Although these words now seem completely outdated, they were written just 25 years before the establishment of the *ad hoc* tribunals and the resurgence of modern international criminal law.[198] Grounded in the history of the second half of the nineteenth century, Schwarzenberger's restatement of the law accurately reflects the post-Civil War debates about sanctioning violations of the laws of war, and explains why war crimes trials are actually grounded in a more distant notion of collective responsibility. In historicising the notion of war crimes, this chapter allows us to fully appreciate the qualitative leap that international criminal justice has taken in the last 20 years.

---

[197] Georg Schwarzenberger, International Law as Applied by International Courts and Tribunals, vol. 2: The Law of Armed Conflict, Stevens and Sons, London, 1968, pp. 453–54.

[198] See also Sunga, 1992, p. 19, *supra* note 6. Writing in the early 1990s, Sunga still quoted Schwarzenberger for the proposition that "[t]he legal foundation of war crimes jurisdiction in international customary law is the right of belligerents to enforce the laws of war [...] under international customary law, war crimes jurisdiction is optional. Belligerents are at liberty to impose any punishment considered appropriate".

10

The Grave Breaches Regime
of the 1949 Geneva Conventions:
Origins, Developments and Prospects

GUO Yang[*]

10.1. Introduction

Criminal punishment for violations of the laws of war dates to the earliest codifications of international humanitarian law, although treaty provisions before the 1949 Geneva Conventions made only little reference to individual criminal liability. The emergence of the 'grave breaches regime' in 1949 was a watershed in the development of international criminal law, although at the time there was a clear intention to contain it within the boundaries of international humanitarian law. It nonetheless represented a decisive step towards international justice following the drafting of the Charter of the International Military Tribunal ('IMT Charter') and the Nuremberg trials that took place in the aftermath of the Second World War.

The grave breaches regime consists of two categories of rules: substantial rules of definition of grave breaches prescribed by the four Geneva Conventions of 1949 and expanded by the Additional Protocol I of 1977; and procedural rules of their penal sanction provided by the Geneva

---

[*] **GUO Yang** is Senior Political Adviser at the Regional Delegation for East Asia of the International Committee of the Red Cross (ICRC). He holds a Ph.D. in international law from China University of Political Science and Law. He originally worked as a legal officer in the Treaty and Law Department of the Ministry of Foreign Affairs, People's Republic of China. In this role he served as a legal adviser of the Chinese Delegation to the *Ad Hoc* Committee on Deliberation of the Optional Protocol to the Convention against Torture, *Ad Hoc* Committee of the United Nations Convention against Transnational Organized Crime, as well as the 57th and 58th sessions of the General Assembly of the United Nations (Third Committee). The author wishes to express his deep appreciation to Richard Desgagné, Regional Legal Adviser of the ICRC Regional Delegation for East Asia for his support in preparing this chapter. The views expressed here are those of the author and do not necessarily reflect those of the ICRC.

Conventions.[1] The regime for the repression of grave breaches today is embedded within the system of modern international criminal law – constituting a bridge between international criminal law and international humanitarian law.

This chapter reviews the grave breaches regime from its inception in 1949, its development and expansion within the Geneva Convention system, as well as its development and enforcement through the jurisprudence of international courts and tribunals. It covers the sources and origins of the main elements that define the grave breaches regime – the definition of the grave breaches themselves, the basis and the modes of liability, the duty to enact legislation, the duty to prosecute or extradite and universal jurisdiction – and their place in the modern international justice system, in the light of the contemporary features of armed conflicts and demands of justice.

10.2. Origins and Historical Development of the Grave Breaches Regime

10.2.1. The Lieber Code

The codification of modern international humanitarian law started in the middle of the nineteenth century but the early treaties in this regard focused on states' obligations towards each other.[2] The punishment of individuals guilty of violations of the laws of war, as it was known at the time, remained in the domain of custom. However, penal sanctions for

---

[1]   Convention (I) for the Amelioration of the Condition of the Wounded and Sick in Armed Forces in the Field, Geneva 12 August 1949, Arts. 49–50 ('Geneva Convention I'); Convention (II) for the Amelioration of the Condition of the Wounded, Sick and Shipwrecked Members of Armed Forces at Sea, Geneva 12 August 1949, Arts. 50–51 ('Geneva Convention II'); Convention (III) Relative to the Treatment of Prisoners of War, Geneva, 12 August 1949, Arts. 129–30 ('Geneva Convention III'); Convention (IV) Relative to the Protection of Civilian Persons in Time of War, Geneva, 12 August 1949, Arts. 146–47 ('Geneva Convention IV'); and Protocol Additional to the Geneva Conventions of 12 August 1949, and Relating to the Protection of Victims of International Armed Conflicts (Protocol I), 8 June 1977 ('Additional Protocol I').

[2]   See the Declaration Respecting Maritime Law, Paris, 16 April 1856; and the Declaration Renouncing the Use, in Time of War, of Explosive Projectiles Under 400 Grammes Weight, Saint Petersburg, 29 November/11 December 1868, in Adam Roberts and Richard Guelff, *Documents on the Laws of War*, 3rd ed., Oxford University Press, Oxford, 2000, pp. 47–59. See also Convention for the Amelioration of the Condition of the Wounded in the Armies in the Field, Geneva, 22 August 1864.

violation of laws of war were established for civil war in a domestic code entitled General Orders No. 100, Instruction for the Government of Armies of the United States in the Field in 1863. This instruction, commonly known as the Lieber Code, was prepared by Francis Lieber with the approval of President Abraham Lincoln and was promulgated for the armies of the Northern states in the American Civil War.[3] The previous chapter by Patryk I. Labuda elaborates the background of the Lieber Code in greater detail.

The Lieber Code consisted of 157 articles and provided detailed rules on the entire range of land warfare, from the conduct of hostilities and the treatment of the civilians to the treatment of specific groups of persons such as prisoners of war, the wounded and so on.[4] Some of the problems addressed by the Lieber Code are still very much relevant to the situations of contemporary armed conflicts such as guerrilla warfare, the status of rebels, the applicability of the laws of war to internal armed conflicts and, what is especially important for the purpose of this chapter, the penal sanctions for violations of laws of war.[5] The Lieber Code gave a detailed elaboration on martial law in occupied territory. It not only prohibited action clearly contrary to the interest of the army such as desertion, treason and refusal to obey legitimate orders but also set up absolute prohibitions against cruelty (the infliction of suffering for the sake of suffering or for revenge), maiming or wounding except in fight, torture, murder, rape, use of poison, wanton violence, or wanton devastation of a district, and finally it forbade all crimes punishable by all penal codes (Articles 16, 22, 44, 47, 70, 71, 80). The violation of these prohibitions frequently demanded severe penal sanctions including the death penalty, which was to be guided by the principles of justice, honour and humanity (Article 4). In order to ensure the effectiveness of these rules, the Lieber Code granted military courts the competence to carry out martial law (Article 12). In short, the penal sanctions were highlighted by the Lieber Code for the sake of maintaining discipline and creating a perception of

---

[3] Frits Kalshoven and Liesbeth Zegveld, *Constraints on the Waging of War: An Introduction to International Humanitarian Law*, 4th ed., Cambridge University Press, Cambridge, 2011, pp. 8–9.

[4] Instructions for the Government of Armies of the United States in the Field, 24 April 1863 ('Lieber Code') (http://www.legal-tools.org/doc/842054/).

[5] Yves Sandoz, "The History of the Grave Breaches Regime", in *Journal of International Criminal Justice*, 2009, vol. 7, no. 4, p. 659.

integrity and legitimacy in the interests of the army.[6] Although an internal document for civil war, the Lieber Code served as a model and inspiration for later efforts in the codification of laws of war and can thus be considered a predecessor to the grave breaches regime.

10.2.2. From the Lieber Code to the First World War

As history indicates, new norms of international law on armed conflicts usually follow major humanitarian upheavals. The failure to apply the 1864 Geneva Convention during the 1870–71 Franco-Prussian War sparked efforts to strengthen the rules of international humanitarian law. In particular, Gustave Moynier, the president of the International Committee of the Red Cross, made two distinct suggestions: first, to unify the nature and scale of penalties for violations of the Geneva Convention; and second, of an even more revolutionary nature, to establish an international judicial organ to investigate breaches and decide questions of guilt. The international community accepted the first idea in the form of a model law developed by the Institut de droit international, but the second was rejected.[7]

The 1874 International Declaration concerning the Laws and Customs of War ('Brussels Declaration') aimed to set up comprehensive rules of armed conflicts modelled on the Lieber Code. But it did not enter into force because states were not prepared to accept it as a binding document. What is interesting for the purpose of the present chapter is that a delegate at the conference negotiating the Brussels Declaration suggested, as Monyier did, that states should co-ordinate their internal legislation to ensure the punishment of violations of laws of war, which, together with the model law, might be considered a first step towards a common definition of grave breaches. Due to the failure of the Brussels Declaration to become legally effective, the Institut de droit international adopted the Laws of War on Land in 1880, also known as the Oxford Manual.[8] This proposed the criminalisation of violations of the laws of war in states' do-

---

[6] *Ibid.*, p. 662.

[7] Jean S. Pictet (ed.), *Geneva Convention for the Amelioration of the Condition of the Wounded and Sick in Armed Forces in the Field: Commentary*, International Committee of the Red Cross, Geneva, 1952, pp. 353–55. See also Sandoz, 2009, pp. 662–63, *supra* note 5.

[8] Institut de Droit International, "Manuel des lois de la guerre sur terre" [Manual on the Laws of War on Land], 9 September 1880.

mestic law but without reference either to standardisation of rules of criminalisation or to international judicial mechanisms. No changes were made in this regard with the publication of the Manual on the Laws of Naval War in 1913.[9]

The Hague Conventions of 1899 and 1907 contained a lot of prohibitions but they did not require states to provide penal ordinances for the repression of violations. However, the revised 1906 Geneva Convention suggested that states adopt legislation necessary to prevent and punish the gravest violations of the Convention, namely pillage and the ill treatment of the wounded and sick of the armed forces, and abuse of the Red Cross flag or armlet. Several states did promulgate domestic law to punish those infractions. The injunction in the 1906 Geneva Convention not only responded to the original proposal made by Monyier and the delegates at Brussels Conference in co-ordinating states' domestic penal sanctions but also paved the way for a distinction between breaches and grave breaches by focusing on the gravest violations of the Convention.[10]

10.2.3. Commission on the Responsibility of the Authors of the War and on Enforcement of Penalties and the Versailles Treaty

The large scale of atrocities committed during the First World War compelled the Allies to establish a Commission on the Responsibility of the Authors of the War and on Enforcement of Penalties ('Commission on Responsibility') after the war. A significant portion of the Commission's work focused on the prosecution of war crimes and its precise mandate, in this regard, was to establish "the facts as to breaches of the laws and customs of war committed by the forces of the German Empire and their Allies on land, on sea, and in the air, in the course of the present [1914–1919] war".[11] Based on the factual information available to the Commission on Responsibility, a comprehensive list of violations of the laws and customs of war that merited criminal punishment was drafted, which addressed not only violations of "Geneva law, that is the rules protecting

---

9   Institut de Droit International, "Manuel des lois de la guerre maritime" [Manual of the Laws of Naval War], 9 August 1913. See also Sandoz, 2009, pp. 663–64, *supra* note 5.

10   Pictet, 1952, pp. 355–56, see *supra* note 7; Sandoz, 2009, p. 665, see *supra* note 5.

11   Carnegie Endowment for International Peace, *Violations of the Laws and Customs of War*. Report of Majority and Dissenting Reports of American and Japanese Members of the Commission on Responsibilities, Conference of Paris, 1919, Division of International Law, pamphlet no. 32.

victims of war such as civilians and prisoners of war, but also the Hague law, namely the rules on means and methods of warfare".[12] What is more interesting is that in its report the Commission on Responsibility made it clear that the official status of a person, even a head of state, did not exempt him from responsibility, and thus it developed the so-called concept of 'passive responsibility' for international criminal law, that is the failure to prevent violations when one is in position to do so, especially in a hierarchical chain of command. As for the question of jurisdiction over those war crimes, the Commission on Responsibility proposed trial of the criminals before national courts, with the exception of four categories of crimes to be placed before an *ad hoc* high tribunal. However, due to an objection by the American delegation, the penalties that materialised into Articles 228 and 229 of the Versailles Treaty did not set up international jurisdiction for violations of the laws and customs of war and the accused could only be brought before military tribunals of the related powers.[13] Due to the weakness of the Versailles Treaty, which was perceived as victor's justice, and thus brought no serious implementation of the penal articles from Germany and its allied states, the first major international effort to bring criminals to justice failed. But the United Nations War Crimes

---

[12] Sandoz, 2009, pp. 667–68, see *supra* note 5. The acts included in the list are: murder and massacres; systematic terrorism; putting a hostage to death; torture of civilians; deliberate starvation of civilians; rape; abduction of girls and women for the purpose of enforced prostitution; deportation of civilians; internment of civilians under inhuman conditions; forced labour of civilians in connection with military operations of the enemy; usurpation of sovereignty during military occupation; compulsory enlistment of soldiers among the inhabitants; attempt to denationalise the inhabitants of occupied territory; pillage; confiscation of property; exaction of illegitimate or of exorbitant contributions and requisitions; debasement of the currency, and issue of spurious currency; imposition of collective penalties; wanton devastation and destruction of property; deliberate bombardment of undefended places; wanton destruction of religious, charitable, educational and historic buildings and monuments; destruction of merchant ships and passenger vessels without warning and without provision for safety of passenger or crew; destruction of fishing boats and of relief ships; deliberate bombardment of hospitals; attack on and destruction of hospital ships; breach of other rules relating to the Red Cross; use of deleterious and asphyxiating gases; use of explosive or expanding bullets, and other inhuman appliances; direction to give no quarters; ill-treatment of wounded and prisoners of war; employment of prisoners of war on unauthorised works; misuse of flag of truce; and poisoning of wells.

[13] However, Article 227 of the Versailles Treaty required a special tribunal to be established for the trial of ex-Kaiser Wilhelm II for a supreme offence against international morality and the sanctity of treaties (crime of aggression), whose judges were appointed by the United States, Britain, France, Italy and Japan. Treaty of Peace between the Allied and Associated Powers and Germany, 28 June 1919, Arts. 227–28 ('Versailles Treaty').

Commission ('UNWCC') took Commission on Responsibility's list of crimes as a basis for its work after the Second World War, and the idea of an international criminal court and code continued to exercise influence in the quest for a means to curb international violence.[14] This supports the view that "there is little argument about the existence of war crimes under international law" from the time of the Commission on Responsibility onwards.[15]

10.2.4. The United Nations War Crimes Commission

In the Moscow Declaration of 1943 the Allies affirmed their determination to prosecute Nazis for war crimes and the UNWCC was established as a result. It consisted of three committees, the third of which focused on the legal concept of war crimes. The list of violations of laws and customs of war prepared by the Commission on Responsibility in 1919 was adopted as basis for the UNWCC's work.[16] The discussion within the UNWCC finally led to the codification of Article 6 of the IMT Charter, in which the war crimes were defined as

> violations of the laws or customs of war [...] shall include, but not be limited to, murder, ill-treatment or deportation to slave labor or for any other purpose of civilian population of or in occupied territory, murder or ill-treatment of prisoners of war or persons on the seas, killing of hostages, plunder of public or private property, wanton destruction of cities, towns or villages, or devastation not justified by military necessity.[17]

Similar provisions were adopted for the International Military Tribunal for the Far East and modified for military tribunals run by the occupying regime as well as for subsequent prosecutions by German courts for several years. Hundreds of war criminals were tried and sentenced in these tribunals.[18] Compared to the list of war crimes drafted by the Commission on Responsibility, Article 6 of the IMT Charter is more concise but

---

[14] Pictet, 1952, p. 357, see *supra* note 7; Sandoz, 2009, pp. 665–71, see *supra* note 5.

[15] William A. Schabas, *An Introduction to the International Criminal Law Court*, 4th ed., Cambridge University Press, Cambridge, 2011, p. 122.

[16] *Ibid.*, p. 5; Sandoz, 2009, p. 672, see *supra* note 5.

[17] Charter of the International Military Tribunal (IMT), Art. 6, 8 August 1945 (https://www.legal-tools.org/doc/64ffdd/).

[18] Schabas, 2011, p. 7, see *supra* note 15.

less detailed. But there is no substantial difference in essence, thus "high-lighting a historical continuity in the development of war crimes that would also flow into the development of the grave breaches regime".[19]

10.2.5. The 1949 Geneva Conventions and Additional Protocol I of 1977

The events of the Second World War convinced the International Committee of the Red Cross ('ICRC') that any future convention on laws of war must include provisions on the repression of violations. At the request of the International Red Cross Conference and after consultations with government experts, the ICRC made a thorough study of the question of repression of violations of laws and customs of war, and in 1948 drafted four new articles on the penalties applicable to persons guilty of violations of the 1906 Geneva Convention. Under these articles, states were required to take legislative measures to ensure either criminal or disciplinary punishment of all kinds of violations, but the grave breaches of the Geneva Conventions would be punished as crimes pursuant to the principle of *aut dedere aut punier* (extradite or prosecute). The draft text was finally submitted to the 1949 Diplomatic Conference for the Establishment of International Conventions for the Protection of War Victims as a basis for discussion, and was adopted with minor changes.[20]

Thus articles entitled "Grave Breaches" were formally introduced into the four conventions: Geneva Convention I (Article 50), Geneva Convention II (Article 51), Geneva Convention III (Article 130) and Geneva Convention IV (Article 147). The acts of the grave breaches are listed as follows:

> wilful killing; torture or inhuman treatment; biological experiments; wilfully causing great suffering; causing serious injury to body or health; extensive destruction and appropriation of property, not justified by military necessity and carried out unlawfully and wantonly; compelling a prisoner of war or a protected civilian to serve in the armed forces of the hostile Power; wilfully depriving a prisoner of war or a protected person of the rights or fair and regular trial prescribed

---

[19] Sandoz, 2009, p. 673, see *supra* note 5.

[20] Final Record of the Diplomatic Conference Convened by the Swiss Federal Council for the Establishment of International Conventions for the Protection of War Victims, Geneva, 21 April–12 August 1949. See also Pictet, 1952, pp. 357–60, see *supra* note 7.

in the Conventions; unlawful deportation or transfer; unlawful confinement of a protected person; taking of hostages.[21]

It was maintained that this list should not be regarded as exhaustive.[22] The expressions 'grave crimes' or 'war crimes' were recommended
to replace 'grave breaches', but this suggestion was refused because even
though the listed acts were described as crimes in the penal laws of almost
all countries, the word 'crimes' had different legal meanings in different
countries and the Diplomatic Conference was not tasked to work out international penal law.[23]

Besides the introduction of a universal definition of the grave
breaches, the 1949 Geneva Conventions further obliged state parties to
enact effective penal sanctions, to search and try or extradite, and to exercise universal jurisdiction over those responsible for grave breaches.[24]
These provisions are considered by Yves Sandoz to be "a decisive step
towards international justice and the beginnings of a universal fight
against impunity for war crimes".[25]

The Additional Protocol I of 1977 was supposed to supplement the
1949 Geneva Conventions for the war victims.[26] In terms of penal sanctions, Additional Protocol I added several grave breaches to the list set up
earlier, especially by criminalising violations of the Hague Conventions
on Laws and Customs of War on Land, some of which had been included
in Article 6 of the IMT Charter. Additional Protocol I further clarified that
grave breaches of the Geneva Conventions and the Protocol would be regarded as war crimes in Article 85(5). By deciding that grave breaches
constitute war crimes, the drafters gave the former an additional meaning,
providing them with criminal consequences in international law.[27]

According to Article 85(1) of Additional Protocol I, provisions on
the repression of grave breaches of the Geneva Conventions should apply
to the repression of grave breaches of the Protocol as well. Therefore, the

---

[21] Some of the grave breaches differ in other Conventions.

[22] Pictet, 1952, p. 371, see *supra* note 7.

[23] *Ibid.*, pp. 366, 371; Sandoz, 2009, p. 675, see *supra* note 5.

[24] Geneva Convention I, Art. 49; Geneva Convention II, Art. 50; Geneva Convention III, Art. 129; Geneva Convention IV, Art. 146, see *supra* note 1.

[25] Sandoz, 2009, p. 675, see *supra* note 5.

[26] Additional Protocol I, Art 1, para. 3, see *supra* note 1.

[27] Marko Divac Öberg, "The Absorption of Grave Breaches into War Crimes Law", in *International Review of the Red Cross*, 2009, vol. 91, no. 873, p. 167.

grave breaches/war crimes defined by Additional Protocol I are subject to universal jurisdiction among the state parties as the grave breaches defined by the Geneva Conventions.[28] Compared to the list prepared by the Commission on Responsibility and Article 6 of the IMT Charter, the conception of grave breaches shows continuity and development of these two earlier documents. The adopted article was considered to be an important step towards an improved application of humanitarian law.[29]

That being said, we should bear in mind that there exist two qualifications on the grave breaches regime provided by the Geneva Conventions and Additional Protocol I. The first is that the grave breaches have to be committed against persons or property protected by the Conventions and the Protocol, which is narrowly defined by the former and expanded a little by the latter.[30] Second, grave breaches are applicable only to international armed conflicts, namely armed conflicts between states as defined by the common Article 2 to the Geneva Conventions or armed conflicts of national liberation as defined by Article 1(4) of Additional Protocol I. Thus no treaty provisions on penal sanctions were established for violations of common Article 3 to the Geneva Conventions and Additional Protocol II of 1977, both of which apply to non-international armed conflict.[31]

---

[28] Yves Sandoz, Christophe Swinarski and Bruno Zimmermann (eds.), *Commentary on the Additional Protocols of 8 June 1977 to the Geneva Conventions of 12 August 1949*, Martinus Nijhoff, Geneva, 1987, para. 3467, p. 992. Additional Protocol I, Art. 85(1) reads: "The provisions of the Conventions relating to the repression of breaches and grave breaches, supplemented by this Section, shall apply to the repression of breaches and grave breaches of this Protocol". As of March 2015, there are 174 states parties to the Protocol.

[29] *Ibid*, para. 3465, p. 991.

[30] José Francisco Rezek, "Protection of the Victims of Armed Conflicts: I. Wounded, Sick and Shipwrecked Persons", in United Nations Educational, Social and Cultural Organization and Henry Dunant Institute (eds.), *International Dimensions of Humanitarian Law*, Martinus Nijhoff, Dordrecht, 1987, pp. 153–203; Claude Pilloud, "Protection of the Victims of Armed Conflicts: II Prisoners of War", *idem.*, pp. 167–85; Oji Umozurike, "Protection of the Victims of Armed Conflicts: III Civilian Population", *idem.*, pp. 187–203.

[31] Protocol Additional to the Geneva Conventions of 12 August 1949, and relating to the Protection of Victims of Non-International Armed Conflicts, 8 June 1977 ('Additional Protocol II'); Sandoz, 2009, pp. 675–77, see *supra* note 5.

10.2.6. From *Ad Hoc* Criminal Tribunals to a Permanent International Criminal Court

Horrified by ethnic cleansing during a series of armed conflicts caused by the disintegration of Yugoslavia in 1991, the international community established the International Criminal Tribunal for the former Yugoslavia ('ICTY') in 1993 through UN Security Council resolution 827.[32] A year later, in response to the tragedy caused by ethnic conflict in Rwanda, the Security Council adopted resolution 955 to create another international *ad hoc* body, the International Criminal Tribunal for Rwanda ('ICTR') with jurisdiction over genocide and other violations of international humanitarian law.[33] The criminal jurisdiction of the two *ad hoc* tribunals covers "serious violation of international humanitarian law", which, in these cases, includes war crimes, crime against humanity and genocide.[34] As for war crimes, Article 2 of the ICTY Statute addresses grave breaches of the Geneva Conventions, which replicates the relevant provisions of the Geneva Conventions, while Article 3 deals with violations of the laws and customs of war, which uses the language of the 1907 Hague Regulations concerning the Laws and Customs of War on Land.[35] What is more inter-

---

[32] United Nations Security Council resolution 827, adopted on 25 May 1993, S/RES/827 (https://www.legal-tools.org/doc/dc079b/). Statute of the International Criminal Tribunal for the Former Yugoslavia, 25 May 1993 ('ICTY Statute') (updated September 2009) (https://www.legal-tools.org/doc/b4f63b/).

[33] Statute of the International Criminal Tribunal for Rwanda, 8 November 1994 ('ICTR Statute') (https://www.legal-tools.org/doc/8732d6/).

[34] Kalshoven and Zegveld, 2011, p. 241, see *supra* note 3.

[35] ICTY Statute, see *supra* note 32. Article 2 reads:

The International Tribunal shall have the power to prosecute persons committing or ordering to be committed grave breaches of the Geneva Conventions of 12 August 1949, namely the following acts against persons or property protected under the provisions of the relevant Geneva Convention:

(a) wilful killing;
(b) torture or inhuman treatment, including biological experiments;
(c) wilfully causing great suffering or serious injury to body or health;
(d) extensive destruction and appropriation of property, not justified by military necessity and carried out unlawfully and wantonly;
(e) compelling a prisoner of war or a civilian to serve in the forces of a hostile power;
(f) wilfully depriving a prisoner of war or a civilian of the rights of fair and regular trial;
(g) unlawful deportation or transfer or unlawful confinement of a civilian;
(h) taking civilians as hostages.

Article 3 reads:

esting is that Article 3 was interpreted by the ICTY as including serious violations of common Article 3 of the Geneva Conventions due to customary law.[36]

As the crisis in Rwanda was seen as internal conflict from the outset, Article 4 of ICTR Statute explicitly makes serious violations of common Article 3 to the Geneva Conventions and Additional Protocol II of 1977 punishable crimes.[37] The recognition of war crimes in internal conflict by these two tribunals was considered historic since it bridged part of the gap left by the Geneva Conventions and Additional Protocol I. As a result, the decisions have contributed significantly to diminishing the rel-

---

The International Tribunal shall have the power to prosecute persons violating the laws or customs of war. Such violations shall include, but not be limited to:

(a)   employment of poisonous weapons or other weapons calculated to cause unnecessary suffering;

(b)   wanton destruction of cities, towns or villages, or devastation not justified by military necessity;

(c)   attack, or bombardment, by whatever means, of undefended towns, villages, dwellings, or buildings;

(d)   seizure of, destruction or wilful damage done to institutions dedicated to religion, charity and education, the arts and sciences, historic monuments and works of art and science;

(e)   plunder of public or private property.

[36]   Sandoz, 2009, p. 678, see *supra* note 5.

[37]   ICTR Statute, see *supra* note 33. Article 4 reads:

The International Tribunal for Rwanda shall have the power to prosecute persons committing or ordering to be committed serious violations of Article 3 common to the Geneva Conventions of 12 August 1949 for the Protection of War Victims, and of Additional Protocol II thereto of 8 June 1977. These violations shall include, but shall not be limited to:

(a)   Violence to life, health and physical or mental well-being of persons, in particular murder as well as cruel treatment such as torture, mutilation or any form of corporal punishment;

(b)   Collective punishments;

(c)   Taking of hostages;

(d)   Acts of terrorism;

(e)   Outrages upon personal dignity, in particular humiliating and degrading treatment, rape, enforced prostitution and any form of indecent assault;

(f)   Pillage;

(g)   The passing of sentences and the carrying out of executions without previous judgment pronounced by a regularly constituted court, affording all the judicial guarantees which are recognized as indispensable by civilized peoples;

(h)   Threats to commit any of the foregoing acts.

evance of the distinction between international armed conflicts and non-international armed conflicts for the punishment of violations.[38]

Following the establishment of the ICTY and ICTR, several mixed tribunals were set up, which combined international and domestic elements. The Extraordinary Chambers in the Courts of Cambodia ('ECCC') was established in 2004 by agreement between the UN and the government of Cambodia to try senior Khmer Rouge leaders for genocide, crimes against humanity, grave breaches of the Geneva Conventions, destruction of cultural property during armed conflicts as well as domestic crimes of homicide and torture. The inclusion of grave breaches implies that the ECCC could deal with crimes that occurred during the armed conflict between Cambodia and Vietnam which lasted for decades. The Special Court for Sierra Leone was established in 2002 by agreement between the UN and the government of Sierra Leone. Besides other international and domestic crimes, its Statute also grants the Court jurisdiction over violations of the common Article 3 of the Geneva Conventions and Additional Protocol II.[39]

Taking the advantage of the favourable political momentum created by the ICTY and the ICTR, the UN decided to pursue its work towards the establishment a permanent international criminal court, taking two draft statutes drawn up by the International Law Commission in the 1950s as a basis. The UN General Assembly convened an *ad hoc* committee for further discussions on the issue, which met twice in 1995, followed by a preparatory committee. After two years the preparatory committee finally produced a consolidated statute text which was submitted for consideration by the Diplomatic Conference of Plenipotentiaries on the Establishment of an International Criminal Court in 1998 in Rome. On 17 July 1998 the conference, after heated debate, adopted the Rome Statute of International Criminal Court ('ICC Statute').[40] The ICC Statute entered into force on 1 July 2002 upon ratification by 60 states. On 11 March

---

[38] Kalshoven and Zegveld, 2011, p. 243, see *supra* note 3.

[39] Statute of the Special Court for Sierra Leone, 16 January 2002 (https://www.legal-tools.org/doc/aa0e20/). Kalshoven and Zegveld, 2011, p. 258–60, see *supra* note 3.

[40] Rome Statute of the International Criminal Court, 17 July 1998, in force on 1 July 2002, United Nations, Treaty Series, vol. 2187, No. 38544 ('ICC Statute').

2003 the International Criminal Court ('ICC') was established in The Hague, the Netherlands.[41]

According to Article 5 of its Statute, the ICC has jurisdiction over the crime of genocide, crimes against humanity, war crimes and the crime of aggression.[42] The list of war crimes identified in the ICC Statute is extensive and much more detailed than any of the previous instruments. As it stands, Article 8 divides war crimes into four categories, two of them addressing international armed conflicts and the other two non-international armed conflicts. The first category in Article 8(2)(a) incorporates grave breaches of the Geneva Conventions, but the use of the formula 'namely' indicates that the list of grave breaches in the Statute is exhaustive. The second category in Article 8(2)(b) covers other serious violations of the laws and customs applicable in international armed conflict. This sub-paragraph consists of 25 items of acts principally based on 1907 Hague Regulations on Laws and Customs of War on Land and Additional Protocol I. As with Article 8(2)(a) this list is probably exclusive since it is also qualified by the formula 'namely'. It is also worth noting that weapons of mass destruction, such as chemical weapons or nuclear weapons, are not included as result of political compromise, an outcome that was considered a great disappointment by some states. Article 8(2)(c) and 8(2)(e) address war crimes under armed conflict not of an international character. Article 8(2)(c) integrates serious violations of common Article 3 of the Geneva Conventions and Article 8(2)(e) is largely drawn from Additional Protocol II. These provisions represent a great success for negotiations at the Rome Conference and are considered a progressive development over the antecedents for their expressed coverage of non-international armed conflicts.[43]

---

[41] See also Schabas, 2011, pp. 15–21, see *supra* note 15; Kalshoven and Zegveld, 2011, p. 246, see *supra* note 3.

[42] ICC Statute, Art. 5, see *supra* note 40.

[43] Leila Nadya Sadat, *The International Criminal Court and the Transformation of International Law: Justice for the New Millennium*, Transnational Publishers, Ardsley, NY, 2002, pp. 160–65. See also Schabas, 2011, p. 115, *supra* note 15.

10.3. Analysis of the Content of the Grave Breaches Regime

10.3.1. Grave Breaches Provided by the Geneva Conventions

The grave breaches established by the 1949 Geneva Conventions include wilful killing; torture or inhuman treatment; biological experiments; wilfully causing great suffering; causing serious injury to body or health; extensive destruction and appropriation of property, not justified by military necessity and carried out unlawfully and wantonly; compelling a prisoner of war or a protected civilian to serve in the armed forces of a hostile power; wilfully depriving a prisoner of war or a protected person of the rights or fair and regular trial prescribed in the Conventions; unlawful deportation or transfer; unlawful confinement of a protected person; and the taking of hostages. Wilful killing constitutes a grave breach when protected persons are deliberately killed by someone who has an obligation to respect their 'protected' status, and there is no need for more than one person to be killed to satisfy this breach.[44] This breach also covers cases where death occurs through omission, where the omission has been wilful and with an intention to cause death.[45]

For the purpose of the Geneva Conventions, torture must be given its legal meaning here, namely the inflicting of severe pain or suffering on a person to obtain confession or information. Inhuman treatment is not specifically defined in the Geneva Conventions. The purpose of this prohibition is to preserve human dignity of the protected persons. It includes causing serious mental harm or physical injury, as well as attack on human dignity. Measures such as cutting protected persons off from the outside world, especially from their families, or grave injury to their human dignity could be considered inhuman treatment.[46] These two types of actions have been made the subject of a subsequent specific international treaty, the Convention against Torture and Other Cruel, Inhuman or De-

---

[44] Julian J.E. Schutte, "The System of Repression of Breaches of Additional Protocol I", in Astrid J.M. Delissen and Gerard J. Tanja (eds.), *Humanitarian Law of Armed Conflict: Challenges Ahead: Essays in Honour of Frits Kalshoven*, Martinus Nijhoff, Dordrecht, 1991, p. 185.

[45] Jean S. Pictet (ed.), *Commentary, IV Geneva Convention Relative to the Protection of Civilian Persons in Time of War*, International Committee of the Red Cross, Geneva, 1958, p. 597.

[46] *Ibid.*, p. 598.

grading Treatment or Punishment ('Torture Convention') of 10 December 1984.[47] What should be noted here is that both are subject to universal criminal jurisdiction under the Geneva Conventions, while the Torture Convention makes a distinction between torture and other cruel or inhuman treatment in that the latter actions are not made subject to universal jurisdiction and extraditable offences.[48] Biological experiments, highlighted by the Geneva Conventions as a particular form of torture or inhuman treatment, do not prohibit the use of new methods of treatment by medical doctors justified by medical reasons and based on concern to improve the person's state of health.[49] This type of action is further elaborated in Article 11 of Additional Protocol I.

"Wilfully causing great suffering" is differentiated from torture or biological experiments in that it covers acts and omissions that affect the body or health of protected persons which can be inflicted as punishment, in revenge or for other motives. "Serious injury to body or health" is a concept quite normally encountered in criminal law and usually uses the length of time the victim cannot work as a criterion of seriousness.[50] "Unlawful deportation or transfer" should be interpreted in conjunction with Articles 45 and 49 of Geneva Convention IV. The unfortunate experiences of the Second World War made this prohibition necessary. Most national laws punish "unlawful confinement" as unlawful deprivation of liberty. However, taking into consideration of the extended powers granted to the occupying powers, the unlawful nature of confinement could therefore be very difficult to prove.[51]

---

[47] Convention against Torture and Other Cruel, Inhuman or Degrading Treatment or Punishment, adopted on 10 December 1984, entry into force on 26 June 1987. Article 1 reads:

For the purposes of this Convention, the term "torture" means any act by which severe pain or suffering, whether physical or mental, is intentionally inflicted on a person for such purposes as obtaining from him or a third person information or a confession, punishing him for an act he or a third person has committed or is suspected of having committed, or intimidating or coercing him or a third person, or for any reason based on discrimination of any kind, when such pain or suffering is inflicted by or at the instigation of or with the consent or acquiescence of a public official or other person acting in an official capacity. It does not include pain or suffering arising only from, inherent in or incidental to lawful sanctions.

[48] Schutte, 1991, pp. 183–84, see *supra* note 44.

[49] Pictet, 1958, p. 598, see *supra* note 45.

[50] *Ibid.*, p. 599.

[51] *Ibid.* See also Schutte, 1991, p. 180, *supra* note 44.

"Compelling to serve in hostile forces" is also punished as illegal recruitment or coercion under national law. But it seems unsatisfactory for the purpose of the Geneva Conventions since the authorities' involvement in the action puts rather a different complexion on the case.[52] This provision should be interpreted with Article 50 of Geneva Convention III and Article 40 of Geneva Convention IV, which provide the kinds of work to which the protected persons may be subject. And the "forces" in this provision should also be considered to cover not only armed forces but also other institutions empowered to use force or violence.[53]

"Wilfully depriving rights of a fair and regular trial" should also be interpreted with other articles in the Geneva Conventions specifying the conditions for the trial of protected persons, namely Articles 84, 99, 105 and 106 of Geneva Convention III and Articles 66, 70, 71, 72 and 73 of Geneva Convention IV. As for prisoners of war, the rights of a fair and regular trial include the right to be tried by a military court or at least by a court which offers essential guarantees of independence and impartiality. As for interned civilians, they enjoy similar judicial guarantees as prisoner of war and their rights to legal assistance and sufficient opportunity to prepare their defence are elaborated in more detail in Geneva Convention IV than in Geneva Convention III. Thus this breach can be split into different offences, such as making a protected person appear before an exceptional court, without notifying the protecting power, without defending counsel and so on.[54]

"Taking hostage" is also a crime recognised and punished by most penal codes. Its legal description has been further elaborated by the International Convention against the Taking of Hostages of 18 December 1979.[55] The threat either to prolong the hostage's detention or to put him

---

[52] Pictet, 1958, p. 600, see *supra* note 45.
[53] Schutte, 1991, p. 182, see *supra* note 44.
[54] *Ibid.*, pp. 181–82. See also Pictet, 1958, p. 600, *supra* note 45.
[55] Geneva Convention IV, art. 1 reads:

> Any person who seizes or detains and threatens to kill, to injure or to continue to detain another person (hereinafter referred to as the "hostage") in order to compel a third party, namely, a State, an international intergovernmental organization, a natural or juridical person, or a group of persons, to do or abstain from doing any act as an explicit or implicit condition for the release of the hostage commits the offence of taking of hostages ("hostage-taking") within the meaning of this Convention.

to death is considered a feature of this breach, which makes it a special intent crime.[56]

The expression "extensive destruction and appropriation of property not justified by military necessity and carried out unlawfully and wantonly" was inspired by Article 6(2)(b) of the IMT Charter and finds its predecessor in Article 23(g) of the Hague Regulations concerning the Laws and Customs of War on Land. It is considered a surprising integration of Hague law into the Geneva Conventions. The only suitable reference in the Geneva Conventions is Article 53 of Convention IV which prohibits destruction by an occupying power of property except under absolute military necessity. As for appropriation, the only related reference seems to be Article 32(2) of Geneva Convention IV which prohibits pillage against protected persons.[57]

Thus, according to the related articles, this grave breach covers a number of different offences. 1) Destruction: Geneva Convention IV forbids the destruction of civilian hospitals and their property or damage to ambulances or medical aircraft. Furthermore, an occupying power may not destroy in an occupied territory real or personal property except where such destruction is rendered absolutely necessary by military operations. 2) Appropriation. In order to appropriate property, an enemy must have occupied the territory. It should be noted that the requisitioning of civilian hospitals and their material and the requisitioning of foodstuffs are subject in occupied territory to a series of restrictive conditions. To constitute a grave breach, such destruction and appropriation must be extensive and an isolated incident would not be sufficient. Even though most national penal codes punish the unlawful destruction and appropriation of property and most military penal codes punish pillage, the destruction and appropriation mentioned here are dependent on the necessities of war. It seems, therefore, that the appropriation and destruction mentioned in Geneva Convention IV must be treated as a special offence.[58]

As noted, this conduct constitutes grave breaches only if it has been directed against persons or objects protected by the Geneva Conventions.

International Convention against the Taking of Hostages, 18 December 1979, UN doc. A/34/46.

[56] Pictet, 1958, p. 600, see *supra* note 45.

[57] Schutte, 1991, p. 180–81, see *supra* note 44.

[58] Pictet, 1958, p. 600, see *supra* note 45.

Geneva Convention I defines protected persons as the wounded and sick of any of the categories provided in Article 13 and medical personnel referred to in Articles 24 and 26. Articles 19 and 35 define the protected objects. Geneva Convention II defines protected persons as the wounded, sick and shipwrecked of any of the categories listed in Article 13 as well as personnel referred to in Articles 36 and 37. The protected objects are hospital ships mentioned in Articles 22, 24, 25 and 27. To be qualified as protected persons or objects, all must have fallen into the hands of enemy.[59] Protected persons under Geneva Convention III are persons listed in Article 4 when they fall into the hands of the enemy. In Geneva Convention IV interned civilians and civilians in occupied territory qualify as protected persons, subject to the nationality requirements under Article 4.

Additional Protocol I also has the category of protected persons. Article 44 expands the categories of persons entitled to prisoners of war status. Persons listed in Article 45 should also be treated as prisoners of war before their status has been finally determined. Stateless persons and refugees are also protected persons within the meaning of Parts I and III of Geneva Convention IV by virtue of Article 73. Another category of protected persons covers wounded, sick and shipwrecked civilians not entitled to the treatment of prisoners of war as well as those find themselves shipwrecked in waters other than the sea. All these persons are considered protected persons only if they belong to the adversary party and refrain from hostilities. The description of medical or religious personnel and medical units or medical transport is also broader in Additional Protocol I than that in Geneva Conventions I and II. For example, under the Protocol they include the medical and religious personnel attached to civil defence organisations.[60]

10.3.2. Grave Breaches Provided by Additional Protocol I

10.3.2.1. Article 85(3)

As for the list of grave breaches, the first outstanding expansion made by Additional Protocol I is the integration of Hague law in Article 85(3), which defines certain serious violations of the provisions on the general

---

[59] Geneva Convention I, Art. 35 and Geneva Convention II, Art. 37, see *supra* note 1.
[60] Schutte, 1991, pp. 186–87, see *supra* note 44; Sandoz *et al.*, 1987, paras. 3647–70, p. 991, see *supra* note 28.

protection of civilians against effects of hostilities and concerning means and methods of warfare as grave breaches.[61] The opening sentence of Article 85(3) refers to the fourth paragraph of Article 11. This latter article aims to clarify and develop the protection of protected persons against medical procedures not indicated by their state of health, and particularly against unlawful medical experiments. The breach defined in that provision has its own constitutive elements different from those laid down in this paragraph and it also departs from the corresponding provisions of the Geneva Conventions in that it qualifies as grave breaches certain activities directed against persons in the power of a party other than the party to which they belong, irrespective of their status, that is whether they are a protected person or not. The conduct described in Article 11 of Additional Protocol I may be considered "inhuman treatment" or "wilfully causing serious injury to body or health".[62]

There are some common constitutive elements applicable to all the sub-paragraphs Article 85(3).

- Wilfully: the accused must have acted consciously and with intent, that is, with his mind on the act and its consequences, and willing them. The requirement of consequences implies that attempts to commit these acts cannot amount to grave breaches. It is not necessary for the intent to be directed at producing the specific consequences and it is sufficient that the conduct be performed wilfully in the sense that the per-

---

[61] Additional Protocol I, Art. 85(3) reads:

In addition to the grave breaches defined in Article 11, the following acts shall be regarded as grave breaches of this Protocol, when committed wilfully, in violation of the relevant provisions of this Protocol, and causing death or serious injury to body or health:

(a) making the civilian population or individual civilians the object of attack;

(b) launching an indiscriminate attack affecting the civilian population or civilian objects in the knowledge that such attack will cause excessive loss of life, injury to civilians or damage to civilian objects, as defined in Article 57, paragraph 2 (a) (iii);

(c) launching an attack against works or installations containing dangerous forces in the knowledge that such attack will cause excessive loss of life, injury to civilians or damage to civilian objects, as defined in Article 57, paragraph 2 (a) (iii);

(d) making non-defended localities and demilitarized zones the object of attack;

(e) making a person the object of attack in the knowledge that he is hors de combat;

(f) the perfidious use, in violation of Article 37 of the distinctive emblem of the red cross, red crescent or red lion and sun or of other protective signs recognized by the Conventions or this Protocol.

[62] Schutte, 1991, p. 189, see *supra* note 44.

petrator knows the character of the item under attack. But conducts referred to under sub-paragraphs (b) and (c) require knowledge of results of excessive losses or damages. This encompasses the concepts of "wrongful intent" or "recklessness", in other words the attitude of an agent who, without being certain of a particular result, accepts the possibility of it happening. On the other hand, ordinary negligence or lack of foresight is not covered, that is when a man acts without having his mind on the act or its consequences although failing to take the necessary precautions, particularly failing to seek precise information, constitutes culpable negligence punishable at least by disciplinary sanctions.[63]

- In violation of the relevant provisions: this element requires that the conduct described shall be interpreted with specific provisions of Parts III and IV.

- Causing death or serious injury to body or health: for all the conducts described by the sub-paragraph to be qualified as grave breaches, certain consequences are required. "The effect must be such that, even if it does not cause death, it will affect people in a long-lasting or crucial manner, either as regards their physical integrity or their physical and mental health."[64]

Grave breach under Article 85(3)(a) is related to Article 51(2) of Additional Protocol I that prohibits making the civilian population or individual civilians the object of attack. The concept of "attack" is defined by Article 49 as acts of violence performed either in offence or defence.[65] Article 85(3)(b) concerns "indiscriminate attacks" defined and prohibited by Article 51(4) and 51(5), which are attacks not directed against civilians but affecting them incidentally.[66] In this regard, it should be noted that even though indiscriminate attacks are prohibited, only those causing excessive incidental damages to civilians or civilian objects constitute grave breaches. The criteria for judging whether the loss is excessive are to weigh up "the concrete and direct military advantage anticipated" and "incidental losses" expected, which are set out by Article 57(2)(a)(iii).[67] It

---

[63] *Ibid,* pp. 189–90; Sandoz *et al.*, 1987, para. 3474, p. 994, see *supra* note 28.

[64] Sandoz *et al.*, 1987, para. 3474, p. 995, see *supra* note 28.

[65] *Ibid.*, para. 3475, p. 995.

[66] *Ibid.*, para. 3477, p. 995.

[67] *Ibid.*, paras. 3478, 3431, pp. 995–96.

would be impossible to judge *in abstracto* under what circumstances the losses are excessive and they can only be assessed on a case-by-case basis. There should also be sufficient evidence to show that the perpetrator understood or accepted the calculated risk of causing excessive losses beforehand.[68]

Article 85(3)(c) is related to Article 56 of Additional Protocol I, which grants special protection to works and installation containing dangerous force, such as dams, dykes and nuclear electrical generating stations. The special protection granted to them makes them immune from attack even if they are military objectives if the attack may cause the release of dangerous forces and severe losses among civilian population. The special protection even applies to other military objectives located at or in the vicinity of them if the attack against those military objectives may cause the release of dangerous forces from the works or installation and severe losses among civilians population. The special protection ceases only those works or installations or military objective located at or in the vicinity of them are used in regular, significant and direct support of military operations and the attack is the only feasible way to terminate that support. In order for this provision to make sense, those works and installations must first be military objectives since attacks against those works or installations of civilian nature have already been covered by Article 85(3)(a). The other constitutive elements are similar to those in Article 85(3)(b). Thus one may conclude that this provision does not add anything substantial to sub-paragraph (b).[69]

The norms underlying Article 85(3)(d) are Articles 59 (non-defended localities) and 60 (demilitarised zones) of Additional Protocol I. The former may be established by unilateral declaration or agreement among parties to the conflict while the latter can only be established by agreement. Non-defended localities should not be made the object of attack and parties to a conflict should not extend their military operations to demilitarised zones if those are against the agreement establishing the zone. For grave breach to be established under this provision, the perpe-

---

[68] Schutte, 1991, p. 189, see *supra* note 44.

[69] *Ibid.*, p. 191; Sandoz *et al.*, 1987, paras. 3482–86, pp. 996–97, see *supra* note 28.

trator should have known such localities or zones had this particular status and had not lost it.[70]

Article 85(3)(e) relates to Article 41 on safeguarding an enemy *hors de combat*. A person who is in the powers of an adversary party and clearly expresses his intention to surrender or has been rendered unconscious or incapacitated by wounds or sickness is considered *hors de combat* provided he abstains from hostilities. It is prohibited to attack such persons. There would be a breach of the rule if the perpetrator knew or should have known the person he was attacking was *hors de combat*. But for it to be a grave breach the perpetrator must have actual knowledge that the person is *hors de combat*.[71] Usually, the persons are those whose status of "protected persons" has not been determined under Geneva Conventions III and IV or Article 45 of Additional Protocol I. Once their protected status is decided they will be under the protection of Article 85(2) of Additional Protocol I.[72]

Article 85(3)(f) relates to perfidious use of emblems or protective signs recognised by the Geneva Conventions and Additional Protocol I. These emblems and signs include a red cross, red crescent, oblique red bands on a white ground (for hospital and safety zones), blue triangle on an orange ground (for civil defence), three bright orange circles (for works or installations containing dangerous forces), and signs agreed upon between parties to the conflict such as for non-defended localities and demilitarised zones.

Articles 54 and 45 of Geneva Conventions I and II prohibit abuse of the Red Cross, red crescent and red lion and sun emblems but do not qualify their perfidious use as a grave breach. However, the perfidious use of internationally recognised emblems had been embodied in the Hague Regulations concerning the Laws and Customs of War on Land in Article 23(f). Additional Protocol I inherited this provision and further defined in Article 37 the term of perfidy as acts inviting the confidence of an adversary to lead him to believe that he is entitled to, or is obliged to accord protection under international humanitarian law, with intent to betray that confidence. But it should be noted that only perfidy for the purpose of

---

[70]   Schutte, 1991, p. 191, see *supra* note 44; Sandoz *et al.*, 1987, paras. 3487–90, p. 997, see *supra* note 28.

[71]   Sandoz *et al.*, 1987, paras. 3491–92, p. 998, see *supra* note 28.

[72]   Schutte, 1991, p. 192, see *supra* note 44.

killing, injury or capture of an adversary is prohibited. And for it to be a grave breach it must also result in the consequences defined in the opening sentence.[73]

It is argued that distinctive signals, signs, emblems or uniforms of the United Nations or of neutral or other states not party to the conflict, or other internationally recognised protective emblems, signs or signals including the flag of truce and the protective emblem of cultural property shall be added to the list of the protected emblems or signs.[74]

Finally, there seem to be some differences between "launching an attack" used in Article 85(3)(b) and (c) and "making someone or something the object of attack" used in other sub-paragraphs, in terms of the scope of perpetrators covered. The former appears to target the commander who orders the attack or those having authority to determine the objectives of the attack while the latter allows for a wider interpretation to include everyone taking part in hostilities.[75]

10.3.2.2. Article 85(4)

The provisions in Article 85(4) differ from those in Article 85(3) in that they do not require particular consequences as constitutive elements and they are also less connected to specific rules of the Geneva Conventions and Additional Protocol I. As for content, Article 85(3) deals with activities on the battlefield and is related to Hague law, but Article 85(4) is mainly concerned with persons in the power of the enemy under Geneva law, except for Article 85(4)(d). And some of the breaches described by Article 85(4) follow inevitably from policy decision of the party to the conflicts, rather than purely individual initiatives.[76] The provision reads:

> [T]he following shall be regarded as grave breaches of this Protocol, when committed wilfully and in violation of the Conventions or the Protocol:
>
> (a) the transfer by the Occupying Power of parts of its own civilian population into the territory it occupies, or the deportation or transfer of all or parts of the population of

---

[73] Sandoz *et al.*, 1987, paras. 3495, 3499, p. 998–99, see *supra* note 28.

[74] *Ibid.*, paras. 3496–498, pp. 998–99. Additional Protocol I, Arts. 37 and 38, see *supra* note 1.

[75] Schutte, 1991, p. 190, see *supra* note 44.

[76] Sandoz *et al.*, 1987, paras. 3500–1, p. 999, see *supra* note 28.

the occupied territory within or outside this territory, in violation of Article 49 of the Fourth Convention;

(b) unjustifiable delay in the repatriation of prisoners of war or civilians;

(c) practices of 'apartheid' and other inhuman and degrading practices involving outrages upon personal dignity, based on racial discrimination;

(d) making the clearly-recognized historic monuments, works of art or places of worship which constitute the cultural or spiritual heritage of peoples and to which special protection has been given by special arrangement, for example, within the framework of a competent international organization, the object of attack, causing as a result extensive destruction thereof, where there is no evidence of the violation by the adverse Party of Article 53, sub-paragraph (b), and when such historic monuments, works of art and places of worship are not located in the immediate proximity of military objectives;

(e) depriving a person protected by the Conventions or referred to in paragraph 2 of this Article of the rights of fair and regular trial.

The conduct described in Article 85(4)(a) is largely covered by grave breaches defined in Article 147 of Geneva Convention IV, whose underlying norm is Article 49 of Geneva Convention IV. Thus the provision in this sub-paragraph dealing with transfer or deportation of the population in occupied territory is just a repetition of the grave breach defined by Geneva Convention IV. The new element in this sub-paragraph is the transfer by the occupying power of its population into the occupied territory, which is prohibited by Article 49 of Geneva Convention IV but not considered a grave breach because of the population concerned are not "protected persons" under the Convention.[77] It may be inspired by the settlement policies of the Israeli government with respect the occupied territory since the Six-Day War of 1967.[78]

Article 85(4)(b) is considered to be inspired by experiences of delays in the repatriation of prisoners of war after the armed conflicts between India and Pakistan in 1971. According to Articles 109 and 118 of

---

[77] *Ibid.*, paras. 3502–4, p. 1000.

[78] Schutte, 1991, p. 193, see *supra* note 44.

Geneva Convention III the seriously wounded or sick prisoners of war should be repatriated during hostilities and all the prisoners of war should be repatriated without delay after the cessation of active hostilities except in case of criminal proceedings and serving sentences. According to Article 35 of Geneva Convention IV civilians in enemy territory are entitled to leave the territory unless their departure is contrary to the national interest of the state. Thus parties to the conflict have an obligation to repatriate prisoners of war but they do not have the same obligation towards protected civilians. In this regard, Article 85(4)(b) seems to have no substantive meaning for civilians.[79]

Article 85(4)(c) is considered a departure from other grave breaches in terms of drafting format. First, it does not link to any specific rules or norms within the Geneva Conventions or Additional Protocol I since the term "apartheid" has never been used and the practice of apartheid never defined. Second, it does not relate the status of protected persons to the victim of the practices concerned.[80] Thus, in order to maintain its legal relevance to the grave breaches regime, this provision should be understood to refer to "torture or inhuman treatment against protected persons", which are already grave breaches of the Geneva Conventions and this provision just aims at emphasising the shocking motive of apartheid practice.[81] It should also be noted that this Article 85(4)(c) only condemns the practice of apartheid and not its policy. The latter is subject exclusively to crimes against humanity.[82]

Article 85(4)(d) is linked with Article 53 of Additional Protocol I on the protection of cultural property. By introducing additional constitutive elements, this sub-paragraph limits cultural property to those "clearly recognised", under special protection by special arrangement, not used in support of a military effort and not located in the immediate proximity of the military objective. For an attack against those properties to be qualified as grave breach, it must result in extensive destruction as well. Taking into consideration these elements, some of which are subject to further clarification such as clearly recognised and special protection, one might

---

[79] Sandoz *et al.*, 1987, paras. 3505–9, pp.1000–1, see *supra* note 28; Schutte, 1991, p. 193, see *supra* note 44.

[80] Schutte, 1991, pp. 193–94, see *supra* note 44.

[81] *Ibid.*, p. 194; Sandoz *et al.*, 1987, paras. 3514–15, p. 1002, see *supra* note 28.

[82] Sandoz *et al.*, 1987, paras. 3512, p.1002, see *supra* note 28.

wonder if it really adds much substance to the grave breach of "the extensive and destruction of protected property" covered by Geneva Convention IV and completed by Article 85(3)(b).[83]

Article 85(3)(e) is largely covered by similar grave breaches under the Geneva Conventions but its added value is to ensure judicial guarantees in Article 75 of Additional Protocol I are embodied into those of the Conventions since Article 75 contains a more elaborate interpretation of the notion of "fair trial" than the relevant provisions of Geneva Conventions III and IV.[84] If one or more of those guarantees in the proceedings are not observed, the procedural process in its entirety can be considered unfair and irregular.[85]

10.3.3. Customary Status of Grave Breaches

There can be no doubt that the definitions of the grave breaches, as contained in the Geneva Conventions, are part of customary international law. This is due to the universal ratification of the Geneva Conventions and state practice concerning grave breaches. This argument is further supported by the inclusion of the grave breaches defined by the Geneva Conventions in the ICTY Statute and the ICC Statute. The report of the UN Secretary-General concerning the establishment of the ICTY clearly states that the application of the principle *nullum crimen sine lege* requires that the ICTY should apply the rules of customary international humanitarian law.[86] In addition, when the ICC Statute was being negotiated there was a general agreement among states that the crimes identified in the Statute were to reflect existing customary law and not create new law.[87] Grave breaches as defined by the Geneva Conventions have therefore become customary international law.[88] However, the same might not be said

---

[83] Schutte, 1991, p. 195, see *supra* note 44.

[84] Sandoz *et al.*, 1987, para. 3519, p. 1003, see *supra* note 28.

[85] Schutte, 1991, pp. 195–96, see *supra* note 44.

[86] UN Secretary-General, Report Submitted Pursuant to Paragraph 2 of Security Council Resolution 808 (1993), 3 May 1993, UN doc. S/25704.

[87] Philippe Kirsch, "Foreword", in Knut Dörmann, *Elements of War Crimes under the Rome Statute of the International Criminal Court: Sources and Commentary*, Cambridge University Press, Cambridge, 2003, p. xiii.

[88] Jean-Marie Henckaerts, "The Grave Breaches Regime as Customary International Law", in *Journal of International Criminal Justice*, 2009, vol. 7, no. 4, pp. 689–91.

about all the grave breaches provided by Additional Protocol I except those integrated by the ICC Statute.[89]

10.3.4. Analysis of Procedural Rules

According to the related provisions of the Geneva Conventions, the states parties undertake to enact any legislation necessary to provide effective penal sanctions for persons committing, or ordering to be committed, any of the grave breaches, and should be under obligation to search for persons alleged to have committed, or to have ordered to be committed, such grave breaches, and should bring such persons, regardless of their nationality, before their own courts. They may also, if they prefer, and in accordance with the provisions of their own legislation, hand such persons over for trial to another high contracting party concerned, provided such a high contracting party has made out a *prima facie* case.[90] Therefore, states parties are obliged to take the following procedural measures to tackle grave breaches.

10.3.4.1. Enacting Effective Penal Sanctions

The obligation to enact effective penal sanctions finds its origin in the 1929 Geneva Convention relative to the Treatment of Prisoners of War but has been made more imperative by the 1949 Geneva Conventions.[91] It first requires states to criminalise all the acts listed by the graves breaches provisions in their domestic law. Even though the Geneva Conventions generally apply in situations of armed conflict, the obligation of the legislation is seemingly to be undertaken in peacetime before a situation of armed conflict arises. Article 80 of Additional Protocol I also requires states to take all necessary measures for the execution of their obligations without delay. As mentioned by the International Court of Justice on a similar obligation in the case of *Belgium v. Senegal*, this obligation of leg-

---

[89] *Ibid.*, pp. 691–92.

[90] Geneva Convention I, Art. 49; Geneva Convention II, Art. 50; Geneva Convention III, Art. 129; Geneva Convention IV, Art. 146, see *supra* note 1.

[91] Geneva Convention Relative to the Treatment of Prisoners of War, Art. 29, 27 July 1929, just requires states to make legislative proposals if their domestic penal code is insufficient. But the 1949 Geneva Conventions provide that states "undertake" to make penal sanctions.

islation has to be implemented as soon as a state is bound by the Convention and it has in particular a preventative and deterrent character.[92]

Second, the penal sanction set up by domestic legislation should be "effective". In order for it to be effective the legislation should specify the nature and extent of the penalty for each infraction, "taking into account the principle of due proportion between the severity of the punishment and the gravity of the offence".[93] Due to their seriousness, imprisonment is recognised as key to punishing grave breaches and other serious violations of international humanitarian law.[94] For the sake of effectiveness, it is especially important to equally apply those sanctions to all the perpetrators, irrespective of the party to which they belong in order to avoid the criticism of victor's justice.

The modalities of liability established by the provisions are commission or ordering. Other modalities, justifications, excuses and defence are all left to states' national criminal law.[95] In this regard, states may need to take into consideration developments of international criminal law on war crimes, which are addressed below.

As for the practical format of legislation, some states prefer to apply their existing military or ordinary criminal law to the grave breaches since their domestic laws have already covered those breaches and provide adequate sanctions. Those provisions are thus superfluous and it is not necessary to introduce new crimes. However, even though most of the grave breaches are already criminal acts under domestic law this is not true for all of them, such as perfidious use of the Red Cross emblem, and the sanctions for them under domestic law may not be adequate.[96] Furthermore, allowing states to rely simply on their ordinary domestic criminal law would make the obligation meaningless, which is an interpretation against the purpose and object of the treaty and thus a violation of treaty

---

[92] International Court of Justice, Questions relating to the Obligation to Prosecute or Extradition, *Belgium v. Senegal*, Judgment, ICJ Reports 2012, para. 75.

[93] Pictet, 1952, p. 364, see *supra* note 7.

[94] ICRC, Preventing and Repressing International Crimes: Towards an "Integrated" Approach Based on Domestic Practice: Report of the Third Universal Meeting of National Committees of the Implementation of International Humanitarian Law, vol. 1, ICRC, Geneva, 2014, pp. 61–66.

[95] Pictet, 1952, p. 364, see *supra* note 7.

[96] Christine van den Wyngaert, "The Suppression of War Crimes under Additional Protocol I", in Delissen and Tanja, 1991, p. 200, see *supra* note 44.

law. In practice, international tribunals such as the ICTY and ICTR could still try a person who had been tried before a national court for serious violation of international humanitarian law if those violations were categorised as ordinary crimes before the national court.[97] This reaffirmed that the special elements of grave breaches could not be fully captured by a domestic equivalent crime.[98]

Another option chosen by states aims at criminalising all serious violations by providing a general reference to the relevant international law including international humanitarian law. Thus all breaches or serious violations of international humanitarian law were made punishable by a simple reference to relevant treaties or customary law and no national implementing legislation was needed, even when the related law was amended or modified. This option is simple and economic. But the disadvantage is that generic criminalisation may violate the principle of legality required by criminal law and it leaves too much room for judicial interpretation.[99]

A third option adopted by states is to enact specific legislation, which usually integrates the full list of grave breaches from the treaty into a stand-alone act or specific part within the domestic law framework and lays down the range of penalties or redefines the description of conduct constituting grave breaches. Common law countries usually follow this approach.[100] This approach is very much in line with the principle of legality as every criminal activity and its punishment are clearly defined and predictable. Some scholars consider that only specific national legislation can satisfy these obligations within different traditions of criminal law, and the stand-alone code would seem to best meet the principle of legality and at the same time adequately underlines the exceptional nature and gravity of grave breaches.[101] But it creates a large workload for states

---

[97] ICTY Statute, Art. 10(2)(a), see *supra* note 32; ICTR Statute, Art. 9(2)(a), see *supra* note 33.

[98] Knut Dörmann and Robin Geiß, "The Implementation of Grave Breaches into Domestic Legal Orders", in *Journal of International Criminal Justice*, 2009, vol. 7, no. 4, pp. 708–10.

[99] ICRC, 2014, p. 33, see *supra* note 94. For example, Article 9 of the Chinese Criminal Law (1997) requires that it applies to those crimes provided by international treaties to which China is a party. See also Dörmann and Geiß, 2009, pp. 711–10, see *supra* note 98.

[100] ICRC, 2014, pp. 33–35, see *supra* note 94.

[101] Dörmann and Geiß, 2009, pp. 708, 717, see *supra* note 98.

and may lack the flexibility to accommodate new developments of the law.

A fourth option for states is a mixture of the two approaches outlined above through general criminalisation supplemented by specific provisions on certain crimes. This option is considered a quite balanced approach that allows respect for the principle of legality and specificity without the necessity of enacting a whole new legislation whenever a state becomes party to a treaty.[102]

10.3.4.2. Establishing Universal Jurisdiction and the Obligation *Aut Judicare Aut Dedere*

Universal jurisdiction is defined as "criminal jurisdiction based solely on the nature of the crime, without regard to where the crime was committed, the nationality of the alleged or convicted perpetrator, the nationality of the victim, or any other connection to the state exercising such jurisdiction".[103] Universal jurisdiction can be a mandatory or permissive provision of treaty or customary law. The 1949 Geneva Conventions represent landmarks in the development of international law as the first treaty-based recognition of universal jurisdiction over war crimes applicable to all states.[104]

Related articles of the four Geneva Conventions oblige states parties to search for and bring suspects of grave breaches before their own courts regardless of their nationality,[105] which has been interpreted as a requirement of universal jurisdiction over grave breaches.[106] Even though the treaty provisions only provide for the irrelevance of a suspect's nationality, the irrelevance of the place of commission of the offence can be implied. Because if it is not the case, it would mean states can only have jurisdiction over grave breaches allegedly committed on their own territories, the explicit mention of the irrelevance of nationality will be made

---

[102] ICRC, 2014, p. 36, see *supra* note 94.

[103] Stephen Macedo (ed.), *The Princeton Principles on Universal Jurisdiction*, Program in Law and Public Affairs, Princeton University, Princeton, NJ, 2001.

[104] Roger O'Keefe, "The Grave Breaches Regime and Universal Jurisdiction", in *Journal of International Criminal Justice*, 2009, vol. 7, no. 4, pp. 811–10.

[105] Geneva Convention I, Art. 49; Geneva Convention II, Art. 50; Geneva Convention III, Art. 129; Convention IV, Art. 146, see *supra* note 1.

[106] Sandoz *et al.*, 1987, para. 3403, see *supra* note 28.

redundant for a state that already can punish any offence occurring in its own territory regardless of the nationality of the perpetrator. Based on these observations, it is understandable that the nationality of victims needs not be mentioned. Finally, it should be emphasised again that the obligation is imposed on all states parties and not just to those that are parties to armed conflicts. Thus putting all these factors together, the obligation to exercise criminal jurisdiction imposed by the grave breaches regime is not dependent on any prescriptive nexus of nationality, territoriality, passive personality or the protective principle, and thus those provisions create an obligation to exercise universal criminal jurisdiction over grave breaches. This interpretation is supported by the *travaux préparatoires* and state practice in implementing the Geneva Conventions.[107] In practice, states should vest their courts with jurisdiction over grave breaches on the basis of universal jurisdiction and, if the opportunity arises, exercise this jurisdiction by search, investigation and prosecution.[108] As the commentary of the Geneva Conventions indicates, this obligation implies activities on the states once they are aware that a suspect is present in their territory.[109] In this regard, states are bound to carry out search, investigation, pre-trial detention, prosecution and trial.[110]

The next provision specifies that states may also, if they prefer, and in accordance with the provisions of their own legislation, hand such persons over for trial to another high contracting party concerned, provided such a high contracting party has made a *prima facie* case. This permissive provision, combined with the mandatory universal jurisdiction, is known as an obligation *aut judicare aut dedere*. It can be noted that the *judicare* element is separate and independent from the *dedere* element under the grave breaches regime, and that states have free choice in adjudication or extradition. In this regard, the interest of states of passive personality (victim states) does not prevail over that of states of active personality (states of perpetrators). And there is no exception to the principle of free choice even when the state of custody orders the grave breach.[111]

---

[107] O'Keefe, 2009, pp. 813–15, see *supra* note 104.

[108] *Ibid.*, pp. 816–17.

[109] Pictet, 1952, pp. 365–66, see *supra* note 7. See also Claus Kreß, "Reflections on the *Iudicare* Limb of the Grave Breaches Regime", in *Journal of International Criminal Justice*, 2009, vol. 7, no. 4, p. 800.

[110] Kreß, 2009, pp. 800–1, see *supra* note 109.

[111] *Ibid.*, pp. 797–99.

As for the handing over of the accused to an international tribunal, the Geneva Conventions are not considered to pose any obstacles to it.[112] But a state's right of free choice under the grave breaches regime might be qualified by priority competence of an international criminal court pro vided by treaties to which the custodial state is a party.[113]

10.3.4.3. Procedural Rules and Customary Law

The procedural rules of legislation, trial or extradition and universal juris-diction are also customary rules. According to customary law, states have obligations to investigate and prosecute those alleged to have committed war crimes.[114] It is thus a corollary that states need to first put a proper legislative framework in place. So the obligation of legislation could even be taken as an integral part of the customary law obligation to repress war crimes. According to the International Law Commission's Report, the ob-ligation *aut dedere aut judicare* for certain categories of crimes is a duty not only from a treaty law perspective but also from generally binding customary norms. It is generally agreed that those categories of crimes should include serious violations of international humanitarian law such as war crimes or grave breaches. State practice also supports the custom-ary law status of this obligation.[115] As for universal jurisdiction, it has long been recognised that states have the right to vest universal jurisdic-tion over war crimes. But the Geneva Conventions go further to make it obligatory to vest universal jurisdiction over grave breaches. Based on existing state practices, especially the universal acceptance of the Geneva Conventions, the rule of universal jurisdiction over grave breaches also reflects customary law.[116] Finally, all these procedural rules are not just technical but fundamental to the "respect for the human person and ele-mentary considerations of humanity", the criterion suggested by the Inter-national Court of Justice for customary international law.[117]

---

[112] Pictet, 1952, see *supra* note 7.

[113] Kreß, 2009, pp. 799–800, see *supra* note 109.

[114] Jean-Marie Henckaerts and Louise Doswald-Beck, *Customary International Humanitarian Law*, vol. 1: *Rules*, Cambridge University Press, Cambridge, 2005, rule 158.

[115] Henckaerts, 2009, pp. 696–98, see *supra* note 88.

[116] *Ibid.*, pp. 698–99.

[117] *Ibid.*, p. 693–700.

10.4. Grave Breaches and War Crimes under International Criminal Law

War crimes are defined as serious violations of customary or treaty rules of international humanitarian law which entail, under customary or conventional law, individual criminal responsibility of the person breaching the rules.[118] War crimes have been punished at domestic level probably since the beginning of criminal law and, moreover, they were the first to be prosecuted pursuant to international law.[119] With the adoption of the ICC Statute in 1998, we now have the most substantial codifications in history of war crimes under the international criminal law, which is supposed to reflect customary international law.[120] This section compares the list of war crimes conducted under Article 8 of the ICC Statute with those of grave breaches under the Geneva Conventions and Additional Protocol I, and elaborates on the dynamic relations between international humanitarian law and international criminal justice. Article 8 of the ICC Statute lists war crimes in four categories, two of which, Article 8(2)(a) and 8(2)(b), address war crimes under international armed conflict, while the other two, Article 8(2)(c) and 8(2)(e), deal with non-international armed conflict.

10.4.1. War Crimes in International Armed Conflict

10.4.1.1. Grave Breaches of the Geneva Conventions

The first category of war crimes under Article 8(2)(a) comprises "grave breaches of the Geneva Conventions of 12 August 1949". This subparagraph integrates the same grave breaches from the Geneva Conventions and thus they are subject to the same conditions and interpretations for their application. For example, they apply to international armed conflict and only concern protected persons as defined in the respective Geneva Conventions.[121]

---

[118] Antonio Cassese, *International Criminal Law*, Oxford University Press, Oxford, 2003, p. 47.

[119] Schabas, 2011, p. 110, see *supra* note 15.

[120] Kirsch, 2003, p. xiii, see *supra* note 87.

[121] Otto Triffterer (ed.), *Commentary on the Rome Statute of the International Criminal Court*, 2nd ed., C.H. Beck, Hart, Nomos, Baden-Baden, 2008, pp. 300–1; Schabas, 2011, pp. 119–21, see *supra* note 15.

The laws of armed conflict "are not static, but by continual adaptation follow the needs of a changing world".[122] This adaptation has been to a large part realised through the jurisprudence of tribunals and courts. Some 45 years after their adoption the grave breaches were first applied by the ICTY, which adopted a dynamic approach to their interpretation and application. First, the ICTY's Appeals Chamber confirmed for the first time that grave breaches were limited to international armed conflict.[123] However, the ICTY expanded their reach through an extension of the concept of an "international conflict for the purpose of determining individual criminal responsibility".[124] The ICTY established an innovative test of "overall control" to determine the relation between an intervening foreign state and non-state groups such as armed forces, militias or paramilitary units, which may turn a *prima facie* internal armed conflict into an international one. As the ICTY stated, the overall control criteria may be satisfied if the state "has a role in organising, coordinating or planning the military actions of the military group, in addition to financing, training and equipping or providing operational support of that group".[125] This interpretation was hugely significant in its effects of broadening the scope of application of grave breaches to include situations which might be considered a civil war and the test has since been followed by the ICTY and "a new path has been charted for international criminal jurisdictions".[126] We need to wait to see whether the ICC follows this test, while some scholars have suggested that it should do so.[127]

---

[122] International Criminal Tribunal for the former Yugoslavia ('ICTY'), *Prosecutor v. Kunarac et al.*, Appeals Chamber, Judgment, IT-96-23 and IT-96-23/I-A, 12 June 2002, para. 67 (https://www.legal-tools.org/doc/029a09/).

[123] ICTY, *Prosecutor v. Duško Tadić at al.*, Appeals Chamber, Decision on the Defence Motion for Interlocutory Appeal on Jurisdiction, IT-94-1-A, 2 October 1995 (https://www.legal-tools.org/doc/866e17/). However, some scholars are of the opinion that this confirmation defied recent trends in state practice illustrating a change in customary international law. See Natalie Wagner, "The Development of the Grave Breaches Regime and of Individual Criminal Responsibility by the International Criminal Tribunal for the former Yugoslavia", in *International Review of the Red Cross*, 2003, vol. 85, no. 850, p. 358.

[124] Ken Roberts, "The Contribution of the ICTY to the Grave Breaches Regime", in *Journal of International Criminal Justice*, 2009, vol. 7, no. 4, p. 747.

[125] ICTY, *Prosecutor v. Duško Tadić*, Appeals Chamber, Judgment, 15 July 1999, IT-94-1-A, para. 137 (https://www.legal-tools.org/doc/8efc3a/).

[126] Roberts, 2009, p. 749, see *supra* note 124.

[127] Triffterer, 2008, p. 302, see *supra* note 121; Dörmann, 2003, p. 24, see *supra* note 87.

Second, the ICTY also required that the prosecutor prove the accused's knowledge of the facts pertinent to the internationality of the conflict,[128] which has been absorbed as constituting an element of war crimes under the ICTY Statute.[129] The requirement of the nexus between the alleged crimes and the armed conflict was also established by the ICTY and has been absorbed as constituting an element of "in the context of and [...] associated with an international armed conflict" for the war crimes under the ICTY Statute.[130]

In addition, the ICTY also expanded the concept of "protected persons" through a purposive interpretation of the scope of protection under Article 4 of Geneva Convention IV. It argued that Article 4 does not make its applicability dependent on formal bonds and purely legal relations indicated by nationality. Rather, it hinges on the substantial relations evidenced by allegiance and effective and satisfactory diplomatic representation or protection since Article 4, if interpreted in the light of its object and purpose, is directed to the protection of civilians to the maximum extent possible.[131] Thus nationals may still have protected person status if they cannot rely on the protection of the state of which they are citizens because they belong to national minorities.[132] This innovation corresponds to the realities of modern conflict that are more likely to be interethnic than between states.[133] It also seems to have been accepted by the ICC since the Elements of Crimes require the perpetrator only to know the fact that the victim belonged to the adversary party to the conflict, rather than the nationality of the victim.[134]

As for the conducts listed as grave breaches, the ICTY has also had the chance to flesh out some individual grave breaches. For example, the ICTY brought life to the grave breach of unlawful confinement of a civilian by interpreting the interaction between different articles of Geneva Convention IV, such as Articles 5, 42 and 43. Thus the detention or confinement of civilians is unlawful either 1) when a civilian has been de-

---

[128] Roberts, 2009, p. 749, see *supra* note 124.

[129] Dörmann, 2003, p. 17, see *supra* note 87.

[130] Roberts, 2009, p. 750–52, see *supra* note 124; Dörmann, 2003, p.17, see supra *note* 87.

[131] Roberts, 2009, p. 753–54, *ibid*; Wagner, 2003, p. 360, see *supra* note 123.

[132] Schabas, 2011, p. 121, see *supra* note 15; Triffterer, 2008, p. 302, see *supra* note 121.

[133] Roberts, 2009, p. 754, see *supra* note 124; Wagner, 2003, p. 361, see *supra* note 123.

[134] ICC Statute, Elements of Crimes, Art. 8(2)(a)(i), para. 3, n. 33, see *supra* note 40; Triffterer, 2008, p. 302, see *supra* note 121.

tained in contravention of Article 42 of Geneva Convention IV, that is, they are detained without reasonable grounds to believe that the security of the detaining power makes it absolutely necessary, or 2) where the procedural safeguards required by Article 43 of Geneva Convention IV are not complied with in respect of detained civilians, even where their initial detention may have been justified.[135] It is also suggested that the ICC follow this interpretation.[136]

Another example of the ICTY's contribution to grave breaches relates to torture. The ICTY has breathed new life into this grave breach. Taking the definition of torture under the Torture Convention as guidance, the ICTY developed a definition of torture for the purpose of international humanitarian law by adjudicating that 1) the prohibited purpose of torture should not be exhaustive since an "exhaustive categorization would merely create opportunity for the evasion of the letter of the prohibition", and 2) the public official requirement found in Article 1 of the Torture Convention is not a requirement under customary international law in relation to the individual criminal responsibility for torture outside of the framework of the Torture Convention.[137] This development seems to have been followed by the ICC Statute as well.[138]

A conclusion may therefore be drawn that the judicial practice on war crimes under international criminal law has developed and will continue to develop the content of the grave breaches contained in the 1949 Geneva Conventions.

10.4.1.2. Other Serious Violations of Customs and Laws of War

The 1907 Hague Regulations and the grave breaches and other prohibitory or protective provisions of Additional Protocol I are the major sources of the 26 types of conduct that form the second category of war crimes defined by Article 8(2)(b) of the ICC Statute as "other serious violations of the laws and customs applicable in international armed conflict within the established framework of international law".[139] This prompts two

---

[135] Roberts, 2009, p. 759–60, see *supra* note 124.

[136] Triffterer, 2008, p. 321, see *supra* note 121.

[137] Roberts, 2009, p. 754–58, see *supra* note 124.

[138] Triffterer, 2008, p. 306–7, see *supra* note 121; Dörmann, 2003, pp. 44, 61, see *supra* note 87.

[139] Schabas, 2011, p. 122, see *supra* note 15; Triffterer, 2008, p. 323, see *supra* note 121.

questions: Are there any grave breaches defined by Additional Protocol I missing from this provision? Are there any new war crimes established on the basis of other provisions of Additional Protocol I?

Three grave breaches established by Additional Protocol I are clearly missing from this category of war crimes in the ICC Statute: launching an attack against works or installations containing dangerous forces in the knowledge that such attack will cause excessive losses to civilians or civilian objects in Article 85(3)(c); unjustified delay in the repatriation of prisoners of war or civilians in Article 85(4)(b); and apartheid and other inhuman and degrading practices in Article 85(4)(c).[140]

With regard to the practice of apartheid or other inhuman and degrading practices, it might amount to war crimes as an outrage on personal dignity, as well as humiliating and degrading treatment under Article 8(2)(b)(xxi).[141] And it could also be charged as a crime against humanity under Article 7 of the ICC Statute. But the threshold for the latter charge is quite high since it requires that the crime be committed as "part of a widespread or systematic attack directed against a civilian population".

The grave breach of an attack against works and installations containing dangerous forces could be covered by Article 8(2)(b)(iv) on excessive incidental damages.[142] It is hard to find a similar alternative offence in the ICC Statute for grave breaches of unjustified delay of repatriation of prisoners of war or civilians. It has been argued that this breach may constitute a war crime under customary international law,[143] but would not be subject to the jurisdiction of the ICC. The reason for these differences may be the less unanimous acceptance of Additional Protocol I in comparison with the Geneva Conventions and that some states may have concerns on some of the norms contained by the Protocol.[144]

War crimes under Article 8(2)(b) that are based on or related to articles of Additional Protocol I other than those of grave breaches include: directing attacks against civilian objects (ii), launching attacks causing excessive damage to the environment (iv), killing or wounding treacher-

---

[140] Sandoz, 2009, p. 679, see *supra* note 5.

[141] Henckaerts and Doswald-Beck, 2005, pp. 588–89, see *supra* note 114.

[142] *Ibid.*, p. 590.

[143] *Ibid.*, p. 588.

[144] Schabas, 2011, p. 122, see *supra* note 15; Triffterer, 2008, p. 288, see *supra* note 121.

ously (xi), declaring no quarter (xii), using human shields (xxiii), starvation of civilians (xxv), and conscripting or enlisting child soldiers (xxvi).

The war crime of directing attacks against civilian objects is based on Article 52(1) of Additional Protocol I, which provides that "civilian objects shall not be the object of attack or reprisals". This war crime is also considered a reflection of customary law.[145] The definitions of civilian objects and military objectives in Article 52 are also the same under customary law. It is argued that the customary status of reprisal against civilian objects is not firmly established. Thus reprisal against civilians remains a treaty prohibition binding only states parties.[146]

The war crime of treacherous killing or wounding is based on Article 23 of the Hague Regulations and is linked to Article 37 of Additional Protocol I, which defines perfidy. The elements of this war crime make it clear that it should be understood as prohibiting the killing or wounding an adversary by resort to perfidy defined by Article 37 of Additional Protocol I.[147] This crime is also a customary crime.[148] On the other hand, perfidious use of the distinctive emblems is a grave breach under Article 85(3)(f) of Additional Protocol I.

The war crime of declaring no quarter is based on Article 23(d) of the Hague Regulations and is linked to Article 40 of Additional Protocol I, which prohibits ordering "that there shall be no survivors, to threaten an adversary therewith or to conduct hostilities on this basis". The elements for this crime indicate that it covers both the declaration and the order of no quarter. But it is not clear whether a threat of no quarter is also covered. There was some opposition to including "to conduct hostilities on the basis of no quarter" into this crime during negotiations over the ICC Statute. Article 40 of Additional Protocol I is considered to reflect customary rules but the related war crime is just "declaring that no quarter will be given".[149] However, this restrictive view will not overly limit the ICC's jurisdiction since the conduct of hostilities on the basis of no quarter may amount to a war crime of killing persons *hors de combat.*[150]

---

[145] Henckaerts and Doswald–Beck, 2005, p. 581, see *supra* note 114.

[146] Triffterer, 2008, pp. 329–30, see *supra* note 121.

[147] *Ibid.*, p. 384–85.

[148] Henckaerts and Doswald-Beck, 2005, p. 575, see *supra* note 114.

[149] *Ibid.*, pp. 161, 575.

[150] Triffterer, 2008, pp. 392–93, see *supra* note 121.

The war crime of using human shields is based on Article 51(7) of Additional Protocol I, which prohibits the use of civilians to shield points, areas or military objectives. Articles 23 and 28 of Geneva Convention IV and Article 12 of Additional Protocol I prohibit the use of prisoners of war and medical units for the same purpose. This prohibition and its violation as a war crime are considered customary law.[151] According to the elements of the crime, the use of human shields implies positive action from the party to take advantage of the location of the protected persons or an intentional co-location of military objectives and protected persons to shield military objectives or operations.[152] This prompts the question of "voluntary human shields", namely persons who have freely chosen to place themselves near military objectives in the hope that their presence will delay or prevent an attack.[153] In this regard, it should be made clear that there is no 'use' in voluntary human shields from the party, thus no charge could be raised under this provision. It is further argued that voluntary shield civilians maintain their civilian status since their action does not amount to direct participation in hostilities, and thus they are still protected from direct attack.[154] However, due to the voluntary nature of taking the risk of being close to a military objective, to the conflict, the threshold of incident damages of the proportionality test may be enhanced.[155]

The war crime of starvation of civilians is based on Article 54 of Additional Protocol I, which prohibits use of "starvation of civilians as a method of warfare" and "to attack, destroy, remove or render useless objects indispensable to the survival of the civilian population". The last part of the crime of "impeding relief supplies" is based on Articles of 23, 55 and 59 of Geneva Convention IV. This provision was considered a new rule at the time of the adoption of Additional Protocol I but since then has been made customary rule through state practice.[156] And conduct under

---

[151] Henckaerts and Doswald-Beck, 2005, pp. 337, 584, see *supra* note 114.

[152] *Ibid.*, p. 340; Triffterer, 2008, p. 454, see *supra* note 121.

[153] Triffterer, 2008, p. 455, see *supra* note 121.

[154] Nils Melzer, *Interpretive Guidance on the Notion of Direct Participation in Hostilities under International Humanitarian Law*, International Committee of the Red Cross, Geneva, 2009, pp. 56–57.

[155] *Ibid.*, p. 57; Triffterer, 2008, p. 456, see *supra* note 121.

[156] Henckaerts and Doswald-Beck, 2005, p. 581, see *supra* note 114.

this crime may constitute other war crimes, such as an attack against civilian objects, destruction of objects of the adversary and so on.[157]

The war crime of conscripting or enlisting child soldiers or using children under the age of 15 to participate actively in hostilities is based on Article 77(2) of Additional Protocol I, which provides that "the Parties to the conflict shall take all feasible measures in order that children who have not attained the age of fifteen years do not take a direct part in hostilities and, in particular, they shall refrain from recruiting them into their armed forces". The wording "participate actively" is considered broader than "take direct part in" since the former covers the latter as well as other active participation in military activities linked to combat.[158] The terms 'conscription' and 'enlist' were used to replace recruitment as some states have concerns that recruitment might include recruitment campaigns addressed to children under the age of 15, and the adjective "national" was added to "armed forces" in order to meet the concerns of several Arab states that feared the term might cover young Palestinians joining the *intifada* revolt.[159] This crime is considered a customary crime as well.[160]

Finally, for conduct under Article 85(3) to amount to grave breaches they must cause death or serious injury to body or health. This is not the case for war crimes under the ICC Statute except Article 8(2)(b)(x).

10.4.1.3. Mode of Liability

The grave breaches regime under the Geneva Conventions limits individual criminal responsibility to the author of the crime and to persons who ordered the crime. Other forms of responsibility were left to the judge who would apply national law. However, customary international humanitarian law has evolved since then and it is now generally recognised that individuals are not only criminally responsible for committing or ordering a grave breach or serious violation of humanitarian law but also for assisting in, facilitating or aiding or abetting, planning or instigating such crimes,[161] which is codified in Article 25 of the ICC Statute.

---

[157] Triffterer, 2008, pp. 470–71, see *supra* note 121.

[158] *Ibid.*, p. 471.

[159] *Ibid.*, p. 473; Schabas, 2011, p. 122, see *supra* note 15.

[160] Henckaerts and Doswald-Beck, 2005, p. 580, see *supra* note 114.

[161] *Ibid.*, p. 554.

10.4.2. War Crimes in Non-International Armed Conflicts

As already noted, there is no grave breaches regime under treaty law for armed conflict not of an international nature. There is only one provision in the 1949 Geneva Conventions, known as common Article 3, which refers to non-international armed conflict. Additional Protocol II to the Geneva Conventions expanded common Article 3 but does not extend the grave breaches regime to serious violations of its provisions.[162] Thus during the negotiation of the ICC Statute, the inclusion of war crimes for non-international armed conflict was difficult to achieve. But given the fact that armed conflict of a non-international character is more frequent today and that it is difficult to prove the international nature of much armed conflict, it became mandatory for most delegations that at least some acts should constitute war crimes in non-international armed conflict.[163]

In the final analysis, the ICC Statute classified war crimes in non-international armed conflict into two categories, namely serious violation of common Article 3 of the Geneva Conventions in Article 8(2)(c) and other serious violations of the laws and customs applicable in armed conflict not of an international character in Article 8(2)(f).

10.4.2.1. Serious Violations of Common Article 3 of the Geneva Conventions

The International Court of Justice considered common Article 3 as a minimum yardstick in cases of civil strife.[164] The ICTY and ICTR also explicitly confirmed that under customary international law violations of common Article 3 entail individual criminal responsibility. Other international or mixed tribunals and some domestic legislation have also followed suit.[165]

As the chapeau of Article 8(2)(c) indicates, its war crimes address "serious violations of Common Article 3". It is considered that any violation of the provisions always constitutes serious violations and would thus

---

[162] Schabas, 2011, p. 131, see *supra* note 15.

[163] Triffterer, 2008, p. 476, see *supra* note 121.

[164] International Court of Justice, *Nicaragua v. United States of America*, 27 June 1986, ICJ Report 14.

[165] Triffterer, 2008, pp. 485–86, see *supra* note 121; Schabas, 2011, p. 132, see *supra* note 15.

fall into the material jurisdiction of this paragraph.[166] As for persons protected under this provision, Article 8(2)(c) simply reiterates the groups of individuals mentioned in common Article 3, namely "persons taking no active part in hostilities, including members of armed forces who have laid down their arms and those placed hors de combat by sickness, wounds, detention or any other cause".[167] It should be noted that the list following the word "including" is not exhaustive. According to the Elements of Crimes, it refers to person or persons who were either *hors de combat*, or were civilians, medical personnel or religious personnel taking no active part in the hostilities. The notion of "taking no active part in the hostilities" is considered to have the same meaning as that of not "taking direct part in hostilities".[168] The notion "namely" used in the chapeau indicates that the list of acts in (i)–(iv) is exhaustive, and thus a serious violation of other paragraphs of common Article 3 is not a crime under the ICC Statute.[169] The punishable acts under this provision include murder, mutilation, cruel treatment and torture, outrages upon personal dignity, taking hostages and summary executions. They represent a common denominator of core human rights.[170]

10.4.2.2. Other Serious Violations of the Laws and Customs Applicable in Armed Conflict not of an International Character, Article 8(2)(e)

The crimes under Article 8(2)(e) of the ICC Statute are largely based on Additional Protocol II or borrowed from those provisions for international armed conflict. It addresses the war crimes of attacking civilians: 1) attacking objects or persons using the distinctive emblems; 2) attacking personnel or objects involved in humanitarian assistance or peacekeeping mission; 3) attacking protected objects; 4) pillaging; 5) rape, sexual slavery, enforced prostitute, forced pregnancy, enforced sterilisation and sexual violence; 6) using, conscripting and enlisting children; 7) displacing civilians; 8) treacherously killing or wounding; 9) denying quarter; 10) mutilation, medical or scientific experiments; 11) destroying or seizing

---

[166] Triffterer, 2008, pp. 486, see *supra* note 121.

[167] *Ibid.*, p. 487.

[168] *Ibid.*, p. 488.

[169] *Ibid.*

[170] Schabas, 2011, p. 132, see *supra* note 15.

the enemy's property; 12) employing poison or poisoned weapons; 13) employing prohibited gases, liquid, material or devices; 14) employing prohibited bullets. The wording and elements of most of the above crimes are similar to those related provisions of Article 8(2)(b) for international armed conflicts with some minor changes due to the specificities of non-international armed conflicts. But the following differences are worth noting.

The war crime of attacking civilians under Article 8(2)(e)(i) is based on Article 13(2) of Additional Protocol II and it has the same wording and elements as Article 8(2)(b)(i) for international armed conflict.[171] It should be noted that unlike war crimes under international armed conflicts, attacks against civilian objects are not classified as war crimes under this section. The reason is that Additional Protocol II does not have a provision prohibiting attacks against civilian objects, and thus prohibition of attacks against civilian objects would not be considered a customary rule.[172]

Even though the wording of Article 8(2)(e)(vi) of sexual or gender crimes is largely identical to that of Article 8(2)(b)(xxii), the former highlights its basis in common Article 3 while the latter in the grave breaches of the Geneva Conventions. This difference is quite understandable due to distinct rules applicable to international armed conflict and non-international armed conflict. Also given the specificities of internal armed conflict, the war crime of using child soldiers applies to all armed forces rather than just national armed forces.[173]

10.5. Conclusion

In the wake of the Second World War states established a grave breaches regime in the 1949 Geneva Conventions that signalled a veritable revolution for the concept of war crimes. Although war crimes were prosecuted and punished at Nuremberg and before, the grave breaches regime was the first treaty codifying war crimes. It represented a determination that

---

[171] In this regard, in non-international armed conflicts, besides members of state armed forces, only those civilians who do not take direct part in hostilities are taken to be civilians for the purpose of conduct of hostilities. Melzer, 2009, pp. 31–36, see *supra* note 154.

[172] Triffterer, 2008, pp. 494, see *supra* note 121. But the ICRC's Customary Study argues that this prohibition constitutes a customary rule.

[173] *Ibid.*, pp. 495–96.

from then on war criminals should be sought everywhere, called to answer to national courts and punished in accordance with pre-existing law.[174]

However, after its inception more than 60 years ago, the grave breaches regime remained, for most of the time, totally inoperative. The reasons for this are partly technical, born of the legal complexities and uncertainties in the regime, which only furnishes keywords to designate a criminal act, thereby leaving a range of indispensable criminal concepts under a cloud of obscurity. But the more substantial reason for its non-operation lies in international politics and the hard facts of military situations. The fear on the part of states of retribution against nationals detained by adversaries prevented them from prosecuting enemies in their custody for war crimes, and the universal jurisdiction vested on third states was generally subject to allegiances to competing superpowers.[175]

With the end of Cold War, the international community breathed life into the grave breaches regime through various international criminal courts and tribunals, which also stimulated domestic legislation on war crimes. Not only have these tribunals clarified the concepts of grave breaches but they also developed convincing solutions for textual limitation of them, such as the concept of international armed conflict and protected persons. What is more, those tribunals confirmed and developed war crimes for non-international armed conflicts on the basis of common Article 3 of the Geneva Conventions and Additional Protocol II, thus fixing the most serious deficiency of the regime, which limited its application only to international armed conflicts.[176]

Today, the grave breaches have been embedded within international criminal law as indicated by the ICC Statute, but as a separate category of war crimes from those violations of laws and customs of war, even though the latter were practically all covered in the Geneva Conventions and Additional Protocol I. This segregation stems from the historical tendency of states in the development of war crimes to simply add layer upon layer of new law without repealing earlier overlapping or redundant equivalents.

---

[174] James G. Stewart, "The Future of the Grave Breaches Regime", in *Journal of International Criminal Justice*, 2009, vol. 7, no. 4, p. 856

[175] *Ibid.*, pp. 856–57.

[176] *Ibid.*, p. 859; see also Dieter Fleck, "Shortcomings of the Grave Breaches Regime", in *Journal of International Criminal Justice*, 2009, vol. 7, no. 4, pp. 833–54.

But this division between grave breaches and other war crimes might lead to a dramatic decline in the use of grave breaches due to its complex technicalities and political sensitivities in proving an internationalised armed conflict. Thus other war crimes are perceived as better alternatives.[177]

Can the grave breaches regime still maintain its autonomous status compared with other war crimes? Even though grave breaches share a lot of commonalities with other war crimes under international criminal law with regard to types of armed conflict, acts and omissions and personal scope (types of perpetrators), and the latter further completes the former with *mens rea* and modes of liabilities,[178] a total abandonment of the grave breaches regime seems both undesirable and improbable. First, as shown above, certain grave breaches have no equivalent in other categories of war crimes. Second, even though a perceived threat to state sovereignty that the ICC might take over its criminal cases has motivated states to enact war crimes legislation according to the ICC Statute, the fact that significantly fewer states are party to the ICC than to the Geneva Conventions and Additional Protocol I actually prevents the grave breaches regime from being redundant.[179] Finally, the procedural obligations of legislation, search and investigation and, more importantly, the mandatory universal jurisdiction provided by treaty law have given the grave breaches regime a unique character to sustain its usefulness as a domestic tool against impunity for war crimes.

For all these reasons, the grave breaches regime seems destined to endure, but as part of an increasingly complex mosaic of law governing war crimes.[180] The laws of armed conflict "are not static, but by continual adaptation follow the needs of a changing world". We could positively anticipate that war crimes will be further clarified and unified by the jurisprudence of international tribunals, especially that of the ICC, in the future. This could reinforce the grave breaches regime.

---

[177] Stewart, 2009, pp. 860–63, see *supra* note 174.

[178] Öberg, 2009, pp. 170–78, see *supra* note 27.

[179] As of 16 March 2015, the Geneva Conventions have 196 states parties; Additional Protocol I has 174; and the ICC Statute has 123. See also *ibid.*, p. 180.

[180] Stewart, 2009, p. 870, see *supra* note 174.

11

From State to Individual: Evolution and Future Challenges of the Transposition of International Humanitarian Law into International Criminal Trials Against Individuals

Philipp Ambach[*]

11.1. Introduction

One of the core crimes common to all statutes of modern international criminal courts and tribunals is war crimes. This crime, intrinsically linked to the parties' conduct during wartime, has its origin in most relevant part in legal texts and conventions of the twentieth century. The Convention respecting the Laws and Customs of War on Land and its Annex, the Regulations concerning the Laws and Customs of War on Land of 18 October 1907 ('Hague Regulations'), the four Geneva Conventions of 1949 and their 1977 Additional Protocols contain the constitutive elements of modern war crimes provisions in the statutes of, most prominently, the United Nation's ('UN') international *ad hoc* tribunals for the former Yugoslavia and for Rwanda, the Special Court for Sierra Leone ('SCSL'), the Extraordinary Chambers in the Courts of Cambodia ('ECCC') and, most comprehensively, the International Criminal Court ('ICC').

These international conventions set out the applicable law during armed conflict (*ius in bello*) and more precisely define the permissible means and methods of warfare and the protection of persons not or no longer taking part in hostilities. These treaties were exclusively addressed at states, creating certain obligations and responsibilities upon them alone. However, these conventions also provided the historical and conceptual

---

[*] Dr. jur. **Philipp Ambach** is Special Assistant to the President of the International Criminal Court. He previously worked as a legal officer at the UN *ad hoc* Tribunals ICTY and ICTR. The views expressed are those of the author alone and do not necessarily reflect the views of the International Criminal Court.

origin for those provisions that describe criminal conduct leading to *individual* criminal responsibility under international law in international and non-international armed conflict.

This chapter analyses how the body of norms in the field of international humanitarian law, as it developed in the late nineteenth and twentieth centuries, has been transposed into the context of individual criminal responsibility before international criminal courts and tribunals for the most serious violations of international humanitarian law. This transposition has demanded – and continues to do so – a great deal of courage and foresight by those who apply the law in order to properly map and define the crimes, mindful of the overarching objective to regulate conduct in war and protect those in armed conflict that need protection most dearly.

The chapter examines how central provisions on serious violations of international humanitarian law, singled out in the Geneva Conventions as well as their Additional Protocol I of 1977 as "grave breaches",[1] have been fitted into the notion of war crimes in the *ad hoc* international courts and tribunals as well as the ICC, alongside a large body of provisions under the law and customs of war, as well as in non-international armed conflict. The discussion outlines the conceptual measures that both the drafters of the statutes and the judges applying these provisions have taken to transpose the foundational elements of grave breaches of international humanitarian law to the strict legal confines of a war crime under international law engendering individual criminal responsibility.

It is argued that it took bold and almost revolutionary steps in judicial law-finding on two main occasions during the twentieth century to first make the law of war crimes a reality and subsequently to extend it to the context of civil war. Having examined these steps, the chapter concludes with a brief assessment of whether, and if so how, the ICC and its jurisprudence can be instrumental in the enforcement of international hu-

---

[1] Convention (I) for the Amelioration of the Condition of the Wounded and Sick in Armed Forces in the Field. Geneva, 12 August 1949, Art. 50 ('Geneva Convention I'); Convention (II) for the Amelioration of the Condition of Wounded, Sick and Shipwrecked Members of Armed Forces at Sea. Geneva, 12 August 1949, Art. 51 ('Geneva Convention II'); Convention (III) relative to the Treatment of Prisoners of War. Geneva, 12 August 1949, Art. 130 ('Geneva Convention III'); Convention (IV) relative to the Protection of Civilian Persons in Time of War. Geneva, 12 August 1949, Art. 147 ('Geneva Convention IV'); Protocol Additional to the Geneva Conventions of 12 August 1949, and relating to the Protection of Victims of International Armed Conflicts (Protocol I), 8 June 1977, Arts. 11 and 85 ('Additional Protocol I').

manitarian law in our times, where the rapid change of symmetries, methods and means of warfare poses a constant threat to the guarantee of the rule of law in armed conflict.

11.2. Brief History of International Humanitarian Law

11.2.1. General Origins

War crimes are inseparably linked to international humanitarian law.[2] While most of the underlying offences are also covered as ordinary criminal offences under national law, it is the link to an armed conflict that elevates them to international crimes. Prohibitions under international humanitarian law provide the exclusive substantive source for a war crime since only a violation of the law applicable in armed conflict can constitute such a crime.[3] This nexus to armed conflict also provides the essential difference to other international crimes such as the crime of genocide and crimes against humanity – these being independent crimes under international law not requiring a nexus to armed conflict.[4]

---

[2] International Criminal Tribunal for the former Yugoslavia ('ICTY'), *Prosecutor v. Duško Tadić*, Appeals Chamber, Decision on the Defence Motion for Interlocutory Appeal on Jurisdiction, IT-94-1-AR72, 2 October 1995, para. 87 ('Tadić case') (https://www.legal-tools.org/doc/866e17/); Gerhard Werle and Florian Jessberger, *Principles of International Criminal Law*, 3rd ed., Oxford University Press, Oxford, 2014, para. 1030, p. 392.

[3] Jean-Marie Henckaerts and Louise Doswald-Beck, *Customary International Humanitarian Law*, vol. 1: *Rules*, Cambridge University Press, Cambridge, 2005, pp. 572–73; Tadić case, Decision on Jurisdiction, paras. 94, 143, *ibid.*

[4] See Michael Bothe, "War Crimes", in Antonio Cassese, Paola Gaeta and John R.W.D. Jones (eds.), *The Rome Statute of the International Criminal Court: A Commentary*, vol. 1, Oxford University Press, Oxford, 2002, p. 387. While crimes against humanity originally could only be committed "in execution of or in connection with" a war crime or crime against peace, see Art. 6(c) of the 1946 Charter of the International Military Tribunal at Nuremberg ('IMT Charter') (https://www.legal-tools.org/doc/64ffdd/), international customary law does no longer require a nexus to armed conflict; Extraordinary Chambers in the Courts of Cambodia ('ECCC'), *Co-Prosecutors v. Nuon Chea and Khieu Samphan*, Trial Chamber, Decision on Co-Prosecutors' Request to Exclude Armed Conflict Nexus Requirement From the Definition of Crimes Against Humanity, 002/19-09-2007/ECCC/TC, 26 October 2011, para. 10 ff., holding that the nexus requirement was no longer part of the material elements of the crime in 1975, *id.*, para. 33 ('Nuon and Khieu case') (https://www.legal-tools.org/doc/01ab87/); Tadić case, Decision on Jurisdiction, para. 140, see *supra* note 2. The nexus requirement in the ICTY Statute is a mere jurisdictional element of the crime; see United Nations Security Council resolution 808 (1993), adopted on 22 February 1993, UN doc. S/RES/808 (1993), Art. 5 ('ICTY Statute'); ICTY, *Prosecutor v. Duško Tadić*, Appeals Chamber, Judgment, IT-94-1-A, 15 July 1999, para.

Essentially, for an individual's conduct to amount to a war crime, two prongs need to be established:

(a) the conduct needs to be a violation of international humanitarian law; and

(b) the violation needs to generate individual criminal responsibility under international treaty or customary law.[5]

International humanitarian law refers to a set of rules that seek to limit the effects of armed conflict by protecting persons who are not or no longer participating in hostilities, on the one hand, and by restricting and regulating the means and methods of warfare available to the warring parties, on the other.[6]

Certain conduct in armed hostilities was already forbidden in ancient times. The Old Testament contained a prohibition on killing prisoners of war.[7] Laws in ancient India outlawed the use of certain weapons and the killing of civilians and combatants who have surrendered themselves or who are *hors de combat*.[8] Islamic law contained provisions protecting civilians during armed conflict and prohibiting excessive and wanton destruction of property. In ancient Greece and under the Roman Empire there were a number of rules regulating armed hostilities.[9] Also

---

249 ('Tadić case') (https://www.legal-tools.org/doc/8efc3a/); ICTY, *Prosecutor v. Dragoljub Kunarac, Radomir Kovač and Zoran Vuković*, Appeals Chamber, Judgment, IT-96-23 and IT-96-23/1-A, 12 June 2002, para. 83 ('Kunarac case') (https://www.legal-tools.org/doc/029a09/); International Criminal Tribunal for Rwanda ('ICTR'), *Prosecutor v. Laurent Semanza*, Appeals Chamber, Judgment, ICTR-97-20-A, 20 May 2005, para. 269 (https://www.legal-tools.org/doc/a686fd/).

[5] Henckaerts and Doswald-Beck, 2005, p. 572–73, see *supra* note 3; Tadić case, Decision on Jurisdiction, paras. 94, 143, see *supra* note 2. See also Michael Cottier, "Article 8(2)(b)(viii)", in Otto Triffterer (ed.), *Commentary on the Rome Statute of the International Criminal Court: Observers' Notes, Article by Article*, 2nd ed., C.H. Beck, Hart, Nomos, Munich, 2008, p. 275.

[6] Mary Ellen O'Connell, "Historical Development and Legal Basis", in Dieter Fleck (ed.), *The Handbook of International Humanitarian Law*, 3rd ed., Oxford University Press, Oxford, 2013, paras. 115 ff.

[7] 2 Kings 6: 21–23 (King James' version).

[8] Patrick Olivelle, *Manu's Code of Law: A Critical Edition and Translation of the Mānava-Dharmaśāstra*, Oxford University Press, Oxford, 2005, ch. 7, verses 90–92; Nagendra Singh, "Armed Conflicts and Humanitarian Laws of Ancient India", in Christophe Swinarski (ed.), *Studies and Essays on International Humanitarian Law and Red Cross Principles*, Kluwer Law International, The Hague, 1985, pp. 531–36.

[9] O'Connell, 2013, para. 107, see *supra* note 6; see also Werle and Jessberger, 2014, paras. 1032–34, see *supra* note 2.

---

through the Middle Ages, with Europe being an example, certain means and methods of warfare were prohibited. Codes of conduct in hostilities among knights applied to various forms of conflict.[10] There are many examples of similar rules in other cultures around the world.[11]

The Age of Enlightenment formalised warfare to the extent that war became an official matter between states and their armies,[12] but it was not until the second half of the nineteenth century that the first significant steps towards a more comprehensive codification of law governing armed conflict were taken. A national, albeit historically significant document in this regard was the so-called Lieber Code of 1863. Drafted by the German-American law professor Francis Lieber on the order of President Abraham Lincoln and intended for the armed forces of the United States during the American Civil War, the Lieber Code contained rules governing how soldiers should conduct themselves in wartime and prohibited certain means and methods of warfare. In particular, it required the humane treatment of civilians in the areas in which armed conflict was taking place, and generally forbade the execution of prisoners of war ("no quarter").[13] While the Lieber Code's applicability was confined to the territory of the United States, it had an inspirational effect beyond its borders, strongly influencing the further codification of the laws of war and the adoption of similar national codes by other states. In addition, it sparked initiatives at the international level: in 1868, a number of mostly European states, Russia and the Ottoman Empire issued the Saint Petersburg Declaration,[14] marking the first formal international agreement pro-

---

[10] *Ibid.*, Werle and Jessberger, para. 1034, see *supra* note 2.

[11] O'Connell, 2013, paras. 107 ff., see *supra* note 6.

[12] Leslie C. Green, *The Contemporary Law of Armed Conflict*, 3rd ed., Manchester University Press, Manchester, 2008, pp. 35 ff.

[13] General Orders No. 100: Instructions for the Government of Armies of the United States in the Field, promulgated on 24 April 1863 ('Lieber Code'), printed in Dietrich Schindler and Jiří Toman, *The Laws of Armed Conflicts*, Martinus Nijhoff, Dordrecht, 1988, pp. 3–23. See, however, Art. 60, second sentence, containing an exception to the rule: "No body of troops has the right to declare that it will not give, and therefore will not expect, quarter; but a commander is permitted to direct his troops to give no quarter, in great straits, when his own salvation makes it impossible to cumber himself with prisoners". This exception was subsequently dropped in more modern codifications of the rule.

[14] Declaration Renouncing the Use, in Time of War, of Explosive Projectiles Under 400 Grammes Weight, Saint Petersburg, 29 November/11 December 1868 ('Saint Petersburg Declaration'), reprinted in Schindler and Toman, 1988, pp. 102 ff., see *supra* note 13.

hibiting the use of certain weapons in war.[15] Of note is the fact that states for the first time formally agreed "that the only legitimate object which States should endeavour to accomplish during war is to weaken the military forces of the enemy" and that the employment of arms "which uselessly aggravate the sufferings of disabled men, or render their death inevitable" would exceed this purpose and "be contrary to the laws of humanity".[16]

11.2.2. The Birth of Geneva and Hague Law

Today's war crimes can be subdivided along two main axes: the first distinguishes between international and non-international armed conflict;[17] the second distinguishes between law protecting persons not or no longer taking active part in hostilities, on the one hand, and rules prohibiting certain methods and means of warfare, on the other. The development and sources of these latter strands of law are briefly outlined, followed by a discussion of their application in light of the character of the armed conflict.

11.2.2.1. The Law of The Hague

Following earlier efforts to find common elements for an international convention on the laws of war in Saint Petersburg in 1868 as well as during the Brussels Conference in 1874,[18] both greatly inspired by the provisions of the Lieber Code, the conferences in The Hague in 1899 and 1907

---

[15] The Declaration confirms the customary rule according to which the use of arms, projectiles and material of a nature to cause unnecessary suffering is prohibited; International Committee of the Red Cross ('ICRC'), Treaties and States Parties to Such Treaties: Introduction to the Saint Petersburg Declaration.

[16] Saint Petersburg Declaration, see *supra* note 14.

[17] See ICC Statute, Art. 8; while Art. 8(2)(a) and (b) covers crimes committed in international armed conflicts, the less detailed sections (c) and (e) list war crimes applicable in non-international armed conflict; Rome Statute of the International Criminal Court, Entered into Force 1 July 2002 ('ICC Statute'). This distinction would, however, appear to be losing significance due to an increasing convergence in the bodies of law applicable in each conflict. See Cottier, 2008, para. 2, *supra* note 5; Werle and Jessberger, 2014, paras. 1071, 1076, *supra* note 2.

[18] The Project of an International Declaration concerning the Laws and Customs of War of 27 August 1874 was, however, never ratified since not all the 15 European states participating in the Brussels Conference were willing to accept it as a binding convention. See the text in Schindler and Toman, 1988, pp. 22–34, *supra* note 13.

brought those initiatives to a historic conclusion. At these conferences, states set a new international standard for the protection of soldiers and the general conduct in war, laid down in the Regulations concerning the Laws and Customs of War on Land ('Hague Regulations'). These legal texts were attached to the Hague Conventions on war on land of 1899 and 1907.[19] The Hague Regulations comprehensively set out minimum rights of prisoners of war. They also established the fundamental principle that "[t]he right of belligerents to adopt means of injuring the enemy is not unlimited".[20] In elaboration of this principle, the Hague Regulations also prohibited weapons "of a nature to cause superfluous injury" or "calculated to cause unnecessary suffering".[21] The provisions of the Hague Regulations constitute the so-called Hague law on the means and methods of warfare[22] and are considered as embodying rules of customary international law.[23]

Since these treaties were adopted at a time when international law was considered to apply only between states, even humanitarian texts such as the Hague Regulations did not contain any provisions explicitly criminalising violations of the treaty, let alone establishing individual criminal responsibility. Seen from today's perspective, the exclusion of the individual from these international legal instruments represented the main obstacle for criminalisation of individuals responsible for state-led policies of illegal military activities.

---

[19] Convention (II) respecting the Laws and Customs of War on Land and its annex: Regulations concerning the Laws and Customs of War on Land, The Hague, 29 July 1899 ('Hague Regulations 1899'); Convention (IV) respecting the Laws and Customs of War on Land and its annex: Regulations concerning the Laws and Customs of War on Land, The Hague, 18 October 1907 ('Hague Regulations 1907'). The 1899 Convention and the Regulations were revised at the Second International Peace Conference in 1907. See the text in Schindler and Toman, 1988, pp. 69–93, *supra* note 13.

[20] Hague Regulations 1899 and Hague Regulations 1907, Art. 23, see *supra* note 19. This principle is repeated in Additional Protocol I to the 1949 Geneva Conventions, Art. 35(1), see *supra* note 1.

[21] Hague Regulations 1899 and Hague Regulations 1907, Article 23(e), see *supra* note 19. See also Additional Protocol I, Art. 35(2), see *supra* note 1.

[22] Cottier, 2008, para. 2, *supra* note 5; Werle and Jessberger, 2014, para. 1042, *supra* note 2.

[23] International Military Tribunal ('IMT'), Prosecutor v. Hermann Wilhelm Göring et al., Judgment, 1 October 1946, in The Trial of German Major War Criminals: Proceedings of the International Military Tribunal sitting at Nuremberg, Germany, Part 22, 22 August –1 October 1946, pp. 445 ff. ('IMT Judgment') (https://www.legal-tools.org/doc/f41e8b/); Cottier, 2008, para. 2, see supra note 5.

The inexhaustible inventiveness of human minds when it comes to cruelty in war has continued to manifest itself ever since, despite the existence and general acceptance of the Hague Regulations. Efforts of lawmakers to keep pace are evident in the various additions that have been made to Hague law through international treaties, in particular regarding the prohibition of certain weapons. The atrocities committed during the First World War provide a sad example of this: the protracted use of poisonous gas during the war triggered the adoption of the 1925 Geneva Protocol prohibiting the use of chemical and biological weapons in international armed conflicts.[24] Two more recent examples are the Chemical Weapons Convention[25] and the Mine-Ban Convention[26]

11.2.2.2. The Early Law of Geneva

Contemporaneous to the events leading to the Hague conferences, international efforts on the protection of persons affected by war were triggered through the Battle of Solferino in Italy between Austrian and French-Sardinian military in 1859. Horrified by the suffering of soldiers wounded and left to die on the battlefields, the Swiss businessman Henry Dunant wrote a book titled *A Memory of Solferino* in which he described his gruesome observations. His continued activism led to the founding of the International Committee of the Red Cross ('ICRC') in 1863 and eventually to the 1864 Geneva Convention for the Amelioration of the Condition of the Wounded in Armies in the Field ('1864 Geneva Convention').[27] This convention seeks to protect persons not or no longer partaking in armed conflict and provides the legal basis for humanitarian assistance in conflict zones carried out by humanitarian organisations such as the ICRC, as

---

[24] Protocol for the Prohibition of the Use in War of Asphyxiating, Poisonous or Other Gases, and of Bacteriological Methods of Warfare, Geneva, 17 June 1925, League of Nations Treaty Series, vol. 94, pp. 66–74. The 1925 Geneva Protocol is a protocol to the Hague Conventions of 1899 and 1907.

[25] Convention on the Prohibition of the Development, Production, Stockpiling and Use of Chemical Weapons and on their Destruction, Paris, 13 January 1993, No. 33757, United Nations Treaty Series, vol. 1974, p. 45.

[26] Convention on the Prohibition of the Use, Stockpiling, Production and Transfer of Anti-Personnel Mines and on their Destruction, Ottawa, 18 September 1997 No. 35597, United Nations Treaty Series, vol. 2056, p. 211.

[27] Convention for the Amelioration of the Condition of the Wounded in Armies in the Field. Geneva, 22 August 1864 ('1864 Geneva Convention').

well as their protection.[28] The 1864 Geneva Convention was replaced by the Geneva Conventions of 1906,[29] 1929[30] and 1949[31] on the same subject and marks the birth of so-called Geneva law which in turn represents a fundamental source of modern war crimes law.

11.3. Conceptual Revolution in Criminalising International Humanitarian Law Violations

The then unimaginable atrocities of the First World War triggered an international impetus to draw from international humanitarian law its most serious violations and to prosecute individuals for their commission.

11.3.1. War Crimes Prosecutions After the First World War

On 29 March 1919 the Commission on the Responsibility of the Authors of the War and on Enforcement of Penalties ('Commission on Responsibility'), convened by the victorious Allied powers, issued its report submitted to the Preliminary Peace Conference,[32] in which it elaborated a list of violations of international humanitarian law for which it sought the prosecution of individual perpetrators in war crimes trials before national courts. The Commission on Responsibility enumerated altogether 32 individual crimes committed in connection with the war, including, *inter alia*, murder, terror, cruel treatment of the civilian population including their use as human shields, deportation of civilians, execution of hostages and prisoners of war, intentional shelling of open towns and hospital ships, arbitrary destruction of property and pillage – all crimes within the repertoire of modern war crimes law.[33] In a similar vein, Article 228 of the Versailles Treaty acknowledged the right of the Allied and Associated Powers to bring before military tribunals persons accused of having

---

[28] *Ibid.*, Arts. 1–3, 7.

[29] Convention for the Amelioration of the Condition of the Wounded and Sick in Armies in the Field, Geneva, 6 July 1906.

[30] Convention for the Amelioration of the Condition of the Wounded and Sick in Armies in the Field, Geneva, 27 July 1929.

[31] Geneva Convention I, see *supra* note 1.

[32] Commission on the Responsibility of the Authors of the War and on Enforcement of Penalties, Report Submitted to the Preliminary Peace Conference, 29 March 1919, re-printed in *American Journal of International Law*, 1920, vol. 14, nos. 1/2, pp. 95–154.

[33] *Ibid.*, pp. 113 ff. and Annex I. For a contemporaneous list of war crimes see ICC Statute, Art. 8(2), *supra* note 17; see also Werle and Jessberger, 2014, para. 8, *supra* note 2.

committed "acts in violation of the laws and customs of war" and even contemplated setting up a special international tribunal to try the former German Kaiser, Wilhelm II.[34] However, neither proper war crimes prosecutions nor the international tribunal ever materialised, and the list of crimes drawn up by the Commission on Responsibility was never made operational in a courtroom. A number of national trials held before the German *Reichsgericht* in Leipzig, conducted largely to appease the Allied powers, ended as ineffective show trials.[35] One of the first attempts to transpose provisions from the Hague Regulations and the 1864 Geneva Convention (including accepted rules of sea warfare) to the context of individual criminal liability thus resulted in failure.

11.3.2. War Crimes Prosecutions After the Second World War

11.3.2.1. The First Revolution: Article 6(b) of the Charter of the International Military Tribunal

At the end of the Second World War, the four victorious powers over the Nazi regime came together in London and adopted the London Agreement,[36] establishing the International Military Tribunal ('IMT') at Nuremberg to try those most responsible for the atrocities committed under the auspices of the Nazi regime. The Statute of the IMT ('IMT Charter') contained the first war crimes provision of an international judicial body

---

[34] Treaty of Peace between the Allied and Associated Powers and Germany, and Protocol, Versailles, 28 June 1919 ('Versailles Treaty'). Art. 227 of the treaty accused Wilhelm II of a "supreme offence against international morality and the sanctity of treaties" before a special internationally staffed tribunal. This tribunal, however, never came to existence since William II remained in the Netherlands which never extradited him.

[35] See also Heiko Ahlbrecht, *Geschichte der völkerrechtlichen Strafgerichtsbarkeit im 20. Jahrhundert*, Nomos, Baden-Baden, 1999, pp. 42 ff. In addition, the applicable law before the *Reichsgericht* was German national criminal law and was thus of little or no significance for the codification of war crimes as crimes under international law.

[36] Agreement by the Government of the United States of America, the Provisional Government of the French Republic, the Government of the United Kingdom of Great Britain and Northern Ireland and the Government of the Union of Soviet Socialist Republics for the Prosecution and Punishment of the Major War Criminals of the European Axis, 8 August 1945, His Majesty's Stationery Office, London, 1945, reprinted in *American Journal of International Law*, 1945, vol. 39, suppl. 257 ('London Agreement').

creating individual criminal liability. Article 6(b) of the IMT Charter[37] established the Tribunal's jurisdiction over

> violations of the laws or customs of war. Such violations shall include, but not be limited to, murder, ill treatment or deportation to slave labor or for any other purpose of civilian population of or in occupied territory, murder or ill-treatment of prisoners of war or persons on the seas, killing of hostages, plunder of public or private property, wanton destruction of cities, towns or villages, or devastation not justified by military necessity.[38]

The Charter of the International Military Tribunal for the Far East ('IMTFE Charter') contained a similar, albeit less comprehensive war crimes provision.[39]

Article 6(b) of the IMT Charter marked a revolutionary step by its drafters: for the first time, war crimes were clearly identified and were made punishable as a crime generating individual criminal responsibility under international law. In fact, the IMT Charter, as well as its application in the *Göring et al.* trial, in which 21 of the most responsible Nazi perpetrators were tried, has often been invoked as the birth of international criminal law.[40] Article 6(b) established, for the first time, the direct link from a prohibition of certain conduct under international humanitarian law to its criminalisation, generating criminal liability of the individual. Numerous subsequent trials of individuals by the occupying powers in post-war Germany adopted this and other provisions of the IMT Charter.[41]

---

[37] Although it was Art. 228 of the Versailles Treaty that introduced the term "acts in violation of the laws and customs of war" as a criminal offence into international treaty law, it merely referred to punishment by national (military) courts under national law. However, the statement that those violations and individual punishment thereof was a matter of international concern represented a novelty; Bothe, 2002, p. 382, see *supra* note 4.

[38] IMT Charter, Art. 6(b), see *supra* note 4.

[39] Charter of the International Military Tribunal for the Far East, Tokyo, 19 January 1946, Art. 5, establishing the Tribunal's jurisdiction over "Conventional War Crimes: Namely, violations of the laws or customs of war" ('IMTFE Charter') (https://www.legal-tools.org/doc/a3c41c/).

[40] Werle and Jessberger, 2014, para. 15, see *supra* note 2.

[41] These trials were held pursuant to Control Council Law No. 10, Punishment of Persons Guilty of War Crimes, Crimes Against Peace and Against Humanity, 20 December 1945, 3 Official Gazette Control Council for Germany 50–55, 1946 ('CCL No. 10') (https://www.legal-tools.org/doc/ffda62/). See Principles of International Law Recognized in the Charter of the Nüremberg Tribunal and in the Judgment of the Tribunal, 1950, doc. A/1316.

The final content of Article 6(b) had been inspired by the preparatory works of the United Nations War Crimes Commission ('UNWCC'), which had been established in 1942 to collect evidence regarding war crimes committed in over 30,000 international criminal cases.[42]

As for the individual crimes listed in the provision, a rather cautious approach of the IMT drafters can be observed in criminalising a select number of prohibitions contained in national military manuals, previous international conventions such as the Lieber Code,[43] and the 1907 Hague Regulations.[44] These represented war crimes provisions that the IMT considered had crystallised into customary law by the time of the Second World War.[45] The list of war crimes is significantly less extensive than the findings of the Commission on Responsibility after the First World War. However, this restrictive approach had the benefit that war crimes in the IMT Charter were on solid grounds as to their existence under customary international law in 1939 (that is, at the beginning of the Second World War), and of being manifestly reflected in *opinio juris* through numerous national and international legal instruments and in state practice before national (military) courts.[46] Hence, with a view to the non-retroactivity principle (*nullum crimen sine lege scripta*), the existence of crimes codified in Article 6(b) was firmly founded in international texts and national laws providing for individual criminal responsibility for these crimes.[47]

---

[42] The UNWCC was composed of 17 nations. M. Cherif Bassiouni, *Introduction to International Criminal Law*, rev. 2nd ed., Brill, Leiden, 2013, p. 549; see also Dan Plesch and Shanti Sattler, "Changing the Paradigm of International Criminal Law: Considering the Work of the United Nations War Crimes Commission of 1943–1948", in *International Community Law Review*, 2013, vol. 15, no. 2, pp. 203–23; Richard J. Goldstone, "Foreword: The United Nations War Crimes Commission Symposium", in *Criminal Law Forum*, 2014, vol. 25, nos. 1/2, pp. 9–15. The public archive of the UNWCC is available in the ICC Legal Tools Database.

[43] See, for instance, the provision on murder and ill-treatment. Henckaerts and Doswald-Beck, 2005, rules 89, 90, pp. 311ff., see *supra* note 3.

[44] Hague Regulations 1907, Arts. 23–28, 47, 56, see *supra* note 19.

[45] IMT Judgment, see *supra* note 23.

[46] See Report of the Secretary-General Pursuant to Paragraph 2 of Security Council Resolution 808 (1993), UN doc. S/25704, 3 May 1993, para. 42 ('Secretary-General's Report on Resolution 808').

[47] Werle and Jessberger, 2014, para. 26, see *supra* note 2.

11.3.2.2. Part Two of the Revolution: The Grave Breaches Provisions of the Geneva Conventions

In the wake of the Second World War, states were urgently aware of the fact that the international legal framework addressing atrocities committed during times of war was far from complete. International treaties and conventions addressing international humanitarian law merely spelled out conduct that was considered a violation of the applicable legal regime but did not (yet) criminalise such violations. Other atrocity crimes had not even been codified in international conventions, such as the crime of genocide.[48] Further, a comprehensive framework protecting civilians in armed conflict was missing despite general agreement that civilians need protection in armed hostilities and may not be a legitimate military target.

As a first comprehensive response to the identified lacunae in 1949 the four Geneva Conventions came into force, revising and adapting previous relevant conventions.[49] All four Conventions contain rules that apply in times of armed conflict[50] and seek to protect persons who are not or no longer taking part in hostilities: the wounded and sick in armed forces in the field and at sea, prisoners of war and civilians. Geneva Convention IV in particular was a direct response to the horrendous crimes committed against the civilian population during the Second World War, and for the first time comprehensively codified the protection of civilians in international armed conflict.[51]

The revolutionary aspect of these conventions is the grave breaches provision in each of the four Conventions, sanctioning the most severe infractions of the Conventions committed against persons or values protected therein. The following grave breaches are similar to all four conventions:

---

[48] Convention on the Prevention and Punishment of the Crime of Genocide, adopted by the General Assembly of the United Nations on 9 December 1948, UN Treaty Series No. 1021 (1951), pp. 278 ff.

[49] Geneva Convention I; Geneva Convention II; Geneva Convention III; Geneva Convention IV, see *supra* note 1.

[50] The Geneva Conventions' Common Article 2 stipulates that they apply wherever there objectively exists an armed conflict: "even if the state of war is not recognized by one of the [belligerent parties]". See also ICTR, *Prosecutor v. Jean Paul Akayesu*, Trial Chamber, Judgment, ICTR-96-4-T, 2 September 1998, paras. 602–10 ('Akayesu case') (https://www.legal-tools.org/doc/b8d7bd/).

[51] Werle and Jessberger, 2014, para. 1039, *supra* note 2.

> wilful killing, torture or inhuman treatment, including bio-
> logical experiments, wilfully causing great suffering or seri-
> ous injury to body or health, and extensive destruction and
> appropriation of property, not justified by military necessity
> and carried out unlawfully and wantonly.[52]

Geneva Convention III[53] and Geneva Convention IV[54] contain further specific prohibitions.

All grave breaches prohibitions are linked to a legal regime laid down in all four Geneva Conventions, obliging member states either to prosecute perpetrators of these crimes or to extradite the suspect(s) to third countries willing to undertake such a prosecution.[55] In other words, the Conventions explicitly link certain prohibitions under international humanitarian law to a mandatory regime of individual criminal accountability – "to provide effective penal sanctions for persons committing [grave breaches]". In doing so, the drafters of the Conventions followed a trend set by the IMT Charter in identifying key provisions that not only merit follow-up through judicial proceedings but also confer a legal obligation on states, and thus the international community, to act. At the same time, the grave breaches provisions clarified that not every violation of international humanitarian law incurs individual criminal liability. Today, the Geneva Conventions are ratified by all states and form part of the body of customary international law.[56]

However, the Geneva Conventions failed to take the further step of contemplating the possibility of an international criminal tribunal competent to try individuals for such crimes – despite the fact that such an idea

---

[52] Geneva Convention I, Art. 50; Geneva Convention II, Art. 51; Geneva Convention III, Art. 130; Geneva Convention IV, Art. 147, see *supra* note 1.

[53] Geneva Convention III, Art. 130 prohibits in addition "compelling a prisoner of war to serve in the forces of the hostile Power", see *supra* note 1.

[54] Geneva Convention IV, Art. 147 prohibits in addition "unlawful deportation or transfer or unlawful confinement of a protected person, compelling a protected person to serve in the forces of a hostile Power, or wilfully depriving a protected person of the rights of fair and regular trial prescribed in the present Convention, taking of hostages", see *supra* note 1.

[55] For Geneva Convention I, see Arts. 50 (grave breaches) and 49 (penal sanction regime); for Geneva Convention II, see Arts. 51 (grave breaches) and 50 (penal sanction regime); for Geneva Convention III, see Arts. 130 (grave breaches) and 129 (penal sanction regime); and for Geneva Convention IV, see Arts. 147 (grave breaches) and 146 (penal sanction regime), see *supra* note 1.

[56] Secretary-General's Report on Resolution 808, para. 37, see *supra* note 46.

had already been considered by the General Assembly of the newly established United Nations for the crime of genocide in reaction to the work of the IMT.[57] Also, the term 'war crimes' was not used in any of the conventions.

11.3.2.3. The 1977 Additional Protocols

While the grave breaches provisions represented a cornerstone for the transposition of certain violations of international humanitarian law to war crimes law, the dynamics and rapidly diversifying geometry of modern warfare made a number of remaining gaps plainly visible. One of the important gaps arose from the fact that armed conflicts were moving steadily away from traditional interstate wars and into more complex patterns; internal armed conflicts became more frequent with limited or concealed involvement of other (state) actors.

The 1977 Additional Protocols were meant to modify and amplify the Geneva Conventions in response to these new forms of armed conflict. Additional Protocol I contains further provisions on the protection of victims of international armed conflicts.[58] Of relevance, it stipulates that armed resistance against colonial domination, foreign occupation and "racist regimes" also qualifies as international armed conflict, thereby applying the framework of the Geneva Conventions to armed conflicts between state authorities and armed groups fighting for their right of self-determination on the territory of that state.[59] Additional Protocol I also contains a number of additional provisions on means and methods of warfare, elaborating on general principles from the Hague Conventions[60] and thus incorporating Geneva law and Hague law together in a single legal document. Furthermore, Additional Protocol I reiterates fundamental

---

[57] Of note, the 1948 Genocide Convention, Art. 6 provided for such an "international penal tribunal as may have jurisdiction with respect to those Contracting Parties which shall have accepted its jurisdiction". See UN doc. A/RES3/260 (1948), where the General Assembly tasks the International Law Commission to study the "desirability and possibility of establishing an international judicial organ for the trial of persons charged with genocide". See also M. Cherif Bassiouni (ed.), *The Statute of the International Criminal Court: A Documentary* History, Transnational Publishers, Ardsley, NY, 1998, p. 741 ff.; Werle and Jessberger, 2014, para. 58, *supra* note 2.

[58] Additional Protocol I, see *supra* note 1.

[59] *Ibid.*, Art. 1(4).

[60] See *ibid.*, Art. 35, reiterating basic principles laid down in Arts. 22, 23 of the Hague Regulations 1907.

principles of *ius in bello* such as the principles of distinction, military necessity and proportionality.[61] Finally, Additional Protocol I provides some important additions to the Geneva Conventions' grave breaches provisions in its Articles 11 and, most importantly, 85, spelling out a number of crimes that had not been explicitly covered by either the IMT Charter or the Geneva Conventions' grave breaches provisions.[62] As an important clarifying note, Article 85(5) of Additional Protocol I stipulates that "grave breaches of the [Conventions and Additional Protocol I] shall be regarded as war crimes", thus incorporating the prohibitions into the context of individual criminal responsibility.

Additional Protocol II of 1977[63] addresses an ambit of application of international humanitarian law that had hitherto received only marginal attention, namely the field of non-international armed conflict. The Geneva Conventions had already laid the foundation for the architecture of international humanitarian law in non-international armed conflict: Article 3 common to the four Geneva Conventions ('Common Article 3') extended many of the fundamental principles and prohibitions in the Geneva Conventions to non-international armed conflicts, overriding obstacles of national sovereignty that had previously prevented international humanitarian law from applying to intrastate conflicts. Internal or civil wars were traditionally considered as internal matters of states, covered by state sovereignty and preventing any intervention by other states in the often bloody countering of intrastate insurgencies.[64] The basic premise underlying Common Article 3 was therefore truly revolutionary in nature.

---

[61] For example, Additional Protocol I, Arts. 35 (military necessity); 48, 52(2) (distinction); 51(5)(b), 57 (proportionality), see *supra* note 1. See, on these principles, Henckaerts and Doswald-Beck, 2005, part I, *supra* note 3; Robert Cryer, Håkan Friman, Darryl Robinson and Elizabeth Wilmshurst, *An Introduction to International Criminal Law and Procedure*, 3rd ed., Cambridge Univesity Press, Cambridge, 2014, section 12.1.3.

[62] Yves Sandoz, Christophe Swinarski and Bruno Zimmerman (eds.), *Commentary on the Additional Protocols of 8 June 1977 to the Geneva Conventions of 12 August 1949*, International Committee of the Red Cross, Geneva, 1987, para. 3472.

[63] Protocol Additional to the Geneva Conventions of 12 August 1949, and relating to the Protection of Victims of Non-International Armed Conflicts (Protocol II), 8 June 1977 ('Additional Protocol II').

[64] See, on the non-intervention principle, International Court of Justice ('ICJ'), Case Concerning Military and Paramilitary Activities in and against Nicaragua, *Nicaragua v. United States* (Merits), 27 June 1986, ICJ Reports 1986, p. 106, para. 202 ('Nicaragua case'); ICJ, Armed Activities on the Territory of the Congo, *Democratic Republic of the Congo v.*

Despite being the only provision in the Geneva Conventions applicable to non-international armed conflict, Common Article 3 contains several fundamental rules, including the humane treatment of persons taking no active part in hostilities[65]; care for the wounded, sick and shipwrecked; and the ICRC's right to offer its services to the parties to the conflict.[66] The International Court of Justice held that Common Article 3 provides a "minimum yardstick" for all armed conflicts and reflects "elementary considerations of humanity".[67] However, Common Article 3 has one essential weakness which impeded the transposition of this provision to the criminal law context: it was excluded from the regime criminalising grave breaches and obliging states to prosecute those infractions nationally.

Additional Protocol II develops and supplements Common Article 3 by spelling out a comprehensive list of prohibited acts against persons taking no direct part in hostilities, which are already covered for international armed conflict by the 1907 Hague Regulations, the Geneva Conventions and Additional Protocol I.[68] It therefore extends some fundamental international humanitarian law guarantees into the ambit of non-international armed conflict.[69] In determining its scope of applicability,[70] Additional Protocol II gave further contours to the definition of non-international armed conflict such as the requirement of a certain belliger-

---

Uganda (Merits), 19 December 2005, ICJ Reports 2005, p. 168. See also Cryer *et al.*, 2014, section 12.1.7., *supra* note 61.

[65] This includes, *inter alia*, the prohibition of violence to life and person, cruel treatment, torture, taking of hostages, humiliating treatment and extrajudicial executions. See Geneva Conventions I–IV, Common Art. 3(1)(a)–(d), *supra* note 1.

[66] The ICRC's involvement entails a level of monitoring of such internal crisis situations, which may have had the effect of reminding the belligerent parties of certain minimal rules and protections applicable in *any* armed conflict.

[67] Nicaragua case, p. 114, para. 218, see *supra* note 64.

[68] Additional Protocol II, Art. 4, see *supra* note 63.

[69] *Ibid.*

[70] *Ibid.*, Art. 1(1), finding that it applies to all armed conflicts between a member state's armed forces and "dissident armed forces or other organised armed groups which, under responsible command, exercise such control over a part of its territory as to enable them to carry out sustained and concerted military operations and to implement this Protocol". The territorial control requirement, is however not part of international customary law and thus establishes a rather unfortunate jurisdictional limitation of Additional Protocol II.

---

ent intensity[71] – a threshold requirement which has since been accepted by the UN *ad hoc* tribunals and the ICC.[72] However, Additional Protocol II stopped short of elevating the enumerated prohibitions in its Article 4 to grave breaches or establishing a duty on states to prosecute (or extradite), thus perpetuating what has been described as a "glaring and preposterous"[73] disparity between the law applicable in international armed conflict and that which applies to internal armed conflict.

The Additional Protocols represented important progress in the further conceptual development of international humanitarian law and the extension of its protective reach, in particular to non-international armed conflict. However, with the Cold War in full swing, geopolitical realities at the time did not allow for an advancement of the transposition of relevant prohibitions to the international criminal law context.

11.4. Conceptual Revolution in Criminalising International Humanitarian Law Violations in Non-International Armed Conflict

11.4.1. The Statutes of the ICTY and ICTR

The establishment of the UN *ad hoc* tribunals just after the end of the Cold War – the International Criminal Tribunal for the former Yugoslavia ('ICTY') in 1994 and International Criminal Tribunal for Rwanda

---

[71]   *Ibid.*, Art. 1(2): "This Protocol shall not apply to situations of internal disturbances and tensions, such as riots, isolated and sporadic acts of violence and other acts of a similar nature, as not being armed conflicts".

[72]   ICC Statute, Art. 8(2)(d) and (f), see *supra* note 17; and ICC, Situation in the Democratic Republic of the Congo, *Prosecutor v. Thomas Lubanga Dyiolo*, Trial Judgment pursuant to Article 74 of the Statute, ICC-01/04-01/06-2842, 14 March 2012, paras. 534 ff. (https://www.legal-tools.org/doc/677866/); ICTY, *Prosecutor v. Limaj et al.*, Trial Judgment, IT-03-66-T, 30 November 2005, para. 90 (https://www.legal-tools.org/doc/4e469a/); ICTY, *Prosecutor v. Haradinaj et al.*, Trial Judgment, IT-04-84-T, 3 April 2008, para. 60 (https://www.legal-tools.org/doc/025913/); ICTY, *Prosecutor v. Ljube Boškoski et al.*, Trial Judgment, IT-04-82-T, 10 July 2008, paras. 199–203 (https://www.legal-tools.org/doc/939486/); Tadić case, Decision on Jurisdiction, paras. 70 ff., see *supra* note 2; ICTR, *Prosecutor v. Clement Kayishema and Obed Ruzindana*, Trial Judgment, ICTR-95-1, 21 May 1999, para. 171 (https://www.legal-tools.org/doc/0811c9/); ICTR, *Prosecutor v. Alfred Musema*, Trial Judgment, ICTR-96-13, 27 January 2000, para. 248 (https://www.legal-tools.org/doc/1fc6ed/).

[73]   Antonio Cassese and Paola Gaeta (rev.), *Cassese's International Criminal Law*, 3rd ed., Oxford Univesity Press, Oxford, 2013, p. 71.

('ICTR') in 1995 – in and of itself can be called a 'revolutionary' development. They represent the first truly international criminal tribunals ever established; in contrast, the IMT represented a creation of only the four victorious Allied powers and was therefore not truly international. Furthermore, the *ad hoc* tribunals' statutes contain provisions not only for war crimes but also for crimes against humanity and genocide. The notion of 'international core crimes' gained shape and content. In addition, both tribunals and their jurisdictions contributed substantially to filling the legal vacuum in non-international armed conflict[74] and ultimately to the transposition of crimes accepted in interstate conflict to the context of civil wars.

The ICTR was established by the UN Security Council in response to the Rwandan genocide, which was in overwhelming part an internal armed conflict.[75] Article 4 of the ICTR Statute established individual criminal jurisdiction over prohibitions under Common Article 3 of the Geneva Conventions as well as Article 4 of Additional Protocol II,[76] thereby for the first time in history extending the legal regime of war crimes into non-international armed conflict. The Statute of the ICTY, established by the UN Security Council a year earlier, did not contain such a provision. While the Secretary-General of the UN had clarified that the ICTY would "have the task of applying existing international humanitarian law",[77] the Security Council decided to take a "more expansive approach to the choice of the applicable law" for the ICTR than for the ICTY in that it included war crimes provisions applicable in non-international armed conflict in Article 4 of the ICTR Statute "regardless whether they were considered part of customary international law or

---

[74] Akayesu case, Trial Judgment, paras. 602–10, see *supra* note 50.

[75] See Preliminary Report of the Independent Commission of Experts established in accordance with Security Council Resolution 935 (1994), annexed to Letter dated 1 October 1994 from the Secretary-General addressed to the President of the Security Council, UN doc. S/1994/1125, 4 October 1994, paras. 91–94; see also Secretary-General's Report on Practical Arrangements for the Effective Functioning of the International Tribunal for Rwanda, UN doc. S/1995/134, 13 February 1995, paras. 11–12 ('Secretary-General's Report on ICTR').

[76] Additional Protocol II, Art. 4(2) has been almost entirely been taken over into ICTR Statute, Art. 4 excluding only the prohibition of "slavery and the slave trade in all their forms" of Additional Protocol II, Art. 4(2)(f), see *supra* note 63; see United Nations Security Council resolution 955 (1994), adopted on 8 November 1994, UN doc. S/RES/955 (1994) ('ICTR Statute').

[77] Secretary-General's Report on Resolution 808, para. 34, see *supra* note 46.

whether they have customarily entailed the individual criminal responsibility of the perpetrator of the crime".[78] Both UN *ad hoc* tribunals have
since confirmed repeatedly that the criminalisation of acts in Article 4 of
the ICTR Statute represents international customary law.[79]

The ICTY war crimes provision represents the logical next step
from the IMT Charter in that it contains two provisions: the first is Article
2, which transposes the Geneva Conventions' grave breaches to the ambit
of international criminal law by establishing individual criminal responsibility for their commission.[80] The second provision, encapsulated in Article 3, is akin to Article 6(b) of the IMT Charter in that it reflects in relevant part the 1907 Hague Regulations on prohibited means and methods
of warfare. However, neither the ICTY Statute nor the Secretary-
General's report on the establishment of the ICTY determines the applicability of the ICTY's war crimes provision in non-international armed
conflict.[81] Such determination has therefore been left to the Tribunal's
jurisprudence.

Not long after the Tribunal's inception, the scope of war crimes applicable in non-international armed conflict under the ICTY Statute was
clarified by the Appeals Chamber in its interlocutory decision on jurisdiction in the *Tadić* case.[82] The Appeals Chamber determined that general
rules and principles protecting civilians or civilian objects from the hostilities (Geneva law) as well as rules regarding means and methods of warfare (Hague law) have gradually been extended to non-international
armed conflict.[83] It held that "[w]hat is inhumane, and consequently pro-

---

[78] Secretary-General's Report on ICTR, para. 12, see *supra* note 75.

[79] Akayesu case, Trial Judgment, paras. 608–9, 616, see *supra* note 50; ICTR, *Prosecutor v.
Georges Anderson Nderubumwe Rutaganda*, Trial Judgment, ICTR-96-3, 6 December
1999, paras. 86–90 (https://www.legal-tools.org/doc/f0dbbb/); ICTR, *Prosecutor v. Laurent Semanza*, Trial Judgment, ICTR-97-20, 15 May 2003, para. 353 (https://www.legal-
tools.org/doc/7e668a/); ICTY, *Prosecutor v. Duško Tadić*, Trial Judgment, IT-94-1, 7 May
1997, para. 609 ('Tadić case') (https://www.legal-tools.org/doc/0a90ae/); Tadić case, Decision on Jurisdiction, paras. 116, 134, see *supra* note 2.

[80] See Secretary-General's Report on Resolution 808, paras. 37–40, see *supra* note 46.

[81] *Ibid.*, paras. 41–44. The Report does, however, make clear that the provisions outlined in
the proposed (and later accepted) ICTY Statute, Arts. 2 and 3 represent "without doubt"
international customary and/or treaty law; *id.*, paras. 33–36.

[82] Tadić case, Decision on Jurisdiction, see *supra* note 2.

[83] *Ibid.*, paras. 119, 127. On Hague and Geneva law see Kai Ambos, *Internationales
Strafrecht*, 4th ed., 2014, para. 6.

---

scribed, in international wars, cannot but be inhumane and inadmissible in civil strife".[84] It then concluded that, while a number of rules applicable in international armed conflict have extended to internal conflicts, there was no "full and mechanical transplant" of those rules into the internal context.[85]

On this basis, the ICTY Appeals Chamber held that serious violations of the customary rules applicable in non-international armed conflict may also generate individual criminal responsibility – a finding embodied by Article 4 of the ICTR Statute and later endorsed by the SCSL.[86] It follows from this finding that the extension of international humanitarian law into internal armed conflict is mirrored by a corresponding extension of individual criminal liability for the violation of these laws wherever state practice and *opinio juris* provide the necessary indicia for it.[87] This is in fact what the ICTY Appeals Chamber established, holding in its *Tadić* jurisdiction decision that Article 3 of the ICTY Statute, listing serious violations of laws and customs of war, is applicable "regardless of whether the [violations] occurred within an internal or an international armed conflict".[88]

---

[84] Tadić case, Decision on Jurisdiction, para. 119, see *supra* note 2: "[E]lementary considerations of humanity and common sense make it preposterous that the use by States of weapons prohibited in armed conflicts between themselves be allowed when States try to put down rebellion by their own nationals on their own territory".

[85] *Ibid.*, para. 126: "[R]ather, the general essence of those rules, and not the detailed regulation they may contain, has become applicable to internal conflicts"; see also ICTY, *Prosecutor v. Kupreškić et al.*, Trial Chamber, Judgment, IT-95-16, 14 January 2000, paras. 521 ff. ('Kupreškić case') (https://www.legal-tools.org/doc/5c6a53/).

[86] Tadić case, Decision on Jurisdiction, para. 134, *supra* note 2; see also SCSL, *Prosecutor v. Augustine Gbao et al.*, Trial Chamber, Judgment, SCSL-04-15-T, 2 March 2009, paras. 60–65 ('Gbao case') (https://www.legal-tools.org/doc/7f05b7/); SCSL, *Prosecutor v. Moinina Fofana, Allieu Kondewa and Sam Hinga Norman*, Appeals Chamber, Decision on Preliminary Motion on Lack of Jurisdiction Materiae: Nature of the Armed Conflict, SCSL-2004-14, 25 May 2004, para. 24 ('CDF case') (https://www.legal-tools.org/doc/a36f4a/); ICTR, *Prosecutor v. Joseph Kanyabashi et al.*, Trial Chamber, Decision on the Defence Motion on Jurisdiction, ICTR-96-15-T, 18 June 1997, para. 35 (https://www.legal-tools.org/doc/a0cb5c/); Akayesu case, Trial Judgment, paras. 610, 616, see *supra* note 50.

[87] Tadić case, Decision on Jurisdiction, paras. 128–35, see *supra* note 2; ICTY, *Prosecutor v. Mučić et al.*, Appeals Chamber, Judgment, IT-96-21, 20 February 2001, paras. 159–74 ('Čelebići case') (https://www.legal-tools.org/doc/051554/). See also Report of the Secretary-General on the establishment of a Special Court for Sierra Leone, 4 October 2000, UN doc. S/2000/915, para. 14. See also Werle and Jessberger, 2014, para.1070, see *supra* note 2.

[88] Tadić case, Decision on Jurisdiction, para. 137, see *supra* note 2.

By virtue of the Appeals Chamber's seminal findings in the *Tadić* decision, the ICTY opened the door for the applicability of Hague law in non-international armed conflict – a set of provisions that Article 4 of the ICTR Statute (based on Geneva law) had not explicitly covered. Taking the statutes of both tribunals together, it can be concluded that they opened the horizon for individual criminal responsibility for international crimes, derived from both Geneva and Hague law, in non-international armed conflict – and did so relatively comprehensively.

11.4.2. A Tool to Fill the Gaps: The *Tadić* Test

The ICTY *Tadić* jurisdiction decision went beyond simply declaring Article 3 of the ICTY Statute applicable in both international and non-international armed conflict. The Appeals Chamber also established a general test determining under which circumstances an offence amounts to a 'serious violation' of international humanitarian law and consequently can be prosecuted as a war crime under Article 3 of the ICTY Statute,[89] regardless of the character of the armed conflict concerned. This test consists of the following four prongs:

(i) the violation must constitute an infringement of a rule of international humanitarian law;

(ii) the rule must be customary in nature or, if it belongs to treaty law, the required conditions must be met [...];[90]

(iii) the violation must be "serious", that is to say, it must constitute a breach of a rule protecting important values, and the breach must involve grave consequences for the victim [...];

---

[89] The Statutes of the ICTY, ICTR and ICC require a violation to be "serious" to amount to a war crime; ICC Statute, Art. 8(2)(b), (c), (e), see *supra* note 17; ICTY Statute, Art. 1, see *supra* note 4; ICTR Statute, Art. 1, see *supra* note 76; United Nations Security Council, Resolution 1315 (2000), Adopted on 14 August 2000, UN doc. S/Res/1315 ('SCSL Statute'), Art. 1(1); Henckaerts and Doswald-Beck, 2005, p. 569, see *supra* note 3: national legislation and state practice shows that violations of international humanitarian law are treated as serious – and therefore as war crimes – if and when they "endanger protected persons or objects or if they breach important values". See also Čelebići case, Appeals Judgment, para. 126, *supra* note 87.

[90] In case of a violation of treaty law, the latter must be 1) unquestionably binding on the parties at the time of the alleged offence; and 2) not in conflict with or derogating from "peremptory norms of international law"; Tadić case, Decision on Jurisdiction, para. 143, see *supra* note 2.

(iv) the violation of the rule must entail, under customary or
conventional law, the individual criminal responsibility
of the person breaching the rule.[91]

While the first two prongs underline the fact that war crimes are
based on and intrinsically connected to a violation of international humanitarian law, the third prong sets a gravity requirement both in terms of the
protected values and regarding the effect of the crime on the victim. This
threshold requirement follows from the general assumption that for an
infraction of international humanitarian law to generate individual criminal liability it needs to be of a minimum gravity and directed against the
most essential values that the violated law seeks to protect.[92] To illustrate
the validity of this threshold requirement, the *Tadić* Appeals Chamber
explained that

> a combatant simply appropriating a loaf of bread in an occu-
> pied village would not amount to a "serious violation of in-
> ternational humanitarian law" although it may be regarded as
> falling foul of the basic principle laid down in Article 46,
> paragraph 1, of the Hague Regulations (and the correspond-
> ing rule of customary international law) whereby "private
> property must be respected" by any army occupying an ene-
> my territory.[93]

Further, the violation must have had a serious impact ("grave consequences") on the victim, thereby establishing what might be regarded as
a result requirement regarding the violation. The Chamber may have been
guided in this by the language of Additional Protocol I. Its Article 85(3)
establishes a result requirement for a number of grave breaches "when
committed wilfully, in violation of the relevant provisions of this Protocol, and *causing death or serious injury to body or health*".[94]

The fourth prong is a reminder that at the outset international humanitarian law consisted of rules applicable among states only.[95] The

---

[91] *Ibid.*, para. 94.

[92] Theodor Meron, "The Humanization of Humanitarian Law", in *American Journal of International Law*, 2000, vol. 94, no. 2, pp. 239, 260 ff.; Henckaerts and Doswald-Beck,
2005, pp. 569–70, see *supra* note 3.

[93] Tadić case, Decision on Jurisdiction, para. 94, see *supra* note 2.

[94] Additional Protocol I, Art. 85(3), see *supra* note 20 (emphasis added). See also Bothe,
2002, p. 384, see *supra* note 4.

[95] Meron, 2000, pp. 239, 243, see *supra* note 92.

general acknowledgement that these rules also generate rights and duties for the individual is fairly recent; the existence of an international rule conferring individual rights or duties has to be carefully established by assessing relevant *opinio juris* and state practice in the specific circumstances of the case.[96] In this respect the Appeals Chamber held that individual criminal responsibility pursuant to the fourth *Tadić* prong "can be inferred from, *inter alia*, state practice indicating an intention to criminalise the prohibition, including statements by government officials and international organisations, as well as punishment of violations by national courts and military tribunals".[97]

To date, the grave breaches provisions of the Geneva Conventions and of Additional Protocol I are, besides the Rome Statute of the International Criminal Court, the only examples of conventional rules explicitly conferring individual criminal responsibility for serious violations of international humanitarian law.[98] The *Tadić* test therefore represents a means to complement the non-exclusive war crimes provision in the ICTY Statute with further crimes that have attained customary status. Both UN *ad hoc* tribunals and the SCSL have consistently applied the *Tadić* test in their case law, significantly clarifying – and increasing – the ambit of war crimes in international and non-international armed conflict.[99]

---

[96] Cassese and Gaeta, 2013, p. 67, see *supra* note 73; Meron, 2000, pp. 239, 243, see *supra* note 92; O'Connell, 2013, paras. 135, 137, see *supra* note 6; Werle and Jessberger, 2014, para. 1066, see *supra* note 2.

[97] ICTY, *Prosecutor v. Stanislav Galić*, Appeals Chamber, Judgment, IT-98-29, 30 November 2006, para. 92 ('Galić case') (https://www.legal-tools.org/doc/c81a32/), citing, *Tadić* case, Decision on Jurisdiction, para. 128, see *supra* note 2.

[98] While the statutes of ICTY and ICTR explicitly refer to relevant prohibitions under humanitarian law (in fact the Geneva Conventions and their Additional Protocols) and attach individual criminal responsibility, these statutes do not represent multilateral treaties but are contained in resolutions of the UN Security Council (ICTY: S/RES/827 (1993), 25 May 1993, para. 2 with reference to the report of the Secretary-General (S/25704 and Add.l) pursuant to paragraph 2 of resolution 808 (1993); ICTR: S/RES/955 (1994), 8 November 1994, para. 1 and Annex). Similarly, the statutes of SCSL, ECCC and STL do not represent multilateral treaties. Only the Rome Statute of the International Criminal Court represents such a treaty document (UN doc. A/CONF.183/9). See also Cassese and Gaeta, 2013, p. 67, see *supra* note 73.

[99] See, for example, Galić case, Appeals Judgment, paras 91 ff., *supra* note 97; Kunarac case, Appeals Judgment, para. 66, see *supra* note 4; ICTY, *Prosecutor v. Kvočka et al.*, Trial Chamber, Judgment, IT-98-30/1, 2 November 2001, para. 123 ('Kvočka case') (https://www.legal-tools.org/doc/34428a/); ICTY, *Prosecutor v. Momčilo Perišić*, Trial Chamber, Judgment, IT-04-81 6 September 2011, para. 75 (https://www.legal-

The *Tadić* Appeals Chamber decision on jurisdiction, on par with Article 4 of the ICTR Statute, therefore truly revolutionised the law applicable in non-international armed conflict; even the ICRC did not claim that war crimes in non-international armed conflict existed prior to the tribunals' statutes and jurisprudence.[100] Subsequent jurisprudence from other international courts has also shown that there is increasing convergence between the rules applicable in non-international armed conflict and those applicable in international conflict. The SCSL Appeals Chamber, for example, found that regarding Article 3 of the SCSL Statute ("Violations of Article 3 common to the Geneva Conventions and of Additional Protocol II") any distinction "is no longer of great relevance *as these crimes are prohibited in all conflicts*".[101] Reiterating the earlier findings of the ICTY in *Tadić*, it held that crimes committed in the context of an internal armed conflict form part of the broader category of crimes acknowledged during international armed conflict.[102]

---

tools.org/doc/f3b23d/); ICTY *Prosecutor v. Stanišić and Simatović*, Trial Chamber, Judgment, IT-03-69-T, 30 May 2013, para. 950 (https://www.legal-tools.org/doc/066e67/); SCSL, *Prosecutor v. Moinina Fofana, Allieu Kondewa and Sam Hinga Norman*, Appeals Chamber, Decision on Preliminary Motion Based on Lack of Jurisdiction (Child Recruitment), SCSL-2004-14-AR72(E), 31 May 2004, para. 26 ff. ('CDF case') (https://www.legal-tools.org/doc/27e4fc/). For the ICC with its exhaustive war crimes provision any such extension of the pool of applicable war crimes remains impossible.

[100] Preliminary Remarks by the ICRC on the Setting-up of an International Tribunal for Prosecution of Persons Responsible for Serious Violations of International Humanitarian Law Committed on the Territory of the Former Yugoslavia, UNSCR res. 808 (1993), 25 March 1993, quoted in Christopher Greenwood, "The Development of International Humanitarian Law by the International Criminal Tribunal for the Former Yugoslavia", in *Max Planck Yearbook of United Nations Law*, 1998, vol. 2, p. 131: "international humanitarian law applicable to non-international armed conflicts does not provide for international penal responsibility".

[101] CDF case, Decision on Nature of Armed Conflict, para. 25, see *supra* note 86 (emphasis added). Similarly, the ICTY Appeals Chamber held in Čelebići case, Appeals Judgment, para. 150, see *supra* note 87, that "something which is prohibited in internal conflicts is necessarily outlawed in an international conflict where the scope of the rules is broader".

[102] *Ibid.*, CDF case, Decision on Nature of Armed Conflict, citing Frits Kalshoven and Liesbeth Zegveld, *Constraints on the Waging of War: An Introduction to International Humanitarian Law*, International Committee of the Red Cross, Geneva, 2001, p. 188; Rodney Dixon, Karim A.A. Khan and Richard May (eds.), *Archbold: International Criminal Courts: Practice, Procedure and Evidence*, 3rd ed., Sweet & Maxwell, London, 2003, paras. 11–26.

11.5. "Judicial Law-Making" of the UN *Ad Hoc* Tribunals?

Both UN *ad hoc* tribunals had, particularly in their earlier years, a multitude of novel and previously unresolved legal problems to tackle with the aim of defining and, where appropriate, enlarging the scope of protection for victims of mass atrocities.[103] The resolution of these problems often demanded a progressive stance towards the status of customary international law in the interpretation of the relevant sources. One example is the Appeals Chamber's finding in *Tadić* extending the scope of application of war crimes to non-international armed conflict.[104] Another example is the ICTY's determination that a test of "overall control" suffices to prove third-party state interference in a conflict that is geographically confined to another state and thus "elevates" the armed conflict to an international level.[105] In doing so, the ICTY diverged from previous International Court of Justice ('ICJ') jurisprudence in the *Nicaragua* case establishing an "effective control" test for third-party state interference for the purpose of State responsibility.[106]

In addition, the broadening of the concept by the ICTY of "protected persons" from the Geneva Conventions to encompass citizens of the

---

[103] Robert Heinsch, Die Weiterentwicklung des humanitären Völkerrechts durch die Strafgerichtshöfe für das ehemalige Jugoslawien und Ruanda, Berliner Wissenschafts-Verlag, Berlin, 2007, pp. 82–185; J.R.W.D. Jones and Steven Powles, International criminal practice: the International Criminal Tribunal for the Former Yugoslavia, the International Criminal Tribunal for Rwanda, the International Criminal Court, the Special Court for Sierra Leone, the East Timor Special Panel for Serious Crimes, War crimes prosecutions in Kosovo, Transnational Publishers, Ardsley, NY, 2003; L.J. van den Herik, The Contribution of the Rwanda Tribunal to the Development of International Law, Martinus Nijhoff, Leiden, 2005.

[104] Tadić case, Decision on Jurisdiction, para. 134, see *supra* note 2; Čelebići case, Appeals Judgment, para. 170, see *supra* note 87.

[105] Tadić, Appeals Judgment, paras. 131, 137, see *supra* note 4, confirmed by ICTY, *Prosecutor v. Zlatko Aleksovski*, Appeals Chamber, Judgment, IT-95-14-/1-A, 24 March 2000, para. 145 ('Aleksovski case') (https://www.legal-tools.org/doc/176f05/). For an evaluation of the "overall control" test, see Danesh Sarooshi, "Command Responsibility and the Blaškić case", in *International and Comparative Law Quarterly*, 2001, vol 50, pp. 452–65; Marco Sassòli and Laura M. Olson, "The Judgment of the ICTY Appeals Chamber on the merits in the Tadić Case: New Horizons for International Humanitarian and Criminal Law?", in *International Review of the Red Cross*, 2000, no. 839, pp. 733–69; see also James G. Stewart, "Towards a Single Definition of Armed Conflict in International Humanitarian Law: A Critique of Internationalized Armed Conflict", in *International Review of the Red Cross*, 2003, no. 850, pp. 313–49.

[106] Nicaragua case, Judgment, p. 14, see *supra* note 64.

---

state's own nationality by relying on "ethnic allegiance" instead of nationality as the determining criterion can be seen as an illustration of the Tribunal's amplification of the protective shield of international humanitarian law through a dynamic interpretation of the *status quo* of the governing law.[107] This last finding was in contrast even to the ICRC commentary at the time, which still provided that in order to be a protected person under the Geneva Conventions one needed to have the nationality of the enemy state.[108]

Further examples of the Tribunals' progressive jurisprudence can be found in the determination of individual crimes committed in violation of the laws and customs of war. An illustrative case is the crime of rape; although referred to in the definition of crimes against humanity, it was not explicitly listed as a war crime in Articles 2 and 3 of the ICTY Statute.[109] However, the results of investigations in the early years of the ICTY did not justify an indictment for crimes against humanity due to the absence of tangible proof of an attack directed against a civilian population; yet, at the same time, there was ample proof of sexual violence.[110] In the *Furundžija* case the Tribunal held that "the prohibition of rape in armed conflicts has been long recognised in international treaty law as well as in customary international law"[111] and thus added the crime of rape to the

---

[107] Tadić case, Appeals Judgment, paras. 163–69, see *supra* note 4, confirmed in Aleksovski case, Appeals Judgment, para. 153, see *supra* note 105, and various other decisions. For a discussion of this new standard, see Sassòli and Olson, 2000, p. 744, *supra* note 105.

[108] J.S. Pictet (ed.), Commentary on Geneva Conventions of 12 August 1949, vol. IV, Geneva Convention IV relative to the Protection of Civilian Persons in Time of War (International Committee of the Red Cross, Geneva, 1952, Art. 4, p. 46: "Even when the definition of protected persons is set out in this way, it may seem rather complicated. Nevertheless, disregarding points of detail, it will be seen that there are two main classes of protected person: (1) 'enemy nationals' within the national territory of each of the Parties to the conflict and (2) 'the whole population' of occupied territories (excluding nationals of the Occupying Power)".

[109] ICTY Statute, Art. 5(g), see *supra* note 4.

[110] Richard J. Goldstone, "Prosecuting Rape as a War Crime", in *Case Western Reserve Journal of International Law*, 2002, vol. 34, no. 3, pp. 277, 285; Goldstone, 2014, p. 13, see *supra* note 42.

[111] ICTY, *Prosecutor v. Anto Furundžija*, Trial Chamber, Judgment, IT-95-17/1, 10 December 1998, para. 168 ('Furundžija case') (https://www.legal-tools.org/doc/e6081b/); ICTY, *Prosecutor v. Mučić et al.*, Trial Chamber, Judgment, IT-96-21, 20 February 2001, paras. 476–79 ('Čelebići case') (https://www.legal-tools.org/doc/6b4a33/); ICTY, *Prosecutor v. Anto Furundžija*, Appeals Chamber, Judgment, IT-95-17/1, 27 July 2000, para. 210 ('Furundžija case') (https://www.legal-tools.org/doc/660d3f/); ICTY *Kvočka et al.*, Appeals

list of war crimes under Article 3 of the ICTY Statute.[112] Also, the Trial Chamber categorised forced oral penetration as rape rather than as sexual assault, thereby further developing the definition of rape as a crime under international law.[113] The *Furundžija* Trial Chamber also broadened the definition of torture under international (customary) law.[114]

In a similar vein, the ICTR jurisprudence has expanded the scope of protection for victims of mass atrocities. Thus, regarding the scope and definition of the crime of genocide, the ICTR held in in the *Akayesu* and *Gacumbitsi* cases, among others, that rape and sexual violence could constitute genocide when the specific conditions of genocide were fulfilled – that is, specific intent to destroy a group in whole or in part – despite Article 2 of the ICTR Statute and the Genocide Convention being devoid of any language expressly supporting such a finding.[115] Furthermore, the progressive definition of rape in *Akayesu*[116] has been hailed as one of the ICTR's greatest achievements.[117]

A more recent example relevant to war crimes law before the ICTY concerns the crime of terror. On the basis of Article 51(2) of Additional Protocol I and Article 13(2) of Additional Protocol II, the *Galić* Appeals Chamber held that the crime of "acts or threats of violence the primary purpose of which is to spread terror among the civilian population" constitutes a serious violation of the laws or customs of war under its Article 3.[118] In applying the *Tadić* test, it found that customary international law imposed individual criminal liability for violations of the prohibition of terror against the civilian population as outlined in Article 51(2) of Addi-

---

Chamber, IT-98-30/1-A, February 2005, para. 395. In addition, in the Čelebići case the ICTY Trial Chamber held that rape could constitute the war crime of torture when the specific conditions of torture were fulfilled: *id.*, paras. 475–94.

[112] Of note, rape, enforced prostitution and any form of indecent assault are war crimes under the Statutes of the ICTR, Art. 4(e), see *supra* note 76 and of the SCSL, Art. 3(e), see *supra* note 89.

[113] Furundžija case, Trial Judgment, para. 178, see *supra* note 111.

[114] *Ibid.*, paras. 162, 253.

[115] Akayesu case, Trial Judgment, paras. 732–34, see *supra* note 50; ICTR, *Prosecutor v. Sylvestre Gacumbitsi*, Trial Chamber, Judgment, ICTR-2001-64-T, 17 June 2004, paras. 291–93 (https://www.legal-tools.org/doc/b4e8aa/).

[116] Akayesu case, Trial Judgment, para. 598, see *supra* note 50.

[117] Catharine A. MacKinnon, "The ICTR's Legacy on Sexual Violence", in *New England Journal of International and Comparative Law*, 2008, vol. 14, no. 2, p. 101.

[118] Galić case, Appeals Judgment, para. 69, see *supra* note 97.

---

tional Protocol I and Article 13(2) of Additional Protocol II.[119] It added
that the crime "encompasses the intent to spread terror when committed
by combatants in a period of armed conflict".[120] In *Dragomir Milošević*
the Appeals Chamber reiterated that the *Tadić* gravity threshold (serious
ness of the violation on the victim) may be physical but could also be of a
psychological nature, for instance imputed through threats of violence and
a corresponding psychological impact on the victim (community).[121] In
essence, with the 'crime of terror' the ICTY added a 'new' crime to its
statutory repertoire of war crimes, referring in particular to international
humanitarian law provisions stating the prohibition on the one side, and
national military manuals on the other, to establish the customary existence of the crime.[122] Reflecting its dynamic understanding of its statutory
war crimes provision, the *Kunarac* Appeals Chamber recalled the judgment of the IMT, holding that the laws of war "are not static, but by continual adaptation follow the needs of a changing world".[123]

Finally, although the present section has focused on the jurisprudence of the ICTY and ICTR, it has not been these tribunals alone that
have continued to delineate and shape international crimes with the available sources in international law. Other international tribunals have similarly contributed to such progress. The Appeals Chamber of the SCSL
held in the *Brima et al.* case that the specific harm inflicted upon a "bush
wife" by way of a blend of sexual slavery, rape, torture and deprivation of
liberty cannot be captured in just one or more specific (sexual) crimes
listed under the SCSL Statute's crimes against humanity provision.[124] It
therefore found that the holding of "bush wives" by way of forced marriage was a distinct stand-alone crime against humanity under "other in-

---

[119] *Ibid.*, paras. 91–98.

[120] *Ibid.*, paras. 69, 102–4 (elements of the crime).

[121] ICTY, *Prosecutor v. Dragomir Milošević*, Appeals Chamber, Judgment, IT-98-29/1-A, 12 November 2009, paras. 32–35 (https://www.legal-tools.org/doc/44327f/).

[122] Galić case, Appeals Judgment, para. 88, see *supra* note 97.

[123] Kunarac, Appeals Judgment, para. 67, see supra note 4, citing Trial of the Major War Criminals before the International Military Tribunal, Nuremberg, 14 November 1945 to 1 October 1946, vol. 1, Nuremberg, p 221. It went on to find that acts such as rape, torture and outrages upon personal dignity "are prohibited and regarded as criminal under the laws of war and that they were already regarded as such at the time relevant to [the indictment in the relevant case]".

[124] SCSL, *Prosecutor v. Alex Tamba Brima et al.*, Appeals Chamber, Judgment, SCSL-04-16-A, 22 February 2008, para. 195 ('Brima case') (https://www.legal-tools.org/doc/4420ef/).

humane acts".[125] More relevant to war crimes, the SCSL Appeals Chamber in *CDF* confirmed that the prohibition of child recruitment has crystallised as a war crime under international customary law.[126] The ECCC held that at the time relevant to the indictments before the chambers − the mid-1970s − there was no longer a requirement that crimes against humanity be committed in connection to an armed conflict.[127]

The international courts' and tribunals' progressive approach in applying and interpreting relevant international law has triggered a debate among scholars and practitioners alike, often reflected in the terms "judicial law-making" and "creative jurisprudence", as to whether judges at the UN *ad hoc* tribunals might have gone beyond simply applying the law and in fact proceeded to creating new law.[128] Article 38(1) of the ICJ Statute − a provision not paralleled in the UN *ad hoc* tribunals' Statutes but with authoritative value in international law − contains the traditional trio of sources of international law: international conventions, customary international law and general principles of international law.[129] According to this provision, judicial decisions of international courts and tribunals can only be seen as "subsidiary" sources of international law, meaning that they can only *state* the law, not *make* the law (*iudicis est ius dicere*

---

[125] *Ibid.*, para. 195; Gbao case, Trial Judgment, paras. 1465–73, see *supra* note 86.

[126] CDF case, Decision on Child Recruitment, paras. 26–53, see *supra* note 99.

[127] Nuon and Khieu case, Decision on Definition of Crimes Against Humanity, para. 10 ff., see *supra* note 4, holding that the nexus requirement was no longer part of the material elements of the crime in 1975, *id.*, para. 33; see also *supra* note 5.

[128] Shane Darcy and Joseph Powderly, *Judicial Creativity at the International Criminal Tribunals*, Oxford University Press, Oxford, 2010; William Schabas, "Customary Law or Judge-made Law: Judicial Creativity at the UN Criminal Tribunals", in José Doria, Hans-Peter Gasser and M. Cherif Bassiouni (eds.), *The Legal Regime of the International Criminal Court: Essays in Honour of Professor Igor Blishchenko*, Martinus Nijhoff, Leiden, 2009, pp. 77–101; Mia Swart, "Judicial Lawmaking at the *ad hoc* Tribunals: The Creative Use of the Sources of International Law and 'Adventurous Interpretation'", in *Zeitschrift für ausländisches öffentliches Recht und Völkerrecht*, 2010, vol. 70, p. 459. See also Joseph Powderly, "Distinguishing Creativity from Activism: International Criminal Law and the 'Legitimacy' of a Judicial Development of the Law", in William A. Schabas, Yvonne McDermott and Naimh Hayes (eds.), *The Ashgate Research Companion to International Criminal Law: Critical* Perspectives, Ashgate, Farnham, 2013.

[129] Statute of the International Court of Justice, 26 June 1945, Art. 38(1)(d) is generally regarded as declaratory of customary international law; Kupreškić case, Trial Judgment, para. 540, see *supra* note 85.

sed non dare).[130] This provision is reflective of the traditional view that states are the sole entities under international law with a law-making capacity – and that they cannot be obliged to accept more law as binding on them than they have explicitly agreed to. The subsidiary character of judicial decisions prevents them from becoming independent formal sources of international law.[131]

The tribunals themselves have consistently regarded their jurisprudence as mere interpretation and application of *existing* customary international law,[132] rather than a new and, following the model of Article 38(1) of the ICJ Statute, the fourth formal source of public international law. The main argument drawn from Article 59 of the ICJ Statute – at least with regard to the jurisprudence of the ICJ – is that the common law principle of binding precedent (*stare decisis*) should not apply to decisions of international bodies.[133] This position has been reflected by both ICTY and ICTR in their jurisprudence:

---

[130] Charles de Montesquieu, *The Spirits of the Law*, vol. 1, New York, Macmillan 1949 [1748], p. 152, quoted by Mohamed Shahabuddeen, *Precedent in the World Court*, Cambridge University Press, Cambridge, 1996, p. 234; see also Robert Heinsch, "Judicial 'Law-Making' in the Jurisprudence of the ICTY and ICTR in Relation to Protecting Civilians from Mass Violence: How Can Judge-made Law Be Brought into Coherence with the Doctrine of the Formal Sources of International Law", in Philipp Ambach, Frédéric Bostedt, Grant Dawson and Steve Kostas (eds.), *The Protection of Non-Combatants during Armed Conflict and Safeguarding the Rights of Victims in Post-Conflict Society: Essays in Honour of the Life and Work of Joakim Dungel*, Brill, Leiden, 2015, pp. 247, 251.

[131] Ian Brownlie, *Principles of Public International Law*, 6th ed., Oxford University Press, Oxford, 2003, p. 19; Georg Dahm, Jost Delbrück and Rüdiger Wolfrum, *Völkerrecht*, 1989, vol. 1, no. 1, p. 77; Knut Ipsen, *Völkerrecht*, Beck, 2004, § 21, margin number 1; Hersch Lauterpacht, *The Development of International Law by the International Court*, Stevens and Sons, London, 1958, pp. 20 ff.; Riccardo Monaco, "Sources of International Law", in Rudolf Bernhard (ed.), *Encyclopedia of Public International Law*, vol. IV, North Holland, Amsterdam, 2000, p. 474.

[132] ICTY, *Prosecutor v. Enver Hadžihasanović*, Appeals Chamber, Decision on Interlocutory Appeal Challenging Jurisdiction in Relation to Command Responsibility, IT-01-47, 16 July 2003, para. 55 (https://www.legal-tools.org/doc/608f09/); ICTY, *Prosecutor v. Tihomir Blaškić*, Appeals Chamber, Judgment, IT-95-14, 29 July 2004, para. 113 (https://www.legal-tools.org/doc/88d8e6/); see also ICTY, *Prosecutor v. Šainović et al.*, Appeals Chamber, Decision on Dragoljub Ojdanic's Motion Challenging Jurisdiction – Joint Criminal Enterprise, IT-99-37-AR72, 21 May 2003, para. 9 (https://www.legal-tools.org/doc/d51c63/), holding that the ICTY's power to convict an individual for a crime under the ICTY Statute "depends on its existence *qua* customary law". Indicative of this see *supra* section 11.2.4.2.

[133] Heinsch, 2015, pp. 297, 308 ff., see *supra* note 130.

> [T]he authority of precedents (*auctoritas rerum similiter ju-dicatarum*) can only consist in evincing the possible exist-ence of an international rule. More specifically, precedents may constitute evidence of a customary rule in that they are indicative of the existence of *opinio iuris sive necessitatis* and international practice on a certain matter, or else they may be indicative of the emergence of a general principle of international law.[134]

However, a restrictive view ascribing to international jurisprudence a mere "evidence" function for existing international (criminal) law and thus confining the judges' role to one of merely stating universally accepted law does not accurately reflect the true value of decisions of these courts and tribunals with regard to the development and definition of international norms.[135] While the tribunals may have at times been satisfied with "extremely limited case law"[136] – and therefore state practice – to confirm a rule under international customary law, it must be appreciated that the role of judges also contains interpretative elements and involves the exercise of discretion. In particular where state practice has not developed in a coherent way or is even contradictory, there is a legitimate role for a judge of an international tribunal to assess the case at hand and bring it to a conclusion in a way that the judge finds to be in accordance with international law – even if that conclusion describes what could be regarded as (an element of) a new provision under international law. Judges are not unconstrained by international law: at a minimum, the decision "must be seen to emanate reasonably and logically from existing and previously ascertainable law".[137] An international court or tribunal cannot elaborate a new rule that is in contradiction to existing international

---

[134] Kupreškić case, Trial Judgment, para. 540 see *supra* note 85.

[135] Heinsch, 2015, pp. 297, 309, see *supra* note 130; K. Ipsen, *Völkerrecht* (2004), § 21, margin number 1.

[136] André Nollkaemper, "The Legitimacy of International Law in the Case Law of the International Criminal Tribunal for the former Yugoslavia", in Thomas A.J.A. Vandamme and Jan Herman Reestman (eds.), *Ambiguity In the Rule of Law: The Interface between National and International Legal Systems*, Europa Law Publishing, Groningen, 2001, p. 17.

[137] Robert Jennings, "The Judicial Function and the Rule of Law in International Relations", in *International Law at the Time of its Codification: Essays in Honour of Roberto Ago*, vol. 3, A. Giuffrè, Milan, 1987, p. 145, quoted in Heinsch, 2015, p. 312, see *supra* note 130.

law.[138] However, in resolving potential conflicts or filling important lacunae, the value of judicial decisions goes beyond one of a mere "subsidiary means", especially with regard to their practical importance for future comparable situations and cases.[139] The jurisprudence of the ICTY and ICTR, and also of other international(ised) courts, in the last two decades has confirmed this observation.

The dynamism of international courts to become the proponents of new international legal rules, which have in turn been verified and validated by ensuing state practice or even treaty codification,[140] has doubtlessly had a beneficial effect for protection of victims of mass atrocities. That result alone would speak for the legitimacy of the means. However, further confirmation for a more conceptual legal validity can be found in the fact that much of the tribunals' 'dynamic' interpretation of the applicable law corresponds to Article 8 of the ICC Statute, demonstrating that decisions and judgments of international courts and tribunals do represent a material source of law – even if not formally acknowledged as such in traditional texts.[141]

In conclusion, the international courts' and tribunals' jurisprudence over the past 20 years has greatly contributed to the codification and definition of international criminal law, transposing a number of key principles from the rules of international humanitarian law into the context of

---

[138] For the ICTY, this flows from the Secretary-General's indication that the ICTY is "applying existing international humanitarian law", Secretary-General's Report on res. 808, paras. 29, 34, see *supra* note 46. This is in particular so for war crimes, *id.*, para. 35. For the ICC this follows from the ICC Statute, Art. 21(1)(b), see *supra* note 17.

[139] See Aleksovski case, Appeals Judgment, para. 107, *supra* note 105, there the ICTY held that in similar cases or legal problems "the Appeals Chamber should follow its previous decisions, but should be free to depart from them for cogent reasons in the interests of justice". See also Heinsch, 2015, p. 308, see *supra* note 130.

[140] By way of example the Geneva Conventions' grave breaches provisions were inspired by provisions in Art. 6(b) of the IMT Charter which, in turn, had *no* direct precedent in international treaty law, see *supra* note 4. Similarly, Art. 8 of the ICC Statute was heavily inspired by the Tribunals' jurisprudence, as witnessed for example by the sections of crimes in non-international armed conflict, the gender crimes provisions as well as the provision on child soldiers, see *supra* note 17.

[141] See also Heinsch, 2015, p. 312 ff., *supra* note 130, proposing to categorise international judicial decisions in a general graduation of in-between steps of the traditional sources under international law, as a "quasi-formal" source in that "that while judicial decisions are not on the same level as international conventions and customary international law, on a factual level they have almost the same impact" (p. 313).

individual criminal responsibility under international law. This process can be brought into conformity with general rules under international law if one accepts that these judicial decisions 'concretise' existing law by adding details to a certain body of law (for example, the definition of rape to the body of sexual offences in international law), elaborate law which has already been in the process of (trans)formation (for example, the acknowledgement of war crimes in non-international armed conflict) and at times even unify divergent views and practices into a new approach.[142]

11.6. Article 8 of the ICC Statute: The Next Revolution?

Article 8 of the ICC Statute represents the most complete war crimes provision of an international court to date. It comprehensively lists a large number of war crimes which exist under customary international law in both international and non-international armed conflict. In addition, as a number of the crimes encompassed in Article 8 do not find a direct equivalent in previous statutes of international courts, the provision doubtlessly represents a step forward in the codification of substantive international criminal law. Many prohibitions that had developed and concretised itself under international humanitarian law are being defined as crimes – in particular through the Elements of Crimes, for example for some means of warfare in internal conflict in Article 8(2)(e)(xiii)–(xv).[143] Some commentators hold that in this respect the ICC Statute itself represents a dynamic interpretation of customary international law,[144] much like some of the UN *ad hoc* tribunals' jurisprudence. However, while representing an important step, each provision of Article 8 still needs to be read and inter-

---

[142] Heinsch speaks of "of 'crystallizing' (customary) international law", *ibid.*, p. 312, referring in analogy to ICJ, North Sea Continental Shelf cases, *Germany v. Denmark/Netherlands*, Judgment, 20 February 1969, ICJ Reports 1969.

[143] The statutory provisions agreed upon in 1998 did not yet contain any explicit provision of the above war crimes regarding certain means of warfare for non-international armed conflict. It was only during the Review Conference of the Assembly of States Parties pursuant to Article 123(1) of the ICC Statute that some relevant provisions were added; Resolution ICC-ASP/8/Res.6, Review Conference, 26 November 2009, Annex III. On the proposals previous to the Kampala Review Conference see Assembly of State Parties, 8th Session, Report of the Bureau on the Review Conference, ICC-ASP/8/43/Add.1, 10 November 2009.

[144] See Michael Cottier, "Rome Statute and War Crimes", in ELSA International (ed.), *International Law as We Enter the 21st Century: International Focus Programme 1997–1999*, Spitz, Berlin, 2001, p. 179.

preted in light of international humanitarian law from which all provisions of Article 8 originate.[145] This is particularly so since the ICC Elements of the Crimes are at times of limited assistance as they merely provide some interpretative guidance for a number of elements of each offence while also leaving some lacunae.[146]

Article 8 contains in its first paragraph a jurisdictional threshold requirement in the form of a "policy element" of the crime under the ICC Statute.[147] While this requirement is not of a mandatory nature – as the term "in particular" implies[148]– it expresses the drafters' conviction that only war crimes of a sufficient gravity and scale should be adjudicated by the ICC and thus provides the prosecutor with a "practical guideline".[149] Article 8(2) addresses the material law and is organised along the distinction between international and non-international armed conflict. Along a second axis, Article 8 distinguishes broadly between law derived from the Geneva Conventions, on the one hand, and provisions related to the Hague law system, determining prohibited means and methods of warfare. This subdivides Article 8 into quadrants regarding the material crimes, the first two covering international armed conflicts and the latter two non-international armed conflicts. Article 8(2)(a) covers grave breaches of the Geneva Conventions, much like Article 2 of the ICTY Statute. Article

---

[145] This is stipulated in the Elements themselves: ICC Statute, Art. 8, Introduction, para. 2, see *supra* note 17. In addition, Art. 8(2)(b) and (e) stipulates that the serious violations of international humanitarian law listed under the respective sub-paragraphs need to be "within the established framework of international law" which suggests that the outer limit of interpretation of these rules is where a provision would be in contravention of existing humanitarian law.

[146] See also Cottier, 2008, para. 7, see *supra* note 5.

[147] ICC Statute, Art. 8(1), see *supra* note 17: "[…] in particular when committed as part of a plan or policy or as part of a large-scale commission".

[148] ICC, Situation in the Democratic Republic of the Congo, Appeals Chamber, Judgment on the Prosecutor's Appeal against the Decision of Pre-Trial Chamber I Entitled "Decision on the Prosecutor's Application for Warrant of Arrest, Article 58", ICC-01/04, 13 July 2006, para. 70 ('Situation in DRC, Judgment on Arrest Warrant Appeal') (http://www.legal-tools.org/doc/8c20eb/).

[149] ICC, Situation in the Central African Republic, *Prosecutor v. Jean-Pierre Bemba Gombo*, Pre-Trial Chamber, Decision Pursuant to Article 61(7)(a) and (b) of the Rome Statute on the Charges of the Prosecutor Against Jean-Pierre Bemba Gombo, ICC-01/05-01/08, 15 June 2009, para. 211 (https://www.legal-tools.org/doc/07965c/); Situation in DRC, Judgment on Arrest Warrant Appeal, para. 70, see *supra* note 148; Cottier, 2008, para. 9 ff., see *supra* note 5; William A. Schabas, *An Introduction to the International Criminal Court*, 3rd ed., Cambridge University Press, Cambridge, 2007, p. 115.

8(2)(b) contains a long list of other serious violations of the laws and customs applicable in international armed conflict, including elements of Additional Protocol I, the 1907 Hague Regulations and other relevant international texts. Article 8(2)(c) applies in non-international armed conflict and lists the prohibitions encompassed by Common Article 3 of the Geneva Conventions. Finally, Article 8(2)(e) enumerates a number of other serious violations under international humanitarian law applicable in non-international conflict, in most relevant part the law on the protection of persons and property, means and methods of warfare, and elements from Additional Protocol II.[150]

The ICC Statute has decisively enhanced the level of protection for victims in armed conflict. Examples include the extensive provisions on gender crimes in both international and non-international armed conflict,[151] and the provision on child soldiers, which mirror the relevant SCSL provision and jurisprudence in this field.[152] Furthermore, the ICC provisions on crimes committed in non-international conflict go a long way to solidifying the emerging consensus in this field.

However, the ICC Statute is also marked by a rigidity that stands in contrast to the *ad hoc* tribunals, whose war crimes provisions provide for the possibility that existing crimes under customary international law that have not been explicitly listed be nevertheless brought within the tribunals' jurisdiction.[153] The *Tadić* Appeals Chamber clarified that the war

---

[150] For an overview, see Cottier, 2008, para. 8, *supra* note 5.

[151] ICC Statute, Art. 8(2)(b)(xxii) and (e)(vi), see *supra* note 17; see also Office of the Prosecutor of the International Criminal Court, Policy Paper on Sexual and Gender-Based Crimes, June 2014.

[152] ICC Statute, Art. 8(2)(b)(xxvi) and (e)(vii), see *supra* note 17; SCSL, *Prosecutor v. Moinina Fofana, Allieu Kondewa and Sam Hinga Norman*, Appeals Chamber, Judgment, SCSL-2004-14, 28 May 2008, para. 139 ('CDF case') (https://www.legal-tools.org/doc/b31512/); SCSL, *Prosecutor v. Alex Tamba Brima et al.*, Trial Chamber, Judgment, SCSL-2004-16, 20 June 2007, para. 731 (https://www.legal-tools.org/doc/87ef08/); CDF case, Decision on Child Recruitment, paras. 18–29, 53, see *supra* note 99; SCSL, *Prosecutor v. Charles Ghankay Taylor*, Trial Chamber, Judgment, SCSL-03-01-T, 18 May 2012, para. 438 and fn. 1052 (https://www.legal-tools.org/doc/8075e7/); Henckaerts and Doswald-Beck, 2005, pp. 508, 593, see *supra* note 3.

[153] See ICTY Statute, Art. 3, *supra* note 4, and ICTR Statute, Art. 4, *supra* note 76: "Such violations shall include, but [shall] not be limited to: [...]". In the *Čelebići* case, the ICTY Appeals Chamber stated that the expression in its Art. 3 "laws and customs of

---

crime provision in Article 3 of the ICTY Statute may be taken to cover "all violations of international humanitarian law other than the 'grave breaches' of the four Geneva Conventions falling under Article 2".[154] In contrast, Article 8 of the ICC Statute is formulated in an exhaustive manner. Any serious violation of international humanitarian law not within the ICC's explicit jurisdictional confines in Article 8 will have to be added by way of an amendment of the ICC Statute. At the same time, the ICC Statute makes clear that the body of offences generating individual criminal liability under international (customary) law may be larger than what is expressly codified in the ICC Statute.[155] The absence of an explicit provision on the crime of terror, indiscriminate attacks as a method of war, or the use of chemical or biological weapons as a means of war illustrates this.[156] In addition, it can be argued that the list of ICC crimes applicable in non-international armed conflict was incomplete from its very inception[157] – as illustrated by the multiple amendments of Article 8(2)(e) during the 2010 Review Conference, criminalising the use of poison or poisoned weapons (lit. (e)(xiii)) and of asphyxiating, poisonous or other gases, and all analogous liquids, materials and devices (lit. (e)(xiv)) as well as the use of bullets which expand or flatten easily in the human body (lit. (e)(xv)) in non-international armed conflict.[158]

---

war" includes *all* laws and customs of war in addition to those explicitly listed in the Article. Čelebići case, Appeal Judgment, para. 111, see *supra* note 111.

[154] Tadić case, Decision on Jurisdiction, paras. 87, 89, see *supra* note 2. "Article 3 functions as a residual clause designed to ensure that no serious violation of international humanitarian law is taken away from the jurisdiction of the International Tribunal. Article 3 aims to make such jurisdiction watertight and inescapable", *id.*, para. 91.

[155] ICC Statute, Arts. 10, 22(3). See Bruce Broomhall, "Article 22", in Triffterer, 2008, see *supra* note 5.

[156] However, the use of such weapons will in most cases also be indiscriminate in application and thus a war crime. In addition, it is argued that lit. (b)(xvii) and (xviii) cover these crimes for international armed conflict and lit. (e)(xiii) and (xiv) for non-international armed conflict. See Dapo Akande, "Can the ICC Prosecute for Use of Chemical Weapons in Syria?", in *EJIL: Talk!*, 23 August 2013 (http://www.ejiltalk.org/can-the-icc-prosecute-for-use-of-chemical-weapons-in-syria/).

[157] But see Alain Pellet, "Applicable Law", in Cassese *et al.*, 2002, p. 1056, *supra* note 4, who sees the definitions of crimes as laid down in Arts. 6 to 8 of the ICC Statute "in some respects" as a "step backwards compared with the case law and customary law itself".

[158] Assembly of State Parties resolution RC/Res.5, Amendments to article 8 of the Rome Statute, RC/11, 10 June 2010, para. 1 and Annex I.

The ICC Statute's rigidity and its cumbersome amendment procedure in its Article 121 bear the risk that the ICC will, in particular in the future, not or no longer reflect current developments in customary international law, in particular in fields where state practice and international treaties may have helped new law to crystallise, such as regarding the criminalisation of prohibited means and methods of warfare in non-international armed conflict. On the other hand, the ICC Statute's rigidity also prevents it from being influenced by temporary political pressures or being drawn into contentious legal territory, in particular regarding issues of state sovereignty, which have not yet been comprehensively charted by international agreements, courts, academia and civil society.[159] In addition, a reopening of statutory provisions codifying fundamental rules such as the Nuremberg Principles could have a destabilising effect beyond the Rome Statute itself and should therefore be avoided.

In conclusion it can be safely said that the ICC will, by virtue of its rather rigid legal framework, not be able to shape the constantly evolving body of international criminal law in the same manner as the UN and other *ad hoc* tribunals did and continue to do.[160] It will therefore not be a 'revolutionary' body in the current landscape of international criminal law but rather one that guarantees the *status quo*. It remains to be hoped that ICC States Parties will permit it at least in cautious steps to amend its Article 8 following developments in the modern geometry of warfare.

11.7. Conclusion

Even with all four Geneva Conventions and the 1977 Additional Protocols in place, the development of modern armed conflict remains very dynamic and the law as it stands will never comprehensively anticipate and account for all conduct that ought to be prohibited. While in particular Additional Protocols I and II sought to connect Geneva and Hague law and amplify their ambit of protection, both also recognised the need for future evolution by reiterating the validity of the so-called Martens

---

[159] See Roger S. Clark, "Article 121", in Triffterer, 2008, paras. 1 ff, see *supra* note 5.

[160] See, for example the ruling of the Special Tribunal for Lebanon's Appeals Chamber on the definition of the crime of terrorism as an international crime: Special Tribunal for Lebanon, Appeals Chamber, Interlocutory Decision on the Applicable Law: Terrorism, Conspiracy, Homicide, Perpetration, Cumulative Charging, Case No. STL-11-01/I /AC/R176*bis*, 16 February 2011, paras. 42 ff. (https://www.legal-tools.org/doc/4c16e9/).

Clause,[161] whereby in situations not covered by the applicable international law in force, persons remain under the general protection of the principles of international law derived from established custom, principles of humanity and the dictates of the public conscience. In other words, the fact that an act of war is not covered in the existing law does not render it legal.[162]

The Statutes of the various international *ad hoc* tribunals and the ICC attest to the essential fact that war crimes can only be committed where international humanitarian law – be it treaty law or customary international law – applies and has been violated.[163] This general principle is as valid today as it was a century ago; the challenge now is to define *when* and *where* international humanitarian law applies in the modern geometry of warfare. The war against terror and the fundamental question regarding the geographical scope of armed conflict[164] is a clear example of the fact that modern wars will require constant adjustments to the present regime. Targeted killings, signature strikes, the increased resort to the use of drones in war and cyber warfare pose new challenges to the definition, application and probably even creation of new standards and provisions under international humanitarian law and, in consequence, war crimes law. War crimes law will continue to crystallise and adapt to the new realities of armed conflict.

---

[161] The Martens Clause goes back to Fyodor Fyodorovich Martens, the Russian delegate at the Hague Conferences of 1899, and has been codified in the preamble of the 1899 and 1907 Hague Conventions. See, for an in-depth discussion of the clause and its significance in the context of modern international humanitarian law, Theodor Meron, "The Martens Clause, Principles of Humanity, and Dictates of Public Conscience", in *American Journal of International Law*, 2000, vol. 94, no. 1, pp. 78–89; Rupert Ticehurst, "The Martens Clause and the Laws of Armed Conflict", in *International Review of the Red Cross*, 1997, no. 317, pp. 125–34.

[162] Additional Protocol I, Art. 1(2), see *supra* note 1, covering international armed conflict; Additional Protocol II, Preamble, para. 4, see *supra* note 63, covering non-international armed conflict. The Martens Clause therefore has an important residual function preventing legal vacuum for grave violations of international humanitarian law, following a similar logic as ICTY Statute, Art. 5(i), see *supra* note 4, for crimes against humanity.

[163] Henckaerts and Doswald-Beck, 2005, pp. 572–73, see *supra* note 3; Tadić case, Decision on Jurisdiction, paras. 94, 143, see *supra* note 2.

[164] See Noam Lubell and Nathan Derejko, "A Global Battlefield? Drones and the Geographical Scope of Armed Conflict", in *Journal of International Criminal Justice*, 2013, vol. 11, no. 1, pp. 65–88.

The ICC Statute system will not be the carrier of revolutionary developments in this respect but rather be a solid source of application of war crimes law fostering the *status quo* in a time where we see not only progression of the law applicable in armed conflict but also initiatives seeking its regression; where states attempt to respond to threats to their national security with pragmatic solutions that may stand in conflict with fundamental rules under humanitarian law. In this regard, the existence of the ICC, which as an institution serves to consolidate and solidify the law, is an essential tool in the current and future political reality to secure the protection of victims in armed conflict and to continue the fight against impunity.

12

The Evolution of Persecution
as a Crime Against Humanity

Helen Brady[*] and Ryan Liss[**]

12.1. Introduction

The story behind the recognition of persecution as a crime of international concern is a key chapter in the development of international criminal law. In short, acceptance by policy, legislative and judicial actors that widespread or systematic discrimination should be the concern of the international community – not simply the territorial state – was instrumental in defining the parameters of the contemporary international criminal law framework. Ongoing international efforts by these actors to repress persecutory conduct were a primary impetus – if not the primary impetus – behind the delineation of the category of crimes against humanity, of which the crime of persecution is a part. It was, ultimately, by proscribing this category of international crimes that international actors pushed the focus of international accountability beyond the regulation of war alone.[1]

---

[*] **Helen Brady** is Senior Appeals Counsel and Head of the Appeals Section at the Office of the Prosecutor of the International Criminal Court.

[**] **Ryan Liss** is a doctoral candidate at Yale Law School, a visiting scholar at the Institute for International Law and Justice, New York University School of Law, a Trudeau Foundation Scholar, and Canadian Social Science and Humanities Research Council Doctoral Fellow. The views expressed in this chapter are solely the co-authors' and should not be attributed to the Office of the Prosecutor or the International Criminal Court. The authors are indebted to Barbara Goy, Matt Cross, and Joanna Langille for their valuable suggestions on a draft of this chapter, and to the participants in the Historical Origins of International Criminal Law Project and the Yale Law School Doctoral Colloquium for their helpful questions and comments. The authors would also like to thank the editorial staff at the Torkel Opsahl Academic EPublisher for their thoughtful comments and revisions. All errors are the authors' own.

[1] Though, as discussed below, an association with war was initially required for an act of persecution to be prosecutable as an international crime as states searched for an appropriate means to distinguish between acts of persecution of international concern, and acts of discrimination that were of purely domestic concern.

Moreover, beyond pointing to its functional role in defining the parameters of international criminal law, examining the codification and adjudication of persecution as a crime against humanity over the past century also highlights important normative insights concerning the field of international criminal law as a whole. Throughout this history, persecution has played a fascinating dual role, viewed at once as a quintessential international crime and a crime on the very precipice between the national and the international.

In the common form of the offence, a perpetrator harms or encroaches upon the fundamental human rights of a person because of that person's membership, affiliation or identification with a group. On the one hand, persecution seems to be an emblematic international crime by some definitions. Those engaged in persecution have as their aim, as one judgment has described it, "the removal of [members of the targeted group] from the society in which they live alongside the perpetrators, or eventually even from humanity itself".[2] To this extent, persecutory acts attack what David Luban has argued are the two fundamental aspects of being human: one's individuality (as persecution reduces an individual to his or her membership within a group), and one's ability to associate and identify with others (as persecution attacks the group itself).[3] It is the fact that crimes against humanity attack these characteristics, Luban asserts, which justifies a humanity-wide concern with such crimes. While Luban's comment is intended to explain international concern with crimes against humanity as a whole, arguably the crime of persecution attacks these core aspects of 'humanness' more directly than any other crime against humanity.

On the other hand, drafters, tribunals, courts, prosecutors and defendants alike have emphasised that persecution as a crime against humanity is situated on the cusp between matters of international and domestic concern. The history of persecution highlights efforts of these actors to parse out the two domains – seeking to delineate the boundary be-

---

[2] International Criminal Tribunal for the former Yugoslavia ('ICTY'), *Prosecutor v. Kupreškić et al.*, Trial Judgment, IT-95-16-T, 14 January 2000, para. 634 ('Kupreškić case') (https://www.legal-tools.org/doc/5c6a53/). See also ICTY, *Prosecutor v. Kordić and Čerkez*, Trial Judgment, IT-95-14/2-T, 26 February 2001, para. 214 (https://www.legal-tools.org/doc/d4fedd/).

[3] David Luban, "A Theory of Crimes Against Humanity", in *Yale Journal of International Law*, 2004, vol. 29, pp. 116–17.

tween discriminatory conduct of exclusively domestic concern and that rising to the level of persecution as an international crime, and thus of international concern. In doing so, these actors have proposed a variety of different criteria by which to distinguish what is of concern only on a domestic level from that which is of international concern, for example, the act's association with armed conflict; the severity of the act; its association with a systematic or widespread attack; its association with a government or organisational policy; and its association with other categories of international crimes,[4] each of which provides some insight into what it means to define an act as an 'international crime'.

This chapter sets out the history of persecution as a crime against humanity from its pre-Nuremberg roots to its contemporary iterations. In doing so, the chapter endeavours to emphasise that, throughout this history, persecution has been a site of contestation and affirmation – both structural and normative – of the parameters of international criminal law as a whole. Further, as this history shows, many of these issues concerning the limits of international criminality were first considered by the drafters of international legal instruments, and the tribunals and courts hearing cases in the immediate aftermath of the Second World War. The answers they proposed have, ultimately, been extremely influential on efforts to resolve the same tensions today.

In making this argument, this chapter begins in section 12.2. with an examination of the historical origins of persecution as an international crime. We survey the various antecedents of the crime in the international community's long-standing concern with persecutory conduct by a state against its own citizens as evidenced through such phenomena as: humanitarian intervention; the practice of making state recognition contingent on promises of minority protection; and the recognition of the "laws of humanity" as a residual domain of international regulation. We then turn to the efforts to adopt a juridical response to persecutory conduct in the wake of First World War, and to the League of Nations' peacetime minor-

---

[4] The majority of these criteria have been invoked as limitations on crimes against humanity as a whole. However, attempts to determine the boundaries of persecution as an international crime specifically have brought many of these to the fore. For instance, as discussed below, the particularities of persecution caused drafters of the Rome Statute of the International Criminal Court ('ICC Statute') to provide jurisdiction to the International Criminal Court only over those acts of persecution connected to another crime under the Statute, while an equivalent requirement was ultimately rejected for all other crimes against humanity.

ity rights regime that followed soon after. Subsequently, we examine efforts to establish a framework of international criminal law in the aftermath of the Second World War and the role that the concern with persecution played at both the United Nations War Crimes Commission ('UNWCC') and the London Conference in expanding international jurisdiction beyond the regulation of war proper. The analysis then moves to the post-Second World War jurisprudence that emerged as tribunals and national courts sought to give shape to the offence of 'persecution as a crime against humanity', grappling with the aforementioned tensions throughout this process. Finally, we conclude section 12.2. with a brief review of the subsequent developments prior to the re-emergence of international criminal law as a matter of primary international concern in the early 1990s, examining the Cold War era jurisprudence of national courts and the rise of international human rights law.

In section 12.3., we turn to the treatment of persecution as a crime against humanity in the contemporary jurisprudence, with a particular focus on the influence of the post-Second World War decisions on the modern case law. In doing so, this section will examine the jurisprudence of the International Criminal Tribunal for the former Yugoslavia ('ICTY'), the International Criminal Tribunal for Rwanda ('ICTR') and the Extraordinary Chambers in the Courts of Cambodia ('ECCC'), reviewing these institutions' legal instruments and their efforts to flesh out the terms of persecution under customary international law. We then move to the International Criminal Court ('ICC'), assessing the treatment of persecution as an international crime in the Court's legal instruments (namely the ICC Statute and the Elements of Crimes), and the approach to the offence in the Court's initial jurisprudence.

Ultimately, in light of the crucial but under-examined role of persecution in the development of the field, we argue that tracing the history of persecution as an international crime provides useful insight both for the contemporary adjudication of persecution as a crime against humanity, and for a nuanced understanding of the field of international criminal law more broadly.

12.2. The Origins of Persecution in International Criminal Law

The acceptance by state delegates, judges and others that persecution constitutes a matter of international concern has had a significant impact on the framework of international criminal law. However, the impact of historic responses to persecution on the development of international criminal law was neither immediate nor preordained. Rather, the influence of international concern with persecution has evolved over time – throughout which persecution has been the subject of both contestation and affirmation as a proper subject matter of international criminal jurisdiction.

In this section, we examine this history from the roots of international concern with persecutory conduct to the codification and adjudication of the offence of persecution in the wake of the Second World War. In doing so, we examine various threads of the origin of persecution as a matter of international concern, before turning to the first multilateral efforts to respond to such conduct in the wake of the First World War (through attempts to criminalise such conduct) and the interwar period (through the institution of the League of Nations' minority rights regimes). Allied efforts at criminalisation at this stage fell short, however, unable in many ways to overcome the view that such matters were an issue of solely domestic concern. League efforts to institute a minority rights framework likewise fell short; the League's project was not applied universally (Western European states, including Germany, were excluded) and its channels of enforcement were lacking. The failure of the League's efforts were, ultimately, evidenced in the rise of the mass persecution of groups on, *inter alia*, racial, religious and political grounds in the lead-up to and throughout the Second World War.

The Second World War spurred a return to international efforts to criminalise mass persecution. The view that such conduct should be the subject of international criminal jurisdiction pushed various state delegations (most notably the United States) to expand the focus of international criminal law beyond the regulation of war proper. This position, however, was by no means universally embraced. Moreover, despite eventual agreement that such conduct should be addressed by international law, the precise boundary between when such conduct was an issue of domestic concern and when it rose to the level of an international crime remained a matter of deep contestation. Even the United States, whose delegates argued strongly for international jurisdiction over persecutory conduct, viewed such acts undertaken in peacetime to be a matter for the territorial state alone to address.

The parameters of the offence set out in the post-war legal instruments and jurisprudence were ultimately the result of debates concerning the very limits of sovereignty and the relationship between the state and international law. We conclude this section by noting that efforts to proscribe international criminal jurisdiction faded to an extent as a result of Cold War tensions in the decades following the Second World War; however, the interests which the criminalisation of persecution (and the category of crimes against humanity as a whole) sought to recognise found something of a legacy in the development of international human rights law.

12.2.1. "An Ever-Increasing Tide": The Origins of Persecution as a Matter of International Concern

The concept of persecution as an international crime crystallised in the wake of the Second World War. However, the roots of persecution as a matter of international concern run deeper. Justice James Brand[5] observed as much in 1949, after the immediate post-war prosecutions were largely complete. In his words:

> The manifestations of international concern over racial, religious, and political persecutions by governments of their own nationals constitute an ever-increasing tide which reached the full only in connection with the atrocities committed by the Nazis in the Second World War.[6]

The recognition of persecution as a crime against humanity, Brand asserted, was just the culmination of this long-standing international concern. This section briefly traces the pre-Nuremberg history of the development of mass discrimination as a concern of the international community to provide context for the eventual rise of persecution as an international crime.

---

[5] Justice Brand served on the US Nuremberg Military Tribunals.
[6] James T. Brand, "Crimes Against Humanity and the Nurnberg Trials", in *Oregon Law Review*, 1949, vol. 28, no. 2, p. 111.

12.2.1.1. Early Antecedents: Humanitarian Intervention, Recognition and the "Laws of Humanity"

The character of persecution as a long-standing matter of international concern is most evident in the centuries-long history of humanitarian intervention prior to the drafting of the United Nations ('UN') Charter.[7] Throughout this period, states referred to "fundamental notions of humanity [...] governing the conduct of states", which they invoked, *inter alia*, to justify "intervention to assist minorities persecuted by their own government".[8] The connection was not lost on those engaged in the effort to establish juridical expression of the prohibition on persecution in the wake of the Second World War. Harley Shawcross, the chief British prosecutor at Nuremberg, for instance, emphasised the link in his opening statement:

> The right of humanitarian intervention on behalf of the rights of man trampled upon by a State in a manner shocking the sense of mankind has long been considered to form part of the law of nations.[9]

---

[7] On the long history of humanitarian intervention dating back as far as the sixteenth century see Brendan Simms and D.J.B. Trim (eds.), *Humanitarian Intervention: A History*, Cambridge University Press, Cambridge, 2011. Notably, the legal status of humanitarian interventions since the adoption of the UN Charter is much more controversial: see Oona A. Hathaway, Julia Brower, Ryan Liss, Tina Thomas and Jacob Victor, "Consent-Based Humanitarian Intervention: Giving Sovereign Responsibility Back to the Sovereign", in *Cornell International Law Journal*, 2013, vol. 46, p. 499. The concept of humanitarian intervention was (and is) admittedly open to abuse, as demonstrated, for instance, by Adolph Hitler's reliance on the principle to justify the invasion of Czechoslovakia to prevent persecution against "racial Germans". The connection between this conduct and the criminalization of persecution was in fact noted by US Nuremberg Military Tribunal III in the *Justice* case: see Nuremberg Military Tribunal ('NMT'), *United States of America v. Josef Altstoetter et al.*, Judgment, December 1947, in *Trials of War Criminals Before the Nuernberg Military Tribunals*, vol. III, 1951, p. 982 ('Justice case') (https://www.legal-tools.org/doc/04cdaf/). To an extent, the prosecution of perpetrators of crimes against humanity can be seen as a judicial substitute for such military interventions.

[8] Steven R. Ratner and Jason S. Abrams, *Accountability for Human Rights Atrocities in International Law: Beyond the Nuremberg Legacy*, Clarendon Press, Oxford, 1997, p. 45. See also Brand, 1949, pp. 108–9, *supra* note 6, noting specific instances of humanitarian intervention dating back to 1827, and analogising these examples to "international concern over the commission of crimes against humanity".

[9] International Military Tribunal ('IMT'), *Trial of the Major War Criminals*, Transcript, 4 December 1945, in *Trial of the Major War Criminals Before the International Military Tribunal*, 1947, vol. III, p. 92 ('IMT Transcript'). See also Brand, 1949, p. 109, *supra* note 6 (discussing the quote).

Thus, as Shawcross went on to observe, in setting out individual criminal responsibility for acts of persecution and other crimes against humanity, "the [London] Charter merely develops a pre-existing principle".[10]

The modern origins of humanitarian intervention were initially grounded in the protection of religious kin who constituted a minority in a foreign state.[11] Yet, while religious affinity remained a common basis for such intervention, over time the concept developed a broader association with protecting minorities against inhumane treatment more generally. Increasingly, those invoking the concept pointed to "the suffering [of individuals as] human beings, rather than only as suffering co-religionists".[12]

Notably, the form of such intervention was not exclusively by military force. In the nineteenth century, for instance, major powers increasingly made their recognition of newly emergent states contingent on guarantees of rights for religious minorities.[13] Often, but not exclusively, based on a conception of religious kinship between the state granting recognition and the relevant minority population, the practice points to the increasing recognition of the protection of minority populations as a matter of international (or at least transnational) concern.

As Ruti Teitel has noted, over time the concept of 'humanity' evidenced in intervention's shift from protecting co-religionists to protecting any suffering minority, spread throughout various aspects of the law of nations.[14] The invocation of the concept, however, was far from unproblematic; it was, for instance, often relied upon not to protect oppressed peoples but to justify imperial dispersion of European norms and as a ba-

---

[10] *Ibid.*, IMT Transcript, p. 92.

[11] See D.J.B. Trim, "'If a prince use tyrannie towards his people': Intervention on Behalf of Foreign Populations in Early Modern Europe", in Simms and Trim, 2011, p. 29, *supra* note 7, discussing the origins of the practice in sixteenth- and seventeenth-century Europe along "confessional lines" in the wake of the Reformation, and *id.*, pp. 30–31, noting that while some similar practices can be discerned in classic antiquity or the Middle Ages, "there are so many fundamental differences" between these periods that the analogy is of limited value.

[12] *Ibid.*, p. 38.

[13] Mark Mazower, "Minorities and the League of Nations in Interwar Europe", in *Daedalus*, 1997, vol. 126, no. 2, p. 51.

[14] See Ruti G. Teitel, *Humanity's Law*, Oxford University Press, Oxford, 2011, pp. 19–33.

sis for colonisation more directly.[15] Teitel, nevertheless, points to the increasing proliferation of a degree of "humanity's law" over the past century and a half, incorporating concern for the individual into the framework of international law, as a positive development.

Several scholars have located the conceptual antecedents of crimes against humanity (including persecution) in part in the laws of war and a residual body of regulation giving one instantiation to the dispersion of the "laws of humanity" identified by Teitel.[16] The Martens Clause in the preamble to the Hague Conventions of 1899 and 1907 is often considered as the first broad conventional recognition of such a body of law in international law. The 1899 articulation of the principle provided that, in situations not specifically addressed by the Hague Conventions and their accompanying regulations,

> populations and belligerents remain under the protection and empire of the principles of international law, as they result from the usages established between civilized nations, from the laws of humanity, and the requirements of public conscience.[17]

In subsequent decades, statesmen, scholars and international lawyers alike would draw on the notion of the existence of a residual scope of international regulation requiring some baseline protection for civilians to address the plight of persecuted peoples through the framework of international law.

---

[15] *Ibid.*, pp. 23–25; Luke Glanville, "The antecedents of 'sovereignty as responsibility'", in *European Journal of International Relations*, 2011, vol. 17, pp. 243–47, discussing the related role of the standard of "civilisation". Relatedly, see *infra* fn. 20–22 and accompanying text.

[16] See, for example, Egon Schwelb, "Crimes Against Humanity", in *British Yearbook of International Law*, 1946, vol. 23, pp. 179–80; M. Cherif Bassiouni, *Crimes Against Humanity: Historical Evolution and Contemporary Application*, Cambridge University Press, Cambridge, 2011, pp. 87–88; Roger S. Clark, "Crimes Against Humanity at Nuremberg", in George Ginsburgs and Vladimir Nikolaevich Kudriavtsev (eds.), *The Nuremberg Trial and International Law*, Martinus Nijhoff Publishers, Dordrecht, 1990, p. 178; Darryl Robinson, "Defining 'Crimes Against Humanity' at the Rome Conference", in *American Journal of International Law*, 1999, vol. 93, no. 1, p. 44.

[17] Hague Convention (II) with Respect to the Laws and Customs of War on Land and its annex: Regulation concerning the Laws and Customs of War on Land, 29 July 1899, 32 Stat. 1803, Preamble. See also Hague Convention (IV) Laws and Customs of War on Land, 18 October 1907, 36 Stat. 2277, Preamble.

12.2.1.2. A First Articulation: First World War

This phenomenon – invoking the "laws of humanity" as a basis to prohibit a spectrum of mistreatment of civilians – is seen most clearly in the efforts to hold individuals responsible for atrocities perpetrated during the First World War. In a pattern that would be repeated in the following decades, evidence of extensive persecution of a population by its own government (in the form of mass discriminatory killings and deportations) was a primary driving force behind the decision to pursue international accountability. In 1915, as the Great War was underway, Turkish officials oversaw a relapse of long-standing discrimination against the country's Armenian population.[18] In May 1915, in response to mounting evidence of discrimination against and massacres of the Armenian population,[19] France, Russia and the United Kingdom called for the responsible individuals to be held accountable. In a joint declaration, the Allies asserted that,

> [i]n view of these *crimes of Turkey against humanity and civilization*, the Allied governments announce publicly to the Sublime Porte that they will hold personally responsible [for] these crimes all members of the Ottoman Government and those of their agents who are implicated in such massacres.[20]

Various moments, sources and ideas have been identified as the origin of the concept and phrase 'crimes against humanity'.[21] Ultimately,

---

[18] See, for example, Vahakn N. Dadrian, *The History of the Armenian Genocide: Ethnic Conflict from the Balkans to Anatolia to the Caucasus*, Berghahn Books, New York, 2003, p. xviii; Samantha Power, *A Problem from Hell: America and the Age of Genocide*, Basic Books, New York, 2013, ch. 1.

[19] By the time of the Declaration, the persecutory campaign had already resulted in approximately 200,000 deaths and would leave an approximately one million dead by the end of the war.

[20] Quoted in Timothy L.H. McCormack, "Selective Reaction to Atrocity: War Crimes and the Development of International Criminal Law", in *Albany Law Review*, 1997, vol. 60, no. 3, p. 700, fn. 102 (emphasis added).

[21] See, for example, Patrick Weil, "The Politics of Memory: Bans and Commemorations", in Ivan Hare and James Weinstein (eds.), *Extreme Speech and Democracy*, Oxford University Press, Oxford, 2009, pp. 566–67; Geoffrey Robertson, *Crimes Against Humanity*, 4th ed., New Press, New York, 2013, p. 21, citing Theodore Roosevelt's 1904 State of the Union address, in which he referred to: "there are occasional crimes committed on so vast a scale and of such peculiar horror as to make us doubt whether it is not our manifest duty to endeavor at least to show our disapproval of the deed and our sympathy with those who have suffered by it [...] in extreme cases action may be justifiable and proper".

however, the 1915 Allied Declaration seems by all accounts to be the most direct link to the contemporary usage.[22]

Several scholars have pointed to the Declaration as the origin, not only of crimes against humanity generally but the concept of persecution as an international crime specifically.[23] Roger Clark, for instance, emphasises the discriminatory component driving the Allies to identify the impugned conduct as a matter of international concern. In his words, "th[e] idea of crimes against humanity and civilization", for the three states issuing the Declaration, "included killings of a minority ethnic group in a country by the group in political power".[24] As Clark goes on to note, while the Declaration's authors seem to source "their intellectual antecedents [...] in the laws of war", the offence they identified was, nonetheless, "distinct from war crimes".[25] More explicitly, ICTY Judge Fausto Pocar points to the Declaration and the contemporaneous international attention given to the Armenian massacres as the moment when "[p]ersecution was first identified as a crime against humanity".[26]

As Ken Roberts has noted, efforts to recognise "persecutory acts" as violations of the laws of humanity are also evident in the work of the post-war Allied Commission on the Responsibility of Authors of the War and on Enforcement of Penalties ('Commission').[27] The Commission en-

---

[22] See United Nations War Crimes Commission, *History of United Nations War Crimes Commission and the Development of the Laws of War*, His Majesty's Stationery Office, London, 1948, p. 189 ('UNWCC Report'). Notably, the phrase "crimes [...] against humanity and civilization" was arrived at after the British delegate expressed concern that the initial draft referring to "crimes committed by Turkey against Christianity and civilization" would "strike an anti-Muslim note"; in response, the Russian foreign minister "substituted 'humanity', which won unanimous approval". Robertson, 2013, *ibid.*, p. 25.

[23] Others have also identified it as a point of origin for international concern with genocide specifically. See, for example, Ken Roberts, "Striving for Definition: The Law of Persecution from its Origins to the ICTY", in Hirad Abathi and Gideon Boas (eds.), *The Dynamics of International Criminal Justice: Essays in Honour of Sir Richard May*, Martinus Nijhoff, Leiden, 2006, p. 258. As discussed below, the origin of these two concepts is tightly intertwined.

[24] Clark, 1990, p. 178, see *supra* note 16. But see Roberts, 2006, p. 258, *supra* note 23, citing Clark as an example of a scholar "labelling" this conduct as genocide.

[25] Clark, 1990, p. 178, see *supra* note 16. Clark suggests that the Declaration's authors sourced their idea in the Martens Clause.

[26] Fautso Pocar, "Persecution as a Crime Under International Criminal Law", in *Journal of National Security Law and Policy*, 2008, vol. 2, p. 356.

[27] Roberts, 2006, pp. 258–59, see *supra* note 23. See Commission on the Responsibility of the Authors of War, "Report of Commission on the Responsibility of the Authors of the

deavoured to assess the terms, basis and means of post-war accountability that should be pursued for the actions of the Central Powers and their allies. In its final report, the Commission proposed that the individuals responsible be held personally liable by way of criminal proceedings for violations both of the "laws and customs of wars" and the "laws of humanity".[28] While a formal definition of laws of humanity was not included in the Commission's report, Egon Schwelb observes that an indication of what the drafters intended to capture can be gleaned from the annex accompanying the report. The annex sets out examples the Commission noted of the wartime violations of the laws and customs of war and the laws of humanity. While "the overwhelming majority" of the incidents could "be classified as charges of war crimes in the narrower sense" a number of crimes seemed to go beyond this scope.[29] In Schwelb's words, "[t]hese charges refer mainly to the massacres of Armenians by the Turks and the massacre, persecutions, and expulsions of the Greek-speaking population of Turkey both European and Asiatic".[30]

While a majority of the Commission supported trials for violations of the laws of humanity, there was not unanimity. The two American delegates set out a series of reservations to the final report in which they noted that, *inter alia*, the Commission's invocation of "the laws of humanity" prevented their delegation from "consenting" to the report's recommendations.[31] The Americans argued that the reference to violations of the laws

War and on Enforcement of Penalties", in *American Journal of International Law*, 1920, vol 14, p. 94 ('Report of Commission on Responsibility').

[28] Report of Commission on Responsibility, 1920, pp. 116–18, 121–22, see *supra* note 27, while asserting that "[e]very belligerent has, according to international law, the power and authority to try the individuals alleged to be guilty of [such] crimes", the Commission recommended setting up a "high tribunal" staffed by members of the Allied nations for certain cases. See also Schwelb, 1946, pp. 180–81, *supra* note 16, discussing the report; Roberts, 2006, pp. 258–59, *supra* note 23, the same; Bassiouni, 2011, pp. 89–90, *supra* note 16 the same.

[29] Schwelb, 1946, p. 181, see *supra* note 16.

[30] *Ibid.* See Commission on the Responsibility of the Authors of the War and on Enforcement of Penalties, Violations of the Laws and Customs of War Reports of and Dissenting Reports of American and Japanese of the Commission of Responsibilities, Conference of Paris, 1919, p. 30 ('Full Report of Commission on Responsibility with Annex'). See also Ratner and Abrams, 1997, pp. 45–46, *supra* note 8, noting that in the Commission's discussions, "[t]he Turkish massacre of Armenians received prominent attention"; Roberts, 2006, p. 259, see *supra* note 23, discussing Schwelb's quote.

[31] Report of Commission on Responsibility, 1920, p. 144, see *supra* note 27.

of humanity went "beyond the terms of the [Commission's] mandate" which only called for consideration of violations of the laws and customs of war.[32] In any event, the delegation noted:

> The law and principles of humanity vary with the individual, which, if for no other reason, should exclude them from consideration in a court of justice, especially one charged with the administration of criminal law.[33]

The United States maintained this position as the debate moved from the Commission to the Peace Conference itself. Ultimately, the final penalty provisions in the Treaty of Versailles (and the parallel peace treaties entered into with the other Central Powers) tracked the American vision for individual accountability. Among other things, the "phrase 'the laws of humanity' [did] not appear" in the final treaties.[34]

The one exception was the Treaty of Sèvres, signed with Turkey. The particularly egregious instances of persecution of Turkey's minority populations[35] received special attention from the Allies. While a reference to the "laws of humanity" was absent from the Treaty of Sèvres (as it was from the other peace treaties), its penalty provisions included an obligation for the Turkish government to surrender individuals "responsible for the massacre committed during the continuance of the state of war on the territory which formed part of the Turkish Empire".[36] However, despite initial domestic trials in Turkey for individuals involved in the massacre of Armenians and several arrests by British officials of individuals suspected of involvement in the massacres, domestic public pressure and pro-

---

[32] *Ibid.*, p. 134.

[33] *Ibid.*, and p. 144, noting: "As pointed out by the American representative on more than one occasion, war was and is by its very nature inhuman, but acts consistent with the laws and customs of war, although these acts are inhuman, are nevertheless not the object of punishment by a court of justice". See also Ratner and Abrams, 1997, p. 46, *supra* note 8, discussing the reservation; Schwelb, 1946, pp. 181–82, *supra* note 16, the same.

[34] See Schwelb, 1946, p. 182, *supra* note 16, noting the result of the negotiations in the Treaties of Versailles, Saint-Germain-en-Laye, Trianon and Neuilly-sur-Seine. Mohamed M. El Zeidy, *The Principle of Complementarity in International Criminal Law: Origin, Development and Practice*, Martinus Nijhoff, Leiden, 2008, pp. 16–26, discussing the drafting of these treaties.

[35] As Schwelb discusses, the persecution concerned both those "of Armenian or Greek race" on Turkish territory. Schwelb, 1946, p. 182, see *supra* note 16. Also see Full Report of Commission on Responsibility with Annex, 1919, p. 30, *supra* note 30.

[36] Treaty of Peace with Turkey signed at Sèvres, 10 August 1920, Cmd. 964, Treaty Series No. 11, His Majesty's Stationery Office, London, 1920, Article 230, http://treaties.fco.gov.uk/docs/pdf/1920/TS0011.pdf, last accessed 8 September 2015.

test in Turkey defeated subsequent efforts.[37] The Allies' insistence on such trials pursuant to the 1915 Declaration, led by the United Kingdom, eventually faded. In 1923 the Treaty of Sèvres was replaced by the Treaty of Lausanne, which substituted the demand for trials with a grant of amnesty.[38]

It is unlikely that these developments rise established a customary international law precedent for the eventual post-Second World War prosecutions.[39] However, it is nevertheless clear that whether or not establishing a criminal prohibition, these post-First World War events demonstrate the existence of conceptual antecedents of persecution as a matter of international concern.

12.2.1.3. The Interwar Period and Persecution as an Issue of International Concern

12.2.1.3.1. The League of Nations Minority Protections Regime

In the wake of the First World War the treatment of minority populations emerged as a central issue of international concern. With the experience of the Armenian massacre, rising tensions between government and minority groups in countries such as Poland and the proliferation of potentially vulnerable minority populations in other newly independent states of Eastern and Central Europe, there was a sense that something needed to be done. Consequently, throughout the interwar period the League of Nations strove – albeit with limited success[40] – to reconceptualise the relationship between minorities and the state as a matter that concerned international society at large. Embracing the interwar enthusiasm for interna-

---

[37] Power, 2013, pp. 14–15, see *supra* note 18; Ron Slye and Beth Van Schaack, *International Criminal Law: Essentials*, Wolters Kluwer Law & Business, New York, 2009, p. 25; El Zeidy, 2008, pp. 22–26, see *supra* note 34.

[38] Treaty of Peace with Turkey, and other instruments, signed at Lausanne, 24 July 1923, Cmd. 1929, Treaty Series No. 16, His Majesty's Stationery Office, London, 1923, Articles 138, 140, referring to the declaration of amnesty, http://treaties.fco.gov.uk/docs/pdf/1923/TS0016-1.pdf, last accessed 8 September 2015. Notably, the prior penalties provisions were absent in the Treaty of Lausanne. See also El Zeidy, 2008, p. 25, *supra* note 34, discussing these events.

[39] See, for example, Robinson, 1999, p. 44, *supra* note 16, commenting on whether these developments provide a precedent for the category of crimes against humanity more generally.

[40] See, for example, Mazower, 1997, pp. 51–52, 54, *supra* note 13.

tionalism and consistent with the League's somewhat paternalistic self-image, the League demanded that the states of Eastern Europe ratify treaties establishing minimum standards for the treatment of minority populations. To ensure these standards were met, the League regime also created a forum for claims of abuse.[41]

However, Western European states – Germany included – absented themselves from the League's minority rights framework, imposing no analogous treaty obligations. In 1943, Quincy Wright noted that whatever the shortcomings of the League regime as it existed, in the absence of a specific treaty it provided no protection for Germany's minorities. As he observed, "there was no formal ground on which the League of Nations could protest against the beginning of the persecutions in Germany". In Wright's view there remained "a general principle that a State was free to persecute its own nations in its own territory as it saw fit".[42] Moreover, though Germany was not bound by the League's minority rights regime, at the core of the Nazi legal ideology was a direct rejection of the League's effort to embed minority rights in international law. As Mark Mazower observes, "Nazi legal theorists attacked Geneva's 'juridification' of international relations and its pathetic belief in a 'common rule of law' applicable to peoples of differing racial worth".[43]

In many ways, the League's effort to protect minority populations against discriminatory treatment by their own state through the intervention of international law was revolutionary. However, as the "beginning of the persecutions" of Jews and others referred to by Wright intensified in Germany and expanded beyond that country's borders, the result of the League's partial[44] and half-hearted implementation[45] of its vision was brought into full relief.

---

[41] *Ibid.*, pp. 50–51, 54, stating that the standards imposed, and the channels for lodging complaints, but for a few successful instances, were largely impotent.

[42] *Ibid.*, p. 56, quoting Quincy Wright in World Citizens Association, *World's Destiny and the United States*, Citizens Association, Chicago, 1941, pp. 102–5.

[43] *Ibid.*, p. 55, citing John H. Herz, "The National Socialist Doctrine of International Law and the Problems of International Organization", in *Political Science Quarterly*, 1939, vol. 54, no. 4, pp. 536–54.

[44] That is, only applying to a select group of states and not establishing a universal standard.

[45] Mazower, 1997, pp. 50–55, see *supra* note 13.

12.2.1.3.2. Informal Developments Concerning the Protection of Minorities

While the development of the League's minority rights regime was underway, others – through less formal channels – sought to continue the immediate post-war endeavour to criminalise mass discriminatory conduct. Among the best-known efforts are those of a young Polish prosecutor, Raphael Lemkin. Though better known for his post-Second World War contributions to the codification of genocide as an international crime, Lemkin's efforts began years prior. Famously, Lemkin sought to present a draft convention proposing "universal repression", through criminalisation, of the destruction of the "physical and cultural existence of groups" to a conference of international lawyers in 1933.[46] In the text, he defined physical destruction as "barbarity", and cultural destruction as "vandalism".

The Polish government – seeking to curry favour with a rising Adolf Hitler – prevented Lemkin from attending the conference. However, his proposal was presented in his absence, and he subsequently advocated the underlying idea across Europe as the conditions in Nazi Germany worsened.[47] There was little immediate response to Lemkin's efforts; nevertheless, his work was central in maintaining a discussion concerning the possibility of criminalising mass discrimination. He would later become influential in post-Second World War efforts to proscribe the relevant offence under international law – delineating, as discussed below, the (closely related) alternative to the idea of persecution in the offence of 'genocide'.[48]

12.2.2. "These Crimes Shall Not Escape Retribution": International Responses to Persecution in the Drafting of the Post-Second World War International Criminal Law Instruments

Faced with mounting evidence of mass persecution of, and atrocities aimed at Jewish, Polish and other identified racial, political or religious populations at the hands of the Nazi regime, diplomats, scholars and lead-

---

[46] Power, 2013, pp. 19–22, see *supra* note 18.

[47] *Ibid.*

[48] See, for example, *infra* section 12.2.2.3.

ers turned their attention back to the possibility of international criminal law and away from the League's minority protection regimes.

As Schwelb observes, declarations early in the war demonstrate that the Allies intended to pursue a regime of individual accountability for those responsible for these acts. This involved promises of retribution for the broader category of atrocity offences rejected in the wake of the First World War, and not simply for war crimes "in the narrower sense, i.e. violations of the laws and customs of war, perpetrated on Allied territory, or against Allied citizens".[49] For example, he points to the 17 December 1942 declaration issued by 13 Allied states and exiled governments[50] in response to what he describes as the "barbarous and inhuman treatment to which the Jews were subjected in German-occupied Europe". The declaration noted reports that

> the German authorities not content with denying to persons of Jewish race in all the territories over which their barbarous rule has been extended, the most elementary human rights, are now carrying into effect Hitler's oft-repeated intention to exterminate the Jewish people in Europe.

And it went on to affirm that

> [t]he above-mentioned Governments and the French National Committee condemn in the strongest possible terms this bestial policy of cold-blooded extermination. [...] They reaffirm their solemn resolution that those responsible for these crimes shall not escape retribution and to press on with the necessary practical measures to this end.[51]

In the years that followed, such declarations would guide states, as they sought to ensure their actions met the standards they had set out in their words.

---

[49] Schwelb, 1946, p. 183, see *supra* note 16.

[50] The declaration was authored by Belgium, Czechoslovakia, Greece, Luxembourg, the Netherlands, Norway, Poland, the United States, the United Kingdom, the Soviet Union, Yugoslavia and the French National Committee.

[51] Declaration excerpted in Robert H. Jackson, *Report of Robert H. Jackson, United States Representative to the International Conference on Military Trials*, United States of America Department of State, London, 1949, pp. 9–10. See also Schwelb, 1946, pp. 183–84, *supra* note 16, discussing the declaration; Roberts, 2006, pp. 260–61, see *supra* note 23, discussing this declaration as set out in Schwelb's article. It is worth noting that Schwelb suggests that this declaration was carefully worded to specifically apply to occupied territory and not to crimes committed on German territory itself; however, this reading is not certain on the language of the declaration.

12.2.2.1. The Issue of Persecution at the UN War Crimes Commission

As one such measure taken to actualise their declared commitment to retribution and accountability through the "organised channels of justice",[52] the states of the newly christened United Nations established the UNWCC in October 1943.[53]

The issue of whether the UNWCC's remit should be limited to 'war crimes' in the strict sense, or whether it should embrace other atrocities, arose early in the life of the institution.[54] Among the primary drivers of this effort to extend the UNWCC's jurisdiction was a desire to respond to the pervasive persecutory treatment of groups by the Nazi regime. As the American representative asserted at a March 1944 meeting of the Legal Committee, the UNWCC's mandate included the need to consider "atrocities which were committed by the Nazis against German Jews and Catholics, as well as other offences perpetrated on religious or racial grounds in pursuance of Nazi ideology".[55] To this end the American delegate introduced a resolution categorising such acts as "crimes against humanity"; it read in full:

> It is clearly understood that the words 'crimes against humanity' refer, among others, to crimes committed against stateless persons or against any person because of their race

---

[52] See, for example, UNWCC Report, 1948, pp. 89–90, 109, *supra* note 22, quoting Punishment for War Crimes, the Inter Allied Declaration Signed at St James's Palace on 13th January and Relative Documents (1942), Declaration of St. James' Palace, 13 January 1942.

[53] The UNWCC did not include any representatives of the Soviet Union, as the Soviets protested against the rejection of their demand that each Soviet Republic receive individual membership in the UNWCC. Notably, the UNWCC is broadly believed to have been created largely to divert attention from the alliance's failure to respond to ongoing violations of the laws of war. See, for example, Robert Cryer, *Prosecuting International Crimes: Selectivity and the International Law Regime*, Cambridge University Press, Cambridge, 2005, pp. 37–38. See also Ann Tusa and John Tusa, *The Nuremberg Trial*, Macmillan, 1983, p. 62, discussing the role of the creation of the UNWCC in domestic British politics.

[54] UNWCC Report, 1948, p. 174, see *supra* note 22: "[T]he rule was stressed during the first days of the Commission's activities, that narrow legalisms were to be disregarded and the field of the violations of the laws of war extended so as to meet the requirements of justice, was applied in respect of this class of crimes". See Clark, 1990, pp. 179–80, *supra* note 16.

[55] UNWCC Report, 1948, *ibid*. See also Roberts, 2006, p. 261, *supra* note 23, discussing this comment.

or religion; such crimes are judicable by the United Nations
or their agencies as war crimes.[56]

Such crimes, the delegate argued, were "crimes against the foundation of civilisation, irrespective of place and time, and irrespective of the question as to whether they did or did not represent violations of the laws and customs of war".[57] For the American delegate, a persecutory element was at the core of the proposed concept of crimes against humanity.[58] This desire to ground a prohibition on persecutory acts – defined by a discriminatory intent – in international law would persist in the debate that followed. Ultimately, it would remain a primary motivation for the very recognition of the category of crimes against humanity.

The proposal, however, met with disagreement over whether addressing such acts fell within the mandate of the UNWCC; states questioned whether a UNWCC tasked to investigate 'war crimes' had jurisdiction to consider the proposed category of offences.[59] Following debate within the Legal Committee, the delegates concluded that the jurisdiction of the UNWCC should be interpreted in a manner consistent with the various collective and individual declarations of the Allies. These declarations, the Legal Committee concluded, evidenced an intention to pursue accountability for acts beyond war crimes strictly defined.[60]

However, members of the Legal Committee recognised the need to establish some limits on which offences in this broader category the UN-WCC should address. The Czechoslovakian representative, for instance, observed that the Allies' prior declarations should not be read to capture

---

[56]   UNWCC, Committee II [*sic*], Resolution moved by Mr. Pell on 16th March 1944, III/I, 18 March 1944 (https://www.legal-tools.org/doc/2aa8b6).

[57]   UNWCC Report, 1948, p. 175, see *supra* note 22.

[58]   See Roberts, 2006, p. 262, *supra* note 23.

[59]   See, for example, UNWCC Report, 1948, p. 175, *supra* note 22. Note that Roberts suggests that the critiques turned on whether international law should intervene into the internal affairs of the German state; however, the UNWCC report indicates that the reticence – at least in the forum of the UNWCC – was based on the terms of its mandate. See Roberts, 2006, p. 262, *supra* note 23.

[60]   See UNWCC Report, 1948, pp. 175–76, *supra* note 22. See also UNWCC, Committee III, Scope of the Retributive Action of the United Nations According to their Official Declarations. (The Problem of "War Crimes" in connection with the Second World War. Explanatory and Additional Note by Dr. Ecer to his Report (Doc. III/4), III/4(a), 12 May 1944, pp. 12–13, reviewing some of the declarations to this effect ('UNWCC, Ecer Memo') (https://www.legal-tools.org/doc/6335bd/); Roberts, 2006, p. 262, see *supra* note 23, discussing these developments.

"mere crimes" but only those "which have some connection with the war".[61] Crimes against humanity "committed because of race, religion and nationality" were so connected because they were in a sense "the real cause of all other crimes, as the source of the war".[62] This effort to distinguish crimes against humanity from "mere crimes" would continue to surface throughout the drafting and jurisprudential debate that followed. The focus on crimes against humanity "connected with the war" would remain a common, but controversial, approach as theories of jurisdiction over the offence developed. Likewise, this effort to distinguish crimes against humanity in general, and persecution specifically, from "mere crimes" would remain a primary challenge for contemporary efforts to delineate international criminal jurisdiction, as discussed below.[63]

With agreement within the Legal Committee on the need for jurisdiction beyond war crimes, the Committee proposed a resolution to be considered by the UNWCC as a whole articulating the terms of its jurisdiction. The resolution proposed four categories of crimes that would compose the scope of the UNWCC's concern: crimes committed for the purpose of launching war; crimes committed in Allied countries or against either members of the armed forces or civilians of Allied nations; crimes committed to prevent restoration of peace; and finally,

> crimes committed against any person without regard to nationality, stateless persons included, because of race, nationality, religious or political belief, irrespective of where they have been committed.[64]

Notably, in the proposed resolution, this final category of crimes was not categorised formally as 'crimes against humanity'.[65] Nevertheless, it was concerned with the same subject matter addressed in the earlier American definition of crimes against humanity: confirming jurisdiction beyond the traditional confines of war crimes to ensure a response to

---

[61] UNWCC, Ecer Memo, 1944, p. 7, see *supra* note 60, reviewing some of the declarations to this effect; Roberts, 2006, p. 262, see *supra* note 23, discussing these developments.

[62] UNWCC, Ecer Memo, *ibid.*

[63] See, for example, *infra* section 12.3.2.1. and section 12.3.3.1.

[64] UNWCC, Scope of the Retributive Action of the United Nations, Resolution Proposed by Committee III, C.20, 16 May 1944 (https://www.legal-tools.org/doc/23d4bd/).

[65] *Ibid.* Nor were any of the other crimes formally categorised in the proposal. But see Roberts, 2006, p. 262, *supra* note 23, suggesting that this category of crimes was classified as 'crimes against humanity' in the proposal.

persecutory conduct. That is, the proposed category extended jurisdiction beyond cases concerning mistreatment of Allied citizens (whether combatants or civilians) to cases concerning mistreatment of persons regardless of their nationality, where the crime evidenced a discriminatory intent on the basis of race, nationality, religion or political belief.[66]

Nevertheless, in August and November 1944, British officials stressed that – while not desiring to "place any unnecessary restriction" on the UNWCC's work and noting the importance of responding to atrocities committed on discriminatory grounds – the UNWCC should be concerned with 'war crimes' in the proper sense. Thus, they argued, its jurisdiction should be restricted to crimes that concerned Allied nationals.[67] Further discussion on the issue of persecution (and crimes against humanity generally) was subsequently placed on hold within the confines of the UNWCC.[68]

12.2.2.2. The Issue of Persecution at the London Conference

Outside of the UNWCC, the four major Allied powers – the United States, the United Kingdom, the Soviet Union and France – held their own bilateral and multilateral meetings to consider the issues that would arise in post-war Germany, including the need for accountability. Despite initial British reluctance on the issue,[69] the four powers agreed to meet in London in June 1945 to discuss what role an international tribunal would play in such plans.[70] Notwithstanding the debate that had already transpired within the UNWCC, the discussion concerning the response to the persecutory acts of the Axis effectively returned to first principles at the London Conference. Nevertheless, ensuring that persecution was recognised as a crime remained central to the debate in London. Again, seeking a response to such acts was a primary driving force behind the effort to

---

[66] See Roberts, 2006, p. 262, *supra* note 23: "This preliminary definition seemed to suggest that a racial, national, religious or political intent was a requisite element in the commission of all types of crimes against humanity, not simply persecution".

[67] UNWCC, Correspondence between the War Crimes Commission and H.M. Government in London Regarding the Punishment of Crimes Committed on Religious, Racial or Political grounds, C.78, 13 February 1945, pp. 2–6 (https://www.legal-tools.org/doc/d2523e/); UNWCC Report, 1948, p. 176, see *supra* note 22. See also Clark, 1990, p. 180, *supra* note 16, discussing the British position, and quoting the British statement.

[68] See UNWCC Report, 1948, p. 176, *supra* note 22; Clark, 1990, p. 180, see *supra* note 16.

[69] Tusa and Tusa, 1983, p. 71, see *supra* note 53.

[70] *Ibid.*, p. 75.

---

establish[71] international criminal accountability beyond the regulation of war.

In the lead up to the London Conference, Justice Robert Jackson (the lead American negotiator and later lead American prosecutor) submitted a report to the President of the United States.[72] The report, which was adopted as the official American position, highlighted the fact that responding to persecution and oppression remained a principal concern of the United States. As Jackson asserted in his report:

> Our people were outraged by the oppressions, the cruelest forms of torture, the large scale murder, and the wholescale confiscation of property which initiated the Nazi regime within Germany. They witnessed persecution of the greatest enormity on religious, political and racial grounds, the breakdown of trade unions, and the liquidation of all religious and moral influences. This was not the legitimate activity of a state within its own boundaries, but was preparatory to the launching of an international course of aggression and was with the evil intention, openly expressed by the Nazis, or capturing the form of the German state as an instrumentality for spreading their rule to other countries. Our people felt that these were the deepest offenses against that International Law described in the Fourth Hague Convention of 1907 as including the "laws of humanity and the dictates of the public conscience".[73]

---

[71] While it seems the debate was guided in part by an effort to recognise or codify existing international criminal prohibitions (see, for example, the discussion among delegates in Jackson, 1949, pp. 334–35, *supra* note 51), as Jackson himself acknowledged in the course of Conference meetings, they also took on a role "settling" the law the tribunal was to apply in various instances in light of the "disputed state of the law of nations". See *idem.*, p. 329.

[72] Earlier in the year, prior to the agreement to meet in London, the Americans had set out a preliminary proposal for trials. Crimes with a persecutory intent were not captured in this initial American proposal for trials of those engaged in the Axis war effort. However, in setting out the crimes of concern, the draft left residual space to "charge and try defendants under [the] Agreement for violations of law other than those recited above, including but not limited to atrocities and crimes committed in violation of the domestic law of any Axis Power or satellite or any of the United Nations". *Ibid.*, p. 24, citing San Francisco Proposal of April 1945. Notably, the offence conceived of was – unlike the other offences set out in the proposal – not sourced in international law, but domestic law of the Axis or UN states. Clark, 1990, p. 182, see *supra* note 16.

[73] Jackson, 1949, p. 49, see *supra* note 51 (emphasis added). He also went on to "restate in more technical lawyer's terms the legal charges against the top Nazi leaders", which in-

Jackson's statement on this point is notable for several reasons. For one, as with efforts in the wake of the First World War, Jackson sought to ground the legal prohibition on persecutory conduct and other atrocities in the Martens Clause's standard of the "laws of humanity". In addition, reflecting an issue that had already arisen in the UNWCC and would continue to guide the debate in London, Jackson pointed to why such conduct rose to the level of international concern: because it was "preparatory to the launching of an international course of aggression".

Some aspects of these views were evident in the initial American proposal prepared for the London Conference, yet there were some notable differences. The 14 June proposal proscribed "[a]trocities and offenses, including atrocities and persecutions on racial or religious grounds, committed since 1 January 1933 in violation of any applicable provision of the domestic law of the country in which committed".[74] Notably, despite the earlier view of such conduct as "the deepest offenses against [...] *International Law*", the June proposal envisaged the prosecution of persecution and other atrocity offences under domestic criminal law. In addition, the need for a connection to the war suggested by Jackson's earlier report was not evident. This distinction was highlighted by the fact that jurisdiction over this category of offences (in contrast to other categories in the proposal) explicitly extended to conduct dating back to January 1933 – that is, when Hitler first came to power in Germany, six years before the onset of war.[75] Finally, as would be a pattern in the drafts circulated at the Conference, the grounds of relevant discrimination enumerated had varied, as "political grounds" mentioned in Jackson's report were absent from the proposal.

Within days of the opening of the London Conference, the British delegation proposed a series of amendments to the American proposal. As noted above, the American proposal located the prohibition on persecution and atrocity (beyond those in violation of the traditional laws of

---

cluded "b) Atrocities and offenses, including atrocities and persecutions on racial and religious grounds, committed since 1933. This is only to recognize the principles of criminal law as they are generally observed in civilized states. These principles have been assimilated as a part of International Law at least since 1907". *Idem.*, p. 50.

[74] *Ibid.*, p. 57. Notably, "atrocities and offenses [...] constituting violations of international law, including the laws, rules and customs of land and naval warfare"; however, persecutions were not mentioned explicitly in the international law provision. See also Clark, 1990, p. 182, *supra* note 16, discussing this proposal.

[75] See Clark, 1990, p. 182, *supra* note 16, discussing this proposal.

war[76]) in the domestic criminal law of the country where the offence was committed. In contrast, the British proposal located the relevant prohibitions squarely in international law as "criminal violations of international laws". However, the British proposal contained an alternative restriction: the British draft only provided jurisdiction over conduct that was undertaken in "pursuance of a common plan or enterprise aimed at aggression against, or domination over, other nations".[77] The provision provided in full that the tribunal's jurisdiction would include

> [a]trocities and persecutions and deportations on political, racial or religious grounds, in pursuance of the common plan or enterprise referred to in sub-paragraph (*d*) hereof [(i.e. aimed at aggression or domination)] whether or not in violation of the domestic law of the country where perpetrated. [78]

Interestingly, not only did the British proposal frame the relevant acts as violations of international law in complete opposition to American proposal, it also asserted that such violations were criminal in spite of their status under domestic law.[79] In addition, the British proposal extended the requirement of a discriminatory element not only to persecutions proper but to "atrocities" and "deportations" as well. In short, once again the proposal to extend the scope of international criminal law beyond war crimes was animated at its core by an effort to recognise the Nazis' persecutory acts (broadly defined) as criminal under international law.

Over the subsequent weeks of the London Conference, the delegations continued to exchange proposals. A French proposal suggested holding responsible those who "directed [...] the policy of atrocities and persecutions against civilian populations".[80] The proposal – in particular its treatment of aggression – was viewed as too broad.[81] A British proposal submitted a few days after referred to the tribunal's jurisdiction over "systematic atrocities against or systematic terrorism or ill-treatment or murder of civilians".[82] Notably, while a reference to persecution was absent

---

[76] That is, traditional violations of the laws of war concerning acts aimed at the opposing belligerent's combatants or civilians, rather than one's own nationals or others.

[77] Jackson, 1949, pp. 86–87, Article 12(d) and (e), see *supra* note 51.

[78] *Ibid.*, Article 12(e).

[79] Clark, 1990, p. 183, see *supra* note 16.

[80] Jackson, 1949, p. 293, see *supra* note 51.

[81] *Ibid.*, pp. 299–300.

[82] *Ibid.*, p. 312.

from this proposal, the prior British requirement that the acts be associated with a common plan had now been substituted with an alternative limiting device, which would later re-emerge in the American Control Council Law No. 10 jurisprudence: the requirement that the relevant atrocities be *systematic* in nature. A requirement that the relevant conduct be systematic (or in the alternative widespread) would ultimately be recognised as a requisite contextual element of crimes against humanity under customary international law. As such, it would eventually be incorporated in all contemporary codifications of the offence including those set out in the Statutes of the ICTR and the ICC Statute.[83]

A Soviet proposal submitted shortly after the British draft also lacked a direct reference to persecution. It provided jurisdiction over "[a]trocities against the civilian population including murder and ill-treatment of civilians, the deportation of civilians to slave labour and other violations of the laws and customs of warfare". Significantly, in categorising these offences as "violations of the laws and customs of warfare", the Soviet proposal, in short, restricted the tribunal's jurisdiction to war crimes as traditionally conceived.[84]

At a conference session on the day the Soviet proposal was circulated, Jackson asserted that the proposal "does not reach all that we want to reach and reaches a good deal we would not want to reach".[85] In particular, the American delegation specifically sought to capture the persecutory acts undertaken by the Axis, including the actions of Germany against its own citizens.[86] Despite this aim, Jackson stressed that "it has been a general principle of the foreign policy of our Government from time immemorial that the internal affairs of another government are not ordinarily our business". Bringing to the fore the primary tension that would persist throughout international efforts to criminalise persecution in the next half-century,[87] Jackson sought to parse out the distinction between discriminatory conduct that rose to the level of an international offence, and that which should be the concern of domestic processes alone. It was not per-

---

[83]   See *infra* section 12.3.2.1. and section 12.3.3.1.

[84]   Jackson, 1949, p. 327, see *supra* note 51. See also Clark, 1990, pp. 184–86, *supra* note 16, discussing how the Soviet definition of atrocities effectively amounted to traditional war crimes.

[85]   Jackson, 1949, pp. 330–31, see *supra* note 51.

[86]   Later in his comments he refers to jurisdiction over such acts as allowing "prosecution of those things which I agree […] are absolutely necessary in this case". *Ibid.*, p. 333.

[87]   See, for example, *infra* section 12.3.2.1. and section 12.3.3.1.

secutory acts in the abstract that justified international intervention; rather, he noted – consistent with the earlier British proposal and the comments in Jackson's own report to President Harry Truman – such intervention was only justified due to the connection between the offences and the waging of the war. As he stated:

> [T]he way Germany treats its inhabitants, or any other country treats its inhabitants, is not our affair any more than it is the affair of some other government to interpose itself in our problems. *The reason that this program of extermination of Jews and the destruction of the rights of minorities becomes an international concern is this: it is a part of a plan for making an illegal war.* Unless we have a war connection as a basis for reaching them, I would think we have no basis for dealing with atrocities. They were a part of the preparation of war for or for the conduct of the war in so far as they occurred inside of Germany and that makes them our concern.[88]

Interestingly, Jackson acknowledged the relevant pressing domestic considerations for the American delegation when addressing the provision on "atrocities, persecutions, and deportations on political, racial, or religious grounds". In his words: "We have some regrettable circumstances at times in our own country in which minorities are unfairly treated". While he felt the need to bring the Nazi's persecutory conduct before the international tribunal, he stressed that "it is justifiable that we interfere or attempt to bring retribution to individuals or to states only because the concentration camps and the deportations were in pursuance of a common plan or enterprise of making an unjust or illegal war in which we became involved".[89] Significantly, as noted below, this would not be the only time when concerns about setting precedents that could reach racially discriminatory laws or other aspects of racial inequality in the United States were acknowledged as a relevant factor by American representatives engaged in pursuing international justice in the wake of the Second World War.

That evening, the British circulated a new draft of the crimes provision, based on the Soviet proposal. The sub-paragraph on jurisdiction over atrocities beyond war crimes effectively merged the language of the earli-

---

[88] Jackson, 1949, pp. 330–31, see *supra* note 51 (emphasis added). See also Clark, 1990, pp. 185–86, see *supra* note 16, discussing this statement.

[89] Jackson, 1949, p. 333, see *supra* note 51.

er British drafts with that proposed by the Soviets. While the first half referred to the discrete acts set out in the Soviet proposal ("including (inter alia) murder and ill-treatment of civilians and deportation of civilians to slave labour"), it went on to add "and persecutions on racial or religious grounds" as per the British drafts. However, as with the earlier British drafts, jurisdiction only extended to persecutions "where such persecutions were inflicted in pursuance of the aggression or domination".[90] It is notable, on the one hand, that the Soviet requirement that such offences be violations of the laws of war was now absent – indicating a broader category of offences was conceived – and, on the other hand, that the British limitation (of acts connected to aggression) only applied to acts of persecution. Only acts of persecution were seen as requiring some jurisdictional limitation at this point; other non-war crime 'atrocities' did not require such a constraint. The two categories, which persisted in the final version of the provision, would soon after be described by the UNWCC as setting out "murder-type" crimes against humanity, and "persecution-type" crimes against humanity.[91]

In the final week of negotiations that followed, several drafts were circulated as the delegates responded to the pressure to reach consensus. While the draft provision on atrocities was subject to a series of further revisions, it remained substantially consistent in form, combining a prohibition on both "murder-type" and "persecution-type" conduct. Among the changes that took place, the limited focus on acts "in pursuance" of aggression or domination was temporarily replaced with a requirement that the acts be "in pursuance of the common plan or conspiracy", consistent with an American proposal.[92] Subsequently, in the penultimate draft circulated by the American delegation, this limitation was replaced once again with the broader standard of "in furtherance of or in connection with any crime within the jurisdiction of the International Tribunal".[93] In addition, the language that initially clearly confined the nexus clause to acts of persecution in the British proposal (and not "murder-type" conduct) was revised somewhat ambiguously, seeming to apply a cabining

---

[90] *Ibid.*, p. 359, Article 6(b).
[91] UNWCC Report, 1948, p. 178, see *supra* note 22. Ratner and Abrams, 1997, p. 17, see *supra* note 8; Roberts, 2006, p. 263, see *supra* note 23.
[92] See Jackson, 1949, pp. 374 and 390, *supra* note 51.
[93] *Ibid.*, p. 395.

standard to the whole provision.[94] Further, the reference to such acts falling within the jurisdiction of the tribunal "whether or not in violation of the domestic law of the country where perpetrated", which was earlier considered by the London Conference, was reincorporated by the American delegation.[95] And, in the penultimate draft, the American delegation added a title "Crimes Against Humanity" to the category of offences.[96] While the same title had been proposed by the American delegate to the UNWCC more than a year prior, Jackson attributed the suggestion to use titles to "an eminent scholar of international law"[97] – believed by some to be Hersch Lauterpacht.[98]

The only significant change between the penultimate American draft and the provision in Article 6(c) of the English-language version of the Charter of the International Military Tribunal ('IMT Charter') signed just over a week later on 8 August 1945 was the inclusion of a semi-colon between the description of "murder-type" and "persecution-type" conduct. The final provision read in full,

> Crimes Against Humanity: namely, murder, extermination, enslavement, deportation, and other inhumane acts committed against any civilian population, before or during the war; or *persecutions on political, racial or religious grounds* in execution of or in connection with any crime within the jurisdiction of the Tribunal, whether or not in violation of the domestic law of the country where perpetrated.[99]

This controversial semi-colon suggested the requirement that the offence be related to another crime within the tribunal's jurisdiction and the declaration that the offence was a crime before the tribunal, notwithstand-

---

[94] See, for example, this change first made at *ibid.*, p. 390: "These include but are not limited to murder and ill-treatment of civilians and deportations of civilians to slave labour and persecutions on political, racial or religious grounds committed in pursuance of the common plan or conspiracy referred to in paragraph (*d*) below".

[95] *Ibid.*, p. 395.

[96] *Ibid.*

[97] *Ibid.*, p. 416.

[98] See Martti Koskenniemi, "Hersch Lauterpacht and the Development of International Criminal Law", in *Journal of International Criminal Justice*, 2004, vol. 2, no. 3, p. 811; Clark, 1990, pp. 189–90, see *supra* note 16.

[99] Charter of the International Military Tribunal ('IMT Charter'), in Jackson, 1949, p. 423, see *supra* note 51, setting out the content of the Nuremberg Charter prior to its amendment by the Berlin Protocol (emphasis added) (https://www.legal-tools.org/doc/64ffdd/).

ing the content of domestic law, only applied to persecution, and not the other acts falling within the category of crimes against humanity.[100] The semi-colon was ultimately removed by way of the Berlin Protocol signed by the four chief prosecutors two months later, with the suggestion that its last-minute inclusion was an error.[101]

In the result, the final version of the provision restricted jurisdiction over all crimes against humanity (and not simply persecution) to those carried out in connection with another crime within the IMT's jurisdiction.[102] However, contrary to the initial proposals concerning crimes against humanity at the London Conference and within the UNWCC, the requirement that discrimination be demonstrated on one of the three enumerated grounds was limited to the offence of persecution and was not extended to "murder-type" crimes against humanity.

As discussed below, debate as to the appropriate application of these constraints has persisted over the subsequent half-century. While various contemporary tribunals have held that the nexus requirement no longer remains necessary under customary international law, the ICC Statute retains an attenuated form of the requirement with regard to persecution specifically while excluding it for crimes against humanity generally.[103] Likewise, while proof of discrimination has generally only been required in establishing charges of persecution in contemporary legal instruments and jurisprudence, the ICTR Statute includes a general requirement of discrimination in the *chapeau* elements applicable to all crimes against humanity.[104]

More immediately, however, in the months following the London Conference the drafters of various other post-Second World War legal instruments endeavoured to engage with the appropriate application of these constraints, and in doing so sought to locate the threshold between

---

[100] Clark, 1990, p. 190, see *supra* note 16.

[101] Berlin Protocol in Jackson, 1949, p. 429, see *supra* note 51. Clark, 1990, pp. 190–92, see *supra* note 16. However, as Roberts notes, "the removal of the semi-colon was never interpreted as extending the requisite political, racial or religious motivate to all forms of crimes against humanity in conformity with previous drafts". Roberts, 2006, p. 263, see *supra* note 23.

[102] While the intention of the chief prosecutors was to extend the limitation to all crimes against humanity, even in the absence of the semi-colon the plain text of the provision could still have been read to apply the relevant constraints to persecution alone.

[103] See *infra* section 12.3.3.1.

[104] See, for example, *infra* section 12.3.2.1.3.

crimes of international concern and crimes of strictly domestic concern. These post-war efforts are discussed in the following subsection.

12.2.2.3. Approaches to Persecution Beyond London

Several related efforts to delineate persecution as a crime under international law followed shortly after the London Conference. While they tracked a substantially similar formula, some distinctions are worth noting.

Control Council Law No. 10 ('CCL No. 10') was signed in December 1945 by the four occupying powers in Germany within five months of the London Conference, and exactly one month after opening statements began before the International Military Tribunal ('IMT') at Nuremberg. The law was intended, *inter alia*, to "establish a uniform legal basis in Germany for the prosecution of war criminals and other similar offenders, other than those dealt with by the International Military Tribunal".[105] The provision concerning crimes against humanity was modelled closely after Article 6 of the IMT Charter. However, most notably, it did not require a connection with another crime as a threshold requirement for jurisdiction. The provision read in full:

> Crimes against Humanity. Atrocities and offenses, including but not limited to murder, extermination, enslavement, deportation, imprisonment, torture, rape, or other inhumane acts committed against any civilian population, *or persecutions on political, racial or religious grounds* whether or not in violation of the domestic laws of the country where perpetrated.[106]

While the absence of the nexus requirement is the only major distinction[107] between the provision and its IMT Charter equivalent, this difference was quite significant and would inform fundamental distinctions

---

[105] Control Council Law No. 10, Punishment of Persons Guilty of War Crimes, Crimes Against Peace and Against Humanity, 20 December 1945, 3 Official Gazette Control Council for Germany 50–55, 1946, Preamble ('CCL No. 10') (https://www.legal-tools.org/doc/ffda62/).

[106] *Ibid.*, Article II(1)(a) (emphasis added).

[107] The text of CCL No. 10 also dropped the IMT Charter's reference to acts "before the war". However, in the text's statute of limitations provision, the drafters of CCL No. 10 indicated an intent to provide jurisdiction to the zonal tribunals that covered January 1933 to July 1945. *Ibid.*, Article II(5).

in the resulting jurisprudence that remain evident in the contemporary interpretation of the offence.

Within a few weeks of the CCL No. 10's entry into force, the focus of post-war justice efforts expanded beyond the European arena to the Pacific. The United States and specifically the Supreme Commander of the Allied Powers in the East, General Douglas MacArthur, moved swiftly to replicate the Nuremberg model.[108] As noted above, the IMT Charter and Tribunal had been an intensely collaborative effort of the four major European powers. In contrast, the creation of the International Military Tribunal for the Far East ('IMTFE' or 'Tokyo Tribunal') was the result of a unilateral proclamation by MacArthur in January 1946, though the terms of its Charter set out by the United States did incorporate minor subsequent amendments proposed by the other Allies engaged in the Pacific forum, as well as the Philippines and India.[109] Again, the definition of crimes against humanity found at Article 5(c) of the IMTFE Charter, including the reference to persecution, was derived largely from the IMT Charter. The provision provided jurisdiction over:

> Crimes against Humanity: namely, murder, extermination, enslavement, deportation, and other inhumane acts committed before or during the war, or persecutions on political or racial grounds in execution of or in connection with any crime within the jurisdiction of the Tribunal, whether or not in violation of the domestic law of the country where perpetrated.[110]

There are, however, two noteworthy differences from its Nuremberg predecessor: (1) "religion" was excluded as a possible ground of persecutory conduct; (2) and "it [was] not expressly stated that 'crimes against humanity' are committed 'against any civilian population'".[111]

---

[108] Solis Horwitz, "The Tokyo Trial", in *International Conciliation*, 1950, vol. 28, pp. 480–82.

[109] *Ibid.*, pp. 482–83.

[110] Charter of the International Military Tribunal for the Far East ('IMTFE Charter'), 19 January 1946, Article 5(c) (https://www.legal-tools.org/doc/a3c41c/).

[111] Also of note is the promulgation of the Pacific Regulations for the US Military Commissions in the region, see UNWCC Report, 1948, p. 215, *supra* note 22.

12.2.3. Persecution on Trial: International Responses to Persecution in Post-Second World War Jurisprudence

Notably, for all the debate involved in their drafting (or perhaps because of it) the provisions proscribing persecution as a crime against humanity in the various post-war legal instruments provided little substance to guide the adjudication of the offence. Consequently, the various tribunals, commissions and courts tasked with interpreting the provision started largely from first principles. The resulting decisions established parameters for the offence that, over the last 20 years, have been instrumental in guiding the adjudication of persecution as a crime against humanity before the contemporary international criminal courts and tribunals.[112]

However, the post-war jurisprudence also leaves much wanting. The Judgment of the IMT at Nuremberg ('Nuremberg Judgment') provided no explicit definition of persecution. Moreover, there is some inconsistency in the IMT's use of the term throughout: while characterising certain acts as "persecution" in convicting some defendants, the IMT failed to clearly invoke the term with regard to the conduct of others which seemed to meet the same standard (while still finding them guilty of crimes against humanity generally).[113] In addition, the discussion of each defendant's guilt for war crimes is seldom distinguished from their guilt for crimes against humanity; as Roger Clark observes, "[t]he discussion of the two offenses is indeed quite jumbled up".[114]

Turning to the jurisprudence of the other post-war tribunals, though persecution was included within the definition of crimes against humanity in the IMTFE Charter, the Indictment did not allege any instances of per-

---

[112] See generally *infra* section 12.3.

[113] See, for example, the failure of the IMT to characterise Kaltenbrunner's, Frick's and Rosenburg's conduct explicitly as "persecution" while it seemed to meet the threshold the Tribunal set elsewhere. IMT, *International Military Tribunal v. Martin Borman et al.*, Judgment, 1 October 1946, in *Trial of the Major War Criminals Before the International Military Tribunal*, 1947, vol. I, pp. 291–93, regarding Kaltenbrunner; pp. 295–96, regarding Rosenburg; pp. 300–1, regarding Frick ('IMT Judgment') (https://www.legal-tools.org/doc/45f18e/). Notably, subsequent jurisprudence and scholars have nevertheless treated the findings of guilt concerning some of these individuals as a precedent for persecution. See, for example, ICTY, *Prosecutor v. Duško Tadić et al.*, Opinion and Judgment, IT-94-1-T, 7 May 1997, para. 706 ('Tadić case') (https://www.legal-tools.org/doc/0a90ae/).

[114] Clark, 1990, p. 194, see *supra* note 16.

secution.[115] Unsurprisingly, the Judgment of the IMTFE does not provide any guidance on the interpretation of the offence.[116] The various judgments of the US military zonal tribunals sitting in Nuremberg ('Nuremberg Military Tribunals' or 'NMT') under CCL No. 10, and of the various national tribunals, courts and commissions in the immediate wake of the war provide some further guidance.[117] There is nevertheless a degree of disagreement in the interpretation of the concepts of persecution and crimes against humanity generally among these decisions that is not always acknowledged, and questions concerning the interpretation of the offence that were not addressed.

Despite these shortcomings, the roots of the contemporary approach to persecution as a crime against humanity can be seen in the immediate post-war jurisprudence. This section reviews some of decisions setting out these foundational principles, as the parameters of the international crime of persecution – a term with a long conceptual history but shorter doctrinal one – began to take shape. At its core, the post-war tribunals characterised as persecution varying sorts of underlying conduct (ranging from other enumerated crimes against humanity to conduct that was not independently criminal) when undertaken in a manner that intentionally discriminated against a group on enumerated grounds.

Like the drafters before them, the post-war tribunals wrestled with how to limit the parameters of persecution, to distinguish conduct of in-

---

[115] See IMTFE, Indictment, No. 1, 1946 ('IMTFE Indictment') (https://www.legal-tools.org/doc/59771d/).

[116] See Yuma Totani, "The Case against the Accused", in Yuki Tanaka, Tim McCormack and Gerry Simpson (eds.), *Beyond Victor's Justice? The Tokyo War Crimes Trial Revisited*, Martinus Nijhoff, Leiden, 2010, p. 154. Notably, while not charging persecution, the Indictment does charge crimes against humanity; however, the IMTFE Judgment also refrained from assessing guilt for crimes against humanity and rather focused on crimes against peace and war crimes. See IMTFE Indictment, see *supra* note 115.

[117] This analysis excludes, *inter alia*, the decisions of British courts. These courts grounded their jurisdiction in the Royal Warrant, which provided jurisdiction only over war crimes and not crimes against humanity. War Office, Special Army Order, Royal Warrant 0160/2498 A.O. 81/1945, Regulations for the Trial of War Criminals, 18 June 1945 (https://www.legal-tools.org/doc/386f77/). See also British Military Court, Luneburg, *United Kingdom v. Joseph Kramer et al.*, 17 September 1945–17 November 1945 in UN-WCC, *Law Reports of Trials of War Criminals*, vol. II, London, 1947, pp. 1, 150–51; the British Military Court hearing the case concerning the Belsen concentration camp noted that all parties recognised that jurisdiction was grounded in the Royal Warrant which differed from the IMT Charter, *inter alia*, insofar as the former "is limited to the trial of war crimes proper and excludes crimes against humanity".

ternational concern from that of solely domestic concern. While the IMT required that the persecutory conduct be connected to the armed conflict in some respect through the connection to another offence within the Tribunal's jurisdiction, this requirement was a matter of disagreement among the NMTs. In addition, several NMTs incorporated a new requirement for crimes against humanity generally (including persecution) not explicitly set out in CCL No. 10: that the conduct be widespread, systematic and pursuant to government policy or acquiescence.

In surveying the post-war jurisprudence this section begins by discussing the *actus reus* of the crime (including the question of what underlying acts were considered persecutory, and the issue of a nexus to other crimes), then turns to the *mens rea* of the offence, and finally provides a brief comment on the relationship between the crimes of genocide and persecution as a crime against humanity. Notably, what follows is not an exhaustive review of the post-war decisions; rather it endeavours to trace the development of the offence in the leading cases. In doing, the analysis seeks to highlight, in particular, efforts to establish parameters of the offence that distinguished the international crime of persecution from what the drafters had referred to as "mere crimes" of domestic concern. This phenomenon is most clearly evident in the discussion of the "nexus requirement" below; however, its influence can be discerned throughout the other areas of the jurisprudence addressed as well.

12.2.3.1. The *Actus Reus* of Persecution

12.2.3.1.1. The Underlying Persecutory Acts or Omissions

As noted above, neither the legal instruments governing the post-war tribunals nor the jurisprudence these tribunals produced set out a comprehensive definition of persecution as a crime against humanity. Moreover, the IMT was particularly inconsistent in its use of the term, complicating the task of drawing robust precedential standards on this point from its Judgment.[118]

---

[118] In the analysis of the IMT Judgment that follows, we rely on instances where the IMT explicitly classified an act as persecution and not simply as a crime against humanity (despite the presence of circumstances that suggested that a specific persecution conviction could be supported). As discussed above, some courts and scholars have taken an alternative position relying on the IMT Judgment as providing precedent for the contemporary in-

Nevertheless, some observations can be made concerning the character of the underlying acts or omissions relied upon by the tribunals for a persecution conviction. Among other things, the tribunals often portrayed persecution as a cumulative or contextualised crime – situating a given impugned act in a broad series of persecutory acts. In addition, while the tribunals did not set out explicit standards concerning underlying conduct, they tended to rely on underlying acts or omissions of varying character for persecution convictions. Such acts included conduct that independently met the definition of a crime against humanity or a war crime, acts that were themselves criminal but were neither crimes against humanity nor war crimes, and finally conduct that in the absence of a discriminatory element would not otherwise have qualified as criminal acts. Finally, while controversial, some scholars as well as modern international criminal courts and tribunals have derived a minimum threshold from the post-war jurisprudence of acts of a similar severity to other crimes against humanity. Much of the jurisprudence examining these factors – though at times only selective aspects of it – would be influential on the jurisprudence of the contemporary international criminal tribunals and courts, as these institutions engaged with the same fundamental question of what conduct constitutes the *actus reus* of persecution.[119]

12.2.3.1.1.1. Cumulative Approach

Perhaps unsurprisingly, given the nature of the charges before them, the post-war tribunals seldom considered a single act of persecution in isolation; rather, they often situated the persecutory conduct of a defendant within an ongoing series of discriminatory events. Before addressing the guilt of individuals and organisations for persecution, for instance, the IMT set out the relevant context in a background section entitled "Persecution of the Jews". The IMT observed that "[t]he persecution of the Jews at the hands of the Nazi Government has been proved in the greatest detail before the Tribunal. It is a record of consistent and systematic inhumanity on the greatest scale".[120] In an oft-quoted excerpt, the IMT went on to state:

---

terpretation of persecution even where the IMT failed to explicitly invoke the term. See *supra* note 113 and accompanying text.

[119] See, for example, *infra* section 12.3.2.1. and 12.3.3.1.

[120] IMT Judgment, p. 247, see *supra* note 113.

> With the seizure of power, the persecution of the Jews was intensified. A series of discriminatory laws was passed, which limited the offices and professions permitted to Jews; and restrictions were placed on their family life and their rights of citizenship. By the autumn of 1938, the Nazi policy towards the Jews had reached the stage where it was directed towards the complete exclusion of Jews from German life. Pogroms were organised, which included the burning and demolishing of synagogues, the looting of Jewish businesses, and the arrest of prominent Jewish businessmen. A collective fine of 1 billion marks was imposed on the Jews, the seizure of Jewish assets was authorised, the movement of the Jews was restricted by regulations to certain specified districts and hours. The creation of the ghettos was carried out on an extensive scale, and by an order of the Security Police Jews were compelled to wear a yellow star to be worn on the breast and back.[121]

This discriminatory treatment, the IMT recounted, developed further into a practice of deportation, human experimentation, extermination, slave labour and other similar acts once the war had begun.[122] Notably, as discussed further below, the IMT subsequently found that the majority of the acts set out in the above excerpt did not to fall within its jurisdiction over persecution as a crime against humanity insofar as – having occurred before the invasion of Poland in 1939 and the onset of the war – they were unrelated to another crime within the IMT Charter. Nevertheless, the IMT seemed compelled to include an account of these acts in the Judgment, establishing the sequence of persecutory conduct within which the acts it subsequently considered fell.

Similarly, in the *Ministries* case, the US NMT approached wartime persecution as a cumulative series of events. As the Tribunal noted, "[t]he persecution of the Jews went on steadily from step to step and finally to death in foul form". The Tribunal went on to further describe the "steps" comprising the persecutory conduct stating:

> The Jews of Germany were first deprived of the rights of citizenship. They were then deprived of the right to teach, to practice professions, to obtain education, to engage in business enterprises; they were forbidden to marry except among

---

[121] *Ibid.*, pp. 248–49.
[122] *Ibid.*, pp. 249–53.

themselves and those of their own religion; they were subject to arrest and confinement in concentration camps, to beatings, to mutilation and torture; their property was confiscated; they were herded into ghettos; they were forced to emigrate and to buy leave to do so; they were deported to the East, where they worked to exhaustion and death; they became slave labourers; and finally over six million were murdered.[123]

In the *Justice* case the US NMT emphasised why such a cumulative or contextual approach was necessary. Noting that the events could not be understood in isolation the Tribunal observed, "[t]he record contains innumerable acts of persecution of individual Poles and Jews, but to consider these cases as isolated and unrelated instances of perversion of justice would be to overlook the very essence of the offence charged in the indictment".[124] As the Tribunal observed, "it is alleged that they participated in carrying out a governmental plan and program for the persecution and extermination of Jews and Poles, a plan which transcended territorial boundaries as well as the bounds of human decency".[125]

12.2.3.1.1.2. Threshold Gravity of Underlying Acts

There remains the question, however, of what acts or omissions – whether as part of a series of persecutory acts or in isolation – the tribunals viewed as appropriately constituting the underlying acts for a conviction of persecution as a crime against humanity. The Nuremberg Judgment is silent on this point, not directly addressing the severity or gravity of acts that would support a conviction.

---

[123] NMT, *United States of America v. Ernst von Weizsaecker et al.*, Judgment, 11–13 April 1949, in *Trials of War Criminals Before the Nuernberg Military Tribunals*, vol. XIV, 1951, p. 471 ('Ministries case') (https://www.legal-tools.org/doc/eb20f6/).

[124] Justice case, vol. III, p. 1063, see *supra* note 7.

[125] *Ibid.* See further the UNWCC's commentary on the case: UNWCC, *Law Reports of Trials of War Criminals*, vol. VI, London, 1948, pp. 82–83. It is worth noting, however, that as the Tribunal observed, part of the reason why the cumulative nature of the events was relevant in the case before it was the nature of the charges: setting out participation in a "governmental plan and program for [...] persecution". This suggests that the cumulative approach to assessing persecution may not always be applicable, but may be more or less relevant depending on the particular nature of the events. The issue of the NMT's development of the contextual elements of crimes against humanity (including the relevance of a plan or policy) is discussed further below.

In contrast, a number of the US NMTs addressed the threshold gravity an underlying act must reach to support a conviction for persecution. As contemporary scholars and jurisprudence have noted, the most direct articulation of such a threshold can be found in the *Flick* case's rejection of discriminatory "compulsory taking of industrial property" as a basis for conviction of persecution as a crime against humanity.[126] After noting that the Nuremberg Judgment did not expressly support treating such acts as crimes against humanity,[127] the US NMT held that

> [n]ot even under a proper construction of the section of [Control Council] Law No. 10 relating to crimes against humanity, do the facts warrant conviction. The "atrocities and offenses" listed therein "murder, extermination," etc., are all offenses against the person. Property is not mentioned. Under the doctrine of *ejusdem generis* the catch-all words "other persecutions" must be deemed to include only such as affect the life and liberty of the oppressed peoples. Compulsory taking of industrial property, however reprehensible, is not in that category.[128]

Chambers of the contemporary international criminal courts and tribunals have subsequently relied upon this statement to conclude that "at a minimum, acts of persecution must be of an equal gravity or severity to the other acts enumerated under [the definition of crimes against humanity]".[129] As Kevin Jon Heller has noted, however, the reasoning in the *Flick* case is problematic insofar as, *inter alia*, it depends "on a significant misstatement of Article II(1)(c) [of CCL No. 10]".[130] The articulation of the "murder-type" crimes against humanity in the provision is not followed by a reference to "*other* persecutions" but rather to "persecutions".

---

[126] See, for example, Kupreškić case, Trial Judgment, para. 619, *supra* note 2; Extraordinary Chambers in the Courts of Cambodia ('ECCC'), *Prosecutor v. Kaing Guek Eav alias Duch*, Appeal Judgement, 001/18-707-2007-ECCC/SC, 3 February 2012, paras. 254–55 ('Duch case') (https://www.legal-tools.org/doc/681bad/).

[127] NMT, *United States of America v. Friedrich Flick et al.*, Judgment, 22 December 1947, in *Trials of War Criminals Before the Nuernberg Military Tribunals*, 1951, vol. VI, p. 1215 ('Flick case') (https://www.legal-tools.org/doc/861416/).

[128] *Ibid.* This reasoning was subsequently adopted in the *IG Farben* case. NMT, *United States of America v. Carl Krauch et al.*, Judgment, in *Trials of War Criminals Before the Nuernberg Military Tribunals*, vol. VIII, 1951, pp. 1129–1130 ('Farben case').

[129] See, for example, Kupreškić case, Trial Judgment, para. 619, *supra* note 2.

[130] Kevin Jon Heller, The Nuremberg Military Tribunals and the Origins of International Criminal Law, Oxford University Press, Oxford, 2011, pp. 247–48.

In Heller's words, "[t]he difference was critical: although the expression 'other persecutions' might have implied that Article II(1)(c) intended to criminalize persecutions 'of the same kind' as the atrocities and offenses, the more generic term 'persecutions' gives rise to no such impression".[131]

As discussed below, the specific application of the *Flick* holding to compulsory takings as a sufficient underlying act for persecution was challenged in other cases before the US NMT. Moreover, while *Flick*'s threshold analysis appears to have been based on a misreading of the text of CCL No. 10, the contemporary interpretation of the *Flick* holding as requiring that underlying acts amount to "gross or blatant denials of fundamental human rights"[132] seems to be supported, *inter alia*, by the drafting history of the relevant post-Second World War legal instruments. As noted above, in London, Jackson (the most adamant proponent of the inclusion of persecution in the definition of crimes against humanity) stressed that the American delegation sought to address, in particular, the "destruction of the rights of minorities".[133]

12.2.3.1.1.3. War Crimes and Crimes Against Humanity as Underlying Acts

Though the post-Second World War jurisprudence does not include an extensive consideration of the precise gravity threshold that underlying acts or omission must meet, some indication can be gleaned from a review of the types of acts that the tribunals relied upon to support persecution convictions. Namely, they relied upon both underlying acts that amounted

---

[131] *Ibid.*, p. 248.

[132] See, for example, Kupreškić case, Trial Judgment, para. 619, *supra* note 2; Duch case, Appeal Judgement, paras. 254–55, see *supra* note 126.

[133] Jackson, 1949, pp. 330–31, see *supra* note 51. While one may be reticent to place too much weight on this statement, the reference to "destruction of rights" does indicate that something more severe than mere discriminatory treatment was intended to be captured. Moreover, this statement is a helpful indication of the intended content of persecution as a free-standing offence, as other comments focused substantially on the extermination and deportation of minorities with discriminatory intent. It should be noted, however, that the excerpted comment from Jackson should not be read as excluding jurisdiction over compulsory takings of property. First, Jackson also indicated that such takings fell within the scope of concern. See *id.*, p. 49, noting in his initial report to Truman that among the acts which were of concern was the "wholescale confiscation of property which initiated the Nazi regime within Germany". Second, the right to property is among those considered as "fundamental" within American conceptions of rights; see, for example, Constitution of the United States of America, Fifth Amendment, 15 December 1791; Constitution of the United States of America, Fourteenth Amendment, 9 July 1868.

to crimes against humanity and war crimes, as well as conduct not meeting this standard. This section surveys some of the decisions falling into the first category; the section that follows surveys decisions in which conduct not amounting to crimes against humanity and war crimes was invoked to support a conviction for persecution.

The notion discussed here (that is, whether a crime against humanity or a war crime *could* be relied upon as the underlying act or omission for a persecution charge) should be distinguished from another matter discussed below, that is the issue of whether a nexus between persecution and other such crimes was *required* for the tribunal to assert jurisdiction. It is also worth emphasising that the proposals put forward during the drafting negotiations requiring discriminatory intent for all crimes against humanity were ultimately not adopted. Thus, while "murder-type" crimes against humanity were relied upon as the underlying acts for persecution charges, a persecutory intent was not required to substantiate a conviction for a "murder-type" crime against humanity.

Examples of reliance on other war crimes and crimes against humanity (namely, deportation, slave labour and extermination) as the underlying acts or omissions grounding persecution convictions against organisations[134] and individuals alike can be found throughout the Nuremberg Judgment.[135] In its discussion of the criminal responsibility of the Gestapo and Sicherheitsdienst ('SD') or secret service, the IMT noted the involvement of these organisations in "anti-Semitic persecution", which included "emigration and evacuation" of Jews from Germany, and in measures "bringing about a complete solution to the Jewish problem in German-dominated Europe", involving deportation of Jews to the East and "the wholesale massacre of Jews" behind the lines of the Eastern front.[136] Likewise, in finding the SS criminally responsible for, *inter alia*,

---

[134] Pursuant to the IMT Charter, the IMT had jurisdiction over both individuals and organisations. See IMT Charter in *Trial of the Major War Criminals Before the International Military Tribunal*, vol. I, 1947, p. 10, Articles 6 and 9–10 (https://www.legal-tools.org/doc/64ffdd/).

[135] As noted above, it is sometimes difficult to discern the precise basis for the IMT's reasoning in the Judgment due to the degree to which its discussion of war crimes and crimes against humanity overlap. However, the following notes those instances where the Judgment refers specifically to "persecution" in its reasoning, and attempts to parse out those acts discussed in connection with this observation or those concerning which the Judgment notes a particular discriminatory nature.

[136] IMT Judgment, pp. 265–66, see *supra* note 113.

crimes against humanity, the IMT pointed to that organisation's "particularly significant role in the persecution of Jews". This role, the IMT noted, included involvement in the "evacuation of Jews from occupied territories" and overseeing the "massacre of the Jews" generally, and in the Warsaw Ghetto in particular.[137] In addressing the guilt of the Nazi leadership for persecution, the IMT observed that the leadership corps was used to minimise resistance back home concerning deportation and extermination happening in the East. In doing so, the IMT noted in its Judgment, "the machinery of the Leadership Corps [was used] to keep German public opinion from rebelling at a program which was started to involve condemning the Jews of Europe to a lifetime of slavery".[138]

The same is evident in the IMT's discussion of the guilt of individual defendants. Baldur von Schirach – a Nazi official in occupied Vienna – was not found guilty of conspiracy to wage war, and was not charged with war crimes nor crimes against peace. However, the IMT concluded he was guilty of crimes against humanity including persecution on the basis of his involvement, *inter alia*, in the deportation of the Jewish population of Vienna to the East with awareness of the conditions there.[139] The IMT likewise noted Arthur Seyss-Inquart "advocated persecution of Jews" and was involved, *inter alia*, with overseeing the mass deportation to Auschwitz of the Jewish population of the Netherlands where he held a leadership position.[140] Finally in concluding that Martin Bormann, a central figure in the Nazi leadership, "was extremely active in the persecution of the Jews" the IMT pointed, among other things, to his involvement in planning for the deportation of Jews from Vienna and in promoting the use of "ruthless force" to secure "the permanent elimination of Jews in Greater German territory".[141]

In setting out the basis for the conviction of individual defendants, the IMT often relied upon conduct constituting crimes against humanity or war crimes in addition to other categories of conduct discussed below,

---

[137] *Ibid.*, p. 271.

[138] *Ibid.*, pp. 259, 261.

[139] *Ibid.*, p. 319. The IMT's reference to both murder-type and persecution-type crimes against humanity in establishing its jurisdictional basis for his conviction at the top of page 319 suggests that they viewed his guilt as including persecution.

[140] *Ibid.*, p. 329. Notably, the IMT's explicit reference to persecution in the discussion of Seyss-Inquart's conduct is in relation to his actions in Poland. The IMT does not invoke the term explicitly in relation to his acts in the Netherlands.

[141] *Ibid.*, pp. 339–20.

together amounting to a series of persecutory measures. In its discussion of Hans Frank's guilt for the persecution of Jews in Poland, for instance, the IMT emphasised his involvement in overseeing a programme under which "[t]hey were forced into ghettos, subjected to discriminatory laws, deprived of goods necessary to avoid starvation, and finally systematically and brutally exterminated".[142]

The jurisprudence of the US NMTs demonstrates a similar reliance on war crimes and crimes against humanity as the underlying acts behind persecution convictions. For instance, in its discussion of persecution in the *Ministries* case, the NMT noted a series of events which involved both: (1) acts which independently amounted to crimes against humanity or war crimes (as the NMT ended its description of the events by noting "[the Jewish population of Germany] [was] deported to the East, where they worked to exhaustion and death; they became slave labourers; and finally over six million were murdered"[143]); and (2) acts which did not. In the *RuSHA* case, the NMT based its findings of guilt under the count of "Persecution and Extermination" of the Jewish and Polish population on, *inter alia*, its earlier discussion of mass deportation.[144] Likewise in the *Pohl* case, the NMT found the defendant Baier guilty for persecution on the basis of his involvement in the exploitation of slave labour of Jewish prisoners.[145]

A review of the post-Second World War cases before national courts demonstrates a similar approach, relying on conduct constituting war crimes or crimes against humanity as the underlying acts of persecution convictions. In the case concerning, Artur Greiser, for instance, the Supreme National Tribunal of Poland entered a conviction on the basis of

---

[142] *Ibid.*, pp. 297–98.

[143] Ministries case, vol. XIV, p. 471, see *supra* note 123. It is worth noting however, that these acts were discussed in the general contextual section, and not with regard to the specific conviction of particular defendants.

[144] NMT, *United States of America v. Ulrich Greifelt et al.*, Judgment, in *Trials of War Criminals Before the Nuernberg Military Tribunals*, vol. V, 1950, p. 152 ('RuSHA case') (https://www.legal-tools.org/doc/2bc719/).

[145] NMT, *United States of America v. Oswald Pohl et al.*, Judgment, in *Trials of War Criminals Before the Nuernberg Military Tribunals*, vol. V, 1950, pp. 1046–47 ('Pohl Case') (https://www.legal-tools.org/doc/84ae05/). The NMT noted that Baier did not himself physically manhandle Jews, or other detainees of the Reich; however, it was through his exploitation of the existing regime of slave labour that Baier perpetuated persecution of the Jews.

all the charges set out in the indictment, which included, *inter alia*, persecution of Jewish and Polish populations through deportation to concentration camps.[146]

12.2.3.1.1.4. Non-Enumerated Conduct as Underlying Acts

While often relying on conduct amounting to crimes against humanity or war crimes as the underlying acts or omission underpinning a persecution conviction, the post-war tribunals did not *require* that the underlying conduct met this threshold. In various instances, the tribunals based convictions for persecution as a crime against humanity on: (1) underlying acts that – while not falling within the enumerated conduct constituting crimes against humanity or war crimes in the relevant post-war legal instrument – were nevertheless criminal in nature;[147] and (2) underlying acts that were not independently criminal in the absence of a discriminatory intent.

Turning again to the IMT's initial articulation of the policy of persecution set out in its Judgment (as excerpted earlier), it noted a number of non-criminal acts such as "a boycott of Jewish enterprises", the passage of discriminatory laws resulting in restrictions on Jewish involvement in German political and economic life and leading eventually to the deprivation of citizenship, as well as restrictions on movement, ghettoisation and the imposition of a requirement to wear identifying marks.[148] A similar

---

[146] Supreme National Tribunal of Poland, *Trial of Gauleiter Artur Greiser*, 21 June 1946–7 July 1946, in UNWCC, *Law Reports of Trials of War Criminals*, vol. XIII, London, 1949, pp. 70, 72, setting out the charges against the accused, and pp. 104–5, confirming the charges as set out, with the exception of personally murdering and committing grievous bodily harm, noting: "In respect of this group of charges which were related to crimes committed against the life, health and property of Poles and Jews, and against the freedom of worship, culture and language of the Polish population, said to have been directed by the accused, the Tribunal stated that the documents laid before it and the evidence of the witnesses have proved in their entirety the charges put forward in that part of the Indictment". Notably, the Tribunal's judgment must be taken in context to the extent that, as Mark Drumbl notes, "[t]he substantive law applied by the Tribunal took the form of a hodge-podge of special decrees, pre-existing municipal law, and the London Agreement". Mark A. Drumbl, "'Germans are the Lords and Poles are the Servants': The Trial of Arthur Greiser in Poland, 1946", in Kevin Jon Heller and Gerry Simpson (eds.), *The Hidden Histories of War Crimes Trials*, Oxford University Press, Oxford, 2013, p. 417.

[147] That is, acts which would criminalised under most if not all criminal codes of the world – such as murder, theft, assault, and similar acts.

[148] IMT Judgment, p. 180–81, see *supra* note 113. It is worth noting again, however, that – while characterising such acts as "persecution" – it concluded it did not have jurisdiction over the majority of such conduct as it took place prior to the onset of that war (leading to an absence of the requisite nexus discussed below).

spectrum of conduct can be seen in the excerpt above from the NMT's *Ministries* case setting out the overall scope of the persecution. The NMT pointed to, *inter alia*, the exclusion of Jews from professions and from education, restrictions on their rights to marry, confiscation of property and other economic deprivations, discriminatory arrests, as well as the passing of discriminatory laws and the discriminatory application of existing laws.[149]

This is likewise evident in the post-war tribunals' assessment of the guilt of individual defendants. The IMT at Nuremberg emphasised the involvement of several defendants in creating a regime of economic and legal discrimination against the Jewish population.[150] For instance, in discussing Hermann Wilhelm Göring's guilt for, *inter alia*, persecution of the Jewish population, the IMT pointed to his imposition of a collective "billion-mark fine" on all German Jews and imposition of a range of discriminatory laws.[151] In its Judgment, the IMT emphasised the economic nature of the measures Göring imposed on the Jewish population, noting such conduct was tied to the question of "how to get their property and how to force them out of the economic life of Europe".[152]

---

[149] Ministries case, vol. XIV, p. 471, see *supra* note 123. See also Justice case, vol. III, pp. 1063–64, *supra* note 7, setting out a similar series of acts the NMT viewed as persecutory.

[150] While not using the term persecution explicitly, in the IMT's analysis concerning Walter Funk's guilt for war crimes and crimes against humanity the Tribunal notes his involvement in the Nazi programme of economic discrimination against Jews, and the fact that he advocated the elimination of Jews from economic life in Germany. IMT Judgment, pp. 305-306, see *supra* note 113. Though we have sought to only rely on instances where the IMT explicitly invoked the term persecution in its analysis, it is worth noting that these acts would not be relevant in establishing guilt under war crimes and crimes against humanity but for its potential contribution to a finding of persecution. Likewise, in discussing Arthur Seyss-Inquart's guilt for war crimes and crimes against humanity, the Tribunal points to, *inter alia*, his imposition of "a series of laws imposing economic discrimination against the Jews" as Reich Commissioner for the Netherlands. IMT Judgment, p. 329, see *supra* note 113. While referring to persecution in relation to Seyss-Inquart's conduct in Poland, the Tribunal does not invoke the term in its discussion of his conduct in the Netherlands. Similarly, Wilhelm Frick was found guilty for war crimes and crimes against humanity on the basis, *inter alia*, of his role in "draft[ing], sign[ing], and administer[ing] many laws designed to eliminate Jews from German life and economy, including prohibiting the Jewish population from various professions, confiscating their property, and placing them outside the existing legal system", IMT Judgment, p. 300, see *supra* note 113.

[151] IMT Judgment, p. 282, see *supra* note 113, noting also that "he was [...] the creator oppressive program against the Jews and other races at home and abroad".

[152] *Ibid.*

Recognition of economic discrimination as a basis for persecution convictions is also evident in the jurisprudence of the US NMT. Notably, this jurisprudence is divided on whether expropriation of industrial property in particular amounted to an underlying act for the purpose of a persecution conviction. As noted in the excerpt from the *Flick* case quoted above, the Tribunal viewed expropriation of industrial property as insufficient to qualify as an underlying act of persecution on the basis, *inter alia*, of the principle of *ejusdem generis*.[153] This holding was subsequently adopted in the *Farben* case.[154] However, as Kevin Jon Heller has noted, other Tribunals at Nuremberg reached different conclusions on this point. In the *Ministries* case, for instance, Richard Darré, the Minister of Food and Agriculture, was convicted for, *inter alia*, his involvement in the extensive programme of expropriation of Jewish agricultural property.[155] The Tribunal described the intent of the programme as "not only to bar Jews from agriculture, but also to rob them of a large part of the value of their property".[156]

Despite the conflicting jurisprudence on the question of expropriation of industrial property, the NMTs widely accepted that theft or takings of personal property could constitute an underlying act for the crime of persecution.[157] The *Flick* case noted that "[a] distinction could be made

---

[153] Flick case, vol. VI, p. 1215, see *supra* note 127.

[154] Farben case, vol. VIII, pp. 1129–30, *supra* note 128.

[155] Ministries Case, vol. XIV, pp. 556–7, see *supra* note 123. See also Heller, 2011, p. 248, see *supra* note 130, discussing the Ministries case holding on this point. Admittedly, the classification of agricultural property in the first half of the twentieth century as industrial rather than personal property may not be such a clean distinction in light of the character of farming at the time.

[156] *Ibid.* While the Tribunal does not refer to this act as persecution specifically, a number of factors support its characterisation as such. First, the impugned conduct involved acts on German territory against German Jews (and thus beyond the Tribunal's characterisation of war crimes of pillaging, etc.). Second, the Tribunal stressed that "[u]nquestionably the proceeds of the Aryanization of farms and other Jewish property were in aid of and utilized in the program of rearmament and subsequent aggression". The effort to connect the conduct with German aggression more broadly suggests that the Tribunal viewed itself as convicting under crimes against humanity rather than war crimes, and thus needed to establish the presence of a nexus to another crime under the Tribunal's jurisdiction (as per the *Ministries* Tribunal's view of the nexus requirement discussed below). Finally, in its analysis the Tribunal emphasised the discrimination against Jews involved in the conduct, suggesting that it was endeavouring to set out the requirements of a persecution conviction.

[157] Heller, 2011, p. 248, see *supra* note 130, discussing the *Pohl*, *RuSHA* and *Ministries* cases on this point.

between industrial property and the dwellings, household furnishings, and food supplies of a persecuted people".[158]

The *Justice* case examined the nature of such "lesser forms of racial persecution" based on underlying acts or omissions falling short of extermination, deportation and other international crimes. The Tribunal noted that, along with the programme of "actual extermination of Jews and Poles", "lesser forms of racial persecution were universally practiced by governmental authority and constituted an integral part in the general policy of the Reich".[159] The Tribunal convicted members of the judiciary of persecution for their "discriminatory application of the law" against Jewish and Polish individuals.[160] Similarly in the *Ministries* case, the Tribunal recognised Lammer's culpability for "judicial persecution" through his role in the perversion of the judicial system to undermine the "ordinary and commonly recognized rights to fair trial" for "Jews and other enemies and opponents of national socialism".[161] The *Justice* Tribunal noted that discriminatory acts which were not criminal in themselves – such as "the denial to Jews of the right to proceed in civil litigation without advancement of costs" – may appear "to be a small matter compared to the extermination of Jews by the millions under other procedures".[162] Nevertheless, the Tribunal observed, such acts are "a part of the government-organized plan for the persecution of the Jews, not only by murder and imprisonment but by depriving them of the means of livelihood and of equal rights in the courts of law".[163]

The post-Second World War tribunals also grounded persecution convictions in acts of incitement, treating the actions of individuals who, through their words drove others to engage in persecution, as constituting persecution as a crime against humanity itself. For instance, the IMT, in its discussion of the guilt of Julius Streicher, the publisher of "an anti-Semitic weekly newspaper" and radio personality, for crimes against humanity, stressed his role in "incit[ing] the German people to active perse-

---

[158] Flick case, vol. VI, p. 1214, see *supra* note 127.

[159] Justice Case, vol. III, pp. 1063–64, see *supra* note 7.

[160] See Roberts, 2006, p. 266, *supra* note 23, discussing the case. See, for example, Justice case, vol. III, p. 1156, see *supra* note 7, concerning the conviction of the defendant Rothaug.

[161] Ministries Case, vol. XIV, pp. 602–5, see *supra* note 123.

[162] Justice Case, vol. III, p. 1114, see *supra* note 7.

[163] *Ibid.*

cution".[164] Notably, the IMT held that, despite Streicher's involvement with the Nazi party, "[t]here is no evidence to show that he was ever within Hitler's inner circle of advisers";[165] his guilt was not based on his contribution to the party in an official capacity, but rather through his consistent and public dissemination of anti-Semitic rhetoric and support for extermination as "Jew-Baiter Number One".[166] On this basis, in one of its most explicit statements of guilt for persecution,[167] the IMT concluded:

> Streicher's incitement to murder and extermination at the time when Jews in the East were being killed under the most horrible conditions clearly constitutes persecution on political and racial grounds in connection with War Crimes, as defined by the Charter, and constitutes Crimes against Humanity.[168]

A case alleging persecution through speech acts was also brought against Hans Fritzsche for his conduct as head of the German Home Press Division and later head of the Radio Division of the Propaganda Ministry during the war.[169] As discussed below, the IMT ultimately found Fritzsche not guilty; however, its conclusion seems to be based more on the absence of specific intent than the insufficiency of the *actus reus* underlying the charges.[170]

A similar basis for a persecution conviction can be seen in the *Ministries* case's reasoning concerning the guilt of Otto Dietrich. Dietrich, as Reich press chief, had substantial control over the content of the popular media throughout the war. The Tribunal noted that the directives he is-

---

[164] IMT Judgment, p. 302, see *supra* note 113. See also Gregory S. Gordon, "Hate Speech and Persecution: A Contextual Approach", in *Vanderbilt Journal of Transnational Law*, 2013, vol. 46, no. 2, p. 303, discussing the post-Second World War persecution speech cases.

[165] IMT Judgment, p. 302, see *supra* note 113.

[166] *Ibid.*, pp. 302–4.

[167] As noted earlier, in other instances it is hard to parse out the IMT's analysis concerning persecution specifically and other acts of crimes against humanity and war crimes generally.

[168] IMT Judgment, p. 304, see *supra* note 113.

[169] *Ibid.*, pp. 336–38.

[170] See *infra* section 12.2.3.2. The IMT implicitly relied upon speech acts, among other conduct, in the finding the Nazi leadership guilty of persecution. As noted above, the IMT emphasised the role of the leadership in minimising resistance at home – "to keep German public opinion from rebelling" – in response to deportation and extermination happening in the East. However, such conduct is arguably best viewed as finding guilt on the basis of party liability (whether through aiding and abetting or another means) for persecution through deportation and extermination itself. See *ibid.*, pp. 259, 261.

sued to the press and periodicals concerning the inclusion of anti-Semitic content and exclusion of Jewish writers "were not mere political polemics, they were not aimless expressions of anti-Semitism, and they were not designed only to unite the German people in the war effort". Rather, the Tribunal found, "[t]heir clear and expressed purpose was to enrage Germans against the Jews, to justify the measures taken and to be taken against them, and to subdue any doubts which might arise as to the justice of measures of racial persecution to which Jews were to be subjected". On this basis, the Tribunal convicted Dietrich of crimes against humanity.[171] The decisions of these tribunals on the relationship between persecution, speech and incitement would subsequently be influential in the development of a line of contemporary jurisprudence at the ICTR on these same themes.[172]

It is worth noting that despite the present effort to delineate the forms of conduct upon which the post-Second World War tribunals relied in reaching convictions for persecution, it is hard to discern which conduct was treated as *per se* sufficient to ground a conviction. As noted above, the jurisprudence tends to rely on a cumulative series of persecutory acts, thereby complicating any effort to identify a given act as independently sufficient. For example, in discussing Frank's involvement in the persecution of Jews through his role as Governor General of occupied Poland, the IMT pointed to the fact that the Jewish population was "forced into ghettos, subjected to discriminatory laws, [and] deprived of the food necessary to avoid starvation".[173] As noted above, the IMT went on to note how this progressive regime of persecutory acts eventually escalated to "extermination". In short, Frank's guilt for persecution was established on the basis of discriminatory but non-criminal acts, as well as acts which themselves rose to the level of war crimes and crimes against humanity.

---

[171] Ministries Case, vol. XIV, pp. 575–76, see *supra* note 123; as the Tribunal observed, "[b]y [providing such justifications] Dietrich consciously implemented, and by furnishing excuses and justifications, participated in, the crimes against humanity regarding Jews". See also Gregory S. Gordon, "The Forgotten Nuremberg Hate Speech Case: Otto Dietrich and the Future of Persecution Law", in *Ohio State Law Journal*, 2014, vol. 75, no. 3, pp. 585–88, discussing the basis for Dietrich's conviction.

[172] See *infra* section 12.3.2.1.1.

[173] IMT Judgment, pp. 297–98, see *supra* note 113.

Similar patterns can be seen in the conviction of Hans Albin Rauter before the Netherlands Special Court in The Hague. The Court found Rauter, the second in command of occupied Netherlands, guilty of persecution against the Jews on the basis of a wide range of discriminatory non-criminal acts. These included orders that Jews

> wear a Star of David in public, and were forbidden to take
> part in public gatherings, to make use of public places for
> amusement, recreation or information, to visit public parks,
> cafes and restaurants, to use dining and sleeping cars, to visit
> theatres, cabarets, variety shows, cinemas, sports clubs, in-
> cluding swimming baths, to remain in or make use of public
> libraries, reading rooms and museums. A special curfew was
> introduced for all Jews between the hours of 8 p.m. and 6
> a.m. Later orders banned them from railway yards and the
> use of any public or private means of transport.[174]

However, the court noted in particular that these measures "subject-ed [the Jewish population] to discriminatory treatment and gradually seg-regated [them] from the rest of the populatio"n, which facilitated their being detected and apprehended at a later date for slave labour and even-tual extermination".[175] It is ultimately unclear to what extent the discrimi-natory, but non-criminal underlying acts, were sufficient to substantiate a persecution conviction in the absence of their relation to the eventual de-portation, slave labour and extermination of members of the targeted group.

12.2.3.1.2. Persecution and a Nexus to Other Crimes within the Court's Jurisdiction

The question of whether a conviction for persecution requires that a nexus be established between an alleged act of persecution and another interna-tional crime remains one of the most controversial elements of the post-Second World War jurisprudence. As discussed above, the issue of a nex-us was broadly debated in the negotiations in London, with the four Allied powers ultimately determining that the IMT's jurisdiction would be lim-ited to crimes against humanity that took place "in execution of or in con-

---

[174] Netherlands Special Court in The Hague, *Trial of Hans Albin Rauter*, 4 May 1948, in UNWCC, *Law Reports of Trials of War Criminals*, vol. XIV, London, 1949, pp. 89, 93. As the UNWCC notes, the trial was undertaken pursuant to a mix of substantive law that in-cluded Dutch law and international law as defined in the Nuremberg Charter. *Id.*, p. 111.
[175] *Ibid.*, pp. 89, 93.

nection with any crime within the jurisdiction of the Tribunal". The semi-colon that appeared in the final draft of the crimes against humanity pro-vision suggested that this requirement only extended to the offence of per-secution; however, as noted earlier, the Berlin Protocol passed months later removed the semi-colon, arguably extending the nexus requirement to the crimes against humanity provision as a whole.[176]

In contrast, an explicit nexus requirement was not included in the terms of CCL No. 10. While the drafting history is not as well document-ed as the London Conference, there are some indications that the exclu-sion was intentional, with evidence of internal discussion among Ameri-can officials supporting the position that the jurisdiction of the zonal tri-bunals should not be limited to crimes against humanity with a nexus to war crimes or crimes against peace.[177] In light of the deletion of the semi-colon in the Nuremberg Charter and the absence of a relevant differentia-tion between "murder-type" and "persecution-type" crimes against hu-manity in CCL No. 10, the discussion of the nexus requirement for perse-cution is effectively a discussion of a nexus requirement for crimes against humanity as whole. Thus, despite this Chapter's focus on persecu-tion, this section will review the jurisprudence addressing the nexus re-quirement more generally.

The jurisprudence suggests – consistent with the drafting history – that the nexus requirement was substantially driven by three related con-siderations. First, as we have emphasised throughout this Chapter, the de-bate concerning the nexus requirement represents the process by which state officials, legal actors and scholars assessed and recognised the nature of the contemporary relationship between international law and sover-eignty. The jurisprudence often demonstrates tension concerning the ques-tion of whether there remained a need to protect the state's jurisdiction over internal matters from international law, such that intervention could only be justified by the need to regulate truly inter-state matters (that is international armed conflict). Second, and closely related to the first point, the various tribunals invoked the nexus requirement as a means to ensure respect for the legality principle: as the argument went, while internation-

---

[176] See *supra* notes 99–101 and accompanying text.

[177] See Heller, 2011, p. 240, *supra* note 130 (discussing exchanges among American officials during the drafting process, including a favourable response to a draft provision which provided jurisdiction over crimes against humanity dating back to 1933 "whether or not connected with the crimes set out in (a) or (b) [on crimes against peace and war crimes]").

al law had previously set standards that governed conduct in war despite domestic standards to the contrary, it had not done so with regard to peacetime conduct. Hence, whatever the merits of establishing international criminal standards for such future conduct, post-war prosecutions should be limited to conduct related in some manner to the war itself. Finally, the nexus requirement also provided some parameters to limit the otherwise potentially broad reach of the concept of crimes against humanity and the criminalisation of persecution. The significance of this final role for the nexus requirement is emphasised by the attempt of those tribunals that rejected it to find a substitute limitation. As further considered in the subsequent section, these considerations (in particular the first and the third) would arise again in the context of the contemporary international criminal courts and tribunals. Then, as now, persecution was at the crux of these debates – in many ways on the threshold between the domestic and international – through which state delegates, judges, lawyers and scholars wrestled with the question of what makes an international crime 'international'.

Despite the explicit nexus requirement in the IMT Charter,[178] the Nuremberg Judgment acknowledged a degree of flexibility as to what was meant by the requirement of "in execution of or in connection with" any crime within the jurisdiction of the Tribunal. This evident, for instance, in IMT's examination of the nexus requirement in its preliminary discussion of the "The Law Relating to War Crimes and Crimes against Humanity". While noting that that a "policy of persecution, repression, and murder of civilians in Germany *before the war of 1939*" and the "persecution of Jews" by Germany during this period was "established beyond all doubt", the IMT refused to make findings of guilt based upon this conduct. As it observed:

> To constitute Crimes against Humanity, the acts relied on before the outbreak of war must have been in execution of, or in connection with, any crime within the jurisdiction of the Tribunal. The Tribunal is of the opinion that revolting and horrible as many of these crimes were, it has not been satisfactorily proved that they were done in execution of, or in connection with, any such crime. The Tribunal therefore

---

[178] Interestingly, in its Judgment, the IMT quoted the text of the pre-Berlin Protocol version of the crimes against humanity provision in which the semi-colon remained. See IMT Judgment, p. 253, see *supra* note 113. However, in the Tribunal's reasoning it extended the nexus requirement to the provision as a whole. *Id.*, p. 254.

cannot make a general declaration that the acts before 1939 were Crimes against Humanity within the meaning of the Charter.[179]

It is important to note that the IMT's reasoning suggests that its comments should perhaps be understood as interpreting a jurisdictional limitation set out by the IMT Charter rather than directed at the substantive requirements necessary to prove a crime against humanity generally.[180]

Whether it was a substantive or jurisdictional standard, the IMT provided some indication of what the nexus requirement demanded in its reasoning concerning the guilt of specific defendants. Its conclusions effectively restricted crimes against humanity to a by-product of war – consistent with Jackson's expressed view during the drafting process as to what made the offence one of international concern.[181] In short, such conduct was only a matter of international concern because of its association with an armed conflict. However, in finding both the defendants Streicher and von Schirach guilty of persecution despite their acquittal on charges of conspiracy to wage war, and the absence of war crimes or crimes against peace charges brought against them, the IMT indicated that the nexus did not require that the defendants have committed the related crimes personally.

Notably, Streicher's impugned conduct took place on German territory and the IMT found that he was not directly involved in the war effort. However, the IMT concluded that Streicher's incitement to discriminate against and exterminate Jews was sufficiently related to a war crime because it took place while "Jews in the East were being killed under the most horrible conditions".[182] Interestingly, the relevant acts in the East effectively played a dual role as a war crime (killing of civilians in occu-

---

[179] *Ibid.*, p. 254 (emphasis added).

[180] The IMT noted shortly before that it "is of course bound by the Charter". *Ibid.*, p. 253. In noting that it could not declare the pre-war acts to be crimes against humanity "within the meaning of the Charter", the Judgment on this point implies that it was arguably noting what acts it could assert jurisdiction over pursuant to its constituting statute, not a comment concerning crimes against humanity more broadly. See also Clark, 1990, pp. 195–96, *supra* note 16, discussing this point.

[181] See *supra* note 88 and accompanying text.

[182] IMT Judgment, p. 304, see *supra* note 113. Notably, the IMT's specific reference to "Jews in the East" (that is, in occupied territory) established the connection to the war crime of killing civilians in the course of an occupation or armed conflict.

pied territory) fulfilling the nexus requirement, as well as persecutory crimes against humanity as incited by Streicher's statements.

In a more straightforward connection, the IMT found von Schirach's persecutory conduct in Austria (including overseeing deportation of Jews) to be sufficiently related to another crime within the Charter, as "Austria was occupied pursuant to a common plan of aggression". As the IMT observed, "[i]ts occupation is, therefore, a 'crime within the jurisdiction of the Tribunal', as that term is used in Article 6(c) of the Charter [setting out the nexus requirement]".[183] Thus, Schirach's conduct, having taken place in his role as a member of the occupying government in Austria, was by necessity related to another crime in the IMT Charter.

While the absence of a nexus requirement in CCL No. 10 has been noted in contemporary jurisprudence,[184] the treatment of the matter by the NMTs was not as simple as it is often portrayed. As Heller notes, despite the absence of a requirement in the text, American officials were reticent to pursue cases concerning pre-war crimes against humanity, in part out of concern for what such a precedent would mean in light of ongoing discrimination against various groups in the United States. As Telford Taylor, the US Chief Counsel throughout the CCL No. 10 cases at Nuremberg, wrote in internal correspondence (echoing the above quoted concerns of Jackson[185]), "departures from democratic systems as may exist in some countries and discrimination, even quite aggravated systems as may exist against negroes in certain countries, should not[,] even[] in these enlightened times, constitute crimes at international law".[186] Nevertheless, the American prosecutors before the US NMT did put forward charges of pre-war crimes against humanity in two cases,[187] and the issue was ultimately addressed by the Tribunals in five cases.[188]

Despite its absence in CCL No. 10, three tribunals found a nexus to the war was required to ground their jurisdiction over crimes against hu-

---

[183] *Ibid.*, pp. 318–19.

[184] See, for example, Kupreškić case, Trial Judgment, para. 577, *supra* note 2.

[185] See *supra* note 89 and accompanying text.

[186] See Heller, 2011, p. 235, *supra* note 130. As Heller notes, the State Department subsequently articulated a similar view, instructing Taylor that (while accepting the legality) "as a matter of policy" the US should not prosecute crimes against humanity that did not meet the nexus standard.

[187] Flick case, vol. VI, pp. 21–23, see *supra* note 127; Ministries case, vol. XII, pp. 38–43, see *supra* note 123. See also Heller, 2011, p. 235, *supra* note 130.

[188] Heller, 2011, p. 236, see *supra* note 130.

manity, including the tribunals which heard the only two cases where pre-war acts were charged. The NMT in *Flick*, in which the prosecution had charged pre-war crimes against humanity, was not convinced that CCL No. 10's silence on the matter was dispositive. In the Tribunal's view, the absence of the IMT's nexus language was insufficient in itself to grant jurisdiction over a peacetime offence. Moreover, the Tribunal pointed to the reference in Article 1 of CCL No. 10 which stated that the IMT Charter was to be made an "integral part" of the law set out in CCL No. 10. On this basis, the *Flick* Tribunal concluded that where CCL No. 10 was silent, the Charter's approach (nexus and all) should be presumed.[189]

In the *Ministries* case, in which peacetime crimes against humanity were also charged, the Tribunal granted a defence motion to dismiss the charges concerning pre-war acts. In finding that it did not have jurisdiction over such acts, the Tribunal focused, *inter alia*, on the presumption that, in drafting CCL No. 10, the occupying powers did not intend to offend the principle of legality by establishing any new criminal offences; rather, their intent, the Tribunal concluded, must be presumed to codify offences already established under international law.[190] The Tribunal went on to state that "there can be no question but that the relationship between human rights and a just and lasting peace is very close and interlocking [and that] [...] if a nation's domestic policy is characterized by aggression at home, its foreign policy will probably also be characterized by aggression". However, it concluded, "the foregoing arguments and observations do not, however, establish that crimes against humanity perpetrated by a government against its own nationals, are of themselves crimes against international law".[191] While calling for the drafting of treaties that established such a standard, the Tribunal concluded that establishing this standard was not its role and dismissed charges relating to pre-1939 crimes against humanity as failing to have a sufficient connection to crimes against peace or war crimes.[192] However, as Heller observes, "the

---

[189] Flick case, vol. VI, pp. 1212–13, see *supra* note 127.

[190] The Ministries NMT quoted the statement of the IMT to this effect: "The Charter is not an arbitrary exercise of power on the part of the victorious nations, but in the view of the Tribunal as will be shown, it is the expression of international law existing at the time of its creation". It observed that this statement "clearly appl[ied] with equal persuasiveness to the question of this Tribunal's jurisdiction under Control Council Law No. 10". Ministries case, vol. XIII, p. 116, see *supra* note 123.

[191] *Ibid.*, p. 117.

[192] *Ibid.*

Ministries tribunal was willing to criminalize peacetime atrocities and persecutions that *did* satisfy the nexus requirement".[193] It refrained from dismissing charges related to, and ultimately convicted the defendant Darré for, theft of Jewish property that took place months before the onset of war. It reasoned that "the proceeds of the Aryanization of farms and other Jewish property were in aid of and utilized in the program of rearmament and subsequent aggression".[194]

While no pre-Second World War charges were brought before the US NMT in the *Pohl* case, in *obiter dicta* it nonetheless raised some of the same concerns previously raised by Jackson and Taylor relating to the extension of international accountability to the peacetime domain. It concluded, ultimately, that a nexus was required so as not to infringe upon German sovereignty. In the view of the Tribunal, there existed no basis for international law to intervene into the peacetime domestic affairs of a state, no matter how severe its treatment of its own citizens. However, this changed with the initiation of international conflict, justifying the nexus requirement: "when attempt is made to make the provisions [of an abusive] decree extra-territorial in their effect and to apply their totalitarian and autocratic police measures to non-Germans and in non-German territory, they thereby invaded the domain of international law".[195]

In contrast, the Tribunals hearing the *Justice* and *Einsatzgruppen* cases explicitly rejected the nexus requirement in *obiter dicta*, despite the fact that there were no relevant charges before them.[196] The Tribunal in the *Justice* case relied upon a textual approach, emphasising that

> it must be noted that Control Council Law No. 10 differs materially from the Charter. The latter defines crimes against humanity as inhumane acts, etc. committed, "in execution of, or in connection with, any crime within the jurisdiction of the tribunal", whereas in C.C. Law 10 the words last quoted are deliberately omitted from the definition.[197]

The analysis by the Tribunal in the *Einsatzgruppen* case went beyond the terms of CCL No. 10 itself. It emphasised that, "humanity [...]

---

[193] Heller, 2011, p. 242, see *supra* note 130.

[194] Ministries case, vol. XIV, p. 557, see *supra* note 123. Heller, 2011, p. 242, see *supra* note 130.

[195] *Pohl* case, vol. V, pp. 991–92, see *supra* note 145.

[196] See Heller, 2011, p. 236, *supra* note 130, discussing these cases.

[197] Justice case, vol. III, p. 974, see *supra* note 7.

has no political boundaries and no geographical limitations", and pursuant to the "laws of humanity", the Tribunal "has jurisdiction to try all crimes against humanity as long known and understood under the general principles of criminal law".[198]

Significantly, having dismissed the nexus requirement, the Tribunals in the *Justice* and *Einsatzgruppen* cases proposed an alternative cabining principle to constrain the potentially broad category of crimes against humanity, and to therefore distinguish conduct of domestic concern from that rising to the level of an international crime. They set out contextual elements requiring that – to be considered a crime against humanity – the relevant conduct must be widespread and systematic and take place pursuant to a policy established by the government.[199] In dismissing the nexus requirement, the Tribunal in the *Einsatzgruppen* case set out what, in its view, set crimes against humanity apart. It was not their connection to war, but rather the fact that

> [c]rimes against humanity are acts committed in the course of wholesale and systematic violations of life and liberty. It is to be observed that insofar as international jurisdiction is concerned, the concept of crimes against humanity does not apply to offenses for which the criminal code of any well-ordered state makes adequate provision. They can only come within the purview of this basic code of humanity because the state involved, owing to indifference, impotency or complicity, has been unable or has refused to halt the crimes and punish the criminals.[200]

Similarly, before observing that crimes against humanity under CCL No. 10 were not restricted to those connected to war, the Tribunal in the *Justice* case emphasised that there were, nonetheless, limitations on what constitutes such an offence. As the Tribunal observed:

---

[198] NMT, *United States of America v. Otto Ohlendorf et al.*, Judgment, in *Trials of War Criminals Before the Nuernberg Military Tribunals*, vol. IV, 1951, pp. 497–99 ('Einsatzgruppen case') (https://www.legal-tools.org/doc/ca2575/).

[199] While not making this connection concerning an alternative cabining principle, Heller provides a helpful analysis of the discussion of the contextual elements in these cases. Heller, 2011, pp. 242–45, see *supra* note 130. Heller also noted that while contextual elements were not dealt with explicitly in the IMT Judgment, it does suggest that crimes against humanity are distinguished from war crimes on the basis that the former are "committed on a vast scale". See IMT Judgment, p. 254, see *supra* note 113; Heller, 2011, p. 242, see *supra* note 130.

[200] Einsatzgruppen case, vol. IV, p. 498, see *supra* note 198.

> Our jurisdiction to try persons charged with crimes against humanity is limited in scope, both by definition and illustration, as appears from C. C. Law 10. It is not the isolated crime by a private German individual which is condemned, nor is it the isolated crime perpetrated by the German Reich through its officers against a private individual. It is significant that the enactment employs the words "against any civilian population" instead of "against any civilian individual." The provision is directed against offenses and inhumane acts and persecutions on political, racial, or religious grounds systematically organized and conducted by or with the approval of the government.[201]

In short, having rejected the nexus to war crimes and crimes against peace as a cabining principle, the two tribunals set out alternative constraints delineating the parameters of this category of crimes.[202] These alternative constraints would ultimately be adopted in the ICC Statute and in contemporary jurisprudence, with the ICTY and ICTR requiring as an element of crimes against humanity under customary international law that the relevant acts be part of a widespread or systematic attack against a civilian population.[203]

As the views of the post-Second World War tribunals on the nexus requirement were closely connected to their respective views on the question of legality, a brief word is appropriate regarding the varying approaches to the issue of legality of charges of persecution as a crime against humanity. While the IMT addressed the issue of *nullum crimen* in the context of the charges of crimes against the peace,[204] it was silent on the issue of whether crimes against humanity generally and persecution specifically challenged the principle of legality.[205] However, the matter was considered by several of the US NMTs.

---

[201] Justice case, vol. III, p. 973, see *supra* note 7.

[202] Similar ideas concerning the need for such contextual requirements are evident, though not as robustly developed, in other cases before the NMTs, including: Ministries case, vol. XIV, p. 522, see *supra* note 123; NMT, *United States of America v. Karl Brandt et al.*, Judgment, in *Trials of War Criminals Before the Nuernberg Military Tribunals*, 1949, vol. II, p. 181 ('Medical case') (https://www.legal-tools.org/doc/c18557/). See also Heller, 2011, pp. 243–44, *supra* note 130, discussing the relevant principles in these and other cases.

[203] See, for example, *infra* section 12.3.2.1.2. and section 12.3.3.1.1.

[204] IMT Judgment, p. 219, see *supra* note 113.

[205] But see *supra* notes 9–10 and accompanying text, discussing Shawcross's submissions on this point before the IMT.

As noted above, the Tribunal in the *Ministries* case found that it did not have jurisdiction over charges of peacetime crimes against humanity on the basis of a presumption that the drafters of CCL No. 10 did not intend to offend the principle of legality.[206] While international regulation of wartime offences had been long recognised, the intervention of international law into the domain of peacetime crimes, the Tribunal concluded, was without sufficient precedent. In contrast, the Tribunal in the *Justice* case rejected the application of the *nullum crimen* principle to international criminal fora, adopting the reasoning of the IMT at Nuremberg in its approach to crimes against peace. It asserted, however, that even if some obligation of fair notice of the intent to punish existed, this had been met by the international community through, *inter alia*, the various wartime declarations made by the Allies.[207]

Perhaps most interestingly, however, the *Einsatzgruppen* Tribunal's legality analysis focused on the crime of persecution specifically, endeavouring to establish the issue as a long-standing matter of international concern. On this point the Tribunal observed:

> Can it be said that international conventions and the law of nations gave no warning to these accused that their attacks against ethnic, national, religious, and political groups infringed the rights of mankind? We do not refer to localised outbursts of hatred nor petty discrimination which unfortunately occur in the most civilised of states. When persecution reach the scale of nationwide campaigns designed to make life intolerable for, or to exterminate large groups of people, law dare not remain silent […]. The Control Council simply reasserts existing law when naming persecutions as an international offense.[208]

The Tribunal considered that fair notice had been given to the defendants by way of progressive international measures endeavouring to respond to persecution. Admittedly, the appropriateness of relying on these prior actions as a basis for fair notice of criminal charges is debatable. Nevertheless, it is interesting to note that the Tribunal saw itself as engaged in a long-standing international effort to respond to the phenome-

---

[206] Ministries case, vol. XIII, p. 116, see *supra* note 123.

[207] Justice case, vol. III, pp. 977–978, see *supra* note 7.

[208] Einsatzgruppen case, vol. IV, p. 49, see *supra* note 198.

non of persecution. For the Tribunal, the origins of international criminal law extended beyond precedents of prior criminalisation and prosecutions.

12.2.3.1.3. Enumerated Grounds and "Discrimination in Fact"

The IMT Charter and CCL No. 10 both provided jurisdiction over acts of persecution committed on political, racial or religious grounds. In contrast, while no charges of persecution were ultimately brought before the IMTFE, its Charter limited jurisdiction to acts of persecution committed on political or racial grounds, excluding persecution on religious grounds, which was less prevalent in the Pacific arena.

The Nuremberg Judgment involves little direct consideration of the grounds on which persecution can occur. The IMT focused its discussion of persecution on that directed toward the Jewish population – in particular the treatment of Jews in occupied territory. While the Judgment's analysis of the grounds upon which this persecution took place is sparse, some guidance can be gleaned from the discussion of the defendant Streicher's guilt. In explaining how Streicher's actions constituted persecution as a crime against humanity,[209] the Tribunal noted that in light of the connection between Streicher's actions and the extermination of Jews taking place in the East, his conduct "clearly constitutes persecution on *political and racial* grounds".[210] While there is no further analysis of this point, it can be presumed that the IMT considered other acts of persecution of the Jewish population to have taken place on the same two grounds.

Persecution of a variety of other groups (spanning religious, racial and political grounds) was also noted in the Indictment of the major war criminals before the IMT. Included in the Indictment were references to persecution by the Nazis of church officials[211] and pacifists[212] (in the de-

---

[209] That is, despite the fact that he was not convicted of war crimes or crimes against peace.

[210] IMT Judgment, p. 304, see *supra* note 113 (emphasis added).

[211] IMT, *Trial of the Major War Criminals*, Indictment, 7 June 1946, in *Trial of the Major War Criminals Before the International Military Tribunal*, 1947, vol. I, p. 33, setting out allegations in the description of the common plan involving "persecution of priests, clergy, and members of monastic orders whom they deemed opposed to their purposes" ('IMT Indictment').

[212] *Ibid.*, setting out allegations in the description of the common plan concerning persecution against "pacifist groups, including religious movements dedicated to pacifism", which the Indictment referred to as "particularly relentless and cruel".

scription of the common plan), and other political opponents[213] (in setting out the charges of crimes against humanity). However, none of these other groups was addressed by the Tribunal in its analysis of the guilt of individual defendants for persecution as a crime against humanity.[214] There are two principal exceptions to this lacuna in the Judgment. The first is a general reference in the contextual section of the Judgment to "[t]he policy of persecution, repression, and murder of civilians in Germany before the war of 1939, who were likely to be hostile to the Government"[215] – presumably a reference to persecution on political grounds. The second is a reference in the discussion of Martin Bormann's guilt for crimes against the peace to the fact that "[h]e devoted much of his time to the persecution of the churches and of the Jews within Germany".[216] However, in the subsequent discussion of Bormann's guilt for persecution as a crime against humanity, the IMT referred exclusively to persecution directed toward the Jewish population.

While the primary focus of the instances of persecution addressed by the US NMTs was again the treatment of the Jewish population, the tribunals' judgments also contain a broader recognition of groups towards whom the persecution was directed. The Tribunal in the *Justice* case, for instance, convicted defendants for their contribution to "racial persecutions" directed toward both Jews and Poles.[217] The *Ministries* case convicted defendants for persecution against various groups, including against members of the church on the basis of religion and politics.[218] Significantly, in the *Ministries* case, while only formally recognising acts of persecution on the grounds enumerated in CCL No. 10, the Tribunal acknowledged that persecution was not restricted to these bases. In its discussion of the evolution of the persecution of the Jews in Germany, the Tribunal noted in *obiter dicta*:

---

[213] *Ibid.*, p. 66, noting in the counts under crimes against humanity, "these persecutions were [...] also directed against persons whose political belief or spiritual aspirations were deemed to be in conflict with the aims of the Nazis".

[214] It is worth noting again, however, that some instances of discriminatory conduct were discussed in these sections without the Tribunal invoking the term 'persecution'.

[215] IMT Judgment, p. 254, see *supra* note 113. Notably, as discussed above, the IMT found it did not have jurisdiction over these acts as they took place prior to the onset of war. There is no further discussion of such political persecution after 1939.

[216] *Ibid.*, p. 339.

[217] Justice case, vol. III, p. 1063, see *supra* note 7.

[218] Ministries case, vol. XIV, pp. 520–27, see *supra* note 123.

> It makes little difference whether the subject of mass hate be a *political party, race, religion, class, or another nation*. The technique is the same, the results are identical, and the hate thus engendered inevitably brings on resistance and in the end ruin upon those who start and participate in it.[219]

In recognising the breadth of the potential targets of "mass hate", the Tribunal foreshadowed the eventual expansion of the grounds of persecution set out in the ICC Statute.[220]

While requiring that discrimination take place on an enumerated ground, from our review of the post-war jurisprudence, the issue of whether or not "discrimination in fact" must be established – as per the later ongoing debate on this issue in ICTY case law[221] – does not seem to have arisen. The fact that the individual affected was part of the group toward which the discriminatory treatment was directed seems to have been presumed throughout the cases at issue.

12.2.3.2. The *Mens Rea* of Persecution

The post-Second World War tribunals did not explicitly address what *mens rea* was necessary to support a conviction of persecution as a crime against humanity. Nevertheless, the tribunals often emphasised the presence of a discriminatory intent towards the targeted group, and as the reasoning in relation to acquitted defendants suggests, the absence of such a discriminatory intent was a key factor in decisions to acquit.

As the IMT at Nuremberg suggested in its general discussion of the practice of persecution against the Jewish population, from 1938 onwards, "Nazi policy towards the Jews had reached the stage where it was directed towards the complete exclusion of Jews from German life".[222] As the IMT further noted, each measure of the official policy of persecution was specifically targeted: they were aimed at the Jewish population as a group, with the intention of that group's economic and social exclusion, and eventual extermination. Similarly, in the IMT's analysis of Hans Frank's guilt for persecution of the Jews, for instance, it alluded to the significance of the discriminatory intent behind his conduct. The IMT began by discussing his involvement in forcing the Jewish population into ghettos,

---

[219] *Ibid.*, p. 470.

[220] See *infra* section 12.3.3.1.2.

[221] See *infra* section 12.3.2.1.3.

[222] IMT Judgment, p. 248, see *supra* note 113.

subjecting them to discriminatory laws and depriving them of food, and his role in overseeing a systematic regime of extermination. The Judgment went on to quote one of Frank's statements affirming his discriminatory intent; as the IMT noted, the defendant told the cabinet of the occupation government of Poland of which he was in charge: "We must annihilate the Jews, wherever we find them and wherever it is possible, in order to maintain there the structure of the Reich as a whole".[223]

The IMT's analysis on the *mens rea* of the various defendants is not sufficiently thorough or explicit to make definitive conclusions concerning what it relied upon to support a conviction in each instance. However, guidance can be gleaned from those instances where it entered an acquittal. In its Judgment, the IMT concluded that Hans Fritzsche, a high-ranking official within the Reich Propaganda Ministry, should be found not guilty of persecution as a crime against humanity. In doing so, the IMT emphasised, *inter alia*, the absence of a discriminatory intent behind his actions. The IMT found that Fritzsche did make several anti-Semitic comments in his speeches, including broadcasting the statements "that the war had been caused by Jews" and said their fate had turned out "as unpleasant as the Führer predicted". Nevertheless, the IMT noted when acquitting the defendant that it was "not prepared to hold that [Fritzsche's comments] were intended to incite the German people to commit atrocities on conquered peoples [...]. His aim was rather to arouse popular sentiment in support of Hitler and the German war effort".[224] Significantly, the IMT did not simply find that Fritzsche had an alternative motive (that is, to arouse popular sentiment), but that he lacked discriminatory intent (that is, did not intend to incite atrocities against a conquered peoples).

Similarly, as the US NMT found in the *Justice* case, a conviction for persecution could not be grounded in a defendant's involvement in passing facially non-discriminatory wartime criminal laws[225] that severely increased the penalties imposed simply because such laws "could be and

---

[223] *Ibid.*, p. 298.

[224] *Ibid.*, p. 338.

[225] In particular laws concerning "habitual criminals", "cases of looting in the devastated areas of Germany", "crimes against the war economy" and "crimes [...] undermining [...] the defensive strength of the nation" (that is, limitations on free speech); Justice case, vol. III, p. 1025, see *supra* note 7.

were applied in a discriminatory manner".[226] Rather, a discriminatory intent was necessary behind the impugned actions themselves. To this end, the defendant Franz Schlegelberger was convicted of persecution for his role in implementing procedures that transformed the Ministry of Justice and the judicial system into a channel of discriminatory application of the laws.[227] Notably, the Court found that Schlegelberger was not using his position in the Ministry of Justice to impose these discriminatory measures because of a particular animus held by the defendant himself; rather he acted in this manner in order to "maintain the Ministry of Justice in the good graces of Hitler and prevent its utter defeat by Himmler's police". This, however, did not undermine his guilt. It was not necessary to establish that Schlegelberger agreed with the policy to impose discriminatory legislation, as long as he intended the legislation to discriminate.[228]

12.2.3.3. Genocide and Persecution

The relationship between the international crimes of genocide and persecution as a crime against humanity is an interesting and complicated one – with some scholars suggesting that any distinction has effectively disappeared.[229] In some ways, however, they offer two different but related visions of the same harm: in short, a crime against the individual as a member of a group (persecution) or a crime against the group itself (genocide). The latter category was not explicitly included in the IMT Charter. How-

---

[226] *Ibid.*, p. 1027: "All of the laws to which we have referred could be and were applied in a discriminatory manner and in the case of many, the Ministry of Justice and the courts enforced them by arbitrary and brutal means, shocking to the conscience of mankind and punishable here. We merely hold that under the particular facts of this case we cannot convict any defendant merely because of the fact, without more, that laws of the first four types were passed or enforced."

[227] *Ibid.*, p. 1086, noting that he used "Ministry of Justice as a means for exterminating the Jewish and Polish populations, terrorizing the inhabitants of occupied countries, and wiping out political opposition at home". See also *id.*, p. 1066, noting his involvement in proposing legislation creating discriminatory penal standards for Jewish and Polish populations.

[228] *Ibid.*, p. 1087, finding him guilty despite observing that, "We believe that he loathed the evil that he did, but he sold that intellect and that scholarship to Hitler for a mess of political pottage and for the vain hope of personal security".

[229] Caroline Fournet and Clotilde Pegorier, "'Only One Step Away from Genocide': The Crime of Persecution in International Criminal Law", in *International Criminal Law Review*, 2010, vol. 10, no. 5, p. 713.

ever, Raphael Lemkin, who had coined the term 'genocide'[230] – renaming his earlier concept of 'barbarity' – secured a position as an adviser to the US War Department through which he successfully lobbied for the concept's inclusion in the Nuremberg Indictment as a subset of crimes against humanity.[231]

While the term was not invoked in the Nuremberg Judgment, it was ultimately recognised as an international crime (specifically a crime against humanity) by the US NMT in the *Justice* case.[232] The Tribunal described genocide as "illustrative" of crimes against humanity that had been "described as racial persecutions" in the indictment.[233] Moreover, the Tribunal pointed to the offence as an example of conduct, which due to its character constitutes an international crime even lacking a connection to other international crimes, and notwithstanding the content of domestic law of the state where the act was committed.[234]

Subsequently, as noted below, genocide would – unlike the category of crimes against humanity as a whole – receive conventional codification in the 1948 Genocide Convention. Consistent with the suggestion of the *Justice* case, on the basis of the "magnitude and its international repercussions" the drafters of the Convention would recognise genocide as a crime "under international law" even in the absence of a connection to war (or to war crimes and crimes against peace).[235]

---

[230] Raphael Lemkin, *Axis Rule in Occupied Europe: Laws of Occupation, Analysis of Government, Proposals for Redress*, Carnegie Endowment for International Peace, Washington, DC, 1944, ch. 9. See also Power, 2013, pp. 40–45, see *supra* note 18.

[231] Ana Filipa Vrdoljak, "Human Rights and Genocide: The Work of Lauterpacht and Lemkin in Modern International Law", in *European Journal of International Law*, 2010, vol. 20, no. 4, p. 1191; IMT Indictment, p. 47, see *supra* note 211.

[232] Justice Case, vol. III, pp. 963, 983, 1128, 1156, see *supra* note 7. See Heller, 2011, pp. 249–50, *supra* note 130, discussing the varying treatments of genocide in the indictments and judgments of the US Nuremberg Military Tribunals cases.

[233] Justice Case, vol. III, p. 963, see *supra* note 7.

[234] *Ibid.*, p. 983. See Heller, 2011, p. 250, *supra* note 130, as the Tribunal stated: "As the prime illustration of a crime against humanity under C. C. Law 10, which by reason of its magnitude and its international repercussions has been recognized as a violation of common international law, we cite 'genocide'".

[235] See Convention on the Prevention and Punishment of the Crime of Genocide, 12 January 1951 ('Genocide Convention') (https://www.legal-tools.org/doc/498c38/).

12.2.4. Subsequent Developments:
Persecution in International and National Law

In the immediate wake of the Second World War there were several other noteworthy developments relevant to the proscription of persecution as an international crime. Most significant was the codification of the crime of genocide in resolutions of the General Assembly and the Genocide Convention. The latter, notably, recognised an additional basis of prohibited discriminatory treatment beyond the other post-war legal instruments: measures against an "ethnical" group.[236] Moreover, as discussed above, the Genocide Convention – consistent with the holding in the *Justice* case – recognised genocide as an international crime even in the absence of a connection to other international crimes.

The General Assembly affirmed the Principles of the Nuremberg Charter,[237] and the International Law Commission ('ILC') adopted the Principles of the IMT Charter and Nuremberg Judgment, affirming the offence of persecution as set out in the Charter.[238] And finally, the ILC's Draft Code of Offences against the Peace and Security of Mankind ('Draft Code') codified persecution as an international crime, removing the nexus requirement, and incorporating in part the contextual elements adopted by the US NMT in the *Justice* and *Einsatzgruppen* cases (specifically requiring state involvement or acquiescence). The Draft Code also recognised two further grounds (social and cultural) of possible discriminatory treatment.[239] Nevertheless, as has been noted often, the development of international criminal law generally, and with it persecution as an international crime, slowed down as the Cold War tempered the international appetite for such an undertaking.

However, several significant developments continued to take place over the intervening decades, particularly before national courts and

---

[236] *Ibid.* See Fournet and Pegorier, 2010, p. 713, see *supra* note 229, offering a view on the close connection between genocide and persecution, including a discussion of the origin of the former.

[237] UN General Assembly, Affirmation of the Principles of International Law Recognized by the Charter of the Nürnberg Tribunal, GA res. 95 (I), UN doc. A/236 (1946).

[238] International Law Commission, "Principles of International Law Recognized in the Charter of the Nürnberg Tribunal and in the Judgment of the Tribunal", in *Yearbook of the International Law Commission*, 1950, vol. II, pp. 374–77.

[239] International Law Commission, "Draft Code of Offences against the Peace and Security of Mankind", in *Yearbook of the International Law Commission*, 1954, vol. II, p. 150, Article 2(11).

through the growth of international human rights law. This section briefly surveys some of these developments.

12.2.4.1. Persecution in Subsequent National Cases

The most notable national decision concerning persecution in the intervening years was the 1961 conviction of Adolf Eichmann, a high-level Reich official, under a 1950 Israeli law providing Israeli courts with jurisdiction over international crimes committed during the Second World War. In the Judgment issued by the District Court of Jerusalem, and upheld by the Supreme Court of Israel, Eichmann was convicted of a range of war crimes, crimes against humanity (including murder, extermination, enslavement, starvation and deportation), the crime of being a member of an organisation declared to be criminal by the IMT, and an additional category set out in the Israeli law: "crimes against the Jewish people", effectively an articulation of the offence of genocide when directed specifically against the Jewish population. The District Court also found Eichmann guilty of persecution on the basis that, in carrying out all the aforementioned crimes against humanity and crimes against the Jewish people, "he persecuted Jews on national, racial, religious and political grounds".[240]

The Judgment is significant for a variety of reasons. First, the District Court's Judgment confirmed that (1) crimes against humanity and, notably, acts of genocide could amount to underlying acts supporting a conviction for persecution; and (2) in such instances, a defendant could be convicted of both the underlying act as a self-standing offence and for persecution in carrying out those acts.[241] Notably, the Judgment also recognised Eichmann's acts of persecution as amounting to war crimes – in addition to crimes against humanity – where they took place on occupied territory.[242] Second, the Israeli law under which the *Eichmann* case proceeded, as confirmed by the Judgment, recognised an additional ground of discrimination beyond those set out in the post-Second World War legal

---

[240] District Court of Jerusalem, *Attorney-General of Israel v. Eichmann*, Judgment, 12 December 1961, in *International Law Reports*, 1962, vol. 36, pp. 273–75 ('Eichmann District Court Judgment'). See also Supreme Court of Israel, *Attorney-General of Israel v. Eichmann*, Judgment, 29 May 1962, in *International Law Reports*, 1962, vol. 36, p. 277, confirming the decision.

[241] Eichmann District Court Judgment, pp. 273–75, see *supra* note 240.

[242] *Ibid.*, p. 275.

instruments: discrimination on national grounds.[243] This precedent, along with the similar recognition of additional grounds in the Genocide Convention and the ILC's Draft Code, would ultimately be reflected in the ICC Statute's expanded definition of persecution as discussed below.[244]

In addition to the immediate post-Second World War cases and a few notable cases throughout the 1950s and 1960s such as *Eichmann*, there was a 'third wave' of renewed interest in prosecuting crimes committed in the Second World War in domestic courts in the 1980s.[245] Several such judgments were rendered convicting defendants of persecution among other crimes. Perhaps most famous among these is the conviction of the German national Klaus Barbie, *inter alia*, for his involvement in the persecution of Jews in Vichy France. In affirming the indictment against him for persecution as a crime against humanity, the French Court of Cassation in a 1985 decision described his involvement as "persecution against innocent Jews carried out for racial and religious motives with a view to their extermination, in furtherance of the 'final solution'".[246] Notably, where the IMT at Nuremberg had described Streicher's persecution of Jews as taking place on racial and political grounds, the Court of Cassation viewed Barbie's conduct as taking place on racial and religious grounds, highlighting that persecution of one group by multiple actors (even as part of the same overarching plan or policy) may be considered as having taken place on several different grounds.

Consistent with the standard established by the US NMT in *Justice* and *Einsatzgruppen*, the Court of Cassation in *Barbie* also held that establishing a charge of crimes against humanity (including persecution) requires demonstrating that the conduct was carried out in a systematic manner and in association with a state policy.[247] However, the Court went

---

[243] *Ibid.*

[244] See *infra* section 12.3.3.1.2.

[245] See Mark A. Drumbl, *Atrocity, Punishment and International Law*, Cambridge University Press, Cambridge, 2007, p. 111.

[246] Court of Cassation (France), *Fédération Nationale des Déportés et Internés Résistants et Patriotes and Others v. Barbie*, Judgment, 20 December 1985, in *International Law Reports*, 1985, vol. 78, pp. 124, 139 ('Barbie Judgment'). As the Court of Cassation noted, no appeal was lodged against Barbie's conviction on these grounds. Barbie was subsequently convicted on the terms of the indictment. *Id.*, p. 148.

[247] *Ibid.*, pp. 124, 139: "Such crimes were constituted by inhumane acts and persecution committed in a systematic manner in the name of a State practising a policy of ideological supremacy, not only against persons by reason of their membership of a racial or religious

beyond the NMT precedents, and required that the state policy be one of "ideological supremacy" against a racial or religious community or opponents of the policy itself. In effect, the Court required that, *not only incidents of persecution* but the *underlying policy itself* must contain a discriminatory element. The Court of Cassation affirmed this approach seven years later in an appeal concerning the indictment against Paul Touvier. Touvier, a French national, had been in charge of intelligence in the area surrounding Lyon for the Vichy-era military police. In confirming crimes against humanity charges in the indictment against Touvier relating to his involvement in the murder of six Jews in 1944, the Court noted what separated such offences from "common law crimes":

> [C]rimes against humanity must form part of the execution of a concerted plan, and be accomplished in the name of a State systematically practicing a policy of ideological hegemony; the crime must also be committed against people because they belong to a particular racial or religious group or because they belong to a group that opposes this policy of ideological hegemony.[248]

The drafters of the ICTR Statute subsequently adopted a similar approach, requiring proof of discrimination for all crimes against humanity and not simply for persecution. However, as discussed below, in practice the *ad hoc* tribunals have not required proof of discrimination for crimes

---

community, but also against the opponents of that policy, whatever the form of their opposition".

[248] Court of Cassation (France), *France v. Touvier*, Judgment, 27 November 1992, as translated in Michael E. Tigar, Susan C. Casey, Isabelle Giordiani and Sivakumaren Mardemootoo, "Paul Touvier and the Crime Against Humanity", in *Texas International Law Journal*, 1995, vol. 30, pp. 285, 298. Notably, at the time of the *Barbie* case, the Court was relying on a 1964 version of the French Penal Code, which established the definition of crimes against humanity by direct reference to the IMT Charter. While the prosecution against Touvier was initiated (in 1973) under this prior Code, by the time his case reached the Court of Cassation a new 1992 Penal Code was in place. While the text of the provision is somewhat ambiguous, the definition of crimes against humanity contained in the new Code seems to require that any crime against humanity be "inspired by political, philosophical, racial or religious reasons, and organized according to a concerted plan against a group within the civilian population". See *id.*, pp. 293–94, describing the change in the law and including an excerpt from the 1992 Penal Code. See also Leila Nadya Sadat, "The French Experience", in M. Cherif Bassiouni (ed.), *International Criminal Law: International Enforcement*, vol. 3, Koninklijke Brill NV, Leiden, 2008, pp. 329, 331, providing an excerpt of the 1964 provision.

against humanity other than persecution, and such a requirement has not been incorporated in the ICC Statute.[249]

The case of Andrija Artuković before the Zagreb District Court in 1986 for his conduct in the Second World War is also notable, if for no other reason than it was subsequently invoked by the ICTY in its effort to assess the parameters of persecution as a crime against humanity.[250] Artuković, who had been part of the Croatian independence movement in the course of the war, was convicted, *inter alia*, "for persecutions, concentration camps and mass killings of Serbs, Jews, Gypsies, as well as Croats who did not accept the [independence] ideology".[251] His conviction for persecution was based, *inter alia*, on passing laws that were discriminatory based on racial identity, deporting individuals to internment camps.[252] Significantly, the *Artuković* case also affirms the principle that both acts which themselves constitute self-standing international crimes (that is, deportation), and those which are not independently criminal (that is, passing discriminatory laws) can be considered as underlying acts for a persecution conviction. As with the immediate post-war jurisprudence, these acts were considered cumulatively thereby complicating any effort to discern a distinct threshold of what conduct is independently sufficient to support a persecution conviction. The *Artuković* case is notable among cases addressing Second World War acts for its recognition of the wide array of groups – spanning racial, religious, political and (significantly) national affiliation – that were the target of persecutory conduct.

12.2.4.2. Persecution and the Rise of International Human Rights

Another significant development over this period that subsequently influenced the contemporary interpretation of the crime of persecution was the rise of the international human rights regime. In many ways crimes against humanity – persecution specifically – and the broader human rights movement that developed in earnest in the wake of the Second World War, have been mutually reinforcing. The crystallisation of the

---

[249] See *infra* section 12.3.2.1.

[250] See Kupreškić case, Trial Judgment, paras. 602, 613, *supra* note 2.

[251] *Andrija Artuković*, Zagreb District Court, Doc. No. K-1/84-61, 14 May 1986, Translation, p. 23, as quoted and translated in Kupreškić, Trial Judgement, para. 602, see *supra* note 2. See also US District Court for the Central District of California, Matter of Extradition of Artuković, 628 F. Supp. 1370, 6 February 1986, addressing the extradition of Artuković from the United States to the former Yugoslavia.

[252] *Ibid.*, p. 16 in Kupreškić case, Trial Judgment, para. 613, see *supra* note 2.

principle that international law's protection of the individual extends to treatment within a state – not shielded by the veil of state sovereignty – was driven in part by the post-war acceptance of the concept of crimes against humanity. The underlying tension between traditional conceptions of sovereign discretion and the intervention of international law into domestic affairs is, as discussed above, quite evident in the drafting history of the relevant post-war instruments and in the post-war tribunals' jurisprudence. In many ways, the post-Second World War human rights movement nascent at the same time carried the legacy of this principle forward. In place of the stalled efforts to establish robust international criminal law proscription throughout the Cold War, interest shifted to the protection of the individual through internationally guaranteed human rights (though, admittedly the development of this domain was significantly affected in its own right by the Cold War).[253] The international recognition of such rights was codified in, *inter alia*, the Universal Declaration of Human Rights,[254] the International Covenant on Civil and Political Rights ('ICCPR')[255] and the International Covenant on Economic Social and Cultural Rights ('ICESCR')[256] among other instruments.[257]

---

[253] Admittedly, the common narrative of the post-war rise of international human rights is not without challenge. See, for example, Samuel Moyn, *The Last Utopia: Human Rights in History*, Harvard University Press, Cambridge, MA, 2012, ch. 5. However, in describing a rise of internationally recognised human rights, we observe that, at the very least, the post-Second World War period saw the proliferation of codifications of human rights instruments at both the international and regional level, as well as institutions tasked with the enforcement of rights articulated in those instruments. Moreover, this area is admittedly a complex field with a robust, emerging histography of its own. What is offered here is simply a cursory description of the developments in the field of human rights for context.

[254] UN General Assembly, Universal Declaration of Human Rights, GA res. 217A (III), UN doc. A/810 at 71, 1948 (https://www.legal-tools.org/doc/de5d83/).

[255] International Covenant on Civil and Political Rights, 16 December 1966 (https://www.legal-tools.org/doc/2838f3/).

[256] International Covenant on Economic, Social and Cultural Rights, 16 December 1966 (https://www.legal-tools.org/doc/06b87e/).

[257] International concern with the protection of individuals from persecution is also embodied in the international refugee framework that developed in the aftermath of the Second World War. See, for example, Convention Relating to the Status of Refugees, 28 July 1951 (https://www.legal-tools.org/doc/9b8e7a/); Protocol Relating to the Status of Refugees, 13 January 1967, 606 UNTS 267. On the development of the principle of non-refoulement in the wake of the Second World War, see Ryan Liss, "A Right to Belong: Legal Protection of Sociological Membership in the Application of Article 12(4) of the ICCPR", in *New York University Journal of International Law and Politics*, 2014, vol. 46, no. 3, pp. 1117–18.

The growth of human rights standards throughout this period was in turn influential on the development of international criminal law generally and on the offence of persecution specifically – both as it developed throughout the Cold War,[258] and when the field of international criminal law re-emerged in earnest as a matter of central international concern in the 1990s. This influence is evident, for instance, in the report of the ILC on its 1996 Draft Code of Offences. The Draft Code set out a provision delineating persecution as an international offence, which included an expanded list of the recognised grounds of discrimination beyond those set out in the post-Second World War instruments (namely prohibiting discrimination on the basis of political, racial, religious and ethnic groups). In its commentary, the ILC noted that what was intended to be captured by the offence was broad, and deeply informed by the human rights protections codified in, *inter alia*, the UN Charter and the ICCPR's provision on non-discrimination.[259] As the ILC noted: "The inhumane act of persecution may take many forms with its common characteristic being the denial of the human rights and fundamental freedoms to which every individual is entitled without distinction as recognized in the Charter of the United Nations (Arts. 1 and 55) and the International Covenant on Civil and Political Rights (Art. 2)".[260]

The notion that the crime of persecution may be used as a means to protect fundamental human rights was ultimately further realised in the re-emergence of the crime of persecution as the offence at the core of the

---

[258] See, for example, International Convention on the Suppression and Punishment of the Crime of Apartheid, 18 July 1976 (https://www.legal-tools.org/doc/d9644f/), Preamble and Art. II, recognising the criminalisation as inspired by the primary human rights instruments, and setting out deprivations constituting the crime of apartheid in a manner consistent with fundamental rights as recognised in the primary international human rights treaties; Convention against Torture and Other Cruel, Inhuman or Degrading Treatment or Punishment, 10 December 1984 (https://www.legal-tools.org/doc/326294/), Preamble, recognising the criminalisation of torture as inspired by the primary international human rights treaties.

[259] International Law Commission, Report of ILC, 48th Sess., 6 May–26 July 1996, UN doc. A/51/10, p. 49.

[260] ILC, 1996, p. 49, see *supra* note 259. Article 2 of the ICCPR provides at paragraph 1 that "Each State Party to the present Covenant undertakes to respect and to ensure to all individuals within its territory and subject to its jurisdiction the rights recognized in the present Covenant, without distinction of any kind, such as race, colour, sex, language, religion, political or other opinion, national or social origin, property, birth or other status." International Covenant on Civil and Political Rights, Article 2(1), see *supra* note 255.

ICTY's jurisprudence, and through its codification in the ICC Statute.[261] The reinvigorated development of persecution as a crime against humanity over the past two decades has been animated by the same principles underpinning the long-standing international concern with the crime. This contemporary expression of the international effort to protect individuals from mass discrimination through the criminalisation of persecutory conduct is the focus of the subsequent section.

12.3. Persecution and the Modern International Criminal Courts and Tribunals

12.3.1. The Re-emergence of the Crime of Persecution in the 1990s

Some 50 years after the IMT and IMTFE Charters first proscribed the crime of persecution as a crime against humanity, the crime went through a kind of renaissance at the two *ad hoc* tribunals, the ICTY and the ICTR. Like the IMT and IMTFE Charters, and CCL No. 10, Article 5(h) of the ICTY Statute and Article 3(g) of the ICTR Statute criminalise persecution as a crime against humanity. However, the contemporary iterations differ from their post-Second World War predecessors by not requiring a nexus with another crime within the Court's jurisdiction, and for the ICTR, by not requiring a nexus to an armed conflict. Both tribunals, in particular the ICTY, have adjudicated the crime of persecution in many cases, thereby contributing greatly to its jurisprudential development.

As the preceding analysis has shown, though the IMT at Nuremberg and the courts established pursuant to CCL No. 10 convicted a number of individuals for persecution as a crime against humanity, the elements of the crime were often not clearly defined. This changed dramatically at the ICTY and ICTR. Not only have these courts rendered a large number of convictions for persecution but they have also developed a rich body of jurisprudence in their adjudication of trials and appeals. Indeed for the ICTY, persecution could be considered the 'flagship crime' – the crime which has best reflected the nature and scope of the ethnic cleansing in

---

[261] It is important to note, as observed by the ICTY Trial Chamber in *Kupreškić*, that the human rights law is not itself the law upon which a conviction for persecution is based. See Kupreškić case, Trial Judgment, para. 589, *supra* note 2. Rather international criminal law under customary international law (and eventually as codified in the ICC Statute) itself developed in a manner consistent with the terms of the fundamental rights recognised under international human rights law and international refugee law.

the former Yugoslavia in the early 1990s, and which has been the most represented in terms of numbers of charges brought and convictions rendered. As noted by William Fenrick: "Just as genocide has become the offence which represents what happened in Rwanda during 1994, so the crime against humanity of persecution has come to typify what happened in the territory of the former Yugoslavia".[262] Of the 110 accused persons charged and tried by the ICTY, 71 were charged with persecution.[263] To date 58 defendants have been convicted of persecution following trial and appeal.[264] At the ICTR, where the 'defining' crime has been genocide, the number of persecution charges and convictions has not been as high. Nevertheless, there have been some notable cases: of the 76 accused persons charged and tried by the ICTR,[265] 19 were charged with persecution, and to date 14 defendants have been convicted of this crime after trial and appeal.[266]

Persecution has no 'counterpart' in the category of war crimes and is largely unknown as a domestic crime in national criminal justice systems (save where the ICC Statute's crimes have been domestically incorporated). For this reason, one of the tremendous contributions of the IC-

---

[262] William J. Fenrick, "The Crime Against Humanity of Persecution in the Jurisprudence of the ICTY", in *Netherlands Yearbook of International Law*, 2001, vol. 32, p. 89.

[263] These figures do not include contempt cases, nor charges against persons who died before being transferred to the ICTY (Bobetko, Drljaca, Alilović, Ražnatović, J. Janjić, Miljković, Borovnica, Gagović and N. Janjić), persons who died before their trial proceedings started (Đukić, Talić, Alagić), or persons who died before their trials had concluded (Kovačević, Dokmanović, Milošević). Nor do they include proceedings against persons who were transferred to national courts and hence not tried by the ICTY (Ademi and Norac, Trbić, Kovačević, Ljubičič, Mejacić *et al.*, Stanković and Janković, Todović and Rašević).

[264] The following cases are still on appeal at the time of writing: Stanišić and Župljanin; Stanišić and Simatović; Tolimir; and Prlić *et al.* A Trial Judgment is pending against Šešelj and Karadžić. Trial proceedings are still underway against Mladić and Hadžić.

[265] These figures do not include contempt cases, nor charges against persons who died before their trial commenced (Musabyimana), persons who died before their trial had concluded (Nzirorera) or persons whose cases were transferred to national authorities (Kayishela, Munyagishari, Munyarugarama, Munyeshyaha, Ndimbati, Ntaganzwa, Ryandikayo, Sikuburabo and Uwikinde). The figures also do not include one accused who was tried, *inter alia*, on a charge of persecution but where the prosecution withdrew the charge in its closing submissions (Kamuhanda).

[266] An Appeal Judgment is still pending in Nyiramasushuko *et al.* (Kanyabashi, Ndayambaje, Nsabimana, Ntahobali and Nyiramasushuko). Three fugitives remain at large and if arrested will be tried by the ICTR's successor institution, the UN Mechanism for International Criminal Tribunals (Bizimana, Kabuga, Mpiranya).

TY and the ICTR to international criminal law has been the development of the substantive content of this crime.

The definition of persecution in the ICC's Statute and Elements of Crimes owes its genesis both to precedents from the post-Second World War period and jurisprudence of the ICTY and ICTR. The ECCC has also contributed to the crime's evolution through the definition of the crime in Article 5 of the Law on the Establishment of the ECCC ('ECCC Special Law') and Article 9 of the Agreement between the UN and the Royal Government of Cambodia ('ECCC Agreement'), and the court's case law. While Article 2(h) of the Statute of the Special Court for Sierra Leone ('SCSL Statute') proscribes persecution, due to the nature of the conflict and crimes committed therein, no charges were brought for this offence at the SCSL.

In section 12.3.2., we examine the most important developments concerning the crime of persecution before the modern *ad hoc* and hybrid international criminal courts and tribunals. In the subsequent section 12.3.3. we review the crime of persecution in the ICC Statute and emerging case law from the ICC. This analysis is approached with a focus on the historical origins of the crime discussed above, and with a view to track the core tensions inherent in the offence's development as a crime at the cusp of the national and international.

12.3.2. The Renaissance of Persecution as a Crime Against Humanity: The *Ad Hoc* and Hybrid International Courts and Tribunals

Persecution as a crime against humanity was addressed by the ICTY in *Tadić*, its first case. In the Trial Judgment issued in 1997, the Trial Chamber described persecution as "[t]he violation of the right to equality in some serious fashion that infringes on the enjoyment of a basic or fundamental right [...], although the discrimination must be on one of the listed grounds to constitute persecution under the Statute".[267] It required two elements for the crime: the occurrence of a persecutory act or omission, and a discriminatory intent for that act or omission on one of the listed grounds, specifically race, religion, or politics.[268]

---

[267] Tadić case, Trial Judgment, para. 697, see *supra* note 113.

[268] *Ibid.*, para. 715.

The ICTY explored the crime in greater depth in *Kupreškić*. In that case, six accused were charged with persecution based on the allegation that, over a six-month period, they had persecuted Bosnian Muslim inhabitants of the Ahmići-Šantići region of Bosnia and Herzegovina through the systematic killing of Bosnian Muslim civilians, destruction of their homes and property, and their detention and expulsion from the region.[269] In its judgment rendered in 2000, the Trial Chamber carefully analysed the historical evolution of persecution, from which it sourced a comprehensive definition of the crime. In short, the *Kupreškić* Trial Chamber concluded that the *actus reus* of persecution was "the gross or blatant denial, on discriminatory grounds, of a fundamental right, laid down in international customary or treaty law, reaching the same level of gravity as the other acts prohibited in Article 5 [crimes against humanity]".[270] The Trial Chamber did not try to exhaustively identify which rights constituted 'fundamental rights' upon which a charge of persecution could be based; rather, consistent with the historic precedents, the Trial Chamber recognised that discriminatory acts could involve conduct such as murder, extermination and other serious acts against a person as already enumerated in Article 5, as well as a variety of other discriminatory acts involving attacks on political, social and economic rights. It found that the charged acts of killings, detention and expulsion, and the comprehensive destruction of homes and property amounted to persecution[271] and convicted the five accused accordingly.[272]

---

[269] Kupreškić case, Trial Judgment, para. 33, see *supra* note 2.

[270] *Ibid.*, paras. 586–620, 621. The Trial Chamber referred to, *inter alia*, the IMT Charter and Control Council Law No.10; international cases such as the Nuremberg Judgment (including the convictions of Streicher and von Schirach) and the *Justice*, *Flick*, *Einsatzgruppen*, *Ministries* and *RuSHA* cases; national cases such as *Eichmann* and *Artuković*; and the ILC Draft Code. See *supra* section 12.2.3.1.

[271] Kupreškić case, Trial Judgment, paras. 628–31, see *supra* note 2. In finding that certain property or economic rights can be considered so fundamental that their denial is capable of constituting persecution, the Trial Chamber noted the Nuremberg Judgment where several defendants such as Göring, Funk and Seyss-Inquart were charged and/or convicted of economic discrimination; see para. 630. See *supra* section 12.2.3.1.1.4.

[272] *Ibid.*, paras. 784, 791, 804, 816, 829. The convictions against three of the accused (Zoran, Mirjan and Vlatko Kupreškić) for persecution and other crimes were later overturned by the Appeals Chamber and no retrial was ordered, on the basis that the persecution charge had been insufficiently pleaded, and because of an insufficiency of evidence. See ICTY, *Prosecutor v. Kupreškić et al.*, Appeal Judgment, IT-95-16-A, 23 October 2001, paras. 246, 304, 397 ('Kupreškić case') (https://www.legal-tools.org/doc/c6a5d1/).

This definition was also adopted in the ICTR's first cases on persecution, *Ruggiu* in 2000 and *Nahimana* in 2003.[273] In *Ruggiu*, the prosecution charged the accused, a journalist and broadcaster at *Radio-Télévision Libre des Milles Collines* ('RTLM'), with persecution for propagating "the Hutu extremist ideology, by systematically inciting ethnic hatred and violence against the entire Tutsi minority".[274] As discussed further below, in convicting Ruggiu for persecution as a crime against humanity (and other crimes) following his guilty plea, the Trial Chamber compared the gravity of his crimes to that of Streicher before the IMT at Nuremberg. The Chamber stated that, like Streicher, Ruggiu had "infected people's minds with ethnic hatred and persecution".[275]

From these early ICTY and ICTR cases, the skeletal framework of persecution as a crime against humanity started to form. The *actus reus* required an act or omission that (1) discriminated in fact; (2) denied or infringed upon a fundamental right laid down in customary international law or treaty law; and (3) where not specified as a crime under the relevant provision on crimes against humanity, the cumulative effect of the underlying acts of persecution reached a level of gravity equivalent to that for other crimes against humanity. The *mens rea* required that the underlying act or omission was (1) carried out deliberately/intentionally and (2) with the intention to discriminate on political, racial, or religious grounds. As further discussed below, these essential requirements can each be sourced in the post-Second World War cases and precedents,[276] and have been applied at the ICTY and ICTR since they were first articulated.[277]

---

[273] ICTR, *Prosecutor v. Georges Ruggiu*, Trial Judgment, ICTR-97-32-I, 1 June 2000, para. 21 ('Ruggiu case') (https://www.legal-tools.org/doc/486d43/); ICTR, *Prosecutor v. Ferdinand Nahimana et al.*, Trial Judgment, ICTR-99-52-T, 3 December 2003, para. 1072 ('Nahimana case') (https://www.legal-tools.org/doc/45b8b6/). Another early case at the ICTR involving persecution charges was *Prosecutor v. Laurent Semanza*, Trial Judgment, ICTR-97-20-T, 15 May 2003, paras. 467–72 ('Semanza case') (https://www.legal-tools.org/doc/7e668a/). However the Trial Chamber did not find persecution proven in that case.

[274] Ruggiu case, Indictment, paras. 4, 9 and 5, see *supra* note 273.

[275] *Ibid.*, Trial Judgment, para. 19. See *supra* section 12.2.3.1.1.4.

[276] See generally *supra* section 12.2.3.

[277] See for example, ICTY, *Prosecutor v. M. Stanišić and Župljanin*, Trial Judgment, IT-08-91-T, 27 March 2013, para. 66 ('Stanišić and Župljanin case') (https://www.legal-tools.org/doc/2ed57f/); ICTY, *Prosecutor v. Zdravko Tolimir*, Trial Judgment, IT-05-88/2-T, 12 December 2012, paras. 846, 848 ('Tolimir case') (https://www.legal-

The following sections examine both the source and the development of these essential elements, which later also resurfaced (although with a different articulation in some respects) in the definition of persecution adopted by the ICC and the hybrid courts – the SCSL and ECCC.

12.3.2.1. The *Actus Reus* of Persecution under Customary International Law

12.3.2.1.1. The Gravity Threshold of Underlying Persecutory Acts or Omissions and the Forms of Underlying Acts

In *Tadić*, the Trial Chamber considered the Nuremberg Judgment (specifically, the convictions against Bormann, Frank, Funk, Seyss-Inquart, Frick and Göring), US NMT jurisprudence such as the *Flick*, *Einsatzgruppen*, *Pohl* and *Justice* cases, and national cases such as *Eichmann*, to conclude that persecution encompasses a variety of acts, including those of a physical, economic or judicial nature, that violate an individual's equal enjoyment of his basic rights.[278] Case law from the ICTY and ICTR over the next 18 years have affirmed that the acts or omissions amounting to persecution can take a variety of forms.

12.3.2.1.1.1. Gravity Threshold

The definition of persecution was further refined in the *Kupreškić*, *Krnojelac* and *Kvočka* cases at the ICTY. The *Kupreškić* Trial Chamber held that a persecutory act is a gross or blatant denial, on discriminatory grounds, of a fundamental right, laid down in international customary or treaty law, reaching the same level of gravity as other acts prohibited in Article 5.[279] It emphasised that there is no list of established fundamental rights, and that the question must be resolved on a case-by-case basis. It noted:

> Although the realm of human rights is dynamic and expansive, not every denial of a human right may constitute a crime against humanity.
>
> [...]

---

tools.org/doc/445e4e/); ICTY, *Prosecutor v. Popović et al.*, Trial Judgment, IT-05-88-T, 10 June 2010, para. 964 ('Popović case') (https://www.legal-tools.org/doc/481867/).

[278] Tadić case, Trial Judgment, para. 710, see *supra* note 113. See *supra* section 12.2.3.1.1 and section 12.2.4.1.

[279] Kupreškić case, Trial Judgment, para. 621, see *supra* note 2.

Accordingly, it can be said that at a minimum, acts of persecution must be of equal gravity or severity to the other acts
enumerated under Article 5.[280]

The Trial Chamber noted that this legal criterion had been set out in
Flick, in the US NMT's rejection of expropriation of industrial property
as insufficient to support a persecution conviction.[281] As discussed above
– while not noted by the Trial Chamber in *Kupreškić* – the reasoning in
Flick was based on a misreading of the text of CCL No. 10, and its application of the gravity threshold to the appropriation of industrial property
was challenged in other post-Second World War cases. Nevertheless, the
crux of the gravity threshold arguably captured a principle intended by the
drafters of the post-war instruments.[282]

Subsequent to *Kupreškić*, ICTY and ICTR Trial Chambers have
continued to apply the equal gravity test.[283] For example, the *Kordić* Trial
Chamber held that persecution required that the act denying a fundamental right (1) be gross and blatant, and (2) reach the same level of seriousness as other acts under Article 5.[284] It acknowledged that the test could
exclude some acts from the "realm of criminal persecution", and called
this a "wholly valid result".[285] The *Krnojelac* Trial Judgment did not con-
cur that there was a separate requirement that the denial of the fundamental right be "gross and blatant",[286] but rather saw the *Kupreškić* definition
as establishing a test of seriousness: only gross or blatant denials of fun-

---

[280] *Ibid.*, paras. 618–19.

[281] *Ibid.*, fn. 897, citing Flick case, vol. VI, p. 1215, see *supra* note 127. See also *supra* note
128 and accompanying text, setting out the relevant excerpt from *Flick*, and section
12.2.3.1.1.2., discussing the excerpt and the post-Second World War gravity standard.

[282] See *supra* section 12.2.3.1.1.2.

[283] ICTY, *Prosecutor v. Milomir Stakić*, Trial Judgment, IT-97-24-T, 31 July 2003, para. 736
('Stakić case') (https://www.legal-tools.org/doc/32ecfb/); ICTY, *Prosecutor v. Naletilić
and Martinović*, Trial Judgment, IT-98-34-T, 31 March 2003, para. 635 ('Naletilić and
Martinović case') (https://www.legal-tools.org/doc/f2cfeb/); *Prosecutor v. Milorad Krnojelac*, Trial Judgment, IT-97-25-T, 15 March 2002, para. 434 ('Krnojelac case')
(https://www.legal-tools.org/doc/1a994b/); *Prosecutor v. Kordić and Čerkez*, Trial Judgment, IT-95-14/2-T, 26 February 2001, para. 195 ('Kordić and Čerkez case')
(https://www.legal-tools.org/doc/d4fedd/); Nahimana case, Trial Judgment, para. 1072, see
supra note 273; Semanza case, Trial Judgment, para. 347, see *supra* note 273; Ruggiu
case, Trial Judgment, para. 21, see *supra* note 273.

[284] Kordić and Čerkez case, Trial Judgment, para. 195, see *supra* note 283.

[285] *Ibid.*, para. 196.

[286] Kupreškić case, Trial Judgment, para. 434, fn. 1303, see *supra* note 2.

damental rights would have the requisite gravity for the crime of persecution.

The ICTY Appeals Chamber subsequently endorsed the equal gravity requirement. The *Krnojelac* Appeal Judgment affirmed that "[t]he acts underlying the crime of persecution, whether considered in isolation or in conjunction with other acts, must constitute a crime of persecution of gravity equal to the crimes listed under Article 5 of the Statute".[287] Despite the potential ambiguity in this wording, the gravity assessment in *Krnojelac* and in cases following has concerned the underlying *acts* rather than the crime of persecution as a whole.[288]

While not every denial or infringement of a right will be sufficient to qualify as persecution as a crime against humanity, the ICTY and ICTR have produced a rich body of case law illustrating a broad range of acts and omissions that, individually or cumulatively, have amounted to persecution. Conscious that a fixed definition of fundamental rights would not serve the interests of justice, and indeed would be immaterial,[289] these Tribunals instead have recognised a wide variety of rights.

These rights have included rights to life, physical and mental integrity, security and liberty, as well as property, economic and judicial rights. For instance, persecution has been constituted by: deportation, forcible transfer and displacement;[290] wanton destruction and plundering;[291] de-

---

[287] ICTY, *Prosecutor v. Milorad Krnojelac*, Appeal Judgment, IT-97-25-A, 17 September 2003, para. 199 ('Krnojelac case') (https://www.legal-tools.org/doc/46d2e5/). See also ICTY, *Prosecutor v. Tihomir Blaškić*, Appeal Judgment, IT-95-14-A, 29 July 2004, para. 135 ('Blaškić case') (https://www.legal-tools.org/doc/88d8e6/); ICTY, *Prosecutor v. Kordić and Čerkez*, Appeal Judgment, IT-95-14/2-A, 17 December 2004, para. 102 ('Kordić and Čerkez case') (https://www.legal-tools.org/doc/738211/); ICTY, *Prosecutor v. Milan Lukić and Sredoje Lukić*, IT-98-32/1-T, Trial Judgment, 20 July 2009, para. 993 ('Lukić and Lukić case') (https://www.legal-tools.org/doc/af5ad0/).

[288] Krnojelac case, Appeal Judgment, para. 199, see *supra* note 287.

[289] Kupreškić case, Trial Judgment, para. 623, see *supra* note 2; Stakić case, Trial Judgment, para. 773, see *supra* note 283.

[290] Blaškić case, Appeal Judgment, para. 153, see *supra* note 287; ICTY, *Prosecutor v. Radoslav Brđanin*, Trial Judgment, IT-99-36-T, 1 September 2004, para. 1025 ('Brđanin case') (https://www.legal-tools.org/doc/4c3228/); Stakić case, Trial Judgment, para. 769, see *supra* note 283; ICTY, *Prosecutor v. Kvočka et al.*, Trial Judgment, IT-98-30/1-T, 2 November 2001, para. 186 ('Kvočka case') (https://www.legal-tools.org/doc/34428a/); ICTY, *Prosecutor v. Milan Martić*, Trial Judgment, IT-95-11-T, 12 June 2008, paras. 427, 430, 432 ('Martić case') (https://www.legal-tools.org/doc/06634c/); ICTY, *Prosecutor v. Blagojević and Jokić*, Trial Judgment, IT-02-60-T, 17 January 2005, paras. 602, 616–18, 621 ('Blagojević and Jokić case') (https://www.legal-tools.org/doc/7483f2/); ICTY, *Prosecutor v. Radislav Krstić*, Trial Judgment, IT-98-33, 2 August 2001, para. 537 ('Krstić

struction of property including cultural and religious buildings;[292] unlawful arrest, detention and confinement of civilians;[293] murder of civilians;[294] detention of civilians, and their being killed, beaten, used as human shields, subjected to overcrowding, physical or psychological abuse
and intimidation, inhumane treatment and deprivation of adequate food
and water;[295] torture, cruel, inhuman, humiliating or degrading treatment;[296] rape and sexual abuse;[297] slavery and servitude;[298] terrorising the

case') (https://www.legal-tools.org/doc/440d3a/); *Prosecutor v. Stanišić and Simatovic*,
IT-03-69-T, Trial Judgment, 30 May 2013, para. 1243 ('Stanišić and Simatovic case')
(https://www.legal-tools.org/doc/066e67/); Popović case, Trial Judgment, para. 989, see
supra note 277.

[291] ICTY, *Prosecutor v. Tihomir Blaškić*, Trial Judgment, IT-95-14, 3 March 2000, para. 227,
('Blaškić case') (https://www.legal-tools.org/doc/e1ae55/); Kordić and Čerkez case, Trial
Judgment, para. 205, see *supra* note 283; Naletilić and Martinović case, Trial Judgment,
para. 701, see *supra* note 283; Martić case, Trial Judgment, paras. 363, 378, 399, see *supra*
note 290; Stakić case, Trial Judgment, paras. 809–10, see *supra* note 283; Krstić case, Trial Judgment, paras. 537, 653, see *supra* note 290; Popović case, Trial Judgment, para. 987,
see *supra* note 277.

[292] Blaškić case, Trial Judgment, para. 227, see *supra* note 291; *Brđanin* case, Trial Judgment,
para. 1023, see *supra* note 290; Stakić case, Trial Judgment, paras. 764, 813, see *supra*
note 283; Kvočka case, Trial Judgment, para. 186, see *supra* note 290; Kordić and Čerkez
case, Trial Judgment, para. 205, see *supra* note 283; Kupreškić case, Trial Judgment, para.
631, see *supra* note 2; Tadić case, Trial Judgment, para. 707, see *supra* note 113; Lukić
and Lukić case, Trial Judgment, para. 996, see *supra* note 287; Stanišić and Župljanin
case, Trial Judgment, paras. 88–89, see *supra* note 277.

[293] Naletilić and Martinović case, Trial Judgment, para. 642, see *supra* note 283; Krnojelac
case, Trial Judgment, para. 438, see *supra* note 283; Kvočka case, Trial Judgment, paras.
186, 189, see *supra* note 290; Kordić and Čerkez case, Trial Judgment, para. 302, see *supra* note 283; Blaškić case, Trial Judgment, para. 220, see *supra* note 291; Kupreškić case,
para. 629, see *supra* note 2; ICTY, *Prosecutor v. Blagoje Simić et al.*, Trial Judgment, 17
October 2003, IT-95-9-T, paras. 62–63 ('Simić case') (https://www.legal-
tools.org/doc/aa9b81/); Martić case, Trial Judgment, paras. 411, 416, see *supra* note 290;
Lukić and Lukić case, Trial Judgment, para. 996, see *supra* note 287.

[294] Martić case, Trial Judgment, paras. 358, 363, 370, 377, 383, 403, see *supra* note 290;
Krstić case, Trial Judgment, para. 537, see *supra* note 290; Stanišić and Simatovic case,
Trial Judgment, para. 1241, see *supra* note 290; ICTR, *Prosecutor v. Pauline Nyiramasuhuko et al.*, Trial Judgment, ICTR-98-42-T, 24 June 2011, paras. 6099, 6101, 6103, 6106,
6108 ('Nyiramasuhuko case') (https://www.legal-tools.org/doc/e2c881/).

[295] Blaškić case, Appeal Judgment, para. 155, see *supra* note 287; Brđanin case, Trial Judgment, para. 1005, see *supra* note 290; Martić case, Trial Judgment, paras. 427, 432, see
supra note 290; Stakić case, Trial Judgment, paras. 786–90, see *supra* note 283.

[296] Brđanin case, Trial Judgment, paras. 1014–20, see *supra* note 290; Blaškić case, Trial
Judgment, para. 220, see *supra* note 291; Martić case, Trial Judgment, para. 411, see *supra*
note 290; Lukić and Lukić case, Trial Judgment, para. 996, see *supra* note 287; Popović
case, Trial Judgment, para. 975, see *supra* note 277.

civilian population;[299] denial of employment, freedom of movement, proper judicial process and proper medical care;[300] arbitrary searches of homes and the denial of equal access to public services;[301] and forced labour assignments requiring civilians to take part in military operations or exposing them to dangerous or humiliating conditions amounting to cruel and inhumane treatment.[302]

12.3.2.1.1.2. Enumerated Crimes as Underlying Acts

In many persecution cases at the ICTY and ICTR, the underlying persecutory acts have themselves amounted to crimes under the relevant Statute. In other words, accused persons at these tribunals have very often faced charges of persecution based on conduct which independently constituted the crimes against humanity of murder, torture, rape, enslavement and other inhumane acts. Charged in this manner, persecution essentially captures an aggravated form of the underlying crime: for example, murder as persecution is murder committed on a discriminatory basis, torture as persecution is torture committed on a discriminatory basis and so on.[303]

---

[297] Brđanin case, Trial Judgment, paras. 1012–13, see *supra* note 290; Stakić case, Trial Judgment, paras. 791–806, see *supra* note 283; Kvočka case, Trial Judgment, para. 183, see *supra* note 290; ICTY, *Prosecutor v. Dragan Nikolić*, Sentencing Judgment, IT-94-2-T, 18 December 2003, para. 111 ('Nikolić case') (https://www.legal-tools.org/doc/f8722c/).

[298] Blaškić case, Trial Judgment, para. 220, see *supra* note 291.

[299] Blagojević and Jokić case, Trial Judgment, paras. 589, 614, 621, see *supra* note 290; Krstić case, Trial Judgment, paras. 537, 653, see *supra* note 290. See also Tolimir case, Trial Judgment, para. 857, *supra* note 277; Popović case, Trial Judgment, para. 981, *supra* note 277.

[300] Brđanin case, Trial Judgment, paras. 1031, 1049, see *supra* note 290; Stakić case, Trial Judgment, paras. 770, 772, see *supra* note 283; Stanišić and Župljanin case, paras. 91–92, see *supra* note 277.

[301] ICTY, *Prosecutor v. Momcilo Krajišnik*, Trial Judgment, IT-00-39-T, 27 September 2006, paras. 736–41 ('Krajišnik case') (https://www.legal-tools.org/doc/62a710/), discussing the Nuremberg Judgment and decisions under Control Council Law No. 10 regarding crimes against humanity for various acts committed against Jews including the denial of equal access to public services and the invasion of privacy through arbitrary searches of homes; Stanišić and Župljanin case, para. 92, see *supra* note 277.

[302] Simić case, Trial Judgment, paras. 85, 1022, see *supra* note 293; Krnojelac case, Appeal Judgment, paras. 201–3, see *supra* note 287.

[303] See also Kai Ambos and Steffen Wirth, "The Current Law of Crimes against Humanity: An Analysis of UNTAET Regulation 15/2000", in *Criminal Law Forum*, 2002, vol. 13, p. 72.

Initially, in *Tadić*, the Trial Chamber found that acts already listed under other sub-headings of Article 5 (crimes against humanity) could not also amount to an act underlying a charge of persecution.[304] It reached this conclusion based on its (ultimately incorrect) view – later overturned on appeal – that all crimes against humanity required discriminatory intent.[305] However, the Trial Chamber found that persecution could encompass acts enumerated elsewhere in the Statute (that is, as war crimes or genocide).[306]

The issue next came up in *Kupreškić*. The accused argued, consistent with *Tadić*, that the other listed crimes against humanity could not constitute an underlying act of persecution. The Trial Chamber found, however, that post-Second World War precedents including the Nuremburg Judgment, judgments delivered pursuant to CCL No. 10 (such as the *Ministries* case and the *RuSHA* case),[307] and national cases (such as *Eichmann*, *Barbie* and others),[308] contradicted the *Tadić* holding.[309] Accordingly, it held that acts enumerated under other sub-headings of Article 5 could support a persecution conviction.[310] Like *Tadić*, it also found that persecution could encompass crimes covered in other parts of the Statute (that is, war crimes and genocide).[311]

12.3.2.1.1.3. Conduct Other Than Enumerated Crimes as Underlying Acts

A more interesting question addressed by ICTY and ICTR cases has been whether acts which are *not* in and of themselves crimes within the Court's jurisdiction could also be underlying persecutory acts. The *Tadić* Trial

---

[304] Tadić case, Trial Judgment, para. 702, see *supra* note 113.
[305] ICTY, *Prosecutor v. Duško Tadić*, IT-94-1-A, Appeal Judgment, 15 July 1999, para. 305 ('Tadić case') (https://www.legal-tools.org/doc/8efc3a/). Notably, as discussed above, this was consistent with the approach of French courts in the late 1980s and 1990s, see *supra* section 12.2.4.1.
[306] Tadić case, Trial Judgment, para. 700, see *supra* note 113.
[307] See *supra* section 12.2.3.1.1.3.
[308] See *supra* section 12.2.4.1.
[309] Kupreškić case, Trial Judgment, paras. 593–607, see *supra* note 2.
[310] *Ibid.*, para. 605.
[311] *Ibid.*, para. 571. See also Kvočka case, Trial Judgment, para. 185, see *supra* note 290; Krnojelac case, Trial Judgment, para. 433, see *supra* note 283; Stakić case, Trial Judgment, para. 735, see *supra* note 283.

Judgment relied on, *inter alia*, the ILC 1991 Report, the ILC 1996 Draft Code, the Nuremburg Judgment, the *Justice* case and the *Eichmann* case to identify acts that could possibly be considered as persecutory.[312] Rather than providing a definitive list of persecutory acts, the Trial Chamber noted that "[p]ersecution can take numerous forms, so long as the common element of discrimination in regard to the enjoyment of a basic or fundamental right is present". It also noted that "persecution does not necessarily require a physical element".[313] While the Chamber recognised there is a limit to the acts which could constitute persecution as a crime against humanity, other than referring to post-Second World War cases which specified particular acts that did not qualify as persecution (such as *Flick*, where the Court determined that offences against industrial property would not constitute persecution),[314] it did not provide express parameters.[315]

However, in a stance restricting the prior position in *Tadić*, the *Blaškić* Appeals Chamber subsequently held that the acts underlying the crime of persecutions must at the time they were committed have constituted a crime against humanity under customary international law, to satisfy the *nullum crimen sine lege* requirement.[316] The Appeals Chamber in *Kordić* followed suit.[317] Their approach implied that to fall within the rubric of persecution the underlying acts themselves must have been crimes against humanity.

The point was clarified by the Trial and Appeals Chambers in *Kvočka*. The case arose from the mistreatment of Bosnian men and women in the Omarska detention camp in northern Bosnia. The underlying acts charged as persecution against the five accused were harassment, humiliation and psychological abuse. The Trial Chamber, referring to post-Second World War cases where acts such as denying bank accounts, educational or employment opportunities, or choice of spouse to Jews on

---

[312] Tadić case, Trial Judgment, paras. 703–10, see *supra* note 113. See *supra* section 12.2.3.1.1.4 and section 12.2.4.1.
[313] Tadić case, Trial Judgment, para. 707, see *supra* note 113.
[314] As noted above, but not addressed by the *Tadić* Trial Chamber, other post-Second World War tribunals disagreed with the *Flick* approach to industrial property. See *supra* section 12.2.3.1.1.2 and section 12.2.3.1.1.4.
[315] Tadić case, Trial Judgment, para. 707, see *supra* note 113.
[316] Blaškić case, Appeal Judgment, paras. 139, 141–42, see *supra* note 287.
[317] Kordić and Čerkez case, Appeals Judgment, para. 103, see *supra* note 287. See also Kordić and Čerkez case, Trial Judgment, paras. 192, 209–10, *supra* note 283.

the basis of their religion amounted to persecution, held that "acts that are not inherently criminal may nonetheless become criminal and persecutorial if committed with discriminatory intent".[318] It read the *Kordić* Trial Judgment's statement that "in order for the principle of legality not to be violated, acts in respect of which the accused are indicted under the heading of persecution must be found to constitute crimes under international law at the time of their commission"[319] to mean that "[j]ointly or severally, the acts alleged in the Amended Indictment must amount to persecution, not that each discriminatory act alleged must individually be regarded as a violation of international law".[320]

The Appeals Chamber in *Kvočka* agreed that the underlying acts of persecution need *not* be criminal in and of themselves. It noted that acts of harassment, humiliation and psychological abuse were not explicitly listed under Article 5 or as offences under other articles of the Statute but could be compared to violations of Common Article 3 of the Geneva Conventions and Article 75 of Additional Protocol I.[321] The Appeals Chamber recalled that "acts underlying persecution under Article 5(h) of the Statute need not be considered a crime in international law".[322]

The Appeals Chamber in *Kvočka* did not explicitly say that it was departing from prior jurisprudence, or provide any authority for its conclusion. But its approach accords with Judge Shahabuddeen's earlier views in his separate opinion in the *Krnojelac* Appeal Judgment. He had explained that the *nullum crimen* principle is respected even when each underlying act of persecution was not independently a free-standing crime. Citing the *Ministries* case and the *Kvočka* Trial Judgment, Judge Shahabuddeen concluded:

> Under paragraph (h) of [article 5 of the Statute], the relevant supporting crime is "persecution", the underlying act or acts being only evidence of the persecution. It is the "persecution" which must have the same gravity as that of enumerated crimes. The underlying act does not have to be a crime listed in article 5 of the Statute. It does not have to be a

---

[318] Kvočka case, Trial Judgment, para. 186, see *supra* note 290.

[319] Kordić and Čerkez case, Trial Judgment, para. 192, see *supra* note 283.

[320] Kvočka case, Trial Judgment, para. 186, see *supra* note 290.

[321] ICTY, *Prosecutor v. Kvočka et al.*, IT-98-30/1-A, Appeals Judgment, 28 February 2005, para. 323 ('Kvočka case') (https://www.legal-tools.org/doc/006011/).

[322] *Ibid.*

crime specified elsewhere in the Statute. Indeed, by itself it does not have to be a crime specified anywhere in international criminal law: it may be a non-crime. [...] But the act, taken separately or cumulatively with other acts, can give rise to the crime of persecution. [...] [T]he Statute is concerned only with cases in which the level of the gravity of the proven persecution matches the level of the gravity of an enumerated crime.[323]

This position is now settled ICTY law and has been followed in later cases. In *Lukić and Lukić*, the Trial Chamber affirmed that there is no comprehensive list of what may constitute the underlying acts of persecution, but they may be crimes listed under Article 5 or other articles of the Statute, or be acts which are not listed in the Statute.[324] Likewise in *Simić*, the Trial Chamber opined that "persecutory act(s) or omission(s) may encompass physical and mental harm, infringements upon individual freedom, as well as acts which appear less serious, such as those targeting property, provided that the victimised persons were specially selected or discriminated on political, racial or religious grounds".[325] In *Brđanin*, the Appeals Chamber held that the denial of the rights to employment, freedom of movement and proper judicial process could constitute underlying acts of persecution (so long as they met the gravity requirement), despite such acts and omissions not being themselves criminalised.[326]

Similarly, the Trial Chamber in *Naletilić and Martinović* found that "[p]lunder of personal belongings may rise to the level of persecution if the impact of such deprivation is serious enough. This is so if the property is indispensable and a vital asset to the owners".[327] As a corollary, in *Blagojević and Jokić*, the Trial Chamber found that the destruction of "non-indispensable" personal belongings such as clothes and wallets did not have a severe enough impact on the victims to reach the threshold of equal gravity as those listed in Article 5 so as to constitute persecution.[328] The Trial Judgment in *Lukić and Lukić* provides another example of

---

[323] ICTY, *Prosecutor v. Milorad Krnojelac*, Appeal Judgment, IT-97-25-A, 17 September 2003, Separate Opinion of Judge Shahabuddeen, paras. 6–7 (https://www.legal-tools.org/doc/7a9f1c/).

[324] Lukić and Lukić case, Trial Judgment, para. 993, see *supra* note 287.

[325] Simić case, Trial Judgment, para. 50, see *supra* note 293.

[326] ICTY, *Prosecutor v. Radoslave Brđanin*, Appeal Judgment, IT-99-36-A, 3 April 2007, paras. 296–97 ('Brđanin case') (https://www.legal-tools.org/doc/782cef/).

[327] Naletilić and Martinović case, Trial Judgment, para. 699, see *supra* note 283.

[328] Blagojević and Jokić case, Trial Judgment, para. 620, see *supra* note 290.

drawing a line at *de minimis* acts required to support a persecution conviction. There, the Trial Chamber was satisfied that the burning down of a Bosnian Muslim civilian's house was of equal gravity to other crimes in Article 3 and 5 of the Statute, but that the accused Milan Lukić's act of stealing a gold necklace from one of the victims was not of sufficient gravity to constitute an underlying act of persecution.[329] The Trial Chamber in *Popović et al.* likewise concluded that the burning of the victims' identity cards and passports did not have a severe enough impact on the victims to reach the threshold of equal gravity to the acts listed in Article 5.[330]

At the ICTR, the Trial Chamber in *Nyiramasuhuko* was unable to conclude that the arrest and transport of Tutsis to a certain location was of equal gravity to other crimes in Article 3 so as to amount to persecution.[331] Notably, in light of the obligation to consider persecutory acts in context – discussed immediately below – this seems a problematic result given that from this location most of the victims were transported to the sites where they were ultimately killed.

The ECCC has followed suit with the *ad hoc* tribunals, holding that non-enumerated conduct may support a charge of persecution if the persecutory acts or omissions are of equal gravity to other crimes against humanity. In the second case before the ECCC, that against Khieu Samphan and Nuon Chea for the Khmer Rouge's displacement of the population from Phnom Penh in April 1975 and certain executions which followed, the Trial Chamber held that persecutory acts may include other underlying offences for crimes against humanity as well as other acts which rise to the same level of gravity or seriousness, including acts which are not necessarily crimes in and of themselves.[332] The Chamber was satisfied that the arrests and murders of former Khmer Rouge officials, and the forcible transfer and enforced disappearance of the "city people", were committed with intent to discriminate on political grounds and were discriminatory in fact, and thus amounted to persecution.[333]

---

[329] Lukić and Lukić case, Trial Judgment, paras. 1021–21, see *supra* note 287.

[330] Popović case, Trial Judgment, paras. 1000–1, see *supra* note 277.

[331] Nyiramasuhuko case, Trial Judgment, para. 6113, see *supra* note 294.

[332] ECCC, *Prosecutor v. Khieu Samphan and Nuon Chea*, Trial Judgment, 002/19-09-2007/ECCC/TC, 7 August 2012, para. 433 ('Khieu and Nuon case') (https://www.legal-tools.org/doc/4888de/).

[333] *Ibid.*, paras. 571–74, 657.

One particularly interesting form that persecution may take is that based on hate speech. In *Nahimana* (the 'Media case'), the ICTR Appeals Chamber rejected the *Kordić* Trial Chamber's holding[334] that hate speech could only amount to persecution if it reached the level of criminal incitement.[335] It held that hate speech could constitute an act of persecution, without itself being criminalised, holding that "this is not a breach of the legality principle, since the crime of persecution as such is sufficiently defined in international law".[336]

In *Nahimana* three accused were charged with persecution (and other crimes) for having used media outlets (RTLM and the *Kangura* newspaper) to disseminate 'hate speech'. That speech included anti-Tutsi propaganda, the promotion of extremist Hutu political ideology and calling out the names and whereabouts of individual victims and demanding their extermination. In addition to persecution, the accused were charged with direct and public incitement to commit genocide based on the broadcasts and publications.

In the Trial Judgment, the Trial Chamber found that hate speech reached the requisite level of gravity for persecution:

> [H]ate speech targeting a population on the basis of ethnicity, or other discriminatory grounds, reaches this level of gravity and constitutes persecution under Article 3(h) of its Statute. [...] Hate speech is a discriminatory form of aggression that destroys the dignity of those in the group under at-

---

[334] Kordić and Čerkez case, Trial Judgment, para. 209, see *supra* note 283. The Trial Chamber in fn. 272 found that it would violate the principle of legality to convict for persecution based on speech alone, noting there was little support for the criminalisation of speech acts falling short of incitement in international and national jurisprudence. It pointed to the *Streicher* case (IMT Judgment, pp. 302–4, see *supra* note 113) where the IMT convicted the accused of persecution because he "incited the German people to active persecution". It noted that the IMT found that his acts (publishing a virulently anti-Semitic journal) "amounted to *incitement* to murder and extermination" (emphasis in original). It also referred to the Akayesu Judgment where the accused was found guilty of direct and public incitement to commit genocide and noted that the only speech act explicitly criminalised under the Statutes of the IMT, Control Council Law No. 10, the ICTY and the ICTR was the direct and public incitement to commit genocide.

[335] ICTR, *Prosecutor v. Ferdinand Nahimana et al.*, Appeal Judgment, ICTR-99-52-A, 28 November 2007, fn. 2264 ('Nahimana case') (https://www.legal-tools.org/doc/4ad5eb/). The Appeals Chamber found the *Kordić and Čerkez* Trial Chamber's reasoning to be "inconsistent with the established case law of the Appeals Chamber, which does not require that the underlying acts of persecution be 'enumerated as a crime elsewhere in the International Tribunal Statute' [...] or regarded as crimes under customary international law".

[336] *Ibid.*, para. 985 and fn. 2255, 2264.

tack. It creates a lesser status not only in the eyes of the group members themselves but also in the eyes of others who perceive and treat them as less than human. The denigration of persons on the basis of their ethnic identity or other group membership in and of itself, as well as in its other consequences, can be an irreversible harm.[337]

The Trial Chamber emphasised that unlike incitement, persecution need not be "a provocation to cause harm. It is itself the harm. Accordingly, there need not be a call to action in communications that constitute persecution. For the same reason, there need be no link between persecution and acts of violence".[338] It drew an analogy with Streicher, who it asserted was convicted by the IMT at Nuremberg of persecution as a crime against humanity for anti-Semitic writings that significantly predated the extermination of Jews in the 1940s.[339]

On appeal, the accused argued that hate speech could not be an act of persecution because it was not criminalised under customary international law. The Appeals Chamber (by a four to one majority) dismissed this argument, relying on the Appeal Judgments in *Kvočka* and *Brđanin*.[340] The majority focused on whether hate speech violated fundamental rights and whether the gravity threshold was met.[341] It found that hate speech *per se* violates the right to human dignity, and hate speech "inciting to violence" violates the right to security (the Chamber also noted that hate speech on its own could not violate rights to life or physical integrity as it would require intermediate actors to cause the harm necessary to amount to a violation of these rights).[342] As for the gravity requirement, the majority found that it did not need to determine whether "mere hate speeches not inciting violence" could rise to the requisite level of gravity, because a cumulative approach had to be taken (as further dis-

---

[337] Nahimana case, Trial Judgment, para. 1072, see *supra* note 273.

[338] *Ibid.*, para. 1073. See *supra* section 12.2.3.1.1.4.

[339] *Ibid.* However, it is worth noting that the IMT, in fact, placed significant emphasis on the temporal connection between Streicher's comments and the extermination of Jews in its final conclusions regarding his guilt. See *supra* section 12.2.3.1.2.

[340] Nahimana case, Appeal Judgment, para. 985 and fn. 2255, see *supra* note 335, relying on Brđanin case, Appeal Judgment, para. 296, see *supra* note 326 and Kvočka case, Appeal Judgment, para. 323, see *supra* note 321.

[341] Nahimana case, Appeal Judgment, paras. 986–87, see *supra* note 335.

[342] *Ibid.*, para. 986.

---

cussed below), taking into account all relevant broadcasts. To this end, it noted that the hate speech in the case

> [was] accompanied by calls for genocide against the Tutsi group and [that] all these speeches took place in the context of a massive campaign of persecution directed at the Tutsi population of Rwanda, this campaign being also characterized by acts of violence (killings, torture and ill-treatment, rapes …) and of destruction of property.[343]

Accordingly, it concluded that the speech taking place in this context meet the gravity threshold.[344]

In *Bikindi*, the Trial Chamber also held that hate speech could amount to a persecutory act. Simon Bikindi, a musician and songwriter, was charged with aiding and abetting persecution and direct and public incitement to commit genocide for the dissemination of his songs which advocated the elimination of the Tutsis over the radio. The Chamber was satisfied that "hate speech may in certain circumstances constitute a violation of fundamental rights, namely a violation of the right to respect for dignity when that speech incites to hate and discrimination, or a violation of the right to security when it incites to violence".[345] The Trial Chamber addressed the question of whether hate speech in isolation could be considered of equal gravity to other crimes in Article 3 of the ICTR Statute. It noted that, since the hate speech would have occurred in the context of a widespread or systematic attack against a civilian population on national, political, ethnic, racial or religious grounds, the facts establishing the existence of the attack could also support a finding of many other underlying acts of persecution. It concluded that "depending on the message conveyed and the context, the Chamber does not exclude the possibility that songs may constitute persecution as a crime against humanity".[346]

The Trial Chamber, however, while convicting Bikindi of direct and public incitement to genocide, failed to convict him for aiding and abetting the persecution of Tutsis. The Chamber concluded that the prose-

---

[343] *Ibid.*, para. 988.

[344] The Appeals Chamber specifically noted that the speeches broadcast by Nahimana's subordinates, "considered as a whole and in their context", were of equal gravity to other crimes against humanity, and found that Nahimana was criminally responsible for those acts. *Ibid.*

[345] ICTR, *Prosecutor v. Simon Bikindi*, Trial Judgment, ICTR-01-72, 2 December 2008, para. 392 ('Bikindi case') (https://www.legal-tools.org/doc/a7213b/).

[346] *Ibid.*, paras. 394–95.

cution had failed to prove that the accused's alleged acquiescence in having his songs played on the radio in the months in which the genocide took place amounted to tacit approval or encouragement which had a substantial effect on the perpetration of the alleged crime.[347]

Ultimately, future cases concerning the crime of persecution based on speech will turn on whether the gravity requirement is substantiated. The historical cases of *Streicher* and *Dietrich* and the ICTR cases of *Nahimana* and *Bikindi* illustrate that a Trial Chamber's factual determination will depend on *which* acts it considers cumulatively to calculate gravity, and how it considers the background and context of the hate speech. These approaches have paved the way for a possible conviction for persecution based, *inter alia*, on hate speech in the pending case of *Šešelj* before the ICTY.[348]

12.3.2.1.1.4. The Cumulative Assessment of Persecutory Acts

As noted above, in making the gravity assessment, the *ad hoc* tribunals have confirmed that underlying persecutory acts should not be considered in isolation; rather they should be examined in context and considered for their cumulative effect.[349] For instance, the *Brđanin* Trial Judgment found that:

---

[347] *Ibid.*, paras. 439–40.

[348] Šešelj has been charged with: "Direct and public denigration through 'hate speech' of the Croat, Muslim and other non-Serb populations in Vukovar, Zvornik and Hrtkovci on the basis of their ethnicities". ICTY, *Prosecutor v. Vojislav Šešelj*, Third Amended Indictment, IT-03-67, 7 December 2007, para. 17(k) (https://www.legal-tools.org/doc/f427f1/). At the time of writing, the evidence phase of his trial had finished and the Trial Chamber was deliberating.

[349] Kupreškić case Trial Judgment, paras. 615, 622, see *supra* note 2. In reaching this conclusion, the Chamber referred to the *Justice* case, which held that "the record contains innumerable acts of persecution of individual Poles and Jews, but to consider these cases as isolated and unrelated instances of perversion of justice would be to overlook the very essence of the offence charged in the indictment". Justice Case, vol. III, p. 1063, see *supra* note 7. It also referred to *Artuković* before the Zagreb District Court, which found that "the obligation of wearing a sign to signify Jewish origin [...] was not only inhuman behavior [with regard] to the whole people, but also a revealing foreboding of death". It is not each individual act, but rather their cumulative effect that matters. Krnojelac case, Trial Judgment, para. 434, see *supra* note 283; Stakić case, Trial Judgment, para. 736, see *supra* note 283; Lukić and Lukić case, Trial Judgment, para. 993, see *supra* note 287. See *supra* section 12.2.3.1.1.1.

> [I]t is in the context of the individual acts and the necessity
> that the acts as well as the violations occasioned by them be
> examined collectively that determines the gravity of the acts
> as a whole, and that it is this gravity which determines
> whether or not the rights violated are therefore 'fundamental'
> for the purposes of the crime of persecution.[350]

The ICTY Chambers have sourced such conclusions in post-Second World War jurisprudence, such as the Nuremberg Judgment, the *Ministries* case and the *Justice* case.[351]

The *Krnojelac* case provides an illustrative example of the importance of taking a cumulative approach to assess whether acts are of 'equal gravity' to other crimes against humanity. When considering acts of forced labour charged as persecution, the Appeals Chamber found that they "must be considered as part of a series of acts comprising unlawful detention and beatings whose cumulative effect is of sufficient gravity to amount to a crime of persecution".[352] It found that the acts of forced labour, unlawful detention and beatings all formed part of the "discriminatory environment" at the Kazneno-Popravni Dom prison where the crimes took place. On this basis, it concluded that persecution based on those acts was as grave as crimes expressly laid down in Article 5 of the Statute.[353] Accordingly, the Appeals Chamber overturned the Trial Chamber's finding that some of the detainees forced to work had not suffered persecution.[354]

The *Kordić* case provides an example of an ICTY Trial Chamber failing to consider acts cumulatively and in context. In that case the Trial Chamber rejected the encouragement and promotion of hatred on political grounds, and the dismissal of Bosnian Muslims from their jobs, as amounting to persecution. It found that the acts were not as serious as other crimes in Article 5. In so finding, the Trial Chamber failed to consider these acts together or with other acts charged as persecution to see if they met the seriousness requirement.[355] By way of contrast, the Trial Chamber in *Brđanin* emphasised that the termination of employment of Bosnian Croats and Muslims occurred concurrently with the plan to eth-

---

[350] Brđanin case, Trial Judgment, fn. 2585, see *supra* note 290.

[351] See *supra* section 12.2.3.1.1.1.

[352] Krnojelac case, Appeal Judgment, para. 199, see *supra* note 287.

[353] *Ibid.,* para. 199.

[354] *Ibid.,* para. 202. Duch case, Appeal Judgment, para. 259, see *supra* note 126.

[355] Kordić and Čerkez case, Trial Judgment, paras. 209–10, see *supra* note 283.

nically cleanse the territory claimed by the Bosnian Serbs. Considered together with the other denials of their rights to freedom of movement, proper judicial process and proper medical care, the charged acts were found to amount to persecution.[356]

The ECCC has also adopted a cumulative approach to its gravity assessments. The ECCC Supreme Court Chamber in *Duch* exhaustively reviewed post-Second World War precedents to find that:

> [T]he crux of the analysis lies not in determining whether a specific persecutory act or omission *itself* breaches a human right that is fundamental in nature. Rather, it lies in determining whether or not the persecutory acts or omissions, when considered cumulatively and in context, result in a gross or blatant breach of fundamental rights such that it is *equal in gravity or severity to other underlying crimes against humanity.*[357]

12.3.2.1.2. The Jettisoning of the Nexus Requirement

The IMT and IMTFE Charters both required that crimes against humanity (including persecution) must be committed in execution of, or in connection with, another crime within the jurisdiction of the Tribunal (that is war crimes or crimes against peace).[358] While CCL No. 10 did not have a nexus requirement, the US NMTs nevertheless required such a nexus in several cases, namely in *Flick, Pohl* and the *Ministries* case.[359] However, from its earliest cases on crimes against humanity generally and persecution specifically, the ICTY has rejected a nexus requirement, holding that it is not required under customary international law.

In *Kupreškić*, the Trial Chamber stated that there was no requirement in customary international law that the crime of persecution be linked to another crime in the Statute.[360] The Trial Chamber noted that when this nexus requirement first appeared in the IMT Charter, it related to *all* crimes against humanity and was a jurisdictional requirement link-

---

[356] Brđanin case, Trial Judgment, paras. 1039, 1041–49, see *supra* note 290.

[357] Duch case, Appeal Judgment, para. 257, see *supra* note 126.

[358] See *supra* section 12.2.2.2 and section 12.2.3.1.1.1.

[359] See *supra* section 12.2.3.1.1.1.

[360] Kupreškić case, Trial Judgment, para. 581, see *supra* note 2.

ing crimes against humanity to the armed conflict.[361] However, after an extensive review of the post-Second World War case law, the Chamber noted that the IMT at Nuremberg exercised jurisdiction over defendants who were convicted of only crimes against humanity (that is, *von Schirach* and *Streicher*) even "when there was only a *tenuous* link to war crimes or crimes against the peace".[362] More dispositive, the Chamber found that as customary international law had developed since 1945, the link between crimes against humanity and war crimes was no longer required.[363] Thus, as it was not required by the Statute or customary international law, the Chamber rejected any requirement of a link between the crime against humanity of persecution and crimes found elsewhere in the Statute.[364] In subsequent cases, Chambers of the ICTY have consistently rejected a nexus requirement for persecution under customary international law.[365] Article 2(h) of the SCSL Statute followed suit: the crime of persecution does not require any nexus or connection with other acts or crimes in the Statute.

The ICTY and ICTR's abandonment of a nexus requirement for crimes against humanity generally and persecution specifically must be considered in light of the addition of a *chapeau* requirement for crimes against humanity that the crimes were committed as part of a widespread or systematic attack directed against any civilian population.[366] This standard – rejecting a nexus to war crimes or other crimes within the court's jurisdiction, but requiring contextual standards concerning the background in which the crimes took place – reflects the approach adopted by the US NMTs in the *Justice* and *Einsatzgruppen* cases. As noted above, both cases rejected the need to prove a nexus to war or war crimes; instead, they each insisted on proof that the conduct was widespread or systematic, and took place pursuant to a government policy. For the NMTs deciding those cases, the contextual element was seen as the true distinguishing feature of crimes against humanity, while also providing parameters to limit this potentially broad category of crimes. The ICTY

---

[361] *Ibid.*, paras. 573–76.

[362] *Ibid.*, para. 576. See *supra* section 12.2.2.2 section 12.2.3.1.1.1.

[363] *Ibid.*, para. 577.

[364] *Ibid.*, para. 581.

[365] Kordić and Čerkez case, Trial Judgment, para. 193, see *supra* note 283.

[366] Tadić case, Appeal Judgment, para. 248, see *supra* note 305; ICTY, *Prosecutor v. Kunarac et al.*, Appeal Judgment, IT-96-23/1-A, 12 June 2002, paras. 85, 90, 93 ('Kunarac case') (https://www.legal-tools.org/doc/029a09/).

and ICTR's abandonment of a nexus requirement for persecution specifically can also be further attributed to the adoption of the 'equal gravity' test as key to determining if certain discriminatory conduct is serious enough to warrant the label of persecution.

The ECCC Supreme Court Chamber in *Duch* likewise held that by 1975 a nexus was not required under customary international law. Notably, the Supreme Court Chamber reached this conclusion despite the statement in Article 9 of the UN-Cambodia Agreement that the ECCC's jurisdiction included crimes against humanity "as defined in the 1998 Rome Statute".[367] (The ICC Statute, as discussed below, contains an attenuated form of the nexus requirement.) The Trial Chamber in the case against *Khieu Samphan and Nuon Chea* took the same position.[368]

In addition to the absence of a nexus requirement, the ICTY has held that customary international law does not require that an act of persecution be committed as part of a *discriminatory* policy or widespread *discriminatory* practice. The cases are also clear that while persecution usually describes a series of acts and not a single act, a single act may nevertheless constitute persecution.[369] Notably, under customary international law, crimes against humanity must be committed as part of a widespread or systematic attack against a civilian population (and at the ICTR this attack must have been carried out on discriminatory grounds to meet the requirements of Article 3 of the Statute). Thus, in practice the persecutory acts underlying a persecution charge will often have been committed against the backdrop of a discriminatory widespread or systematic attack against a particular civilian group defined by their membership on one or more of the identified grounds for discrimination; however, this is not a legal requirement.[370]

As discussed below, for persecution specifically (but not for crimes against humanity generally), the ICC Statute has reverted to a version of

---

[367] Duch case, Appeal Judgment, para. 261, see *supra* note 126.

[368] Khieu and Nuon case, Trial Judgment, para. 432, see *supra* note 332.

[369] Kupreškić case, Trial Judgment, para. 624, see *supra* note 2; ICTY, *Prosecutor v. Mitar Vasiljević*, Trial Judgment, IT-98-32-T, 29 November 2002, para. 246 ('Vasiljević case') (https://www.legal-tools.org/doc/8035f9/). See also ICTY, *Prosecutor v. Mitar Vasiljević*, Appeal Judgment, IT-98-32-A, 25 February 2004, para. 113 (https://www.legal-tools.org/doc/e35d81/); Blaškić case, Appeal Judgment, para. 135, see *supra* note 287; Kordić and Čerkez case, Appeal Judgment, para. 102, see *supra* note 287.

[370] Kupreškić case, Trial Judgment, para. 615, see *supra* note 2.

the nexus requirement adopted in the Nuremberg Judgment and the CCL No. 10 cases of *Flick*, *Pohl* and *Ministries*: while it does not require a nexus to war crimes, it does require that the crime of persecution be carried out "in connection with any act referred to in this paragraph [(enumerating crimes against humanity)] or any crime within the jurisdiction of the Court".[371]

12.3.2.1.3. Recognised Grounds of Discrimination and the Element of "Discrimination in Fact"

One key aspect of persecution as a crime against humanity under customary international law is that the persecutory conduct must have been committed on discriminatory grounds.[372] At the ICTY and ICTR, the grounds for discrimination are limited to three: political, racial and religious grounds,[373] the same grounds which were proscribed in the IMT Charter, and CCL No. 10.[374]

Early on, the *Tadić* Trial Judgment confirmed that even though Article 5 of the Statute referred to "persecutions on political, racial *and* religious grounds", it is necessary only to prove one (rather than all) discriminatory bases to support a conviction for persecution;[375] each of the listed grounds is independently sufficient.[376] Notably, the wording of the ICTY and ICTR Statutes on this point differs from the post-war instruments; while the *ad hoc* tribunals' Statutes set out a conjunctive list of discrimi-

---

[371] Rome Statute of the International Criminal Court, Entered into Force 1 July 2002, Article 7(1)(h) ('ICC Statute').

[372] Article 3 of the ICTR Statute also requires for crimes against humanity that the attack directed against the civilian population be committed on discriminatory grounds. United Nations Security Council, Resolution 955 91994, Adopted on 8 November 1994, UN doc. S/RES/955 (1994) ('ICTR Statute'). ICTR Courts have read this as a jurisdictional requirement only and not something required as a substantive element under customary international law: ICTR, *Prosecutor v. Jean Paul Akayesu*, Appeal Judgment, ICTR-96-4-A, 1 June 2001, paras. 461–69 ('Akayesu case') (https://www.legal-tools.org/doc/c62d06/).

[373] United Nations Security Council resolution 808 (1993), Adopted on 22 February 1993, UN doc. S/RES/808 (1993), Article 5(h) ('ICTY Statute'); ICTR Statute, Article 3(g), see *supra* note 372.

[374] See *supra* section 12.2.2.2 and section 12.2.2.3.

[375] Tadić case, Trial Judgment, para. 713, see *supra* note 113.

[376] Naletilić and Martinović case, Trial Judgment, para. 638, see *supra* note 283; Stakić case, Trial Judgment, para. 732, see *supra* note 283; Simić case, Trial Judgment, para. 52, see *supra* note 293.

natory grounds, the list in the IMT Charter and CCL No. 10 was disjunctive.[377]

Significantly, both ICTY and ICTR have recognised ethnicity as a prohibited ground of discrimination despite its exclusion from the enumerated list. The *Brđanin* Trial Chamber concluded that the concept of 'race' includes ethnicity.[378] The Trial Chamber in *Nahimana* reached the same conclusion, but using somewhat different reasoning. Specifically, the Chamber held:

> As the evidence indicates, in Rwanda the targets of attack were the Tutsi ethnic group and the so-called moderate Hutu political opponents who supported the Tutsi ethnic group. The Chamber considers that the group against which discriminatory attacks were perpetrated can be defined by its political component as well as its ethnic component. At times the political component predominated [...] RTLM, Kangura and CRD [...] essentially merged political and ethnic identity, defining their political target on the basis of ethnicity and political positions relating to ethnicity. [...] In these circumstances the Chamber considers that the discriminatory intent of the Accused falls within the scope of the crime against humanity of persecution on political grounds of an ethnic character.[379]

This reasoning – equating political and ethnic grounds of discrimination – seems somewhat legally problematic; nonetheless, it appears to

---

[377] The IMT Charter and Control Council Law No. 10 required that persecutions take place on political, racial *or* religious grounds. See *supra* section 12.2.2.2 and section 12.2.2.3.

[378] Brđanin case, Trial Judgment, para. 992, fn. 2484, see *supra* note 290. See also: Kordić and Čerkez case, Appeal Judgment, para. 111, see *supra* note 287; Kvočka case, Appeal Judgment, paras. 366, 455, see *supra* note 321; ICTY, *Prosecutor v. Šainović et al.*, IT-05-87-T, Trial Judgment, 26 February 2009, vol. I, para. 176: "In practice, discrimination on the basis of ethnicity has been accepted as a ground upon which the requirement is satisfied" ('Šainović case') (https://www.legal-tools.org/doc/9eb7c3/); Stanišić and Župljanin case, Trial Judgment, para. 68, see *supra* note 277.

[379] Nahimana case, Trial Judgment, para. 1071, see *supra* note 273; ICTR, *Prosecutor v. Théoneste Bagosora et al.*, Trial Judgment, ICTR-98-41, 18 December 2008, para. 2209. ('Military I') (https://www.legal-tools.org/doc/6d9b0a/). Cf. Semanza case, Trial Judgment, para. 471, see *supra* note 273: the Trial Chamber took a restrictive approach to the three listed grounds, and found that the prosecution had not proved that the killings were committed on political grounds.

be animated by the broader trend leading to the expanded recognition of grounds of discrimination in the ICC Statute, as discussed below.[380]

Similarly consistent with this trend, Article 2(h) of the SCSL Statute included ethnicity in addition to the three grounds of race, religion or politics. Article 5 of the ECCC Law, in contrast, adopted only the three traditional discriminatory grounds of race, religion and politics. While Article 9 of the UN-Cambodia Agreement – referring to the ECCC's jurisdiction over crimes against humanity as defined in the ICC Statute – may suggest that the list of discriminatory grounds at the ECCC includes the additional grounds articulated in Article 7 of the ICC Statute, the ECCC Supreme Court Chamber in *Duch* read the provision more narrowly. It noted that, while crimes against humanity may be committed on a variety of discriminatory grounds other than those enumerated, such a physical or mental disability, age or infirmity or sexual preference, the ECCC's jurisdiction is circumscribed by the discriminatory grounds expressly included under Article 5 of the ECCC Law namely, "persecutions on political, racial or religious ones".[381]

The group-orientated nature of the offence is reflected in the requirement that the act or omission underlying a charge of persecution must "discriminate in fact" – meaning that the result either has a discriminatory impact upon individuals actually belonging to the group targeted or the result otherwise discriminates in a manner that corresponds with the perpetrator's intent. ICTY and ICTR Chambers have considered a variety of factors to make this determination, including the discriminatory context of the attack against the civilian population,[382] and the discriminatory circumstances surrounding the commission of the acts.[383]

Different approaches have emerged over the years at the ICTY on the requirement that the *actus reus* discriminate in fact. Chambers have sought to determine whether this element: (1) simply demands that the act be carried out on discriminatory grounds; or alternatively (2) whether it also requires that the victim of the discriminatory treatment actually belong to the group targeted on an enumerated ground. This ambiguity arose because the Statute does not expressly state that an act amounting to per-

---

[380] See *infra* section 12.3.3.2.

[381] Duch case, Appeal Judgment, para. 237, see *supra* note 126. See *supra* section 12.2.3.3.

[382] Krnojelac case, Appeal Judgment, paras. 184–85, see *supra* note 287.

[383] *Ibid.*, para. 202; Military I, Trial Judgment, para. 3208, see *supra* note 379.

secution must take place against a member of the listed group.[384] Rather, Article 5(h) only requires that the conduct take place on discriminatory grounds. Due the silence in the Statute, and the absence of post-Second World War jurisprudence directly addressing the issue,[385] ICTY Chambers were forced to assess the issue from first principles.

In *Kvočka*, in apparent contradiction with the definitions of persecution adopted in *Tadić*, *Kupreškić* and *Kordić*,[386] the Trial Chamber found that discrimination occurred when a person was the target of discriminatory treatment on the basis of the accused's *suspicion* that the victim belonged to a targeted group. The *Kvočka* Chamber held that it was irrelevant whether such suspicion turned out to be inaccurate.[387] In reaching this conclusion the Trial Chamber held that "discriminatory grounds form the requisite criteria, not membership in a particular group".[388] As one commentator, Ken Roberts, has noted, on this test the prosecution need not show that the act in fact harmed a member of the targeted group to find persecution.[389]

However, the *Krnojelac* Trial Chamber, the next to address the crime of persecution, rejected the *Kvočka* approach. The Chamber limited its consideration to discriminatory acts that had in fact taken place against Muslims and non-Serbs. In dismissing charges of persecution based on an accused's mistaken belief of a victim's membership in a targeted group, the Chamber held that

---

[384] This is to be contrasted with the crime of genocide, which expressly requires that the genocidal act be committed against members of one of the listed groups: see ICTY Statute, Article 4, *supra* note 373, ICTR Statute, Article 2, *supra* note 372. Furthermore, unlike a group targeted for genocide, a group targeted for persecution may be defined in terms of positive or negative criteria: Kvočka case, Trial Judgment, para. 19, see *supra* note 290; Kvočka case, Appeal Judgment, para. 366, see *supra* note 321. See also Roberts, 2006, p. 275, *supra* note 23: "[I]t is not at all clear why genocide would necessitate a result corresponding to the intent, while persecution would not. Logically, it would appear that both offences should be applied in the same manner".

[385] See *supra* section 12.2.3.1.3.

[386] Tadić case, Trial Judgment, para. 715, see *supra* note 113; Kupreškić case, Trial Judgment, para. 621, see *supra* note 2; Kordić and Čerkez case, Trial Judgment, paras. 189, 203, see *supra* note 283.

[387] Kvočka case, Trial Judgment, para. 195, see *supra* note 290.

[388] *Ibid.*, para. 197.

[389] Roberts, 2006, p. 273, see *supra* note 23.

the existence of a mistaken belief that the intended victim will be discriminated against, together with an intention to discriminate against that person because of that mistaken belief, may amount to the inchoate offence of *attempted* persecution, but no such crime falls within the jurisdiction of this Tribunal.[390]

The Trial Chamber noted that the prior jurisprudence had required a discriminatory element as part of the *actus reus*, that is, the act or omission must in fact have had discriminatory consequences rather than merely having been undertaken with discriminatory intention. It opined that the *Kvočka* approach could lead to the illogical result that an accused could be convicted of persecution without anyone actually having been persecuted.[391] Further, the Trial Chamber stressed that, while the Statute did not expressly require that the discrimination take place against a member of the targeted group, such a standard was the necessary implication of a requirement that an act or omission occur on a discriminatory basis.[392] It observed that, ultimately, the *Kvočka* approach – finding that discriminatory grounds even without discriminatory effect fulfilled the requisite criteria – failed to account for the interests intended to be protected by the crime.[393] Finally, it also noted that the *Kvočka* approach would blur the distinction between persecution and other crimes against humanity (such as murder, torture and so on), which have as their object the protection of all civilians regardless of their group association.[394]

The *Naletilić and Martinović* Trial Chamber returned to the issue with a new perspective. While it too required proof of discrimination in fact, unlike *Krnojelac* (which required that the persecutory act take place against a member of the targeted group on an objective basis), the *Naletilić and Martinović* Trial Chamber allowed the perpetrator's own belief to define who constituted a member of the targeted group.

---

[390] Krnojelac case, Trial Judgment, para. 432 and fn. 1292, see *supra* note 283 (emphasis in original). For a discussion of this discrepancy in approach, see Daryl Mundis, "Current Developments at the *Ad Hoc* International Criminal Tribunals", in *Journal of International Criminal Justice*, 2003, vol. 1, no. 3, p. 203.

[391] Krnojelac case, Trial Judgment, para. 432, see *supra* note 283

[392] *Ibid.*

[393] *Ibid.*, para. 432 and fn. 1294.

[394] *Ibid.*, para. 432 and fn. 1293. This was followed in Vasiljević case, Trial Judgment, paras. 245, 251, see *supra* note 369.

The *Naletilić and Martinović* Trial Chamber disagreed with the "overly narrow interpretation" of the term "targeted group" in *Krnojelac*.[395] Following the *Kvočka* Trial Judgment, it held that the targeted group should not be viewed as consisting solely of persons who *personally* carry the racial, religious or political criteria of the group. Rather, the parameters of the targeted group must be interpreted broadly, and may include persons who are *"defined by the perpetrator as belonging* to the victim group due to their close affiliations or sympathies for the victim group".[396] This was consistent with the principle behind the offence "as it is the perpetrator who defines the victim group while the targeted victims have no influence on their status".[397] In such cases, a factual discrimination occurs as "the victims are *discriminated in fact* for who or what they are on the basis of the perception of the perpetrator".[398] As Roberts has noted, on the *Naletilić* definition, once the specific intent to discriminate against a certain person is established, it will be impossible for the *actus reus* to be qualified as anything but discriminatory in fact.[399]

The issue was finally resolved at the ICTY by the Appeals Chamber in *Krnojelac*. While the Appeals Chamber confirmed the Trial Chamber's definition of persecution, it disagreed with the Trial Chamber's holding that the targeted group must be defined objectively rather than from the perpetrator's perspective. Countering the Trial Chamber's example,[400] the Appeals Chamber opined that if a Serb deliberately murdered a Serb on the basis of a misplaced belief that the victim was Muslim, the Serb victim may still be the victim of the crime of persecution. The Chamber concluded that "the act committed against [the victim in this instance constitutes] discrimination in fact, *vis-à-vis* the other Serbs who were not subject to such acts, effected [by] the will to discriminate against a group on grounds of ethnicity".[401] The definition of persecution in the *Krnojelac*

---

[395] Naletilić and Martinović case, Trial Judgment, para. 1572, see *supra* note 283.

[396] *Ibid.*, para. 636 (emphasis in original).

[397] *Ibid.*

[398] *Ibid.* This approach was followed in Stakić case, Trial Judgment, para. 734, see *supra* note 283.

[399] Roberts, 2006, p. 280, see *supra* note 23.

[400] Krnojelac case, Trial Judgment, para. 432, fn. 1293, see *supra* note 283.

[401] Krnojelac case, Appeal Judgment, para. 185, see *supra* note 287. Roberts criticises this approach as falling victim to a definitional trap: that is, on this definition, once the discriminatory intent vis-à-vis a certain victim is proven, so too will the discriminatory consequences, regardless of whether the victim is objectively part of the targeted group. He al-

Trial Judgment, as clarified and adopted in the *Krnojelac* Appeal Judgment, has subsequently been followed in by the ICTY Trial Chambers[402] and Appeals Chamber.[403]

The ECCC Supreme Court Chamber in *Duch* likewise concluded that "discrimination in fact", or the demonstration of actual discriminatory consequences, was a necessary element of the *actus reus* of persecution.[404] It agreed with the *Duch* Trial Chamber that an act or omission is discriminatory in fact when "a victim is targeted because of the victim's membership in a group *defined by the perpetrator* on specific grounds, namely on political, racial or religious basis".[405] Accordingly it affirmed the Trial Chamber's finding that the targeted group in that case included "all real or perceived political opponents [to the CPK] including their close relatives or affiliates".[406]

However, the Supreme Court Chamber stressed that the requirement of "discriminatory in fact" must be connected to the requirement that the victim *actually* belong to a sufficiently identifiable political, racial or religious group. In doing so, it expressly favoured the *Krnojelac* Trial Judgment over the *Krnojelac* Appeals Judgment (and subsequent ICTY cases). Accordingly, it disagreed with the *Duch* Trial Chamber's conclusion that persecution would be established even when the perpetrator was objectively mistaken as to the victim's membership in the targeted

---

so argues that by its approach, the Appeals Chamber must have "clearly rejected" the notion that the crime's object is the protection of members of targeted political, racial and religious groups, but without saying what the purpose of the crime is. Roberts, 2006, pp. 281–82, see *supra* note 23.

[402] See, for example, Brđanin case, Trial Judgment, paras. 992–93, *supra* note 290; Blagojević and Jokić case, Trial Judgment, paras. 579, 583, see *supra* note 290; Martić case, Trial Judgment, paras. 117–18, see *supra* note 290; Šainović case, Trial Judgment, para. 177, see *supra* note 378.

[403] See, for example, Vasiljević case, Appeal Judgment, para. 113, *supra* note 369; Blaškić case, Appeal Judgment, para. 131, *supra* note 387; Kordić and Čerkez case, Appeal Judgment, para. 101, *supra* note 287; ICTY, *Prosecutor v. Lukić (Milan) and Lukić (Sredoje)*, Appeal Judgment, IT-98-32/1-A, 4 December 2012, para. 455 ('Lukić and Lukić case') (https://www.legal-tools.org/doc/da785e/).

[404] Duch case, Appeal Judgment, paras. 267, 271, see *supra* note 126.

[405] Duch case, Appeal Judgment, para. 272, see *supra* note 126 (emphasis in original), quoting ECCC, *Prosecutor v. Kaing Guek Eav alias Duch*, 001/18-07-2007/ECCC/TC, Trial Judgment, 26 July 2010, para. 377 ('Duch case') (https://www.legal-tools.org/doc/dbdb62/).

[406] *Ibid.*, para. 273, quoting the Duch Trial Judgment, para. 390, see *supra* note 405.

group.[407] While agreeing that the perpetrator determines the criteria for targeting on political grounds, it opined that persecutory intent by itself does not establish persecution unless the victim was a member of a "discernible targeted group".[408] The relevant persecutory consequences must, effectively, be experienced by the group, in that denying the individual victim's fundamental rights has a discriminatory impact on the group as a whole. Where the act or omission done with persecutory intent is committed against an individual who does not belong to the targeted group, the consequence of the act may be real for the victim in the sense of the denial of a fundamental right, but not discriminatory in fact as required for persecution.[409]

Thus, for the ECCC Supreme Court Chamber, there can be no "discrimination in fact" when the perpetrator mistakenly believes that a victim actually belongs to the defined target group, or when the perpetrator targets victims irrespective of whether they meet the discriminatory criterion, that is, when the targeting is indiscriminate.[410] Applying this approach, the Supreme Court Chamber overturned the Trial Chamber's conviction of Duch for persecution as a crime against humanity in relation to those individuals who had been detained, interrogated, enslaved and executed at S-21 prison as a result of indiscriminate targeting by the accused rather than discrimination on political grounds. It substituted convictions against the accused for extermination, enslavement, imprisonment, torture and other inhumane acts as crimes against humanity for his involvement in the relevant conduct.[411]

12.3.2.1.4. Pleading Persecution and Fair Notice to the Accused

The crime of persecution also raises important issues concerning pleading. While persecution is an 'umbrella crime', which may encompass a variety of types of persecutory conduct, an indictment for persecution must plead all the underlying acts of persecution relied upon for the

---

[407] *Ibid.*, para. 275, see *supra* note 126, disagreeing with the Duch Trial Judgment, para. 377, see *supra* note 405.
[408] *Ibid.*
[409] *Ibid.*, para. 276.
[410] *Ibid.*, para. 277.
[411] *Ibid.*, para. 284.

FICHL Publication Series No. 22 (2015) – page 530

charge. As the Trial Chamber in *Stanišić and Zupljanin* recently emphasised:

> While the crime of persecution may be considered as an
> "umbrella" crime, the principle of legality requires that the
> Prosecution nonetheless charge particular acts or omissions
> amounting to persecution, rather than persecution in general.
> Persecution cannot, because of its nebulous character, be
> used as a catch-all charge, and it is not sufficient for an in-
> dictment to charge a crime in generic terms.[412]

Accordingly, the prosecution cannot simply rely on a general
charge of persecution in an indictment – this would be inconsistent with
the principle of legality and would not give the accused sufficient notice.[413] Rather, particular acts must be charged as persecution in sufficient
detail to notify the accused as to what they are charged with and to enable
them to prepare their defence. Indeed in *Kupreškić et al.*, the Appeals
Chamber reversed the convictions of two accused for persecution on the
basis that the charge had been insufficiently pleaded in the indictment.[414]
Each underlying persecutory acts need not be contained in a separate
charge; rather such acts can be, and usually are, included within the one
charge.[415]

12.3.2.2. The *Mens Rea* of Persecution under Customary International Law

Another hallmark of persecution under customary international law is that
it requires proof of discriminatory intent. In addition to proving the *mens
rea* for the *chapeau* elements of crimes against humanity[416] and the under-

---

[412] Stanišić and Župljanin case, Trial Judgment, para. 67, see *supra* note 277.
[413] Kupreškić case, Trial Judgment, para. 626, see *supra* note 2; Vasiljević case, Trial Judgment, para. 246, see *supra* note 369; Stakić case, Trial Judgment, para. 735, see *supra* note 283; Simić case, Trial Judgment, para. 50, see *supra* note 293; Kordić and Čerkez case, Appeal Judgment, paras. 132–36, see *supra* note 287.
[414] Kupreškić case, Appeal Judgment, paras. 98, 124–25, see *supra* note 272; Blagojević and Jokić case, Trial Judgment, para. 581, see *supra* note 290.
[415] *Ibid.*, Kupreškić case, Appeal Judgment.
[416] Since persecution is a crime against humanity, the acts of the physical perpetrators must form part of a widespread or systematic attack directed against any civilian population. The corresponding *mens rea* requirement is knowledge that there is an attack against the civilian population and knowledge, or taking the risk, that the acts form part of this attack: see Šainović case, Trial Judgment, vol. I, paras. 143, 153, 162, *supra* note 378.

lying act of persecution,[417] the prosecution must prove that the acts were done with the specific intent to discriminate on one or more of the listed grounds, that is race, religion or politics.[418]

Persecution is the only crime against humanity in the ICTY Statute to require a discriminatory intent.[419] As discussed above, much of the impetus for the recognition of crimes against humanity as a distinct category of international crime can be historically traced to concerns to repress and punish persecutory conduct. To this extent, early proposed definitions of crimes against humanity were effectively a definition of persecutory conduct.[420] However, in the final text of the IMT Charter – and subsequent post-war legal instruments – discrimination was only required for "persecution-type" crimes against humanity, but not for "murder-type" crimes against humanity.[421]

---

[417] At the ICTY and ICTR, this includes both direct and indirect intent (awareness of a high degree/substantial likelihood of risk that the crime will occur). See, for example, Krajišnik case, Trial Judgment, para. 782, *supra* note 301, in relation to destruction of cultural property as an underlying act of persecution; and Šainović case, Trial Judgment, vol. I. para. 206, see *supra* note 378, in relation to wanton destruction or damage to religious sites and cultural monuments as an underlying acts of persecution.

[418] Kordić and Čerkez case, Trial Judgment, para. 212, see *supra* note 283; *Blaškić* case, Trial Judgment, para. 235, see *supra* note 291. ICTY and ICTR cases also recognise ethnic grounds. The crime of genocide also requires a *dolus specialis*, namely an intent to destroy a national, racial, ethnical or religious group, as such. While in both cases the perpetrator singles out the victim because of their membership (or perceived membership) of a particular group, in the case of persecution the perpetrator does not necessarily seek to destroy the group as such. However, what starts as persecution may evolve into genocide.

[419] However, at the ICTY some crimes against humanity can be carried out on a discriminatory basis. For example, one of the prohibited purposes of torture as a crime against humanity under customary international law may be an intention to discriminate against the victim on any grounds. However discrimination is not always required to prove torture under customary international law; torture may also be carried out to obtain information, to intimidate or to punish: see Kunarac case, Appeal Judgment, paras. 142, 144, *supra* note 366; ICTY, *Prosecutor v. Anto Furundžija*, Trial Judgment, IT-95-17/1-T, 21 July 2000, para. 162 (https://www.legal-tools.org/doc/e6081b/). Note that the ICC's definition of torture as a crime against humanity did not include the requirement that torture be carried out for a prohibited purpose, but kept this requirement for torture as a war crime. Compare ICC Statute, Article 7(2)(e) (torture as a crime against humanity) with Article 8(2)(a)(ii)-1 and Article 8(2)(c)(i)-4 (torture as a war crime in international and non-international armed conflicts), see *supra* note 371.

[420] See *supra* section 12.2.2.1 and section 12.2.2.2.

[421] See *supra* section 12.2.2.2.

Notably, however, at the ICTR the distinction between persecution and other crimes against humanity is somewhat less clear. Under the ICTR Statute discriminatory intent forms part of the *chapeau* require-ments of the attack directed against the civilian population that must be established for *all* crimes against humanity. Specifically, Article 3 of the Statute provides that the enumerated crimes must have been part of a widespread or systematic attack against a civilian population on national, political, ethnic, racial or religious grounds. It should be noted that, at the ICTR, the discriminatory aspect refers only to the attack as a whole and that each of the crimes against humanity – except for persecution – need not have been undertaken with discriminatory intent.

Discriminatory intent exists when a person targets someone on the basis of his or her membership (or believed membership) in a specific group. As explained by the *Naletilić* Trial Chamber, "a discriminatory basis exists where a person is targeted on the basis of religious, political or racial considerations, i.e. for his or her membership in a certain victim group that is targeted by the perpetrator group".[422] The *Simić* Trial Cham-ber further explained, "the victimised persons […] [are] specifically se-lected or discriminated on political, racial or religious grounds".[423]

12.3.2.2.1. The Meaning of Specific Intent to Discriminate

In contrast to the Nuremburg Judgment and cases decided under CCL No. 10,[424] ICTY and ICTR cases have examined the *mens rea* element for per-secution in detail. In *Krnojelac*, the Trial Chamber described the intent for persecution as carrying out the persecutory act deliberately "with the in-tention to discriminate on one of the listed grounds, specifically race, reli-gion or politics".[425] Such intent has been characterised as "discriminatory intent" in the jurisprudence,[426] the *Stakić* Trial Chamber has described it as a form of *dolus specialis*.[427] Significantly, the prosecution must prove the discriminatory intent for each of the acts or omissions underlying the

---

[422] Naletilić and Martinović case, Trial Judgment, para. 636, see *supra* note 283.

[423] Simić case, Trial Judgment, para. 50, see *supra* note 293.

[424] See *supra* section 12.2.3.2.

[425] Krnojelac case, Trial Judgment, para. 431, see *supra* note 283. See also Vasiljević case, Trial Judgment, para. 248, *supra* note 369; Naletilić and Martinović case, Trial Judgment, para. 638, *supra* note 283.

[426] Kvočka case, Appeal Judgment, para. 346, see *supra* note 321.

[427] Stakić case, Trial Judgment, para. 737, see *supra* note 283.

charge of persecution.[428] In other words, the intent relates to the specific acts charged as persecution rather than the attack in general, even though the latter may also have a discriminatory aspect.[429]

The Trial Chambers in *Vasiljević* and *Simić* held that the perpetrator must intend to discriminate; it is not sufficient that he or she is aware that his or her conduct is discriminatory – the perpetrator must consciously intend to discriminate.[430] In *Blaškić*, the Appeals Chamber held that a conviction for persecution requires proof of the specific intent to cause injury to a human being because he or she belongs to a particular community or group.[431] The Appeals Chamber also confirmed that it is not necessary to establish that the perpetrator possessed a *persecutory* intent over and above a discriminatory intent. In other words, he or she need not have formulated or implemented a particular discriminatory plan or policy such as the removal of targeted persons from society or humanity.[432] The *Blaškić* holding on this point is analogous to the decision of the US NMT in the *Justice* case convicting Schlegelberger for persecution. As discussed above, while Schlegelberger intended to act discriminatorily, he

---

[428] Popović case, Trial Judgment, para. 969, see *supra* note 277, citing Blagojević and Jokić case, Trial Judgment, para. 584, see *supra* note 290; Simić case, Trial Judgment, para. 51, see *supra* note 293; Vasiljević case, Trial Judgment, para. 249, see *supra* note 369. See also Blaškić case, Appeal Judgment, para. 164, *supra* note 287: "the *mens rea* of the perpetrator carrying out the underlying physical acts of persecutions" requires evidence of discriminatory intent; Krnojelac case, Appeals Judgment, para. 184, *supra* note 287, stating that the prosecution must prove the "relevant acts were committed with the requisite discriminatory intent".

[429] Krnojelac case, Trial Judgment, para. 436, see *supra* note 283.

[430] Vasiljević case, Trial Judgment, para. 248, see *supra* note 369; Simić case, Trial Judgment, para. 51, see *supra* note 293; Lukić and Lukić case, Trial Judgment, para. 994, see *supra* note 287. In Krnojelac case, Trial Judgment, para. 435, see *supra* note 283, the Trial Chamber stated: "while the intent to discriminate need not be the primary intent with respect to the act, it must be a significant one". See also Kvočka case, Trial Judgment, paras. 194–98, see *supra* note 290.

[431] Blaškić case, Appeal Judgment, para. 165, see *supra* note 287; Kupreškić case, Trial Judgment, para. 607, see *supra* note 2; Semanza case, Trial Judgment, para. 350, see *supra* note 273; Nahimana case, Trial Judgment, para. 1071, see *supra* note 273.

[432] Blaškić case, Appeal Judgment, para. 165, see *supra* note 287. See also Kupreškić case, Trial Judgment, paras. 610–14, *supra* note 2; Vasiljević case, Trial Judgment, para. 248, *supra* note 369; Krnojelac case, Trial Judgment, para. 435, *supra* note 283; Stakić case, Trial Judgment, para. 739, *supra* note 283; Simić case, Trial Judgment, para. 51, *supra* note 293; Lukić and Lukić case, Trial Judgment, para. 994, *supra* note 287; Stanišić and Župljanin case, Trial Judgment, para. 69, see *supra* note 277.

---

did so based on non-discriminatory motives, that is, for professional advancement.[433]

ICTY and ICTR cases have clarified that personal motives such as settling old scores or seeking personal gain do not necessarily exclude discriminatory intent.[434] So long as the discriminatory intent is established, crimes against humanity can be committed for purely personal reasons. The Appeals Chamber in *Đorđević* has highlighted this point in relation to rape and sexual violence crimes charged as persecution:

> [P]ersonal motive does not preclude a perpetrator from also having the requisite specific intent. The Appeals Chamber emphasizes that the same applies to sexual crimes, which [...] must not be treated differently from other violent acts simply because of their sexual component.[435]

There are obvious similarities between the crimes of persecution and genocide, their respective *mens rea* standards being one. As the ICTY Trial Chamber observed, "when persecution escalates to the extreme form of wilful and deliberate acts designed to destroy a group or part of a group, it can be held that such persecution amounts to genocide".[436] Likewise the Trial Chamber in *Tolimir* noted that the crime of persecution as a crime against humanity belongs to the same *genus* as the crime of genocide, as both encompass targeting of persons belonging to a particular group. However, it distinguished the *mens rea* for persecutions from that required for genocide on the basis the former is not accompanied by the intention to destroy the targeted group.[437]

In *Duch*, the ECCC Supreme Court Chamber upheld the Trial Chamber's definition of the *mens rea* of persecution as requiring the deliberate perpetration of an act or omission with the specific intent to per-

---

[433] See *supra* section 12.2.3.2.

[434] Kvočka case, Appeal Judgment, para. 463, see *supra* note 321.

[435] ICTY, *Prosecutor v. Vlastimir Đorđević*, Appeal Judgment, IT-05-87/1-A, 27 January 2014, para. 887 ('Đorđević case') (https://www.legal-tools.org/doc/e6fa92/), citing Kvočka case, Appeal Judgment, para. 370, see *supra* note 321: the Appeals Chamber determined that the Trial Chamber reasonably held that Radić acted with the required discriminatory intent when he committed rape and sexual violence against the non-Serb women notwithstanding his personal motives for committing these acts; and Kunarac case, Appeal Judgment, para. 153, see *supra* note 366: the Appeals Chamber held that even if a perpetrator's motivation is entirely sexual, it does not follow that the perpetrator does not have the intent to commit an act of torture.

[436] Kupreškić case, Trial Judgment, para. 636, see *supra* note 2.

[437] Tolimir case, Trial Judgment, para. 849, see *supra* note 277.

secute on racial, religious or political grounds, finding that this was supported by post-Second World War jurisprudence.[438] It upheld the Trial Chamber's conclusion that the accused "shared the intent motivating the CPK policy to eliminate all political enemies as identified by the Party Centre, and to imprison, torture, execute or otherwise mistreat S-21 detainees on political grounds".[439] In conformity with the *Blaškić* Appeals Judgment, the Supreme Court Chamber held that whether the accused "internalised the goals of the CPK behind the persecution policy or only wanted to prove himself as a loyal and efficient member of the Party" was immaterial to the finding that he possessed the requisite intent.[440] This conclusion is, again, consistent with US NMT's conclusions in the *Justice* case regarding Schlengberger.[441]

12.3.2.2.2. Proving Discriminatory Intent

The main issue relating to the *mens rea* element for persecution concerns its proof. While in some cases direct evidence may prove an accused's *mens rea* – for example, an accused's derogatory statements[442] – in most cases discriminatory intent is inferred from the surrounding circumstances. In early cases such as *Tadić*, *Kvočka* and *Krstić*, the Trial Chambers were quite liberal in inferring discriminatory intent from the surrounding context of the attack in which the acts were committed.[443]

However, in *Krnojelac* the Trial Chamber rejected the notion that it is sufficient to look at the attack to prove that each individual act charged amounts to persecution. Instead the Chamber required evidence of the discriminatory nature of each persecutory act, from which it could infer discriminatory intent.[444] The *Vasiljević* Trial Chamber followed suit,

---

[438] Duch case, Appeal Judgment, paras. 236, 240, see *supra* note 126, confirming the Duch Trial Judgment, para. 380, see *supra* note 405. See, for example, *supra* section 12.2.3.2.

[439] Duch case, Appeal Judgment, para. 240, see *supra* note 126, quoting the Duch Trial Judgment, para. 392, see *supra* note 405.

[440] Duch case, Appeal Judgment, para. 240, see *supra* note 126, confirming the Duch Trial Judgment, para. 396, see *supra* note 405.

[441] See *supra* section 12.2.3.2.

[442] Brđanin case, Trial Judgment, para. 1001, see *supra* note 290; Lukić and Lukić case, Trial Judgment, para. 1025, see *supra* note 287.

[443] Tadić case, Trial Judgment, para. 652, see *supra* note 113; Krstić case, Trial Judgment, paras. 536–38, see *supra* note 290; Kvočka case, Trial Judgment, para. 195, see *supra* note 290; Military I case, Trial Judgment, para. 2208, see *supra* note 379.

[444] Krnojelac case, Trial Judgment, para. 436, see *supra* note 283.

agreeing that it was not sufficient to infer specific intent for acts carried out within a discriminatory attack from the attack alone:

> This approach may lead to the correct conclusion with respect to most of the acts carried out within the context of a discriminatory attack, but there may be acts committed within the context that were committed either on discriminatory grounds not listed in the Statute, or for purely personal reasons. Accordingly, this approach does not necessarily allow for an accurate inference regarding intent to be drawn with respect to all acts that occur within that context.[445]

Notably, the approach initially adopted in *Tadić*, *Kvočka* and *Krstić* had the potential for over-inclusiveness, as it may treat all acts within a discriminatory context as persecutory. In contrast, however, the approach subsequently adopted in *Krnojelac* and *Vasiljević* was potentially too narrow, and could result in excluding acts for lack of direct evidence even though they took place within an overall discriminatory context.

In *Stakić*, the Trial Chamber tried to resolve the two approaches by focusing on the role of the accused within the context of the attack. The Chamber noted that in *Krnojelac* and *Vasiljević* the accused were closely related to the commission of the crimes: the former, as the warden of the prison where the persecutory acts of torture and beatings had occurred, and the latter, as a direct participant in the underlying acts. The *Stakić* Trial Chamber agreed that in such cases, proof would be required to establish that the direct perpetrator acted with discriminatory intent in relation to the specific act.[446] However, where, as in *Stakić*, the accused was in the position of a superior:

> [T]o require proof of the discriminatory intent of both the accused and the acting individuals in relation to all the single acts committed would lead to an unjustifiable protection of superiors [....] [Accordingly,] proof of a discriminatory attack against a civilian population is a sufficient basis to infer the discriminatory intent of an accused for the acts carried out as part of the attack in which he participated as a (co-) perpetrator.[447]

Indeed, in cases of indirect perpetration, the *Stakić* Trial Chamber opined, there was no need to prove that the direct perpetrator acted with a

---

[445] Vasiljević case, Trial Judgment, para. 249, see *supra* note 369.

[446] Stakić case, Trial Judgment, para. 741, see *supra* note 283.

[447] *Ibid.*, para. 742.

discriminatory intent; all that had to be proven was that there was a discriminatory attack against the non-Serb population.[448]

The *Krnojelac* Appeals Judgment provided a sounder (and safer) approach to inferring discriminatory intent from a surrounding attack:

> The Appeals Chamber may not hold that the discriminatory nature of the beatings can be inferred directly from the general discriminatory nature of an attack characterized as a crime against humanity. [...] Even so, the Appeals Chamber takes the view that discriminatory intent may be inferred from such a context as long as, in view of the facts of the case, circumstances surrounding the commission of the alleged acts substantiate the existence of such intent. Circumstances which may be taken into consideration include the operation of the prison (in particular the systematic nature of the crimes committed against a racial or religious group) and the general attitude of the offence's alleged perpetrator as seen through his behaviour.[449]

In *Krnojelac*, the Appeals Chamber inferred the accused's discriminatory intent from the Trial Chamber's finding that "the detention of the non-Serbs in the KP Dom [prison], and the acts and omissions which took place therein, were clearly related to the widespread and systematic attack against the non-Serb civilian population in the Foca municipality".[450] Further, it found that the only reasonable conclusion was that the beatings and acts of forced labour were inflicted upon the non-Serb detainees because of their political or religious affiliations and were therefore committed with the requisite discriminatory intent.[451]

The *Blaškić* and *Kordić* Appeal Judgments both subsequently adopted this approach. They agreed that discriminatory intent cannot automatically be inferred from the general discriminatory nature of the surrounding attack,[452] but that such a context *may* provide evidence of the discriminatory intent of an accused.[453] Discriminatory intent may only be

[448] *Ibid.*, para. 746.
[449] Krnojelac case, Appeal Judgment, para. 184, see *supra* note 287. See also Tolimir case, Trial Judgment, para. 850, *supra* note 277.
[450] *Ibid.*, Krnojelac case, Appeal Judgment, para. 186.
[451] *Ibid.*, paras. 186 and 202.
[452] *Ibid.*, para. 110; Blaškić case, Appeal Judgment, para. 164, see *supra* note 287. See also Brđanin case, Trial Judgment, para. 997, *supra* note 290.
[453] Krnojelac case, Appeal Judgment, para. 184, see *supra* note 287.

inferred from the context if the circumstances surrounding the commission of the alleged acts substantiate the existence of such intent.[454] The systematic nature of the crimes committed against a particular racial or religious group, and the perpetrator's general attitude as demonstrated by his or her behaviour, may also be considered.[455]

The need to take a cumulative approach to the evidence becomes particularly evident when considering rape and sexual violence as the underlying acts of persecution. The Trial Chambers in *Đorđević* and *Šainović* failed to find that acts of rape and sexual violence committed by Serb perpetrators against Kosovar Albanian women and girls amounted to persecution.[456] While the respective Trial Chambers had found that killings, forcible transfer of civilians and property crimes committed in the course of the forcible expulsion of Kosovar Albanians from Kosovo were done on a discriminatory basis, they failed to infer that the rapes and acts of sexual violence committed were persecutory from the surrounding circumstances. On appeal, the Appeals Chamber in *Šainović* overturned the Trial Chamber's finding. The Appeals Chamber, relying on *Blaškić* and *Krnojelac*, found that the Trial Chamber had failed to draw the proper inferences from the context and circumstances surrounding the commission of the crimes.[457] It found that the only reasonable inference to be drawn from the totality of the evidence was that the rapes were committed with discriminatory intent, and amounted to persecution.[458]

Similarly in *Đorđević*, the Appeals Chamber found that the Trial Chamber had failed to properly evaluate the circumstances surrounding the sexual assault of Kosovar Albanian women and the broader context in which the crimes had occurred. Specifically, it held that the Trial Cham-

---

[454] *Ibid.*, para.110.

[455] Kvočka case, Appeal Judgment, para. 460, see *supra* note 321.

[456] Šainović case, Trial Judgment, vol. 2, para. 1245, see *supra* note 378; ICTY, *Prosecutor v. Vlastimir Đorđević*, Trial Judgment, IT-05-87/1-T, 23 February 2011, paras. 1796–97 ('Đorđević case') (https://www.legal-tools.org/doc/653651/).

[457] ICTY, *Prosecutor v. Šainović et al.*, Appeal Judgment, IT-05-89-A, 23 January 2014, paras. 579–80 ('Šainović case') (https://www.legal-tools.org/doc/81ac8c/).

[458] *Ibid.*, paras. 584, 586, 591, 593, 595, 597, 599. The Appeals Chamber also found that persecution through sexual assaults was foreseeable to the three accused and that they willingly accepted the risk, and thus by their participation in a joint criminal enterprise were responsible for committing persecution based on rapes and sexual assaults: at paras. 1581, 1582, 1591, 1592, 1602. However, in the circumstances of the case, the Appeals Chamber declined to enter new convictions against the accused on appeal in relation to the rapes and sexual assaults as persecution: para. 1604.

ber had failed to properly consider that the relevant acts had taken place in the course of the forced displacement of the Kosovar Albanian population by Serbian forces pursuant to a joint criminal enterprise, which had been implemented by a systematic campaign of terror and violence aimed at forcing the Kosovar Albanians to leave Kosovo.[459] The Appeals Chamber examined the surrounding context, in particular the fact that the crimes of rape and sexual assault had occurred while the victims were, on discriminatory grounds, being deported or detained prior to deportation. On this basis the Appeals Chamber concluded that such crimes were carried out with discriminatory intent and as such amounted to persecution.[460]

12.3.3. The Crime of Persecution in the ICC: Regression and Expansion

Article 7(1)(h) of the ICC Statute proscribes the crime of persecution as follows:

> Persecution against any identifiable group or collectivity on political, racial, national, ethnic, cultural, religious, gender as defined in paragraph 3, or other grounds that are universally recognised as impermissible under international law, in connection with any act referred to in this paragraph or any crime within the jurisdiction of the Court.

Article 7(2)(g) of the ICC Statute further elaborates that "persecution means the intentional and severe deprivation of fundamental rights contrary to international law by reason of the identity of the group or collectivity".

Following the Rome Conference in 1998 during which the ICC Statute was drafted, a Preparatory Commission was established; it met from 1999 to 2002 to draft several important legal instruments relating to the ICC framework, including, from 1999 to 2000, the Elements of Crimes, one of the primary sources of law for the ICC. The Elements define the elements of persecution in detail as follows:

---

[459] Đorđević case, Appeal Judgment, para. 877, see *supra* note 435.

[460] *Ibid.*, paras. 886, 898, 90. Having found that the possibility that sexual assault with discriminatory intent might be committed was sufficiently substantial as to be foreseeable to Đorđević, and that he willingly took the risk when he participated in the joint criminal enterprise ('JCE'), the Appeals Chamber (by a four to one majority) found Đorđević responsible pursuant to JCE for persecution through sexual assaults, and entered a new conviction against him on appeal: paras. 926–29.

1. The perpetrator severely deprived, contrary to international law, one or more persons of fundamental rights;

2. The perpetrator targeted such person or persons by reason of the identity of a group or collectivity or targeted the group or collectivity as such;

3. Such targeting was based on political, racial, national, ethnic, cultural, religious, gender as defined in article 7, paragraph 3, of the Statute, or other grounds that are universally recognised as impermissible under international law;

4. The conduct was committed in connection with any act referred to in article 7, paragraph 1, of the Statute or any crime within the jurisdiction of the Court;

5. The conduct was committed as part of a widespread or systematic attack directed against a civilian population; and

6. The perpetrator knew that the conduct was part of or intended the conduct to be part of a widespread or systematic attack directed against a civilian population.

As the final two elements concerning persecution are general features of all crimes against humanity (indeed features distinguishing crimes against humanity from ordinary domestic crimes), they will not be discussed in detail.[461] The states establishing the ICC took the *chapeau* elements for crimes against humanity a step further, adding in Article 7(2)(a) of the ICC Statute the requirement that the attack directed against a civilian population be "pursuant to or in furtherance of a State or organisation-

---

[461] Such general elements reflect the customary international law standard, articulated by the ICTY, ICTR, SCSL and ECCC, that a conviction for crimes against humanity requires establishing that all enumerated crimes – including persecution – have been committed as part of a widespread or systematic attack against a civilian population, and that the perpetrator intended or knew that his conduct was part of that attack. Tadić case, Trial Judgment, para. 648, see *supra* note 113. Only the attack, and not the accused's individual acts, need be widespread or systematic: see Kunarac case, Appeal Judgment, para. 96, *supra* note 366, referring to ICTY, *Prosecutor v. Kunarac et al.*, Trial Judgment, IT-96-23/1-T, 22 February 2001, para. 431 (https://www.legal-tools.org/doc/fd881d/). Widespread denotes scale and number of victims: see ICTR, *Prosecutor v. Jean Paul Akayesu*, Trial Judgment, ICTR-96-4-T, 2 September 1998, para. 580 (https://www.legal-tools.org/doc/b8d7bd/). Systematic denotes "the organised nature of the acts of violence and the improbability of their random occurrence": see Stakić case, Trial Judgment, para. 625, *supra* note 283; *Kunarac* case, Appeal Judgment, para. 95, *supra* note 366.

al policy to commit such attack".[462] The inclusion of a state or organisational policy, in addition to a widespread or systematic attack against a
civilian population, is similar to the standard adopted by the *Einsatzgrup-*
pen and *Justice* cases to constrain the potentially broad category of crimes
against humanity – including persecution – in lieu of a nexus to war
crimes or crimes against peace.[463]

Persecution as a crime against humanity did not feature in the first
few cases before the ICC – *Lubanga, Katanga and Ngudjolo* and *Bemba*.
As a result no trial judgments have yet been rendered on the crime and the
case law is rather sparse. However, this is likely to change in the future.
Persecution has been charged against 13 persons in several pending cases,
including two accused currently in trial (*Ruto and Sang*) and three accused committed to stand trial (*Gbagbo, Blé Goudé* and *Ntaganda).* The
following analysis focuses on the elements of persecution as a crime
against humanity at the ICC, against the backdrop of the evolution of these elements in the historical and modern courts and tribunals.

12.3.3.1. The *Actus Reus* Elements of Persecution in the ICC

12.3.3.1.1. An Attenuated Nexus Requirement and the Dropping of an Equal Gravity Requirement

Article 7(1)(h) and Element 4 of Article 7(1)(h) in the Elements of Crimes
expressly require that the denial of fundamental rights occur in connection
with any act underlying crimes against humanity or with any other crime
within the jurisdiction of the ICC.[464] To an extent, this nexus requirement

---

[462] ICC Statute, Article 7(2)(a), see *supra* note 371. See ICC, *Prosecutor v. William Samoei Ruto and Joshua Arap Sang*, Decision on the Confirmation of Charges Pursuant to Article 61(7)(a) and (b) of the Rome Statute, ICC-01/09-01/11-373, 23 January 2012, para. 163 ('Ruto and Sang case') (https://www.legal-tools.org/doc/96c3c2/).

[463] See *supra* section 12.2.3.1.2.

[464] The 'nexus' requirement is a purely objective one: footnote 22 to the Elements of Crimes clarifies that "no additional mental element is necessary for this element [4] other than that inherent in element 6 [the perpetrator knew that the conduct was part of or intended to be part of a widespread or systematic attack directed against a civilian population]". Accord- ingly, the perpetrator need only know of the overall context of the attack directed against the civilian population in which he carried out his (persecutory) acts or omissions. He or she need not also have to be aware of any specific 'connected' acts. For a similar reading of the nexus requirement, see Ambos and Wirth, 2002, pp. 72–74, *supra* note 303. See also Georg Witschel and Wiebke Rückert, "Article 7(1)(h) – Crime against Humanity of Perse-

reflects a version of the requirement contained in the IMT and IMTFE Charters and insisted upon in various CCL No. 10 judgments, such as *Flick*, *Pohl* and the *Ministries*. As noted above, however, such a nexus was neither required by the express terms of CCL No. 10, and was explicitly rejected in two cases decided under CCL law No. 10, namely the *Einsatzgruppen* and *Justice* cases. In contemporary jurisprudence, the ICTY, ICTR and ECCC have dismissed the need for a nexus requirement.[465]

However, the ICC Statute nexus requirement differs in two significant ways from the Nuremberg variant. First, while in the IMT Charter and Judgment and some CCL No. 10 cases *all* crimes against humanity had a nexus requirement, under the ICC Statute the requirement only applies to the crime of persecution. In addition, while in these historical instruments and cases the nexus was essentially one to war — by way of a connection to war crime or crimes against peace — in the ICC the nexus also extends to any act underlying the enumerated crimes against humanity and genocide, in addition to war crimes, and potentially the crime of aggression.

Effectively, such requirements render unnecessary any requirement for 'equal gravity' with other acts amounting to crimes against humanity or other crimes within the ICC Statute. First, the persecutory conduct must occur in connection with acts amounting to another crime against humanity, war crime or act of genocide within the Court's jurisdiction. And further, since persecution is a crime against humanity, the persecutory conduct must have occurred as part of a widespread or systematic attack against a civilian population committed pursuant to or in furtherance of a state or organisational policy.[466] In other words, the ICC's definition

---

cution", in Roy S. Lee (ed.), *The International Criminal Court: Elements of Crimes and Rules of Procedure and Evidence*, Ardsley: Transnational Publishers, 2001, p. 97.

[465] See *supra* section 12.2.3.1.2., discussing the treatment of the nexus requirement in the Second World War jurisprudence, and section 12.3.2.1.2., discussing the treatment of the nexus requirement in contemporary jurisprudence.

[466] Paragraph 2 to the Introduction to Crimes against Humanity in the Elements of Crimes provides:

> The last two elements for each crime against humanity describe the context in which the conduct must take place. These elements clarify the requisite participation in and knowledge of a widespread or systematic attacks against a civilian population. However, the last elements should not be interpreted as requiring proof that the perpetrator had knowledge of all characteristics of the attack or the precise details of the plan or policy of the State or organisation.

of persecution represents an amalgam of *all* the cabining requirements articulated in the post-Second World War instruments and cases save for a rigid nexus to war.

The adoption of a nexus requirement can be attributed to the concern expressed by some delegations to the Rome Conference that the term 'persecution' was too vague and elastic and in need of additional limitations.[467] Several countries were concerned that any discriminatory practices could be labelled 'persecution' and prosecuted by the Court. The inclusion of a requirement of a nexus to other acts in Article 7 or other crimes in the ICC Statute was intended to ensure that criminal conduct properly classified was captured by the definition.[468] For concerned states, the nexus requirement was a way to restrict the ICC from intervening into certain laws, policies or practices that could potentially be labelled discriminatory, but which did not occur in the context of war crimes or crimes against humanity. Parallels can be seen between such discussions and those that took place in the discussions and drafting of the IMT Charter.[469]

Due to the inclusion of the nexus requirement, the crime of persecution at the ICC could arguably be seen as an 'ancillary' crime, whereas at the ICTY and ICTR it is very much a separate and distinct crime in its own right. However, as Robert Cryer *et al.* observe, "the requirement should not pose a significant obstacle for legitimate prosecutions of persecution, since it is satisfied by a linkage to even one other recognised act (a killing or other inhumane act), which one would expect to find in a situation warranting international prosecution".[470] Herman von Hebel and Darryl Robinson, two delegates heavily involved in the negotiations on crimes against humanity, note that the act connected to the persecution need not have been committed as part of a widespread or systematic attack and conclude that "the possibility of connection to any inhumane act

---

[467] Robinson, 1999, p. 54, see *supra* note 16. See also Robert Cryer, Håkan Friman, Darryl Robinson and Elizabeth Wilmshurst, *An Introduction to International Criminal Law and Procedure*, 2nd ed., Cambridge University Press, Cambridge, 2010, p. 260.

[468] See Witschel and Rückert, 2001, p. 95, see *supra* note 264.

[469] See *supra* section 12.2.3.1.2.

[470] Cryer *et al.*, 2010, p. 260, see *supra* note 467.

ensures that persecution will not be a mere auxiliary offence or aggravating factor".[471]

In a similar vein, Kai Ambos and Steffen Wirth note that

> the persecutory conduct must only be connected to a (single) murder and not to a murder which is part of a widespread or systematic attack consisting of other enumerated inhumane acts [...]. In other words, the multiplicity of grave human rights violations (which are not, as such, enumerated among the inhumane acts), e.g. severe attacks on personal property, can be transformed into the crime of persecution by a single connected murder.[472]

They argue that if a murder is committed with discriminatory intent, that persecutory murder need not be connected to another murder or crime since the connection requirement would be met by the identity of the persecutory act (murder) and the connected act (murder).[473]

12.3.3.1.2. The Fundamental Rights Protected and the Standard to Assess their Deprivation

Similar to the definition under customary international law, the crime of persecution at the ICC requires an intentional and severe deprivation of fundamental rights (akin to the "gross and blatant denial of fundamental rights" standard required by the ICTY and ICTR).

What is the meaning of "fundamental rights" in Article 7(2)(g) of the ICC Statute? The lack of definition in the Statute led to much debate in the Preparatory Commission negotiations on the Elements of Crimes. Some delegates wanted to ensure that persons would not be held criminally liable at the ICC for failing to observe values or norms recognised in some states but not others. They wanted to clarify the term, stating "such fundamental rights should be those which are recognised and accepted on a universal level, that is to say, those rules applicable *vis-à-vis* the State, either because they constitute international custom as a source of international law or because the State has accepted them through its conventional

---

[471] Herman von Hebel and Darryl Robinson, "Crimes within the Jurisdiction of the Court", in Roy S. Lee (ed.), *The International Criminal Court: The Making of the Rome Statute: Issues, Negotiations, Results*, Kluwer Law International, The Hague, 1999, pp. 101–2.

[472] Ambos and Wirth, 2002, pp. 71–72, see *supra* note 303.

[473] *Ibid.*, p. 72.

obligations".[474] After much debate, delegations agreed, however, to include a reference to "universally recognised as impermissible under international law" only in relation to any new grounds of persecution not enumerated in Article 7(1)(h), but not specifically in relation to the concept of fundamental rights in Element 1 of Article 7(1)(h). The concept of universal recognition was also incorporated into the first paragraph of the Elements of Crimes' Introduction to Crimes against Humanity – but not as a specific requirement for persecution.[475]

As for the standard to be applied when assessing the deprivation of fundamental rights, Machteld Boot has proposed, in line with case law from the *ad hoc* tribunals, that the word "severe" should not be interpreted to refer to the character of an act of persecution as such, but rather to the character of the deprivation of rights.[476] Element 1 of Article 7(1)(h) of the Elements of Crimes and Article 7(2)(g) of the ICC Statute further requires that such severe deprivation of fundamental rights be "contrary to international law". The debate at the Preparatory Commission on whether to include this phrase was resolved by adding footnote 21 to Element 1, stating that "this requirement is without prejudice to paragraph 6 of the General Introduction to the Elements of Crimes". The latter provides that "the requirement of 'unlawfulness' found in the Statute or in other parts

---

[474] Summary of Statements made in Plenary in Connection with the Adoption of the Report of the Working Group on the Rules of Procedure and Evidence and the Report of the Working Group on Elements of Crime, Preparatory Commission document PCNICC/2000/INF/4, 13 July 2000, p. 3.

[475] See Preparatory Commission document PCNICC/2000/L.1/Rev.1/Add.2. Paragraph 1 of the Introduction to Crimes against Humanity provides:

> Since article 7 pertains to international criminal law, its provisions, consistent with article 22, must be strictly construed, taking into account that crimes against humanity as defined in article 7 are among the most serious crimes of concern to the international community as a whole, warrant and entail individual criminal responsibility, and require conduct which is impermissible under generally applicable international law, as recognized by the principal legal systems of the world.

[476] Machteld Boot, "Genocide, Crimes against Humanity, War Crimes, Nullum Crimen Sine Lege and the Subject Matter Jurisdiction of the International Criminal Court", in *School of Human Rights Research Series*, 2002, vol. 12, p. 519, referring to Krstić case, Trial Judgment, para. 535, see *supra* note 290 and Kupreškić case, Trial Judgment, para. 622, see *supra* note 2.

of international law, in particular international humanitarian law, is generally not specified in the Elements of Crimes".[477]

The ICC will need to determine which rights are "fundamental" – and thereby protected by the crime of persecution – on a case-by-case basis. In addition to those recognised by the *ad hoc* tribunals,[478] fundamental rights could also potentially include the right to have or choose a religion; the right to adequate food, housing and health; and the right to obtain education. The Court may gain inspiration from instruments such as the 1948 Universal Declaration of Human Rights, the International Covenant on Civil and Political Rights and the International Covenant on Economic, Social and Cultural Rights among others.[479]

To date the prosecution's charging of persecution at the ICC has been based on acts that are arguably more 'traditional' violations of fundamental rights, namely, the right to life, the right to physical and mental integrity, the right to remain in one's own home and community and the right to property (manifest as acts of murder, deportation and forcible transfer, rape and sexual violence, inhumane acts, destruction or pillaging of property) and which are also in and of themselves criminal under the ICC Statute. This appears to reflect an effort to (uncontroversially) meet both the nexus requirement and the requirement that the deprivation of the fundamental rights be severe. For example, in the case of *Ruto and Sang*, presently in trial, charges were confirmed against the present Deputy President of Kenya and a radio broadcaster for persecution against persons perceived to be supporters of the Party of National Unity ('PNU'), a political party.[480] The persecution alleged is based on killing and forcibly displacing PNU supporters in several locations in Kenya during the post-election violence in 2007–2008.

Charges of persecution were also brought in the *Kenya Situation* against Uhuru Kenyatta, Francis Muthaura and Mohammed Ali, based on murder, rape and other forms of sexual violence, other inhumane acts and deportation or forced transfer. While charges against Ali (including persecution) were dismissed, charges (including persecution) against Muthaura, a senior member of government, and Kenyatta, the current President of

---

[477] Witschel and Rückert, 2001, p. 96, see *supra* note 264.

[478] See *supra* section 12.3.2.1.

[479] See *supra* section 12.2.4.2.

[480] Ruto and Sang case, Decision on the Confirmation of Charges, paras. 271–74, 347, see *supra* note 462.

Kenya, were confirmed.[481] The Pre-Trial Chamber found substantial grounds to believe that intentional and discriminatory targeting of civilians based on political grounds had occurred, the victims having been targeted by reason of their identity as perceived Orange Democratic Movement supporters.[482]

Charges including persecution were confirmed against the former President of Côte d'Ivoire, Laurent Gbagbo, in June 2014.[483] In the *Gbagbo* Confirmation Decision, the Pre-Trial Chamber confirmed charges for persecution based on killings, rapes and injuries inflicted by pro-Gbagbo forces in several incidents in and around Abidjan, the victims having been targeted by reason of their identity as perceived political supporters of the then leader of the opposition (and now President) Alassane Ouattara.[484] The former Minister for Youth, Charles Blé Goudé, has likewise been committed for trial on persecution charges,[485] and an arrest warrant containing persecution charges is presently outstanding against Simone Gbagbo, Laurent Gbagbo's wife, and member of his inner circle.[486] In all three cases, the alleged underlying acts of persecution are murder, rape and other acts of sexual violence and inhumane acts, with the victims allegedly being discriminated against on political grounds.

In *Ntaganda*, persecution charges (among others) have been confirmed against the accused.[487] These persecution charges are based on the

---

[481] ICC, *Prosecutor v. Uhuru Muigai Kenyatta and Mohammed Hussein Ali*, Decision on the Confirmation of Charges Pursuant to Article 61(7)(a) and (b) of the Rome Statute, ICC-01/09-02/11-382-Red, 23 January 2012 (https://www.legal-tools.org/doc/4972c0/).

[482] *Ibid.*, paras. 281–83, 416. Following recantation of witnesses' evidence, the prosecution dropped its case against Muthaura. In 2014, following further recantation by witnesses and a lack of co-operation by Kenya, the prosecution withdrew the charges against Kenyatta.

[483] ICC, *Prosecutor v. Laurent Gbagbo*, Decision on the Confirmation of Charges against Laurent Gbagbo, ICC-02/11-01/11-656-Red, 12 June 2014 ('Gbagbo case') (https://www.legal-tools.org/doc/5b41bc/).

[484] *Ibid.*, paras. 204–6.

[485] ICC, *Prosecutor v. Charles Blé Goudé*, Decision on the confirmation of charges against Charles Blé Goudé, ICC-02/11-02/11-186, 11 December 2014, paras. 122–23 (https://www.legal-tools.org/doc/0536d5/).

[486] ICC, *Prosecutor v. Simone Gbagbo*, Warrant of Arrest for Simone Gbagbo, ICC-02/11-02-01/12, 29 February 2012 (https://www.legal-tools.org/doc/1ac0b4/).

[487] ICC, *Prosecutor v. Bosco Ntaganda*, Decision Pursuant to Article 61(7)(a) and (b) of the Rome Statute on the Charges of the Prosecutor Against Bosco Ntaganda, ICC-01/04-02/06, 9 June 2014, paras. 36, 97, 142, 146, 156, 159, 165 (https://www.legal-tools.org/doc/a9897d/).

---

underlying crimes of murder, attempted murder, attacks on civilians, rape, sexual slavery, forcible transfer, attacking protected objects, pillaging and destroying enemy property which occurred during two attacks perpetrated on ethnic grounds against the non-Hema population in towns and villages in Ituri in 2002 2003. In its Confirmation Decision, the Chamber considered that all of the charged acts constituted severe deprivation of fundamental rights, namely, the right to life, the right not to be subjected to torture or cruel, inhumane or degrading treatment and the right to private property.[488]

In *Mbarushimana*, arising from the Situation in the Democratic Republic of the Congo, the suspect was charged with war crimes and crimes against humanity, including persecution, in the North and South Kivu regions of the country. The prosecution alleged in the document containing the charges that perpetrators targeted women and men perceived as affiliated with the Forces Armées de la République Démocratique du Congo based on their political affiliation, through torture, rape, inhumane acts and inhuman treatment.[489] However, none of the charges against Mbarushimana (including those concerning persecution) were confirmed. The Pre-Trial Chamber was not satisfied that the prosecution had established a culpable link between the crimes on the ground and the suspect. Furthermore, since it was not satisfied that there was a state or organisational policy to commit an attack against the civilian population (to satisfy the *chapeau* elements of crimes against humanity), the Pre-Trial Chamber found it unnecessary to make any findings as to the underlying crimes against humanity including persecution.[490]

In the Situation in Libya, Saif Gaddafi and Abdullah al-Senussi have also been charged with crimes against humanity including persecution. In confirming their arrest warrants, the Pre-Trial Chamber found reasonable grounds to believe that acts of persecution based on political grounds were committed in several locations in Libya (based on the victims' political opposition, whether actual or perceived, to Muammar Gad-

---

[488] *Ibid.*, para. 58.

[489] ICC, *Prosecutor v. Callixte Mbarushimana*, Prosecution's Document Containing the Charges and List of Evidence submitted pursuant to Article 61(3) and Rule 121(3), ICC-01/04-01/10, 3 August 2011, para. 96 and count 13 (https://www.legal-tools.org/doc/9d5b62/).

[490] ICC, *Prosecutor v. Calixte Mbarushimana*, Decision on the Confirmation of Charges, ICC-01/04-01/10-465 Red, 16 December 2011, paras. 105, 267 ('Mbarushimana case') (https://www.legal-tools.org/doc/63028f/).

dafi and his regime).[491] The alleged persecution was perpetrated through killings, inhumane acts and imprisonment.[492]

Charges of persecution have also been included in the arrest warrants currently outstanding against Ahmad Harun,[493] Ali Kushayb[494] and Abdel Hussein,[495] for crimes committed in Darfur, Sudan. These persecution charges against the Sudanese Minister of State for Humanitarian Affairs, a senior Militia/Janjaweed leader, and the Sudanese Minister of Defence and former Minister of the Interior, consist primarily of acts against the Fur group in Darfur, including murder, attacks on the civilian population, destruction of property, forcible transfer, rape, outrages against personal dignity, pillaging and inhumane acts.

12.3.3.1.3. The Targets of the Crime

The potential targets of the crime of persecution under the ICC Statute are set out in Articles 7(1)(h) and 7(2)(g), which refer to persecution against any identifiable "group or collectivity". In addition, when defining persecution in the Elements of Crimes, the drafters recognised in Element 2 that the target of the crime could be either individual members of a group or the group itself. While the terms "group" and "collectivity" appear interchangeable, when a number of groups are attacked, the sum of these groups could appropriately be referred to as a collectivity.

Element 2 requires that the reason why a person, group, or collectivity was targeted is because of the identity of the group or collectivity as such. It provides that "the perpetrator targeted such person or persons by

---

[491] ICC, *Prosecutor v. Saif Al-Islam Gaddafi and Abdullah Al-Senussi*, Decision on the "Prosecutor's Application Pursuant to Article 58 as to Muammar Mohammed Abu Minyar Gaddafi, Saif Al-Islam Gaddafi and Abdullah AlSenussi", ICC-01/11-01/11, 27 June 2011 (https://www.legal-tools.org/doc/094165/).

[492] Following an unsuccessful admissibility challenge, Libya has been ordered to transfer Gaddafi to the Court. In relation to al-Senussi, the Pre-Trial Chamber found that in light of ongoing criminal proceedings in Libya, the case against him is inadmissible in the ICC and has closed the case.

[493] ICC, *Prosecutor v. Ahmad Harun*, Pre-Trial Chamber I, Warrant of Arrest for Ahmad Harun, ICC-02/05-01/07, 27 April 2007 (https://www.legal-tools.org/doc/7276ad/).

[494] ICC, *Prosecutor v. Ali Kuyshab*, Pre-Trial Chamber I, Warrant of Arrest for Ali Kushayb, ICC-02/05-01/07, 27 April 2007 (https://www.legal-tools.org/doc/cfa830/).

[495] ICC, *Prosecutor v. Abdel Raheem Muhammad Hussein*, Pre-Trial Chamber I, Warrant of Arrest for Abdel Raheem Muhammad Hussein, ICC-02/05-01/12, 1 March 2012 (https://www.legal-tools.org/doc/ab0d6e/).

reason of the identity of a group or collectivity or targeted the group or collectivity as such".[496] In future cases, the ICC will need to resolve the exact relationship between the person targeted and the group. At the Preparatory Commission, various proposals were discussed including requiring a relationship based on membership in a group, support for a group or identification with a group. As consensus could not be reached, the element was drafted to reflect Article 7(2)(g)'s wording as closely as possible, leaving future case law to address any ambiguities.[497]

The wording of Element 2 of Article 7(1)(h) and Article 7(2)(g) – "by reason of the identity of a group or collectivity" – may suggest that the discrimination must take place against a person who is *in fact* a member of one of the listed groups. However, it remains to be seen whether such wording will quell the type of debate at the ICC that ensued at the ICTY and ECCC as to whether a person who is targeted by a perpetrator in the mistaken belief that he or she is a member of the group can form part of the victim group of the persecutory conduct. Since the ICC allows for the possibility of attempted crimes (unlike at the *ad hoc* tribunals), such a person could in any event be considered the victim of attempted persecution.

The ICC's jurisdiction covers a *significantly* expanded list of "discriminatory grounds" to that in the other modern international courts and tribunals and the post-Second World War tribunals. As Article 7(1)(h) and Element 3 of the Elements of Crimes provide, the targeting must be based on "political, national, ethnic, cultural, religious, gender [...] or other grounds universally recognised as impermissible under international law". This broad list can no doubt be attributed to the rise of the international human rights movement beginning in the 1940s, which led to the drafting of several human rights treaties and conventions with expansive non-discrimination provisions such as the ICCPR.[498]

The inclusion of gender as a ground of persecution was a significant achievement of the Rome Conference.[499] Although the prosecution has

---

[496] Witschel and Rückert, 2001, pp. 96–97, see *supra* note 264. See also Preparatory Commission documents: PCNICC/1999/WGEC/DP.36, PCNICC/1999/WGEC/DP.39 and PCNICC/1999/DP.4/Add.1.

[497] Witschel and Rückert, 2001, p. 97, see *supra* note 264.

[498] See *supra* section 12.2.4.2. As discussed above this connection was made directly in the ILC Report on its 1996 Code.

[499] The inclusion was not entirely new in the international arena: the UN High Commissioner for Refugees ('UNHCR') had approved in 1991 the idea that a person could claim refugee

not yet charged persecution on the grounds of gender,[500] it has stated in its recently adopted *Policy Paper on Sexual and Gender-Based Crimes* that "[t]he crime against humanity of persecution is an important recognition within the Statute that will help confront the issue of impunity for systematic persecutions on the basis of gender or 'other grounds' that are universally impermissible under international law".[501]

One particularly contentious issue at the Rome Conference was whether "gender" could be interpreted to include sexual orientation or identity. Some delegations favoured a broad approach to the term, while others feared a broad interpretation.[502] The debate grew so heated that "gender" became the only ground of discrimination to be defined in the Statute: Article 7(3) provides that the term "gender" refers to "the two sexes, male and female, within the context of society. The term 'gender' does not indicate any meaning different from the above". Whether this definition could include persecution on the grounds of sexual orientation is something upon which opinions diverge,[503] and may be something for the Court to decide in future cases.

---

status on the basis of gender persecution: See UNHCR, Guidelines on the Protection of Refugee Women, UN doc. EC/SCP/67, 1991, discussed in Valerie Oosterveld, "Gender, Persecution, and the International Criminal Court: Refugee Law's Relevance to the Crime against Humanity of Gender-Based Persecution", in *Duke Journal of Comparative & International Law*, 2006, vol. 17, pp. 50–56, 62–89.

[500] But see ICC, *Prosecutor v. Callixte Mbarushimana*, Decision on the Prosecutor's Application for a Warrant of Arrest against Callixte Mbarushimana, ICC-01/04-01/10-1, 28 September 2010, p. 10 (https://www.legal-tools.org/doc/04d4fa/) confirming charges against the accused for, *inter alia*, the crime against humanity of persecution "by intentionally and in a discriminatory manner targeting women and men seen to be affiliated to the FARDC on the basis of their gender, through torture, rape, inhumane acts and inhuman treatment in various locations in North and South Kivu Provinces of the DRC". The persecution charge was subsequently incorporated into the document containing the charges as persecution based on political grounds, and confirmed on that basis: see ICC, *Prosecutor v. Callixte Mbarushimana*, Prosecution's Document Containing the Charges and List of Evidence submitted pursuant to Article 61(3) and Rule 121(3), ICC-01/04-01/10, 3 August 2011, para. 96 and count 13 (https://www.legal-tools.org/doc/9d5b62/), and Mbarushimana case, Decision on the Confirmation of Charges, paras. 105, 267, see *supra* note 490.

[501] Office of the Prosecutor of the International Criminal Court, *Policy Paper on Sexual and Gender-Based Crimes*, International Criminal Court, 2014, para. 33.

[502] For a description of the debate and its outcome, see Cate Steains, "Gender Issues", in Lee 1999, pp. 371–75, see *supra* note 471.

[503] Boot, 2002, p. 522, see *supra* note 476; Oosterveld, 2006, pp. 56–62, 79–81, see *supra* note 499.

Another open question is the scope of "other grounds universally recognised as impermissible under international law". Debate at the Preparatory Commission on whether to include the phrase "universally recognised" for this element was resolved with the adoption of the phrase "universally recognised as impermissible under international law".[504] Commentators have observed that "universally recognised" should be interpreted simply as "widely recognised", and does not require that all states in the world recognise the particular ground for it to be impermissible.[505] The ICC will need to determine in future cases the exact scope of this potentially broad mandate. For example, will the crime of persecution embrace discriminatory grounds such as language, opinion, colour, social origin, property, birth, mental or physical disability, economic or age related grounds? As these grounds are included in the Universal Declaration of Human Rights, the ICCPR and the ICESCR, they could be said to be established in international law, and as such could potentially amount grounds "universally recognised as impermissible under international law".[506]

12.3.3.2. The *Mens Rea* Elements of Persecution at the ICC

Article 7(1)(h) and Elements 2 and 3 of the definition of persecution in the Elements of Crimes provide that the perpetrator *targeted* persons by reason of the identity of a group or collectivity, or *targeted* the group or collectivity as such, and that such targeting *was based on* one or more of the enumerated discriminatory grounds. This wording articulates a higher standard of criminal intent, akin to *dolus specialis* or intent in the narrow sense of 'purpose' or 'aim'.

Accordingly, in addition to proving the *mens rea* for the underlying offence and for the *chapeau* elements of crimes against humanity, the prosecution must prove a discriminatory intent. For example, in the *Gbagbo* Confirmation Decision the Pre-Trial Chamber found substantial grounds to believe that the accused intended the discriminatory use of violence against known or perceived supporters of his political opponent

---

[504] See Preparatory Commission document PCNICC/2000/L.1/Rev.1/Add.2.

[505] Witschel and Rückert, 2001, p. 96, see *supra* note 264. See also Machteld Boot and Christopher Keith Hall, "Persecution", in Otto Triffterer (ed.), *Commentary on the Rome Statute of the International Criminal Court: Observers' Notes, Article by Article*, Baden-Baden, Nomos, 1999, p. 150.

[506] See *supra* section 12.2.4.2.

Ouattara.[507] Likewise, in the *Ntaganda* Confirmation Decision, the Pre-Trial Chamber was satisfied that the evidence showed there were substantial grounds to believe that the perpetrators carried out the crimes against the non-Hema civilian population by reason of their ethnic origin,[508] and that the accused acted with discriminatory intent in relation to the two attacks.[509] The discussion is rather scant, but it appears that, similar to the ICTY and ICTR case law, the Chamber was prepared to draw the necessary inferences regarding Ntaganda's discriminatory intent from the nature of the attacks.

12.4. Conclusion

Persecution could be considered the quintessential international crime on some definitions, or at the very least the quintessential crime against humanity. In the most common form of the offence, a perpetrator severely harms or encroaches upon the fundamental human rights of a person because of that person's membership, affiliation or identification with a group. The targeted person and their group may be defined by criteria that are chosen by the victim (for example, politics, religion) or criteria that are more immutable or stable (for example, race, ethnicity, gender). Whatever the grounds upon which the individual is targeted, the harm of the offence goes, in essence, to the heart of what it is to be human – that is, the combination of a person's very individuality and his or her ability to associate and identify with others; the crime of persecution simultaneously reduces a person to their identification with or membership in a group, and attacks the group itself.[510] The crime of persecution as a crime against humanity is really aimed at protecting these fundamental features of humankind, of 'humanness'.

While cognizant of the significance of persecution as crime against humanity, in endeavouring to define the offence, states, drafters, courts, prosecutors and defendants alike have at the same time been sensitive to locating the proper boundary between discriminatory conduct which

---

[507] Gbagbo case, Decision on the Confirmation of Charges, para. 236, see *supra* note 483.

[508] ICC, *Prosecutor v. Bosco Ntaganda*, Pre-Trial Chamber II, Decision Pursuant to Article 61(7)(a) and (b) of the Rome Statute on the Charges of the Prosecutor Against Bosco Ntaganda, ICC-01/04-02/06, 9 June 2014, para. 58 (https://www.legal-tools.org/doc/5686c6/).

[509] *Ibid.*, para. 126.

[510] See Luban, 2004, pp. 116–17, see *supra* note 3.

should be a matter for domestic concern, and that which should be addressed and sanctioned by the international community as an international crime. The tension between the recognition of the importance of the values protected by persecution, and the demarcation of the domains of domestic and international concern, has been a constant theme throughout the history of this crime.

Interestingly, as the above review has shown, the search by states for an appropriate way to address the persecution of minorities by their own governments after the First World War and in the interwar years was one of the key conceptual forces that led to the birth of crimes against humanity in general. By the time the IMT Charter was concluded, crimes against humanity had expanded beyond the notion of discriminatory acts alone to include a wider set of offences than merely persecutory-type conduct. Nevertheless, the roots of crimes against humanity and those of the crime against humanity of persecution specifically remained firmly intertwined.

In the effort to establish boundaries between the national and international, drafters and judges have over time embraced a variety of threshold criteria. In the post-Second World War efforts to proscribe crimes against humanity (including persecution) as an international crime and to adjudicate individual criminal responsibility for these crimes, both the IMT and several CCL No. 10 Tribunals required that a nexus to war or war crimes be shown for both crimes against humanity generally, and persecution specifically. Eventually the *ad hoc* tribunals established in the 1990s would conclude that such a nexus was not required under customary international law for all crimes against humanity, including persecution. At the same time, the ICTY and ICTR borrowed alternative standards from the CCL No. 10 case law that had abandoned the nexus requirement for crimes against humanity, and insisted instead that the underlying acts of crimes against humanity be committed in the context of a widespread or systematic attack directed against a civilian population. Drawing from the historical precedents, the *ad hoc* tribunals also insisted that the underlying persecutory acts involve a gross or blatant denial or infringement of fundamental rights, be equally grave as the other enumerated crimes against humanity, and be done with discriminatory intent on discriminatory grounds.

The drafters of the ICC Statute further delineated the definition of persecution (and crimes against humanity in general). Not only did they follow the *chapeau* requirement for crimes against humanity of a widespread or systematic attack against a civilian population, but they also required that such an attack be pursuant to a state or organisational policy. Further cabining the potentially broad scope of the crime of persecution, the drafters reintroduced an (attenuated) nexus element for the crime of persecution, requiring that the persecutory conduct be committed in connection with another act falling under the definition of crimes against humanity or another crime in the ICC Statute. In addition, the Statute's drafters included in the definition the requirement that the relevant conduct involve an intentional and severe denial or infringement of the fundamental rights of an individual based on his or her membership in a group, done with discriminatory intent. At the same time the drafters took a more expansive view of the reasons why a person or group may be targeted through the inclusion of a non-exhaustive list of discriminatory grounds. This was no doubt a reflection of the rise of human rights in general over the past century.

In the effort by states and courts to properly define crimes against humanity and persecution, these various cabining devices have been used to endeavour to capture conduct that is best labelled persecution as a crime against humanity while they have, at the same time, been used to distinguish criminal conduct of international concern from discriminatory practices perceived to be best left to the purview of the state concerned. The question of where to draw that line has not always been straightforward or without controversy. Nevertheless, as we have argued, the evolution of persecution throughout the past century – and likely its development going forward – provides insights into the evolving parameters of the domain of international criminal law itself.

13

Examining the Origins of
Crimes against Humanity and Genocide

Sheila Paylan[*] and Agnieszka Klonowiecka-Milart[**]

Genocide and crimes against humanity, as we know them today, are two legal concepts that overlap in significant ways. However, they have assumed clear independence as separate crimes under international criminal law. For instance, one may be convicted for both genocide and crimes against humanity cumulatively for the same set of facts. Unlike certain specified crimes against humanity that have been determined by international criminal tribunals to be incapable of cumulative convictions (such as murder being subsumed by extermination), neither genocide nor any crime against humanity may subsume one another.

There is some debate as to whether such divergence was, at the origin of the creation of both terms, intentional. Both terms came into existence to describe similar mass atrocities: the Ottoman government's systematic extermination of its minority Armenian subjects from their histor-

[*] **Sheila Paylan** serves as a Legal Officer and Greffier of the Supreme Court Chamber of the Extraordinary Chambers of the Courts of Cambodia ('ECCC'). She has previously worked in the Trial Chambers, Appeals Chamber, and the Office of the President of the International Criminal Tribunal for Rwanda. She is a graduate of McGill University, Canada, with degrees in both Common Law and Civil Law, and holds a postgraduate certificate in international justice, as well as a postgraduate diploma in human rights, from the University of London.

[**] **Agnieszka Klonowiecka-Milart** currently serves as an international judge at the Supreme Court Chamber of the ECCC. Previously she was a United Nations-appointed international judge at the Supreme Court of Kosovo, adjudicating, among other things, charges of genocide and war crimes arising from the conflict in 1998–1999. She started her legal career as an Assistant Professor at the Law Faculty, Marie Curie Sklodowska University, Lublin, Poland. She entered the judiciary in 1991. Since 1998 she has been active in the area of the international rule of law, including UN judicial and legal reform programmes in Bosnia-Herzegovina and Afghanistan. The authors wish to thank Siobhan Coley-Amin and Alexander Foster for their assistance with an earlier draft of this chapter. The views expressed here reflect those of the authors and are not intended to represent or reflect the views of the United Nations.

ic homeland within the territory constituting the present-day Republic of Turkey from 1915 to 1918; and the systematic extermination of six million Jews by the Nazi regime and its collaborators, which took place throughout Nazi Germany and German-occupied territories in Europe between 1941 and 1945.

That these two legal terms emerged in the twentieth century should not be taken to correlate with the historical emergence of the underlying acts of genocide or crimes against humanity. Indeed, accounts of genocide and crimes against humanity may be traced as far back as antiquity, even arising out of Greek mythology; Homer quotes King Agamemnon's quintessential pronouncement of root-and-branch genocide:

> We are not going to leave a single one of them alive, down
> to the babies in their mothers' wombs – not even they must
> live. The whole people must be wiped out of existence, and
> none be left to think of them and shed a tear.[1]

While it is unclear whether this pronouncement had any basis in fact, there are more factually reliable, and widely known, cases that might fall under the modern definition of genocide and crimes against humanity. These include the destruction of Carthage, the destruction of the Albigenses and Waldenses, the Crusades, the march of the Teutonic Knights, the destruction of the Christians under the Ottoman Empire, the massacres of the Herreros in southern Africa, the 1894–1896 massacres of the Armenians, followed by their extermination in 1915–1918, the slaughter of Christian Assyrians in 1933, the destruction of the Maronites, and the pogroms against the Jews in Czarist Russia and Romania. Indeed, as the world's most famous genocide scholar, Raphael Lemkin, stated: "By destroying six million Jews, several million Slavs, and almost all the Gypsies of Europe, the Nazis have focused our attention more sharply on this phenomenon, which was not new in itself".[2]

It can thus be said that, irrespective of a variety of root causes and rationalisations, humanity has always nurtured conceptions of social difference that generate a sense of group belonging and group exclusion. Being a member of a group may enable a person to cope with a threatened

---

[1] Quoted in Frank Chalk and Kurt Jonassohn, *The History and Sociology of Genocide: Analyses and Case Studies*, Yale University Press, New Haven, NJ, 1990, p. 58.
[2] See Raphael Lemkin, "Genocide as a Crime under International Law", in *United Nations Bulletin*, 15 January 1948, vol. 4, p. 70.

identity and serve the need for connectedness to other human beings. Within a group, shared enmity towards another group may intensify feelings of belonging and strengthen group identity.[3] Such sentiment and antagonism, in turn, may often lead to violent action towards the other group. In this way, the origins of crimes against humanity and genocide, historically or anthropologically speaking, can be traced back for centuries.

Nonetheless, despite the long-standing existence of the acts predicating crimes against humanity and genocide, efforts to prohibit such acts as international crimes did not arise until after the First and Second World Wars. The origins of the criminal prosecution of genocide and crimes against humanity began with the recognition at the beginning of the twentieth century that the persecution of certain groups was not only morally reprehensible but should also incur legal responsibility.

13.1. Influence of the First World War

On 24 May 1915 the allied governments of France, Britain and Russia made a joint declaration denouncing a series of massacres against Armenians in the Ottoman Empire, which had begun to occur in the context of the First World War ('1915 Declaration'). This marked the most notorious instance in recorded history of the use of a phrase that was to become one of the most powerful concepts of international law – "crimes against humanity".[4] The 1915 Declaration reads as follows:

> For about a month the Kurd and Turkish populations of Armenia has been massacring Armenians with the connivance and often assistance of Ottoman authorities. Such massacres took place in middle April at Erzerum, Dertchun, Eguine, Bitlis, Mouch, Sassoun, Zeitoun, and through Cilici[a]. Inhabitants of about one hundred villages near Van were all murdered. In that city, [the] Armenian quarter is besieged by Kurds. At the same time in Constantinople [the] government ill-treats inoffensive Armenian population. *In view of these new crimes of Turkey against humanity and civilization* the Allied governments announce publicly to the Sublime Porte that they will hold personally responsible [for] these crimes

---

[3] Ervin Staub, *The Roots of Evil: The Origins of Genocide and Other Group Violence*, Cambridge University Press, Cambridge, 1989, p. 49.

[4] William A. Schabas, *Genocide in International Law*, Cambridge University Press, Cambridge, 2000, pp. 16–17.

> all members of the Ottoman government and those of their
> agents who are implicated in such massacres.[5]

Such a pronouncement differed drastically from any previously made in the international legal or political arena. Instead of conforming to the status quo and religiously observing state sovereignty and immunity of heads of state, the pronouncement made a specific threat of individualised sanctions and accountability for government officials involved in atrocities against their own citizens. The language of the pronouncement has been traced to the so-called Martens Clause, which was first inserted, at the suggestion of the Russian delegate at the Hague Peace Conference of 1899, in the preamble of the 1899 Hague Convention II with respect to the Laws and Customs of War on Land, and then restated (in a slightly modified form) in the preamble of the 1907 Hague Convention IV on the same matter. It reads as follows:

> Until a more complete code of the laws of war has been is-
> sued, the High Contracting Parties deem it expedient to de-
> clare that, in cases not included in the Regulations adopted
> by them, the inhabitants and the belligerents remain under
> the protection and the rule of the principles of the law of na-
> tions, as they result from the usages established among civi-
> lized peoples, *from the laws of humanity, and the dictates of
> the public conscience.*[6]

Since 1907 the Martens Clause has been hailed as a significant turning point in the history of international humanitarian law. It arguably represents the first recognition of the existence of international legal rules embodying humanitarian considerations, and the notion that these rules are no less binding than those motivated by military or political concerns. Before the Martens Clause, international treaties and declarations had

---

[5] Dispatch sent on 29 May 1915 by US Secretary of State, William Jennings Bryan, to the US Embassy in Constantinople (now Istanbul), Turkey to be forwarded to the Turkish government. Document No. RG 59, 867.4016/67, US National Archives (emphasis added).

[6] Convention Respecting the Laws and Customs of War by Land (Hague IV), 18 October 1907, [1910] United Kingdom Treaty Series 9, preamble (emphasis added). See also Convention with Respect to the Laws and Customs of War on Land (Hague II), 29 July 1899, 32 Stat. 1803, Treaty Series 403, preamble: "Until a more complete code of the laws of war is issued, the High Contracting Parties think it right to declare that in cases not included in the Regulations adopted by them, populations and belligerents remain under the protection and empire of the principles of international law, as they result from the usages established between civilized nations, from the laws of humanity and the requirements of the public conscience".

simply proclaimed the importance of humanitarian considerations, leaving each belligerent to decide for itself whether its acts were humane and calling upon states to uphold moral principles.[7] By contrast, the Martens Clause proclaimed the existence of principles or rules of customary international law arising not only from state practice, but also from humanity and the public conscience.[8]

The Armenian genocide is conventionally held to have started on 24 April 1915, the day Ottoman authorities rounded up and arrested some 250 Armenian intellectuals and community leaders in Constantinople (now Istanbul). Armenians of the Ottoman Empire had already been subjected to massacres in the mid-1890s, with estimates of the dead ranging from 80,000 to 300,000.[9] The massacres were carried out during the reign of Abdul Hamid (Abdulhamit) II (1876–1909), the last Sultan effectively to rule over the Ottoman Empire, and accordingly are commonly known as the Hamidian massacres. The origins of the massacres and hostility to the Armenians lay in the gradual – and eventually, by the First World War, sudden and final – decline of the Ottoman Empire in the last quarter of the nineteenth century. This coincided with Armenians of the empire, long considered second-class citizens, calling for civil reforms and better treatment from their government from the mid-1860s onwards.[10] Their success in gaining promise of reform through international pressure – for example, through European intervention during the 1878 Congress of Berlin culminating in the 1878 Treaty of Berlin, Article 61 of which provided for reforms – was not met with action or implementation, but rather violent reprisals from the Sultan who was not prepared to relinquish any power. He began to express the belief that the woes of the Ottoman Empire stemmed from "the endless persecutions and hostilities of the Christian world".[11]

The massacres marked a new threshold of violence in the Ottoman Empire, particularly because they occurred in peacetime with none of the exigencies of war normally invoked as a legal justification for such action. They would, however, fall short of 'genocide' in the modern sense.

---

[7] Antonio Cassese, "The Martens Clause: Half a Loaf or Simply Pie in the Sky?", in *European Journal of International Law*, 2000, vol. 11, no. 1, p. 188.

[8] *Ibid.*, pp. 188–89.

[9] Taner Akçam, A Shameful Act: The Armenian Genocide and the Question of Turkish Responsibility, Metropolitan Books, New York, 2006, p. 42.

[10] *Ibid.*, p. 36.

[11] *Ibid.*, p. 43.

The Sultan's intention was not to destroy of the Armenian group *per se*, but rather to dissuade the Armenians from entertaining any notions of seeing reforms introduced under Western pressure. By undermining their expectations and the sense of self-reliance they hoped to develop in order to cope with the aggravated disorder and misrule in the empire's eastern provinces, the Sultan sought to strike a severe blow to Armenian efforts to organise politically. The impunity with which the Hamidian massacres were carried out exposed the serious vulnerability of the Armenian population as the Ottoman Empire went into further decline. The Hamidian massacres had set a precedent. All of its elements would be reproduced during the Armenian genocide.[12]

Significant as it was as an expression of *opinio juris*, the 1915 Declaration did little more than appease the conscience of Europe. The 1915 Declaration was neither followed by any action nor did it stop the atrocities. It did, however, render the Ottoman government determined to "keep the news [of the annihilation of the Armenians], as long as possible, from the outside world".[13] Following the arrests on 24 April 1915, the Armenian genocide was then carried out over the next four years and implemented in two phases: the wholesale killing of the able-bodied male population through massacre and subjection of army conscripts to forced labour, followed by the deportation of women, children, the elderly and infirm on death marches leading to the Syrian desert.[14] Driven forward by military escorts, the deportees were deprived of food and water and subjected to systematic robbery, rape and massacre. The intent to destroy the Armenian group in whole had by then reached its zenith. Even loyal Armenians were categorised as disloyal and treated as such.[15] In his memoirs, the

---

[12] Rouben Paul Adalian, "Hamidian (Armenian) Massacres", in Israel W. Charny (ed.), *Encyclopedia of Genocide*, vol. 1, ABC-CLIO, Santa Barbara, CA, 1999, pp. 287–88.

[13] Henry Morgenthau, *Ambassador Morgenthau's Story*, Wayne State University Press, Detroit, 2003, p. 224 (originally published by Doubleday, Garden City, NY, 1918).

[14] Arnold Toynbee, "A Summary of Armenian History up to and Including the Year 1915", The Treatment of Armenians in the Ottoman Empire 1915-16: Documents Presented to Viscount Grey of Fallodon, Secretary of State for Foreign Affairs, G.P. Putnam's Sons, for His Majesty's Stationery Office, New York and London, 1916, pp. 637–53.

[15] Ugur Ümit Üngör, *The Making of Modern Turkey: Nation and State in Eastern Anatolia, 1913–1950*, Oxford University Press, Oxford, 2011, pp. 67–68: "The Armenian Catholic Bishop Ignatius Maloyan had become anxious about the worsening situation and seems to have written a letter to his co-religionists, in case something happened to him. Maloyan urged his parish to remain calm and loyal to the government […]. On 5 May 1915 Talaat authorized the Third Army to disarm all Armenian gendarmes in Diyarbekir province. This

American Ambassador to Constantinople at the time, Henry Morgenthau, recounts one of several conversations with Mehmet Talaat (one of the triumviri of the Committee of Union and Progress that *de facto* ruled the declining Ottoman Empire during the First World War, and widely considered to be the main mastermind and perpetrator of the Armenian genocide)[16] to try to convince him to end the Armenian massacres:

> "It is no use for you to argue," Talaat answered, "we have already disposed of three quarters of the Armenians; there are none at all left in Bitlis, Van, and Erzeroum. The hatred between the Turks and the Armenians is now so intense that we have got to finish with them. If we don't, they will plan their revenge. [...] We will not have the Armenians anywhere in Anatolia. They can live in the desert but nowhere else." I still attempted to persuade Talaat that the treatment of the Armenians was destroying Turkey in the eyes of the world, and that his country would never be able to recover from this infamy. [...] I had many talks with Talaat on the Armenians, but I never succeeded in moving him to the slightest degree. [...] He seemed to me always to have the deepest personal feeling in this matter, and his antagonism to the Armenians seemed to increase as their sufferings increased. One day, discussing a particular Armenian, I told Talaat that he was mistaken in regarding this man as an enemy of the Turks; that in reality he was their friend. "No Armenian," replied Talaat, "can be our friend after what we have done to them".[17]

The total number of Armenians killed as a result has been estimated at between 1 and 1.5 million (out of a population of approximately 2 million). This death toll does not take into account the large numbers of Armenians, especially women and children, who were forced to convert to Islam as a structural element of the annihilation of the Armenian people.[18]

---

way, even loyal Armenians were categorized as disloyal and treated as such" (internal citations omitted).

[16] See, *inter alia*, Akçam, 2006, pp. 165, 186–87, *supra* note 9.

[17] Morgenthau, 2003, pp. 232–33, see *supra* note 13.

[18] See Ara Sarafian, "The Absorption of Armenian Women and Children Into Muslim Households as a Structural Component of the Armenian Genocide", in Omar Bartov and Phyllis Mack (eds.), *In God's Name: Genocide and Religion in the Twentieth Century*, Berghahn Books, Oxford, 2001, pp. 209–17. See also Norman M. Naimark, *Fires of Hatred: Ethnic Cleansing in Twentieth-Century Europe*, Harvard University Press, Cambridge, MA, 2002, p. 42.

Following the Armenian genocide, Britain, Italy and France signed the 1920 Treaty of Sèvres on the part of the victorious Allies[19] – their peace treaty with Turkey – envisaging both the establishment of military tribunals to prosecute war crimes and international trials to prosecute the massacres. In particular, Article 226 of the Treaty of Sèvres provided as follows:

> The Turkish Government recognizes the right of the Allied Powers to bring before military tribunals persons accused of having committed acts in violation of the laws and customs of war. Such persons shall, if found guilty, be sentenced to punishments laid down by the law. This provision will apply notwithstanding any proceedings or prosecution before a tribunal in Turkey or in the territory of her allies.[20]

By contrast, Article 230 of the Treaty of Sèvres provided that:

> The Turkish Government undertakes to hand over to the Allied Powers the persons whose surrender may be required by the latter as being responsible for the massacres committed during the continuance of the state of war on territory which formed part of the Turkish Empire on August 1, 1914.
>
> The Allied Powers reserve to themselves the right to designate the tribunal which shall try the persons so accused, and the Turkish Government undertakes to recognise such tribunal.
>
> In the event of the League of Nations having created in sufficient time a tribunal competent to deal with the said massacres, the Allied Powers reserve to themselves the right to bring the accused persons mentioned above before such tribunal, and the Turkish Government undertakes equally to recognise such tribunal.[21]

By providing for separate modes of punishment for the massacres and for the war crimes, the Treaty of Sèvres demonstrated that the massacres – that is, "these new crimes of Turkey against humanity and civilization" – were viewed as distinct from war crimes. The Treaty also provided for the restitution of all properties stolen from "Turkish subjects of non-

---

[19] The Treaty of Peace between the Allied and Associated Powers and Turkey, 10 August 1920 ('Treaty of Sèvres'), reprinted in *American Journal of International Law*, 1921, vol. 15, supp., pp. 179 ff.

[20] *Ibid.*, Art. 226.

[21] *Ibid.*, Art. 230.

Turkish race who have been forcibly driven from their homes by fear of massacre or any other form of pressure since January 1, 1914".[22]

However, the Treaty of Sèvres was never ratified, as it was seen to be very harsh in its terms, similarly to the 1919 Treaty of Versailles ending the war between the Allies and Germany.[23] Among other things, though recognising the inability of Turkey to make "complete reparation" for its responsibility for the First World War,[24] the Treaty of Sèvres imposed on Turkey the obligation to pay "for all loss or damage [...] suffered by civilian nationals of the Allied Powers, in respect of their persons or property, through the action or negligence of the Turkish authorities during the war and up to the coming into force of the present Treaty".[25]

These and other crippling terms – such as carving up the remaining territories of the Ottoman Empire among the Allies, gaining control over Turkey's finances, and turning the Dardanelles Strait into international waters – angered and embittered many Turks, including Mustafa Kemal Atatürk. Atatürk, a military officer and leader of the Turkish national movement, insisted on safeguarding Turkey's interests and independence and would subsequently successfully lead the 1919–1922 Turkish War of Independence, thereby defeating the Allies and forcing them back to the negotiating table.[26] This culminated in replacing the Treaty of Sèvres with the 1923 Treaty of Lausanne, which restored large territories to the Turks, and omitted not only any provision on punishment equivalent to Articles 226 or 230 of the Treaty of Sèvres but also any mention of the Armenians. The Treaty of Lausanne was instead accompanied by a declaration of amnesty for all offences committed from 1 August 1914 to 20 November

---

[22]   *Ibid.*, Art. 144.

[23]   The Treaty of Peace between the Allied and Associated Powers and Germany, 28 June 1919 ('Versailles Treaty') (https://www.legal-tools.org/doc/a64206/).

[24]   See Treaty of Sèvres, Art. 231, *supra* note 19: "Turkey recognizes that by joining the war of aggression which Germany and Austria-Hungary waged against the Allied Powers she has caused the latter losses and sacrifices of all kinds for which she ought to make complete reparation. On the other hand, the Allied Powers recognize that the resources of Turkey are not sufficient to enable her to make complete reparation".

[25]   *Ibid.*, Art. 235.

[26]   Donald Bloxham, The Great Game of Genocide: Imperialism, Nationalism, and the Destruction of the Ottoman Armenians, Oxford University Press, Oxford, 2005, pp. 101–2, 147.

1922.[27] The former British Prime Minister David Lloyd George called it an "abject, cowardly, and infamous surrender".[28]

As a result, no international prosecution of the perpetrators of the Armenian genocide ever occurred. At the national level, a series of courts martial were held in 1919–20 in Constantinople at which the leadership of the Committee of Union and Progress and selected former officials were court martialled for, *inter alia*, subversion of the constitution, wartime profiteering and the massacres of both Armenians and Greeks.[29] They were, however, disingenuous, only serving as a stage for political battles to help the Liberal Union Party root out the Committee of Union and Progress from the political arena.[30] Some Ottoman officials were held as prisoners of war on Malta to be tried in the international tribunal envisaged by the Treaty of Sèvres. However, as indicated above, those trials never took place, instead an exchange for British prisoners of war was done as a result of Article 119 of the Treaty of Lausanne. The British Foreign Secretary Lord Curzon said the subsequent release of many of the Turkish prisoners was "a great mistake".[31] Nevertheless, despite efforts to avoid criminal or pecuniary responsibility for the massacres and mass theft of Armenian properties – culminating in full-blown denial of the Armenian genocide today[32] – Atatürk publicly acknowledged that the atrocities committed against the Armenians were "a shameful act".[33]

---

27 The Treaty of Peace with Turkey Signed at Lausanne, 24 July 1923, *The Treaties of Peace, 1919–1923*, vol. 2, Carnegie Endowment for International Peace, New York, 1924. See also *ibid.*, pp. 166–69.

28 David Lloyd George, *The Truth about Peace Treaties*, Gollancz, London, 1938, p. 1351.

29 Taner Akçam, *Armenien und der Völkermord: Die Istanbuler Prozesse und die Türkische Nationalbewegung*, Hamburger Edition, Hamburg, 1996, p. 185.

30 Klaus Detlev Grothusen, Die Türkei in Europa, Beiträge des Südosteuropa-arbeitskreises der Deutschen Forschungsgemeinschaft zum IV. Internationalen Südosteuropa-*Kongreß der Association Internationale d'Études du Sud-East Européen*, Ankara, 13–18 August 1979, p. 35.

31 FO 371/7882/E4425, folio 182, The National Archives, UK: "The less we say about these people [the Turks detained at Malta] the better. [...] I had to explain why we released the Turkish deportees from Malta skating over thin ice as quickly as I could. There would have been a row I think. [...] The staunch belief among members [of Parliament is] that one British prisoner is worth a shipload of Turks, and so the exchange was excused".

32 The topic of the Turkish government's denial of the Armenian Genocide falls outside the scope of the present chapter. For more on the subject, see, *inter alia*, Yair Auron, *The Banality of Denial: Israel and the Armenian Genocide*, Transaction Publishers, Piscataway, 2004; Richard G. Hovannisian (ed.), *Remembrance and Denial: The Case of the Armenian Genocide*, Wayne State University Press, Detroit, 1999; Vahakn Dadrian, *Key Elements in*

The story of the Leipzig trials is not entirely dissimilar, with initial plans being set out in the Treaty of Versailles, though some important differences arise. For instance, Article 227 of the Treaty of Versailles provided that the ex-Kaiser was to be "publicly arraigned" for "a supreme offence against international morality and the sanctity of treaties" before an international tribunal. As such, the proceedings were not intended to be criminal in the municipal sense, but rather of a moral character, because aggression was not seen to be an international crime at the time. Nevertheless, similarly to the failed promise of international prosecution in the 1915 Declaration and the Treaty of Sèvres, Article 227 of the Treaty of Versailles was never implemented as the Netherlands refused to extradite the ex-Kaiser and hand him over to the Allies.[34]

The absence of an effective international penal response to those "crimes of Turkey against humanity and civilization" thus limited the significance of the phrase to an acknowledgement that customary international law arguably recognised certain crimes against humanity, though not explicitly called as such. The absence of an actual prosecution of crimes against humanity also left the substantive content of the crime unclear.[35] Nonetheless, the Treaty of Sèvres became an important precedent for the international community when formulating its response to atrocities committed by Axis countries during the 1930s and 1940s. Indeed, over the next two decades after the First World War, criminal law specialists began considering and drawing up proposals for prosecution and representation of international crimes. For instance, the International Law Association and the International Association for Penal Law studied the possibility of establishing an international criminal jurisdiction.[36]

---

the Turkish Denial of the Armenian Genocide: A Case Study of Distortion and Falsification, Zoryan Institute, Arlington, 1999.

[33] Akçam, 2006, pp. 12–13, 335–36, 348, see *supra* note 9.

[34] See Robert Cryer, Prosecuting International Crimes: Selectivity and the International Criminal Law Regime, Cambridge University Press, Cambridge, 2005, pp. 33–34.

[35] Charles Chernor Jalloh, "What Makes a Crime Against Humanity a Crime Against Humanity", in *American University International Law Review*, 2013, vol. 28, no. 2, p. 392.

[36] Report on the Question of International Criminal Jurisdiction by Ricardo J. Alfaro, Special Rapporteur, 1950, UN doc. A/CN.4/15, paras. 18–25. These efforts resulted in the adoption of a convention in 1937 by the League of Nations contemplating the creation of an international criminal court to prosecute persons accused of offences under the Convention for the Prevention and Punishment of Terrorism. See Convention for the Creation of an International Criminal Court, League of Nations OJ spec. supp. no. 156 (1936), LN doc.

13.2. Developments Between the Wars

The interwar period was thus marked with mostly a lull or reluctance to follow through on promises of sanctions and actually implement ideas of criminalising state behaviour that, although clearly reprehensible, infringed the general and cardinal rule against violating state sovereignty.[37] Indeed, most views on the abortive response to the Armenian genocide are based on what geopolitical interests were at the time. Donald Bloxham describes the interwar period in relation to genocide and crimes against humanity aptly as follows:

> Britain was the only one of the [Allied] powers that showed any sign of taking seriously the 1915 declaration, the subsequent provisions for trial of the Paris Peace Conference, and then articles 226–30 of Sèvres. France and Italy simply used the question as another bargaining counter. Yet British progress was impeded by the desire to amend relations with the nationalists and the fact that the [Turkish] nationalists themselves held a number of British armistice control officers as hostages. As far as prosecution of the murderers of the Armenians was concerned, there was also a legal problem. While crimes against POWs were indictable under the traditional rubric of the "laws and customs of war", the prosecution of a state's mass murder of its own civilians had not yet found a legal name or been framed in appropriate legislation, and was arguably not subject to the jurisdiction of external powers. Sèvres was vague about both the law and the forum that would be used for such a trial, and the British law officers had always been reluctant to experiment, an approach that would be precisely duplicated in debates from 1944 about trying Germans for crimes against German Jews. *Legally speaking, in the inter-war world, genocide, as long as*

C.547(I).M.384(I).1937.V (1938). However, an insufficient number of states ratified the convention, and so it never came into force.

[37] In his memoirs recounting his diplomatic efforts to convince Talaat to stop the Armenian massacres, Morgenthau wrote: "Technically, of course, I had no right to interfere. According to the cold-blooded legalities of the situation, the treatment of Turkish subjects by the Turkish Government was purely a domestic affair; unless it directly affected American lives and American interests, it was outside the concern of the American Government. When I first approached Talaat on the subject, he called my attention to this fact in no uncertain terms", see Morgenthau, 2003, p. 226, see *supra* note 13.

> *it affected only the citizens of the perpetrator state, was*
> *simply seen as that state's "internal affair".*[38]

The moral imperative to the international community's reaction to the Armenian genocide should not be underestimated; however, the very horrors that prompted action in the first place may have caused a distancing from those horrors which dissuaded further action in the aftermath. The world stood by helplessly, never having witnessed such enormous crimes in modern times[39] and perhaps unable to grasp the scope of the atrocities, even after the end of the First World War. Global media coverage missed an opportunity for reflection at the time of the Armenian genocide by depicting the Turk as the barbarous "other", bloodthirsty and sadistic, and allowing for Western- or European-centric constructions justifying war and intervention. In this way, it is argued that Europeans never imagined themselves capable of perpetrating such atrocities against their own people, and therefore deemed it unnecessary to legislate against such crimes for future purposes.

Failure to actually institute the prosecution at either the international and national levels marks the culture of impunity that would rear its ugly head in the Second World War, starting with Hitler's August 1939 address to his military commanders at the Obersalzberg on the need for ruthlessness in the coming invasion of Poland. In his address, Hitler assured the audience that they would not be held to account since no one now remembered the annihilation of the Armenians.[40] Raphael Lemkin, who coined the term "genocide", has stated that he did so with the fate of the Armenians in mind,[41] explaining in an interview televised in 1949 that "it happened so many times. First to the Armenians, then after the Armenians, Hitler took action".[42]

---

[38] Bloxham, 2005, p. 163, see *supra* note 26 (emphasis added).

[39] The Armenian genocide is widely acknowledged by genocide scholars to have been one of the first modern, systematic genocides. See, *inter alia*, Niall Ferguson, *The War of the World: Twentieth-Century Conflict and the Descent of the West*, Penguin, New York, 2006, p. 177.

[40] Bloxham, 2005, p. 217, see *supra* note 26.

[41] See, *inter alia*, Auron, 2004, p. 9, *supra* note 32: "when Raphael Lemkin coined the word genocide in 1944 he cited the 1915 annihilation of Armenians as a seminal example of genocide"; Schabas, 2000, p. 25, see *supra* note 4: "Lemkin's interest in the subject dates to his days as a student at Lvov University, when he intently followed attempts to prosecute the perpetration of the massacres of the Armenians".

[42] Allessandra Stanley, "A PBS Documentary Makes Its Case for the Armenian Genocide, With or Without a Debate", in *New York Times*, 17 April 2006.

Lemkin became interested in the subject while a student of linguistics at the University of Lwów (since 1945, Lviv, Ukraine), when he learned of Soghomon Tehlirian's assassination of Mehmet Talaat in 1921 in Berlin. Tehlirian was a survivor of the Armenian genocide who lost his entire family. When Atatürk put an end to the promise of an international tribunal, a Boston-based Armenian plot called Operation Nemesis formed in response to seek vigilante justice against those most responsible for the Armenian genocide. Tehlirian took part in the plot, and was assigned to assassinate Talaat, who had been living peacefully as a private citizen in Germany after fleeing Turkey with his co-conspirators in 1918. Tehlirian successfully assassinated Talaat in broad daylight, and his subsequent trial came to the attention of Lemkin, who queried one of his professors as to why Talaat was not tried but Tehlirian was. The professor answered: "Consider the case of a farmer who owns a flock of chickens. He kills them and this is his business. If you interfere, you are trespassing". Lemkin, struck by the answer, retorted: "It is a crime for Tehlirian to kill a man, but it is not a crime for his oppressor to kill more than a million men? This is most inconsistent".[43]

The Second World War and the atrocities brought by the Nazis made it apparent and imperative that such deeds no longer go ignored or unpunished. Similarly to the 1915 Declaration, the United States, Britain and the Soviet Union – that is, the new Allied powers of the Second World War – issued a declaration on 17 December 1942 officially noting the mass murder of European Jewry and resolving to prosecute those responsible for violence against civilian population.[44] On 20 October 1943 a United Nations War Crimes Commission was established to investigate war crimes committed by Nazi Germany and its allies. On 1 November 1943 the Allied powers issued another joint declaration that the German war criminals should be judged and punished in the countries in which their crimes were committed, but that "the major criminals, whose offenc-

[43] Samantha Power, *"A Problem From Hell": America and the Age of Genocide*, HarperCollins, New York, 2003, p. 17.

[44] The statement was read to British House of Commons in a floor speech by the Foreign Secretary Anthony Eden, and published on the front page of the *New York Times* and many other newspapers. See "Allies Condemn Nazi War on Jews", in *New York Times*, 18 December 1942.

es have no particular geographical localization", would be punished "by the joint decision of the governments of the Allies".[45]

By April 1945 the Allied powers had thus finally agreed on the principle of prosecuting Nazi war criminals. Nonetheless, there remained much work ahead in setting up the trials.[16] Though some political leaders advocated summary executions instead of trials, the Allied powers agreed to set up an International Military Tribunal ('IMT') to be held in Nuremberg.[47] The Charter of the IMT ('IMT Charter') was issued on 8 August 1945 and set down the laws and procedures by which the Nuremberg trials were to be conducted.[48] Lemkin was involved in the process, becoming one of the legal advisors to US Supreme Court Justice Robert Jackson, the chief American prosecutor at Nuremberg and the head of the American delegation to the London Conference that framed the IMT Charter.[49] Although the word "genocide" appears in the drafting history of the IMT Charter, its final text used the term "crimes against humanity" to deal with the persecution and physical extermination of national, ethnic, racial and religious minorities.[50] In particular, Article 6 of the IMT Charter established the jurisdiction of the Tribunal over three crimes, provided as follows:

> The following acts, or any of them, are crimes coming within the jurisdiction of the Tribunal for which there shall be individual responsibility:
>
> (a) *Crimes against Peace*: namely, planning, preparation, initiation or waging of a war of aggression, or a war in violation of international treaties, agreements or assurances, or

---

[45] Moscow Conference of Foreign Secretaries, Secret Protocol, Annex 10, Declaration of German Atrocities (Signed by Roosevelt, Churchill and Stalin), 1 November 1943 ('Moscow Declaration'), *A Decade of American Foreign Policy: Basic Documents, 1941–49*, Government Printing Office, Washington, DC, 1950.

[46] Daniel Marc Segesser and Myriam Gessler, "Raphael Lemkin and the International Debate on the Punishment of War Crimes (1919–1948)", in Dominik J. Schaller and Jürgen Zimmerer (eds.), *The Origins of Genocide: Raphael Lemkin as a Historian of Mass Violence*, Routledge, London, 2009, p. 19.

[47] Agreement for the Prosecution and Punishment of the Major War Criminals of the European Axis, 8 August 1945, 82 UNTS 279 ('London Agreement') (https://www.legal-tools.org/doc/844f64/).

[48] Charter of the International Military Tribunal, Annex to the London Agreement, 8 August 1945 ('IMT Charter') (https://www.legal-tools.org/doc/64ffdd/).

[49] Segesser and Gessler, 2009, p. 19, see *supra* note 46.

[50] William Schabas, "Origins of the Genocide Convention: From Nuremberg to Paris", in *Case Western Reserve Journal of International Law*, 2008, vol. 40, nos. 1/2, p. 42.

participation in a common plan or conspiracy for the accomplishment of any of the foregoing;

(b) *War Crimes*: namely, violations of the laws or customs of war. Such violations shall include, but not be limited to, murder, ill-treatment or deportation to slave labor or for any other purpose of civilian population of or in occupied territory, murder or ill-treatment of prisoners of war or persons on the seas, killing of hostages, plunder of public or private property, wanton destruction of cities, towns or villages, or devastation not justified by military necessity;

(c) *Crimes against Humanity*: namely, murder, extermination, enslavement, deportation, and other inhumane acts committed against any civilian population, before or during the war; or persecutions on political, racial or religious grounds in execution of or in connection with any crime within the jurisdiction of the Tribunal, whether or not in violation of the domestic law of the country where perpetrated.

Leaders, organizers, instigators and accomplices participating in the formulation or execution of a common plan or conspiracy to commit any of the foregoing crimes are responsible for all acts performed by any persons in execution of such plan.

Crimes against humanity were subsequently included in the 1945 Control Council Law No. 10,[51] the 1946 Charter of the International Military Tribunal for the Far East ('IMTFE Charter')[52] and the Nuremberg Principles, which states unanimously affirmed by UN General Assembly resolution 95 (I) on 11 December 1946,[53] and which were later formulated by the International Law Commission pursuant to UN General Assembly resolution 177 (II) (a) in 1950.[54]

---

[51] Control Council Law No. 10, Punishment of Persons Guilty of War Crimes, Crimes Against Peace and Against Humanity, 20 December 1945, 3 Official Gazette Control Council for Germany 50–55, 1946, Article II(1)(c) (https://www.legal-tools.org/doc/ffda62/).

[52] Charter of the International Military Tribunal for the Far East, 19 January 1946, Art. 5(c) ('IMTFE Charter') (https://www.legal-tools.org/doc/a3c41c/).

[53] Affirmation of the Principles of International Law recognized by the Charter of the Nürnberg Tribunal, UNGA res. 95 (I), 11 December 1946.

[54] Report of the International Law Commission on its Second Session, 5 June–29 July 1950, to the General Assembly, Fifth Session, Supplement No. 12, Doc. A/1316, reprinted in

The evolution of the term "genocide", however, as cognate to "crimes against humanity" as it may be, took a different path. While prosecutors used the term occasionally in their submissions to the Nuremberg Tribunal, "genocide" did not appear in the final judgment, issued on 1 October 1946.[55] The Tribunal also limited its judgment to wartime crimes against humanity, given that Article 6(c) of the IMT Charter required a nexus with other crimes under the jurisdiction of the Tribunal.[56] There are no documents explaining the rationale for adding this requirement at the last moment in the London Agreement. However, it served to restrain the jurisdiction of the IMT.

The failure or omission of the IMT to prosecute or condemn peacetime genocide or crimes against humanity proved to be a great disappointment for Lemkin, who is described as having suffered tremendous concern that the Tribunal did not go far enough in dealing with genocidal actions. Lemkin was not alone in expressing displeasure with the decision to leave unpunished Nazi atrocities committed before the outbreak of the war.[57] The overall discontent with the decision created enough momentum to cause the United Nations General Assembly to adopt resolution 96 (I) on 11 December 1946, which affirmed "that genocide is a crime under international law which the civilized world condemns", and mandated the preparation of a draft convention on the crime of genocide. Although describing genocide as a crime of "international concern", resolution 96 (I) was silent as to whether genocide could be committed in peacetime or in war.[58] This was because the majority of the General Assembly was not prepared to recognise universal jurisdiction for the crime of genocide.[59] Nevertheless, the stage was set to begin a process that ended with the

---

Yearbook of the International Law Commission 1950, vol. 2, United Nations, New York, 1957, pp. 374–78 ('Report of the International Law Commission').

[55] IMT, *International Military Tribunal v. Martin Borman et al.*, Judgment, 1 October 1946 (https://www.legal-tools.org/doc/45f18e/).

[56] A reading of Article 6 of the IMT Charter, as transcribed in the text of this article above, shows that the crimes against humanity, as defined at Article 6(c), needed to be committed "before or during the war [...] in execution of or in connection with any crime within the jurisdiction of the Tribunal", that is, crimes against peace or war crimes, as defined by Article 6(a) and (b), respectively, which in turn were linked to an armed conflict. The same applies to Article 5(c) of the IMTFE Charter.

[57] Schabas, 2008, p. 35, see *supra* note 50.

[58] UN General Assembly resolution 96 (I), The Crime of Genocide, 11 December 1946, UN doc. A/231 ('Resolution on the Crime of Genocide').

[59] Schabas, 2008, p. 36, see *supra* note 50.

adoption on 9 December 1948 of the Convention on the Prevention and Punishment of the Crime of Genocide ('Genocide Convention').[60] Entering into force on 12 January 1951, namely 90 days after the 20th ratification,[61] the Genocide Convention is one of the most widely ratified international instruments today,[62] and forms part of customary international law.

Lemkin was one of three experts selected by the United Nations Secretary-General Trygve Lie to assist in the preparation of the draft convention, but once the official UN process began Lemkin stepped aside, having the sharp political foresight that he could be more valuable on the outside and proceeding to lobby each UN member state involved.[63] Although his dreams of the creation of such an instrument may be said to have come true – he is indeed reported to have been brought to tears on the day that the Convention was adopted[64] – the final version of the legal definition of genocide is a watered down form of the definition Lemkin propounded during the drafting of the Genocide Convention, originally proposed in his book *Axis Rule*. It provides as follows:

> Article II: In the present Convention, genocide means any of the following acts committed with intent to destroy, in whole or in part, a national, ethnical, racial or religious group, as such:
>
> a. Killing members of the group;
> b. Causing serious bodily or mental harm to members of the group;
> c. Deliberately inflicting on the group conditions of life calculated to bring about its physical destruction in whole or in part;
> d. Imposing measures intended to prevent births within the group;
> e. Forcibly transferring children of the group to another group.
>
> Article III: The following acts shall be punishable:

---

[60] UN General Assembly, Prevention and Punishment of the Crime of Genocide, 9 December 1948, A/RES/3/260 ('Genocide Convention') (https://www.legal-tools.org/doc/498c38/).

[61] *Ibid.*, art. 13.

[62] At the time of writing, the Genocide Convention had 146 Parties and 41 Signatories.

[63] Power, 2003, pp. 54–55, see *supra* note 43.

[64] Segesser and Gessler, 2009, p. 20, see *supra* note 46.

a. Genocide;

b. Conspiracy to commit genocide;

c. Direct and public incitement to commit genocide;

d. Attempt to commit genocide;

e. Complicity in genocide.

Lemkin had consistently envisioned genocide as being of tripartite character – physical, biological and cultural. By way of illustration, he published the following in the *United Nations Bulletin* in January 1948:

> There are three basic phases of life in a human group: physical existence, biological continuity (through procreation), and spiritual or cultural expression. Accordingly, the attacks on these three basic phases of the life of a human group can be qualified as physical, biological, or cultural genocide. It is considered a criminal act to cause death to members of the above-mentioned groups directly or indirectly, to sterilize through compulsion, to steal children, or to break up families. Cultural genocide can be accomplished predominantly in the religious and cultural fields by destroying institutions and objects through which the spiritual life of a human group finds expression, such as houses of worship, objects of religious cult, schools, treasures of art, and culture. By destroying spiritual leadership and institutions, forces of spiritual cohesion within a group are removed and the group starts to disintegrate. This is especially significant for the existence of religious groups. Religion can be destroyed within a group even if the members continue to subsist physically.[65]

Although he did not believe the world to be ready for a permanent international criminal court,[66] he did proclaim the necessity of rendering genocide subject to universal jurisdiction and immune from any requirement of a nexus with armed conflict:

> International law is strictly divided into two bodies, the law of war and the law applicable in time of peace. Crimes under international law (*delicta juris gentium*) are a quite different matter from crimes connected with war. Within the first category come such crimes as piracy, trade in women and children, trade in slaves, the drug traffic, trading in obscene publications, and forgery of currency. These crimes are punished

---

[65] Lemkin, 1948, p. 71, see *supra* note 2.

[66] Power, 2003, pp. 55–56, see *supra* note 43.

according to the principle of 'universal repression,' meaning that a criminal can be validly punished by the court of the country where he is apprehended, irrespective of the place where the crime was committed. For example, an individual who has traded in women in Stockholm can be validly tried by a court in Paris. Such a criminal cannot claim any right to asylum. International law invokes the solidarity of the states in punishing such crimes and makes the soil burn under the feet of such offenders. [...]

Indeed, genocide must be treated as the most heinous of all crimes. It is the crime of crimes, one that not only shocks our conscience but affects deeply the best interests of mankind.[67]

Lemkin thus seemed certain that the entirety of his propounded view of genocide would prevail. However, the inclusion of cultural genocide in the scope of the Convention was ultimately voted down by the UN General Assembly's Sixth Committee, and universal jurisdiction was rejected during negotiations, with strong opposition by France, the Soviet Union and the United States.[68] Article 6 of the Genocide Convention only recognises territorial jurisdiction – "by a competent tribunal of the State in the territory of which the act was committed" – as well as the jurisdiction of an "international penal tribunal as may have jurisdiction with respect to those Contracting Parties which shall have accepted its jurisdiction". Nevertheless, universal jurisdiction over genocide – as well as war crimes and crimes against humanity – has since come to be widely treated as an accepted feature of customary international law.[69]

Lemkin might also have found some solace over his distress in the IMT Charter's and Judgment's lacuna when, despite the silence of resolution 96 (I) on the criminalisation of peacetime genocide, the nexus re-

---

[67] Lemkin, 1948, p. 70, see *supra* note 2.

[68] See Draft Convention on Genocide Submitted to the Sixth Committee by the French Delegation, *Historical Survey of the Question of International Criminal Jurisdiction*, appendix 15, United Nations General Assembly, International Law Commission, New York, 1949, pp. 144–45, Doc. A/CN.4/7/Rev.1. See also UN GOAR, Sixth Committee, 3rd session, pt. 1, Summary Records, 1948, pp. 394–406.

[69] See, *inter alia*, Madeleine H. Morris, "Universal Jurisdiction in a Divided World: Conference Remarks", in *New England Law Review*, 2001, vol. 35, no. 2, p. 347.

quirement was not included in the Genocide Convention after all.[70] Concession was also made to allow "forcible transfer of children from one group to another" as a punishable act, as was the inclusion of "[d]eliberately inflicting on the group conditions of life calculated to bring about its physical destruction in whole or in part", both of which pay clear heed to the methods of destruction during the Armenian genocide.

13.3. Contemporary Developments

13.3.1. Crimes Against Humanity

Because of the Cold War that followed the Nuremberg and Tokyo trials, it was not until the early 1990s that the concepts of genocide and crimes against humanity were put to the test again in practice, in response to the imploding wars in Rwanda and (the former) Yugoslavia. In setting up the International Criminal Tribunal for the Former Yugoslavia ('ICTY'), it seemed at first that the nexus requirement between armed conflict and crimes against humanity in international law would remain. Article 5 of the 1993 ICTY Statute was indeed partly modelled on the IMT Charter, containing a definition of crimes against humanity that required them to be "committed in armed conflict, whether international or internal in character".[71] However, in late 1994 Article 3 of the Statute of the International Criminal Tribunal for Rwanda ('ICTR') was enacted with a definition of crimes against humanity that explicitly breaks the link with armed conflict by excluding it from the definition.[72] Under Article 3 of the ICTR

---

[70] Genocide Convention, Article 1, see *supra* note 60: "The Contracting Parties confirm that genocide, whether committed in time of peace or in time of war, is a crime under international law which they undertake to prevent and to punish".

[71] Statute of the International Tribunal for the Former Yugoslavia, 25 May 1993, SC Res. 827, UN SCOR 48th sess., 3217th mtg., UN doc. S/RES/827, art. 5 ('ICTY Statute') (https://www.legal-tools.org/doc/b4f63b/). However, in the Secretary-General's Report to the Security Council on the establishment of the ICTY, when commenting on the subject matter jurisdiction of the tribunal under Article 5, he noted that "[c]rimes against humanity […] are prohibited regardless of whether they are committed in an armed conflict, international or internal in character". UN Secretary-General, Report of the Secretary-General Pursuant to Paragraph 2 of Security Council Resolution 808, 3 May 1993, UN doc. S/1993/25704, para. 47.

[72] Statute of the International Criminal Tribunal for Rwanda, 11 November 1994, SC Res. 955, UN SCOR 49th sess., 3453rd mtg., UN doc. S/Res/955, article 3 ('ICTR Statute') (https://www.legal-tools.org/doc/8732d6/). In the Secretary-General's Report to the Security Council on the establishment of the ICTR, the Secretary-General noted that the "stat-

Statute, the requirement is that crimes such as murder, extermination, enslavement, rape and so on be "committed as part of a widespread or systematic attack against any civilian population on national, political, ethnic, racial or religious grounds". In 1995 the ICTY Appeals Chamber followed suit by declaring that the requirement that crimes against humanity be associated with an armed conflict was inconsistent with customary law.[73] It explained that the Security Council had included the nexus in Article 5 of the ICTY Statute as a jurisdictional limit only.[74] According to William A. Schabas, the more plausible explanation is that the lawyers in the United Nations Secretariat who drafted the Statute believed the nexus to be part of customary law, and the Security Council did not disagree.[75]

In any event, the following definition of crimes against humanity of the Rome Statute of the International Criminal Court ('ICC Statute') parts with the nexus requirement. Article 7(1) states:

> For the purpose of this Statute, 'crime against humanity' means any of the following acts when committed as part of a widespread or systematic attack directed against any civilian population, with knowledge of the attack:
>
> a. Murder;
>
> b. Extermination;

---

ute of the Rwanda Tribunal […] was an adaptation of the statute of the Yugoslav Tribunal to the circumstances of Rwanda" and that there was "no reason to limit [Article 3's] application" with reference to the "temporal scope of the crime" by including the language "when committed in armed conflict, whether international or internal in character" as was done in the ICTY Statute. UN Secretary General, Report of the Secretary-General Pursuant to Paragraph 5 of Security Council Resolution 955, 13 February 1995, UN doc. S/1995/134, p. 9, fn. 5.

[73] ICTY, *Prosecutor v. Duško Tadić*, Appeals Chamber, Decision on the Defence Motion for Interlocutory Appeal on Jurisdiction, IT-94-1, 2 October 1995, para. 141 (https://www.legal-tools.org/doc/866e17/). See also, for example, ICTY, *Prosecutor v. Duško Tadić*, Appeals Chamber, Judgment, IT-94-1, 15 July 1999, para. 251 (https://www.legal-tools.org/doc/8efc3a/).

[74] ICTY, *Prosecutor v. Vojislav Šešelj*, Appeals Chamber, Decision on the Interlocutory Appeal Concerning Jurisdiction, IT-03-67, 31 August 2004, para. 13 (https://www.legal-tools.org/doc/a64634/).

[75] See Schabas, 2008, p. 50, *supra* note 50, referring to Secretary-General, Report of the Secretary-General Pursuant to Paragraph Two of the Security Council Resolution 808, 3 May 1993, delivered to the Security Council, UN doc. S/25704, para. 47, agreeing that "crimes against humanity were first recognized by the Charter".

c. Enslavement;

d. Deportation or forcible transfer of population;

e. Imprisonment or other severe deprivation of physical liberty in violation of fundamental rules of international law,

f. Torture;

g. Rape, sexual slavery, enforced prostitution, forced pregnancy, enforced sterilization, or any other form of sexual violence of comparable gravity;

h. Persecution against any identifiable group or collectivity on political, racial, national, ethnic, cultural, religious, gender as defined in paragraph 3, or other grounds that are universally recognized as impermissible under international law, in connection with any act referred to in this paragraph or any crime within the jurisdiction of the Court;

i. Enforced disappearance of persons;

j. The crime of apartheid;

k. Other inhumane acts of a similar character intentionally causing great suffering, or serious injury to body or to mental or physical health.[76]

The nexus has thus definitively disappeared from the definition of crimes against humanity as we know it today. Whereas the definition of genocide has not changed in the slightest since its inception in 1948, the definition of crimes against humanity has struggled to find solid footing, undergoing some form of change every time it is defined anew. If one takes the view that genocide is a subset, or an aggravated form, of the broader category of crimes against humanity, it seems conceptually illogical to dispense with the nexus requirement for one crime and not the other, even if one takes the view that genocide and crimes against humanity are wholly different in that the former protects groups whereas the latter protects the individual. The drive to create the Genocide Convention in the first place arose in large part out of the international community's concern that the Nuremberg Judgment was too limited in its jurisdiction by reason of the nexus requirement within the IMT Charter.

Crimes against humanity feature another element that is subject to development and judicial debate. At the time the concept was created un-

---

[76] Rome Statute of the International Criminal Court, 1 July 2002, Art. 7(1).

der international law, crimes against humanity required a contextual element whereby the relevant crime had to be committed pursuant to a state policy. This was initially a core part of the definition of crimes against humanity. After the Second World War, for example, the IMT Charter specified that crimes against humanity referred to state crimes – the perpetrators had to have committed crimes "acting in the interests of the European Axis countries".[77] Similarly, national courts that implemented crimes against humanity in domestic jurisdictions emphasised the state contextual element.[78]

Since Nuremberg, however, there has been a development towards a broader approach to the State contextual element, shifting the focus away from the requirement to have a State or State-like organisation responsible.[79] This is reflected in case law from the ICTY, the Special Court for Sierra Leone and the International Criminal Court ('ICC').[80] Article 7(2)(a) of the ICC Statute now explicitly states the widespread and systematic attack directed against the civilian population should be carried out "pursuant to or in furtherance of a State or organizational policy to commit such an attack". This has been interpreted by the majority of the Pre-Trial Chambers of the ICC, applying a broad definition to the word "organizational" in the phrase "State or organizational policy", finding that the key question is the capacity of the organisation to carry out crimes against humanity.[81] Therefore "State or organizational policy" does not just refer to a *de jure* state but can be the policy of a non-state entity.[82]

---

[77] William Schabas, "State Policy as an Element of International Crimes", in *Journal of Criminal Law and Criminology*, 2008, vol. 98, no. 3, p. 954.

[78] Tilman Rodenhäuser, "Beyond State Crimes, Non-State Entities and Crimes against Humanity", in *Leiden Journal of International Law*, 2014, vol. 27, no. 4, p. 918.

[79] *Ibid.*, pp. 918–20.

[80] See, for example, ICTY, *Prosecutor v. Limaj et al.*, Judgment, IT-03-66-T, 30 November 2005 (https://www.legal-tools.org/doc/4e469a/); Special Court for Sierra Leone, *Prosecutor v. Alex Tamba Brima et al.*, Judgment, SCSL-04-16-T, 20 June 2007 (https://www.legal-tools.org/doc/87ef08/); ICC, *Prosecutor v. Germain Katanga, Jugement rendu en application de l'article 74 du Statut*, ICC-01/04-01/07, 7 March 2014 (https://www.legal-tools.org/doc/9813bb/).

[81] ICC, Situation in the Republic of Kenya, Pre-Trial Chamber, Decision pursuant to Article 15 of the Rome Statute on the Authorization of an Investigation into the Situation in the Republic of Kenya, ICC-01/09, 31 March 2010 (https://www.legal-tools.org/doc/338a6f/).

[82] Rodenhäuser, 2014, p. 920, see *supra* note 78.

This may drag the scope of the crimes away from its original aim. Schabas reasons that "a principal rationale for prosecuting crimes against humanity as such has been the fact that such atrocities generally escape prosecution in the State that normally exercises jurisdiction". He argues that a contextual state requirement (albeit defined broadly to incorporate state-like entities) is more in keeping with the historical aim of prosecuting such crimes under international law.[83] However, a broader approach to the definition of "organisation", examining the capacity of the organisation rather than state-like characteristics, is supported by other contextual elements of crimes against humanity.[84] Tilman Rodenhäuser argues that the required degree of organisation can be deduced from other contextual elements, such as if the attack is "widespread and systematic", "directed against any civilian population" and "pursuant to or in furtherance of a [...] policy".[85]

13.3.2. Genocide

On the other hand, the definition of genocide as it currently stands is also seen as too narrow, particularly with the special intent (*dolus specialis*) requirement "to destroy, in whole or in part, a national, ethnical, racial or religious group, as such".[86] Not only does it seem conceivably impossible to prove intent to exterminate a group until at least a significant part of it has already been wiped out, but it would further be necessary to ensure that the group was targeted by virtue of its 'group-hood' (as opposed to a coincidence that the victims happened to belong to a group of national, ethnic, racial or religious character).

During the drafting work on the Genocide Convention, although debate raged about the specific groups to be included, protection to political, social, gender, or other such groups was excluded from the Convention. Critics have argued that the omission of political, economic, social, gender and other groups is illogical and incompatible with the Convention's lofty mission.[87] The limitation of protected groups to just the de-

---

[83] Schabas, 2008, p. 978, see *supra* note 77.

[84] Rodenhäuser, 2014, pp. 922–23, see *supra* note 78.

[85] *Ibid.*, pp. 923–27.

[86] Genocide Convention, Art. 2, see *supra* note 60.

[87] William Schabas, "Groups Protected by the Genocide Convention: Conflicting Interpretations from the International Criminal Tribunal for Rwanda", in *ILSA Journal of International & Comparative Law*, 2000, vol. 6, no. 2, p. 376.

fined four has also been criticised by academics and human rights activists as narrowing the reach of genocide to near non-applicability.[88] Nonetheless, countervailing concerns about the "dilution" of the genocide definition have also been raised by academics like Schabas, who argues that recent history "has disproven the claim that the genocide definition was too restrictive to be of any practical application".[89] Schabas argues that there is value in society defining a crime so heinous that it will occur only rarely, and that a formal amendment risks trivialising the horror of the real crime when it is committed.[90]

Indeed, after its adoption in 1948 and entry into force in 1951, the Genocide Convention lay dormant for 50 years. The first time that the Genocide Convention was interpreted and applied by an international court was in the case of *The Prosecutor v. Jean-Paul Akayesu* before the ICTR,[91] which adopted the definition of genocide as enunciated in the Convention verbatim in its constitutive statute.[92] Akayesu was the former mayor (*bourgmestre*) of Taba commune in the Prefecture of Gitarama, Rwanda, and was convicted of genocide, direct and public incitement to commit genocide, and crimes against humanity.[93] The trial judgment, which was upheld on appeal,[94] was pivotal in many respects, two of which bear specific mention here. First, in convicting Akayesu for genocide, the ICTR Trial Chamber held that that rape and sexual violence could constitute acts of genocide insofar as they were committed with the intent to destroy, in whole or in part, a targeted group, as such.[95] The Trial Chamber reasoned that "[s]exual violence was an integral part of the process of destruction, specifically targeting Tutsi women and specifically contributing to their destruction and to the destruction of the Tutsi group as a whole".[96]

---

[88] See Schabas, 2008, p. 46, *supra* note 50.

[89] Schabas, 2000, p. 386, see *supra* note 87.

[90] *Ibid.*, pp. 386–87.

[91] ICTR, *Prosecutor v. Jean-Paul Akayesu*, Judgment, ICTR-96-4-T, 2 September 1998 (https://www.legal-tools.org/doc/b8d7bd/) ('Akayesu Trial Judgment').

[92] ICTR Statute, Art. 2, see *supra* note 72.

[93] Akayesu Trial Judgment, para. 1, 745, see *supra* note 91.

[94] ICTR, *Prosecutor v. Jean-Paul Akayesu*, Appeals Chamber, Judgment, ICTR-96-4-A, 1 June 2001 (https://www.legal-tools.org/doc/c62d06/).

[95] Akayesu Trial Judgment, paras. 731–33, see *supra* note 91.

[96] *Ibid.*, para. 731.

Second, the Trial Chamber had to determine whether the Tutsis fell under one of the protected groups outlined in the definition of genocide, because at no point did the Genocide Convention's drafters actually define "national, ethnical, racial or religious" groups, and these terms have been subject to considerable subsequent interpretation. The Trial Chamber categorised the Tutsis as an ethnic group,[97] which it defined as "a group whose members share a common language or culture".[98] A problem arises in that Rwanda's Hutus and Tutsis share the same language and culture. The Trial Chamber thus took the initiative of stretching the definition of genocide further, reasoning that the *travaux préparatoires* of the Genocide Convention showed an intention by the drafters to accord protection to "any stable and permanent group".[99]

The decision of another Trial Chamber at the ICTR took an alternative approach to defining the Tutsis as a protected ethnic group. In the *Kayishema et al.* case, the Trial Chamber noted that an "ethnic group could be a group identified as such by others, including perpetrators of the crimes".[100] Since it is often the offender who defines the individual victim's status as a member of a group protected by the Genocide Convention,[101] this subjective approach tends to align with the realities of a perpetrator's determination of group membership. The Nazis, for example, had detailed objective criteria establishing who was Jewish and who was not, and in Rwanda Tutsis were often betrayed by their identity cards when there was no other way to determine their status.[102] Accordingly, the Trial Chamber concluded that the Tutsis were an ethnic group based on the existence of their government-issued official identity cards describing them as such.[103]

In the ICC Statute, the ICTR's interpretation of the definition of genocide in *Akayesu* protecting "stable and permanent groups" was not similarly endorsed as the ICTY's interpretation of the nexus requirement (or lack thereof) was in the definition of crimes against humanity. Indeed, despite the above-mentioned criticism over the narrowness of the defini-

---

[97] *Ibid.*, para. 124.

[98] *Ibid.*, para. 513.

[99] *Ibid.*, paras. 511, 516.

[100] ICTR, *Prosecutor v. Clément Kayishema et al.*, Judgment, ICTR-95-1-T, 21 May 1999 para. 36 ('Kayishema Trial Judgment') (https://www.legal-tools.org/doc/0811c9/).

[101] Schabas, 2000, p. 386, see *supra* note 87.

[102] *Ibid.*

[103] Kayishema Trial Judgment, paras. 522–30, see *supra* note 100.

tion of genocide as in the Genocide Convention, states have rarely showed any inclination to consider amendment. According to Schabas, they were given a golden opportunity at the 1998 Rome Conference to fix any gaps in Article 2 of the Genocide Convention, but declined to do so.[104] In debate in the Committee of the Whole at the Rome Conference, only Cuba argued for amendment of the definition to include social and political groups.[105] Otherwise, there was a chorus of support for the original text of the definition of genocide adopted by the General Assembly.[106]

13.4. Conclusion

The world was confronted with not unprecedented, yet nevertheless shocking, demonstrations of human cruelty in the First and Second World Wars, most notably with the Armenian genocide and the Jewish Holocaust. Although the Armenian genocide led to the acknowledgement that crimes against humanity committed in peacetime violated customary international law, the complete absence of an international penal response rendered efforts to suppress and punish the Armenian genocide unsuccessful. Efforts to suppress the Jewish Holocaust were similarly unsuccessful, but by the end of the Jewish Holocaust efforts to punish could no longer be ignored.

In contrast to the shelving of the Armenian genocide, by the end of the twentieth century the international community appears to have shifted perspectives towards a willingness to end impunity for genocide and crimes against humanity with the establishment of such institutions as the *ad hoc* international criminal tribunals for Rwanda and the former Yugoslavia, the International Criminal Court, the Special Court for Sierra Leone and the Extraordinary Chambers in the Courts of Cambodia. The statutes and jurisprudence of these courts show that, despite the fate of the Armenians having gone unpunished, the concepts of genocide and crimes against humanity have nonetheless continued to evolve along the lines

---

[104] Schabas, 2008, p. 46, see *supra* note 50.

[105] Conference of Plenipotentiaries on the Establishment of an International Criminal Court, Consideration of the Question Concerning the Finalization and Adoption of a Convention on the Establishment of an International Criminal Court in Accordance with General Assembly Resolutions 51/207 of 17 December 1996 and 52/160 of 15 December 1997, 20 November 1998, UN doc. A/CONF.183/C.1/SR.3, para. 100.

[106] See Schabas, 2008, p. 46, *supra* note 50; Report of the International Law Commission, see *supra* note 54.

conceived in the 1915 Declaration and the Treaty of Sèvres, namely with a view to consolidating such crimes as a distinct and discrete legal category, increasingly distinguishable from war crimes.

However, this apparent shift in international efforts towards ending impunity did not arise from purely altruistic motives, and the decision to create legal crimes punishing mass atrocities amounting to genocide and crimes against humanity arose mainly out of geopolitical interests. The legal concepts of genocide and crimes against humanity have therefore also developed in accordance with reigning geopolitical interests of the time. The result is that the legal tools created have been rendered largely impotent in the face of actually preventing or consistently and exhaustively punishing the crimes of genocide and crimes against humanity. The Genocide Convention has imposed an obligation on state parties to not only punish, but to prevent, the occurrence of genocide. Yet, preventable and ongoing mass atrocities continue to occur and re-occur due to poor or lagging international decision-making, with the Rwandan genocide of 1994 being the most notorious case in point.

More recent efforts to address the lameness of the legal framework to address such crimes and fill critical gaps in the international system that allow such tragedies to go unchecked have been placed in diplomatic channels such as with the creation of the UN Office of the Special Adviser on the Prevention of Genocide, which also includes a Special Adviser on the Responsibility to Protect. The mandates of the two Special Advisers include alerting relevant actors to the risk of genocide, war crimes, ethnic cleansing and crimes against humanity, enhancing the capacity of the United Nations to prevent these crimes, including their incitement, and working with member states, regional and sub-regional arrangements, and civil society to develop more effective means of response when they do occur. A more robust and focused effort to strengthen and harmonise the current legal framework to prevent and punish such crimes independently of prevailing geopolitical interests would be a crucial component in achieving these goals.

14

Individual Criminal Responsibility for Violations of
Jus ad Bellum under Customary International Law:
From Nuremberg to Kampala

Meagan S. Wong[*]

14.1. Introduction

In 2010 an event of historic significance took place at the Review Conference of the Rome Statute of the International Criminal Court ('ICC Statute') in Kampala. The Assembly of States Parties to the ICC Statute adopted by consensus resolution RC/Res.6 ('Kampala Amendments'), which contained amendments with respect to the crime of aggression.[1] The Kampala Amendments include, *inter alia*, a definition of the crime (Article 8*bis*) along with the conditions for which the ICC may exercise jurisdiction (Article 15*bis* and 15*ter*). Annexed to the Kampala Amendments are Elements of Crimes pertaining to the crime of aggression and Understandings regarding the amendments.

The Kampala Amendments are representative of the first definition of the crime of aggression in a multilateral instrument under international

---

[*] **Meagan S. Wong** is a Ph.D. Candidate at Leiden University. She was previously a Visiting Scholar at the Lauterpacht Centre for International Law, University of Cambridge (2012-13) and a visiting doctoral student at Oxford University (2011-12). She has an LL.M. from University College London and LL.B. (Hons) from Leeds University. She has been called to the Bar of England and Wales (Middle Temple).

[1] Resolution RC/Res.6 on the Crime of Aggression, Review Conference of the Rome Statute, adopted on 11 June 2010, Depositary Notification C.N.651.2010 Treaties-8 ('Kampala Amendments'). See Carsten Stahn, "The 'End', the 'Beginning of the End' or the 'End of the Beginning'? Introducing Debates and Voices on the Definition of 'Aggression'", in *Leiden Journal of International Law*, 2010, vol. 23, no. 4, pp. 875–82; Christian Wenaweser, "Reaching the Kampala Compromise on Aggression: The Chair's Perspective", in *Leiden Journal of International Law*, 2010, vol. 23, no. 4, p. 883–87; Niels Blokker and Claus Kreß, "A Consensus Agreement on the Crime of Aggression: Impressions from Kampala", in *Leiden Journal of International Law*, 2010, vol. 23, no. 4, p. 889–95; Claus Kreß and Leonie von Holtzendorff, "The Kampala Compromise on the Crime of Aggression", in *Journal of International Criminal Justice*, 2010, vol. 8, no. 5, p. 1179–1217.

---

law. Therefore, the ICC embodies the potential for an international court to enforce criminal sanctions against individuals for the crime of aggression.[2] As such, situations of aggression may be prosecuted at the ICC if it is satisfied that the underlying act committed by the aggressor state is an act of aggression in violation of *jus ad bellum,* which is of sufficient gravity to be considered a crime of aggression.

Not every violation of *jus ad bellum* by a state will give rise to individual criminal responsibility. A violation of *jus ad bellum* must be of a certain threshold to give rise to individual criminal responsibility. This threshold is encapsulated in the state act element of the crime. Hence, the state act element of the crime of aggression can be understood as the violation of *jus ad bellum* that the alleged aggressor state must satisfy in order that the individual criminal responsibility of the defendant can be assessed. This assessment of alleged criminal conduct of the defendant can only be considered upon determination that the alleged aggressor state has committed a violation of *jus ad bellum* that has amounted to an act of aggression. In other words, individual criminal responsibility is predicated upon the state responsibility of the aggressor state, as there is an intrinsic link between the act of aggression and the crime of aggression.

This chapter focuses upon the definition of the crime of aggression, with particular reference to the state act element of the crime. The latter should be understood as a substantive component within the definition of the crime of aggression, and not merely a procedural prerequisite. The underlying objective of the present analysis is to examine how the state act element of the crime of aggression has developed in international law by comparing the definition of the crime in the Charter of the International Military Tribunal (crimes against peace) at Nuremberg ('IMT Charter') and the Kampala Amendments (crime of aggression). During the trial at the International Military Tribunal ('IMT'), international law had only

---

[2] The jurisdiction of the ICC remains to be activated. Pursuant to Article 15*bis*(3) and Article 15*ter*(3): "The Court shall exercise jurisdiction over the crime of aggression in accordance with this article, subject to a decision to be taken after 1 January 2017 by the same majority of States Parties as is required for the adoption of an amendment to the Statute"; Rome Statute of the International Criminal Court, 17 July 1998, in force on 1 July 2002, United Nations, Treaty Series, vol. 2187, no. 38544. The amendments to Article 8 reproduce the text contained in depositary notification C.N.651.2010 Treaties-6, while the amendments regarding Articles 8*bis*, 15*bis* and 15*ter* replicate the text contained in depositary notification C.N.651.2010 Treaties-8; both depositary communications are dated 29 November 2010 ('ICC Statute').

just begun to shift from a decentralised system to a centralised system governed by the framework of collective security under the Charter of the United Nations ('UN Charter').[3] Under this new dispensation, a legal framework pursuant to the UN Charter would replace the normative framework that governed and prohibited the use of interstate force prior to the formation of the UN. The state act element of crimes against peace in the IMT Charter is reflective of the normative framework that prohibits the use of interstate force under a decentralised system, while the state act element of the crime of aggression in the Kampala Amendments must be read in accordance with the legal framework under the UN Charter. It should be appreciated that these two definitions represent different paradigms of international law.

The chapter first presents a preliminary insight as to how *jus ad bellum* and international criminal law interplay in a situation of aggression. This serves to place in context how the crime of aggression and the act of aggression are intrinsically linked. The starting point of the analysis examines the state act element of the crime as defined in the IMT Charter as crimes against peace under Article 6(a). The discussion then examines how the IMT interpreted the state act element of the crime with respect to the acts committed by Germany. The aim is to identify the components of the state act element of crimes against peace.

The next step is to appraise whether the state act element of crimes against peace pursuant to the principles of international law recognised by the IMT Charter and the Judgment of the Tribunal ('Nuremberg Principles') have attained customary international law status. It is generally accepted that the Nuremberg Principles are regarded as substantive aspects of customary international law. From the outset, it should be clarified that the same may not be said with respect to the definition of the crime of aggression in the Kampala Amendments.[4] Therefore, the customary international law norms that criminalise aggression are consistent with the definition of crimes against peace pursuant to the Nuremberg Principles.

---

[3]   Charter of the United Nations and Statute of the International Court of Justice, 26 June 1945 ('UN Charter') (https://www.legal-tools.org/doc/6b3cd5/).

[4]   Kampala Amendments, Art. 8*bis*(1) and Annex III, Understandings, para. 4, see *supra* note 1; ICC Statute, Art. 10, see *supra* note 2. See also Marko Milanovic, "Aggression and Legality: Custom in Kampala", in *Journal of International Criminal Justice*, 2012, vol. 10, p. 165–87.

The chapter then examines the crime of aggression pursuant to the Kampala Amendments with particular reference to the state act element of the crime. As will be seen, the state act element of the crime is of much higher specificity than the definition in the IMT Charter. The underlying requirements of the state act element of the crime for the purposes of prosecution at the ICC will be discussed.

The final part of this chapter conducts a comparison between the definitions in the IMT Charter and the Kampala Amendments with respect to the state act element of the crime. First, a comparison is made as to whether the scope of acts of aggression that give rise to individual criminal responsibility has evolved under international law in the light of the paradigm shift. In other words, whether there have been any changes to the threshold for the violations of *jus ad bellum* for the purposes of qualifying an act of aggression as a crime of aggression. Second, there is an assessment of whether the state act element of the definition of the crime of aggression pursuant to the Kampala Amendments reflects or departs from customary international law.

14.2. Individual Criminal Responsibility for Violations of *Jus Ad Bellum*: Understanding the Crime of Aggression

The crime of aggression differs from other international crimes, such as genocide, crimes against humanity and war crimes because it is intrinsically linked to an act of aggression committed by an aggressor state. As already noted, the prerequisite of the act of aggression as a substantive part of the crime of aggression is known as the state act element. Aggression is inherently and essentially an act of state, which is generally understood as a violation of *jus ad bellum* by the aggressor state against the aggressed state. *Jus ad bellum* is the legal framework that governs the use of force between states, conferring obligations on states to refrain from recourse to force against other states. An act of aggression implies that the aggressor state has *prima facie* breached its obligations under the primary norms of *jus ad bellum* to refrain from an act of aggression against the aggressed state. The breach of obligations by the aggressor state must be established before it can be assessed whether the defendant can be found responsible for the crime of aggression.

Criminalisation of aggression is the process whereby international criminal law places norms directly on individuals to refrain from conduct relating to the state act of aggression. When an individual commits the crime of aggression, he/she breaches obligations with respect to these norms under international criminal law. As such, the breach of these norms leads to individual criminal responsibility for the crime of aggression. This is how *jus ad bellum* and international criminal law interplay. Both legal frameworks are applicable in a situation of aggression, which is why the crime of aggression arises simultaneously with an act of aggression.

14.3. The International Military Tribunal at Nuremberg and Crimes Against Peace

The definition for crimes against peace is encapsulated in Article 6(a) of the IMT Charter: "planning, preparation, initiation or waging of a war of aggression, or a war in violation of international treaties, agreements or assurances".[5] This definition can be divided into two substantive components. First, the state act element is a "war of aggression" or a "war in violation of international treaties, agreements or assurances". Second, the elements of individual conduct refer to the "planning, preparation, initiation or waging" (of the state act element). For the purposes of this chapter, planning, preparation, initiation or waging can be considered as "modes of perpetration", which serve to connect the state act element of the crime to the individual, as it is only through participation in one of these modes of perpetration that an individual can actually facilitate an act of aggression committed by a state.

The state act element of the crime should be determined prior to contemplating the conduct of the perpetrator. Indeed, this was the approach of the IMT with respect to crimes against peace. It first sought to determine the presence of the state act element prior to examining whether the defendants had participated in the modes of perpetration that gave

---

[5]   Charter of the International Military Tribunal, *Trial of the Major War Criminals Before the International Military Tribunal, Nuremberg, 14 November 1945–1 October 1946*, vol I. Official Documents, pp. 10–16. Nuremberg, Germany, 1947, Art. 6(a) ('IMT Charter') (https://www.legal-tools.org/doc/64ffdd/).

rise to the state act element.[6] In other words, the IMT first determined whether the acts specified in the Indictment under Count 2 amounted to wars of aggression and/or wars in violation of international treaties, agreements and assurances committed by Germany before considering the involvement of the defendant.[7]

The IMT presented an extensive review of facts in its Judgment relating to the aggressive behaviour of Germany. This is very insightful with regard to understanding how the IMT made a determination of the state act element of crimes against peace. The facts can be broadly categorised in three sections. The first section examined the Nazi regime in Germany: the origins and aims of the Nazi party; its seizure and consolidation of power; and measures of rearmament.[8] This provides the context behind the IMT's view that "war was seen to be inevitable, or at the very least, highly probable" if the purposes of National Socialist movement were to be accomplished.[9]

The second section focused on the common plan of conspiracy and aggressive war.[10] The IMT found it necessary to "look more closely at some of the events which preceded these acts of aggression",[11] primarily because "the aggressive designs of the Nazi Government were not accidents arising out of the immediate political situation in Europe and the world; they were a deliberate and essential part of Nazi foreign policy".[12] The IMT proceeded to examine the facts with respect to the preparation and the planning of aggression, drawing attention to four meetings that

---

[6]   "Judicial Decisions: International Military Tribunal (Nuremberg), Judgment and Sentences", in *American Journal of International Law*, 1947, vol. 41, pp. 192–214 ('Nuremberg Judgment and Sentences').

[7]   Count Two of the Indictment states: "The wars referred to in the Statement of Offense in this Count Two of the Indictment and the dates of their initiation were the following: against Poland, 1 September 1939; against the United Kingdom and France, 3 September 1939; against Denmark and Norway, 9 April 1940; against Belgium, the Netherlands, and Luxembourg, 10 May 1940; against Yugoslavia and Greece, 6 April 1941; against the U.S.S.R., 22 June 1941; and against the United States of America, 11 December 1941"; Indictment of the International Military Tribunal, *The Trial of German Major War Criminals by the International Military Tribunal Sitting at Nuremberg Germany*, 1947 ('IMT Indictment'). See also *ibid.*, pp. 186–214.

[8]   Nuremberg Judgment and Sentences, pp. 175–86, see *supra* note 6.

[9]   *Ibid.*, p. 187.

[10]   *Ibid.*, pp. 186–92.

[11]   *Ibid.*, p. 186.

[12]   *Ibid.*, p. 187.

took place on 5 November 1937, 23 May 1939, 22 August 1939 and 23 November 1939. These meetings were significant because Hitler had made important declarations with respect to his aggressive purposes.[13]

The third section provided an extensive review of the facts relating to Germany's actions with respect to Austria, Czechoslovakia, Poland, Denmark, Norway, Belgium, the Netherlands, Luxembourg, Yugoslavia, Greece, the Soviet Union and the United States.[14] It is this identification of facts that is most relevant to the analysis of this chapter and, as such, will be referred to in understanding how the IMT determined the state act element of the crime.

14.3.1. Crimes Against Peace: The State Act Element

The state act element of crimes against peace is "a war of aggression or a war in violation of international treaties, agreements and assurances". As the conjunctive 'or' is used, this implies that individual criminal responsibility can be determined upon either a "war of aggression" or a "war in violation of international treaties, agreements and assurances". Indeed, as the IMT was satisfied that Germany had committed aggressive wars against 12 nations, it found it unnecessary to discuss whether these aggressive wars were also wars in violation of international treaties, agreements, or assurances.[15] Nevertheless, the common underlying criterion between these two variants of the state act element is that the act of state must amount to war.[16]

14.3.1.1. A War of Aggression

A war of aggression was not defined in the IMT Charter. It can thus be inferred that it was left for the discretion of the IMT to determine whether Germany had committed a war of aggression against the relevant nation. The first point to appreciate is that an act of aggression is different from a war of aggression and the IMT made this distinction clear. The seizures of Austria and Czechoslovakia were considered acts of aggression,[17] while it

---

[13] *Ibid.*, p. 188.

[14] *Ibid.*, pp. 192–214.

[15] *Ibid.*, p. 214.

[16] "The Tribunal had explicitly stated that 'war is essentially an evil thing'. Its consequences are not confined to the belligerent States alone, but affect the whole world", *ibid.*, p. 186.

[17] *Ibid.*, pp. 192–97.

was held that Germany had committed wars of aggression against the other 12 nations. What, then, is the difference between an act of aggression and a war of aggression?

14.3.1.1.1. Acts of Aggression

In March 1938, Austria was seized by Germany. The IMT held that "the invasion of Austria was a pre-meditated aggressive step in furthering the plan to wage aggressive wars against other countries".[18] However, prior to this Hitler had announced on 21 May 1935 that Germany had no intention to either attack or interfere with the internal affairs of Austria.[19] Peaceful assurances were made, such as a public avowal of peaceful intentions in early May 1936, and a bilateral agreement had even been entered into between Austria and Germany on 11 July 1936, in which the latter recognised the full sovereignty of the former.[20]

The Austrian Chancellor, Kurt von Schuschnigg, was persuaded to seek a conference with Hitler, which took place in Berchtesgaden on 12 February 1938. At that meeting Hitler threatened Schuschnigg with an immediate invasion of Austria. The Chancellor agreed to grant political amnesty to various Austrian Nazi sympathisers convicted of crimes and to appoint one of the defendants, Arthur Seyss-Inquart, as Minister of the Interior and Security with control of the police. Schuschnigg subsequently attempted to hold a plebiscite on 13 March 1938 on the question of Austrian independence, which was ultimately withdrawn as a consequence of an ultimatum given by Hitler. On 11 March 1938, further ultimatums were made, which included a demand for Schuschnigg's resignation and that Seyss-Inquart should replace him as Chancellor. The Austrian President, Wilhelm Miklas, eventually agreed to the appointment.[21]

On 12 March 1938, Hitler gave the final order for German troops to cross the border at dawn, and instructed his appointed Chancellor to use

---

[18] *Ibid.*, p. 192.

[19] *Ibid.*

[20] The Austro-German Agreement of 11 July 1936 stated: "(1) The German Government recognizes the full sovereignty of the Federated State of Austria in the spirit of the pronouncements of the German Fuhrer and Chancellor of 21 May 1935. (2) Each of the two Governments regards the inner political order (including the question of Austrian National-Socialism) obtaining in the other country as an internal affair of the other country, upon which it will exercise neither direct nor indirect influence". *Ibid.*

[21] *Ibid.*, pp. 192–93.

formations of Austrian Nazis to depose the President and seize control of the government. At daybreak, German troops marched into Austria with no resistance.[22] The next day a law was passed for the "reunion" of Austria, as the province of Ostmark, into the German Reich. The IMT held that "the methods employed to achieve the object were those of an aggressor. The ultimate factor was the armed might of Germany ready to be used if any resistance was encountered".[23]

With respect to Czechoslovakia, it was already clear at a secret conference held on 5 November 1937 between Hitler and his military and foreign policy leadership that Germany had definitely decided upon the seizure of territories.[24] False assurances were made to a Czechoslovakian minister in Berlin on 11 and 12 March 1938. However, on 28 May 1938, Hitler ordered that preparations should be made for military action against Czechoslovakia by 2 October, and he subsequently signed a directive on 30 May 1938 which declared his "unalterable decision to smash Czechoslovakia by military action in the near future".[25]

The IMT found that plans were made to occupy Czechoslovakia before the Munich Conference on 29 September 1938.[26] At this Conference, which was attended by Hitler, Mussolini, and the British and French Prime Ministers, the Munich Pact was signed, stipulating that Czechoslovakia was required to acquiesce in the cession of the Sudetenland to Germany. However, Hitler demonstrated no intention of adhering to the Munich Pact as he issued a directive on 21 October 1938 to the armed forces on their future tasks, which stated that "it must be possible to smash at any time the remainder of Czechoslovakia if her policy should become hostile towards Germany".[27]

Hitler suggested summoning the Czechoslovak President, Emil Hácha, and his Foreign Minister for a meeting in Berlin on 14 March 1939, at which some of the Nuremberg defendants were present. Hácha was presented with an ultimatum to sign an agreement at once consenting to the incorporation of the Czechoslovak people into the German Reich,

---

[22] *Ibid.*, p. 193.

[23] *Ibid.*, p. 194.

[24] *Ibid.*

[25] *Ibid.*, p. 195.

[26] *Ibid.*, p. 195–96.

[27] *Ibid.*, p. 196.

otherwise Bohemia and Moravia would face destruction as German troops had already received orders to invade and that any resistance would be broken with physical force. This also included a threat that Prague would be completely destroyed from the air. The President and Foreign Minister signed the agreement at 04:30. The next day German troops occupied Bohemia and Moravia, which was followed by a German decree incorporating Bohemia and Moravia into the Reich as a protectorate.[28]

In examining the facts presented by the IMT, it becomes apparent that there was no actual use of armed force by Germany or armed resistance or counterforce by Austria or Czechoslovakia.[29] However, international agreements between Germany and Austria and Czechoslovakia respectively were violated, along with false assurances of good relations. Despite the lack of armed force, both countries were annexed by Germany. The internal political structures of both countries were changed and they were incorporated into Germany as the result of duress from the series of threats backed with the use of force.

My view is that the threat of use of force was the aggressive element. As the acts of aggression committed against Austria and Czechoslovakia were not considered wars of aggression or wars in violation of international treaties, agreements or assurances, they were not included in the Indictment under Count 2 for crimes against peace.[30] Therefore, no defendants were convicted for crimes against peace against Austria and Czechoslovakia. From this, it can be reaffirmed that the state act element is indeed an essential component of the definition for crimes against peace.

14.3.1.1.2. Wars of Aggression

As already noted, the IMT found that Germany committed wars of aggression against the following 12 countries: Poland, the United Kingdom, France, Denmark, Norway, Belgium, the Netherlands, Luxembourg, Yu-

---

[28] *Ibid.*, p. 196–97.

[29] *Ibid.*, p. 192–97.

[30] Nevertheless, the acts of aggression against Austria and Czechoslovakia could be considered as part of the participation in a common plan or conspiracy to commit crimes against peace, which is why these acts were included in Count One of the Indictment. IMT Indictment, see *supra* note 7.

goslavia, Greece, the Soviet Union and the United States.[31] The facts pertaining to each situation are now examined.

Poland was the first war of aggression identified by the IMT.[32] Germany and Poland had signed two agreements: the Arbitration Treaty between Germany and Poland at Locarno (1925) and the German-Polish Declaration of Non-Aggression (1934). Hitler himself had made several speeches about maintaining peace and harmony between Germany and Poland.[33] However, on 24 November 1938 a directive from the Oberkommando der Wehrmacht was issued to the German armed forces to make preparations for an attack upon Danzig.[34] Yet more speeches were made assuring mutual relations between Poland and Germany on the 25 and 30 January 1939. Nevertheless, directives to the armed forces were issued on 3 and 11 April 1939.[35]

On 23 May 1939 Hitler announced his decision to attack Poland. He provided his reasons and discussed the effect the decision might have on other countries. This included an admission that it was necessary for Germany to enlarge her "living space" (*Lebensraum*) and secure food supplies:

> There is therefore no question of sparing Poland, and we are left with the decision to attack Poland at the first suitable opportunity. We cannot expect a repetition of the Czech affair. There will be war. Our task is to isolate Poland. The success

---

[31] Nuremberg Judgment and Sentences, p. 197–214, see *supra* note 6.

[32] *Ibid.*, p. 197.

[33] *Ibid.*, pp. 197–98.

[34] The directive stated: "Preparations are also to be made to enable the Free State of Danzig to be occupied by German troops by surprise", *ibid.*, p. 198.

[35] The directive of 3 April 1939 stated: "The Fuhrer has added the following directions to Fall Weiss [the military code name for the German invasion of Poland]. (1) Preparations must be made in such a way that the operation can be carried out at any time from 1 September 1939 onwards. (2) The High Command of the Armed Forces has been directed to draw up a precise timetable for Fall Weiss and to arrange by conferences the synchronized timings between the three branches of the Armed Forces". The directive of 11 April 1939 stated: "Quarrels with Poland should be avoided. Should Poland however adopt a threatening attitude towards Germany, 'a final settlement' will be necessary, notwithstanding the pact with Poland. The aim is then to destroy Polish military strength, and to create in the East a situation which satisfies the requirements of defense. The Free State of Danzig will be incorporated into Germany at the outbreak of the conflict at the latest. Policy aims at limiting the war to Poland, and this is considered possible in view of the internal crisis in France, and British restraint as a result of this", *ibid.*, pp. 189–99.

of the isolation will be decisive. [...] the isolation of Poland is a matter of skilful politics.[36]

The records of the meeting reveal that Hitler realised there was a possibility of Britain and France coming to Poland's assistance. He was of the opinion that if the isolation of Poland could not be achieved, Germany should first attack Britain and France, or should concentrate primarily on the war in the West, in order to defeat Britain and France or to destroy their effectiveness. In the next couple of weeks other meetings were held and directives were issued in preparation for the war.

On the 22 August 1939, in a speech to the commanders-in-chief, Hitler announced the war on Poland.[37] There were unsuccessful appeals to Hitler to refrain from war with Poland from Britain, the Holy See and France.[38] On the 25 August 1939 Britain signed a pact of mutual assistance with Poland, which caused Hitler to hesitate and postpone the invasion of Poland which was initially due to start on 26 August.[39] These developments started negotiations between Britain and Poland, which the IMT held "were not entered in good faith or with any desire to maintain peace, but solely in the attempt to prevent Great Britain and France from honoring their obligations to Poland".[40]

On 31 August 1939, Hitler issued his final directive announcing that the attack on Poland would start on 1 September. He subsequently gave instructions as to what action would be taken if Britain and France should enter the war in defence of Poland.[41] The IMT held:

> [B]y the evidence that the war initiated by Germany against Poland on 1 September 1939 was most plainly an aggressive war, which was to develop in due course into a war which embraced almost the whole world, and resulted in the commission of countless crimes, both against the laws and customs of war, and against humanity.[42]

---

36 *Ibid.*, p. 200.
37 *Ibid.*
38 *Ibid*, pp. 201–2.
39 *Ibid.*, p. 202.
40 *Ibid.*, p. 203.
41 *Ibid.*
42 *Ibid.*

The IMT stated that "the aggressive war against Poland was but the beginning. The aggression of Nazi Germany spread quickly from country to country".[43]

The next countries to suffer were Denmark and Norway. The former had entered into a Treaty of Non-Aggression with Germany on 31 May 1939.[44] However, Germany invaded Denmark on 9 April 1940.[45] Norway was sent assurance by Germany on 2 September 1939 to respect its territory.[46] But on 9 April 1940, Norway was invaded by Germany.[47] The IMT found that "as early as October 1939, the question of invading Norway was under consideration".[48]

The defence at the IMT put forward an argument that Germany was compelled to attack Norway to forestall an Allied invasion, and thus its actions were preventative.[49] However, the IMT rejected this line of reasoning: "It is clear that when the plans for an attack on Norway were being made, they were not made for the purposes of forestalling an imminent Allied landing, but, at the most, that they might prevent an Allied occupation at some future date", and that "Norway was occupied by Germany to afford her bases from which a more effective attack on England and France might be made, pursuant to plans prepared long in advance of the Allied plans which are not relied on to support the argument of self-defence".[50] The IMT thus concluded that "in the light of all the available evidence, it is impossible to accept the contention that the invasions of Denmark and Norway were defensive, and in the opinion of the Tribunal they were acts of aggressive war".[51]

---

[43] *Ibid.*

[44] The Treaty stated that the parties to the Treaty were "firmly resolved to maintain peace between Denmark and Germany under all circumstances", *ibid.*

[45] *Ibid.*

[46] The terms of the assurance stated: "The German Reich Government is determined in view of the friendly relations which exist between Norway and Germany under no circumstance to prejudice the inviolability and integrity of Norway, and to respect the territory of the Norwegian State", *ibid.*

[47] *Ibid.*, p. 204.

[48] *Ibid.*, p. 205.

[49] *Ibid.*

[50] *Ibid.*, p. 206.

[51] *Ibid.*, p. 207.

The IMT found that "the plan to seize Belgium and the Netherlands was considered in August 1938, when the attack on Czechoslovakia was being formulated, and the possibility of war with France and England was contemplated".[52] In May 1939, when Hitler foresaw the possibility at least of a war with Britain and France in consequence of the attack against Poland, he said: "Dutch and Belgian air bases must be occupied. [...] Declarations of neutrality must be ignored".[53]

In relation to Belgium, the Netherlands and Luxembourg, Hitler had assured these three nations that he would respect their neutrality, and he had repeated this assurance on 6 October 1939. Nevertheless, on 10 May 1940, German forces invaded the Netherlands, Belgium and Luxembourg. At a conference on 23 November 1939, Hitler stated:

> The progress of the war depends on the possession of the Ruhr. If England and France push through Belgium and Holland into the Ruhr, we shall be in the greatest danger. [...] Certainly England and France will assume the offensive against Germany when they are armed. England and France have means of pressure to bring Belgium and Holland to request English and French help. In Belgium and Holland the sympathies are all for France and England. [...] If the French Army marches into Belgium in order to attack us, it will be too late for us. We must anticipate them. [...] We shall sow the English coast with mines which cannot be cleared. [...] My decision is unchangeable; I shall attack France and England at the most favorable and quickest moment. Breach of the neutrality of Belgium and Holland is meaningless. [...] If we do not break the neutrality, then England and France will. Without attack, the war is not to be ended victoriously.[54]

The IMT held that "the invasion of Belgium, Holland, and Luxembourg was entirely without justification. It was carried out in pursuance of policies long considered and prepared, and was plainly an act of aggressive war. The resolve to invade was made without any consideration than the advancement of the aggressive policies of Germany".[55]

---

[52] *Ibid.*

[53] *Ibid.*

[54] *Ibid.*, p. 208.

[55] *Ibid.*, p. 209.

On 1 June 1939, Hitler had provided Yugoslavia with assurances that Germany would respect its boundaries.[56] Yet Germany had tried, albeit unsuccessfully, to persuade Italy to enter the war on its side against Yugoslavia.[57] On 28 October 1940, Italy invaded Greece. Hitler tried to persuade Mussolini that "Yugoslavia, must if at all possible be won over by other means, and in other ways".[58] On 12 November and 13 December 1940, Hitler issued directives with respect to the invasion of Greece.[59]

At a meeting on 20 January 1941 between Hitler and Mussolini, the former stated that the massing of troops in Romania served three purposes: as an operation against Greece; as protection of Bulgaria against Russia and Turkey; and as a safeguard for the guarantee to Romania.[60]

On 3 March 1941, British armed forces landed in Greece to assist in resistance against the Italians.[61] On 18 March, Hitler was asked for confirmation that the "whole of Greece will have to be occupied, even in the event of a peaceful settlement", to which he replied, "the complete occupation is a prerequisite of any settlement".[62]

On 25 March 1941, Germany once again reassured its determination to respect the sovereignty and territorial integrity of Yugoslavia at all times, when the latter adhered to the Tripartite Pact. However, the next day Yugoslav ministers were removed in Belgrade by a coup d'état, and the new government repudiated the Pact. In response, Hitler stated that Yugoslavia was an "uncertain factor in regard to the contemplated attack

---

[56] Hitler said in a public speech on the occasion of the visit to Germany of the Prince Regent of Yugoslavia: "the firmly established reliable relationship of Germany to Yugoslavia now that owing to historical events we have become neighbors with common boundaries fixed for all time, will not only guarantee lasting peace between our two peoples and countries, but can also represent an element of calm to our nerve-racked continent. This peace is the goal of all who are disposed to perform really constructive work", *ibid.*

[57] In a conversation between Hitler and the Foreign Minister of Italy, Galeazzo Ciano, and one of the defendants, the former said: "Generally speaking, the best thing to happen would be for the neutrals to be liquidated one after the other. This process could be carried out more easily if on every occasion one partner of the Axis covered the other while it was dealing with the uncertain neutral. Italy might well regard Yugoslavia as a neutral of this kind", *ibid.*

[58] *Ibid.*

[59] *Ibid.*, p. 209–10

[60] *Ibid.*, p. 210

[61] *Ibid.*

[62] *Ibid.*

on Greece and even more so with regard to the attack upon Russia".[63] He announced that he was determined, irrespective of the possible loyalty of the new government, for preparations to be made to destroy Yugoslavia militarily and as a national unit. This would be done with "unmerciful harshness".[64] Germany invaded Greece and Yugoslavia on 6 April 1941 without warning and the Luftwaffe bombed Belgrade.

The IMT found that "so swift was this particular invasion that there had not been time to establish any 'incidents' as a usual preliminary, or to find and publish any adequate 'incidents' as a usual preliminary, or to find and publish any adequate 'political' explanations". Thus, it was held that

> it is clear from this narrative that aggressive war against Greece and Yugoslavia had long been in contemplation, certainly as early as August of 1939. The fact that Great Britain had come to the assistance of the Greeks, and might thereafter be in a position to inflict great damage upon German interests was made the occasion for the occupation of both countries.[65]

Germany signed the non-aggression pact with the Soviet Union on 23 August 1939. The IMT was satisfied that the Soviet Union had conformed to the terms of this pact. Germany, for its part, began to make preparations in secret for an attack on the Soviet Union in the late summer of 1940.[66] Hitler issued a directive on 18 December 1940 that called for the completion of all preparations connected with the realisation of the attack on the Soviet Union by 15 May 1941.[67]

Prior to this directive, surveys had been made of the economic possibilities of the Soviet Union, including its raw materials, its power and transport system and its capacity to produce arms. Military-economic units were created in accordance to these surveys, which were to achieve the most complete and efficient economic exploitation of the occupied territories in the interest of Germany. Furthermore, a framework was designed pertaining to the future political and economic organisation of the

---

[63] *Ibid.*

[64] *Ibid.*, p. 211.

[65] *Ibid.*

[66] *Ibid.*

[67] The directive stated: "The German armed forces must be prepared to crush Soviet Russia in a quick campaign before the end of the war against England. [...] Great caution has to be exercised that the intention of the attack will not be recognized", *ibid.*

occupied territories. These plans had outlined the destruction of the Soviet Union as an independent state and the conversion of Estonia, Latvia, Bielorussia (Belarus) and other territories into German colonies. Germany had also managed to draw Hungary, Romania and Finland into the war against the Soviet Union.[68]

The IMT found that "on 22 June 1941, without any declaration of war, Germany invaded Soviet territory in accordance with the plans so long made".[69] It also found that "Germany had the design carefully thought out, to crush the U.S.S.R as a political and military power, so that Germany might expand to the east according to her own desire".[70] It was held that "the plans for the economic exploitation of the U.S.S.R for the removal of masses of the population, for the murder of the Commissars and political leaders, were all part of the carefully prepared scheme launched on 22 June without warning of any kind, and without the shadow of legal excuse. It was plain aggression".[71]

Germany declared war on the United States four days after the attack launched by the Japanese on the US fleet in Pearl Harbor on 7 December 1941.[72] Germany, Italy and Japan had signed the Tripartite Pact on 27 September 1940. The IMT found that on 28 November 1941, 10 days before the attack on Pearl Harbor, one of the defendants, on behalf of Germany, encouraged Japan to attack Britain and the United States, assuring that Germany would join the war against the United States immediately. Japanese representatives told Germany and Italy that Japan was preparing to attack the United States and asked for their support. They agreed, to which the IMT pointed out that "in the Tripartite Pact, Italy and Germany had undertaken to assist Japan only if she were attacked".[73] The IMT held:

> Although it is true that Hitler and his colleagues originally did not consider that a war with the United States would be beneficial to their interest, it is apparent that in the course of 1941, that view was reviewed, and Japan was given every encouragement to adopt a policy which would almost cer-

---

68 *Ibid.*, p. 212.
69 *Ibid.*
70 *Ibid.*
71 *Ibid.*, p. 213.
72 *Ibid.*
73 *Ibid.*, p. 214.

tainly bring the United States into the war. And when Japan attacked the United States fleet in Pearl Harbor and thus made aggressive war against the United States, the Nazi Government caused Germany to enter that war at once on the side of Japan by declaring war themselves on the United States.[74]

It should be pointed out that the war of aggression committed by Germany against the United States was different from the other wars of aggression in two respects. First, Germany had made an official declaration of war. Second, there was no actual use of military force by Germany against the United States. It is presumed therefore that the declaration of war was sufficient to satisfy the IMT of the state act element of the crime.

From this extensive review of the facts, the following points can be deduced with respect to understanding the constitutive elements of a war of aggression. First, the underlying requirement appears to be that there must be an actual initiation of the use of force by the alleged aggressor state. Despite the breach of bilateral agreements and other means of peaceful assurances, and the threat of the use of force against Austria and Czechoslovakia, these aggressive measures that had caused annexation and incorporation into German territory were not sufficient to be considered a war of aggression in the absence of use of force.

Second, the use of force may be accompanied by a number of clear objectives: annexation and occupation of territory and annihilation (Poland); furthering purposes of aggression against other countries (Belgium, the Netherlands, Luxembourg, Yugoslavia, Greece); gaining military advantage over other adversaries by preventing them from assisting a previously aggressed state (Denmark, Norway); expansion of territory (Soviet Union); and the formal declaration of war in support of a third state's war of aggression (United States). The clear trend appears to be that a war of aggression typically involved the initiation of the use of force by the aggressor state, accompanied by an objective leading to a partial or full occupation of the invaded territory, with the exception of the war of aggression against the United States where there was a formal declaration of war for the purposes of assisting in Japan's war of aggression.

My view is that a war of aggression comprises two components: an objective component and a subjective component. The former refers to the

---

[74] *Ibid.*

initiation of the use of force, which can be determined objectively, while the latter encompasses the objectives used for advancing the aggressive purposes of the war, for example the partial or full occupation of the invaded territory, objectives of annihilation, purposes of further aggression against other countries or gaining military advantages over aggressed alliances. This can be identified as the "aggressive intent" or the *animus aggressionis*. In contrast to the first component, the *animus aggressionis* is subjective.

In this regard, after the war, the UN General Assembly proposed to the International Law Commission ('ILC') to work on a Draft Code of Offences Against the Peace and Security of Mankind ('Draft Code'). The ILC Special Rapporteur, Jean Spiropoulos, in his second report on the Draft Code explained the concept behind the *animus aggressionis*:

> In the absence of a positive definition of aggression provided for by an international instrument and applicable to the concrete, this case, international law, for the purpose of determining the "aggressor" in an armed conflict, it is assumed to refer to the criteria contained in the "natural" notion of aggression.[75]

The "natural" notion, according to Spiropoulos, consisted of both an objective and subjective criteria. The former occurs when a state commits an act of violence, while the latter when the violence committed must be due to aggressive intention.[76] The link between the objective and subjective can be seen here:

> The mere fact that a State acted as first does not, per se, constitute "aggression" as long as its behavior was not due to: aggressive intention (Subjective element of the concept of aggression). That the *animus aggressionis* is a constitutive element of the concept of aggression needs no demonstra-

---

[75] Second Report on a Draft Code of Offences Against the Peace and Security of Mankind by Mr. J. Spiropoulos, Special Rapporteur, A/CN.4/44, Annex, para. 152, in *Yearbook of the International Law Commission*, 1951, vol. II ('Second Report on a Draft Code').

[76] Spiropoulos submitted that only if both objective and subjective criteria are taken together may it be possible to decide "which State, in an international armed conflict, is to be considered as 'aggressor under international law'. The (natural) notion of aggression is a concept per se, which is inherent to any human mind and which as a primary notion, is not susceptible of definition. Consequently whether the behavior of a State is to be considered as an 'aggression under law' has to be decided not on the basis of a specific criteria adopted a priori but on the basis of the above notion which, to sum it up, is rooted in the 'feeling' of the Government concerned", *ibid.*, para. 153.

tion. It follows from the very essence of the notion of aggression as such.[77]

The submission that the *animus aggressionis* is an integral part of the meaning of a war of aggression can be supported by the IMT's findings with respect to Germany's actions against the United States. Despite the lack of armed force, the declaration of war nevertheless represented the *animus aggressionis* – the intention to assist a third state in an aggressive war. It can be further inferred a war of aggression does not necessarily need to encompass both the objective and subjective elements, as the latter appears to suffice.

14.3.1.2. A War in Violation of International Treaties, Agreements and Assurances

Although the IMT did not find it necessary to determine this variant of the state act element of the crime, wars in violation of international treaties, agreements or assurances are nevertheless still a part of the substantive definition of crimes against peace. Therefore, it is worth mentioning the international treaties, agreements or assurances that the IMT acknowledged were of principal importance: the Hague Conventions, the Versailles Treaty, treaties of mutual guarantee, arbitration and non-aggression between Germany and the other powers, and the Kellogg-Briand Pact.[78]

As the acts of aggression and wars of aggression were committed by Germany prior to the formation of the United Nations, the aforementioned international instruments are indicative of the normative framework that pertained to the prohibition of the use of force under international law. Therefore, the violation of these international instruments that result in war is indicative of a breach of the prohibition of the use of force. From this, it can be inferred that it is the violation of the prohibition of the use of force, which constitutes the state act element of crimes against peace.

14.3.2. The Nuremberg Principles and Customary International Law

The UN General Assembly resolution 95(1) of 1946 affirmed the principles of international law recognised by the IMT Charter and the Judgment

---

[77] *Ibid.*

[78] Nuremberg Judgment and Sentences, pp. 214–16, see *supra* note 6.

of the IMT as the Nuremberg Principles. Although this may be representative of the early stages of acceptance by the international community of these general principles as norms of customary international law, at the time of their adoption this remained only an affirmation of the principles. The General Assembly also adopted resolution 177 (II) (1947), which mandated the formulation of the principles of international law to the ILC, and directed it, *inter alia*, to formulate the principles of international law recognised in the IMT Charter and Judgment.[79] The ILC questioned whether its role should ascertain the extent to which the principles contained in the IMT Charter and Judgment constituted principles of international law. It concluded:

> Since the Nürnberg principles had been affirmed by the General Assembly in resolution 95 (I) of 11 December 1946, the task of the Commission was not to express any appreciation of these principles as principles of international law but merely to formulate them.[80]

At this point, the customary international law status of the envisaged Nuremberg Principles was still not clear. Nevertheless, the ILC embarked on the task of formulating these principles, and subsequently adopted them at its second session in 1950.[81] It should be noted that the Nuremberg Principles as elaborated by the ILC were never formally adopted by the General Assembly. General Assembly resolution 488 (V) (1950) invited the "Governments of Member States to furnish their observations accordingly".[82]

The Nuremberg Principles that are of key relevance to the present analysis are Principle I, which stipulates that "any person who commits an act which constitutes a crime under international law is responsible there-

---

[79] United Nations, General Assembly resolution 177 (II), Formulation of the Principles Recognized in the Charter of the Nürnberg Tribunal and in the Judgment of the Tribunal, 21 November 1947.

[80] International Law Commission, Report of the International Law Commission to the General Assembly on the Work of the First Session, 12 April–9 June 1949, ch. III, UN doc. A/CN.4/SER.A/1949 (1949), in *Yearbook of the International Law Commission*, 1949, vol. I, p. 282.

[81] For commentaries on the principles, see Second Report on a Draft Code, *supra* note 75.

[82] See Observations of Governments of Member States relating to the Formulation of the Nürnberg Principles Prepared by the International Law Commission, A/CN.4/45 and Corr. 1, Add. 1 and Corr. 1 and Add. 2, in *Yearbook of the International Law Commission*, 1951, vol. II.

for and liable to punishment"; and Principle VI(a) which holds that crimes against peace are punishable as a crime under international law. It should be noted that the definition of crimes against peace mirrored Article 6(a) of the IMT Charter.

In parallel to the work on formulating the Nuremberg Principles, the ILC was, as already noted, also directed to work on compiling a Draft Code of Crimes against the Peace and Security of Mankind. The first draft of 1951 comprised five articles, of which the crimes defined in Article 2 were considered as crimes under international law, for which the responsible individuals should be punished.[83] It is worth mentioning that crimes against peace were mentioned as aggression in the Draft Code under Article 2(1) as "any act of aggression, including the employment by the authorities of a State of armed force against another State for any purpose other than national or collective self-defence or in pursuance of a decision or recommendation by a competent organ of the United Nations".[84] Here, the shift in terminology from "crimes against peace" to "act of aggression" can be seen. Although there is no definition for the act of aggression, Article 2(1) nevertheless appears to reflect the framework of *jus ad bellum* and principles of collective security pursuant to the UN Charter.[85]

Although the legal effects of the Draft Code and the UN General Assembly Resolutions are not so clear, the positive opinions that were generally expressed by governments with respect to the Nuremberg Principles and these multilateral international instruments were nevertheless indicative of the political will of states to embrace them as a substantive source of law. Thus, positive opinions, affirmations and multilateral international instruments suggest the formation of customary international rules with respect to the Nuremberg Principles. Neither is it clear when the actual crystallisation of the Nuremberg Principles as customary international law occurred. It appears to have been a rather gradual process. As such, it must be understood that the principles within the IMT Charter and Judgment did not create any form of instant customary international law rules. Rather, the principles were affirmed and gradually accepted by the

---

[83] Draft Code of Crimes against Peace and Security of Mankind with Commentaries, in *Yearbook of the International Law Commission*, 1951, vol. II, para. 59, p. 135.

[84] *Ibid.*

[85] See Report by J. Spiropoulos, Special Rapporteur, UN doc. A/CN.4/25 (1950), in *Yearbook of International Law Commission*, 1950, vol. II, p. 262.

international community through positive declarations and multilateral instruments.

At present, it is generally accepted that the Nuremberg Principles, and thus crimes against peace, have attained customary international law status. It is also generally accepted that the customary international law rule pertaining to the crime of aggression has not developed past Nuremberg. Although the ICC Statute had incorporated the crime of aggression under Article 5(1), the legal nature of the Statute as a multilateral instrument limits the jurisdiction of the ICC to its state parties.[86] Therefore, the definition of the crime of aggression is only for the purposes of prosecution at the ICC, and should not be regarded as a substantive definition of the crime in the sense of a customary international law rule.[87]

Under customary international law, the state act element of the crime of aggression is a war of aggression or a war in violation of international treaties, agreements or assurances. In the light of the Nuremberg Judgment, this can be understood as the initiation of the use of force, accompanied by *animus aggressionis* and a violation of the prohibition of the use of force. How would these two variants be applicable with respect to the current paradigm of international law?

There have been changes with respect to terminology. First, the crime of aggression appears to have replaced crimes against peace. Yet the change in terminology carries no real ramifications as they both refer to the same crime. As such, crimes against peace and the crime of aggression can be used interchangeably.[88] Second, it appears that international law has shifted away from the use of the word "war". It can be observed that war is not mentioned in the substantive provisions of the UN Charter. Nevertheless, despite the change in terminology, the substantive value of

---

[86] There are instances where the ICC may exercise jurisdiction over individuals who are nationals of non-state parties. See Dapo Akande, "The Jurisdiction of the International Criminal Court over Nationals of Non-Parties: Legal Basis and Limits", in *Journal of International Criminal Justice*, 2003, vol. 1, no. 3, p. 618–50.

[87] See Marko Milanovic, "Is the Rome Statute Binding on Individuals? (And Why We Should Care)", in *Journal of International Criminal Justice*, 2011, vol. 9, no. 1, p. 25–32.

[88] In the *R v. Jones*, Lord Bingham of Cornhill stated that it had not been suggested that there was "any difference of substance" between a crime against peace and a crime of aggression and that as a matter of convenience he would refer to the latter, see [2006] UKHL 16, 29 March 2006.

a war of aggression or a war in violation of international treaties, agreements or assurances is retained under customary international law.[89]

The latter is relatively more straightforward. As discussed above, the international treaties, agreements or assurances reflect the normative framework that prohibits the use of force. In contemporary public international law, the core international treaty that regulates the use of interstate force is the UN Charter. In particular, Article 2(4) of the UN Charter stipulates:

> All Members shall refrain in their international relations from the threat or use of force against the territorial integrity or political independence of any state, or in any other manner inconsistent with the Purposes of the United Nations.

Thus, a war in violation of international treaties, agreements or assurances in the light of the current paradigm of international law can be understood as a war in violation of the UN Charter and the other instruments under international law that create the normative framework that prohibits aggression, for example, General Assembly resolutions 2625 (XXV) of 1970 ('resolution 2625') and 3314 (XXIX) of 1974 ('resolution 3314').[90]

As noted above, there has been a shift in terminology: war is not defined in the UN Charter. It can be presumed that the violation of the legal framework prohibiting the use of force must be of sufficient magnitude that it may be normatively perceived as war for the act to be considered as aggression.

What about a war of aggression? Articles 1 and 39 of the UN Charter do not mention a war of aggression but instead refer to an act of aggression. Resolution 3314, which provides a normative definition of aggression, refers to an act of aggression. My view is that the change in terminology from war to act should not detract from the constitutive elements of a war of aggression that formulate the state act element of the crime of aggression under customary international law.[91] In other words,

---

[89] See Carrie McDougall, *The Crime of Aggression under the Rome Statute of the International Criminal Court*, Cambridge University Press, Cambridge, 2013, p. 151.

[90] UNGA resolution 2625 (XXV), Declaration on Principles of International Law concerning Friendly Relations and Co-operation among States in accordance with the Charter of the United Nations, 24 October 1970, UN doc. A/RES/25/2625; and UNGA resolution 3314 (XXIX), Definition of Aggression, 14 December 1974.

[91] *Ibid.*, p. 153.

irrespective of the change in terminology, the state act element of the crime of aggression under customary international law is the initiation of the use of force of the alleged aggressor state, and the *animus aggressionis*. The aggressive intent is not only a subjective concept but also a rather natural concept. Therefore, in the light of a positive approach to the current legal framework pertaining to the use of force, the significance that the *animus aggressionis* holds with respect to ascertaining the legality of the use of force is questionable. A positive approach would tend to only examine the legality of the use of force by the alleged aggressed state under the framework of *jus ad bellum* without considering the *animus aggressionis*. A non-positive approach, on the other hand, may value the *animus aggressionis* as part of the deciding whether the use of force by the alleged aggressor state was for a "just" purpose or not.[92]

Determining the legality of the use of force or the existence of an act of aggression is subject to the methodological interpretation of the existing rules of *jus ad bellum*. Nevertheless, it should be clarified that the consideration of the *animus aggressionis* is for the purposes of establishing the state act element of the crime to prosecute an individual for crimes against peace, and not for determining the existence of an act of aggression committed by the alleged aggressor state for the purposes of invoking legal consequences under state responsibility. The latter can be done in an objective manner without the need to consider any mental element of the aggressor state.[93]

14.4. The Kampala Amendments and the Crime of Aggression

The definition of the crime of aggression in the Kampala Amendments is found in Article 8*bis*. It is worth reproducing the definition in its entirety.

Crime of aggression:

---

[92] See Erin Creegan, "Justified Uses of Force and the Crime of Aggression", in *Journal of International Criminal Justice*, 2012, vol. 10, no. 1, pp. 59–82.

[93] See Draft Articles on State Responsibility for Internationally Wrongful Acts, Art. 2, adopted by the ILC at its 53rd Session, 2001, and submitted to the General Assembly as part of the ILC's report covering the work of that session (A/56/10), in *Yearbook of the International Law Commission*, 2001, vol. II, pp. 34 ff. André Nollkaemper, "Concurrence Between Individual Responsibility and State Responsibility In International Law", in *International and Comparative Law Quarterly*, 2003, vol. 52, no. 3, p. 633.

1. For the purpose of this Statute, "crime of aggression" means the planning, preparation, initiation or execution, by a person in a position effectively to exercise control over or to direct the political or military action of a State, of an act of aggression which, by its character, gravity and scale, constitutes a manifest violation of the Charter of the United Nations.

2. For the purpose of paragraph 1, "act of aggression" means the use of armed force by a State against the sovereignty, territorial integrity or political independence of another State, or in any other manner inconsistent with the Charter of the United Nations. Any of the following acts, regardless of a declaration of war, shall, in accordance with United Nations General Assembly resolution 3314 (XXIX) of 14 December 1974, qualify as an act of aggression:

   (a) The invasion or attack by the armed forces of a State of the territory of another State, or any military occupation, however temporary, resulting from such invasion or attack, or any annexation by the use of force of the territory of another State or part thereof;

   (b) Bombardment by the armed forces of a State against the territory of another State or the use of any weapons by a State against the territory of another State;

   (c) The blockade of the ports or coasts of a State by the armed forces of another State;

   (d) An attack by the armed forces of a State on the land, sea or air forces, or marine and air fleets of another State;

   (e) The use of armed forces of one State which are within the territory of another State with the agreement of the receiving State, in contravention of the conditions provided for in the agreement or any extension of their presence in such territory beyond the termination of the agreement;

   (f) The action of a State in allowing its territory, which it has placed at the disposal of another State, to be used by that other State for perpetrating an act of aggression against a third State;

    (g) The sending by or on behalf of a State of armed
bands, groups, irregulars or mercenaries, which carry
out acts of armed force against another State of such
gravity as to amount to the acts listed above, or its
substantial involvement therein.

It should be noted that Article 8*bis*(1) explicitly states that the definition is only for the purposes of the ICC Statute. Thus, the definition should not be regarded as a substantive source of international law. This is reaffirmed in Annex III, Understanding 4:

> It is understood that the amendments that address the definition of the act of aggression and the crime of aggression do so for the purpose of this Statute only. The amendments shall, in accordance with article 10 of the Rome Statute, not be interpreted as limiting or prejudicing in any way existing or developing rules of international law for purposes other than this Statute.[94]

It is also important to understand that the definition of the crime of aggression in Article 8*bis* serves to establish individual criminal responsibility of the defendant, and not to invoke consequences under state responsibility for the aggressor state.[95] The ICC deals exclusively with the former, which means that any legal consequences that can be invoked against the aggressor state for the act of aggression should be assessed in a different international forum.

14.4.1. The Crime of Aggression: The State Act Element

The state act element pursuant to Article 8*bis*(1) is "an act of aggression which, by its character, gravity and scale, constitutes a manifest violation of the Charter of the United Nations". The elements of the crime pertaining to individual conduct comprise two separate components: "the planning, preparation, initiation or execution" and "by a person in a position effectively to exercise control over or to direct the political or military action of a State".[96] Therefore, under Article 8*bis*(1), there are three conditions that must be satisfied. First, the alleged aggressor state has committed "an act of aggression which by its character, gravity and scale con-

---

[94] Kampala Amendments, Annex III, Understandings, para. 4, see *supra* note 1.

[95] ICC Statute, Art. 25(4), see *supra* note 2.

[96] Kampala Amendments, Annex I, Amendments, Art. 8*bis*, Crime of Aggression, see *supra* note 1.

stitutes a manifest violation of the Charter of the United Nations". Second, the defendant must be "in a position to effectively exercise control over or to direct the political or military action of a State". And third, the defendant must participate in one or more of the modes of perpetration.

As mentioned at the outset, the focus of the present analysis is on the state act element of the crime. Nevertheless, it should be briefly noted that there are two differences from the definition in the IMT Charter with respect to the elements of individual conduct. First, the mode of perpetration "waging" has been replaced with "execution". Second, there is an additional element with respect to the position of the defendant in the political or military structure of the aggressor state. This element is more commonly known as the "leadership element", and it forms part of the substantive definition of the crime of aggression at the ICC.[97] As such, only an individual who satisfies the leadership element may be prosecuted for the crime of aggression.

The link between the state act element of the crime and the elements of the crime pertaining to the conduct of the individual is the actual existence of an act of aggression, which, by its character, gravity and scale, constitutes a manifest violation of the UN Charter. In the absence of such an act of aggression, the conduct of the individual cannot be assessed. This is reaffirmed in Element 3 of the crime:

> The act of aggression – the use of armed force by a State against the sovereignty, territorial integrity or political independence of another State, or in any other manner inconsistent with the Charter of the United Nations – was committed.[98]

From this, it is inferred that the ICC can only determine the elements of individual conduct if it is satisfied that an actual act of aggression has occurred. With respect to the initiation and waging of an act of aggression, this is relatively straightforward. However, the planning and preparation of aggression refers to conduct by the individual which is undertaken prior to the actual act of aggression by the aggressor state. Element 3 clarifies that the ICC may not make any findings that the defendant has planned and prepared an act of aggression in the absence of an

---

[97] Kevin Jon Heller, "Retreat from Nuremberg: The Leadership Requirement in the Crime of Aggression", in *European Journal of International Law*, 2007, vol. 3, no. 2, p. 477–97.

[98] Kampala Amendments, Annex II, Amendments to the Elements of Crimes, Element 3, see *supra* note 1.

actual act of aggression. This means that a defendant may not be prose-cuted for the planning and preparation of an act of aggression that had not actually been committed by the alleged aggressor state.

According to Article 8*bis*(1), only the acts of aggression which by their character, gravity and scale constitute a manifest violation of the UN Charter may be prosecuted at the ICC as a crime of aggression. The mani-fest violation of the UN Charter is indicative of a threshold that is appli-cable to the act of aggression. Thus, not every situation of aggression can be considered as a crime of aggression for the purposes of prosecution at the ICC. Likewise, not every instance of use of force in violation of *jus ad bellum* may be considered as an act of aggression for the purposes of Ar-ticle 8*bis*(1). Unlike the IMT Charter and the Draft Code, the Kampala Amendments have defined an act of aggression with respect to the state act element of the crime. The definition of an act of aggression for the purposes of Article 8*bis*(1) is contained in Article 8*bis*(2).

14.4.2. Article 8*bis*(2): An Act of Aggression

Article 8*bis*(2) can be divided into two separate sections. The first sen-tence is the *chapeau* clause:

> For the purposes of paragraph 1, "act of aggression" means the use of armed force by a State against the sovereignty, ter-ritorial integrity or political independence of another State, or in any other manner inconsistent with the Charter of the United Nations.

The second sentence provides examples of acts that may be consid-ered as acts of aggression:

> Any of the following acts, regardless of a declaration of war, shall, in accordance with United Nations General Assembly Resolution 3314 (XXIX) of 14 December 1974, qualify as an act of aggression.

This is followed by a list of acts that which mirrors the acts con-tained in Article 3 of resolution 3314. This enumerated list serves as ex-amples of acts that may qualify as acts of aggression.[99] It can be noted that the definition of an act of aggression under Article 8*bis*(2) is taken

---

[99] *Ibid.*, Annex I, Amendments, Art. 8*bis*(2). See also Informal Intersessional Meeting of the Special Working Group on the Crime of Aggression, Princeton University, New Jersey, 8–11 June 2006, ICC-ASP/5/SWGCA/INF.1, para. 10 ('Princeton Report 2006').

verbatim from Articles 1 and 3 of resolution 3314. There is, however, one slight but significant difference, which is that the second sentence of Article 8*bis*(2) modifies Article 3 of resolution 3314 by replacing "subject to and in accordance with the provisions of Article 2" with "in accordance with UN GA 3314".

Bearing in mind that the purpose of resolution 3314 is to serve as guidance to the Security Council in determining an act of aggression under Article 39 of the UN Charter, Article 2 is one of the provisions that makes reference to the discretion of the Security Council to determine an act of aggression.[100] By not incorporating any specific reference to Article 2 of resolution 3314 into Article 8*bis*(2), it can be inferred that the Security Council is precluded from playing a role in determining an act of aggression as part of the substantive definition of the crime for the purposes of prosecution at the ICC.[101] It should be clarified that this is indeed a separate matter from the role of the Security Council with respect to determining aggression as a condition for the exercise of jurisdiction under Article 15*bis* and Article 15*ter*.

Yet a valid question can be raised as to whether Article 2 is nevertheless implicitly incorporated by virtue of the reference to resolution 3314 in Article 8*bis*(2). This question is directly relevant to whether resolution 3314 has to be read in its entirety with respect to Article 8*bis*(2).[102] Reading resolution 3314 in its entirety would give effect to the discretion of the Security Council under Article 2 to conclude that the use of force concerned or its consequences are not of sufficient gravity to make a finding of an act of aggression. Article 4 of resolution 3314 also acknowledges the discretion of the Security Council to determine that other acts may constitute aggression, in addition to the enumerated list of acts under Article 3. It should also be noted that Article 4 explicitly notes that the enumerated list under Article 3 is not exhaustive. This point will shortly be

---

[100] Resolution 3314, Art. 2, see *supra* note 90, states: "The first use of armed force by a State in contravention of the Charter shall constitute prima facie evidence of an act of aggression although the Security Council may, in conformity with the Charter, conclude that a determination that an act of aggression has been committed would not be justified in the light of other relevant circumstances, including the fact that the acts concerned or their consequences are not of sufficient gravity".

[101] Stefan Barriga, "Negotiating the Amendments on the Crime of Aggression", in Stefan Barriga and Claus Kreß (eds.), *Crime of Aggression Library: The Travaux Préparatoires of the Crime of Aggression*, Cambridge University Press, Cambridge, 2012, p. 27.

[102] *Ibid.*, pp. 25–27.

returned to. At present, the issue is whether the reference to resolution 3314 should be interpreted as incorporating the other provisions into the reading of Article 8*bis*(2).

In my view, the drafting of the phrase "in accordance with Resolution 3314" in lieu of "subject to and in accordance with the provisions of article 2" is indicative of a deliberate decision to exclude any potential role of the Security Council to determine an act of aggression for the purposes of ascertaining the state act element of the crime. Indeed, to give effect to the exclusion of the role of the Security Council in determining an act of aggression, Articles 2 and 4 of resolution 3314 must be non-applicable. The only logical approach is to read Article 8*bis*(2) without incorporating resolution 3314 as a whole. Furthermore, if it were intended for other provisions of resolution 3314 to be incorporated into Article 8*bis*(2), the relevant provisions could have also been included in the draft together with Articles 1 and 3.

It is submitted that Article 8*bis*(2) should be read without the incorporation of resolution 3314 as a whole. In support of this, the Report of the Special Working Group on the Crime of Aggression observes that "the point was made that the reference to General Assembly resolution 3314 did not import the content of that resolution as a whole".[103] As such, only Articles 1 and 3 of resolution 3314 are to be given effect in Article 8*bis*(2).

The question that arises is whether the list of acts in Article 8*bis*(2) is exhaustive in nature. Although Article 4 of resolution 3314 is not meant to give effect to Article 8*bis*(2), in the context of the original resolution, it is stated that the list of acts in Article 3 is not exhaustive. As such, the Security Council had discretion to determine acts that fall outside this list as acts of aggression. It is only logical that the enumerated list in Article 8*bis*(2) is not exhaustive if the original provision that it is based upon is not exhaustive in nature. However, in terms of fulfilling a substantive component of a definition of a crime for the purposes of determining individual criminal responsibility it is also understandable that different standards may need to apply. This is especially so with respect to Article 22 of the ICC Statute, and the general principle of legality.

---

[103] Report of the Special Working Group on the Crime of Aggression, February 2009, ICC-ASP/7/20/Add.1, Annex II, para. 17 ('SWGCA Report 2009').

The debate surrounding this question need not be discussed here. My understanding is that the answer is not entirely conclusive, thus the question still remains.[104] Nevertheless, my view is that the enumerated list in Article 8*bis*(2) is not necessarily exhaustive.[105] This will allow the ICC to have some discretion in determining an act of aggression. Acts that fall outside the enumerated list may nevertheless be considered as an act of aggression provided they meet the definition within the *chapeau* clause, that is, "the use of armed force by a State against the sovereignty, territorial integrity or political independence of another State, or in any other manner inconsistent with the Charter of the United Nations".[106] Therefore, it is the *chapeau* clause which is of more significance with respect to determining an act of aggression.

The use of resolution 3314 as a premise for the definition of an act of aggression in the Kampala Amendments has nevertheless been subject to criticism.[107] Objections include, *inter alia*, the fact that resolution 3314 was drafted for the purposes of guiding the Security Council under Article 39 of UN Charter to make a determination of an act of aggression, and not for the purposes of criminal responsibility.[108] Be that as it may, resolution 3314 represents the normative definition of aggression under international law. Thus, adopting a text, which was already agreed upon by the international community in the light of a General Assembly resolution, was perhaps the most logical decision of those involved in the negotiation pro-

---

[104] Barriga, 2012, p. 28, see *supra* note 101.

[105] See Informal Intersessional Meeting of the Special Working Group on the Crime of Aggression, Princeton University, New Jersey, 11–14 June 2007, ICC-ASP/6/SWGCA/INF.1, para. 51 ('Princeton Report 2007').

[106] *Ibid.*, para. 48; SWGCA Report 2009, para. 34, see *supra* note 103; McDougall, 2013, p. 103, see *supra* note 89; Claus Kreß and Leonie von Holtzendorff, 2010, p. 1191, see *supra* note 1.

[107] Claus Kreß, "Time for Decision: Some Thoughts on the Immediate Future of the Crime of Aggression: A Reply to Andreas Paulus", in *European Journal of International Law*, 2011, vol. 20, no. 4, p. 1136–37. Some delegations preferred to make no reference to resolution 3314 at all; see Princeton Report 2007, para. 41, *supra* note 105.

[108] See Report of the Special Working Group on the Crime of Aggression, February 2007, ICC-ASP/5/35, para. 22 ('SWGCA Report 2007a'); Report of the Special Working Group on the Crime of Aggression, ICC-ASP/6/20/Add.1, June 2008, Annex II, para. 32 ('SWGCA Report 2008'); SWGCA Report 2009, para. 17, see *supra* note 103; Report of the Special Working Group on the Crime of Aggression, 13 December 2007, ICC-ASP/6/SWGCA1/, para. 23 ('SWGCA Report 2007b').

ceedings, as defining an act of aggression from the scratch would have been a considerable task.[109]

The important point to remember is that the definition of the act of aggression in Article 8*bis*(2) is not the state act element of the crime *per se*. Thus, it is not Article 8*bis*(2) which gives rise to individual criminal responsibility, but rather it is Article 8*bis*(1). Article 8*bis*(2) serves as the preliminary step to fulfilling the state act element of the crime under Article 8*bis*(1).

14.4.3. Article 8*bis*(1): Examining the Threshold

Presuming that every violation of *jus ad bellum* by the alleged aggressor state may amount *prima facie* to an act of aggression, the threshold within Article 8*bis*(1) implies that some acts of aggression are more serious than others and should give rise to individual criminal responsibility.[110] This threshold is acknowledged as a manifest violation of the UN Charter.

But, what is a manifest violation of the UN Charter? There is no reference to this in any other international instrument. As such, the threshold is a new construct and will thus be subject to interpretation. In accordance with traditional methods of interpretation, the most ordinary definition of manifest is "to show something clearly, through signs or actions" or "clearly be shown or visible" or, even more simply, to be "obvious". It can be inferred that the most ordinary meaning of the threshold is that the act of aggression must be a clear, visible and obvious breach of the UN Charter. Thus, it can be further inferred that alleged violations of the UN Charter, which involve the more contentious – or grey – areas of *jus ad bellum*, are excluded from Article 8*bis*(1) simply by virtue of fail-

---

[109] In the SWGCA Report 2008, see *supra* note 108, para. 31, it was stated that some delegations considered draft Article 8*bis*(2) to constitute the best compromise, as it fulfilled several requirements: it was precise enough to respect the principle of legality; it covered only the most serious crimes; it was sufficiently open to cover future forms of aggression; and it was clearly understood that this definition only served the purpose remained free to continue to apply their own standards to the crime of aggression. The reference to resolution 3314 was considered appropriate, as that resolution was a carefully negotiated instrument that reflected current customary international law. See also SWGCA Report 2007b, para. 14, *supra* note 108; and Robert Heinsch, "The Crime of Aggression after Kampala: Success or Burden for the Future?", in *Goettingen Journal of International Law*, 2012, vol. 2, no. 2, p. 725.

[110] Princeton Report 2006, paras. 18, 20, see *supra* note 99.

---

ing to be a clear, visible and obvious breach of the UN Charter. In other words, situations of alleged aggression where the underlying legality of the use of force falls within a grey area of *jus ad bellum* are excluded from being considered as the state act element of the crime of aggression.

It is written in the special introduction to the Elements of the Crime of Aggression that the term 'manifest' is an objective qualification.[111] This in itself is instructive, as it implies that the qualification should be made without considering subjective factors. However, it is not particularly insightful with respect to understanding the meaning of the threshold. The fifth Element of the Crime stipulates: "The act of aggression, by its character, gravity and scale, constituted a manifest violation of the Charter of the United Nations". From this, it can be inferred that the components "character, gravity and scale" should be taken into consideration with respect to determining a manifest violation of the UN Charter. Once again, none of these terms is defined. Also, neither of these terms appears in relation to the prohibition of the use of force under Article 2(4) in any other international instrument. According to the most ordinary meaning of these components, character is the distinctive nature of something; gravity means heaviness or weight, or of extreme importance or seriousness; scale means a proportion between two sets of dimensions or a distinctive relative size, extent or degree.

From this, it can be inferred that the state act element of the crime of aggression pursuant to the Kampala Amendments consists of an act of aggression, which by its distinctive nature is of sufficient importance or seriousness, heaviness or weight, and is of a large proportion or distinctive degree, which constitutes a clear, visible and obvious violation of the UN Charter. As can be seen, the phrase containing the qualifying terms "character, gravity and scale" adds considerable depth to the threshold of a "clear, visible and obvious" violation of the UN Charter.

This raises the question of whether all three components have to be present for an act of aggression to constitute a manifest violation of the UN Charter. It appears *prima facie* that the use of the conjunctive "and" implies that all three factors must be present.[112] However, is this really true? Understanding 7 states that

---

[111] Kampala Amendments, Annex II, Amendments to the Elements of Crimes, Introduction 3, see *supra* note 1.

[112] Heinsch, 2012, pp. 713–43, see *supra* note 109.

in establishing whether an act of aggression constitutes a manifest violation of the Charter of the United Nations, the three components of character, gravity and scale must be sufficient to justify a "manifest" determination. No one component can be significant enough to satisfy the manifest standard by itself.[113]

The first sentence implies that all three components must be present for the qualification of a manifest violation to be made. It can perhaps be further inferred that each individual component must be sufficient in itself to give rise to the qualification of a manifest violation.[114] However, the second sentence appears to shed a different light, as it can be read to support a submission that two components *may* sufficiently serve as the qualifiers with respect to determining a manifest violation of the UN Charter. Thus, in the absence of one of the components, the ICC is not necessarily precluded from finding that the act of aggression pursuant to Article 8*bis*(2) has amounted to a manifest violation of the UN Charter.

Yet it is significant to point out that the second sentence of Understanding 7 should not be read to suggest that two components *are* sufficient make a finding of a manifest violation of the UN Charter. My view is that the act of aggression pursuant to Article 8*bis*(2) should be assessed in the light of all three components. However, in a situation when one of the components is absent, this will not preclude the ICC from finding that the act of aggression has amounted to a manifest violation of the UN Charter in the light of the two components that are present.

As the normative threshold for an act of aggression under *jus ad bellum* is the use of armed force in "contravention of" or "in a manner inconsistent" with the UN Charter,[115] the threshold of a manifest violation would inherently exclude violations of *jus ad bellum* under Article 2(4) of

---

[113] Kampala Amendments, Annex III, Understandings, para. 7, see *supra* note 1.

[114] Claus Kreß, who was the focal point for the negotiations relating to the Kampala Amendments' Understandings, explains that "the idea behind this sentence was to exclude the determination of manifest illegality in a case where one component is most prominently present, but the other two not at all. It was thought that use of the word 'and' in the formulation of the threshold requirement in draft art 8 bis (1) excluded a determination of manifest illegality in such a case and that the understanding should properly reflect this fact", see Claus Kreß, Stefan Barriga, Leena Grover and Leonie Von Holtzendorff, "Negotiating the Understandings on the Crime of Aggression", in Barriga and Kreß, 2013, p. 96, see *supra* note 101.

[115] UN Charter, Art. 2(4), see *supra* note 3; resolution 3314, Arts. 1 and 2, see *supra* note 90.

the UN Charter that are of insufficient magnitude to be considered as aggression, as well as actual acts of aggression. Therefore, it is presumed that there is only a very narrow scope of acts of aggression that can be considered as a crime of aggression. The ramifications of this are that there are only very few situations of aggression where the relevant individual that satisfies the leadership element under Article 8*bis*(1) may be prosecuted for the crime of aggression at the ICC. By limiting the ICC's jurisdiction to only the most serious acts of crime thereby excludes "cases of insufficient gravity and falling within a grey area".[116]

Indeed, the normative threshold for determining an act of aggression under international law appears to be lower than the threshold under Article 8*bis*(1) for the crime of aggression. This has given rise to concern in the international community that there may be two thresholds relating to aggression under international law.[117] In particular, there is concern that the threshold required for the crime of aggression at the ICC is higher than an act of aggression under international law.[118] However, it should be emphasised that the act of aggression and the crime of aggression are two separate misconducts under international law, governed by two different legal frameworks. The breach of the primary rules of each legal framework gives rise to different consequences under the secondary norms of responsibility. An act of aggression will give rise to state responsibility, while a crime of aggression will give rise to individual criminal responsibility.

Thus, state responsibility and individual criminal responsibility are two separate sets of secondary rules, where the legal consequences can be invoked irrespective of and without prejudice to each other. My view is that this should help to dispel any apprehension with respect to "two competing definitions of aggression in public international law" or "the newer ICC definition eclipsing the jus ad bellum definition".[119] Regardless of whether the act of aggression may be considered as a crime of aggression under Article 8*bis*(1), the aggressor state had nevertheless

---

[116] SWGCA Report 2008, para. 24, see *supra* note 108.

[117] See Mary Ellen O'Connell and Mirakmal Niyazmatov, "What is Aggression? Comparing the *Jus ad Bellum* and the ICC Statute", in *Journal of International Criminal Justice*, 2012, vol. 10, no. 1, p. 189–207.

[118] Daniel D. Ntanda Nsereko, "Aggression under the Rome Statute of the International Criminal Court", in *Nordic Journal of International Law*, 2002, vol. 71, p. 503.

[119] O'Connell and Niyazmatov, 2012, p. 200, see *supra* note 117.

breached its duty to comply with primary obligations under *jus ad bellum*. As such, in an appropriate forum consistent with international dispute settlement, the aggressed state has a right under international law to invoke legal consequences pertaining to the responsibility of the aggressor state. Although there may not be individual criminal responsibility, it is not entirely true that there is no form of international responsibility for acts of aggression or lesser violations of the UN Charter.

For the purposes of establishing individual criminal responsibility at the ICC for the crime of aggression, the legal position in relation to the state act element of the crime can be summarised as follows. In every situation of alleged aggression, there are two steps in determining whether the wrongful act can be considered as a crime of aggression that may be prosecuted at the ICC. First, the alleged aggression must satisfy the criteria under Article 8*bis*(2) to be considered an act of aggression. Upon satisfaction, the second step is to assess the act of aggression in accordance with the threshold under Article 8*bis*(1). If it is satisfied that the act of aggression by its character, gravity and scale constitutes a manifest violation of the UN Charter, the state act element of the crime is established.

14.5. Comparing Crimes Against Peace and the Crime of Aggression: From Nuremberg to Kampala

At the IMT Trial the state act element of the crime was a war of aggression or a war in violation of international treaties, agreements and assurances. The underlying criterion that the act must constitute a war was demonstrated by the approach of the IMT whereby the acts of aggression committed against Austria and Czechoslovakia did not give rise to individual criminal responsibility for crimes against peace. In Article 8*bis*(1) of the Kampala Amendments, the state act element of the crime encompasses an act of aggression (subject to the applicable threshold). However, this should not be read to infer that the state act element of the crime of aggression has been watered down in international law from a war of aggression to an act of aggression. Instead, the change in nomenclature is reflective of the shift in paradigm within international law where reference is no longer made to war. The correct approach is to compare the underlying substantive components of each definition with respect to the state act element of the crime.

As discussed above, there were two substantive components to a war of aggression at Nuremberg: 1) the objective component, which is the initiation of the use of force of the aggressor state; and 2) the subjective component, which is the *animus aggressionis* of the state. As the war of aggression against the United States appeared to only encompass the *animus aggressionis* of Germany, this suggests that both aspects are not necessarily cumulative. Admittedly, this appears to be rather vague, as there is no definitive formula with respect to whether both components need to be present in all situations of aggression, or whether certain circumstances may require only one of the components to be present. Nevertheless, for the purposes of the present analysis, it is presumed that both components are applicable.

The state act element of the definition of the crime in the Kampala Amendments is now evaluated in light of these two components. With respect to the initiation of the use of force, the act is subject to a two-part process in order to satisfy the state act element of the crime of aggression. The use of force must first be tested against Article 8*bis*(2) as to whether it amounts to an act of aggression. It is then further subjected to the threshold under Article 8*bis*(1) of the Kampala Amendments. As for the latter, the question is whether the *animus aggressionis* has been excluded entirely from the state act element of the crime of aggression in the Kampala Amendments. As there is no explicit mention of the *animus aggressionis* in Article 8*bis*, it may be inferred that it is not a substantive component in determining the state act element.

The *animus aggressionis* is a natural concept, which may not be entirely consistent with the concept of the principle of legality. It is understandable that the Kampala Amendments exclude the concept of the *animus aggressionis*. This can be inferred from examining the threshold under Article 8*bis*(1). As the threshold is specific in nature and requires an objective evaluation, this would appear to exclude the *animus aggressionis*. Yet, it is worth pointing out that the *animus aggressionis* was also not explicitly mentioned in the IMT Charter either, but had played a role in the Tribunal's determination of the state act element of the crime. Thus, it should not be ruled out entirely that the *animus aggressionis* may nevertheless be taken into consideration when determining whether the use of force amounts to an aggression under Article 8*bis*(2) or whether the act of aggression amounts to a manifest violation of the UN Charter.

As it is a natural sentiment, whether the *animus aggressionis* is considered in the determination process is entirely dependent upon the methodological approach adopted by the relevant interpreter. As already mentioned, a positive approach will exclude any considerations of the *animus aggressionis*, while a non-positive approach may value the *animus aggressionis* in determining whether the act in question amounts to a manifest violation of the UN Charter. Regardless of which methodological approach to interpreting the legal framework of *jus ad bellum* is preferred, it is clear that the state act element of the crime of aggression in the Kampala Amendments is more specific than the state act element of crimes against peace in the IMT Charter.

The next question is whether the more specific definition entails a narrower or broader scope of violations of *jus ad bellum* that may be potentially prosecuted at the ICC than at Nuremberg. The comparison is between: 1) the initiation of the use of force, and the *animus aggressionis;* and 2) an act of aggression, which by its character, gravity and scale constitutes a manifest violation of the UN Charter. My view is that it is difficult to make an immediate assessment for two broad reasons.

First, the shift in terminology between war of aggression and act of aggression extends slightly further beyond mere nomenclature. The change in terminology is also reflective of the shift in paradigm from a decentralised system of international law to the present centralised system enshrined in the UN Charter. Prior to the formation of the UN Charter, it is questionable whether there was an existing legal framework that prohibited the use of force. With only a normative framework in place, the IMT had to assess the acts committed by Germany in accordance with different standards than those the ICC would rely on today. What about a war of aggression? Should the wars of aggression committed by Germany against the 12 nations be evaluated in the light of Article 8*bis*(1), it is questionable as to whether all of them would satisfy the state act element of the crime. For instance, it is certain that the war of aggression against the United States would not meet the threshold, as a declaration of a war of aggression would not suffice to meet the threshold. In this regard, it can be said that the threshold in the Kampala Amendments is higher than the IMT Charter. However, this may not be entirely accurate as it may be argued that the normative value of a war encompasses even greater magnitude of armed force than a manifest violation of the UN Charter. Be that as it may, the point is that the two different frameworks that prohibit interstate force applicable to the IMT Charter and the Kampala Amendments make it difficult to make a direct assessment as to which threshold is higher.

Second, the jurisdiction of the ICC with respect to the crime of aggression remains to be activated. Any contemplation at this point with respect to prosecution of the crime of aggression is conceptual. As such, the present comparison between Nuremberg and Kampala is also conceptual. In this regard, the state act elements in both of the definitions do not necessarily fall far from each other in the sense that they both constitute serious uses of force by the aggressor state. What can be said with certainty is that the definition of the state act element of the crime is more specific in the Kampala Amendments than the IMT Charter. By virtue of the two-step process involved in determining whether the act in question satisfies the state act element of the crime, it is likely that a narrower scope of acts would be able to comply with the requirements set forth in the overall test. In the light of this, it is only logical to submit that a narrower scope of situations of violations of *jus ad bellum* may be prosecuted at the ICC than at Nuremberg or domestic courts.

This narrower scope would imply that the state act element of the crime of aggression in the Kampala Amendments is narrower than customary international law. However, this is not necessarily a negative outcome. By having a definition that is narrower than customary international law, there will be less of a basis for a defendant to challenge the principle of legality, as the act would fall into the broader compass of the former. This is especially relevant in circumstances where the ICC will not ordinarily have jurisdiction, for example, in situations of Security Council referrals over a non-state party,[120] or a state party that has opted out of the Kampala Amendments.[121]

The counter-argument is that the state act element of the crime of aggression in Kampala is broader than customary international law. This is premised on Article 8*bis*(2) capturing "an extremely broad range of conduct", and the threshold in Article 8*bis*(1) seeming "highly unlikely that in requiring a certain level of seriousness and evident illegality it sets the bar as high as importing a *de facto* requirement that a 'war' has taken

---

[120] By virtue of Kampala Amendments, Art. 15*bis*(5), see *supra* note 1, the ICC may not exercise jurisdiction over a non-state party.

[121] *Ibid.*, Art. 15*bis*(4).

place".[122] If the definition of the crime of aggression for the purposes of the ICC is broader than customary international law, then there is potential for the defendant to challenge the principle of legality in the situations mentioned above where the ICC will not ordinarily have jurisdiction.

In any event, regardless of which view is adopted, there is merit in a more specific definition of the crime of aggression despite whether the state act element of the crime is broader or narrower than the one applicable at Nuremberg. As already noted, any comparison at this point is largely conceptual. It remains to be seen how the ICC will determine the state act element. Upon such determination, a clearer comparison can be made with the IMT Charter.

14.6. Conclusion

The present study has highlighted the significance of the state act element as an integral component of the substantive definition of the crime of aggression. The norms of customary international law that criminalise acts of aggression have been traced to its origins in the Nuremberg Principles. At the IMT Trial the initiation of the use of force by Germany with an *animus aggressionis* against other nations gave rise to individual criminal responsibility for crimes against peace. Moving forward to the ICC after Kampala, an act of aggression, which by its character, gravity and scale constitutes a manifest violation of the UN Charter, may be prosecuted as a crime of aggression.

As there is yet to be an actual prosecution at the ICC for the crime of aggression, any comparison with the IMT Trial remains rather conceptual. A direct comparison is further confounded by the fact that the state act element encapsulated in the definition of crimes against peace reflects a decentralised system of international law, while the state act element in the Kampala Amendments was drafted in the light of a centralised system of collective security.

The only logical conclusion is that the higher specificity and two-tiered test with respect to the state act element of the crime in the Kampala Amendments suggest that only very few violations of *jus ad bellum* may fit the requirement under Article 8*bis*(2) to be considered as an act of aggression, and even fewer acts of aggression pursuant to Article 8*bis*(2)

---

[122] McDougall, 2013, p. 154, see *supra* note 89.

may be considered as a crime of aggression under Article 8*bis*(1). From this, it is submitted that the scope of acts that can be prosecuted at the ICC for the crime of aggression is narrower than at Nuremberg.

Although the state act element within the Kampala Amendments does not appear to reflect customary international law entirely, the definition of the crime does not appear to depart entirely from the Nuremberg Principles either. Indeed the Kampala Amendments may play an instrumental role in developing the rules of customary international law that criminalise aggression. Indeed, this will unfold with time. As the jurisdiction of the ICC over the crime of aggression remains to be activated, it is premature to evaluate the effectiveness of the definition in the light of prosecution at the ICC and the overall objectives of international criminal justice. In the interim, it should be appreciated that despite any apprehension with respect to the Kampala Amendments, it is a remarkable achievement that arose from a long, dedicated endeavour to criminalise aggression for the purposes of an international court to have jurisdiction over the crime.

15

Shaping the Definition of Complicity in International Criminal Law: Tensions and Contradictions

Marina Aksenova[*]

15.1. Introduction

This chapter explores the historical evolution of the concept of complicity in international criminal law. The main argument is that complicity is just one example of the legal construction resulting from tensions characteristic of international criminal law in general. A historically orientated approach allows us to see the difficult choices faced by the creators of the first international Tribunals at Nuremberg and Tokyo as well as the subsequent developments shaping the field. Judge Henri Donnedieu de Vabres, who represented France at the International Military Tribunal ('IMT'), noted the extraordinary nature of the new institution created in the aftermath of the unconditional surrender of Germany on 5 June 1945.[1] Only high-level officials stood trial at Nuremberg, many of them occupying purely bureaucratic posts within the system. Complicity as a traditional criminal law concept for attributing criminal responsibility to those who do not physically perpetrate the crime was at the heart of the tension

---

[*] **Marina Aksenova** is a Postdoc at iCourts, Centre for Excellence for International Courts, University of Copenhagen, Denmark. She holds a Ph.D. in law from the European University Institute, Florence, Italy. She has interned at the Extraordinary Chambers in the Courts of Cambodia, Phnom Penh, and served as a research assistant for the Agency for Fundamental Rights' study "Border Police Human Rights Training in the EU".

[1] Henri Donnedieu de Vabres, "Le procès de Nuremberg devant les principes modernes du droit penal international" [The Nuremberg Trial and the Modern Principles of International Criminal Law], in *Recueil des Cours de l'Academie de droit international de la Haye*, vol. 70, 1947, pp. 477–582, reprinted in Guénaël Mettraux (ed.), *Perspectives on the Nuremberg Trial*, Oxford University Press, Oxford, 2008, pp. 213–73.

stemming from the need to declare individual guilt while capturing the collective nature of wrongdoing.[2]

International criminal law was born out of necessity. Necessity drove the occupying powers to discard the traditional notion of sovereignty and prosecute individuals for criminal acts stipulated in the IMT Charter.[3] Necessity did not entail chaos, however. De Vabres pointed out that the judges avoided arbitrariness when interpreting and applying the IMT Charter. They filled the inevitable lacunae by the principles of international law with the reference to the IMT Charter. The IMT Charter was the constitution of Nuremberg and served as a solid framework for further development of international criminal law. Decades have gone by, and international criminal law judges still engage in a struggle to respond adequately to the "aspirations of the universal conscience" and to "pursue traditional through innovative spirit".[4]

This chapter aims at understanding how the community of lawyers and scholars approached the problem of individual responsibility for mass crimes in the presence of legal gaps as well as the means through which they arrived at complicity as a mode of criminal participation. The question is whether the traditional modes of liability were suitable in resolving the problem of attributing responsibility for mass atrocities. Judge B.V.A. Röling of the International Military Tribunal for the Far East ('IMTFE') referred to international crimes as "system criminality" – a term underlining the complexity of networks involved in collective offending.[5]

The history of individual criminal responsibility for violations of international law starts at Nuremberg with the establishment of the IMT

---

[2]   In this regard, the International Criminal Tribunal for the former Yugoslavia ('ICTY') Trial Chamber in the *Čelebići* case correctly noted that the principle of individual criminal responsibility implies that even those who do not physically commit the crime in question are still liable for other forms of participation. See ICTY, *Prosecutor v. Mučić et al.*, Trial Chamber, Judgment, IT-96-21-T, 16 November 1998, para. 319 ('Čelebići case') (https://www.legal-tools.org/doc/6b4a33/).

[3]   Charter of the International Military Tribunal annexed to the London Agreement of 8 August 1945 for the Prosecution and Punishment of Major War Criminals of the European Axis ('IMT Charter') (http://www.legal-tools.org/doc/64ffdd/).

[4]   De Vabres, 1947, p. 217, see *supra* note 1.

[5]   See Elies van Sliedregt, *Individual Criminal Responsibility in International Law*, Oxford University Press, Oxford, 2012, p. 20.

pursuant to the London Agreement of 8 August 1945.[6] The IMT Charter attached to the London Agreement was one of the first international legal instruments targeting persons, as opposed to states. Article 6 established the jurisdiction of the IMT over persons acting in the interests of the European Axis countries, "as *individuals* or as *members of organizations*".[7] Control Council Law No. 10, passed a few months later, provided a framework for the subsequent prosecution of war criminals in occupied Germany.[8] The Charter of the IMTFE established in Tokyo focused on Japanese war criminals.[9] The text of the IMTFE Charter largely replicated the IMT Charter.

Right from the beginning, the principle of individual criminal responsibility for the violations of international law struggled with the complexity of the offences in question. The famous pronouncement of the IMT – "[c]rimes against international law are committed by men, not by abstract entities"[10] – stands in contrast with the constructions developed by this Tribunal to capture the collective nature of crimes committed by Nazi Germany: conspiracy, criminal organisation and inference of guilt based on the official position of the accused in the apparatus of power. Likewise, the Judgment of the IMTFE relied heavily on the notion of conspiracy and group responsibility of members of the Japanese government for violations of the law of war.[11]

---

[6]   Agreement by the Government of the United States of America, the Provisional Government of the French Republic, the Government of the United Kingdom of Great Britain and Northern Ireland and the Government of the Union of Soviet Socialist Republics for the prosecution and punishment of the major war criminals of the European Axis, 8 August 1945, in *Trial of the Major War Criminals Before the International Military Tribunal, Nuremberg, 14 November 1945–1 October 1946*, vol I., Nuremberg, 1947, pp. 8–9 ('London Agreement') (https://www.legal-tools.org/doc/844f64/).

[7]   IMT Charter, Art. 6, see *supra* note 3 (emphasis added).

[8]   Control Council Law No. 10, Punishment of Persons Guilty of War Crimes, Crimes Against Peace and Against Humanity, 20 December 1945, Art. 2(2) (http://www.legal-tools.org/doc/ffda62/).

[9]   Charter of the International Military Tribunal for the Far East, Art. 6, 19 January 1946, as amended 26 April 1946 ('IMTFE Charter') (https://www.legal-tools.org/doc/a3c41c/).

[10] International Military Tribunal ('IMT'), *Prosecutor v. Hermann Wilhelm Göring et al.*, Judgment, 1 October 1946 ('Nuremberg Judgment') (https://www.legal-tools.org/doc/f41e8b/).

[11] International Military Tribunal for the Far East ('IMTFE'), *United States of America et al. v. Araki Sadao et al.*, Judgment, 12 November 1948 ('Tokyo Judgment') (https://www.legal-tools.org/doc/3a2b6b/). See Neil Boister, "The Application of Collective and Comprehensive Criminal Responsibility for Aggression at the Tokyo International

---

Three main vectors of the historical evolution of complicity can be identified: the Nuremberg and Tokyo trials, the subsequent trials of war criminals before the Nuremberg Military Tribunals and domestic courts, and, finally, the efforts of the International Law Commission ('ILC') in codifying the Nuremberg Principles and drafting the Code of Crimes against the Peace and Security of Mankind.[12] Complicity was barely used by the IMT and IMTFE save for the opinions of the French judges sitting in both Tribunals. Rather, conspiracy was the instrument employed by these two Tribunals to address the questions of collective criminality. The subsequent trials relied on the two sets of rules relating to criminal responsibility: provisions implementing Control Council Law No. 10 and national criminal law.[13] The rules enacted in the British and American zones were based on Control Council Law No. 10, while other states, such as France and Norway, relied exclusively on their domestic law in trying war criminals.[14] Even those states that relied on Control Council Law No. 10 drew heavily on their domestic law in determining the main criminal law concepts. Complicity crystalized in the case law emanating from these trials, in particular in the French and British zones.

Finally, going outside a purely judicial analysis, the United Nations General Assembly decided through resolution 177 (II) of 21 November 1947 to entrust the ILC with a twofold task: first, to formulate the principles of international law recognised in the IMT Charter and the Nuremberg Judgment; and second, based on those principles, to prepare a Draft Code of Offences against the Peace and Security of Mankind ('Draft Code').[15] In fulfilling its mandate, the ILC contributed significantly to understanding the scope and the meaning of complicity in international criminal law. The Special Rapporteur of the ILC assigned with drafting the Code of Crimes against the Peace and Security of Mankind, Doudou Thiam, insightfully pointed out that in the context of international crimes,

---

Military Tribunal", in *Journal of International Criminal Justice*, 2010, vol. 8, no. 2, pp. 425–47.

[12] Draft Code of Crimes against the Peace and Security of Mankind adopted by the International Law Commission in 1996, Report of the ILC to the General Assembly, Forty-Eighth Session, UN GAOR, 51st Sess., Suat No. 10 UN A/51/10, 1996 ('Draft Code').

[13] Van Sliedregt, 2012, pp. 30–31, see *supra* note 5.

[14] *Ibid.*

[15] UNGA resolution 177 (II), Formulation of the Principles Recognized in the Charter of the Nürnberg Tribunal and in the Judgment of the Tribunal, 21 November 1947, UN doc. A/RES/177(II).

the "traditional moulds are broken", and "the classic dichotomy of principal and accomplice, which is the simplest schema, is no longer applicable because of the plurality of actors".[16]

The ultimate question is how the legal instrument of complicity was born in international criminal law and what preconditions it implies. The main claim of this chapter is that the concept of complicity emerged through the following three tensions inherent in international criminal law: domestic versus international law, collective wrongdoing versus individual criminal responsibility, and substantive crimes versus forms of participation. The second part of the chapter defines complicity and conspiracy for reasons of clarity, while the subsequent sections address each of the tensions that helped in shaping the content and the definition of complicity.

15.2. Complicity and Conspiracy: Definitions

It is important to give some essential definitions prior to embarking on the exploratory journey. Complicity is a mode of liability doctrine that attributes criminal responsibility to those who do not physically perpetrate the crime.[17] This is a generic definition that applies to both domestic and international criminal law. The functional core of complicity is constructing a link between the accomplices' contribution and the criminal act of another person. This legal instrument assists in addressing the situations when someone does not "pull the trigger of a gun", but significantly contributes to the crime. Various domestic legal systems recognise different types of complicity: aiding and abetting and instigating being the most common. Aiding and abetting presupposes knowledge of the crime, intention to assist and a contribution that is significant enough to impact on the offence. Instigation differs from aiding and abetting in that the instigator prompts the commission of the crime by influencing the principal offender and creating an inclination towards to the offence.

Conspiracy is different from complicity because it is a distinct crime and not just a mode of liability. Conspiracy exists in both English and American law as an offence consummated upon entering into the ar-

---

[16] Doudou Thiam, Special Rapporteur, Eighth Report on the Draft Code of Crimes against the Peace and Security of Mankind, UN doc. A/CN.4/430 and Add. 1, § 23, para. 30.

[17] For more on complicity in international criminal law, see Marina Aksenova, *Complicity in International Criminal Law*, Hart Publishing, 2016, Oxford (forthcoming).

rangement to commit criminal acts. Conspiracy typically requires an agreement between two or more conspirators that at least one of them will commit a substantive offence.[18] Conspiracy is a legal instrument widely used in American criminal law for holding someone responsible if they agree with another person to commit an offence, without regard for whether the other person is returning the agreement. An overt act performed in furtherance of the accord is typically also required to maintain the conviction.[19]

In *Pinkerton v. United States* (1946) the US Supreme Court held that each member of a conspiracy can be liable for substantive offences carried out by co-conspirators in furtherance of the conspiracy, even when there is no evidence of their direct involvement in – or even knowledge of – such offences provided they were "reasonably foreseen as a necessary or natural consequence of the unlawful agreement".[20] The practical outcome of the *Pinkerton* rule is that conspiratorial complicity destroys the distinction between accomplices and perpetrators since the effect of finding membership in the conspiracy is making the defendant a co-perpetrator of substantive offences committed in furtherance of the conspiracy.[21] The *Pinkerton* case has been widely criticised both in the US and abroad.[22] The rule has never been incorporated in the US Model Penal Code but applied in a number of cases.[23] Conspiracy remains highly contested crime in the prosecutions of the Guantánamo detainees by the US Military Commissions. These courts refer to international law when US domestic law does not cover certain conduct. The US DC Court of Appeals recently voiced an opinion in *Al Bahlul v. United States* that international law of war offences does not include conspiracy, thus vacating *Al Bahlul*'s inchoate conspiracy conviction.[24] The implications of this new

---

[18] American Law Institute, Model Penal Code, section 5.03(1).

[19] Paul H. Robinson, "United States", in Kevin Jon Heller and Markus D. Dubber (eds.), *The Handbook of Comparative Criminal Law*, Stanford University Press, Stanford, CA, 2011, pp. 579–80.

[20] United States Supreme Court, *Pinkerton* v. *United States* (1946) 328 US 640.

[21] George P. Fletcher, *Rethinking Criminal Law*, Little, Brown, Boston, 1978, p. 674.

[22] Harmen van der Wilt, "Joint Criminal Enterprise: Possibilities and Limitations", in *Journal of International Criminal Justice*, 2007, vol. 5, no. 1, pp. 91–108.

[23] Fletcher, 1978, pp. 634 ff., see *supra* note 21.

[24] United States Court of Appeals, *Ali Hamza Ahmad al Bahlul v. United States*, No. 11-1324 (DC Cir. 2014) Court of Appeals for the DC Circuit, 12 June 2015.

---

ruling are still to be determined. What is clear, however, is the charge of conspiracy was found to be incompatible with international law.

15.3. Domestic versus International Law

When it comes to the first contradiction of national and international law, it is important to remember that from the very beginning international criminal law was significantly influenced by domestic penal law systems.[25] The drafters of the IMT Charter came from different legal and political cultures. The need to compromise shaped not only the language of the constituent documents but also the charges against the accused and the final judgments. The Charters were the products of a political compromise between the Allied powers.[26] A number of conflicts, mostly rooted in national variations, characterised the London Conference where the IMT Charter was adopted. The US Chief Prosecutor at Nuremberg, Robert H. Jackson, stressed, among other things, the ideological dissimilarities between the Soviet and the Western European legal traditions and the differences between the common law adversarial proceedings and the Continental inquisitorial criminal trial.[27]

The struggle among legal traditions coupled with various extra-legal considerations did not stop at the stage of the drafting of the IMT and IMTFE Charters. Framing the charges and, in particular, defining the link between the accused and the crime, were highly influenced by the Anglo-Saxon concept of conspiracy. The first count of the IMT indictment – general conspiracy incorporating all actions of the accused deemed to be criminal from the formation of the Nazi Party in 1919 to the

---

[25] Solis Horwitz, "The Tokyo Trial", in *International Conciliation*, 1950, no. 465, Carnegie Endowment for International Peace, p. 540.

[26] Richard Overy notes that the British delegation initially insisted on summary executions for the perpetrators of war crimes while the Soviets and the Americans were in favour of trial in front of a military tribunal, but with different understanding of what the trial entailed (the Soviet authorities regarded the trial as a show trial). The final list of the defendants to be prosecuted before the IMT represented a series of compromises as well: the Allied powers assembled an eclectic list of persons, who represented the dictatorial regime in different capacities. See Richard Overy, "The Nuremberg Trials: International law in the Making", in Philippe Sands (ed.), *From Nuremberg to The Hague: The Future of International Criminal Justice*, Cambridge University Press, Cambridge, 2003, pp. 1–29.

[27] Robert Jackson, "Nuremberg in Retrospect: Legal Answer to International Lawlessness", in *American Bar Association Journal*, 1949, vol. 35, pp. 813–16 and 881–87, reprinted in Mettraux, 2008, pp. 358–59, see *supra* note 1.

end of the war in 1945 – was the solution proposed by Jackson on the basis of a memorandum by the US military lawyer Murray Bernays.[28] The Nuremberg prosecution team charged, under count one, conspiracy to commit crimes against peace, war crimes and crimes against humanity, as defined in Article 6 of the IMT Charter. This Article called for individual criminal responsibility for the following acts:

> (a) Crimes against peace: namely, planning, preparation, initiation or waging of a war of aggression, or a war in violation of international treaties, agreements or assurances, or participation in a common plan or conspiracy for the accomplishment of any of the foregoing;
>
> (b) War crimes: namely, violations of the laws or customs of war. Such violations shall include, but not be limited to, murder, ill-treatment or deportation to slave labor or for any other purpose of civilian population of the occupied territory, murder or ill-treatment of prisoners of war or persons on the seas, killing of hostages, plunder of public or private property, wanton destruction of cities, towns or villages, or devastation not justified by military necessity;
>
> (c) Crimes against humanity: namely, murder, extermination, enslavement, deportation, and other inhumane acts committed against any civilian population, before or during the war; or persecutions on political, racial or religious grounds in execution of or in connection with any crime within the jurisdiction of the Tribunal, whether or not in violation of the domestic law of the country where perpetrated.
>
> Leaders, organizers, instigators and accomplices participating in the formulation or execution of a common plan or conspiracy to commit any of the foregoing crimes are responsible for all acts performed by any persons in execution of such plan.

Continental lawyers at Nuremberg objected to the grand conspiracy charge and rejected the idea of conviction without proof of the specific crimes perpetrated by the defendant.[29] As a result of this disagreement,

---

[28] Nuremberg Judgment, p. 222, see *supra* note 10; Overy, 2003, pp. 14–16, see *supra* note 26; van Sliedregt, 2012, p. 22, see *supra* note 5.

[29] Overy, 2003, p. 19, see *supra* note 26.

the IMT felt compelled to narrow the scope of the charge in two respects. First, it rejected the prosecution's idea of a single conspiracy capturing all the criminal conduct of the defendants, and instead held that the evidence established the existence of many separate plans. The Tribunal declined to accept Hitler's *Mein Kampf* as the evidence of a common plan.[30]

Second, the IMT distinguished between conspiracy to commit acts of aggressive war as a substantive crime flowing from Article 6(a) of the IMT Charter and conspiracy in the sense of Article 6(c) aimed at establishing the responsibility of persons participating in a common plan. The IMT proceeded with charges under count one only in relation to the substantive crime of conspiracy to wage aggressive war.[31] As a result of curtailing the conspiracy charge, three of the defendants – von Papen, Schacht and Fritzsche – were acquitted on all four counts of the indictment.[32] The IMT entered convictions for this charge only in relation to seven defendants who were "informed and willing participants of German aggression".[33]

The Tokyo prosecution team, like the Nuremberg prosecutors, opted for the all-encompassing count of conspiracy (count one), but also supplemented it with a number of subsequent counts, breaking down the grand conspiracy into constituent parts. The reason for these extra counts was to secure convictions if the umbrella charge failed, as happened at Nuremberg.[34] The IMTFE prosecution extended conspiracy over a period of over 18 years and defined its objective in broad terms of securing "the military, naval, political, and economic domination of East Asia and the Pacific and Indian Oceans, and for all countries and islands therein and bordering thereon".[35] However, in contrast with the Nuremberg Judgement that rejected the existence of grand conspiracy, the first broad count of the Tokyo indictment proved to be successful, rendering the subsequent sub-conspiracy counts redundant. The majority Judgment supported the broad interpretation of conspiracy to wage aggressive war – all of the defendants, except General Matsui Iwane and Foreign Minister Shigemitsu

---

[30] Nuremberg Judgment, p. 222, see *supra* note 10.
[31] *Ibid.*, pp. 223–24.
[32] Overy, 2003, p. 28, see *supra* note 26.
[33] For example, Rudolf Hess; Nuremberg Judgment, p. 276, see *supra* note 10.
[34] Neil Boister and Robert Cryer, *The Tokyo International Military Tribunal: A Reappraisal*, Oxford University Press, Oxford, 2008, p. 207.
[35] *Ibid.*; Tokyo Judgment, pp. 48, 421, see *supra* note 11.

Mamoru, were convicted on count one as "leaders, organizers, instigators, or accomplices" in the conspiracy.[36] The IMTFE established that "the conspiracy existed for and its execution occupied a period of many years", and that "[a]ll of those who at any time were parties to the criminal conspiracy or who at any time with guilty knowledge played a part in its execution are guilty of the charge contained in Count I".[37]

Complicity, as an alternative mechanism for addressing system criminality, never arose in the Nuremberg and Tokyo Judgments notwithstanding the fact that Article 6(c) of the IMT Charter and Article 5(c) of the IMTFE Charter specifically provided for the liability of accomplices participating in the execution of a common plan or conspiracy to commit any of the aforementioned crimes. However, the separate and dissenting opinions of individual judges from different jurisdictions reflected divergent views on the issue. These separate voices serve as the best indicators of the complexity of the legal landscape of the time. Complicity surfaced in the opinions of the French judges, primarily because of the importance of this mode of responsibility in France. Judge de Vabres of the IMT insisted that complicity would have been a more appropriate form of dealing with group criminality because of its wider acceptance in the variety of legal systems and its focus on the subjective indicators of individual culpability, rather than external evidence of common agreement. De Vabres thought that the French counterpart of conspiracy – complicity – was more consistent with modern doctrines that insist on the idea of individualised punishment.[38] He insisted that the last paragraph of Article 6(c) of the IMT Charter adopted the French notion of complicity and endorsed the principles of ordinary criminal law.[39] De Vabres stressed that the lack of solidarity and equality among the conspirators made it difficult to distinguish the guilt of each individual perpetrator.[40]

---

[36] Tokyo Judgment, pp. 49, 773, see *supra* note 11. See Gordon Ireland, "Uncommon Law in Martial Tokyo" in *Yearbook of World Affairs*, 1950, vol. 4, p. 80; Boister and Cryer, 2008, pp. 217–19, see *supra* note 34.

[37] Tokyo Judgment, pp. 49, 770, see *supra* note 11; Boister and Cryer, 2008, p. 223, see *supra* note 34.

[38] Boister and Cryer, 2008, p. 243, see *supra* note 34. De Vabres, however, acknowledged the tempting nature of conspiracy as a charge, giving to the Hitlerian enterprise "the cover of a romantic prestige that is not without seductive appeal".

[39] *Ibid.*, p. 250.

[40] De Vabres, 1947, pp. 244–45, see *supra* note 1.

The other criticism of the doctrine of conspiracy is that it is specific to common law and unknown to German and French law.[41] De Vabres explained that the charge of conspiracy stemmed from the same social necessity to capture the acts of a multitude of individuals that is present in both Continental and English law. The technical means of addressing this legal problem in Continental law are, however, different. French law uses the notion of complicity or accessory participation in relation to the intended crime. The French point of view is subjective in that it captures the moral or psychological element connecting separate conducts which aim at the same result, namely the commission of the common crime. In contrast, the English notion of conspiracy focuses on the external objective indicators of the existence of a common plan.

Just like the French judge at Nuremberg, the French judge at the IMTFE – Henri Bernard – insisted on the broader use of complicity. His point of view was that the Japanese Emperor should have been punished as a principal author of the Pacific War and all the defendants standing trial at Tokyo could only be considered his accomplices.[42] Judge Röling from the Netherlands held a different view on this matter, which he based on cultural differences. He considered that the decision not to try the ceremonial head of state – the Emperor – was correct. The allegations were that the Emperor was the mastermind of the war, but Röling pointed towards the very complicated structure of the Japanese government and the differences in Japanese speech. There was, for example, a misunderstanding of some of the Emperor's words such as: "If the war starts, shall we win?". This is the Japanese way of expressing that he was against it, but many critics interpreted this line otherwise.[43]

The subsequent proceedings against former Nazis were conducted under the Control Council Law No. 10 and national penal laws of the trying states. France, for example, used its domestic criminal law during these prosecutions. Thus, it is not surprising that French courts relied almost exclusively on the complicity/perpetratorship dichotomy when determin-

---

[41] *Ibid.*, pp. 242–51.

[42] IMTFE, *United States of America et al. v. Araki Sadao et al.*, Dissenting Judgment of the Member from France of the International Military Tribunal for the Far East (Bernard), 12 November 1948, p. 22 (https://www.legal-tools.org/doc/d1ac54/). See also Ireland, 1950, p. 64, fn. 22, *supra* note 32.

[43] B.V.A. Röling and Antonio Cassese, *The Tokyo Trial and Beyond: Reflections of a Peacemonger*, Polity Press, Cambridge, 1993, p. 42.

ing the modes of responsibility of the accused.[44] In the trial of *Gustav Becker et al.*, the Permanent Military Tribunal in Lyon convicted the former German customs officers in French Savoy for illegal arrest and ill treatment of French citizens, which resulted in the death of the three victims later in Germany. Two of the accused were convicted as perpetrators, while the remaining 17 individuals were convicted as their accomplices.[45] The court stipulated: "It is a principle of penal law that accomplices are held responsible in the same manner as actual perpetrators, and this principle is recognized in the field of war crimes as it is in that of common penal law".[46]

Prosecutions in the British and American zones pursuant to rules based on the Control Council Law No. 10 were also highly "domesticated". The British courts used the national concept of "common design" to determine whether the accused were "concerned in" committing the specific war crimes while the courts located in the US zone adhered to the common law "concerted approach" to criminal participation and focused on the link between the accused and the crime on a case-by-case basis. For example, the term "concerned in the killing" was clarified in the case of *Werner Rohde et al.* decided by the British Military Court in Wuppertal. The Judge Advocate in this case held that:

> [T]o be concerned in a killing it was not necessary that any person should actually have been present. [...] If two or more men set out on a murder and one stood half a mile away from where the actual murder was committed, perhaps to keep guard, although he was not actually present when the murder was done, if he was taking part with the other man with the knowledge that other man was going to put the killing into effect then he was just as guilty as the person who fired the shot or delivered the blow.[47]

In this case the Court convicted several officials working at the Natzweiler-Stuthof concentration camp of killing four captive women

---

[44] Van Sliedregt, 2012, p. 35, see *supra* note 5.

[45] French Permanent Military Tribunal, Lyon, *France v. Becker et al.*, in United Nations War Crimes Commission, *Law Reports of the Trials of the War Criminals*, vol. 7, His Majesty's Stationery Office, London, 1948, p. 70.

[46] *Ibid.*

[47] British Military Court, Wuppertal, *United Kingdom v. Rohde et al.*, in United Nations War Crimes Commission, *Law Reports of the Trials of the War Criminals*, vol. 15, His Majesty's Stationery Office, London, 1948, p. 56.

prisoners. The roles of the accused varied but none was charged with actually killing the women concerned: the medical officer at the camp admitted to giving lethal injections; the prisoner working in the crematorium
acknowledged preparing the oven for the occasion; while another accused, a functionary at the camp, followed the order to bring the harmful
drug and overheard the conversations relating to the execution of the four
prisoners.[48]

Finally, the work of the ILC on defining the modes of responsibility
for the Draft Code of Crimes against the Peace and Security of Mankind
was predicated on the exploration of domestic legal systems. The Special
Rapporteur, Doudou Thiam, looked at complicity in various jurisdictions
in an attempt to define the concept in international law. Thiam identified
the gap in international criminal law in attributing responsibility for the
crimes committed by a plurality persons.[49] He attempted to fill this gap by
investigating the notion of complicity in domestic and international law
and delimiting its scope. Thiam explored domestic law and found that the
scope of the concept and its content varied from country to country: complicity may include physical acts (aiding and abetting, provision of
means) and intellectual or moral assistance (counsel, instigation, orders).
In some countries, those who provide intellectual assistance are labelled
"indirect perpetrators", while in others "originators".[50] Moreover, the
boundary between the concepts of perpetrator, co-perpetrator and accomplice shifts depending on the legislation in question.[51] When it came to
complicity in international law, Thiam acknowledged the need for a broad
definition of criminal participation corresponding to the complexity of
international justice. One of the reasons for this is the difficulty of assigning the actors to one category or another and determining the precise role
played by each in the context of international law.[52] Based on the work of

---

[48] *Ibid.*, p. 55.

[49] Fourth Report on the Draft Code of Offences against the Peace and Security of Mankind
by Mr. Doudou Thiam, Special Rapporteur, 11 March 2986, UN doc. A/CN.4/398 and
Corr. 1–3, para. 89, p. 61 ('Fourth Report').

[50] Eighth Report on the Draft Code of Crimes against the Peace and Security of Mankind by
Mr. Doudou Thiam, Special Rapporteur, 8 March and 6 April 1990, UN doc. A/CN.4/430
and Add. 1, paras. 7–13, p. 29 ('Eighth Report').

[51] Fourth Report, para. 99, p. 64, see *supra* note 49.

[52] Eighth Report, para. 22, p. 30, see *supra* note 50.

the Special Rapporteur, the ILC adopted a new version of the Draft Code in 1991[53] and a further version in 1996.[54]

There is one concluding observation in relation to the role of domestic law in shaping complicity in international criminal law. It is the frequency with which the first war crimes courts referred to the wide domestic acceptance of a certain rule in order to secure its international legitimacy. For example, the IMT alluded to the "criminal law of most nations" in support of the rule that following the unlawful order does not absolve the defendant from responsibility.[55] The United Nations War Crimes Commission held that British rules regarding complicity in crimes are found in substance in the majority of legal systems.[56] This trend shows the historical importance of the general principles of law recognised by civilised nations as a source of international criminal law.

15.4. Collective Wrongdoing versus Individual Criminal Responsibility

The second tension between individual criminal responsibility and collective wrongdoing stems from the need for some medium between the crime and the offender in international criminal law. This is because very few men standing trial for mass crimes directly order or perpetrate certain offences. The ILC Special Rapporteur emphasised the difficulty of applying the traditional domestic law principal/accomplice dichotomy to international offences. He acknowledged that the latter require a broader definition of complicity to cover the complexity of the legal context associated with international crimes.

The IMTFE settled for conspiracy as a tool designed to capture collective criminality. Conspiracy declared an agreement to commit mass atrocities criminal without the need to prove underlying offences. The leadership position was determinative, in the eyes of the IMTFE judges, of whether the accused belonged to a conspiracy or was responsible for

---

[53] Report of the International Law Commission on the Work of its Forty-third Session, 29 April–19 July 1991, UN doc. A/46/10.

[54] Report of the International Law Commission on the Work of its Forty-eighth Session, 6 May–26 July 1996, UN doc. A/51/10.

[55] Nuremberg Judgment, p. 221, see *supra* note 10.

[56] United Nations War Crimes Commission, *Law Reports of the Trials of the War Criminals*, vol. 11, His Majesty's Stationery Office, London, 1949, p. 72 ('Law Reports, vol. 11').

the crimes committed under his supervision. The IMT relied on conspiracy to a lesser extent than its Tokyo counterpart. The Nuremberg response to the problem of attribution of responsibility for the acts committed by distant others was to focus on the factual contribution of the accused to the common plan and his official position within the Nazi hierarchy. The IMT therefore avoided a legalistic discussion about the modes of participation of each accused.

The prosecutions of former Nazis by national authorities in the aftermath of the IMT signified a shift from the fact-based approach to criminal participation of Nuremberg and Tokyo to a more nuanced and developed body of law regarding the ways in which the defendant was involved in a crime. These trials were driven, to a large extent, by national law. Thus, many ambiguities characteristic of the domestic legal systems affected the way various modes of participation were used. For example, the British court in *Schonfeld* struggled to distinguish participation in the common design and aiding and abetting. In the trial of *Franz Schonfeld and Others* the British Military Court in Essen faced the task of determining whether several members of the German Security Police (*Sicherheitspolizei*) were concerned in the killing of three unarmed members of the Allied air force, who were hiding in the house provided by members of the Resistance.[57] Instead of puting into effect the arrest, the defendants shot the pilots. The court convicted four of the defendants and acquitted the remainder.[58] The evidence clearly established that the actual shooting was carried out by only one of the defendants, but the court convicted three more individuals of the same crime based on their actual or constructed presence at the scene of the crime (entering the pilots' house together with the direct perpetrator). All four persons convicted of war crimes were sentenced to death.

The precise basis for conviction in *Schonfeld* is unclear.[59] The Judge Advocate made several conflicting observations: first, he held that if the object of the visit to the house was initially lawful, that is, to arrest the pilots, the three others were not guilty of the charge of "being con-

---

[57] British Military Court, Essen, United Kingdom v. Franz Schonfeld and Nine Others, ibid., p. 64.

[58] *Ibid.*, p. 67.

[59] Rupert Skilbeck, "Cases: Schonfeld and Others", in Antonio Cassese (eds.), *The Oxford Companion to International Criminal Justice*, Oxford University Press, Oxford, 2009, p. 905.

cerned with the killing" that resulted from one of them starting to shoot. They were innocent so long that they did not aid or abet the direct perpetrator. Second, if the three men aided and abetted the shooter, they would be guilty. And, finally, if the rule regarding "common design" were found to be applicable, the others present would be guilty of murder whether or not they aided or abetted the offence.[60] The Judge Advocate referred to the theory of actual or constructive presence at the scene of the crime, used by the traditional English law doctrine to establish a boundary between the two forms of participation. Notwithstanding the reference to this theory in the judgments, the British courts failed to consistently apply it in cases like *Rohde* or *Schonfeld* and instead settled for a half-hearted compromise.

The US Military Tribunals adopted the unitary model of criminal participation, thereby placing all modes of responsibility on an equal footing. This does not mean, however, that the judges paid no attention to the way in which the defendants became involved in the crimes. Quite the opposite; the US courts developed the fault and conduct requirement of the individual criminal responsibility. For example, the *Justice* case stressed the importance of the personal knowledge of the accused,[61] while *Pohl* guarded against assuming criminality solely on the basis of official capacity.[62] The *Pohl* Tribunal also highlighted the importance of positive action in establishing a defendant's consent to the commission of the crimes. By focusing on legal requirements of responsibility the US Tribunals sitting in Nuremberg distanced themselves from the approach adopted at the IMT and IMTFE.

---

[60] The Judge Advocate went on to explain the difference between various modes of participation in English law: accessory before the fact is always absent from the scene of the crime; a principal in the first degree is an actual perpetrator; and a principal in the second degree is present at the commission of the offence and aids and abets its commission. Law Reports, vol. 11, pp. 69–70, see *supra* note 56.

[61] Nuremberg Military Tribunal, *United States of America v. Josef Alstötter et al.*, Judgment, 4 December 1947, in *Trials of War Criminals Before the Nuremberg Military Tribunals Under Control Council Law No. 10*, vol. III, US Government Printing Office, p. 62 ('Justice case') (https://www.legal-tools.org/doc/04cdaf/).

[62] Nuremberg Military Tribunal, United States of America v. Oswald Pohl et al., Judgment, 3 November 1947, in Trials of War Criminals Before the Nuremberg Military Tribunals Under Control Council Law No. 10, vol. V, US Government Printing Office, pp. 176–77 ('Pohl case') (https://www.legal-tools.org/doc/84ae05/).

The trials of industrialists in the aftermath of the war are yet another example of the tension stemming from the complexity of crimes in question. Corporations represent the middle ground between the state and the person. As demonstrated in the *Krupp case*, for example, these corporations are perfectly capable of committing violations of international law.[63] However, the attribution of responsibility for these violations to a particular individual within the firm is challenging. Nonetheless, the American and British courts undertook this task and acknowledged the responsibility of firms' officers for breaching the laws and customs of war.

15.5. Substantive Crimes versus Forms of Participation

The third tension between complicity as a mode of participation and complicity as a substantive crime flows directly from the collective nature of the offences in question. The distinction between the wrongdoing and the manner in which individuals become involved is not always clear in international criminal law. One can trace how judicial reasoning evolved in this regard. The first international criminal Tribunals hardly referred to the form of liability of each accused, despite their being explicitly mentioned in the IMT and IMTFE Charters. The Nuremberg and Tokyo Judgments did not explicitly distinguish between primary perpetrators and other crime participants and instead adopted a rather fact-based approach to attributing responsibility.[64] As Kai Ambos notes, "the Nuremberg approach can be called pragmatic rather than dogmatic".[65] One can find two explanations for this peculiarity: first, the lack of theoretical framework during the first international criminal trials; and second, the adoption of an inchoate offence of conspiracy, rather than various forms of complicity, as a method of capturing the collective nature of crimes.

---

[63] Nuremberg Military Tribunal, United States of America v. Alfried Felix Alwyn Krupp von Bohlen und Halbach et al., Judgment, 31 July 1948, in Trials of War Criminals Before the Nuremberg Military Tribunals Under Control Council Law No. 10, vol. X ('Krupp case'), (https://www.legal-tools.org/doc/ad5c2b/).

[64] Elies van Sliedregt, *The Criminal Responsibility of Individuals for Violations of International Humanitarian Law*, TMC Asser Press, The Hague, 2003, p. 39; Kai Ambos, "Individual Criminal Responsibility", in Gabrielle Kirk McDonald and Olivia Swaak-Goldman (eds.), *Substantive and Procedural Aspects of International Criminal Law*, vol. 1: *Commentary*, Kluwer Law International, The Hague, 2000, pp. 8–9.

[65] Ambos, 2000, p. 8, see *supra* note 64.

In 1950 the ILC first codified complicity in the commission of a crime against peace, a war crime or a crime against humanity as a substantive crime under international law.[66] Arguably this was the result of the lack of a distinction between the modes of participation and the substantive offences at Nuremberg. The ILC's position regarding complicity changed only with the adoption of the 1991 Draft Code of Crimes against the Peace and Security of Mankind which recognised that complicity is a mode of participation and belongs to the section on general principles of law.[67] The same 1991 Draft Code provided the definition of complicity for the first time since the beginning of the ILC's work on the issue in the early 1950s. This shift, leading to a deeper and more nuanced understanding of complicity, was likely the result of the scrupulous work on the issue by the ILC's Special Rapporteur in the 1980s.[68] The other reason for this change of attitude towards complicity was the legacy of the post-IMT prosecutions of war criminals pursuant to the Control Council Law No. 10. These trials rejected the fact-based approach of Nuremberg and Tokyo and stressed the importance of defining the link between the accused and the crime. The final 1996 Draft Code contained a detailed list of the modes of criminal participation, paving the road to the relevant provision of the Rome Statute of the International Criminal Court ('ICC Statute').[69]

15.6. Conclusion

International criminal law was born out of necessity. Law and politics came together in a moment of universal revulsion and outrage to create a space for international prosecutions. The Charters of the IMT and IMTFE provided the future trials with a basic framework, but the novelty of the whole enterprise left a lot of legal lacunae to be filled by practice. Individual criminal responsibility is one vivid example of the concept that re-

---

[66] Principles of International Law Recognized in the Charter of the Nuremberg Tribunal and in the Judgment of the Tribunal, 1950, Principle VII, *Yearbook of the International Law Commission*, vol. II., United Nations, New York, 1950.

[67] Report of the International Law Commission on the Work of its Forty-third Session, 29 April–19 July 1991, UN doc. A/46/10.

[68] At its 34th session, in 1982, the International Law Commission appointed Doudou Thiam as Special Rapporteur for the topic. The Commission, from its 35th session in 1983 to its 42nd session in 1990 received eight reports from the Special Rapporteur. *Ibid.*, p. 80.

[69] Report of the International Law Commission on the Work of its Forty-eighth Session, 6 May–26 July 1996, UN doc. A/51/10.

quired refinement and redefinition throughout the history of international criminal law. Article 6 of the IMT Charter and Article 5 of the IMTFE Charter extended jurisdiction of these Tribunals to individuals, thus breaking away from the traditional conception of state sovereignty as standing in between the collective international enforcement and a person. At the same time, the Charters only briefly mentioned the modes of liability as a concluding remark in the above-mentioned articles: "Leaders, organizers, instigators and accomplices participating in the formulation or execution of a common plan or conspiracy to commit any of the foregoing crimes are responsible for all acts performed by any person in execution of such plan".

The first international judges and prosecutors had to solve many practical questions, while being true to the respective Charters and satisfying the aspirations of international law. Domestic law often played a gap-filling role in the situations when no legal solution grounded in international law was available. This was a reasonable approach and this is why conspiracy was the first legal instrument to tackle the problem of collective offending. Promoted by American scholars, this doctrine allowed for criminalising agreement to commit acts of aggressive war without requiring any underlying activity. It provided evidentiary relief, but caused a lot of discomfort among Continental lawyers, who saw this doctrine as an imposition of guilt by association. This is the reason conspiracy mostly failed at the IMT. It survived at the IMTFE, but was criticised in some strong dissenting opinions. The cosmopolitan nature of international criminal law comes to light in this failure of conspiracy as a crime under international law. The community of lawyers and judges arriving from different legal cultures and traditions had to legitimise the whole process and, without near-universal approval, the new legal solutions were likely to be doomed. The recent *Al Bahlul* judgment by the US DC Court of Appeals, which rejects conspiracy as a crime under international law, supports this proposition.

The chapter has shown how complicity made its way onto the stage of international criminal law. This mode of liability is more nuanced than conspiracy in that it focuses on the individual and may often serve as a usual tool for attaching criminal responsibility. Complicity barely surfaced in the Nuremberg and Tokyo Judgments, but started gaining ground during the prosecutions pursuant to Control Council Law No. 10. The work of the UN Special Rapporteur contributed significantly to understanding the modes of liability in general and complicity in particular. One needs to underscore the role of the UN and the ILC in developing the tools for further international prosecutions. The Draft Code of Crimes against the Peace and Security of Mankind that embodied decades-long developments of international criminal law served as a basis for the ICC Statute.

The chapter has discussed the following tensions that led to the dislocation of complicity from the periphery to the centre of international criminal law: those between the domestic and international law, the substantive crimes and modes of liability, and the collective wrongdoing and individual criminal responsibility. These tensions are inherent in the discipline as a whole for they reflect the choices that judges, prosecutors and defence counsel regularly make when handling the cases of insurmountable scope and gravity, when working with international colleagues, and when deciding on how to qualify certain acts and the ways in which the accused became involved in them.

16

The Evolution of Conspiracy as a Mode of Collective Criminal Liability Since Nuremberg

Zahra Kesmati[*]

16.1. Introduction

By looking at the very nature of serious international crimes one realises that committing such crimes through the contribution of individuals is a prerequisite under international criminal law. Serious international crimes such as war crimes, crimes against humanity and genocide share a common feature: they are typically large scale, planned and executed through systematic structures, usually pursuant to a common plan.[1] As the Appeals Chamber in Tadić case at the International Criminal Tribunal for the former Yugoslavia ('ICTY') states, serious crimes under international criminal law "do not result from the criminal propensity of single individuals but constitute manifestations of collective criminality: the crimes are often carried out by groups or individuals acting in pursuance of a common criminal design".[2] Given that such mass crimes usually involve intensive efforts of many individuals and multiple layers of culpability, the hypothesis of having a single defendant in such atrocities is almost impossible. Therefore, allocating responsibility among those individuals and the question of how to punish those involved in committing an international

---

[*] **Zahra Kesmati** holds a Ph.D. in international law from Allame Tabatabaee University, Tehran, Iran. She previously worked as a researcher for the Islamic Human Rights Commission (2001–2002). She was selected as a Distinguished Student by the Iranian Ministry of Science, Research and Technology in 2000 and as Distinguish Student by Allame University in 2001. She currently works in the Claims Division of International Affairs of the National Iranian Oil Company.

[1] Héctor Olásolo, *The Criminal International Responsibility of Senior Political and Military Leaders as Principals to International Crimes*, Hart Publishing, Oxford, 2010, p. 1.

[2] International Criminal Tribunal for former Yugoslavia, *Prosecutor v. Duško Tadić et al.*, Appeals Chamber, Judgment, IT-94-1, 15 July 1999, para. 191 ('Tadić Appeal Judgment') (http://www.legal-tools.org/doc/8efc3a/).

crime has gained immense importance within the theories of criminal re-sponsibility.[3]

International criminal responsibility for collective criminal actions has been recognised in case law and jurisprudence, stretching from Nuremberg to the most current proceedings of the *ad hoc* tribunals and the International Criminal Court ('ICC'). As Jens Ohlin argues, there are "three doctrines for imposing individual liability for collective endeavors which have been recognised in international case law and jurisprudence: conspiracy, joint criminal enterprise and co-perpetration".[4]

Conspiracy can be conceived in two major forms. First, conspiracy can be considered as an *inchoate* criminal offence as in common law.[5] Under this conception, conspiracy is a distinct crime, separate from the target crime that conspirators agree upon and plan to commit. The common law requires only an agreement in order for the conspirators to be guilty of the substantive crime of conspiracy.[6] In case of "pure agreement" conspiracy functions as a rule of an inchoate crime instead of attribution.[7] The second conception of conspiracy can be traced back to the Pinkerton liability rule. In its most expansive form, the Pinkerton rule states that "any conspirator in a continuing conspiracy is responsible for the illegal acts committed by his cohorts in furtherance of the conspiracy, within the scope of the conspiracy and reasonably foreseeable by the conspirators as a necessary or natural consequence of the unlawful agreement".[8] Under the latter conception, conspiracy can provide liability when other substantive crimes have been committed by one of the co-

---

[3] Alison Marston Danner and Jenny S. Martinez, "Guilty Associations: Joint Criminal Enterprise, Command Responsibility, and the Development of International Criminal Law", in *California Law Review*, 2005, vol. 93, no. 1, p. 1.

[4] Jens David Ohlin, "Joint Intentions to Commit International Crimes", in *Chicago Journal of International Law*, 2010, vol. 11, no. 2, p. 695.

[5] Neal Kumar Katyal, "Conspiracy Theory", in *Yale Law Journal*, 2003, vol. 112, p. 1307.

[6] Joshua Dressler, *Understanding Criminal Law*, 6th ed., LexisNexis, New Providence, NJ, 2012, p. 493.

[7] Mark A. Summers, "Attribution of Criminal Liability: A Critical Comparison of the U.S. Doctrine of Conspiracy and the ICTY Doctrine of Joint Criminal Enterprise from an American Perspective", in *Croatian Annual of Criminal Law and Practice*, 2011, vol. 18, p. 183.

[8] Mathew A. Pauley, "The *Pinkerton* Doctrine and Murder", in *Pierce Law Review*, 2005, vol. 4, no. 1, p. 6.

conspirators.[9] According to this concept, an individual is held criminally liable for agreeing to commit unlawful acts and offences for his co-conspirators. Liability based on conspiracy can also be raised under this broad conception of conspiracy theory. Within this an individual can be held liable for offences that he would not participate in, as long as the offence was predictable given a common plan.[10] Therefore, conspiracy-based liability requires: 1) a conspiratorial agreement or a common plan; 2) a crime committed by any of the co-conspirators; such that 3) the crime is one of the obvious goals of the agreement. This chapter focuses on conspiracy as a mode of liability, but also touches on its use as an inchoate crime where there is a need to clarify.

Historically, the conspiracy doctrine was established within international law to aid prosecution of key war criminals.[11] Conspiracy was considered a response to the inability of the 'causation doctrine' to deal with situations in which multiple individuals were jointly responsible for the commission of a crime.[12] Generally, this was raised to ease the burden of producing evidence in post-war situations where witnesses and physical evidence were difficult to obtain.[13] Accordingly, it was considered an essential legal device for the prosecution of criminal groups during the Second World War. The authors of the Charter of the International Military Tribunal ('IMT') stated that "it will never be possible to catch and convict every Axis war criminal [...] under the old concepts and procedures".[14] Therefore they specifically looked to the doctrine of conspiracy to facilitate doing so.[15] As Aaron Fichtelberg notes: "Some individuals who are intimately involved with the discrete criminal acts may be a great distance geographically, temporally or even causally from the actual

---

[9] Ibid.

[10] George P. Fletcher, Rethinking Criminal Law, Oxford University Press, Oxford, 2000, pp. 218–20.

[11] Danner and Martinez, 2005, p. 1, see supra note 3.

[12] Elies van Sliedregt, "Joint Criminal Enterprise as a Pathway to Convicting Individuals for Genocide", in International Criminal Justice, 2007, vol. 5, no.1, pp. 196–97.

[13] Anthony Dinh, "Joint Criminal Enterprise at the ECCC: The Challenge of Individual Criminal Responsibility for Crimes Committed under the Khmer Rouge", in Cambodia Tribunal Monitor, 18 June 2008.

[14] Quoting Colonel Murray Bernays of the US War Department, cited in Ciara Damgaard, Individual Criminal Responsibility for Core International Crimes: Selected Pertinent Issues, Springer-Verlag, Berlin, 2008, p. 132.

[15] Ibid.

crime and thus may have no direct relation to the harm that the crimes caused".[16] The main purpose of this theory was to net "big fish"[17] as the District Court in the Eichmann trial noted: "On the contrary, in general, the degree of responsibility increases, as we draw further away from the man who uses fatal instrument with his own hands and reach the higher ranks of command".[18]

Although conspiracy may not be expressly an essential tool of accountability before the ICTY and ICC, new versions of the conspiracy doctrine including joint criminal enterprise and co-perpetration have been recognised by ICTY jurisprudence, the ICC Statute and recent proceedings elucidating that they are basically the product of conspiracy theory blended with doctrines of accomplice liability.

The purpose of this chapter is not to determine whether the three collective doctrines conform to the principle of culpability. Rather, it intends to evaluate the development of conspiracy as a mode of liability within the evolution of international criminal jurisprudence. The discussion tries to determine whether this concept has been transformed into new variants such as joint criminal enterprise and co-perpetration, and clarify the evolution of collective liability theories relating to conspiracy under international jurisprudence. The chapter also explores the commonalities and differences of these theories.

The discussion traces the conspiracy doctrine from the IMT at Nuremberg and subsequent Nuremberg trials, to the jurisprudence of the *ad hoc* tribunals of the ICTY, the International Criminal Tribunal for Rwanda ('ICTR') and the ICC. Section 16.2. provides an overview of what role conspiracy-based liability played in shaping the IMT Charter and Nuremberg trials as well as trials conducted pursuant to Control Council Law No. 10 ('CCL 10'). Section 16.3. analyses the ways that conspiracy has been articulated in key international documents. Sections 16.4. and 16.5. consider the ICTY and ICTR case law by looking into the relationship between conspiracy and joint criminal enterprise, and examine the extent to which conspiracy has influenced the development of liability theories,

---

[16]   Aaron Fichtelberg, "Conspiracy and International Criminal Justice", in *Criminal Law Forum*, 2006, vol. 17, no. 2, p. 152.

[17]   Bradley F. Smith, *The American Road to Nuremberg: The Documentary Record 1944–1945*, Hoover Institution Press, Stanford, CA, 1982, p. 98.

[18]   Supreme Court of Israel, *Adolf Eichmann v. The Attorney General of the Government of Israel*, Criminal Appeal No. 336/61, Judgment, 29 May 1962, para. 197.

especially joint criminal enterprise. Section 16.6. turns to co-perpetration
and common purpose liability under the ICC Statute and their links with
conspiracy.

16.2. Conspiracy at the Nuremberg Trials

After the Second World War the victorious powers concluded an agreement to establish a tribunal at Nuremberg for the prosecution of war criminals whose offences could not be attributed to a certain geographical territory.[19] Conspiracy formed part of Nuremberg documents and proceedings "at the instigation of the Americans because of its unique features of
combating collective criminality in common law jurisdictions".[20] Murray
Bernays was the American lawyer who designed and "planned the legal
framework and procedures for the Nuremberg War Crimes Trials after
World War II, basing the trials on the legal foundation of conspiracy and
publically trying the war crimes defendants through well-established legal
methods, resorted to the United States domestic law of criminal conspiracy".[21] Indeed Bernays proposed the initial idea of including conspiracy in
the IMT Charter. He maintained that conspiracy might provide an appropriate basis for catching and convicting "a large number of guilty people
against whom there might not have been direct evidence of having carried
out the atrocities, but they participated in the common enterprise".[22] In his
famous memorandum Bernays wrote:

> The Nazi Government and its Party and State agencies [...]
> should be charged before an appropriately constituted inter-
> national court with conspiracy to commit murder, terrorism,
> and the destruction of peaceful populations in violation of
> the laws of war [...] once the conspiracy is established, each
> act of every member thereof during its continuance and in

[19] International Military Tribunal, *The Trial of German Major War Criminals: Proceedings of the International Military Tribunal Sitting at Nuremberg, Germany*, Judgment, part 22, 1 October 1946 ('Nuremberg Judgment') (http://www.legal-tools.org/doc/45f18e/).

[20] Juliet R. Amenge Okoth, *The Crime of Conspiracy in International Criminal Law*, Asser Press, The Hague, 2014, p. 80.

[21] Jacob A. Ramer, "Hate by Association: Joint Criminal Liability for Persecution", in *Kent Journal of International and Comparative Law*, 2007, vol. 7, no. 1, p. 40; see also Smith, 1982, pp. 33–37, *supra* note 17.

[22] Smith, 1982, p. 35, see *supra* note 17.

furtherance of its purposes would be imputable to all other members thereof.[23]

He supported the idea that using conspiracy to prosecute Nazi defendants would be adequate to establish the guilt of all participants. Eventually Bernays found that "a conspiracy to wage aggressive war could rightfully include everything the Nazi regime had done since coming to power on 30 January 1933". Moreover, conspiracy removed the central legal problem that defendants could claim obedience to higher orders as a defence.[24]

However, Herbert Wechsler, who served at Nuremberg as assistant Attorney General on the part of the United States, rejected this idea by explaining that "maybe international law did not similarly recognize the criminality of conspiracies".[25] As regards the meaning of the term 'conspiracy', Wechsler further added that "Bernays himself was confused between conspiracy as a crime and conspiracy as a mode of complicity in substantive offences, committed by one of the conspirators".[26] Telford Taylor, one of the primary architects of the IMT, also disagreed with the view of Bernays: "The Anglo-American concept of conspiracy was not part of European legal systems and arguably not an element of the internationally recognized laws of war".[27]

In preparation for the IMT the American delegation proposed to use conspiracy at the London Conference in 1945. Since the concept was absent in the continental criminal systems, it caused much controversy and provoked divergent approaches between common law and civil law countries.[28] At the conference "the French viewed conspiracy entirely as a bar-

---

[23] *Ibid.*

[24] NAII, RG 107, Stimson Papers, Memorandum on War Crimes, 9 October 1944: Letter from Stimson to Stettinius (Secretary of State), 27 October 1944, enclosing "Trial of European War Criminals: The General Problem", pp. 1–5, cited in Richard Overy, "The Nuremberg Trials: International Law in the Making", in Philippe Sands (ed.), *From Nuremberg to The Hague: The Future of International Criminal Justice*, Cambridge University Press, Cambridge, 2003, p. 16.

[25] Norman Silber and Geoffrey Miller, "Toward 'Neutral Principles' in the Law: Selections from the Oral History of Herbert Wechsler", in *Columbia Law Review*, 1993, vol. 93, no. 4, p. 894.

[26] *Ibid.*

[27] Telford Taylor, *The Anatomy of the Nuremberg Trials: A Personal Memoir*, Alfred A. Knopf, New York, 1992, pp. 35–36.

[28] Danner and Martinez, 2005, p. 115, see *supra* note 3.

barous legal mechanism unworthy of modern law, while the Soviet attack on conspiracy was that it was too vague and so unfamiliar to the French and themselves, as well as to the Germans, that it would lead to endless confusion".[29] The concept of imputed liability for unlawful acts of co-conspirators was known in common law jurisdictions at the time, and consisted of an agreement between two or more persons with the intention of carrying out a crime and playing a role in furtherance of the agreement. "Its justificatory existence is apparently of a preventive nature."[30]

This kind of liability for co-conspirators had not been embraced in any civil law jurisdictions. Despite French and Soviet objections to the conception,[31] conspiracy was ultimately included in Nuremberg proceedings due to the United States' supremacy during the post-war period. Justice Robert H. Jackson, the chief American negotiator of the IMT Charter and chief prosecutor at the IMT, proposed two varied concepts of conspiracy at the London Conference: the *inchoate* concept that had been inherited from English law and was included in Article 6(a); and the *parties* concept which was traced back to Pinkerton rule,[32] crystallised into the last and general provision of Article 6. It is obvious that the main elements of conspiracy based liability were extracted "as a matter of general principles" from the Pinkerton rule, and at Nuremberg "conspiracy was mainly employed as a form of participation rather than as an inchoate crime".[33]

The focus of the following sections is to examine the role conspiracy has played in shaping the Nuremberg Proceedings. Accordingly, the discussion is divided into three parts devoted to the IMT Charter, the IMT trial and the CCL 10 trials to clarify how conspiracy was historically conceptualised in this process.

---

[29] Stanislaw Pomorski, "Conspiracy and Criminal Organizations", in George Ginsburgs and V.N. Kudriavtsev (eds.), *The Nuremberg Trial and International Law*, Martinus Nijhoff, Dordrecht, 1990, pp. 213–16.

[30] Ilias Banktekas and Susan Nash, *International Criminal Law*, 3rd ed., Routledge-Cavendish, London, 2007, p. 34.

[31] Danner and Martinez, 2005, p. 115, see *supra* note 3.

[32] US Supreme Court, *Pinkerton v. United States*, 328 U.S. 640, 1946.

[33] Banktekas and Nash, 2007, p. 34, see *supra* note 30.

16.2.1. The International Military Tribunal Charter

The Charter of the IMT annexed to the London Agreement, which formed the statutory and legal basis for the IMT, included conspiracy within its *ratione personae* and subject matter jurisdiction. Article 6 of the IMT Charter provided:

> The following acts, or any of them, are crimes coming within the jurisdiction of the Tribunal for which there shall be individual responsibility:
>
> (a) Crimes against peace: namely, planning, preparation, initiation or waging a war of aggression, or a war in violation of international treaties, agreements or assurances, or participation in a common plan or conspiracy for the accomplishment of any of the foregoing;
>
> (b) War crimes: namely, violations of the laws or customs of war. Such violations shall include, but not be limited to, murder, ill-treatment or deportation to slave labor or for any other purpose of civilian population of or in occupied territory, murder or ill-treatment of prisoners of war or persons on the seas, killing of hostages, plunder of public or private property, wanton destruction of cities, towns or villages, or devastation not justified by military necessity;
>
> (c) Crimes against humanity: namely, murder, extermination, enslavement, deportation, and other inhumane acts committed against any civilian population, before or during the war; or persecutions on political, racial or religious grounds in execution of or in connection with any crime within the jurisdiction of the Tribunal, whether or not in violation of the domestic law of the country where perpetrated.
>
> Leaders, organizers, instigators and accomplices participating in the formulation or execution of a common plan or conspiracy to commit any of the foregoing crimes are responsible for all acts performed by any persons in execution of such plan.[34]

---

[34] Charter of the International Military Tribunal, Article 6, 8 August 1945 ('IMT Charter') (https://www.legal-tools.org/doc/64ffdd/).

The initial perception of Article 6 was that only participation in a conspiracy for the perpetration of a *crime against peace* could be prosecuted and similar conspiracy provisions were not included in the definitions of *war crimes* or *crimes against humanity*. By looking closely at the final paragraph it becomes clear that it covers "leaders, organizers, instigators and accomplices" who have taken part in the formulation or execution of a "common plan or conspiracy" to commit any of those crimes. It is obvious that this wording is directly concerned with the *ratione personae* jurisdiction of the IMT.[35] This paragraph provided for attribution of liability to persons who did not personally execute the listed crimes but nevertheless participated or contributed to their formulation or execution in other capacities.

It seems that Article 6 of the IMT Charter did not distinguish between principal and accessorial liability. As Kai Ambos pointed out, "the IMT […] embraced a unitary model which did not distinguish between the perpetration of a crime (which gives rise to principal liability) and participation in a crime committed by third person (which gives rise to accessorial liability)".[36] However, Article 6 distinguishes conspirators according to the nature of their contributions in up to four different categories of individuals participating in the common plan or conspiracy: the leaders, the organisers, the instigators and accomplices.

As noted, Article 6 contains two provisions relating to "common plan or conspiracy". First, the term "conspiracy" appears in Article 6(a) in the phrase "participation in a common plan or conspiracy". Conspiracy within this concept was included within the provision defining crimes against peace (Article 6(a)), but not within the provisions defining war crimes and crimes against humanity (Articles 6(b)) and 6(c)).[37] Article 6(a) seems to provide the substantive offence of crimes against peace *and* "participation in a common plan or conspiracy for the accomplishment of any [crimes against peace]", while Article 6(b) and (c) included the substantive offences of war crimes and crimes against humanity without any

---

[35] Edoardo Gereppi, "The Evolution of Individual Criminal Responsibility under International Law", in *International Review of the Red Cross*, 1999, vol, 81, no. 835, pp. 531–53.

[36] Kai Ambos, *La Parte General del Derecho Penal Internacional: Bases Para un a Elaboración Dogmática* [The General Part of International Criminal Law: Bases for a Dogmatic Development], Uruguay, Konrad-Adenauer-Stiftung, Berlin, 2005, p. 75, cited in Olásolo, 2009, p. 21, see *supra* note 1.

[37] Banktekas and Nash, 2007, p. 35, see *supra* note 30.

corresponding conspiracy within their texts.[38] Although the wording of Article 6(a) suggests that a crime against peace may be perpetrated through a conspiracy to commit war crimes and crimes against humanity, its inclusion in Article 6(a) was clearly aimed at formulating a particular form of perpetration – the crime of aggression.

Second, the reference to "common plan or conspiracy" is also found in the last paragraph of Article 6. Some scholars maintain that the inclusion of this phrase twice within the same Article raises some confusion.[39] The interpretation of the last paragraph and its connection with the previous paragraphs are matters that demand consideration. As Article 31(1) of the Vienna Convention on the Law of the Treaties states: "A treaty shall be interpreted in good faith in accordance with the ordinary meaning to be given to the terms of the treaty in their context and in the light of its object and purpose".[40] It has been argued that its textual interpretation and the order and placement of the provision in the Charter support the view that the last paragraph of Article 6 modifies each of the paragraphs numbered (a), (b) and (c).[41] Kevin Jon Heller refers to the last paragraph of Article 6 as a "catch-all" provision.[42] He submits that a form of responsibility/mode of participation contained in the last paragraph of Article 6 attaches to all three previous categories of crimes, that is, crimes against peace, crimes against humanity and war crimes.[43] Indeed Article 6 closed with a general conspiracy provision that applied to all three offences. Accordingly, the final provision does not support an inchoate conspiracy charge, its language is more consistent with conspiracy-based mode of liability.

On the other hand, and as noted, the main provisions of Article 6 of the IMT Charter refer to participating in the formulation or execution of a

---

[38] *Ibid.*

[39] Jonathan A. Bush, "The Prehistory of Corporations and Conspiracy in International Criminal Law: What Nuremberg Really Said", in *Columbia Law Review*, 2009, vol. 109, no. 5, pp. 1094–1262.

[40] Vienna Convention on the Law of Treaties, 23 May 1969.

[41] Roger S. Clark, "Nuremberg and the Crime against Peace" in *Washington University Global Studies Law Review*, 2007, vol. 6, no. 3, pp. 527–50.

[42] Kevin Jon Heller, *The Nuremberg Military Tribunals and the Origins of International Criminal Law*, Oxford University Press, Oxford, 2011, p. 276.

[43] *Ibid.*

"common plan or conspiracy".[44] It seems that this equates the concept of common plan which contains main elements such as plurality of persons, common design, participation in a common design and shared intent, with the notion of conspiracy.

Apart from the concept of conspiracy, another controversial theory of liability that was considered before the IMT was that of criminal organisations. The concept of criminal organisations has been considered to be equivalent to criminal conspiracy. Article 9 of the ITM Charter provides: "At trial of any individual of any group or organization the Tribunal may declare (in connection with any act of which the individual may be convicted) that the group or organization of which the individual was a member was a criminal organization". Article 10 further reinforces Article 9 by providing that once the Tribunal declared an organisation criminal, this would be final and the "competent national authority of any Signatory shall have the right to bring individuals to trial for membership therein".

As noted by the IMT: "A criminal organization is analogous to a criminal conspiracy in that the essence of both is co-operation for criminal purposes".[45] Like conspiracy, the concept of criminal organisation was established to create criminal responsibility for situations involving mass organised criminality with many participants. It was an ambitious attempt by the prosecution to overcome any evidentiary or procedural burden that it would otherwise encounter in proving every individual's role in the crimes perpetrated by the Nazi regime. In fact the prosecution maintained that it was part of the conspiracy concept. It was noted that as soon as an organisation was declared criminal, its members would become responsible for the criminal acts of one another, like in a conspiracy. As conspiracy was intended to "net the big fish", criminal organisation was to be used for "netting the smaller fish".

16.2.2. Trial at International Military Tribunal

The IMT trial started in 1945 with the indictment of 24 major war criminals and six organisations. The indictment contained four counts: 1) participation in a common plan or conspiracy for the accomplishment of a crime against peace, war crimes and crimes against humanity; 2) plan-

---

[44] IMT Charter, see *supra* note 34.
[45] Nuremberg Judgment, p. 82, see *supra* note 19.

ning, initiating and waging wars of aggression and other crimes against peace; 3) war crimes; and 4) crimes against humanity.[46]

The first count echoed the exact wording of Article 6, charged the defendants with participating as "leaders, organizers, instigators, or accomplices in the formulation or execution of a common plan or conspiracy".[47] The first count clarified the particulars of the nature and development of a common plan and conspiracy which had been founded in Germany under the Nazis and covered 25 years from the time of establishment of the Nazi Party in 1920 to the end of the war in 1945. This addressed the Nazi Party as the core of the common plan or conspiracy. It recognised that the Nazi Party was the "instrument of cohesion among the defendants" from which they executed the purpose of conspiracy, and further the most important thing is that participation in affairs of the Nazi Party and the government was evidence of the participation in the conspiracy.[48] When defence counsel objected to conspiracy, the IMT recognised that there was no definition of conspiracy in the IMT Charter. In its judgment the Tribunal stated its understanding of conspiracy: "the conspiracy must be clearly outlined in its criminal purpose. It must not be too far removed from the time of decision and of action".[49]

Although defendants were charged under the first count with conspiracy to carry out all the three listed crimes in Article 6, the Tribunal did not recognise the two later conspiracies on crimes against humanity and war crimes. It declared that contrary to the prosecution's view, the Charter did not provide for conspiracy to commit war crimes and crimes against humanity. The Tribunal held that although the last paragraph of Article 6 seemed to create the perception that it provided for conspiracy with respect to all crimes, this provision did not actually generate new or separate crimes. The Tribunal instead asserted that the provision was only designed to establish responsibility of persons participating in the common plan to wage a war of aggressions.[50]

On the other hand, the Tribunal found five important principles within Article 6 of the Charter: 1) it imposes "individual responsibility"

---

[46] *Ibid.*
[47] *Ibid.*, p. 14.
[48] *Ibid.*, p. 56.
[49] *Ibid.*, p. 57.
[50] *Ibid.*, p. 55.

for acts constituting crimes against peace; 2) crimes against peace contain planning, preparation, initiation or waging of illegal war; 3) crimes against peace also include participation in a common plan or conspiracy to commit illegal war; 4) an illegal war consists of either a war of aggression or a war in violation of international treaties; accordingly the prosecution had to address whether the war planned, prepared, initiated and waged by the Nazi conspirators were illegal; and 5) individual criminal responsibility of a defendant is imposed by this provision not merely by reasons of direct, immediate participation in the crime. The IMT asserted: "It is sufficient to show that a defendant was a leader, an organizer, instigator, or accomplice who participated either in the formulation or in the execution of a common plan or conspiracy to commit crimes against peace". The judgment further stated "that the responsibility of conspirators extends not only to their own acts but also to all acts performed by any persons in execution of the conspiracy".[51] Thus under Article 6 "all the parties to a common plan or conspiracy are the agents of each other and each is responsible as principal for the acts of all the others as his agents". Referring to this provision the IMT recognised the conspiratorial nature of the planning and preparation of the Nazi aggression and the individual participation of named persons in the Nazi conspiracy for aggression leading to the attacks during from 1933 to 1939. The count of conspiracy to wage aggressive war dealt with crimes committed immediately before the Second World War began. The Tribunal decided to investigate the law on common plan or conspiracy together with the second count of planning and waging war, justifying that the same evidence had been produced to support both counts.[52]

The IMT indictments and judgments used the terms 'common plan' and 'conspiracy' interchangeably.[53] For example, count one of the IMT indictment is entitled "The Common Plan or Conspiracy", suggesting that the terms are synonymous, or are, at the very least, similar to one another. The IMT judgment also frequently used the expression "common plan or conspiracy" and equates the concept of common plan with the notion of

---

[51] *Ibid.*, p. 14.

[52] *Ibid.*, p. 55.

[53] Damgard, 2008, p. 185, see *supra* note 14.

conspiracy.[54] The IMT justified that both had been carried out in a systematic and organised manner and decided that it would still proceed to find the guilt of the defendants under both counts,[55] while it seemed that the joint planning and preparation of such war by the defendants was the only evidence showing the existence of a conspiracy.

As noted, the IMT observed that the Nazi Party was an instrument for carrying out the aims of their conspiracy. Accordingly it recognised the existence of a plan under a dictatorial regime and rejected the defence argument that a plan cannot exist in a dictatorship. The Tribunal stated that a plan executed by several persons, though plotted by single person, was still a plan, and the participants could not escape from liability by alleging that they had been directed to do so by its author.[56] The IMT declared that by co-operating with the architect of the main plan with full knowledge of his aims, the defendants had made themselves members of the plan.[57]

It is well understood that the IMT was unwilling to embrace any form of vicarious liability that was not closely tied to an underlying offence under Article 6; therefore some level of *actus reus* and *mens rea* was necessary for defendants. Unlike in some American jurisdictions,[58] where the accused can be held strictly liable for any and all crimes committed by conspirators, the IMT sought to restrict liability to individuals who knew or should have known about their role in committing war crimes.[59] Indeed the IMT required a very high threshold of participation and knowledge of the plan and limited the charge of conspiracy only for those who participated in preparatory acts materialising into the actual acts of aggression.[60] Nevertheless the evidentiary threshold of the IMT

---

[54] Nuremberg Judgment, pp. 12, 23, 56, see *supra* note 19. See also Elies van Sliedregt, *The Criminal Responsibility of Individuals for Violations of International Humanitarian Law*, TMC Asser Press, The Hague, 2003, p. 17.

[55] Nuremberg Judgment, *ibid.*, p. 64.

[56] Ibid.

[57] Ibid.

[58] Raha Wala, "From Guantanamo to Nuremberg and Back: An Analysis of Conspiracy to Commit War Crimes under International Humanitarian Law", *Georgetown Journal of International Law*, 2010, vol. 41, no. 3, p. 693.

[59] Bush, 2009, p.1100, see *supra* note 39.

[60] Banktekas and Nash, 2007, pp. 50–53, see *supra* note 30.

was high, requiring that knowledge of the conspiracy be proven directly and beyond reasonable doubt.[61]

The IMT found guilty under the charges of participation in a common plan or conspiracy, with great caution, only eight of the 24 indicted war criminals.[62] These eight defendants were regarded as having had a close link with Hitler's policy and were also a part of his inner circle of advisers. They had attended the conference at which Hitler had expressed his plans. Therefore the Tribunal considered them to be Hitler's co-conspirators. Their liability for conspiracy was based on the substantial role they played in the formulation and execution of plans, with full knowledge of the unlawful nature of the war and with the common intent that force be used along with their position to contribute to the decision to invade.[63]

16.2.3. Control Council Law No. 10 Trials

CCL 10 adopted by the Allied Control Council in post-war Germany provided the occupying authorities with the instruments to try suspected war criminals in their respective occupation zones. The crimes defined in Article II of CCL 10 were to a great extent similar to those set out in the Article 6 of the IMT Charter, with conspiracy only being specifically mentioned under the commission of crimes against peace.[64] The following overview is strictly with respect to the post-war tribunals' interpretation of the conspiracy-based liability.

The CCL 10 trials regarding conspiracy and common plan can be divided into three categories. The first category involved groups of individuals acting together to perpetrate a crime and, most often, included the killing of victims. An example could be the so-called Almelo trial in which four individuals worked together to execute two victims but where only one person pulled the trigger each time, while the others merely stood watch or dug the graves.[65] The British Military Court convicted all

---

[61] *Ibid.*

[62] Nuremberg Judgment, pp. 101–154, see *supra* note 19.

[63] *Ibid.*

[64] Control Council Law No. 10, Punishment of Persons Guilty of War Crimes, Crimes against Peace and against Humanity, Article II, 20 December 1945 (https://www.legal-tools.org/doc/ffda62/).

[65] British Military Court for the Trial of War Criminals, Trial of Otto Sandrock and Three Others (Almelo Trial), 24–26 November 1945, in United Nations War Crimes Commis-

four individuals for murder. The Court found that the charged persons' intention to affect the result and their participation in the execution of the plan rendered them individually liable for murder. This liability would persist even if all of the charged persons did not personally effectuate the crime. The judge ruled that

> there was no dispute that all three (Sandrock, Schweinberger and Hegemann in the case of Pilot Officer Hood, and Sandrock, Schweinberger and Wiegner in the case of van der Wal) knew what they were doing and that they had gone to the wood for the very purpose of having the victims killed. If people were all present together at the same time, taking part in a common enterprise which was unlawful, each one in their own way assisting the common purpose of all, they were all equally guilty in law.[66]

In this case the Court also considered the problem of collective responsibility, with reference to a British Royal Warrant that had been issued on 4 August 1945:

> Where there is evidence that a war crime has been the result of concerted action upon the part of a unit or group of men, then evidence given upon any charge relating to that crime against any member of such unit or group, may be received as prima facie evidence of the responsibility of each member of that unit or group for that crime.
>
> In any such case all or any members of any such unit or group may be charged and tried jointly in respect of any such war crime and no application by any of them to be tried separately shall be allowed by the Court.[67]

The main elements of this category included: 1) the existence of a common plan to commit a crime, 2) involving a plurality of persons who all shared the intent to commit the crime, and 3) the participation of the charged person in the execution of the plan. The essence of this category is that participants in the plan were responsible for the crime, despite the fact that not all of them physically perpetrated the crime. The problem raised is that this category does not define the degree of participation nec-

---

sion, *Law Reports of the Trials of War Criminals*, vol. 1, His Majesty's Stationery Office, London, 1947, p. 35.

[66] *Ibid.*, p. 43.

[67] Ibid.

essary to invoke this form of liability nor does it define any limits on the scope of the plan for which this liability can be applied.

The second category involves convictions of individuals who fulfilled different roles at concentration camps and bore responsibility for the crimes perpetrated at those camps so long as they were aware of the abuses and willingly took part in the functioning of the institution. The case that can be considered as an example is from the Dachau concentration camp.[68] The indictment stated that the accused "acted in pursuance of a common design to commit the acts hereinafter alleged and as members of the staff of the Dachau Concentration Camp [...] did [...] willfully, deliberately and wrongfully aid, abet and participate in the subjection of civilian nations".[69] The definition of common design was given at the Dachau trial as "a community of intention between two or more persons to do an unlawful act".[70] This definition does not differ materially from the definition of conspiracy offered in a standard criminal law textbook of the time: "the agreement of two or more persons to effect any unlawful purpose whether as their ultimate aim or only as a means to it".[71] The Dachau judgment stated that the elements required were: "1) that there was in force [...] a system to ill-treat the prisoners and commit the crimes listed in the charges, 2) that each accused was aware of the system, 3) that each accused, by his conduct 'encouraged, aided and abetted or participated' in enforcing this system".[72]

The other case that may fall into this category is that of Oswald Pohl and 17 co-defendants.[73] The defendants were charged with maintaining and administering concentration camps in a manner so as to cause in-

---

[68] General Military Government Court of the United States Zone, The Dachau Concentration Camp Trial; Trial of Martin Gottfried Weiss and Thirty-nine Others, Case No. 60, 15 November–13 December 1945, in United Nations War Crimes Commission, *Law Reports of the Trials of War Criminals*, vol. 11, His Majesty's Stationery Office, London, 1949, p. 5 ('Dachau case').

[69] *Ibid.*, The Charges, p. 5.

[70] *Ibid.*, p. 14.

[71] Courtney Stanhope Kenny, *Outlines of Criminal Law*, 15th ed., Cambridge University Press, Cambridge, 1936.

[72] Dachau case, p. 13, see *supra* note 75.

[73] United States Military Tribunals, United States v. Oswald Pohl, et al., Judgment, 3 November 1947, Trials of War Criminals Before the Nuremberg Military Tribunals Under Control Council Law No. 10, vol. V, US Government Printing Office (http://www.legal-tools.org/doc/84ae05/).

jury, disease, starvation, torture and death of the inmates. The indictment filed against the defendants contained four counts: 1) participation in a common design or conspiracy; 2) war crimes carried out through the administration of concentration camps and extermination camps; 3) crimes against humanity also carried out through the administration of concentration camps and extermination camps; and 4) membership in a criminal organisation.[74] According to counts one and four, all the defendants acted according to a common design unlawfully, wilfully and knowingly conspired and agreed with each other and with various other persons, to commit war crimes and crimes against humanity. Count one states: "all of the defendants herein, acting pursuant to a common design, unlawfully, wilfully, and knowingly did conspire and agree together and with each other and with divers other persons, to commit War Crimes and Crimes against Humanity".[75] Count one also declares that

> all of the defendants [...] participated as leaders, organizers, instigators, and accomplices in the formulation and execution of the said common design, conspiracy, plans, and enterprises to commit, and which involved the commission of War Crimes and Crimes against Humanity, and accordingly are individually responsible for their own acts and for all acts performed by any person or persons in execution of the said common design, conspiracy, plans, and enterprise.[76]

Although the Tribunal acknowledged that administration of concentration camps involved a broad criminal programme requiring co-operation of many persons, it decided to disregard certain parts of count one in as far as it charged conspiracy as a separate crime. The Tribunal declined to strike out the whole of count one, choosing to retain parts of it that referred to the unlawful participation in the formulation and execution of common plan.

The third category involved individuals who were convicted for crimes committed by others and for which there was no apparent evidence that a shared intent existed regarding the crime. These cases generally involved mob actions that resulted in the unlawful killing of Allied prison-

---

[74] United States Military Tribunals, *United States v. Oswald Pohl, et al.*, Indictment, Case No. 4, 13 January 1947, Office of Military Government for Germany, Nuremberg (https://www.legal-tools.org/doc/b4a1c8/).

[75] *Ibid.*, p. 4.

[76] *Ibid.*, p. 7.

ers of war. In the Essen lynching case that tried Erich Heyer and six others, there was no evidence that a shared intent to kill the prisoners existed (only the intent to abuse them) nor that the defendants physically caused the deaths.[77] The prosecution argued that no such intent was necessary when everyone knew that the prisoners were doomed: "every person in that crowd who struck a blow was both morally and criminally responsible for the deaths".[78] The British Military Court convicted all the defendants for murder.

Each category discussed here – groups of individuals acting together to perpetrate a crime, individuals who fulfilled different roles at concentration camps and bore responsibility for the crimes perpetrated at those camps, and individuals who were convicted for crimes committed by others and for which there was no apparent evidence that a shared intent – requires, at the least, that a form of criminal recklessness existed within the common plan doctrine. Additionally, each category determines conspiracy as a form of participation and requires the existence of a common plan to commit the offences, awareness of the system by the accused, and that the accused be involved in the operation of the system.

16.3. Conspiracy in International Documents

This section addresses how conspiracy has been articulated in well-known international legal documents. The Hague Conventions of 1899 and 1907 and the Geneva Convention IV of 1949 do not include conspiracy to commit war crimes within the lists of grave breaches, or in other provisions that proscribe conduct.[79] Additional Protocol I to the Geneva Conventions does address vicarious liability, but only under a principle of command responsibility, suggesting that exclusion of other liability theories was intentional.[80]

---

[77] British Military Court for the Trial of War Criminals, Trial of Erich Heyer and Six Others (Essen Lynching Case), 18–19 and 21–22 December 1945, in United Nations War Crimes Commission, *Law Reports of the Trials of War Criminals*, vol. 1, His Majesty's Stationery Office, London, 1947, p. 88–92.

[78] *Ibid.*, p. 89.

[79] Convention IV relative to the Protection of Civilian Persons in Time of War, 12 August 1949, arts. 146–47.

[80] Protocol Additional to the Geneva Conventions of 12 August 1949, and relating to the Protection of Victims of International Armed Conflicts (Protocol I), 8 June 1977, arts. 86–87.

In its first session, the United Nations General Assembly adopted a resolution affirming the principles of the London Charter and the IMT judgment as well as the Nuremberg Principles, and established the International Law Commission ('ILC'), which was tasked with codifying international law.[81] The ILC first published its codification of the Nuremberg Principles in 1950, which did not include the conspiracy-based liability provision for war crimes that the London Charter contained. Instead it included "complicity" in war crimes and other offences, but listed participation in a common plan or conspiracy to commit crimes against peace as a separate crime.[82]

The ILC's 1996 Draft Code of Crimes against the Peace and Security of Mankind with commentaries ('Draft Code') makes clear that the conspiracy provision was only intended to apply to high-level military commanders and government officials.[83] Therefore mid-level officials and their subordinates would need to be held liable through other liability theories. More generally, the 1996 Draft Code (Article 2(3)(e)) provides responsibility when an individual "[d]irectly participates in planning or conspiring to commit such a crime which in fact occurs".[84] Sub-paragraph 3(e) intends to ensure that high-level government officials or military commanders who formulate a criminal plan or policy, as individuals or as co-conspirators, are held accountable for the major role that they play which is often a decisive factor in the commission of the crimes covered by the Draft Code.

The crimes set forth in the Draft Code, due to their very nature, often require the formulation of a plan or a systematic policy by senior government officials and military commanders. Such a plan or policy may require more detailed elaboration by individuals in mid-level positions in the governmental hierarchy or the military command structure, who were

---

[81] United Nations General Assembly Resolution, GA Res. 94(I), UN doc. A/94, 11 December 1946, establishing the International Law Commission; GA Res. 95(I), UN doc. A/95, 11 December 1946, affirming the Nuremberg Principles; GA Res. 177(II), UN doc. A/177, 21 November 1947, tasking the International Law Commission with codifying the Nuremberg Principles.

[82] "Principles of International Law Recognized in the Charter of the Nuremberg Tribunal and in the Judgment of the Tribunal", in *Yearbook of the International Law Commission*, 1950, vol. 2, no. 13, pp. 374–78.

[83] "Draft Code of Crimes against the Peace and Security of Mankind", *Yearbook of the International Law Commission*, 1996, vol. 2, pp. 18–19.

[84] *Ibid.*, p. 18.

responsible for ordering the implementation of the general plans or policies formulated by senior officials. The criminal responsibility of the mid-level officials who ordered their subordinates to commit the crimes is provided for in Article 2(3)(b). Such a plan or policy may also require a number of individuals in low-level positions to take the necessary action to carry out the criminal plan or policy. The criminal responsibility of the subordinates who actually committed the crimes is provided for in Article 2(3)(a). Thus, the combined effect of sub-paragraphs (a), (b) and (e) is to ensure that the principle of criminal responsibility applies to all individuals throughout the governmental hierarchy or the military chain of command who contributed in one way or another to the commission of a crime set out in the code.[85]

Irrespective of these provisions, George P. Fletcher notices that over the last half-century "every relevant international treaty on international humanitarian law or international criminal law ha[s] deliberately avoided the concept and language of conspiracy".[86] While conspiracy as a substantive offence has generally been rejected at the international level, it was included in the 1948 Convention on the Prevention and Punishment of the Crime of Genocide ('Genocide Convention').[87] Conspiracy to commit genocide is explicitly illegal under the Genocide Convention. The Genocide Convention is the treaty with the most prominent use of conspiracy as a substantive crime. "The *travaux preparatories* revealed that inclusion of conspiracy was justified by the serious nature of the crime of genocide, which made the criminalization of mere preparatory acts such as agreement to commit it imperative."[88] As Taylor Dalton states: "The Genocide Convention includes the charge of conspiracy as a direct response to Nazi Germany's actions against the Jewish population".[89] Article 3 of the Genocide Convention states:

> The following acts shall be punishable:
>
> (a) Genocide;

---

[85] *Ibid.*

[86] George P. Fletcher, "Hamdan Confronts the Military Commissions Act of 2006", in *Columbia. Journal of Transnational Law*, 2007, vol. 45, no. 2, p. 448.

[87] Ohlin, 2010, p. 702, see *supra* note 4.

[88] Sliedregt, 2003, p. 32, see *supra* note 54.

[89] Taylor R. Dalton, "Counterfeit Conspiracy: The Misapplication of Conspiracy as a Substantive Crime in International Law", in *Cornell Law School Graduate Student Papers*, 2010, no. 24, p. 16.

(b) Conspiracy to commit genocide;

(c) Direct and public incitement to commit genocide;

(d) Attempt to commit genocide;

(e) Complicity in genocide.[90]

The crime of conspiracy to commit genocide reflects the drafters' desire to criminalise even the planning of genocide.[91] Many of the provisions in the Genocide Convention, particularly Article 3, have become a part of customary international law since it has been adopted in the statutes establishing the ICTY and ICTR, even though it was not included in the ICC Statute.[92] The 1998 International Convention for Suppression of Terrorist Bombing did not recognise conspiracy, but seemed to have included the main concept of conspiracy, namely common purpose. Article 2 states that a person is considered to have committed an offence it they contribute "to the commission of one or more offences as set forth [...] by a group of persons acting with a common purpose; such contribution shall be intentional and either be made with the aim of furthering the general criminal activity or purpose of the group or be made in the knowledge of the intention of the group to commit the offence or offences concerned".[93] This formulation of liability was adopted by the subsequent ICC Statute.

Generally, conspiracy-based liability, as Ohlin says, "does not exist in the relevant international instruments dealing with international crimes – at least not under this doctrinal name".[94] However, other modes of liability based on collective conduct, for example the doctrine of joint criminal enterprise, share many of the characteristics of conspiracy and continue to be used in international criminal jurisprudence.[95] This is discussed next.

---

[90] Convention on the Prevention and Punishment of the Crime of Genocide, 9 December 1948, Art. 3.

[91] Dalton, 2010, p. 8, see *supra* note 89.

[92] Antonio Cassese, *International Criminal Law*, 2nd ed., Oxford University Press, Oxford, 2008, pp. 189–209.

[93] International Convention for the Suppression of Terrorist Bombings, UNTS 256, adopted 15 December 1997.

[94] Jens David Ohlin, "Attempt to Commit Genocide", in Paola Gaeta (ed.), *The UN Genocide Convention: A Commentary*, Oxford University Press, Oxford, 2009, p. 209.

[95] Cassese, 2008, pp. 189–90, see *supra* note 92.

16.4. Conspiracy in International Criminal Tribunal for the Former Yugoslavia

While conspiracy as a mode of liability is absent from the ICTY, planning, which seems to have some similar elements with conspiracy, exists in Article 7(1) of the ICTY Statute on individual criminal responsibility.[96] Planning is the first form of participation under this article. It usually encompasses those who are on the top of a hierarchy, and likely to be applied to 'leaders' in a governmental or a military structure. The *actus reus* of planning is composed of three elements: an act of planning, the commission of a crime, and a causal link between the act and the crime. A significant difference between planning and conspiracy is that while the planning of a crime may be committed by a single person, conspiracy requires at least two. Planning involves "one or several persons contemplating designing the commission of a crime at both the preparatory and execution phases".[97] The existence of a plan, whether this is formal or informal, must be demonstrated by direct or circumstantial evidence. The level of participation of the accused in the plan is an additional important factor. According to the Brđanin Appeals Chamber, planning liability arises only if it was "demonstrated that the accused was substantially involved at the preparatory stage of that crime in the concrete form it took, which implies that he possessed sufficient knowledge thereof in advance".[98]

The *mens rea* for planning requires that the accused intended the crime in question materialised through the plan. With regard to direct intent, the Kordić Appeals Chamber stated that "a person who plans an act or omission with the awareness of the substantial likelihood that a crime will be committed in the execution of that plan" has the requisite *mens rea* for planning, since this is regarded as accepting that crime.[99] This would

---

[96] United Nations, Updated Statute of the International Criminal Tribunal for the Former Yugoslavia, Resolution 827, 25 May 1993 (https://www.legal-tools.org/doc/b4f63b/).

[97] International Criminal Tribunal for Rwanda, *Prosecutor v. Jean-Paul Akayesu*, Trial Judgment, 2 September 1998, ICTR-96-4-T, para. 480 ('Akayesu Trial Judgment') (https://www.legal-tools.org/doc/b8d7bd/).

[98] International Criminal Tribunal for the Former Yugoslavia, *Prosecutor v. Radoslav Brđanin*, Appeal Judgment, 3 April 2004, IT-99-36-T, para. 267 ('Brđanin Appeal Judgment') (http://www.legal-tools.org/doc/782cef/).

[99] International Criminal Tribunal for the Former Yugoslavia, *Prosecutor v. Kordić*, Appeal Judgment, IT-95-14/2, 17 December 2004 (https://www.legal-tools.org/doc/738211/). See also Banktekas and Nash, 2007, p. 27, see *supra* note 30.

be referred to as an oblique intent which does not seem to be supported by conspiracy doctrine. Therefore, joint participation in planning a crime is only the earliest evidence of a conspiracy.

The Anglo-American concepts of conspiracy have been incorporated into the ICTY and ICTR and have been blended with the civil law doctrines of accomplice liability to create the doctrine of joint criminal enterprise. The question that may arise in this regard is whether joint criminal enterprise theory provides individual responsibility for contributions to group criminality in the same way that conspiracy does or does joint criminal enterprise have a more stringent threshold for *mens rea* and *actus reus*. In other words, could we consider joint criminal enterprise as an extension or manifestation of conspiracy?

Joint criminal enterprise is one of the concepts that has been developed under international criminal law to deal with the issue of collective criminal actions.[100] As noted, at Nuremberg the terms 'common plan' and 'common design' were used to refer to conspiracy. Similar terms have been used interchangeably to describe joint criminal enterprise by the ICTY. Although joint criminal enterprise was not included in the ICTY Statute, it was first proposed in the Tadić Appeal Judgment as a form of commission.[101] The ICTY Appeals Chamber in the Krnojelac case concluded that the doctrines of conspiracy and joint criminal enterprise were related, noting that a "joint criminal enterprise exists where there is an understanding or arrangement amounting to an agreement between two or more persons that they will commit a crime".[102] The accused may also be held responsible not only for the crimes that he committed or participated in with intent and knowledge but also for crimes performed by other participants, when crimes are a natural and foreseeable consequence of the purpose of the criminal enterprise. Indeed, as Kai Ambos notes, "[t]he Chamber looked for a theory of international criminal participation that takes sufficiently into account the *collective, widespread and systematic context* of such crimes".[103] Statistics show that 64 per cent of the indict-

---

[100] Okoth, 2014, see *supra* note 20.

[101] Tadić Appeal Judgment, see *supra* note 2.

[102] International Criminal Tribunal for former Yugoslavia, *Prosecutor v. Milorad Krnojelac*, Judgment, 15 March 2002, IT-97-25, para. 80 (Krnojelac Judgment) (https://www.legal-tools.org/doc/1a994b/).

[103] Kai Ambos, "Joint Criminal Enterprise and Command Responsibility", in *Journal of International Criminal Justice*, 2007, vol. 5, p. 159.

ments submitted to the ICTY between 25 June 2001 and 1 January 2004 relied on this doctrine.[104]

While the purpose of the conspiracy as a mode of liability as "the method of choice for targeting senior military and political leaders"[105] and to facilitate the burden of producing evidence in post-war situations where witness and physical evidence were likely difficult to obtain, it seems that joint criminal enterprise is the developed form of conspiracy that has "most often been used in the *ad hoc* tribunals as part of the conceptual development of a mode of liability in international criminal law".[106] The main element of both joint criminal enterprise and conspiracy is a common plan or an agreement, whether explicit or tacit, which is based on a common purpose. The participants in both theories are united within their common purpose to achieve an ultimate goal. They act on a common enterprise/plan with a common intention.

The Tadić Appeals Chamber distinguished joint criminal enterprise relying on the post-Second World War case law's three categories of collective criminality.[107] The first *basic* form ('JCE I') requires liability for a common intention and/or purpose. In both joint criminal enterprise and conspiracy there is a common criminal purpose, whether we label it an enterprise or agreement, and under both theories the defendant must have had the specific intent that the crime to be carried out is explicitly a part of the common criminal purpose; under both all defendants must intend that the target crime of the joint criminal enterprise must be committed. The second category is the *systematic* form ('JCE II') which creates liability for participation in an institutionalised common plan and incidental criminal liability based on foresight. The third category is known as the *extended* joint enterprise ('JCE III'), that is to say the co-perpetrators are actually involved in acts beyond the common plan but which are the natural and foreseeable consequence of the main plan.[108]

It is well established that the roots of joint criminal enterprise liability can be found in the Nuremberg jurisprudence, which considered the reciprocal attribution of the doctrine of common designs in that a plan or

---

[104] Danner and Martinez, 2005, p. 107, see *supra* note 3.
[105] Danner and Martinez, 2005, p. 107, see *supra* note 3.
[106] Dalton, 2010, p. 16, see *supra* note 89.
[107] Tadić Appeal Judgment, paras. 185 ff., see *supra* note 2.
[108] Ambos, 2007, p. 160, see *supra* note 103.

collective enterprise serves as the basis for attribution. In the aforementioned CCL 10 cases, the three categories of conspiracy largely correspond to the three forms of JCE.

There are remarkable resemblances between joint criminal enterprise and conspiracy. The objective elements of joint criminal enterprise requires 1) a plurality of persons, 2) a common plan, design or purpose, which implies 3) the existence of a group of persons who agree to carry out a crime. This equates it to a conspiracy.[109] While the common plan forms part of the *actus reus* for joint criminal enterprise, the agreement is the *actus reus* for conspiracy, both resulting from the decision of at least two or more persons working together to achieve a criminal objective. The extended form of joint criminal enterprise, JCE III, attributes liability to an accused for criminal acts he did not personally perform or even have knowledge of as long as they were natural and foreseeable. Here we can see the footprint and impact of the Pinkerton case. The legal justification of this form of joint criminal enterprise is its resemblance to the legal bases of the Pinkerton doctrine, which holds individuals responsible for foreseeable crimes by co-conspirators. It is obvious that the prosecution does not need to prove an express agreement or common plan; their existence may be inferred from the conduct of a group of persons acting jointly. The resemblances between the two concepts gives the impression that perhaps the ICTY was seeking to remove a gap resulting from the failure to provide for a conspiracy theory that would include all the crimes within the Statute, by adopting a concept of conspiracy with a different name, that would be applicable to all crimes and become a convenient tool for the prosecution.[110]

The Appeals Chamber in the Tadić case not only identified the three separate categories of joint criminal enterprise but also distinguished two different elements – subjective and objective – of each category.[111] The objective elements include three items: 1) a plurality of persons which requires the involvement of two or more persons; 2) existence of a common plan, design or purpose; and 3) contribution to further the com-

---

[109] Beatrice I. Bonafè, *The Relationship between State and Individual Responsibility for International Crimes*, Martinus Nijhoff, Leiden, 2009, p. 178.

[110] Antonio Cassese, "The Proper Limits of Individual Responsibility under the Doctrine of Joint Criminal Enterprise", in *Journal of International Criminal Justice*, 2007, vol. 5, no. 1, p. 110.

[111] Tadić Appeal Judgment, para. 209, see *supra* note 2.

mon criminal plan involving the perpetuation of one of the crimes.[112] The subjective elements also require that "all of the co-perpetrators possess the same intent to effect the common purpose".[113] In the Brđanin case the Appeals Chamber tried to develop objective elements of joint criminal enterprise by stating that: 1) in respect of the plurality of persons, it is not necessary to identify each member of the criminal groups by name; 2) regarding the common purpose the prosecutor must prove that the purpose is effectively common for all members and prove a significant contribution of the accused in the execution of the purpose of joint criminal enterprise; and 3) with respect to attributing the crimes of the external perpetrators to the members of enterprise it is necessary to prove at least the existence of a link between the direct perpetrators and their acts and at least one members of the enterprise.[114]

Accordingly, in addition to planning, the ICTY has linked joint enterprise to conspiracy to commit war crimes and it seems that conspiracy has been transformed into a joint criminal enterprise liability theory after Nuremberg. The conclusion may be that joint criminal enterprise is similar to conspiracy as a form of participation, with the former typically includes more stringent *mens rea* and *actus reus* requirements than conspiracy, although it similarly relies on a criminal agreement.

The ICTY has also tried defendants for conspiracy to commit genocide as an inchoate crime, pursuant to Article 4(3) of the ICTY Statute. For instance Zdravko Tolimir, the assistant commander for intelligence and security of the Bosnian Serb Army, was tried for, *inter alia*, genocide and conspiracy to commit genocide for events that took place in Srebrenica.[115] Additionally, in the Popović case four defendants were charged with, *inter alia*, genocide and conspiracy to commit genocide. The charges alleged that the men entered a "joint criminal enterprise to murder all

---

[112] *Ibid.*, para. 227.

[113] International Criminal Tribunal for former Yugoslavia, *Prosecutor v. Kvočka et al.*, Appeals Chamber Judgment, 28 February 2003, IT-98-30/1, para. 82 (https://www.legal-tools.org/doc/006011/).

[114] Brđanin Appeal Judgment, paras. 364–437, see *supra* note 98.

[115] International Criminal Tribunal for the former Yugoslavia, *Prosecutor v. Zdravko Tolimir*, Third Amended Indictment, Count One, 4 November 2009, IT-05-88/2 (https://www.legal-tools.org/doc/026f86/).

the able-bodied Muslim men from Srebrenica", with the purpose "to destroy, in part, a national, ethnic, racial, or religious group".[116]

It should be mentioned that the ICTY distinguished conspiracy as an inchoate crime from joint criminal liability, for example in the Milutinović case, where Dragoljub Ojdanić challenged the court's jurisdiction:

> Whilst conspiracy requires a showing that several individuals have agreed to commit a certain crime or set of crimes, a joint criminal enterprise requires, in addition to such a showing, that the parties to that agreement took action in furtherance of that agreement. In other words, while mere agreement is sufficient in the case of conspiracy, the liability of a member of a joint criminal enterprise will depend on the commission of criminal acts in furtherance of that enterprise.[117]

16.5. Conspiracy in the International Criminal Tribunal for Rwanda

More cases of conspiracy as an inchoate crime were tried before the ICTR. Article 2 of the ICTR Statute gives the Tribunal power to prosecute persons suspected of committing genocide. Conspiracy is only mentioned here with respect to the crime of genocide.[118] The ICTR's judgments have so far addressed the issue of conspiracy in 14 cases.[119] Conspiracy to commit genocide was first defined in the Musema case as "an agreement between two or more persons to commit the crime of genocide".[120] The agreement between members of conspiracy may be explicit or implicit, as expressed in the later Nahimana case: "the existence of a formal or ex-

---

[116] International Criminal Tribunal for the former Yugoslavia, *Prosecutor v. Popović et al.*, Indictment, 4 August 2006, IT-05-88, paras. 31, 35 (https://www.legal-tools.org/doc/ce4324/).

[117] International Criminal Tribunal for former Yugoslavia, *Prosecutor v. Milutinović et al.*, Appeals Chamber, Decision on Dragoljub Ojdanić's Motion Challenging the Jurisdiction – *Joint Criminal Enterprise*, 21 May 2003, IT-99-37-AR72, para. 23 (http://www.legal-tools.org/doc/d51c63).

[118] Statute of the International Criminal Tribunal for Rwanda, Art. 2, 31 January 2010 (https://www.legal-tools.org/doc/8732d6/).

[119] Okoth, 2014, p. 130, see *supra* note 20.

[120] International Criminal Tribunal for Rwanda, *Prosecutor v. Alfred Musema*, Judgment, 27 January 2000, ICTR-96-13, para. 191 ('Musema Judgment') (https://www.legal-tools.org/doc/6a3fce/).

press agreement is not needed to prove the charge of conspiracy".[121] It is important that the members of the group act together in a concerted and co-ordinated way within a unified framework. The Nahimana Chamber noted that the prosecution should adduce evidence that the accused conspired with others to commit genocide. This form of agreement is considered the main element of a conspiracy charge. The ICTR in the Musema and Nahimana cases thus addressed the issue of criminal conspiracy as it pertains to the crime of genocide.[122] In the Kambanda case, the defendant was accused of both genocide and conspiracy to commit genocide.[123]

In the Musema case, the Trial Chamber held that an individual can be found guilty solely for the crime of conspiracy to commit genocide even if no genocide takes place.[124] It is not therefore surprising that the Trial Chamber in the Musema case, after defining genocidal conspiracy as "an agreement between two or more persons to commit the crime of genocide", argued that since it is the agreement that is punishable, it is irrelevant whether or not it results in the actual commission of genocide.[125] It is obvious, moreover, that in this manner genocidal conspiracy is treated as an inchoate crime, rather than as a form of liability. As to the existence of a conspiratorial agreement, the Nahimana trial judgment concluded that this may be inferred:

> Conspiracy can be comprised of individuals acting in an institutional capacity as well as or even independently of their personal links with each other. Institutional coordination can form the basis of a conspiracy among those individuals who control the institutions that are engaged in coordinated action.[126]

The *mens rea* for conspiracy to commit genocide is similar to that of the crime of genocide. The persons involved must all share the *dolus*

---

[121] International Criminal Tribunal for Rwanda, *Prosecutor v. Ferdinand Nahimana et al.*, Judgment, 3 December 2003, ICTR-99-52, para. 1045 ('Nahimana Judgment') (https://www.legal-tools.org/doc/45b8b6/).

[122] International Criminal Tribunal for Rwanda, *Prosecutor v. Ferdinand Nahimana et al.*, Appeals Chamber Judgment, 28 November 2007, ICTR-99-52 (https://www.legal-tools.org/doc/04e4f9/).

[123] International Criminal Tribunal for Rwanda, *Prosecutor v. Jean Kambanda*, Judgment, ICTR-97-23-S, 4 September 1998 (https://www.legal-tools.org/doc/49a299/).

[124] Musema Judgment, para. 74, see *supra* note 120.

[125] *Ibid.*

[126] Nahimana Judgment, para. 1048, see *supra* note 121.

specialis of genocide, namely, the intent to destroy in whole or in part a national, ethnical, racial or religious group as such. The *mens rea* includes a general awareness of the existence of the conspiracy by its members, they participate knowingly in it along with others, and the knowledge of their role in furtherance of their common purpose, which is to commit genocide. The agreement between members of a conspiracy may be explicit or implicit, as expressed in the Nahimana case.

The ICTR is, nonetheless, divided as to whether upon the occurrence of a genocide the accused should be convicted of both genocide and conspiracy or just one of the two, on the basis of the same facts. The Musema trial judgment took a negative approach to this question,[127] while in the Niyitegeka case the Trial Chamber was inclined to punish the accused for both.[128]

16.6. Consipracy in International Criminal Court

Unlike the ICTY and ICTR Statutes, the ICC Statute leaves out conspiracy as an inchoate crime, even with regards to the crime of genocide. The term 'conspiracy' is not expressly referred to in any way in the ICC Statute. The question remains whether Article 25(3)(a) and (d) of the ICC Statute could be regarded as a substitute for conspiracy as a mode of liability. This section looks at the link between conspiracy and the collective responsibility doctrines under the ICC.

During the debates over whether to include conspiracy in the ICC Statute, two proposals were raised: "one where the conspirators simply plan but do not carry out the conspiracy themselves and another where it is the conspirators that perpetrate the overt act".[129] Initial drafts of the Statute "oscillated between the traditional common-law approach to conspiracy",[130] which considers conspiracy as an inchoate crime, and the modern approach, which considers conspiracy as a mode of participation in a crime. The compromise solution was Article 25(3)(a) and (d) of the

---

[127] Banktekas and Nash, 2007, p. 35, see *supra* note 30.

[128] International Criminal Tribunal for Rwanda, *Prosecutor v. Eliezer Niyitegeka*, Judgment, 16 May 2003, ICTR-96-14 (https://www.legal-tools.org/doc/325567).

[129] Banktekas and Nash, 2007, p. 36, see *supra* note 30.

[130] Albin Eser, "Mental Elements – Mistake of Fact and Mistake of Law", in Antonio Cassese, Paola Gaeta and John R.W.D Jones (eds.), *The Rome Statute of the International Criminal Court: A Commentary*, vol. 1, Oxford University Press, Oxford, 2002, p. 913.

ICC Statute on individual criminal responsibility, which has similar characteristics to the Nuremberg concept of 'common plan'.[131] It seems that some sort of conspiracy-based liability has been recognised by the ICC Statute, by replacing conspiracy with the idea of "a crime by a group of persons".[132] This implicitly permits joint and common liability as a mode of liability where it provides that a person shall be criminally responsible for an international crime if he "[c]ommits such a crime, whether as an individual, jointly with another or through another person, regardless of whether that other person is criminally responsible".[133] The Statute thus seems to be able to encompass conspiracy with a different level of *mens rea* since it appears to refer to co-perpetration.

The ICC Pre-Trial Chamber in the Lubanga case took the position that with regards to co-perpetration under Article 25, the ICC Statute requires action "with intent" as a required mental element within the Statute.[134] The prosecutor charged Lubanga "with criminal responsibility under Article 25(3)(a) of the Statute, which covers the notions of direct perpetration (commission of a crime jointly with another person) and indirect perpetration (commission through another person, regardless of whether that other person is criminally responsible)".[135] The prosecution also referred to Article 25(3)(d) of the ICC Statute in addition to Article 25(3)(a) arguing that it "believed that 'common purpose' in terms of Article 25(3)(d) could properly be considered as a third applicable mode of criminal liability".[136] The Pre-Trial Chamber, with reference to Article 25(3)(a), held that although the common plan must include an element of criminality, it does not need to be specifically directed at the commission of a crime. It is sufficient:

> i) that the co-perpetrators have agreed (a) to start the implementation of the common plan to achieve a non-

---

[131] United Nations, Rome Statute of the International Criminal Court, Art. 25, p. 18, 1 July 2000 (https://www.legal-tools.org/doc/7b9af9/).

[132] *Ibid.*, Art. 25(3)(d).

[133] *Ibid.*, Art. 25(3)(a).

[134] International Criminal Court, *Prosecutor v. Thomas Lubanga Dyilo*, Pre-Trial Chamber, Décision sur la confirmation des charges, ICCC-01/04-01/06, 29 January 2007, para. 410 ('Lubanga case') (https://www.legal-tools.org/doc/b7ac4f/).

[135] *Ibid.*

[136] William A. Schabas, *An Introduction to the International Criminal Court*, 3rd ed., Cambridge University Press, Cambridge, 2007, p. 212.

criminal goal, and (b) to only commit the crime if certain conditions are met; or

ii) that the co-perpetrators (a) are aware of the risk that implementing the common plan (which is specifically directed at the achievement of a non-criminal goal) will result in the commission of the crime, and (b) accept such and outcome.[137]

It seems that the Pre-Trial Chamber tried to explain that individual responsibility arises when an offence is committed by a "plurality of persons".[138] This is based on the assumption that "any person making a contribution can be held vicariously responsible for the contributions of all the others and as a result can be considered as a principal to the whole crime".[139] The contribution has to be one that, in some way, helps the group's activities towards the commission or attempted commission of a crime. Article 25(3)(d) of the ICC Statute provides for the criminal responsibility of a person who "in any other way contributes to the commission or attempted commission of such a crime by a group of persons acting with a common purpose".[140] It is borrowed almost verbatim from Article 2(3) of the International Convention for the Suppression of Terrorist Bombing, establishing complicity in collective criminality. It appears to provide derivative liability for accomplices.

The Lubanga Pre-Trial Chamber concluded that Article 25(3)(d) "is closely akin to the concept of joint criminal enterprise or the common purpose doctrine adopted by the jurisprudence of the ICTY".[141] It also referred to this as being a "residual form of accessory liability which makes it possible to criminalise those contributions to a crime who cannot be characterised as ordering, soliciting, inducing, aiding, abetting or assisting within the meaning of article 25(3)(b) or article 25(3)(c) of the Statute, by reason of the state of mind in which the contributions were made".[142] According to the accomplice liability theory, defendants are

---

[137] Lubanga case, para. 344, see *supra* note 134.
[138] *Ibid.*, para. 327.
[139] *Ibid.*, para. 326.
[140] Kevin Jon Heller, "Lubanga Decision Roundtable: More on Co-Perpetration", *Opinio Juris*, 16 March 2012, available at: http://opiniojuris.org/2012/03/16/lubanga-decision-roundtable-more-on-co-perpetration/.
[141] Lubanga case, para. 335, see *supra* note 134.
[142] *Ibid.*, para. 337.

prosecuted especially because they are considered participants in a criminal action with a unity of purpose or a commonality of intention. The essential element of the contribution is thus intention. In fact, Article 25(3)(d) provides that the contribution be intentional and that it either 1) be made with the aim of furthering the criminal activity of group or 2) be made in the knowledge of the intention of the group to commit the crime.[143] The emphasis of Article 25(3) of the ICC Statute on 'contribution' rather than on conspiracy is thus in a certain sense a development in international criminal law.

16.7. Conclusion

Initially the conspiracy doctrine was established in international law to aid the prosecution of the main war criminals of the Second World War. Conspiracy may also be considered to be a response to the inability of the causation doctrine to deal with situations in which multiple individuals were jointly responsible for the commission of a crime. Because of its unique features of combating collective criminality it was considered an ideal tool for prosecutors. Post-Second World War jurisprudence rejected conspiracy as an inchoate crime, but as a mode of liability it was included in international proceedings under different names.

Conspiracy-based liability no longer exists in the relevant international instruments dealing with international crimes and humanitarian law at least not called as such. However, the ICTY developed the joint criminal enterprise theory based on Nuremberg and subsequent jurisprudence, despite the criticisms made against it. Joint criminal enterprise has become a collective liability theory in modern international criminal law. The mode of liability of planning also bears certain resemblances to conspiracy. It is obvious that conspiracy has not been recognised as an inchoate crime in the ICC, but the constitutive elements of conspiracy-based liability forms the basis for Article 25(3)(a) and (d) of the ICC Statute, which establishes both principal liability according to the collective mode of liability, namely "jointly with another" under Article 25(3)(a) and accessorial liability under Articles 25(3)(d) in collective criminality.

---

[143] Andrea Sereni, "Individual Criminal Responsibility", in Flavia Lattanzi and William A. Schabas (eds.), *Essays on the Rome Statute of the International Criminal* Court, vol. 2, Editrice il Sirente Piccola Società Cooperativa a r.l., p. 111.

Therefore the doctrines of joint criminal enterprise, co-perpetration and common purpose/plan liability might be considered as new forms and extensions of the conspiracy doctrine. The common denominator that links the three doctrines is the existence of a criminal agreement or a common plan among the participants, as an externalised evidence, that the parties intend for the crime to be committed.

The Evolution of Command Responsibility in International Criminal Law

Chantal Meloni[*]

17.1. Overview of the Principle of Individual Criminal Responsibility for Mass Crimes

The effective attribution of criminal responsibility to individuals involved in the commission of heinous mass crimes – such as those that come under the jurisdiction of the International Criminal Court ('ICC') – is one of the challenges that the international community has had to contend with for the last 60 years, if not longer.[1] Notwithstanding the enormous difficulties relating to the "macro-criminal" dimension of international crimes, it soon became clear that only the timely attribution of individual criminal responsibility to those implicated at various levels in the commission of the crimes could be an effective reaction to the massive violations of human rights.[2] It was also immediately evident that the need to bring single individuals to justice was particularly important with regard to those oc-

---

[*] **Chantal Meloni** is a criminal lawyer and academic at the University of Milan, Italy, where she teaches international criminal law. She holds a Ph.D. in comparative criminal law from the University of Pavia, Italy. In 2006–7, she worked at the International Criminal Court as Legal Assistant to the judges of Pre-Trial Chamber. In 2010 she was awarded an Alexander von Humboldt fellowship for a research project on "The protection of the right to life in asymmetrical conflicts" at Humboldt University of Berlin, Germany. In the context of this project she was in Gaza in 2010 with the Palestinian Centre for Human Rights. Her research interests focus on international criminal law, especially on accountability mechanisms, individual responsibility for international crimes and on the protection of victims of international crimes. She is the author of *Command Responsibility in International Criminal Law* (TMC Asser, The Hague, 2010) and co-editor of *Is There a Court for Gaza? A Test Bench for International Justice* (TMC Asser/Springer, The Hague, 2012).

[1] Hans Kelsen, "Collective and Individual Responsibility in International Law with Particular Regard to the Punishment of War Criminals", in *California Law Review*, 1943, vol. 31, no. 5, p. 533–71.

[2] Gerhard Werle, "Menschenrechtsschutz durch Völkerstrafrecht", in *Zeitschrift für die gesamte Strafrechtswissenschaft*, 1997, vol. 109, no. 4, p. 822.

---

cupying positions of authority, the "most senior leaders", in other words those with powers of command.

Nowadays it is generally recognised that one of the most effective means for ensuring the promotion of and compliance with international (humanitarian) law lies in bringing to justice those military and political leaders who are normally behind the commission of genocides, crimes against humanity and war crimes.[3] However, the practical difficulties in bringing to trial high-ranking individuals are never easy to overcome at the political and judicial level.

After the First World War, with the signing of the Treaty of Versailles, there was already a first attempt to incriminate a head of state, namely the German Kaiser Wilhelm II of Hohenzollern, as the commander-in-chief for the crimes committed during the war by the German army.[4] It was proposed to put him on trial before a (international) tribunal managed by the Allied powers, while the trials of the other individuals accused of war crimes were assigned to the jurisdiction of the German Supreme Court sitting in Leipzig. As it is well known, the indictment of the Kaiser remained on paper only because the Netherlands refused to extradite him, and out of hundreds of suspects contained in the original list of other individuals only 12 were finally put on trial in Leipzig.[5] However, the importance of what happened after the First World War should not be underestimated. The report presented by the Commission on the Responsibility of the Authors of the War[6] and the Treaty of Versailles marked a significant step towards the recognition of the criminal responsibility of

---

[3] International Criminal Tribunal for the former Yugoslavia ('ICTY'), *Prosecutor v. Milan Martić*, Trial Chamber, Decision, IT-95-11, 8 March 1996, para. 21.

[4] Treaty of Peace between the Allied and Associated Powers and Germany, 28 June 1919, Arts. 227–28 ('Versailles Treaty') (https://www.legal-tools.org/doc/a64206/). On the Treaty of Versailles after the First World War and the attempt to establish an international tribunal see, among others, Heiko Albrecht, *Geschichte der völkerrechtlichen Strafgerichtsbarkeit im 20. Jahrhundert*, Nomos, Baden-Baden, 1999, pp. 28 ff.

[5] On the Leipzig trials, see the interesting testimony by Claud Mullins, *The Leipzig Trials: An Account of the War Criminals' Trial and A Study of German Mentality*, H.F. & G. Witherby, London, 1921.

[6] The Commission on the Responsibility of the Authors of the War and the Enforcement of Penalties was established with the task of investigating the responsibilities for the international law violations and crimes committed during the war. Report Presented to the Preliminary Peace Conference, Versailles, 29 March 1919, Pamphlet No. 32, Division of International Law, Carnegie Endowment for International Peace, Washington, DC, reprinted in *American Journal of International Law*, 1920, vol. 14, no. 1, pp. 95–154.

individuals under international law. It was also the first recognition of the irrelevance of immunities and official positions for the commission of international crimes. It is notable that some of the first references to the command responsibility doctrine can already be found at that time. Within the commission of inquiry some delegations proposed to proceed against the "highly placed enemies" on the basis of the so-called doctrine of abstention pursuant to which who "ordered, or with knowledge thereof and with power to intervene, abstained from preventing or taking measures to prevent, putting an end to or repressing, violations of the laws or customs of war" was liable for punishment.[7]

Surely the times were not ready for all this. The American and the Japanese representatives strongly opposed this proposal. If, on the one hand they admitted the possibility of trying highly placed enemies for their commissive behaviour (as a matter of principle), on the other they rejected the possibility of holding someone responsible for war crimes on the mere basis of his omission.[8] In fact it is only after the Second World War, with the jurisprudence of the Nuremberg and Tokyo Tribunals, that the principle of individual criminal responsibility received explicit recognition in international law. International criminal law began to develop on these premises and it is within this framework that the command responsibility doctrine was finally established as a fundamental tool to attribute crimes to the upper echelons.

---

[7] Weston D. Burnett, "Command Responsibility and A Case Study of the Criminal Responsibility of Israeli Military Commanders for the Pogrom at Shatila and Sabra", in *Military Law Review*, 1985, vol. 107, p. 82. See also W.H. Parks, "Command Responsibility for War Crimes", in *Military Law Review*, 1973, vol. 62, pp. 12 ff.

[8] In particular, the American representatives' reservation was very clearly articulated: "It is one thing to punish a person who committed, or possessing the authority, ordered others to commit an act constituting a crime; it is quite another thing to punish a person who failed to prevent, to put an end to, or to repress violations of the laws or customs of war. In one case the individual acts or orders to act, and in doing so committs a positive offence [sic]. In the other he is to be punished for the acts of others without proof being given that he knew of the commission of the acts in question or that, knowing them, he could have prevented the commission". Memorandum of Reservations Presented by the Representatives of the United States to the Report of the Commission on Responsibilities, Annex II, 4 April 1919, reprinted in *American Journal of International Law*, 1920, vol. 14, p. 127.

17.2. Development of the Command Responsibility Doctrine in International Criminal Law

As Mirjan Damaška once wrote, command responsibility is an "umbrella term".[9] In a broad sense, it indicates a series of ways in which an individual in a position of command can be considered responsible for the actions of his subordinates. In its broadest meaning, the term indicates the responsibility of the commander who fails to fulfil his duties as a military superior. This kind of responsibility is not limited to the failure of the commander to exercise control properly over his troops; it can also be triggered, for example, by exposing the troops under his command to excessive and unnecessary risks.[10] Pursuant to such a responsibility – which can be of various natures, although it is normally disciplinary – the military commander may be punished irrespective of the behaviour of his soldiers, and in particular irrespective of their commission of any crime.[11]

In the strictest sense, command responsibility indicates instead the criminal responsibility of the superior for the crimes committed by his subordinates.[12] The expression was used originally in the military context and eventually also expanded to the non-military field. In this regard, the expression *superior responsibility* is more appropriate, as it also includes individuals in non-military positions.[13]

17.2.1. The Military Origins

The origins of command responsibility are indeed very remote. Scholars have identified the first example of command responsibility in some provisions contained in what is considered to be the most ancient military treatise of the world, *The Art of War* by Sun Tzu, a Chinese military man-

---

[9] Mirjan Damaška, "The Shadow Side of Command Responsibility", in *American Journal of Comparative Law*, 2001, vol. 49, no. 3, p. 455.

[10] *Ibid.*

[11] Kai Ambos, "Superior Responsibility", in Antonio Cassese, Paola Gaeta, John R.W.D. Jones (eds.), *The Rome Statute of the International Criminal Court: A Commentary*, Oxford University Press, Oxford, 2002, pp. 823 ff.

[12] For a more thorough analysis of the notion and its different meanings, see Chantal Meloni, *Command Responsibility in International Law*, TMC Asser, The Hague, 2010, pp. 1 ff.

[13] Although less precise than superior responsibility, command responsibility, which is commonly used in scholarly works and jurisprudence, is also used throughout this chapter to indicate the responsibility both of military commanders and civilian superiors for the crimes committed by their subordinates.

ual dating back to 500 BCE. It provided that: "When troops flee, are insubordinate, distressed, collapse in disorder or are routed, it is the fault of the general"; "If the words of command are not clear and distinct, if orders are not thoroughly understood, the general is to blame".[14] The responsibility of the commander for his troops has been recognised ever since in the various military manuals at the domestic level, which does not mean that the commander was criminally responsible for the subordinates' illegal actions. It was rather a form of disciplinary military responsibility for breaching his duties as a military superior.[15]

The modern doctrine of command responsibility under international law has its roots in the principle of "responsible command".[16] This is a fundamental principle of humanitarian law that requires that an army be commanded by a person responsible for his subordinates.[17] The Fourth Hague Convention on the Laws and Customs of War on Land of 1907 already recognised that those who have the power of command in an army are responsible for the violations committed by the forces under their command.[18]

Both command responsibility and the principle of responsible command aim to promote and ensure compliance with the rules of international (humanitarian) law,[19] but the two notions are distinct.[20] In con-

---

[14] Parks, 1973, pp. 3–4, see *supra* note 7.

[15] Leslie Green, "Command Responsibility in International Humanitarian Law", in *Transnational Law and Contemporary Problems*, 1995, vol. 5, no. 2, p. 319.

[16] On the origins of the doctrine, see A. B. Ching, "Evolution of the command responsibility doctrine in light of the Čelebići decision of the International Criminal Tribunal for the Former Yugoslavia, in *North Carolina Journal of International Law & Commercial Regulation*, 1999, pp. 167 ff. See also Guénaël Mettraux, *The Law of Command Responsibility*, Oxford University Press, Oxford, 2009.

[17] See William J. Fenrick, "Article 28 – Responsibility of Commanders and other Superiors", in Otto Triffterer (ed.), *Commentary on the Rome Statute of the International Criminal Court*, 1st ed., Nomos, Baden-Baden, 1999, p. 516.

[18] Convention (IV) respecting the Laws and Customs of War on Land and its annex: Regulations concerning the Laws and Customs of War on Land. The Hague, 18 October 1907 (https://www.legal-tools.org/doc/fa0161/). See Parks, 1973, pp. 11 ff., *supra* note 7; and Ilias Bantekas, "The Contemporary Law of Superior Responsibility", in *American Journal of International Law*, 1999, vol. 93, no. 3, p. 573.

[19] ICTY, *Prosecutor v. Enver Hadžihasanović et al.*, Trial Chamber, Decision on Joint Challenge to Jurisdiction, IT-01-47, 12 November 2002, para. 66 (https://www.legal-tools.org/doc/c46fc0/).

[20] See, on the point, Boris Burghardt, *Die Vorgesetztenverantwortlichkeit im völkerrechtlichen Straftatsystem*, Berliner Wissenschafts-Verlag, Berlin, 2008, pp. 80 ff.

trast to command responsibility, the principle of responsible command does not entail *per se* any form of punishment or liability. The two perspectives are complementary: the one regards the duties that are entailed in the idea of command, whereas the other concerns the liability that arises from the breach of those duties. Therefore one can say that "command responsibility is the most effective method by which International Criminal Law can enforce responsible command".[21]

17.2.2. The Tokyo Trial and the Yamashita Trial

Eventually this doctrine developed further and it is no longer confined to the military field. Nowadays there is no doubt that command responsibility extends also to non-military superiors with respect to the commission of international crimes.[22] There were already some precedents in the application of this doctrine to non-military superiors in the jurisprudence after the Second World War. In particular, the International Military Tribunal for the Far East ('IMTFE') in the Tokyo Trial[23] resorted to a form of liability for omission in order to convict the members of the Japanese government for the war crimes committed by the Japanese army. These convictions were strongly criticised as forms of collective or strict liability, where the personal guilt of the defendants was not properly established.[24] At the same time, however, there is a positive legacy of the Tokyo Trial, in that the IMTFE established the existence of duties of preven-

---

[21] ICTY, *Prosecutor v. Enver Hadžihasanović et al.*, Appeals Chamber, Decision on Interlocutory Appeal Challenging Jurisdiction in Relation to Command Responsibility, IT-01-47, 16 July 2003, para. 16 ('Hadžihasanović case') (https://www.legal-tools.org/doc/608f09/). See also Mettraux, 2009, p. 55, *supra* note 16.

[22] For more details, see Meloni, 2010, pp. 159 ff., *supra* note 12.

[23] The Tribunal was formed on 19 January 1946 by means of a Special Proclamation to Establish an International Military Tribunal for the Far East by the Supreme Allied Commander in the Far East, General Douglas MacArthur (https://www.legal-tools.org/doc/242328/). See Neil Boister and Robert Cryer, *The Tokyo International Military Tribunal: A Reappraisal*, Oxford University Press, Oxford, 2008.

[24] Notable in this regard is the vibrant dissenting opinion of the Dutch Judge, B.V.A. Röling. International Military Tribunal for the Far East ('IMTFE'), *United States of America et al. v. Araki Sadao et al.*, Opinion of Mr. Justice Roling Member for the Netherlands, 12 November 1948 (https://www.legal-tools.org/doc/fb16ff/), reprinted in B.V.A. Röling and C.F. Ruter (eds.), *The Tokyo Judgment: The International Military Tribunal for the Far East (I.M.T.F.E.), 29 April 1946–12 November 1948*, Amsterdam University Press, Amsterdam, 1977, pp. 1043–1148.

tion (of international crimes) analogous to those of military commanders, directed specifically at political leaders and members of the government.[25]

Much criticism has also been brought against the conviction of General Yamashita Tomoyuki who was sentenced to death by an American military court set up by order of General Douglas MacArthur in 1945 for massacres committed against Filipino civilians by his troops.[26] Yamashita, it was said, was not convicted for having done something but for "having been something". In fact the charges against him were not that he had ordered the crimes committed but that he failed to prevent them from being committed.[27] The biggest problem in this case was that Yamashita's knowledge of the crimes was not properly proved.[28] His conviction was based upon a sort of imputed knowledge. The judges affirmed that he "must have known of the crimes". In fact, the reasoning of the judges was that the crimes were so extensive and widespread that they must either have been wilfully permitted by the accused or secretly ordered.[29] Nevertheless, the importance of the case lies in the fact that for the first time a military commander had been made accountable for the crimes committed by his subordinates on the sole basis of his failure to discharge his military duty to control his troops.

The US Supreme Court, before which the case was heard immediately after Yamashita's conviction by the military court,[30] established the principle that an army commander has a legal duty to take appropriate

---

[25] In this sense, see W.J. Fenrick, "Some international Law Problems Related to the Prosecutions before the International Criminal Tribunal for the Former Yugoslavia", in *Duke Journal of Comparative & International Law*, 1995, vol. 6, pp. 103–25.

[26] Among the many works that refer to the Yamashita case as one of the most important precedents on command responsibility, see Burnett, 1985, pp. 71 ff., *supra* note 7; Green, 1995, pp. 329 ff., *supra* note 15; Matthew Lippman, "The Uncertain Contours of Command Responsibility", in *Tulsa Journal of Comparative and International Law*, 2001, vol. 9, pp. 4 ff; Andrew D. Mitchell, "Failure to Halt, Prevent or Punish: The Doctrine of Command Responsibility for War Crimes", in *Sydney Law Review*, 2000, vol. 22, no. 3, pp. 384–85; Parks, 1973, pp. 22 ff., see *supra* note 7; M.L. Smidt, "Yamashita, Medina, and Beyond: Command Responsibility in Contemporary Military Operations", in *Military Law Review*, 2000, vol. 164, pp. 155 ff.

[27] The phrase is from Harry E. Clarke, Yamashita's defence counsel, commenting on the charge. See Richard L. Lael, *The Yamashita Precedent: War Crimes and Command Responsibility*, Scholarly Resources, Wilmington, DE, 1982.

[28] For more analysis on this point, see Meloni, 2010, pp. 46 ff., *supra* note 12.

[29] Parks, 1973, pp. 30 ff., see *supra* note 7. See also Burnett, 1985, pp. 92–94, *supra* note 7.

[30] US Supreme Court, *In Re Yamashita*, 327 US 1, 16 1946, 4 February 1946, in *Law Reports*, vol. IV, pp. 38 ff.

measures to prevent the violations of the laws of war and that he may be charged with personal responsibility for his failure to take such measures when violations result. Referring to the provisions of Articles 1 and 43 of the Regulations annexed to the Fourth Hague Convention of 1907, of Article 19 of the Tenth Hague Convention and of Article 26 of the Geneva Red Cross Convention of 1929, the judges affirmed the principle that a commander has the duty to control his subordinates' conduct, ensuring that they respect the law, and that violation of this duty is a violation of the laws of war. This principle, as we shall see, was to become the foundation for numerous other trials in the period after the Second World War and beyond.

17.2.3. The Nuremberg Trial and the Subsequent Proceedings

At Nuremberg there was no need to resort to command responsibility as a mode of liability based on omission, given the abundance of evidence of the criminal orders (and thus of commission) set by the Nazis. In fact, neither the Charter of the International Military Tribunal ('IMT Charter')[31] nor Control Council Law No. 10[32] contained any specific provisions on command responsibility. Nevertheless, some provisions referring to the "duty of superiors" were included in the regulations adopted by the single states with the aim of providing homogeneous rules for holding the trials (against German war criminals) before their domestic courts.[33]

Among the so-called subsequent proceedings held by US Military Tribunals in Nuremberg from 1947 to 1949 we can find some relevant cases involving the command responsibility of German war criminals, all of them regarding military commanders. In particular, the *High Command* trial[34] and the *Hostage* trial[35] were of the utmost importance for the devel-

---

[31] Charter of the International Military Tribunal annexed to the London Agreement of 8 August 1945 for the Prosecution and Punishment of Major War Criminals of the European Axis ('IMT Charter') (http://www.legal-tools.org/doc/64ffdd/).

[32] Control Council Law No. 10, Punishment of Persons Guilty of War Crimes, Crimes Against Peace and Against Humanity, 20 December 1945 (http://www.legal-tools.org/doc/ffda62/). Control Council Law No. 10 was adopted by the major Allied powers – the United States, Britain, France and Soviet Union – after Germany's unconditional surrender.

[33] For further discussion, see Smidt, 2000, pp. 155 ff., *supra* note 26.

[34] Military Government for Germany, USA, United States of America v. Wilhelm von Leeb et al., Judgment, 28 October 1948, in Trials of War Criminals Before the Nuernberg Military Tribunals Under Control Council Law No. 10, October 1946–April 1949, vol. 11, US

opment of the doctrine because they rejected the standard of strict liability which had been adopted in *Yamashita*. More precisely, the American judges set the following standard for command responsibility to be established:

> There must be a personal dereliction. That can occur only where the act is directly traceable to him [the commander] or where his failure to properly supervise his subordinates constitutes criminal negligence on his part. In the latter case, it must be a personal neglect amounting to a wanton, immoral disregard of the action of his subordinates amounting to acquiescence. Any other interpretation of international law would go far beyond the basic principles of criminal law as known to civilized nations.[36]

In short, these cases are important because they clarified that there must be "personal neglect", "knowledge" or "acquiescence" by the commander in order to hold him criminally responsible for the crimes of the subordinates that he failed to properly supervise. As we can note, it was not yet a full elaboration of the command responsibility doctrine as intended today, but the premises were already set after the Second World War for this responsibility to be further developed.

17.2.4. The Cold War and the First Codification of Command Responsibility

The period of the Cold War – the years between the end of the Second World War in 1945 and the fall of the Berlin Wall in 1989 – was not particularly significant with regard to the development of international criminal law in general and for the doctrine of command responsibility in particular. Command responsibility had an echo in some important national proceedings. It was raised in the Adolf Eichmann trial, which was held

---

Government Printing Office, Washington, DC, 1949, pp. 512 ff. ('High Command case') (https://www.legal-tools.org/doc/c340d7/). See also Parks, 1973, pp. 38–58, *supra* note 7; and Burnett, 1985, pp. 99–109, *supra* note 7.

35   Military Government for Germany, USA, United States v. Wilhelm List et al., Judgment, 19 February 1948, in Trials of War Criminals Before the Nuernberg Military Tribunals Under Control Council Law No. 10, October 1946–April 1949, vol. 11, US Government Printing Office, Washington, DC, 1949, pp. 1230–1319 (https://www.legal-tools.org/doc/b05aa4/). See Parks, 1973, pp. 58–64, *supra* note 7; and Burnett, 1985, pp. 109–14, *supra* note 7.

36   High Command case, pp. 543–44, see *supra* note 34, quoted in Parks, 1973, p. 43, see *supra* note 7.

before the Israeli District Court in Jerusalem and before the Israeli Supreme Court in 1961–1962.[37] Eichmann, in his position as the chief of the Gestapo in Berlin, was the person responsible for the implementation of the "final solution", the Nazi plan for the extermination of the Jews. He was therefore convicted – and sentenced to death – on the basis of his commissive responsibilities rather than on command responsibility *stricto sensu*.[38]

Superior responsibility did play a role during and following the Vietnam War, with US soldiers tried on the basis of the American Uniform Code of Military Justice.[39] In particular, the command responsibility doctrine was debated and applied in the case against Lieutenant William Calley and his superior Captain Ernest Medina, and against Major General Samuel Koster for the massacre at Mỹ Lai.[40]

At the international level, however, the situation of political tension brought the projects regarding the codification of international criminal law and the creation of a permanent international criminal law court substantially to a standstill, even though these projects had been warmly supported at the international level in the wake of the indignation and emotion over the horrors of the Second World War. In any case, neither the first Draft Codes of the Offences against the Peace and Security of Mankind nor the Draft Statute for an International Criminal Law, drawn up by the International Law Commission ('ILC') between 1950 and 1954, contained any provisions dedicated to command responsibility.[41] Neither the

---

[37] The Judgments in English of the Israeli District Court and Supreme Court against Eichmann are published in *International Law Reports*, vol. 36, 1968, pp. 18–276 and 277–344.

[38] On the Eichmann trial, see the testimony by Hanna Arendt, *Eichmann in Jerusalem: A Report on the Banality of Evil*, Viking Press, New York, 1963. For the relevant criminal law aspects of the trial, see Kai Ambos, *Der allgemeine Teil des Völkerstrafrechts: Ansätze einer Dogmatisierung*, Dunkler & Humblot, Berlin, 2001, pp. 182–90.

[39] See Burnett, 1985, p. 121, *supra* note 7. In any case these were mostly disciplinary procedures.

[40] See William V. O'Brien, "The Law of War, Command Responsibility and Vietnam", in *Georgetown Law Journal*, 1972, vol. 60, pp. 605 ff. See also Parks, 1973, pp. 1 ff., *supra* note 7; William G. Eckardt, "Command Criminal Responsibility: A Plea for A Workable Standard", in *Military Law Review*, 1982, vol. 97, pp. 1 ff.; Burnett, 1985, p. 71 ff., *supra* note 7; Green, 1995, pp. 319 ff., *supra* note 15; Lippman, 2001, pp. 1 ff., *supra* note 26.

[41] For a complete documentary reconstruction of the works of the International Law Commission, see M. Cherif Bassiouni (ed.), *The Statute of the International Criminal Court: A Documentary History*, Transnational Publishers, Ardsley, NY, 1998. For a comparison of

Genocide Convention of 1948 nor the four Geneva Conventions of 1949 contained any provision on command responsibility. This absence is indicative of the fact that at the time no agreement had been reached at the international level over the notion and formulation of the doctrine.

As a matter of fact the first international instrument that codified command responsibility was the 1977 Additional Protocol I to the 1949 Geneva Conventions. Notably, the provision of Article 86 already contained *in nuce* all the elements of the current doctrine:

> The fact that a breach of the Conventions or of this Protocol was committed by a subordinate does not absolve his superiors from penal or disciplinary responsibility [...] if they knew or had information which should have enabled them to conclude that he was committing [...] such a breach and if they did not take all feasible measures within their power to prevent or repress the breach.[42]

As outlined by the commentary drawn up by the International Committee of the Red Cross, three elements have to be fulfilled for a superior to be responsible for an omission in relation to a crime committed by a subordinate:

a) The superior concerned must be the superior of that subordinate;

b) The superior knew, or had information, which should have enabled him to conclude that a breach was being committed or was going to be committed;

c) The superior did not take the measures within his power to prevent it.[43]

---

the criminal law principles contained in the three Draft Codes presented by the ILC, in 1954, 1991 and 1996, see Ambos, 2001, pp. 443 ff., *supra* note 38.

[42] Protocol (I) Additional to the Geneva Conventions of 12 August 1949, and relating to the Protection of Victims of International Armed Conflicts, 8 June 1977, Art. 86 ('Additional Protocol I') (http://www.legal-tools.org/doc/d9328a/). The two Additional Protocols of 1977 to the four Geneva Conventions of 1949 were the outcome of the Diplomatic Conference on the Reaffirmation and Development of International Humanitarian Law Applicable in Armed Conflicts, established by the Swiss Government, depositary of the Geneva Conventions, in 1974. Additional Protocol I, which came into force on 7 December 1978, is applicable to the international armed conflicts involving the state parties that have ratified the Geneva Conventions and the Protocol (*id.*, Art. 1).

[43] Jean de Preux, "Article 87: Duty of Commanders", in Yves Sandoz, Christophe Swinarski and Bruno Zimmermann (eds.), *Commentary on the Additional Protocols of 8 June 1977*

These elements have to be analysed in connection with the provision of the following Article 87,[44] containing the duties of the military commander at the basis of command responsibility.[45] From the combined provision of the two norms it emerges that the commander who knows about the crimes being committed has the duty to take such steps in order to prevent and, where necessary and appropriate, to punish the breaches of the Convention or of the Protocol committed by his subordinates. Each commander therefore has in the first place the *duty to prevent* the breaches and stop their occurrence (to suppress). If the breaches have already been committed, in the second place he has the *duty to punish* them (which can simply mean that the superior has the *duty to report* the crimes to the competent authorities). As a measure aimed at preventing or suppressing breaches of humanitarian law, Article 87(2) of Additional Protocol I also provides for the duty of the commander to ensure that members of the armed forces under his command are aware of their obligations under the Conventions of Geneva and their Protocols. This duty of commanders is to be "commensurate with their level of responsibility".[46]

What emerges clearly from these provisions is the functional idea inspiring the whole doctrine of command responsibility, namely that military commanders are in the best position to guarantee respect for humanitarian law, for example by imposing respect for discipline on their soldiers, limiting the unjustified use of force, and ensuring an accurate flow of information and an adequate system of reporting. The concept of responsible command finds its full expression in the work of the drafters of the Protocol, who recognised the primary role of military commanders in pursuing the effective implementation of Geneva law.[47] Commanders are thus regarded as an instrumental tool – at the national and international levels – in the prevention of the commission of war crimes. To this aim,

---

to the Geneva Conventions of 12 August 1949, International Committee of the Red Cross, Geneva, 1987, pp. 1012–13.

[44] Additional Protocol I, Art. 87(1), see *supra* note 42, reads as follows: "The High Contracting Parties and the Parties to the conflict shall require military commanders, with respect to members of the armed forces under their command and other persons under their control, to prevent and, when necessary, to suppress and to report to competent authorities breaches of the Conventions and of this Protocol".

[45] See, in this regard, de Preux, 1987, pp. 1019 ff., *supra* note 43.

[46] Ibid.

[47] *Ibid.*, p. 1022.

they are charged with precise duties of control and prevention, and corresponding responsibilities, in case these duties are breached.

In light of the above, Additional Protocol I marks a fundamental step towards the definitive recognition of the doctrine of command responsibility in international law. Although it is debated whether Additional Protocol I as a whole has achieved customary law status,[48] this seems certain with regard to Article 86(2), which, as the jurisprudence of the International Criminal Tribunal for the former Yugoslavia ('ICTY') also confirmed,[49] may be recognised as a rule of international customary law.[50] Notwithstanding the fact that Article 86 generically refers to "superiors", because the following Article 87 expressly addresses only military commanders – by specifying their duties – these provisions are mainly interpreted as applicable only to the military field.[51]

17.2.5. The *Ad hoc* Tribunals and the Implementation of Superior Responsibility outside the Military Field

With the fall of the Berlin Wall, the changed political climate at the beginning of the 1990s allowed a renaissance of the international criminal justice projects that had long been at a standstill. In particular, the United Nations Security Council created two subsidiary organs on the basis of Chapter VII of the UN Charter as measures "to maintain and restore international peace and international security".[52] With resolution 827 of 25 May 1993 the Security Council set up the ICTY for the purpose of judging those responsible for crimes committed during the 1990s Balkans con-

---

[48] On the customary law status of the Additional Protocols, see Christopher Greenwood, *Essays on War in International Law*, Cameron May, London, 2006, pp. 179 ff.

[49] ICTY, *Prosecutor v. Zejnil Delalić et al.*, Appeals Chamber, Judgment, IT-96-21, 20 February 2001, paras. 195, 231 ('Čelebići case') (https://www.legal-tools.org/doc/051554/); ICTY, *Prosecutor v. Dario Kordić and Mario Čerkez*, Trial Chamber, Judgment, IT-95-14/2, 26 February 2001, para. 441 ('Kordić case') (http://www.legal-tools.org/doc/d4fedd/).

[50] Burghardt, 2008, pp. 42, 77 and 85 ff., see *supra* note 20.

[51] See Fenrick, 1995, pp. 119–20, *supra* note 25. Contra Michael Bothe, Karl J. Partsch and Waldemar Solf (eds.), *New Rules for Victims of Armed Conflicts*, Martinus Nijhoff, The Hague 1982, pp. 523 ff. In the latter's view Additional Protocol I, Art. 86, which is directed at military commanders, could be extended to civilian superiors if these exercise a power over their subordinates that is substantially analogous to that of a military commander.

[52] Charter of the United Nations and Statute of the International Court of Justice, 26 June 1945, Art. 39 ff.

---

flict.[53] With resolution 955 of 8 November 1994 the International Criminal Tribunal for Rwanda ('ICTR') was established, with jurisdiction over the genocide perpetrated in Rwanda in 1994.[54]

According to the Statutes of the *ad hoc* Tribunals[55] a person is to be considered individually responsible for a crime under the jurisdiction of the Tribunals – war crimes, crimes against humanity or genocide – if he or she planned, instigated, ordered or committed it, or if s/he otherwise aided and abetted in its planning, preparation or execution.[56] Moreover, both Article 7(3) of the ICTY Statute and Article 6(3) of the ICTR Statute expressly provided for superior responsibility in the following terms:

> The fact that any of the acts referred to in Articles 2 to 5 of the present Statute was committed by a subordinate does not relieve his superior of criminal responsibility if he knew or had reason to know that the subordinate was about to commit such acts or had done so and the superior failed to take the necessary and reasonable measures to prevent such acts or to punish the perpetrators thereof.

As we can note, these provisions referred generally to the "superior". As a matter of fact, at the outset of their activity the *ad hoc* Tribunals had to decide whether command responsibility could apply also to civilians or not. After some uncertainty, the judges acknowledged the applicability of the doctrine to civilian superiors; indeed, there is now abundant jurisprudence on this point, produced by both Tribunals.[57] In particular it

---

[53]   UN Security Council Resolution 827, Adopted 22 February 1993, UN doc. S/RES/827 (1993) (https://www.legal-tools.org/doc/dc079b/) to which the Statute of the International Tribunal for the former Yugoslavia is annexed ('ICTY Statute') (https://www.legal-tools.org/doc/b4f63b/).

[54]   UN Security Council resolution 955, Adopted 8 November 1994, UN doc. S/RES/955 (1994) (https://www.legal-tools.org/doc/f5ef47/) to which the Statute of the International Tribunal for Rwanda is annexed ('ICTR Statute') (http://www.legal-tools.org/doc/8732d6/).

[55]   The Statutes of the ICTY and ICTR are substantially identical, as the latter is built on the model of the former, apart from some differences in the definition of the crimes which were dictated by the necessity to take into account the different situations under the jurisdiction of the Tribunals. Therefore, generally, what holds true for the ICTY Statute is implied as being valid also for the provisions of the ICTR Statute.

[56]   ICTY Statute, Art. 7(1), see *supra* note 53 and ICTR Statute, Art. 6(1), see *supra* note 54.

[57]   More thoroughly on the jurisprudence of the *ad hoc* Tribunals, see Meloni, 2010, pp. 77 ff; in particular on the differences regarding the non-military superiors, pp. 128–31, see *supra* note 12.

---

is worth mentioning the so-called *Čelebići* case before the ICTY,[58] which set for the first time the distinctive elements of command responsibility and more broadly of "superior responsibility" as a mode of criminal liability in international criminal law. However, the jurisprudence of the *ad hoc* Tribunals also reveals the difficulties in applying this mode of liability outside the military field.

The first problem relates to the verification of the subordination relationship outside the military sphere. In the jurisprudence of the *ad hoc* Tribunals it is in fact not clear whether the requirements and the degree of responsibility with regard to a civilian superior are the same as those of a military commander.[59] Several civilian superiors, in particular politicians, were charged before the ICTR and convicted for superior responsibility. In this regard, the judges found that the evidence necessary for establishing a civilian superior's possession of effective authority (and control) can be different from the military commander standard.[60] Paradigmatic of these differences and of the difficulties in proving the civilian superior's effective authority and control was the *Kordić* case before the ICTY.[61] Kordić was a politician at the regional level in central Bosnia, who had been charged under Article 7(3) of the ICTY Statute for the crimes committed against the Bosnian Muslims in the region of the Lašva Valley in 1992 and 1993. According to the judges, he enjoyed "tremendous influence and power" in his territory. However, the Tribunal did not accept the prosecutor's argument that the defendant possessed *de facto* control over the armed forces that committed the crimes and therefore acquitted Kordić of his responsibility under Article 7(3).[62] Fundamental was the distinction introduced by the judges between "effective control" and "substantial influence" that the defendant exercised over the perpetrators of the crimes: unlike the power of control, substantial influence (even if "tremendous", as in this case) is not sufficient for ascribing responsibility for omission to the superior, in particular if the person concerned is a civilian.[63]

---

[58]   ICTY, *Prosecutor v. Zejnil Delalić et al.*, Trial Chamber, Judgment, IT-96-21, 16 November 1998, para. 356 ('Čelebići case') (http://www.legal-tools.org/doc/d09556/).

[59]   Čelebići case, Appeals Chamber, Judgment, para. 240, see *supra* note 49.

[60]   ICTR, *Prosecutor v. Ignace Bagilishema*, Appeals Chamber, Judgment, ICTR-95-1A, 3 July 2002, paras. 50 ff. (https://www.legal-tools.org/doc/ebc505/).

[61]   Maria Nybondas, "Civilian Superior Responsibility in the *Kordić* Case", in *Netherlands International Law Review*, 2003, vol. 50, no. 1, pp. 59 ff.

[62]   Kordić case, Trial Chamber, Judgment, see *supra* note 49.

[63]   *Ibid.*, para. 413. Several other ICTY and ICTR judgments consistently followed this view.

Moreover, another problem emerges with regard to the content of the measures required by the jurisprudence for a civilian superior to prevent or punish the crimes of the subordinates.[64] As for the duty to prevent, while in the military field a superior can directly intervene in the course of action of his subordinates, normally disposing of disciplinary powers and having the power to issue binding orders, the same generally does not hold true for civilian superiors. Therefore the preventative measures in the civilian context will be integrated mostly by means of protesting or reporting (to the competent authorities). In fact, the differences between military commanders and civilian superiors become even greater with regard to the duty to punish. Indeed, there is normally no power to sanction outside the military sphere. This was affirmed in the *Aleksovski* case:

> Although the power to sanction is the indissociable corollary of the power to issue orders within the military hierarchy, it does not apply to the civilian authorities. It cannot be expected that a civilian authority will have a disciplinary power over subordinates equivalent to that of the military authorities in an analogous command position. To require a civilian authority to have sanctioning powers similar to those of a member of the military would so limit the scope of the doctrine of superior authority that it would hardly be applicable to civilian authorities.[65]

Thus it is clear that the measures that a civilian superior can adopt are normally weaker than the corresponding ones in the military field. The risk that, notwithstanding the measures adopted, the crime is nevertheless committed and the culprits not punished is higher in this respect, even if the superior took all possible (available) measures.

Finally, with regard to the mental element of superior responsibility, it is interesting to note that, even if the *ad hoc* Tribunals' Statutes did not introduce any difference in the standard required for military and civilian superior, some judgments did in fact introduce such a difference, taking the ICC Statute provision as a point of reference in this regard.[66]

---

[64] See for instance ICTY, *Prosecutor v. Zlatko Aleksovski*, Trial Chamber, Judgment, IT-95-14/1, 25 June 1999, para. 78 (http://www.legal-tools.org/doc/52d982/).

[65] *Ibid.*

[66] ICTR, *Prosecutor v. Clement Kayishema and Obed Ruzindana*, Trial Chamber Judgment, ICTR-95-1, 21 May 1999, paras. 227-228 (https://www.legal-tools.org/doc/0811c9/).

17.3. Article 28 of the ICC Statute

The applicability of command responsibility to non-military superiors has been made explicit for the first time in a written provision by the drafters of the Rome Statute of the International Criminal Court ('ICC Statute') of 1998.[67] Article 28 dictates similar but not identical rules for military commanders – or others effectively acting as military commanders – and for civilian superiors. Article 28 of the ICC Statute is divided into two parts. While subsection (a) concerns military commanders, or those who effectively act as such, subsection (b) deals with the responsibility of civilian superiors, identified in a residual way *vis-à-vis* the provision subsection (a). Such a provision is the result of a proposal put forward by the United States delegation, which considered it correct to provide for a separate rule to take into account the difference between the powers of control of a military commander and those of a civilian superior. The latter indeed was thought to enjoy a lesser degree of control and influence over his or her subordinates.[68]

Both forms of superior responsibility are built on common elements, but there are also significant differences, most prominently with regard to the knowledge requirement, that is, the mental element. Whereas in order to be held responsible it is required that the military commander either knew, or owing to the circumstances at the time should have known, that his/her subordinated forces were committing or about to commit such crimes, for the civilian superior it is required that he/she either knew or consciously disregarded information which clearly indicated that the subordinates were committing or about to commit such crimes. Moreover, in the case of a non-military superior, the crimes must concern activities that were within the effective responsibility and control of the superior.

By means of Article 28, the drafters of the ICC Statute have provided for a far more complete and detailed provision on superior responsibility than all previous instruments, requiring a very precise establishment of its constitutive elements. However, and despite the *ad hoc* Tribunals' extensive jurisprudence, many issues regarding the doctrine of command responsibility are still open for interpretation. In fact, the application of this form of liability is not yet clear, which might explain to a certain ex-

---

[67] Rome Statute of the International Criminal Court, 17 July 1998, entered into force 1 July 2002, United Nations Treaty Series, vol. 2187, No. 38544 ('ICC Statute').

[68] See in this regard, Ambos, 2002, pp. 848 ff., see *supra* note 11.

tent why the ICC only resorted once to this mode of liability during the first 12 years of its activity.

This is not the place for a detailed analysis of each individual element of command responsibility under Article 28 of the ICC Statute.[69] Yet some brief observations can be made on the *Bemba* case, the first proceedings dealing with command responsibility before the ICC, which is going to be very significant for the evolution of this doctrine in international criminal law.

17.3.1. The First Case Before the ICC: *Bemba*

The first (and so far only) interpretation of Article 28 of the ICC Statute was in the context of the decision confirming the charges against Jean-Pierre Bemba Gombo of 15 June 2009.[70] Originally, the prosecutor had charged the suspect with criminal responsibility as a co-perpetrator under Article 25(3)(a) of the ICC Statute.[71] However, following a request by the Chamber in this sense,[72] the prosecutor submitted an amended charging document where the responsibility of Bemba for the alleged crimes was framed "in the alternative" as command or superior responsibility under Article 28(a) or (b) of the ICC Statute. As a result of the three-day hearing,[73] Bemba was set to stand trial for murder, rape and pillaging, as war crimes and crimes against humanity, due to his alleged responsibility as a commander. The trial started in November 2010 and the Trial Chamber

---

[69] For an extensive analysis on the point, see Meloni, 2010, p. 139, *supra* note 12.

[70] ICC, Situation in Central African Republic, *Prosecutor v. Jean-Pierre Bemba Gombo*, Pre-Trial Chamber II, Decision Pursuant to Article 61(7)(a) and (b) of the Rome Statute on the Charges of the Prosecutor Against Jean-Pierre Bemba Gombo, ICC-01/05-01/08, 15 June 2009 ('Bemba case') (https://www.legal-tools.org/doc/07965c/).

[71] On the concept of co-perpetration before the ICC, and more generally on Article 25(3)(a) of the ICC Statute, see Gerhard Werle, "Individual Criminal Responsibility in Article 25 ICC Statute", in *Journal of International Criminal Justice*, 2007, vol. 5, no. 4, p. 953. See also Stefano Manacorda and Chantal Meloni, "Indirect Perpetration versus Joint Criminal Enterprise: Concurring Approaches in the Practice of International Criminal Law?", in *Journal of International Criminal Justice*, 2011, vol. 9, no. 1, p. 159.

[72] "It appears to the Chamber that the legal characterisation of the facts of the case [might] amount to a different mode of liability under Article 28 of the Statute". See ICC, Situation in Central African Republic, *Prosecutor v. Jean-Pierre Bemba Gombo*, Pre-Trial Chamber III, Decision Adjourning the Hearing pursuant to Article 61(7)(c)(ii) of the Rome Statute, ICC-01/05-01/08-388, 3 March 2009, para. 46 ('Bemba case') (http://www.legal-tools.org/doc/81d7a9/).

[73] The confirmation of charges hearing against Bemba was held from 12 to 15 January 2009.

Judgment was not yet out at the time of writing. In the decision confirming the charges, Bemba was described as the *de jure* commander-in-chief of the political-military Mouvement de Libération du Congo ('MLC') in Central African Republic. To reach this conclusion, the Pre-Trial Chamber judges considered that Bemba had the following powers: to issue orders that were complied with; to appoint, promote, dismiss, arrest, detain and release other MLC commanders; and, to ultimately prevent and repress the commission of crimes. Bemba was believed to have retained his effective authority and control over MLC troops throughout the military intervention in Central African Republic, having the material ability to contact his commander of operations and to make the decision to withdraw his troops from the field. The judges found sufficient evidence to believe – for the purpose of the confirmation of charges – that the accused knew that MLC troops were committing or were about to commit crimes,[74] and that he failed to take all necessary and reasonable measures within his power to prevent or repress the commission of crimes because "he disregarded the scale and gravity of crimes and opted for measures that were not reasonably proportionate to those crimes".[75]

Article 28 of the ICC Statute has been interpreted by the ICC Pre-Trial Chamber as a form of criminal responsibility based on a legal obligation to act, which is composed of very specific elements, in part different for the military and for the non-military superior. Having determined that Bemba fell under the notion of military or military-like commander, the Chamber limited itself to the analysis of the first paragraph of Article 28.[76] The judges held that the category of military-like commanders may encompass superiors who have control over irregular forces, such as rebel groups, paramilitary units, including armed resistance movements and militias structured in military hierarchy and having a chain of command. Thus, the expressions *effective command and control* and *effective authority and control* are to be interpreted as alternatives having the same meaning but referring to distinct groups of commanders. While command is applicable to *de jure* military commanders (*stricto sensu*), authority refers to military-like or *de facto* commanders. In this sense, the words *command* and *authority* were interpreted not to imply a different standard of

---

[74] Bemba case, Decision, para. 489, see *supra* note 70. This paragraph lists the factors from which the Chamber derived Bemba's actual knowledge about the occurrence of the crimes.

[75] *Ibid.*, para. 495.

[76] *Ibid.*, para. 407.

control. The ICC judges referred to ICTY case law to define the concept of "effective control", which lies at the very heart of the doctrine of command responsibility. Following the *ad hoc* Tribunals' definition, the notion of effective control was described as the material ability to prevent and punish the commission of the offences. The Chamber also listed several factors that can indicate the existence of the superior-subordinate relationship.[77]

With regard to *successor command responsibility* – one of the controversial issues before the ICTY[78] – the ICC Chamber correctly established that there must be temporal coincidence between the superior's detention of effective control and the criminal conduct of his subordinates. The judges acknowledged the existence of a minority opinion in the case law of the *ad hoc* Tribunals. According to this minority opinion, it is sufficient that the superior had effective control over the perpetrators at the time at which the superior is said to have failed to exercise his or her powers to prevent or to punish[79] (regardless of whether he or she had the control at the time of the commission of the crime, as the majority of the ICTY jurisprudence instead requested), but they rejected it on the basis of the language used by Article 28 of the ICC Statute. Indeed the provision at issue requires that the subordinates' crimes be committed "as a result of his or her failure to exercise control properly", thus requiring that the suspect had effective control "*at least* when the crimes were about to be committed".[80]

As for the element of causality – another strongly debated issue before the *ad hoc* Tribunals[81] – the Chamber interpreted Article 28 as requiring a causal link between the superior's dereliction of duty and the under-

---

[77] *Ibid.*, paras. 415–17.

[78] ICTY, *Prosecutor v. Enver Hadžihasanović et al.*, Trial Chamber, Judgment, IT-01-47, 15 March 2006, para. 199 (http://www.legal-tools.org/doc/8f515a/), and Hadžihasanović case, Appeals Chamber, Decision on Interlocutory Appeal, para. 55, see *supra* note 21.

[79] Reference is made to ICTY, *Prosecutor v. Naser Orić*, Appeals Chamber, Judgment, Declaration of Judge Shahabudden and Partially Dissenting Opinion and Declaration of Judge Liu, IT-03-68, 3 July 2008, paras. 65–85 ('Orić case') (http://www.legal-tools.org/doc/e053a4/).

[80] Bemba case, Decision, para. 419, see *supra* note 70.

[81] Čelebići case, Trial Chamber, Judgment, paras. 398–99, see *supra* note 58. See, in doctrine, Otto Triffterer, "Causality, a Separate Element of the Doctrine of Superior Responsibility as Expressed in Article 28 Rome Statute?", in *Leiden Journal of International Law*, 2002, vol. 15, no. 1, pp. 179 ff.

---

lying crimes.[82] The element of causality as such was only referred to the commander's duty to prevent the commission of future crimes. The judges nonetheless found that the failure to punish, being an inherent part of the prevention of future crimes, would be in a way causal *vis-à-vis* the subordinates' crimes, in the sense that the failure to take measures to punish the culprits is likely to increase the risk of commission of further crimes in the future.[83] Having considered that "the effect of an omission cannot be empirically determined with certainty" and thus that "there is no direct causal link that needs to be established between the superior's omission and the crime committed by subordinates",[84] the Chamber found that because a *conditio sine qua non* causality requirement (or "but for test") would be impossible to fulfil with regard to a conduct of omission, it is only necessary to prove that the commander's omission increased the risk of the commission of the crimes charged in order for the causality nexus to be fulfilled.[85] However, the reasoning of the judges lacks some clarity as to the assessment of causality, which is surely hypothetical in cases of omission, but is actually hypothetical also with regard to commission. The hypothetical nature of the assessment shall thus not be the decisive argument to adopt the "risk increasement test" and reject the "but for test".[86]

Regarding the mental element of command responsibility, the Chamber clarified that strict liability is not admitted under Article 28 of the ICC Statute. Two standards of culpability are possible for military commanders: actual knowledge ("knew") or negligence ("should have known"). Actual knowledge cannot be presumed but can be obtained by

---

82 Bemba case, Decision, para. 423, see *supra* note 70.

83 Reference is made in the *Bemba* decision to similar findings contained in the ICTY jurisprudence, and in particular in the *Hadžihasanović* case. However, as we have already clarified on other occasions, this finding is tricky because tends to confuse the responsibility of the superior for the subordinates' crimes that *have already been committed* with the *risk of commission of future crimes*. It shall be recalled that no responsibility arises pursuant to the command responsibility doctrine for the mere lack of control of the superior over the subordinates, as long as the crimes are not actually committed. See Meloni, 2010, pp. 165–67, *supra* note 12.

84 Bemba case, Decision, para. 425, see *supra* note 70.

85 *Ibid.*, para. 426: "To find a military commander or a person acting as a military commander responsible for the crimes committed by his forces, the Prosecutor must demonstrate that his failure to exercise his duty to prevent crimes inreased the risk that the forces would commit these crimes".

86 On the point see Kai Ambos, "Critical Issues in the *Bemba* Confirmation Decision", in *Leiden Journal of International Law*, 2009, vol. 22, no. pp. 721–22.

way of direct or circumstantial evidence, as decided by the *ad hoc* Tribunals. The Chamber, however, oddly noted that the knowledge required respectively under Article 30(3) and Article 28(a) of the ICC Statute would be different, since the former is applicable to the forms of participation as provided for in Article 25 of the Statute, while, under Article 28, the commander *does not participate* in the commission of the crime.[87] This finding is unconvincing. Regardless of whether command responsibility is considered to be a form of participation in the subordinates' crimes or a distinct mode of liability, it is unclear why the cognitive element, knowledge, under Article 30 of the ICC Statute should be different from knowledge under Article 28 of the ICC Statute.[88] More convincingly, in our view, it can be argued that it is not the knowledge but rather its object (also called *mental object*) that is different under the two provisions: in the case of Article 30 the mental object is the crime as such, whereas under Article 28 what the superior needs to know is the criminal conduct of his or her subordinates.[89]

In order to define the "should have known standard" the ICC judges referred again to ICTY jurisprudence.[90] The Chamber acknowledged that a difference exists between the "had reason to know" and the "should have known" standard, but unfortunately did not consider it necessary to elaborate any further. In any case, what emerges clearly is that under the should have known standard the superior is found to be *negligent* in failing to acquire knowledge of his subordinates' illegal conduct. In the view of the Court, the should have known standard requires "an active duty on the part of the superior to take the necessary measures to secure knowledge of the conduct of his troops and to inquire, regardless of the availability of information at the time of the commission of the crimes".[91] However, among the *indicia* relevant for the determination of this negligence standard, the Chamber mentioned the same circumstances which were also mentioned with reference to the proof of actual knowledge

---

[87] Bemba case, Decision, para. 479, see *supra* note 70.

[88] Ambos, 2009, pp. 719–21, see *supra* note 86.

[89] Meloni, 2010, p. 188, see *supra* note 12.

[90] In particular reference is made to the *Blaškić* case, see Bemba case, Decision, para. 432, *supra* note 70.

[91] *Ibid.*, para. 433.

through circumstantial evidence.[92] This practice of referring to the same factors to establish the actual knowledge or the *negligent* ignorance – typical of the ICTY jurisprudence[93] – risks confusing distinct *mens rea* standards, obliterating any differences that may exist.

Another debatable finding of the *Bemba* decision is the Chamber's consideration of the superior's failure to punish the subordinates' past crimes as an indication of the risk of commission of future crimes, thus warranting the conclusion that the superior knew or at least should have known about the crimes.[94]

With regard to the conduct element of command responsibility, the Chamber considered that the three duties arise for the superior at different stages:

a) before the commission of the crime(s) the superior has the duty to prevent them;

b) during their commission he has the duty to repress the crimes; and

c) after the crimes have been committed the superior has the duty to punish or submit the matter to the competent authorities.

The Chamber further observed that the duty to repress encompasses the duty to stop ongoing crimes and the duty to punish the forces after the commission of crimes.[95] In turn, the duty to punish is an alternative to the duty to refer the matter to the competent authorities. In the first case the superior has the power himself to take the necessary measures, while in the second case the superior does not have the ability to do so and can, therefore, only submit the matter to the competent authorities.

The powers also vary according to the position of the superior in the chain of command. From this schema the judges drew the conclusion that "a failure to fulfil one of these duties is itself a separate crime under Article 28(a) of the Statute" and therefore that a military commander can be

---

[92] Such circumstances are: 1) that the superior had general information to put him on notice of crimes committed or of the possibility of occurrence of unlawful acts; and 2) that such available information was sufficient to justify further inquiry. *Ibid.*, para. 434.

[93] Meloni, 2010, p. 114, see *supra* note 12.

[94] Reference was made to the Special Court for Sierra Leone, specifically SCSL, *Prosecutor v. Augustine Gbao et al.*, Trial Chamber, Judgment, 04-15-T, 2 March 2009, para. 311 (https://www.legal-tools.org/doc/7f05b7/).

[95] ICC, Bemba Decision, para. 439, see *supra* note 70.

held responsible for one or more breaches of duty under Article 28(a) in relation to the same underlying offence.[96] The Chamber correctly held that a failure to prevent the crimes could not be cured by fulfilling the subsequent duty to repress or submit the matter to the competent authorities. However, to impose cumulative convictions on the same superior for the same subordinates' crimes on the basis of the different duties is not convincing from two points of view: first, because such a notion is inconsistent with an understanding of command responsibility as a mode of liability (as it actually is under Article 28 and as the Court confirmed in this decision); and second, because it does not appear to be respectful of the criminal law principles on concurrence of offences.[97]

With regard to the possible overlapping of Articles 25(3) and 28 of the ICC Statute, the first jurisprudence of the ICC excluded the possibility of trying an individual for the same facts under both modes of liability. In the *Bemba* case, the amended charging document submitted to the Pre-Trial Chamber by the prosecutor charged the suspect "primarily" with criminal responsibility as a co-perpetrator under Article 25(3)(a) or "in the alternative" under command or superior responsibility as provided by Article 28(a) or (b) of the Statute.[98]

At the outset of their reasoning, the judges found that in order to establish the responsibility of the suspect, Article 28 represents an alternative to Article 25, thus excluding the possibility of cumulative charges (and of cumulative convictions) under different modes of liability for the same crimes. This position is to be welcomed, especially in light of the rights of the defence, which were often neglected by the *ad hoc* Tribunals' practice of cumulative and imprecise charges at the indictment stage. Moreover, the ICC Pre-Trial judges clearly affirmed that an assessment of the responsibility under Article 28 should only be secondary to an assessment of responsibility under Article 25. If there were evidence of any active involvement of the suspect in the commission of the crimes, the charges against him should be brought under the latter provision rather

---

[96] *Ibid.*, para. 436.

[97] On the *concursus delictorum*, see Ambos, 2009, p. 723, *supra* note 86.

[98] See ICC, Situation in Central African Republic, *Prosecutor v. Jean-Pierre Bemba Gombo*, Office of the Prosecutor, Annex 3 to "Prosecution's Submission of Amended Document Containing the Charges, Amended List of Evidence and Amended In-Depth Analysis Chart of Incriminatory Evidence", ICC-01/05-01/08-395-Anx3, 30 March 2009 (http://www.legal-tools.org/doc/d7f72e/).

than under Article 28.[99] In sum, it emerges that command responsibility and responsibility for commission regarding the same defendant for the same facts are never cumulative. This conclusion, along with the circumstance that the elements of command responsibility under Article 28 are not easy to prove at trial, already indicates that, similarly to what happened before the ICTY with the joint criminal enterprise doctrine,[100] command responsibility before the ICC will be often absorbed into a form of liability covered by Article 25(3) of the ICC Statute.

17.4. Difficulties in the Interpretation of the Command Responsibility Doctrine

From the standpoint of criminal law command responsibility presents a number of problems. Many of the elements composing this form or responsibility are still not clear and subject to debate. To a certain extent, this is not surprising since this doctrine is a genuine creation of international criminal law and traces its origin through the process and evolution of international law.[101] By contrast, the forms of commission and modes of participation for international crimes normally originate from related concepts known in domestic criminal law. The difficulties relating to the interpretation of command responsibility are also due to the fact that we are dealing with a form of liability that incriminates not an action but a failure to act. Responsibility for omission has always been a very critical issue in penal law: one thing is to punish a person for what she did, quite another is to punish him/her for something that she did not do. In particular, not every system acknowledges the principle that omitting to prevent a criminal event under certain conditions can amount to its commission.[102]

---

[99] *Ibid.*, para. 342: "An examination of Mr. Jean-Pierre Bemba's alleged criminal responsibility under Article 28 of the Statute, would only be required if there was a determination that there were no substantial grounds to believe that the suspect was, as the Prosecutor submitted, criminally responsible as a co-perpetrator within the meaning of Article 25(3)(a) of the Statute for the crimes set out in the Amended DCC (document containing the charges)". See also *id.*, paras. 402–3.

[100] Indeed charges brought under the joint criminal enterprise doctrine are generally easier to proof. See Mark J. Osiel, "Modes of Participation in Mass Atrocity", in *Cornell International Law Journal*, vol. 38, no. 3, 2005, p. 793.

[101] In this sense, Ambos, 2001, p. 667, see *supra* note 38; Gerhard Werle and Florian Jessberger, *Principles of International Criminal Law*, 3rd ed., Oxford University Press, Oxford, p. 221.

[102] See the thorough study by Michael Duttwiler, "Liability for Omission in International Criminal Law", in *International Criminal Law Review*, 2006, vol. 6, no. 1, pp. 1–61.

17.4.1. Responsibility for Omission and the Duty to Act of the Superior

The problem clearly emerged during the negotiations for the adoption of the ICC Statute. The Draft Statute for the International Criminal Court presented at the Diplomatic Conference contained a provision dedicated expressly to general responsibility for omission.[103] The old Article 28 of the Draft provided that the criminal conduct relevant for the purposes of responsibility for crimes within the competence of the Court could assume the features both of an action and of an omission, thus establishing the equivalence between the superior's failure to prevent a crime that he had the legal duty to prevent and its commission.[104] However, this provision was eliminated during the negotiations, as it was impossible to reach an agreement between the various delegations, in particular on account of the firm opposition of the French delegation whose legal system does not envisage any equivalence clause between criminal action and omission.[105] Thus the only rule left in the ICC Statute regarding liability for failure to act is the actual Article 28, specifically dictated for command responsibility.

Nevertheless, what clearly emerges out of those legal systems that do recognise liability for omission as a general principle of their criminal legal order is that liability by omission can only be triggered by the failure to prevent something when under a duty to do so.[106] It is necessary to stress this last point, which is unfortunately often forgotten in the legal analysis and sometimes also in the judgments. Indeed, no one can be held responsible for something that he or she did not do, unless he or she was under a legal obligation to do it. Of course, this holds true also with regard to command responsibility. Therefore the first thing in assessing whether an individual can be held responsible under this doctrine is to verify whether he or she was under a legal duty to do what he or she omit-

---

[103] On the previous projects on the issue, among which was the Siracusa Draft of 1996, see Kerstin Weltz, Die Unterlassungshaftung im Völkerstrafrecht: eine rechtsvergleichende Untersuchung des französischen, US-amerikanischen und deutschen Rechts, Iuscrim, Freiburg im Breisgau, 2004, pp. 230–32.

[104] Draft Statute for the International Criminal Court, Art. 28, 14 April 1998, UN doc. A/CONF.183/2/Add.1.

[105] Weltz, 2004, pp. 237 ff., see *supra* note 103.

[106] For more analysis on the issue of responsibility for omission in international criminal law, see Meloni, 2010, pp. 220 ff., *supra* note 12.

ted to do, specifically to prevent or punish the crimes of the subordinates. This requirement is contained in the so-called first element of command responsibility, namely in the superior–subordination relationship. By properly verifying whether the person at issue was in fact a "superior" or a "commander" the assessment that the person was under a legal obliga tion to prevent the illegal behaviour of his subordinate can be satisfied.[107]

It is undisputed in jurisprudence that "the absence of a formal appointment is not fatal to a finding of command responsibility".[108] On the other hand, the possession of *de jure* authority is not sufficient. As affirmed by the ICTY judges in *Čelebići*: "The formal status of superior or the formal designation as a commander should not be considered to be a necessary prerequisite for command responsibility to attach".[109] The problem that the judges had to face was clear: in the context of the former Yugoslavia, where the formal structures of command had broken down and new, improvised informal structures had been established, the possession of *de facto* powers which were not formally recognised was the rule and not the exception. Thus, the jurisprudence of the ICTY defined the concept of superior in a factual rather than formal manner, making this element dependent on the defendant's *de facto* ability to act. In a nutshell, it was said that it is a superior the one who has effective control over the subordinates. At the same time, the effective control was defined as the ability to prevent or punish the crimes committed by the perpetrators. This created a loop that often resulted in the impossibility of establishing the existence of the superior–subordinate relationship and ultimately of command responsibility.[110]

On the contrary, the duty to act – deriving from the position of superior – and the proof of the material ability to act – of the superior – should be kept separate. Only when it is established that the person was a superior (*de jure* or *de facto*) can his or her ability to act be verified.[111] Thus it is important to emphasise that the superior has to have had both

---

[107] For a full elaboration on the point, see *ibid*, pp. 154 ff.

[108] Čelebići case, Appeals Chamber, Judgment, para. 197, see *supra* note 49.

[109] *Ibid.*, paras. 206, 251.

[110] For a more thorough analysis of the ICTY jurisprudence, Burghardt, 2008, pp. 112–80, see *supra* note 20.

[111] For a more in-depth analysis, see Meloni, 2010, pp. 94 ff., *supra* note 12. With regard to this jurisprudence, which considers the doctrine of command responsibility applicable also in the absence of a pre-existing duty to act, see also Mettraux, 2009, pp. 48–51, *supra* note 16.

the legal duty and the material possibility to prevent or punish the crimes. It is correct to say that a superior is a person who – in a hierarchical relationship (which can be *de jure* or *de facto*) – has a position of command or authority that gives him or her effective control over the behaviour of other individuals. It is not the other way around. In fact a person who has the material ability to prevent or punish, and therefore effective control over the behaviour of other individuals, is not necessarily a superior (for the sake of the applicability of the command responsibility doctrine), because he can lack the duty to act.

Effective control is a necessary requirement that must be proved both for *de jure* and for *de facto* commanders.[112] Thus, for example, if several chains of command exist, responsibility is to be attributed to the superior who actually exercised the powers to command and control over those who committed the crimes. This is now clear in the ICC Statute that uses the expressions "effective command and control" and "effective authority and control", where authority is to be intended as the normative analogy of command outside the military field.[113]

If command is the typical military power to issue compelling orders, authority can be defined as the power of a superior to issue instructions to subordinates in pursuance of a certain activity. In this context it means something not as strong and as absolute as command. Therefore, while command is the typical and connoting element of the superior–subordinate relationship pertaining to formally appointed military commanders, authority refers to those who lack the official qualification of military commanders but effectively act as such.

Article 28(b) of the ICC Statute introduces a further requirement in order for command responsibility to attach to civilian superiors, namely that the underlying crimes committed by the subordinate "concerned activities that were within the effective responsibility and control of the superior". Hence outside the military field, besides the existence of a relationship of subordination between the superior and the perpetrator of the crime, a further connection is required between the superior and the specific activity in whose sphere the crime was committed. This requirement seems appropriate in a context where the sources of the legal duty to act

---

[112] See, among many, Orić case, Appeals Chamber, Judgment, para. 91, *supra* note 78.

[113] Specifically on the application of command responsibility to civilian superiors, Nybondas, 2003, pp. 59 ff., see *supra* note 61.

of the superior are less easily identifiable and have a weaker foundation than in the military sector.

17.5. Possible Evolution of Command Responsibility: A Proposal to Clarify and Distinguish the Basic Forms of Command Responsibility

As already noted, the application of command responsibility at the judicial level is still subject to critical questions. Here we can just mention some of the major issues: Does the superior need to share the same intent of the subordinates with regard to the crimes committed by them and, if not, what exactly is he requested to know? Is a causal nexus required between the failure to act of the superior and the crime of the subordinate? Can a superior be responsible for the crimes committed by the subordinates before he assumed control over them? In our view, most of these issues can be reduced to one, namely to the uncertain nature of command responsibility. In other words, the question is whether we are dealing with a form of responsibility pursuant to which the superior is held accountable for the subordinates' crimes (thus war crimes, crimes against humanity, genocide) as he had participated in their commission or, instead, whether the superior is responsible of a specific offence of dereliction of duty.

For instance, to request a causal nexus between the omission of the superior and the subordinates' crime would be consistent with an understanding of command responsibility as a mode of liability pursuant to which the superior is made answerable for the crimes of his subordinates and convicted for those very crimes. In contrast, causality would not be required if the superior is held responsible only for his failure to act, namely for his dereliction of duty.

The issue is surely a most complicated one and it is beyond the scope of this chapter to analyse it in great detail. But the matter is very concrete and not at all abstract, as the jurisprudence of the ICTY shows. Indicative of the practical consequences of framing command responsibility as a separate crime, rather than as mode of liability, was the *Orić* case before the ICTY. In that case the judges convicted the accused – a former commander of the Srebrenica armed forces – to two years' imprisonment, instead of the 18 years requested by the prosecutor, for failure to prevent the crimes committed by his soldiers. In the words of the prosecutor, the "two years' sentence is manifestly inadequate because it is based on a fundamental error in the nature of Orić's criminal responsibility by classifying Orić's crimes as a failure to discharge his duty as a superior, rather than as a mode of liability".[114] To be clear: Orić was not convicted for war crimes, as his subordinates were, but for a separate crime of dereliction of duty.[115]

The ICC of course does not have to follow the jurisprudence of the *ad hoc* Tribunals. As we have seen, the language adopted by the drafters of the ICC Statute is much more precise and the incipit of Article 28 makes it clear that command responsibility is considered a mode of liability and not as introducing a separate offence of the superior. Nevertheless, difficulties also arise from the formulation of Article 28 of the ICC Statute if interpreted as a mode of liability pursuant to which the superior is made responsible for the crimes of his subordinates. Hypothetically, would it be correct to make a commander accountable for the war crimes committed by his soldiers that he inculpably ignored and could not prevent but that he subsequently failed to punish? Even if we do not want to define the nature of command responsibility we cannot escape from the following question: For what exactly is the superior to be punished? In the end, it is a matter of rules of attribution of criminal responsibility. Indeed no one can be blamed for a crime unless that crime is attributable to him or her. Now the question is: How and when can a crime be attributed to someone?

General principles of criminal law provide for the criteria at both the subjective and objective levels in order to hold someone responsible for a crime. There is not always agreement among scholars on such criteria, but at least the minimal standards are clear. At the subjective level it is clear that (international) criminal law refuses strict liability. This means that a mental element is required (in the form of intent or in exceptional cases of negligence) and that the possibility of holding someone responsible for crimes committed by others shall be excluded unless there is a personal culpability that makes that individual accountable for that specific crime. Now, for the purpose of command responsibility the possible *mens rea* of the superior can be quite different.

---

[114] See ICTY, *Prosecutor v. Naser Orić*, Prosecution Appeal Brief, IT-03-68, 16 October 2006, paras. 152 ff.

[115] This issue is thoroughly dealt with in Chantal Meloni, "Command Responsibility. Mode of Liability for the Crimes of Subordinates or Separate Offence of the Superior?", in *Journal of International Criminal Justice*, 2007, vol. 5, no. 3, pp. 619–37.

The ICC Statute provides that a military or military-like commander be responsible if he or she "knew or owing the circumstances at the time should have known that the forces were committing or about to commit such crimes". With regard to civilian superiors the ICC Statute sets a higher standard requiring that the superior "knew or consciously disregarded information which clearly indicated that the subordinates were committing or about to commit such crimes". This means that we can have a whole spectrum of different cases, ranging from the gravest scenario, where the superior knew and intentionally omitted to take action, to the commander who ignored the crimes but should have known about them and therefore negligently failed to act, passing from the reckless superior who disregarded the information.

Similarly, with regard to the conduct of the superior, this can take very different contours. The superior in fact is required to take all of the necessary and reasonable measures within his or her power in order to prevent/repress or submit the matter to the competent authorities. The aim of the measures will change, of course, depending on the moment when the superior acquires knowledge of the risk of commission of crimes by his subordinates. A superior who knew and had the possibility to prevent a crime will not be considered to have discharged his or her duty by punishing *ex post* the culprits. The conduct must in any case be culpable. This means that if the superior did not have the material possibility to prevent or repress the commission of the crimes he cannot be responsible. The ICC Statute explicitly endorses this requirement in that it speaks of "necessary and reasonable measures within his or her power".

Therefore, in determining what the superior is to be held accountable for, it is erroneous to consider command responsibility to be a unitary form of responsibility. Indeed, around a central corpus of common elements there are at least four different basic forms of responsibility which can be differentiated on the basis of their objective and subjective elements. We have cases of 1) intentional failure to prevent or 2) of negligent failure to prevent, and cases of 3) intentional failure to punish or of 4) negligent failure to punish (where *punish* is intended to include both repress and submit the matter to the authorities).

Although the ICC Statute regulates all of the previously mentioned forms of command responsibility in a single provision, each of these forms should be considered separately because of their very different features and requirements. As a matter of fact, the forms of command responsibility regarding the superior's intentional or negligent failure to punish present a completely different structure to those concerning the failure to prevent. In these cases the superior's failure to take the necessary and reasonable measures clearly follows the commission of the crime by the subordinates. Thus no causal nexus can exist between the failure to act of the superior and the underlying crime. At most a link can be established, and in fact is required by the norm ("as a result"), between the superior's failure to exercise control properly and the subordinates' commission of the crimes but structurally the subordinates' crime cannot be linked to the failure to exercise the duty to punish.

We reach an opposite conclusion if we take into account the failure to prevent. The intentional failure to prevent a crime resembles a form of complicity, where the superior participates in the crimes of his subordinates.

In sum, it can be said that command responsibility is not a specific crime of omission nor is it a form of participation in the subordinates' crimes. It is indeed a mode of criminal liability for international offences, which can imply different consequences depending on the features of each case. The situation of a superior who knew about the crimes in time, had the possibility of preventing them and intentionally decided not to take any action is completely different from the one of the superior who ignored the fact that subordinates were committing the crimes, had no possibility of preventing them but then negligently failed to act in order to punish them. Such differences require distinct treatments, including at the stage of sentencing, given the incomparable gravity of the one situation *vis-à-vis* the other. This methodology is, in our view, necessary if we want to reconcile command responsibility with the fundamental principles of individual and culpable responsibility, which are at the base of every liberal and democratic criminal system, including the international one.

18

___

The History of the Defence of Superior Orders and its Intersection with International Human Rights Law

Hitomi Takemura[*]

18.1. Introduction

The defence of superior orders is claimed by a subordinate who commits a violation of international humanitarian law by following an order that was given by his or her superior. International crimes are not isolated offences that are committed by lone individuals. Rather, due to their scale and systematic nature, international crimes are committed through organisational structures. Thus, the question of whether individuals bear criminal responsibility when they execute an order is a critical issue that is related to international crimes. With the exception of the Rome Statute of the International Criminal Court ('ICC Statute'), international criminal legal instruments are normally silent on the topic of defence. However, they deal explicitly with the defence of superior orders.[1]

Today, the debate surrounding defence seems to be almost settled. If the defence of superior orders in the context of international criminal law can theoretically be claimed by a subordinate with regard to an international crime, then there remains almost no possibility to successfully claim such a defence before international criminal tribunals and the Inter-

---

[*] **Hitomi Takemura** is an Associate Professor of International Law at the School of Foreign Studies, Aichi Prefectural University, Japan. She received an LL.M. in public international law and international criminal law from Leiden University, an LL.M. in international law from Hitosubashi University, and a Ph.D. in law at the Irish Centre for Human Rights, National University of Ireland. She worked as an intern at the Appeal Chamber of the International Criminal Tribunal for Rwanda (July–December 2004) and for the International Criminal Court (March–August 2005).

[1] Kai Ambos, *Treatise on International Criminal Law*, vol. 1: *Foundation and General Part*, Oxford University Press, Oxford, 2013, p. 376.

national Criminal Court ('ICC'). This is because the seriousness of the subject-matter jurisdiction and the seniority of the personal jurisdiction of the international criminal tribunals contribute to the absolute denial of the defence of superior orders. In a similar vein, the ICC is supposed to deal with only the most serious violations of international humanitarian law. Therefore, an *a priori* judgment is made that the crime of genocide and crimes against humanity are *always* manifestly unlawful under Article 33(2) of the ICC Statute, as elaborated below. Moreover, the seniority of the defendants before these international criminal tribunals and courts generally prevented them from pleading the defence of superior orders.

Nevertheless, this chapter seeks to introduce the concise history and current legal situation surrounding the defence of superior orders, and this will be presented, for the most part, in chronological order. Such a historical approach is in line with aspirations of the fundamentally important Historical Origins of International Criminal Law ('HOICL') research project. A historical survey of the defence of superior orders can be regarded as a good example of serving the purpose of the HOICL – that is, constructing common ground and transcending the disagreements surrounding the contentious issues of international criminal law. The defence of superior orders used to be one of the most intensely debated problems in international criminal law; however, this debate seems to have been settled, at least in the realm of international criminal jurisdiction. The Trial Chamber of the International Criminal Tribunal for the former Yugoslavia ('ICTY') claimed that individuals even have a duty to disobey manifestly illegal orders under international law in tandem with the restriction of the defence of superior orders in international criminal law.[2]

In concert with the emergence of the individual's duty to disobey manifestly illegal orders, claims of selective conscientious objection have also arisen recently.[3] This chapter attempts to correlate the individual's

---

[2] International Criminal Tribunal for the Former Yugoslavia ('ICTY'), *Prosecutor v. Dražen Erdemović*, Trial Chamber, Sentencing Judgment, IT-96-22-T, 29 November 1996, para. 18 (http://www.legal-tools.org/doc/eb5c9d/).

[3] While the right to conscientious objection to military service in general (absolute conscientious objection) has now become established, the right to selective conscientious objection is admittedly not well established under national laws. See Peter Rowe, "Members of the Armed Forces and Human Rights Law", in Andrew Clapham and Paola Gaeta (eds.), *The Oxford Handbook of International Law in Armed Conflict*, Oxford University Press, Oxford, 2014, p. 541.

duty to disobey manifestly illegal orders under international law with the human right to selective conscientious objection. The argument is simple. If one wants to have a narrow defence of superior orders, one needs to further develop the human right to conscientious objection. Recent state practices illustrate that individuals tend to claim their human right not to participate in or become involved with an armed conflict that is contrary to international law against their own states. First, this chapter focuses on the history of superior orders in international criminal law. It then explores the current international law situation with regard to the issue of conscientious objectors. Finally, there has been an emergence of state practices concerning the individual's right to refuse to contribute to manifestly illegal wars and the issue of the state's duty to protect its nationals from participating in a manifestly unlawful war under international law. These state practices may endorse an emerging vertical relationship between individuals and their duties under international law by means of underscoring the importance of human dignity as an overarching imperative for states.

This chapter necessarily involves an aspect of the study of international human rights law, and it focuses on its interplay with the individual's duties with regard to international criminal law. It is arguably safe to describe this approach as interdisciplinary even though it falls within the realm of a common field of public international law. This interdisciplinary approach is directed toward the spirit of the HOICL project, which questions both the paradigm of the historical narrative of international criminal law and the existing stereotypical approach to issues of international criminal law.

18.2. History of the Development of Superior Orders

The history of the defence of superior orders is as old as the history of international criminal trials. One of the earliest medieval attempts at international criminal justice took place in 1474.[4] This was the *ad hoc* re-

---

[4] Military Government for Germany, USA, United States of America vs. Wilhelm von Leeb et al., 28 October 1948, Trials of War Criminals Before the Nuernberg Military Tribunals Under Control Council Law No. 10, October 1946–April 1949, vol. 11, US Government Printing Office, Washington, DC, 1949, p. 476: "We also refer to an article from the Manchester Guardian of 28 September 1946, containing a description of the trial of Sir Peter of Hagenbach held at Breisach in 1474. The charges against him were analogous to 'Crimes

gional trial of the Governor of Breisach, Peter von Hagenbach, who raised the plea of obedience to the orders of his superior at his trial for murder, arson and rape.[5] Despite his plea of superior orders, Hagenbach was convicted and was deprived of his knighthood for crimes he had owed a duty to prevent.[6] He was found to have "trampled under foot the laws of God and of man".[7]

Having acknowledged this experimental, medieval, transregional criminal justice, the issue of superior orders has been recognised as an issue of public international law only since the twentieth century, and especially since the First World War. Practically speaking, prior to the First World War the problem of superior orders did not play a major role because the so-called act of state doctrine had reigned until that time.[8] Under this doctrine, only states could be held liable in international law, while the responsibility of individuals was essentially irrelevant. Nevertheless, some jurisprudence exists from the period after the First World War. The Treaty of Versailles, signed on 28 June 1919, called for the trials of the former German Kaiser, Wilhelm II, and persons accused of having committed acts in violation of the laws and customs of war.[9] However, the treaty failed to include a provision on the defence of superior orders and left the matter for the tribunal to decide,[10] and, as is well known, the international tribunal never took place because of the refusal of the Netherlands to extradite Wilhelm II.

By the time the United Nations War Crimes Commission was established on 20 October 1943 to undertake the prosecution of war crimes

against Humanity' in modern concept. He was convicted" ('High Command case') (https://www.legal-tools.org/doc/c340d7/).

[5] Georg Schwarzenberger, *International Law as Applied by International Courts and Tribunals*, vol. 2: The Law of Armed Conflict, Stevens and Sons, London, 1968, pp. 462–66.

[6] William H. Parks, "Command Responsibility for War Crimes", in *Military Law Review*, 1973, vol. 62, p. 5.

[7] Schwarzenberger, 1968, p. 466, see *supra* note 5; Leslie C. Green, "Fifteenth Waldemar A Solf Lecture in International Law", in *Military Law Review*, 2003, vol. 175, p. 311.

[8] Albin Eser, "'Defences' in War Crime Trials", in Yoram Dinstein and Mala Tabory (eds.), *War Crimes in International Law*, Kluwer Law International, The Hague, 1996, p. 254.

[9] Treaty of Peace between the Allied and Associated Powers and Germany, 28 June 1919, Arts. 227–28 ('Versailles Treaty') (https://www.legal-tools.org/doc/a64206/).

[10] Commission on the Responsibility of the Authors of the War and on Enforcement of Penalties, Report Presented to the Preliminary Peace Conference, Versailles, 29 March 1919, reprinted in *American Journal of International Law*, 1920, vol. 14, p. 117.

committed by Nazi Germany and its allies, the debate on the issue of obedience to superior orders converged on the subjective criteria for considering it a general principle of criminal law, *mens rea*, and the objective criterion for considering the obedience to superior orders, which is manifest illegality of conduct. Ultimately, Article 8 of the Charter of the International Military Tribunal ('IMT Charter') adopted a severe position for the defence of superior orders – that is, the so-called absolute liability principle. Acquittal is not mentioned in Article 8; there is reference only to the mitigation of punishment as a possibility. The provision of Article 6 of the Charter of the International Military Tribunal for the Far East ('IMTFE Charter') is also similar to the IMT Charter, though technically its wording gave the judges of the IMTFE some leeway to take into account the fact of obedience to superior orders in the context of other defences, such as duress or a mistake of law.[11]

Broadly speaking, the defence of superior orders is not an available defence at *ad hoc* international tribunals.[12] Articles 7(4) of the ICTY Statute, Article 6(4) of the International Criminal Tribunal for Rwanda ('ICTR') Statute, Article 6(4) of the Special Court for Sierra Leone ('SCSL') Statute, Article 29 of the Law on the Establishment of Extraordinary Chambers in the Courts of Cambodia ('ECCC') for the Prosecution of Crimes Committed during the Period of Democratic Kampuchea, Article 3(2) of the Statute for the Special Tribunal for Lebanon ('STL'), and Section 21 of the Law of the Special Panels for East Timor are derived almost verbatim from Article 8 of the IMT Charter and categorically deny superior order as a defence. Even though the SCSL Statute, the STL Statute, the Law on the Establishment of the ECCC and the Law of the Special Panels for East Timor were all adopted after the ICC Statute, they did not follow its provision of the defence of superior orders. Suzannah Linton and Caitlin Reiger suggest that the drafters of Section 21 of Regulation 2000/15 of the Special Panels for East Timor obliged the special pan-

---

[11] Yoram Dinstein, *The Defence of 'Obedience to Superior Orders' in International Law*, A.W. Sijthoff, Leiden, 1965, p. 157; Elies van Sliedregt, The Criminal Responsibility of Individuals for Violation of International Humanitarian Law, TMC Asser, The Hague, 2003, p. 320.

[12] Alexander Zahar, "Superior Orders", in Antonio Cassese (ed.), *The Oxford Companion to International Criminal Justice*, Oxford University Press, Oxford, 2009, p. 525.

els to examine customary international law to determine the contents of the legal rules of superior orders.[13]

In national jurisdictions, the principle of manifest illegality before national tribunals has become mainstream since the end of the Cold War.[14] The defence of superior orders in the national context is a complete defence if the superior's order is not manifestly unlawful and the defendant did not know of the order's illegality.[15] In contrast, at the international level, the absolute liability approach towards the defence of superior orders has been preferred by international criminal tribunals.

The negotiation of the provision of the defence of superior orders was controversial throughout the drafting of the ICC Statute. The provision in the ICC Statute eventually took a middle position between the histories of international and national legislations and jurisprudences. Under Article 33(1) of the ICC Statute, the defence may be invoked under three cumulative conditions: 1) the person was under a legal obligation to obey the orders of the government or the superior in question; 2) the person did not know that the order was unlawful; and 3) the order was not manifestly unlawful. Article 33(2) further provides that "[f]or the purpose of this article, orders to commit genocide or crimes against humanity are manifestly unlawful". Since the resolution adopted in Kampala to amend the ICC Statute and introduce the crime of aggression to the jurisdiction of the

---

[13] Suzannah Linton and Caitlin Reiger, "The Evolving Jurisprudence and Practice of East Timor's Special Panels for Serious Crimes on Admissions of Guilt, Duress and Superior Orders", in *Yearbook of International Humanitarian Law*, 2001, vol. 4, p. 198.

[14] According to the International Committee of the Red Cross Rules on Customary International Humanitarian Law, Rule 154, Obedience to Superior Orders: "In finding that superior orders, if manifestly unlawful, cannot be a defence, several courts based their judgements on the fact that such orders must be disobeyed. Besides the practice related to the defence of superior orders, practice specifying that there is a duty to disobey an order that is manifestly unlawful or that would entail the commission of a war crime is contained in the military manuals, legislation and official statements of numerous States. This rule is confirmed in national case-law". See also Jean-Marie Henckaerts and Louise Doswald-Beck (eds.), *Customary International Humanitarian Law*, vol. 1: *Rules*, Cambridge University Press, Cambridge, 2009, pp. 563–64.

[15] See Paola Gaeta, "The Defence of Superior Orders: The Statute of the International Criminal Court versus Customary International Law", in *European Journal of International Law*, 1999, vol. 10, p. 176, fn. 7. Gaeta enumerates national/military laws, such as in Denmark, Germany, Israel, the Netherlands, Spain, Switzerland and Norway. Even in countries like Greece and Italy, which have legislation of the absolute liability principle, the conditional liability approach has been affirmed by case law.

ICC is silent on the issue of the defence of superior orders, the availability of the defence to the crime of aggression is debatable. Still, the Elements of the Crimes of Aggression require that the act of aggression, by its character, gravity and scale, constitute a manifest violation of the Charter of the United Nations ('UN Charter') and that the perpetrator was aware of the factual circumstances that established such a manifest violation of the Charter.[16] Therefore, it would be difficult for perpetrators to claim the order to commit a crime of aggression that was not manifestly unlawful by definition.[17] The leadership nature of the crime also, by definition, becomes an obstacle to applying the defence of superior orders to the perpetrators of the crime of aggression.[18]

18.3. Models of the Defence of Superior Orders Adopted in its Historical Development

Reflecting on the history of the defence of superior orders, five schools of thought concerning this problem are discernible. The first, and the theory which is mostly in decline, is the doctrine of *respondeat superior*.[19] According to this doctrine, obedience to superior orders is automatically and *a priori* an absolute defence to a criminal prosecution. The person who bears the responsibility must be the superior and not the subordinate. In 1906 one of the most prominent international law scholars at the time, Lassa Oppenheim, published the first edition of his treatise on international law, which advocated this doctrine.[20] However, the doctrine did not gain ground at the time of the post-Second World War trials.

Second, as an antithesis to *respondeat superior*, the doctrine of absolute liability has come into being. This doctrine claims that the fact of obedience to orders does not create a defence *per se*. In other words, orders from a superior do not justify an unlawful act but can be considered in mitigation. Generally speaking, the absolute liability doctrine is said to

---

[16] Resolution RC/Res.6 on the Crime of Aggression, Review Conference of the Rome Statute, adopted on 11 June 2010, Depositary Notification C.N.651.2010 Treaties-8.

[17] See, for example, Carrie McDougall, *The Crime of Aggression under the Rome Statute of the International Criminal Court*, Cambridge University Press, Cambridge, 2013, p. 198.

[18] *Ibid.*, p. 197.

[19] This doctrine is sometimes also termed the "doctrine of passive obedience" or "*Befehl ist Befehl*".

[20] Lassa Oppenheim, *International Law: A Treatise*, 2 vols., Longman, Green and Co., London, 1905.

have been supported by international legislation and jurisprudence prior to the ICC Statute, while the conditional liability doctrine is generally adopted by national legal systems.[21] The absolute liability doctrine is used, though not by many states, on several national levels,[22] whereas the conditional liability doctrine now appears in Article 33 of the ICC Statute.

Third, the absolute liability doctrine may have been a suitable instrument, specifically for trying the major war criminals whose acts were, by nature, manifestly unlawful.[23] Recently, the general tendency of the treatment of the defence of superior orders is that the illegality of orders is subject to the manifest illegality test. This approach, which is called the manifest illegality principle, is taken by the ICC Statute. Although this approach is primarily an objective test for soldiers who obey illegal orders, many advocates think that the ultimate objective of this test is to ascertain the subjective knowledge of the defendant regarding the illegality of the order.[24] They believe that the subordinate can be acquitted if he or she believed honestly or in good faith that he or she had to obey the order. This is known as the *mens rea* principle. Even though obedience to superior orders may not be a defence *per se*, it may be acknowledged in conjunction with the other circumstances of a given case within the ambit of a defence that is based on a lack of *mens rea*, such as the result of compulsion or mistake.

Fourth, in drafting instruments of international tribunals, there is a preference to follow the doctrine of superior orders as a ground of mitigation. This position holds that obedience to a superior order is not a defence *per se* and should be regarded as a factual detail or, at least, as grounds for mitigation. This approach is derived from the absolute liability principle. This position was recognised by the IMT Charter at Nuremberg and was subsequently affirmed by the statutes of *ad hoc* international criminal tribunals.

---

[21] Gaeta, 1999, pp. 174–75, see *supra* note 15. See also van Sliedregt, 2003, pp. 329, 332, see *supra* note 11.

[22] According to Gaeta, the absolute liability approach has been taken in Argentina, Austria, Iran, Romania and the United Kingdom. Gaeta, 1999, p. 179, fn. 21, see *supra* note 15.

[23] See Sarah T. Cornelius, "The Defence of Superior Orders and Erich Priebke", in *Patterns of Prejudice*, 1997, vol. 31, no. 1, p. 10.

[24] See, for example, Annemieke van Verseveld, *Mistake of Law: Excusing Perpetrators of International Crimes*, TMC Asser, The Hague, 2012, p. 98.

Fifth, some international criminal lawyers claim that, notwithstanding a clear rejection of obedience to superior orders as an absolute *justificatory* defence for an accused acting under military authority in armed conflict, this substantive defence to war crimes by virtue of a legal *excuse* ought to be maintained.[25] This school of thought could be termed "the doctrine of justification and excuse".

In the case of justification, an action that would *per se* be considered contrary to law is regarded as lawful and does not amount to a crime. However, in the case of excuse, an action contrary to the norm remains unlawful. Nonetheless the wrongdoer is not punished because of a lack of *mens rea* and/or special circumstances approved by law and society. In other words, superior orders to commit a crime can never *justify* the committal of a crime in executing the order. However, there remains the possibility of using this defence *not by itself* but when the order is considered within the framework of other defences, such as duress or coercion, as an *excuse*.[26]

18.4. The Actuality of the Defence of Superior Orders Based on Recent International Practice

After Nuremberg and until the adoption of the ICC Statute, it may be no exaggeration to say that the rejection of the defence of superior orders had been regarded as customary international law since the relevant provisions of the defence of superior orders of the statutes of these tribunals adopted the absolute liability doctrine, as noted earlier. The defence of superior orders became a problem as early as the first case of conviction and sentence before the ICTY – the *Erdemović* case. In its Appeals Judgment, the judges independently dealt with the issue of the defence of superior orders. For instance, Judge Cassese held that

> there is no necessary connection between the two. Superior
> orders may be issued without being accompanied by *any*

---

[25] Mordechai Kremnitzer, "The World Community as an International Legislator in Competition with National Legislators", in Albin Eser and Otto Lagodny (eds.), *Principles and Procedures for a New Transnational Criminal Law*, Max Planck Institute, Freiburg im Breisgau, 1992, p. 345; and see also Geert-Jan Alexander Knoops, *Defenses in Contemporary International Criminal Law*, Transnational Publishers, Ardsley, NY, 2001, p. 170.

[26] Otto Triffterer, "Article 33 Superior Orders and Prescription of Law", in Otto Triffterer (ed.), *Commentary on the Rome Statute of the International Criminal Court: Observer's Notes, Article by Article*, Nomos, Baden-Baden, 1999, pp. 580–81.

threats to life or limb. In these circumstances, if the superior order is manifestly illegal under international law, the subordinate is under a duty to refuse to obey the order. If, following such a refusal, the order is reiterated under a threat to life or limb, then the defence of duress may be raised, and superior orders lose any legal relevance.[27]

The Joint Separate Opinion of Judges McDonald and Vorah allegedly supported the *mens rea* principle,[28] though the primogenitor of the doctrine, Yoram Dinstein, complained that his work was not directly cited and that no approbation was made in their joint separate opinion.[29] After the *Erdemović* case, the ICTY distinguished between duress and the defence of superior orders, since the latter is absolutely denied in Article 7(4) of its Statute. For instance, in *Bralo*, the Trial Chamber of the ICTY recognised that "[d]uress and superior orders are separate, but related concepts and either may count in mitigation of sentence".[30]

As a consequence of following the provision of the IMT Charter with minor alterations, the ICTY does not regard superior orders as a defence. Moreover, the fact of the existence of manifestly unlawful superior orders has not been easily taken into consideration in the mitigation of sentences, even though the fact of following superior orders is one of the mitigating factors explicitly referred to in both the ICTY and the ICTR Statutes. If the nature of the order is manifestly unlawful, then the fact that the individual obeyed such orders, as opposed to acting on his or her own initiative, does not merit the mitigation of punishment.[31] In 2010 the Appeals Chamber of the ICTY held that the fact that the accused was or-

---

[27] ICTY, *Prosecutor v. Dražen Erdemović*, Appeals Chamber, Judgment, Separate and Dissenting Opinion of Judge Cassese, IT-96-22-A, 7 October 1997, para. 15 (emphasis in original) (https://www.legal-tools.org/doc/a7dff6/).

[28] ICTY, *Prosecutor v. Dražen Erdemović*, Appeals Chamber, Judgment, Joint Separate Opinion of Judge McDonald and Judge Vohrah, IT-96-22-A, 7 October 1997, para. 34 (https://www.legal-tools.org/doc/f91d89/).

[29] Yoram Dinstein, *The Defence of 'Obedience to Superior Orders' in International Law*, repr. ed., Oxford University Press, Oxford, 2012, p. xix.

[30] ICTY, *Prosecutor v. Miroslav Bralo*, Trial Chamber, Judgment, IT-95-17-S, 7 December 2005, p. 19, para. 53 ('Bralo case') (https://www.legal-tools.org/doc/e10281/); ICTY, *Prosecutor v. Miroslav Bralo*, Appeals Chamber, Judgment on Sentencing Appeal, IT-95-17-A, 2 April 2007, p. 11, para. 22 (https://www.legal-tools.org/doc/14a169/).

[31] ICTY, *Prosecutor v. Darko Mrđa*, Trial Chamber, Sentencing Judgment, IT-02-59-S, 31 March 2004, p. 17, para. 67 (https://www.legal-tools.org/doc/d61b0f/).

dered to lead the operation did not exonerate him from criminal responsibility if, in the execution of the order, he or she, in turn, instructed other persons to commit a crime.[32] The manifestly unlawful nature of superior orders influenced considerations of the mitigation of the sentence, and the Trial Chamber of the ICTY stated: "The Chamber also finds that any orders given to Bralo to kill civilians and destroy homes would have been manifestly unlawful, such that they have no mitigatory value in the determination of sentencing the present case".[33] In addition to the manifestly unlawful nature of superior orders, the senior status of the accused in the army and the repeated execution of crimes all contributed to no consideration of the existence of superior orders in regard to mitigating factors in *Bagosora* before the ICTR.[34]

The SCSL appears to be even stricter than the ICTY with regard to mitigating circumstances. Although Kanu raised superior orders as one of the mitigating circumstances, the Trial Chamber treated it as a question of duress. On rejecting the fact of obedience to superior orders as a mitigating factor, the Trial Chamber II of the SCSL held that "[t]here is no evidence that Kanu acted under duress. The fact that Kanu voluntarily reiterated criminal orders previously issued by Brima cannot be considered as mitigation".[35]

The ECCC treated the defence of superior orders and duress separately when it considered them as defences and mitigating circumstances.[36] Neither the Trial Chamber nor the Supreme Court Chamber of the

---

[32] ICTY, *Prosecutor v. Ljube Boškoski and Johan Tarčulovski*, Appeals Chamber, Judgment, IT-04-82-A, 19 May 2010, p. 63, para. 167 (https://www.legal-tools.org/doc/54398a/).

[33] Bralo case, Trial Chamber, Sentencing Judgment, p. 20, para. 54, see *supra* note 30.

[34] International Criminal Tribunal for Rwanda, *Prosecutor v. Théoneste Bagosora et al.*, Trial Chamber, Judgment and Sentence, ICTR-98-41-T, 18 December 2008, p. 573, para. 2274 (https://www.legal-tools.org/doc/6d9b0a/). In *Bagosora*, whereas the Trial Chamber recognised that Nsengiyumva and Ntabakuze were at times following superior orders in executing their crimes, given their own senior status and stature in the Rwandan army, the Chamber was convinced that their repeated execution of these crimes as well as the manifestly unlawful nature of any orders they received to perpetrate them reflected their acquiescence in committing them, and no mitigation was warranted on this ground.

[35] Special Tribunal for Sierra Leone, *Prosecutor v. Alex Tamba Brima, Brima Bazzy Kamara, Santigie Barbar Kanu*, Trial Chamber, Sentencing Judgment, SCSL-04-16-T, 19 July 2007, p. 32, para. 122 (https://www.legal-tools.org/doc/e912c3/).

[36] Extraordinary Chambers in the Courts of Cambodia ('ECCC'), *Co-Prosecutors v. Kaing Guek Eav alias Duch*, Trial Chamber, Judgment, 001/18-07-2007/ECCC/TC, 26 July 2010, para. 608: "Though often pleaded in conjunction with superior orders, duress may

ECCC in *Duch* recognised the defence of superior orders and superior orders as a mitigating circumstance, since Kaing Guek Eav alias Duch was found to have known that the orders were unlawful.[37] However, the approach taken by the Trial Chamber should be noted. It examined whether the accused knew the unlawfulness of following orders to commit war crimes in accordance with Article 33 of the ICC Statute, though Article 29(4) of the ECCC law adopts an absolute liability approach by providing for "the fact that a Suspect acted pursuant to an order of the Government of Democratic Kampuchea or of a superior shall not relieve the Suspect of individual criminal responsibility".[38]

Since the international community and international criminal tribunals have limited resources, they tend to focus on the senior perpetrators of systematic criminality of the gravest international crimes. Consequently, for such senior leaders, there is a limited possibility of obedience to superior orders, since they usually belong to the top of the system criminality. However, there seems to be no customary international law governing how to handle cases concerning a subordinate's obedience to superior orders of a nature that is not manifestly unlawful.[39] The fact of obedience to superior orders may be considered in defences other than the defence of superior orders. These include mistakes of law, mistakes of fact and/or duress, as set forth in Articles 32 and 31(1)(d) of the ICC Statute, respectively, though the conditions of these defences are again very rigid and limited.

While the constitutional texts of the international criminal tribunals, with the exception of the permanent ICC, presuppose the manifest illegality of their subject matter crimes and categorically deny the defence of superior orders, national courts appear to maintain conditional responsi-

---

also serve as an independent mitigating factor" ('Duch case') (https://www.legal-tools.org/doc/dbdb62/).

[37] *Ibid.*, paras. 552, 606-608. ECCC, *Co-Prosecutors v. Kaing Guek Eav alias Duch*, Supreme Court Chamber, Appeal Judgment, 001/18-07-2007/ECCC/SC, 3 February 2012, para. 365 (https://www.legal-tools.org/doc/681bad/).

[38] The footnote of the Trial Chamber Judgment cited Article 100 of the 1956 Penal Code, the relevant national law during the 1975 to 1979 period, which stipulates: "In the case of illegal orders given by a lawful authority, the judge shall determine, on a case-by-case basis, the criminal responsibility of those executing the orders" (unofficial translation). Duch case, Trial Chamber, Judgment, fn. 962, see *supra* note 36.

[39] Gerhard Werle and Florian Jessberger, *Principles of International Criminal Law*, 3rd ed., Oxford University Press, Oxford, 2014, p. 251, para. 667.

bility under the manifest illegality principle and presume the manifest illegality of orders involving crimes under international law.[40]

The denial of the defence of superior orders is also seen in international human rights instruments, such as Article 2 of the Convention against Torture and Article VIII of the Inter-American Convention on the Forced Disappearance of Persons.[41] General Comment No. 20 by the Human Rights Committee in relation to Article 7 – the prohibition of torture – of the International Covenant on Civil and Political Rights states that "no justification or extenuating circumstances may be invoked to excuse a violation of article 7 for any reasons, including those based on an order from a superior officer or public authority".[42]

18.5. How the Right of Conscientious Objection May Be Relevant

The next question is how the influence and growth of a particular human rights norm may alter the legal understanding of superior orders – namely, the right of conscientious objection. Considering the intersection between human rights law and international criminal law as they have historically developed is important given their shared aims of protecting the individual and important public values. This is also important for practical, on-the-ground reasons. The manifest illegality test of the defence of superior orders ultimately demands reasonable pre-consideration on the part of the individual when he or she follows an order from his or her superior. In reality, however, the feasibility of such a pre-consideration may be seriously circumscribed due to the environment surrounding those who must obey orders. No law should compel any individual to observe a norm that is practically unreasonable.

In this context, the system of conscientious objection may assist soldiers to defend their judgments on each war and each order that is giv-

---

[40] *Ibid.*, para. 668, p. 251.

[41] Convention against Torture and Other Cruel, Inhuman or Degrading Treatment or Punishment, General Assembly resolution 39/46, Annex, 39 UN GAOR Supp. No. 51, UN doc. A/39/51, 10 December 1984; Inter-American Convention on Forced Disappearance of Persons, OAS Treaty Series No. 68, 33 ILM 1429, 9 June 1994.

[42] Human Rights Committee, General Comment 20, Article 7 (Forty-fourth session, 1992), Compilation of General Comments and General Recommendations Adopted by Human Rights Treaty Bodies, UN doc. HRI/GEN/1/Rev.1, 1994.

en. Of course, the defence of superior orders and the notion of conscientious objection are two different concepts. Yet, the duty to disobey manifestly illegal orders may be legally fulfilled by means of the human rights system of conscientious objection. The corollary of denying the defence of superior orders in the context of manifest illegality may be not only deny a legitimate defence when soldiers are prosecuted but also demand that soldiers abstain from obeying manifestly illegal orders altogether. The duty to refuse to obey a manifestly illegal order was clearly established by the President of the ICTY in the *Erdemović* case. As Rule 154 of the customary international rules enumerated by the International Committee of the Red Cross demands, "[e]very combatant has a duty to disobey a manifestly unlawful order" today.[43]

Despite this duty of the individual to uphold international humanitarian law, it is not clear how he or she can fulfil this duty within his or her own nation by means of claiming conscientious objector status. Such a duty of the individual under international criminal law and international humanitarian law would be efficiently performed only if the international community recognises and supports the right to conscientious objection in the normative body of international human rights law. In modern history, conscientious objection is regarded as being as old as the history of conscription. The waning of conscription in European countries is proportional to the rise of conscientious objectors. While the supervising bodies of international and regional human rights law have witnessed numerous individual cases of conscientious objection, there is no "international" human rights treaty that clearly sets out the individual's right to conscientious objection. Consequently, the right to conscientious objection under international law has remained somewhat obscure.

The Charter of Fundamental Rights of the European Union is the first regional and, therefore, to some extent, international human rights instrument that recognises explicitly the right to conscientious objection as a part of the right to freedom of conscience. In addition, Article 12(1) of the Ibero-American Convention on Young People's Rights, which entered into force on 1 March 2008, recognises that youths have the right to make a conscientious objection to obligatory military service.

---

[43] Henckaerts and Doswald-Beck, 2009, p. 563, see *supra* note 14.

Both Article 8(3)(c)(ii) of the International Covenant on Civil and Political Rights[44] ('ICCPR') and Article 4(3)(b) of the European Convention on Human Rights ('ECHR'),[45] on the one hand, relate to freedom from slavery and forced labour, respectively, and both categorically preclude military service and any national service required by the law of conscientious objectors in countries in which conscientious objection is recognised.[46] On the other hand, both Article 18 of the ICCPR and Article 9 of the ECHR enshrine freedom of thought, conscience and religion without referring explicitly to the right to make a conscientious objection to military service. Therefore, the long-standing positions of both the Human Rights Committee of the ICCPR and the ECHR initially took the view that their human rights conventions did not provide for the right to conscientious objection, especially taking into account Articles 8 (3)(c)(ii)[47] and 4(3)(b), respectively.[48] However, their positions have gradually changed over the last three decades.

The Human Rights Committee of the ICCPR adopted the General Comment No. 22 on Article 18 of the freedom of thought, conscience and

---

[44] International Covenant on Civil and Political Rights, General Assembly resolution 2200A (XXI), 21 UN GAOR Supp. (No. 16) at 52, UN doc. A/6316, 16 December 1966, 999 UNTS 171, entered into force 23 March 1976.

[45] European Convention for the Protection of Human Rights and Fundamental Freedoms, 4 November 1950, 213 UNTS 221, entered into force 3 September 1953.

[46] Article 8(3)(c) of the International Covenant on Civil and Political Rights stipulates: "(c) For the purpose of this paragraph the term 'forced or compulsory labour' shall not include: [...] (ii) Any service of a military character and, in countries where conscientious objection is recognized, any national service required by law of conscientious objectors". Article 4(3)(b) of the European Convention on Human Rights stipulates: "(3) For the purpose of this article the term 'forced or compulsory labour' shall not include: [...] (b) any service of a military character or, in case of conscientious objectors in countries where they are recognised, service exacted instead of compulsory military service".

[47] Human Rights Committee, *L.T.K. v. Finland*, Communication no. 185/1984, UN doc. CCPR/C/25/D/185/1984, 9 July 1985.

[48] *Grandrath v. Germany*, no. 2299/64, Commission report of 12 December 1966, Yearbook ECHR, 10, p. 626; *G.Z. v. Austria*, no. 5591/72, Commission decision of 2 April 1973, Collection 43, p. 161; *X. v. Germany*, no. 7705/76, Commission decision of 5 July 1977, Decisions and Reports (DR) 9, p. 201; *Conscientious Objectors v. Denmark*, no. 7565/76, Commission decision of 7 March 1977, DR 9, p. 117; *A. v. Switzerland*, no. 10640/83, Commission decision of 9 May 1984, DR 38, p. 222; *N. v. Sweden*, no. 10410/83, Commission decision of 11 October 1984, DR 40, p. 203; *Autio v. Finland*, no. 17086/90, Commission decision of 6 December 1991, DR 72, p. 246; *Peters v. the Netherlands*, no. 22793/93, Commission decision of 30 November 1994, unreported; *Heudens v. Belgium*, no. 24630/94, Commission decision of 22 May 1995, unreported.

religion on 30 July 1993. It recognised that the right to conscientious objection may be derived from the article by holding that "[t]he Covenant does not explicitly refer to a right to conscientious objection, but the Committee believes that such a right can be derived from article 18, inasmuch as the obligation to use lethal force may seriously conflict with the freedom of conscience and the right to manifest one's religion or belief".[49]

In 2012 the Human Rights Committee of the ICCPR recognised the violation of Article 18(1) of the ICCPR by Turkey in a communication with regard to conscientious objectors who were Jehovah's Witnesses. In this case, the committee

> reiterates that the right to conscientious objection to military service is inherent to the right to freedom of thought, conscience and religion. It entitles any individual to an exemption from compulsory military service if the latter cannot be reconciled with the individual's religion or beliefs. The right must not be impaired by coercion. A State party may, if it wishes, compel the objector to undertake a civilian alternative to military service, outside of the military sphere and not under military command. The alternative service must not be of a punitive nature, but must rather be a real service to the community and compatible with respect for human rights.[50]

The Human Rights Committee thus interprets Article 18 of the ICCPR and recognises the right to conscientious objection to military service independent from Article 8(3)(c)(ii).

In recent cases, the Human Rights Committee has treated the right to conscientious objection to military service as part of the absolutely protected right to hold a belief, although the committee had analysed the applicants' rights to conscientious objection to military service as an instance of the manifestation of belief in practice until the cases of 2010, which are subject to limitation under Article 18(3).[51]

---

[49] Human Rights Committee, General Comment 22, Article 18 (Forty-eighth session, 1993). Compilation of General Comments and General Recommendations Adopted by Human Rights Treaty Bodies, UN doc. HRI/GEN/1/Rev.1 at 35, 1994, para. 11.

[50] *Cenk Atasoy and Arda Sarkut v. Turkey*, Communication nos. 1853/2008 and 1854/2008, UN doc. CCPR/C/104/D/1853-1854/2008, 29 March 2012.

[51] See Joint Opinion of Committee Members Yuji Iwasawa, Gerald L. Neuman, Anja Seibert-Fohr, Yuval Shany and Konstantine Vardzelashvili (concurring), *Young-kwan Kim et al. v. Republic of Korea*, Communication no. 2179/2012, UN doc. CCPR/C/112/D/2179/2012, 15 October 2014.

Likewise, Strasbourg's attitudes toward the right to conscientious objection to military service have softened. On 7 July 2011 the Grand Chamber of the European Court of Human Rights made a break with the past decisions of the Commission and held that "article 9 should no longer be read in conjunction with article 4 § 3 (b). Consequently, the applicant's complaint is to be assessed solely under article 9".[52] Although the Court did not explicitly read the right to conscientious objection to military service into Article 9, it held that

> article 9 does not explicitly refer to a right to conscientious objection. However, it considers that opposition to military service, where it is motivated by a serious and insurmountable conflict between the obligation to serve in the army and a person's conscience or his deeply and genuinely held religious or other beliefs, constitutes a conviction or belief of sufficient cogency, seriousness, cohesion and importance to attract the guarantees of article 9.[53]

In this case, the applicant, who was a Jehovah's Witness, complained that his conviction for refusing to serve in the army had violated Article 9, and the Court found that the applicant's conviction constituted an interference, which was not necessary in a democratic society within the meaning of Article 9 of the ECHR.[54]

There are two categories of conscientious objector (conscientious objection): one is an absolute conscientious objector (absolute conscientious objection), and the other is a selective conscientious objector (selective conscientious objection). Selective conscientious objectors are opposed to certain military actions. Taking account of individuals' duties to disobey manifest illegal orders under international law, the *jus ad bellum* and *jus in bello* violations should be relevant to selective conscientious objection. The international community once supported selective conscientious objection by means of a UN General Assembly resolution. In its resolution 33/165, the General Assembly recognised "the right of all persons to refuse service in military or police forces which are used to enforce *apartheid*".

---

[52] European Court of Human Rights, *Bayatyan v. Armenia*, Grand Chamber, Judgment, no. 23459/03, 7 July 2011, para. 109.

[53] *Ibid.*, para. 110.

[54] *Ibid.*, para. 128.

The *jus in bello*-based claim of conscientious objection is likely to fail due to the practical difficulties of presenting evidence of *jus in bello* before obeying an order. In the context of asylum seekers, the "real risk" of participating in illegal acts (Norway) or the likelihood of being closely involved in actions that offend the basic rules of human conduct (the United Kingdom) has to be proved in order to claim the status of refugee as a conscientious objector. Another difficulty in relation to the *jus ad bellum* and *jus in bello* basis may be that the relationship between the two is sometimes very obscure. This may be even more so in the case of foot soldiers.

After all, despite the clear existence of the individual's duty to observe international humanitarian law, including both *jus ad bellum* and *jus in bello*, in reality it may be very unlikely for a conscientious objector to claim his or her status successfully on the sole basis of duties under international humanitarian law before domestic courts. In addition, the international community does not have the capacity and resources to adjudicate claims of the apparent illegality of the use of force and the means of warfare.

The coexistence and historical development of both the duty of disobeying manifestly illegal orders under international law and the right of conscientious objection to military service may sound illogical; however, the two should not necessarily be seen as mutually exclusive. The system of conscientious objection may sometimes be the only resort for soldiers who are facing manifestly illegal orders under international law. The United Nations Human Rights Commission encouraged "States, as part of post-conflict peace-building, to consider granting, and effectively implementing, amnesties and restitution of rights, in law and practice, for those who have refused to undertake military service on grounds of conscientious objection" in its resolution 2004/35 in April 2004.[55] Respect for the individual's right to conscientious objection to military service by both states and the international community may provide the cornerstone of peace and stability in situations which outrage the conscience of mankind, such as any that involve a serious violation of international humanitarian law.

---

[55] Human Rights Commission, 2004/35, 19 April 2004, para. 4. Adopted without a vote. See chap. XI – E/2004/23 – E/CN.4/2004/127.

18.6. State Practices Concerning Individuals' and States' Duties Not to Participate in Manifestly Illegal Armed Conflict under International Law

Domestic cases dealing with an individual's or state's duty not to participate in manifestly illegal armed conflict under international law have emerged. The case of *Germany v. N.* dealt with the question of whether a soldier may refuse to participate in a military software project supporting Operation Iraq Freedom, the so-called Iraq War, which he believed to be illegal under international law.[56] The soldier had engaged in an information technology project that aimed to improve co-operation between Germany and other North Atlantic Treaty Organization ('NATO') countries in their operations. When Operation Iraqi Freedom began in March 2003, he told his captain and the medical officer of his unit about his legal and moral concerns regarding Germany's role in the conflict. Thereafter, he found himself unable to comply with military duties, and he was released from his post. Disciplinary proceedings were subsequently initiated against him on charges of disobedience. Although the military court (*Truppendienstgericht*) found him guilty, the Federal Administrative Court (*Bundesverwaltungsgericht*) discharged him based on its finding that the military duty of obedience and loyal service does not demand blind or unconditional devotion to superiors.[57] The Court found that "an order is not binding if it functions as part of a war of aggression that would disturb the peaceful coexistence of nations, or if it contravenes fundamental rules of international law such as the UN ban on the use of force", although the Court did not decide whether this was such a case.[58] Upon examining the soldier's expression of conscience, the Court considered both the soldier's personal convictions and the legal uncertainties surrounding the military intervention in Iraq under the UN Charter without valid Security Council resolutions authorising the use of force by NATO.[59] In the Court's opinion, "when the major decided not to obey the

---

[56] German Federal Administrative Court (*Bundesverwaltungsgericht*), *Germany v. N.*, Decision No. 2 WD 12.04, 21 June 2005. Ilja Baudisch, "German Federal Administrative Court Decision on a Soldier's Right to Refuse to Obey Military Orders for Conscientious Reasons: Germany v. N. Decision No. 2 WD 12.04", in *American Journal of International Law*, 2006, vol. 100, no. 4, p. 911.

[57] Ibid.

[58] *Ibid.*, p. 912.

[59] Ibid.

order, he faced the danger of being entangled in an illegal conflict and therefore could lawfully demand another employment without violating his duties as a soldier".[60]

In the United Kingdom House of Lords' case of *R v. the Prime Minister and others*, the appellants alleged that the government had failed to exercise due diligence to satisfy itself of the legality under international law of the military action when the government decided to take part in the military operations in Iraq and then begin the British occupation of Iraq in light of Article 2 of the ECHR (as set out in Schedule 1 of the Human Rights Act 1998). It was also alleged that Article 2 of the ECHR obliged the government to establish an independent public inquiry into the legality of the invasion of Iraq in 2003 under international law.[61] The members of the House of Lords unanimously dismissed the appeal.[62] The leading judgment by Lord Bingham stated that "article 2 has never been held to apply to the process of deciding on the lawfulness of a resort to arms, despite the number of occasions on which member states have made that decision over the past half century and despite the fact that such a decision almost inevitably exposes military personnel to the risk of fatalities".[63] Bingham raised three main reasons for his decision: 1) the lawfulness of military action has no immediate bearing on the risk of fatalities;[64] 2) the draftsmen of the ECHR could not have envisaged that it could have provided a suitable framework or machinery for resolving questions about the resort to war;[65] and (3) subject to limited exceptions and specific extensions, the application of the ECHR is territorial, and the rights and freedoms are ordinarily to be secured to those within the borders of the state and not outside.[66]

---

[60] *Ibid.*, p. 914.

[61] United Kingdom House of Lords, *R (Gentle) v. The Prime Minister and others*, Judgment, 9 April 2008, [2008] UKHL 20, [2008] 1 AC 1356 (HL).

[62] *Ibid.*

[63] United Kingdom House of Lords, Judgments – R (on the application of Gentle (FC) and another (FC)) (Appellants) v. the Prime Minister and others (Respondents), Session 2007–2008 [2008] 1 AC 1356, pp. 1366–67, para. 8.

[64] *Ibid.*, p. 1367, para. 8.

[65] *Ibid.*, p. 1369, para. 13.

[66] Ibid., pp. 1383–84, para. 66. R (Gentle) v. The Prime Minister and others, 2008, see supra note 61.

Although Baroness Hale found that neither the state nor the European Court of Human Rights can rule upon the legality of the use of force against Iraq because it is beyond their competence,[67] she wished that "we could spell out of art 2 a duty in a state not to send its soldiers to fight in an unlawful war. States should protect their soldiers from the consequences of having in practice to obey orders whether or not they are lawful".[68] Whereas Hale thought that "it might reasonably be expected that they would decline to commit their troops to an unlawful war",[69] she thought the European Court of Human Rights would not construct out of Article 2 a duty not to send soldiers to fight in an unlawful war.[70] In her view, the lawfulness of war is an issue between states – not between individuals or between individuals and the state – and the ICC Statute has not changed this relationship, since the ICC's jurisdiction over the crime of aggression did not exist at the time of delivery of judgment even before the Review Conference of the Statute of the International Criminal Court.[71]

Nonetheless, Hale at least recognises that when a state expects its soldiers to obey their superiors' orders irrespective of their own views on the lawfulness of those orders, then, under the ICC Statute, there will be a correlative duty of the state to its soldiers to ensure that those orders are lawful.[72] Her judgment suggests that this would be a state duty under the ICC Statute and probably not an individual human right to disobey orders from a state to take part in an illegal war nor a state duty under the right to life of the ECHR.

Even though the duty of a state to ensure the individual human right to life by not engaging in the illegal use of force under international law has not yet been found in state practices, it would be an overstatement that states have no responsibility at all. In *Al-Skeini v. UK*, the European Court of Human Rights found that the state has a duty to investigate effectively any death arising out of the use of force by that state, even in overseas situations in which the state officials exercise "control and authority" over

---

[67] *Ibid.*, p. 1381, para. 58.

[68] *Ibid.*, p. 1381, para. 55.

[69] *Ibid.*, p. 1381, para. 56.

[70] *Ibid.*, p. 1381, para. 57.

[71] *Ibid.*

[72] *Ibid.*, para. 50.

foreign nationals.[73] The emerging awareness of the state's obligation to protect the right to life in an extraterritorial jurisdiction in which the state in question exercises authority may be recognised through such an international practice.

It may be true that "[t]he standard of responsibility of the state is not to protect the lives of its soldiers under all circumstances. War is, after all, a dangerous business".[74] This is all the more reason for states to refrain from becoming involved with the illegal use of force at the level of *jus ad bellum*. For consideration of *jus in bello*, states owe a great responsibility to the chain-and-command structure which enables them to make sure that military orders are in conformity with international humanitarian and human rights laws. Eventually, soldiers' concerns would be cleared. At the same time, under such circumstances, the right to life of civilians would be duly respected.

18.7. Conclusion

Since the Iraq War of 2003 selective conscientious objection has attracted increasing attention. Since modern soldiers are more educated than their predecessors, they have begun to raise a voice of conscience when they have doubts about a cause and/or means of a war.[75] Recent studies have shown that "national authorities deal very differently and often inconsistently with" selective conscientious objection.[76] The United Kingdom, Israel and Germany do not recognise selective conscientious objection in law. However, the United Kingdom and Germany "acknowledge that conscripted or professional service members may object to participation in specific operations on grounds of conscience" subject to case-by-case considerations.[77]

---

[73] European Court of Human Rights, *Al-Skeini and others v. the United Kingdom*, Grand Chamber, Judgment, Strasbourg, Application No. 55721/07, 7 July 2011.

[74] Rowe, 2014, p. 539, see *supra* note 3.

[75] Andrea Ellner, Paul Robinson and David Whetham, "Introduction: 'Sometime they'll give a war and nobody will come'", in Andrea Ellner, Paul Robinson and David Whetham (eds.), *When Soldiers Say No: Selective Conscientious Objection in the Modern Military*, Ashgate, Farnham, 2014, p. 5.

[76] Andrea Ellner, Paul Robinson and David Whetham, "The Practice and Philosophy of Selective Conscientious Objection", in Ellner *et al.*, 2014, p. 239, see *supra* note 75.

[77] *Ibid.*

Even though the right to selective conscientious objection to military service has not yet been widely recognised, international practices at least show that the Human Rights Committee of the ICCPR and the European Court of Human Rights are more attentive to conscientious objectors to military service, demanding that an alternative service be provided for conscientious objectors in lieu of military service. The trajectory of the restriction of the defence of superior orders under international criminal law and the duties of individuals to disobey manifestly illegal orders as its corollary or prerequisite benefit from an emerging history of selective conscientious objection and vice versa.

International legal practices absolutely deny the availability of the defence of superior orders and the existence of obedience to superior orders as mitigating circumstances, or they at least tend to presuppose the manifest illegality of superior orders to commit a serious violation of international law. Under such circumstances, each soldier should be regarded as a moral agent rather than "the obedience of an automaton".[78] In this respect, the developments of international criminal law, especially the principle of the conditional liability doctrine, the principle of the manifest illegality of the defence of superior orders, seemingly enhance norm consciousness among individuals and states.

This chapter attempts to infuse new life into the no longer contentious problem of the defence of superior orders by forming a bridge between individuals' obligations under international criminal law to disobey manifestly illegal orders and the international human right to disobey orders that contravene international law. This attempt would invite a fresh perspective on the history of the defence of superior orders and eventually contribute to the HOICL project. International society is becoming increasingly individual-centric; thus, a vertical relationship is emerging between international society and individuals.[79] The exercise of state sover-

---

[78] See Mark W.S. Hobel, "'So Vast an Area of Legal Irresponsibility'? The Superior Orders Defense and Good Faith Reliance on Advice of Counsel?", in *Columbia Law Review*, 2011, vol. 111, p. 583, fn. 45. "Any limited acceptance of a superior orders defence must hold the individual accountable for examining the contents of an order given, even if such an examination is quick and completed in accordance with the contingencies of the moment", *ibid.*, p. 592.

[79] Kai Ambos, "Punishment without a Sovereign? The *Ius Puniendi* Issue of International Criminal Law: A First Contribution towards a Consistent Theory of International Criminal Law", in *Oxford Journal of Legal Studies*, 2013, vol. 33, no. 2, pp. 293–315.

eignty is constantly and severely checked through the lenses of international criminal law and international human rights law by treaty bodies or international society in general. Individuals are becoming increasingly visible, even in the field of international law, though they have traditionally been covered by the veil of state sovereignty. The defence of superior orders teaches human beings a fundamental lesson about fostering the ability to think about even the complex issues of international law, such as the legality of the use of force, on their own.

19

International Criminal Law Issues in the Fight against Terrorism: The Criminalisation of Conspiracy in Japan and South Korea

Hae Kyung Kim[*]

19.1. Introduction

The threat of terrorism has been on the rise in recent times. In particular, terrorists have tried to become more effective by causing massive damage using unexpected methods at unexpected times. In addition, with the advance of globalisation, both terrorism victims and terrorists themselves have become more multinational, and the scope of investigations devised in response and compensation has also enlarged. While this issue has been present since acts of terrorism such as hijackings proliferated, especially from the 1960s onwards, the 11 September 2001 attacks in the United States made clear the increasing multinational nature of both victims and perpetrators, as well as the potential for the expansion of massive and non-discriminatory damage (comprising nearly 3,000 deaths in that instance). More recently, the terrorist organisation Islamic State that dominates areas it controls through a combination of hostage terrorism and fear has expanded the territory it controls in Syria and northern Iraq and uses terrorist videos to mobilise more fighters.

---

[*] **Hae Kyung Kim** is an Associate Professor at the University Research Center, Nihon University, Japan and also teaches on the Law in Japan Programme at Meiji University School of Law. Previously, she held faculty positions with the School of Pacific and Asian Studies, University of Hawaii and the Columbian College of Arts and Sciences, George Washington University, USA. She received her Ph.D. and M.A. in International Studies at Waseda University. Her current research examines how the control of terrorism influences international financial trade in Japan, South Korea and the United States. This research project is funded by the Grants-in-Aid for Scientific Research from Japan's Ministry of Education, Culture, Sports, Science and Technology. She is the author of *A Study on the Preventive Measures against Terrorism: The Present State of International Law and the Proposal for the Future* (Waseda University Press, 2011).

These developments mean that as terrorism becomes more prevalent the way that governments work to combat terrorists and co-operate with the related agencies of foreign countries becomes more important. As part of these efforts, since the creation of the Convention on Offences and Certain Other Acts Committed on Board Aircraft (better known as the Tokyo Convention)[1] in 1963 there have been 13 further international conventions dealing with the means and implementation of acts of terrorism, leading to the International Convention for the Suppression of Acts of Nuclear Terrorism of 2005.[2] Along with these initiatives, the United Nations General Assembly adopted the International Convention for the Suppression of the Financing of Terrorism in 1999, targeting the funding that can be considered the "oxygen" for terrorism.[3] The following year the General Assembly adopted the Convention against Transnational Organized Crime that deals with the prevention of international crime, including money laundering.[4] The conventions stipulated penalties and countermeasures as means of tackling terrorism, targeting participation in and conspiracy with organised crime organisations, money laundering, the obstruction of justice and corruption (involving public officials).

This chapter focuses on conspiracy as defined in the Convention against Transnational Organized Crime and discusses how the acceptance of this Convention and the concept of conspiracy it embodies have been received in Japan and South Korea in light of 1) the international environment, 2) the characteristics of the bureaucracy in both countries, and 3) their basic national policies in this field. While case studies from Japan form the major part of the analysis, a comparison with South Korea has been included because the structure and content of the domestic law in both countries are similar due to the influence of Japan's colonial rule on South Korea. Such a comparative method is useful in clarifying the rea-

---

[1] Convention on Offences and Certain Other Acts Committed on Board Aircraft, signed 14 September 1963, entered into force 4 December 1969, 704 United Nations Treaty Series 219.

[2] International Convention for the Suppression of Acts of Nuclear Terrorism, signed 13 April 2005, entered into force 7 July 2007, United Nations Treaty Series, vol. 2445, p. 89, UN doc. A/RES/59/290.

[3] International Convention for the Suppression of the Financing of Terrorism, adopted 9 December 1999, United Nations Treaty Series, vol. 2178, p. 197, UN doc. A/RES/54/109.

[4] Convention against Transnational Organized Crime, adopted 15 November 2000, entered into force 29 September 2003, United Nations Treaty Series, vol. 2225, p. 209, UN doc. A/55/383 ('CTOC').

sons why Japan has postponed the ratification of the Convention due to the requirement of establishing conspiracy as a crime.

With regard to the criminalisation of conspiracy, concerns are often expressed even in countries where criminal punishment is applied, as has been stressed by Benjamin E. Rosenberg, formerly the chief trial counsel for the New York Attorney General.[5] In order to criminalise conspiracy, it is necessary to specifically determine the scope of mental or physical involvement in the crime. Because it is normally difficult to present evidence of participation in a conspiracy (since it is necessary to rely on confessions by accomplices) and judgments are based on prior assessment because the actual acts have not yet taken place, this means that the judgment as to whether or not a crime has taken place can be unclear. This in turn is a factor that divides opinions concerning the criminalisation of conspiracy.

Japan provides an interesting case study of these concerns. While there were frequent arrests in Japan before the Second World War for suspicion of orchestrating illegal organisations (campaign groups that criticised the imperial family or the private ownership system) without any concrete evidence, in the post-war legal system the criminalisation of conspiracy has not been recognised other than in relation to crimes concerning insurrection (Penal Code, Articles 77 and 78) or revisions to domestic law in order to ratify international conventions on terrorism.[6] For this reason, severe resistance to the criminalisation of conspiracy can be seen in Japan.

This chapter provides an overview of this situation and then examines discussions in Japan concerning new efforts to establish conspiracy as a crime in order to ratify the Convention against Transnational Organized Crime – from the perspective of the government and civic groups as well as the viewpoint of international law scholars and practitioners. The discussion then introduces the situation in South Korea, where, like Japan, the Convention has not yet been ratified, in order to clarify the key issues that arise when developing domestic law to accompany the adoption of international law. The analysis suggests that if government policy is embedded in the historical context behind domestic criminal law, and these

---

[5] Benjamin E. Rosenberg, "Several Problems in Criminal Conspiracy Laws and Some Proposals for Reform", in *Criminal Law Bulletin*, 2007, vol. 43, no. 4, p. 427.

[6] Japan, Penal Code, Law No. 45, 1907, as amended, Arts. 77, 78 ('Japan, Penal Code').

provisions come into conflict with international criminal law, then this case study will offer useful ideas for considering how to reconcile these policies.

19.2. Terrorism Prevention and Excessive Information Collection by the United States

Countries around the world are becoming more vigilant towards terrorism. The interest of intelligence agencies that had focused on the movements of hypothetical enemies is now shifting to focus on the prevention of domestic terrorism. While each individual act of terrorism may not shock the security of a given country, once an act of terrorism occurs it compromises the country's credibility. And with the advance of globalisation, such damage is also becoming more multinational. For this reason, concern with terrorism has increased significantly since the beginning of the twenty-first century.

The 9/11 terrorist attacks were a major turning point that served to increase such concerns. The ongoing response of the United States to these risks covers an extremely wide scope, as this response is in some ways a continuation of the intelligence activities that were conducted during the Cold War before the 1990s. As the intelligence and national security expert, Mark M. Lowenthal, states: "Collection derives directly from requirements".[7] Desire is essential for the collection of information. Another way of stating this is that with rising concerns about terrorism there is also an increased imperative to collect information involving the daily life of the public. In particular, when the government of the United States viewed the widespread monitoring of telephones, email and so on as necessary to prevent terrorism at its early stages, it not only monitored members of the general public suspected of being implicated in crime but also became involved in mobile phone surveillance of the leader of a close ally.[8]

While the domestic Foreign Intelligence Surveillance Act of 1978 does not apply to Americans, whether someone is an American or a foreigner is not called into question for acts that represent a violation of Arti-

---

[7] Mark M. Lowenthal, *Intelligence: From Secrets to Policy*, CQ Press, Washington, DC, 2006, p.59.

[8] Mark Mazzetti and David E. Sanger, "Tap on Merkel Provides Peek at Vast Spy Net", in *New York Times*, 30 October 2013, p. A1.

cle 17 of the International Covenant on Civil and Political Rights.[9] However, due to major improvements in the information processing capabilities of analysis equipment, it is now possible to shift away from gathering crime information on only those who fall within a limited scope and adopt call recording and batch monitoring of emails of those with suspicious or important information. Furthermore, due to the fact that if a large volume of information is gathered it will contain important data, there have been many cases of privacy infringement as a result of gathering more information than necessary. Lowenthal also states that "[i]n the United States, collection outruns processing and exploitation".[10] If such a situation becomes excessive, it can cause a greater loss of confidence in the state than the actual occurrence of terrorism itself warrants. These concerns are then recognised as a reality as the result of the dissemination of various news stories, accusations,[11] reports[12] and so on.

19.3. Convention against Transnational Organized Crime

The Convention against Transnational Organized Crime aims for the international community as a whole to respond to crimes that cannot be dealt with through the criminal justice system of a single country, given the globalised nature of crime. In addition, it is widely recognised that international judicial co-operation cannot be established in order to achieve the objectives of the Convention unless the following tasks are addressed: 1) defining set criminal acts (a consensus on what constitutes serious crimes, money laundering, obstruction of justice and so on); 2) defining jurisdiction; 3) stipulating the confiscation of criminal proceeds; and 4) stipulating criminal extradition.

Especially now, when terrorism has become such a clear international threat, and even if the judicial process takes place after the fact, this means that terrorists will have achieved their objective of making a political statement or advancing their ideology by creating fear among citizens

---

[9] International Covenant on Civil and Political Rights, adopted 16 December 1966, United Nations Treaty Series, vol. 999, 1976, Art. 17, p. 177.

[10] Lowenthal, 2006, p. 60, see *supra* note 7.

[11] Glenn Greenwald, No Place to Hide: Edward Snowden, the NSA, and the U.S. Surveillance State, Metropolitan Books, New York, 2014.

[12] Gerhard Schmid, Report on the Existence of a Global System for the Interception of Private and Commercial Communications (ECHELON Interception System) (2001/2098(INI)), European Parliament, PE 205.391, A5-0264/2001, 11 July 2001.

and governments. For this reason, it is necessary to criminalise acts *before* terrorism takes place in order to prevent violence before the commission of the act. The important point here is deciding at which point actions should be criminalised. Even if a criminal act is aborted, it is necessary to go through several stages in order to perform an illegal act. For example, the execution phase of terrorism passes through the stages of 1) agreeing to conduct the act, 2) establishing a criminal group, 3) securing funds and 4) preparing materials. In this case, the Convention against Transnational Organized Crime enables criminalisation at the initial stage of agreeing to conduct the act. This stage is conspiracy, and the specific basis for it is described in Article 5(1)(a):

> Article 5. Criminalization of participation in an organized criminal group
>
> 1. Each State Party shall adopt such legislative and other measures as may be necessary to establish as criminal offences, when committed intentionally:
>
>   (a) Either or both of the following as criminal offences distinct from those involving the attempt or completion of the criminal activity:
>
>   (i) Agreeing with one or more other persons to commit a serious crime for a purpose relating directly or indirectly to the obtaining of a financial or other material benefit and, where required by domestic law, involving an act undertaken by one of the participants in furtherance of the agreement or involving an organized criminal group;
>
>   (ii) Conduct by a person who, with knowledge of either the aim and general criminal activity of an organized criminal group or its intention to commit the crimes in question, takes an active part in:
>
>   a. Criminal activities of the organized criminal group;
>
>   b. Other activities of the organized criminal group in the knowledge that his or her partic-

> ipation will contribute to the achievement of
> the above-described criminal aim.[13]

As can be inferred from the expression "Either or both of the following", the Article stipulates that conspiracy and participation in a criminal organisation are in fact interchangeable. It thus follows that it would be acceptable to adopt legislation for criminalising either conspiracy or participation in a criminal organisation in order to ratify the Convention against Transnational Organized Crime. In fact, ratifying countries such as the United States and United Kingdom have fulfilled the standards of the Convention by criminalising conspiracy, while Germany and France have fulfilled its standards by criminalising participation in a criminal organisation.

In Japan, because the concept of conspiracy is already present in Article 78 of the Penal Code, covering plots for insurrection, and Article 4 of the Explosives Control Act, that deals with conspiracy to use explosive materials, the Ministry of Justice views conspiracy as a more familiar concept than participation in a criminal organisation.[14] The Japanese legal system, including the Penal Code, has been influenced by both Anglo-American law and Continental law, so much so that Katsunori Kai has called the Penal Code "ultra-hybrid" in that it has been influenced by Germany, France, the United Kingdom, the United States and other countries.[15] In discussions on the legal system, while it is believed that criminalisation of participation in a criminal organisation could be accepted, because the Japanese government submitted a bill to criminalise conspiracy in order to ratify the Convention against Transnational Organized Crime discussions have tended to focus on the conspiracy provision.

---

[13] CTOC, Art. 5(1), see *supra* note 4.

[14] Japan, Penal Code, Art. 78, see *supra* note 6; Japan, Explosives Control Act, Act No. 149 of 1950, Art. 4. Ministry of Justice, Japan, "Reason for Not Selecting the Criminalisation of Participation in a Criminal Organisation" (http://www.moj.go.jp/keiji1/keiji_keiji35-5.html).

[15] Katsunori Kai, "Hikakuhouteki kanten karamita nihonkeihou no tokucho: Ultra-hybrid keiho toshiteno nihon keihou: Ida houkoku heno comment" [Characteristics of Japan's Penal Code from a Comparative Legal Perspective: Japan's Penal Code as an Ultra-hybrid Penal Code: Comment on the Ida Report], in Waseda University Institute of Comparative Law (ed.), *Nihonhou no nakano gaikokuhou: Kihonhou no hikakuhouteki kousatsu*, Waseda University Institute of Comparative Law, Tokyo, 2014.

19.4. Circumstances in Japan in Relation to the Criminalisation of Conspiracy

The risk of terrorism is a frequent topic of discussion in Japan. The world's attention focused on Japan in 1995 following Aum Shinrikyo's sarin gas attack on the Tokyo underground. Since then Japan has received several terrorist threats from al-Qaeda after announcing that it would support the so-called War on Terror led by the United States. For this reason, while the methods to be deployed in order to prevent terrorism are being discussed, opinions on how best to go about this are mixed due to strong concerns that the government will go too far with wiretapping and other monitoring measures that are essential for the criminalisation of conspiracy. Here we look at two opinions with regard to this point.

19.4.1. Confrontation between the Government and Civic Groups

Article 43 of the Penal Code primarily stipulates that "[t]he punishment of a person who commences a crime without completing it may be reduced; provided, however, that voluntary abandonment of commission of the crime, shall lead to the punishment being reduced or the offender being exculpated".[16] In other words, an attempted crime does not apply as long as an act is not commenced, excluding the specific crimes described above.

Under these circumstances, when the Japanese government signed the Convention against Transnational Organized Crime in December 2000 it selected the criminalisation of conspiracy in order to ratify the Convention. It then submitted cabinet-sponsored legislative bills to this effect to the Diet on three occasions, starting in 2003. However, each bill was abandoned. When a new resubmission was made in October 2005 as a cabinet-sponsored bill it was abandoned less than a year later. While the topic was subsequently raised at various times, including studies on making a submission to the Diet as an amended bill for the Act for Punishment of Organised Crimes, Control of Crime Proceeds and Other Matters, a concrete bill submission was not achieved.

In these circumstances, much attention was attracted when the cabinet of Prime Minister Koizumi Junichirō submitted a bill for the Partial Amendment to the Penal Code regarding the Internationalisation and Or-

---

[16] Japan, Penal Code, Art. 43, see *supra* note 6.

ganisation of Crimes and Advancement of Information Processing to the Diet in 2005. While the bill included 1) the new criminalisation of bribery of a witness, 2) offences for handling criminal proceeds as serious crimes, 3) the development of penalty provisions for bribery and related crimes committed abroad, and 4) the development of penalties for acts interfering with forcible execution, most attention was taken by references to the criminalisation of conspiracy. Particularly important was the Act on Punishment of Organised Crimes, Control of Crime Proceeds and Other Matters that was enacted in 1999 in response to the expanded scale and internationalisation of organised crimes, such as drug- and firearm-related crimes pursued criminal organisations, and the sarin gas attack on the Tokyo underground which caused a significant deterioration in public safety.[17] The new bill proposed the establishment of Article 6(2) concerning crimes that are subject to penal servitude or imprisonment of at least four years that would criminalise as conspiracy specified criminal acts. The contents of the bill are as follows:

> Individuals that act in conspiracy with an organization to execute the acts that constitute the crimes stated in each item below as group activities shall be sentenced with the penalty stipulated in each item. However, this penalty shall be reduced or waived for parties that voluntarily surrender before commencing the act.
>
> 1. Crimes for which the death penalty or life or maximum term penal servitude or imprisonment of ten years or more is stipulated: penal servitude or imprisonment of up to five years;
>
> 2. Crimes for which maximum term penal servitude or imprisonment of four years to ten years is stipulated: penal servitude or imprisonment of up to two years.

There was much criticism regarding this bill and it was actively debated in the Diet, the media and academic circles, as the government proposal was revised twice[18] while the opposition party also submitted a bill.

---

17. Japan, Act on Punishment of Organised Crimes, Control of Crime Proceeds and Other Matters, Law No. 136 of 1999.

18. The revised points were: 1) the charting of types of crime; 2) the inclusion of preparations for criminal acts within the scope of penalties; 3) limitations on punishments for parties that voluntarily surrender (related to crimes for which the death penalty or life or maximum-term penal servitude or imprisonment of five years or more is stipulated); 4) prohibi-

Outside parliament, the reaction of civic groups including bar associations was also very significant. In particular, the Japan Federation of Bar Associations played a leading role in the movement to debate the new bill. In September 2006 it released an opinion opposing the criminalisation of conspiracy, identifying four major criticisms.[19]

The primary claim of the Japan Federation of Bar Associations is that, based on the existing legal system, the authority of the state is put into motion only when there is an infringement of the law or a risk of such an infringement, and that this is what constitutes a modern, liberal criminal justice system. In particular, in the punishment of crimes in the penal system, the general rule is to punish acts that have already been committed, only punish attempts when necessary, and punish the concept of preparation before acts are commenced only in extremely rare exceptions for very serious crimes. The Japan Federation of Bar Associations claims that if the agreement to commit a crime were to be criminalised, it would newly enable arrests for over 600 acts, which would risk changing the principles of Japan's penal system. The second claim is that in the past the government argued during the deliberations on the Convention against Transnational Organized Crime at the United Nations that criminalising conspiracy would be contrary to the principles of domestic law. Furthermore, it was also stated that there were no provisions for the criminalisation of participation in a criminal organisation either.[20] Third, the Japan Federation of Bar Associations claims that it would be possible to handle parts of the Convention as a reservation and to make an interpretative declaration. They point out that it would be possible to handle Article 34(2) of the Convention as a reservation and introduce the criminalisation of conspiracy limited to crimes of a transnational nature.[21] Fourth, with re-

---

tion of infringement on the freedom thought and conscience; and 5) prohibition of limitations on the legitimate activities of labour unions and other organisations.

[19] Japan Federation of Bar Associations, "JFBA Opposes Criminalization of Conspiracy", 14 September 2006.

[20] First Session of the Ad Hoc Committee on the Elaboration of a Convention against Transnational Organized Crime, Proposals and Contributions Received from Governments, Vienna, 19–29 January 1999, A/AC.254/5/Add.3.

[21] CTOC, Art. 34(2), see *supra* note 4:

The offences established in accordance with articles 5, 6, 8 and 23 of this Convention shall be established in the domestic law of each State Party independently of the transnational nature or the involvement of an organized criminal group as described in article 3, paragard to the selection of Article 5(1)(a)(i) of the Convention against Transnational Organized Crime for all serious crimes involving organised criminal groups, as called for in Article 5(3),[22] there is already a law in place in Japan for punishment before attempting crimes established through agreement, and for this reason the Japan Federation of Bar Associations argues that it is unnecessary to revise the law in the first place.

While the Japan Federation of Bar Associations has made these legal comments, at the same time it also questioned the government's Japanese-language translation of the title of the Convention, suspicious that the government intended to make it easier to gain public consent for the criminalisation of conspiracy. Typically, the government prepares the translation of conventions and the translated title is used in both public and private documents. However, in the case of the translation of the word "transnational" in the Convention, while the government uses the word *kokusai* (international), the Japan Federation of Bar Associations and other organisations use the word *ekkyo* (transnational). In a standard English–Japanese dictionary, the *ekkyo* means to go across borders and is used for the word "transnational" while the word *kokusai* that means "international". *Kokusai* focuses on international co-operation, and for Japan that has an affinity with the thinking of the United States and Europe and is thus positioned as a positive term. For this reason, those opposed to the criminalisation of conspiracy suspect that by using the word *kokusai* the government is attempting to create the impression that the Convention is a positive thing. For this reason, the word *ekkyo* is often used in the Japanese title of documents, written from the perspective of opposition to the criminalisation of conspiracy. As a result, this is a source of confusion for those unaware of the background behind this choice of words.

---

graph 1, of this Convention, except to the extent that article 5 of this Convention would require the involvement of an organized criminal group.

[22] *Ibid.*, Art 5(3):

States Parties whose domestic law requires involvement of an organized criminal group for purposes of the offences established in accordance with paragraph 1(a)(i) of this article shall ensure that their domestic law covers all serious crimes involving organized criminal groups. Such States Parties, as well as States Parties whose domestic law requires an act in furtherance of the agreement for purposes of the offences established in accordance with paragraph 1(a)(i) of this article, shall so inform the Secretary-General of the United Nations at the time of their signature or of deposit of their instrument of ratification, acceptance or approval of or accession to this Convention.

19.4.2. Debate Between International Law Scholars and the Federation of Bar Associations

There has thus been a debate between the government and the Japan Federation of Bar Associations. As part of this debate, the international law scholar Furuya Shuichi released a study in 2008 focusing on an international law-based interpretation of the claim of the associations.[23] In response, a refutation was released by Kakuyama Tadashi, the former vice chairman of the Japan Federation of Bar Associations in 2009.[24] While Furuya argues that "it is clear when considering the Convention from the perspective of international law that the criminalisation of conspiracy (or participation in a criminal organisation) has to be introduced",[25] Kakuyama claims that the criminalisation of conspiracy would present "universal human rights issues".[26] There are both strong and weak points used to reach each of these conclusions. Because this debate clarifies many of the issues concerning the acceptance of the Convention against Transnational Organized Crime and international conventions in general domestic law, we introduce both arguments and examine their characteristics.

19.4.2.1. The Perspective of International Law: Furuya's Argument

Furuya's study examined the opinion released by the Japan Federation of Bar Associations in 2006. His main point is that, first and foremost, ratifying countries must criminalise either conspiracy or participation in a criminal organisation, or both, in domestic law. Furuya claims that the rationale for this is the Legislative Guides for the implementation of the Convention created by the United Nations.[27] The associations and other organisations use paragraph 51 of the Legislative Guides that states as a

---

[23] Shuichi Furuya, "Kokusai soshiki hanzai boshi joyaku to kyobozai no rippoka – kokusaiho no shiten kara" [UN Convention against Transnational Organized Crime and the Criminalization of Conspiracy: From the Viewpoint of International Law], in *Keisatsugakuronshu*, 2008, vol. 61, no. 6.

[24] Tadashi Kakuyama, "Kokusai soshiki hanzai boshi joyaku to kyobozai no rippoka no yohi" [The United Nations Convention against Transnational Organized Crime and the Necessity of Legislation Criminalizing Conspiracy], in *Jiyuutoseigi*, 2009, vol. 60, no. 8.

[25] Furuya, 2008, p.146, see *supra* note 23.

[26] Kakuyama, 2009, p.118, see *supra* note 24.

[27] United Nations Office on Drugs and Crime Division for Treaty Affairs, Legislative Guides for the Implementation of the United Nations Convention against Organized Crime and the Protocols Thereto, United Nations, 2004 ('Legislative Guides').

basis for opposing the criminalisation of conspiracy: "The options allow for effective action against organised criminal groups, without requiring the introduction of either notion – conspiracy or criminal association – in States that do not have the relevant legal concept". For his part, Furuya suggests that this argument can be refuted due to the fact that the phrase "without requiring the introduction of either notion" in the Legislative Guides is unclear. His claim is that Article 5 of the Convention against Transnational Organized Crime clearly stipulates the implementation of the criminalisation of conspiracy and/or criminal association as domestic law, and that this is also clarified in the wording from paragraphs 48 to 51 and the interpretation of the French version of the Legislative Guides: "*sans qu'il soit nécessaire d'introduire l'un ou l'autre concept*",[28] meaning "either or both". Furthermore, Furuya focuses on the statement "in accordance with fundamental principles of its domestic law" in Article 34(1) of the Convention, and responds to the claim that it would not be necessary to establish conspiracy as a crime if criminalisation is conducted in accordance with the basic principles of Japan's domestic law. Furuya's view is that, in consideration of the background leading to the establishment of the Convention, this means that the necessary measures should be taken in accordance with the legislative process of each country when establishing legislation as designated by the Convention and this does not refer to the basic principles of domestic law. Thus the scope of duties in Article 34 cannot be reduced.

Second, Furuya claims that the criminalisation of conspiracy in accordance with the Convention against Transnational Organized Crime cannot be limited to international crimes. There are parties opposed to the criminalisation of conspiracy, because paragraph 59 of the interpretative notes related to Article 34 of the Convention stipulates implementation as follows:

> The paragraph is intended to indicate to States Parties that, when implementing the Convention, they do not have to include in their criminalisation of laundering of criminal proceeds (article 6), corruption (article 8) or obstruction of justice (article 23) the elements of transnationality and in-

---

[28] Office des Nations Unies contre la drogue et le crime, Division des traités, Guide legislative pour l'application de la Convention des Nations Unies contre la criminalité transnationale organisée Office des Nations Unies contre la drogue et le crime, United Nations, 2004, para. 51, p. 19.

volvement of an organised criminal group, nor in the criminalisation in an organised criminal group (article 5) the element of transnationality.[29]

Critics therefore argue that the international nature of crimes serves
as the basis for the criminalisation of conspiracy including in domestic
law. In response to this, Furuya's view is that because there is a statement
to the effect that *transnationality* should be included, this can be understood as an expression of ambiguity stemming from confusion in the negotiating process or overhasty drafting. Furthermore, using the statements
in paragraphs 18, 31, 45 and 68, and the fact that the same phrasing is repeatedly used in the Legislative Guides, Furuya takes the position that it is
clear that transnationality is not included in criminalisation in the Convention.

Third, in response to the idea of ratification with a reservation and
an interpretative declaration, Furuya claims that this would not be possible in the case of Japan. Furuya argues that handling the whole of Article
5 as a reservation would not be possible as this would eliminate or change
the legal effect of the Convention. Furthermore, with regard to making an
interpretative declaration and reservation to the effect of "ratification for
major crimes of a transnational nature" in response to Article 34(2) that
states it "shall be established in the domestic law of each State Party independently of the transnational nature or the involvement of an organised
criminal group", Furuya claims that because it is clear that, based on the
interpretation of the Convention, the scope of crimes does not include
transnationality as previously stated, no other interpretation would be possible.

Finally, Furuya makes a specific comment regarding reservations.
In response to the Convention, the United States commented that federal
criminal law regulates acts concerning commerce between states and with
foreign countries. As a consequence, it has made a reservation for cases in
which it is not possible to fulfil the obligations of the Convention for
crimes within states that fall within the jurisdiction of state law. While the
reservation made by the United States does not designate a specific provi-

---

[29] United Nations General Assembly, Report of the Ad Hoc Committee on the Elaboration of
a Convention against Organized Crime on the work of its first to eleventh sessions, Interpretative notes for the official records (travaux préparatoires) of the negotiation of the
United Nations Convention against Transnational Organized Crime and the Protocols, UN
doc. A/55/383/Add.1, 3 November 2000, para. 59, p. 11.

sion, it is believed to be a reservation concerning Article 34(2). In response to this, Furuya views the reason for this reservation as understandable because it is an issue that involves the fundamentals of the constitutional legal system of the United States, that is, a federal system. In contrast, because the reservation that would be made by parties in opposing the criminalisation of conspiracy in Japan would only be based on political grounds, due in part to the Convention being contrary to the tradition of Japan's penal system, Furuya claims that such a reservation would be contradictory to the intentions and objectives of the Convention against Transnational Organized Crime.

19.4.2.2. Opposition to Conspiracy as a Crime: Kakuyama's Argument

In response to Furuya's argument against the Japan Federation of Bar Associations, Kakuyama has provided a refutation. First, he claims that Japan already has a method for preventing crime prior to its commission established by a domestic agreement on all serious crimes involving organised criminal groups, as identified in Article 5(3). The points raised by Kakuyama are as follows: 1) the preparation of a crime, conspiracy and so on have already been criminalised as serious crimes; 2) there are precedents and legal theories in which parties that only participated in the decision-making process and did not participate in the execution have been viewed as having jointly executed the crime; 3) there are penalty provisions for conspiracy involving terrorism; and 4) there are strict penalty provisions for possession of firearms whether or not there is criminal intent. Kakuyama claims that there is no need to criminalise conspiracy and participation in a criminal organisation if these factors and the wording of paragraph 51 of the Legislative Guides are taken into consideration. Furthermore, he argues that the correct understanding of paragraph 43 of the Legislative Guides is that the meaning and spirit of the Convention are more important than the phrasing, and that legislation should be made in accordance with the legal system of each respective country.[30] Kakuyama

---

[30] Legislative Guides, para. 43, p. 18, see *supra* note 27:

National drafters should focus on the meaning and spirit of the Convention rather than attempt simply to translate Convention text or include it verbatim in new laws or amendments. The drafting and enforcement of the new offences, including legal defences and other legal principles, are left to the States parties (see art. 11, para. 6). Therefore, they must ensure that the new rules are consistent with their domestic legal tradition, principles

claims that from this perspective it is difficult to make rigidly uniform interpretations based on the Convention itself, and these circumstances are described by the Legislative Guides as well. In addition, in response to the difference in interpretation of the French version of the Legislative Guides mentioned by Furuya, Kakuyama claims this is representative of the ambiguous nature of the Legislative Guides themselves.

Second, Kakuyama argues that it would be possible to make transnationality a requirement for applicable crimes. As already noted, Furuya did not focus on the interpretative notes for the Convention against Transnational Organized Crime due to their ambiguity, and used the Legislative Guides as the rationale for his argument. Kakuyama views this stance as arbitrary. On top of that, because the purpose of the Convention itself is stated in Article 1 as "to promote cooperation to prevent and combat transnational organised crime more effectively", and because making a reservation limited to transnationality would fall under Article 19(c) of the Vienna Convention on the Law of Treaties that states "in cases not falling under sub-paragraphs (a) and (b), the reservation is incompatible with the object and purpose of the treaty", a reservation in this case would fulfil this criterion.

Third, Kakuyama makes a claim regarding phrasing concerning the relationship between the basic principles of domestic law and the obligations of the Convention. According to Furuya, the reservation towards the Convention by the United States was recognised because there were obligations that could not be performed due to constitutional law, despite having made every effort as a federal government. In contrast, Kakuyama claims that establishing penal laws that excessively infringe on the freedom of thought, expression and association in Japan's response to the Convention would not be possible in accordance with the country's constitution. With regard to this point, if one views undocumented basic principles of domestic law as having actual legal significance, this is synonymous with the inclusion of constitutional constraints, and Kakuyama points out that Furuya also recognised this principle in his paper.[31]

19.4.2.3. Summary

---

and fundamental laws. This avoids the risk of conflicts and uncertainty about the interpretation of the new provisions by courts or judges.

[31] Furuya, 2008, p.164, see *supra* note 23.

It is now possible to assess the statements made in the two arguments. In terms of the primary issue concerning whether to select the criminalisation of conspiracy or participation in a criminal organisation upon ratification of the Convention against Transnational Organized Crime, if one reads the actual Convention, no other option is presented. A clear judgment can be made without having to refer to the discussions in the Legislative Guides. Of course, because there are countries that have ratified the Convention without establishing new domestic law, it is difficult to assess what the reality is. However, looking at the law itself, if the Convention is ratified it calls for the criminalisation of either conspiracy or participation in a criminal organisation.

Regarding the debate on limiting transnationality, as Furuya commented – "it is not clear, and opinions are divided in Japan in debates concerning this issue"[32] – it is difficult to make a clear judgment.

In terms of the relationship between the principles of domestic law and reservations on the Convention, if there are conflicts between the interpretations and basic policies of Japan's domestic law and the Convention it would be difficult to view the establishment of a reservation as solely a government policy issue. The reason this issue was widely debated in Japan is that the idea became widespread that the Convention differed from Japan's legal principles and basic policies. (This perspective also relates to the comparison with South Korea, examined below.)

Lastly, what is being considered in the statements of the Japan Federation of Bar Associations and Kakuyama are the concerns towards the criminalisation of conspiracy, and that an argument is not being made against responding to international organised crime. Their fundamental claim is that it would be risky to criminalise conspiracy in a manner that is not consistent with Japan's penal law system, and that what should be done should be discussed in order to avoid the establishment of such laws while at the same time also ratifying the Convention.

19.5. Comparison of Japan and South Korea: Criminalisation of Conspiracy

The situation in South Korea can serve as a comparison for the debate around the criminalisation of conspiracy in order to ratify the Convention

---

32 *Ibid.*, p. 158.

against Transnational Organized Crime in Japan. Because South Korea was once under Japanese colonial rule, the country's elite studied in Japanese higher education institutions and formed a legal community out of this experience. For this reason, the Japanese legal system has left a strong mark on that of South Korea, even after independence. The content of legal provisions and overall structure are very similar for the nationality laws of both countries that are covered in this chapter.[33] Furthermore, there is an affinity between South Korea and Japan in terms of the awareness of the risk of terrorism due to factors such as terrorist attacks by North Korea and both countries being designated as a target by al-Qaeda due to their support for the War on Terror. The differences in Japanese and South Korean responses towards the criminalisation of conspiracy, despite their comparable legal systems and a similar awareness of the risks of terrorism, make clear not only the characteristics of Japan but also issues in the process of ratifying international criminal law and developing it into domestic law.

19.5.1. Circumstances in South Korea Relating to the Criminalisation of Conspiracy

South Korea signed the Convention against Transnational Organized Crime in 2000, just like Japan, but has yet to ratify it. Among the 34 member countries of the Organisation for Economic Co-operation and Development ('OECD'), this is a position unique to South Korea and Japan; the other 32 countries have already ratified the Convention.[34]

Article 25(1) of South Korea's Criminal Act (or Penal Code) concerning a criminal intention stipulates: "When an intended crime is not completed or if the intended result does not occur, it shall be punishable as an attempted crime".[35] And concerning conspiracy and preparation Article 28 stipulates: "When a conspiracy or the preparatory action for a crime has not reached the commencement stage for the commission of the

---

[33] Hae Kyung Kim, "Kankoku no kokusekiho niokeru tabunka kazoku no hoteki kadai – nihon tono hikaku no shiten kara" [The Legal Issues of the Multicultural Family through the Korean Nationality Act: A Comparison with Japan], in *Ajia Taiheiyo Toukyu*, 2013, vol. 20, pp. 347–48.

[34] CTOC, Status of Ratification, Acceptance, Approval, Accession, Succession, see *supra* note 4.

[35] Republic of Korea, Criminal Act, Act No. 293, 18 September 1953, as amended, Art. 25(1).

crime, the person shall not be punishable, except as otherwise provided by Acts".[36] In this manner, it is stipulated that attempted crime should not be punishable as long as actions are not commenced, in the same manner as the law in Japan. The National Security Law that was first enacted in 1948, just three and a half months after the foundation of the Republic of (South) Korea, was established for the purpose of securing the safety of the nation and the survival and freedom of its citizens by regulating anti-state activities that could threaten the security of the country.[37] Article 3 imposes penalties on preparations for and conspiracy with anti-state activities. This constitutes the special provisions in Article 28 of the Criminal Act. In other words, just as in Japan, in South Korea's legal system acts must be commenced to be recognised as attempted crimes, and crimes with the intention to overturn the state are recognised as conspiracy crimes.

Looking broadly at these conditions, one might think that the Convention against Transnational Organized Crime has not been ratified as a result of an inability to accept the criminalisation of conspiracy due to the similarities in basic legal policy in both South Korea and Japan. However, the actual circumstances are different. According to the penal law scholar, Shin Eui Gi, the reason that South Korea has not ratified the Convention is as follows:

> In 2000 the United Nations adopted the Convention against Transnational Organized Crime and its additional protocols, and while South Korea signed the Convention, it has still not ratified the Convention because domestic law has not been developed yet. In order to implement this Convention, the task is to develop domestic law and in turn formulate comprehensive legislation to prevent all organized crimes, not only international organized crime, and to eliminate organized crime by doing so.[38]

---

[36] *Ibid.*, Art. 28.

[37] Republic of Korea, National Security Act, Law No. 3318 (1980), as revised by Law No. 4373 (1991).

[38] Eui Gi Shin, "Gugje jojigbeomjoe bangji hyeobyag ui gugnae ihaengbangan yeongu" [Legislative Introduction Programme of the United Nations Convention against Transnational Organized Crime], in *Hangug hyeongsa jeongchaeg yeonguwon* [Korean Institute of Criminology] *Yeongu chongseo*, 2005, 05–27, p. 25.

In other words, there is not much of a sense of a "crisis" regarding international organised crime in South Korea. And for this reason legislation in line with international demands has yet to be developed.

Furthermore, there is no significant awareness in South Korea of the circumstances surrounding conspiracy crimes as a pressing issue for the country. For example, an article in the newspaper *Kukmin Ilbo* on the development of a bill criminalising conspiracy in Japan expressed some concerns: "What does the Japanese government intend to do by going so far as to deceive its citizens in order to criminalise conspiracy? It looks to be an excessively punitive law that will cover a total of 619 types of crimes".[39] However, the article did not go as far as saying that the same thing would happen in South Korea if it ratified the Convention against Transnational Organized Crime. In other words, it could be said that there is not much momentum in the legal system or public opinion in South Korea towards discussing the criminalisation of conspiracy or ratifying the Convention.

Two salient points can be considered here: 1) the kind of stance South Korea has towards monitoring its own citizens and crimes related to conspiracy compared to Japan; and 2) whether South Korea is more hesitant towards the criminalisation of organised crime activities compared to Japan (or other countries). South Korea enacted the National Security Act before the Criminal Act. The National Security Act was modelled on Japan's Peace Preservation Act that has come into force in 1925 and which was directed explicitly against political opponents.[40] There has been much criticism that, in a similar way, the Korean National Security Act was used in the period from the 1960s to the 1980s against people and organisations that opposed the military-dominated government. Then, following the achievement of democratisation in the 1990s, there were frequently proposals from reformist politicians for the abolition or amendment of the National Security Act. A decision was made on its constitutionality by the Constitutional Court in 2004 and by the Supreme Court in 2010 to retain the law;[41] and even in public opinion polls, people calling for the its abolition are in a minority.[42]

---

[39] "Gongmojoe" [Conspiracy], in *Kukmin Ilbo*, 22 November 2006.

[40] Japan, Peace Preservation Act, 12 April 1925.

[41] Constitutional Court of Korea, Petition for the Unconstitutionality of Article 7 Paragraph 1 of the National Security Law, etc., 26 August 2004, Law Reports, vol. 16, no. 2, p. 297. Supreme Court of Korea, Obstructing and Injuring Special Official Duty Execution, Ob-

We can also compare South Korea with Japan in terms of the monitoring of citizens through an examination of the Protection of Communications Secrets Act.[43] In the past, wiretapping was used in South Korea in order to crack down on dissidents. The Communications Secrecy Protection Act was established in 1993 in response to criticism of these past abuses. While the basic intent of the law is to protect the secrecy and freedom of the communications of citizens, as an exception it stipulates the scope of crimes for which wiretapping by state institutions is permitted and the court approval procedures when conducting wiretapping. However, there is also an emergency monitoring system that makes it possible to commence wiretapping without the court's permission as long as notice is provided within 36 hours. In addition, wiretapping is also permitted for those crimes stipulated in the National Security Act, including treason, conspiracy against the country by granting military privileges, crimes involving diplomatic relations, crimes involving public safety, crimes involving explosives, and crimes involving drinking water. In contrast, Japan's Act on Communications Interception During Criminal Investigations only stipulates four types of crime subject to wiretapping in Article 3(1): 1) drug-related crimes; 2) firearms-related crimes; 3) collective stowaways; and 4) searches for murders conducted by organisations. It is clear that the scope of wiretapping in South Korea is quite broad in comparison.[44]

South Korea has been proactive in relation to ratifying international legal provisions regarding money laundering. During the 1990s it developed legislation in reference to the legal system in Japan that had been developed in advance of these systems.[45] South Korea received recom-

---

structing General Traffic, Violation of National Security Law (Praising, Incitement, Etc.), Violation of Laws Concerning Assembly and Demonstration, 23 July 2010, Judgment 2010–1189, based on decision of all court members.

[42] "Yeolonjosa: Gugga boanbeob gaejeong 66%, pyeji 14%" [Public Opinion Poll: National Security Law Reform 66%, Abolition 14%], in *Chosun Ilbo*, 7 September 2004.

[43] Republic of Korea, Protection of Communications Secrets Act, Presidential Decree No. 14289, 28 June 1994.

[44] Japan, Law Regarding the Interception of Communications for Criminal Investigations, Law No. 137, 18 August 1999, Art. 3(1).

[45] Hae Kyung Kim, "Kankoku niokeru Money Laundering kanrenho no tokusei: Kokusaiteki yosei heno tenkan ga motarashita koka" [Characteristics of Money Laundering Laws in South Korea: Effects Resulting in the Conversion to International Demands], in *Horitsuronso*, 2015, vol. 87, nos. 4/5.

mendations from the intergovernmental Financial Action Task Force on Money Laundering ('FATF') that regulates international money laundering. With the passing of the Act on Reporting and Use of Information Concerning Certain Financial Transactions[46] and the Act on Regulation and Punishment of Concealment of Crime Proceeds[47] in 2001, South Korea made clear a stance in responding to international demands rather than basing its statutes on Japanese law. On the other hand, in June 2014 the FATF made the following comment concerning Japan: "failure to remedy the numerous and serious deficiencies identified in FATF's third mutual evaluation report adopted in October 2008".[48] In contrast, South Korea has received no such recommendations. In other words, in the field of money laundering, South Korea is developing legal systems in line with international standards. Thus it can be said that South Korea is being proactive towards the criminalisation of organised crime. Furthermore, looking at the status of the ratification of the 13 conventions relating to the prevention of international terrorism, as of March 2015 both South Korea and Japan have ratified all these conventions, demonstrating a cooperative stance towards international terrorism prevention systems. In other words, the characteristics of South Korea are apparent in the differences between money laundering and other terrorism countermeasures and international organised crime countermeasures.

From this point of view, in terms of the criminalisation of conspiracy, while South Korea does have a legal system similar to that in Japan, the wiretapping that is a prerequisite for the criminalisation of conspiracy is broadly recognised as legitimate in South Korea. In contrast, there are South Korean concerns about Japan having such tendencies, and there is some hesitation in relation to the ratification of the Convention against Transnational Organized Crime. It can thus be seen that the South Korean situation is different to that in Japan, where the importance of dealing with organised crime and international co-operation is understood, but

---

[46] Republic of Korea, Act on Reporting and Use of Information Concerning Certain Financial Transactions, Act No. 6516, 27 September 2001, as amended.

[47] Republic of Korea, Act on Regulation and Punishment of Concealment of Crime Proceeds, Act No. 6517, 27 September 2001, as amended.

[48] Financial Action Task Force on Money Laundering, "FATF Calls on Japan to enact adequate anti-money laundering and counter terrorist financing legislation", n.d. ('FATF'). Financial Action Task Force on Money Laundering, *Third Mutual Evaluation Report: Money Laundering and Combating the Financing of Terrorism: Japan*, FATF Secretariat, Paris, 2008.

where differences between the penal law system and policy prevent the Convention being ratified, with the criminalisation of conspiracy as the largest issue. However, it is an oversimplification to say that while the protection of human rights is valued in Japan it is disregarded in South Korea. For this reason, we need to examine how this situation can be interpreted from the perspective of the law in terms of what kind of impact a state's basic policy, including constitutional law, has on the acceptance of international criminal law.

19.5.2. Differences in Basic State Policies in Japan and South Korea

The basis of the analysis of state policies here is a sociological interpretation. The reason for this is that when looking at the different responses towards the criminalisation of conspiracy in Japan and South Korea, a comparison of the provisions in legislation alone may not clarify matters. As already shown, while the content of penal law and basic principles were viewed as issues in Japan, a different response occurred in South Korea despite the fact that it has similar state laws and legislation. Therefore, a sociological approach can help to understand the social factors that result in different interpretations of similar provisions.

19.5.2.1. Basic Policy in Post-War Japan

Since Japan's Penal Code came into effect in 1908, a number of revisions have been made up to the present. While the reasons for revisions include the diversification of crime, changes in techniques and responses to various conventions, the most significant amendment was conducted in October 1947 following the Second World War. The purpose of this revision was to make the Penal Code consistent with the spirit of the Constitution of Japan that came into effect in May 1947. However, there have been no revisions made concerning clauses on attempted crimes, and these clauses have been kept as they were. In other words, it was not until modern times that the position of attempted crimes in the Penal Code became established.

However, in pre-war Japan, conspiracy at the stage before attempted crimes was broadly criminalised. The freedom of thought and conscience (Article 19) and the freedom of assembly and association as well as speech, press and all other forms of expression (Article 21) that are currently protected by the Constitution were not recognised at that time.[49] Those who opposed the government, and socialists, communists and anarchists in particular, were subject to oppression. This was particularly the case for the Peace Preservation Act that was enforced in 1925, which criminalised and levied penalties on participation in a criminal organisation.[50] Because targets would adopt an organised defence, the government conducted acts such as wiretapping, internal infiltration, and using informants mainly through police agencies such as the Special Higher Police in order to find their targets. It was not uncommon for arrestees to be tortured, and there were many cases of deaths.

Because of this historical background, reflections on the period before the war, as well as the existence of the Peace Preservation Act and Special Higher Police, are extremely sensitive issues in Japan.[51] As a consequence, there is strong opposition to the use of wiretaps and informants in order to prove conspiracy crimes. In addition, this sense of risk does not simply stop at the penal law system, as many also believe that search activities associated with the criminalisation of conspiracy and of the forming of criminal organisations would be incompatible with the spirit of the current Constitution. These perspectives have given momentum to the opposition movement. In terms of specific examples, the Japan Federation of Bar Associations has branches across the country, many of which have made statements in opposition to the criminalisation of conspiracy. Some organisations have pointed out the connections between the criminalisation of conspiracy and the Peace Preservation Act,[52] and the assertions of civic groups and the mass media tend to be increasingly adopting this point of view. Furthermore, the Japan Federation of Bar Associations has made a statement in opposition to all criminalisation of conspiracy, arguing that such an initiative runs the risk of infringing on the fundamental

---

[49] Japan, Penal Code, Arts. 19, 21, see *supra* note 6.

[50] Japan, Peace Preservation Act, see *supra* note 40.

[51] The Peace Preservation Act and Special Higher Police were abolished and disbanded in accordance with a human rights directive issued in October 1945 immediately after the arrival of the General Headquarters, the Supreme Commander for the Allied Powers that temporarily administered Japan following the Second World War and also played a leading role in the formulation of the Constitution.

[52] Yamaguchi Bar Association, "Voice of Chairman in Opposition to the New Establishment of Conspiracy as a Crime", 7 December 2005; and Hyogo-Ken Bar Association, "Repeated Opinion in Opposition to the New Establishment of Conspiracy as a Crime", 3 October 2005.

human rights stipulated by the Constitution, such as the freedom of thought and the freedom of association.

Considering these circumstances, it is apparent that opposition to the criminalisation of conspiracy in Japan is strongly related to respect for fundamental human rights that serves as the basic constitutional concept that was established following the Second World War. In other words, as can be seen in Kakuyama argument, opposition to the criminalisation of conspiracy in Japan can be viewed as a Constitution-related issue.

19.5.2.2. Basic Policy in South Korea Following Independence

When considering social conditions in South Korea related to the law and historic background from modern to contemporary times, one should understand that for nearly half a century the country underwent hardships and people had barely enough to survive. Specifically, South Korea was under Japanese colonial rule from 1910 to 1945, had a short period of independence as the Korean peninsula was then divided between the North and South from 1948 onwards, and had to deal with the Korean War from 1950 to 1953. Furthermore, even as conflicts over the North–South divide continued, South Koreans shared a sense of pride in their ongoing independence and also in the rapid economic development that they achieved in the face of these conditions.

In relation to the ratification of the Convention against Transnational Organized Crime, South Korea is wary of the criminalisation of conspiracy in Japan, and at the same time the scope of wiretapping in its own political system is broader than it is in Japan. Second, while there is hesitation in South Korea towards organised crime countermeasures, the country is more proactive in the development of laws in response to money laundering than Japan. How can these differences be explained?

First, it is necessary to think about the impact of North Korea when considering the focus on wiretapping and other measures in South Korea. One of the reasons for the establishment of the National Security Act was the fact that while South Korea was being established, there were uprisings by armed forces within the South that supported North Korea. This led to the state having to fight its own citizens, resulting, it is said, in tens of thousands of deaths. In an attempt to achieve stability, the Rhee Syngman administration (1948–1960) enacted the National Security Law five years ahead of the Criminal Act of 1953. From this, one can discern a policy aimed at prioritising ideological unification of the state and stability over the creation of a penal law system.

Subsequently, the Korean War fought between North and South Korea and their respective allies from 1950 began to grow in scale, leading to the involvement of United Nations forces and the Chinese military. The war led to the destruction of the country, in response to which an agreement was signed in 1953 between the commander-in-chief of the United Nations Command, on the one hand, and the supreme commander of the Korean People's Army and the commander of the Chinese People's Volunteer Army, on the other, concerning a military armistice in the peninsular, the Korean Armistice Agreement. The preamble of the Armistice states: "the objective of establishing an armistice which will insure a complete cessation of hostilities and of all acts of armed force in Korea until a final peaceful settlement is achieved".[53] However, a peaceful settlement between the two countries has still not been achieved, and intermittent fighting and clashes continue. Examples include the North Korean army making a failed attempt to invade the official residence of the South Korea's prime minister in 1968, a North Korean submarine landing on South Korean territory and a North Korean army attack in 1996, a North Korean missile launch in 2010, as well as several small- to medium-scale exchanges of gunfire in the border areas. For this reason, although over 60 years have passed since the signing of the Korean Armistice Agreement, people in South Korea are still very wary about the North.

As a result of these concerns, there is still military conscription in South Korea and there are frequent evacuation drills conducted on a nationwide scale for everyone living in the South. Unsurprisingly, more people in South Korea feel that wiretapping and monitoring in accordance with the National Security Act and other laws that are countermeasures against North Korea are in fact reasonable. An incident that clearly demonstrates this occurred in 2014. A leading member of the left-wing Unified Progressive Party who was elected to the National Assembly in 2012 was accused of plotting an insurrection and violating the National Security Act for conspiring with party members to work together with North Korea to destroy core facilities in the South and overthrow the government. In December 2014 this opposition party was ordered to disband

---

[53] Armistice Agreement for the Restoration of the South Korean State, 27 July 1953, Preamble.

by the Constitutional Court and the National Election Commission cancelled its party registration. As a result, the Unified Progressive Party was instantly dissolved and five opposition party members lost their seats as members of the National Assembly. Although some of the details of the incident are unclear, this incident indicates that association with North Korea may take precedence in decisions by the Constitutional Court. In this regard, Article 8(1) of the Constitution states: "All citizens enjoy the freedom of speech and the press, and of assembly and association". In contrast, Article 21(4) states: "If the purposes or activities of a political party are contrary to the fundamental democratic order, the Government may bring action against it in the Constitutional Court for its dissolution, and, the political party is dissolved in accordance with the decision of the Constitutional Court".[54] In other words, opposition to North Korea has an extremely important position in South Korean politics and law, even within the Constitution as the basic of the country.

It is also necessary to consider South Korea's recognition of Japan. The preambles of laws generally state matters such as the purpose for establishing the law and basic principles; and the first sentence of the preamble expresses the starting point for the basic principles of the country. Looking at the preamble of the South Korean Constitution, one can understand its stance towards Japan. The preamble begins with the following statement: "We, the people of Korea, proud of a resplendent history and traditions dating from time immemorial, upholding the cause of the Provisional Republic of Korea Government born of the March First Independence Movement of 1919".[55] The March First Independence Movement of 1919 refers to the movement of independence from Japan. In other words, just as the first sentence of the preamble of the Japanese Constitution which states "never again shall we be visited with the horrors of war through the action of government" expresses the determination to break away from the pre-war Japanese government,[56] the foundational document of South Korea focuses on independence from Japan, which was an imperial country. Another way of putting this is that there is wariness in South Korea towards Japan regressing to what it was before the Second World War. This awareness combined with suspicion towards North Ko-

---

[54] Republic of Korea, Constitution, adopted 17 July 1948, Arts. 8(1) and 21(4).
[55] *Ibid.*, Preamble.
[56] Japan, Constitution, 3 May 1947, Preamble.

rea. This has led to what at first seems to be a conflicting attitude of South Korean people of tolerance towards wiretaps, and concerns towards Japan deciding to act in the same manner.

Why is South Korea proactive towards money laundering counter-measures, but not equally proactive towards international organised crime countermeasures? South Korea changed its money laundering counter-measures in response to increased concerns in 2000 that it would be des-ignated by the FATF as one of the non-cooperative countries and territo-ries.[57] Because international restrictions apply concerning various finan-cial transactions once a country is listed as such, South Korea feared that such a designation would have a negative impact on its external credit-worthiness. What was most serious for South Korea was the FATF's per-ception that it was non-cooperative in the global fight against money laundering and terrorist financing. As already noted, the FATF is an inter-governmental organisation that regulates money laundering, including terrorism countermeasures, and while it is positioned as a separate organi-sation from the OECD, there is an FATF Council within the OECD Council. Furthermore, compared to the member countries of the OECD that include middle-sized and emerging economies such as those of East-ern Europe, Chile and Israel, the FATF member countries consist of ad-vanced countries and large countries that include China, Hong Kong, Sin-gapore, Brazil, Russia and India. For this reason, being designated a non-cooperative country represented a threat to South Korea's prestige as an advanced country.

For South Korea, which had aimed to cast off its status as a middle-sized or emerging economy by joining the OECD in 1996 and joining the FATF in 2009, its long-held desire was to be recognised as an advanced country at the global level. Among other things, this would be seen as proof of superiority over North Korea and of overcoming the negative image of being formerly under Japanese colonial rule. With the inaugura-tion of President Kim Young-sam in February 1993 – the first civilian administration in over 30 years – the goals of establishing a new South Korea and becoming an advanced country were set, including the launch-

---

[57] "Hangug, jageum setagbangji bihyeobjo gugga jijeong ganeungseong" [Possibility of South Korea Being Designated as a Non-cooperation State in Money Laundering Preven-tion], in *Chungang Ilbo*, 12 February 2001.

ing of a new five-year plan (1993–1997) with the goal of achieving advanced country status.[58]

Later presidents also pursued this trajectory. For example, in the inaugural speech of President Lee Myung-bak in 2008, he first highlighted all the hardships the country had experienced since its foundation, and then stated: "That is how one of the poorest countries in the world has come to bid for its place among the 10 largest economies in the world ... and stand shoulder to shoulder with the most advanced countries". In addition, the title of the speech itself was "Together We Shall Open a Road to Advancement".[59] In other words, being an advanced country is a source of pride for the people of South Korea and actions aimed at becoming a FATF member for more substantial recognition as an advanced country have been consistent with the country's overall goals. Furthermore, meeting the criteria for the money laundering countermeasures called for by the FATF can also be seen as meeting international demands, and they could be considered as easy to accept for this reason. Conversely, in the case of ratification of the Convention against Transnational Organized Crime, as indicated by the adoption of the convention in the United Nations General Assembly, what is being called for is not external legal force, but merely a stance as a country towards organised crime.

On the other hand, Japan's countermeasures towards international money laundering have not been very positively received internationally, as previously noted. According to the FATF, the issues concerning Japan are as follows:

> The most important deficiencies deal with the incomplete criminalization of terrorist financing, the lack of satisfactory customer due diligence requirements and other obligations in the area of preventive measures applicable to the financial and non-financial sectors, the incomplete mechanism for the freezing of terrorist assets, and the failure to ratify and fully implement the Palermo Convention.[60]

Based on this, it is apparent that Japan has not met international demands with regard to this matter. While the FATF has issued

---

[58] Gugga gilogwon, "Sin gyeongje 5gaenyeon gyehoeg (93–97)" [New Economic Five-Year Plan (93–97)], 1993.

[59] Lee Myung-bak, Inaugural Address, "Together We Shall Open a Road to Advancement", 25 February 2008.

[60] FATF, n.d., see *supra* note 48.

recommendations to Japan in the past, this has led to business people responding with the view that it is not necessary to follow foreign pressures because Japan has its own economic practices.[61] From this response, one can infer the way of thinking in which external interference with its own development strategies is not viewed favourably because Japan has already established a position as a major economic power. In addition, since Japan has been a member country since the launch of the FATF, some people believe that while not following FATF recommendations may have a negative impact on Japan's international reputation it will not lead to a loss of its creditworthiness. For this reason, Japan has not conducted money laundering countermeasures in the same way that South Korea has, and Japan has supported conventions related to the prevention of international terrorism.

Looking at the situation in Japan and South Korea it is apparent that matters not clearly stipulated in laws and basic principles have a significant effect on the ratification of conventions and the acceptance of international measures and demands. In particular, both Japan and South Korea underwent critical junctures as nations in the late 1940s, and the national guidelines created in response to the demands of the citizens at that time have value as unwritten law. Of course, while simple legal frameworks that are undeveloped should be revised, for the ratification of the Convention against Transnational Organized Crime it will likely be necessary for both countries to create domestic law in accordance with the basic legal philosophy that holds in each country.

19.6. Conclusion

Concerns about international terrorism have grown recently. As a result, the number of countries ratifying the Convention against Transnational Organized Crime has increased. The criminalisation of conspiracy or of the forming of criminal organisations has been adopted as a valid strategy in response to terrorism. To be sure, advanced responses could be effective against the current form of terrorism that tends to randomly target large numbers of people. However, in Japan's response to the criminalisa-

---

[61] Hae Kyung Kim, "Kokusai torihiki niokeru fuseina shikin ido kisei nikansuru ichikosatsu: Tero taisaku juyo niokeru nihon no kadai" [A Study on the Regulation of Illicit Fund Movement in International Trades: Continuing Issues for Japan in Accommodating Anti-terrorism Measures], in *Horitsuronso*, 2014, vol. 86, nos. 4/5, p. 37.

tion of conspiracy, it is clear that there are issues regarding the acceptance of international law in domestic law. Generally, international law represents the norms of the international community, and it is effective in indicating the policy towards concepts that should be achieved. On the other hand, for Japan, which has a basic state policy based on past reflections, accepting the criminalisation of conspiracy is viewed as a step backwards with regard to an awareness of human rights. This means that there is some discordance with the general position of international law. As can be seen in the establishment of the International Criminal Court, international criminal law is becoming more and more efficacious. When considering the position of international law as public prescriptive law, the questioning of the convention triggered by the basic principles of domestic law in Japan suggests that the development of international criminal law does not only advance, as revalidation is called for at times.

In response to this situation, there is debate as to whether all provisions should be fully accepted in accordance with the provisions of international law or whether reservation should be recognised. However, looking at the current situation in Japan, it would be difficult to recognise the establishment of conspiracy as a crime exactly as called for in the provisions, and the creation of a new bill as stated in the Convention against Transnational Organized Crime would again cause much debate. But if the situation remains as it is, it will mean that Japan will not have a legal system sufficient for preventing in advance international terrorism and other organised crimes of a transnational scale, and that it would be easier for organisations considering such crimes to make Japan their base. The United Nations and international community that have adopted the Convention against Transnational Organized Crime need to compare and consider that risk with the current state of Japan in which the domestic law issue relating to the criminalisation of conspiracy has continued unresolved for more than a decade. In other words, the question is whether to prioritise the risk that international terrorism and transnational organised crime pose to countries around the world or to prioritise calling for a resolution of the debate regarding Japan's legal system. Considering the current situation, in order to improve the effectiveness of international countermeasures, recognising a reservation by Japan and countering international organised crime and terrorism could be an effective option.

20

Mitigating Circumstances in
International Criminal Sentencing

ZHANG Binxin[*]

20.1. Introduction

Since the establishment and operationalisation of the International Criminal Tribunal for the former Yugoslavia ('ICTY') and the International
Criminal Tribunal for Rwanda ('ICTR'), many elements of international
criminal law have undergone significant development. Sentencing, however, remains a rather underdeveloped area. It still possesses few clear
guidelines, and is surrounded by inconsistency and unpredictability. This
chapter deals with one particular aspect in international criminal sentencing, namely mitigating circumstances. It attempts to sketch the evolution
of the practice and law of mitigating circumstances from the post-Second
World War international war crimes trials to two recent convictions and
sentencing of the International Criminal Court ('ICC').

  This chapter examines the various mitigating circumstances considered in the judicial discourse of international criminal courts and tribunals
in different eras, including war crimes trials after the Second World War,
trials at the ICTY and ICTR, and finally the ICC. By means of this historical investigation, the analysis traces the development of the law in this
area and identifies key trends. From this, it can be observed that the scope
of mitigating circumstances considered by international courts and tribunals has expanded considerably. More importantly, behind this is an amplification of the underlying ideologies of international criminal justice
and their goals and aims. In the early trials, the main focus in determining
sentencing was the culpability of the accused person and proportionality
of sentences. More recent practice, however, has paid more attention to

---

[*] **ZHANG Binxin** is an Assistant Professor at Xiamen University Law School and the inaugural PKU-CILRAP Research Fellow. Her main research interest is international criminal
law and procedure. She has co-authored a book on war crimes and published several articles and book chapters on issues related to international criminal law and procedure. She
holds a Ph.D. in international law from Renmin University of China.

broader goals, such as the accused's contribution to the reconciliation of a given society. Yet there is no consistent approach as to which is the priority among the different, and at times contradictory, ideologies, and thus also no clear and consistent guidelines on the weight to be attached to the different mitigating circumstances. As a result, this tends to exacerbate the confusion and uncertainty in international criminal sentencing, making it even more inconsistent and unpredictable.

20.2. Post-Second World War Trials

The post-Second World War cases generally had limited discussions on the determination of sentences. The governing legal instruments, being very brief on a whole, also contained very few guidelines on sentencing and mitigating circumstances. The only mitigating circumstance explicitly stipulated in the Charter of the International Military Tribunal ('IMT Charter') was superior orders. According to Article 8 of the IMT Charter, superior orders could not be a full defence, but "may be considered in mitigation of punishment if the Tribunal determines that justice so requires". Article 6 of the Charter of the International Military Tribunal for the Far East (the 'IMTFE Charter') contained an identical provision.

In the case law, there were very few deliberations about general grounds for mitigation apart from superior orders. There were occasional discussions on mitigation. These discussions touched upon some different elements, but they lacked both consistency and any categorisation. One rare occasion when the Tribunal discussed in general terms mitigating circumstances was the *Hostage* case in which the US Military Tribunal stated:

> Throughout the course of this opinion we have had occasion to refer to matters properly to be considered in mitigation of punishment. The degree of mitigation depends upon many factors including the nature of the crime, the age and experience of the person to whom it applies, the motives for the criminal act, the circumstances under which the crime was committed, and the provocation, if any, that contributed to its commission.[1]

---

[1] Nuremberg Military Tribunal, United States of America v. Wilhelm List et al., Judgment, Case No. 7, 19 February 1948, in Trials of War Criminals Before the Nuremberg Military Tribunals Under Control Council Law No. 10, vol. XI, US Government Printing Office, Washington, DC, p. 1317 ('Hostage case') (http://www.legal-tools.org/en/doc/b05aa4/).

The Tribunal then went on to pronounce the sentences of the convicted persons, without further explaining how the mitigating circumstances were considered in the sentencing. It is thus unclear what each of the factors mentioned meant exactly. It could be said that the Tribunal, as well as other tribunals after the Second World War, felt no necessity to spell out clearly what were the specific factors they considered for mitigation, and what facts of the cases corresponded to those factors. They simply took the liberty to impose a sentence based on their overall evaluation of the facts.

Nevertheless, it is still possible to identify, from the post-Second World War case law, some grounds for mitigation that were or seemed to have been considered by the tribunals. Apart from superior orders, the factors that were relatively frequently considered included the mental state of the convicted person towards the commission of the crime, and his/her personal circumstances, such as age and health status.

20.2.1. Superior Orders

Although superior orders were the only mitigating circumstance explicitly provided for in the IMT Charter, the Nuremberg Tribunal actually did not consider following superior orders as a mitigating circumstance. On the contrary, it unequivocally stated in the *Keitel* case that "[s]uperior orders, even to a soldier, *cannot be considered in mitigation* where crimes so shocking and extensive have been committed consciously, ruthlessly, and without military excuse or justification".[2] In the same vein, in the *Jodl* case the IMT stated: "Participation in such crimes as these has never been required of any soldier and he cannot now shield himself behind a mythical requirement of soldierly obedience at all costs as his excuse for commission of these crimes".[3] These pronouncements suggest that the IMT added some strict conditions on the consideration of superior orders as mitigating circumstances. When the crimes concerned are very serious, committed consciously and without military excuse or justification, superior orders cannot be considered as mitigating circumstances. This explains why the IMT did not actually accept superior orders in mitigation,

---

[2] International Military Tribunal, *Trial of the Major War Criminals Before the International Military Tribunal, 14 November 1945–1 October 1946*, vol. 22, International Military Tribunal, Nuremberg, 1948, p. 536 (emphasis added) ('Trial of the Major War Criminals').

[3] *Ibid.*, p. 571.

despite the explicit provision in its Charter. The crimes before the IMT were of such a nature that it did not find such conditions existed.

Although not considered by the IMT, superior orders were indeed considered as mitigating circumstances in many other post-Second World War cases. In the *Peleus* trial, the British Military Tribunal considered superior orders and the fact of resisting superior orders in sentencing. According to the official commentary, these considerations seem to be the reasons for reduced or lighter sentencing.[4] In the *Sawada* trial the United States Military Commission in Shanghai imposed a light sentence on the three convicted persons. The Commission obviously took into consideration the fact that "[t]he offences of each of the accused resulted largely from obedience to the laws and instructions of their Government and their Military Superiors. They exercised no initiative to any marked degree".[5] While recognising that such circumstances did not constitute full defence, the Commission held that "they do compel unusually strong mitigating consideration".[6]

When superior orders were considered a mitigating circumstance, the fact that the defendant resisted the illegal orders was often given much weight, even though the orders were still carried out in the end. In the *Hostage* case, the defendant Hubert Lanz received 12 years' imprisonment. The Tribunal took into account the fact that Lanz refused to carry out unlawful orders of shooting large numbers of Italian soldiers and officers, and that he demanded that court-martial proceedings were to be conducted to determine guilty officers.[7] Although by his actions Lanz only managed to reduce the number of killings, and the Tribunal held that the "killing of the reduced number was just as much a criminal act […] for which the defendant is responsible", Lanz's resistance to the unlawful orders seems to have been taken into account in his sentencing.[8] Similar-

---

[4]   British Military Court, Hamburg, *United Kingdom v. Eck et al.*, in United Nations War Crimes Commission, *Law Reports of Trials of War Criminals*, vol. 1, His Majesty' Stationery Office, London, 1947, p. 21 ('Peleus case') (https://www.legal-tools.org/doc/f6aa9f/).

[5]   United States Military Commission, Shanghai, *United States of America v. Sawada et al.*, in United Nations War Crimes Commission, *Law Reports of Trials of War Criminals*, vol. 5, His Majesty's Stationery Office, London, 1948, p. 7.

[6]   Ibid.

[7]   Hostage case, Judgment, p. 1312, see *supra* note 1.

[8]   *Ibid.*, pp. 1313, 1319.

ly, in the *Einsatzgruppen* trial, Erwin Schulz received a relatively light sentence as the court noted that "confronted with an intolerable situation, he did *attempt* to do something about it".[9] Thus, it appears that what the Tribunal took into consideration was the person's *efforts* in resisting illegal orders. The actual result of the resistance was not the main concern for the purpose of sentencing.

20.2.2. Mental State

In the Nuremberg Judgment, the IMT often considered how "actively" the defendant participated in the crimes, and whether the crime was committed "knowingly and voluntarily". It is obvious that these considerations may also pertain to the criminal liability of the accused, but in the Nuremberg Judgement they were considered when determining sentences, and sometimes explicitly as mitigating circumstances.

In the *Funk* case, the Tribunal sentenced the defendant to life imprisonment because in spite of his "important official positions, Funk was never a dominant figure in the various programs in which he participated", which the Tribunal considered as "a mitigating fact".[10] The role a defendant played in the criminal act clearly pertains to his or her criminal liability. However, here what the Tribunal seems to stress is that Funk did not play a central role in spite of his "important official positions". In other words, he could have (or even should have given his official position) played a central role, but he *chose* not to. What really mattered as a mitigating fact was not so much that he did not play a dominant role, but that he *did not want to* play such a role. This latter aspect was perhaps what the Tribunal found to have distinguished him from Jodl, who testified that he was opposed to an unlawful order "on moral and legal grounds, but could not refuse to pass it on".[11] Thus, what the Tribunal truly meant by "a mitigating fact" was the person's mental state of unwillingness or at least a reluctance to conduct the crime, combined with the conduct of refraining from committing the criminal act.

---

[9] Nuremberg Military Tribunal, *United States of America v. Otto Ohlendorf et al.*, Opinion and Judgment, in Trials of War Criminals Before the Nuremberg Military Tribunals Under Control Council Law No. 10, vol. IV, US Government Printing Office, Washington, DC, pp. 519–21 (emphasis added) ('Einsatzgruppen case') (https://www.legal-tools.org/doc/74e839/).

[10] Trial of the Major War Criminals, vol. 22, p. 552, see *supra* note 2.

[11] *Ibid.*, p. 570.

Similarly, in the *Speer* case, another one of the rare cases where the IMT considered mitigating circumstances, the Tribunal noted:

> Speer's establishment of blocked industries did keep many laborers in their homes and that in the closing stages of the war he was one of the few men who had the courage to tell Hitler that the war was lost and to take steps to prevent the senseless destruction of production facilities. [...] He carried out his opposition to Hitler's scorched earth program [...] by deliberately sabotaging it at considerable personal risk.[12]

Here Speer not only opposed to Hitler's orders but also took substantial steps to alleviate the results of the crimes, and did all this "at considerable personal risk". It is thus not clear exactly which mitigating factors were considered in this case, as there was a combination of efforts to help victims, resistance to superior orders and even the "deliberately sabotaging" of such orders. However, a comparison of Speer with the *Seyss-Inquart* case reveals that the IMT attached significant weight to the mental state of the person. In the *Seyss-Inquart* case, although the Tribunal recognised that "in certain cases Seyss-Inquart opposed the extreme measures [...] he was largely successful in preventing the Army from carrying out a scorched earth policy, and urged the Higher SS and Police Leaders to reduce the number of hostages to be shot", it seems to consider this insufficient to warrant mitigation.[13] The Tribunal sentenced Seyss-Inquart to death as he remained "a knowing and voluntary participant" in the crimes of which he was convicted.[14] Thus, actual acts of opposition and even success in preventing damages are not enough; it is the mental state of the convicted person that really matters.

20.2.3. Personal Circumstances

The mitigating factors mentioned in the *Hostage* case included "the age and experience of the person", which pertain to the personal circumstances of the convicted person. Various factors relating to personal circumstances were considered in the post-Second World War cases, including diminished mental status and health conditions.

---

[12]   *Ibid.*, p. 579.

[13]   *Ibid.*, p. 576.

[14]   *Ibid.*

At Nuremberg, Rudolf Hess raised the issue of his unstable mental status. The Tribunal recognised it "may be true" that he "acts in an abnormal manner, suffers from loss of memory, and has mentally deteriorated during this Trial".[15] However, he was still found to be able to stand trial and was convicted in spite of the aforementioned finding, as there was "no suggestion that Hess was not completely sane when the acts charged against him were committed".[16] Nevertheless, he was sentenced to life imprisonment, arguably a relatively light sentence considering the crimes of which he was convicted and the general sentencing practice of the Nuremberg Tribunal. The Tribunal did not make any explicit explanations, so this cannot be certain, but Hess's diminished mental status might well have played a part in the determination of his sentence.

The health condition of the defendant was also often taken into consideration. In the *Ministries* case, the Tribunal recognised that the defendant Stuckart was in a serious physical condition. His various diseases required that he should be in "more or less constant hospitalization in the future".[17] Thus, the Tribunal found that "confinement would be equivalent to the death sentence".[18] As the Tribunal did not find Stuckart's crime warranted a death sentence, it sentenced him to a term of imprisonment equivalent to the time he had already been in custody.[19]

Similarly, in the *Krupp* case, several defendants had to be excused from attendance because of their health. The Tribunal also expressed concerns that these defendants "should not be exposed by incarceration to dangerous consequences to their health".[20] The Tribunal still sentenced these defendants to imprisonment, as it found itself not in a position to determine whether the health condition of the defendants would actually "cause fatal or other extremely serious consequences".[21] However, it rec-

---

[15] *Ibid.*, p. 530.

[16] Ibid.

[17] Nuremberg Military Tribunal, *United States of America v. Ernst von Weizsaecker et al.*, Judgment, 11 April 1949, in Trials of War Criminals Before the Nuremberg Military Tribunals Under Control Council Law No. 10, vols. XII–XIV US Government Printing Office, Washington, DC, p. 869 ('Ministries case') (http://www.legal-tools.org/doc/eb20f6/).

[18] Ibid.

[19] *Ibid.*, pp. 869–70.

[20] Nuremberg Military Tribunal, *United States of America v. Krupp von Bohlen et al.*, Judgment, 31 July 1948, in Trials of War Criminals Before the Nuremberg Military Tribunals Under Control Council Law No. 10, vol. X, US Government Printing Office, Washington, DC, p. 1452 ('Krupp case') (https://www.legal-tools.org/doc/f6aa9f/).

[21] Ibid.

ommended that the Military Governor should make examinations and alter the sentences if necessary.[22]

20.3. *Ad Hoc* Tribunals

The Statutes of the *ad hoc* Tribunals are much more comprehensive compared to the IMT and IMTFE Charters. However, their provisions on penalties and sentencing guidelines are still very brief and general. In terms of factors that should be taken into account when imposing sentences, the ICTY and ICTR Statutes only mention generally that these should include "such factors as the gravity of the offence and the individual circumstances of the convicted person".[23] Apart from this general provision, the Statutes also provide specifically that acting pursuant to an order, while not able to relieve criminal responsibility, "may be considered in mitigation of punishment if [...] justice so requires".[24] This is identical with the provisions in the IMT and IMTFE Charters.

In its jurisprudence, the ICTY and ICTR's considerations of mitigating factors were much more comprehensive than the post-Second World War cases. In terms of superior orders as expressly provided in their Statutes, the Tribunals increasingly linked them with the issue of duress and seldom used superior orders as an independent mitigating factor. They also took into consideration many other factors that were not provided for in the Statutes. The jurisprudence of the *ad hoc* Tribunals developed a relatively consistent practice in terms of what circumstances could be considered in mitigation, although the weight given to different circumstances remained at the sole discretion of the respective chambers and was subject to considerable inconsistency.

Other than superior orders, as explicitly specified in the Statutes, other factors often considered by the *ad hoc* Tribunals in mitigation included individual circumstances like age and family situation of the person. There were also many new developments in the *ad hoc* Tribunals' case law, including the consideration as mitigating circumstances of co-

---

[22] Ibid.

[23] United Nations, Statute of the International Criminal Tribunal for the Former Yugoslavia, adopted 25 May 1993, Art. 24(2) ('ICTY Statute') (https://www.legal-tools.org/doc/b4f63b/); United Nations, Statute of the International Criminal Tribunal for Rwanda, adopted 8 November 1994, Art. 23(2) ('ICTR Statute') (https://www.legal-tools.org/doc/8732d6/).

[24] ICTY Statute, Art. 7(4), see *supra* note 23; ICTR Statute, Art. 6(4), see *supra* note 23.

operation with the prosecution, a guilty plea, an expression of remorse, voluntary surrender, the absence of a previous criminal record and so on.[25] The developments of new grounds for mitigation are particularly noteworthy as they are not simply an expansion of possible mitigating circumstances but reflect more fundamental ideological shifts in sentencing and international criminal justice generally.

20.3.1. Superior Orders and Duress

In the jurisprudence of the ICTY, the issue of superior orders is often connected with duress. The ICTY *Erdemović* case is a well-known example of how the Tribunal treated the issue of superior orders. Although the ICTY Statute identified superior orders as a possible mitigating factor, and made no mention of duress, the Tribunal treated duress as a mitigating factor and superior orders only as a factual situation that contributed to the existence of duress.[26] In reaching its conclusion, the Tribunal stressed the "real risk" of being killed the accused faced "had he disobeyed the order".[27] In their Separate Opinion in *Erdemović*, Judges McDonald and Vohrah also pointed out the connection between superior orders and duress, arguing that they are often engaged by the same factual circumstances.[28]

The ICTY recognised that superior orders and duress are two separate legal issues and superior orders could be an independent mitigating factor.[29] However, it imposed such strict conditions on the application of superior orders as a mitigating factor that it is seldom seen in the case law. In *Mrdja*, the Trial Chamber found that the evidence presented in the case could not sustain an argument of duress, and thus it had to consider superior orders as an independent mitigating factor.[30] The Trial Chamber found that no mitigation could be granted because "the orders were so

---

[25] ICTY, *Prosecutor v. Miroslav Deronjić*, Trial Chamber, Sentencing Judgment, IT-02-61, 30 March 2004, para. 156 ('Deronjić case') (https://www.legal-tools.org/doc/95420f/).

[26] ICTY, *Prosecutor v. Drazen Erdemović*, Trial Chamber, Sentencing Judgment, IT-96-22, 5 March 1998, p. 18 ('Erdemović case') (https://www.legal-tools.org/doc/72fd40/).

[27] *Ibid.*, p. 19.

[28] ICTY, *Prosecutor v. Drazen Erdemović*, Appeals Chamber, Joint Separate Opinion of Judge McDonald and Judge Vohrah, IT-96-22, 7 October 1997, para. 34 ('Erdemović case') (https://www.legal-tools.org/doc/f91d89/).

[29] ICTY, *Prosecutor v. Darko Mrdja*, Trial Chamber, Sentencing Judgment, IT-02-59-S, 31 March 2004, para. 65 ('Mrdja case') (https://www.legal-tools.org/doc/d61b0f/).

[30] *Ibid.*, paras. 66–67.

manifestly unlawful".[31] As this was the sole reason given for this finding, the Trial Chamber's approach seems to be that superior orders can only be considered an independent mitigating factor when the orders are not manifestly illegal.

In terms of duress as a mitigating circumstance on its own, the ICTY's case law required real risk or threats, as well as the accused person's attempt to resist or dissociate him/herself from the crime. In *Mrdja*, the Trial Chamber did not accept duress as a mitigating circumstance because there was no evidence that the accused "wanted to dissociate himself from the massacre at the time of its commission".[32] This is clearly different from the factual situation in the *Erdemović* case, where duress was accepted as a mitigating circumstance. In *Erdemović*, the accused expressly refused to commit the crime, and only committed the killing after being threatened with execution. The *Erdemović* ruling was also expressly endorsed by the ICTR in *Rutaganira*, where the Trial Chamber cited *Erdemović* and reiterated that duress could not be "a complete defence to a soldier charged with a crime against humanity and/or war crime involving the killing of innocent human beings", but could be considered as a mitigating circumstance.[33]

20.3.2. Individual Circumstances

When determining the sentences, the ICTY and ICTR read various factors into "individual circumstances" as mentioned in their Statutes, including age and the family background of the accused.

In the *Erdemović* case, the accused's young age was taken into account as a mitigating factor. The ICTY held that because of his character, Erdemović was "reformable and should be given a second chance to start his life afresh upon release".[34] Here, it was not the young age alone that was treated as a mitigating factor, but actually the "reformable" character of the accused and the need to allow him enough time to "start his life afresh" that played a decisive role. Also considered was the accused's family background, including the young age of his child and the hardship

---

[31] *Ibid.*, para. 67.

[32] *Ibid.*, para. 66.

[33] ICTR, *Prosecutor v. Vincent Rutaganira*, Trial Chamber, Judgment and Sentence, ICTR-95-1C-T, 14 March 2005, para. 161 (https://www.legal-tools.org/doc/cd2a8f/).

[34] Erdemović case, Sentencing Judgment, p. 13, see *supra* note 26.

his family would endure because of his serving a prison sentence.[35] When discussing these circumstances, the Chamber at the same time referred to the accused's character and his reluctance in engaging in the criminal acts. It is thus clear that the Tribunal's consideration of family background and age was linked with the character of the convicted, and they were accepted as mitigating factors because the convicted was deemed "reformable".

Similar considerations can also be found in ICTR case law. In *Serushago,* the Trial Chamber considered in mitigation the accused's age and family background, that he was only 37-years-old and that he had six children.[36] Similar to the ICTY, the Trial Chamber also considered at the same time other factors including the accused's co-operation with the prosecutor and his showing remorse publicly.[37] Taken together, these factors, in the Trial Chamber's view, "would suggest possible rehabilitation".[38]

Thus, the Tribunals' consideration of age, family background and other individual circumstances was mainly for the purpose of determining whether the accused would be "reformable". It is rehabilitation that underlies such factors as mitigating circumstances.

20.3.3. New Developments

Apart from those cases discussed above, the *ad hoc* Tribunals also took into consideration many other factors as mitigating circumstances in their case law, factors that were not considered in the post-Second World War trials. These newly recognised factors include co-operation with the prosecution, a guilty plea, remorse, a contribution to prevent historical revisionism and so on. The rationale behind these factors includes promoting reconciliation, contributing to the historical truth and saving the Tribunals' energy and resources. These considerations were clearly absent in the post- Second World War case law, and actually only became prevalent in the later jurisprudence of the *ad hoc* Tribunals. They demonstrate the multiple goals that today's international criminal institutions are seeking to pursue or at least are bearing in mind in their operations.

---

[35] *Ibid.*

[36] ICTR, *Prosecutor v. Omar Serushago*, Trial Chamber, Sentence, ICTR-98-39-S, 5 February 1999, para. 39 (https://www.legal-tools.org/doc/e2dddb/).

[37] *Ibid.*

[38] Ibid.

The Rules of Procedure and Evidence of both the ICTY and the ICTR provide explicitly for only one mitigating factor, that is, "substantial co-operation with the Prosecutor".[39] The ICTY considered two aspects with respect to such co-operation in its jurisprudence. One is the substantive value of the co-operation, such as providing new information and giving evidence in other cases.[40] The other is the extent of the co-operation and the attitude of the accused. In *Erdemović*, for example, the Tribunal stressed the fact that "the accused co-operated without asking for anything in return".[41]

The ICTY also considered a guilty plea a mitigating factor. In the *Erdemović* case, the first case before the ICTY in which an accused was convicted on the basis of a guilty plea, the Trial Chamber gave three reasons for considering a guilty plea as a mitigating circumstance: that "[a]n admission of guilt demonstrates honesty"; that it would encourage those already indicted or unknown perpetrators to come forth; and that it would save "the time and effort of a lengthy investigation and trial".[42]

Closely related to a guilty plea is another mitigating factor frequently considered in the *ad hoc* Tribunals' case law, that is, remorse on the part of the accused. In *Erdemović*, the ICTY took into account the "genuine and real" sorrow and remorse the accused felt when determining his sentence.[43] In *Plavšić*, the Trial Chamber considered remorse as connected with the accused's guilty plea, and even observed that the accused, by her guilty plea, could be considered to have already demonstrated remorse.[44] It considered remorse and "the substantial saving of international time and resources as a result of a plea of guilty before trial" together warranted a reduced sentence.[45] Particularly noteworthy, however, is that the Trial Chamber did not stop there. It went on to consider what it called "a further and significant circumstance [...] namely the role of the guilty

---

[39]   ICTY and ICTR Rules of Procedure and Evidence, Rule 101(B)(ii).

[40]   Erdemović case, Sentencing Judgment, see *supra* note 26, pp. 17–18.

[41]   *Ibid.*, p. 17.

[42]   *Ibid.*, p. 16.

[43]   *Ibid.*, pp. 16–17.

[44]   *Prosecutor v. Biljana Plavšić*, Trial Chamber, Sentencing Judgment, IT-00-39 and 40/1-S, 27 February 2003, para. 73 ('Plavšić case') (https://www.legal-tools.org/doc/f60082/).

[45]   Ibid.

plea of the accused in establishing truth in relation to the crimes and furthering reconciliation in the former Yugoslavia".[46]

Plavšić was the first case before the ICTY where the consideration of a guilty plea as a mitigating circumstance was justified on the ground of furthering reconciliation.[47] As discussed above, earlier in the *Erdemović* case, the reasons the Trial Chamber gave for considering a guilty plea as a mitigating circumstance were mainly related to the saving of resources. The Trial Chamber only went beyond this in its *dicta*, explaining the "sentencing policy of the Chamber". There the Trial Chamber further stressed the importance of discovering the truth and the contribution of a confession to the discovery of truth. The Chamber observed that the ICTY's mandate was not only "to investigate, prosecute and punish" international crimes but it also had a duty "to contribute to the settlement of the wider issues of accountability, reconciliation and establishing the truth", and "[d]iscovering the truth is a cornerstone of the rule of law and a fundamental step on the way to reconciliation".[48]

Plavšić went further than this by directly relying on "establishing truth" and "furthering reconciliation" as justifications for a guilty plea as a mitigating circumstance. Later cases followed this approach and recognised that a guilty plea, and the admission of guilt and responsibility generally, would contribute to the process of reconciliation.[49] In *Deronjić*, the Trial Chamber, apart from recognising a guilty plea as an acknowledgment of responsibility and furtherance of reconciliation, also pointed out that a guilty plea could protect victims "from having to relive their experiences and re-open old wounds".[50] Notably, it only mentioned the effect of saving the Tribunal's resources at the very last, and only "[a]s a side-effect, albeit not really a significant mitigating factor".[51] This is almost a complete reverse of the earlier *Erdemović* approach.

---

[46] Ibid.

[47] Shahram Dana, "The Limits of Judicial Idealism: Should the International Criminal Court Engage with Consequentialist Aspirations?" in *Penn State Journal of Law & International Affairs*, 2014, vol. 3, p. 93.

[48] Erdemović case, Sentencing Judgment, para. 21, see *supra* note 26.

[49] Deronjić case, Sentencing Judgment, para. 134, see *supra* note 25; *Prosecutor v. Dragan Nikolić*, Trial Chamber, Sentencing Judgment, IT-94-2-S, 18 December 2013, para. 246 ('Nikolić case') (https://www.legal-tools.org/doc/f8722c/).

[50] Deronjić case, Sentencing Judgment, para. 134, see *supra* note 25.

[51] Ibid.

In still later case law, reconciliation was considered a separate mitigating factor, no longer necessarily attached to a guilty plea. In *Nikolić*, the ICTY Trial Chamber highlighted the accused's "readiness and willingness to contribute to the truth-finding mission of the Tribunal" and his "attempt to achieve reconciliation".[52] The accused expressed a hope that his confession could ultimately help to bring about "reconciliation and peaceful coexistence".[53] He also expressed willingness to actually meet the victims and offered to provide information to them. The Trial Chamber thus found the accused willing to contribute to reconciliation and took this into account in mitigation.[54]

Apart from reconciliation, other broader considerations the ICTY took into account when determining sentencing and accepting mitigating circumstances included the contribution to the establishment of the historical truth. The Trial Chamber in *Deronjić* considered "contribution to prevention of revisionism of crimes committed in Srebrenica" a separate mitigating factor. The Trial Chamber held that the accused's acknowledgment of the Srebrenica massacre and his admission of preparing revisionist documents denying the massacre were important both for future cases before the Tribunal and to "negate the arguments of future revisionists".[55] The Trial Chamber not only considered the accused's contribution to prevent revisionism a mitigating factor but also attributed "significant weight to this factor in mitigating" the accused's sentence.[56]

This review of the some of the ICTY jurisprudence reflects the Tribunal's changing attitudes with respect to the purpose of sentencing, and indeed the purpose of its entire operation. In later ICTY cases, there is clearly an increasing emphasis on contributing to broader goals like reconciliation, the protection of victims and the establishment of the historical truth. This change has significantly influenced the factors taken into account in mitigation and the weight attached to each factor. As the *Blaškić* Trial Chamber pointed out, "in determining the sentence, the weight attributed to each type of circumstance depends on the objective

---

[52] Nikolić case, Sentencing Judgment, para. 249, see *supra* note 49.
[53] Ibid.
[54] Ibid.
[55] Deronjić case, Sentencing Judgment, para. 259, see *supra* note 25.
[56] *Ibid.*, para. 260.

sought by international justice".[57] However, what if there are multiple, and at times contradictory, objectives sought, and the priority among them has not been clearly spelled out?

For the *Blaškić* Trial Chamber, the priority was very clear. The Chamber mentioned four different objectives of the sentence, namely, retribution, protection of society, rehabilitation and deterrence.[58] It then invoked previous ICTY case law to stress the utter importance of deterrence.[59] To the Trial Chamber, the specific personal circumstances should be accorded less significance when determining sentencing.[60] Thus, although recognising rehabilitation as an objective of sentences, and also finding the accused's character "reformable", the Chamber ruled that the weight to be attached to the personal factors should be "limited or even non-existent".[61]

Similarly, in the *Kambanda* case before the ICTR, the Trial Chamber clearly considered retribution and deterrence as the two main objectives of sentencing.[62] The accused in this case pleaded guilty and cooperated comprehensively with the prosecution by providing "invaluable information" and agreeing to testify for the prosecutor in other cases.[63] While recognising these facts constituted mitigating circumstances, the Trial Chamber found that they were negated by the aggravating circumstances, including especially Kambanda's "high ministerial post".[64] Kambanda was sentenced to the highest penalty of life imprisonment.[65] In making its decision, the Chamber stressed that the "degree of magnitude of the crime is still an *essential criterion* for evaluation of sentence", and that "[a] sentence must reflect the *predominant standard* of proportionality between the gravity of the offence and the degree of responsibility of

---

57   ICTY, *Prosecutor v. Tihomir Blaškić*, Trial Chamber, Judgment, IT-95-14-T, 3 March 2000, para. 765 (https://www.legal-tools.org/doc/e1ae55/).

58   *Ibid.*, para. 761.

59   *Ibid.*, paras. 761–63.

60   *Ibid.*, para. 765.

61   *Ibid.*, paras. 781–82.

62   ICTR, *Prosecutor v. Jean Kambanda*, Trial Chamber, Judgment and Sentence, ICTR-97-23-S, 4 September 1998, para. 28 (https://www.legal-tools.org/doc/49a299/).

63   *Ibid.*, para. 47.

64   *Ibid.*, para. 62.

65   *Ibid.*, verdict.

the offender".[66] There was thus a clear emphasis on retribution as a sentencing objective.

However, in later cases, when broader ideologies were added into the sentencing parameters, it seemed to be increasingly difficult for the Tribunals to maintain consistency. In the *Plavšić* case, the contribution to reconciliation was given much weight, and was so particularly because of Plavšić's high position. The ICTY Trial Chamber, in its Sentencing Judgment, cited expert witnesses and stressed that Plavšić's status as a former high-ranking political leader made her confession crucially significant for the process of reconciliation in the region.[67] The Trial Chamber then concluded that Plavšić's "acknowledgement of responsibility, particularly in the light of her former position as President of Republika Srpska, should promote reconciliation".[68] It thus decided to "give significant weight to the plea of guilty by the accused", accompanied by her expression of remorse and contribution to reconciliation, as a mitigating factor.[69] Plavšić's 11-year sentence was considered by many to be too lenient, especially given the ICTY's practice of considering superior position an aggravating factor and imposing severer sentences on high-ranking accused persons.[70] It also stands in sharp contrast with the *Kambanda* case. At the same time, in other cases where a contribution to reconciliation was also considered as a mitigating circumstance it was not given as much weight as in the *Plavšić* case.[71]

Indeed, what constitutes mitigating circumstances and how much weight is to be given to such circumstances are subject to "a considerable degree of discretion" of the Tribunal that hears the case.[72] However, there still needs to be some degree of consistency and guidelines. While the consideration of each specific circumstance may depend on the particular situation of each case, the general sentencing policy and objectives at the level of principle should be consistent.

---

[66] *Ibid.*, para. 57-58.

[67] Plavšić case, Sentencing Judgment, paras. 69, 76, see *supra* note 44.

[68] *Ibid.*, para. 80.

[69] *Ibid.*, para. 81.

[70] Dana, 2014, pp. 102, 106. see *supra* note 47.

[71] *Ibid.*, pp. 104–5.

[72] ICTY, *Prosecutor v. Dragomir Milošević*, Appeals Chamber, Judgment, IT-98-29/1-A, 12 November 2009, para. 316 (https://www.legal-tools.org/doc/44327f/).

20.4. International Criminal Court

The ICC Statute and its Rules of Procedure and Evidence together contain the most comprehensive provisions on sentencing and mitigating circumstances to date. In its two convictions thus far, the ICC has had an opportunity to pronounce on some of the issues concerning mitigating circumstances.

20.4.1. ICC Statute and Rules of Procedure and Evidence

The Rome Statute of the ICC ('ICC Statute') provides that in determining the sentence, the Court "shall [...] take into account such factors as the gravity of the crime and the individual circumstances of the convicted person".[73] This is the same as the Statues of the *ad hoc* Tribunals. However, the ICC Rules of Procedure and Evidence contain much more detailed provisions in this regard compared to those of the *ad hoc* Tribunals. Rule 145 provides a list of additional factors that can be taken into account when determining the sentence, including

> the extent of the damage caused, in particular the harm caused to the victims and their families, the nature of the unlawful behaviour and the means employed to execute the crime; the degree of participation of the convicted person; the degree of intent; the circumstances of manner, time and location; and the age, education, social and economic condition of the convicted person.[74]

In terms of mitigating circumstances, Rule 145 lists the following:

(i) The circumstances falling short of constituting grounds for exclusion of criminal responsibility, such as substantially diminished mental capacity or duress;

(ii) The convicted person's conduct after the act, including any efforts by the person to compensate the victims and any cooperation with the Court.[75]

This is also a non-exhaustive list, and the two listed circumstances are not specific in nature, but rather categories of circumstances that can include many different situations. The only explicitly mitigating circum-

---

[73] Rome Statute of the International Criminal Court, entered into force, 1 July 200, Art. 78(1) ('ICC Statute') (https://www.legal-tools.org/doc/7b9af9/).

[74] International Criminal Court, Rules of Procedure and Evidence, adopted on 9 September 2002, ICC-ASP/1/3 (Part.II-A), Rule 145(1)(c) (https://www.legal-tools.org/doc/8bcf6f/).

[75] *Ibid.*, Rule 145(2)(a).

stance provided for in the Rules of Procedure and Evidence of the *ad hoc* Tribunals, that is, "substantial co-operation with the Prosecutor", was replaced by "any cooperation with the *Court*" and listed as an example of the general category of "the convicted person's conduct after the act". Another specifically mentioned example in this category is "any efforts by the person to compensate the victims". Clearly, mitigating circumstances that can be taken into account by the ICC are not limited to these alone. The factors mentioned in Rule 145(1)(c) might serve as mitigating circumstances, just as they may also be considered in aggravation, depending on the circumstances of the case. As both provisions are non-exhaustive, the ICC might also take into account additional factors not mentioned in these provisions.

One of the explicitly listed categories of mitigating circumstances is "the circumstances falling short of constituting grounds for exclusion of criminal responsibility". The Rules of Procedure and Evidence give "substantially diminished mental capacity or duress" as examples of such circumstances.[76] Other grounds for exclusion of criminal responsibility include a certain state of intoxication, self-defence,[77] and a mistake of fact or mistake of law under certain particular circumstances.[78]

Worth highlighting in particular is the issue of superior orders. Since Nuremberg, it has been a settled principle that superior orders cannot serve as a full defence but only as a mitigating circumstance. The IMT was even reluctant to actually consider it a mitigating circumstance regardless of the explicit provision in its Charter. The *ad hoc* Tribunals were also very strict in considering it in mitigation. In their case law, superior orders on their own were seldom considered as a mitigating circumstance, but often served as a factual circumstance in the finding of duress. The ICC Statute, however, went as far as giving superior orders the status of a full defence, albeit under exceptional circumstances. Article 33 of the ICC Statute stipulates that following superior orders

> shall not relieve that person of criminal responsibility unless:
>
> (a) The person was under a legal obligation to obey orders of the Government or the superior in question;

---

[76] *Ibid.*, Rule 145(2)(a)(i).

[77] ICC Statute, Art. 31, see *supra* note 75.

[78] *Ibid.*, Art. 32.

(b) The person did not know that the order was unlawful; and

(c) The order was not manifestly unlawful.

[…] orders to commit genocide or crimes against humanity are manifestly unlawful.

As "circumstances falling short of constituting grounds for exclusion of criminal responsibility" can be considered as mitigating circumstances, the fact of following superior orders, falling short of fulfilling the above-listed conditions, may also be considered as mitigating circumstances.

The ICC Statute's treatment of superior orders finds its roots in the post-Second World War cases. In the *Hostage* case, the Tribunal stressed that soldiers were only required to obey lawful orders, and thus following unlawful orders could not shield a subordinate from criminal responsibility. On the other hand, the Tribunal also stated:

> We are of the view, however, that if the illegality of the order was not known to the inferior, and he could not reasonably have been expected to know of its illegality, no wrongful intent necessary to the commission of a crime exists and the interior will be protected.[79]

The ICTY seemed to be stricter in this regard, as it found in *Mrdja* that superior orders could not be considered in mitigation because the orders were manifestly unlawful.[80] Thus, for the ICTY superior orders should not be manifestly unlawful even for being considered as a mitigating circumstance, and should not, under any circumstances, serve as a full defence according to the ICTY Statute.[81]

20.4.2. Mitigating Circumstances in the *Lubanga* and *Katanga* Cases

In the *Lubanga* case of the ICC's Situation in the Democratic Republic of Congo, the only mitigating circumstance the Trial Chamber took into consideration in its determination of sentencing was the accused's co-operation with the Court. Notably, the Trial Chamber considered this factor in the light of the defence argument about an abuse of process on the part of the prosecution. The Chamber noted, as a mitigating circumstance,

---

[79] Hostage case, Judgment, p. 1236, see *supra* note 1.

[80] Mrdja case, Sentencing Judgment, para. 67, see *supra* note 29,

[81] ICTY Statute, Art. 7(4), see *supra* note 23.

Lubanga's co-operation with the Court, "notwithstanding some particularly onerous circumstances, which included" the prosecution's repeated failure in terms of disclosure and evidence and its inappropriate use of a public interview.[82] Thus, although the controversial issue of alleged abuse of process by the prosecution was rejected and not accepted as a reason to reduce the sentence,[83] it was nevertheless considered in the determination of the sentence to the benefit of Lubanga.

Trial Chamber II in the *Katanga* case considered various possible mitigating circumstances, but in the end only upheld two, that is, Katanga's young age and his family situation, as well as his active support of the process of the disarmament and demobilisation of child solders.[84] Many other factors were also recognised as mitigating circumstances, but not upheld in this case because the evidence did not support the existence of such circumstances. The age, family situation, as well as the reputation and character of the accused were considered under the heading of "personal circumstances".[85] Katanga's young age and his family situation were found to be likely to promote his reintegration.[86] The Chamber further considered Katanga's reputation in his community and his relationship with the civilian population, which it found to be "both benevolent and protective", and held that these circumstances could also be considered in mitigation.[87] Notably, the Chamber made clear that considering the nature of the crimes, these mitigating circumstances would not play a "determinative role" but would only be given "very relative weight".[88] The Chamber was also explicit in stating that the other mitigating factor in this case, namely Katanga's contribution to the disarmament and demobilisation of child soldiers, was "much more important".[89]

---

[82]   ICC, Situation in the Democratic Republic of Congo, *Prosecutor v. Thomas Lubanga Dyilo*, Trial Chamber, Decision on Sentence pursuant to Article 76 of the Statute, ICC-01/04-01/06, 10 July 2012, para. 91 (https://www.legal-tools.org/doc/c79996/).

[83]   *Ibid.*, para. 90.

[84]   ICC, Situation in the Democratic Republic of Congo, *Prosecutor v. Germain Katanga*, ICC-01/04-01/07, Trial Chamber II, Décision relative à la peine (article 76 du Statut), 23 May 2014, para. 144 (https://www.legal-tools.org/doc/7e1e16/).

[85]   *Ibid.*, para. 78 ff.

[86]   *Ibid.*, para. 85.

[87]   *Ibid.*, para. 88.

[88]   Ibid.

[89]   *Ibid.*, para. 144.

When considering the factor of remorse, the *Katanga* Trial Chamber discussed in more general terms the weight that it might bear in sentencing. In this particular case, the Chamber found that the evidence could not establish an expression of sincere remorse or compassion on the part of the accused.[90] However, the Chamber stated generally that both "sincere compassion for the victims" and "sincere remorse" can possibly be considered in sentencing.[91] It further declared that the expression of compassion should "be given a much lower weight" than remorse.[92] This approach seems to be different from the previous case law, in which the tribunals or courts were often ambiguous about how much weight was given to each different mitigating circumstance. The discussion of this issue in general terms is even more rare. If this practice is followed by later cases, it might contribute to the consistency of the ICC's sentencing practice. On the other hand, the weight to be given to each different circumstance should, in large part, depend on the particular circumstances of the case concerned. Too much generalisation is neither pragmatic nor reasonable. There is indeed a fine balance between the setting up of some guidelines to maintain consistency and the need to reserve space for flexibility and ample consideration of the particular circumstances of each case.

Other factors considered in *Katanga* as mitigating circumstances included real and sincere efforts to promote peace and reconciliation,[93] co-operation with the Court[94] and violation of the fundamental rights of the convicted.[95] Thus, similar to the *ad hoc* Tribunals, the ICC also took into consideration factors pertinent to the reintegration of the convicted person, and to the peace and reconciliation process, which, in the *Katanga* case, included a contribution to the demobilisation of child soldiers.

20.5. Conclusion

From the early practice of international criminal sentencing in the post-Second World War era to that of the *ad hoc* Tribunals and now the ICC, many developments are evident. In terms of mitigating circumstances in sentencing, early legal instruments contained only occasional provisions.

---

[90] *Ibid.*, para. 121.
[91] *Ibid.*, para. 117.
[92] Ibid.
[93] *Ibid.*, para. 91.
[94] *Ibid.*, paras. 127–28.
[95] *Ibid.*, para. 136.

They were considerably developed by the *ad hoc* Tribunals' abundant jurisprudence, while the ICC Statute and Rules of Procedure and Evidence reflect the greatest efforts so far to clarify and lay down some consistent parameters in this regard.

A notable trend that can be discerned from this history is that the factors considered in mitigation have increased considerably, and the rationale behind these different factors has also expanded to reflect various ideologies and goals of international criminal justice. In the post-Second World War cases and early practice of the *ad hoc* Tribunals, although there was a lack of any theoretical pronouncements, it is clear that the main consideration was the culpability of the accused. Circumstances that related to the extent to which the accused could exert their free will, their attempts to resist illegal orders and to assist victims were all discussed extensively in these cases.

To focus on culpability is perhaps the most traditional and "natural" approach when it comes to the determination of sentencing, including considerations of mitigating circumstances. Later practice in international criminal justice, however, developed new grounds for mitigation, which reflect more fundamental shifts of ideology not only in sentencing but also in international criminal justice generally. If the focus on culpability can be said to relate to the circumstances surrounding the commission of the crime *per se*, later practice has paid increasing attention to events and the accused's attitude *after* the commission of the crime. New factors considered in this regard include the accused's co-operation with the prosecution or the court, expressions of remorse, contributions to prevent historical revisionism, contributions to reconciliation and so on.

In justifying the considerations of these different factors in mitigation, the tribunals and courts have invoked a wide range of rationales. Among the more traditional ones are the efficiency of international criminal justice and the rehabilitation of the accused, while more recently advanced rationales include the contribution to reconciliation and the peace process, and the desire to produce a verifiable historical record. This reflects an expansion of the general goals and ideologies of international criminal justice. These different ideologies may involve specific problems and concerns. The contribution to reconciliation, for example, has been criticised as being too speculative and susceptible to manipulation.[96]

---

[96] Dana, 2014, pp. 97–98, see *supra* note 47.

While similar or other criticisms could be made in relation to each mitigating circumstance and its rationale, a more general and far-reaching problem with this expansion of considerations and ideologies is that there is no clear priority among them. The practice of the tribunals and courts is very unclear and inconsistent in this regard. Different approaches have been taken in different cases, and the judges seldom offer any explanation of their choices in any particular case.

The ICC, in its early sentencing practice in the *Katanga* case, appears to make an effort to pronounce on the different weight to be granted to different mitigating circumstances in more general terms. This effort could be a positive sign. But to pronounce on the weight of each different factor is both unrealistic and difficult to justify, without a clear theoretical basis. To really establish consistency in this regard, future practice needs to identify priorities among the different ideologies underlying different sentencing considerations. As the primary function of criminal proceedings is no doubt about determining and punishing criminal acts, sentencing guidelines, including factors considered in sentencing and the weight to be granted to each factor, should also reflect this. While the specific factors and the weight to be attached to them can only be decided in individual cases, on a more general and fundamental level the priority among different ideological foundations should be clearly pronounced and maintained.

INDEX

A

A Memory of Solferino, 396
absolute liability, 721
accomplice liability, 652, 672, 680
Act on Communications Interception
  During Criminal Investigations, 7 59
Act on Punishment of Organised Crimes,
  Control of Crime Proceeds and Other
  Matters, 746, 747
Act on Regulation and Punishment of
  Concealment of Crime Proceeds, 759
Act on Reporting and Use of Information
  Concerning Certain Financial
  Transactions, 759
ad hoc international criminal court, 233
ad hoc tribunals, 61, 353, 414, 424, 650,
  778, 792
Additional Protocol I to the Geneva
  Conventions, 343, 350–52, 361–69,
  379, 403, 404, 667, 693, 695
Additional Protocol II to the Geneva
  Conventions, 106, 354, 355, 384, 404,
  405, 406
Adeimantus, 53
adharma, 15
adhyaksha, 21
admiralty courts, 3, 7, 63–91
Admiralty Court, Dutch, 83
Admiralty, English Court of, 67–69, 76,
  83, 87, 88
Admiralty, Scottish High Court of, 79
Aegospotami proceedings, 5 6
Aeschines, 54
Aetolian League, 48
Agamemnon, 558
aggression, act of, 588, 590, 591, 608,
  610, 611, 615–19, 621, 622, 623, 720
aggression, crime of, 587–90, 594–96,
  609, 611, 622, 623, 627, 628, 720
  leadership element, 614
  state act element, 9, 609, 613–15, 626,
    627
aggression, war of, 593–606, 610
  state act element, 624
Agha, Ahmed, 199
Ahmad, Pasha, 189, 197, 244
Ahrens, Friedrich, 270
aiding and abetting, 633
Akayesu case, 416, 582
Aksenova, Marina, 9, 629
Al Bahlul v. United States, 634, 647
Albigenses, destruction of the, 558
Aleksovski case, 698
Alexander II, 168
Alford, Roger, 171
Ali, Mohammed, 547
Alien Tort Statute, 105
Allen, Denis, 258
Allen, S.G., 151
Allied Commission on the Responsibility
  of Authors of the War and on
  Enforcement of Penalties, 439, 440
Allied Control Council, 663
Allied Declaration, 439
Almelo trial, 663
al-Qaeda, 746, 756
al-Senussi, Abdullah, 549
Al-Skeini v. UK, 735
amātya, 22
Ambach, Philipp, 8, 389
Ambos, Kai, 545, 645, 657, 672
American Civil War, 8, 93, 103, 106,
  304, 313, 322, 338, 345, 393
American Revolutionary War, 87
American Uniform Code of Military
  Justice, 692
amnesty law, 59
Anders, Władysław, 271, 272, 273
Andersonville prison, 103
Andocides, 57
Anglo-Spanish Court of Mixed
  Commission, 235
Anglo-Spanish War, 69
animus aggressionis, 605, 609, 611, 624,
  625, 627
Antigone, 45

anti-Semitism, 476
Anurak, Luang, 137
apartheid, 368, 380
Arendt, Hannah, 297
Aretha-śāstra, 14
Arginusae trial, 56
Arginusae, Battle of, 56
Argives, 35
Aristotelian school, 42
Armenian genocide, 9, 439, 442, 558,
    561–63, 566, 570, 584
arna, 14
Arnaudeau, Eugène, 323
Artaxerxes, 37
Arthaśāstra, 17, 24
Artuković case, 497
Artuković, Andrija, 497
āśrama, 14
āśramadharma, 16
asteya, 19
Atatürk, Mustafa Kemal, 565, 566
Athenians, 47, 50, 53, 56
attack, concept of, 363
Aum, Shinrikyo, 745
Auschwitz, 469
aut dedere aut judicare, 373–75
aut dedere aut punier, 350
Axis Rule, 574

B

Bagosora case, 725
Baker-Baker, William Henry, 151
Barbie case, 510
Barbie, Klaus, 495
Barzini, Luigi, 163, 165
Bazilevsky, Boris, 277, 278, 280
Beaumont, Richard, 295
Béclard, L., 215, 222, 223
Bedenck, Albert, 275
Belgium v. Senegal, 370
bellum iustum, 64
Bemba case, 542, 700–707
Bemba Gombo, Pierre, 700
Berger, L., 154
Bergsmo, Morten, 1
Beria, Lavrenty P., 251
Berlin Conference, 172, 173, 177
Bernard, Henri, 639

Bernays, Murray, 636, 653
Bertie, Reginald Henry, 144
Bey, Husni, 216
Bey, Nuri, 204
Biddle, Francis, 250, 260, 266, 291
Bikindi case, 517, 518
Bikindi, Simon, 517
Bingham, Thomas, 734
Blagojević and Jokić case, 513
Blaškić case, 511, 534, 536, 539, 538,
    784
Blé Goudé, Charles, 548
Bloxham, Donald, 568
Bluntschli, Johann Caspar, 333
Boer War, 330
Boot, Machteld, 546
Bormann, Martin, 469, 488
Bosnian Serb Army, 675
Boxer Protocol, 133, 176
Boxer Rebellion, 3, 120, 131, 133, 154,
    176
Boxer Rebellion Trial, 176
Boxer Rebellion Tribunal, 179
Boxers, 161, 162, 164, 176
boyourouldis, 187
Brady, Helen, 9, 11, 429
Brahmin, 21
Bralo case, 724
Brand, James, 434
Brđanin case, 513, 518, 519, 524, 675
Brima et al. case, 417
Brimelow, Thomas, 259
British Court of Inquiry, 144, 146, 154
British Crown Courts, 153
British Manual of Military Law, 144
British Military Court, 145, 146, 147,
    663, 667
British Military Tribunal, 774
British War Crimes Executive, 285, 293
Brockman-Hawe, Benjamin E., 8, 173,
    181
Broughton Mainwaring, Rowland, 151
Brussels Conference, 321, 322, 327, 331,
    347, 394
Brussels Declaration, 168, 346
Brytan, Samuel, 319
Buddhism, 14
Buddhist doctrine of non-violence, 14
Buis, Emiliano J., 2, 7, 27

E

F

G

Geneva Convention III, 359, 361, 368, 402
Geneva Convention IV, 113, 359, 360, 361, 367, 368, 378, 401, 402, 667
Geneva Conventions, 343, 350–52, 357, 373, 375, 386, 401, 414, 426, 693
Common Article 3, 105, 354, 355, 384, 404, 405, 407
génocidaires, 93
genocide, 5, 109, 491, 557–85, 581
Gentili, Alberico, 67
George, David Lloyd, 566
German-Polish Declaration of Non-Aggression, 597
Germany v. N. case, 733
Gestapo, 468, 692
Gia Long, 126
giri-durga, 18
Gorbachev, Mikhail, 251
Gordon, Gregory S., 2, 7, 119
Göring et al. trial, 399
Göring, Hermann, 263, 266, 268, 269, 472
Goucher, Candice, 171
grave breaches, 8, 343, 350, 357–70, 376–79, 380, 383, 384, 386, 387, 401, 402, 403, 412
Green family, 155
Green, Thomas, 79
Greiser, Artur, 470
Grosgurin, Inspector, 127, 137
Grotius, Hugo, 67, 88, 89
Guantánamo, 634
guerrilla warfare, 345
gunadharma, 16
GUO Yang, 8, 343
Gustav Becker et al. case, 640

H

Hácha, Emil, 595
Hagenbach trial, 167
Hague Conferences, 321, 395
Hague Convention II, 560
Hague Convention IV, 560, 687, 690
Hague Convention X, 690
Hague Conventions, 325, 347, 351, 395, 437, 606, 667
Hague law, 395, 410

Hague Peace Conference, 168, 560
Hague Regulations, 379, 396, 400
Hague Regulations concerning the Laws and Customs of War on Land, 353, 360, 395
Hale, Brenda, 735
Halil, Arap, 154
Hall, William E., 331, 335
Halleck, Henry W., 307, 313
Hamidian massacres, 562
Hamilton-Temple-Blackwood, Frederick, 238
Hammurabi, 24
Hariri, Rafik, 178
Hart, Gideon, 319
Harun, Ahmad, 550
hate speech, 515
Hedges, Charles, 80
hegemón, 39, 40
hegemonía, 41, 60
Hellenica, 50
Heller, Kevin Jon, 466, 482, 658
Henderson Chapman, Thomas, 144
Henry VIII, 67, 76
Henslow, E., 151
Heracleidae, 49
Heraians, 34
Herodotus, 49
Herreros, massacre of the, 558
Hess, Rudolf, 289, 777
Heyer, Erich, 667
High Command trial, 690
High Court of Justice, 97, 99, 101
Hindu law, 16, 24
Hinduism, 14
Historical Origins of International Criminal Law, 1, 716, 737
Hitler, Adolf, 569, 593, 594, 597, 663
Holt, Joseph, 104, 106
hors de combat, 365, 385, 392
Hostage case, 772, 774, 776, 789
Hostage trial, 690
hostis humani generis, 74, 234
House of Commons, 97, 98
House of Lords, 7 34
Howard, Francis, 145
Hull, Elisabeth, 338
Human Rights Committee, 254, 729, 730, 737

international law, individualisation of,
338
International Law Association, 567
International Law Commission, 9, 493,
605, 607, 632, 641, 646, 668, 692
International Military Commission, 3,
146, 168
Candia, 148–53
Canea, 153–54
Crete, 179
International Military Tribunal, 3, 8, 9,
52, 94, 112, 113, 116, 180, 250, 254,
297, 398, 400, 458, 460, 462, 463,
469, 471, 472, 474, 476, 477, 479,
480, 481, 486, 487, 489, 490, 571,
573, 588, 591–93, 623, 625, 627, 631,
637, 644, 653, 659–63, 668, 773, 775,
788
Charter, 63, 72, 114, 255, 343, 349,
351, 360, 398, 400, 456, 459, 479,
532, 571, 580, 591, 593, 626, 630,
635, 636, 638, 646, 651, 653, 656–
59, 663, 690, 718, 772
International Military Tribunal for the Far
East, 112, 349, 459, 461, 630, 631,
637, 642, 644, 688
Charter, 399, 459, 460, 572, 631, 635,
638, 646, 719, 772
International Peace Bureau, 170
international penal law, 330
International Red Cross Conference, 350
interned civilians, 359, 361
Iraq War, 733, 736
Irving, David, 257
Islamic law, 392
Islamic State, 739
isonomía, 30, 33, 41, 60
iudicis est ius dicere sed non dare, 419
Iverson, Jens, 7 , 93
Iwane, Matsui, 637

J

Jackson, Robert, 114, 116, 250, 255, 260,
287, 293, 296, 450, 453, 467, 480,
571, 635, 655
Jainism, 14
James II of Aragon, 78

Japan Federation of Bar Associations,
748, 762
Jaruzelski, Wojciech, 251
Jay, John, 87
Jenkins, Leoline, 79
Jewish Holocaust, 9, 584
Jīmūtavāhana, 24
Jodl case, 773
Johnson, Andrew, 106
joint criminal enterprise, 4, 10, 650, 672,
673–75
joint criminal enterprise theory, 672, 681
joint criminal enterprise, 4
Jumblat, Said Bey, 200, 205, 219, 227
Junichirō, Koizumi, 746
jury system, 21
jus ad bellum, 590, 608, 611, 615, 619,
620, 621, 627, 732
violation, 588, 590
jus gentium, 84
jus in bello, 46, 389, 404, 732
jus post bellum, 60
jus postliminii, 89, 88
justum bellum, 84
just war, 17, 43, 73
Justice case, 465, 474, 483, 484, 486,
488, 490, 492, 493, 495, 519, 521,
534, 536, 543, 644
Justice case, 505, 542
justification and excuse, doctrine of, 723

K

Kai, Katsunori, 745
Kakuyama Tadashi, 750, 753
Kambanda case, 677, 785, 786
Kampala Amendments, 9, 587, 589, 611–
23, 624, 626, 627, 628
Kampuchean United Front for National
Salvation, 108
Katanga case, 542, 790–91, 793
Katyn massacre, 6, 8, 249–97
Kautilya, 14, 18
Kayishema et al. case, 583
Kazneno-Popravni Dom prison, 519
Keitel case, 773
Kellogg-Briand Pact, 73, 606
Kenya Situation, 547
Kenyatta, Uhuru, 547

N

O

respondeat superior, doctrine of, 721
responsibility, passive, 348
responsibility, superior, 686, 692, 697, 699
responsible command, prinicple of, 687
retaliation, 4, 304–13
retaliation, subsidiary, 336
Review Conference of the Rome Statute of the International Criminal Court, 587
Revolutionary People's Tribunal, 110
Rig Veda, 13
Roberts, Frank, 295
Roberts, Ken, 439, 526
Robinson, Darryl, 544
Robinson, Harry, 144
Rodenhäuser, Tilman, 581
Rohde case, 644
Röling, B.V.A., 630, 639
Roman Empire, 392
Rome Conference, 356, 540, 544
Rosenberg, Alfred, 262
Rosenberg, Benjamin E., 741
rta, 19
Rudenko, Roman, 260, 265, 290
Ruggiu case, 504
rule of law, 21
RuSHA case, 470, 510
Russell, John, 211, 212, 228
Russo-Japanese War, 322
Russo-Turkish War, 128
Rutaganira case, 780
Ruto and Sang case, 547
Rwandan genocide, 407

S

sabhāpati, 21
sacred law, 22
Šainović case, 539
Saint Petersburg Declaration, 168, 393
Sakul, Kahraman, 174
Sanford, George, 285
Sarva Dharma Sama Bhava, 13
śāstra, 14
saucham, 19
Sauckel, Fritz, 289
sautra, 14
Savory, Douglas, 261

Sawada trial, 774
Schabas, William, 6, 8, 113, 249, 578, 581, 582, 584
Schacht, Hjalmar, 637
Schlegelberger, Franz, 491
Schonfeld case, 643, 644
Schulz, Erwin, 775
Schwarzenberger, Georg, 340
Schwelb, Egon, 440, 445
Scott, William, 87
Scott-Fox, David, 293
Second Boer War, 322
Second World War, 401, 433, 434, 493, 569, 570
Seidl, Alfred, 289
self-defence, 43, 44
sentencing, 11, 771–93
Serushago case, 781
Servatius, Robert, 289
Šešelj case, 518
Seven Years' War, 82
Seyss-Inquart case, 776
Seyss-Inquart, Arthur, 469, 594
Shawcross, Hartley, 261, 435
Shen Chia-pen, 159, 164, 165
Shin Eui Gi, 757
Shudra, 21
Sicherheitsdienst, 468
Sicherheitspolizei, 643
Siemers, Walter, 269, 289
signature strikes, 427
Simić case, 513, 533, 534
Singh, Nagendra, 13
Sinha, Manoj Kumar, 6, 13
slavery, 307, 309
smṛti, 15, 16, 24
Solferino, Battle of, 167, 396
SONG Tianying, 1
Sophocles, 45
Sparta, 38, 39
Spartan allied tribunal, 54
Spartans, 27, 35, 46, 53
Special and Temporary Court, 135
Special Court for Sierra Leone, 355, 409, 413, 417, 580, 725
  Statute, 413, 502, 521, 525
Special Panels for Serious Crimes on East Timor, 179
Special Tribunal for Lebanon, 3, 178

TOAEP TEAM

OTHER VOLUMES IN THE
FICHL PUBLICATION SERIES

Morten Bergsmo, Mads Harlem and Nobuo Hayashi (editors):
Importing Core International Crimes into National Law
Torkel Opsahl Academic EPublisher
Oslo, 2010
FICHL Publication Series No. 1 (Second Edition, 2010)
ISBN 978-82-93081-00-5

Nobuo Hayashi (editor):
National Military Manuals on the Law of Armed Conflict
Torkel Opsahl Academic EPublisher
Oslo, 2010
FICHL Publication Series No. 2 (Second Edition, 2010)
ISBN 978-82-93081-02-9

Morten Bergsmo, Kjetil Helvig, Ilia Utmelidze and Gorana Žagovec:
The Backlog of Core International Crimes Case Files in Bosnia and Herzegovina
Torkel Opsahl Academic EPublisher
Oslo, 2010
FICHL Publication Series No. 3 (Second Edition, 2010)
ISBN 978-82-93081-04-3

Morten Bergsmo (editor):
Criteria for Prioritizing and Selecting Core International Crimes Cases
Torkel Opsahl Academic EPublisher
Oslo, 2010
FICHL Publication Series No. 4 (Second Edition, 2010)
ISBN 978-82-93081-06-7

Morten Bergsmo and Pablo Kalmanovitz (editors):
Law in Peace Negotiations
Torkel Opsahl Academic EPublisher
Oslo, 2010
FICHL Publication Series No. 5 (Second Edition, 2010)
ISBN 978-82-93081-08-1

Morten Bergsmo, César Rodríguez Garavito, Pablo Kalmanovitz and Maria Paula Saffon (editors):
Distributive Justice in Transitions
Torkel Opsahl Academic EPublisher
Oslo, 2010
FICHL Publication Series No. 6 (2010)
ISBN 978-82-93081-12-8

Morten Bergsmo, César Rodriguez-Garavito, Pablo Kalmanovitz y Maria Paula Saffon (editores):
Justicia Distributiva en Sociedades en Transición
Torkel Opsahl Academic EPublisher
Oslo, 2012
FICHL Publication Series No. 6 (2012)
ISBN 978-82-93081-10-4

Morten Bergsmo (editor):
Complementarity and the Exercise of Universal Jurisdiction for Core International Crimes
Torkel Opsahl Academic EPublisher
Oslo, 2010
FICHL Publication Series No. 7 (2010)
ISBN 978-82-93081-14-2

Morten Bergsmo (editor):
Active Complementarity: Legal Information Transfer
Torkel Opsahl Academic EPublisher
Oslo, 2011
FICHL Publication Series No. 8 (2011)
ISBN 978-82-93081-55-5 (PDF)
ISBN 978-82-93081-56-2 (print)

Sam Muller, Stavros Zouridis, Morly Frishman and Laura Kistemaker (editors):
The Law of the Future and the Future of Law
Torkel Opsahl Academic EPublisher
Oslo, 2010
FICHL Publication Series No. 11 (2011)
ISBN 978-82-93081-27-2

Morten Bergsmo, Alf Butenschøn Skre and Elisabeth J. Wood (editors):
Understanding and Proving International Sex Crimes
Torkel Opsahl Academic EPublisher
Beijing, 2012
FICHL Publication Series No. 12 (2012)
ISBN 978-82-93081-29-6

Morten Bergsmo (editor):
Thematic Prosecution of International Sex Crimes
Torkel Opsahl Academic EPublisher
Beijing, 2012
FICHL Publication Series No. 13 (2012)
ISBN 978-82-93081-31-9

Terje Einarsen:
The Concept of Universal Crimes in International Law
Torkel Opsahl Academic EPublisher
Oslo, 2012
FICHL Publication Series No. 14 (2012)
ISBN 978-82-93081-33-3

莫滕·伯格斯默 凌岩（主编）：
国家主权与国际刑法
Torkel Opsahl Academic EPublisher
Beijing, 2012
FICHL Publication Series No. 15 (2012)
ISBN 978-82-93081-58-6

Morten Bergsmo and LING Yan (editors):
State Sovereignty and International Criminal Law
Torkel Opsahl Academic EPublisher
Beijing, 2012
FICHL Publication Series No. 15 (2012)
ISBN 978-82-93081-35-7

Morten Bergsmo and CHEAH Wui Ling (editors):
Old Evidence and Core International Crimes
Torkel Opsahl Academic EPublisher
Beijing, 2012
FICHL Publication Series No. 16 (2012)
ISBN 978-82-93081-60-9

YI Ping:
戦争と平和の間——発足期日本国際法学における「正しい戦争」
の観念とその帰結
Torkel Opsahl Academic EPublisher
Beijing, 2013
FICHL Publication Series No. 17 (2013)
ISBN 978-82-93081-66-1

Morten Bergsmo and SONG Tianying (editors):
On the Proposed Crimes Against Humanity Convention
Torkel Opsahl Academic EPublisher
Brussels, 2014
FICHL Publication Series No. 18 (2014)
ISBN 978-82-93081-96-8

Morten Bergsmo (editor):
Quality Control in Fact-Finding
Torkel Opsahl Academic EPublisher
Florence, 2013
FICHL Publication Series No. 19 (2013)
ISBN 978-82-93081-78-4

Morten Bergsmo, CHEAH Wui Ling and YI Ping (editors):
Historical Origins of International Criminal Law: Volume 1
Torkel Opsahl Academic EPublisher
Brussels, 2014
FICHL Publication Series No. 20 (2014)
ISBN 978-82-93081-11-1

Morten Bergsmo, CHEAH Wui Ling and YI Ping (editors):
Historical Origins of International Criminal Law: Volume 2
Torkel Opsahl Academic EPublisher
Brussels, 2014
FICHL Publication Series No. 21 (2014)
ISBN 978-82-93081-13-5

All volumes are freely available online at http://www.fichl.org/publication-series/. Printed copies may be ordered from distributors indicated at http://www.fichl.org/torkel-opsahl-academic-epublisher/distribution/, including from http://www.amazon.co.uk/. For reviews of earlier books in this Series in academic journals, please see http://www.fichl.org/torkel-opsahl-academic-epublisher/reviews-of-toaep-books/.

Lightning Source UK Ltd.
Milton Keynes UK
UKOW06n1828201215

265109UK00008B/101/P